Tax Planning for Owner-Managed Companies

2017/18

Tax Planning for Family and Owner-Managed Companies

2017/18

By Peter Rayney FCA CTA (Fellow) TEP
Peter Rayney Tax Consulting Ltd

Bloomsbury Professional

Bloomsbury Professional
An imprint of Bloomsbury Publishing Plc

Bloomsbury Professional Ltd	Bloomsbury Publishing Plc
41–43 Boltro Road	50 Bedford Square
Haywards Heath	London
RH16 1BJ	WC1B 3DP
UK	UK

www.bloomsbury.com

BLOOMSBURY and the Diana logo are trademarks of

Bloomsbury Publishing Plc

© Bloomsbury Professional Ltd 2017

British Library Cataloguing-in-Publication Data

A catalogue record for this book is available from the British Library.

ISBN:	PB:	978 1 52650 136 3
	Epdf:	978 1 52650 138 7
	Epub:	978 1 52650 137 0

Typeset by Phoenix Photosetting Ltd, Chatham, Kent
Printed and bound by CPI Group (UK) Ltd, Croydon, CR0 4YY

To find out more about our authors and books visit www.bloomsburyprofessional.com. Here you will find extracts, author information, details of forthcoming events and the option to sign up for our newsletters.

Preface

There are few areas of taxation that do not impact on family or owner-managed companies and their shareholders. Consequently, this book covers a wide range of tax planning matters. Its growth in size reflects the substantial increase and growing complexity in our tax legislation. This year's edition is fully up-to-date with the relevant 2017 legislative changes, as well as new practical points, emerging case law and developments in HMRC practice.

In this book I have taken a slightly unique approach of summarising the key planning points from the separate viewpoints of the company itself, the shareholders who work for the company (usually as directors), the non-working shareholders and in some instances the employees. Only by taking that approach can the complete picture be seen – the planning checklists appear at the end of all relevant chapters. Numerous worked examples are provided to illustrate the practical tax and commercial implications for a host of typical situations (all references to characters and companies in the examples are, of course, entirely fictitious!).

Clearly there will be occasions when what is tax efficient for the company itself will not necessarily be effective for the shareholders in their capacity as individual taxpayers. This conflict need not always present a major problem, but proper regard must be had to the interests of all parties before embarking upon any tax planning exercise.

It is intended that this book will provide the complete picture on family/owner-managed company tax planning for professional advisers such as tax consultants, accountants and solicitors, and to the owners and financial directors of these types of company themselves. This book has been extensively updated since it was first published in 1995 and draws heavily on my extensive practical experience in dealing with owner-managed companies.

The book naturally enough starts with consideration of the family/owner-managed company, its structure and its operation (I have assumed that the (private) limited company is the most appropriate vehicle for the business). Consideration is then given to the corporate structure, followed by an overview of appropriate tax strategy. The book also provides a brief guide to the computation of a company's corporation tax liability for both trading and investment companies, the revised company loss relief rules, and the impact of HMRC's penalty regime.

I then look at specific areas affecting the family/owner-managed company, including:

- the various methods of extracting funds from the company and the impact of the recent dividend tax increases;

- remuneration strategies, treatment of employee benefit trusts and the impact of the 'disguised remuneration' legislation;

- the treatment of benefits and expenses, including the company car regime;

- treatment of personal service companies under the IR35 regime and the new 'off-payroll' working rules; and

- full consideration of the recent radical changes to the pension regime as it affects owner-managers and helpful planning strategies.

The main employee share schemes and arrangements are also discussed, with full coverage of Enterprise Management Incentive (EMI) share option schemes. I also consider the ways in which shares can be passed to employees who are not members of the family. Detailed practical consideration is given to the potential impact of the 'restricted securities' regime in the context of relatively straightforward unapproved share awards and options.

Succession planning is a vital issue for long established family or owner-managed companies and I therefore cover the relevant tax and commercial angles extensively in Chapter 17 (Succession Planning and Passing on the Family Company). It must be recognised that the next generation may not have the desire or, possibly, the ability to take over the running of the business. In such cases, a sale of the company or a management buy-out (perhaps through a purchase of own shares) must be contemplated.

Most owner managers will subsequently benefit from the Entrepreneurs' relief (ER) regime, which provides them with an effective 10% CGT rate on exit. The ER regime for share sales and related planning issues in relation to different deal structures is reviewed extensively in Chapter 15. Valuing a family company is a minefield when either passing on a family/owner-managed company or selling it to outsiders. The principles of commercial and fiscal share valuations are therefore discussed in some detail (see Chapter 10).

This book also covers other important tax aspects of family and owner-managed companies. These include financing issues, expanding the business by way of acquisitions, corporate reconstructions and demergers and how to wind-up the company in a tax-efficient manner as well as securing the best possible relief for any shareholder losses.

A family or owner-managed company can be an invigorating environment, and it is one that has a major role to play in the UK economy. This is evidenced by the many tax breaks that have been given to the owner-managed business sector in recent years.

The successful company has seen a number of changes (eg the growing use of non-executive directors and the increase in demands for a specialised service or product). With proper tax planning strategies being adopted, the family or owner-managed company can look forward to continuing success. It is hoped that this book will be an indispensable guide for those involved in advising and running family and owner-managed companies.

This book includes the relevant changes included in the Finance Bill 2017–19 but was published shortly before it received Royal Assent.

I must give special thanks to my partner, Patricia Caputo, and my friends, Claire Beaumont, Ellie Brown, Gillian Fitzgerald and Kate Upcraft (Kate Upcraft Consultancy Ltd) for their help and support with the updating work and final editing checks for this edition of the book.

As ever, I owe a considerable debt of gratitude to the commitment and professionalism of the team at Bloomsbury Professional and their encouragement, with particular thanks to Jane Bradford for her sterling work. I must also express my sincere appreciation for the loving support and enthusiastic encouragement provided by Patricia.

If you like this book, please tell your friends and colleagues. If you have any comments or suggestions for future editions – please email me (peter@ prtaxconsulting.co.uk).

Peter Rayney

October 2017

Whilst every care has been taken to ensure the accuracy of the contents of this work, no responsibility for loss occasioned to any person acting or refraining from action as a result of any statement in it can be accepted by the authors or the publisher.

For Patricia

Contents

Contents

Contents

Contents

Contents

Table of Statutes

[All references are to paragraph number]

Table of Statutory Instruments

[All references are to paragraph number]

Table of Cases

[All references are to paragraph number]

Table of Cases

D

M

T

Chapter 1

The Family and Owner-Managed Company, Tax Planning Concepts, and Tax Avoidance

IMPORTANCE OF FAMILY AND OWNER-MANAGED COMPANIES

1.1　　Many empirical studies show that family-owned businesses are still the dominant form of business organisation, accounting for over two-thirds of all UK companies.

According to research commissioned by *The Institute for Family Business* in 2016, there are around 4.6 million family businesses in the UK. These family businesses provide an estimated 11.9 million jobs, accounting for 36% of overall employment in the UK.

It is estimated that family businesses contributed some £125 billion of tax receipts in 2014, equating to approximately 19% of total government tax revenues.

Apart from their vital contribution to the UK economy, the family business sector provides an important platform for developing entrepreneurial talent and start-ups.

Many family businesses are household names, such as Bestway Group, JC Bamford (commonly known as JCB), Laing O'Rourke and Clarks Shoes. Even many prominent public companies, such as Sainsbury's, retain a strong family connection through substantial shareholdings or representation at board level. Many other private companies are the product of management buy-outs, management buy-ins and 'public to private' transactions.

DEFINING A FAMILY OR OWNER-MANAGED COMPANY

1.2　　Perhaps the most important feature of family and owner-managed companies is that control of the company (both at shareholder and board levels) is concentrated in the hands of just a few individuals or a single 'dominant' chief executive.

According to a group of European family business experts a leading definition of a family business is as follows:

'A firm, of any size, is a family business, if:

(1)   The majority of decision-making rights is in the possession of natural person(s) who established the firm, or in the possession of natural person(s) who has/have acquired the share capital of the firm, or in the possession of their spouses, parents, children or children's direct heirs.

(2)   The majority of the decision-making rights are indirect or direct.

(3)   At least one representative of the family or kin is formally involved in the governance of the firm.

Listed companies meet the definition of a family enterprise if the person who established or acquired the firm (share capital) or their families or descendants possess 25% of the decision-making rights.'

This definition was adopted in the *European Commission Final Report Of The Expert Group on Family Business Relevant Issues* in 2009.

This book is aimed at the complete spectrum of family and owner-managed businesses (although it is not intended to deal with 'listed' family companies).

At a more basic level, we could define a family company as one in which a single family holds more than 50% of the voting shares and effectively controls the business by occupying the key positions in the senior management/executive team. More importantly perhaps, this working definition will also include companies that are themselves acknowledged to be family businesses (for example in promotional literature and even in advertising campaigns).

In many cases, family companies will be characterised by more than one generation being involved in the business. While many families are involved in the day-to-day running of the business, many others take a more 'hands-off' approach by involving professional 'non-family' managers.

Many of the tax planning techniques covered in this book will apply to companies where there are family connections which are not sufficient to give voting control.

The 'owner-managed company' nomenclature represents a much wider class of private company. Generally, it will be a company controlled by a small group of individuals (who are not necessarily *family* members), often originating from management buy-out or buy-in transactions. That said, many of the issues faced by firms that consider themselves 'non-family' companies, such as ownership, succession and business strategy tend to be the same as those faced by any other business.

CLOSE COMPANIES

1.3   According to HMRC, close companies make up a significant proportion of the companies in the UK.

The important 'close company' definition used in the tax legislation is likely to cover the vast majority of family and owner-managed companies. There are a number of special tax provisions, which only apply to a 'close company', and these are covered in this book. Essentially, a close company is one that is controlled by its directors *or* by five or fewer participators (shareholders) [*CTA 2010, s 439*].

KEY CHARACTERISTICS AND DYNAMICS OF FAMILY AND OWNER-MANAGED COMPANIES

1.4   The family or owner-managed company has considerable flexibility since it is free from the scrutiny of investment analysts and the shareholder accountability of 'plcs'. That said, if a private company has institutional or 'third party' shareholding or venture capital finance, the consequential shareholder or loan agreements are likely to place certain (sometimes significant) restrictions on the owner manager's operation of the business.

The decision making process in family and owner-managed companies is generally much quicker, which brings many operational benefits and enhances relationships with employees.

Many family companies succeed because they foster a unique sense of belonging and enhanced common purpose across the whole workforce. Indeed, family companies are particularly pre-eminent in the service sector, notably within hotels, retail stores, restaurants and similar businesses, where the 'personal touch' is essential.

Almost all family businesses have grown from the vision and 'hard graft' of the founder and in many cases the employees will have a very special loyalty to the business and the family owner managers. The inherent strengths of family businesses are commitment, culture and pride that often combine to produce a competitive edge.

1.5   On the other hand family businesses are often introspective and steeped in tradition. Many believe they have cornered a 'niche' and are best placed to defend their position as they have been making the same product(s) for long enough to know their market 'inside-out'. However, such attitudes can make the family business particularly vulnerable since they fail to make the necessary adjustments demanded by a rapidly changing technological and economic environment. In many cases, reluctance to embrace change is due to the perceived adverse effects that it may have on individual family members.

It follows that tax planning for the family or owner-managed company and their proprietorial shareholders should always be based on a clear understanding of, and be compatible with, the particular family dynamics and the culture of the business.

SUCCESSION PLANNING

1.6 Probably the most significant (and often heated) issue facing many family companies is succession.

Based on research carried out by Moore Stephens in 2016, the average age of SME owners is 54.5 years old with around two thirds being over the age of 50.

Leading business schools have found that around 70% of family businesses struggle with succession planning. Owner managers regularly find it difficult to give up control and often fear that their 'children' might damage the business.

The failure rate is very high. It is estimated that only 30% of family businesses make it to the second generation of family ownership, with some 13% surviving to the third generation, and just 3% beyond that. This statistic is often referred to as the '30:13:3 rule'.

There are possibly many explanations for this – for example, the 'current' generation have more job opportunities, greater geographic job mobility or may value 'life beyond work' (especially if they have seen the family work very hard for little reward!).

According to recent research, less than one in five UK family firms continue to 'reserve' managerial positions for members of the family. This perhaps removes the common perception that all family businesses tend to be suspicious of outsiders. In the author's view, 'outsiders' and non-executive directors can inject considerable fresh thinking, objectivity and professionalism into what is often an inward-looking environment.

Succession planning has to be managed very carefully indeed and may involve making some tough decisions. The key issues for the owner manager are:

- Whether members of the family have the necessary acumen and skills to develop and run the business (and do they want to)?

- Can the existing family members achieve the true potential of the business?

- Would it be better to bring in an 'outsider' to take over the company (perhaps under a 'management buy-in')?

1.7 In many cases, owner-managers are willing to hand over management to the next generation but retain either 100% or majority ownership control. The 'owner-manager' parent often uses their ownership 'control' of the company to influence or interfere with the running of the company. This highlights perhaps their greatest fear – loss of power.

Given the high incidence of marriage failures, many owner managers are very concerned about their hard-earned business wealth being compromised in a divorce settlement. Many families will therefore insist that their children enter into pre-nuptial settlements when they marry. This can be an awkward issue and needs to be handled in a diplomatic and professional manner.

Sometimes succession issues may also create friction between the various family members which, in turn, can have an adverse effect on the business. Succession planning should start many years before the owner manager plans to retire – it is a process rather than an event. This should be clearly communicated to those family members involved in the business as well as the shareholders. In some cases it may be appropriate for family members to work in another business to ensure they have the right skills and knowledge before (re)joining the family firm. Much of the emotional 'heat' can be taken out of this 'succession' process by using relevant business advisers or, possibly, the company's own independent 'non-executive' directors.

The owner manager should produce a written succession plan, specifying their 'retirement date', and adhere to it! – this would avoid the frustration and demotivation of many 'next-in-line' successors caused by the incumbent owner manager's (often) frequent deferral of their retirement from the business. The relevant tax issues involved in passing on the company to the next generation, etc. are fully dealt with in Chapter 17.

The vast majority of owner managers are able to benefit from the generous Entrepreneurs' relief (ER) (which gives a CGT tax rate of 10% on qualifying gains up to £10 million). In many cases, they will tend to seek an exit from their business rather than take a chance that their children will be able to carry on the business. In the author's experience, relatively few people now follow their parents into the family business.

The general strategy for the majority of owner-managed companies today seems to be to grow the business for a successful trade sale or management buy-out 'exit'.

FINANCIAL MANAGEMENT AND CASH FLOW

1.8   All companies must constantly plan and monitor their financial position. The development of the business is invariably dictated by the availability of finance and the budgeting and control of cash flow is essential. Especially in the early phase of a business, the ability to 'keep the bank manager happy' will often be critical to its survival. Consequently, cash flow will often be a key driver in evaluating the efficacy of any business tax planning exercise.

Many family and owner-managed companies in the 'start-up' phase will need to be especially vigilant to the danger of growing too fast, since they will not usually have the necessary borrowing facilities in place or capital base to provide the requisite level of working capital.

TAX PLANNING AND TAX AVOIDANCE

Interaction with family dynamics

1.9   This book particularly concentrates on tax planning strategies for the family and owner-managed company. It must be appreciated that there are a number of special factors that apply to such companies where any plan of action is being proposed – whether the plan is related to tax or any other topic. The special features, relationships, and 'emotional' interests within a family company should never be overlooked when giving tax advice to the company and its owners. Otherwise, putting forward what might seem to be sound tax planning techniques could sooner or later create resistance or major problems.

It is always true to say, no matter who the taxpayer may be, that the 'tax tail should not wag the commercial dog'. Whilst tax is an important factor in the decision-making processes it should never be considered in isolation.

Some planning techniques will centre on the structure of the company and its shareholders. Other strategies will be brought about by that company's activity. Broadly speaking a family or owner-managed company can carry out either a 'trading' or 'investment' activity. Various tax reliefs will be available depending on the nature of these activities.

Owner managers of *trading* companies will invariably benefit from a 10% CGT entrepreneurs' relief (ER) rate on their share disposal gains (up to a lifetime limit of £10 million). Amongst other things, the ER rules impose a minimum voting 5% shareholding requirement (except for certain EMI shareholdings). Consequently, many small minority shareholdings are unlikely to qualify for ER and will therefore usually pay CGT at the main current rate of 20% (see 15.33–15.42 for detailed coverage of ER.)

Investment company shareholders will generally incur a 20% CGT rate on significant share sales.

Various reliefs and incentives are given to all companies but will be of particular interest to family or owner-managed companies where there is an in-built facility to match reward with ownership.

Tax planning and development of the 'Ramsay' doctrine

Duke of Westminster and the nature of tax avoidance

1.10   The ability to make appropriate tax planning arrangements was first 'blessed' by the courts way back in 1935 in the legendary *Duke of Westminster* case. This involved an arrangement made by Hugh Grosvenor, 2nd Duke of Westminster, to reduce his surtax bill. He agreed to pay his staff under seven year deeds of covenant on the understanding that they would *not* claim additional wages for their future work. The House of Lords upheld this 'scheme' with Lord Tomlin famously opining that:

> 'Every man is entitled if he can to order his tax affairs so that the tax attaching under the appropriate Acts is less than it would otherwise be' (*Duke of Westminster v CIR* (1935) 19 TC 490).

The clear principle arising from this 'watershed' case was that taxpayers were entitled to organise their tax affairs so as to minimise their tax liabilities. This meant that the courts would look at the legal form of the relevant transactions as opposed to their substance, unless the documents were effectively a 'sham'. However, the general anti-abuse rule (GAAR) now places a statutory limitation on the 'Duke of Westminster' principle. This limit is effectively reached where the relevant tax planning arrangements 'go beyond anything which could reasonably be regarded as a reasonable course of action' (see 1.19). Furthermore, the UK tax legislation is also 'peppered' with so-called 'mini-GAARs', which prevent various relieving provisions applying where the transactions etc. are mainly motivated by tax avoidance.

Historically, tax avoidance schemes have broadly entailed arrangements or plans to avoid the payment of tax, which include artificial steps for which there is no commercial justification. In *CIR v Willoughby* [1997] STC 995 (at page 1003h), Lord Nolan said that:

> 'The hallmark of tax avoidance is that the taxpayer reduces his liability to tax without incurring the economic consequences that Parliament intended to be suffered by any taxpayer qualifying for such reduction in his tax liability'. He distinguished this from tax mitigation, which is evidenced by the taxpayer taking advantage of a fiscally attractive option afforded to him by the legislation so that he 'genuinely suffers the economic consequences that Parliament intended to be suffered by those taking the option'.

> This statement is analogous to HMRC's working definition of tax avoidance, which is 'using the tax law to get a tax advantage that Parliament never intended'

Emergence of the *Ramsay* doctrine

1.11   With tax avoidance, the taxpayer's objective is to have a taxable event without paying the relevant tax and without (technically) breaking the law. The high tax rates during the 1960s and 1970s encouraged the growth of a sophisticated tax avoidance industry, which relied on the principles that had been established in the *Duke of Westminster* case.

However, the House of Lord's landmark decision in *WT Ramsay v CIR* [1981] STC 174 marked the death knell for these types of tax avoidance arrangements. In essence, *Ramsay* applied to pre-arranged tax avoidance schemes that were largely of a 'circular' or 'self-cancelling' nature where the parties broadly ended up in the same economic position from which they started, apart from the intended tax saving and professional costs.

In *Ramsay* the taxpayer created a non-taxable gain which was matched by an allowable CGT loss. If each step in this scheme was viewed separately, the taxpayer would have created a deductible loss that sheltered the CGT on the gain. However, if the scheme was looked at as a 'whole', there was no loss since it was matched by a (non-taxable) contrived gain and on this basis the loss claim failed. Thus, under the so-called *Ramsay* approach, the courts could tax the relevant parties according to the real economic substance of the transaction. By looking at the scheme as a whole rather than its individual steps, the courts are able to negate the purported tax advantage.

Furniss v Dawson – extension of the *Ramsay* doctrine

1.12   The so-called *Ramsay* doctrine was further extended in *Furniss v Dawson* [1984] STC 153 and *Craven v White* [1988] STC 476 (and other cases) to tax avoidance transactions where the parties ended up in a different position from that in which they started. In *Furniss v Dawson*, Lord Brightman defined the relevant principles as follows:

'First, there must be a pre-ordained series of transactions …

Secondly, there must be steps inserted which have no other commercial (business) purpose apart from the avoidance of a liability to tax …

If those two ingredients exist, the inserted steps are to be disregarded for fiscal purposes.'

The courts also placed some important limitations on the application of the doctrine so that it could only be applied to tax planning steps that are implemented at a time when there was a near certainty of the end result. This is important since, if tax planning is undertaken where there are uncertain elements as to the final result, it should have a good chance of success.

Subsequent major cases, including *MacNiven v Westmoreland Investments Ltd* [2001] STC 237, have placed further technical refinements on the *Ramsay* principle, with some contending that they contradict the formulation laid down by Lord Brightman in *Furniss v Dawson*. In *Westmoreland Investments*, the end result of the scheme was that nothing had changed. However, their Lordships were not prepared to allow a statute to be interpreted artificially by the Revenue, merely because the taxpayer gained a tax advantage. In deciding whether a particular form of tax avoidance is acceptable or unacceptable, Lord Hoffmann opined that you have to apply '… the statutory language to the facts of the case. The court must therefore interpret the relevant statute and apply it to the particular circumstances of the case'.

More recently, the courts have clearly shown a disapproval of contrived and aggressive tax schemes, such as demonstrated by the decisions in *Drummond v HMRC* [2008] STC 2707 and *Underwood v HMRC* [2009] STC 239.

The *Ramsay* doctrine has also been employed as part of the judicial analysis to strike down a number of 'high-profile' film partnership schemes, which involved a number of entertainers and celebrities. In *Acornwood LLP and others v HMRC* [2016] UKUT 0361 (TCC), the Upper Tribunal (UT) concluded that the 'Icebreaker' schemes involving numerous LLPs failed. The LLPs were involved with many 'blockbuster' films, such as *Avatar* and *The Life Of Pi*. The scheme users claimed they were active members of their respective LLPs and claimed tax relief on greater losses than the amounts they had invested. While the FTT accepted the LLPs were trading (exploiting intellectual property rights), their main aim was to secure tax relief for its members. Thus, it ruled that most of the expenses claimed did not meet the 'wholly and exclusively' test and were disallowed.

The Court of Appeal dealt with a scheme that involved acquiring the rights to certain Disney films. These were then sub-leased back to a different Disney entity for a guaranteed income stream (*Eclipse Film Partners No 35 LLP* [2015] EWCA Civ 95). HMRC had challenged the £117 million worth of tax relief claims on the basis that no trading activity was being carried on. The court concluded that the economic reality of the arrangements was that of a fixed-term investment, although some contingent receipts might be received later if the films were successful. It also found that there were no decided cases that justified the view that Eclipse 35's activity was inherently a trade. The Supreme Court subsequently refused leave to appeal. Those involved in the scheme may have to repay between four and six times their original stake!

Judicial inconsistencies in applying *Ramsay*

1.13   In practice, the interpretation of the *Ramsay* doctrine has given rise to various uncertainties. This is largely due to many 'apparently' inconsistent decisions previously reached by the House of Lords and Supreme Court. Tax advisers therefore had to take a view as to whether certain earlier decisions can be ignored.

In *Mayes v HMRC* [2011], Lord Justice Mummery seemed to offer some simplification when he said that there was no need to consider cases before *Barclays Mercantile Business Finance (BMBF) v Mawson* [2005] STC 1. This approach was considered by the Supreme Court in *HMRC v Tower MCashback LLP 1* [2011] UKSC 19 to be too simplistic.

Nevertheless, Lord Walker seems to agree that the *BMBF* ruling should be the main starting point. But he also indicates that at least three cases before remain generally relevant:

- *Ramsay* itself as the 'fountain head';

- *MacNiven v Westmoreland Investments Limited*, which offers a more detailed discussion than BMBF; and

- *Collector of Stamp Revenue v Arrowtown Assets Ltd* [2003] HKCFA 46, which provides 'many helpful insights'.

Other *Ramsay*-based decisions on specific areas remain relevant to those topics. Thus, in relation to *Tower MCashback's* case, this meant the rulings in *Ensign Tankers (Leasing) Ltd v Stokes* [1992] 1 AC 655 and the Privy Council decision in *Peterson v Commissioner of Inland Revenue* [2005] STC 448 were relevant. These cases dealt with whether expenditure has been incurred for capital allowances purposes when the expenditure is provided by means of non-recourse loans or other 'soft' financing arrangements.

In *Greene King and another v HMRC* [2016] EWCA Civ 782, the Court of Appeal concluded that an artificial loan relationship scheme failed to achieve its intended benefit of achieving a tax mismatch within the Greene King group.

Purposive interpretation of the law

1.14 An important emerging principle is the need to look at the *purpose* of the legislation rather than taking a literal approach to its interpretation. In recent years, the courts have repeatedly decided to construe a particular taxing statute in such a way so as to 'tease-out' the wishes or intention of Parliament in the context of the relevant transactions.

For example, in the *BMBF* case the House of Lords said 'The present case … illustrates the need for a close analysis of what, on a purposive construction, the statute actually requires'.

Subsequently, the Court of Appeal adapted a purposive approach in *Prizedome Ltd, Limitgood Ltd v The Commissioners of Her Majesty's Revenue and Customs* [2009] EWCA Civ 177. The case involved an elaborate attempt to circumvent the corporate 'pre-entry loss' provisions. In finding for HMRC, Lord Justice Mummery observed: 'This interpretation makes no sense and cannot have been intended by Parliament.' Ascertaining the intention of Parliament brings its own problems.

More recently, the courts have continued to adopt a purposive approach. For example, in *PA Holdings Ltd v HMRC* [2011] EWCA Civ 1414, the Court of Appeal held that payments of dividends through a special tax avoidance structure could be treated as earnings. Interestingly, it held that although the group's employees received their bonuses in the form of (legally declared) dividend payments, this did not change their character. It also held that the *Ramsay* principle could apply to the arrangements and determine that the payments constitute employment income (see 5.3).

The purposive approach was also followed in the *Glasgow Rangers* employee benefit trust case (see 5.13A–5.13E for detailed analysis of this case).

Cases involving financial instruments

1.15   There have been a number of cases involving linked financial instruments designed to achieve a tax advantage on the basis that each instrument should be taxed under its own separate tax rules (which would typically give rise to a tax-relievable loss). The decision in *Scottish Provident Institution v HMRC* [2004] UKHL 52 demonstrates that such highly-linked instruments would be treated as a single transaction under *Ramsay*, thus nullifying any purported tax loss.

This principle was followed in *Peter Schofield v HMRC* [2010] UKFTT 196 (TC), which involved the artificial creation of a capital loss using four linked option contracts. The First Tier Tribunal had little difficulty in concluding that the four options should be viewed as a composite transaction and thus no actual capital loss arose.

Many avoidance cases tend to rely on the creation of an 'artificial' term in the legal documentation which provides there is a remote chance of the scheme not being implemented as planned. In *Astall v HMRC* [2010] STC 137 the taxpayer attempted to bring a loan note within the relevant discounted security rules by inserting a clause permitting its early redemption. The taxpayer's contended that since the amount payable on an early redemption would have involved a deep gain, it should be treated as a relevant discounted security. However, since the exercise of this option was very unlikely, HMRC argued that it should be ignored when construing the terms of the loan note. The Special Commissioner agreed, concluding that the position should be viewed realistically and it was practically certain in this case that the redemption right would not be exercised.

The High Court also agreed with the Special Commissioner's findings, confirming that the *Ramsay* and *BMBF* dicta required all relevant possibilities to be viewed in such a way as to restrict them to the 'real ones'. Although this can often be a very subjective issue, the courts usually tend to lack sympathy when looking at tax avoidance cases such as this!

The *Pepper v Hart* ruling – resolving ambiguities in legislation

1.16   In cases of ambiguity, *Pepper v Hart* [1992] STC 898 held that reference can be made to Parliamentary debate (Hansard) provided a clear statement was made by a relevant minister addressing the point under consideration when the legislation was introduced. (This principle might also extend to the explanatory

11

notes produced on new legislation by HM Treasury.) However, in many cases there are no clear ministerial statements – for example, the particular 'fact pattern' under consideration may not have been contemplated by Parliament/ HM Treasury. In such cases, the judges may then end up having to 'second-guess' the intention of Parliament!

HMRC approach to tax avoidance and morality issues

1.17   Over the last decade or so, HMRC has used various 'weapons' to increase the pressure on the tax avoidance industry whilst at the same time, strengthening its ability to negate tax avoidance.

Almost every year, we have seen numerous 'targeted anti-avoidance rules (TAARs) being introduced into key legislative provisions. The disclosure of tax avoidance schemes (DOTAS) regime, introduced in 2004, also provides HMRC with an early warning into tax avoidance schemes, enabling the 'unacceptable' ones to be swiftly blocked (see 1.20)

HMRC also seeks to provide a deterrent through the 'spotlights' page on its website – www.hmrc.gov.uk/avoidance/spotlights.htm. This provides HMRC's views about specific schemes and arrangements, which it considers are flawed as a matter of law and are therefore likely to be challenged.

HMRC believes that most of the marketed schemes currently being promoted would fail if challenged in the courts. This is backed up by some compelling statistics. In recent years, HMRC have 'won' around 80% of the tax avoidance cases that have come before the courts and tribunals, with many cases being settled before going to appeal (source; HMRC *Tackling marketed tax avoidance schemes – summary of responses* (March 2014)).

In 2013, HMRC also introduced a further weapon to tackle abusive tax avoidance arrangements – the General Anti-Abuse Rule (GAAR) – which is extensively covered in 1.18 to 1.19A. This was followed up in 2014 by legislation enabling HMRC to issue notices to collect tax in dispute in cases where the courts have already ruled against a similar scheme (see 1.17B).

HMRC can also issue advance payment notices (APNs) to pay the tax where they relate to a scheme that is subject to DOTAS or HMRC succeeds in counteracting the scheme following a ruling by the GAAR advisory panel – see 1.19B). Furthermore, 'enablers' of tax avoidance schemes can be 'hit' with stringent penalties (based on the level of fees that have been charged in connection with the schemes).

In summary, HMRC now has the ability to tackle anyone involved in the 'supply chain' of tax avoidance schemes that have effectively been defeated at a tribunal!

In the current economic climate, tax avoidance has become a major political and moral issue, with many large companies, high profile individuals and celebrities coming under intense media and public scrutiny. Indeed, the then

Prime Minister, David Cameron, felt obliged to comment that 'some of these schemes we have seen are quite morally wrong'. Similarly, in his Budget 2012 speech, George Osborne (the then Chancellor of the Exchequer) firmly expressed the view that 'aggressive' tax avoidance is 'morally repugnant'.

We have also witnessed some pretty scathing (albeit sometimes misinformed) coverage in the media on a range of tax avoidance issues. An article in *The Times* in June 2012 entitled 'Pay tax according to conscience, not the law' advised that '…instead of asking their accountants if a tax avoidance scheme is legal, the rich should ask themselves: is it moral?'

The acceptability of tax avoidance arrangements clearly invokes a wide range of moral and ethical judgements. However, the prevailing view is that schemes that are designed solely to enable companies and individuals to reduce their tax liabilities are not 'acceptable', even if the relevant arrangements technically comply with the 'letter of the law'.

Companies and (high-profile) individuals will also now look at the potential reputational risks and damage before embarking on 'tax avoidance' schemes.

Guidance for the tax profession – Professional conduct in relation to taxation ('PCRT')

1.17A   The various professional bodies (including the ICAEW, ICAS, CIOT and STEP) have now provided guidance on the professional adviser's approach to tax planning and avoidance (see *Professional Conduct in Relation to Taxation (PCRT)* – latest version published 1 November 2016 (effective from 1 March 2017) – see *www.tax.org.uk/professional-standards/professional-rules/professional-conduct-relation-taxation*).

The PRTC guidance states that 'members' must not create, encourage or promote tax planning arrangements or structures that:

- set out to achieve results that are contrary to the clear intention of Parliament in enacting relevant legislation; and/or

- are highly artificial or highly contrived and seek to exploit shortcomings within the relevant legislation.

The PRTC provides useful advice on what is considered (acceptable) tax planning and (unacceptable) tax avoidance, although it recognises that there is no widely accepted definition of these terms. The PRTC emphasises that it is not intended to stop legitimate tax advice and planning, and accepts that the 'borderline' will always be one of judgement.

FA 2014 'accelerated payment notice' (APN) regime

1.17B   In the *FA 2014*, HMRC intensified its battle against the tax avoidance industry by the introduction of the 'accelerated payment notice' (APN) provisions. Historically, users of tax avoidance schemes had been able to retain the tax in dispute with HMRC, thus giving a considerable cash flow advantage. This benefit alone has provided an incentive to enter into 'unacceptable' tax avoidance schemes. However, since 22 July 2014, this has been countered by legislation that enables HMRC to issue an APN.

HMRC can send these notices to those who have entered into tax avoidance schemes that have been 'defeated' in the courts. The APN requires taxpayers to make appropriate amendments to their returns and/or settle the amount in dispute. HMRC can charge penalties for failing to comply with the notice. Typically, an APN demands that some or all of the disputed tax is paid on account while the relevant tax dispute is litigated in a tax tribunal.

Furthermore, the APN regime also extends to taxpayers involved in tax avoidance schemes that:

- fall to be disclosed under DOTAS (see 1.20–1.33), or

- HMRC counteracts under the GAAR, following an opinion of the GAAR Advisory Panel that the relevant arrangements are not a reasonable course of action (see 1.19A).

The main problem with the DOTAS 'trigger' for issuing APNs is that many advisers have tended to adopt a prudent approach with DOTAS reporting. Consequently, many DOTAS notifications are being made on a 'protective' basis so to prevent the risk of penalties being levied for a failure to notify (see 1.23A). In *R (on the application of Dunne) v HMRC* [2015] EWHC 1204 it was argued that HMRC should not be able to issue APNs on the strength of 'protective' DOTAS notifications, but this matter was not considered further.

Anecdotal evidence shows that HMRC are mainly using the APN rules to deal with those using a registered DOTAS. However, HMRC made a serious error in 2015, when it issued some 2,000 APNs to those involved in the 'Montpelier' IR35 Manx Partnership arrangements. The APNs should *not* have been issued as the relevant 'Montpelier' scheme was not on the DOTAS register, and hence, somewhat embarrassingly, HMRC had to withdraw the notices!

Before issuing an APN, HMRC must issue the relevant enquiry notice/tax assessment. Once the APN is issued, the taxpayer must pay the tax in dispute within 90 days, or a further 30 days if the taxpayer requests that HMRC should reconsider the amount of the payment notice. Penalties apply for late payment. If the relevant issue remains under appeal, the legislation does not permit any postponement of the disputed tax.

If the taxpayer subsequently shows that the 'disputed' tax was not payable, HMRC will repay the relevant amount with interest supplement. On the other hand, if HMRC succeeds, it will retain the tax. The final amount of tax due is likely to be different from the amount demanded through the APN, so there will be a balancing payment.

There would appear to be no risk-free method of avoiding or mitigating the obligation to make payments under an APN. The APN does not provide any statutory right of appeal to a specialist tribunal. Therefore, the only potential challenges are to seek a judicial review or contend that the APN is invalid. Recent court decisions suggest that taxpayers are only likely to prevent HMRC collecting the tax demanded by the APN where they can demonstrate financial hardship as demonstrated in the *Dunne* case (see above).

The APN regime now provides the ultimate deterrent to those who still seek to engage in highly aggressive (and artificial) tax planning. Many argue that the extension of APNs to DOTAS schemes could be retrospective since it will catch those who may have entered into schemes a long time ago. From that viewpoint, these provisions are highly contentious but with public sentiment now firmly against tax avoidance, HMRC would contend that this is all 'fair game'!

The APN regime is proving to be a powerful weapon. HMRC reported in August 2016 that tax of more than £2.5 billion has been paid on APNs and more than 50,000 notices have been issued.

GENERAL ANTI-ABUSE RULE (GAAR)

Background to the introduction of the General Anti-Abuse rule (GAAR)

1.18   In December 2010, the government announced that it wished to go further to tackle tax avoidance. It invited Graham Aaronson QC to lead a study group to consider the merits of introducing a general *anti-avoidance* rule. His findings were published on 21 November 2011.

Mr Aaronson's main conclusion was that a narrowly targeted GAAR would be desirable and it should be aimed at blocking the most 'egregious' tax avoidance arrangements – ie those that are highly abusive and artificial... 'which are widely regarded as intolerable'. The study concluded that the GAAR should contain important safeguards for taxpayers who sought to structure their tax affairs on a reasonable commercial basis.

Mr Aaronson proposed that the GAAR should only apply to 'abnormal arrangements' defined as those which 'considered objectively [and] viewed as a whole ... have no significant purpose apart from achieving an abusive tax result' *or* which have '... features which would not be included in the arrangement if it did not also have as its sole purpose, *or* as one of the main purposes, achieving an abusive tax result'.

For these purposes Mr Aaronson's report broadly defined an 'abusive tax result' as any reduction or deferral of tax *unless* the arrangements were considered to be the result of 'the reasonable exercise of choices' afforded by the tax legislation *or* there was no intention to achieve the advantageous tax result.

In the Budget 2012, the Government confirmed that it would adopt Mr Aaronson's recommendations with the view to introducing a GAAR in FA 2013. However, the FA 2013 provisions go further than Mr Aaronson's original proposals.

First, without any explanation, the Government has rebranded the new legislation as the General *Anti-Abuse* Rule.

Second, the Government has extended the GAAR to a wider range of taxes than those proposed by Mr Aaronson. Thus, the GAAR applies to income tax, CGT, corporation tax, IHT, Stamp duty land tax (SDLT) and the annual tax on enveloped dwellings (ATED). However, VAT is excluded due to 'potentially difficult interactions with the [European] doctrine of abuse of law'.

GAAR legislation

1.19 *FA 2013* enacted the GAAR, which applies from 17 July 2013. Broadly speaking, HMRC can apply the GAAR to make appropriate 'adjustments' to negate the effect of the purported tax savings derived from 'abusive tax arrangements' [*FA 2013, s 206*]. For these purposes, tax arrangements' means arrangements, which, it would be reasonable to conclude from all the circumstances, were entered into for the purpose of obtaining a tax advantage.

However, such arrangements are *not* considered abusive, and therefore fall outside the scope of the GAAR, where they satisfy the so-called 'double-reasonableness' test.

This test is framed negatively and so would *not* be satisfied where the entering into or carrying out of the relevant arrangements

> '…cannot reasonably be regarded as a reasonable course of action, having regard to all the circumstances including the relevant tax provisions, the substantive results of the arrangements, and any other arrangements of which the arrangements form part'

For these purposes, the 'relevant tax provisions' are construed widely to include the statutes, any express or implied principles on which the statutes are based, their policy objectives, and any shortcomings in the statutes etc. that the arrangements are intended to exploit.

The legislation helpfully lists the factors that should be taken into account in assessing whether the relevant arrangements are 'reasonable'

- Is the outcome consistent with the principles and policy objectives of the relevant tax legislation?

- Do the arrangements include any contrived or abnormal steps?

- Are the arrangements intended to exploit any shortcomings in the tax legislation?

- Do the result of the arrangements result in an amount of income, profits or gains for tax purposes that is significantly less than the income, etc. for economic purposes – or a tax loss that is significantly greater than the economic loss?

Furthermore, where the relevant arrangements accord with established practice and HMRC has 'indicated its acceptance of that practice', those arrangements will not be regarded as abusive. It is therefore important to refer to HMRC's detailed updated Guidance dated 15 April 2013 (see 1.19A below).

If HMRC considers that the GAAR applies (ie broadly, the relevant arrangements are considered abusive), it has the power (subject to certain procedural safeguards) to do whatever is 'just and reasonable' to counteract the tax advantages arising from the relevant arrangements [*FA 2013, s 209*]. What is 'just and reasonable' would depend on the specific facts of the case and the relevant tax law being exploited. For example, this could mean denying relief for any non-economic or artificial losses that had been created.

Some consider the GAAR legislation to be too broad and lacking in clarity. The result is that the GAAR legislation brings added complexity; yet the dividing line between acceptable and unacceptable tax planning still seems to be as hazy as ever! Tax advisers will therefore have to exercise careful judgement when determining the 'spirit' of contemplated arrangements and their compliance with the GAAR, whilst seeking to obtain the best result for their clients.

HMRC's GAAR Guidance

1.19A Given its practical importance, various useful statements from HMRC's Guidance note are summarised below:

- The underlying premise of the GAAR is that the levying of tax is the principal mechanism used by the state to pay for the services and facilities that it provides for its citizens. All taxpayers should therefore pay their fair contribution.

- The primary objective of the GAAR is to deter taxpayers from entering abusive arrangements and to deter would-be promoters from promoting them. The DOTA rules have no direct impact on the application of the GAAR (see 1.20).

- If taxpayers need to enter into contrived steps to avoid an inappropriate tax charge (for example, so as to avoid a tax charge on an amount exceeding the economic gain), HMRC would not normally see this as abusive. Hence, such arrangements would fall outside the scope of the GAAR.

- The GAAR fundamentally applies to arrangements that are regarded as 'abusive'. Meeting the so-called 'double-reasonableness' test filters out non-abusive arrangements. HMRC indicates that the 'double reasonableness' test recognises that there are some arrangements which some would regard as a reasonable course of action whilst others would not.

- The legislation does not prioritise the guiding factors (see 1.19 above) for the 'double reasonableness' test. However, where the principles and policy objectives are discernible, these will normally be particularly important factors. If they were not – for example, in cases where the draftsman had not considered the relevant possibility – the main focus would shift to the second and third factors.

- Importantly, the GAAR excludes arrangements that are in accordance with practices accepted by HMRC. In applying the appropriate weight to HMRC pronouncements, greater weight is given to clear statements made in HMRC's published tax bulletins, internal manuals, or correspondence with certain representative bodies. Lesser weight is given to correspondence received by an accountancy firm that did not concern the relevant taxpayer. The nature of HMRC's acceptance of the practice would also be influential.

- Companies and individuals must apply the GAAR when completing their tax returns. If they fail to reflect the application of the GAAR when completing their return, there may be a potential exposure to penalties (see 4.59). For example, penalties could apply if it is reasonable for the taxpayer to believe that a 'GAAR adjustment' is required but they failed to make one. If there is uncertainty about the application of the GAAR, a 'white space' disclosure is recommended (see 4.57).

- The GAAR advisory panel plays a pivotal role in the operation of the GAAR. HMRC cannot issue a notice under the GAAR to counteract a tax scheme unless the relevant arrangements have first been referred to the panel for its opinions and a sub-panel has given its opinion. As at September 2017 the panel has issued one Opinion Notice (18 July 2017). This involved a 'contrived series' of arrangements for rewarding employees in the form of gold bullion and with an obligation to an employee benefit trust being taken on by employees. Unsurprisingly, each of the sub-panel members concluded that entering into and carrying out these arrangements was 'not a reasonable course of action in relation to the tax provisions'.

- The panel does not decide whether the GAAR in fact applies, and its views are not binding on either the taxpayer or HMRC.

  The panel also publishes reports on its work, and contributes to the development of guidance on the GAAR

- The GAAR is not subject to any HMRC clearance process. However, the Guidance confirms that the GAAR cannot be invoked where HMRC has confirmed that tax avoidance is not one of the main purposes of a proposed transaction under an advance statutory clearance procedure.

Similarly, the GAAR could not be used where HMRC has granted clearance under a provision that carries a wide tax avoidance test (such as in relation to an 'exempt' company purchase of own shares (see 13.46 and 13.53). However, where clearances have a narrow ambit, then HMRC would be free to consider the application of the GAAR to other taxes.

The full HMRC Guidance can be found at www.hmrc.gov.uk/avoidance/gaar-part-abc.pdf.

DISCLOSURE OF TAX AVOIDANCE SCHEMES (DOTAS) REGIME

Background to the DOTAS rules

1.20   Prior to the introduction of DOTAS there had been a growing trend in the 'marketing' of innovative aggressive tax planning schemes. During 2003 alone, the (then) Revenue effectively 'closed' down a number of fairly artificial schemes, including those creating tax deductions through the use of gilt strips, capital redemption policies and life-insurance policies. Such schemes were regarded as particularly 'unpalatable' and were closed as soon as they became known to HMRC.

However, there was a considerable delay between the wide implementation of such schemes and HMRC finding out about them. Under the normal self-assessment return processes, HMRC would not normally have received information about tax avoidance schemes until a long time after they had been implemented. HMRC also explained that large amounts of tax were lost simply because such arrangements were not 'picked-up' during their review of income and corporate tax returns (due to inadequate disclosure and so on).

The original intention behind the Disclosure of Tax Avoidance ('DOTAS') legislation (found in *FA 2004, ss 306–319* (together with supplementary sets of regulations) was to provide HMRC with an 'early-warning' system for new and innovative tax planning schemes, enabling the Government to block those which it deemed to be unacceptable. Furthermore, DOTAS allows HMRC to swiftly block disclosed tax avoidance schemes during the course of their implementation, which is likely to dissuade most potential users of 'aggressive schemes'.

Under DOTAS, tax avoidance schemes are given a scheme reference number (SRN). This must be reported on the tax returns of those using the relevant scheme, thus enabling HMRC to make a prompt enquiry into the case rather than rely on the more uncertain discovery assessment rules (see 4.57).

There is plenty of evidence to suggest that the DOTAS rules have proved to be a very effective weapon in curbing and stamping out the use of aggressive tax avoidance schemes.

1.21 The *FA 2014* strengthened the DOTAS regime even further by giving HMRC 'contentious' powers to deal with its backlog of cases involving tax avoidance schemes. Before these rules were introduced, users of tax avoidance schemes were normally able to wait until HMRC succeeded in a case against them before the tax tribunal. The *FA 2014* provisions removed this cash flow advantage by giving HMRC powers issue accelerated payment notices (APNs) to force tax avoidance scheme-users' to pay the disputed tax up front (see 1.17B).

Promoter conduct notices

1.21A The *FA 2014* gave HMRC additional powers, which are aimed at deterring clients from dealing with 'aggressive' promoters – often referred to as the POTAS (Promoters of Tax Avoidance) regime. The aim is to regulate and improve the behaviour of such promoters.

HMRC can issue a 'conduct notice' to promoters who meet certain defined 'threshold conditions'. They are laid out in *FA 2004, Sch 34* and include being designated a deliberate tax defaulter, a 'dishonest' tax agent, being charged with a relevant criminal offence (such as cheating the public revenue or fraud), or where the promoter is subject to disciplinary action by a professional body or regulatory authority.

The *FA 2016* also introduces further conditions that can trigger a 'conduct notice', such as where a promoter has been 'defeated' by HMRC in tax avoidance arrangements at least three times within the previous three years (*FA 2014, s 237(1ZA), (1ZB)*).

Only HMRC officials within Counter-avoidance are authorised to issue conduct notices, which can last for up to two years. HMRC will seek to use these conduct notices to obtain full details about a particular tax-planning product, its intermediaries and users. HMRC expects to 'resolve' most cases informally (agreeing acceptable standards etc) with the cooperation of the relevant promoter rather than issuing conduct notices.

HMRC can also impose behavioural conditions on the promoter, which can seriously limit the promoters' activities. If the conditions are breached, HMRC can obtain permission from a first-tier tax tribunal to issue a much more burdensome 'monitoring notice'.

Monitored promoters must notify their clients when they enter this category, with further requirements then falling on intermediaries and clients. In many cases this will make it difficult for the promoters to carry on in business.

Operating the DOTAS legislation

1.22 The original 2004 DOTAS rules applied to tax arrangements concerning employment or certain financial products, which were identified as high-risk areas for HMRC. Since then they have been substantially widened.

The revised DOTAS rules now apply to the whole spectrum of income tax, corporation tax and capital gains tax, National Insurance Contributions ('NICs'), and schemes that seek to avoid an Inheritance Tax (IHT) charge on transfers of assets into trusts .

Special DOTA rules also apply to SDLT (covered in 1.34) and ATED (see 12.32). The VAT DOTAS rules are contained in the 2015/16 and earlier editions of this book.

The DOTAS rules seek to ensure that a tax/NIC saving arrangement is disclosed where:

- it will, or might be expected to, enable someone to obtain a tax/NIC advantage (*FA 2004, s 318*);

- the tax/NIC advantage is (or might be expected to be) the main benefit/ one of the main benefits of that arrangement [*FA 2004, s 306(1)(c)*]; and

- the relevant scheme falls within at least one of the presented 'hallmarks' set out in the legislation (see 1.26–1.30 below).

The broad effect of the 'hallmark' tests (revised in February 2016) is to limit disclosure to those tax and NIC avoidance schemes that are highly innovative in the way they produce a tax/NIC saving. HMRC has confirmed that the DOTAS rules also operate for 'tax benefits' that are intended to be obtained in relation to legislation that has yet to be implemented.

1.23 Relevant disclosures must be made by the 'scheme promoter or introducer' (widely defined) within five days of the scheme being 'made available'. Because HMRC felt that many promoters were delaying their disclosure notification until the scheme was almost about to be implemented, an earlier trigger point was introduced. This requires promoters/introducers to notify HMRC within five days of the date the scheme is first marketed (even in general terms) to clients or potential clients.

In the case of 'in-house' schemes, where the people using the scheme have designed and implemented it themselves, the scheme must be disclosed within 30 days of it being implemented.

Most professional firms tend to adopt a prudent approach here. Thus, if a client *could* be advised about a particular scheme/arrangement (because sufficient detailed research or analysis has been done), then it is likely to be considered 'disclosable'.

Promoters are broadly defined as those who design, implement, or are involved in the organisation and management of, relevant tax schemes or arrangements made available to taxpayers [*FA 2004, s 307*]. Many promoters will be responsible for designing a tax avoidance scheme or making firm approaches to taxpayers with the view to making such schemes available for their use. Both UK and overseas based promoters are subject to the DOTAS rules but only to the extent that the scheme is expected to provide a UK tax advantage.

FA 2010 also added the concept of an 'introducer', who generally 'market' tax schemes or products (see also 1.25).

Promoters and introducers are generally required to register such schemes with HMRC's Anti-Avoidance Group (AAG) on the declaration form AAG1 within the period specified above. (The AAG is responsible for the development, maintenance and delivery of HMRC's anti-avoidance strategy.)

The registration on form AAG1 must provide brief details of the scheme, the type of transactions involved, the expected tax consequences and the statutory tax rules that are being relied upon. HMRC will then issue a scheme registration number (SRN) for the 'scheme' (generally) to the promoter.

FA 2004, s 312 broadly requires the promoter to pass the SRN to the users of the relevant tax scheme or arrangement (and any other parties that may benefit from it). In many cases, this must be done within 30 days of the receipt of the SRN from HMRC. The SRN must be disclosed by taxpayers using the scheme on their relevant income tax, corporation tax, or IHT returns. If no tax return is required to be filed or in certain other cases, the SRM must be disclosed on forms AAG4 or AAG4 (SDLT).

FA 2010 introduced a new requirement for promoters to give HMRC details of those clients provided with an SRN (see 1.24).

1.23A   Severe penalties can imposed for failing to notify a scheme under DOTAS. An initial penalty of up to £600 per day applies from the failure to notify up to the date the tribunal determines the penalty. If the tribunal considers that this penalty does not create a sufficient deterrent, it can increase it up to a maximum of £1,000,000. HMRC can levy a further penalty of up to £600 per day if the failure continues.

HMRC generally seeks to enforce penalties unless the promoter has exercised reasonable judgement in deciding that no disclosure is required or where the promoter can demonstrate a 'reasonable excuse'.

HMRC has the necessary power to investigate compliance under the DOTAS provisions, such as to make enquiries into whether a scheme is fully disclosable [*FA 2004, s 313A*] or to request more detailed disclosure [*FA 2004, s 308A*].

Providing details of clients

1.24   Promoters must provide HMRC with quarterly details of clients that have been issued with an SRN within 30 days of the end of the relevant quarterly return period.

The requirement to provide 'client lists' was introduced to address HMRC's concerns that they are not generally able to assess the extent to which a particular tax scheme has been used until they receive disclosures of SRNs provided with individual tax returns. Since promoters now have to submit details of clients 'receiving' SRNs, HMRC can quantify the take-up' of a particular scheme more quickly, enabling it to take swift counter-action where appropriate.

Following *FA 2013*, clients are also required to provide the promoter with certain information for inclusion in the promoter's client list. HMRC also has the power to seek additional further details from a promoter where the client is an intermediary rather than the end user of the scheme

Introducer obligations

1.25 Some accountants, tax advisers and other financial advisers sell tax schemes to their clients as introducers. In many cases, they will have been provided with details of a particular tax scheme by a promoter.

HMRC have the power to require 'introducers' (such as accountants etc) to provide the names and addresses of those who have provided them with details of a proposed or actual scheme. *FA 2004, s 213C* makes it clear that HMRC must first serve a notice on the introducer to provide the information. Failing to comply with the notice will give rise to a penalty of up to £5,000 (with daily penalties up to £600).

Summary of 'hallmarks'

Confidentiality

1.26 This hallmark applies where an element of the arrangements gives rise to an expected tax advantage, and a promoter might reasonably expect the mechanics of that 'tax advantage' to be kept confidential from other promoters. This hallmark also applies if the way in which the tax advantage arises should be kept confidential from HMRC (so that the relevant element of the arrangements could be reused in future).

For example, the use of a confidentiality letter would usually 'trigger' this hallmark, except where the scheme in question is reasonably well known in the tax profession.

This hallmark does not apply to small or medium-sized businesses where there is no 'promoter' of the scheme.

Premium fee

1.27 A scheme falls under this hallmark if it might reasonably be expected that a promoter *would be able to* obtain a premium fee from someone reasonably experienced in receiving services of the type being provided. This is a hypothetical test, so that it does not depend on whether such a fee is actually received. A premium fee would be one that is *significantly* attributable to obtaining the relevant tax advantage – this would therefore catch success-based fees and contingent fees. It is not meant to relate to fees generated simply by those taking up a tax-saving scheme.

New sub-categories have been added to deal with bespoke arrangements (subject to a £1 million minimum fee threshold) and certain collective investment schemes.

Standardised tax products

1.28   This hallmark is designed to capture what HMRC refer to as 'mass marketed schemes'. These are 'shrink-wrapped' or 'plug and play' tax schemes (giving rise to a 'main tax benefit') that are easily replicated. The scope of this particular 'hallmark', such as whether there is a tax product that is made available generally, is determined by various tests.

In February 2016, the scope of this hallmark was widened, largely because promoters had been resisting disclosure of schemes that contained minor changes for individual clients.

Thus, in its revised format, the 'hallmark' is met if it is reasonable to expect that an informed observer (having studied the standardised arrangements and having regard to all relevant circumstances) would conclude the relevant conditions are met. The aim is to look to the substance of the relevant arrangements. Thus, the key test is whether the main purpose of the 'standardised' scheme is to obtain a tax advantage or an expectation of obtaining one (*Tax Avoidance Schemes (Prescribed Descriptions of Arrangements) (Amendment) Regulations 2016, SI 2016/99, reg 10*).

Furthermore, after 23 February 2016, the original grandfathering exemption for pre-1 August 2006 standardised tax products is abolished, thus extending the scope of the hallmark.

Normal commercial arrangements and various approved HMRC schemes (such as EIS, SEIS, VCT, and approved share schemes) are exempt from disclosure unless they are part of wider tax avoidance arrangements.

Financial products

1.28A   The 'financial products' hallmark (introduced on 23 February 2016) targets schemes that contain a direct link between the use of a financial product and the benefit of a tax advantage. It uses an 'informed observer' test, enabling matters outside the legislation to be considered, such as commercial factors and HMRC guidance.

Having regard to all relevant factors, the financial product would be 'disclosable' where an informed observer would conclude that one of the main benefits of including the financial product is the gaining of the tax advantage (and satisfy either conditions 3 or 4 within (*SI 2016/99, reg 19*).

The list of financial products provided is extensive, and includes loans and shares. HMRC's accept there are numerous examples of non-abusive transactions/products that would be exempt from disclosure (see *HMRC – Technical consultation on draft hallmarks for Disclosure of Tax Avoidance regime – February 2016*) at 5.18 and 5.20).

Certain tax shelters

Loss schemes

1.29 The 'loss schemes' hallmark captures schemes designed to generate trading losses for individuals (who can then offset the losses against their income tax and capital gains tax liabilities) where they exceed the economic loss suffered. This hallmark applies where more than one individual is expected to implement the arrangements, and (since 23 February 2016) *one of the* main benefits of such arrangements is to generate a loss for potential use against income tax or CGT liabilities.

Since 23 February 2016, the hallmark also incorporates an 'informed observer' test (see 1.28). Thus, when looking at the arrangements as a whole and all relevant circumstances, disclosure is required where the scheme would not have been entered into had it not produced the offset-able tax losses (*SI 2016/99, reg 11*).

This was extended in 2010 to also cover schemes designed to generate corporate losses. Genuine business losses do not fall within the hallmark.

Leasing arrangements

1.30 This hallmark broadly applies to arrangements which include a 'short-term' plant or machinery lease for a term of two years or less, where the value of any leased asset is at least £10,000,000 (or where the value of all of the leased assets is at least £25,000,000). This is a complex hallmark, and the relevant detailed rules are set out in *Tax Avoidance Schemes (Prescribed Descriptions of Arrangements) Regulations 2006, SI 2006/1543, regs 13–17*.

Inheritance tax and DOTAS

1.31 The Government intends to extend the DOTAS regime to 'unacceptable' IHT planning generally.

In HMRC's consultation document (*Strengthening the Tax Avoidance Disclosure Regimes for Indirect Taxes and Inheritance Tax*) published on 20 April 2016, a draft SI indicates that two tests must be satisfied for DOTAS reporting for IHT (and Indirect Taxes). These are:

- the main purpose of the arrangements is to obtain a tax advantage; and

- they must be 'contrived or abnormal'.

There are a number of exceptions for mainstream insurance-based schemes. HMRC are currently considering the responses to the consultation document. If legislated, the main difficulty will be determining whether the relevant planning arrangements are 'contrived or abnormal'. HMRC has indicated that 'plain vanilla' IHT planning arrangements would not be reportable under the extended DOTAS.

However, at the time of writing, the DOTAS reporting rules only apply to arrangements that are designed to avoid Inheritance Tax (IHT) on transfers into trusts (but no other aspect of IHT charges).

These targeted IHT DOTAS rules are solely aimed at lifetime transfers into trust that are structured to avoid an IHT charge. The normal use of reliefs and exemptions, such as Business Property Relief, Agricultural Property Relief, and the 'normal expenditure out of income' exemption should not be caught. Similarly, planning that was generally available before 6 April 2011 is 'grandfathered' and falls outside the scope of the IHT DOTAS rules. However, the 'grandfathering' exemption is likely to be dropped under the proposed changes noted above.

Disclosing 'DOTAS' schemes

1.32   Given the tax authorities' wish to ensure that everyday tax advice and arrangements do not trigger a disclosure obligation, the relevant hallmarks included in the updated version of the regulations are now more tightly targeted at innovative or sophisticated avoidance schemes.

Where a particular arrangement has been disclosed under DOTAS and given an HMRC scheme reference number or SRN, this does not imply any form of acceptance or clearance by HMRC – so HMRC does not necessarily approve the relevant scheme or accept that it works. HMRC has said in their guidance notes that: 'on its own the disclosure of a tax arrangement has no effect on the tax position of any person who uses it. However, a disclosed tax arrangement may be rendered ineffective by Parliament, possibly with retrospective effect'.

Based on recent experience with HMRC, it would appear that to avoid a 'discovery' (ie an enquiry outside the normal time limit), full details of the relevant scheme or arrangement must be given on the tax return (see 4.57). In HMRC's view, following *Langham v Veltema* it is *not* sufficient just to enter the scheme reference disclosure number.

More recently, the *FA 2014* changes marked a 'game-changing' step in dealing with users of tax avoidance schemes. HMRC can now issue APNs to schemes disclosed under DOTAS, giving HMRC a substantial advantage in dealing with the tax avoidance industry (see 1.17B and 1.21)

HMRC is proposing substantial penalties for advisers who 'enable' tax avoidance and profit from doing so. As currently drafted, these proposals have been strongly criticised as being too widely drafted and could potentially apply to many professional service providers. Similarly, it is felt that penalties could be levied on advisers who give perfectly reasonable and legitimate advice, which may deter advice being provided in complex cases.

Legal professional privilege

1.33   There has been considerable debate on the extent to which disclosure is prevented on the grounds of legal professional privilege, which applies to confidential communications between solicitors and their clients for the purpose of obtaining legal advice. The House of Lords has recognised legal professional privilege as a fundamental human right.

The disclosure rules were designed to provide details about the relevant tax scheme and not the identity of the particular taxpayer or their circumstances. Nevertheless, in July 2004, the Law Society indicated that they would not be able to comply with the disclosure regime on the grounds of legal professional privilege.

HMRC's legislative response to this has been that if a particular disclosure would be covered by 'legal professional privilege', then the responsibility for disclosing the arrangements falls on the client/taxpayer. The client/taxpayer also has the option of (unambiguously) waiving privilege to enable the (solicitor) promoter to make the appropriate disclosure.

Stamp duty land tax disclosure regime

1.34   Following changes introduced in 2012, the SDLT DOTAS scheme now applies to commercial and residential property of *any value*

SDLT disclosures are made where there is a substantial risk of tax avoidance and broadly follow the normal direct tax disclosure rules (See 1.22–1.23).

The SDLT rules are effectively 'bolted-on' to the existing primary DOTAS legislation for direct tax. Thus, the main benefit of the SDLT scheme (or one of them) must be to obtain a tax advantage. However, the direct tax disclosure regime's 'hallmark' criteria (see 1.26–1.30) do *not* apply to SDLT schemes.

No disclosure is required where the SDLT scheme incorporates one or more of the main steps listed in the Appendix to the SDLT regulations, *unless* the scheme depends on *combinations* of steps or *multiple* use of the same step. These steps include the use of Special Purpose Vehicles, claiming SDLT reliefs, and transferring businesses as a going concern [*Stamp Duty Land Tax Avoidance Schemes (Prescribed Descriptions of Arrangements) Regulations 2005, SI 2005/1868*].

HMRC has taken particular interest in the use of SDLT sub-sale arrangements (which have largely been blocked in *FA 2013*). Consequently, the SDLT DOTAS rules were extended to certain 'sub-sales' schemes that existed before 1 April 2010. These must also be disclosed so that HMRC can find out who is using them.

When a scheme is disclosed, HMRC allocates a scheme reference number (SRN) to the promoter, who must issue the number to the client. Promoters will also provide HMRC with periodic information about those clients provided with an SRN.

Users of notified SDLT schemes must provide details of the scheme reference number or SRN on Form AAG 4 (SDLT).

Extracting Funds from the Company

SHOULD SURPLUS PROFITS BE RETAINED OR EXTRACTED?

Main issues

2.1   Family and owner-managed companies can freely decide how much of their profits should be returned to the shareholders or retained within the business. The 'working' shareholders will need to extract a basic level of income from the company to satisfy their personal requirements. Hitherto, the comparatively lower income tax rates tended to encourage companies to extract surplus profits. Companies that relied on bank borrowings or institutional finance may, however, have been prescribed financial limits on the amount of dividends and other payments which can be made to the owner-manager shareholders.

From a commercial perspective, the company's cash flow and working capital requirements must be considered when determining the timing and amount of funds to be taken out. Given that the extraction of funds (see 2.5) gives rise to a tax charge, which will be particularly expensive where large sums are involved, there is little point in taking them out by bonus, dividend, etc unless they are required by the owner-manager for their personal/family's needs. With the current high levels of income tax rates many owner-managers are likely to retain more profits within their companies. Within these constraints, some owner-managers may still wish to regularly remove 'surplus' cash from the business so as to remove it from any further business risk (subject to the requirements of the *Insolvency Act 1986*, for example, the 'two year' look-back period for 'preferential' or 'under-value' transactions under *IA 1986, ss 238 and 239*).

A further factor to consider is the potential double charge to tax, which arises where profits retained in the company are invested in appreciating assets. The appreciation in asset values could potentially be taxed both in the company and when the value is realised by the shareholders, perhaps on a sale or liquidation of the company. However, if the company is eventually sold for a price based on a multiple of earnings, the value of the shares may bear little relationship to the level of retained profits. Furthermore, the 'double charge' effect would not be a problem where the company's shares are to be passed down as a family heirloom on death. Owners of personal service companies are effectively forced to extract 'tainted' income and additional factors will come into play (see Chapter 6).

Entrepreneurs' relief (ER) and Investors' relief (IR)

2.2   Owner managers of trading companies enjoy particularly favourable CGT treatment, with a current 'exit' ER CGT rate of 10% (up to a cumulative lifetime gains, limit of £10 million). (The detailed ER rules are examined in 15.33–15.43B.) However, since 6 April 2016, all other 'non-ER' significant gains are taxable at 20% (except those arising on the sale of residential property).

The *Finance Act 2016* introduced Investors Relief (IR), which provides a 10% CGT-rate of the disposal of qualifying shares after three years. Like ER, the IR 10% CGT rate is subject to a separate £10 million lifetime gains limit. As a general rule, 'business angels' should normally be eligible for IR but employees and 'paid' directors cannot qualify. See 15.45 to 15.46B for review of the IR rules.

Retention of profits

2.3   With a current ER limit of £10 million, the overall tax costs of realising retained profits as a capital gain (for example, by liquidation or sale – see 2.4) have remained identical to the pre-6 April 2008 business taper regime (assuming the (cumulative) gains are below £10 million).

Retained profits only suffer corporation tax at the company's marginal tax rate and may ultimately be realised at low CGT rates.

The ability to reinvest profits within company structures at relatively low tax rates has encouraged many sole traders and partnerships to incorporate their businesses. For 2017/18, unincorporated businesses earning substantial profits will generally suffer a marginal 47% combined income tax/Class 4 NIC rate on their profits, regardless of whether the profits are 'ploughed-back' within the business or extracted.

All companies pay corporation tax at 19% from 1 April 2017 (previously 20% since 1 April 2015). Thus, the total effective rate of taking profits as a capital sum is 27.1% (ignoring the impact of any base cost, etc) calculated as follows:

	£
Profit	100
Corporation tax at 19%	(19)
Retained profit = chargeable gain	81)
CGT @ 10% (assuming ER)	(8.1)
Net realisation	72.9
Total effective tax rate	28%

If ER is not available at the time the retained profits are taken as a 'capital distribution', the overall effective rate increases to 35.2% (assuming a 20% CGT rate). The rates on retained profits compare very favourably with the current top income tax rates.

Taking profits as capital gains

2.4   Unless the owner-manager is making a complete, or almost complete, 'exit' from the company, it may be difficult to find an effective method of converting profits into a capital sum. Taking the profits as a capital distribution on a subsequent winding-up is not a realistic option if the business is continuing (see also 16.27–16.30). This means that the individual will have to sell their shares either back to the company or by way of an external sale.

Given the relatively wide gap between CGT and dividend tax rates, HMRC are likely to use the Transaction in Securities rules where shares in close companies are sold to a commonly controlled company, Employee Benefit Trust, pension fund, etc but not normally on commercially driven sales to third parties. However, unless there is *complete certainty* that transaction will satisfy the post-sale 'no-connection' test, it is recommended that the advance clearance procedure in *ITA 2007, s 701* is used to obtain assurance that HMRC is satisfied that the transaction is not driven by the avoidance of income tax (see 15.82–15.91).

If the company is likely to be sold, the level of its *retained* profits will not normally influence its sale price, which is normally based on a multiple of its post-tax earnings. With the relatively low rates of CGT, however, it is tempting to 'gross up' the price for the retained earnings rather than strip them out as a pre-sale dividend (see 15.105).

Taking all the above factors into account, a balanced approach between retention and extraction of profits will generally be required in practice. Ultimately, the decision must depend on whether the shareholders need the money for their personal requirements and whether they are able to obtain a better 'return' on the funds than the company.

Extracting funds or value from the company

2.5   It is possible to extract funds or value from the company in a number of ways, although (*a*) to (*c*) below are usually available only for those shareholders who work in the company as a director or employee. The most important methods of extracting value are listed below (the references indicate where a detailed discussion of the topic may be found in this book):

(*a*)   directors' remuneration or bonuses and paying salaries to other family members (see 2.9–2.37 and Chapter 5);

(*b*)   provision of benefits in kind and company shares (see Chapters 7 and 8);

(*c*)   pension contributions (see Chapter 10);

(*d*)   dividends (see 2.12–2.18, 2.25–2.27 and Chapter 9);

(*e*)   charging rent on personally owned property which is used in the company's trade (see 2.38–2.42);

(*f*)   selling assets to the company for value (see 2.43–2.45);

(*g*)   charging interest on loans to the company (see 2.46–2.47 and 11.9);

(*h*)   loans or advances from the company (see 2.48–2.60);

(*i*)   purchase of own shares (see 13.41–13.59); and

(*j*)   Repayment/reduction of share capital (see 13.60–13.60C).

(*k*)   liquidation of the company (see Chapter 16).

The overall tax cost of the various methods of extraction will vary and it is important to determine the tax efficiency for each method of extracting funds/value.

2.6   On an on-going basis, the working shareholders may well, in addition to drawing a normal salary, decide whether to extract surplus profits by means of a bonus or dividend. This aspect is considered in further detail at 2.9–2.37. In addition, owner-managers will often ensure that adequate provision is made for their future pension and that tax efficacious benefits in kind are provided. Owner-managers may also consider extracting funds through a loan account, but this too involves a tax cost.

CAPITAL RECEIPTS VERSUS INCOME RECEIPTS

Basic planning techniques

2.7   A purchase of the company's own shares, liquidation or sale of a company tend to be the most common 'exit-routes' for shareholders when they wish to leave the company, retire or realise capital value.

In the context of a purchase by the company of its own shares, it is usually possible to structure the transaction either as a capital gains receipt within *CTA 2010, s 1033*, or as a distribution.

Similarly, if the company is about to be wound up, value can be extracted by means of an income dividend if the amount is paid prior to liquidation. Amounts distributed during the winding up should be a capital distribution (liable to CGT) for the shareholder. However, where the liquidation is mainly driven by 'unacceptable' phoenixing to extract the company's retained profits at beneficial CGT rates, the *FA 2016* 'anti–phoenix' Targeted Anti-Avoidance Rule ('TAAR') is likely to apply. If the liquidation falls within the TAAR, the liquidation distributions would be taxed at dividend *income tax* rates (as opposed to CGT). Please see 16.30–16.30B for detailed coverage of the 'anti-phoenix' TAAR.

Comparing income and capital gain positions

2.8   It is particularly important to compare the tax liabilities under the income and capital route *well in advance* of these transactions in order to determine the most tax-efficient route.

For individual shareholders, an income distribution in 2017/18 will generally carry a tax charge of 32.5% or (where the taxpayer's income exceeds the £150,000 top tax rate bracket), 38.1%.

The tax efficiency of taking a capital gain will therefore depend on the shareholder's potential effective CGT rate (maximum of 20% with reduction to 10% if ER or IR is available).

Any planning steps which are then necessary, for example, to characterise the transaction as income, can then be implemented with minimal risk of an HMRC attack under the *Furniss v Dawson* doctrine (*Furniss v Dawson* [1984] STC 153) (see 1.12). The potential application of the GAAR may also be a consideration, where HMRC consider the relevant planning to be abusive or egregious (see 1.19).

BONUS VERSUS DIVIDENDS

Impact of National Insurance Contributions (NIC)

2.9   Although the working shareholders can reward themselves in a number of ways, the main choice often lies between whether to pay a bonus or a dividend. The high levels of NIC rates have meant that more owner-managers tend to draw a substantial part of their profits in the form of dividends. Profits extracted as 'earnings' (ie salary or bonus) are now subject to significant NIC charges. For 2017/18, the first £157 per week (or, if earnings are calculated on an annual basis, £8,164 per year) does not suffer employers' NIC. Above this 'secondary threshold', the company pays NIC on all earnings at 13.8%. Most P11D benefits in kind are subject to a NIC Class 1A charge of 13.8% (without any threshold).

For 2017/18, directors and employees suffer NIC at the rate of 12% on their earnings and benefits between £157 and £866 per week (or, if earnings are calculated on an annual basis, £8,164 and £45,000. An additional employee NIC charge of 2% is levied where the individual's total earnings/benefits exceed the 2017/18 upper earnings limit of £45,000. This means that a 2% employees' NIC charge arises on all earnings, etc above the £45,000 threshold with no restrictions.

For 2017/18, companies will still be able to deduct (up to) £3,000 from their first remittance of employer's NIC's providing the director is *not* the sole employee (see 5.5A).

For those owner-managers with the 'work till you drop' ethos, it is perhaps worth noting that employees' NIC ceases to be payable on their earnings after they have reached 'pensionable age'. This is currently 65 years old for men, 60 years old for women born before 6 April 1950, and 65 for women born after 5 April 1955 (with a sliding scale operating between those dates). From December 2018, the state pension age will start to increase for both men and women (see 10.39 for details).

However, employers' (ie secondary) NICs continue to be paid on an individual's earnings beyond their pensionable age.

An employer's NIC charge under Class 1A applies to the majority of benefits in kind, including company cars and private fuel. The Class 1A NIC charge is based on the total benefits taxed as 'employment income' under the *ITEPA 2003* rules.

National Minimum/Living Wage

2.10   Owner-managers will need to adhere to the National Living Wage (NLW) and National Minimum Wage (NMW) legislation. The NLW effectively replaced the NMW on 1 April 2016 for employees aged 25 and over. The NMW continues to apply for those employees who have not reached their 25th birthday. HMRC is responsible for policing the minimum wage legislation on behalf of the Department for Business, Innovation and Skills (BIS).

The NLW and NMW legislation only applies where an individual has a contract of employment. In law, the directors' rights and duties are defined by that office. They can be removed from office by a simple majority of the votes cast at a general meeting of the company. Clearly, if the director *actively* works in the business, receives a salary, and enjoys other rights accorded to employees, an employer/employee relationship will be established.

In contrast, an employee's rights and duties are expressed in a contract of employment, which need not be in writing and can be an implied or oral contract.

Due to the informal nature of the arrangements in many small companies, there may be some uncertainty as to whether an employment contract exists between the company and its controlling director. The question of whether an office holder is employed will clearly depend on the facts of each case. Where there is no explicit contract, the NMW and NLW rules are unlikely to apply, even where the director carries out a wide range of activities, which might include 'working in the company's shop'. In such cases, the work would be regarded as done in the director's capacity as an office holder.

Indeed, BIS confirms that if there is no written employment contract or other evidence of an intention to create an employer/worker relationship, it will not seek to contend that there is an unwritten or implied employment relationship between a director and his company.

However, a prudent course of action would be for 'owner-manager' directors to pay themselves (and of course their staff) sufficient remuneration to satisfy the requirements of the NLW and NMW legislation.

The current NLW/NMW rates are as follows:

Age	From 1 April 2017 Hourly rate
Employees aged 25 and over (NLW)	£7.50
Employees aged 21–24	£7.05
Development rate (employees aged 18–20)	£5.60
Young workers rate (aged 16–17)	£4.05
Apprentices under 19, or over 19 and in first year	£3.50

Dividends cannot be treated as remuneration for this purpose, nor can benefits in kind, other than the provision of living accommodation.

Employers that do not comply with the NLW/NMW will have to pay the 'underpaid' amount to its workers at current minimum wage rates. HMRC will issue a Notice of Underpayment (NoU) to start this process.

Breaking the NLW/NMW law can be an expensive business, since non-compliance is subject to penalties of up to 200% of the underpaid amount (with a 50% reduction if paid within 14 days). The overall maximum penalty is 'capped' at £20,000 for each worker.

The Government will 'name and shame' most exploitative employers, which may cause reputational damage to their businesses. For example, nearly 350 of the worst offending employers' were published on the government's website in February 2017. Compliance with the NLW/NMW should therefore be taken very seriously!

Determining appropriate amount to extract from company

2.11   Most discussions about profit extraction usually start by focusing on the amount available to be paid out to the owner-manager(s). This is generally influenced by one or more of the following factors:

- the amount required for future retention in the business (to satisfy future working capital or capital investment purposes);

- the level of the company's distributable reserves and 'free' cash flow;

- any provisions or restrictions laid down in Shareholder Agreements or a company's Articles, particularly where venture capital finance has been used;

- the desire to 'de-risk' part of the 'surplus cash' generated by the business by taking it out of the company;

- the shareholders' personal 'income' requirements and tax position (and the impact of the 45% income tax rate!);

- 'one-man-band' type service companies may be affected by IR35 (see Chapter 6) and 'spousal' settlement considerations in fixing the level of 'remuneration' to be paid out, although the House of Lords decision in the *Arctic Systems* case gives potentially vulnerable taxpayers greater comfort in this area (see 9.32–9.36).

Having broadly determined the appropriate level of profits that can be 'extracted' by the owner-manager(s), attention then usually shifts to deciding whether the amount should be paid out as a bonus and/or dividend.

Comparison between bonus and dividends

2.12   If the company pays tax at the small profits' rate it is nearly always beneficial to extract surplus funds by means of a dividend as the now relatively high cost of NICs is avoided. The substitution of dividends for remuneration is not regarded as an abnormal pay practice for NIC purposes (*Social Security and Benefits Act 1992, Sch 1, para 4(c)*). It is possible, however, that the National Insurance Contributions Office (NICO) may seek to challenge dividends which have not been declared in accordance with the relevant *Companies Act* formalities. If the correct legal procedures are not followed, it can be asserted that a payment is not a 'valid' dividend and hence must be 'NIC-able' earnings (see 9.2).

The recent Court of Appeal ruling in *HMRC v PA Holdings Ltd* [2011] EWCA Civ 1414 demonstrates that the judiciary may seek to treat purported dividend payments as employment income where aggressive tax avoidance schemes have been used (see 5.3 and 9.13).

2.13   The dividend regime radically changed on 6 April 2016. For 2017/18 the key aspects for owner managers are summarised as follows:

- Dividends do not carry any form of tax credit.

- Owner-managers have a £5,000 dividend tax allowance (decreasing to £2,000 from 6 April 2018), which essentially represents a 'nil rate' band for their dividend income.

- Dividend income represents the highest slice of income and is allocated to the tax bands *before* the £5,000 dividend 'nil-rate' band.

- Subject to personal allowances and the £5,000 dividend 'nil-rate' band, dividends are taxed at the following rates:

Total taxable income	Tax rate applied
Below basic rate income threshold – £33,500	7.5%
Between basic rate threshold and £150,000	32.5%
Above £150,000	38.1%

2.14   Some owner-managers may be tempted to extract their income entirely in the form of dividends, but it is often sensible to extract a reasonable level of salary. In any event, if the owner-manager has no other taxable income, it is often beneficial to pay at least a sufficient salary to maintain NIC records such that each year is a qualifying year for state pension 'accrual' purposes.

Various tax comparisons between extracting surplus profits as a bonus or a dividend for 2017/18 are shown in the worked examples below. The various factors listed at 2.26 may also influence the decision, depending on the relevant circumstances of each case.

Bonus versus dividend comparison – 2017/18

2.15   Example 1 (assuming a marginal income tax rate of 40%) and Example 2 (assuming a marginal income tax rate of 45%) below illustrate that it will often be beneficial to extract surplus profits as a dividend for 2017/18 (despite the recent increase in dividend tax). However, this is subject to the other factors cited at 2.26.

It should be noted that, where a company pays a bonus, there is an additional NIC cost – but corporate tax relief is given on the total cost of the bonus and related NIC, ie the company does not pay corporation tax on this part of its profits. On the other hand, a dividend is not tax deductible and hence profits earmarked for a dividend suffer corporation tax.

Example 1

2017/18 – Bonus versus dividend comparison (owner manager's marginal tax rate of 40%)

Greaves Limited is likely to have surplus profits available of £100,000 for the year ended 31 March 2018, which could be paid to its sole shareholder, Mr Jimmy, as a bonus or dividend. Mr Jimmy already draws a monthly salary of £4,000 (ie in excess of the basic rate threshold upper earnings limit), and therefore his marginal tax rate is 40%.

The relevant tax and NIC effects are compared below.

			Bonus		Dividend
	£		£	£	£
Available profits			100,000		100,000
Less: Employer's NIC –					
£87,873 @ 13.8%			(12.127)		
Corporation tax @ 19%					(19,000)
			87,873		81,000
Income tax thereon					
Bonus	87,873	@ 40%	(35,149)		
Employees' NIC @ 2% (rate on earnings above upper limit)	87,873	@ 2%	(1,758)		
Dividend:					
Tax	76,000*	@ 32.5%			(24,700)
Net cash available			50,966		56,300

	£	Bonus £	£	Dividend £
Tax and NIC liabilities				
Employer's NIC		12,127		
Corporation tax				19,000
PAYE and NIC				
(£35,149 + £1,758)		36,907		
Dividend tax liability				24,700
		49,034		43,700
Effective overall tax rate		49.0%		43.7%

Tax saved by paying a dividend = £5,334 (£49,034 less £43,700).
* Dividend of £81,000 less £5,000 dividend 'nil rate' band

Example 2

2017/18 – Bonus versus dividend comparison (owner manager's marginal tax rate of 45%)

Bonds Limited is likely to have surplus profits available of £100,000 for the year ended 31 March 2018, which could be paid to its sole shareholder, Mr Billy, as a bonus or dividend. Mr Billy already draws a monthly salary of £15,000 and therefore his marginal income tax rate is 45%.

The relevant tax and NIC effects are compared below.

	£	Bonus £	£	Dividend £
Available profits		100,000		100,000
Less: Employer's NIC –				
£87,873 @ 13.8%		(12,127)		
Corporation tax @ 19%				(19,000)
		87,873		81,000

	£		Bonus £	£	Dividend £
Income tax thereon					
Bonus	87,873	@ 45%	(39,543)		
Employees' NIC @ 2% (rate on earnings above upper limit)	87,873	@ 2%	(1,758)		
Dividend					
Tax	76,000*	@ 38.1%			(28,956)
Net cash available			46,572		52,044
Tax and NIC liabilities Employer's NIC			12,127		
Corporation tax					19,000
PAYE and NIC					
(£39,543 + £1,758)			41,301		
Dividend tax liability					28,956
			53,428		47,956
Effective overall tax rate			53.4%		48.0%

Tax saved by paying a dividend = £5,472 (£53,428 less £47,956).
* Dividend of £81,000 less £5,000 dividend 'nil rate' band

Shareholders paying tax at the basic rate

2.16   For 2017/18, where the shareholder only pays tax at the basic rate, their dividend income would simply be subject to income tax at 7.5%. This should still give a reasonable tax 'extraction' rate (especially where the £5,000 dividend nil-rate band is available)

Example 3

2017/18 – Dividend tax and £5,000 nil rate band (basic rate tax payer)

Terry's expected taxable income during the year ended 5 April 2018 is as follows:

- Employment income – £11,500

- Dividend from Blues Ltd – £15,000

Terry's income tax liability is £750, calculated as follows:

	Total	*Personal Allowance*		*Basic rate band*
	£	£	£	£
Employment income	11,500	11,500		
Less: Personal allowance		(11,500)		
Dividend	15,000			15,000
Dividend nil-rate band	(5,000)			(5,000)
Taxable	10,000	nil		10,000
Taxed at 7.5%				750

2.17　The above examples have been simplified to show the relevant tax that would be payable at relevant marginal rates. There will, of course, be many cases where tax/NIC is payable over two or more rate bands and detailed calculations will be required. With the post-5 April 2016 changes, dividends should still be preferred but will offer less tax savings than before.

As a result of the large 'gap' between individual and corporate tax rates, companies will become increasingly attractive as a vehicle to earn and retain income. Many highly profitable sole traders, partnerships and LLPs have either recently incorporated or are considering incorporation in the near future. However, the sale of goodwill of an unincorporated business to a company no longer qualifies for entrepreneurs' relief (ER) (for post-2 December 2014 disposals). Thus, the transfer of goodwill would normally be taxed at 20% (rather than the 10% ER CGT rate).

COMPANIES WITH TAX LOSSES

2.18　If the company has tax losses, the payment of a bonus will increase the tax-adjusted trading loss. If there is scope to carry back the loss against the previous year, corporation tax relief is effectively obtained. The rate of relief would depend on the level of the prior year's profits. If there is no scope to relieve the bonus by loss carry-back (or group relief), then it will be included as part of the company's carried forward trading losses and the tax relief is effectively deferred until the losses are offset against future trading profits.

Carried forward trading losses arising after 1 April 2017 are subject to more generous offset rules. In such cases, companies can offset their unused losses against profits from different types of income (and profits of other group companies). However, 'very large' companies may be subject to certain restrictions in the amount of losses they can offset (see 4.40)

Repayment interest would accrue on tax repaid for the previous year, from nine months after the end of that period.

In contrast, a dividend would not create an additional loss.

The 'bonus versus dividend' equation therefore depends, amongst other things, on the effective rate of company tax relief and the amount of any repayment interest.

WHEN SHOULD THE 'BONUS V DIVIDEND' COMPARISON BE MADE?

2.19   It is generally preferable for the computational 'bonus versus dividend' profit extraction comparison to be made *before* the year end. From the owner-manager's viewpoint, there may of course be a timing point regarding the particular tax year into which the bonus/dividend should fall (particularly if there is a need to avoid the top tax rate).

2.20   The position with bonuses is more flexible since it is also possible to make a provision in the year end statutory accounts and obtain tax relief in that period, provided the bonus is paid within nine months of the year end (see 2.22). In the vast majority of cases, such a provision must comply with FRS 102/FRS 105, which requires a legal or constructive obligation to pay the bonus to exist at the balance sheet date (see 4.5). In practical terms, this means that the anticipated results should be considered before the year end and an agreement should be in place for any required bonuses. It may also be preferable to look at the anticipated results of the company for other reasons. For example, this would enable the directors to consider the amount of any pension contributions which must be paid before the year end to ensure that tax relief is obtained in the current period. This means that reliable management accounting figures should be available.

DETAILED IMPLICATIONS OF PAYING A BONUS

Corporation tax relief

2.21   In the case of a trading company, the remuneration or bonus should be deductible against profits. It is very rare for an Inspector to challenge the level of remuneration paid to working director shareholders. The amounts paid to owner-managers will generally stand up to scrutiny as being a commercial rate, given their role in the company and the responsibility involved. In contrast, HMRC often seeks to limit the tax deduction for directors' fees paid by investment companies to a very modest amount (see 4.43 note (*i*)). In such cases, extracting funds via a dividend is likely to be more tax efficient.

If the Inspector challenges the corporation tax deduction for the remuneration and denies relief for the amount considered to be excessive, this amount will still be subject to PAYE tax and NICs. However, by concession, HMRC is prepared to refund the PAYE tax paid on this amount, provided the excess amount is formally waived by the director and the amount is actually reimbursed to the company (see *ICAEW Tax Faculty Technical Release TAX 11/93*). However, any NIC liability will still stand as the NICO does not apply this concession.

Relief for accrued remuneration

2.22   A special rule applies to remuneration which is accrued or unpaid at the end of a company's accounting period, such as a provision for a bonus. Such remuneration can only be deducted against the company's taxable profits for that period if it is paid within nine months after the period end [*CTA 2009, ss 1288* and *1289*]. The date when remuneration is deemed to be paid is defined in *ITEPA 2003, s 18* (this rule also applies for PAYE purposes (see 5.5)).

In the case of directors, the date of payment will often be the time when payment is actually made, or when the director becomes legally entitled to the amount (although the statutory definition also includes other events). In practice, HMRC will accept that a bonus is 'paid' when it is credited to a director's current account.

Unless a director has a service agreement, his remuneration can only be determined when it is approved by the shareholders at the company's AGM, which will normally be the date on which the company's annual accounts are signed. However, where appropriate, reliance can be placed on the decision in *Re Duomatic* [1969] 1 All ER 161 (applied more recently in *Cane v Jones* [1981] 1 All ER 533). This case decided that, where the directors agree in their capacity as shareholders the amount to be paid to them as directors' remuneration, this agreement will have the same effect as a resolution passed at the AGM. Consequently, where the AGM is likely to occur after the end of the nine-month period, it should still be possible to trigger a 'payment' of the bonus within the nine-month period by agreement of the director shareholders, which should be formally minuted. It will be appreciated that bonuses provide a convenient way of reducing a company's taxable profits after the year end.

2.23   If the shareholder director is fortunate enough to have a healthy credit balance on their loan/current account, they can draw amounts from the account during the accounting period without attracting any PAYE or NIC charges. The loan/current account can then be 'topped up' by a bonus following the year end and the exercise repeated next year.

The tax deduction rules for accrued bonus/remuneration may be used to obtain earlier corporation tax relief for amounts to be paid within the nine months following the year end. Provided the statutory accounts have not been signed-off, a provision can be made for bonuses paid (or to be paid) within nine months of the year end. Care must be taken that any such provision is FRS 102/ FRS 105 complaint. This would require there to be a 'present obligation' at the balance sheet date to pay a bonus. This could be evidenced by minutes of a board meeting held prior to the year end, or even by the fact that such bonuses are regularly made. A provision written into the accounts after the year end (which does not satisfy current UK GAAP) would be open to challenge from HMRC, since it could seek to disallow the deduction in the year. HMRC are increasingly looking at accounting and accounting standards as part of their enquiries.

When providing for accrued directors' remuneration in the accounts, it is normal practice to provide also for the PAYE and NIC (including employer's NIC) liabilities in the accounts to which the remuneration relates. If this practice is not adopted the amount would be provided gross and when the directors' final remuneration is approved (at the AGM, if not earlier), the net remuneration would then be credited to the relevant director's accounts. At that date, the PAYE and NICs must then be accounted for (*ICAEW Tax Faculty Guidance Note TAX 11/93*).

PAYE and cash flow

2.24 The payment of the bonus will, of course, attract a PAYE/NIC liability. PAYE at the basic rate (and higher rate, if applicable) and Class 1 NICs are normally payable 14 days after the end of the month in which the bonus is 'paid' or 'made available' [*SI 2003/2682, reg 69*]. If the director receives a relatively low monthly salary and a high bonus payment once a year, further NICs are likely to become due on the annual re-calculation (this is because the NICs accounted for will have been subject to the monthly 'upper earnings limit', as shown in 5.16 – Example 4).

If the tax due on the bonus was incorrect (for example, if the PAYE code was wrong), there may be additional tax to pay when the individual submits their tax return (at the latest by 31 January following the relevant tax year). However, provided the unpaid amount is less than £3,000 and the tax return is submitted early (say) by 31 October after the tax year for a paper return and 31 December after the tax year (if filed online), HMRC will adjust the PAYE code for the following tax year enabling that tax to be collected on a gradual basis over the next tax year.

With a bonus, the owner-manager only receives the net amount after deducting PAYE and NIC. By contrast, where a dividend is paid, the owner-manager receives the full cash amount and does not have to pay the higher rate tax until a later date. Payments of tax on the dividend are made in accordance with the normal self-assessment rules. This requires interim tax payments to be made on 31 January in the tax year and on 31 July following the tax year (based on the previous year's tax liability), with a final payment being due on the following 31 January. Where a regular payment of dividends is established, the tax may become factored into the interim payments. Some owner-managers alternate between bonuses and dividends to prevent tax on dividends being factored into their payments on account.

In some cases, it may be beneficial to defer the payment of a dividend from say March to 6 April or later, as this may defer the higher rate liability (particularly if the director/shareholder's interim tax payments are based on a low prior year tax liability).

The tax cash flow implications therefore need to be considered, which will vary according to the individual circumstances of each case. When interest costs have been taken into account, this may affect the 'bonus v dividend' comparisons considered above.

REAL TIME INFORMATION (RTI)

2.24A   Under RTI, details of payments of earnings to directors must now be sent to HMRC every time a payment is made. The report must be made in the form of a Full Payment Submission (FPS). Further coverage of the RTI system can be found at 5.11A.

With the introduction of the RTI system for reporting PAYE it is even more important for owner-managers to be clear about the status of all payments made to them at the time they are made. Furthermore, evidence must be retained to support the relevant treatment.

For example, if amounts drawn by a director (and debited to their loan account) are later considered to be a salary/bonus, they will not have been reported 'on or before the payment is made' in accordance with the RTI rules, which may lead to penalties being imposed by HMRC.

Care must be taken to ensure that amounts drawn by a director and debited to their loan account are *not* regarded as a payment on account of earnings, which would be reportable under RTI. HMRC will not consider such amounts to be earnings in the absence of evidence as to their exact true nature (HMRC EIM 42280). It should also be noted that HMRC appears to be making increased use of the rule in *ITEPA 2003, Ch 3* which provides that any personal expenses paid by the company should be treated as (advance) payments of earnings. If *ITEPA 2003, Ch 3* catches these payments, they would be subject to PAYE and NICs. For owner managers it is therefore important to place on record that overdrawn loan accounts are to be cleared by dividends or personally by the director and are not paid as expenses.

Under the RTI regime, many owner-managed companies have had to develop greater financial discipline. As part of this process, companies should produce proper *contemporaneous* evidence to support dividends, salaries and bonuses.

One sensible approach is for owner managers to develop an agreed payment plan at the start of the tax year. Assuming the company has sufficient reserves, it would be sensible to bring the loan account in credit by paying an appropriate dividend at the start of the year. The owner manager can then draw down regular amounts during the year (whilst keeping their loan account in credit). A one-off salary payment can be made in the last month of the tax year, which would avoid regular monthly RTI reporting. Consideration might also be given to applying for annual RTI reporting.

ICAEW RTI Helpsheet 3 published in April 2013 contains further guidance relating to the impact of RTI on directors' remuneration (see 5.11B).

PAYMENT OF DIVIDENDS

2.25   In the context of a family or owner-managed company, the company's directors decide on the maximum level of the annual dividend that should be paid, based on the company's annual accounts and general financial position. Their proposed dividend is then put forward to the shareholders (in many cases, the same or largely the same individuals as the directors), who vote (by ordinary resolution) whether to pay the suggested figure or a *lower* amount.

Dividends are paid proportionately to the number of shares held (of the same class), although it is possible for shareholders to waive all or some of their dividend entitlement. Some companies have different classes of shares enabling them to alter the level of dividend paid on each separate class. It is only possible to pay dissimilar levels of dividend on different classes of shares. Once the vote has been passed, the dividend becomes 'declared' when it is then strictly regarded as having been made for tax purposes (see 9.18).

Directors usually have the power to make interim dividends before the final dividend is made. It is, therefore possible to pay dividends on a regular basis. However, many owner-managers find it easier just to pay one 'large' dividend, which is then credited to their current account with the company, upon which they can draw through the year. In practice, HMRC treats the 'crediting' of a dividend to a loan/current account as having been paid for tax purposes.

Further detailed coverage of the procedures for paying and taxing dividends is given in Chapter 9.

BONUS VERSUS DIVIDEND – OTHER FACTORS

2.26   The 'bonus versus dividend' decision will often be influenced by a number of other factors, the main ones being set out below:

(*a*) **Pension provision** – In the past, owner-managers often enjoyed considerable flexibility regarding the level of contributions they were able to make. However, they can currently only enjoy tax relief on pension contributions of up to £40,000 in the relevant tax year (plus any unused 'allowance' brought forward from the three previous years) (see 10.25 and 10.25A).

The 'annual allowance' limit applies to both personal and *company* contributions. It cannot therefore be side-stepped by routing pension contributions through the company.

Personal contributions only rank for income tax relief if the payer has sufficient 'relevant earnings' since relief is available on up to 100% of their relevant earnings for the tax year. However, if they have little or no earnings, relief is always given on gross contributions of up to a maximum of £3,600. Thus, where the owner-manager decides to draw little or no salary, they will still be able to fund a personal pension scheme at a rate of up to £3,600 (gross) per year. It should be noted that dividend income does not count as relevant earnings.

Owner-managers will need to have a reasonable level of salary/bonuses/ benefits to make worthwhile (tax relievable) pension contributions. Thus, where additional pension provision is required, it will often be necessary to pay appropriate bonuses. The bonus would not attract any income tax if it can be sheltered by a matching pension contribution (made within the relevant limit). However, a personal pension payment would *not* shelter the employers' and employees' NIC liability on the bonus. These NIC costs can be avoided where the company undertakes to pay the individual's pension contributions (instead of the bonus). Although the company is discharging a pecuniary benefit of the individual, this does not give rise to a taxable benefit.

Detailed commentary of the pension contributions relief system is provided in Chapter 10.

(*b*) **Protecting social security and basic state retirement benefits** – Dividends do not attract NICs and therefore a certain level of remuneration is required to secure certain earnings-related social security benefits and the National Insurance Retirement Pension ('NIRP'). It is only necessary for an individual's earnings to be above the lower earnings limit (£113 per week for 2017/18) to qualify and, therefore, a small salary should always be paid (also possibly to satisfy the National Living Wage requirements – see 2.10). In fact, provided the earnings exceed the lower earnings limit but are below the primary earnings threshold (£157 per week for 2017/18) basic state retirement benefits can be protected without incurring any NIC liability.

(*c*) **Share valuations** – A history of dividend payments might increase the value of minority shareholdings for tax purposes. This is because the valuation of a minority shareholding may be determined by the expectation of dividend income. Share valuations for controlling shareholders are unlikely to be affected (see 14.38–14.39 and 14.50–14.53).

(*d*)　**Spread of shareholdings** – as shareholders receive dividends in proportion to their holdings, the amount of dividends received by each shareholder may not provide a fair reward for the working shareholders and may prove too generous for the non-working or 'passive' shareholders. On the other hand a bonus can be a problem where the company's shareholdings have become widely spread over time. A 'dividend waiver' may be the answer here, provided it does not create any 'settlement' problems (see 9.22–9.27). Use of a separate class of shares for the non-working shareholders might be a more elegant solution on a long term basis (see 9.28).

(*e*)　**Personal borrowing and other issues** – some lenders may not understand the methodology of profit extraction used by owner-managed companies and only focus on 'remuneration/salary' (as opposed to bonuses and dividends) when providing mortgages, loans, etc. Remuneration is also used to calculate redundancy pay and remains important for income protection plans. PHI cover can be provided to take salary/bonus as well as dividends into account.

EXTRACTING SURPLUS PROFITS – SOME CONCLUSIONS

2.27　The various worked examples in this chapter largely concentrate on the extraction of 'surplus' profits where a reasonable level of salary has already been paid. It is often considered beneficial to pay a modest level of salary. However, where tax-efficiency is paramount, there is no substitute for doing the relative computations to compare the combined effective tax rates (for the company and its owner-manager(s)).

Since 1 April 2015, all companies pay tax at the same rate of tax, which is 19% from 1 April 2017 (20% between 1 April 2015 to 31 March 2017). This is subject to limited exceptions – see 3.15. On the basis of effective tax rates, the payment of dividends should be marginally preferable. Dividends also offer the added potential of a longer deferment in the payment of income tax.

Where shareholders only pay tax at the lower or basic rates, dividends will invariably be more tax efficient.

However, the above broad generalisations may be overturned by various other factors. Thus, a relatively high bonus payment might be required to enable the owner-manager to augment their personal pension fund with tax allowable contributions (subject to the annual allowance limits). In certain situations, the payment of a bonus may provide a useful way of keeping a company outside the quarterly instalment regime for corporation tax.

In summary, family and owner-managed companies should consider a sensible combination of bonuses and dividends and, in appropriate cases, pension contributions. The precise mix would depend on the particular circumstances of each company and its shareholders.

REMUNERATION PAID TO OTHER MEMBERS OF THE FAMILY

2.28   As a general rule, tax will be saved if income can be paid to other members of the owner-manager's family in order to use their annual personal allowances and benefit from their lower marginal tax rates. Inspectors are likely to scrutinise salaries paid to members of the family to see whether they are paid at or above the market rate for the duties performed. Where the amount clearly exceeds the commercial rate, the Inspector will seek to disallow the 'excess' element on the grounds that it has *not* been incurred wholly and exclusively for the purposes of the company's trade. In practice, the agreement of an 'allowable' amount is likely to be negotiated.

TRANSFERRING INCOME TO THE SPOUSE

Income tax for spouse or civil partner

2.29   For the sake of brevity, but at the risk of appearing sexist(!), the following commentary (in particular) is couched exclusively in terms of the husband being the one who owns and runs the company and puts income into his wife's hands. However, the comments below apply equally to those situations where the wife owns the company and the roles are reversed. (The same considerations also apply to same-sex couples, either married or registered as civil partners.)

Under independent taxation, each spouse has their own personal allowance and personal basic rate bands. It is generally beneficial to bring the spouse in as a director or employee and pay them a salary, provided the following conditions are met:

(a)   the salary is taxable at a lower rate of tax (than that suffered by the owner-manager on his income);

(b)   this income tax saving is not exceeded by the additional NIC liability (see 2.39); and

(c)   the company is able to obtain a tax deduction for the salary (see 2.41).

2.30   *Extracting Funds from the Company*

In all such cases, it is recommended that the remuneration (or dividend – see 2.43) should not be paid into a joint bank account, but one in the spouse's sole name. The same benefits may also apply to bringing in a civil partner as an employee/director.

2.30   Many spouses only work on a 'part-time' basis. However, part-time workers also fall within the National Living Wage (NLW) legislation. Hence, the amount paid to the spouse (providing they are over 25 years old) must not be lower than the current rate of £7.50 per hour requirement (see 2.10 for further details). However, if the spouse works for the company without any remuneration at all, she may well not be an employee, and hence the NLW legislation will not apply as the relationship may be explained by a desire to assist the company voluntarily (ICAEW Tax Guide 7/00).

Universal credit

2.31   The 'Universal Credit' system replaces almost all social security benefits and tax credits system. (Please see 2013/14 and earlier editions of this book for details of the previous WTC and CTC rules.)

Details of the Universal Credit are set out in the *Welfare Reform Act 2012*. Universal credit for working people is administered and 'underpinned' by the RTI system (see 2.24A and 5.11A).

Universal credit replaces the following:

- Income-based Jobseeker's Allowance
- Income-related Employment and Support Allowance
- Income Support
- Child Tax Credits
- Working Tax Credits
- Housing Benefit

Universal Credit is firmly targeted at jobseekers and low paid workers and so it offers few benefits to most owner managers. It will supply a standard allowance plus additional amounts for disability, housing, children and other caring responsibilities. Claimants under the current benefits system are guaranteed to be no worse off under the Universal Credit system.

The amount payable will be restricted by reference to income thresholds for earned and unearned income at rates of 65% to 100% for unearned income. Most owner managers would have a withdrawal rate of 100% where they extract profits by way of dividends and thus are unlikely to receive any benefits under the Universal Credit system.

Spouse's NIC liabilities

2.32   The income tax benefits of giving a salary to a spouse are often reduced by the NIC cost. In 2017/18, if the spouse earns £157 or more per week (or more than £8,164 on an annual basis), *employees'* NICs are payable at 12% on earnings between £157 and £866 per week (£8,164–£45,000 per year). The first £157 per week is free of NICs. Contracting out is no longer possible from 6 April 2016.

When the spouse's total annual earnings reach the upper earnings limit of £45,000, a 2% NIC 'surcharge' is levied on any amount exceeding the limit.

For 2017/18, *employer's* NICs are levied at the standard rate of 13.8% for earnings exceeding £157 per week with no maximum limit. (The first £157 per week (£8,164 per year) is NIC free.)

An annual salary of up to £8,164 can therefore be paid in 2017/18 without any income tax or NIC liability.

TAX DEDUCTION FOR REMUNERATION PAID TO SPOUSE

2.33   The optimum amount to be paid to the spouse must therefore be carefully considered. Unless the spouse works for the company on a full-time basis, HMRC will require the amount to be substantiated in relation to the duties performed. Inspectors often critically assess the amount of remuneration paid to a wife in relation to the work she performs. It may be helpful to draw up a job specification listing all the wife's duties (for example, secretarial, certain administrative duties, etc) together with some indication of the time commitment. There must also be some evidence of payment to the spouse. Unsurprisingly, in *Moschi v Kelly* [1952] 33 TC 442, tax relief for the wife's wages was denied since they were charged to the owner's own drawings account!

If the wife is appointed as a director, then the legal obligations and responsibilities assumed in that position alone should justify a reasonable level of remuneration. Provided the amount paid to the wife reflects the work she *actually* carries out, the company should have no difficulty in obtaining a tax deduction. (Similar considerations apply to remuneration paid to a civil partner, etc.)

A further advantage of paying remuneration to the wife is that it can be used to support company pension contributions to provide her with a pension in her own right, subject to the spouse's overall package meeting the 'wholly and exclusively' requirement (and the pension payment being within the annual allowance – see 10.23).

A spouse could also pay tax-deductible personal pension contributions up to 100% of her salary.

The *Copeman v William Flood & Sons Ltd* case

2.34   Where HMRC considers the level of remuneration to be excessive, they will challenge it using the decision in *Copeman v William Flood & Sons Ltd* (1940) 24 TC 53. (Similar issues apply to the tax deductibility of company pension contributions – see 10.31.) This case enables them to disallow the 'excess' part of the remuneration charged in the accounts on the grounds that this element was not paid wholly and exclusively for the purposes of the company's trade (*CTA 2009, s 54*).

In the *Copeman* case, the Revenue contested the deduction for remuneration of £2,600 paid in 1938 to a pig dealer's daughter, for dealing with telephone queries. This would be equivalent to remuneration of well over £75,000 in current day values! The case was remitted to the Commissioners to determine the amount which should be disallowed.

Waiving 'disallowed' remuneration

2.35   If HMRC succeed in substituting a lower figure for the tax deductible remuneration, the wife would strictly be taxable on the *full amount* of the remuneration. However, provided the 'excess' element is formally waived and paid back to the company, HMRC will generally restrict the income tax charge to the *deductible* element of the remuneration (*Employment Income Manual, para 42730*).

If the spouse is also a shareholder, the Inspector may treat any non-waived 'disallowed' amount as a distribution, which should not increase the tax liability. However, HMRC will still retain any NIC liability.

Paying dividends to a spouse

2.36   If the wife does little or no work for the company, no relief can really be justified. In these cases, it is generally better to structure the shareholdings so that the spouse receives dividend income instead. Provided fully-fledged ordinary shares are provided to the spouse, HMRC is unlikely to challenge it now, following its defeat in *Garnett v Jones* [2007] STC 1536 – the so-called *Arctic Systems* case. On the other hand, if the shares issued only contain dividend rights (such as non-voting preference shares), HMRC will probably be able to counter the relevant arrangements, as they successfully did in *Young v Pearce* [1996] STC 743 (see 9.10).

Dividend-splitting may also be considered by those owner-managers affected by the 'top' (2017/18) dividend tax rate of 38.1%. In many cases, owner-managers will seek to pay their spouses part of 'their' dividend entitlement to avoid paying this tax rate on their dividends.

HMRC was very keen to introduce legislation to negate these types of income-shifting/income splitting arrangements as soon as the *Arctic Systems* ruling went against it. However, the Treasury seems to have lost the appetite to introduce appropriate new legislation to counter income splitting between married couples. It is recommended that any spousal dividend should be paid into their own bank account (rather than an account in joint names).

Following the changes to the dividend tax regime in 2016/17, spousal dividend planning still remains. For example, a 'non-tax paying' spouse could take a *tax-free* dividend of £16,000 (ie an amount equal to their personal allowance and dividend nil-rate band).

Most owner-managers prefer taking advantage of the 7.5% 'basic-rate' band. Thus, assuming spouses have no other taxable income, they could receive a dividend in 2017/18 of £45,000 at a tax cost of only £2,137, as calculated below:

	£
Cash dividend	45,000
Personal allowance	(11,500)
Taxable dividend	33,500
Basic rate band is £33,500 but	
First £5,000 – nil rate	–
Next £28,500 @ 7.5%	2,137
Tax Liability	2,137

Where spouses take dividends, they would have little or no relevant earnings for pension purposes. However, it is still possible for them to make annual tax-deductible gross pension contributions of up to £3,600 gross (£2,880 net of basic rate tax relief relieved at source), provided this can be justified in terms of their 'commercial' pay package.

Example 4

Salary or dividend for spouse

Mr Astle is the controlling shareholder of Astle Ltd, which is based in the West Midlands. His wife holds 20% of the ordinary shares in Astle Ltd.

Mr Astle is deciding whether to pay £20,000 to his wife as a salary (before NICs) or dividend for the year to 31 March 2018. She has no other income.

Mrs Astle performs secretarial and administrative duties for the company which should be sufficient to justify corporation tax relief for the salary.

	£	Salary £	Dividend £
Available Profits		20,000	20,000
Less Employer's NIC (13.8% on			
£18,565 – £8,164)		(1,435)	
Gross pay		18,565	
Less Employees' NIC 12% × (£18,565 – £8,164)		(1,248)	
Corporation tax at 19%			(3,800)
		17,317	16,200
Less Income tax thereon			
On Salary			
Salary	18,565		
Less PA	(11,500)		
Taxable	7,065		
Income tax (£7,065 at 20%)		(1,413)	
On Dividend			
Cash	16,200		
Less PA	(11,500)		
Taxable dividend	4,700		
Within dividend nil rate band of £5,000		–	–
Post-tax receipt		15,904	16,200

EMPLOYING THE CHILDREN

2.37　The owner-manager's children may also work for the company at weekends, or in their school/college/university holidays. The company will need to comply with the appropriate legislation and by-laws for employing children aged under 16. Children cannot be employed in a factory and those under 13 cannot be employed except for light duties in limited circumstances.

The National Living Wage (NLW) rules must be adhered to for children aged 25 or over and the National Minimum Wage (NMW) rules for children aged between 16 and 24 (see 2.10 for current applicable rates).

If the children have taken out student loans, then the company may be liable to make appropriate deductions from their salary towards repayment of their loan. No student loan deductions are currently required where the salary is less than £17,775 per year in 2017/18.

The wages received by the children can be paid tax free up to their personal allowance, with any excess being liable at the basic rate or higher rate, as appropriate. Once again, HMRC will seek to establish the commercial justification for the payment in relation to the work done by the children. Payments made to the owner-manager's children which constitute 'disguised pocket money' will be disallowed (see *Dollar v Lyon* [1981] STC 333). There will, of course, be cases where a fairly reasonable amount can be substantiated as a genuine trading expense of the company. For example, the author is aware of a case where a teenage son of an owner-manager was paid a justifiable commercial wage for trial testing computer games that had been developed by the business. In such cases, such amounts will clearly be allowable as a trading expense.

Under the current pension regime, pension contributions of up to £3,600 gross (£2,880 net of the basic rate tax relief contributed at source by HMRC) can be made for each child, even in the absence of any relevant earnings (see 10.30).

CHARGING RENT ON PERSONALLY OWNED ASSETS USED BY THE COMPANY

Rationale for holding property personally and tax treatment of rent

2.38   A number of owner-managers leave the trading property outside the company to mitigate the effect of the potential 'double-tax' charge and to create wealth outside the company (free from the claims of its creditors (subject to personal guarantees), etc).

In such cases, the owner-manager can extract funds from the company by charging the company a market rent for the use of the property. The rent may be paid under a formal lease agreement between the owner-manager and the company. If the property is jointly-owned, for example, by the owner-manager and their spouse, then the rent would be paid to both in the appropriate shares.

SDLT is payable where (and to the extent that) the chargeable consideration for the lease exceeds £150,000 (for commercial property). A 2% charge applies for chargeable consideration falling within the '£150,001 to £250,000' band, with any excess over £250,000 being charged at 5%.

In broad terms, the chargeable consideration represents the net present value of the future rental income, with special rules applying to variable and/or contingent rents (see 12.29). It is not possible to mitigate the SDLT charge by charging a low rent, since a deemed market rental value applies where the property is let to a 'connected company' (as will generally be the case). If the SDLT charge is prohibitive, it may be worth considering granting a simple 'licence to occupy' the property since this is an *exempt* interest in land for SDLT purposes. In broad terms, a licence to occupy represents a non-exclusive right of occupation so it is important that any documentation does not grant the company the sole exclusive right to occupy the property [*FA 2003, s 48(2)(b)*].

The rent paid by the company would be deductible against its profits (provided it represents a market rent) and the rent received would be taxable in the owner-manager's hands as property income (but no NIC liability would arise). The owner-manager can deduct, as property business expenses, the normal expenses of running the let property, including repairs (not capital improvements), service expenses, insurance, security costs and relevant professional fees. Interest paid on personal loans taken out to purchase or improve the property will also be tax-deductible (subject to the income tax relief restriction for interest costs which is being phased in from 2017/18).

Where the owner-manager has borrowed money to purchase the property, he would normally charge rent to secure immediate tax relief for the interest [*ITTOIA 2005, s 272*]. Clearly, if only part of the building is let, then only a corresponding part of the costs can be deducted as property business expenses.

Where personally held property is subsequently sold alongside a disposal of the owner-manager's shares, it may be possible to claim Entrepreneurs' Relief (ER) on the property gain under the associated disposal rules. Provided the owner-manager has 'ER capacity' after relief has been claimed against the share sale, a 10% ER CGT rate can be applied to the property gain. Since 18 March 2015, shareholders' must sell at least a 5% stake in the company to qualify for 'associated disposal' relief (see 15.45).

In such cases, the gain qualifying for ER would be denied or restricted where the owner-manager has previously charged a rent for the use of the property (see 15.45).

INTEREST ON BORROWINGS AND CAPITAL ALLOWANCES

2.39   In some cases, the owner-manager may not charge a rent, but will arrange for the company to pay the interest on their personal borrowings that were taken out to purchase or improve the property. Such 'interest' would be deductible in computing the company's trading profits as it represents consideration for occupying the property for trading purposes. Following normal accountancy principles, the company's interest payment on the owner-manager's behalf is counted as a property business receipt in the owner-manager's hands, but this would be offset by the owner-manager's actual obligation to pay the interest (subject to the proposed phasing out of full income tax relief (see 2.38)). (If the company does not pay rent or interest, the owner-manager cannot secure any income tax relief for the interest.)

Other allowable deductions include capital allowances on integral features and plant attached to the building.

VAT issues

2.40 Provided the property is used for normal commercial (non-residential) purposes, the owner-manager can elect to opt to tax it. Where the owner-manager is personally VAT registered, VAT would be added to the rent charged to the company (as well as on any service charges). An option to tax would almost certainly be required where VAT was charged on the purchase price paid for the property (or on any substantial improvements). Provided the election is in place, this will enable the owner-manager to recover VAT on any expenses incurred in relation to the property in their capacity as a landlord. However, it also means that if the property is sold, VAT would have to be charged on the sale proceeds (unless it was possible to use the 'transfer of going concern' exemption (see 12.34).

Provided the company is fully taxable (for VAT purposes), VAT charged on the rents would be fully recovered. Thus, overall, charging VAT on the rent is likely to be cash neutral whilst enabling VAT to be reclaimed on property improvements and running expenses.

Where the owner-manager is only likely to suffer minimal VAT costs, it may not be worthwhile to opt to tax (unless of course VAT was charged on the original purchase cost which needs to be recovered).

Extraction of profits via rent

2.41 The tax effect of extracting profits via a rent is similar to the payment of remuneration, except that no PAYE or NIC is payable.

Example 5

Rent charged to company for use of owner-manager's property

Mr Downing owns the entire share capital of The Downing Cross Company Ltd. The factory used by the company was, however, purchased by Mr and Mrs Downing in equal shares many years ago.

For the year ended 31 March 2018 the company was charged a rent of £30,000. Mr and Mrs Downing's claim for allowable property expenses were £3,000 each. They had no finance costs.

Assuming that, for the year ended 31 March 2018, the company's taxable profits before charging the rent were £260,000, the tax consequences are as follows:

	Company	Mr Downing	Mrs Downing
	£	£	£
Taxable profits before rent	260,000		
Less: Rent charged	(30,000)	15,000	15,000
Taxable profit (after rent charge)	230,000		
Less: Corporation tax @ 19%	(43,700)		
Post-tax profit	186,300		
Less: Allowable property expenses		(3,000)	(3,000)
Taxable rent		12,000	12,000
Company tax saving on rent			
£30,000 @ 19%	5,700		
Income tax payable:			
Marginal tax rate @ 40%		6,000	
Marginal tax rate @ 20%			3,000

Subsequent sale of property

2.42   If the owner manager subsequently sells the property, any capital gain will generally be taxed at the main current CGT rate of 20%.

Where the property is being sold along with an ER-eligible disposal of shares in the company, the owner manager *may* be able to obtain a 10% rate on any unused ER entitlement against the property gain under the 'associated disposal' rules (subject to any restriction for rent charges) (see also 2.38 and 15.45).

SELLING AN ASSET TO THE COMPANY FOR VALUE

Background

2.43   The controlling shareholder may personally own the company's trading premises. This means that the property should not be exposed to the company's creditors on a winding up, although in many cases, banks or other lenders will secure a charge on the property. Consequently, as far as the commercial risk is concerned, there may be little difference whether the property is owned by the company or shareholder.

Owner-managers might consider extracting a capital sum from their company by selling the (personally-owned) property to the company. The disposal would generate a capital gain in their hands, which will now generally be taxed at 20%. (Note that 'associated disposal' ER relief is not available for 'separate property sales – see 15.45.)

SDLT may be payable on the purchase by the company (see 12.25 for current SDLT rates). In such cases, SDLT would normally be levied on the market value of the property irrespective of the actual sale price paid by the company (see 2.45). The transfer of the property to the company may also improve the owner-manager's business property relief position for IHT purposes (see 17.106).

Care is necessary to ensure that the property is not sold at an over-value, since the excess amount could be taxed as employment income (or as a shareholder distribution) (see 9.10) [*CTA 2010, s 1000*].

CGT treatment

2.44   An immediate chargeable gain can be avoided by selling the property to the company at its original base cost (which will be the March 1982 value where the property was held by the owner-manager at that date). Although the disposal computed by reference to market value, the 'unrealised element' of the gain can be held over under the business asset gift relief provisions in *TCGA 1992, s 165* (which must be claimed on form IR295). This relief is not affected by any previous rent charges. By concession, it is not necessary to agree the market value of the gifted asset with HMRC. The 'transferor' owner-manager and the company must request this treatment in writing (SP8/92).

Where the owner-manager sells the asset at its original base cost/March 1982 value, the company will effectively acquire it at that amount (see 13.14–13.22 for the operation of CGT hold-over relief).

Where the asset is sold to the company at its original base cost or a lower amount, this will be the acquisition cost on the company's balance sheet. However, it is possible to bolster the company's balance sheet by subsequently revaluing the asset. The uplift in valuation would be credited to a revaluation surplus account within shareholders' funds.

VAT and SDLT

2.45   The owner-manager will normally be connected with the company within *CTA 2010, s 1122*, since they either control it in their own right or together with their family members. Consequently, the 'deemed market value' rule in *FA 2003, s 53* will apply for SDLT purposes, irrespective of the actual consideration paid by the company. The amount of SDLT payable on the acquisition of the property by the company will therefore depend on its market value (which is treated as the 'chargeable consideration' – see 12.28). However, if the property was previously owned by a 'connected' family partnership, the special partnership SDLT provisions take precedence over the deemed 'market value' rule, which may result in a reduction or elimination of the SDLT charge.

The SDLT chargeable consideration normally includes any VAT chargeable on the sale and it appears that HMRC requires any potential VAT to be added to the 'deemed' market value consideration for these purposes.

Where the property is subject to a VAT option to tax (see 2.40), the owner-manager will need to charge VAT on the purchase price (which is normally recoverable by the company). Some care is required over the timing of the transaction to ensure that the company is able to recover the input VAT before it is paid over by the owner-manager. Although the property may have been previously let to the company at a commercial rent, the sale cannot be treated as a transfer of a going concern since the same letting business would not be carried on by the company (the property would then become 'owner-occupied').

CHARGING INTEREST ON LOANS TO THE COMPANY

Commercial implications

2.46   Where owner-managers make a loan to the company or have a credit balance on their current account, there is nothing to stop them charging the company with interest on the loan. The interest rate charged should be at a commercial rate, which (depending on the company's financial position and creditworthiness) could be several base points above the bank base lending rate. This would recognise the 'risk' element of non-recovery if the company gets into financial difficulty, although it may be possible to secure the lending (for example) against the company's property. If the interest charged by a shareholder-director materially exceeds a commercial rate, HMRC may seek to treat the 'excess' amount as a salary (seeking PAYE and NIC) or dividend distribution.

ACCOUNTING FOR OWNER MANAGER'S LOAN TO COMPANY

2.46A   FRS 102 requires all financing transactions to be accounted for on a consistent basis. Consequently, where owner managers make an interest-free or below market interest loan to 'their' companies, this is seen as giving additional financial benefits to the company as compared with arm's length borrowing transactions.

Loans with a fixed repayment term (of longer than 12 months) are shown as a non-current liability on the balance sheet. Unless the company is 'small' (see 2.46B below), FRS 102 requires interest-free loans (or loans below commercial interest rates), to be valued at their amortised cost i.e. the present value of the future payments discounted at a market rate of interest for a similar debt instrument. Consequently, the loan must be discounted to its present value. In subsequent periods, the interest is unwound by debiting the profit and loss account.

This treatment produces an initial gain and notional finance charges for accounting purposes, which are dealt with through the profit and loss account. There is an exception if the loan is provided from an owner manager, when the initial gain is recognised as a capital contribution from the owner manager. This reflects the economic substance of the transaction and would be recorded with shareholders 'capital'.

For loans made in accounting periods starting *after 31 December 2015,* the initial gain and the subsequent notional interest adjustments are completely ignored for tax (*CTA 2009, s 446A*).

These accounting complications do not arise where the loan is repayable on demand *or* where interest is charged at a commercial rate.

2.46B   Different rules apply where the company is 'small'. For these purposes, a company is 'small' (for accounting periods starting after 31 December 2015), if it falls below at *least two* of the following thresholds for the current/previous year or the previous two years (or for the first year of incorporation):

Turnover	£10.2 million	For 12 months or, where appropriate, pro-rata
Total gross assets	£5.1 million	
Employees	50	Monthly average of employees

* Parent companies of a group must meet at least two of the above 'net' basis limits *and* turnover (£12.2 million) and gross assets (£6.2 million) on a 'gross' basis (ie without eliminating intra-group transactions).

Where a company is small, it can opt to account under FRS 105 which does not require the above 'valuation' treatment.

However, many small companies have adopted FRS 102. Thankfully, in May 2017, the Financial Reporting Council amended FRS 102 enabling *small companies* to report shareholder loans (or loans from any close family member of a shareholder) to be reported at their transaction value (as opposed to the present value)!

Company's tax deduction for interest

2.47   Under the 'loan relationship' rules, the company normally obtains relief for interest charged in its accounts on an accruals basis, ie on the amount charged against its profits. However, any loan to a close company from an individual shareholder (or an associate of a shareholder) is subject to the 'late interest' rule (see 3.12 for definition of a close company). (Although the *Finance Act 2015* repealed much of the late interest rules, they still apply for loans from owner managers and other individual shareholders.)

Under these rules, the corporate tax deduction for any interest that remains unpaid more than 12 months after the accounting period end, is deferred until the interest is actually paid [*CTA 2009, ss 373* and *375*].

A close company therefore only gets relief for the interest on a loan from its owner-manager on an accruals basis provided it is paid in, or within 12 months after the end of, the relevant accounting period.

If the period of the loan exceeds (or can be extended beyond) one year, the interest would be treated as 'annual interest'. Since the interest is paid to an individual, the company must deduct lower rate tax (of 20%) at source when the interest is paid. (Only interest on bank and building society loans can be paid 'gross' from 6 April 2016.) This interest is reported and paid over to HMRC on Form CT 61. The recipient shareholder-director is taxed on the ('grossed up') interest *received* (with credit being given for any tax deducted at source). The interest does not constitute earnings and therefore no NICs are payable.

In some cases, it may be possible to secure a timing advantage by exploiting the late interest rule within the constraints of the rules. For example, a company could accrue interest on an owner-manager's loan account in its accounting period ended 31 March 2018 with the interest being paid in (say) June 2018. Thus, the interest would still be deductible against the company's profits for the year ended 31 March 2018 (with the benefit of the tax reduction being obtained on 1 January 2019). On the other hand, the recipient would be taxed on a 'received' basis in 2018/19, with the income tax liability being payable on 31 January 2020.

Example 6

Charging interest on a director's loan account

Mr Cresswell is a 75% shareholder of Aaron 3 Ltd. Over the years, he has ploughed back most of his dividend income to provide additional working capital for the company.

During the year ended 31 March 2018, the balance outstanding on his loan account with the company was £300,000 on which he charged interest at 8% per year.

The company's taxable profits (*before* charging interest on Mr Cresswell's shareholder loan account) for the year ended 31 March 2018 were £780,000.

The tax position for the company and Mr Cresswell is as follows:

Year ended 31 March 2018	
Company	£
Taxable profits before interest	780,000
Less: Interest charge	
£300,000 × 8% =	(24,000)
Taxable profit after interest charge	756,000
Corporation tax @ 19%	(143,640)
Profit after tax	612,360
Company tax saving on interest	
£24,000 @ 19%	£4,560

The company will only obtain tax relief in the year ended 31 March 2018 provided the interest is actually paid to Mr Cresswell by 31 March 2019. Relief will not be given if the interest is simply 'rolled-up' as a credit to his loan account and remains outstanding at 31 March 2019.

Mr Cresswell	
Interest received net of tax deducted by company	
£24,000 less £4,800 (ie 20% × £24,000)	19,200
Less: Income tax payable	
£24,000 @ (say) 40% = £9,600 less £4,800 (tax deducted at source by company)	(4,800)
Net amount received	14,400

LOANS FROM THE COMPANY

Companies Act restriction

2.48   Since 1 October 2007 private companies have been able to make loans to directors (provided they have been approved by shareholders) [*CA 2006, s 197*]. Loans to those connected with the director are also subject to the same 'shareholder approval' rules. (Connected persons under the *CA 2006* include spouses, minor and adult children, parents, and so on.)

The *CA 2006* does not require any approval for small loans/quasi-loans (£10,000) and minor credit transactions (£15,000).

If the company fails to obtain the required resolution of its shareholders, the loan is voidable under *CA 2006, s 213*. This means that the company could rescind the loan and recoup its money.

Scope of *CTA 2010, s 455* charge

2.49   Strictly, the *CTA 2010, s 455* charge only arises on loans made to 'participators' (invariably shareholders) of a close company, and the vast majority of owner-managed companies will be 'close' for these purposes (see 1.3).

Consequently, owner managers will normally be subject to a *CTA 2010, s 455* charge of 32.5% (25% for pre-6 April 2016 loans) where the company makes a loan or advance to them which is not repaid within nine months of the company's year-end (see 2.58).

The charge can also apply where a loan is made to an 'associate' of the shareholder, such as a spouse, parent, grandparent, child, grandchild, brother or sister, as well as a business partner [*CTA 2010, s 448(2)*].

For FRS 102-related accounting issues for (overdrawn) directors' loan accounts, see 2.56 and 2.57).

Changes introduced in *FA 2013* have widened the scope of *s 455* in relation to loans made to 'related' partnerships and trusts after 19 March 2013 (see 2.56A).

Furthermore, *FA 2013* also introduced:

• special rules to deal with 'bed and breakfasting arrangements (see 2.63A); and

• an anti-avoidance charge on 'benefits' enjoyed by shareholders (under arrangements that would not otherwise be caught by *CTA 2010, s 455*) – see 2.64.

There is a separate rule which deems a *CTA 2010, s 455* liability to arise where a participator (or associate) incurs a debt to the company – for example, where the shareholder buys a 'personal' asset on credit in the company's name [*CTA 2010, s 455(4)*]. This particular trap can also occur with management charges that remain due to a 'parallel' partnership service company (for longer than six months (see exemption (*b*) below)). Any debt incurred by the partnership would fall within *CTA 2010, s 455(4)* (see *Grant v Watton; Andrew Grant Services Ltd v Watton* [1999] STC 330).

There are various exemptions from the *s 455* tax liability, but they are of little assistance to most family and owner-managed companies:

(*a*) loans up to £15,000 in total are exempt where the borrower works full time for the company and does not own more than 5% of the ordinary share capital [*CTA 2010, s 456(4)*];

(*b*) indirect loans involving the supply of goods on credit by the close company are exempt provided this is made in the normal course of trade (except where the credit given exceeds six months) [*CTA 2010, s 456(2)*];

(*c*) the tax charge does not apply where the company is a lending institution which makes the loan or advance in the ordinary course of its business [*CTA 2010, s 456(1)*]. HMRC only regards this exemption as being available where the company is carrying on the business of money lending and this is part of its general business activities.

Although *CTA 2010, s 455* is generally regarded as a 'deposit' tax (since it is repayable when the loan/advance is repaid), it is still treated as 'an amount of corporation tax' and thus is liable to interest and penalties in the normal way (see 4.59–4.63). It is therefore important that all *CTA 2010, s 455* loans are disclosed on the CT 600 return, even if the relevant tax liability is discharged by repayment of the loan within nine months of the company's year-end (see 2.64A).

Loans to 'related' trusts and partnerships/LLPs

2.50 A *CTA 2010, s 455* charge will now firmly catch loans made to the trustees of a settlement in which at least one of the trustees or beneficiaries (actual or potential) is a participator (or an associate of an individual of a participator).

FA 2013 ensures that loans made to a trust are caught by *CTA 2010, s 455*, irrespective of whether the trust holds shares in the company. All that is required is that either:

● (at least) one trustee; or

● a beneficiary of the trust

is a shareholder of the 'lending' company. .

For loans made after 19 March 2013, the *FA 2013* confirms that a loan or advance to a partnership/LLP in which *at least one* participator (or their associate) is a partner/member is caught by *CTA 2010, s 455*. Furthermore, the new *CTA 2010, s 455(1)(c)* also catches loans made to a partnership/LLP that includes at least one corporate partner/member. A *s 455* charge can therefore easily apply where there is no significant overlap between the company's shareholders and the partners/members.

Unfortunately, the *FA 2013* provisions do not include any 'commercial purpose' exemption, which had been widely called for. *CTA 2010, s 455* will therefore apply to commercially based loan arrangements, such as where a 'related' close company makes a loan to a property development LLP to fund a new development.

Partners or members often inject funding into the partnership/LLP through their capital accounts, which reflects the nature of their investment or proprietorial interest in the relevant firm. Since partners do not have a right to demand repayment of their capital account, many would strongly argue that this cannot be viewed as a 'loan or advance' within the meaning of *CTA 2010, 455(1)(c)*. Consequently, where a corporate partner/member makes a capital contribution to a partnership/LLP, it should *not* be subject to a *CTA 2010, s 455* charge.

Example 7

Application of *CTA 2010, s 455* to loans made to partnerships/LLPs

Mr Allen is a 40% shareholder in Gills Ltd and a 50% member of Allen LLP, as shown below:

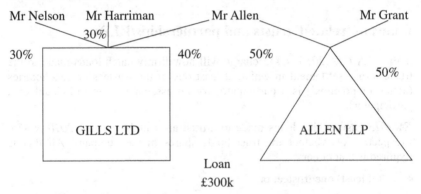

In June 2017 Gills Ltd made a loan of £300,000 to Allen LLP to provide additional working capital.

The loan of £300,000 to Allen LLP would be caught by *s 455*. This is because Mr Allen is both a partner (member) of the LLP and a participator in the 'lending' company (Gills Ltd).

Beneficial loan charge

2.51 Since owner managers will also be within the scope of the directors'/ employment/benefit, any loan made to them by the company will also fall within the scope of the beneficial loan provisions. Thus, if the company does not charge any interest on the loan (or the interest charge is less than the official rate), a taxable benefit will arise on the 'interest' benefit [*ITEPA 2003, s 175*]. These provisions are fully explained at 7.60.

Mechanics of *CTA 2010, s 455* charge

2.52   The aim of this legislation is to levy tax on what would otherwise be an easy method of extracting cash from the close company on a tax-free basis. *CTA 2010, s 455* requires the company to account for tax at the rate of 32.5% on the loan/advance. For loans/advances made before 6 April 2016, *CTA 2010, s 455* tax is charged at 25%.

The *CTA 2010, s 455* tax therefore represents a stand-alone charge which is deposited with HMRC. If the loan or overdrawn account is repaid in whole or in part (or is released (see 2.64)), the appropriate portion of the *CTA 2010, s 455* tax is discharged or refunded [*CTA 2010, s 458(2)*]. Any repayment from HMRC must be claimed within four years from the end of the *financial year* in which the loan is repaid/released.

For companies that are not subject to the Quarterly Instalment Payment (QIP) regime, the *CTA 2010, s 455* liability falls due nine months after the end of their company's accounting period (in line with their normal due date for payment of tax). However, if the company pays its tax under the QIP regime, any (undischarged) *CTA 2010, s 455* liability must be factored into its instalment payments (see 4.50–4.53).

Some owner-managers may wish to consider extracting funds from company by making a substantial loan to mitigate their income tax liabilities. There will be a one-off *CTA 2010, s 455* charge equal to 32.5% (25% for pre-6 April 2016 loans/advances) and an annual employment benefit charge based on the official rate of interest.

Thus, the *CTA 2010, s 455* charge on a £100,000 loan advanced on 1 June 2017 would be £32,500 (assuming the amount remains outstanding more than nine months after the company's year-end) and the tax on the 'interest' benefit would be just £1,200 for a 40% taxpayer (ie £100,000 × 3% × 40%).

If the loan is repaid before the *CTA 2010, s 455* tax is due for payment, the liability is discharged and the tax does not have to be paid over. However, if the loan remains outstanding after the nine month due date, HMRC will seek the *s 455* tax and charge interest from the due date until the tax is paid.

When the loan is subsequently repaid, the repayment of the *CTA 2010, s 455* tax is deferred until nine months after the *end of the CTAP in which the loan is repaid or reduced,* with repayment interest arising on any delayed repayment. Given this lead time for repayment of the *CTA 2010, s 455* tax, owner managers should always try to avoid triggering a *CTA 2010, s 455* liability by repaying their loans within nine months of the balance sheet date.

Director's overdrawn loan accounts

2.53   HMRC insist that the company's record keeping should ensure that balances of directors' loan accounts are accurate and kept up to date. HMRC are concerned that poorly kept records "may result in non-business expenditure incurred by the directors being incorrectly recorded or mis-posted in the business records and claimed in error as an allowable expense". Particular risk areas include the payment of personal bills, such as credit cards, personal expenses paid by company, and personal entertaining.

2.54   In practice, there is usually a potential *CTA 2010, s 455* exposure on overdrawn director-shareholder's current or loan accounts. In many cases, an overdrawn loan account may not be established until sometime after the balance sheet date, eg when the accounts are completed or following certain audit adjustments. It is therefore important to establish the proper balance before the 'nine-month' due date for the *CTA 2010, s 455* tax. This will enable the owner-manager to decide whether to clear the balance by voting an additional bonus or declaring an appropriate dividend. Dividends must be properly declared and documented to demonstrate that the debt due to the company has been repaid (see 9.20). Repayment via cheque to the company is the most robust way of demonstrating repayment.

2.55   If an overdrawn balance remains after the 'nine month' due date, the *CTA 2010, s 455* tax falls due and interest will begin to accrue. Where regular advances/loans are made to a company's shareholder director, HMRC will often contend that these have the character of 'earnings' and seek to apply PAYE and NIC on the relevant amounts. Proper loan documentation will help to rebut such challenges. To avoid HMRC seeking (unexpected) PAYE and NIC liabilities on regular withdrawals, where the owner-manager wishes to extract regular amounts from the company, it may be better for them to pay regular 'quarterly' dividends instead (see also 2.24A and 5.11A).

In cases where frequent advances have been accepted as loans under an HMRC enquiry, there may be insufficient evidence as to the amounts that have been cleared by subsequent repayment(s). Inspectors normally seek to apply the rule in *Clayton's* case (1816 MR Ch Vol 1, 572), which provides that repayments are set against the oldest debts first. Given that loans or advances may have been subject to different *CTA 2010, s 455* tax rates, it may be preferable to allocate the repayments against the loans/advances liable to the 32.5% rate in priority to those subject to the 25% charge.

Inspectors will not accept that separate 'director's' accounts can be aggregated or netted off each other since the *CTA 2010, s 455* charge arises where a close company 'makes any loan or advances any money' to a shareholder. HMRC seems to accept that genuine book entries (with supporting documentation) can be made where a credit balance is used to repay a debit balance. However, the *ICAEW Tax Faculty Guidance Note TAX 11/93* recommends that a company should draw a cheque to pay off the whole or part of the credit balance with another cheque being paid into the company to clear the debit balance. This will therefore provide firm evidence of the date the loan is repaid.

Interaction of FRS 102 and directors' loan accounts

2.56   Many owner-managed companies are now required to adopt FRS102. (Micro-entities can adopt the simplified FRS 105 (for accounting periods starting after 31 December 2015.)

The application of FRS 102 could have implications for the way in which directors' loan accounts are accounted for going forward.

There is an argument that the build-up of entries in the directors loan account over an accounting period is not a financing transaction, provided the loans are intended to be settled within a year. In practice, transactions between the directors and 'their' companies are often entered into on an informal basis. Therefore, to avoid the potential complexities of FRS 102 accounting treatment, owner-managers should specifically record that their loan accounts are repayable on demand. The loan accounts can then be recorded at 'cost' under FRS 102 (as was historically the case).

On the other hand, if the transactions on a directors' loan account are considered to be 'financing transactions', FRS 102 requires the balances to be accounted for under the amortised cost basis using the effective interest method. However, this can normally be avoided if a commercial rate of interest is charged. In such cases, there should be no (material) difference between the initial recognition amount and the amount received/settled on maturity. Furthermore, if the rate of interest charged is at least equal to HMRC's official rate, no tax charge arises under the 'beneficial loan' legislation (see 2.51 and 7.62).

2.57   If no interest is charged (or is charged at less than a commercial rate) the loan account balance must be recorded at present value. This is likely to give rise to a 'shortfall' between the face value of the loan and its present value. In this case, the resultant debit would be treated in the company's books as a 'distribution' (para 11.13 of FRS 102). This reflects the benefit of the interest-free/cheap interest being provided to the shareholder.

Example 8

Treatment of 'long-term' interest-free loan to a director-shareholder

Andre is a 100% shareholder of Ayew Ltd, which draws up accounts to 31 March each year. On 1 April 2017, the company provides a £20,000 interest-free loan to him repayable on 31 March 2020. A comparable market interest rate is 6%.

The accounting entries would be:

	Dr	Cr
Director's loan account	£16,792*	
Discount (= distribution)	£3,207	
Cash		£20,000
* This is the present value of £20,000 received in three years time at a discount rate of 6%		

Under normal corporation tax 'loan relationship' rules, the discount would normally be regarded as a (deductible) non-trading debit. However, for loans arising after 31 December 2015, the 'discount' would not be deductible for corporation tax purposes.

2.57A The 'individual' directors/shareholders tax treatment is *not* based on the FRS 102 accounting treatment. Consequently, any taxable benefit is calculated using the beneficial loan rules (see 2.51 and 7.62). Also the *CTA 2010, s 455* charge is still based on the actual amount of the loan or advance (see 2.49).

'Bed and breakfasting' of loan accounts

2.58 HMRC introduced specific legislation to counter the use of 'bed and breakfasting' arrangements in *FA 2013*. (See 2015/16 and earlier editions of this book for pre-*FA 2013* treatment of 'bed and breakfasting' arrangements.)

Under the *FA 2013* changes, which apply for loans repaid after 19 March 2013, *CTA 2010, s 458* repayment relief can be denied in two different situations:

The 30-day repayment restriction

The new *CTA 2010, s 464C(1)* will apply where within a 30-day period:

- a shareholder has made repayments of 'their' *CTA 2010, s 455* loan (exceeding £5,000) ('relevant repayments'); and

- In a *subsequent accounting period*, new loans/advances (exceeding £5,000) are made to the same person or their associate (relevant chargeable payments).

This therefore catches the clearest form of bed and breakfasting arrangement. In such cases, *CTA 2010, s 458* repayment relief is only given *if and to the extent* that the *relevant repayments exceed the relevant chargeable payments*. In effect, the legislation only recognises the 'real' repayment (since repayments are matched with the amounts that have been re-lent shortly after the end of the relevant accounting period are).

An illustrative diagram showing the operation of the '30-day' rule is given below:

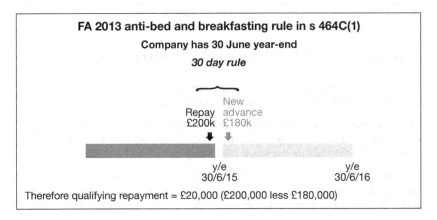

> **FA 2013 anti-bed and breakfasting rule in s 464C(1)**
>
> **Company has 30 June year-end**
>
> ***30 day rule***
>
> Repay £200k · New advance £180k
>
> y/e 30/6/15 · y/e 30/6/16
>
> Therefore qualifying repayment = £20,000 (£200,000 less £180,000)

However, importantly, this restriction does *not* apply if the amount repaid gives rise to an income tax liability in the individual shareholder's hands (*CTA 2010, s 464C(6)*). This would typically arise where a bonus is voted for or dividend is paid to 'clear' the shareholder-director's loan account, as is often the case in practice.

In practice, HMRC accept that the crediting of an interim dividend to a loan account represents 'payment' at the time the relevant book entry is made, since the amount is then 'placed unreservedly at the disposal of the directors/ shareholders as part of their current accounts with the company' (see 9.20). Some company law purists would argue with that approach, contending that a payment requires a transfer of cash.

On a strict analysis of *CTA 2010, s 464C(6)*, the 'repayment' itself *must* give rise to the income tax charge. The Chartered Institute of Taxation (CIOT) (see *TAX Adviser, May 2014*) pointed out to HMRC that it is the entitlement to the bonus or dividend itself that gives rise to the income tax charge. Worryingly, recent correspondence between the CIOT and HMRC suggests that HMRC are taking a strict interpretation of this 'exemption'. It appears that HMRC considers that the exemption would only apply if the loan account were cleared by a book entry 'crediting' the relevant bonus or dividend from the (lending) company.

Many would argue that an appellate tribunal would adopt a purposive approach so that the 'income tax payment' requirement would be met where, for example, a company actually pays a *cash* dividend to a director, who then uses these monies to repay a loan account.

HMRC have confirmed that the exemption would not apply where the loan account is cleared by, for example, rent or interest payments received from the company (although it is difficult to see how this view is supported by the legislation).

Example 9

Operation of *CTA 2010, s 464C(1)* restriction

Thierry is a (UK resident) executive director of, and also a 75% shareholder in Henry Ltd, which makes up accounts to 31 March each year.

The company has incurred some large personal expenses on Thierry's behalf during the year ended 31 March 2017, with the result that Thierry owes the company £25,000 before the week leading up to its 31 March 2017 year-end.

Thierry arranges to repay the £25,000 from his personal funds, with his cheque clearing the company's bank account on 28 March 2017. However, on 2 April 2017, he arranges for the company to advance a new loan of £20,000 to him.

Since the £25,000 repayment on 28 March 2017 was made within 30 days of a new loan of £20,000 (falling in the subsequent accounting period), it is matched with the new £20,000 loan first, so that only the excess amount is eligible for *CTA 2010, s 458* repayment relief, as follows:

	£
Repayment	25,000
Matched with new loan	(20,000)
Qualifying repayment	5,000
Therefore repayment of *s 455* tax = £5,000 × 32.5%	£1,625

There is no restriction in the repayment claim if the amount repaid gives rise to an income tax charge on the relevant shareholder or their associate. Thus, if Thierry had credited a dividend of £25,000 from Henry Ltd to his loan account, it would be treated as a full repayment of the loan, and the company would obtain the full *CTA 2010, s 455* tax repayment of £6,250. This is logical since HMRC will collect income tax from Thierry on the dividend payment.

The arrangements rule

The 'complementary' provision in *CTA 2010, s 464C(3)* potentially applies where the total amount of a shareholder's *CTA 2010, s 455* loan exceeds £15,000 before any repayment. If it does, the provisions in *CTA 2010, s 464C(4)* are triggered when a repayment is made, provided:

- arrangements had been made for one or more chargeable payments to be made to replace some, or all, of the amount repaid...' and

- the amount of those chargeable payments exceeds £5,000.

In other words, this provision broadly requires that arrangements (which is a wide-ranging term) be in place (typically by the company and/or the relevant shareholder) to 'replace' some or all of the repayment. In such cases, the amount qualifying for repayment relief under *CTA 2010, s 458* is computed as:

Loan repayment(s)	X
Less: New loans/advances for which arrangements are in place	(X)
Qualifying repayment	X

It should be a little easier to prove whether there are arrangements actually in place for the company to grant fresh loans/advances. However, (as the CIOT Technical Team put it) 'any arrangement for a re-borrowing is likely to have involved a negotiation between the participator and the company that took place inside the head of the shareholder-director'. It is to be hoped that HMRC will adopt a sensible approach when applying this provision.

As with the '30 day' rule (see above), *CTA 2010, s 464C(3)* does *not* apply if the 'repayment' transaction gives rise to a taxable bonus or dividend (or waiver). Thus, if the loan is credited with a bonus (which is subjected to PAYE/NIC), this 'credit' will give rise to a valid repayment claim under *CTA 2010, s 458*.

Example 10

Operation of *CTA 2010, s 464C(3), (4)* restriction

Winston holds 100% of the issued share capital of Reid Ltd, which makes up accounts to 30 September each year.

The management accounts show that Winston owed the company some £50,000 at 31 August 2017, which had been built up over the last 11 months.

Winston wishes to clear the loan account to avoid the *CTA 2010, s 455* liability. However, he cannot personally afford to repay it at present. Winston therefore asks his friend's company, Vaz Tê Ltd, for a short-term loan on the understanding that he would repay it within two months by taking a new loan from his company.

There is a significant risk that HMRC would contend that the 'arrangement' with Vaz Tê Ltd would be caught by *CTA 2010, s 464C(3)* and thus deny any claim for repayment relief.

On the other hand, Winston could clear his loan account with a dividend payment of (say) £70,000 on (say) 27 November 2017. Since his loan account was cleared by a taxable dividend, the repayment will qualify for *CTA 2010, s 458* relief (*CTA 2010, s 464C(6)*). As the loan would be 'cleared' by a taxable amount within nine months of the 30 September 2017 year-end, the *s 455* tax would be discharged under *CTA 2010, s 458*.

Winston would not be liable to pay the income tax on his dividend (in 2017/18) until 31 January 2019.

CTA 2010, s 464A anti-avoidance charge on 'benefits' provided to shareholders

2.59   The *FA 2013* introduced a completely new weapon for dealing with 'indirect benefits' (as opposed to loans) enjoyed by close company shareholders. *CTA 2010, s 464A* imposes a 32.5% deemed 'corporation tax' charge on the relevant close company where:

- it is a party to tax avoidance arrangements (which are widely defined); and

- as a result of those arrangements, a 'benefit' is directly or indirectly conferred on a shareholder of the company (or their associate).

Where the shareholder receives the benefit before 6 April 2016, it is charged at the 25% tax rate.

The *CTA 2010, s 464A* charge will *not* apply where the benefit conferred on the participator would be subject to the 'normal' *CTA 2010, s 455* tax charge or an income tax charge.

HMRC considers that the *CTA 2010, s 464A* charge would be invoked in certain 'hybrid' partnerships where:

- an individual partner's capital account becomes overdrawn (after 19 March 2013); and

- that overdrawn account has effectively been financed by the undrawn profits (or capital introduced) of a corporate partner.

HMRC's explanatory notes indicate that the main target of this provision is to levy a tax charge where *individual* partners benefit as a result of the retention of profits in the partnership/LLP by a corporate partner. This 'benefit', which would otherwise be tax-free, would typically arise where individual partners reduce their own capital account or take sufficient drawings to overdraw their current/capital accounts.

In such cases, the (close) corporate partner could be liable to an *CTA 2010, s 464A* charge on the individual partner's overdrawn capital/current account (or, if lower, the amount funded by the corporate member).

Given that *CTA 2010, s 464A* can only be triggered where there are tax avoidance arrangements, we would expect the 32.5%/25% tax charge to be restricted to those cases where there is *deliberate* 'transfer of value' to 'related' individual partners via the partnership/LLP arrangements.

CTA 2010, s 464B contains a mechanism for repayment of the *CTA 2010, s 464A* tax charge if payments are returned to the company. However, such cases are likely to be rare since (in contrast to a loan), the 'benefit' conferred on the shareholder does not give rise to any repayment obligation.

It is hoped that HMRC would not use these widely drawn provisions as a carte blanche to attack normal commercial arrangements where individual partners/members simply draw profits earned in accordance with their profit share entitlements – it should be possible to show there is no tax avoidance motive here. Similarly, *CTA 2010, s 464A* should not apply where an individual partner's/member's drawings are 'financed' entirely from their own capital account (ie without relying on the capital account of a fellow corporate partner/ member).

Example 11

Scope of *CTA 2010, s 464A* charge

Gareth is a 75% shareholder in Bale Ltd (a close trading company).

Both Gareth and Bale Ltd became equal partners in 'The Bale Partnership' on 1 April 2011, which draws up accounts to 30 September each year.

Under the terms of the partnership agreement, Bale Ltd and Gareth share profits in the ratio of 75%:25% respectively.

During the year ended 30 September 2017, the partnership generated profits of £1,500,000, which were shared as follows:

	£
Bale Ltd (75%)	1,125,000
Gareth (25%)	375,000
Total	1,500,000

Bale Ltd's profits are credited to its capital account and are left retained in the partnership business. On the other hand, Gareth has drawn over £800,000 from the business and, by the end of September 2017, his partnership capital account is overdrawn by some £400,000.

HMRC are likely to contend that *CTA 2010, s 464A* should apply to Gareth's overdrawn capital account.

The assertion would be that:

- the 'overdrawn' element represents a benefit conferred on Gareth; and

- this has been funded by Bale Ltd's undrawn profits.

The *CTA 2010, s 459* charge – deemed close company loans for certain arrangements

2.59A   The normal *CTA 2010, s 455* charging rules are supplemented by a special *CTA 2010, s 459* charge, which may apply where a *s 455* charge does not normally bite.

In broad terms, a 32.5% (25% pre-6 April 2016) tax charge may be triggered under *CTA 2010, s 459*, where:

- under arrangements made by someone,

- a close company makes a loan that is *not* within the normal *CTA 2010, s 455* charge; and

- a person (other than the close company) makes a payment to a participator (or their associate), which is *not* subject to an income tax charge (*CTA 2010, s 459(3)*).

In such cases, the loan is treated as having been made to the 'participator' under *CTA 2010, s 455*.

CTA 2010, s 459 primarily aims to catch certain 'back-to-back arrangements' – such as where a close company deposits cash with (say) a bank on the understanding that the bank will make an advance or loan to a participator of that close company. These arrangements would firmly fall within this legislation.

However, the wording of *CTA 2010, s 459* is sufficiently wide to catch ('financial assistance' type) loans made in connection with certain type of company takeover (especially management buy-out deals), as illustrated below:

3. Newco makes a payment to the sellers of Target which is not subject to income tax in their hands (they are participators of Target since they would be on the share register of Target when the deal is completed.

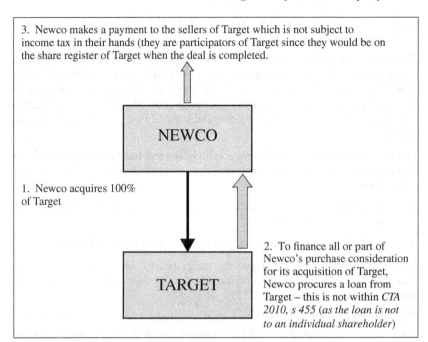

1. Newco acquires 100% of Target

2. To finance all or part of Newco's purchase consideration for its acquisition of Target, Newco procures a loan from Target – this is not within *CTA 2010, s 455* (*as the loan is not to an individual shareholder*)

In practice, it is often possible to 'plan out' of the potential *CTA 2010, s 459* charge by arranging for Target to make an appropriate dividend to Newco (rather than a loan). The 'tax-free' dividend monies received by Newco are then used to discharge the purchase consideration payable to the sellers of Target. Since there is *no* loan to Newco, *CTA 2010, s 459* cannot apply.

HMRC continues to confirm that where the relevant conditions (as summarised above) are satisfied, it will seek to apply the *CTA 2010, s 459* provisions.

CTSA reporting obligations for *CTA 2010, ss 455* and *464A* tax

2.60   Under corporation tax self-assessment, the *CTA 2010 s 455* tax must be reported on the corporation tax return form CT600 and various details of loans made to participators, etc must be given on the supplementary page CT600A (even if the *CTA 2010, s 455* liability has been discharged by repayment or waiver). Companies that are liable to pay their corporation tax in instalments must include any anticipated or actual *CTA 2010, s 455* tax in their instalment liabilities (see 4.48). The same obligations also apply to any *CTA 2010, s 464A* tax (see 2.59)

The CT600 return form must normally be submitted within 12 months from the end of the company's accounting period. Late returns attract a flat rate penalty of £100 increasing to £200 if the return is more than three months late. (These penalties become £500 and £1,000 respectively, if the company was subject to a flat penalty charge in each of its two preceding accounting periods.)

Companies must take care to ensure they report all *CTA 2010, s 455* loans correctly since they are potentially exposed to HMRC penalties. Penalties are now charged according to the underlying taxpayer behaviour that gave rise to the error. Thus, HMRC will charge a greater penalty where it can show that the understatement of the tax liability was deliberate (as opposed to an innocent error).

Penalties are based on the relevant amount of tax that has been understated, the nature of the taxpayer's behaviour and the extent of disclosure. For example, a penalty of:

- *up to 30%* will arise on any understated *CTA 2010, s 455* tax due to lack of reasonable care: or

- *up to 70%* on any deliberately understated *CTA 2010, s 455* tax.

For these purposes, in arriving at the understated *CTA 2010, s 455* tax, no reduction is made for any offset under *CTA 2010, s 458(2)* (where the loan has been subsequently repaid (see 2.52)).

The relevant penalty would be substantially reduced where the taxpayer makes full disclosure or takes active steps to correct the mistake. No penalty should arise where the taxpayer makes a genuine mistake. See 4.59–4.64 for full details of penalty regime.

Example 12

CTA 2010, s 455 tax and interest on overdrawn director's loan

Mr Noble, a shareholder in Claret & Blue Captain Ltd (a close company), overdrew his director's loan account by £20,000 in November 2017. This amount was still outstanding at the end of the company's accounting period on 31 December 2017, although it was entirely cleared by the payment of a bonus on 30 June 2018.

The company's accounts, corporation tax computations and return form CT600 for the year ended 31 December 2017 were submitted to HMRC in September 2018.

The company must complete the supplementary page CT600A and submit it with the return. In Part 1, the company must show the loan of £20,000 made to Mr Noble during the period, but would also claim relief from the *s 455* liability (in Part 2) as the loan was repaid by 30 September 2018 – ie within nine months of the end of the accounting period.

Mr Noble would also be subject to an employment income charge on the benefit of the interest-free loan. The company would also be subject to a Class 1A NIC charge on the same amount.

WAIVER OF LOANS TO SHAREHOLDERS

Income tax charge on shareholder

2.61 An income tax charge arises if the company releases or simply writes off a loan to a shareholder (or an associate of a shareholder) [*ITTOIA 2005, s 415*]. The loan must be formally waived (which must be documented by a formal legal deed), as opposed to merely not being collected by the company.

Since 6 April 2016, loans formally waived or released no longer get the benefit of the 10% tax credit. Instead, the amount of the loan waived/released is taxed at the post-5 April 2016 'distribution' tax rates. The amount waived is treated as dividend income under *ITA 2007, s 19(1)(d)*. Thus, loan waivers can also benefit from the £5,000 'dividend' nil-rate band (see also see 9.12B).

Thus, depending on the level of the shareholder's other income, the deemed 'dividend income' is taxed as the top slice of their total income in 2017/18 as shown below (ignoring the £5,000 dividend nil rate band):

Amount of loan waived/ released	Tax rate applied
Up to £33,500	7.5%
£33,501 to £150,000	32.5%
More than £150,000	38.1%

Where the shareholder is a director (or an employee), the *ITTOIA 2005, s 415* charge also takes priority over any employment income tax charge on the waiver under *ITEPA 2003, s 188* (due to the statutory priority rule in *ITEPA 2003, s 188*). However, HMRC has been recently trying to assert that the waived amount should be regarded as earnings under general principles (see 2.62)

It is fairly clear that if a waiver or release was in contemplation at the time the original 'loan' was made, then it is unlikely to be treated as a loan in the first place – there would be strong arguments for treating the payment as 'income' which would be characterised according to the underlying facts!

Provided any HMRC challenge to treat the loan waiver as 'earnings' can be successfully rebutted (see 2.62), the loan waiver, release, or write-off should be taxed as dividend income under *ITA 2007, s 19*.

Please see 2015/16 and earlier editions of this book for treatment of loans waived/released before 6 April 2016.

HMRC contention that amount waived is earnings

2.62 In recent times, HMRC has been trying to challenge loan waivers on the grounds that the amount waived was earnings based on basic principles within *ITEPA 2003, s 62* (as opposed to the deemed *ITEPA 2003, s 188* employment charge (see 2.61 above)

Many advisers remain unconvinced by HMRC's view on this. However, in the case of *Stewart Fraser Ltd v HMRC* [2011] UKFTT 46 (TC), the company had written off a loan to a shareholder-director. The taxpayer contended that the write-off was made in his capacity as a shareholder rather than a director, and therefore not considered to be earnings. Nevertheless HMRC successfully contended that the write-off was 'earnings' which gave rise to an NIC liability.

In giving their evidence, HMRC said that it considered that:

'Had they (the loans) been waived for him in his capacity as a shareholder then HMRC would have expected to see this discussed and approved at a shareholders' meeting involving all the shareholders.'

Following this useful statement, it would therefore be advisable for waivers/ write-offs of loans to participators to be approved at a general meeting of the shareholders or by an elected written resolution under *Companies Act 2006, ss 292* and *293*.

NIC treatment of loan waivers

2.63 Although the *ITTOIA 2005, s 415* charge takes precedence over the *ITEPA 2003, s 188* 'employment income' charge for income tax purposes, any such release is likely to be treated as 'earnings' for NIC purposes. 'Earnings' is widely defined for NIC purposes to include 'any remuneration or profit derived from the employment' (*SSCBA 1992, s 39(1)(a)*). HMRC's view is that given this wide coverage, the release of a director's loan would be seen as rewarding the director for services rendered and would thus be liable to Class 1 NICs.

However, following the ruling in the *Stewart Fraser* case (see 2.62 above), it may be possible to side step an NIC charge by following appropriate corporate procedures. In the *Stewart Fraser* case, the company lost its appeal that the loan write-off was made in Mr Fraser's capacity as a shareholder. The Tribunal could find no evidence for this since the *directors* had approved the write-off, not the shareholders. To demonstrate that Mr Fraser's loan had been waived in his capacity as a shareholder, HMRC would have expected to see this discussed and approved at a meeting of all the shareholders. Thus, applying this reasoning, provided a loan waiver is approved at a general meeting of the shareholders (or by a written shareholders resolution (see 2.62)), it should be possible to avoid an NIC charge.

Clearly, if the shareholder is neither a director nor an employee, there can be no question of an NIC charge being levied on the release.

Novation of loans

2.64 The case of *Collins v Addies* [1992] STC 746 held that the novation of a shareholder loan gives rise to a release. The company had advanced a loan to its two director shareholders and the company was subsequently sold. As part of the sale, the purchaser of the company agreed to take over these debts. Thus, the shareholder loans were novated so that the target company released the shareholders from their debts and the purchaser agreed to take them over. The court held that novation of the £68,000 debt constituted a taxable release under what is now *ITTOIA 2005, s 415*.

As illustrated by this case, the debtor (borrower) cannot assign the debt. A novation takes place under which the existing debtor is released from the debt and a new 'lender' (assignee) takes on a new debt (with the debtor). *ITTOIA 2005, s 415* will therefore catch situations where the creditor assigns the loans to someone else.

Recovery of *CTA 2010, s 455* tax

2.65 Where a loan is released or waived, the company can recover from HMRC any tax paid under *CTA 2010, s 455*. The amount is due for repayment nine months after the accounting period in which the loan is waived (see 2.59).

Note that a loan waiver (upon which an *ITTOIA 2003, s 415* liability would arise) would enable the *CTA 2010, s 455* tax to be repaid in a 'bed and breakfasting' arrangement and the special rules in 2.58 would not apply.

Corporation tax treatment of loan waiver

2.66 A properly executed release of a loan (provided it is properly accounted for under GAAP) would reduce the amount of loan that is due to be paid which would be written-off against the company's profits.

However, the *FA 2010* introduced legislation preventing almost all owner-managed companies from claiming a loan relationship (non-trading) tax deduction for the release or write-off of a loan made to a shareholder (or associate thereof) (*CTA 2009, s 321A*). This rule (which applies to close companies) affects amounts that are written-off after 23 March 2010. Nevertheless, despite these changes, it remains possible for companies to deduct amounts written-off in respect of other loans (where the borrower is not a shareholder or one of their 'associates').

Before 24 March 2010, the loan relationship legislation [*CTA 2009, s 324(1)*] contained an apparent loophole, since it permitted relief to be claimed on the write-off of shareholder loans as well as other 'third party' loans. However, in practice, HMRC have been known to resist claims for 'non-trading' debt relief under the loan relationship rules, contending that they are (already) blocked by various anti-avoidance provisions, such as *CTA 2009, s 444* (transactions not conducted on an arms' length basis).

Example 13

ITTOIA 2003, s 415 tax liability on release of shareholder loan

In June 2016, Hotspur Ltd (which is a close company) advanced an interest-free loan of £90,000 to Mr Alli, who is a 30% shareholder of the company. He does *not* work for Hotspur Ltd.

The loan remained outstanding nine months after the 31 December 2016 year end and therefore *CTA 2010, s 455* tax of £29,250 (32.5% × £90,000) was paid to HMRC on 1 October 2017.

In November 2017, the company decided to waive the £90,000 loan due from Mr Alli. Mr Alli and Hotspur Ltd entered into a formal deed to release the debt.

Hotspur Ltd

Since the company is 'close' and Mr Alli is a shareholder ('participator'), the *CTA 2009, s 321A* restriction applies to the amount written-off. Thus, the consequent loan relationship debit of £90,000 is not deductible for corporation tax purposes.

The *CTA 2010, s 455* tax of £29,250 also becomes repayable (which must be claimed), being due for repayment on 1 October 2018, ie nine months after the end of the accounting period in which the loan is waived – the year ended 31 December 2017.

Mr Alli

Assuming Mr Alli's total income (including the waiver) exceeds £150,000, his *ITTOIA 2005, s 415* charge in 2017/18 will be as follows:

	£
Amount waived less dividend 'nil-rate' band (£90,000–£5,000)	85,000
Tax at 38.1%	32,385

It is important to note that if Mr Alli were a *director or employee* of Hotspur Ltd, the *ITTOIA 2005, s 415* charge would still prevail, but HMRC would also seek to impose a Class 1 NIC charge. Recently HMRC has contended that amounts of loans waived should be treated as earnings under *ITEPA 2003, s 62* – see 2.63 above.

BENEFITS IN KIND TO NON-WORKING SHAREHOLDERS

2.67   Certain expenses or benefits provided to a close company shareholder (or an associate of a shareholder) are treated as a distribution under *CTA 2010, s 1064*. Without these special provisions it would be possible to provide benefits to a non-working shareholder on a tax-free basis.

This 'deemed distribution' treatment does not apply where the expense or benefit is already taxed under the employment income rules in *ITEPA 2003*. Consequently, in practice, these rules would effectively apply to non-working shareholders being provided with living accommodation and other benefits or services (to the extent that they are not made good by the shareholder or their associate). These rules do not include pensions or lump sums payable on death or retirement.

The value of the distribution is taken to be the same amount that would have applied if the amount had been treated as an employment-related benefit (see Chapter 7). The recipient shareholder would be taxed on this amount in accordance with the relevant 'dividend taxation' rules (see Chapter 9).

The amount of the 'distribution' cannot be deducted against profits for corporation tax purposes

If a non-working shareholder was provided with a car, the distribution would be based on the scale benefit charge computed under the rules in 7.8–7.10. This would not be the same figure as the depreciation and running costs that would have to be disallowed in calculating the company's taxable profits (since being incurred for a non-working shareholder, they would not generally be for the purposes of the trade).

PLANNING CHECKLIST – STRATEGIES FOR EXTRACTING FUNDS FROM THE COMPANY

Company

- The extraction of funds is often influenced by the company's cash flow and working capital position.

- Where appropriate, shareholders can loan funds back to the company to restore liquidity and provide working capital.

- Dividend payments can easily be timed for optimum income tax efficiency in the hands of the shareholder(s).

- Corporate tax relief for bonuses can be effectively back-dated by making provision in the statutory accounts under the nine-month rule. However, care must be taken to ensure such provisions also comply with current UK GAAP, such as FRS 102/FRS 105.

Working shareholders

- Generally require a sensible mix of remuneration/bonuses and dividends. Adopting a profit extraction model of 'low salary/high dividends will often be tax-efficient.

- Some owner-managers wish to extract surplus cash funds from the company to remove them from any further business risk.

- To avoid high income tax rates on substantial salaries and bonuses, owner managers could consider providing 'cheap' loans from the company. Such loans would only suffer employment tax at 1.2%/1.35% (ie official rate 3% × 40%/45%) for a complete tax year. The loans can be repaid when appropriate, although a *CTA 2010, s 455* charge will also arise if the loans are not repaid within nine months of the company year-end in which they were made.

- A *CTA 2010, s 455* liability is now likely to be triggered where an owner managed company makes a loan to a 'related' partnership or LLP (even where it is being made for genuine trading purposes). Similarly, a *CTA 2010, s 455* charge may also arise on loans to the trustees of a 'connected' trust.

- To avoid having to discount the value of directors' loan accounts under FRS 102, it is recommended to make the loans repayable on demand.

- Following *FA 2013*, the 'bed and breakfasting' of *CTA 2010, s 455* loans is no longer effective as a means of avoiding the *CTA 2010, s 455* tax or securing its repayment. However, these rules do enable the *CTA 2010, s 455* tax to be avoided/repaid where the loan account is cleared by means of a taxable bonus, dividend (or waiver of the loan).

- Owner managers should consider bringing their loan accounts into credit by paying a dividend or 'large' bonus early in the tax year, thus enabling amounts to be drawn at a later date with no tax repercussions or RTI issues.

- It may be possible to avoid incurring Class 1 NICs on the waiver of directors overdrawn loan accounts by ensuring that this is approved at a general meeting of all the shareholders (or by a shareholders' written resolution)

- Dividends still remain attractive for shareholders who are only liable to lower or basic rate income tax. A small salary is usually worthwhile to provide a 'credit' for state pension purposes.

- Owner-managers can mitigate income tax on their earnings to the extent that they are paid out as pension contributions. Income tax relief for pension contributions is subject to the annual £40,000 'annual allowance' restriction. Also take into account any potential unused relief from the previous three years.

- Where the company's trading premises are personally owned by the controlling shareholder, it may be desirable to sell them to the company to obtain a tax-efficient extraction of cash.

Other employees

- Employees generally look for good remuneration packages with tax-efficient benefits (although there is now an increasing preference for cash).

- In appropriate cases, an incentive-based bonus scheme should be considered.

Non-working shareholders

- Dividends are much more tax-efficient as the company cannot claim tax relief for 'remuneration', particularly for non-working spouses. However, some care must be exercised to avoid the dividend being taxed on the owner-manager(s) under the settlement legislation.

- Consider paying pension contributions of up to £2,808 net (tax relief of up to £792 is added at source by HMRC) for non-working shareholders.

Chapter 3

Shareholding and Corporate Structures

SHARES VERSUS DEBT

Overview

3.1   This chapter reviews the issues involved in deciding how a family or owner-managed company's shareholding should be split and the way in which its trading activities may be structured.

The owner-managers and other parties can inject funds into the company in two ways:

(*a*)   by a subscription for shares; and/or

(*b*)   by lending money to the company.

It is far easier to obtain repayment of funds injected on loan account. Cash paid for shares can normally only be returned on a winding up, a company's purchase of its own shares or under the *Companies Act 2006* share capital reduction provisions (via a special resolution supported by a solvency statement). The company may, of course, issue redeemable preference shares provided that it is authorised to do so by its Articles and the company already has non-redeemable shares in existence.

The relevant tax/commercial considerations involved in choosing the mix between shares and debt are considered in Chapter 11.

Shareholders' rights

3.2   In essence, shares give the holder various membership rights in the company. These rights spring from the *Companies Act 1985* and the *Companies Act 2006* and the company's own Articles or shareholder's agreement, etc. They would include the right to attend and vote at general meetings, receive dividends and a return of their capital on liquidation. The shareholder enjoys these benefits in return for their lack of security. Minority shareholders generally have little say in the management of the company's affairs – their main protection is the potential to bring an 'unfair prejudice' action before the court. The court has the power to impose a variety of remedies, including a purchase of the aggrieved member's shares or a winding-up order.

Lenders' rights

3.3   Money can be loaned to the company in various ways. Where the loan is unsecured, the lender has a contract with the company for the debt. Contract law and the terms of any loan agreement will govern the lender's rights and remedies (for example, the return of the loan and the right to interest payments).

In some cases, an unsecured lender may request a personal guarantee, possibly from one or more directors. Thus, if the company fails to repay the loan, the lender can claim against the guarantor. Many 'owner-manager' loans are interest-free, although the payment of interest on a loan should be considered where there are other 'outside' shareholders and as a way of extracting profits without any NIC cost.

Where a loan is secured, the lender has additional 'security' rights in addition to their contractual ones. Where the lender takes a fixed charge over (invariably) land and buildings, the borrowing company cannot deal with these assets in any way until the loan is fully repaid. On the other hand, a floating charge generally covers the borrowing company's fixed assets (other than land and buildings), debts, and trading stock. Consequently, the company has the ability to deal freely with these assets unless and until the floating charge crystallises. If the lender's security becomes threatened, the debenture/loan agreement will enable them to appoint an administrator/receiver who will then be able to realise the relevant underlying assets for satisfying the loan (and accrued interest). A lender can petition the court to put the company into compulsory liquidation. However, following the *Enterprise Act 2002*, a company in financial difficulty is more likely to appoint an administrator (out of court) to rescue the company as a going concern or achieve a better realisation of its assets (than a liquidation).

STRUCTURING THE SHAREHOLDINGS

Formation of company

3.4   The shareholding structure of the company is best decided on its formation. Typically, the shares will be subscribed for at par when the company has little value. Subsequent changes can of course be made to the shareholding structure.

If the company has been profitable, its shares will have increased in value. Although transfers between shareholder in a family or owner-managed company can often be made without incurring an immediate IHT or CGT liability, there may be other risks. For example, if an individual shareholder dies within seven years of gifting shares, an IHT liability may arise (see 17.10 and 17.11). Similarly, the ability to hold-over the capital gain is dependent on the company qualifying as a 'trading company' and it may also be restricted where the company has some 'chargeable' investment assets (see 13.20).

Given the tightening of the 'employee share' legislation (see Chapter 8) and, in particular, the much wider definition of when shares are deemed to be acquired by reason of a directorship or employment, it would appear that the vast majority of share issues must now be reported. Employee share reporting is made via HMRC's online Employment Related Securities (ERS) service (see 8.83).

Inheritance tax issues

3.5   In a typical family or owner-managed company, the proprietor will often hold the majority of the issued share capital. The current 100% IHT exemption on private trading company shareholdings means that retention of the shares will often be a sensible policy, as the shares will be fully exempt from IHT on death and will also benefit from a tax-free uplift in value for CGT purposes (see 17.17).

The 100% IHT business property (BPR) exemption looks set to remain intact for the foreseeable future and is unlikely to be changed by the current Government. However, IHT should not be the only consideration here. If the proprietor's children or other close family members play an active part in the business, it may be necessary for the owner-manager to pass some shares to them during their lifetime. This will motivate them and perhaps reward their contribution to the increase in the company's value created by their efforts. This will also aid the 'succession planning' process and, of course, the psychological impact can be a significant factor.

In most cases, it should be possible to transfer the shares directly to the intended family recipients. Where shares are gifted to close family members, there should be no 'employment income' tax charge due to the exemption in *ITEPA 2003, s 421B* for 'shares made available in the 'normal course of domestic, family, or personal relationships' (see 8.17).

Alternatively, some shares could be transferred to an 'intermediate' family trust with CGT deferral (under an appropriate hold-over election) and without incurring any immediate IHT liability due to the 100% BPR exemption.

The owner-manager will usually require a substantial holding or perhaps a separate class of shares to satisfy their personal financial needs (through dividends). In many cases, the shares must provide the owner-manager adequate control over the company but effective control need not be relinquished if an appropriate trust is used. These issues are considered further in Chapter 17.

FACTORS THAT MAY INFLUENCE SHAREHOLDING STRUCTURE

Level of control required

3.6 Owner-managers should consider whether or not it is necessary for them to own all the shares. From a capital tax viewpoint, they may consider that this is the best course, given the complete exemption from IHT on death coupled with a tax-free uplift in the share values for CGT.

Owner-managers can, in fact, obtain absolute control by holding at least 75% of the voting rights, since they would then be able to pass special resolutions, sell the business, vary its constitution and put it into liquidation. For effective day-to-day control, such as the appointment and removal of directors, determination of remuneration and dividend policy, it is only necessary to hold more than 50% of the shares.

Owner-managers may be prepared to share effective 'control' with their spouses and family trusts (of which they can be 'first named' trustees (see 17.54)).

Based on many practical experiences, it is always advisable for owner-managers to keep the company's shares tightly held between 'trusted' family members and possibly key management team members. All too often, proprietors end up regretting their (or their parents') decision to issue shares to certain family members (usually to satisfy some emotional obligation!). This is especially problematic when the level of such shareholdings increases following other shares being repurchased by the company, etc.

Particular care should be taken to ensure that the company's Articles of Association provide appropriate protection against shares being transferred outside a 'closely defined' shareholder group.

Financial security and likelihood of a future sale

3.7 Many owner-managers view the business as a way of building up their financial security. When the time comes for them to step down and hand over control, the company should have provided them with sufficient funds for their future requirements. For many, this equates to maximising the amount of shares held. However, even where the company is to pass to the next generation, the owner-manager (with perhaps their spouse) only needs to control the company, ie by having shares carrying more than 50% of the votes. 'Value' can be built up by taking sufficient remuneration, dividends, and ensuring appropriate pension provision is made (see 17.41).

If the owner-manager's main objective is to build up the company for a future sale, or indeed flotation, they should ensure that they have sufficient shares to achieve the desired level of the future sale proceeds.

Providing dividends to the spouse and other family members

3.8 Where the owner-manager's spouse (or civil partner) has little income of their own, it will often be beneficial for the spouse/civil partner to hold some shares to obtain an appropriate level of dividend. This is best done by issuing the appropriate number of ordinary shares to the spouse/civil partner on formation of the company, or the owner-manager subsequently gifting some ordinary shares to them. In some cases, their shares can be re-categorised as a separate class (whilst retaining the same rights). This will provide greater flexibility with future dividend payments. Dividend taxation is covered in chapter 9.

In many cases, shares will be held by spouses to benefit from lower dividend tax rates, typically the 7.5% rate that applies to dividends taxed within the 'basic rate' band (see 9.29 to 9.39).

HMRC will normally accept the payment of spousal dividends following the House of Lords important ruling in the *Arctic Systems* case. Although such arrangements are likely to create a settlement for income tax purposes, the Law Lords held that the spousal dividends could not be taxed in the transferor spouse's hands under the settlements legislation, since the 'inter-spousal' outright gifts exemption in (what is now) *ITTOIA 2005, s 626* applied to fully-fledged ordinary shares (see 9.30).

On the other hand, the use of non-voting preference shares is likely to be a 'non-starter'. As demonstrated in *Young v Pearce* [1996] STC 743, the provision of such shares would be regarded as a settlement but would not be exempted under the outright gifts exemption in *ITTOIA 2005, s 626* since typically the shares would effectively represent a right to income (see 9.38).

Shares can also be provided to other family members to provide dividend income to them. However, the payment of dividends to minor children of the owner-manager (settlor) or trusts set up for their benefit are likely to be caught by the parental settlement rules in *ITTOIA 2005*. Importantly, in such cases, there is no equivalent of the 'outright gifts' exemption available to married couples/civil partners. It is considered unlikely that HMRC could invoke the settlement legislation in other cases (see 9.41).

CGT ENTREPRENEURS' RELIEF (ER)

3.9 Under the current ER legislation, owner-managers can sell their companies/businesses with the first £10 million of 'qualifying business gains' being taxed at 10%, with any excess gains being taxed at 20% (28% before 6 April 2016).

To be eligible for ER, the owner-manager and their fellow shareholders (who must be an officer or employee of the company) must ensure that they own at least 5% of the ordinary share capital (carrying at least 5% of the voting rights) in the 12 months before the share sale/cessation of trade (see 15.34 to 15.46).

INHERITANCE TAX PLANNING

3.10 Some proprietors are only willing to pass 'control' of the company down to the next generation on their death. In such cases, they are likely to maximise their shareholding (and perhaps their spouse's). This would enable them to take full advantage of the 100% IHT Business Property Relief (BPR) exemption (see 17.19) and the CGT free 'step-up' in base cost on death. By contrast, loans held by shareholders do not attract any BPR and, therefore, will be liable to IHT.

EMPLOYEE SHARE SCHEMES

3.11 The proprietor may want to provide shares for his key managers or employees (possibly through an approved share scheme) to foster a true sense of ownership and involvement in the company.

The proportion of shares issued to employees is usually nominal to avoid disturbing the balance of power. It is often both possible and desirable for employee shares to be a separate class of shares – this provides the appropriate flexibility to pay different rates of dividend to separate groups of shareholders. The detailed considerations are set out in Chapter 8.

As the principal aim is to give employees shareholder status, this should be carefully documented to avoid any risk of HMRC seeking to challenge that this is a contrived scheme to disguise bonus payments as dividends, thus avoiding PAYE/NIC.

CLOSE COMPANY LEGISLATION

Definition of a close company

3.12 The vast majority of typical family or owner-managed companies will be 'close companies' for tax purposes. Put simply, a company will be close if it is under the control of:

- five or fewer shareholders; or

- any number of shareholders who are also directors of the company, ie controlled by director-shareholders [*CTA 2010, s 439*].

For these purposes, any shares held by any associate of an individual shareholder must be attributed to that shareholder [*CTA 2010, s 451(4)*]. This would include shares held by a business partner or by relatives of a shareholder, such as his parents, spouse or civil partner, children (both minor and adult), brothers and sisters [*CTA 2010, s 448(1)(a), (2)*]. Similarly, shares held by the trustees of a trust created by the participator (or one of their relatives) or a trust in which the participator has an interest are treated as held by an associate [*CTA 2010, s 448(1)(b)(c)*]. Shares held by a nominee are also counted [*CTA 2010, s 451(3)*].

3.13 One or more people would be taken as having control if they have or are entitled to have more than 50% of the issued share capital, voting power, or company's assets on a winding up. This would catch any arrangements, such as options, to acquire shares at a future date – these are counted at the current date in determining whether the relevant controlling interest is held [*CTA 2010, s 451(4), (5)*].

Disadvantages of close company status

3.14 The wide-ranging nature of the close company definition (see 3.12) means that the vast majority of family and owner managed companies will be treated as 'close' for tax purposes. However, the consequences of being a close company are not as serious as they once were. Currently, the principal tax disadvantages of being a close company are as follows:

(*a*) a 32.5% tax charge arises under *CTA 2010, s 455* when any loan or advance is made to a shareholder of the company (see 2.56–2.65);

(*b*) any benefit provided to a non-working shareholder or 'associate', is taxed as a distribution in the recipient's hands The company is therefore denied a tax deduction for the relevant cost [*CTA 2010, ss 1000(2)* and *1064*] (see 2.66);

(*c*) Shareholders may be unable to obtain interest relief on their personal borrowings to acquire shares in the company, although relief is available for close *trading* or *property rental* companies [*ITA 2007, s 392*] (see 11.9–11.11).

CORPORATION TAX RATES

3.15 Corporation tax is levied by reference to financial years ('FY') – a financial year represents a 12-month period to 31 March. For example, FY 2017 represents the 12 months to 31 March 2018.

As part of the Government's policy to have a single unified rate of corporation tax, since 1 April 2015, all companies (except those with oil and gas ring fence profits) pay tax at the main rate.

3.16 The main rate for FY 2017 is 19%

The unification of the corporate tax rates from FY 2015 enabled the often complex 'associated' companies rules to be abolished. However, to prevent corporate groups manipulating their profits to avoid the accelerated payment of tax under the quarterly instalment payment (QIP) provisions, there is a new simplified 'anti-fragmentation' rule. This introduces the concept of a 'related 51% group company and applies for CTAPs periods beginning after 31 March 2015. These provisions are discussed further in 4.50 to 4.50C.

The main rate for FYs 2015 and 2016 is 20%, FYs 2017 to 2019 is 19%, and FY 2020 is 17%.

Details of the pre-1 April 2015 corporate tax rates and related rules can be found in the 2016/17 and earlier editions of this book.

PAYMENT OF CORPORATION TAX

Quarterly instalment payment (QIP) rules

3.17 Broadly speaking, 'large' companies pay their tax under the quarterly instalment payment (QIP) system. All other (ie 'non-large') companies pay their corporation tax liability nine months after the end of their CTAP.

Since 1 April 2015, a company would generally be liable to pay its corporation tax in quarterly instalments if its taxable profits exceed £1,500,000. This £1,500,000 12-month limit is apportioned by the number of any related 51% group companies (as determined at the end of the *last* CTAP) plus the relevant company. The limit is reduced on a pro-rata basis if the CTAP is less than 12 months.

In simple terms, a 'related 51% group company' would be either a company which controls a 51% subsidiary or a 51%+ subsidiary (see 4.50A for further details).

The operation of the QIP rules is fully dealt with in 4.50–4.54.

CHOOSING AN APPROPRIATE CORPORATE STRUCTURE

Main types of corporate structure

3.18 Where various members of the family or owner-managers carry on a number of trades or ventures, which is the case for many medium or large-sized businesses, it is necessary to choose the most appropriate and efficient operating structure from both the tax and commercial point of view.

Many medium and large-sized family and owner-managed businesses enjoy varying degrees of diversification by carrying on a number of different trades or activities. Over time, such additional activities may need to be bolted-on, either by organic growth, or by acquiring existing businesses. The commercial rationale might be to increase market share, gain economies of scale, acquire different channels of distribution, or simply add value by entering into a new area.

The choice of corporate structure for a diversified family and owner-managed business often lies between the following:

• single divisionalised company (see 3.21);

• parallel companies (see 3.25);

• corporate group structure (see 3.27).

3.19   Given its importance to the shareholders 'exit' planning, entrepreneurs' relief considerations are likely to have a major influence on the ultimate choice of structure. For example, any 'investment-type' activity that could prejudice a shareholder's entrepreneurs' relief should be carried on through a separate company (see 15.36). In the case of a divisionalised company, it may be necessary to keep out, or extract, any high-risk activity that could potentially dissipate the assets of the entire company and lead to its demise.

3.20   Diversified owner-managed businesses must continually review their legal structures to see whether or not these remain appropriate for their various operations. This can only be done by a systematic and rational appraisal of the main commercial, legal and tax implications associated with each type of structure.

The three main legal corporate structures are illustrated in Example 1 below. The main commercial, legal and tax implications for each structure are dealt with at 3.30. Para 3.31 also includes a detailed checklist.

Example 1

Illustration of different operating structures

John and Paul Barnes have decided to incorporate their existing transport and haulage businesses. John manages the warehousing operation and Paul manages the haulage side of the business.

The main types of operating structure are illustrated below:

Divisionalised structure

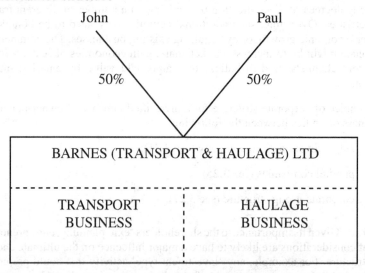

John   Paul

50%   50%

BARNES (TRANSPORT & HAULAGE) LTD

TRANSPORT   HAULAGE
BUSINESS   BUSINESS

(Carries on both businesses)

Parallel company structure

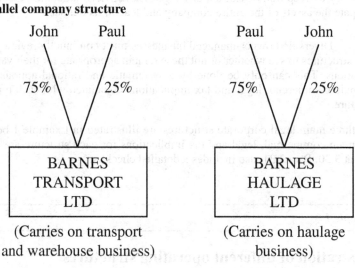

John   Paul   Paul   John

75%   25%   75%   25%

BARNES   BARNES
TRANSPORT   HAULAGE
LTD   LTD

(Carries on transport   (Carries on haulage
and warehouse business)   business)

Corporate group structure

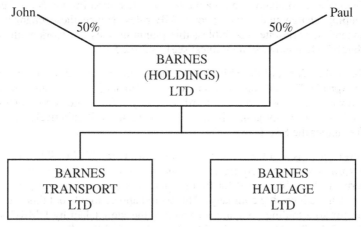

(Both trading companies are wholly owned subsidiaries
of a holding company)

Single divisionalised company

3.21   A total divisionalisation entails the various trading activities being
carried on through a single company, usually operating as a number of separate
divisions or branches. In some cases, a partial divisionalisation may be required
using a number of companies. Each divisional company would combine the
operating activities of the same or similar type of trading activity.

Divisionalisation should bring administration cost savings through
streamlining, etc. However, high risk businesses should usually be excluded
from the divisionalised company and retained in a separate subsidiary company.
This will prevent the assets of the divisionalised company being exposed to
potential claims from creditors of the high-risk business in the event of its
collapse. The author has witnessed the difficulties encountered where one of
the divisionalised businesses (of a single company) made substantial losses
and its closure was being contemplated. The divisionalised company had no
choice but to meet all its liabilities and commitments.

3.22   Before the *FA 2011*, divisionalised structures were at a clear tax
disadvantage as compared with a typical corporate group structure (see 3.27).
The sale of a profitable trading division would have often produced a capital
gains charge (on the sale of goodwill, etc) whereas if the trade had been carried
on through a separate subsidiary company, the gain would generally be tax-free
under the Substantial Shareholding Exemption (SSE) (see 3.32).

However, the *FA 2011* changes to corporate group gains will often mean that a divisionalised company can obtain effective exemption for any *capital* gains degrouping charge under the special SSE rules. (Since these changes did not extend to corporate intangibles, this planning does not work with post-31 March 2002 goodwill/intangibles: see 12.45–12.50.)

To obtain the benefit of the SSE, the company will first hive down the relevant (pre-1 April 2002) trade and assets to a new company (Newco). Subsequently, Newco would then be sold to the third party buyer. Since the degrouping gain is taxed as part of any gain arising on the share sales, it effectively becomes tax-free under the SSE (see 3.38).

However, there is a potential technical difficulty here. *TCGA 1992, Sch 7AC, para 15A(2)* seems to require the chargeable assets (such as goodwill and property) to have been used for trading purposes by a fellow *group* member (other than the investing company). This would appear to rule out this planning option for sole trading companies (which is the view taken by HMRC in its *Capital Gains Tax Manual* at CG53080C). Many feel that this is an oversight in the legislation since seems contrary to the policy reason for this provision.

With most 'hive-down' arrangements, Newco would not have been held by the 'divisionalised' company for the minimum 12-month SSE 'substantial shareholding' period (see 3.32). However, *TCGA 1992, Sch 7AC, para 15A* deems the 'seller' (ie the divisionalised company) to have satisfied this 'holding' requirement whilst the 'hived-down' assets (including goodwill) were used for trading purposes by the group. Furthermore, Newco would also be deemed to have been a trading company for the minimum 12-month 'SSE' period before the sale.

Switching a corporate group to a divisionalised structure

3.23   If a diversified business is currently operating within a corporate group structure, it is usually possible to restructure its operations on a divisionalised basis without any material tax costs. The trade, assets and liabilities of each subsidiary would be transferred (or hived-up) to the parent company (which becomes the divisionalised company).

Each subsidiary will usually transfer its net assets at book value for a cash consideration, which is frequently left outstanding as an inter-company loan because the then dormant subsidiary has no requirement for cash. The assets are normally transferred at their book values (provided the transferring subsidiary has positive reserves, a transfer at its carrying book value does not create a distribution for *Companies Act 2006* purposes – see 13.101.)

Alternatively, the relevant assets could be distributed in specie to the parent company (see 9.8)

CTA 2010, Pt 22, Ch 1 ensures that no capital allowance clawbacks occur (the assets being transferred at their tax written down values). Furthermore, provided that all the relevant liabilities are transferred to the new divisionalised company, any unused trading losses would automatically be transferred with the trade offset in the divisionalised company against the future profits of that *same* trading activity.

No capital gains would arise on the assets transferred as they would be transferred under the no gain/no loss rule under *TGCA 1992, s 171*. The capital gains 'no gain/no loss' still applies to goodwill and other intellectual property (IP) held by the group at 1 April 2002 which continue to rank as 'capital gains' assets in the hands of the (related) transferee company (since this falls outside the scope of *CTA 2009, s 882(1)(a), (3)*).

Goodwill and other IP assets acquired (from third parties) or created by the group after 31 March 2002 are transferred on a 'tax-neutral' basis under the *CTA 2009, Part 8* intangibles regime [*CTA 2009, ss 775, 776, and 848*].

The 'hive-up' transfer of assets should not produce any stamp duty land tax or VAT costs [*FA 2003, Sch 7, para 1* and *VATA 1994, s 43* or *VAT (Special Provisions) Order 1995, art 5*].

The proposed divisionalisation may affect the confidence of the employees, customers, suppliers and bankers. It will therefore be important to give advance notification to all interested parties setting out the particular reasons in each case. A number of important commercial issues will also need to be addressed. For example, borrowing arrangements will have to be re-negotiated and various trading contracts may need to be signed, re-negotiated or novated.

Protection of valuable trading names

3.24   It is possible that well-known and highly valued trade names may be attached to the subsidiary companies which become dormant as a result of the divisionalisation. However, the valuable trading names of subsidiaries can be protected by the divisionalised company entering into 'undisclosed agency' agreements with dormant subsidiaries.

Each dormant subsidiary would act as an agent for an undisclosed principal, ie the divisionalised company. In this way, the valuable name of the dormant subsidiary is retained. The trading results would still be reflected in the divisionalised company (as principal), although the 'outside world' would still believe that it is dealing with the subsidiaries (for example, sales invoices would still be raised in the name of the dormant subsidiary).

Parallel companies

3.25 In a parallel company structure, each trade is run through a separate company. The shareholdings in each company reflect the management responsibility of each underlying business. Typically, the separate companies may together be owned by a group of individuals. This structure also offers more scope for some shares to be owned by senior management.

Probably the main benefit of a parallel company structure arises if one of the companies is sold off. The sale proceeds will be paid directly to the individual shareholders and the shareholders will often be able to secure a 10% ER CGT rate on (currently) their first £10 million of qualifying gains (see 15.33–15.42).

Direct ownership of the shares also tends to give the shareholders greater flexibility in mitigating their CGT liabilities which might include ER claims, potential emigration, EIS CGT deferral relief, and so on (see Chapter 15).

By way of contrast, the overall tax charge is likely to be higher where a company is sold as a subsidiary in a corporate group structure. Although the sale of the subsidiary itself would often be free of tax (assuming that the relevant conditions for the SSE applied (see 3.32)), the sale proceeds are 'locked in' the parent company. If the sale proceeds are required by the shareholders, these are likely to be extracted as a dividend, which would incur a penal income tax charge (see 2.13–2.15 and 9.12).

A *continuing* shareholder cannot extract value as a capital gain since the Transaction in Securities rules in *ITA 2007, s 684* would almost certainly be invoked by HMRC to tax the amount as a quasi-dividend. In such cases, the only available routes would be a capital distribution on winding up the parent company, or a 'capital gains' structured buy-back of shares (not available unless the shareholder 'retires' (see 13.46 – Table 2 (2)).

Converting parallel companies to a corporate group structure

3.26 If it becomes necessary to switch from a parallel company to a corporate group structure, this can normally be done using a share for share exchange. The shareholders of each parallel company will transfer their shares to a new company (or an existing parallel company) in exchange for shares (see Example 2 below). Provided that this reorganisation is undertaken for commercial reasons, the share exchange will avoid CGT under *TCGA 1992, ss 127* and *135*. This means that the new shares are treated as being acquired at the same time and at the same base cost as the shareholders' old shares in the parallel company.

A stamp duty liability may arise (equal to ½% of the value of each parallel company 'sold') unless the strict conditions of *FA 1986, s 77* can be satisfied. This requires the new acquiring company's share capital to 'mirror' precisely that of each acquired parallel company, with the proportions held by each shareholder being the same as they were before the transfer. Where there are different shareholdings, it may be possible save stamp duty on the first share exchange by arranging for the new 'holding' company to acquire the most valuable company first. The shares of the new company will be a 'mirror-image' of the acquired company and should therefore qualify for the *FA 1986, s 77* exemption.

However, since 29 June 2016, where there are arrangements in place for a 'change in control' in the new holding company (as defined in *CTA 2010, s 1124*) at the time of the share exchange, stamp duty relief under *FA 1986, s 77* is denied (*FA 1986, s 77A*) (see also 13.60D).

It is *not* possible to transfer *unlisted shares* in a trading company to another *company* under the protection of a *TCGA 1992, s 165* business asset hold-over claim (see 13.14)

Example 2

Merging two companies via a share for share exchange

Greenwood's Legends Ltd (GLL) and Sam's Irons Ltd (SIL) are 'related' companies, which have common trading links. They now wish to merge.

The shareholdings are summarised below

	GLL *Ordinary shares of* *£1 each*	SIL *Ordinary shares of* *£1 each*
Geoff	40	–
Bobby	40	–
Billy	20	–
Kevin	–	150
Jussi	–	150
Total shares	100	300

GLL is currently valued at £2.5 million and hence, on a sale, the ordinary shares are worth £25,000 each on a sale (£2,500,000/100 shares).

SIL is worth £900,000 – each ordinary share being worth £3,000.

To facilitate the merger of the two companies, it has been agreed that GLL will acquire the entire share capital of SIL at its market value of £900,000.

Thus, GLL will need to issue 36 new £1 ordinary shares to the SIL's shareholders – i.e. 18 new shares to both Kevin and Jussi.

After GLL's acquisition of SIL, GLL's revised shareholdings would be as follows:

	Ordinary shares of £1 each	% holding
Geoff	40	29.41
Bobby	40	29.41
Billy	20	14.70
Kevin	18	13.24
Jussi	18	13.24
Total shares	136	100.00

GLL will then be worth £3.4 million (GLL value of £2 5 million plus value of its 100% subsidiary, SIL, £900,000).

The value of each shareholder's holding before and after the share exchange remains the same. For example, Kevin's 50% holding in SIL was worth £450,000 before the share exchange, being 50% × £900,000). After the share exchange, Kevin's holding in SIL would also be worth £450,000, being £3,400,000 × 18 shares/136 shares).

GLL would pay stamp duty at 0.5% on the £900,000 purchase consideration for SIL's shares.

Corporate group structure

3.27 In a conventional corporate group structure, the individual shareholders will own the shares in the parent company, which in turn will hold the shares in the various trading subsidiaries. The corporate group structure has particular operational tax advantages over the parallel company structure. The combined effect of the various 'group' tax reliefs effectively enables the group to be treated as a single entity for tax purposes, although there are some limitations to this principle.

A further attraction is a group's ability to dispose of its subsidiaries tax-free under the SSE (see 3.32). On the other hand, the tax compliance and administration for a sizeable group can involve considerable costs; a single divisionalised company tends to be more tax efficient.

The availability of the various tax reliefs for groups generally depends on the percentage of the subsidiary's ordinary shares held by the parent. In many cases, the subsidiaries will be wholly owned and hence can benefit from the full range of reliefs. If there are outside minority or joint-venture interests, the availability of certain reliefs will depend on whether the parent has:

- more than 50% of the subsidiary's shares (a 51% subsidiary);
- at least 75% of the subsidiary's ordinary shares (a 75% subsidiary).

A checklist of the main group tax reliefs, showing those available with a 51% and 75% subsidiary, is provided at 3.37.

Entrepreneurs' relief status – holding company of a trading group

Key tests

3.28 It is important to confirm that the holding company qualifies as a 'holding company of a trading group' to ensure that entrepreneurs' relief (ER) is available to the shareholders. The detailed ER rules are set out in 15.34–15.40.

To qualify, a two-stage test must be satisfied:

- the company must be a holding company, ie its business must consist wholly or mainly (more than 50%) of the holding of shares in one or more 51% subsidiaries (ignoring any trade actually carried on by it);

- the group must be a trading group, ie when looking at all the activities actually carried on by the group, they must be of a 'trading' nature. For these purposes, any investment/non-trading activities are ignored provided they are not 'substantial' in relation to the group's total activities [*TCGA 1992, s 165A*].

HMRC's practice is to interpret 'substantial' as meaning 'more than 20%'. There is no definitive measure of this and therefore various indicative measures should be examined when reviewing a company's qualifying ER status, with each case being judged on its own facts.

Thus, if there are non-trading activities, such as property letting to *non-group* members, holding share investments and so on, these must represent less than 20% of whatever measure is appropriate in each case. The possible measures used may include the turnover from non-trading activities, the value of non-trading investments, the underlying costs, or the time spent by the company's directors and employees on non-trading activities.

Since the legislation requires all of the group's activities to be 'taken together', any intra-group transactions, such as where a holding company lets property to a (51%) subsidiary, would be ignored. (See also 15.40–15.43A for further detailed commentary.)

Given the subjective nature of these tests, it is probably better to keep 'tainted' activities in a separate company outside the group.

In less 'clear-cut' cases, companies can apply to HMRC under the non-statutory business clearance procedure to confirm whether the company is a qualifying trading company for ER purposes (see 15.44).

Treatment of joint venture interests

3.29 For share disposals after 17 March 2015, the favourable ER (and business asset gift relief) treatment for joint venture interests *only* applies where the shareholder claiming ER has an effective 5% interest in the underlying 'joint venture' trading company. In such cases, the joint venture company is effectively treated as 'transparent', with the 'investing company/group being deemed to carry on an appropriate proportion of the joint venture company's trade (see 15.43–15.43C for further coverage of this area).

If the ER-claimant does not have the required 5% effective holding in the joint venture company, the investing company's/group's shareholding in the 'joint venture' company is treated as an investment. This will not necessarily mean that the investing company/group fails to qualify as a trading entity for ER, since this will depend on an analysis of the various factors described in 3.28 above and 15.40–15.41.

These rules apply for ER and business asset gift hold-over relief purposes in determining the trading status of the relevant company/group. The SSE legislation has different 'joint venture' rules (see 3.34).

TAX AND COMMERCIAL FACTORS AFFECTING CHOICE OF STRUCTURE

3.30   The selection of a suitable structure depends upon the relative importance of a number of commercial, tax and legal factors.

The commercial consideration of limited liability may outweigh all other considerations, particularly in relation to certain types of trading activity, which are vulnerable to large claims and liabilities. This would point to the use of separate parallel companies or a group structure. However, many banks and other lenders will wish to protect their position by entering into cross-guarantee and personal guarantee arrangements.

Conventional corporate group structures may be attractive given that disposals of subsidiaries are often tax-free under the SSE (see 3.32). However, where the owner-managers wish to extract the sale proceeds from the holding company, an income tax charge would be incurred. If one or more of the companies are likely to be sold, the availability of ER (on the first £10 million of gains) giving a CGT charge of 10% on disposal, gives considerable impetus to a 'parallel company' arrangement.

If one or more trades are making substantial losses, it is normally advisable to ensure their immediate offset, which would point towards a group or divisionalised structure.

In many cases, the optimum shareholding structure may be a 'hybrid' arrangement using a combination of the main structures outlined above. The main tax and commercial considerations are summarised in the checklist – (see 3.31). The detailed tax reliefs available to groups are considered further at 3.37.

OPERATING STRUCTURE CHECKLIST

3.31

	Single company (divisionalised structure)	*Parallel companies*	*Corporate group*
Commercial liability	Risks and liabilities of any one trade may threaten the viability of the other trades (eg the entire company may be forced into receivership as a result of a major claim or liability in one division).	Limited liability for each company subject to any loan cross-guarantee arrangements (collapse of one company does not bring others down).	Limited liability for each company (subject to any cross-guarantee arrangements for borrowings, etc). Parent company is not legally obliged to support an insolvent subsidiary, although may need to do so to avoid adverse commercial publicity.
Audit and administration	Single audit fee for one company. Minimum audit fees, secretarial and legal compliance costs.	Each company requires an audit. Duplication of administrative costs, etc.	Each company requires an audit. Duplication of administrative costs.
	Detailed results of each trade can be hidden within one set of 'combined' accounts, which prevents competitors and potential predators obtaining detailed information about each trade.	Each company needs to prepare accounts.	May need to prepare consolidated accounts.

	Single company (divisionalised structure)	Parallel companies	Corporate group
	Divisionalised accounts may show a much larger-sized business with much greater financial strength (this may assist certain companies in obtaining contracts etc). Brings pressure to harmonise employment terms and conditions, etc for employees and managers of all divisions, which may create problems. Possibility of demotivating key members of management team, eg lower perceived status of divisional manager as compared with company director.		In certain cases, the consolidated accounts create the impression of much greater size and financial backing.
Shareholder control	No direct relationship between shareholdings and management responsibility for each business.	Shareholdings can reflect management responsibility of each business, giving greater control and reward for efforts.	Shares should normally be held in the holding company as this enables company to secure a statutory corporate tax deduction for employee shares under *CTA 2009, Pt 12, Ch 2*.

	Single company (divisionalised structure)	Parallel companies	Corporate group
			Where appropriate, 'subsidiary company' employees can be given a special class of shares in the parent company with the required rights over the *subsidiary*'s profits and assets, etc.
Sale of company/trade	Proceeds are received directly by shareholders and subject to CGT with the possible benefit of ER, therefore no element of double taxation.	Proceeds received directly by shareholders, with possible low CGT liability due to the availability of ER (as for single company)	Subsidiaries can often be sold without a tax charge under the Substantial Shareholdings Exemption (SSE) (see 3.32).
	Provided the trade started before 1 April 2002, it should be possible to sell a division on an exempt basis under SSE by first hiving-down the trade and asset to a new subsidiary *provided there is at least one pre-existing subsidiary.* However, a tax change will be incurred if the sale proceeds are required to be extracted by the ultimate shareholders.	Each business can be sold separately through a company.	Group roll-over relief is also available for asset sales (for property and goodwill, although goodwill/IP roll-over is more restrictive (see 15.11).

Single company (divisionalised structure)	*Parallel companies*	*Corporate group*
This strategy will *not* apply where the goodwill of the trade started or was acquired after 31 March 2002, since a degrouping charge will arise under the intangibles regime'		Shareholders suffer tax charge if proceeds are extracted from the group.

Tax implications

	Single company (divisionalised structure)	*Parallel companies*	*Corporate group*
Corporation tax payment	Single company will be able to pay its corporation tax at the normal nine month due date provided it keeps its profits below £1,500,000	All companies can pay their corporation tax at the normal nine month due date provided each has profits below £1,500,000	Under the Quarterly Instalment Payment regime, companies must pay their corporation tax in quarterly instalments where their taxable profits exceed the relevant apportioned limit (ie £1,500,000, divided by the number of active related 51% group companies plus one). The timing of quarterly instalment payments is accelerated for companies with annual taxable profits in excess of £20m.

	Single company (divisionalised structure)	Parallel companies	Corporate group
Tax reliefs	Very efficient for tax purposes – maximises available reliefs and provides full matching of payments, receipts and gains.	Within each company, the position is the same as that of a single company. Since April 2017, companies can offset their unused post-31 March 2017 trade losses against all future income/profit streams, subject to the 50% offset restriction for profits over £5 million (see 4.40 – 4.40A). However, trading losses and capital losses cannot be surrendered between the companies.	Within each company, the position is the same as that of a single company. Since April 2017, companies can offset carried forward (post-31 March 2017) trade losses against future other income/profit streams or against fellow group companies profits. However, the offset of carried forward losses against future profits is restricted to 50% of the amount of profits over £5 million. The £5 million allowance is a group threshold but it can be allocated amongst group members in the most suitable way (see 4.40-4.40A). Trading losses can also be surrendered between each member of a 75% group (see 4.41 – 4.41A). Various other reliefs are available (see 3.37).

	Single company (divisionalised structure)	*Parallel companies*	*Corporate group*
	In particular, losses of any trade can be relieved by offset against current year's total profits, and: • offset against total profits of previous year; • carried forward against profits of the same trade. Since April 2017, companies can offset their unused post-31 March 2017 losses against all future income/profit streams. However, the offset of carried forward losses against future profits will be restricted to 50% of the amount of profits over £5 million (see 4.40–4.40A).		Group companies can normally elect under *TCGA 1992, s171A* to match their capital gains and capital losses – in effect, enabling capital losses to be relieved against gains made by other group members. (However, it is not possible to use pre-entry capital losses – broadly *pre-acquisition* capital losses of *acquired* subsidiaries).
Capital losses	Chargeable gains will also be offset against allowable capital losses.		

110

THE SUBSTANTIAL SHAREHOLDINGS EXEMPTION (SSE)

Background

3.32   A valuable corporate capital gains exemption is generally available on the sale of trading subsidiaries under the Substantial Shareholdings Exemption (SSE) [*TCGA 1992, Sch 7AC*]. The corollary is that no relief is available for capital losses arising on an SSE-qualifying disposal.

For these purposes, substantial means at least 10% of the ordinary share capital (and other economic rights, such as at least a 10% entitlement in profits available for distribution) [*TCGA 1992, Sch 7AC, para 8*]. Thus, the exemption should apply to most sales of trading subsidiary companies as well as equity interests in joint ventures and other affiliated companies. The SSE will apply equally to disposals of UK and overseas resident companies.

The *Finance (No 2) Act 2017* makes substantial relaxations to the SSE conditions, enabling the SSE to be available to a wider range of groups (see 3.33). Special SSE rules were also introduced to enable qualifying institutional investors to claim SSE but they are not covered here. Please see 2016/17 and earlier editions of this book for details of the pre-1 April 2017 SSE regime.

Furthermore, since 2011 degrouping charges are often exempt under SSE (see 3.38 for detailed rules). However, such SSE protection is not available for degrouping charges on *CTA 2009, Pt 8* intangible assets (ie goodwill and other intangible assets created or acquired after 31 March 2002).

Main qualifying conditions

3.33   It is clearly important to ensure that the relevant main conditions for obtaining the SSE will be satisfied. Since 1 April 2017, there are only two key requirements:

(*a*)   the relevant shareholding investment must qualify as a 'substantial shareholding' held in the investee company *throughout* a 12-month period starting not more than six years before the shares are disposed of (see 3.34); and

(*b*)   the investee ('target') company in which the shares are held must be a *qualifying* trading company/holding company of a trading group from the start of the 12-month 10% 'substantial shareholding' period (in (a) above) and ending with the disposal date (see 3.35).

Since 1 April 2017, no statutory 'trading' requirement is placed on the investing company or group (ie the company/group making the relevant disposal).

The *previous* SSE legislation required the seller company to be a trading company or member of a trading group *immediately* after the disposal. This prevented the ability to claim the SSE in a number of cases. Typically, a group would have been (predominantly) an investment group or a holding company would sell its only trading subsidiary (and not have qualified as a trading company afterwards).

Under the *F (No 2) A 2017* regime, these issues are now irrelevant since the tax 'status' of the investing company ceased to be taken into account for SSE purposes. This is a very welcome change since it is *no longer necessary* to carry out a detailed review of the 'investing' group's activities to determine the availability of SSE.

Substantial shareholding requirement

3.34   The investee/seller company must hold at least 10% of the ordinary share capital of (and 10% of certain economic rights in) the investee/target company (*TCGA 1992, Sch 7AC, paras 7 and 8*). The 10% shareholding requirement must be satisfied throughout any 12-month period starting within six years of the disposal.

In most cases, the selling company will hold at least 10% of the equity in the investee/target company within the 12 months ending with the date of the disposal. However, the 'six-year' look-back enables SSE to be claimed on any disposal so long as the selling company holds at least 10% of the equity for a continuous 12-month period within the six years before the relevant disposal (see Example 3 below).

For the purposes of this test, it is possible to 'look through' any prior no gain/no loss transfer (such as an intra-group transfer) and include the *transferor's* period of ownership. Furthermore, all holdings held by the group are counted for the purposes of the '10% test' [*TCGA 1992, Sch 7AC, paras 9 and 10*].

Example 3

Claiming SSE on disposal of very small (less than 10%) holding

City Group Ltd acquired a 40% shareholding in a precision engineering company, Zabaleta PE Ltd (ZPEL) on 16 January 1985.

It sold a 35% shareholding in ZPEL on 26 May 2017 (with the benefit of the SSE), and retained a very small 5% holding in that company.

On 11 September 2017 City Group Ltd sold its remaining 5% stake in ZPEL.

Provided ZPEL remains a trading company until 11 September 2017, City Group Ltd can also claim SSE on the sale of its 5% interest since it has held at least 10% of the ordinary share capital of ZPEL throughout a 12-month period in the six years ending 11 September 2017.

'Trading company or trading group member' requirement

3.35 For the purpose of determining whether or not companies make up a group, the capital gains group rules in *TCGA 1992, s 170* are followed but with 51% subsidiaries being included (rather than the normal 75% subsidiary test). A 'subgroup' represents companies that would form a (51%) group but where the 'sub-holding' company is a 51% subsidiary of another group company.

The key SSE trading company and trading group definitions are similar to those used for CGT ER purposes [*TCGA 1992, Sch 7AC, paras 20* and *21*] (see 15.36–15.39 for further analysis). However, the SSE regime has less restrictive rules that treat most (10% plus) joint venture interests in trading companies as trading activities (rather than investments) for the purposes of the 'trading test' [*TCGA 1992, Sch 7AC, para 24*].

Under the *F (No 2) A 2017* regime, the *investee/target company* must be a trading company or holding company of a (51%) trading group (sub-group) throughout the 'substantial shareholding' period up to the date of the disposal (see 3.34).

The previous SSE rules provided that the *investee/target* company also had to satisfy this 'trading' test *immediately* after it was sold (requiring the seller to insist on a warranty from the buyer to ensure the condition would be satisfied). Since 1 April 2017, this is no longer the case except in two specific cases:

- When the company is sold to a (non-UK) 'connected' company/ shareholder (ie outside the normal capital gains group).

- Where reliance is placed on the special 'deeming' rule for trade 'hive-downs' in *TCGA 1992, Sch 7AC, para 15A* – see 12.60. The (often) new subsidiary company must therefore continue to trade immediately after its disposal out of the group.

The status of the *seller company/group* is no longer relevant under the post-31 March 2017 regime. Despite this relaxation, the investee/target company must still meet the relatively stringent 'trading' test throughout the 12-month substantial shareholding period *and* (where applicable – see 3.34) up to the relevant disposal date. It will not qualify if there are any 'substantial' non-trading activities and clearly a pure 'investment' subsidiary does not attract SSE.

The legislation does not define 'substantial'. However, HMRC generally seeks to apply a relative test using a 20% benchmark (see *IR Tax Bulletin 62* (see 15.37)). This 20% test is likely to be applied by Inspectors when considering whether SSE is likely to apply on a particular transaction.

In practice, the HMRC would apply the 20% test to various measures, such as income, assets, and management time. In the author's view, although these tests are helpful, they merely provide a pragmatic guide. They should not be followed rigidly and (in some cases) one or more of these criteria may not provide a reliable indicator; for example, the disposition of a company's assets might not reveal the true nature of the company's main activities – assets are not activities, they are merely the result of the activities.

The holding of cash/income can still be treated as trading if the amounts are earmarked for future trading use. Similarly, the holding of surplus cash that is derived from trading cash flows can normally be ignored provided that it is not actively managed as an investment.

3.35A   If HMRC apply an asset test, then the value of a trading company's, or group's, goodwill (which is essentially trading in character) should be included, even though it is not normally reflected on the balance sheet. In broad terms, goodwill represents the amount by which the market value of the company/ group exceeds its tangible net asset value.

Groups are effectively viewed as a 'single entity' for SSE purposes. Thus intra-group transactions are ignored (even if they are of an investment nature – such as the letting of 'trading' properties to subsidiary companies). Similarly, time spent on managing trading subsidiaries would also be disregarded. In dealing with any HMRC challenge in this area, it should always be remembered that the '20%' non-trading limit does not have any statutory backing and would not necessarily be followed by the courts.

Given the substantial amounts that may be involved in an SSE claim, if there are any potential doubts or concerns about an investee/target company's 'trading' status, it is generally prudent to seek an appropriate assurance from HMRC by applying for a non-statutory business clearance. (Before 1 April 2017, the majority of non-statutory clearance applications were often made due to uncertainties about the 'trading' status of the *investing* group – thankfully the *F (No 2) A 2017* relaxations remove the need for such clearance applications!)

HMRC will accept clearance applications where there is a material uncertainty over the SSE status of an impending transaction (see HMRC Business Brief 41/07). The application should cover the various matters on HMRC's checklist (see HMRC website at www.hmrc.gov.uk/cap/annex-a-checklist.pdf).

In the context of an SSE application, this would include the reasons for the transaction, the relevant facts, the company's view of the application of the SSE rules to the disposal and the issues on which HMRC's opinion is sought. It is worth noting that HMRC may reject or not respond to an SSE clearance application if it does not explain in sufficient detail the genuine uncertainty inherent in the availability of SSE.

Example 4

Exempt disposal under the SSE

Terry Holdings Ltd has had three wholly-owned trading subsidiaries for many years as follows:

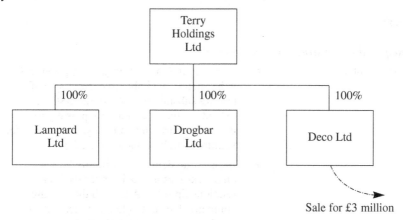

Sale for £3 million

The group is currently valued at some £35 million and has no investment activities.

However, in May 2017, it receives an offer to sell Deco Ltd to Stamford Bridge plc for £3 million. The disposal of Deco Ltd takes place on 18 August 2017, which gives rise to a capital gain of £2.8 million.

The capital gain of £2.8 million arising on the disposal of the shares in Deco Ltd should be exempt under the (post-31 March 2017) SSE rules.

• Since Deco Ltd has been wholly-owned by Terry Holdings Ltd for at least the previous 12 months up to 18 August 2017, it satisfies the 'substantial shareholding' test.

• Deco Ltd ('the company invested in') has been a trading company for the 12 months to 18 August 2017.

CORPORATE GROUP RULES

Tax treatment of group companies

3.36   Most groups of family companies and owner-managed businesses will have wholly owned UK subsidiaries and will therefore enjoy all the main tax reliefs available to groups. However, both the legislation and case law continue to demonstrate that the combined effect of the group rules does not always put the group in the same position as a single company.

Furthermore, if outside minority interests are to be introduced in one or more subsidiaries, care must be taken to ensure that the shareholding structure does not unnecessarily prejudice important tax benefits. The required minimum shareholding qualification varies according to the type of relief.

Main reliefs for group companies – checklist

3.37

Required group structure	*Main reliefs*
51% + subsidiary	• Substantial Shareholdings Exemption (SSE) is frequently available to exempt sale of trading subsidiaries. (*Note*: the SSE also extends to the sale of a 10% plus equity interest in a trading company, such as a joint venture shareholding – see 3.32.)
	• Intra-group debts can normally be released on a 'tax-neutral' basis under the loan relationship rules. Although the lending company does not obtain any tax deduction for the amount waived, the borrowing company's credit to profit and loss is normally tax-free.
	• Companies may participate in 'group payment' arrangements to pay corporation tax in quarterly instalments. The representative company makes the tax payment(s) for the participating group companies, which helps to ensure that the group's tax interest exposure is minimised (see 4.50–4.53).
75% + subsidiary	• Current year tax losses generated by one group member can be surrendered to another by way of group relief (see 4.41) [*CTA 2010, ss 99–106*].
	Since 1 April 2017, brought forward trade losses arising after that date can also be group-relieved, with the offset being restricted to 50% of profits exceeding the apportioned group threshold. The £5 million threshold is allocated amongst group companies as decided by the group – (see 4.41A).

Required group structure   *Main reliefs*

- Consortium relief may be available for a pro rata share of current losses [*CTA 2010, ss 132, 133* and *143–153*].

- Chargeable assets can be transferred between group companies with the deferral of the relevant tax until the asset is sold outside the group, or a degrouping charge arises on the transferee company leaving the group within six years (although degrouping charges may be exempt under the SSE – see 3.38) [*TCGA 1992, ss 171* and *179*].

  Similarly, post-1 April 2002 intangible fixed assets are transferred on a 'tax-neutral' basis between 75% group members, thus preventing any taxable profit arising on the transfer. If the transferee company leaves the group within six years, an intangibles degrouping charge arises within that company (subject to an election to allocate the charge to a fellow group member) [*CTA 2009, ss 775, 776,* and *848*].

- Effective group capital loss relief can be obtained by electing under *TCGA 1992, s 171A.*

- Tax refunds can be surrendered to other group members to minimise the group's net interest on unpaid tax [*CTA 2010, s 963*].

- All group companies are effectively regarded as a single entity for the purposes of roll-over relief. This enables a capital gain realised by one group company to be rolled-over against qualifying assets purchased by another outside the group [*TCGA 1992, s 175*].

- Intangible fixed asset roll-over relief is also available for reinvestment in goodwill and other intangible fixed assets on a group basis [*CTA 2009, ss 754–763*]. (See 12.53 and 15.14).

Required group structure   Main reliefs

- Trades can be transferred between the group companies without the adverse tax consequences of a cessation. Assets on which capital allowances have been claimed would be transferred at their tax written down values and unused trading losses are carried across into the transferee company (subject only to the restrictions applying where the transferor company is technically insolvent) [*CTA 2010, Pt 22, Ch 1*].

- Land and property (subject to stamp duty land tax (SDLT)) and shares (subject to stamp duty) can normally be transferred between group companies without any SDLT/stamp duty liability. However, the SDLT and stamp duty group transfer provisions do not apply where there are arrangements for the transferee company to leave the group, or the consideration for the transfer is being provided directly or non-directly by a third party [SDLT – *FA 2003, Sch 7, para 2*; stamp duty – *FA 1930, s 42; FA 1967, s 27* – see also SP 3/98].

  However, an SDLT degrouping charge arises in respect of *land and property* transferred intra-group where the *transferee* company leaves the group within three years of the intra-group transfer and continues to hold the property [*FA 2003, Sch 7, para 3*].

Capital gains' degrouping charges and interaction with SSE

3.38   Members of the same (75%) group are permitted to transfer chargeable assets between them on a no gain/no loss basis (under *TCGA 1992, s 171*). This recognises that, although each group company is a separate legal entity, the group companies effectively operate together as a single economic unit.

To ensure that this rule cannot be abused by the so-called 'envelope trick', we have degrouping charge legislation in *TCGA 1992, s 179*. Broadly speaking, the degrouping charge rules apply where a chargeable asset has been transferred into a subsidiary within *six years* of it leaving the group (typically via a third party sale). Provided the relevant asset is still held by the subsidiary when it leaves the group, *TCGA 1992, s 179(4)* provides that there is a deemed disposal (and re-acquisition) of that asset. Under the pre-*FA 2011* regime, the degrouping tax charge arose in the 'departing' subsidiary, although an election could have been made to allocate the gain to its fellow (75%) group members. (Similar rules apply to degrouping charges realised under the *CTA 2009, Part 8* intangibles regime)

Whilst the rationale for the degrouping charge is understandable, it has often caused many problems for corporate groups seeking to sell part of their activities some time after a commercial group restructuring exercise. Furthermore, since the introduction of the SSE in 2002, shares in a subsidiary can often be sold 'tax-free' under the SSE (see 3.32 to 3.35A) but that subsidiary could still be exposed to a degrouping tax charge. *FA 2011* addressed these concerns by radically changing the mechanics of the degrouping charge.

The actual degrouping gain/loss is still calculated on the same basis – ie the transferee subsidiary is deemed to sell and reacquire the relevant asset at its market value immediately after the previous intra-group transfer. However, where the transferee leaves the group due to a sale of its shares (or shares in another group company) – as will typically be the case – then the degrouping gain is added to the consideration received for the disposal of the shares. On the other hand, if the deemed degrouping disposal gives rise to a capital loss, this is effectively added to the base cost of the shares being sold (*TCGA 1992, s 179(3D)*). Note that the '*FA 2011*' degrouping charge provisions are not 'mirrored' under the *CTA 2009, Part 8* intangibles regime (see 3.39).

If the subsidiary leaves the group as a result of more than one 'group' share disposal, the degrouping gains/losses can be allocated between the various disposals as the group sees fit (*TCGA 1992, s 179 F*).

One very important consequence of these changes is that where the sale of the subsidiary (or other group company) qualifies for the SSE, this will also effectively ensure that the degrouping gain obtains the benefit of the exemption. The interaction between the SSE and revised degrouping rules is illustrated in example 5 below.

The original method for taxing the degrouping charge will continue to apply where a company leaves the group otherwise than as a result of a share disposal by a UK resident company – for example, as a result of a share issue that 'swamps' the existing 75% group connection.

Example 5

SSE protection for degrouping charges

Bilic Holdings Ltd is the parent company of several 100% owned trading subsidiaries.

In August 2017, Bilic Holdings Ltd sold its 100% shareholding in Enner Ltd for £2.5 million. (The current 'indexed' base cost of the shares is £450,000.)

Enner Ltd had acquired its current office premises from a fellow 75% subsidiary, Noble Ltd, in February 2014 at its then market value of £1.25 million , although for tax purposes it was transferred on a no gain/no loss basis under *TCGA 1992, s 171*. These office premises had originally been purchased by Noble Ltd in August 2003 for £500,000.

The sale of the shares in Enner Ltd qualifies for exemption under the SSE rules. This means that the degrouping gain in respect of its office premises is also exempted since it is added to the capital gains consideration for the Enner Ltd share sale.

The relevant calculations are as follows:

Sale of 100% holding in Enner Ltd	
	£000
Share sale proceeds	2,500
Degrouping gain (see below)	550
Total sale consideration	3,050
Less: Indexed base cost	(450)
Capital gain = Exempt under SSE	2,600
Degrouping charge	
Deemed MV (February 2014) consideration	1,250
Less: Base cost	(500)
Indexation (£500,000 × 0.40)	(200)
Capital gain	*550
*treated as part of consideration for sale of Enner Ltd	
Note that since more than three years have passed since the intra-group transfer, there would be no SDLT degrouping charge (see 3.37).	

Intangibles degrouping charge

3.39   The intangibles legislation applies to goodwill, intellectual property and other intangibles created or acquired by a group *after 31 March 2002*. It has similar (but not the same) degrouping charge rules to those used for 'capital gains' assets under *TCGA 1992, s 179*.

Under the intangibles regime, where a (75%) subsidiary company leaves a group:

- holding 'new' goodwill or intangible assets;

- which it previously acquired within the previous six years from a fellow group company under the 'tax-neutral' rule in *CTA 2009, s 776*,

CTA 2009, s 780 imposes a degrouping charge on the 'departing' subsidiary. The subsidiary is deemed to have realised and reacquired the asset immediately after the original intra-group transfer at its then market value. Consequently, this will normally give rise to a taxable credit, based on the excess of the market value over any available base cost. (On the other hand, if the base cost exceeds the market value, a tax deductible trading debit arises but only if the goodwill/intangibles were acquired between 1 April 2002 and 7 July 2015).

The goodwill/intangible asset is deemed to be re-acquired at market value. Following the *F (No 2) A 2015* restrictions introduced in *CTA 2009, s 816A*, it would appear that no tax relief would be available on 'pre-7 July 2015' goodwill where the 'deemed' re-acquisition occurs after 7 July 2015.

Where a degrouping charge arises after 7 July 2015, it will simply be based on the actual degrouping gain (with no adjustments for tax amortisation). See 2013/14 edition for treatment of pre-8 July 2015 degrouping charges (at 3.39).

The degrouping charge is normally taxed in the relevant 'transferee' subsidiary company as a trading profit immediately before it leaves the group (although it is possible to reallocate the profit/loss to a fellow 75% group company).

Unfortunately, the *FA 2011* SSE changes (see 3.38) have not been extended to the corresponding intangibles degrouping charge in *CTA 2009, s 780*. An intangibles degrouping tax charge would therefore still arise in a subsidiary that was sold within six years of a prior transfer of (*post-March 2002*) goodwill to it, even though SSE is likely to be available to the 'disposing' company.

Given the differing tax treatment between capital gains and intangibles degrouping charges, groups will need to carefully identify whether any goodwill potentially subject to a degrouping charge arose or was acquired before 31 March 2002 or afterwards.

PLANNING CHECKLIST — SHAREHOLDING AND CORPORATE STRUCTURES

Company

- Keep number of companies to a minimum consistent with commercial objectives. However, the number of commonly 'owned' (*but not grouped*) trading companies does not affect the corporation tax charge.

- Activities which carry a high level of commercial risk should be kept in a separate company.

- It is normally possible to sell 'trading' subsidiaries without a tax charge under the SSE. Following the post-31 March 2017 relaxations, it should be easier to qualify for the SSE (since, for example, the tax status of the seller company/group is now irrelevant).

- Under the *FA 2011* degrouping charge provisions, it is often possible to sell a trading subsidiary with SSE protection for the degrouping gain as well as the 'share disposal' gain. However, this beneficial treatment does *not* apply to degrouping charges arising on (post-March 2002) goodwill or intangible assets.

- The company's 'trading' status for SSE and ER purposes should be reviewed regularly.

- The company must ensure that all chargeable events in connection with shares and share options are reported online on form 42, normally by 6 July following the end of the relevant tax year.

Working shareholders

- Owner-manager shareholders should normally be eligible for ER, which provides a low 10% CGT rate on cumulative qualifying gains up to £10 million. ER is only available if the company satisfies the fairly stringent trading criteria throughout the 12 months prior to any share sale.

- Shares *transferred* to the owner manager's children and other family members should be exempt from any employment income tax charges since they are made available in the 'normal course' of domestic and family relationships.

- The award of new shares or the exercise of share options to employees and key managers may be taxed as employment income where they are acquired at less than market value. If these shares are only subject to the standard pre-emption rights, etc, applying to all shareholders, HMRC may still regard them as 'restricted'. It is therefore generally prudent to make a protective *ITEPA 2003, s 431* election to ensure that any future (post-acquisition) growth in the shares falls within the capital gains regime.

- Owner-managers will have effective control of their company by owning more than 50% of voting shares – this may include shares held by trusts in which they are (first-named) trustees.

- To obtain the greatest benefit from the 100% IHT business property relief (BPR) exemption, owner-managers should maximise their own/spouse's shareholding – money introduced by way of loan does not qualify for any IHT relief.

- Separate companies enable ownership to be more directly related to management of different businesses.

- Different classes of shares can be used to give flexibility over future dividend payments.

Other employees

- Employee share incentive arrangements normally increases the employees' identification with the company and offers them the possibility of a large capital profit on future sale (which would be taxable at beneficial CGT rates).

- Owner-managed groups should aim to issue all shares to their employees (including those employed by subsidiary companies) at 'parent company' level to obtain the statutory corporate tax deduction for shares issued to employees under *CTA 2009, Pt 12, Ch 2*.

Non-working shareholders

- 100% BPR is generally available on any shareholding in a trading company or group. This means that BPR can be obtained on both voting and non-voting shareholdings, including preference shares.

- Since 6 April 2016, capital gains are normally taxed at 20% (or possibly 10% for those on low income).

Chapter 4

Trading Company versus Investment Company Computations under CTSA

TAX STATUS OF COMPANY

General tax treatment of trading and investment companies

4.1   It is often necessary to determine whether a company is a trading company or an investment company since this may affect the tax reliefs or exemptions that are available to the company or its shareholders. For example, certain CGT and IHT reliefs may be enjoyed by shareholders of a trading company (or holding company of a trading group – see below), but not by shareholders of an investment company.

In this context, it should be appreciated that the definition of a 'trading company' for CGT Entrepreneurs' Relief (ER), CGT business asset hold-over relief and the corporate Substantial Shareholdings Exemption (SSE) is markedly different from that used for most other tax purposes, particularly corporation tax.

Where family or owner-managed businesses are operated through a holding/subsidiary company structure, the holding company may be treated as carrying on an investment business even though it does little more than hold shares in its trading subsidiaries. However, the various tax reliefs given to the shareholders of trading companies are extended to situations where the shareholders own shares in a holding company of a trading group. Of course, where a holding company carries on a substantial trading activity in its own right, for example, supplying management and administrative support services to its trading subsidiaries for a management charge, it may (depending on the other facts) be treated as a trading company for tax purposes.

The computation of the taxable profits for each type of company is computed in a different way for corporation tax (see 4.2 and 4.3). For simplicity, this chapter covers the corporation tax treatment of both trading and investment companies. Although the legislation no longer insists on a company being an investment company to claim certain corporation tax reliefs, this chapter retains the 'investment company' nomenclature since, in practice, the vast majority of companies carrying on investment businesses will be colloquially known or identified as 'investment companies'.

This chapter also contains a summary of the corporation tax payment rules and the corporation tax self-assessment (CTSA) return, which is given at 4.50–4.54 and 4.55–4.58, respectively. HMRC penalties under CTSA are dealt with in 4.59–4.64.

Trading companies

4.2　　Broadly, for many tax purposes (with the notable exceptions of CGT ER, business asset hold-over relief and the corporate SSE) a trading company is one which exists *wholly or mainly* for the purpose of carrying on a trade.

In many cases, it will be clear that the company exists for trading purposes. In marginal cases, it may be possible to demonstrate that the company is a trading company by applying the 'wholly or mainly' test to the company's turnover, net profits, net assets and management time. Ideally, more than two of the above tests should 'wholly or mainly' relate to the trading activities. HMRC usually regard the expression 'wholly or mainly' as meaning more than 50%.

4.3　　A more stringent definition applies for CGT ER and CGT business asset hold-over relief. Here, the owner manager and the other shareholders only obtain ER if the company exists '*wholly* for the purpose of carrying on one or more trades', although the legislation ignores any *non-trading* activities where they have no substantial (ie 20%) effect on the total business (see 15.36– 15.38). A similar rule applies for corporate SSE, although the SSE regime is more generous in its treatment of underlying joint venture structures (see 3.42 and 3.45).

CORPORATION TAX COMPUTATIONS

Pro-forma computation for trading company

4.4　　A detailed pro-forma corporation tax computation for a typical trading company is set out below, together with accompanying notes. For corporation tax purposes, the assessable profits represent the amount of income and gains arising in the accounting period [*CTA 2009, ss* 2 and *5(2)*]. The pro-forma computation is comprehensive so all items will not necessarily occur in the same period, for example, if the company claims relief for a current year trading loss, there will not be a trading profit, unless the company is carrying on another trade.

Pro-forma Trading Co Ltd

Corporation tax computation based on the accounting period ended …

	£	£	*Notes*
Tax-adjusted trading profit (after deducting capital allowances) (see 4.15–4.34)	X		(a)
Less Trading losses brought forward under *CTA 2010, s 45* (see 4.40)	(X)	X	(b)
Property business income (net of allowable expenses)		X	(c)
Non-trading loan relationship profits (including interest receivable)	X		(d)
Less: Non-trading loan relationship deficit carried back	(X)	X	
Taxable dividends		X	(e)
Other taxable income		X	
Chargeable gains (less allowable capital losses)		X̲	(f)
		X	
Less: Non-trading loan relationship deficit brought forward (against non-trading profits only)		(X)	(g)
		X	
Less: Current year non-trading loan relationship deficit		(X)	(g)
		X	
Less: Current year (and unused post-31 March 2017) trading loss offset (*CTA 2010, s 37(3)(a)*) (see 4.36)		(X)	(h)
		X	and (b)
Less: Charitable donations relief		(X)	(i)
		X	
Less: Group relief (see 4.41)		(X)	(j)
		X	
Less: Trading losses carried back under *CTA 2010, s 37(3)(b)* (see 4.37)		(X̲)	(k)
TAXABLE TOTAL PROFITS		(X)	
Pro-forma computation of corporation tax liability			
Corporation tax on 'profits' @ X% (see 3.15–3.16)		X	(l)
Less: Double tax relief		(X)	
		X	
Less: Income tax on excess of 'taxed' investment income		(X)	
CORPORATION TAX LIABILITY		(X)	(m)

Notes:

(a)   All trading related interest and other trading loan relationship (LR) debits and credits are included in the company's tax-adjusted trading results. An allowable trading LR debit is available for 'impaired' debts (which includes bad and irrecoverable debts), unless they are due from 'connected companies'.

All types of interest payments to other UK companies (and UK banks) are paid gross (ie without any tax being deducted).

Amortisation or any write-off relating to goodwill and other intangibles is dealt with under *CTA 2009, Part 8*. However, this only includes goodwill and other intangibles acquired from third parties or created by the company/group between 1 April 2002 and 7 July 2015. In such cases, the accounting amortisation and write-off is deductible against the trading profits, broadly based on the amounts deducted in the company's accounts under GAAP. However, for goodwill and 'customer-related' intangibles acquired *after 7 July 2015*, the *F(No 2)A 2015* prevents any tax deduction being claimed. The detailed rules are explained at 12.49–12.50.

Any credits or profits arising on post-31 March 2002 goodwill and intangibles are generally taxed as part of the company's trading profits (see 12.49).

All patent royalties are deducted as a trading expense on an accruals basis, normally based on the amount reflected in the accounts (ie on an 'accruals basis') [*CTA 2009, s 728*]. Patent royalties to UK companies are paid gross.

(b)   Unused trading losses brought forward from periods before 1 April 2017 can only be offset against trading profits of the same trade. From 1 April 2017, the amount of loss that can be offset may be subject to various restrictions (see below).

Trading losses arising after 31 March 2017 may be set off against any type of profits or chargeable gains arising in future accounting periods. This significant increase in the flexibility of loss offsets in future periods is covered in more detail in 4.40.

From 1 April 2017, a restriction will apply to the amount of profits that can be sheltered by brought-forward losses. Only 50% of profits above the first £5 million (which may be lower if a company is part of a group) arising in any accounting period may be covered by losses brought forward from any source (see 4.40). This restriction applies regardless of when the brought-forward losses were incurred.

Since 1 April 2017, trading losses are forfeited if a major change in the conduct of the company's trade occurs within five years of a sale of the

company (or other change in ownership) [*CTA 2010, ss 673* and *674*].
A shorter period of three years applies before 1 April 2017 (see 12.59)).

(c) The corporation tax treatment of rental and other income from the
letting of UK or overseas land and property is taxed as a single property
business under *CTA 2009, s 209*. (A UK property business must be kept
separate from an overseas property business, but beyond that there is
no need to keep separate results for each individual property.) Broadly
speaking, the profits and losses of the property business are computed on
an accruals basis using the same principles for calculating taxable trading
profits (see *CTA 2009, ss* 210 and *214*). Capital allowances relating to
a property business (for example, plant provided in the let property) is
deducted as a property business expense. (Relief for a property business
loss is examined in 4.45, note (c).)

(d) Non-trading loan relationship (LR) profits include all non-trading interest
receivable, such as bank, building society and intra-group interest and
other profits arising from the company's non-trading LRs (including
non-trading foreign exchange gains). In the case of a trading company,
interest is invariably received on non-trading account.

However, any non-trading loan interest payable and other non-trading
loan relationship/foreign exchange deficits must be deducted in arriving
at the (net) 'non-trading' LR income [*CTA 2009, s 301(4)*]. Interest on
borrowings used to finance investments would be non-trading. A non-
trading LR deficit may be carried back against the company's 'non-trade'
loan relationship profits of the previous year [*CTA 2009, s 462*] (see also
note (h) below and 4.45, note (e)).

(e) The vast majority of UK and overseas dividends are exempt from UK
corporation tax. The relevant legislation can be found in *CTA 2009,
Part 9A*. It is therefore important to eliminate or reduce any overseas
withholding tax, which cannot be credited for double tax relief purposes
and will therefore be a cost.

Where a foreign-sourced dividend does fall to be taxed, it should be
'grossed-up' for any withholding taxes and (where the company holds
more than 10% of the voting rights of the overseas company) the
'underlying tax'. The underlying tax represents the overseas tax payable
on the profits out of which the dividend was paid [*TIOPA 2010, ss 32* and
57–59]. Double tax relief is claimed for these amounts up to a maximum
limit, representing the UK corporation tax on the grossed-up dividend
[*TIOPA 2010, ss 2–6* and *18*].

(f) Chargeable gains are computed in the normal way with relief given for
indexation. Roll-over relief may be available for gains arising on most
types of fixed assets used in the trade (for example, property occupied for
trading purposes and fixed plant and machinery). Capital gains arising
on the disposal of (pre-1 April 2002) goodwill can only be rolled-over
against the acquisition of 'new' goodwill and intangibles (see 15.14).

Profits arising on the sale (realisation) of post-31 March 2002 acquired/ generated goodwill and other intangibles are included within the company's trading profits, but may be deferred under the intangibles roll-over regime in *CTA 2009, Part 8, Ch 7* (see 12.53 and 12.54).

Capital gains arising on the sale of trading subsidiaries and other qualifying shareholding investments should normally be exempt under the Substantial Shareholdings Exemption (SSE). Broadly speaking, the SSE applies to the disposal of both UK and overseas resident trading companies which have been (at least) 10% owned throughout the 12 months before the disposal (see 3.32).

(g) A non-trading loan relationship (LR) deduction is available for interest payable on loans taken out for non-trading purposes and any losses or deficits arising on non-trading loans (including non-trading foreign exchange losses). The amount eligible for a non-trading deduction must be computed after deducting any non-trading interest income and other non-trading loan related profits.

Under *CTA 2009, ss 456–463*, a non-trading LR deficit can be relieved in one or more of the following ways – see also 11.8:

(i) offset against the company's taxable profits of the same corporation tax accounting period (CTAP)

(ii) surrendered under the group relief provisions for offset against the current year profits of fellow (75%) group members or consortium company claimants

(iii) carried back for offset against the company's non-trading LR profits of the previous year; or

(iv) carried forward for offset against the company's total non-trading profits of the next CTAP (or the following CTAP after that). (The carry-forward relief is fairly restrictive for a trading company as it will not normally have much in the way of non-trading profits, although it might, for example, have a significant one-off capital gain that can be sheltered.) However, greater flexibility on the offset of carried forward non-trading LR deficits is available for deficits arising *after 31 March 2017* (see 4.40).

(h) A current year trading loss (see 4.36) is deducted against profits before deducting qualifying charitable donations [*CTA 2010, s 189*].

(i) Donations to charities are relieved in the CTAP in which they are paid and deducted from the company's total profits after any other relief but before group relief. Qualifying charitable donations broadly comprise payments to charities (which are made 'gross') and the market value of assets gifted to a charity [*CTA 2010, Part 6*].

(j)   Losses claimed from other group companies by way of group relief are deducted in priority to trading losses carried back from a subsequent period [*CTA 2010, s137(4), (5)*].

(k)   If trading losses are carried back under *CTA 2010, s 37(3)(b)* (see 4.37) they are set off before charitable donations relief, which may therefore become unrelieved. If the company is a member of a group, it may be possible to surrender the charitable donations relief by way of group relief.

(l)   The Patent Box regime gives a lower tax rate for certain intellectual property income (see 4.10G–4.10K).

(m)   If a company's taxable profits exceed £1,500,000, it must pay its corporation tax liability under the quarterly instalment payment (QIP) rules. The £1,500,000 limit is apportioned, where appropriate, to take account of active 51% group companies (see 3.23) and periods of less than 12 months (see 4.47–4.53 for further details).

Where a company's profits do not exceed the relevant QIP limit, it will pay its corporation tax nine months after the end of the CTAP.

CALCULATING THE TAX-ADJUSTED TRADING PROFIT

Importance of GAAP

4.5   The principal source of income for a trading company would be its trading profits. The starting point for computing the tax-adjusted trading profit will be the accounting profit, which will have been prepared on generally accepted commercial and accounting principles (eg see *Johnston v Britannia Airways* [1994] STC 763). There is now a statutory requirement for a company's profits to be computed in accordance with generally accepted accounting practice (GAAP), except where this is overridden by legislative provisions [*CA 2006, s 464*].

The vast majority of UK companies now prepare accounts under either EU IFRS or FRS 102.

Companies using the Financial Reporting Standard for Smaller Entities (FRSSE) will mostly move to FRS 102 for their first accounting period starting after 31 December 2015 (see 4.5A). 'Micro-entities' can adopt the new FRS 105, which provides a significantly 'simplified' financial reporting framework, with reduced disclosures. However, even if a company is eligible for the reduced disclosure afforded by FRS 105, it may require a greater level of financial disclosure if it has borrowings, is seeking to raise finance, is growing rapidly, and so on.

A move to new accounting standards should not affect the tax treatment of the vast majority of transactions, but there are a few exceptions (see 4.5A below).

In recent years, the courts have placed considerable weight on generally accepted accounting principles (GAAP) in determining the way in which an item should be treated for tax purposes (in the absence of a contrary statutory rule).

HMRC accept that GAAP determines the period in which income or expenditure is recognised for tax purposes. For example, a provision can only be made where the company has an obligation (legally or constructively by its actions) to incur expenditure as a result of past events. The provision must be estimated with reasonable accuracy. It is accepted that any provision validly made under FRS 102 will be allowed for tax purposes unless the amount relates to disallowable capital expenditure or is treated differently under specific tax legislation. Special rules apply to certain types of provision – for example:

- provisions for future repairs and overhauls of plant and machinery cannot be made unless the obligation to incur the expenditure has crystallised at the balance sheet date;

- provisions for restructuring and reorganisation can only be made at the balance sheet date where the company has a detailed plan and has raised a valid expectation among those affected that it will be implemented;

- provision must be made where a contract becomes onerous, for example, where a company vacates leasehold premises and remains responsible for the lease rents.

The principle of allowing relief for future rentals payable on vacated premises was accepted in *Herbert Smith v Honour* [1999] STC 173. HMRC accept that there is no rule of tax law which prevents provisions for 'anticipated' losses and events, and will also allow provisions for foreseeable losses on long-term work in progress contracts (see IR Press Release dated 20 July 1999).

In the author's experience, HMRC are increasingly looking at provisions in their enquiries and regularly refer provisions (and other items relating to the application of GAAP) to their 'in-house' accountants to comment on their validity under UK GAAP.

The courts now frequently hear evidence from experts confirming how a transaction under scrutiny falls to be treated under GAAP – see, for example, the Court of Appeal case of *Greene King and another v HMRC* [2016] EWCA Civ 782, and the FTT decision in *Stagecoach Group and Stagecoach Holdings v HMRC* [2016] UKFTT 120. In the *Stagecoach Holdings* case, the company failed to satisfy the additional legislative requirement that the accounting treatment should 'fairly represent' a loan relationship loss.

As the concept of materiality does not exist for corporation tax, this may lead to a mismatch between what the company's auditors have agreed is a true and fair figure in the accounts and what HMRC believes to be the case. It is therefore always advisable to consider such provisions thoroughly from a corporation tax perspective, and document them accordingly. (See 4.9 for the treatment of bad debt provisions generally.)

Adoption of IFRS, FRS 102 or FRS 105

4.5A Trading and investment companies must now adopt either (EU) IFRs, FRS 102 or FRS 105. (The FRSSE may only be used for accounting periods starting before 1 January 2016) (see 4.5)

The vast majority of owner-managed companies are using FRS 102, which lays down a comprehensive financial reporting framework (and replaces all pre-existing FRSs and SSAPs). FRS 101 is a modified version of International Accounting Standards (IAS) with adjustments to ensure alignment with the Companies Act 2006 and to allow reduced disclosure requirements. Companies can adopt the 'reduced' disclosure requirements in FRS 101, but must still use FRS 102 for accounting measurement and detailed accounting treatment.

On transition to FRS 102, assets and liabilities at the accounting transition date will be identified, recognised and measured in line with the requirements of the new standards. Profits and losses from the accounting transition date will be recognised in accordance with the new standards.

Various changes were made to the UK tax legislation to enable companies to transition into the IAS and these rules will also apply to assist companies adopting FRS 102. Broadly, the tax legislation enables companies to retain the same *tax* treatment that they previously applied.

The transition to FRS 102 represents a change from one 'valid' basis to another. In such cases, *CTA 2009, Pt 3, Ch 14* states that adjustments should be made that will ensure that all taxable income and deductions are brought into the computation only once.

However, where a company takes the opportunity to correct accounting errors arising in previous years (such as an incorrect method of valuing its stock) these errors must be dealt with separately. Unlike the transition to FRS 102, they will represent a change from an 'invalid' to a 'valid' basis of accounting. Consequently, these 'errors' must be corrected where possible from the year in which they first occurred, with the intervening tax computations being adjusted accordingly either by an amended return and/or letter to HMRC.

Adjustments to company's profit and loss account

4.6 The company's profit and loss account will invariably include non-trading and capital items and various adjustments must be made in order to arrive at the assessable trading profit. However, amounts relating to a company's 'loan relationships' (including interest) and intangible fixed assets (within the Intangible fixed assets regime, including patent royalties) are generally reflected within the trading profit. The tax deductible or taxable amounts are usually based on the amounts reflected in the accounts under generally accepted accounting practice (GAAP).

Certain types of expenditure charged in the accounts are not deductible for tax purposes. For example, depreciation on fixed assets must be added back to the profits. Instead, relief is given by capital allowances, which is the statutory tax relief for capital expenditure (see 4.13–4.34).

On the other hand, since April 2002 companies have been able to deduct any amortisation of goodwill or other intangible fixed assets created or acquired by the company (from an unrelated third party). However, tax deductions for goodwill amortisation are denied for goodwill or customer-related intangibles purchased after 7 July 2015 (see 12.45–12.50A for further details).

Income that is dealt with under a different tax regime or category must be excluded from the accounting profit and dealt with under the relevant rules for that tax regime. Similarly, income that is exempt from tax must be excluded.

A trading loss will arise where the allowable expenses and capital allowances exceed the trading receipts.

Computation of taxable trading profits

4.7 A pro-forma computation for the adjustment of trading profits for tax purposes is given below.

Taxable trading profit computation

		£	£
Net profit on ordinary activities before taxation per accounts			X
Add	Depreciation (but see 12.49–12.50 re amortisation of intangible fixed assets)	X	
	Loss on disposal of fixed assets	X	
	Capital expenditure (eg alterations, improvements) charged to repairs, etc	X	
	Entertaining (client)	X	
	Non-trading interest payable	X	
	Non-trading foreign exchange losses	X	
	Legal and professional charges (eg relating to disposals/purchases of property)	X	
	Donations	X	
	Increase in general provisions	X	
	Pension contributions charged to profit and loss account	X	

		£	£
	Remuneration accrued, but not paid within nine months of end of period	X	
		—	X
Less	Relief for employee share awards and share options (see 8.89)	(X)	
	Adjustment for qualifying research and development expenditure – (see 4.10 below)	(X)	
	Profit on sale of fixed assets/investments	(X)	
	Other capital profits/gains	(X)	
	Dividends received	(X)	
	Income from overseas companies	(X)	
	Bank deposit interest	(X)	
	Building society interest	(X)	
	Other non-trading loan interest receivable	(X)	
	Non-trading foreign exchange profits	(X)	
	Net property rental income	(X)	
	Other investment income	(X)	
	Decrease in general provisions	(X)	
	Pension contributions paid in period	(X)	
	Pension scheme refund	(X)	
	Non-taxable income	(X)	
	Accrued remuneration paid more than nine months after end of previous period	(X)	
	Capital allowances (net of balancing charges)		
	– Plant and machinery (see 4.13–4.34)	(X)	
	– Other	(X)	
			(X)
Tax adjusted trading profit/(loss)			X

'Wholly and exclusively' requirement for trading expenses

4.8   It is well known that a trading company can only obtain relief against its trading profits for those expenses that have been incurred wholly and exclusively for the purposes of its trade [*CTA 2009, s 54*].

The *Corporation Tax Act 2009* makes it clear that partial relief can be given where expenditure is incurred for 'mixed' purposes. In such cases, relief can be claimed for 'any identifiable part or identifiable proportion of the expense which is incurred wholly and exclusively for trading purposes' [*CTA 2009, s 54(2)*].

Relief for impaired/bad debts (and debt releases)

Trade debts

4.9   Companies can generally obtain tax relief for 'impaired' trading debts written-off and specific provisions against doubtful trading debts (which are dealt with under the loan relationship (LR) rules) by virtue of *CTA 2009, s 481(1), (3)(d)*. (Trade debts come within the 'non-lending' relationships within *CTA 2009, s 479*.) As trade debts are within the LR regime, impairment relief cannot be claimed for trade debts between connected companies (see 4.9A).

To ensure impairment relief is claimable, it would generally be necessary to demonstrate that the 'bad or doubtful' debt has arisen in the normal course of the company's trade and the relevant transactions had been commercially motivated. In assessing the amount that may need to be treated as an 'impairment loss' (ie bad or doubtful debt), it is permissible to take account of events and circumstances arising after the balance sheet date (but before the date the accounts are signed off) where they provide further evidence of conditions that existed at the 'balance sheet' date (*IR Tax Bulletin, Issue 12*). Relief can also be claimed where a trade debt is written-off as a result of a formal release by the 'creditor' company.

CTA 2009, s 481(1), (3)(f) ensures symmetry for released debts between connected companies. The release is dealt with entirely under the LR regime, so it is 'tax-free' under the normal 'connected companies' LR rules. (*CTA 2009, s 464(1)* gives loan relationships priority over any other taxing provisions, so *CTA 2009, s 94* no longer applies to 'money' trade debts.) However, an 'unconnected' creditor would generally be taxed on the release under normal LR principles.

A special exemption applies where a debt is released under a statutory insolvency arrangement. In such cases, *CTA 2009, s 322(2)* enables the credit released to profit and loss account to be 'tax-free'. This was extended from 1 January 2015 to cases where, without the release, there would be a material risk of the company being unable to pay its debts within the next 12 months (*CTA 2009, s 322(5B)*).

Funding loans

4.9A   Funding or finance loans are dealt with under the LR regime and therefore follow the same principles as in 4.9. Thus, impairment relief is generally available on doubtful and irrecoverable loans. Similarly, debits arising from 'releases' are tax-deductible.

However, no LR relief is available for the impairment write-off or 'debit release' of a 'connected' company debt [*CTA 2009, s 354*]. This rule applies where a company is connected at any time in the accounting period.

In broad terms, a company is 'connected' with another company where one of the companies controls the other or where they are both under the control of the same company [*CTA 2009, s 466(2)*]. For these purposes, control would be exercised by a company where it is able conduct another company's affairs according to its wishes (whether through the holding of shares, voting power or by powers contained in the articles of association).

An allowable LR debit is given where a debt is released as part of a qualifying 'debt/equity' swap even where the relevant companies become connected in the accounting period in which the swap takes place (see 11.23 to 11.26 for detailed analysis).

ENHANCED RESEARCH AND DEVELOPMENT (R&D) RELIEF

Overview

4.10   Small and medium-sized companies may qualify for enhanced research and development tax (R&D) reliefs. For these purposes, an SME is defined under EU Regulations (2003/361/EC) as modified by *CTA 2009, s 1120* as a company or organisation with fewer than 500 employees *and* either of the following:

- an annual turnover not exceeding €100 million; or
- a balance sheet not exceeding €86 million.

This is not the same SME definition that is used by HMRC for various other tax purposes. If a company is not an SME it may be eligible for R&D relief under the 'large' company regime (see 4.10B).

A company or organisation cannot be considered to be a SME if it is part of a larger enterprise that – taken as a whole – would fail these tests.

When applying these thresholds, the absolute employee, turnover or balance sheet data of *linked* enterprises (broadly 51% group companies are included). However, for partner enterprises (broadly a company which holds at least 25% of the share capital of the relevant company *or* represents a 25% plus shareholding of the relevant company), only a pro-rata proportion of the data is taken into account.

In some cases, the application of the SME definition can be complex, as illustrated in the cases of *Pyreos v HMRC* [2015] UKFTT 123 (which held that venture capital investor companies can be ignored for the purposes of the SME test) and *Monitor Audio Ltd v HMRC* [2015] UKFTT 357 TC04541 (which held that an investment bank could be excluded from being a 'partner enterprise').

Enhanced R&D relief is given for qualifying R&D expenditure qualifying 'revenue' costs incurred on R&D (in accordance with GAAP) that meets the relevant guidelines issued by the Department for Business, Innovation and Skills.

A less generous R&D tax relief is available for large companies. (The large company rules are unlikely to apply to most family and owner managed companies but see 4.10B for brief comments.)

Enhanced R&D reliefs for small and medium-sized companies

4.10A   Since 1 April 2015, small and medium sized companies can claim a 130% (125% pre-1 April 2015) enhancement to their qualifying R&D expenditure, giving a total R&D tax deduction of 230% (225% pre-1 April 2015) of the relevant R&D expenditure.

For example, if a small company incurs qualifying R&D expenditure of £60,000 in its accounting year ending 31 March 2017 then it may include £138,000 as a cost in its corporation tax computation – an extra deduction of £78,000.

Due to EU 'state aid' constraints, there is a total cap of €7.5 million on the corporation tax value of the relief that can be claimed on any one project.

SME companies can claim an actual cash payment where their R&D tax credits produce a trading tax loss and they surrender that loss. For expenditure incurred after 31 March 2015 the amount of the surrenderable loss is the lesser of:

● the amount of the unrelieved trading loss sustained in that period; and

● 230% of the related qualifying R&D expenditure.

Since 1 April 2014, the payable tax credit for R&D expenditure is equal to 14.5% of the surrenderable loss for that period.

A company may only claim the additional deduction for R&D expenditure and/or the payable R&D tax credit, if it is a going concern at the time when the claim is made [*CTA 2009, ss 1046* and *1057*].

Expenditure must be revenue in nature to qualify for the additional relief. Eligible *capital* expenditure on R&D separately qualifies for 100% R&D allowances.

EU law prevents businesses receiving more than one State Aid for a project – the SME enhanced R&D relief is deemed to be State Aid. This means that any further form of State Aid will preclude what might otherwise be a valuable R&D tax relief claim. Companies that carry on various R&D projects should therefore ensure that any claim for a 'Notified State Aid' grant is made for the relevant specific R&D project since this would only preclude R&D relief for that project (rather than all its R&D spending).

Qualifying R&D activities and costs

4.10B HMRC's guidelines state that, 'For there to be R&D for the purpose of the tax relief, a company must be carrying on a project that seeks an advance in science or technology. It is necessary to be able to state what the intended advance is, and to show how, through the resolution of scientific or technological uncertainty, the project seeks to achieve this.'

This can, in some cases, include a project to improve or enhance an existing technology as long as advances in science or technology are being made.

R&D projects can occur in a wide range of businesses, for example the pharmaceutical industry, construction and software development.

Costs eligible for the relief fall into several categories:

- Eligible staff/directors' costs (see 4.10C);

- Consumable or transformable materials;

- Subcontracted R&D costs (see 4.10D);

- Expenditure on external workers; and

- Software.

Many other related overheads relating to the R&D work – such as rent and rates etc – do not qualify for any relief since they are not fully used up or consumed by the R&D activity. No relief is available for the costs of any item produced in the course of the R&D work that is subsequently sold. Claims for materials must therefore be reviewed to ensure that they are not reflected in goods sold.

Eligible staff and directors' costs

4.10C Eligible staff costs include employee's/director's wages and salaries, the related employer's NICs, and company pension contributions. However, no claim can be made for benefits in kind.

In the vast majority of cases, employees will only spend part of their time on qualifying R&D activities. Consequently, the proportion of staff costs claimed for the enhanced R&D relief is based on the time spent on the relevant R&D project(s), normally using time sheets or similar records.

It is also possible to claim for certain 'indirect' staff costs that relate to the relevant R&D project. Under the DTI/BIS guidelines, these would relate to 'activities which form part of a project, but do not directly contribute to the resolution of the scientific or technological uncertainty'. This could include staff training to support the R&D project, staff costs relating to relevant data collection etc, and clerical and administrative work supporting the R&D work (eg time spent ordering relevant materials for the project or drafting project reports).

However, general staff administration (eg central HR and finance staff) costs cannot be claimed (*CTA 2009, s 1124(5), (6)*).

Owner managers who undertake specific work on R&D projects should ensure they take a 'commercial salary' to maximise the potential R&D claim (which would be claimed on a proportionate basis). In such cases, extracting profits via dividends instead would not be helpful.

Subcontract R&D

4.10D   Companies can also claim relief for subcontracted R&D work, albeit on a restricted basis.

Where the subcontractor is an 'unrelated' third party, relief can be claimed for 65% of the amount charged by the subcontractor. A company can also elect to base its claim on the actual costs incurred by the subcontractor but it is normally much better to claim relief on 65% of the amount invoiced by the sub-contractor.

On the other hand, where a 'connected' company provides the subcontract R&D services, relief must be claimed on the actual sub-contractor costs.

R&D enhancement relief in respect of payments to subcontractors can only be claimed when the amount in question has been physically paid, as confirmed in *Gas Recovery and Recycle Ltd v HMRC* (TC 5473).

Example 1

Computation of enhanced R&D relief

Hart Hi-Fi Ltd, is a manufacturer of high-fi equipment and is a qualifying SME for the purposes of the enhanced R&D relief rules.

In April 2017, it started a new R&D project on wafer thin 'micro' hi-fi speakers. The relevant R&D expenditure incurred during the year ended 31 March 2018 was as follows:

	£	
Consumables materials	22,500	
Direct labour costs – R&D staff (including related employer's NIC)	225,400	An analysis shows that 60% of direct labour time is spent on the R&D project
Factory administration staff costs (including related employer's NIC)	89,500	It is estimated that £11,000 can be related to the R&D project
Heating and lighting	17,980	

	£	
External sub-contract worker costs (supplying R&D services for project)	67,800	
Capital expenditure – sound testing equipment	89,230	In fixed asset 'additions'

The 'technical' R&D staff costs are restricted to the percentage of time spent (60%) actively working on the R&D project. It is also possible to claim £11,000 for the administration staff costs that relate to the R&D project.

Only 65% of the costs of externally-provided sub-contract workers are claimable.

It is not possible to include capital expenditure, although it should qualify for 100% research and development capital allowances.

The amount qualifying for the enhanced R&D relief is as follows:

	£
Consumables materials	22,500
R&D staff costs (including related employer's NIC) 60% × £225,400	135,240
Relevant indirect R&D admin costs	11,000
Heat and light	17,980
External sub-contract worker costs 65% × £67,800	44,070
Qualifying R&D costs	230,790

The enhanced R&D relief would therefore be £300,027 (being £230,790 at 130%).

£230,790 would have already been charged against the company's profits, and therefore an additional enhanced R&D deduction of £300,027 would be claimed against the taxable trading profits.

Enhanced R&D relief for large companies

4.10E   Large companies can claim an enhanced R&D deduction of 130% (ie an uplift of 30%) for qualifying expenditure incurred before 1 April 2016. In contrast to the SME regime, if this gives rise to an overall loss there is no repayable credit (see 4.10A above).

The R&D scheme for large companies is supplemented with an 'above the line' (ATL) credit system. This was optional for expenditure incurred after 31 March 2013 but is compulsory for post-31 March 2016 expenditure.

The ATL credit is shown in the accounts and increases the company's EBITDA by 11% (10% before 1 April 2015) of the qualifying R&D expenditure. The ATL credit is then deducted from the corporation tax liability. The overall impact is that R&D relief is effectively given at 8.36% of the qualifying expenditure (based on the FY17 corporation tax rate of 19%). It can generate a repayment, subject to conditions.

Relief

4.10F   Claims for the enhanced R&D relief are made in a company's tax return, and must be made within two years from the end of the relevant accounting period.

The return should include the figure for the enhanced expenditure and, if applicable, the amount of tax losses being surrendered for a payable tax credit.

It is also good practice to include supplementary information with the return to illustrate why the company considers its project or projects to be allowable as R&D. Typically, a short report is produced that:

● explains the relevant R&D project;

● summarises the eligible R&D costs incurred;

● shows how the claim is made up in the return.

Staff costs are often one of the larger elements of a claim. Consequently, companies should maintain a suitable record of staff time spent on R&D projects, since this will be used to determine the qualifying R&D staff costs.

PATENT BOX REGIME

Electing for lower 'patent box' tax rate

4.10G   The patent box regime provides the benefits of lower corporation tax rates on certain types of intellectual property (IP) income. The patent box regime focuses on patents because they have a strong link with the research and development (R&D)/high-tech sector. The relief provides an incentive for UK companies to develop innovative-patented products, and hence should encourage the valuable technicians and workers associated with their development and exploitation to be based in the UK. In many cases, for the smaller company, deciding whether to enter the patent box is likely to require liaison with IP/patent lawyers.

Companies can elect whether or not they wish to apply the patent box rules – they are not mandatory [*CTA 2010, Part 8A*]. The patent box legislation is lengthy (over 40 pages) and complex. An election for patent box treatment must be made within two years from the end of the corporation tax accounting period (CTAP) in which the relevant profits arose, and will normally be made on the company's tax return.

The original regime was phased from 1 April 2013, with an appropriate percentage applied to the profits for each financial year when calculating the available relief. The reliefs available in recent years are as follows:

1 April 2015 to 31 March 2016	80 per cent
1 April 2016 to 31 March 2017	90 per cent
From 1 April 2017	100 per cent

This regime has proved to be relatively short-lived, as it has been withdrawn for new claims for periods ending after 30 June 2016.

The replacement regime is similar but not identical, and companies with multiple patents may need to consider their record-keeping carefully. Existing patent box claims are 'grandfathered' in until 2021 and so there will be a period in which the two systems are both current.

The rules for *periods ending after 30 June 2016* are explained below. For details of the original patent-box regime (which is being 'grandfathered'), please see 2016/17 and earlier editions of this book.

The reduced patent box corporation tax rate (currently set at 10%) is applied by subtracting an additional trading deduction from the profits chargeable to corporation tax [*CTA 2010, s 357A*], which is calculated as:

$RP \times FY\% \times ((MR - IPR) \div MR)$

Where:

- RP is the company's relevant IP profits (see 4.10I).
- FY% is the appropriate percentage for each financial year.
- MR is the main rate of corporation tax.
- IPR is the reduced rate of 10 per cent.

Qualifying conditions

4.10H The Patent Box is available to qualifying companies within *CTA 2010, s 357B* that make profits from exploiting qualifying intellectual property rights. This generally means that the company must own one or more patents or have an exclusive right over them. Broadly, the rules require exclusivity in a national territory or a specific commercial field. The company must actively have developed the patent or a product incorporating the patent.

If the company is a member of a group (which is very widely defined – see *CTA 2010, s 357GD*), it must also meet the 'active ownership' condition for the CTAP in *CTA 2010, s 357B(5)*. This requires the company to perform a significant amount of management activity in relation to its IP rights. The policy aim is to prevent passive IP holding companies taking advantage of the patent box rate.

For the purposes of the patent box, the patent must be granted with the UK patent office, the European patent office, or the relevant patent offices of certain other countries. It is sufficient for the patent to be granted by one of the 'permitted' offices, although special advice is often required since commercial factors may require patents to be filed in several countries.

The patent box only applies from the date the patent is granted but an election can be made to cover the 'patent pending' period. If the company wishes to make a claim under the original regime, the patent must have been applied for *by 30 June 2016*. The claim can then be made for the pre-30 June 2016 period, within the usual time limits. This will bring that patent within the existing rules.

Calculating the relevant IP profits

4.10I   The intention of the rules is to only allow relief to the extent that a company was substantially involved in the original creation or development of the relevant patent, which is known as the 'nexus' principle.

Thus, for periods ending after 30 June 2016, IP profits must be streamed by patent, product, or category. For companies with several patented products, this will require a certain level of record-keeping, which may not be required for any non-tax reason. HMRC accept that it may not be practicable to split the IP income where products comprise a number of IP rights, and will allow companies to allocate the income between IP categories or products. Many owner-managed companies are likely to benefit from using the small patent box profits elections (see 4.10J)

Where products incorporate both original and 'new' regime patents, the income should be split and calculated under each regime separately.

The initial step is to identify the company's relevant IP income (RIPI).

Once the IP income has been calculated for each patent/product (RIPI sub-stream), the 'routine' and 'marketing' adjustments are then applied to each sub-stream amount. The net 'profit' for each RIPI sub-stream is added together to arrive at the relevant IP profits taxed at the patent box rate. See 4.10K for summary of computation steps.

Small patent box profits elections

4.10J   Many owner-managed companies are likely to use the small patent box profits rules to simplify the calculation of their patent box income. Three separate elections can be made to streamline their patent box computations (see *CTA 2010, s 357BN*).

- Global streaming election (under *CTA 2010, s 357BNC*) to aggregate all the company's IP income (ie without having to allocate it to each IP stream) (see 4.10K – Step 2).

- Notional royalty election – (*CTA 2010, s 357CD*), which is available to companies that use patents in their actual processes.

- Small claims figure election to compute the marketing assets return (see 4.10K – Step 5).

To benefit from any of the above elections, the company must only have one trade and its qualifying residual profits (see 4.10K – Step 4) for the relevant accounting period must be *less* than:

- £1,000,000, or

- *if higher*, the 'relevant maximum'.

Where the company has no related 51% group companies (see 4.50) the relevant maximum is £3,000,000. If it is connected with 51% group companies, the relevant maximum is (£3,000,000 (I+N)), where N is the number of 51% group companies that are elected into the patent box regime.

A company will always be able to make any of the elections where its qualifying residual profits for the relevant period are less than £1,000,000. However, if it exceeds this £1,000,000 threshold, *CTA 2010, s 357BN(3)* prevents an election being claimed if the company has used the (post-30 June 2016) patent box regime in any of the previous four years without making that same election.

Main steps for computing relevant IP profits

4.10K   The various steps involved in calculating the relevant IP profits are summarised below:

Step

1   The total taxable income of the trade (excluding financing income) is apportioned into two elements, being:

- RIPI = income from patent sales (including the full amount of income from the sale of products incorporating a patented item), patent licence income, and income from the sale of other IP rights.

- All other income.

2   Once the RIPI is computed, it is then divided into IP sub-streams, with separate sub-streams for each IP right or IP category.

Many owner-managed companies will be able to make a special 'global' streaming election to avoid having to allocate between individual patent/IP streams (see 4.10J).

3   Expenses are allocated between the RIPI sub-streams and the other income.

Each patented item/IP right is looked at separately, and specific costs allocated to it. Expenses can be allocated on a just and reasonable basis, after removing tax-disallowable items, finance expenses and additional deductions for R & D and 'creative' tax reliefs.

4   The routine return for *each* RIPI sub-stream is deducted. This is calculated as 10% of the routine expenses that are allocated to each sub-stream. Routine expenses comprise trading capital allowances, premises costs, personnel costs, plant and machinery costs, professional services and utilities costs).

After the 'routine return' has been deducted, the balance represents the Qualifying Residual Profit (QRP) (or a patent box loss).

5/6   Deduct marketing return (provided there is a 'surplus' after Step 4)

If a company's total QRP is less than £1,000,000 it will normally be able to make a 'small claims' election to calculate the marketing return (but see 4.10J for detailed conditions). By making this election, the marketing return is 25% of the QRP for each sub-stream.

In other cases, the marketing assets return is computed using normal transfer pricing principles (*CTA 2010, s 357CN*).

Step

7   Apply R&D/acquisition restriction where appropriate to each sub-stream.

The claim is restricted to 'local' R&D, using a detailed formula to remove a proportion relating to purchased patents and R&D carried out elsewhere in the group (see *CTA 2010, s 357BL*).

This adjustment effectively restricts the IP income where the company has incurred expenditure on acquiring IP rights or it has sub-contracted R&D work from a connected party (looking back to relevant cumulative expenditure of up to 20 years). Most SMEs carry out their own R&D or sub-contract the R&D to unconnected parties and therefore should not normally be affected by 'the R&D fraction' adjustment.

The resultant figures for each RIPI sub-stream are added together to produce the relevant IP profit, which is taxed in the 'patent box'.

There are special rules to deal with patent losses (not covered here).

TRANSFER PRICING REGIME

Overview

4.11   CT600 self-assessment returns must apply arm's-length transfer prices on all transactions with 'connected persons'. Broadly speaking, the transfer pricing rules mainly apply where a UK company is 'large' (or is part of a 'large' group) as defined under EU guidelines. A company/group is 'large' if it does not fall within the SME definition (see 4.12). The transfer pricing rules are contained in *TIOPA 2010, ss 147–217*.

A 'large' owner managed company must therefore apply 'arm's length' transfer pricing on all transactions with any fellow-group or 'sister' companies – irrespective of whether they are UK or non-UK resident for tax purposes. Examples where arm's length transfer pricing would be used may include:

•   The sale of goods to an overseas subsidiary that acts as a sales distributor in the overseas country. The goods might be sold to the overseas company on a 're-sale' price basis after making appropriate deductions for the overseas company's sale and marketing costs and their resale 'profit margin'. An alternative approach would be to apply a cost-plus method – such as cost to UK company plus (say) 10% to 20%.

•   Provision of management and administrative support to all group companies – a management charge would be rendered to each company on a 'fair and justifiable' basis, bearing in mind the time spent and the salary/staff costs and attributable overheads. The company may devise a standard costing model to arrive at a reasonable hourly rate for management and administrative support services.

- The licensing of intellectual property (IP) to other group companies – a charge may be made on (say) a 'royalty' rate basis on sales or by a 'profit-split' method which allocates the profit from using the IP to each company on a reasonable basis.

- Loans made to overseas companies – the company must charge a commercial rate of interest on the loans – which might, for example, be LIBOR + 4% to 10%, depending on lending risk.

Large companies within the scope of the UK transfer pricing rules must be vigilant and ensure they identify all services that are provided to their fellow 'group' companies, ensuring that a commensurate commercial price is charged to them. This exercise may not always be straightforward as some services may be of an indirect nature or 'hidden'.

As a result of the G20/OECD's Base Erosion and Profit Shifting project, the OECD's Transfer Pricing Guidelines were updated in 2016 and 2017.

Practical experience suggests that HMRC do not generally seek out *UK-to-UK* transfer pricing enquiries where there is little or no UK tax risk (which will often be the case where there is an equal corresponding tax adjustment!).

Dormant company exemption

4.11A There is a limited exemption for companies that were dormant at 31 March 2004 (the 'start-date' for the revised UK transfer pricing regime), with the exception of an intra-group balance. In such cases, provided the company was dormant for at least three months up to 31 March 2004, it will stay outside the scope of the transfer pricing rules so long as it remains dormant.

Thus, interest will need to be charged on intra-group balances with companies that only became dormant after 31 March 2004.

Apply arms-length transfer pricing

4.11B It is accepted that establishing an appropriate 'arm's length' price sometimes involves a degree of judgement and HMRC is generally prepared to discuss particular transfer pricing issues before a CT600 return is made or before the transactions take place.

Companies may wish to avoid reporting commercial transfer pricing in their accounts. This is acceptable to HMRC provided the company makes appropriate transfer pricing adjustments in its tax computation and CT600.

Under CTSA, companies have a statutory obligation to keep and retain appropriate records and support documentation to back up their transfer pricing policies and implementation. This would include the primary accounting records, details of transactions with 'connected companies' and any appropriate tax adjustments to ensure the computations reflect 'arm's length' transfer-pricing. There are stringent penalties for non-compliance – see 4.58.

New rules for 'Country by Country reporting' apply for accounting periods beginning after 31 December 2015. These will not affect the vast majority of owner managed companies as there is a minimum turnover limit of €750 million.

Corresponding adjustments

4.11C   Whenever a transfer pricing adjustment is made in the tax computation of the company providing the goods/services, the UK legislation enables the 'counterpart' UK company to claim a corresponding adjustment (eg an increase in the relevant expenses) to its taxable profits/income in its own tax return [*TIOPA 2010, ss 174–176*]. The counterpart UK resident company must make their corresponding adjustment within two years from the date the 'provider' UK company makes its adjustment.

HMRC cannot, of course, require an overseas tax jurisdiction to make a 'corresponding adjustment' in an *overseas* company's tax return, but double taxation would result if no relief were granted. Consequently, most of the UK's double tax treaties allow a 'mutual agreement' procedure, under which the overseas tax authority (known as the 'competent authority') is required to consider granting corresponding relief. If the case cannot be resolved by the overseas tax authority unilaterally, both HMRC and the overseas tax authority can consult to resolve the case by mutual agreement, but this cannot be guaranteed. The general time limit for seeking 'competent authority' is often based on Article 25 of the OECD Model Treaty, which provides a three year period from the notification of the 'double tax' issue. Cases involving connected EU companies are decided under the European Arbitration Convention [90/463/EEC (the Arbitration Convention)].

UK groups may be affected by transfer pricing adjustments made by an overseas tax jurisdiction. This might be the case where, for example, an overseas company (in a country with which the UK has a double tax treaty) provides support services to a 'connected' UK resident company. In this case, the UK company would have to seek relief by making a competent authority claim. *SP1/11* provides further guidance on the mutual agreement procedure. Small and medium-sized companies are generally exempt from the UK's transfer pricing rules (see 4.12 below).

The new Multilateral Instrument (MLI) signed in Paris in June 2017 includes a minimum standard for improving dispute resolution. This contains an optional measure to allow a corresponding adjustment where the tax authority of one treaty party has imposed a transfer pricing adjustment. The UK has indicated that it will agree this provision, although both treaty partners have to agree before it will apply. The MLI provisions could come in to force as early as 2018.

Exemption for small and medium-sized companies

4.12   Small and medium-sized enterprises (SMEs) do not have to apply statutory transfer pricing principles on their dealings with 'connected' UK companies or on many cross-border transactions with their 'connected' overseas companies.

The exemption to overseas companies applies where the overseas jurisdiction's double tax treaty with the UK contains a non-discrimination article [*TIOPA 2010, ss 166, 167* and *173*]. This exemption would cover EU countries, Australia, Canada, Japan and the USA and many other developed countries (see HMRC website for full details). In practice, this means that SMEs would generally apply transfer pricing on transactions with 'connected' companies based in tax-havens [*TIOPA 2010, s 167(3)*].

A UK resident company may still have to apply arm's length transfer pricing where it transacts with related companies in 'other' jurisdictions as a result of 'their' local transfer pricing rules.

An SME company can also elect to 'disapply' its exemption from the transfer pricing rules for a particular CTAP. Where the election is made, all its relevant transactions will be subject to arm's length transfer pricing [*TIOPA 2010, s 167(2); ICTA 1988, Sch 28AA, para 5B(3)*].

SMEs are defined under special EU regulations (*CTA 2010, s 172* and the *Annex* to the *Commission Recommendation 2003/361/EC* of 6 May 2003). These limits have not increased for many years. However as they are expressed in Euros exchange rate movements must be taken into account when considering the application of these rules each year. The relevant economic/financial criteria are tested on a (consolidated) group basis:

	Small Company	*Medium-sized Company*
Employees (full time equivalent)	Less than 50	Less than 250
AND EITHER		
Turnover	*Less than €10 million*	*Less than €50 million*
OR		
Balance sheet total (ie Gross Asset value)	*Less than €10 million*	*Less than €43 million*

Notes:

1   The above criteria can apply to any form of business enterprise, but only companies are covered here.

2   The tests are considered separately for each period – .to satisfy either the 'small' or 'medium' sized criteria, the company must meet the

'employee headcount' condition and either the 'turnover' or 'balance sheet' conditions.

3   Translations to sterling (£) should be done at the average rate for the period.

4   The appropriate pro-rata share of employees/turnover/gross assets of linked enterprises and relevant partnership interests must be included.

In broad terms, a linked enterprise is one which can be controlled through shareholding, voting or contractual rights. A relevant partnership interest is one where at least 25% of a partnership's capital or voting rights are held.

In the case of medium-sized enterprises only, HMRC also have the power to apply the transfer pricing rules. Where this power is invoked, the UK company would receive a 'transfer pricing' notice for the relevant CTAP requiring appropriate adjustments to its UK profits. Any right of appeal against the notice can only be made on the basis that the company is a 'small enterprise'. It is expected that this power would only be exercised where there is blatant manipulation leading to a significant loss of UK tax.

CAPITAL ALLOWANCES

Background to capital allowances regime

4.13   Capital expenditure incurred cannot be deducted against the taxable trading profit. Expenditure charged to fixed assets in the accounts will invariably be treated as capital expenditure. The periodic write-off of fixed asset expenditure through depreciation charges will be disallowed (although the amortisation of intangibles and goodwill (acquired or created after 31 March 2002 is allowable under *CTA 2009, Pt 8*). Certain capital expenditure may also be charged directly against profits and, for tax purposes, this must also be disallowed. However, provided the capital expenditure falls into one of the defined categories, tax relief will be given through the capital allowances system.

There has been a considerable amount of tinkering with capital allowances over recent years – hardly giving business a stable framework to plan their capital investment. A major change occurred from April 2008 when an Annual Investment Allowance (AIA) was introduced. AIA-eligible expenditure is immediately written off for tax purposes.

Since the AIA was introduced, the expenditure limit has changed frequently. From 1 April 2014 until 31 December 2015, the annual AIA expenditure limit was £500,000. This limit was reduced to £200,000 from 1 January 2016, and remains at this level indefinitely (see also 4.20).

There are complex rules for companies with accounting periods straddling the dates on which the limit changes (see 4.21).

Expenditure in excess of the AIA limit (which may be lower for separate group companies) then qualifies for WDAs or FYAs as appropriate.

4.14 *Trading Company v Investment Company Computations under CTSA*

The main types of capital allowances and the current rates obtainable for each class of expenditure are set out below. Capital allowances must be claimed on the company's tax return [*CAA 2001, s 3*].

Current main rates of capital allowances

4.14

	Note	Initial/first-year allowance (FYA)/AIA	Writing-down allowance (WDA)
Plant and machinery (see also 4.15–4.19)	(*a*) (*b*) (*c*)	100%	18% (standard rate)
			8% (reduced rate)
Annual Investment Allowance (AIA) (see 4.20)	(*c*)	£200,000 (from 1 Jan 2016)	
Enhanced capital allowances			
Low-emission (up to 75 g/km CO_2) cars (see 4.23)	(*d*)	100%	
Natural gas/hydrogen refuelling equipment	(*d*)	100%	
Designated energy efficient or water saving plant (see 4.23)	(*e*)	100%	
Environmentally beneficial plant and machinery (see 4.23)	(*f*)	100%	
Other cars			
Cars – 75 g/km to 130 g/km CO_2 emissions (see 4.25)			18% (main pool)
Cars – over 130 g/km CO_2 emissions (see 4.25)			8% (special rate pool)
'Long-life' plant and machinery (see 4.29)	(*g*)		8%
Renovation of business premises in disadvantaged areas	(*h*)	100%	
Enterprise zones assisted areas plant and machinery	(*i*)	100%	
Research and development		100%	

152

Notes:

(a)   Since 1 April 2012 the annual WDA rate is 18%.

(b)   Expenditure included in the special rate pool attracts a lower WDA of 8%.

The special rate pool includes integral features (see 4.26 for details), thermal insulation (such as roof lining, double glazing and cavity wall insulation), long life assets (see (g) below and 4.29) and cars with CO2 emissions of 130g/km or more (see 4.27).

(c)   Since 1 January 2016, the Annual Investment Allowance (AIA) is given on the first £200,000 spent on qualifying plant and machinery expenditure in a 12-month CTAP.

(For previous AIA limits see 4.20). Where an accounting period straddles periods to which different annual limits apply, there are transitional rules which calculate the amount of AIA that may be claimed (see 4.21).

(d)   Low-emission cars and vehicles qualify for 100% FYAs (regardless of the company's size). These include cars that emit no more than 75 g/km of CO^2 (no more than 95g/km for pre-1 April 2015 purchases), electric cars, and zero emission goods vehicles (see 4.23).

100% FYAs can also be claimed on expenditure on natural gas/hydrogen refuelling equipment, such as storage tanks, pumps, controls, etc. These types of 100% FYAs are available to all companies irrespective of their size.

(e)   Any company can claim 100% FYAs on designated energy efficient or water saving plant. Such plant must meet strict water saving or efficiency criteria. Current eligible items include specified meters and monitoring equipment, flow controllers, leakage detection systems and efficient toilets and taps (see 4.23).

(f)   All companies can claim 100% FYAs on expenditure on designated energy-saving plant and equipment. Products that qualify are contained on the Department of Energy and Change Climate website (www.beis. gov.uk/etl/site/etl.html) which is continuously updated. Static lists are also available at https://www.gov.uk/guidance/energy-technology-list

Eligible categories of energy saving plant and equipment include:

- automatic monitoring and targeting equipment;
- air-to-air energy recovery equipment
- boilers;
- combined heat and power systems;
- compressed-air equipment;
- heat pumps;
- high speed hand motors and driers;
- radiant and warm air heaters;

- heating, ventilation and air conditioning (HVAC) equipment;

- motors and drivers;

- pipework insulation;

- refrigeration display cabinets;

- solar thermal systems; and

- uninterruptable power supplies.

(g)   Expenditure on 'long life' plant is included in the 'special rate' pool (see (b) above). The annual WDA rate on long life plant is therefore 8%.

The long-life asset rules apply to certain types of plant with a working life of 25 years or more, provided the company spends more than the annual *de minimis* limit of £100,000, (apportioned amongst associated companies) for the accounting period. The £100,000 limit is apportioned by reference to '51% group companies' (see 4.50–4.50B).

Plant and machinery which is a fixture in or provided for use in a retail shop, showroom, hotel or office is specifically excluded from 'long-life' asset treatment and is therefore eligible for 'normal' allowances.

(h)   A 100% Business Premises Renovation Allowance (BPRA) is given for capital expenditure incurred on the conversion or renovation of qualifying business premises situated in a 'designated' disadvantaged area. The premises must be situated in a 'disadvantaged' area and must not have been used for at least one year before the renovation work begins – its last use being as office accommodation or for general trading purposes (but not as a dwelling). The 100% allowance is particularly attractive for renovated shops and commercial offices (since they would typically attract little or no relief under the capital allowances legislation).

Only conversion work qualifies for the 100% BPRA (ie it does not include (for example) expenditure on buying the building, extending it (other than to provide access), or on plant and machinery (other than fixtures). No balancing charge/allowance is made if the renovated building continues to be used (or suitable and available for letting) for at least five years (seven years for expenditure incurred before 1 April 2014) after the remedial work [*CAA 2001, ss 360A–360Z4*].

Qualifying expenditure incurred before 5 April 2017 will be eligible (the *Business Premises Renovation Allowances (Amendment) Regulations 2012, SI 2012/868*). However, to fall in line with State Aid requirements, the qualifying expenditure is capped at €20 million for each project. A claim for BPRA is not permitted if another form of State Aid has been or will be received.

The definition of 'qualifying expenditure' for BPRA is restricted so that relief is only available for the actual costs of building and construction work. Costs of arranging finance or architecture or surveying costs do not qualify. Limited relief is given for associated costs of up to 5% of the qualifying expenditure. Expenditure on integral features is excluded.

BPRA claimed on expenditure paid for in advance of the work is clawed back if the relevant work is not completed within 36 months from the date the expenditure is incurred.

(i)   100% first year allowances are available where companies invest in new (not replacement) plant and machinery for use in a trade/business that is primarily situated in a designated enterprise zone (as defined in *Assisted Areas Order 2007, SI 2007/107*). The expenditure must be incurred between 1 April 2012 and 31 March 2020 [*CAA 2001, ss 45K–45N*].

PLANT AND MACHINERY ALLOWANCES

Main conditions

4.15   A company qualifies for plant and machinery allowances provided it carries on a 'qualifying activity' (the most common category being a trade) and incurs 'qualifying expenditure' [*CAA 2001, s 11*]. To qualify:

- a company's expenditure must be of a capital nature on the provision of plant or machinery (wholly or partly) for its qualifying activity; and

- the company must own the asset as a result of incurring the expenditure.

It is a fundamental requirement that capital expenditure must be incurred. Sometimes, there may be problems in determining whether loose tools, utensils and other 'short life' items should be treated as capital or revenue. Based on the ruling in *Hinton v Maden and Ireland Ltd* [1959] 38 TC 391, if the anticipated life of the relevant item is less than two years, the expenditure may normally be written off as a trading expense. If the plant's useful life is likely to exceed two years then it will normally be considered a capital asset on which capital allowances can usually be claimed [*CTA 2009, s 53 (ICTA 1988, s 74(1)(d))*].

Meaning of 'plant'

4.16   The tax legislation does not define the meaning of 'plant' although it does specify items that are deemed to be 'plant' (for example, alterations to an existing building incidental to the installation of plant or machinery [*CAA 2001, s 25*]). It has been left to the courts to establish those items that qualify as plant and as companies have tried to extend the scope of the meaning of plant, there has been a plethora of tax cases on this particular subject.

The leading case of *Yarmouth v France* (1887) 19 QBD 647 established three important conditions for an item to qualify as plant, namely:

(a)   it must be apparatus;

(b)   it must be used for the carrying on of the business;

(c)   it must be kept for permanent use in the business.

Subsequent cases introduced a further qualification that the item must not form part of the premises in or upon which the business is conducted. This fundamental distinction between 'setting' and 'apparatus' is central to most of the cases on the identification of plant. The courts have invariably applied the 'apparatus' test in determining whether the relevant item fulfils a functional role (either active or passive) in the carrying on of a particular trade. For example, those items accepted as plant include office partitioning (moved frequently to meet trading conditions) (*Jarrold v John Good & Sons Ltd* (1962) 40 TC 681) and decorative articles contributing to the atmosphere in a hotel (*CIR v Scottish and Newcastle Breweries Ltd* [1982] STC 296).

Following the ruling in *Scottish and Newcastle Breweries Ltd*, HMRC will generally accept that expenditure on 'ambience' or 'decorative' plant is eligible for capital allowances where they are provided for the enjoyment of the public in a hotel, restaurant or similar trades. Typically, the trade would involve the creating an appropriate 'ambience' for its customer and the plant would be specially chosen to achieve that.

However, in *JD Wetherspoon v HMRC* [2012] 83/2010 UKUT 42 the Upper Tier Tribunal found that panelling was an unexceptional component of a pub and part of the premises. Therefore, the panelling was not 'decorative' plant and consequently not eligible for capital allowances.

In *Wimpey International Ltd v Warland* [1989] STC 273, Lord Justice Fox re-affirmed the well-established 'premises' test. Items will not qualify as plant where they are part of the premises or place in which the business is conducted, as opposed to being an asset with which the business is conducted.

Some important guidance with regard to fitting-out costs of existing premises is provided in the Upper Tier Tribunal ruling in *JD Wetherspoon v HMRC* [2012] UKUT 42 (TCC). This case involved a £33 million refurbishment project undertaken by Wetherspoon. Importantly, capital allowance claims were upheld on a wide range of items on the grounds they were 'incidental' building alterations to permit the installation of plant or machinery. Based on the precise facts, these included the replacement of various floors, drainage installations, tiling to kitchen and toilet walls if they were simply splashbacks, lighting to toilets, panels to hide cisterns and pipework in toilet cubicles and a reinforced kitchen floor. The Tribunal also confirmed the approach normally adopted in practice in relation to the allocation of preliminary costs (such as overheads and professional fees), stating that these costs can usually be apportioned on an appropriate 'pro-rata' basis.

Items that have been held not to be plant under the premises test include:

- a metal canopy over petrol pumps at a petrol filling station (*Dixon v Fitch's Garage Ltd* [1975] STC 480); and

- false ceilings concealing piping and wiring (*Hampton v Fortes Autogrill Ltd* [1980] STC 80).

- a car valeting bay (which was also used to apply glasscoat finishes to vehicles) (*Rogate Services Ltd v HMRC* [2014] UKFTT 312 (TC)).

In the *Rogate Services Ltd* case, the car valeting bay was found to be 'a place of work', where glasscoat could be applied 'advantageously' and could not therefore be plant. Even if it were plant, it would be excluded from being plant on the grounds that it was a building or structure within *CAA 2001, s 21* or *22* (see 4.17).

The First Tier Tribunal concluded that a caravan in which an employee was required to live for the proper performance of his duties did not play a part in the carrying out of those duties. Thus, it held that the caravan was not plant (*P Telfer v HMRC* [2016] UKFTT 614).

Restrictions for buildings and structures

4.17 Case law and HMRC practice have established that, in certain circumstances, structural and other items included in buildings qualify as 'plant' for capital allowance purposes. However, HMRC attempted to restrict any further extension in this area by introducing a statutory code in the *Finance Act 1994* (mainly due to a number of cases brought to the Commissioners by certain large supermarket chains). Broadly, expenditure on buildings (including any assets forming part of a building), structures and on land alterations will *not* qualify as plant unless it falls into one of the various categories specified in List C found in *CAA 2001, s 23*.

List C (see 4.18) attempts to codify those items that case law or HMRC practice has previously treated as plant.

The legislation first specifies those buildings (including assets incorporated within buildings), structures or any works involving land alterations which are deemed *not* to be plant (but may have qualified for industrial buildings allowances prior to 1 April 2011). These items are listed in Lists A and B found in *CAA 2001, ss 21* and *22* which are fully reproduced below.

List A

Assets treated as buildings

1.   Walls, floors, ceilings, doors, gates, shutters, windows and stairs.

2.   Mains services, and systems, for water, electricity and gas.

3.   Waste disposal systems.

4.   Sewerage and drainage systems.

5.   Shafts or other structures in which lifts, hoists, escalators and moving walkways are installed.

6.   Fire safety systems.

List B

Excluded structures and other assets

1.   A tunnel, bridge, viaduct, aqueduct, embankment or cutting.

2.   A way, hard standing (such as a pavement), road, railway, tramway, a park for vehicles or containers, or an airstrip or runway.

3.   An inland navigation, including a canal or basin or a navigable river.

4.   A dam, reservoir or barrage, including any sluices, gates, generators and other equipment associated with the dam, reservoir or barrage.

5.   A dock, harbour, wharf, pier, marina or jetty or any other structure in or at which vessels may be kept, or merchandise or passengers may be shipped or unshipped.

6.   A dike, sea wall, weir or drainage ditch.

7.   Any structure not within items 1 to 6 other than —

   (*a*)   a structure (but not a building) within Chapter 2 of Part 3 (meaning of 'industrial building'),

   (*b*)   a structure in use for the purposes of an undertaking for the extraction, production, processing or distribution of gas, and

   (*c*)   a structure in use for the purposes of a trade which consists in the provision of telecommunication, television or radio services.

Items unaffected by deemed 'non-plant' treatment

4.18   Until recently numerous categories of expenditure were not affected by the deemed 'non-plant' treatment. This still applies to expenditure on thermal insulation which is statutorily treated as plant but this treatment for fire safety, etc has now been repealed (see *CAA 2001, ss 29–32*). List C (reproduced below) also 'carves out' 33 important generic headings from the deemed 'non-plant' rules in Lists A and B above and which may therefore be plant (depending on the facts of the case and case law precedent) [*CAA 2001, s 23*].

List C

Expenditure unaffected by sections 21 and 22

1.   Machinery (including devices for providing motive power) not within any other item in this list.

2.   Gas and sewerage systems provided mainly —

    (a)   to meet the particular requirements of the qualifying activity, or

    (b)   to serve particular plant or machinery used for the purposes of the qualifying activity.

3   [Omitted by *FA 2008, s 73(1)(b)(ii)*.]

4.   Manufacturing or processing equipment; storage equipment (including cold rooms); display equipment; and counters, checkouts and similar equipment.

5.   Cookers, washing machines, dishwashers, refrigerators and similar equipment; washbasins, sinks, baths, showers, sanitary ware and similar equipment; and furniture and furnishings.

6.   Hoists.

7.   Sound insulation provided mainly to meet the particular requirement of the qualifying activity.

8.   Computer, telecommunication and surveillance systems (including their wiring or other links).

9.   Refrigeration or cooling equipment.

10.   Fire alarm systems; sprinkler and other equipment for extinguishing or containing fires.

11.   Burglar alarm systems.

12.   Strong rooms in bank or building society premises; safes.

---

13. Partition walls, where moveable and intended to be moved in the course of the qualifying activity.

14. Decorative assets provided for the enjoyment of the public in hotel, restaurant or similar trades.

15. Advertising hoardings; signs, displays and similar assets.

16. Swimming pools (including diving boards, slides and structures on which such boards or slides are mounted).

17. Any glasshouse constructed so that the required

18. Cold stores.

19. Caravans provided mainly for holiday lettings.

20. Buildings provided for testing aircraft engines run within the buildings.

21. Moveable buildings intended to be moved in the course of the qualifying activity.

22. The alteration of land for the purpose only of installing plant or machinery.

23. The provision of dry docks.

24. The provision of any jetty or similar structure provided mainly to carry plant or machinery.

25. The provision of pipelines or underground ducts or tunnels with a primary purpose of carrying utility conduits.

26. The provision of towers to support floodlights.

27. The provision of —

    (a) any reservoir incorporated into a water treatment works, or

    (b) any service reservoir of treated water for supply within any housing estate or other particular locality.

28. The provision of —

    (a) silos provided for temporary storage, or

    (b) storage tanks.

29. The provision of slurry pits or silage clamps.

30. The provision of fish tanks or fish ponds.

31. The provision of rails, sleepers and ballast for a railway or tramway.

32. The provision of structures and other assets for providing the setting for any ride at an amusement park or exhibition.

33. The provision of fixed zoo cages.

Note: Items 1 to 16 do not include any asset 'whose principal purpose is to insulate or enclose the interior of a building or to provide an interior wall, floor or ceiling which (in each case) is intended to remain permanently in place' [*CAA 2001, s 23(4)*].

Timing of Annual Investment Allowance (AIAs) and other capital allowances

4.19 Plant and machinery may qualify for the annual investment allowance (AIA) or writing down allowances ('WDAs') in the corporation tax accounting period ('CTAP') in which the expenditure is incurred.

As a general rule, capital expenditure is deemed to be incurred for (all) capital allowance purposes on 'the date the obligation to pay becomes unconditional', regardless of whether there is a later date by which payment should be made. This would be determined by reference to the terms of the purchase contract. In some cases, the relevant date may be the date the relevant expenditure is invoiced. However, in many cases, the company may be required to pay for plant or machinery within a certain period after delivery. In such cases, the Revenue considers that the obligation to pay becomes unconditional when the asset is delivered (see IR Tax Bulletin, Issue 9, November 1993, page 97).

However, the 'unconditional obligation to pay' date rule does not apply if:

- the purchase agreement provides for a credit period exceeding four months after the payment obligation becomes unconditional; or

- the payment obligation occurs earlier than under normal commercial practice and this was solely or mainly designed to accelerate the timing of capital allowances [*CAA 2001, s 5*].

ANNUAL INVESTMENT ALLOWANCES (AIAS)

Basic rules for claiming AIA

4.20 The annual investment allowance (AIA) is available to all companies (irrespective of size). The AIA provides 100% relief on most plant and machinery expenditure up to a specified annual limit (*CAA 2001, s 38A*), which has changed frequently. The AIA is available on most plant and machinery expenditure with the notable exception of cars.

Qualifying AIA expenditure also excludes expenditure incurred:

- in the CTAP during which the qualifying activity is permanently discontinued;

- in connection with a change in the nature or conduct of the trade carried on by someone other than the person incurring the expenditure, where obtaining the AIA is one of the main benefits resulting from the change.

The company can only claim the AIA in the same CTAP in which the expenditure is incurred and must have owned the asset at some point during that CTAP (*CAA 2001, s 51A*). See 4.25 for relevant anti-avoidance rules.

The *annual* AIA expenditure limit is calculated on a pro-rata basis where the CTAP is less than 12 months.

The most recent annual limits (see *CAA 2001, s 51A(5)*) are as follows:

From 1 January 2013 to 31 March 2014	£250,000
From 1 April 2014 to 31 December 2015	£500,000
From 1 January 2016 onwards	£200,000

Thus, expenditure on plant and machinery in a particular CTAP (excluding plant qualifying for special 100% FYAs and cars) will qualify for 100% AIAs up to the relevant limit, with any balance qualifying for standard or special rate pool WDAs. It is possible to make a partial AIA claim but any unused allowance cannot be carried forward and is therefore lost.

Companies may allocate the AIA to any qualifying expenditure as they see fit [*CAA 2001, s 51B(2)*]. This provides flexibility, allowing the company to set the AIA against the expenditure which secures the most beneficial advantage. For example, a company may allocate the allowance first against any expenditure which would otherwise attract the lowest rates of relief, such as 'integral features' or long life assets (which attract 8% WDAs) (see 4.26).

Special transitional rules for CTAPs straddling different AIA annual limits

Overview

4.21   Special transitional rules apply to companies where their CTAP straddles one or more of the dates on which the limit changes, some of which are highly (and needlessly) complex! The transitional rules dealing with cases where a 12-month CTAP straddles 31 December 2015 is dealt with in 4.21A below. See 2015/16 edition of this book for earlier transitional provisions.

Example 2

AIA in transitional CTAP for the year ended 30 November 2016

Ogbonna Ltd spent £350,000 on qualifying plant and equipment in the year ended 30 November 2016, as follows:

1 December 2015 to 31 December 2015	£175,000
1 January 2016 to 30 November 2016	£175,000

The relevant AIA limits for the CTAP were:

		£
1 December 2015 to 31 December 2015	1/12 × £500,000 =	41,667
1 January 2016 to 30 November 2016	11/12 × £200,000 =	183,333
AIA limit for CTAP		225,000

The company's AIA claim for the year ended 30 November 2016 would be:

		£
1 December 2015 to 31 December 2015	Restricted to period limit	41,667
1 January 2016 to 30 November 2016	Amount spent	175,000
		216,667

Thus, of the £350,000 qualifying expenditure, only £216,667 would rank for AIAs with the balance of £133,333 being eligible for WDAs.

Special rules for group companies and certain related companies

4.22   Each company has its own AIA allowance. However, only a single AIA is given for a group of companies [*CAA 2001, ss 51C* and *51D*]. In practice, the anti-fragmentation provisions severely limit the application of the AIA for groups.

For these purposes a group of companies exists if one company is a 'parent undertaking' of another company. The term 'parent undertaking' [*Companies Act 2006, s 1162*] essentially applies to a company which holds the majority in the voting rights of another company (ie > 50%), or a company which has a right to exercise a dominant influence over another company either through a 'control' contract or a provision in that company's articles.

The same rules apply where *similar* 'qualifying activities' are carried by two or more 'commonly controlled' companies. For these purposes, the similar activities condition applies if at the end of the accounting period for *either* company more than 50% of its turnover is broadly derived from a similar economic activity (broadly under the same NACE qualification, which is the first level of EU statistical classification under *EU Regulation (EC) 1893/2006* of the European Parliament). However, in practice, such cases are likely to be relatively rare.

Thus, most AIA claims by commonly controlled companies should not be restricted, so that each company would be able to claim its full AIA entitlement.

FIRST YEAR ALLOWANCES (FYAS)

Special 100% FYAs for low emission cars and environmentally-friendly plant

4.23   The following main categories of expenditure are eligible for 100% FYAs (known as 'first year qualifying expenditure') irrespective of the company's size:

- low-emission cars – ie cars with emissions not exceeding 75g/km (95g/km before 1 April 2015) qualify as 'low emission' cars for FYA purposes. (For related employee scale charge rules see 7.15.)

- Zero emission cars and vans (ie those powered entirely by electricity or hydrogen fuel cell) and, for a limited period from 23 November 2016 to 31 March 2019, the installation of electric vehicle charging infrastructure.

- natural gas/hydrogen refuelling equipment;

- designated energy-saving plant and equipment;

- environmentally beneficial new plant or machinery designated as meeting specified water saving or efficiency standards.

Expenditure on low/zero emission cars that are to be leased is excluded from FYAs from 1 April 2013.

FYAs are *not* available for certain assets or in some special circumstances, which are set out as 'general exclusions' in *CAA 2001, s 46(2)*.

4.24   In practice, the most common exclusions tend to be where the expenditure is incurred in the CTAP in which the trade permanently ceases or where the plant and machinery is leased-out.

In this context, it should be noted that the letting of any asset on hire would be regarded as leasing (except where the letting is part of a service – eg the provision of building access services that involves the hire of scaffolding).

However, 100% FYAs are permitted on *leased* natural gas/hydrogen refuelling equipment and other energy saving equipment and environmentally beneficial plant or machinery assets (see above).

It is important to note that long funding leases allow for capital allowances to be claimed by the lessee. Consequently, the lessor's expenditure on plant or machinery would *not* qualify for capital allowances [*CAA 2001, s 70A*].

Anti-avoidance rules for FYAs and AIAs

4.25   There are also various 'anti-avoidance' rules that are designed to prevent FYAs or AIAs being given [*CAA 2001, s 217*] where:

- plant is purchased from a 'connected person' [*CAA 2001, s 214*];

- the sole or main benefit of the transaction is to claim capital allowances [*CAA 2001, s 215*]; and

- plant is acquired in a sale and leaseback transaction [*CAA 2001, s 216*].

If the expenditure on plant or machinery does *not* qualify for FYAs or AIAs, it will be allocated to one of the relevant pools (see below). The majority of such expenditure will flow through to the main pool and attract annual WDAs of 18% [*CAA 2001, s 56(1)*].

SPECIAL CAPITAL ALLOWANCE RULES

Integral features

4.26   The concept of 'integral features' (broadly certain fixtures embedded within buildings) was introduced on 1 April 2008. The policy intention is that such items have a reasonably long life and should not therefore attract an accelerated form of tax relief (through normal WDAs etc). However, the more cynical view is that this was simply a further way of restricting capital allowances claimed on items of plant included in buildings.

The following items of expenditure are classified as expenditure on integral features:

(i)   electrical systems (including lighting systems);

(ii)   cold water systems;

(iii)   space or water heating systems; powered systems of ventilation, air cooling or air purification; and any floor or ceiling comprised in such systems;

(iv) lifts, escalators and moving walkways; and

(v) external solar shading.

Expenditure on integral features is included in a special rate pool (see 4.31) and will only attract WDAs at the lower rate of 8% per year (reducing balance basis).

4.27 Repair and replacement expenditure on integral feature items is generally allowable as a 'revenue' deduction. However, the legislation deems any repairs/replacements of integral features to be capital expenditure if the amount spent over a 12-month period exceeds 50% of the replacement cost of the relevant integral feature. If this 50% limit is exceeded, then the entire repair/ replacement expenditure will be added to the special rate pool and only attracts the 8% WDA (as opposed to an immediate 'revenue' deduction [*CAA 2001, s 33B*]. Although HMRC have indicated that they will take a reasonably relaxed approach to operating this rule, it seems fairly mean! Thus, where companies anticipate that they might exceed the '50% rule', they might consider deferring some of the repair costs so as to fall outside the relevant 12-month period.

Capital allowances on cars

4.28 The capital allowances regime for cars changed radically on 1 April 2009, with the view to encouraging businesses towards more eco-friendly cars.

Companies still qualify for 100% FYAs on cars provided their CO_2 emissions limit does not exceed 75 g/km (50g/km from 1 April 2018). Electric cars and vans also attract 100% FYAs (see 4.23).

The full cost of 'eco-friendly' cars (often referred to as ultra-low emission vehicles (ULEVs)) can therefore be written-off against the company's taxable profits in the year of purchase. (There are some major car manufacturers which have cars on the market with CO_2 ratings not exceeding 75g/km – these include the Mitsubishi Outlander PHEV (42 g/km) and Audi A3 Sportback (hybrid) (37 g/km).)

For other cars (ie those exceeding the critical 75g/km 100% FYA threshold), the capital allowances depends on their emissions rating.

The current treatment (until 31 March 2018) is summarised as follows:

CO_2 emissions	Capital Allowances treatment
75g/km to 130g/km	18% WDAs within the normal 'plant and machinery' pool
Over 130g/km	8% WDAs within the 'special rate' capital allowances' pool

These rules do *not* apply to vans, black-cabs, and motorcycles – they can (usually) be allocated to the main plant and machinery pool (attracting 18% WDAs – see 4.14) or 100% AIAs (see 4.20), as appropriate.

In most cases, *rental payments* on *leased cars* will be deductible for tax purposes in accordance with the amount charged to profit and loss in the accounts, subject to a restriction for less eco-efficient cars (but see 7.38 for further details).

It is worth remembering that company cars with relatively low emission rates tend to be more tax-efficient for the employees, since they attract relatively smaller taxable benefit charges (and commensurately lower Class 1A NICs) (see 7.27). Electric cars are particularly beneficial from this point of view (see also 7.18).

An up-to-date guide to green cars can be found at www.carfueldata.dft.gov.uk, a searchable index which provides useful data including CO_2 ratings and fuel consumption.

Long life assets

4.29   Where the plant is treated as 'long life', it will only be entitled to WDA at the rate of 8% each year. Long life plant is added to the special rate pool, which gives 8% WDAs on a reducing balance basis) [*CAA 2001, s 102(1), (4)*].

Plant is treated as 'long life' if it is reasonable to expect that its useful economic life is 25 years or more when new [*CAA 2001, s 91(1)*]. However, it is important to note that the 'long life' asset rules do not apply where the company's total expenditure on plant is less than £100,000 in the (12-month) accounting period [*CAA 2001, ss 97–99*].

For accounting periods beginning after 31 March 2015, the £100,000 limit is divided by reference to '51% group companies' (see 4.50–4.50B) rather than by reference to 'associated companies'.

The long life asset rules do not apply where the relevant plant is a fixture used in a retail shop, showroom, office or hotel [*CAA 2001, s 93*]. In all such cases, the plant will remain eligible for WDAs at the normal rates.

Short-life assets

4.30   Short-life asset elections are typically made for assets which are likely to be sold or scrapped by the eighth anniversary of the end of the CTAP in which they were acquired, such as computer equipment, tooling, etc. The 'short life asset' cut off is eight years for expenditure incurred after 31 March 2011. Each short-life asset or annual group of 'similar' short-life assets (see *IR Statement of Practice SP1/86*) is included in a separate pool, which often enables a beneficial balancing allowance to be claimed on disposal.

The legislation does not stipulate an eight year asset life requirement at the outset, but no tax benefit would arise from making a short life asset election if the plant or machinery is ultimately used for more than eight years. This is because, if the asset is still retained at the eighth anniversary from the end of the accounting period of its acquisition, it is transferred back to the main capital allowances pool and loses its separate identity.

With an 'eight-year' short life asset window and a main WDA rate of capital allowances of just 18% per year , more short life asset claims are likely to be made as a means of accelerating tax relief for most plant and machinery assets.

Example 3

Short life v main pool treatment

Slaven Ltd incurred £100,000 on 'short life' plant on 1 April 2017. The finance director, Mr Bilic, prepared the following calculations to determine whether a short life asset election would be worthwhile (assuming that the plant would be sold in year seven for 10% of its original cost).

Year	Main Pool	Short life asset
	£'000	£'000
Cost	100.00	100.00
WDA –1	(18.00)	(18.00)
WDA – 2	(14.76)	(14.76)
WDA – 3	(12.10)	(12.10)
WDA – 4	(9.92)	(9.92)
WDA – 5	(8.14)	(8.14)
WDA – 6	(6.67)	(6.67)
Disposal – 7	(10.00)	(10.00)
BA –7	–	(20.41)
WDA – 7	(3.67)	
TWDV c/fwd	16.73	
Total allowances to year 7	83.26	100.00

The above calculations show that, with a short life asset election, the plant would be fully written off for tax purposes in year seven. In contrast, with no election, the plant within the main pool is only about 83% written off, with about 17% still to be relieved over a relatively long period.

COMPUTATIONAL PROCEDURE

Allocation to relevant pools

4.31   A capital allowance computation is prepared for each corporation tax accounting period (CTAP). To claim the allowances, a company must first allocate its qualifying expenditure to one of the relevant pools [*CAA 2001, s 58*].

A company's qualifying capital expenditure on plant and machinery for a CTAP is allocated to a relevant 'pool' being either:

• 	a single asset pool;

• 	a special rate pool; or

• 	the main pool.

A *single asset* pool only includes expenditure relating to *one* single asset, the main category being 'elected' short life assets (see 4.30) [*CAA 2001, s 54(2), (3)*].

The *special rate pool* is used to capture the *total* expenditure relating to integral features, (see 4.26), cars with CO_2 emissions of more than 130 g/km (see 4.27), thermal insulation of an existing building used in a qualifying trade, and 'long life' assets (see 4.29).

The annual WDA for expenditure in the special rate pool is 8%.

All other plant and machinery expenditure is allocated to the *main pool*. The main pool therefore collects and aggregates the vast majority of expenditure. Thus, after allocating the first £200,000 (post-31 December 2015 – see 4.20 for previous annual amounts) eligible for AIAs, the remaining amount attracts the 18% WDAs, which are calculated on a reducing balance basis.

Where the tax written down value of the main and special pools (before the WDA for the period) is £1,000 or less, it can be fully written off as the WDA for the period (*CAA 2001, s 56A*). (The £1,000 *de minimis* amount is computed on a pro-rata basis for CTAPs of less than 12 months.)

Plant and machinery included in the main pool effectively loses its identity and is written down along with the other assets in the pool. Assuming no AIAs, with a WDA of 18% calculated on a reducing balance basis, it can take about ten years to write off 90% of the relevant expenditure.

Thus, if it is likely that the plant will be used for less than eight years, it will be advantageous to make a short-life asset election to place the asset (or group of similar assets) in a separate pool (see 4.30). The potential advantage is that a balancing allowance would be triggered on disposal, thus ensuring that the plant (less its scrap/disposal value) is fully written off for tax purposes over its working life in the business.

Calculation of writing down allowances on the main pool

4.32 The main steps for calculating capital allowances are set out below:

(a) the unrelieved TWDV of qualifying expenditure on the main pool (ie the tax written-down value (TWDV) brought forward) is brought forward from the previous CTAP;

(b) expenditure on plant and machinery, etc for the CTAP (excluding expenditure qualifying for annual investment allowance (AIAs)) is allocated to the main pool. Broadly, when added to the opening TWDV, this gives the 'available qualifying expenditure' (AQE). (Where companies claim FYAs/AIAs on their plant and machinery expenditure, this expenditure is not allocated to a pool for that period.);

(c) the total of any disposal receipts (TDR) for the CTAP is then calculated. The company brings in the disposal receipts for all assets that have triggered a 'disposal event'. Typically, a disposal receipt will represent the sale proceeds arising on the sale of an asset, although the amount is limited (where appropriate) to the original cost of the asset [*CAA 2001, ss 55, 61* and *62*];

(d) WDAs at the rate of 18% for a (12-month) CTAP are then calculated on the amount by which the AQE exceeds the TDR. (The WDA is given in the year of purchase, regardless of the date on which the asset is acquired.) However, if AQE exceeds TDR by £1,000 or less the balance (ie the amount by which AQE exceeds TDR) can be taken as the WDA for the period [*CAA 2001, s 56A(2)*]. No WDAs are available for the period in which the company ceases to trade [*CAA 2001, s 55(2), (4)*];

(e) if the TDR exceeds the AQE, a balancing charge will arise [*CAA 2001, s 55(3)*];

(f) a balancing allowance on the main pool (ie where the AQE exceeds the TDR) only occurs on the permanent cessation of the company's trade or any other qualifying activity [*CAA 2001, ss 55(1), (2), (4)*].

4.33 In contrast to the main pool or class pool, a disposal event on a single asset pool will always result in a balancing allowance or balancing charge:

● a balancing allowance arises where AQE exceeds TDR;

● a balancing charge arises where TDR exceeds AQE.

Plant and machinery allowances computation

4.34 Example 4 illustrates how plant and machinery allowances are calculated.

Example 4

Capital allowances computation

Gerrard Engineering Ltd (which is a singleton company) incurred the following capital expenditure during the year ended 31 December 2017.

	AIA qualifying expenditure	Qualifying for WDAs	Special rate pool	Total
	£	£	£	£
12 Dart 750 Machining centres (see note below)	200,000	103,000		303,000
Clicker press		4,580		4,580
Dell PCs and autocad software –		10,900		10,900
Hyundai i10 car (including extras) – 119 g/km		7,430		7,430
Works delivery van		18,200		18,200
Volvo S80 2.0f Se premium (including extras) – 199g/km			22,975	22,975
	200,000	144,110	22,975	367,085

Note – Only the first £200,000 out of the £303,000 spent on the Machining centres attracts AIAs – with the balance of £103,000 being eligible for WDAs.

During the period, the company sold one of its test rigs for £15,800.

The company's capital allowance computation for the year ended 31 December 2017 is as follows:

	Main pool	Special rate pool	Total	Total allowances
	£	£	£	£
TWDV b/fwd	150,180	–	150,180	
Additions	144,110	22,975	167,085	
AQE	294,290	22,975	317,265	
TDR – Disposal proceeds	(15,800)		(15,800)	
	278,490	22,975	301,465	
WDA – 18% /8%	(50,128)	(1,838)	(51,966)	51,966
AIA Qualifying Expenditure	200,000		200,000	
AIA	(200,000)		(200,000)	200,000
TWDV c/fwd	228,362	21,137	249,499	
Total allowances				251,966

RELIEF FOR COMPANY TRADING LOSSES

4.35 The basic reliefs available for trading losses are summarised below; their order of offset is shown in the pro-forma computation in 4.4 above.

The *Finance (No 2) Act 2017* relaxed the restrictions on the future use of trading (and other) losses arising after 31 March 2017. The rules for the use of pre-1 April 2017 losses remain unchanged.

Current year offset against total profits

4.36 Trading losses arising in a corporation tax accounting period (CTAP) can be offset against the company's other profits of the same period (calculated before charitable donations relief, but *after* deducting any current/prior year non-trading loan relationship deficit). This rule is unaffected by the *Finance (No 2) Act 2017* changes to the company loss rules.

Relief is only available if the trade is operated on a 'commercial' basis with the view to making a profit.

The claim (which is made on the CT600 return) must be made within two years after the end of the loss-making CTAP, although HMRC can extend this period [*CTA 2010, s 37(3)(a)*].

Twelve-month carry-back against total profits

4.37   Where the current year *trading* losses cannot be fully deducted against the profits of the current period, any remaining loss can generally be carried back under *CTA 2010, s 37(3)(b)* against the company's total profits of the CTAP(s) of the previous 12 months. This rule is not affected by the *Finance (No 2) Act 2017* changes.

Although a careful review of losses is often required to ensure their most beneficial use, companies often find that carrying back losses provides beneficial tax repayments (with interest), in particular in recent years where tax rates have been reducing.

If a CTAP straddles the previous 12-month period, then the profits are apportioned and the loss can only be set-off against the part within the previous 12 months.

4.38   The trading losses can only be offset if the company was carrying on the same trade, from which the loss arose, in the previous CTAP. The loss carry-back relief is subject to the same two-year time limit and 'commercial basis' test as the current year offset in 4.36 above.

The loss carry-back claim must be for the full amount of the loss (or if less, the relievable profits). It is not possible to make a partial claim. A carried back loss is offset against a company's profits *after* deducting group relief but *before* charitable donations relief. This means that charitable donations (including covenanted donations and charitable gifts of assets) may become permanently 'disallowed'.

An extended 'three' carry-back can be made where the company ceases to trade. In such cases, trading losses incurred in the 12 months prior to cessation may be carried back against the profits of the CTAPs of the previous *three years* on an unrestricted basis (see 16.8).

The detailed mechanics of the loss carry back relief under *CTA 2010, s 37(3) (b)* (for a CTAP for the year ended 31 March 2017) are illustrated in Example 5 below.

4.39

Example 5

Current year trading loss relief

Hurst Hatricks Ltd incurred a trading loss of £280,600 in its accounting period for the 12 months ended 31 March 2017. It makes up accounts for calendar years.

The 2017 loss of £280,600 can be mainly relieved as follows:

	2015	2016	2017	2017 Loss utilisation
	£	£	£	£
Tax-adjusted trading profit	135,500	189,700	–	(280,600)
Net property rental income	12,400	13,100	14,300	
Chargeable gain		–	65,000	
Non-trading loan relationship deficit	(34,700)	(56,900)	(50,200)	
	113,200	145,900	29,100	
Less *CTA 2010, s 37(3)(a)* current loss offset			(29,100)	29,100
Less *CTA 2010, s 37(3)(b)* loss offset vs 2014		(145,900)		145,900
Less Qualifying charitable donation	(1,500)	–*		
Corporation tax profits	111,700	–	–	
Loss carried forward under CTA 2010, s 45				(105,600)

* Qualifying charitable donations of £1,500 in 2016 become unrelieved.

Carry-forward against future trading profits

4.40   *Losses incurred before 1 April 2017*

Unused trading losses can be carried forward for offset against the first available taxable *profits of the same trade* [*CTA 2010, s 45*]. It follows that if the company's trading activity ceases, any excess losses are effectively forfeited.

From 1 April 2017, the amount of losses that may be offset may be subject to a financial limit (see 4.40A).

Losses arising after 31 March 2017

Finance (No 2) Act 2017 provides greater flexibility on the use of brought-forward trading losses. However, these rules only apply to losses arising after 31 March 2017. However, these also apply to post-31 March 2017 unused non-trading LR deficits, unused UK property business losses, and surplus management expenses.

Under this regime, *brought forward* trading losses and other losses/amounts are available for offset against future profits of any nature and for surrender as group relief. However, the amount that may be offset may be 'capped' (see 4.40A).

This flexible loss offset rule can only be used where the company continues to carry on the same trade but will not be available where its trade has become 'small' or negligible or is conducted on a 'non-commercial' basis (*CTA 2010, s 45A(3)*).

Limits on post-31 March 2017 offset of brought forward losses

4.40A   From 1 April 2017, there is a restriction on the amount of future profits that can be sheltered by brought forward trading (and other) losses. This restriction applies regardless of whether the brought-forward loss arose before or after 1 April 2017

For a *singleton* company, up to £5 million of its total profits (the company 'deductions allowance') for a 12 month period under new *CTA 2010, s 269ZL*, can be fully sheltered by brought forward losses. However, above the £5 million allowance, only 50% of any 'excess' total profits can be reduced by unrelieved losses.

The financial limit on in the amount of brought forward losses that can be offset effectively defers relief. Where a company has both pre-1 April 2017 losses and losses generated after that date, it can elect to choose the order in which they are offset.

Losses that cannot be offset under these rules continue to be carried forward against future profits/income (under the pre-31 March 2017 or post-1 April 2017 loss provisions, as appropriate)

The Treasury claims that 99% of companies will be unaffected by this restriction, either because they do not have losses above £5 million to carry forward or they are not likely to make profits exceeding £5 million in a single year!

Example 6

Offset for brought forward trading losses after 31 March 2017

Chicharito Ltd has been trading profitably for several years. However, in the year ended 31 March 2018, the business experienced serious difficulties. Consequently, after making all possible loss relief claims, it had trading losses carried forward of £568,000 at 31 March 2018.

The company's senior management expect to turn the business round in the year to 31 March 2019. A tax-adjusted profit of £400,000 has been forecast for this period. In June 2018, the company will also sell its freehold warehouse realising an expected chargeable gain of around £350,000.

All the unused trading loss can be relieved in the year to 31 March 2019, as shown below:

	£
Budgeted trading profits	400,000
Gain on warehouse	350,000
Total profits	750,000
Less: Trade losses b/bwd offset	(568,000)
Total taxable profits	182,000

Group relief for losses

4.41 Trading losses (as well as certain other items of relief including non-trading loan relationship deficits, property rental business losses and management expenses) can be surrendered by a member of the group in whole or in part to another group member for offset against the claimant's total profits of its current CTAP (*CTA 2010, Part 5*).

For this purpose, all group companies must be part of a 75% corporate group. It is possible to trace the required 75% ownership through any company, irrespective of its tax residence.

Historically, only UK-resident companies (or UK branches of non-resident companies) could participate in group relief claims. Since 1 April 2006, losses arising in a foreign subsidiary resident within the EU or the EEA may be surrendered to a UK group company by way of group relief, but only in restricted circumstances where the foreign subsidiary has fully exhausted all possible methods of relieving the loss in its 'local' jurisdiction (including carrying the losses forward for offset against future profits). In practical terms, this means that overseas losses (computed on a UK tax basis) may be relieved only where the foreign subsidiary has ceased trading either during the loss-making period or very shortly afterwards.

Increased group relief flexibility from 1 April 2017

4.41A   Losses relating to periods before 1 April 2017 can only be offset by way of group relief against the total profits of a *corresponding CTAP* of the claimant company.

However, group relief is available for brought-forward losses which were generated after 31 March 2017 (see 4.40 above). This is subject to certain anti-avoidance rules which broadly seek to ensure:

- the relevant companies were 'tax-grouped' in the period when the losses originally arose; and

- where the losses are trading losses, the trade continues to be carried on in the surrendering company in the period of offset.

Example 7

Group relief post-31 March 2017

Javier Holdings Ltd has a single 100% subsidiary, Marko Ltd. Both companies make up accounts to 31 March each year.

During the year ended 31 March 2018, Marko Ltd is likely to generate a tax-adjusted trading loss in the region of £580,000, of which some £200,000 will be group relieved to Javier Holdings Ltd for the same period.

Marko Ltd therefore expects to carry forward trading losses of £380,000 at 31 March 2018.

If Marko Ltd breaks even in the year ended 31 March 2019, up to £380,000 of its brought forward losses can be group relieved to its parent company.

INVESTMENT COMPANIES AND COMPANIES WITH INVESTMENT BUSINESSES

Investment businesses

4.42   In practice, the tax rules giving relief for management expenses will generally apply to investment companies, ie those companies that mainly carry on investment activities, such as holding a portfolio of investments in shares or property investment.

Management expenses and any associated capital allowances relating to an *investment business* (there is no requirement for the company to be an 'investment company') can be deducted against the income/profits of that investment business (see 4.43). This means, for example, that holding companies that carry on a trading activity can claim relief for their management expenses relating to their investment business.

An investment business is any business consisting wholly or partly of making investments [*CTA 2009, s 1218*]. Existing case law has interpreted this to mean simply holding investments rather than making them and also includes making a single investment.

In contrast, an investment dealing company, whose object is to make a profit from buying and selling investments would be treated as carrying on an investment dealing trade and would therefore be a trading company. The receipt of any investment income from its investments would be incidental to its main activity.

It is also unlikely that a company in liquidation would be treated as carrying on an investment business. Only rarely will a liquidator carry on a business existing wholly or mainly in the making of investments. The liquidator's main objective is to realise the company's assets to the best advantage.

Tax relief for management expenses

4.43   Any company carrying on an investment business can claim corporation tax relief for the management expenses (and capital allowances) relating to that business. Thus, for example, a company that carries on a trade and makes investments will now be entitled to relieve any management expenses incurred in relation to its investment business.

Under *CTA 2009, ss 1219* and *1225*, management expenses are now deductible on an 'accruals' basis, based on the amount debited to the company's profit and loss account (or the statement of total recognised gains and losses) in accordance with generally accepted accounting practice (GAAP. For further details, see also 4.45 notes (*h*) to (*j*).

Where the corporation tax accounting period does not coincide with the period for which the statutory accounts are drawn up, the debits are apportioned on a time basis (some other method can be used if that is more just and reasonable). Subsequent credits or 'reversals' relating to management expenses are 'credited' against the management expenses for that period, with any 'excess' amount being taxed [*CTA 2009, s 1229*].

Unallowable purposes

4.44   Management expenses are disallowed if they relate to investments held for an 'unallowable purpose' [*CTA 2009, s 1220*]. In the main, this relates to investments that are not held for a business or other commercial purpose, which in practice should be very rare.

The HMRC manuals (CTM 08220) give as an example of unallowable expenditure, any expenses relating to shares in a football club supported by one of the company's directors. However, where the investment was motivated (at least) partly as a way of promoting the company's business, only part of the cost would be disallowed as relating to an 'unallowable purpose'.

The 'unallowable purpose' exclusion also extends to expenditure relating to investment activities run on a mutual basis or by members clubs.

INVESTMENT COMPANIES AND COMPANIES WITH INVESTMENT BUSINESSES – PRO-FORMA TAX COMPUTATION

4.45   Where a company is an investment company or carrying on one or more investment activities, its corporate tax computation will bring together the assessable income and gains from all sources and then deduct from its total profits its management expenses and charges on income, etc.

A pro-forma corporation tax computation is provided below, together with accompanying notes.

Pro-forma Investment Co Ltd

Corporation tax computation based on the accounting period ended

	£	£	Notes
Property business income	X		
Rents receivable			(*a*)
Less: Allowable letting expenses	(X)		
Capital allowances on let property	(X)		(*b*)
		(X)	
		X	(*c*)

	£	£	Notes
Non-trading loan relationship profits and interest (net of any non-trading debits)	X		(d)
Less: Non-trading loan relationship deficit carried back	(X)	X	(e)
Taxable investment income		X	
		X	
Less: Share loss relief on disposals of shares in unquoted trading companies		(X)	(f)
Income		X	
Chargeable gains		X	
Total profits		X	
Less: Capital allowances re investment business		(X)	(g)
Less: Management expenses			
Excess management expenses b/fwd	X		
Amount incurred for period	X		(h) (i)
	X		
Offset against profits	(X)	(X)	
Excess management expenses c/fwd	X		(j)
	X	X	
Less: Current non-trading forex/loan relationship deficit (net of any non-trading loan relationship profits) arising in period		(X) (X)	(k)
		X	
Less: Qualifying charitable donations relief (being qualifying charitable donations and gifts of assets to charities)		(X)	(l)
Total profits before group relief		X	
Less: Group relief		(X)	
TAXABLE TOTAL PROFITS		X	

Notes:

(a) *Property business income* – The receipt of rental income, such as in the case of a property investment company, is taxed on an accruals basis in accordance with generally accepted accounting principles (GAAP) [*CTA 2009, ss 203–206*]. Expenses wholly and exclusively incurred for the rental business are deductible against the rental income (applying the same principles used for calculating taxable trading profits) [*CTA 2009, s 210*]. Similarly, any debit and credit amounts relating to intangible fixed assets within a property rental business are reflected in its taxable results [*CTA 2009, s 748*].

The company must split its expenses between those incurred in managing its investment properties and those of managing the company itself. This may also necessitate an apportionment of expenditure, such as directors' remuneration (see note (*i*) below). The property management expenses are deducted against property income. The expenses of managing the company are deductible as management expenses (see note (*h*) below).

(b) *Capital allowances relating to let property* – Capital allowances relating to let property are deductible as a property business expense (which may increase or create a property business loss).

(c) *Property rental business losses* – If a UK property rental business loss arises, this is offset against the company's *current year taxable profits*. Any unrelieved loss can be carried forward and set-off against future total profits (provided the rental business continues). If the rental business ceases, an investment company can carry forward any unrelieved losses as a management expense.

See 4.40 for offset rules for brought forward property business losses and management expenses that arise after 31 March 2017.

It is also possible to surrender a property rental business loss by way of group relief to the extent that it (together with any *current period* management expenses and qualifying charitable donations) exceeds the surrendering company's *gross* profits. Where an 'excess' amount is available for surrender, the order of offset is charges, then property business losses, then management expenses.

If an overseas property rental business loss arises, this can only be carried forward to set against future profits of the overseas property rental business (*CTA 2010, s 66*). The future offset of unused overseas property losses arising after 31 March 2017 continues to be subject to the same restrictions.

(d) *Non-trading loan relationship profits* – The non-trading loan relationship profits include all non-trading interest receivable, such as bank, building society and intra-group interest and other profits arising from the company's non-trading loan relationships (including non-trading foreign exchange gains).

However, any non-trading loan interest payable (and other *non-trading* loan relationship/foreign exchange deficits) must be deducted in arriving at the 'non-trade' loan relationship income [*CTA 2009, s 301(4)*]. (All interest payable to UK companies/UK banks is paid gross (ie without deducting 20% income tax).)

(e) *Carry-back of non-trading loan relationship deficit* – A claim can be made under *CTA 2006, s 462* to carry back all or part of a non-trading deficit (including foreign exchange losses) against the company's 'non-trade' loan relationship profits of the previous year. This relief is deducted after all other reliefs except group relief for trading losses [*CTA 2009, s 463(5)*].

The offset of post-31 March 2017 non-trading loan relationship deficits carried forward to future periods is dealt with in 4.40.

(f)   *Share loss relief* – Where an 'investment company' realises a capital loss on a disposal of an unquoted trading company's shares, it may elect to offset that loss against its income of the same period and then the previous period. A capital loss arising from a 'negligible value' claim (see 16.47) can also be relieved under these rules. A number of conditions must be satisfied to obtain relief.

For these purposes, the company must be an 'investment company' as defined in *CTA 2009, s 1218*. An investment company is defined as 'any company whose business consists wholly or mainly in the making of investments and the principal part of whose income is derived therefrom'. In *FPH Finance Trust Ltd v CIR* (1944) 26 TC 131, it was held that these tests should be applied over a representative period rather than the accounting period under review. Clearly, the company's main activity must be to hold investments for the receipt of income in the form of interest, dividends and rents (see *Casey v Monteagle Estate Co* [1962] IR 406). In *Jowett v O'Neill and Brennan Construction Ltd* [1998] STC 482, it was held that the simple placing of funds on deposit in a bank account is unlikely to constitute a business or investment activity.

Relief can only be claimed if the investment company originally *subscribed* for the shares (ie it is not available for 'second-hand' shareholdings). The shares must be in an unquoted company which was either trading at the date of the disposal or has ceased to trade within three years of the disposal date (and has not since become an investment company or engaged in certain excluded activities, such as dealing in shares, land or commodities). Broadly speaking, relief is only available to shares in companies that would qualify for EIS relief (see 11.41–11.43). In all cases, the investee company must not be an 'associated company', such as a 51% subsidiary [*CTA 2010, ss 68–90*].

(g)   *Capital allowances* – Capital allowances can be claimed on plant and machinery purchased for the purpose of a company's investments business in the same way as a trading company. This would include, for example, the purchase of office furniture, office equipment, computers, cars, etc [*CAA 2001, ss 11* and *15(1)(g)*]. If the capital allowances exceed the company's income for a period, the excess is added to the company's management expenses for general offset against its total profits. Any unrelieved capital allowances are treated in the same way as excess management expenses.

(h)   *Management expenses* – Any company carrying on an investment business can obtain relief for its relevant management expenses against its total profits (see 4.43). Under *CTA 2009, s 1225*, management expenses are generally based on the amount reflected in the accounts in accordance with GAAP.

Generally, management expenses are those incurred in managing the investments and would therefore include normal office running costs and reasonable directors' remuneration. Capital expenditure is not deductible as a management expense [*CTA 2009, s 1219(3)*], although HMRC accept that it may often be difficult to draw the dividing line on costs relating to the acquisition of investments (see below).

The scope of expenses allowed by the definition is often unclear, particularly in relation to research and the appraisal of potential 'target' companies for investment. The company will not necessarily obtain relief for every expense and positively has to show that an expense falls to be treated as an expense of management. In practice, difficulties often arise in obtaining relief for directors' remuneration (see note (*i*) below) and expenses relating to seeking and changing investments.

For example, brokerage and stamp duties on the purchase or sale of investments are considered to be part of the cost of purchasing or selling an investment and would therefore not be allowed as a management expense (*Capital and National Trust Ltd v Golder* (1949) 31 TC 265). HMRC's guidance notes take the view that expenditure on appraising and investigating investments, such as obtaining preliminary reports for a number of possible investment options, are not regarded as capital and hence would qualify for relief. On the other hand, HMRC has generally taken the view that once a decision has been taken to acquire a particular investment, any costs incurred from that point are capital. Case law suggests that this may not always be the case. For example, professional fees incurred in evaluating and preparing for the purchase of a company that was subsequently aborted were allowed by the Court of Appeal in *Camas plc v Atkinson* [2003] STC 968.

Certain statutory 'management expense' deductions are available which includes the relief for shares awarded to or share options exercised by directors and employees [*CTA 2009, ss 1221, 1013(3) and 1021(3)*] (see Chapter 8 for detailed coverage of relief for employee shares).

(i)   *Directors' remuneration* – Inspectors often seek to limit the 'management expenses' deduction to the amount they consider reasonable, having regard to the duties performed (in contrast, directors of trading companies generally have no difficulty in voting themselves significant levels of remuneration).

In the case of an investment business, HMRC typically argue that only a modest amount relates to the cost of managing the company's investments and the company itself. Where there are likely to be difficulties in obtaining relief for directors' remuneration, the use of dividends should be considered as a means of extracting funds from a company (see 2.12–2.17). If the Inspector disallows excess remuneration, it is possible to eliminate the employment income tax liability (but not the NIC liability) by formally waiving the remuneration and reimbursing the amounts to the company (see 2.21).

In the case of a property investment company, a higher level of remuneration can be justified on the basis that it relates to the management of the properties, which would require a greater degree of management time. In practice, directors' remuneration of between 7.5% and 15% of a company's rental income might be allowed, although a higher amount could be substantiated where the directors are personally involved in collecting rent, supervising maintenance and improvements and negotiating rent reviews, etc. This would be relieved as a property rental business expense rather than a management expense (see note (a) above).

The 'nine-month rule' for accrued remuneration also applies to directors' remuneration deductible as a management expense [*CTA 2009, s 1249*] (see 2.22 and 5.10). This restriction on the level of allowable remuneration an 'investment company' can pay also means that the directors can only make modest provision for pensions.

(j) *Surplus management expenses* – If the company's management expenses exceed its profit (ie effectively, the company has a loss), the surplus management expenses are carried forward to the next CTAP. They will then be treated as management expenses of the next period (and offset against total profits) [*CTA 2009, s 1223(3)*].

Refer to 4.40 for future offset of surplus management expenses arising after 31 March 2017.

Subject to this, excess management expenses can be carried forward indefinitely, unless the company ceases to carry on its investment business or where there is a major change in the conduct of the company's business, etc within five years either side of a change in ownership [*CTA 2010, ss 677 and 678*].

(k) *Current year offset of non-trading loan relationship deficit* – A claim can be made to relieve a non-trading deficit against the company's taxable profits of the same CTAP (known as the 'deficit period') [*CTA 2009, s 461*]. In the case of most investment companies, all interest payable and losses or deficits arising on loans (including foreign exchange losses) will normally be 'non-trading'. The amount eligible for a non-trading deduction must be computed after deducting any non-trading interest income and other non-trading loan related profits (see note (d) above).

(l) *Qualifying charitable donations relief* – This relief is given on qualifying donations to a charity (within *CTA 2010, s 191*) and the market value of certain assets gifted to a charity (under *CTA 2010, s 203*). Charitable donations relief is also available where assets are sold to a charity below their market value – in this case the relief is based on the amount by which the market value exceeds the sale price. Relief is given in the period in which the payments/asset transfer is made.

Annual payments or annuities are claimed as a management expense provided they are incurred for business purposes, subject to the 'unallowable purpose' rule (see 4.44).

Example 8

Investment company tax computation

Carroll Properties Ltd rents out various commercial properties in the east end of London. Its results for the year ended 31 December 2017 were as follows:

	£	£
Rental income		100,000
Bank interest income		5,000
Expenses:		
Property related	29,600	
Management expenses	12,800	42,400
Capital allowances:		
Property related	5,400	
General	9,200	14,600

Carroll Properties Ltd's taxable profits for 2017 would be calculated as follows:

	£	£
Rental income		100,000
Less:		
Property expenses	(29,600)	
Capital allowances	(5,400)	
		(35,000)
Property business income		65,000
Non-trading loan relationship profits		5,000
Total profits		70,000
Less:		
Management expenses		(12,800)
Capital allowances		(9,200)
Taxable total profits		48,000

CLOSE INVESTMENT HOLDING COMPANIES ('CICS')

4.46   A CIC is a special category of company that previously unable to benefit from the small profits rate or small profits marginal relief [*CTA 2010, s 18(b)*]. This is irrelevant for corporation tax purposes *from 1 April 2015 onwards*, since all companies pay the same rate of corporation tax regardless of the size of their profits or type of income (see 3.18).

Interest relief still continues to be unavailable on borrowings to lend monies to or purchase shares in a CIC [*ITA 2007, s 392(2)*] (see 11.9–11.12 and 11.19).

PAYMENT OF CORPORATION TAX

Quarterly instalment payment (QIP) rules

4.47   'Large' companies pay their tax under the quarterly instalment payment (QIP) system. The detailed rules are found in the *Corporation Tax (Instalment Payments) Regulations 1998, SI 1998/3175* as amended by the *Corporation Tax (Instalment Payments) (Amendment) Regulations 2014, SI 2014/2409.*

In simple terms, companies that are within the QIP regime will pay their corporation tax liability for the relevant corporation tax accounting period (CTAP) in months 7, 10, 13 and 16 following the start of that CTAP. For exact payment dates see 4.51.

For QIP purposes, a large company is a company whose profits exceed the corporation tax upper limit (in force at the end of the relevant CTAP).The current upper limit of £1,500,000 (see 3.16). If profits are hovering around the £1,500,000 threshold, there may be a case for providing an additional bonus to the owner manager(s) to avoid the instalment rules!

For accounting periods beginning after 31 March 2015, the £1,500,000 limit is apportioned by reference to '1 + N', with N being the number of 'related 51% group companies' (as determined at the end of the *last* CTAP) and reduced where the CTAP is less than 12 months. Broadly, a company is a 'related 51% group company' of another company in a CTAP if it is a 51% subsidiary of another company (see 4.50).

As the limits are apportioned equally between related 51% group companies, this rule is particularly disadvantageous where the profits arise unevenly between them.

4.48   To assist growing companies, a company which becomes 'large' will not have to pay tax in instalments for that 'first relevant' period (only) provided its profits are less than £10 million (again apportioned for related 51% group companies and/or for CTAP's of less than 12 months). This 'transitional' measure gives companies time to prepare for paying by instalments.

4.49   *For CTAPs starting before 1 April 2015*, the £1,500,000 limit was apportioned by the number of 'associated companies' plus one. The definition of an 'associated company' was complex and much wider, since it included both 'grouped' companies and other companies controlled by a common shareholder(s). For detailed analysis of 'associated companies' see 3.20–3.30 of the 2014/15 edition of this book.

The QIP regime is subject to a de minimis rule. If the total tax liability for the CTAP is less than £10,000, QIPs are not required.

Although HMRC will do their best to issue reminders and payslips to those companies they believe to fall within the QIP regime, the responsibility to make QIPs still falls on each company.

Companies that are not within the QIP regime, must pay their corporation tax liability within nine months after the end of the CTAP.

Example 9

Apportioning limits for QIP purposes

Adrián Holdings Ltd, has three 100% trading subsidiaries and carries on a group administration services trade.

Its recent taxable trading profits are:

	£
Year ended 31 March 2016	100,000
Year ended 31 March 2017	380,000

Adrián Holdings Ltd is forecast to have £450,000 of profits for the year ended 31 March 2018.

All three 100% trading subsidiaries are related 51% group companies. The relevant limits to determine if QIPs apply to the company would be:

- £1,500,000/(3+1)4 = £375,000.

- £10,000,000/(3+1)4 = £2,500,000.

The company's profits exceeded £375,000 at the end of the year ended 31 March 2017. However, because its profits for that CTAP are less than £2,500,000, it is not subject to QIPS for that CTAP and hence will pay its corporation tax liability by 1 January 2018.

Nevertheless, it will be subject to QIPs for the year ended 31 March 2018, unless its actual taxable profits for that CTAP do not exceed £375,000.

Related 51% group company

4.50 For CTAPs starting after 31 March 2015, a much simpler concept of 'related 51% group companies' is used to apportion the £1,500,000 under the QIP regime. Unlike the often-complicated 'associated company' rules, the related 51% group company only applies to corporate groups.

For these purposes, *CTA 2010, s 279F* states that:

> 'A company (B) is a related 51% group company of another company (A) in an accounting period if for any part of that accounting period–
>
> (a)   A is a 51% subsidiary of B,
>
> (b)   B is a 51% subsidiary of A, or
>
> (c)   both A and B are 51% subsidiaries of the same company.'

A company is a 51% subsidiary if more than 50% of its ordinary share capital is beneficially owned directly or indirectly by another company (*CTA 2010, s 1119*).

Related 51% group company – exemptions

Carrying on a business

4.50A The related 51% group company legislation disregards any company that is not carrying on a trade or business at any point in the CTAP.

In the vast majority of cases, it will be very clear that a company is carrying on a business or trade. However, in certain situations, careful consideration may be required to determine whether a company is 'carrying on a business', which has a wider meaning than trading. Although some earlier case law debated the point (see, for example, *CIR v The Korean Syndicate Ltd* 12 TC 181), it seems that the concept of 'carrying on a business' implies some activity being actively carried on. As a general rule, where a company earns an income return from its assets, this indicates that it is carrying on a business and would be therefore be counted as a related 51% group company for the purposes of the relevant limits for QIP purposes.

On the other hand, dormant related 51% group companies that have not carried on any trade or business at any time during the relevant CTAP are ignored.

Interestingly, following *Jowett v O'Neill and Brennan Construction Ltd* [1998] STC 482, where a company only receives bank deposit interest in the CTAP, it was decided that this did *not* constitute the carrying on of an investment business.

This approach was followed in *HMRC v Salaried Persons Postal Loans Ltd* [2006] STC 1315, where a company received rent from a property it had previously occupied for its trade. It was held that the company had not carried on a business – the letting was merely a continuation of the letting of the former trading premises and was not actively managed.

A different decision was reached in *Land Management Ltd v Fox* [2002] STC (SSCD) 152. This case involved a company that let property and made and held investments. The company advanced an interest-bearing loan to a related company and placed funds on deposit at the bank. It was held that these activities amounted to the carrying on of a business.

In a case involving CGT incorporation relief, the Upper Tier Tribunal held that the letting of ten flats, which involved some day-to-day management was a 'business' (*Ramsay v HMRC* [2013] UKUT0226).

Non-trading holding companies

4.50B In fairly restricted cases, *CTA 2010, s 279F(5)* exempts certain 'non-trading holding' companies from being a 'related 51% group company' by deeming them not to carry on a business. Such holding companies are exempted, provided they:

(a)   do not carry on a trade;

(b)   have one or more 51% subsidiaries; and

(c)   are passive.

Broadly speaking, a holding company would be regarded as 'passive' for the relevant CTAP where:

● it has no assets (other than its subsidiaries);

● any dividends received from its subsidiaries have been fully re-distributed to its own shareholders; and

● it has no chargeable gains, management expenses or qualifying charitable donations.

In practice, it is unlikely that many holding companies would satisfy all the relevant conditions for the *CTA 2010, s 279F(5)* exemption.

However, this does not necessarily prevent the group from arguing that, on the facts, the holding company is not carrying on a business and is effectively dormant. This would include cases where the holding company does not carry on any business activity and simply 'passively' holds shares in one or more subsidiaries. However, if it incurs significant costs and/or receives investment income, HMRC will often (successfully) argue that the company is carrying on a business.

QIP timetable

4.51   The tax instalment payments for a 12-month accounting period are made as follows:

First instalment   25%   —   six months and 13 days after the start of the accounting period

Second instalment   25%   —   three months after the first instalment

Third instalment   25%   —   three months after the second instalment

Final instalment   25%   —   three months and 14 days after the *end* of the accounting period

Thus, if the company has a 31 December year-end, its QIPs will fall due on 14 July, 14 October, 14 January and 14 April.

If the corporation tax accounting period lasts less than 12 months, the *last* instalment falls due three months and 14 days from the end of the accounting period. The *other* instalments would be due every three months starting six months and 13 days from the start of the relevant accounting period.

The Government intends to bring forward the dates of quarterly instalment payments for companies with profits of more than £20 million, starting in April 2019, but draft legislation for this has not yet been published. The intention is that payments will be due entirely within the year, falling due in the third, sixth, ninth and twelfth month of the accounting period (assuming a twelve-month CTAP).

Estimating potential corporation tax liability

4.52   To minimise the company's interest exposure, appropriate revisions to the quarterly instalments (and, where appropriate, 'top-up' payments) would be made as the company's view of its *estimated* tax liability for the relevant year changes.

The requirement to estimate the tax liability for the entire period some six months into it requires companies to establish reliable forecasts. However, there may be an unforeseen change in trading patterns or unpredictable events, such as the sale of an investment towards the end of the period or unplanned capital expenditure and so on. Such variations are likely to create material interest costs where the actual liability turns out to be greater.

Penalties may be charged where a company fraudulently or deliberately fails to pay the appropriate instalments, in addition to the standard penalties for failure to pay the company's corporation tax by the filing date of the CTSA return without a reasonable excuse.

Comparing quarterly instalments with actual tax liability

4.53   Once the company has calculated its final tax liability for the period, the tax instalments and balancing payment that it should have made are compared with its QIPs. Interest on underpaid and overpaid amounts can then be calculated. The QIP regime requires companies continually to review their expected tax liabilities and make 'top-up' payments where necessary to reduce their interest costs. Similarly, if the company considers that too much tax has been paid to date (for example, as a result of reduced profits or an anticipated loss), it may make an appropriate reduction in the next instalment or claim a repayment.

Interest will accrue from the first QIP date to the 'nine-month' due date at the base rate plus 1% for *unpaid* tax and base rate less 0.25% for overpaid tax. After the nine-month normal due date, the interest increases to *base rate* plus 2.5% for underpayments and (since 2009) a flat rate of 0.5% for overpayments. The interest payments will be worked out on a last in first out basis. Thus, for example, any repayment will generally consist of the latter payments made by the company.

The base rate reduced in August 2016, resulting in the first reduction of interest rates on late paid corporation tax since 2009.

HMRC's 'Time To Pay' (TTP) regime

4.54   Under the 'Time To Pay' (TTP) initiative, companies can apply to HMRC's dedicated Business Payment Support Service (BPSS) to defer their tax payments over an appropriate suitable pre-agreed period. This facility applies to *all* their tax liabilities, including corporation tax, PAYE, National Insurance, Construction Industry Scheme tax deductions, and VAT. Companies must contact HMRC as soon as it as appears likely that they anticipate a problem in paying their tax.

HMRC will often grant companies a deferred period over which to pay their taxes provided they are satisfied that the company cannot pay them on the due date(s). The TTP arrangements are negotiated on a 'case-by-case' basis taking into account the company's cash flow profile, and can vary from a few months to a longer period (although cases lasting over a year are only agreed in exceptional circumstances). HMRC stress that the same principles are applied to all taxpayers, although the precise arrangements would be tailored to reflect the risk/return associated with different tax liabilities. For higher risk cases, HMRC will demand more supporting information for TTP applications.

HMRC expect the company to put forward a realistic payment proposal and they will allow viable companies to pay over a period they can afford. Currently, HMRC appears to be requesting an 'up-front' lump sum with fairly tight monthly repayment schedules. Where a company's financial position improves, HMRC must be contacted since the company is likely to be asked to increase or clear their tax payments.

HMRC emphasise the need to contact the BPSS before tax payments become overdue – otherwise the local office handling the collection of overdue tax will need to be contacted and surcharges are likely to apply.

The advantage of deferring tax payments through the BPSS is that surcharges and penalties will not apply to deferred payments, though interest will be charged for the period that tax payments remain outstanding.

Companies applying for the 'time to pay' concession must contact the BPSS (0300 200 3835). They must be able to provide their tax reference number, details of the relevant tax that it is seeking to defer and basic details of its cash inflows and outflows. Larger deferrals or complex cases may require more time and further information is generally required before payment arrangements can be agreed. Where a company wishes to defer more than £1 million of tax, it will need an Independent Business Review.

CORPORATION TAX SELF-ASSESSMENT (CTSA) RETURN

CT600 return

4.55   All companies are subject to the corporation tax self-assessment (CTSA) regime which evolved from Pay and File and incorporates much the same rules for filing the return, claims and late filing penalties.

The return form CT600 must normally be filed, together with the accounts and tax computations, within 12 months from the end of the relevant corporation tax accounting period (CTAP).

Most *trading* companies can use the short version of the computational return.

The detailed version of the return must be used where special claims are made (such as group relief), where any entry is £10 million or more, and by investment companies. Loans to shareholders of close companies during the period must be summarised on supplementary page CT600A. Group relief claims and surrenders are detailed on supplementary page CT600C.

The penalty for filing the CT600 return late is £100. This rises to £200 where the return is more than three months late. These penalty rates rise to £500 and £1,000 respectively where the return is filed late for a third consecutive period.

For very late returns tax-related penalties can arise in addition to the flat-rate penalties above. They are calculated as follows:

- Where a return is filed between 18 months and 24 months after the end of the company's accounting period: 10% of any unpaid corporation tax.

- Where a return is still not filed 24 months after the end of the accounting period: a further 10% of any unpaid corporation tax.

The amount of unpaid corporation tax in both these cases is the amount that was not paid by the date the company first became liable to a tax-related penalty.

Revised penalty rules were set out in *FA 2009, Sch 55* to align the penalty regime across various taxes. These rules are being brought in by statutory instrument on a piecemeal basis and have not yet been introduced for corporation tax returns.

The CTSA system

4.56   The CT600 return is a true self-assessment. The onus is on the company to ensure that its tax return is correct and complete. No assessment or determination is issued by HMRC to agree the tax result. The returns are subject to a 'process now, check later' system, with any obvious mistakes arising from the processing of the returns being corrected by HMRC.

However, the taxable profit or loss is automatically treated as final after 12 months from the filing date (ie usually two years from the end of the relevant corporation tax accounting period (CTAP)), unless HMRC initiate an enquiry leading to an amendment of the return within the 12-month period.

Where the return is submitted early, the 12-month enquiry 'window' now starts from when the return is submitted (so the window will close sooner (*FA 1998, Sch 18, para 24(2)*)). However, this rule does not apply to large and medium sized groups (under the *Companies Act 2006*). HMRC will therefore still be able to open an enquiry into the company tax return of any member of a large or medium-sized group within the 12-month period of the statutory filing date, however early the return is delivered. However, HMRC is keen to encourage these larger companies to file early where it is possible for them to do so. Therefore, where it is practical to do so, HMRC's policy is to open all enquiries into a group's returns within 12 months of the delivery of the last individual company tax return from any member of that group.

HMRC's operational note states that this procedural change will apply to those companies dealt with by either HMRC's Large Business Services or Local Compliance (Large and Complex) offices. This is because HMRC is unlikely to have sufficient resources to extend this treatment to other large or medium-sized corporate taxpayers dealt with outside of these two units (mainly medium sized companies).

Companies can generally adjust their returns (post-submission) within the 12-month period following the statutory filing date.

The majority of cases selected for enquiry are chosen on an objective basis, ie that there may be something wrong in the return following various checks made by HMRC on the return information. Also, a small number of cases will be selected at random. For further details of HMRC's procedures and practice for enquiries, see *IR Code of Practice 14*.

HMRC's Discovery powers

Four-year/six-year time limits

4.57 To ensure finality under CTSA, HMRC's ability to 'open-up' previous years CT returns is generally restricted to the 12-month enquiry window discussed in 4.56 above.

However, under *TMA 1970, s 29*, HMRC has the power to make a discovery assessment outside the normal 12-month enquiry window. In practice, HMRC will often seek to raise discovery assessments when it misses the normal enquiry deadline, on the grounds that it was not aware (or sufficiently aware) of the relevant matters giving rise to an increased tax liability.

A counter-balancing protection is given to taxpayers under *TMA 1970, s 29(5), (6)*. Thus, HMRC officers can only make a further assessment outside the normal enquiry period if they could not have been 'reasonably expected, on the basis of the information made available to them before that time' to be aware of the insufficiency of the self-assessment (see 4.57A). Consequently, where taxpayers make full disclosure and no enquiry is made by HMRC, they are 'protected' from a subsequent discovery being made by HMRC, thus providing valuable certainty in their tax affairs.

HMRC can only raise 'discovery' assessments within *four* years of the end of the relevant CTAP where it can show that tax has been under-stated on a CT return as a result of a mistake with *insufficient disclosure* on that return.

However, the time limit for raising discovery assessments is extended in more 'serious' cases involving failure to take reasonable care (six years from the end of the CTAP) or where there has been a deliberate understatement (20 years from the end of the CTAP) (*FA 1998, Sch 18, para 46*).

Assessing the level of disclosure required

HMRC v Charlton & Corfield

4.57A The relevant principles for determining whether sufficient disclosure has been made are covered in a number of cases. Probably one of the most important rulings is provided by *HMRC v Charlton & Corfield* [2013] STC 866 since it reviewed all the various authorities and issues relating to discovery assessments.

Briefly, the facts in the *Charlton* case were as follows:

- The tax returns submitted by the taxpayers provided the scheme reference number (SRN) under the disclosure of tax avoidance schemes (DOTAS) rules (see 1.20 and 1.32). The taxpayers claimed substantial capital losses had arisen under an avoidance scheme involving the purchase and sale of life assurance policies.

- The taxpayers had disclosed full details on the 'white spaces' in their returns. This included detailed information about the transaction (eg dates; the amount invested; amount realised), together with the actual loss claimed and the reasoning supporting the loss claim.

- HMRC had raised enquiries on most other users of the tax scheme (quoting the same SRN) within the normal time limit.

- Several months later, HMRC discovered that no enquiry had been made in relation to *Charlton* and *Corfield* – an enquiry letter had been prepared for *Corfield*, but was never sent out!

- Once HMRC had received a favourable ruling from the Special Commissioner in *Drummond v HMRC* [2007] STC (SCD) 682 (see 1.12) (which involved a very similar scheme), it raised discovery assessments on *Charlton* and *Corfield*.

The Upper Tribunal (UT) held that HMRC had not been entitled to issue discovery assessments. The key test was whether the taxpayers had provided information which would have enabled a hypothetical officer of HMRC to have been aware of the under assessment.

HMRC argued that the existence of the Form AAG1 (which contained details of the scheme and was submitted by the scheme's promoters – see 1.23) should not be regarded as having been made available to it for the purposes of *TMA 1970, s 29(6)*. This was rejected by the Tribunal, which observed:

'...The SRN was included in each Respondent's tax return, but on a different page to the white space disclosures of the scheme and the pages setting out the capital gains computations and the figures for income on the surrender of the policy. We are, however, in no doubt that, first, the existence of the form AAG1 could reasonably have been expected to have been inferred by the hypothetical officer, and secondly that the physical separation of the SRN number from other relevant entries on the tax return would not have prevented an officer from making the necessary link between them so as reasonably to infer the relevance of the form AAG1 to the insufficiencies ...

The circumstances of the form AAG1 in our view make it reasonable for its existence and relevance to be inferred. An officer would be aware of the significance of an SRN, and of the fact that a promoter would have been required under *section 308(1)* of the *Finance Act 2004*, to have provided information, in the form AAG1, to HMRC ... In our view, the form AAG1 is just the sort of information the availability and relevance of which might reasonably be inferred from the inclusion of the SRN in a return which also discloses tax effects consistent with tax planning.

In addition to the information in the form AAG1, the Tribunal also concluded that the hypothetical HMRC officer would have sufficient knowledge of second hand life insurance policies to appreciate the unusual nature of the entries in the taxpayers' returns and they would also be aware of the *Drummond* decision.

In arriving at its decision, the UT made some interesting points on the application of the 'discovery' rules:

- A competent discovery assessment could be made where it 'newly appears to an officer acting honestly and reasonably, that there is an insufficiency in an assessment, for any reason whatsoever, including the correction of an oversight'. Thus, it is not necessary to uncover new facts to enable a discovery outside the normal statutory enquiry window.

- In determining what information is made available to an HMRC officer or should have been inferred by that officer, this is measured by the information that a hypothetical HMRC officer had available to them or could have inferred – not the actual HMRC officer. The key point was what the officer could actually be expected to be aware of, not what they might be expected to do to acquire that awareness.

- The UT referred to the landmark case of *Langham v Veltema* [2004] STC 544. This established that if an HMRC officer would have had to make enquiries to obtain further information, they should not be expected to do so in order to make a subsequent discovery assessment. In the *Veltema* case, Lord Justice Auld succinctly summarised the position as follows:

  'The Inspector is to be shut out from making a discovery assessment under the section only when the taxpayer or his representatives, in making an honest and accurate return or in responding to a s 9A enquiry, have clearly alerted him to the insufficiency of the assessment, not where the Inspector may have some other information, not normally part of his checks, that may put the sufficiency of the assessment into question.'

Therefore, it is not possible to assume that the officer has possession of any specific knowledge elsewhere within HMRC. The hypothetical officer is not the 'embodiment of HMRC as a whole'.

- There should be no presumption that the hypothetical officer would need to consult specialist colleagues to ascertain the relevance of the information provided by the taxpayer.

- It is only necessary to consider the quality and extent of the information provided, not the ability of the officer to understand. The hypothetical officer's personal qualities or level of knowledge were irrelevant, although it can be assumed that they have a 'reasonable' knowledge and understanding.

●   In a complex case, both the nature of the information and the way it is presented will be material in determining its adequacy in order to prevent a valid discovery assessment.

Robert Smith v HMRC

4.57B   In the case of *Robert Smith v HMRC* TC02768, Mr Smith fared much less favourably than the taxpayers in *Charlton*. The *Robert Smith* case also involved an avoidance scheme that triggered a purported capital loss of some £500,000 as a result of the purchase and subsequent sale of a second-hand life insurance policy (whereas the economic loss was only some £50,000).

However, in this case, no DOTAS number was provided and therefore the Tribunal had to consider the level of information actually provided by the taxpayer. Although there was some disclosure, it was certainly not enough. The Tribunal ruled that the relevant disclosure must alert the HMRC officer to an objective awareness of an actual insufficiency.

While HMRC had full details of the relevant 'capital loss' scheme and had placed a message on the HMRC internal intranet that the scheme was to be challenged, this did not count since it did not come from the taxpayer (ie it was not within any of the stated categories in *TMA 1970, s 29(6), (7)*). This followed the precedent firmly established in *Veltema*.

Had a DOTAS number had been provided then it possible that that the decision would have followed *Charlton*.

Corbally-Stourton v HMRC

4.57C   The adequacy of the taxpayer's disclosure on the tax return was also examined in the case of *Corbally-Stourton v HMRC* [2008] SpC 692. In this case, the taxpayer had purchased a 'capital loss' scheme.

The Special Commissioner accepted that the test should be whether a reasonable officer would conclude that it was more probable than not that there had been a loss of tax, as expressed below:

'Thus in my view it is not required that the officer be aware that there was in truth an insufficiency or that he be aware that it was beyond all reasonable doubt that there was an insufficiency, but merely that the information should enable him to conclude on balance that there was an insufficiency. Again a mere suspicion would not be enough, but, a conclusion in relation to which he had some residual doubt may well be sufficient. If he could reasonably have been expected to have come to such a conclusion before (the end of the normal enquiry period) he is precluded from making a discovery assessment'.

However, in this case, although a reasonable level of disclosure had been given on the tax return, it was not enough to satisfy the Special Commissioner that it was 'probably wrong'!

DS Sanderson v HMRC

4.57D Another capital loss scheme, involving a 'beneficial interest in the Castle Trust', was considered in *DS Sanderson v HMRC* [2016] EWCA Civ 19.

In the absence of an agreement on the facts, the Court of Appeal examined three hypothetical scenarios in which a different level of information was available to the HMRC officer.

Firstly, the tax return alone was considered to be insufficient, given the non-disclosure of the self-cancelling nature of the transactions.

Secondly, it was speculative to assume that the officer would have a general knowledge of HMRC's views about the Castle Trust.

And thirdly, it could not be assumed that a hypothetical officer would have specific knowledge of the results of HMRC's investigation into the Castle Trust.

In summary, for adequate disclosure to have been made the officer should be able to infer the information required. This must be reasonably drawn from the tax return, and it cannot be generally inferred that further information might be available elsewhere within HMRC.

Other cases involving discovery

4.57E Assessing the correct level of disclosure is likely to be difficult in many cases. However, some comfort can be obtained from the later Special Commissioners ruling in *Mr & Mrs Bird v HMRC* [2008] (SpC 720). In this case, HMRC was unable to make 'out-of-time' discovery assessments under the parental settlement rules. The Special Commissioner ruled that the taxpayer had *not* been negligent ('negligence' was replaced by carelessness for discovery assessments made after April 2010). He held that the taxpayer could not have realised that the arrangements for allowing his (minor) children to subscribe for shares in his company constituted a settlement for income tax purposes – 'this would demand a sophistication that is beyond what is expected of the assumed reasonable competent taxpayer'.

In contrast, in *Brown and Brown v HMRC* [2012] UKFTT, insufficient details were contained in the taxpayers' tax returns for an inspector to infer that they had undertaken a company purchase of own shares transaction. The tribunal also found that details of the transaction contained in the company's return (accounts) were not available to the inspector for these purposes. Consequently, HMRC was entitled to make a 'discovery' assessment (see also 13.46).

Discovery and Statement of Practice 1/06

4.58   HMRC realise that the ruling in *Veltema* (see 4.57A) presented practical difficulties since 'prudent' tax practitioners will wish to send voluminous amounts of information to protect their own and their client's positions.

Consequently, in SP 1/06, HMRC encourage practitioners/companies to submit the minimum necessary to make disclosure of a (potential) 'insufficiency' in a return. In HMRC's view, sufficient information must be disclosed to enable an inspector to be aware of the relevant issue and the significance of the details provided.

Some figures disclosed on the return may be open to interpretation or uncertain, such as valuations, reserves, provisions, stock valuations and so on. All these items normally require some judgement to be exercised about the correct figure to enter. However, HMRC may regard this figure as insufficient, unless it has been 'fully alerted' to the full circumstances of that entry.

There may also be cases where the taxpayer has reasonably taken a different interpretation from that published as HMRC's view.

Record retention requirements

4.58A   The self-assessment regime requires specific accounting records, documents, vouchers, etc to be retained to enable a complete and correct return. Where companies are within the scope of the transfer pricing regime (see 4.11), documentation must also be retained to demonstrate that transfer pricing on goods and services, etc supplied to and from overseas and UK affiliates as well as between UK and UK affiliates have been conducted on an arm's length basis (see 4.11–4.12).

All supporting records and documents must be kept for six years from the end of the return period or longer if an HMRC enquiry is still in progress. Penalties of up to £3,000 will be levied for failure to comply.

PENALTIES UNDER CTSA

Circumstances giving rise to a penalty

4.59   A penalty can be charged under *FA 2007, Sch 24* where there is either an error in a document or an under-assessment by HMRC. In the context of CTSA, *FA 2007, Sch 24, para 1* states that a penalty will be payable where a company provides a CT600 return or accounts (or any other document relied on for determining its liability to corporation tax, which might be a document submitted in correspondence with HMRC after the submission of a CT600) provided two conditions are satisfied:

- Condition 1 – the return, accounts or relevant document contains an inaccuracy leading to either an understatement of a liability to tax, a false or inflated loss, or a false or inflated claim to a tax repayment; and

- Condition 2 – the inaccuracy is careless or deliberate.

Penalties can arise if a company is careless and fails to take 'reasonable care' (although it is possible for such penalties to be suspended – see 4.61 below). The test of what is 'reasonable' will vary from company to company, and depends on their particular circumstances.

On the other hand, if the company can demonstrate that reasonable care has been taken, it may be possible to appeal against any penalties and reduce them to nil.

Based on the ancient case of *Blyth v Birmingham Waterworks Co* (1856) 11 Ex Ch 781, 'careless' behaviour is seen as a failure to take reasonable care. This case also developed the concepts of a 'reasonable man' and reasonable care. HMRC are therefore obliged to consider the individual circumstances of each person (see HMRC Compliance Handbook at CH 81140).

Every company is expected to maintain sufficient records to provide a complete and accurate return. Where a company is involved in an unfamiliar transaction or area, HMRC stress that it is reasonable to expect the tax implications to be checked out and/or appropriate advice to be taken.

The legislation also extends to the company's tax agent(s) [*FA 2007, Sch 24, para 18*]. However, penalties should not be levied provided reasonable care is taken by the 'agent'. Penalties can also be applied to managers, secretaries or any other persons managing the company's affairs.

Calculation of penalties

4.60 With the introduction of these fixed penalties, there is likely to be less scope for negotiating the penalties with HMRC. Penalties are applied to the 'potential lost revenue' (PLR).

PLR broadly represents the additional tax due or payable to HMRC as a result of correcting an inaccuracy or understatement. Group relief and repayments of *CTA 2010, s 455* tax are ignored in calculating the PLR.

This means, for example, if a company (carelessly) fails to disclose a *s 455* tax charge (see 2.56) on the CT600 return, then the penalty would be applied to the *s 455* tax charge (irrespective of the fact that the *s 455* tax would be recovered when the loan is repaid (see 2.64A). Similarly, groups of companies cannot reduce any tax understatements (and hence penalties) by making group relief claims.

The fixed penalty rates are based on the taxpayer's behaviour that gives rise to an error. These are distinguished into three types of culpability:

- a careless mistake (ie failing to take 'reasonable care');
- a deliberate but not concealed inaccuracy; and:
- a deliberate and concealed inaccuracy.

Clearly penalties can be avoided or minimised by providing correct tax returns, keeping appropriate records to provide complete and accurate returns, taking appropriate tax advice, and promptly disclosing any problems or errors on returns that have already been submitted.

The relevant maximum penalty rates are as follows:

Culpability	Maximum penalty
Careless error	30%
Deliberate error (without concealment)	70%
Deliberate and concealed error	100%

Determining reduction in penalty

4.61 A penalty can be reduced where the error is disclosed to HMRC since varying percentage reductions are applied to the relevant penalty rate for 'prompted' and 'unprompted' disclosures. Thus, lower penalties will be levied for less serious taxpayer behaviour and higher penalties for more serious types of behaviour.

Thus, for example, where a company informs HMRC about an error in a tax return on an *unprompted* basis (ie where the company has no reason to believe HMRC are about to discover it) then it may be possible for the penalty to be completely eliminated.

Penalties will be reduced where HMRC is informed about any errors and the company assists it in working out the additional tax with access to the relevant figures. However, a lower reduction in penalty applies where HMRC effectively 'prompts' the relevant disclosure.

Disclosure is defined in *FA 2007, Sch 24, para 9(1)* as:

(a) telling HMRC about it;

(b) giving HMRC reasonable help in quantifying the item; and

(c) allowing HMRC access to the records to ensure that the error is fully corrected.

The 'quality' of a disclosure includes consideration of the timing, nature and extent of that disclosure [*FA 2007, Sch 24, para 9(3)*]. Effective management of any enquiry or voluntary disclosures will therefore be crucial in reducing any penalty due.

Assuming the inaccuracy does not involve non-UK income arising or assets situated outside the UK, *FA 2007, Sch 24, para 10* provides for a potential reduction in penalties and lays down a minimum penalty for each case, as follows:

Culpability	Maximum penalty	Minimum penalty	
		for unprompted disclosure	for prompted disclosure
Careless error	30%	0%	15%
Deliberate error (without concealment)	70%	20%	35%
Deliberate *and* concealed error	100%	30%	50%

This can be shown diagrammatically as follows:

Penalty range

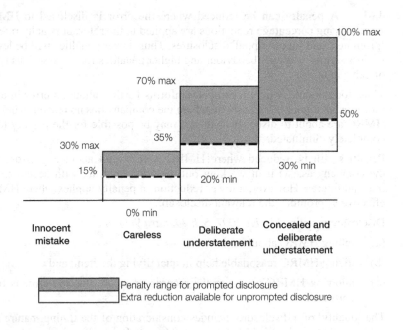

Penalty range for prompted disclosure
Extra reduction available for unprompted disclosure

Penalty computation check-list

4.62   The following computational steps should be used for each *separate* error:

1.	Compute taxable profits, income or capital gain for relevant error	
2.	Calculate Potential Lost Revenue on those taxable profits, income, or gains	
	The Potential Lost Revenue is the additional amount of tax payable as a result of the error being corrected (but group relief and repayments of *CTA 2010, s 455* tax are ignored for this purpose). Where there are multiple errors or where tax has been delayed, see *FA 2008, Sch 24, paras 5–9*)	
	The Potential Lost Revenue =	PLR
3.	Determine relevant behaviour category	
	• Innocent – (so ignore = nil penalty)	
	• Careless	
	• Deliberate but not concealed	
	• Deliberate and concealed	
4.	If *not* an innocent error, identify the highest % penalty for relevant error =	H%
5.	Is the disclosure voluntary/unprompted *or* prompted?	
6.	Identify lowest % penalty for the behaviour =	L%
7.	Maximum disclosure reduction = H less L =	MDR%
8.	Assess quality of disclosure that was made	
9.	Negotiate with HMRC, the % reduction for 'disclosure' =	NR%
10.	The actual reduction in the penalty = MDR% × NR% =	AR%
11.	The applied penalty %=H% less AR%	P%
12.	Actual penalty applied to error = PLR × P%	

Suspension of penalties

4.63   Where a penalty has been charged for failing to take '*reasonable care*' (careless inaccuracy), HMRC may suspend all or part of the penalty for up to two years [*FA 2007, Sch 24, para 14*]. HMRC must issue a written 'penalty suspension' notice which will provide certain conditions for the suspension of the penalty, which may include action to be taken by the company.

Provided all the suspension conditions have been met during the suspension period, HMRC will cancel the penalty. A suspended penalty will become payable if the company breaks one of the suspension conditions or incurs another tax penalty.

In *Ian Hall* [2016] FTT 05166 it was held that a penalty for carelessness, which HMRC refused to suspend on the grounds that the error was not likely to be repeated, should have been suspended. HMRC had failed to show that it had considered the conditions for suspension to apply or provided any evidence to show how it had reached its decision.

Similarly, in *Duncan* [2016] TC 05438, the Tribunal concluded that the penalty should be suspended. Anecdotal evidence suggests that HMRC sometimes seek to deny the suspension of penalties on the grounds that appropriate 'suspension' conditions cannot be set, as demonstrated in the *Duncan* case. Mr Duncan had proposed to use a qualified advisor to prepare his future returns, which would help to ensure his tax returns were free from careless errors and the judge concluded that this was an acceptable 'suspension' condition.

Penalty for failing to notify an under-assessment by HMRC

4.64   Penalties can also be charged where an assessment issued by HMRC understates a liability to tax and reasonable steps are not taken to notify HMRC within 30 days from the date of the assessment in question. In considering whether the steps are reasonable, account is taken of whether the taxpayer knew of the under-assessment or ought to have known. In such cases, the penalty loading is 30% (with the same reduction percentage as for careless errors).

PLANNING CHECKLIST – TRADING COMPANY AND INVESTMENT COMPANIES

SUMMARY OF TAX TREATMENT AND MAIN TAX RELIEFS

	TRADING COMPANY	**INVESTMENT COMPANY**
Relief for expenses	Trading expenses deductible against trading profits, provided incurred wholly and exclusively for the purposes of the trade.	Management expenses (basically all costs of managing company's investments are deducted against total profits on an 'accruals' basis (including capital gains)). (There is no statutory 'wholly and exclusively' restriction, but in practice HMRC tend to apply one.)
Relief for directors' remuneration	Usually no problem in practice for proprietorial directors (although strictly subject to the 'wholly and exclusively' test).	Level of deduction frequently challenged – remuneration generally limited to a (much lower) justifiable figure.

	TRADING COMPANY	**INVESTMENT COMPANY**
Relief for interest costs	All interest deductible on an accruals basis as a trading or non-trading deduction, depending on the purpose of the borrowing.	All interest will normally be deductible on an accruals basis as a non-trading loan relationship debit.
Relief for capital expenditure	Relief given under the capital allowances system.	Relief given under capital allowances system (on same basis as trading company).
Relief for losses	Trading losses can be carried back against total profits for previous year(s) and/or carried forward against future *trading* profits of the same trade (*but see 4.40 for treatment of trading losses incurred after 31 March 2017*).	Excess management expenses (effectively an investment company's 'loss') can be carried forward against total profits (but not carried back).
Roll-over relief	Available on certain categories of asset (such as property, fixed plant) used for trading purposes.	Not available for investment property.
	Gains or profits on the sale of goodwill and other intangible fixed assets may be rolled-over against the purchase of goodwill/ intangible fixed assets.	Gains or profits from the sale of intangible fixed assets used within a property rental or other 'investment' business may be rolled-over against goodwill/ intangible fixed assets.
Share loss relief for capital losses on unquoted shares	No relief.	Can elect to offset loss against income subject to certain conditions.
Availability of shareholder reliefs:		

	TRADING COMPANY	INVESTMENT COMPANY
– Entrepreneurs' relief (ER)	CGT rate of 10% for cumulative qualifying gains up to (currently) £10 million. Excess gains are taxed at 20% (28% before 6 April 2016).	ER not available – Significant gains are likely to be taxed at 20% (28% before 6 April 2016).
– Investors' relief	CGT rate of 10% after three years of share subscription.	IR not available. CGT rate of 20%.
– CGT hold-over relief for gifts or undervalue sales of business assets	Relief normally available, but note 'narrow' trading company definition applies. Relief is restricted where company holds investment property.	Relief not given unless company is a 'holding company of a trading group'.
– Capital treatment for purchase of own shares, IHT business property relief	Relief available (but in most cases reliefs are restricted where company holds investment property).	No relief, unless company qualifies as a holding company of a trading group.
– Substantial Shareholdings Exemption	Can generally be claimed on the sale of a trading company or holding company of trading subgroup.	Before 1 April 2017, only available if the 'investment' holding company qualifies as a member of a trading group. From 1 April 2017, an investment company may be able to claim SSE provided the company being sold is a trading company or holding company of trading subgroup.
– Interest relief on loan to buy shares in company	Yes.	Yes, unless company is a CIC (close investment holding company).

Chapter 5

Remuneration Strategies

BACKGROUND

Factors influencing levels of remuneration

Many family or owner-managed companies do not follow any particular remuneration strategy and simply leave matters to market forces. Whilst a rigid set of rules may well be inappropriate, remuneration planning can be to everyone's advantage.

For owner managers and other working shareholders, the level of remuneration will generally be determined by a number of factors:

(*a*)   dividend strategies as a means of mitigating the impact of costly NICs (see 2.11–2.18 and Chapter 9);

(*b*)   the need to make a suitable pension provision – personal pension contributions are still dependent on sufficient remuneration being taken to 'frank' the tax-relievable contribution, but the attraction of making substantial additional pension contributions has been reduced in recent years. Pension contribution relief is now limited to a maximum annual allowance of £40,000, with the ability to make use of relief carried forward from the previous three years (see Chapter 10) but can, for those with adjusted net income above £150,000, be reduced as low as £10,000

(*c*)   the anti-avoidance IR 35 rules for taxing income of personal service companies (see Chapter 6);

(*d*)   the possible commercial need to retain a specific level of profits;

(*e*)   meeting the national minimum wage (NMW) and national living wage (NLW) requirements (where there is an underlying employment contract) – see 2.10 for the impact of the NLW/NMW on owner-managed companies.

(*f*)   the requirements of a shareholders' agreement, for example, with a venture capitalist investor;

(*g*)   the possible need to keep directors' remuneration within the limits imposed by a lending bank; and

(*h*)   the working shareholders' personal spending requirements.

Many owner managers will also wish to avoid the 'top' 45% tax rate, preferring to keep their combined salary/bonuses/dividends below the £150,000 income threshold.

Furthermore, owner managers often seek to minimise the current high levels of NICs (see 5.4). For the working shareholders, this is likely to involve 'payment' in the form of dividends (see 2.12) and perhaps the payment of company pension contributions for their benefit. The use of salary sacrifices and tax-efficient benefits (see Chapter 7) may also be useful.

The interests of non-working shareholders may often be different, but they will be keen to see the adoption of a properly formulated and consistent strategy. The general staff of the business will have their own agendas too: their first concern will be an appropriate level of basic remuneration, but they will also be interested in fringe benefits and performance-related bonuses.

EBT AND EFRBS ARRANGEMENTS

5.2 Over the past two decades, a number of owner managers have been tempted to use employee benefit trusts (EBTs) and employer funded retirement benefit schemes (EFRBSs) as a means of side-stepping substantial income tax and NIC costs on their remuneration packages. HMRC's response was to introduce 'wide-ranging' anti-avoidance legislation in *FA 2011* – 'Employment income provided through third parties' – to negate the purported tax/NIC advantages of such schemes (see 5.17–5.21).

This legislation is not retrospective but HMRC has already reached settlements for the relevant tax/NIC for a large number of the earlier (pre-*FA 2011*) cases. Further, following HMRC's decisive victory in the Rangers case (*RFC 2012 Plc (in liquidation) (formerly The Rangers Football Club Plc) v Advocate General for Scotland* [2017] UKSC 45, it is now in a very strong position to pursing those who have not yet settled their outstanding EBT/EFRBS tax/NICs liabilities (see 5.13–5.13E).

ALPHABET SHARE ARRANGEMENTS

5.3 Some companies have been substituting 'bonuses' for dividends by using so-called 'alphabet share' arrangements for their employees. Broadly, these involve issuing employees with A, B, C, etc shares carrying an entitlement to such dividends as may be declared by the ordinary shareholders/directors on each separate class, but with minimal other rights.

In the most aggressive form of these arrangements, the alphabet shares' carry no economic or voting rights other than the ability to receive dividends. In such cases, HMRC can contend that the dividends constitute employment income under the special benefits from securities rules in *ITEPA 2003, Ch 4* and *s 447*.

HMRC may seek to apply this legislation where they can show that tax avoidance is involved, which would enable the dividend to be treated as a 'benefit' derived from the shares acquired by virtue of employment. Alternatively, HMRC might be able to successfully challenge these arrangements under the recent GAAR (see 1.19).

HMRC are also likely to press for NICs on the 'dividends' on the basis that they constitute earnings. Alphabet share arrangements are used by 'umbrella companies' which have been subject to anti-avoidance legislation since 2007 (see 6.39).

However, pro-rata dividends paid on fully-fledged ordinary shares of different classes are less likely to be caught by these rules (even where the shares are employment related). In particular, these rules should not apply to different classes of shares issued on incorporation, where the subscribers subsequently become employees/directors. Furthermore, there should be no problem where different classes of shares are used to provide flexibility in making different levels of dividends to owner managers and other 'non-working' shareholders, thus avoiding the need for waivers.

However, the tax position appears less clear where *employees* receive ordinary shares carrying substantive rights with the shares being designated into different classes to enable different levels of dividend to be paid to particular employees or groups of employees, presumably because HMRC would seek to establish an underlying 'tax avoidance' motive (see *ICAEW Tax Faculty Taxline*, March 2005).

In this context, some consider there is a decent argument that dividends paid on the shares of the same class are *not* special benefits – only benefits accruing to a shareholder outside their normal share rights but by virtue of their shareholding should be caught under *ITEPA 2003, Ch 4*.

A further important defence that has continually been put forward by some eminent tax barristers is that the so-called 'dividend-priority' rule in *ITEPA 2003, s 716A* should ensure that such income should still be treated as dividend income. Indeed, this line of reasoning received judicial approval by both the First-Tier and Upper-Tier Tax Tribunals in *PA Holdings Ltd v HMRC* at [2009] UKFTT 95 (TC) and [2010] UKTT 251 (TCC).

However, the Court of Appeal (at [2011] EWCA Civ 1414) decided that PA Holdings' payment of employee bonuses by way of legal dividend payments had the character of earnings and could *not* therefore be dividends. Consequently, Lord Justice Moses considered that the 'dividend-priority' rule was irrelevant here (despite this being an express statutory provision). Once he had decided that the amounts were taxable as earnings, it was not possible to tax them as anything else (ie as a dividend).

Unfortunately, PA Holdings Ltd dropped its appeal to the Supreme Court in April 2013, which has created considerable uncertainty as to how far these principles could apply to mainstream dividend payments by owner managed companies. See also detailed commentary at 9.13 and 9.14.

However, following the increase in dividend tax rates on 6 April 2016, most companies are likely to curb their use of the above arrangements since the tax benefits of using dividends are smaller.

NATIONAL INSURANCE CONTRIBUTIONS (NICS)

Scope of NICs

5.4 Directors and employees are usually liable to primary Class 1 National Insurance Contributions (NICs) on their earnings, which include payments of money and money's worth. (For NIC purposes earnings includes remuneration or profit derived from employment – *SSCBA 1992, s 3*.) This would cover payments in respect of contracts made personally by the director or employee, but which are paid for by the employing company (for example, 'personal' private healthcare or mobile phone contracts).

A simple but effective NIC saving idea is to move contracts into the company's name, such as a telephone contract for the private home phone line such that only Class 1A is due from the employer. Where a contract is in the individual's name but reimbursed by the company, both Class 1 primary and secondary contributions are due.

By contrast, if the contract is directly with the third party and in the company's name, the benefit is reported on the employee's P11D form. This arrangement will only be liable to Class 1A NICs, providing a potential NI saving.

Non-cash vouchers (which can be surrendered for goods and service) are also subject to NICs (subject to certain special exemptions, for example, the popular childcare vouchers although these cannot be newly received from 6 April 2018. Special rules apply to ensure that NICs are applied to readily convertible assets (see 5.13 and 13.36).

In certain cases, tips should not count as earnings for NIC purposes provided they are received directly from the customer (and have not been distributed/allocated first by the employer).

NIC RATES

5.5 For the year ending 5 April 2018, NIC on directors' and employees' earnings (including benefits) are calculated as follows:

- Employees' NICs are levied at the rate of 12% on earnings falling between the annual primary threshold (£8,164 per year) and upper earnings limit (£45,000 per year), with a 2% NIC charge being levied on earnings above the upper earnings limit (without any 'ceiling');

- Employers' NICs of 13.8% are charged on earnings above the annual secondary threshold of £8,164. The employee and employer NIC thresholds are now realigned.

- Employers' NICs are not due for those aged under 21 and apprentices aged under 25 (based on their age as at the pay date) for earnings up to the Upper Secondary/Apprentice Upper Secondary threshold, which for 2017/18 is £45,000.

The basic calculation of Class 1 NICs for directors is covered at 5.26. The lower earnings limit and earnings threshold are applied in relation to each separate employment/office – rather than per earner. It is therefore likely that employees/directors with a number of concurrent employments/directorships will pay a lower amount of NICs (as compared with the NICs that would have been payable had the earnings come from a single employment/directorship). However, there are special rules which are designed to counter any artificial fragmentation arrangements using 'connected' companies etc [*Social Security (Contributions) Regulations 2001, SI 2001/1004, reg 15*].

It should also be noted that NICs are effectively 'credited' for state benefits once earnings exceed the lower earnings limit or LEL (£5,876 per year) whereas (employees') NICs do not become payable until earnings exceed the primary earnings threshold (£8,164 per year). In appropriate cases (eg part-time workers and owner-managers), remuneration levels could be 'fixed' to take advantage of these rules ensuring that employees/directors maintain their entitlement to state benefits.

Employment allowance

5.5A   Since 6 April 2014, qualifying employers are able to claim the NIC employment allowance. The employment allowance offers a maximum £3,000 for 2017/18 (£2,000 until 6 April 2016) reduction in secondary (*employer's*) Class 1 NICs. Thus, the annual amount of relief afforded by the allowance is restricted to the amount of employer's Class 1 due where an employer's total annual liability is less than £3,000 a year.

The NIC allowance is *not* available in respect of any of the following:

- Employees of a public authority or other employers whose business is wholly or mainly of a public nature (other than a charity);

- Employees working on the employer's personal, family or household affairs. However, since 6 April 2015 employers employing a carer, 'care and support employers', are able to claim the allowance.

- In relation to the 'deemed earnings 'of workers supplied by a personal service company (PSC) or a managed service company (MSC) (see 6.4 and 6.48). However, the NIC allowance is given against any *actual* earnings that have a Class 1 NICs liability.

- Since 6 April 2016, where the only individual employed by the company is also the only director. Companies where there is more than one director who is paid at, or above, the primary threshold for the length of their employment still qualify.

Where companies are connected (broadly if one company has control of the other or if they are under common control) the allowance is available to only one of the connected companies. Companies are free to choose which company should get the allowance. Where a company has more than one PAYE scheme, eg one for employees and one for directors, then only one scheme may elect to receive the employment allowance, although if the chosen scheme has less than £3,000 liability at year end and the other scheme (or schemes) have a Class 1 secondary NICs liability, additional employment allowance up to the £3,000 limit may be claimed by letter to HMRC.

The normal retrospective NIC timescale of six years applies. This is useful for owner-managed companies that were unaware of the allowance and have not yet claimed it. However, the Government announced in the March Budget 2017 that HMRC will carry out more compliance activity on the employment allowance to establish if it has been incorrectly claimed by 'single director' and connected companies.

Employers must self-certify their eligibility for the allowance on an Employer Payment Summary (EPS) under RTI (see 5.10A). This election carries forward annually so only need be 'set' on the EPS as 'yes I wish to claim' once. The credit for the employer NICs shown on the FPS is then applied to the first payment of secondary NICs in the tax year, with any surplus being carried forward until it is fully used. It is worth noting that the credit is not applied until the 22nd of the month after the tax month that the liability was incurred ie the deadline for payment of the remittance to HMRC, so the PAYE scheme's business tax account will appear underpaid until this date. The employment allowance marker can be set at any time in the tax year and the total Class 1 secondary NICs liability at that point in the year can be claimed as soon as the eligibility marker is set, even though that may exceed the employer NICs due for that tax month. (HMRC's Basic PAYE Tools software includes the facility for employers to claim the allowance and all commercial software providers also include this.) The employment allowance eligibility marker should not be unset if eligibility is lost mid-year as once there is a secondary NICs liability for a tax year the full allowance is due and is not pro-rated.

An anti-avoidance rule prevents the NIC allowance being given where an employer enters into arrangements where the main purpose, or one of the main purposes, is to secure entitlement to the allowance where it would not otherwise be due. For example, this is likely to prevent for a company establishing a separate 'sole trader' business to obtain an additional £3,000 NIC allowance, where there is no good commercial reason for it to do so.

Apprenticeship levy

5.5B   A new apprenticeship levy was introduced on 6 April 2017. The levy represents a new training tax, only fully or partly recoverable if the business employs apprentices and has employees based in England.

The levy is only be payable by businesses who have 'pay subject to employer national insurance' of £3 million in 2017/18. A monthly offset of £1,250 (£15,000 per year) reduces the levy to zero for any business with less than £3 million of 'NIC-able' pay.

However, where an owner-managed business is 'connected' with another (see 5.5A above), it will only have one levy allowance of £15,000. However, unlike the NIC Employment Allowance (see 5.5A), the levy allowance can be 'shared' amongst the connected companies, with the chosen apportionment reported on the April Employer Payment Summary (EPS).

Consequently, owner-managed companies may be 'connected' with other businesses that have used their £15,000 allowance. In such cases they would have to pay the 0.5% apprenticeship levy on some or all of their 'NIC-able' pay .

TAXATION OF EARNINGS

Basic position for employees and directors

5.6   Tax is charged on the full amount of employment income received during the tax year. For employees (who are resident, ordinarily resident and domiciled in the UK), earnings are treated as received on the earlier of:

(*a*)   actual payment of earnings or on account of earnings; or

(*b*)   entitlement to payment of earnings or to payment on account of earnings.

These timing rules do not necessarily apply to benefits in kind (see Chapter 7).

The basic rules may sound reasonably straightforward, but not surprisingly there are further provisions where *directors* (who are resident and domiciled in the UK) are concerned. For this purpose, a 'director' means:

(i)   in relation to a company whose affairs are managed by a board of directors or similar body, a member of that body;

(ii)   in relation to a company whose affairs are managed by a single director or similar person, that director or person; and

(iii) in relation to a company whose affairs are managed by the members themselves, a member of the company [*ITEPA 2003, s 18(3)*].

Furthermore, a director includes any person in accordance with whose directions or instructions the company's directors are accustomed to act, often referred to as a 'shadow director'. Someone giving advice in a professional capacity is ignored [*ITEPA 2003, s 18(3)*].

Directors' earnings are treated as received on the *earliest* of:

(*a*) actual payment of (or on account of) earnings;

(*b*) entitlement to payment of (or on account of) earnings;

(*c*) the time at which the sums are credited to the company's accounts or records (any restrictions on the right to draw them are ignored);

(*d*) the end of a period of account where earnings are determined before the end of that period;

(*e*) the determination of earnings for a period of account if they are determined after the end of that period [*ITEPA 2003, s 18(1)*].

A director resigning during the tax year does not avoid these special rules for that year [*ITEPA 2003, s 18(2)*].

ADDITIONAL 'TIMING' RULES FOR DIRECTORS

5.7   Earnings are treated as being paid when they are credited to the accounts, even where a legal restriction operates to prevent them being drawn until a later date or event occurs. However, remuneration that enjoys no right of payment unless a pre-determined condition occurs is not treated as paid until the right to payment becomes unequivocal. See also 5.7A for tax relief where bonuses are clawed-back.

When accounts are prepared in readiness for an AGM they will invariably include a provision entry for directors' remuneration (see 5.10 for the corporation tax implications of such a provision). This will not normally constitute pay until the amount has been formally agreed by the Board (when it will become necessary to operate PAYE). However, if the remuneration has been formally agreed and is not credited to an account in the director's name but to another account or record of the company, it will still be deemed to be taxable employment income.

If the shareholders approve the director's remuneration by formal agreement before the AGM, a receipt may be deemed to arise following the decision in *Re Duomatic* [1969] 1 All ER 161. This important rule will often establish a 'taxable' entitlement to director's remuneration before the AGM (see 2.22).

For all payments that are deemed to arise under the rules set out above, PAYE and NIC should be calculated and RTI accounted for in the same way as actual payments.

If the amount of remuneration is determined before the end of the period to which it relates, but by the end of the period some or all of it has not actually been paid, or become due to be paid, or been credited, then payment of the unpaid amount is not regarded as having taken place until the end of the period.

Where the level of remuneration is profit-related, payment thereof is made when all the relevant profit information is known so the amount can be calculated, and not when the actual formula is agreed.

Owner-managers will now pay more attention to the timing of their bonus payments to reduce their exposure to the very high combined PAYE/NIC rates. In some cases, this may mean owner-managers/directors deferring bonus payments to shift them into another tax year (when their marginal tax rates are lower).

In some cases, it might be sensible for the company to provide temporary loans to meet their personal cash flow requirements, since the tax cost of the potential benefit-in-kind charge is relatively low (see 2.24 and 2.57 for further commentary and 7.61 for benefit-in-kind rules on beneficial loans).

RELIEF FOR 'NEGATIVE EARNINGS'

5.7A   In *Julian Martin v HMRC* [2014] UKUT 0429, the Upper Tribunal (UT) held that relief was available for negative earnings under *ITA 2007, s 128* (as provided for by *ITEPA 2003, s 11(3)(a)*). This case establishes that it is possible to obtain relief where all or part of a bonus payment is subsequently clawed-back. It also concluded that it is not possible for the original charge on the earnings received to be amended or reversed.

Based on the contractual arrangement between the parties, the UT concluded that the initial (bonus) payment of £250,000 had been made as consideration for Mr Martin agreeing to enter into his new employment contract. Thus, it was fully taxable in the year it was received and was not a contingent payment on account.

In the *Julian Martin* case, Mr Martin was paid a 'signing-on' bonus when he entered into a new employment contract for a minimum five-year period. (It was agreed that the bonus was paid for signing the contract, not for remaining in employment for five years, so it was earned when the contract was signed.) However, part of this bonus would become repayable if he exercised his right to terminate the contract within the five-year period.

This 'bonus repayment' was triggered when Mr Martin gave early notice. Mr Martin contended that he was entitled to relief against the income tax paid on the original bonus. The UT held that the contractual terms were clear. When Mr Martin became liable to repay a proportion of his bonus, this could not be viewed as a compensation for a repudiatory breach of contract because it was being made in accordance with the terms of the contract. Consequently, the

UT upheld the earlier decision of the FTT that the repayment was 'negative earnings', as it had the characteristic of earnings, albeit paid in the 'wrong' direction! The UT held that, under the employment loss rules, the negative earnings must be deducted in the year they were paid.

Following *the Julian Martin* case, HMRC updated its guidance at EIM00800 to EIM00845. This states that 'negative earnings are payments from the employee to the employer (or exceptionally, a third party) which "…arise directly out of the employment'. HMRC confirms that a payment can be negative taxable earnings only for the period in which it is actually paid. The only exception to this rule is where the payment is made after an employment has ceased, in which case it is treated as being made in the final year of employment.

ITA 2007, s 128 enables an employment loss to be offset against the general income for the same tax year and/or the previous tax year. This relief is now subject to the *FA 2013* 'capping' rules, thus limiting any deduction to the *greater* of £50,000 or 25% of tax. Any unrelievable loss can be treated as an off-settable capital loss (*ITEPA 2003, s 130*).

The *Julian Martin* case did not cover the NICs aspect, and hence it is not certain whether a competent claim can be made for a refund of the relevant Class 1 NICs

PERSONAL SERVICE COMPANIES (PSCs)

5.8   If the business of the owner-managed company involves providing a service, some or all of its income may be caught by the IR 35 provisions (now enacted in *ITEPA 2003, Ch 8*), or the managed service companies rules introduced in the *Finance Act 2007* (see Chapter 6). If this is the case, those provisions will govern the remuneration strategy for the working shareholders and other employees, particuarly from April 2017 if the PSC has clients in the public sector.

CORPORATION TAX RELIEF FOR THE COMPANY

5.9   The remuneration for directors and other employees is generally deductible for the period of account to which it relates, subject to the overriding rule that the amount is commercially justifiable. Where remuneration/bonus remains unpaid at the balance sheet date, *CTA 2009, ss 1288* and *1289* provides that this may still be deductible for the accounting period ending on that date, provided it is actually 'paid' within nine months of the year-end. A similar rule applies for determining the allowable management expenses of investment businesses [*CTA 2009, ss 1249* and *1250*].

The date of payment is defined fairly widely and is the same as the date of receipt for 'employment' income tax purposes, as set out in 5.7 and 5.8 [*CTA 2009, ss 1289(4)* and *1250(4)*].

However, this is subject to the overriding accounting rule in *CTA 2009, s 46*, which requires that profits must be computed in accordance with generally accepted accounting principles ('GAAP'). In this particular context, any provision for bonuses etc. would have to comply with FRS 12 (see 4.5). This means that (amongst other things), the company must have created a current obligation to pay the relevant bonus by the year-end date – for example, by means of an appropriate written agreement or Board minute.

Where the accrued bonus/remuneration is not paid within nine months from the end of the period, the above statutory rules provide that the tax deduction is only given in the (later) period when the amount is paid.

If the company submits its accounts and tax computations before nine months after the end of the period of account, any earnings still unpaid at that time should not be claimed. An adjustment to the tax computations is then made if the remuneration is actually paid within the nine-month period, provided a claim is made under *CTA 2009, s 1289(3)* or *1250(3)* within two years from the end of the period of account concerned.

See 2.21–2.23 for a full discussion of this topic.

THE PAYE SYSTEM AND THE FAMILY OR OWNER-MANAGED COMPANY

Basic position

5.10   The time of payment of earnings for PAYE purposes is specifically defined in *ITEPA 2003, s 686*. The time when payment is made for PAYE purposes is virtually identical to that used in *ITEPA 2003, s 18* (as detailed in 5.7 above).

Real Time Information (RTI) regime

5.10A   Since 6 April 2013, all employers have been filing their payroll and PAYE/NIC information under the Real Time Information (RTI) system. Under RTI, all PAYE/NIC information is submitted *online* to HMRC 'on or before' the contractual payment date that applies to the directors/employees. Thus, if employees are paid weekly, the relevant PAYE information must be filed online on a weekly basis.

Most HMRC RTI guidance refers to 'the date that employees are paid' whereas in fact HMRC require that the FPS payment date is the contractual due date even if that falls at a weekend or bank holiday as long as payment is made on the first banking day prior to the contractual payment date. For example, an earnings payment due on 25 December should be reported as that date, even if it has been physically paid on 24 December. Where payment is brought forward even earlier than the first banking day prior to the bank holiday/weekend, as is commonplace around Christmas, then the payment date must reflect that earlier date

Employers are required to make a *full payment submission* (FPS) when a payment is made to a director or employer, 'on or before' the contractual date of payment. This switch to RTI has created significant work for employers since an FPS requires additional information that has not been required before, including:

(*a*)   hours worked by employee (reported in bands) only based on the contractual hours so not the variance each pay period;

(*b*)   employee's UK/non-UK passport number (though this is not mandatory);

(*c*)   details of employees who have not reached the NIC lower earnings limit (see 5.5); and

(*d*)   'flagging' employees who are not paid regularly (such as seasonal workers).

An employer's first FPS under RTI is generally treated as a *payroll alignment submission* and is used to match the employers' existing payroll details with those already held by HMRC (HMRC records are not updated with the employer-held data). Subsequent FPS's need only include details of employees actually receiving payment but this will be dictated by the payroll software in use

An FPS must normally be filed by the contractual date of payment at the latest. HMRC allow employers an occasional lapse from this rigid timetable of up to three days after the filing due date without this incurring a penalty. However, to ensure a risk-assessed penalty is not invoked for FPSs submitted after any payment date in the file, a 'late reporting reason' must be included to disapply the penalty. This easement will continue until 5 April 2018.

HMRC also operated temporary relaxations for small employers. Until 6 April 2014, employers with fewer than 50 employees could file their FPS by the date of the normal payroll run (but no later than the end of the PAYE tax month). A further 'concession' applies to 5 April 2016, for those employing nine or fewer employees. These very small businesses could report PAYE information monthly, on or before the last pay date each month (rather than the end of the tax month as was the case from 6 April 2014 to 5 April 2015).

An *employer payment summary* (EPS) is used to inform HMRC of any permissible reductions (such as statutory maternity pay) against the totals already submitted on the FPS. If a company has suffered CIS tax deductions on its sub-contractor income, relief is given via the EPS. The EPS submission is also used to 'flag' to HMRC if no directors/employees have been paid in the relevant period or in future periods (thus preventing unnecessary HMRC demands being issued for non-filing of FPS returns. Since April 2017, the

EPS is also used to report the amount of the apprenticeship levy and any levy allowance. The RTI system also enables NIC numbers to be verified either when taking on new employees or for existing records (using a NIC number verification request (NVR)).

Many PAYE forms (such as forms P14 and P35 end of year submissions, form P46 (for starters and leavers)) are no longer required under RTI, since the relevant information is now provided by the FPS. P45 forms are still provided to leavers but HMRC are informed of the date of leaving via the FPS. Forms P60 and P11D continue to be used in the normal way.

At the end of the tax year, employers submit the final FPS and/or EPS for the pay period as normal, indicating that it is the final submission for the relevant tax year. The previous declaration questions that used to appear on the P35 were removed as an RTI year-end requirement for the 2014/15 tax year onwards.

RTI and owner managers

5.10B   Owner managers need to be especially careful that 'their' companies comply with the key RTI requirement to file the FPS (see 5.11A) *on or before* the contractual date that their salary or bonus payments are made.

Where owner managers pay a small salary, it may be easier to approach HMRC to ask to operate an annual PAYE scheme for RTI purposes, but this can only be used if all the strict rules are met. Under an annual scheme, all employees must be paid annually and within the same single tax month. Furthermore, the company is only required to pay HMRC annually. Once registered as an annual scheme, an FPS (see 5.11A) is not required for 11 months of the year where no payments are made to employees. If more than one employee payment (and FPS) is submitted, HMRC will cancel the annual payer status for the year and subsequent years. For flexibility, most 'annual payment' employers will choose March to ensure that all payments can be made in this month. One of the issues with RTI at present is that HMRC can 'lose' annual payer status and begin to levy penalties for months where no FPS or 'Nil' EPS has been filed. To avoid this, annual payers can choose, in April of each year, to submit a 'nil activity' EPS for the whole of the forthcoming tax year to ensure filing obligations are met. The FPS that is sent for the 'PAYE month' will simply replace the 'nil activity' for that particular month.

Alternatively, where an owner manager's loan account is in credit, 'payment' for RTI could safely be triggered by 'crediting' the loan account.

Where the loan account is overdrawn, it would be necessary to actually pay the salary, which could then be lent back to the company, with an appropriate credit being made to the director's loan account. Given that many owner managers draw a salary below the primary threshold, there should be no NIC cost. Provided the company has sufficient reserves, the loan account might also be credited with an appropriate dividend (see 9.20). It is important that these entries are made timeously to provide an audit trail in the event of an HMRC enquiry.

Regular monthly payments could then be made to the owner manager from the loan account. Since they would be simple repayments of the loan, no FPS would be necessary.

Under RTI, an FPS can be filed *at any time* before payment is made. This means that it is possible to run the monthly payroll and submit FPS(s) for a full year in month one. The monthly salary would then be paid in the normal way. It is also possible to run a quarterly payroll in advance of each quarter if payroll software allows this. The only issue with this approach is if HMRC issue a tax code that affects the months that have been sent in advance or the employee's salary alters in any way when a correction would need to be made.

Agency workers

5.10C   *ITEPA 2003, Pt 2, Ch 7* applies to treat payments to workers as earnings (and hence subject to PAYE/NIC) where

- a worker provides services personally to a client via an agency; and

- the client pays that agency for the worker's services.

The key test is the requirement for the worker to be subject to the supervision, direction or control of the client or hirer.

Since 6 April 2014, the agency rules have been widened to counter arrangements by certain agencies that disguise employment as self-employment, which have typically been common in certain sectors such as nursing and childcare. Consequently, the *FA 2014* amendments also take into account the actual arrangements between the relevant parties, irrespective of the contents of any written agreements. Consequently, this enables HMRC to imply there is 'control' where a worker is engaged via an intermediary.

HMRC told the Professional Contractors Group in December 2013 that these arrangements often involve low-paid workers who are 'unaware that they are being engaged on a self-employed basis until they try to claim employment rights'. HMRC confirmed that the revised agency rules should not affect genuine contractors working through their own companies.

Under the post-*FA 2014* regime, intermediaries will bear the tax risk if they treat their 'workers' as self-employed (either mistakenly or intentionally). In contrast to the IR35 rules (see 6.4), HMRC can go directly to the intermediary for the unpaid PAYE and NIC – it does not need to find the 'worker' in the chain.

Employment intermediaries are also subject to record keeping and reporting requirements that require that an RTI return that reports all payments made gross by the intermediary is sent each quarter.

HMRC APPROACH TO PAYE COMPLIANCE

PAYE interest and penalties

5.11   HMRC charge interest on late PAYE/NIC payments. Interest is chargeable on unpaid amounts for each PAYE period (which runs from the 6th of each month to the 5th of the following month) from the 22nd of the following PAYE period (19 April if payment is made by cheque) [*Income Tax (PAYE) Regulations 2003, SI 2003/2682, reg 82*].

HMRC can also levy penalties for late payments of monthly or quarterly PAYE. Penalties, which for 2017/18 are still clerically assessed, start at 1% of the late PAYE, increasing to 4% depending on how many times a payment for a period is made late or not in full. No penalty is charged if only one payment is late in any tax year, provided it is not more than six months late. HMRC can mitigate the penalty if there are 'special circumstances' (but this does not include inability to pay). Thus, it is therefore advisable to retain and document evidence of special reasons causing a PAYE payment to be made late. Companies with severe cash flow problems may be able to apply to HMRC to pay their PAYE in instalments under the 'Time to Pay' initiative (see 4.54).

Interest and penalties on late paid PAYE and NICs are *not* deductible against profits for corporation tax purposes (see *ITEPA 2003, s 684(4)* and *SSCBA 1992, Sch 1, para 6 (4B)*).

Under the RTI penalty provisions in *FA 2013, Sch 50*, there can also be penalties for late or insufficient filing of RTI returns based on the number of employees in each PAYE scheme (reassessed on the second Saturday of each tax month). The monthly penalties are as follows:

Number of employees in PAYE scheme	Monthly penalty £
1–9	100
10–49	200
50–249	300
250 +	400

Employers are permitted one default without penalty each year*, with subsequent defaults attracting a penalty. The 'reasonable excuse' provisions apply. In April 2014 HMRC introduced a new RTI 'Late Reporting Reason' field within the FPS to allow employers to state the reason for the late submission.

Only one penalty can be charged each tax month regardless of how many returns are late or missing. Penalties are charged quarterly in July, October, January and April.

For 2015/16 to 2017/18, penalties are clerically risk-assessed in the same way as late payment. Additional tax-geared penalties of 5% of the amount on the late submitted FPS or amounts underpaid apply where a file or payment is more than three months late.

RTI penalties should always be preceded by an online Generic Notification Notice (GNN). Late or non-filing warnings are issued on the 12th day after the month-end, whilst late payment warnings are issued around the first of the month after the remittance deadline.

The reasonable excuse provisions in *FA 2009, Sch 55, para 23* apply to late/ non filing of RTI returns as well as to pre-RTI employer returns. Insufficiency of funds is not a reasonable excuse unless this is outside of the taxpayer's control. Actions of a third party (such as a tax adviser or agent) are also not a reasonable excuse.

In order for taxpayers to successfully claim a reasonable excuse, they must remedy the failure without unreasonable delay once the excuse has ceased.

Appeals against RTI penalties are made using the online Penalties and Appeals Service (PAS) that can be accessed by both employers and agents through PAYE online.

5.11A There have been many cases considering whether taxpayers' excuses are 'reasonable'. HMRC states that it would consider a reasonable excuse to be 'an unexpected or unusual event that is either unforeseeable or beyond the person's control, and which prevents the person from complying' (HMRC CH26340). HMRC has provided examples of cases which it considers would fall within the 'reasonable excuse' category, and those which would not, on its website and in its guidance notes.

A taxpayer appealed penalties on the basis of reasonable excuse in *TRM Electronics Ltd* [2013] UKFTT 602 (TC)). In this case, the employer's end of year return for 2011/12 was filed online before the due date, but the filing was unsuccessful because the software was operating in test mode. Following this, there were a number of other technological issues, but the taxpayer filed the late return as soon as possible. The FTT upheld its claim for reasonable excuse.

In *Dudman Group Ltd* [2011] UKFTT 771 (TC), nine out of twelve PAYE and NICs payments were made late between May 2010 and April 2011. The company cited the bankruptcy or liquidation of several of its customers as a reasonable excuse for the late payments. HMRC issued penalties totalling £30,000, stating that it did not consider the company had a reasonable excuse. On appeal to the FTT, the Tribunal found in the taxpayer's favour on the grounds that it had made every effort to resolve its cashflow difficulties. Furthermore, the FTT has accepted that taxpayers had a 'reasonable excuse' in a number of other cases where they had cashflow issues originating from bad debts and changes to sole customer payment terms (*Northern Bulk Transport Ltd v HMRC* [2011] UKFTT 787 (TC); *HCM Electrical Ltd v HMRC* [2011] UKFTT 852 (TC); *Trio Offset Ltd v HMRC* [2012] UKFTT 60 (TC)).

However, in *AJM Mansell Ltd v HMRC* [2012] UKFTT 602 (TC), late payment to the taxpayer by its main customer, the Department of Health, was not accepted as a reasonable excuse for late payment of its PAYE and NIC payments in 2010/11. The taxpayer, a pharmacy, was subject to a 4% penalty in relation to the amounts paid late. As well as citing the Department of Health's late payments, the taxpayer also argued that allocating the payments differently to the month after each payment was due would have resulted in a lower penalty. Although the Tribunal found in HMRC's favour, it considered the approach set out in the case of *The Mecca* [1897] AC 286 applied to penalties under the *FA 2009, Sch 56* regime. The *Mecca* case established that where there were different debts to which payments could be allocated, the creditor had the right to determine the allocation of the payments *except* where the debtor specified a certain allocation. Therefore, the penalties in the *AJM Mansell Ltd* case would have been reduced if the taxpayer had specified an alternative allocation of the payments.

5.11B   The question of penalties for late filing of employer returns was examined in *Hok Ltd* [2011] UKFTT 433 (TC); *CRC v Hok Ltd* [2012] STC 225. Hok Ltd failed to file its 2009/10 P35 return by the 19 May 2010 deadline. However, HMRC did not issue a penalty notice until 27 September 2010 by which time the monthly £100 penalty had accumulated to £400. The return was then filed by 15 October 2010 by which time the penalties had reached £500. The taxpayer appealed to the FTT stating that it considered HMRC's delayed issue of the penalty notice to be 'unfair and falling very far below the standard of fair dealing and conscionable conduct to be expected of an organ of the state'.

However, on HMRC's appeal to the Upper Tribunal, the FTT's decision was overturned. The Upper Tribunal held that the FTT could not determine that a penalty should be cancelled on the grounds of unfairness. It may only determine whether a penalty applies based on the specific facts, which significantly limits the FTT's ability to decide whether penalties apply. Following *Hok*, taxpayers have little chance of successfully appealing penalties unless they have complied with the law or have a reasonable excuse for failing to comply. Thus, it is recommended that all events relating to online submission issues should be documented carefully, including records and acknowledgments of online submissions.

PAYE compliance and enquiries

5.11C   With a family or owner-managed company, HMRC are often particularly keen to check that PAYE is being applied to sums received by directors.

Under the current employer compliance regime, when HMRC finds underpayments of PAYE or benefits not declared (such as company cars) for directors and their families, it will often wish to widen the scope of its enquiries. In such cases, HMRC may launch a formal investigation into the director's personal tax affairs, based on the perceived irregularities they have found within the business. Clearly, this could involve a wide-ranging review of the director's tax affairs.

Another weapon available to HMRC which is less commonly used is a *SI 2003/2682, reg 80* determination. This can be used where the Inspector considers that tax is due under PAYE and has not been remitted to the Collector. In the context of family or owner-managed companies, it is often used to collect tax on directors' remuneration voted in the accounts. A *SI 2003/2682, reg 80* determination carries interest that runs from 19 April following the tax year to which it relates [*SI 2003/2682, reg 82*].

Furthermore, if the determination is not paid within 30 days of the determination notice becoming final, HMRC reserve the right to recover the outstanding PAYE liability due from the employee if they have reason to believe that the employee was aware that the company wilfully failed to deduct PAYE [*SI 2003/2682, reg 81*]. The employee is entitled to appeal against the direction notice.

PAYMENT IN ASSETS

5.12   PAYE and NIC have to be accounted for on the provision of a 'readily convertible asset' (RCA) to a director/employee. An RCA means an asset:

(*a*)   which is capable of being realised on a recognised investment exchange, the London Bullion Market, the New York Stock Exchange or on any market specified in PAYE regulations; or

(*b*)   that consists in the rights of an assignee, or any other rights, in respect of a money debt due to the employer or any other person; or

(*c*)   that consists of property subject to a fiscal warehousing regime; or

(*d*)   that represents anything likely (without anything being done by the employee) to give rise to a right to obtain an amount of money that is similar to the cost involved in providing the asset; or

(*e*)   for which trading arrangements exist or are likely to come into existence [*ITEPA 2003, s 702*].

An extended definition of RCAs applies where shares are awarded to or share options are exercised by directors or employees. Although in most cases, shares in owner managed companies are not RCAs (since there is usually no available market to trade the shares), there are special rules which deem shares in a subsidiary (under the control of an unlisted company) to be RCAs, thus making them subject to PAYE and NIC (see 8.39–8.41).

PAYE also has to be accounted for on:

- the provision of a cash voucher, ie a salary cheque;

- the provision of a 'non-cash' voucher capable of being exchanged for goods coming within the RCA definition; and

- credit tokens to obtain money or such goods [*ITEPA 2003, ss 693–695*].

Although a 'high street retail' voucher is a non-cash voucher, it will be be treated as an RCA if it is transferable since it could readily be exchanged for a sum of money similar to the expense incurred in providing it. On the other hand, if the voucher is non-transferable it would probably not be an RCA and will not be subject to PAYE (but would be taxed as earnings).

If the director/employee does not reimburse the employer for the relevant PAYE within 90 days of the tax year end after the relevant date of 'receipt' of the relevant item, this PAYE tax will also be taxed as employment income and entered on the P11D (see Example 1).

Example 1

Payment in assets

Mr Parker receives a bonus of £5,000 from Scott Ltd paid by way of gold bullion on 1 May 2017.

PAYE due, say £2,250 (45%), is paid to the Collector of Taxes by 22 June 2017.

If Mr Parker does not pay £2,250 to his employer by 4 July 2018 (90 days from 5 April 2018) he will be taxed on £7,250 in 2017/18 with a credit for the £2,250 tax.

USE OF EMPLOYEE BENEFIT TRUSTS (EBTs) AND EMPLOYER-FINANCED RETIREMENT BENEFIT SCHEMES (EFRBS)

Pre-*FA 2011* EBT and EFRBS arrangements

5.13 From the mid-1990s, employee benefit trusts ('EBTs') and latterly employer-financed retirement benefit schemes ('EFRBS') increased in popularity, with many schemes being structured to 're-characterise' payments made to owner managers (and employees) without triggering PAYE or NIC liabilities.

However, the 2017 Supreme Court ruling in the *Rangers* case (*RFC 2012 Plc (in liquidation) (formerly The Rangers Football Club Plc) v Advocate General for Scotland* [2017] UKSC 45 dealt a major blow to the tax efficacy of these arrangements. The Supreme Court ruling now confirms that amounts paid into an EBT will normally be taxed as the relevant employee's earnings at that point. This ruling will also apply to the previous use of EFRBS.

The ruling was so decisive to question the continued need for the 'disguised remuneration' legislation, which was introduced in the *Finance Act 2011* (see 5.17).

The *Glasgow Rangers* EBT case

Background

5.13A   Over the past few decades or so EBTs and similar structures have been widely used by owner managed companies. Such arrangements generally relied on a literal construction of tax law (as it then stood) to avoid PAYE and NICs on directors' and senior managers' pay. Of course to the layman (and indeed almost all tax professionals), these arrangements looked like an 'offensive' tax dodge. The Supreme Court judgment in the *Rangers* case handed down on 5 July 2017 is highly significant since it firmly concludes that amounts paid into EBTs are taxable (under PAYE) when the contributions are made to the EBT.

Key facts

5.13B   Between 2001 and 2008, the club's parent company made contributions of £55.5 million and €5.3 million to its Employees' Remuneration Trust. This was referred to as 'the Principal Trust', which had all the characteristics of a typical EBT.

Where the company wished to benefit a particular player/employee, it made a 'pre-agreed' cash contribution to the Principal Trust ('the EBT') in respect of that employee. The company also recommended to the EBT trustee that the amount be resettled on a sub-trust, to be applied in accordance with the employee's wishes.

When new players were recruited, the discussions focused on the 'net of tax' pay they would receive and the existence of the sub-trust mechanism. They were told that a loan from the sub-trust would enable them to receive a greater amount than if they received pay net of normal PAYE/NIC deductions!

In addition to their employment contract (recording an agreed 'lower' salary), the company provided each player with a 'side letter' under which it undertook to carry out the relevant 'sub-trust' arrangements, referring to the sums that had been agreed in prior negotiations. The player also completed a loan application, which was always made for the agreed amount.

Typically, the unsecured loans made to the players/employees were for a term of ten years at a commercial interest rate (LIBOR plus 1.5%–2%).

Between 2001 and 2010, loans of £47.65 million were paid to the players/employees.

The basic EBT arrangements are illustrated below:

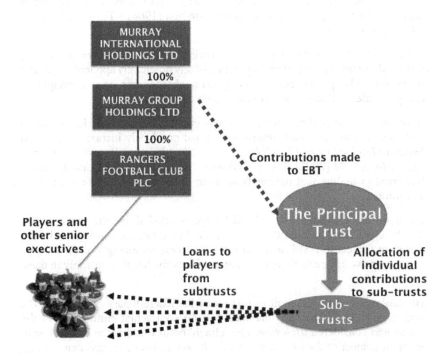

The 'redirection' principle

5.13C   HMRC had introduced an entirely new legal argument before the earlier Scottish Court of Session hearing (see 2015/16 edition of this book for details of this judgment). This is now often referred to as the 'redirection' principle. In essence, this legal doctrine says that any payment which *derives* from an employee's work must be taxed as earnings, even where the employee directs or agrees that it should be paid to a third party. Consequently, the payments/contributions made to the EBT *in respect of* a player/other employee constituted their taxable earnings and therefore should have been subjected to PAYE and NICs.

Findings of the Supreme Court

5.13D In formulating the Supreme Court decision, Lord Hodge (who gave the sole leading judgment) emphasised the wide purpose of the tax legislation taxing earnings from employment. Lord Hodge emphasised that the general 'earnings' charging provisions in *ITEPA 2003, s 62* (and its predecessor) do not contain any specific requirement for the earnings to be received by the relevant employee. Consequently, payments deriving from an employee's labour fall to be taxed as 'their' earnings even where they are assigned (with the employee's agreement or acquiescence) to a third party. This principle is supported by the legal analysis in *Smyth v Stretton* (1904) 5 TC 36 and *Hadlee v CIR* [1993] AC 524).

Lord Hodge observed that where a tax charge arises under general principles, this would normally override the operation of any potentially applicable specific provisions. The precedence of the general charge over any 'overlapping' charging rules will therefore prevent double taxation.

In reaching these findings, it was perhaps inevitable that Lord Hodge had to conclude that the Special Commissioners had previously incorrectly decided *Sempra Metals Ltd v HMRC* [2008] STC (SCD) 1062) and *Dextra Accessories Ltd v Macdonald* [2002] STC (SCD) 413. His view was the Commissioners had erred in finding that payments made to third parties should *not* be taxed as earnings.

Based on the above reasoning, Lord Hodge concluded that the sums paid to the Principal Trust for a footballer constituted their taxable earnings and were therefore subject to PAYE and Class 1 NICs. This reasoning is clearly based on a purposive and realistic interpretation of how the law should apply in these circumstances.

His analysis was no different in respect of the discretionary bonuses for the senior executives. The fact that they had no contractual entitlement to the bonus was considered irrelevant. The 'clinch' point was that the bonuses were given in respect of the executives' work. It could also be argued that the fact the executive had chosen to receive their bonus payments via the sub-trust structure meant that they had acquiesced in the arrangement.

Some conclusions

5.13E HMRC has always maintained that the arrangements provided through EBTs, EFRBS, and similar structures should be taxed as earnings. In practice, there were a number of tax approaches to this depending on the precise facts of each case. Thus, for example, the 'PAYE' trigger point may be taken as the point where an employee is contractually entitled to receive the payment or where funds had been allocated to a 'sub-trust' for the relevant employee's benefit and so on.

HMRC has always encouraged EBT users to take advantage of its employee benefit trust settlement opportunity ('EBTSO'). Under the EBTSO, HMRC would generally collect the relevant PAYE/NIC with interest from the trigger 'payment' date but invariably without penalties. A similar resolution opportunity was offered for EFRBS. These settlement opportunities ended in 2015.

Following the Supreme Court decision in the *Rangers* case, the EBTSO begins to look like a pretty good deal. However, there are still a significant number of EBT/EFRBS cases that have yet to settle their PAYE and NICs with HMRC. Since these will almost invariably be on 'all fours' with the *Rangers* decision, HMRC will now be able to use its Follower and Accelerated Payments Notice weapons to collect the relevant tax in these cases (without any recourse to a tribunal) (see 1.17B). Those involved in these remaining cases really have very little option now but to 'throw in the towel' and settle with HMRC.

In the light of the Supreme Court's unanimous decision, many tax advisers now question the need for the introduction of the 'disguised remuneration' legislation in 2011 (see 5.17). However, it should be remembered that, before the disguised remuneration rules were introduced, HMRC were dealing with the earlier 'unfavourable' decisions in *Sempra* and *Dextra*, which both found that amounts paid to a third party could *not* be taxed as earnings (see above). Furthermore, the FTT in the *Rangers* case had (by a majority decision) accepted the legal validity of the trust structure and the trustee's discretion. The FTT found that the footballers did not beneficially own 'their' sub-trust funds and simply 'enjoyed' loans from the trusts. The Upper Tribunal supported this view.

Against this background, HMRC were fully justified in introducing the disguised remuneration regime, since this provided a comprehensive 'backstop' counter to the abusive use of EBTs and similar structures in case HMRC failed in the higher courts. Of course, in the light of the Supreme Court ruling, a case could be made for abolishing all or most of the disguised remuneration legislation, which has now been rendered otiose.

The Supreme Court ruling serves as a useful reminder that contrived, abusive, and egregious tax avoidance schemes will not be tolerated by HMRC or the tribunals/courts.

Statutory deduction rules for contributions to EBTs/EFRBS

5.14 To counter the 'earlier' potential for tax avoidance using EBTs and similar structures, HMRC strengthened the rules for claiming corporate tax relief on EBT contributions in the *Finance Act 2003*.

Broadly, the *FA 2013* legislation which defers corporation tax relief for contributions made to EBTs until the relevant amounts have been subjected to PAYE and NIC or used to meet qualifying expenses of the trust [*CTA 2009, ss 1290–1296*]. This rule was expressed to apply to 'employee benefit schemes'. For these purposes, an 'employee benefit scheme' is defined widely as a trust, scheme or other arrangement for the benefit of persons who are or include present or former employees of the employer (now in *CTA 2009, s 1291(2)*).

Following the *FA 2003* restrictions on the tax deductibility of contributions to an EBT, similar arrangements for owner managers and employees began to be made through Employer Financed Retirement Benefit Schemes (EFRBS). Many argued that contributions to an EFRBS benefited from a specific exclusion from the *FA 2003* rules, since they qualified as a statutory deduction for a 'qualifying benefit' within (what is now) *CTA 2009, s 1292(5)*.

Broadly speaking an EFRBS is a flexible discretionary trust which enables benefits to be provided after retirement to the 'employee' members of the scheme. After an employee's death, the trustees will have the power to provide a pension or other benefits to the employee's dependants. EFRBS' are more flexible than registered schemes since they are not restricted by the various constraints imposed on 'registered' pension schemes (see 10.49).

However, following the Supreme Court ruling in the *Rangers* case (see 5.13–5.13E) and, since 2011, the disguised remuneration rules (see 5.17–5.20), company contributions made to EBTs/EFRBs will invariably be taxed as earnings when they are made. Thus, if follows, that a coporation tax deduction should also be available at the same time.

Use of EBTs for share schemes

5.15 A large number of EBTs are set up to acquire new or existing shares in the company. Typically, the EBT is a separate trust entity and is funded by contributions from the sponsoring company. The trustees, who should be independent from the company, can decide how to use the trust funds for the beneficiaries, often consulting with the company.

The acquisition of shares may be funded by company contributions or borrowing. The trust often holds the shares for a number of years for distribution in due course to employees. The distribution is either direct or via an employee share scheme. The likely advantages of an EBT for a family or owner-managed company include the following:

- shares may be acquired at a low price for distribution to employees;

- it can be used as a 'warehouse' for problem shareholdings such as those acquired from an outgoing shareholder;

- an internal share market is created, enabling employees to buy and sell shares.

The statutory deduction rules for company EBT contributions do not apply where the EBT is awarding or transferring shares to directors and employees (see *CTA 2009, s 1290(4)*. This is because the company obtains its tax deduction under the employee share acquisition relief rules in *CTA 2009, Pt 12* (see 8.85–8.87).

IHT issues for EBTs

5.16   The EBT beneficiaries are normally the company's/group's current and previous employees and their families and dependants. In such cases, the EBT should fall within the *IHTA 1984, s 86* exemption (see *IHTA 1984, s 58(1) (b)*) from the normal IHT charges that apply to (discretionary) trusts (see 17.91 to 17.94).

The trustees of the EBT generally decide which beneficiaries are to benefit and the amount to be made available to them. Benefits are often provided by outright payments to different employees, cheap loans, and the provision of assets as well as shares.

In the context of a close 'owner-managed' company, shareholders (participators) holding 5% or more of the company's shares are generally *excluded* from benefit. This is because *IHTA 1984, s 13* only exempts the company's contributions from being counted as a 'transfer of value' for IHT purposes where the EBT's 'shareholder' beneficiaries do *not* have 5% or more of the voting rights. (A close company's transfer of value is apportioned amongst its (5% plus) shareholders under *IHTA 1984, s 94*.)

Even where the 5% plus shareholders are excluded from benefit, HMRC will deny the *IHTA 1984, s 13* exemption where they have actually received a benefit from the EBT – for example by way of a loan or a sub-trust for their/ their family's benefit.

However, there should be *no* need to rely on the protection given by *IHTA 1984, s 13* where the company can deduct the contribution for corporate tax purposes [*IHTA 1984, s 12*] and/or it can be demonstrated that the contribution was not intended to give a gratuitous benefit [*IHTA 1984, s 10*].

Under current law, arrangements involving EBTs will invariably give rise to an earnings charge and hence a corresponding corporate tax deduction (see

5.13–5.13E and 5.18–5.19). Thus, the above potential IHT exposure issue is now unlikely to arise.

FA 2011: 'EMPLOYMENT INCOME PROVIDED THROUGH THIRD PARTIES'

Purpose of *FA 2011*

5.17 The aim of the *FA 2011* – 'Employment income provided through third parties' contained in *ITEPA 2003, Pt 7A* (popularly referred to as the 'disguised remuneration' rules) – is to impose a PAYE and NIC charge where third-party arrangements are used to provide what is, in substance, 'a reward, recognition or a loan' in connection with the employee's current, former or future employment. According to HMRC's guidance at EM45000, the *Part 7A* legislation is intended to tackle arrangements that:

- involve third parties (including trusts or other vehicles), and

- seek to avoid or defer the payment of income tax.

In practice, the 'third party' will normally be an EBT or EFRBS. The legislation (which runs to some 68 pages) has an extremely wide-scope and applies from 6 April 2011 but also catches certain 'payments' made between 9 December 2010 and 5 April 2011. Similar NIC regulations are also in force (for arrangements occurring after 5 December 2011).

A major criticism of the 'disguised remuneration' rules is that they can impose a tax/NIC charge before the relevant individual has a legal entitlement to draw the money. This follows from the wide-ranging nature of the 'earmarking' rule (see 5.19 and 5.20).

Since 17 July 2013, HMRC have also been able to use the GAAR to negate the tax advantages of egregious arrangements involving EBTs and EFRBS (see 1.19).

Basic application of the *ITEPA 2003, Pt 7A* rules

5.18 The application of the complex *ITEPA 2003, Pt 7A* can be broken down into three main stages:

(1)	Is there a third party?	The legislation does *not* apply where an employer provides something directly to an employee (unless the employer is acting as a 'trustee' or has given an undertaken to pay contributions to an EFRBS).
(2)	Are the *ITEPA 2003, s 554A* conditions satisfied?	This involves three questions:
		• Is there a 'relevant arrangement' relating to A?
		• 'Is it reasonable to suppose that, in essence'… the relevant arrangement … is (wholly or partly) a means of providing … with the provision of rewards or recognition or loans in connection with A's employment with B'?
		This is often referred to as the 'gateway' test, since the arrangement will only be caught if the director/employee passes through this 'gateway'.
		Thus, if the substance of the arrangements shows that the relevant individual is *not* a director or employee or the payments are *not* related to an employment or directorship, the legislation will not apply.
		• Has a relevant third person taken a relevant step in connection with that arrangement?
		Notes:
		(a) 'A' is a current, former, or prospective employee.
		(b) 'B' is (normally) the employee's company.
		(c) For these purposes, a relevant arrangement is widely defined to include 'any agreement, scheme, settlement, transaction, trust or understanding, whether it is legally enforceable or not' (*ITEPA 2003, s 554Z(3)*).

In most cases, a relevant third person will be the trustees of an EBT or EFRBS, but it can be any other person (which could include an employer acting as trustee).

There are three kinds of relevant step:

(i) *Earmarking* – 'earmarking' is a very broad concept and applies to earmarking (however informally) of a sum or an asset with the view to taking a later step. There is no further statutory definition and hence 'earmarking' is likely to be construed under its normal English meaning, which is 'to set aside (money, etc.) for a particular purpose'.

Under *ITEPA 2003, s 554B*, it does not matter whether any details of the later step have been decided, such as the asset that will be applied, the sum in question, or whether the employee or a 'linked person' has any legal right to have the step taken.

This is effectively legislates HMRC's view that amounts contributed to an EBT sub-trust for the benefit of a *specific individual* represents earnings (which has now been confirmed in the *Rangers* case (see 5.13–5.13E).

(A 'linked person' covers anyone connected with the employee or a close company in which the employee is a participator or a 51% subsidiary of that company.)

Chronologically, 'earmarking' this is likely to be the earliest charging point. The concept of 'earmarking' is especially aimed as 'sub-trusts' or 'sub-funds', where appointments are made from the main trust for the benefit of specific individuals.

A tax charge is imposed at this stage (even though the employee may never receive the 'earmarked' amount!)

ITEPA 2003, s 554Z14 provides relief from the tax charge where, broadly, it can be shown that the relevant employee will *never* benefit. This claim must be made within four years of the 'earmarking' event.

Based on HMRC's guidance, where contributions are made to an EFRBS on a 'pooled' basis (ie so they cannot be attributed to a single member), they would not be caught by the *ITEPA 2003, Pt 7A* legislation (since there is no 'earmarking'). This means that wholly unfunded EFRBS arrangements should be safe for employers looking to provide a general 'top-up' pensions facility.

(ii) *Payment or transfer of an asset* – this refers to the 'payment' to a 'relevant person' (ie, A or any other person chosen by A). This also covers other 'benefits' provided to a relevant person, such as a loan, a transfer of an asset, and the grant of a lease (likely to exceed 21 years) (see *ITEPA 2003, s 554C* for details).

Note that this 'relevant step' catches a 'loan' (as well as an absolute payment of money) which triggers a PAYE/NIC charge.

Since April 2017, schemes resulting in a loan or other debt being owed by an employee to the third party, whatever the intervening steps, will also be caught. Similarly, schemes that attempt to rely on the loan being received by the employee receiving the loan in another capacity (eg shareholder of a close company) will trigger a 'relevant step'.

		Note that this 'relevant step' catches a 'loan' (as well as an absolute payment of money) which triggers a PAYE/NIC charge.
		Since April 2017, schemes resulting in a loan or other debt being owed by an employee to the third party, whatever the intervening steps, will also be caught. Similarly, schemes that attempt to rely on the loan being received by the employee receiving the loan in another capacity (eg shareholder of a close company) will trigger a 'relevant step'.
		Other than in limited cases, no relief from the charge is available if the loan is subsequently repaid.
		(iii) *Making an asset available* – this applies where the relevant third person – makes an asset available (without transferring it) to A (ie the employee) or 'linked person' (see (e)(ii) above); or – makes the asset available to A two or more years after A's employment with B (*ITEPA 2003, s 554D*).
		Although the general 'benefits' rules broadly provides an annual charge on the provision of an asset (other than cars and accommodation) equivalent to 20% of its cost (see 7.6), any charge falling within *Part 7A* is based on 100% of its cost (and the general benefits charge no longer arises). For these purposes, it does not matter whether A enjoys any actual benefit (*ITEPA 2003, s 554D(3)(c)*).
(3)	Do any of the exclusions in *ITEPA 2003, Pt 7A* apply?	Even though points (1) and (2) above are satisfied, it may still be exempted from an employment income/NIC charge if it falls within one of the numerous exclusions, which limit the scope of the legislation quite considerably.

These exclusions are very prescriptive and the main types are summarised below:

– A direct issue of shares by fellow group companies (since a group company is not a relevant third person provided there are no tax avoidance motives) and shares acquired for full value (see 8.17 and 13.29).

– Loans made directly by the employing company/group (since there is no relevant third person) (see 7.61).

– EBTs operating with approved share schemes (CSOPs, EMI schemes, SIPs, and SAYE schemes) provided there are no related tax avoidance arrangements (*ITEPA 2003, s 554E*) (see 8.49–8.82).

– Employee benefits arrangements and shared-car ownership schemes (see Chapter 7). A number of benefits are provided by *third parties* (eg child care vouchers) and would potentially be caught by *ITEPA 2003, Pt 7A*. However, exemption is given under *ITEPA 2003, s 554G* provided the (third-party) employee benefits are generally made available to a substantial proportion (eg at least over 50%) of employees *and* do not have a tax avoidance motive.

– Deferred bonus arrangements, provided the vesting date is within five years and provided there are no tax avoidance arrangements. In such cases, the PAYE/NIC charge is deferred until the bonus is awarded (*ITEPA 2003, s 554H*).

– Long Term Incentive Plans (LTIPs) under which a 'reasonable' amount of shares are earmarked for long term awards, provided there are no tax avoidance arrangements (*ITEPA 2003, s 554J*).

– Exit-based cash or share awards are excluded from an 'earmarking' charge on a similar basis to LTIPs (*ITEPA 2003, s 554K*).

	– Share options and phantom share scheme arrangements are excluded from an 'earmarking' charge (*ITEPA 2003, s 554L*) (see 8.9).
	– Payments or assets from pre-6 April 2011 non-registered or unfunded pension schemes or from pre-6 April 2006 contributions to EFRBSs (which retain their existing income tax treatment (see 10.49).
	– While pension schemes generally come within the ambit of the *ITEPA 2003, Pt 7A* legislation, no tax charge arises on any relevant step taken by registered pension schemes (subject to the annual and lifetime allowances).
	However, there are no special exemptions for qualifying non-UK pension schemes (QNUPs) or qualifying registered overseas pension schemes (QROPs), since they are not 'registered' pension schemes).
	Where an *ITEPA 2003, Pt 7A* charge potentially arises on shares which is also taxable under employment related securities legislation. In such cases, *ITEPA 2003, s 554N* provides that shares are taxed under the employment related securities regime (which takes precedence) (see 8.15–8.38).
	Thus, even if a transactions satisfies (1) and (2) above, there is no *ITEPA 2003, Pt 7A* charge if it falls within one of the 'exclusions' listed in (3).

DEALING WITH EBT/EFRBS LOANS

5.19   EBT loans made after 5 April 2011 (even if they carry commercial interest rates) would be taxable as a relevant step under *ITEPA 2003, Pt 7A* (see 5.18 – Table (2) note (ii)). (There is a narrow exemption for loans made by financial institutions.)

This would mean that the loan is taxed as employment income (and subject to Class 1 NICs), subject to relief for any earlier 'relevant step'. Note that (unlike *CTA 2010, s 455* tax), there is no provision for the tax to be recovered if the loan is subsequently repaid.

Loans made by EBTs/EFRBSs to employees before *9 December 2010* are not caught by the *ITEPA 2003, Pt 7A*.

However, pre-existing EBT arrangements would still be taxed on the basis of case law rulings (see 5.13–5.13E) Alternatively, HMRC can also use the legislation to tax loans made to beneficiaries that remain outstanding on *5 April 2019*, irrespective of when the loan was taken out. Of course, in the light of the favourable (to HMRC!) ruling in the *Rangers* case, this additional legislative provision now appears to be otiose.

EBT loans may also be taxable under the beneficial loan rules in *ITEPA 2003, s 175* (since they will be provided by reason of the individual's employment or office) (see 7.61). However, if the loan is a qualifying one (ie the interest would have been 'tax-deductible' (or would have been if the loan was interest-bearing), then no *ITEPA 2003, s 175* arises.

HMRC have confirmed that the 'writing-off' of a pre-9 December 2010 loan is not a 'relevant step' under the *ITEPA 2007, Pt 7A* rules, but this might itself create taxable earnings.

It may also be the case that altering the terms of an existing pre-9 December 2010 loan is not a 'relevant step'– for example, the trustees may agree to extend the repayment period of the loan. However, HMRC has indicated that any alteration to the terms of a loan would be assessed on a 'case-by-case' basis. In any event, such loans would automatically be taxed at 5 April 2019 if they had not been repaid by then (see above).

As a transitional step, loans made *after 8 December 2010 and before 6 April 2011* were subject to a charge under the *ITEPA 2003, Pt 7A* provisions, *if they were not repaid by 6 April 2012*. If the loans were not repaid by then, the amount of the loan would be taxed (and subject to NICs) in the director's/employee's hands.

PAYE AND NIC TAX CHARGES UNDER *ITEPA 2003, PT 7A*

5.20 Broadly speaking, if an earnings tax charge arises on the contributions made to the EBT, there should not be a further tax charge when the relevant amounts are distributed. This is achieved by a tax credit in *FA 2011, Sch 2, para 59*. This credit mechanism seeks to ensure there is no tax liability on 'exit' if a PAYE charge on the relevant amount has been levied at an earlier stage (or where a settlement has been reached with HMRC to accept an earlier charge). Payments on account and payments under accelerated payment notices and follower notices do *not* form part of the 'para 59' credit.

The tax charge under *ITEPA 2003, Pt 7A* arises when a relevant step is taken. It will be appreciated that there may be several 'relevant steps' in relation to the same amount (for example, an amount might be first 'earmarked followed by a loan of the same amount). In such cases, the tax charge arises at the first of those relevant steps. However, the tax charge on the first relieves any potential tax on a subsequent relevant step in relation to the same arrangements.

PAYE and NIC applies to the value of the relevant step and is payable as part of the monthly PAYE liability. The *ITEPA 2003, Pt 7A* charge takes precedence over the normal PAYE rules and is likely to occur at an earlier stage (eg at the 'earmarking' step).

The tax cost of a *ITEPA 2003, Pt 7A* charge would increase if the employee concerned does not reimburse the PAYE tax within 90 days from the end of the relevant tax year (*ITEPA 2003, ss 222(1)* and *687A*). (Before April 6 2014, the relevant 'reimbursement' period was 90 days after the *ITEPA 2003, Pt 7A* charge arose.) If the PAYE is not reimbursed within the 90 day period, then a further tax charge arises on them under *ITEPA 2003, s 222* (see 8.46). This provision is interpreted strictly and any refund outside the relevant 90-day period will not prevent a charge arising (*Chilcott v HMRC* [2010] EWCA Civ 1538). As a general rule, the rules are particularly penal in that the *ITEPA 2003, Pt 7A* tax charge is not refundable if the 'relevant step' is unwound – for example if the loan is repaid or the asset is transferred back to the provider. The same problem arises where an employee is subject to a tax charge on 'earmarking', yet actually end up receiving nothing. However, in this situation, the tax may be refunded provided the arrangements are altered so that the employee is incapable of benefiting from the earmarked amount and no other person becomes able to benefit from it.

ITEPA 2003, s 554Z8 provides that where actual consideration is given for a relevant step, no charge arises. No charge should therefore arise where assets are replaced by another asset(s) of similar value. However, HMRC has become aware that this provision has been used to extract real value from EBTs. Consequently, from 17 March 2016, relief under *s 554Z8* will *not* be given where there is a direct/indirect connection between the consideration given and tax avoidance arrangements

The above 'para 59' tax credit does not work so well where the EBT retains funds which grow in value through investment. In such cases, *ITEPA 2003, Sch 2, para 59(1)(f)(ii)* generally exempted that investment return from a charge (frequently on the basis that the investment growth has been taxed in the EBT). However, this 'investment return' credit will *not* be given if the tax has *not* been paid on the 'original earnings' by 31 March 2017, perhaps under the HMRC EBT/EFRBS settlement opportunity (which was withdrawn in March 2017 – see 5.13E). This would mean that the 'investment element' in funds distributed out of the EBT would be subject to a PAYE/NIC charge.

Example 3

PAYE/NIC on loan from an EFRBS

Mr Carroll (a UK resident) owns 20% of the entire issued capital of Shoot Ltd, and is also its sales director.

In December 2016, Shoot Ltd set up an EFRBS and paid a contribution of £200,000 to it.

After properly considering a request from the employing company, the trustees of the EFRB made a loan of £80,000 to Mr Carroll in recognition of his work over the past few years.

- The EFRBS would be an arrangement under *ITEPA 2003, s 554A*.

- The trustees of the EFRBS are a 'relevant third person' and the loan is a relevant step within *ITEPA 2003, s 554C*.

- The arrangements therefore meet the necessary conditions in *ITEPA 2003, s 554A*.

The £80,000 loan (the value of the relevant step) is treated as Mr Carroll's employment 'earnings' and hence is subject to PAYE/NIC, with Mr Carroll being liable to reimburse the PAYE tax within 90 days of 5 April 2017 (otherwise an additional tax charge arises under *ITEPA 2003, s 222*).

Example 4

No specific earmarking

In December 2012, Rush Green Ltd set up an EBT for the benefit of all its employees, making a contribution of £200,000 to the trust.

In 2014, the trustees of the trust were asked to set aside some funds for paying staff bonuses to the office staff. However, there were no specific individual employees named on the instructions from the company.

Consequently, since there were no identifiable employees, there is no 'earmarking' and no employment income tax charge arises as a result of the instructions under *ITEPA 2003, Pt 7A*.

USE OF SHARE OPTIONS

Popularity of share option schemes

5.21   Share option schemes have been used for many years as a method of delivering a performance reward to employees at very low cost to the company. However, the use of unapproved share option schemes has snowballed in recent times as smaller companies seek to use share options as a replacement for the high salaries they cannot afford to pay.

Gains on most unapproved option shares would generally be taxed at the current CGT rate of 20% unless entrepreneurs' relief applies (see 8.13)). However, provided the 'up-front' income tax charge can be minimised, unapproved share option arrangements can still be quite attractive (and are still preferable to highly taxed (and NIC-able) remuneration). Where shares represent very small minority holdings, the value agreed with HMRC should in most cases be relatively small (due to the substantial valuation discount applied against the valuation).

Considerable care must be taken to mitigate the sometimes harsh effects of the 'employment-related' restricted securities regime (see Chapter 8). Standard ordinary shares issued by most private companies may not be 'restricted', but given HMRC's current stance, it is recommended that protective *ITEPA 2003, s 431* elections are made. These elections avoid the risk of subsequently incurring an employment income tax charge when the shares are subsequently sold (see 8.32–8.33).

Beneficial statutory corporation tax relief is available for shares provided to employees as well as on the exercise of employee share options. The relief is broadly given on the 'value' taxed as employment income in the employees' hands (replacing any charge that may have flowed through the profit and loss account under GAAP). EMI share options are favourably treated since corporate tax relief is still obtained on the market value of shares on exercise (despite the fact that the employee typically only pays the market value at the time the option is granted) (see 8.86).

Unapproved share option schemes can often give rise to obligations to account for PAYE and National Insurance (rather than the normal payment of tax under the self-assessment system) where the shares are readily convertible assets (RCAs). This is unlikely in most cases since there is no ready available market for the shares, although shares in subsidiary companies are caught as deemed RCAs (see 5.13).

PAYE ON SHARE OPTIONS

5.22   When a director/employee receives shares from their employer or exercises share options granted by their employer, they are taxed on the market value of those shares at the time of receipt or exercise. If the shares are readily convertible assets ('RCAs') (see 5.12), PAYE and NICs must be applied at the time the share option is exercised. The PAYE/NIC is levied on the market value of the relevant shares less any amount paid for them and the option (see Example 5).

Shares in a private company are not normally treated as RCAs unless it the company is about to be sold or is listed on a recognised exchange such as OFEX or AIM (see also 13.36).

The amount of PAYE due when the share options are exercised may be considerable and it may not be possible to deduct this from the employee's pay in a single month. If this is the case, the company must recover the excess PAYE from the employee within 90 days after the year-end in which the shares were received or the option exercised (see 5.12, Example 1 and 8.46). If the company fails to do this, the unpaid tax is taxed as employment income in the employee's hands. The employee will then be charged tax and NICs on this deemed employment income. The company could grant a formal loan to the employee during this period to cover the PAYE tax – this may then fall to be taxed under the beneficial loan provisions (see 7.61). It is worth noting here that if the company cannot recover all of the PAYE from the employee, the company is still legally obliged to pay over the full amount of PAYE to HMRC at the next remittance deadline.

Unless the PAYE tax has been formalised as a loan, there is no provision for HMRC to extend the recovery period in any circumstances, even if the employee pays the PAYE due shortly after 90 days have elapsed.

NICS ON SHARE OPTIONS

5.23 NICs can arise in a number of cases in relation to shares *that are RCAs* (see 5.12) such as where such shares are acquired through unapproved share option arrangements (or a simple award of shares).

In broad terms, the NIC charge is calculated on the market value of the shares when the option is exercised, after deducting the exercise price and any amount paid for the option. The employing company thus has to account for NICs on the profit realised by its employees on exercise of their share options. Thus, where the shares are RCAs and they increase in value, the NIC cost of the share option scheme spirals upwards.

A solution to this sticky problem is for the liability for the NIC charge to be passed to the employee either by joint NIC election or voluntary agreement [*SSCBA 1992, Sch 1, paras 3A, 3B* as amended by the *National Insurance Contributions and Statutory Payments Act 2004 (NICSPA 2004), s 3*]. Companies can make provision in their share plan documentation to put employees under a contractual obligation to enter into a joint NIC election that must be approved by HMRC or a voluntary agreement. NIC elections provide certainty that the legal obligation for the secondary NICs has transferred to the employee. In the case of an agreement, HMRC can still pursue the employer who can only recover the secondary NICs from the employee if they agree to the recovery.

Where employees pick-up the employers' NIC in this way, they can get relief for the NICs due on the exercise of the option against the PAYE due on the same event (see 5.13) [*ITEPA 2003, s 481*]. However, it makes the calculation of the net PAYE due rather more complicated.

NICs can also be levied on certain other 'chargeable events' under *ITEPA 2003, Pt 7*. For example, where (in the absence of an *ITEPA 2003, s 431* election) the value of shares (falling within the 'restricted securities' regime) is artificially increased (by the amendment or lifting of restrictions) – the NIC charge generally arises on the relevant increase in value.

Following the *NICSPA 2004*, employers can also enter into joint elections or voluntary agreements to pass on NICs arising *after* the acquisition of restricted securities (and on the exercise of an option over such shares) and convertible securities. This ability does not extend to all the potential chargeable events under *ITEPA 2003, Pt 7*.

The mechanics of various share option and share incentive schemes are discussed in Chapter 8. Following a consultation exercise, HMRC concluded in October 2016 that NIC options will be retained.

Example 5

Tax on unapproved share option

Mr Ogbonna has *unapproved* share options in Farewell Boleyn Ltd, an unquoted company, with no employment income tax charge on the grant. The exercise price is £2 per share on 20,000 shares. Farewell Boleyn Ltd draws up accounts to 31 December each year.

Farewell Boleyn Ltd is seeking a flotation on AIM. Before then, in August 2016, Mr Ogbonna exercises the share options and acquires the 20,000 shares, which were then worth £16 each.

On the exercise, Mr Ogbonna is taxed under *ITEPA 2003, ss 476–478* on:

$(20,000 \times £16) - (20,000 \times £2) = £280,000$

HMRC will argue that PAYE has to be operated on the £280,000 'profit' as the shares are RCAs (since at the date the option is exercised there is an understanding that trading arrangements are likely to come into existence).

Farewell Boleyn Ltd will be able to claim a corporate tax 'trading' deduction for the 'taxable amount' of £280,000 (see 5.22 and 8.85–8.87).

CORPORATE TAX RELIEF FOR SHARE AWARDS AND THE EXERCISE OF SHARE OPTIONS

5.24   Companies can claim corporation tax relief on the issue of shares to, or the exercise of share options by, directors and employees. In broad terms, the relief is based on the amount charged to income tax in the director's/employee's hands (or in the case of shares provided under an approved share scheme, the amount that would have been taxed). Details of the statutory corporate tax rules for employee shares and share option exercises are provided in 8.85–8.87.

NATIONAL INSURANCE CONTRIBUTIONS FOR DIRECTORS

Earnings periods

5.25   National Insurance contributions (NICs) for employees are payable by reference to the gross earnings for an earnings period (in contrast to the PAYE system, where tax is usually applied on a cumulative basis). NICs are therefore applied to employees' pay based on their weekly or monthly pay interval. This means that the maximum thresholds are applied on a monthly or weekly basis. Since 6 April 2013, the NIC reporting is processed under RTI (see 5.10A).

Special rules apply to directors, who have an 'annual earnings' period, even if they are paid at regular or irregular monthly or weekly intervals. This is to avoid a director receiving a large amount of earnings (or more likely a bonus) as a single payment thereby restricting the amount of NICs due for that month at 12% (as a result of the monthly upper earnings limit after which employee NICs are levied at 2%). There are no equivalent rules for employees who are *not* directors.

In terms of the administrative arrangements, broadly an employing company can choose to make NIC payments on account during the tax year based on the actual intervals of payment of earnings in the same way as for other employees. If they choose to do this they must seek an wriiten agreement from the director that allows for the employer to recover any outstanding NICs liability from the director should they leave mid-year or if an error in calculation occurs – a so-called 'good faith error'

The director's overall NIC liability at year end (or when they relinquish their directorship) is then re-calculated by reference to the complete annual earnings period. Where the director only draws a regular salary, the annual re-calculation exercise is likely to have little impact on the director's/company's total NIC liability. However, if any irregular and/or varying payments have been made, additional NIC will usually be payable.

Where a director is appointed during a tax year, there is a pro-rata annual earnings period. No change is made to the annual earnings period when a director resigns [*Social Security (Contributions) Regulations 2001, SI 2001/1004, reg 8*] but a recalculation takes place at that point to assess if any additional liability is due.

Example 6

NIC calculation for director appointed during the tax year

Mr Pablo (a UK resident) is appointed a director of Slaven's Irons Ltd when there are 20 weeks left in the tax year 2017/18. With a primary threshold of £157 per week and an upper earnings limit of £866 per week, Mr Pablo's pro rata limits are:

20 × £157 = £3,140

and

20 × £866 = £17,320

Slaven's Irons Ltd pays secondary Class 1 NICs above the secondary threshold of £157 per week.

20 × £157 = £3,140

The NIC position for 2017/18 is:

Total earnings	Mr Pablo
£3,140 or less	Nil
£3,141 to £17,320	12% of earnings between £3,141 and £17,320
Over £17,320	2% of earnings above £17,320
Total earnings	*Slaven's Irons Ltd*
£3,140 or less	Nil
Over £3,140	13.8% of earnings above £3,140

Example 7

Payments on account for a director

Mr Kouyate is a director receiving a regular monthly salary of £1,000. His company decides to use a monthly earnings period for 2017/18 as follows:

Monthly secondary (employer) threshold	£680
Monthly primary (employee) threshold	£680
Monthly upper earnings limit	£3,750

He receives a bonus of £10,000, to be paid with his June 2017 salary. The NIC position for 2017/18 is:

	Earnings	Director's NIC	Employer's NIC
	£	£	£
Month 1 (April)	1,000	38.40	44.16
Month 2 (May)	1,000	38.40	44.16
Month 3 (June)	11,000	513.40	1,424.16
By month 11, totals are:	21,000	897.40	1,865.76

The month 12 calculation must consider the total earnings in the annual earnings period:

	Earnings	Director's NIC	Employer's NIC
	£	£	£
Month 12 (cumulative total)	22,000	1,660.32 *	1,909.37**
Less paid on account		(897.40)	(1,865.76)
Due for month 12		762.92	43.61

* £22,000 less annual threshold £8,164 = £13,836 × 12% = £1,660.32
** £22,000 less annual threshold £8,164 = £13,836 × 13.8% = £1,909.37

DIRECTORSHIPS HELD BY MEMBERS OF A PARTNERSHIP

5.26   In some cases, fees are received by directors who are also members of a partnership. This does not alter the fact that the fees come from holding office and should therefore be taxed as employment income with consequent PAYE and NIC obligations. However, by concession (ESC A37), HMRC accept that such amounts can be treated as professional income of the partnership provided:

- The directorship is a normal incident of the profession and the relevant firm;

- The fees only represent a small part of the firm's profits; and

- The fees are pooled for division amongst the partners under the partnership agreement

The firm must provide a written undertaking to HMRC that the directors' fees will be included in its gross income. The same practice is also followed for NIC purposes under *Social Security (Contributions) Regulations 2001, SI 2001/1004, reg 27*.

This concession also extends to directors fees, which are subjected to corporation tax (for example, where a company has the right to appoint a director to the Board of another company), but not where a director has 'control' of that company under *CTA 2010, s 1124*.

Note that the *FA 2013* extended the ambit of the IR35 provisions to directors' fees received by personal service companies (see 6.4A).

OVERSEAS SECONDMENTS

5.27 A number of owner-managed companies will have extended their business operations overseas, possibly having one or more overseas branches and/or subsidiaries. Sometimes this will involve the secondment of UK-based managers or directors to develop the overseas business.

As a general rule, where a UK director or employee is sent to work in another EU member state (or Iceland, Liechtenstein, Norway and Switzerland) for up to 24 months, they can continue to remain within the UK NIC regime. Initially, the application to continue paying UK NICs must be made on form A1 (E101 before May 2010). After that, by mutual agreement of the competent authorities of the home and host countries, the period of protection can be extended for up to five years. In essence, a director or employee seconded overseas can remain within the UK NIC/social security system for up to five years (and would not be subject to further social security contributions in the host EU country). This period would also count towards entitlement to UK pensions, etc.

In other cases, notably secondments to Canada, the USA and Japan, the potential duplication of UK NICs and host country social security contributions would normally be resolved by a reciprocal agreement/social security treaty. In many cases, the agreement/treaty generally gives five years automatic protection from host country contributions, with the UK secondee remaining subject to UK NICs and pension/benefit entitlements.

NON-EXECUTIVE DIRECTORS

5.28 If there are non-executive directors on the board, then, as a general rule, PAYE and NIC should be applied to remuneration and fees paid in the normal way. The tax treatment for reimbursed expenses, such as attending board meetings, depends on the manner in which they are paid. If the expenses are paid in cash by the non-executive director and subsequently reimbursed by the company, the payments made by the company are liable to PAYE and NICs. Where the expenses are met directly by the company and paid to the third party, the payments are reportable on the form P11Ds (although the ESC

A4 effectively exempts travelling expenses incurred on travelling between companies in the same group and other defined situations).

Since 6 April 2013, the IR35 employment tax legislation has applied to office holders, such as directors (see 6.4A) (see *ITEPA 2003, s 49(1)(c)*). Thus, where a personal service company (PSC) owner performs the duties of a non-executive director for a client, the fees would be caught by IR35. Similarly, IR 35 would be invoked where a PSC is appointed as a corporate director and then (typically) the owner of the PSC performs the duties of that office.

In all these cases, the directors' fees etc. would be paid gross to the PSC. However, the fee income would then be subject to the IR 35 deemed salary calculation (including employers'/employees' NICs) in the PSC (see 6.23 and 6.24). However, employees' NICs would not be due where the non-executive director is over the state retirement age (as is often the case!).

Many companies will seek to minimise the current high levels of NICs (see 5.4). For the working shareholders, this may involve 'payment' in the form of dividends and perhaps the payment of company pension contributions for their benefit. The use of salary sacrifices (now known as Optional Remuneration Arrangements or OpRAs) and tax-efficient benefits (see Chapter 7) may also be useful given the relatively high NIC costs.

SHARE AND OTHER INCENTIVE ARRANGEMENTS

5.29   Approved/tax-favoured share option schemes bring many advantages, giving employees a sense of proprietorship thus aligning their interests with those of the owners. Moreover, share schemes can provide employees with the potential to generate tax efficient capital gains provided there is a planned 'exit' strategy. In some cases, shares can be sold to an EBT, or it is possible for the company to buy back the shares where someone leaves.

Employee share schemes may provide a cost-effective mechanism for rewarding directors and employees and are often regarded as a key element of their remuneration package. They include Share Incentive Plans (SIPs), Company Share Option Plans (CSOPs) and EMI schemes – all of which are covered in Chapter 8.

5.30   The range of tax-efficient incentive schemes available to employers also include:

- a discretionary bonus scheme, to fund a tax-efficient investment such as an Individual Savings Account (ISA) or pension scheme;

- a flexible benefits programme (Chapter 7 provides detailed coverage of the tax treatment of the main types of benefits in kind);

- interest-free loans up to £10,000 in total per employee (no income tax charge on the benefit).

TERMINATION PAYMENTS

Basic taxation of termination payments and key exemptions

5.31   Termination payments have become a key focus of HMRC. Inspectors seem to look very closely at any returns where termination payments have been reported and often seek to challenge the tax-exempt treatment of them.

From April 2018, changes are being made to the tax and NICs treatment of termination payments to make the system fairer and simpler. Thus, for example the £30,000 tax exemption will also apply to employer NICs, with the rest of the termination payment being subject to tax and employer (not employee) NICs (see 5.32)

Where an employee is made redundant, or otherwise has their employment terminated, there may be scope for receiving the first £30,000 of any pay-off tax-free (*ITEPA 2003, s 403(1)*). Note, that the remainder above the £30,000 exemption is taxable at the highest part of the taxpayer's income (subject to the application of a number of other potential exemptions, such as for foreign service (*ITEPA 2003, s 413*) or disability/injury (*ITEPA 2003, s 406*).

However, it is only possible to take advantage of the £30,000 exemption where the payment is *not* otherwise taxable as earnings under the general charging rules in *ITEPA 2003, ss 6* and *62*. In other words, the payment must *not* represent earnings derived from the office or employment, but must be triggered by its termination. This crucial point is not always easily resolved, as demonstrated by the large body of case law in this area – see, for example, *Dale v de Soissons* [1950] 2 All ER 460 and *Williams v Simmonds* [1981] STC 715. Thus, payments made while an employee works their notice, or is on 'gardening leave, would be fully taxable as earnings (see 5.36).

Except in the case of a genuine redundancy payment (see 5.33), if the director/employee has a right to the termination payment, then it will invariably be treated as earnings from the office/employment under the general rule in *ITEPA 2003, s 62*. Such rights may be contained in the individual's employment or service contract, letter of appointment, or staff handbook. Similarly, where the director/employee has a reasonable expectation of receiving a termination payment, HMRC always seek to treat this as taxable earnings (see 5.35).

Where the director/employee is also a shareholder, they will often want to sell their shares on ceasing to work (indeed they may be forced to sell them in certain circumstances). Where the size of the director's shareholding is able to exert influence, it is not surprising that Inspectors often attempt to argue that a lump sum 'termination' does not enjoy the *ITEPA 2003, s 403* exemption. Instead, HMRC often seek to treat it as a (non-relievable) distribution by the company or as part of the sale proceeds for the shares.

Termination payments fall into various categories (as outlined below). The nature of the payment will usually have a significant bearing on the tax treatment for the company and director/employee. In practice, it may often be necessary to go behind the actual description of the 'termination' payment and establish the precise reason for and circumstances surrounding it.

There is no 'absolute right' to the £30,000 termination payments or exemption. The relevant documentation (for example, Board minutes, and termination agreement) must reflect the reality of the circumstances in which the payment is being made. In the author's experience, Inspectors frequently challenge claims for the tax exemption and each case must be examined carefully on its own facts to determine whether the claim is defensible. In practice, probably the most 'clear-cut' case is where the director/employee receives damages as compensation for loss of their office or employment (see 5.34). The first tier tribunal decisions in *Reid v HMRC* [2012] UKFTT 182 (TC) and *Johnson v HMRC* [2013] UKFTT 242 (TC) confirm that settlement agreements (previously known as compromise agreements: see 5.34 below) should clearly schedule the constituent parts of the termination payment (see 5.35).

As a general rule, termination payments that are eligible for the £30,000 exemption are recognised for tax purposes when they are received or the recipient becomes entitled to receive them.

Non-cash benefits included in a 'termination package' are deemed to be received when they are used or enjoyed [*ITEPA 2003, s 403(3)(b)*]. All payments made from the same employment and employer must be aggregated for the purpose of the £30,000 exemption (together with those made by associated employers) [*ITEPA 2003, s 404*]. Any benefits in excess of the £30,000 exemption would be taxed under the normal benefit rules.

Employer contributions towards the employee's legal fees in relation to their termination of employment are exempt from tax (*ITEPA 2003, s 413A*). To qualify for this exemption, payments must be incurred exclusively in connection (generally this is interpreted broadly by HMRC) with the termination of the employment. Furthermore, they must be made in respect of a court/tribunal order, or a compromise agreement for the direct payment of fees by the employer to the employee's solicitor. VAT on the employee's legal fees cannot be recovered by the employer.

It is important to note that a termination payment will be completely exempt (ie not just up to the £30,000 threshold) where it is made on account of the employee's death or injury or disability of the employee [*ITEPA 2003, s 406*]. In *Horner v Hasted* 67 TC 439, it was held that to qualify for the exemption the employee must have an identified medical condition which disables or prevents the employee from carrying out the duties of the employment at the time of the termination of the contract, and that the disability payment must be made only on account of that disability. Disability is considered by HMRC to include both sudden affliction and the effects of a chronic or gradual deterioration in health.

However, the Upper Tribunal ruled in *Moorthy v HMRC* [2016] UKUT 13 TCC that this 'exemption' did not cover 'injury to feelings'. Based on the facts, a settlement payment for injury to feelings on termination of employment was held to be taxable as a termination payment under *ITEPA 2003, s 403*. The payment settled all the taxpayer's claims against the employer including claims for age discrimination arising during the redundancy selection process. The Upper Tribunal also found that HMRC were wrong to offer another £30,000 tax-free under *s 406* as 'injury had occurred. It concluded that *ITEPA 2003, s 406* was intended, only to exempt payments related to physical injury or disability not 'injury to feelings'.

The case of *Nichols v Gibson* [1994] STC 1029 confirmed that the taxation of termination payment rules operate independently of the general earnings rules in the employment income tax code. Thus, a termination payment received (in respect of a UK employment) was held to be taxable in the UK even though the employee was not UK resident or ordinarily resident in the tax year of receipt. However, there is a full exemption for a 'substantial' period of foreign service (as defined in *ITEPA 2003, s 413*). If the foreign service period does not qualify for the full exemption, the taxable element of the termination payment (ie after the £30,000 exemption) will qualify for a pro-rata reduction under *ITEPA 2003, s 414*.

Basic NIC treatment of termination payments

5.32 NICs will normally be due where the employee has a contractual right to receive the payment or where there is an established practice of making such payments.

On the other hand, no NIC liability should arise on a genuine termination payment, as this does not relate to 'remuneration or profits derived from an employment'. The NIC exemption for termination payments is completely unrestricted so the full amount of any termination payment should escape NIC liability (but see 5.31 above for April 2018 changes to the employer NIC position).

REDUNDANCY PAYMENTS

5.33 Under the *Employment Rights Act 1996, s 139* 'redundancy' broadly occurs where an employee's dismissal results from the cessation, relocation or reorganisation of the business.

Statutory redundancy payments made under *the Employment Rights Act 1996, s 167(1)* (or Northern Ireland equivalent) are exempt from income tax under *ITEPA 2003, s 309*.

The exemption in *ITEPA 2003, s 309* also applies to an 'approved contractual payment' under an agreement within the *Employment Rights Act 1996, s 157*.

Both statutory redundancy and relevant approved contractual payments are, however, taken into account in exempting the first £30,000 of any overall termination package [*ITEPA 2003, s 309(3)*]. Consequently, if the total termination payment is in excess of the £30,000 exemption threshold, income tax is charged on the excess amount.

Redundancy payments can be made under 'non-statutory' schemes and arrangements (for example, schemes designed to deal with the specific closure of a business division, or the making of 'top-up' payments in addition to statutory payments). Non-statutory redundancy payments are normally treated in the same way as 'statutory' redundancy payments, provided that there is a genuine redundancy in accordance with Statement of Practice SP1/94. Basically, this situation arises where the Inspector is satisfied that the payment falls within the definition of a 'redundancy payment' under the *Employment Rights Act 1996* and that there has been a genuine redundancy. The payment must not represent a terminal bonus for carrying out additional duties.

In *Colquhoun v HMRC* [2010] UKUT 431 the Upper Tax Tribunal held that a payment received for giving up rights in a redundancy scheme falls within *ITEPA 2003, s 403*, even where the termination occurred some time later. Consequently, the payment qualified for the £30,000 exemption

Application may be made to the Inspector for advance clearance to pay lump sum redundancy payments of up to £30,000 free of tax – the written application should include copies of the scheme documentation and any intended letter to be sent to employees.

COMPENSATION FOR LOSS OF OFFICE OR UNFAIR DISMISSAL AND COMPROMISE AGREEMENTS

5.34 It may be possible to show that the payment to the director validly represents compensation for loss of office. If so, the amount of compensation should be determined properly taking the following factors into account:

(*a*) the gross future remuneration lost to the director because of the breach of contract;

(*b*) a discount to reflect the difference in timing between the date the compensation is paid and the date(s) on which the remuneration would actually have been paid under the terms of the contract;

(*c*) a reduction to reflect the prospect of the director obtaining future employment from which they will derive earnings that would wholly or partly replace the earnings they would have received under the contract;

(*d*) a reduction to reflect job seeker's allowance receivable;

(*e*)   an adjustment to reflect the fact that the entire remuneration payable under the contract would have been taxable in the director's hands, whereas only the excess of the compensation payment over £30,000 is actually taxable.

The director or employee will normally be required to sign a 'termination agreement' or 'settlement agreement' where they accept the compensation 'in full and final settlement' of any claims that they may have against the company – as part of these arrangements, the director/employee normally agrees not to litigate against the company. HMRC have previously confirmed that such 'settlement arrangements' do not give rise to a 'restrictive covenant' tax charge under *ITEPA 2003, s 225*. However, HMRC may seek to challenge the composition of the 'package' where it looks excessive.

Prior to 29 July 2013, such agreements were known as 'compromise agreements'. The *Enterprise and Regulatory Reform Act 2013* renamed them 'settlement agreements'.

On the other hand, where an amount is allocated to a specific 'restrictive' undertaking given by the director/employee (not to compete with the company or solicit its employees, or not to litigate against the company etc), this would be taxed under *ITEPA 2003, s 225* as employment income (subject to PAYE). Such payments would also attract NICs.

Where an employment tribunal awards employee compensation, this will generally benefit from the £30,000 exemption. This is unlikely to be the case where the tribunal reinstates the employee, with the employee receiving compensation from the time of their dismissal to the date they were re-instated. However, *Wilson v Clayton* [2005] STC 157 helpfully provides that, following a 'reinstatement' decision, a negotiated compromise payment to compensate for 'unfair dismissal' as a result of the employer withdrawing an essential car user allowance was not taxable (falling within the exemption in what is now *ITEPA 2003, s 401*). This was on the basis that the payment had been made to compensate for unfair dismissal and was therefore made in connection with the termination of the employment.

The case of *Tottenham Hotspur Ltd v HMRC* [2016] UKFTT 389 demonstrates that where payments to employees (in this case the footballers Peter Crouch and Wilson Palacios) are made 'in return for the surrender of the players' rights' under their contracts, this would fall within the beneficial 'termination payment' rules. (This appeal was motivated by the significant savings in employers' NIC that were available in 2011.) Based on the precise facts of the case, The FTT concluded that the contracts had been terminated and the 'termination' payments had been made in consideration for the contractual rights that had been abandoned. This was in contrast to the situation where a lump sum payment had been made in return for a reduction/elimination of future duties under the contract. It was not necessary for their to be an actual breach of the employment contract, as was held in *Henley v Murray* [1941]

31 TC 351. Furthermore, the tribunal considered that it made little difference whether the contract provided for early termination by mutual consent or not.

In some cases, it might be argued that all or part of the payment represents compensation for the injury to the employee's feelings. This was the case in *Walker v Adams* [2004] STC (SCD) 269, where the Special Commissioners decided that part of an Employment Tribunal award relating to 'injury to feelings' was free of tax. Equally a payment made in compensation for discrimination during employment (rather than during the termination (see the case of *Moorthy* in 5.31 above) will be totally tax-free). Where the compensation covers both 'in-service' and termination discrimination, it should be apportioned so that the 'in-service' payment benefits from being tax-exempt.

If it can be proved that a compensation payment relates to damages paid for unlawful conduct, etc on the part of the employing company, this should not be taxable as earnings. Furthermore, even though compensation receipts (derived from assets) are within the charge to CGT under *TCGA 1992, s 22*, they should be exempted under ESC D33 on the basis that there is no underlying asset in such cases.

It is important that 'settlement agreements' should clearly show each constituent monetary amount making up the total termination payment. The taxpayers in *Reid v HMRC* [2012] UKFTT 182 (TC) and *Johnson v HMRC* [2013] UKFTT 242 (TC) (who had both worked for the same company) ran into difficulties with HMRC due to poorly drafted compromise agreements. Both agreements contained 'entire agreement' clauses. As part of their termination payment, each taxpayer received a £30,000 repayment, representing the amount each paid into an enterprise investment scheme (EMI) when they first joined the company. HMRC sought to tax this £30,000 since the compromise agreement provided no evidence to support the fact that it related to a repayment related to the EMI scheme.

Although there was external evidence to support this, the tribunal in *Reid* accepted HMRC's submission that the 'entire agreement' clauses prevented it from doing so. However, in *Johnson*, the tribunal did not follow *Reid* (noting that this decision was not binding on it!). In *Johnson*, it was held that since HMRC was not a party to the compromise agreement, it could not rely on the 'entire agreement' clause. This meant that the external evidence could be considered, which clearly showed that Mr Johnson's £30,000 related to the EMI scheme and hence was not taxable. Nevertheless, despite the contrary nature of these decisions, such difficulties would be avoided by having clearly drafted compromise agreements.

In *Oti-Obihara v HMRC* [2010] UKFTT 568 (TC), a payment was made to a former employee who had made allegations of racial discrimination and harassment against his former employer. The employee and employer reached a settlement that provided for the termination of the employment, the waiver of all claims against the employer, and a lump sum payment. The former employer treated the lump sum as non-taxable, which was challenged by HMRC. On appeal to the FTT, it was held that the payment should be split into an amount, which represented compensation for financial loss arising from the termination, with the remainder being tax-free as compensation for discrimination. Following *Oti-Obihara*, there were grounds for justifiable apportionments to be made of lump sum payments where there are similar circumstances, although this was challenged challenged by the Upper Tribunal in Moorthy (see 5.31 above).

PAYMENTS IN LIEU OF NOTICE (PILONS) AND GARDEN LEAVE

5.35   A payment in lieu of notice ('PILON') can be made in a variety of situations. Four possibilities were identified by Lord Browne-Wilkinson in *Delaney v Staples* [1992] 1 AC 687, these being where:

(*a*)   'garden leave' is taken – where notice is given, but not worked, and a salary for the period is paid as a 'lump sum';

(*b*)   a PILON is provided in the employment contract as an alternative to a period of notice;

(*c*)   a PILON is made on the employer and employee agreeing (at the point of 'termination') that the employment is to cease without proper notice;

(*d*)   the contractual arrangements do not provide for a PILON, but the employer terminates the contract and tenders a PILON.

In such cases, it will be necessary to establish whether the PILON would be taxed as employment income under the general rule in *ITEPA 2003, ss 6* and *7(2)*. This would be done by reviewing the relevant provisions in the employee's contract of employment, together with established practices, which might create a reasonable expectation that a PILON would be received. Thus, if such payments have always been made in the past, a custom will have been established.

In *SCA Packaging Ltd v HMRC* [2007] EWHC 270 (Ch), the company argued that PILONs should escape tax since they were paid under the terms of a trade union-negotiated memorandum inserted into the employees' contracts. However, Justice Lightman held that, even though the PILONs were paid as a result of a collective agreement, they were still received under the terms of the employees' contracts and hence were taxable as earnings. The PILONs were therefore subject to PAYE and NIC in the normal way. On the other hand, if the company had simply terminated the contracts without giving the employees notice, they would have been entitled to damages instead, which would have been eligible for the £30,000 exemption in *ITEPA 2003, s 403*. It is unlikely that the right to make a PILON could be implied into a contract that expressly provided for employees to be given specified notice periods (*John Morrish v NTL Group Ltd* [2007] CISH 56).

HMRC will seek to tax any so-called Auto-PILONs (which are made by employers as an *automatic* response to notice being given by either side). Such payments usually equate to the gross pay due for the relevant notice period.

It is therefore important to ensure that the correct terminology is applied to the payment. It is recommended that employers carry out a 'critical assessment' in each case to assess whether or not the employee works their notice period and, if not, what level of payment should be made.

If it can be shown that the employee is receiving a true damages payment for the early termination of their contract, then it should be eligible for the £30,000 'termination payment' exemption. This was confirmed in *Michael Phillips v HMRC* [2016] UKFTT 0174 (TC) where a payment was described as a payment in lieu of notice (PILON) in a settlement agreement. However, the taxpayer wasn't successful in asking for apportionment over two tax years: as one payment was made it could only be considered for one £30,000 tax exemption.

In such cases, an employer would normally seek to mitigate damages to the minimum level payable. Thus, for example, the PILON should *not* match the gross pay for the notice period but should be reduced to take account of tax and NIC that would have been suffered under the *Gourley* principle. (The House of Lords decided in *British Transport Commission v Gourley* [1955] 3 All ER 796 that damages based on loss of income should be reduced to take account of the tax that would have been suffered on the 'lost' income.)

Where the employee is on garden leave, they are still employed and remain bound by their contract of employment. Consequently, HMRC generally take the view that any payment for garden leave is fully taxable as employment income, since it represents the salary for the notice period. This principle has received judicial blessing in *Richardson v Delaney* [2001] STC 1328 (see also *Ibe v McNally* [2005] STC 1426). Where an employment is terminated within situation (*b*) above, the analysis applied is that the contract is terminated in accordance with its terms. Hence, as the payment is a contractual one, it falls to be taxed as earnings. This reasoning is supported by the Court of Appeal in *EMI Group Electronics Ltd v Coldicott* [1999] STC 803.

If a contract provides discretion for the employer to make PILONs, but it can be demonstrated that the employer has breached the terms of the contract, the amount paid to the employee will be treated as compensation, thus benefiting from the £30,000 exemption. This was established in *Cerberus Software Ltd v Rowley* [2001] IRLR 160. In this case, the employment contract gave the employ the right to terminate the employee's contract by giving six months' notice, provided it made a PILON to the employee. The contract stated that the employer 'may' make a PILON.

The Court of Appeal found that the employer had the choice whether or not to make a PILON as it could either:

- breach the contract and pay damages for that breach rather than pay the PILON; or

- give notice to the employee.

By terminating the employment without notice, the employer was in breach of contract and it was therefore liable to pay damages to the employee, which did not constitute a contractual right of the employee.

HMRC accepts that the conclusion reached in *Cerberus* 'clearly applies wherever the contractual clause is not prescriptive in requiring a payment where notice is not given' (*HMRC Tax Bulletin 63*).

On the other hand, where a PILON is made in situation (*c*) above, it would *not* normally be treated as earnings from the employment, provided there is no existing prior understanding which might point to it being a contractual provision. There is also a strong argument that the payment is being made to avoid the risk of a compensation payment being awarded at an Employment Tribunal. Similarly, any PILON made within the circumstances in (*d*) would represent liquidated damages for breach of contract (for failing to give proper notice) and would therefore be eligible for the £30,000 exemption within *ITEPA 2003, s 403* (see *IR Tax Bulletin 24* (August 1996)).

EX GRATIA PAYMENTS

5.36   Where a working shareholder ceases to work for the company, in certain limited circumstances it may be possible to receive a tax-free payment which is of an 'ex gratia' nature. This should be exempt from tax up to the £30,000 exemption threshold limit (see 5.22), provided it is not made by reference to past services. For example, in the case of *Barclays Bank Plc v HMRC* [2007] STC 747 it was held that benefits received were in reference to past service.

Ex gratia payments are not defined in the legislation and so the meaning of ex gratia for tax purposes derives primarily from case law. In *Mercer v Pearson* [1976] STC 22, an ex gratia payment was defined as one 'which is made voluntarily, that is pursuant to the exercise of a liberty and without the payer acting under the compulsion of a duty'. HMRC contend that genuine ex gratia payments very rarely arise, and will frequently challenge these.

Previously, HMRC's view as stated in Statement of Practice SP13/91, was that ex gratia payments made on retirement or death were receipts from an unapproved retirement benefits scheme and were specifically taxed as employment income under *ITEPA 2003, s 394(1)*. Thus, any ex gratia payment made near or at retirement would not have enjoyed the £30,000 exemption.

SP13/91 has now been withdrawn following the changes to the pension rules from 6 April 2006. Any payments or other benefits made on retirement or death are now considered to be receipts from an Employer-Financed Retirements Benefit Scheme. However, the tax treatment remains largely unchanged – the £30,000 exemption is not applicable, as any ex gratia lump sum payments made on retirement or death will constitute 'relevant benefits' and so will be counted as employment income under *ITEPA 2003, ss 393B* and *394(1)*.

HMRC is vigilant to the fact that some employers may seek to dress up a 'retirement' as a termination in order to take advantage of the termination payment exemption under *ITEPA 2003, s 401* and are likely to look very closely at the underlying facts see whether the 'termination' payment should be taxed under the above rules.

In *DV Thomas v HMRC* [2013] UKFTT 043 (TC), the employer company paid one of its directors £37,200 on his retirement from the company aged 66. The former director did not include this as taxable income on his tax return. Following an enquiry HMRC issued an amendment to charge tax on it. The former director appealed HMRC's amendment to the FTT, which in turn dismissed his appeal. This was on the basis that the payment was taxable under *ITEPA 2003, s 393B* as a 'relevant benefit' that had been provided 'on or in anticipation of the retirement of an employee'.

Severance payments made on redundancy, loss of office or on death or disability due to an accident will generally be exempt and would not be taxed under the above 'retirement' rules.

CONTEMPORANEOUS SALE OF SHARES

5.37 Particular care is required where there are arrangements to make termination payments to directors (especially where they are also controlling shareholders) around the same time as the company is sold or their shares are re-purchased by the company.

In *Allum v Another v Marsh* [2005] STC (SCD) 191 HMRC were able to persuade the Special Commissioner that voluntary payments of £30,000 each(!) made to the shareholders (husband and wife) at the time their shares were re-purchased by the company were taxable as they were made in recognition of services provided. This was probably not helped by the company saying that the payments were made 'following [their] resignation due to retirement ... in appreciation of their services to the company over many years'.

The decision in *Snook (James) & Co Ltd v Blasdale* (1952) 33 TC 244 is also particularly instructive as it provides a further example of how *not* to do things! This case involved an agreement to sell shares, with a provision to pay compensation for loss of office being included in the agreement. It was held that the compensation payments could not be deducted against profits as they were linked to the agreement for the sale of the company.

In such cases, to have any possibility of success, it will be necessary to demonstrate to a (usually 'cynical') Inspector that the termination payment was not linked to the sale of the shares in any way. In such cases, it is important to be able to demonstrate that the termination payment and consideration for the shares were arrived at independently and there was no value shifted to the 'tax-exempt' payment. Where the Inspector succeeds in denying relief, they will often tax the payment as a distribution or as part of the proceeds for the sale of the shares.

EMPLOYER'S PAYE OBLIGATIONS AND PENSION PLANNING

5.38   Where the termination payment is taxable/NIC-able', the company must account for PAYE and employees' NIC/employer's NIC. If the £30,000 exemption is incorrectly applied to the termination payment, the employing company will therefore have to pick up a large PAYE and NIC bill later on, with possible penalties and interest on top!

Many companies will wish to protect their position by operating PAYE and NIC where there is any doubt surrounding the availability of the tax exemption. On the other hand, given that the company will then have to pay 13.8% employer's NIC on the payment, it is important not to be over-prudent in this area and apply PAYE/NIC without proper consideration of the legal principles. If there is some genuine uncertainty about the tax treatment of a proposed termination payment, the employer should consider seeking an advance ruling from HMRC.

In *Norman v Yellow Pages Sales Ltd* [2010] EWCA Civ 1395, the Court of Appeal held that if a termination settlement agreement failed to specify any apportionment between taxable and non-taxable elements (such as injury to feelings – see 5.24), then for the purposes of operating PAYE, the employer company is entitled to apply PAYE on the full amount.

Where a termination payment is made *after the employee's P45 has been issued*, companies must deduct the full amount of tax under PAYE operating code 0T/1 i.e. taxing the sum at 20%, 40% and 45% depending upon the sum paid.

Where all or part of the intended termination payment would fall to be taxed, it might be beneficial for the company to make a large pension payment instead. The pension payment would be earmarked for the employee's benefit, although care would need to be taken to ensure that this fell within the £40,000 annual allowance (also allowing for any unused relief brought forward from the three previous years) (see 10.23) or even as low as £4,000 (£10,000 between 6 April

2015 and 5 April 2017) if the reduced money purchase annual allowance (MPAA) is in point (see 10.27A).

Sometimes, employers may be asked to make the termination payment 'gross' (without any tax or NICs being deducted), on the basis that the employee is giving an indemnity to reimburse any tax and NIC ultimately found to be payable by HMRC. In the writer's experience, it can be difficult to successfully pursue a claim under the indemnity, due to difficulties in tracking down the former employee etc.!

The employer must also report details of termination payments (including benefits) that exceed £30,000 in value. The director/employee must report full details of any termination payment or benefits on their tax return.

PLANNING CHECKLIST – REMUNERATION STRATEGIES

Company

- Consider commercial desirability of retaining a level of profits.

- Surplus profits could be distributed as bonuses to selected personnel, or through pension scheme contributions or other benefits.

- Review any share option scheme for PAYE and NIC implications and remember to claim a corporate tax deduction for any shares or share options provided to employees.

- Remuneration properly provided in year-end accounts should be paid within nine months from the end of the accounting period. Any provision for bonuses in the year end accounts must comply with GAAP. Broadly, this means that the obligation to pay the bonus must have crystallised by the year-end.

- Where workers have been re-categorised as employees, the company should seek to obtain 'credit' for the tax/NIC previously paid by the worker in any negotiated PAYE settlement (under the 2008 regulations post-*Demibourne*).

- Carefully determine whether PAYE/NIC must be applied to any 'relevant steps' taken within an EBT or EFRBS, such as earmarking for or making loans to employees.

- Review all arrangements where employee benefits etc. are provided by third parties to ensure that they are exempted from any PAYE/NIC under the 'disguised remuneration' rules in *ITEPA 2003*.

- HMRC's decisive success in the *Rangers* case means that it now has a very strong basis for seeking PAYE and NIC on all EBT/EFRB arrangements set up before the 'disguised remuneration' legislation. Furthermore, any pre-9 December 2010 EBT loans that remain

---

outstanding on 5 April 2019, will be subject to an immediate PAYE/NICs charge

- Carefully review any proposed termination payment to ensure whether it can be paid without deduction of PAYE or NIC.

Working shareholders

- Dividend strategy may determine the level of profits available for distribution as remuneration.

- Consider whether IR 35 or managed service company provisions apply to any contracts performed through a personal/managed service company. This includes the services of an office holder.

- From 6 April 2017, contracts performed by PSCs for public sector bodies will potentially have PAYE tax and NICs withheld by the relevant body. This needs reflecting in the company's accounts/tax computations so that a double charge to PAYE and NIC doesn't occur (see Chapter 6).

- Ensure that any PAYE arising under the *ITEPA 2003, Pt 7* rules is reimbursed to the company within 90 days of the tax year end to prevent a further employment tax charge arising under *ITEPA 2003, s 222.*

- Consider the required level of earnings for pension funding.

- Ensure that any settlements agreements made on the termination of employment clearly specify the nature of each payment making up the total termination payments.

Other employees

- Look for basic remuneration plus performance-related bonus.

- Check that pay received for hours worked is at least as much as the national minimum wage.

Non-working shareholders

- Consider whether any excess remuneration is commercially justifiable or desirable. In such cases, it is generally better for them to take it as a dividend.

Chapter 6

Personal Service and Managed Service Companies

INTRODUCTION

Personal service companies (PSCs)

6.1 The term 'personal service company' (PSC) was not in common use before 9 March 1999, when Gordon Brown slipped the press release, IR35, into his Spring Budget pack. This infamous press release marked a radical change in tax policy. It enabled the then Inland Revenue to 'look through' an established corporate structure and treat its underlying income as derived from a 'deemed' employment in appropriate cases. This controversial principle is applied where the 'worker' (who owns the company) would have been treated as an employee if they had worked directly for the client, rather than through their 'intermediary' company. In other words, IR35 will apply where the relationship between the worker and the client/engager would be one of employment if the PSC and any other party in the contractual chain did not exist.

The relevant anti-avoidance legislation, which targets the provision of services through an 'intermediary' was introduced in *FA 2000, Sch 12* (now 'consolidated' into *ITEPA 2003, Pt 2, Ch 8*, although it is generally referred to as 'the IR35 rules'). The IR35 regime only bites when the business involves *services* performed by an individual rather than the production or trading of goods. Such personal service companies commonly provided computer or management consultancy, copywriting, designing and construction-type work.

Since 6 April 2016, travel and subsistence expenses cannot be paid tax-free to workers engaged via an employment intermediary, such as a personal service company, where they are subject to supervision, direction or control (SDC).

There have been no further proposals regarding the IR35 regime and the private sector. However, there are significant new proposals affecting the public sector that came into force in April 2017 (see 6.1C). Given the 'unlevel playing field' this creates for contractors, many believe this will be extended to the private sector!

Current working practices and the gig economy

6.1A   Following the Office of Tax Simplification's recommendations, Budget 2011 confirmed that the Government would retain the IR35 rules but with some administrative improvements.

The complexity of today's workforce and the way work is offered and carried out was highlighted in the 188-page report on employment status that the Office of Tax Simplification (OTS) published in March 2015 and the survey results that the Citizen's Advice Bureau issued in August 2015. This found there were nearly 500,000 people working in the UK who ought to be classed as workers rather than self-employed. These 'workers' should be entitled to the full range of employment rights, and a large subset of this group should also be subject to PAYE and NIC.

The OTS found that businesses were now less motivated by the savings in employers' NICs resulting from a 'self-employed' relationship. This has now been outweighed by the risks of non-compliance with employment rights including pensions auto-enrolment. This risk had been mitigated for many businesses by the use of an intermediary (such as a personal service company, agency or managed service company 'umbrella').

Work continued throughout 2016 to improve HMRC's employment status indicator tool which was one of the agreed recommendations from the OTS and to develop the new 'Check Employment Status for Tax' service to support the changes to 'off payroll working' in the public sector from April 2017 (see 6.1C).

6.1B   Those in employment generally suffer a higher tax rate than the self-employed and owner managers. This is largely due to the imposition of the relatively penal rate of employers' NICs. The Government is currently trying to address the loss of tax revenues caused by the increased shift to 'self-employment'. For example, self-employment accounts for 45% of the total employment growth since March/May 2008. The largest 'self-employed' sectors include construction, joinery/plumbing, education, retail, cleaning, taxis, hairdressing, health, IT and agriculture.

The gig economy is a term used to describe the use of independent 'freelancers' and temporary workers as opposed to full time workers. Workers are typically paid for each 'gig' they do, such as delivering food or taxi journeys and so on. The taxation of PSCs is closely related to taxing the so-called 'gig' economy since an increasing number of those in the 'gig' economy are working through PSCs and hence mitigating their tax/NIC liabilities.

A number of recent cases (such as the '*Uber*' employment tribunal case (see 6.22A) and *Pimlico Plumbers* [2017] EWCA Civ 51) have found those operating in the gig economy (many via PSCs) to be 'workers' rather than employees. There is no concept of 'worker' in tax law and so these 'workers' can be engaged by businesses without giving them various protections under employment law.

'Off-payroll working' in the public sector

Background

6.1C   In May 2016, HMRC published a consultation on IR35 reform aimed at the public sector, with the resultant reforms taking place from 6 April 2017.

The 'public sector' includes the NHS, police and fire authorities, local authorities, the BBC, Channel 4, the Bank of England and Universities. However, in a 'last-minute' amendment to the *Finance Act 2017*, retail pharmacies and opticians where locums typically work through PSCs were excluded from the 'public sector' definition.

Under these rules, where a PSC works for a public sector body, the responsibility for applying PAYE/NIC shifts from the PSC to the party paying the PSC. However, if there is a chain of suppliers, the PAYE/NIC must be deducted by the intermediary closest to the PSC. This is generally referred to as 'off-payroll working'.

HMRC have designed a digital tool – the 'Check Employment Status for Tax' – to assist public sector bodies determine whether the PSC provider falls within the IR35 regime (once they have assessed if there a requirement for personal service and an element of control).

If the contract is deemed to be within IR35, the (public sector) engager will have to deduct tax and NI from the payment made to the PSC (see 6.1D).

Since the implementation of the new rules in April 2017, public sector bodies have taken a variety of approaches. The most 'risk averse' bodies have insisted that all PSCs are now treated as employees under an employment contract – this is probably the most expensive option for the public sector body.

Other public bodies have taken the more appropriate approach of considering every contract separately to ensure that 'reasonable care' has been taken to assess status correctly. There will be PSCs operating in the public sector that are not caught by the new rules, for example where they are providing a product rather than personal services

Anecdotally, the early signs are that many contractors are now refusing to work within the public sector and are shifting all their contract work to the private sector. This may well influence the government to extend these rules to the private sector.

265

Payroll processes

6.1D   It would appear simple for the public sector engager to deduct PAYE tax and NICs from the PSC's payment. However, this has proved more complex in practice. Perhaps the major difficulty is trying to establish whether the contract is caught by the new 'off-payroll' rules. This is proving to be particularly challenging for 'smaller' public sector bodies who are not familiar with the current IR35 rules. Furthermore, the 'Check Employment Status for Tax' tool was also delivered very late and appears to be providing inconsistent results.

HMRC's guidance on the payroll processes required is sparse! Where the public sector body accepts it is caught by the 'off-payroll' rules, it must capture sufficient personal information to set up the PSC on its payroll system. This requires the development of some sort of 'starter' checklist that delivers to the public sector body's payroll team, not only personal details about the PSC, but also sufficient information to allocate an NICs table letter and a tax code.

The guidance indicates that NICs table letter A will always be operated (although this will not be the case if the individual working within the PSC is under 21 or over state pension age). In terms of PAYE tax code, the guidance requires that a basic-rate (BR) code is *always* operated. This, of course, will lead to an under-deduction of tax where the worker's marginal tax rate is more than 20%.

The PSC must indicate to the public sector engager the fees that are to be subject to tax and NICs are *net* of VAT and any 'qualifying business expenses' (ie only those expenses that are allowable for an employee under *ITEPA 2003, s 336*). There is no 'IR 35' 5% expense allowance under the 'off payroll' regime.

Once the tax and NI has been withheld from the fees, it is paid over to HMRC as part of the remittance due in respect of employees by the 22nd of the following tax month. The public sector engager should provide a statement to the PSC indicating how the fees have been subjected to tax and NICs, as payment of the PSC's invoice will be a combination of the net fees, VAT and any qualifying expenses.

When the PSC withdraws monies from its company that have been subject to a withholding of tax and NI by the public sector body, this should be done without deduction of tax and NICs (and reported in the appropriate 'FPS' fields that relate to tax- and NI-free payments (see 5.10A).

The PSC should ensure it is not treated as a worker for auto-enrolment purposes. Unfortunately, from the public sector body's perspective, the fees are classed as pay subject to the apprenticeship levy.

Public sector bodies cannot avoid withholding tax and NICs from PSCs by the use of an agency. The agency is required to operate the 'off payroll' rules and would receive the determination of status from the public sector body to do this.

Managed service companies (MSCs)

6.2   PSCs are typically owned by a single employee/director. Their shareholders would control the company including its finances. However, HMRC considered that the IR35 rules for PSCs also applied to so-called managed service companies (MSCs).

MSCs tended to be structured so that the 'worker' is unlikely to be controlling the company or its finances. Instead, the MSC would generally be controlled by a provider – often referred to as the scheme provider. HMRC found it difficult to apply the IR35 rules to MSCs.

By the time HMRC had established that a PAYE/NIC debt existed within an MSC, the company could avoid that liability by winding up or ceasing to trade and moving its 'workers' into a new MSC. Since MSCs tend to have few if any assets, HMRC would be unable to collect any tax liability that they had determined. New legislation was therefore introduced in *Finance Act 2007* (*ITEPA 2003, Pt 2, Ch 9*) – these provisions take MSCs out of the existing IR35 regime and subject them to a separate code (reviewed in 6.40–6.51). Under the *FA 2007*, any debt of an MSC can be collected from certain third parties. Furthermore, the 'workers' may not be able to claim tax relief for their travel costs to and from their end client.

TAX AVOIDANCE

6.3   Individuals working in a wide variety of industries, from IT to door security, find that they are forced to operate through a company rather than as sole traders, in order to gain work. The limited liability company was seen as a convenient vehicle to protect the client from the strict employment tests, which would normally require the client to treat the worker as an employee and apply PAYE and National Insurance to his invoice. A limited company also gives some protection to the assets of the individual from creditors of the business should the venture fail.

The government perceived that businesses which operated as companies for these reasons and paid out a proportion of their profits as dividends rather than remuneration (as described at 2.12), were deliberately avoiding payment of PAYE/NICs and should be stopped. Such businesses were also viewed as avoiding tax by gaining tax relief for expenses borne by the business which would not be deductible for tax purposes if the work was performed through an employment contract taxed as earnings.

In Autumn 2000, an umbrella body of 'knowledge-based workers', known as the Professional Contractors Group (PCG), demonstrated the strength of opposition to the IR35 regime by bringing a judicial review action. However, the PCG lost their action in both the UK courts (High Court and Court of Appeal) in Autumn 2001 (*R (on the application of Professional Contractors Group Ltd) v IRC* [2002] STC 165) and the European Court of Justice (2002).

CONSEQUENCES OF IR35

Deemed earnings rule for PAYE and NIC

6.4   The apparent intended effect of the IR35 rules is to level the playing field between employees and 'contractors' who work alongside them through personal service companies (PSCs), and who may pay lower NICs on an equivalent amount of income. The anti-avoidance provisions in *ITEPA 2003, ss 48–61* – the IR35 rules – look through the PSC and apply PAYE to income caught by the rules (see 6.23).

Similar rules are contained in the *Social Security Contributions (Intermediaries) Regulations 2000, SI 2000/727* which also bring the deemed employment income received by the PSC within the charge to NICs.

In broad terms, the intermediary 'PSC' must compute the deemed earnings of its 'owner-manager'. This is done by quantifying the income from the company's clients (net of VAT) and deducting various permitted expenses. The net amount is deemed to be pay received by the owner-manager at the end of the tax year which is then subject to PAYE tax and NICs.

However, since 6 April 2017, a radically modified regime applies to PSCs working for public bodies. Broadly, under this 'off-payroll' working regime, the public sector 'engager' must deduct PAYE and NICs from the payments made to the PSC (see 6.1C and 6.1D).

The potential application of IR35 must be taken seriously. When HMRC successfully uphold the IR35 status of a company, the amount of back-tax can be substantial, as demonstrated in *Dragonfly Consulting* [2008] EWHC 2113 where the taxpayer lost and was liable to a tax bill of nearly £100,000.

Office holders

6.4A   Until 6 April 2013, the IR35 rules did not apply where the relationship was only that of an 'office holder'. Thus, for example, non-executive directors who invoiced for their directorships from their PSCs did not have to subject this income to PAYE under the IR35 regime (see 5.9).

However, when it came to light that several senior public sector officials were providing their services through an intermediary (and thereby avoiding NIC), the Government decided to extend the IR35 rules so that they now apply to office-holders, eg directors. From 6 April 2013, where a worker provides services as office-holder they are caught by the IR35 regime. This change affected a large number of *non-executive directors* who typically provide their services through companies. From 6 April 2013, they must apply IR35 to the directors' fees/income received by their companies.

HMRC believe that, for NIC purposes, the IR35 rules have always applied to office-holders although they do not seem to have enforced this in practice. Accordingly, HMRC believe that the change in April 2013 only affects the IR35 tax (and not NIC) legislation.

HMRC were encouraged to abolish the term 'office-holder' by the OTS review of employment status in 2015. However, it declined to do so saying its existence was enshrined in many areas of legislation.

What income is caught?

6.5   The IR35 rules apply to income from 'relevant engagements' performed through a PSC which fulfil certain conditions (see 6.8). Such income (after making certain deductions) will be treated as 'deemed' earnings subject to PAYE tax and NIC. It is the money actually received by the PSC which is considered to be proceeds of the relevant engagement. Any commission which is deducted by an agency before payment of the balance on to the PSC is outside the scope of the IR35 rules.

For these purposes, a relevant engagement is one which is:

- performed personally by the 'personal service' worker;

- under a contract arranged between the client and the PSC;

- in circumstances in which the worker would be classified as an *employee* of the client if the services had been provided directly to the client [*ITEPA 2003, s 49(1)*].

Thus, the key defence to an IR35 challenge by HMRC is for the personal service worker to demonstrate that, if the intermediary company had not been interposed, they would have had a 'self-employment' relationship with the ultimate client.

Since 6 April 2013, where a personal service company supplies the services of an office holder (such as a director), the relevant fees/income will be taxed as deemed earnings under the IR35 calculation (see 6.4A and 6.23). For services supplied before 6 April 2013, the IR35 rules did not apply where the 'worker's' only relationship with the end-user was that of an office-holder.

Employed v self-employed

6.6 Individuals who work for a living are classified as either employed or self-employed. Unfortunately, there is no statutory definition of either term, so a number of tests drawn from case law have to be applied to each circumstance to determine whether the working conditions are those of employment or self-employment when all the facts are considered.

To fall outside the IR35 rules it must be shown that the worker would be self-employed and not employed. HMRC provide guidance about the application of IR35 and helpful information is contained in its guidance *IR56 Employed or self-employed?* which is available in the government archive as detail from the former HMRC website.

In spite of this detailed guidance, each PSC must be examined on its own facts based on the points considered below. One of the problems is that each contract undertaken by the PSC must be looked at separately for tax purposes. If the classification of a particular contract is challenged, the Inspector of Taxes will quote selectively from case law to support their stance, often using older cases which have little bearing on modern working practices.

6.7 It is, therefore, not surprising that IR35 has spawned a long line of cases, each of which add further layers of complexity to the 'employed v self-employed' problem. Determining whether someone is employed or self-employed can often be a murky area for small businesses. These difficulties are clearly demonstrated by the case of *Larkstar Data Ltd* [2008] EWHC 3284. The General Commissioners agreed that a contractor was not caught by IR35. However, HMRC appealed to the High Court, which sent the case back to the General Commissioners for a rehearing. The High Court held they had misdirected themselves in law by failing to consider all the evidence put before them by HMRC!

During the course of its 2013 review, HMRC informed the House of Lords' Personal Service Company Select Committee that £550 million of tax would be at stake should the rules be abolished (see 1.1C). The Select Committee questioned the accuracy of this figure, which was purely an estimate of HMRC. Furthermore, the Committee recommended that since the justification for the retention of the IR35 regime relies 'almost entirely upon this calculation of a deterrent effect, we believe that HMRC should publish a detailed assessment to justify maintaining the IR35 legislation.'

IR35 continues to be an arduous burden for those who consider that they may be potentially within its scope.

Conditions for the company

6.8 A PSC is regarded as a 'relevant intermediary' and thus falls within the IR35 provisions where the worker:

- has a *material interest* in the company; *or*

- receives a payment from the company that is not employment income, but could reasonably be taken to represent earnings from a relevant engagement, such as a dividend [*ITEPA 2003, s 51(1)*].

A material interest is:

- the beneficial ownership of, or the ability directly or indirectly to control more than 5% of the PSC's ordinary share capital;

- possession of, or the right to acquire, more than 5% of the PSC's distributions; or

- entitlement to receive more than 5% of the assets available for distribution among the participators [*ITEPA 2003, s 51(4)*].

The worker's interest in the company includes any shares held by his associates. In this context, an associate includes a husband, wife (or civil partner), parent or remoter forebear, child or remoter issue, brother, sister or business partner. Note that for the purposes of the IR35 rules a 'co-habiting' girlfriend or boyfriend is treated as a spouse [*ITEPA 2003, s 61(4)*].

The 'second limb' for payments that 'could reasonably be taken to represent remuneration' is likely to catch a 'composite service' company that employs many workers (assuming the other IR35 conditions are satisfied). In such cases, each employee will normally have a separate class of shares which entitles them to receive dividends based on the amount the company receives from the client for their respective services. Thus, any dividend effectively represents earnings for services provided by the worker to the client.

Interaction with agency legislation

6.8A   HMRC provided a useful note to deal with concerns about the extension of the agency rules to personal service companies. In the agency legislation (see 5.10C), the 'third party' or agency is any structure interposed between the engager/end-user and the worker.

Consequently, the agency includes employment businesses and PSCs. PSCs therefore need to consider the impact of the agency legislation (in the same way as they did before it was widened by *FA 2014* – see 5.10C).

The post-*FA 2014* agency legislation applies to a worker providing their services through a PSC if all the following conditions are satisfied:

- the worker personally provides, or is personally involved in the provision of, services to another person as a consequence of a contract between that person and a third person;

- the manner in which the worker provides the services is subject to supervision, direction or control by any person;

- earnings are received by the worker for providing the services; and

- the earnings do not constitute employment income apart from under the agency legislation.

Consequently, HMRC considers that the post-*FA 2014* agency rules will *not* generally apply where a worker is engaged via a PSC, as *all* the above criteria will not normally be met. For example:

- the worker must receive earnings as a consequence of providing their services. Therefore, dividends paid to the worker as a genuine consequence of their shareholding in the PSC will not normally fall within the agency rules.

- the agency legislation only applies when the worker receives earnings which does not constitute employment income before the provisions of that legislation are applied. Any actual salary paid to the worker by the PSC is already employment income so the agency provisions would not apply to the earnings.

THE TESTS FOR SELF-EMPLOYMENT

In business on own account

6.9   The overriding fact which the courts have sought to establish is whether an individual is in business on their own account. One of the key distinctions is whether the work is being provided under a:

- 'contract of service' – which implies a master/servant (ie employment) relationship; *or*

- contract for services – in this context the 'services' nomenclature generally contemplates a series of services being provided to different customers by an independent self-employed worker/contractor.

The only practical guidance is the case law that emanates from the relevant cases that are taken to appeal. There is no statutory definition of 'self-employment'.

A number of factors must always be considered when reaching a conclusion as to whether someone is engaged in business on their own account (self-employed), as was pointed out by Mummery LJ in *Hall v Lorimer* [1994] STC 23. In *Walls v Sinnett* [1987] STC 236 the judge emphasised that the facts as a whole must be looked at and that something which is compelling in one case may not be so important in another. The case of *Barnett v Brabyn* [1996] STC 716 is interesting because here HMRC argued, unusually but successfully, that the taxpayer was self-employed.

In *Lewis (t/a MAL Scaffolding) and others v HMRC* [2006] (SSCD) 253, the Special Commissioners again adopted this approach, finding that, on the evidence and the balance of probabilities, scaffolders engaged by Mr Lewis were not employees.

An IT contractor was held to be operating under a contract that would have been an employment one but for the interposed IR35 company in *Island Consultants Ltd v HMRC* [2007] SSCD 700. The IT contractor worked on a customer's five-year project under three-month contracts, which were invariably renewed. He was paid a daily rate and did not receive paid holidays, sick pay or pension contributions which might be useful indicators of self-employment (see 6.17). However, the IT contractor had no other customers and the repeated renewal of the contract indicated a longer term relationship with mutual obligations.

In *Datagate Services Ltd v HMRC* [2008] STC (SCD) 453, a computer software consultant (B) was the sole director and shareholder of a company providing computer consultancy services. B's company entered into a contract with another company, TPS, to provide services to a third company, MBDA. The taxpayer B successfully won on appeal. Applying the IR35 concept, which ignores the two PSCs, the Commissioner found that the taxpayer was 'in business on his own account and was not a person working as an employee in someone else's business'.

The case of *Demibourne Ltd v HMRC* [2005] (SSCD) 667 concerned a hotel maintenance man who retired but continued working in the same capacity, albeit as a self-employed contractor. The Special Commissioner held that there was still an employer-employee relationship and hence PAYE should have been operated by the hotel. The Commissioner said that to change from being an employee to becoming 'self-employed' meant significant changes in practice and working arrangements would have been required .... In this case, the Commissioner also ruled that the employer would be responsible for all the PAYE/NIC, with no 'set-off' or credit being made for the tax that had already been paid by the worker under self-assessment. This triggered considerable widespread difficulties in 're-categorisation' cases which have now largely been resolved.

6.10   In both *Battersby v Campbell* [2001] (SSCD) 189 and *FS Consulting Ltd v McCaul* [2002] (SSCD) 138, the Special Commissioner decided that the substance of the contractual arrangements largely pointed towards the existence of a contract of service (ie employment relationship).

However, in the case of *Lime-IT Ltd v Justin (Officer of the Board of Inland Revenue)* [2003] (SSCD) 15, the taxpayer (Miss Fernley) succeeded in demonstrating sufficient indicators of 'self-employment' to persuade the Special Commissioner that she was working on her own account. The Special Commissioner made the following findings:

●   the client company contracted for specific projects with the contract being terminated when the specified work was completed (in fact, the contract was terminated prematurely) (see 6.17 and 6.19). During the contract Miss Fernley worked for four other clients;

- no significant control was exercised over Miss Fernley's activities (see 6.16);

- monthly invoices were rendered with 30-day terms of payment;

- the PSC (Lime-IT Ltd) and Miss Fernley had to provide their own computer equipment (see);

- there was a genuine right of substitution (even though it had not actually been used) (see 6.14);

- there was a large variation in the hours that were actually worked for the client company each week (with no work being carried out in some weeks);

- Miss Fernley was found not to be 'part and parcel' of the client company's organisation (she had a different security pass from employees, her own business cards and could not enjoy employee benefits).

The *Lime-IT* case illustrates the benefits of having a properly prepared and implemented 'contract for services' and also a taxpayer's passionate determination to uphold it!

In *Larkstar Data Ltd* [2008] EWHC 3284 (see 6.7), HMRC contended that IR35 applied to a company that provided the computer consultancy services of Mr Brill primarily to one client for about two and a half years. Mr Brill had to work exclusively at the client's office for security reasons and thus had to use the client's equipment.

However, Mr Brill did not have any 'employment-type' benefits such as sick and holiday pay and there was limited control over how he performed his work. Furthermore, there was a substitution clause in his contract, which if genuine, is a strong determinant in favour of self-employment, but there were some doubts as to whether this could ever be enforced due to security issues. Mr Brill was outside the company's structure and he was seen as a professionally independent 'contractor'. He was also able to take on other clients, which was also helpful as an indicator of 'self-employment'.

The Commissioners considered that there was no evidence of mutuality of obligation which indicated 'independent contracting' (see 6.11). However, on appeal, the High Court found that they had misdirected themselves on this issue. There were two significant aspects here:

(a) Although Mr Brill was a consultant and there was no 'control' by the client how he carried out work, the Commissioners did not properly consider the authorities referred to by HMRC (such as *Cornwall County Council v Prater*) on this aspect.

(b) One of the findings of fact was that Mr Brill was encouraged to work during the client's core hours, on Mr Brill's own evidence. Had they found that Mr Brill was indeed required to work these hours, the Commissioners' may have concluded this pointed towards employment.

The case was therefore referred back for a second hearing before a different set of Commissioners. However, somewhat surprisingly, it was reported in April 2010 that HMRC has dropped the case with an agreed settlement of £129.79!

Mutuality of obligations

6.11 One of the fundamental attributes of an employment contract is the mutuality of obligations.

Thus, if 'employment' status is to be avoided, it is important that the client or end-user is not obliged to offer work to the PSC, nor is the PSC obliged to accept the work if offered. (Contracts that are worded to 'continue until either party gives notice' would seem to imply actual mutual obligations and this type of wording should be avoided.)

In *Ansell Computer Services Ltd v Richardson* [2004] (SSCD) 472, the Special Commissioner held that the lack of mutual obligations pointed to self-employment status. Other factors also supported this view.

In *Ansell*, the worker was a specialist defence industry software contractor and his PSC provided services (via an agency) to Marconi and British Aerospace. These services involved working on specific defence contracts alongside their permanent employees and other freelance contractors. The PSC's contracts were renewed regularly from one year to the next. However, the worker had complete flexibility over the number of hours worked. Although there was an overriding maximum number of hours for the engagement, there was no minimum requirement and the worker was not obliged to 'put in' a particular number of hours each day or week. Other factors supporting 'self-employed' status were the right to appoint a substitute (although this was unlikely to be exercised in practice) and the various practical differences between the freelance workers and the regular employees (such as lack of sick pay/holiday pay, etc).

Ansell usefully demonstrates that each case must be subjectively judged on its own facts. Although there were few indicators of being 'in business on own account', these facets were not really typical for someone engaged on secret projects in secure premises.

6.11A *Cornwall County Council v Prater* [2006] EWCA Civ 102 involved a home tutor engaged by the Council to teach children at home. The home tutor simply performed whatever engagements the council gave to her, without any guarantee of work. However, Justice Mummery held that this made no difference –

> '… once a contract was entered into and while that contract continued, she was under an obligation to teach the pupil and Council was under an obligation to pay her …. That was all that was legally necessary to support the finding that each individual teaching engagement was a contract of service'.

Financial risk

6.12   The degree of financial risk an individual takes with their business is an indication of self-employment. If their own money is invested in the business to buy capital assets or services that the business needs, there is a risk that the business may not generate the funds to cover the outlay.

For example, an individual may undertake a training course in the hope that the cost of the course will be covered by the additional fees they will be able to charge based on their improved knowledge. However, there is no guarantee that they will be able to gain work after the course to repay the investment. Even the issuing of an invoice to secure payment involves a small financial risk as the invoice might not be paid, or there may be some delay in payment.

In *Autoclenz v Belcher* [2011] UKSC 41, the workers were obliged to pay for their own insurance and other expenses. However, there were detailed arrangements for them to purchase their equipment and supplies from the company for a fixed percentage of their income and the company prepared their invoices on their behalf. Amidst other factors, this led the Supreme Court to decide that there was an employment relationship (see also 6.37).

Profit from sound management

6.13   If an individual is paid by the task they may be able to increase the profit made from that job by completing the task in a shorter time. The power to organise the work and perform tasks more efficiently is an indication of self-employment. If there is a real prospect of making a loss on any particular assignment the indication of self-employment is stronger (*Market Investigations Ltd v Minister of Social Security* [1968] 3 All ER 732).

Right of substitution

6.14   The issue of substitution is likely to be crucial for many PSCs. The fact that an individual can choose whether to complete a contract personally or send a substitute is a strong indication of self-employment. It should be stressed that the right to supply a substitute must be a real one which must be agreed by the client.

In the employment tribunal case, *Express and Echo Publications Ltd v Tanton* [1999] IRLR 367, it was enough that the contract allowed the individual to send a substitute to complete the task to conclude that the contract was for services and thus a self-employment rather than an employment. In *First Word Software Ltd v HMRC* [2008] STC (SCD) 389, the individual worked solely for one company for one year on a specified software project, and was still held to be self-employed due to a substitution clause in the contract. Other factors also supported this view. On the other hand, in another employment tribunal case, *Glasgow City Council v Mrs MacFarlane and Mrs Skivington*, the women had a limited right to substitution in their contracts but were still found to be employees.

The Court in *Dragonfly Consultancy Ltd v HMRC* [2008] EWHC 2113 was sceptical about the use of 'substitution' clauses which the end user would not accept. Dragonfly had various consecutive contracts with an agency over a three-year period to supply an IT tester (Mr Bessell – its sole director) to an end user client. However, the High Court held that it was unrealistic to suppose that the end user would ever have agreed to an unqualified right of substitution – they 'wanted Mr Bessell'! The taxpayer's case primarily failed because of the lack of effective right of substitution in the contract – Mr Bessell was effectively required to perform the work personally.

The Special Commissioner in *Castle Construction (Chesterfield) v HMRC* [2009] STC (SCD) 97 was even more sceptical when he commented:

'it is quite common for advisers to insert 'substitution' clauses into contracts, or into the final contract with the client in IR35 ('intermediary') cases, obviously in an effort to diminish the impression that the relationship is one of employment … In many cases, the substitution clauses inserted have been qualified by the requirement that the counter-party must consent to the choice of substitute … I consider that in the present case the clause was broadly nonsense, with no attention to reality … it seems to me that the substitution clause was a fiction, designed by an adviser, or the draftsman of some precedent document, to enhance the 'non-employee' case, and that on the facts of this case, that endeavour fails, and is if anything (by suggesting the need to resort to such artificiality) counter-productive'.

In *Autoclenz v Belcher* [2011] UKSC 41, the Supreme Court found that, on a true construction of the actual working arrangements, the work had to be done by the workers and they could not provide substitutes (even though the written contract gave a right of substitution). In practice, it was concluded that there was no possibility that the workers would provide a substitute. However, the Supreme Court clearly stated that if a genuine right of substitution exists, the worker cannot be an employee (see also 6.37).

Control

6.15   HMRC tend to place a lot of emphasis on this aspect of the working relationship. The Inspector will examine the extent of the client's ability to control the worker. The operation of actual control is largely irrelevant – it is the right to control that is important. If the client can move the worker from task to task and specify how the work is to be done, in addition to where and when the work is to be performed, an extensive right of control is being exercised. Alternatively, if the client has no power to shift the worker on to different tasks but requires regular reports on the task to be submitted, there is only a limited right of control.

Cable & Wireless Plc v Muscat [2006] EWCA Civ 220 was a case begun at the Employment Appeal Tribunal, concerning the unfair dismissal claim of an individual who provided services to Cable & Wireless through a PSC. It was held at the Court of Appeal that the essentials of a contract of employment were the obligation to provide work for remuneration and the obligation to perform it, coupled with control by the 'employer'. It did not matter whether the arrangements for payment were made directly or indirectly – there was an implied contract between the worker and the end-user, and they were entitled to rights as an employee.

This could have a fundamental effect on the IR35 regulations, as implying a contract between the end-user and the worker would bypass any intermediary companies and hence IR35 could not apply. If an implied contract exists, the worker is an employee and would be subject to PAYE tax and NIC in the normal way. There is, therefore, currently uncertainty regarding the application of IR35 in such cases.

Cable & Wireless v Muscat obviously has an impact on both clients and employment agencies. They now face uncertainty as to whether they will be liable for unexpected PAYE tax and NIC (as well as the possibility of employment rights claims from workers previously supposed to be self-employed).

The case of *Pimlico Plumbers Limited v Smith* (UKEAT/2014/0495) considered whether Pimlico had sufficient control over its 125 'contractors'. The workers were required to wear a uniform, to drive vans with the Pimlico logo and could only be contacted by customers through Pimlico. Contracts and estimates were issued in the name of Pimlico and payment was made to Pimlico. Pimlico also monitored the movements of operatives through a GPS system on their vans. Despite this level of control, Mr Smith's written contract said that he was in business on his own account, he took the financial risk on when invoices would be paid, and supplied his own insurance and tools. However, despite this level of business risk, the EAT found he was *not* self-employed since he had limited substitution rights as any 'shift swap' had to be approved by Pimlico.

Provision of equipment or premises

6.16   If a worker provides their own tools and equipment to perform the relevant tasks, they are more likely to be self-employed, particularly if the items provided are large (*Ready Mixed Concrete (South East) Ltd v Minister of Pensions and National Insurance* [1968] 2 QB 497).

If a certain amount of the work is performed at premises controlled by the PSC rather than the client, the contract has more chance of falling outside the IR35 provisions. In *Tax Bulletin, Issue 45*, Example 2 shows that the fact that an engineer working largely at home using his own computer and office equipment is a strong pointer to self-employment. However, the occasional choice to work at home using one's own equipment will not make an employed worker self-employed.

Basis of payment

6.17　It is normal for employees to have paid holidays, sick pay, maternity pay and long service bonuses. HMRC will view any payment of overtime as an indication of employment. A fixed payment for a particular task is an indication of self-employment. However, piecework or commission payments can apply to both employment and self-employment. The lack of employee benefits such as a company sick pay does not necessarily mean that the worker is self-employed, as many short-term employments do not carry these advantages.

Intention

6.18　If there was no intention by either of the parties to create an employment, this will be treated as a pointer to self-employment (*Massey v Crown Life Insurance Co* [1978] ICR 590). If all the other factors of the working relationship are neutral, the intention of the parties may be the decisive factor in 'employment status' cases.

Long-term contract

6.19　HMRC place a high degree of significance on the length of a particular engagement when deciding whether it will fall within the IR35 rules or not. Note that it is the total engagement with the particular client that is normally examined, not the length of each contract. One engagement may be made up of several short contracts, or an initial short contract that is extended.

Standard agency contracts

6.20　Workers who use agencies to obtain contracts for them to work through their own PSC often rely on standard contracts drawn up by those agencies. These contracts tend to require the contractor to:

(*a*)　perform the work at a location specified by the client;

(*b*)　spend at least a given number of hours per week on the task;

(*c*)　be remunerated at an agreed hourly rate or daily rate;

(*d*)　keep a timesheet checked and authorised by the client; and

(*e*)　be subject to the direction of the client.

The *IR Press Release* dated 7 February 2000 stated that where such a standard contract is used for a period of one month or more the Revenue view is that the contract falls within the IR35 rules.

The 'employment' cases of *Franks v Reuters Ltd and First Employment Ltd* [2003] EWCA Civ 417 and *Dacas v Brook Street Bureau (UK) Ltd* and *Wandsworth London Borough Council* [2004] EWCA Civ 217 both held that, where a worker 'worked' through an employment agency, an employment relationship had still been established between the worker and the end-user. In both cases, the worker had worked on a 'long-term' basis for one specific customer and thus had been largely integrated into the end user's business.

This reasoning was followed in *Muscat v Cable & Wireless plc* [2006] EWCA Civ 220, where Mr Muscat's PSC supplied his services to Cable & Wireless through an agency (see 6.15). Subsequently, Cable & Wireless terminated the contract with the agency. The Court of Appeal upheld Mr Muscat's compensation claim for unfair dismissal ruling that he was an employee and implied contracts were imposed to grant him employment rights.

Following these developments, it is quite possible that, where an arrangement falls within IR35, it could now be treated as an actual employment rather than deemed employment. If this is the case, the 'end-user' could well have an obligation to apply PAYE tax and NIC (rather than the PSC 'intermediary'). The changes to IR35 engagements in the public sector from April 2017 outlined above will achieve this move of liability to the end-user (see 6.1C).

Summary and other factors

6.21   Based on the indicators of 'self-employment v employment' set out in 6.4 to 6.20 above, it is helpful to summarise some of the key determinants that should be considered when determining whether IR35 will apply in relation to any particular situation.

- How many clients does the 'worker' have?

- What is the intention of the parties?

- How long does the contract last and what are its terms? (eg is there a notice period, specified hours of work, where and how is the work carried out?)

- Does the contract contain an 'employee-type' pay structure, such as hourly rate, fixed pay, holiday pay, and employee-type benefits?

- Is the worker paid an agreed fee for a particular project stage and are there performance deadlines etc?

- Are any benefits provided similar to employees (company car/van, sick pay bonuses etc)?

- What is the degree of the worker's financial risk in the project and do they have to rectify work at their own cost?

- Does the worker provide their own equipment etc. on site?

- Does the worker have a genuine ability to provide a 'substitute' to carry out the work in their place?

- Is the worker integrated into the client's business?

HMRC will also look at factors outside the immediate working relationship to determine the status of a particular contract. It will look at past contracts, if appropriate, and consider the individual's business characteristics, for example, whether they advertise their services or undertake other expenditure to win work.

Some of these factors were recently explored in *ECR Consulting Ltd v Revenue & Customs* [2011] UKFTT 313 (TC), which found that the contractor did not establish an employment relationship with the end-user:

- *Substitution* – The end-user (VDS) used their contractors on the basis that they could obtain the best advice at the most reasonable price. VDS relied on the Agency to provide the contractors. The Tribunal felt it was immaterial who was appointed, so long as they had the necessary skills.

- *Best price negotiated* – VDS were prepared to negotiate the best price at the time, which was £600 for the first contract and almost half that amount for the second contract. There is a clear finding that it would not have been possible to control an 'employee's' pay in this way and a contract of service would make no such provision.

- *Control* – The Tribunal found that VDS had no 'real' control over the way in which Miss Richardson worked. VDS accepted invoices showing 37.5 hours worked but her internal records showed that the actual working hours varied from week to week. This is consistent with a contract at a fixed agreed price.

- *Mutuality of obligations* – The termination provisions made it clear that there was no obligation on either party to employ the other or work for the other. This was demonstrated when Miss Richardson refused initially to work for VDS and also when VDS subsequently terminated the first contract prematurely. Again, this kind of provision would not have featured in a contract of services.

Business entity tests

6.22 HMRC introduced business entity tests to adopt a risk-based approach to the IR35 legislation provide greater levels of certainty. However, these tests were withdrawn on 6 April 2015.

Interaction with auto-enrolment

6.22A Since July 2012, all employers have progressively been drawn into the obligation to provide a workplace pension to eligible workers. The definition of 'worker' is broader than employee. Thus, for example, as in the case of *Muscat* (see 6.15 above) where an individual is found to be a worker in terms of employment rights, this may have a persuasive effect on HMRC or in any tax tribunal hearing.

This risk has been amplified by the employment tribunal case of *Aslam, Farrar and Others v Uber (Case reference 2202551/2015 & Others),* which concluded that the 'Uber' drivers were workers (as opposed to self-employed contractors) – this case goes to appeal in September 2017. A similar finding was also reached in *Dewhurst v Citysprint UK Ltd ET/2202512/2016.*

No case law has yet established a period of time after a contract has ended that would prevent individuals taking a case to an employment tribunal on the basis that during the engagement they were (at the very least) workers and so should have received holiday pay, sick pay and now more expensively, employer pension contributions.

This risk of re-categorisation as a 'worker' adds another dimension to the issue of employment status as it now involves the Pension Regulator as well as HMRC. The Regulator has stressed that, while the definition of worker has many interactions with HMRC's view of employment, there will be individuals who, whilst correctly not being paid under PAYE, are still classed as 'workers' under employment law and, as such, they must be assessed for auto-enrolment purposes.

A number of exclusions to the auto-enrolment of workers were introduced in April 2016. HMRC and The Pension Regulator have made it clear that PSCs caught by the new 'off payroll' rules are not workers for auto-enrolment purposes since they will have been given a staging date in their own right as an independent business

IR35 DEEMED EMPLOYMENT PAYMENT AND PAYE/NIC CALCULATIONS

Deemed employment payment

6.23 The IR35 provisions treat the net income arising from the company's relevant engagements (see 6.5) as the employment income of the worker who performed the engagement, subject to the permitted deductions listed at 6.24 [*ITEPA 2003, s 54*]. From 6 April 2013, income received from directorships and other offices must also be included as 'IR35 income' (see 6.4A).

It is the money actually received by the PSC that is considered to be proceeds of the relevant engagement. Any commission which is deducted by an agency before payment of the balance on to the PSC is outside the scope of the IR35 rules.

The permitted deductions include any salary and benefits that were paid to the worker (excluding VAT) during the tax year. All these amounts are deducted from the net income from relevant engagements to arrive at the worker's deemed IR35 employment payment. This is treated as paid on 5 April (the last day of the relevant tax year), with PAYE and NICs due 14 days later. The value of any taxable benefits provided directly by the final client to the worker is added when calculating the deemed employment payment.

Permitted deductions

6.24   The permitted deductions are:

(*a*)   a general deduction equal to 5% of the *gross* receipts from relevant engagements (net of VAT) to cover all the other costs of running the company including seeking other work;

(*b*)   normal expenses of employment allowable under *ITEPA 2003, s 336* and other deductions allowed by *ITEPA 2003, Pt 5, Chs 1–5*, such as professional indemnity insurance premiums and professional subscriptions (from 6 April 2016, travel to an engagement is classed as 'home to work' travel and is not allowable- see 6.24A below);

(*c*)   capital allowances on equipment which is wholly, exclusively and necessarily purchased for the performance of a relevant engagement [*CAA 2001, s 262*];

(*d*)   employer's contributions paid to an approved pension scheme or personal pension scheme;

(*e*)   employer's NICs (including Class 1A NICs) due on actual remuneration and benefits in kind (but not where they are covered by the £3,000 NIC employment allowance if it is able to be claimed by the PSC – only the amount actually paid to HMRC can be claimed);

(*f*)   the final amount of employer's NICs due on the deemed employment payment; and

(*g*)   the total of the payments and benefits received by the worker during the year [*ITEPA 2003, s 54*].

'Home to work' travel and subsistence payments

6.24A   Since 6 April 2016, individuals within IR35 who work through a PSC, umbrella company or an agency are subject to special restrictions. They cannot deduct 'home to work' travel and subsistence costs where they are subject to supervision, direction or control (SDC) of anyone in the contractual chain.

This restriction extends to contracts where there is a right to SDC even if it is not exercised. Workers will therefore have to prove they are not under SDC if they wish to claim these travel and subsistence costs, as HMRC will automatically assume that SDC applies.

Since April 2015 intermediaries are required to make a quarterly RTI returns of their 'workers' and amounts paid 'gross' so this will raise the visibility of such payments.

HMRC guidance on SDC can be found at www.gov.uk/government/publications/employment-intermediaries-personal-services-and-supervision-direction-or-control/employment-intermediaries-personal-services-and-supervision-direction-or-control.

6.25   There is no requirement to demonstrate that the costs covered by the 5% deduction for the general expenses of running the PSC have actually been incurred. This additional deduction will be allowed in all cases.

For example, the cost of training paid for by the PSC is not permitted as a separate deduction. Training expenses must be covered by the 5% general deduction, or paid for directly by the customer company (see Statement from the Paymaster General available on HMRC's website – www.hmrc.gov.uk/ir35/pmgltr.htm now in the HMRC archive).

Capital allowances on equipment which does not meet the 'wholly, exclusively and necessarily' test cannot be deducted for the deemed employment income calculation, but they remain deductible for corporation tax purposes. Thus, a PSC that owns a significant amount of equipment may easily make a trading loss (for corporation tax purposes) if all, or most, of its income is derived from relevant engagements.

Example 1

IR35 calculations – comprehensive worked example of deemed employment income and PAYE/NIC

Henry (who is over 21 and not an apprentice!) owns 100% of Thierry Ltd, which makes up its accounts to 5 April each year. All of the income received by the company is from relevant 'employment' engagements in the private sector. The company's results for year to 5 April 2018 are:

	£	£
Income received (net of VAT)		80,000
Expenses:		
'Non-allowable' travelling and subsistence costs	3,020	
Accountancy and company secretarial costs	3,000	
Telephone, internet and stationery	1,500	
Salary paid to Henry	11,500	
Employer's NI on salary (£11,500 – £8,164) × 13.8%	460	
Employer pension contributions	2,500	
Total expenses		21,980
Net profit before tax		58,020

Calculation of deemed employment payment

	£	£
Receipts in the tax year		80,000
Less:		
Salary + NICs paid in year (£11,500 + £460)	11,960	
Employer's pension contribution	2,500	
General expense deduction – 5% × £80,000	4,000	
		18,460
Deemed employment income		61,540

Accounting for deemed employment income and PAYE/NIC

	£	£
Deemed employment income (including secondary NICs)	61,540.00	
Employer's NIC (£ 61,540 × 13.8%/113.8%)	(7,462.67)	7,462.67
Deemed gross employment income	54,077.33	
Employee's Class 1 NICs:		
£45,000 – £11,500 (salary) = £33,500 × 12%	4,020.00	
£20,577.33 × 2%	411.55	4,431.55
PAYE:		
Basic rate: £33,500 × 20% (NB personal allowance 2017/18 is £11,500, ie amount of salary)	6,700.00	
Higher rate: (£54,077 – £33,500) = £20,577 × 40%	8,230.80	14,930.80
Total payment due to HMRC		26,825.02

PAYE payment

6.26   A director whose PSC is subject to the IR35 rules has to report any deemed employment payment on the month 12 Full Payment Submission due by 5 April with a final year end declaration by 19 April. It is accepted that this timetable is tight, so by concession HMRC will allow personal service companies to submit estimated figures for the amount of PAYE and NICs due (and pay this estimate over) on the deemed employment payment by 5 April, with accurate figures submitted by the following 31 January using an Earlier Year Update (EYU) with any balancing payment of PAYE and NICs paid over by the same date.

If no salary payments are made during the year a nil payment Employer Payment Summary (EPS) must be filed each month, or a 'nil activity' EPS in advance for between 1 and 12 months.

Interest on underpaid PAYE and NICs will run from 19 April to 31 January, but penalties will not be charged under *TMA 1970, s 98A* if the above procedures have been complied with and the final figures are provided by 31 January following the tax year end.

The deemed employment payment must be shown on the individual's P60 that they must receive by 31 May.

Deduction for corporation tax

6.27   The deemed employment payment is treated as made on 5 April whether or not it is actually paid, so it can only be deducted from the corporation tax profits for the accounting period covering that 5 April [*FA 2000, Sch 12, para 17(2)*].

This could create cash flow problems for companies with a 31 December or 31 March year end. For such companies, there can be no deduction in the corporation tax computation for any deemed employment income treated as paid on the 5 April following the company year end. For this reason, many companies will want to review the date of their year-end to ensure a matching corporate tax deduction is available in the same period.

Double taxation trap

6.28   If the deemed earnings are actually paid out after 5 April, further PAYE and NICs become due on the actual payment, because paying PAYE and NICs on the deemed employment payment treated as paid on 5 April does not frank a subsequent salary payment. The same salary is thus subject to PAYE and NICs twice. On the other hand, if the deemed employment income is extracted from the company by way of a dividend, the double taxation can be relieved by the company making a claim to reduce the amount of dividend taxed in the shareholder's hands (see 6.32).

Investigation

6.29   It has been reported that HMRC have been drawing together their specialist IR35 teams with a view to addressing concerns about the use of PSCs to avoid employment taxes and NICs.

HMRC can raise an employment income tax and National Insurance charge on any underpaid PAYE and NICs arising on a deemed employment payment, plus interest and penalties, due from 19 April following the end of the tax year during which it was deemed to have been paid. If the company does not meet its obligations to pay over the tax, NICs and penalties due, HMRC can collect the amounts due directly from the employee/shareholder.

VAT

6.30   Any VAT the PSC charges on relevant engagements is not included in the calculation of the deemed employment income of the contractor. If the turnover of the PSC is above the VAT threshold it must register for VAT and account for VAT on all its supplies, including the amounts invoiced for relevant engagements. The PSC may well find itself having to keep two sets of accounting records, one for VAT purposes and one for the IR35 rules, with the latter having a much more restricted range of allowable expenses.

Contractors in the construction industry

6.31   The IR35 rules can apply to PSCs operating in the construction industry, who may also be subcontractors themselves subject to the tax deduction system for the construction industry (CIS).

Under the CIS scheme, the company 'sub-contractor' is paid net of either a 0/20/30 per cent tax deduction by the contractor, depending on the sub-contractor's status. The income from the contract would be included as gross in the deemed earnings payment and hence subject to PAYE and NIC on top of the 'CIS tax' already withheld by the main contractor. However, the pressure on the company's cash flow can be reduced by offsetting the tax withheld from amounts received under the CIS scheme (taxed as deemed IR35 earnings) from the company's own tax payments of corporation tax, PAYE, NICs and so on. Clearly, such potential cash flow issues should not arise if a company can ensure that it is paid on a 'gross' basis under the CIS.

PROBLEMS WITH IR35

Extracting funds

Dividends

6.32   Any dividends paid by a PSC are ignored in the calculation of the deemed employment income under the IR35 rules. If the dividend is paid out of income from relevant engagements, the income will first be subject to PAYE and NICs before being taxed again in the hands of the shareholder. Dividend taxation is dealt with in Chapter 9.

This double tax charge is relieved by the PSC making a claim to reduce the value of the dividend by the amount of the deemed employment income [*ITEPA 2003, s 58*].

Off-payroll working interaction

6.32A   Where a salary is extracted from the PSC that relates to monies paid to the PSC by the relevant public sector body 'engager', this should be taken by the owner free of tax and NIC and reported on this basis on the full payment submission (see 6.1D).

Other employees

6.33   If the PSC employs people who are direct fee earners, the full employment costs are deductible for corporation tax purposes, but are not deductible in the calculation of the deemed employment income to the extent that those costs exceed the permitted 5% allowance. The PSC is obliged to pay PAYE and NICs in full on the employee's wages, but such costs will have to be met out of the deemed employment income of the contractor, so PAYE and NICs will be charged twice on the same income. There is no relief for this double tax charge.

Other contractors

6.34   Where there are two or more employees who perform relevant engagements within a PSC, the receipts need to be divided between them on a 'just and reasonable basis' to determine the deemed employment income of each worker. If the PSC apportions the receipts in a way which HMRC believe is not reasonable, the Inspector can reapportion the money and demand tax from the company according to their own apportionment. The company can appeal against HMRC's decision, but this power introduces another level of uncertainty into the calculation of the deemed employment income.

Mixture of work

6.35   Personal service companies that receive income from relevant engagements as well as other sources need to apportion their gross receipts and expenses between the sources subject to IR35 and those sources outside these rules. This may involve keeping records on a project or contract-by-contract basis.

Example 2

Apportionment between IR35 income and other income

Richard writes software which is marketed through his PSC, Wright IT Ltd. However, as the sales of the software can be volatile Richard also works as an IT contractor through the same company.

An apportionment of income and expenses is likely to be required between the software receipts (which are not deemed employment income under the IR35 rules) and the contracting work (which may be subject to the IR35 regime).

Solutions

Seeking an opinion from HMRC

6.36   Taxpayers who are uncertain about the status of contracts performed through their personal service companies may seek an opinion from HMRC. Such queries should be addressed to the specialised HMRC office:

HM Revenue and Customs IR35 Customer Service Unit S0733 NE98 1ZZ Newcastle Upon Tyne United Kingdom

Tel No: 0300 123 2326 email: ir35@hmrc.gov.uk

A copy of the signed contract should be posted or faxed to the above address, together with relevant information such as:

- details of other work performed recently through the same PSC (with other clients too);

- written statements from the worker and client about how the contract is carried out;

- how the work was procured including copies of adverts, any job specification, tenders made by the client if any;

- any contractual terms not included in the written contract however entered into

- how work is allocated and the role of the workers with the client's organisation and any equipment supplied by the worker

The contractor must also supply his own National Insurance number, the tax reference number of his company and the postcode of its registered office. These details may also be submitted by e-mail to ir35@hmrc.gsi.gov.uk, with the subject line containing the tax reference number of the company followed by the company's postcode.

HMRC aim to provide a reply to requests directed through the IR35 Unit within 28 days of receiving all the details. HMRC will provide a confirmation letter with a unique reference number that will be valid for three years. If, HMRC open an IR35 review, this number can be provided to HMRC and it and will suspend the review while all the relevant information is considered. In the event of any disagreement with HMRC's decision, with an independent review can be requested from another HMRC 'status' officer. Note that HMRC will not give any advice on a *proposed* contract, so the contract must already have been signed and agreed by the parties before an Inspector is prepared to examine its terms.

If there is no written contract governing the terms of the worker's engagement, the worker should write to HMRC setting out the terms and conditions that have been agreed with the client. The client will also need to confirm that it has agreed such terms in a separate letter.

Form of contract

6.37   In the past, the contract between the PSC and the client or end-user has been a key document when determining the tax treatment of the receipts from that contract, unless it was clearly a 'sham' or did not reflect the actual terms of the relationship between the parties.

The Supreme Court decision in *Autoclenz v Belcher* [2011] UKSC 41 represents a marked shift in the law relating to the construction of written contracts between engagers and their workers (see also 6.12 and 6.14). The Supreme Court ruling demonstrates that the courts are able to adopt a more purposive approach and look at the real agreement between the parties and how they have conducted themselves in practice.

In *Autoclenz*, the company considered that its team of car valeters were self-employed and engaged them under explicit contracts of self-employment. On the other hand, the valeters claimed to be workers and so entitled to holiday pay and the National Minimum Wage.

The company disputed their claim and the case was initially taken to the Employment Tribunal. Ultimately, the Supreme Court ruled that the workers were employees, despite the existence of the 'self-employment' contracts.

The normal contract law rule is that the written contract is normally determinative and this principle holds good for commercial contracts. However, the *Autoclenz* judgement shows that the courts have more latitude to disregard the terms included in written contract between engagers and workers. This is because of the parties' unequal bargaining power, and the fact that the written contract is almost invariably provided by the engager.

In *Autclenz*, it was found that the actual written contract did not accurately reflect the actual arrangements between the company and its valeters across a number of the tests of employment. There was no mention in the contracts of any mutuality of obligation but the terms agreed outside of the contract were that Autoclenz was obliged to offer work to the valeters and they were obliged to carry it out, which bore the hallmarks of employment.

6.37A   Both legal and tax issues will be relevant when determining whether a particular arrangement is likely to fall within the IR35 regime. Thus, ideally both a lawyer and a taxation practitioner should review the draft contract. The contract and the actual arrangements between the parties should contain as many attributes providing strong indications of self-employment as possible to escape from the IR35 rules (see the decision in *Lime-IT Ltd v Justin (Officer of the Board of Inland Revenue)* [2003] (SSCD) 15). These would include:

- fixed term – if the job is not completed within the original term or a further task is found, a separate contract should be drawn up;

- short period of engagement – long-term engagements covering periods of more than six months are taken as an indication of employment;

- fixed price – the PSC bears the risk of a reduced profit margin if the work is not completed on time;

- the right to send a substitute;

- the use of equipment and premises provided by the PSC;

- evidence of the intention of the parties not to create an employment;

- no provision for attributes of employment such as sick pay, holiday pay, overtime rates, or benefits such as reserved parking;

- no restrictions on the worker performing other work during or for a period after the term of the contract.

The written contract will be ineffective if the *actual* performance of the work and the relationship between the worker and client tell a different story. This point was confirmed in *Netherlane Ltd v York* [2005] (SSCD) 305. Making the normal IR35 assumption that the services are being provided directly, it is only possible to determine whether the worker is self-employed or is operating under a contract of service by looking at the entire relationship. See also 6.21 for a review of key indicators of employment and self-employment.

Although the actual contractual arrangements are indicative, it is also necessary to look at all the other circumstances in which the services are being performed. In this case, the worker acted as a team leader on the company's premises (for seven days a week) and reported to a named supervisor. There was little evidence that he was in business on his own account (other than by providing his own laptop and mobile phone).

A PAYE audit team investigating a PSC will normally visit the premises where the work is actually carried out to determine the facts of the working arrangement.

Pension contributions

6.38 Where a worker/contractor has operated for many years through his PSC drawing large dividends and a small employment income, his pension fund may be relatively low. This is because dividends cannot be used as a basis to pay a company pension or personal pension contributions.

The deemed IR35 employment income counts as 'earnings' for pensions purposes, which means the worker can pay personal contributions of up to 100% of their earnings, restricted, where appropriate, to the annual 'input' allowance of £40,000 (or lower amount if the input allowance has been tapered down) , which can be increased by any available carried-forward relief under the 'three-year' rule . Any pension contributions made in excess of this limit will trigger a 'clawback' tax charge at the individual's marginal income tax rate applied to the 'excess' over the allowance (see 10.23 to 10.24).

Any *company* pension contributions can be deducted in calculating the deemed earnings for IR35 purposes. Similarly, such contributions can be made without any NIC cost. Under the post-5 April 2011 pensions regime, the worker can arrange for pension contributions to be paid by their company, but these are also subject to the annual allowance rules. For further commentary, see Chapter 10.

Offshore companies

6.39 Working on relevant engagements in the UK through a PSC registered overseas does not avoid the IR35 provisions. The place where the work is performed determines if the individual would be subject to UK PAYE and NICs and if the engagement would be treated as an employment, then it will fall within the IR35 rules.

If an offshore company supplies a contractor to perform a relevant engagement in the UK, but fails to deduct the PAYE and NICs required under the IR35 rules, HMRC may take action to recover the tax due from the contractor. In addition, any assets of the offshore company located in the UK may be seized as part of an action to recover unpaid tax.

MANAGED SERVICE COMPANIES

Background to *FA 2007* legislation

6.40 MSCs are similar to PSCs, in that they are companies through which individuals offer their services to an end client. However, whereas a PSC is likely to have a single shareholder and director, a managed service company (MSC) is likely to act on behalf of a number of individuals and therefore the worker/shareholder is unlikely to be controlling the company or its finances. Typically, workers in an MSC do not exercise any control over the company – control lies in the hands of the provider of the MSC (known as the scheme provider). MSC scheme providers tend to be companies which provide the structure and are responsible for the administration and running of the company.

The *FA 2007* legislation (inserted in *ITEPA 2003, Pt 2,Ch 9*), is HMRC's response to the widespread tax avoidance created through the growth in MSCs – a problem which apparently involves around 240,000 workers including teachers, nurses and train drivers. HMRC estimate that if the new legislation had not been introduced, the potential 'tax revenue' loss in 2007/08 would have been in the region of £350 million.

6.41 MSCs have been used to sidestep the original stringent IR35 rules. They typically involve a 'provider' who sets the company up and runs it on behalf of the workers. The *FA 2007* targets the 'provider' – in HMRC's view, the relevant 'workers' are only operating through a service company because there is a provider who is willing to run and manage the company (for a decent fee!).

HMRC have declared that using the IR35 rules to deal with this growing avoidance problem in the service sector would be far too labour-intensive. This would inevitably involve a time consuming 'contract-by-contract' analysis to determine whether there is a disguised employment. Under the *ITEPA 2003, Pt 2, Ch 9* MSC rules, the countering tax charge is triggered simply by the presence of a provider – without the need to unravel the underlying contracts.

6.42 The legislation therefore aims to identify any companies that are managed by a provider. Although there are a number of different company structures, MSCs often use so called 'alphabet shares' with A shares being issued to worker A, B shares to worker B and so on. This enables the workers net income (after certain deductions) to be channelled to them as tax-efficient dividend income. However, where a company falls within the *FA 2007* regime, this dividend income is deemed to be earnings for both PAYE and NIC purposes (see 6.44). HMRC consider this to be a far more efficient approach and, given the growing avoidance problem, justifies the wider-ranging *ITEPA 2003, Pt 2, Ch 9* regime.

In the past, even where HMRC established that an MSC was caught under the IR35 'intermediaries' legislation, any enforcement action taken to collect the outstanding PAYE/NIC due debt often proved fruitless since these companies generally had few assets. It was also easy for such companies to cease trading and for workers to be moved into a new MSC.

Typical MSC structures

6.43   Various structures have been adopted in practice – but under a typical MSC scheme the workers would obtain their work engagements through an agency (in a similar way to those who operate PSCs). A common 'composite company' structure (which would be targeted by the *FA 2007*) is illustrated below:

Typical Managed Service Company Structure

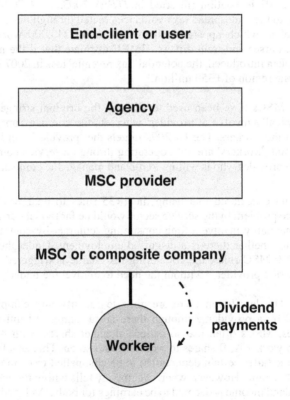

Notes:

1   The agency would typically pay the MSC scheme provider for the work – the contract would be between the agency and the composite company. There would be a separate contract between the scheme provider and the composite company;

2   In the composite company several otherwise 'unrelated' workers (HMRC estimate they typically number between 10 and 20) are made worker/shareholders of the company. Each worker would usually be paid the National Minimum Wage and hold a different class of share. This would enable the company to pay different rates of dividends to each worker (which would be linked to the amount paid by each relevant end client in respect of that worker)

3   The worker is treated as having the employment with the MSC. Under the pre-6 April 2016 rules, this enabled the workers to claim tax relief for the cost of travel from 'home' to the workplace on the basis that this was a temporary place of work. This 'facility' has now generally been blocked (see 6.49).

4   The scheme provider would charge a fee for arranging payments to the composite company. The scheme provider would normally also exercise control of the composite company rather than the workers/shareholders.

Offshore MSCs

6.44   The MSC legislation in *ITEPA 2003, Pt 2, Ch 9* also catches offshore MSCs, where both the relevant services are provided in the UK and the worker is resident in UK. Where these two conditions are met, HMRC considers that the MSC has a place of business in the UK, whether or not it in fact does.

If an offshore MSC fails to apply the legislation, HMRC can determine the PAYE and NICs that should have been accounted for and can recover the liability from the third parties listed in 6.50 should the offshore MSC not meet its liability.

Identifying a 'tainted' Managed Service Company

Key MSC tests

6.45   A MSC company will fall within *ITEPA 2003, Pt 2, Ch 9* where it meets *all* the following criteria:

- Its business consists wholly or mainly of providing a worker's services to others.

- More than half of the company's income is paid out to the worker in some form.

- The method used to pay the worker (principally by way of dividend) increases the net amount received by the worker (as compared with the amount that would have been given if every amount was earnings from an employment).

- An MSC provider (or associate) is *involved* with the company (an MSC provider is defined as a person who carries on a business of promoting or facilitating the use of companies to provide the services of individuals).

6.46 The involvement of an MSC provider is likely to be a very sensitive 'trigger' condition, and for these purposes an MSC (or any associate) will be 'involved' with the relevant company [*ITEPA 2003, s 61B(2)*] if

- It benefits financially on an ongoing basis from the provision of the individual's services; or

- It influences or controls the provision of those services, or the way in which the payments to the individual (or their associate) are made, or the company's finances, or any of its activities; or

- It gives or promotes an undertaking to make good any tax loss.

The meaning of 'associate' for the purposes of *ITEPA 2003, s 61B(2)* is tightly defined as someone who acts in concert with the MSC provider for the purpose of securing that the workers services are provided by a company. Further guidance can be obtained from HMRC's website.

6.47 HMRC has confirmed that it is not its intention to bring accountants and genuine employment agencies within the scope of the 'MSC' regime for MSCs – thus there are 'carve-out' exemptions in *ITEPA 2003, s 61B(3), (4), (5)*. The vast majority of firms providing legal or accounting services in a professional capacity will *not* be treated as an MSC provider. HMRC's MSC guidance of July 2007 clarified that 'professional capacity' only applied to persons professionally qualified (or training for a professional qualification), regulated by a regulatory body. Examples of businesses that HMRC considers to be exempt are:

(1)   a firm of accountants carrying on the business of being accountants;

(2)   a tax adviser carrying on the business of being a tax adviser;

(3)   a company formation agent;

(4)   a chartered secretary;

(5)   an employment agency undertaking its core business of placing workers with end clients;

(6)   service companies like insurance companies and payroll bureaux;

(7)   a trade association operating in the service sector.

However, there can be a fine dividing line between accountants giving advice to individuals in the normal course of their business and those that encourage a particular course of behaviour. For example, HMRC indicates that the exemption will *not* apply to 'a firm of accountants carrying on a discernible part of their business specifically to market and/or provide corporate solutions and services to individuals providing their services to end-clients' – this would be an MSC provider.

Deemed MSC employment income

Calculating the deemed employment income

6.48   From 6 April 2007, *ITEPA 2003, s 61D* treats all 'non-employment' income extracted from the company (which will typically be dividends) as earnings from an employment.

The deemed employment payment is calculated by taking the amount of the payment or benefit and then making a deduction for expenses that would have been deductible if the worker had been employed directly by the client. This net figure is deemed to be inclusive of employer's NIC, so a further recalculation is necessary is required to determine the final amount liable to PAYE and employee's NIC (*ITEPA 2003, s 61E*).

NICs will only be due on deemed employment payments received by individuals from 6 August 2007.

Example 3

ITEPA 2003, s 61E calculation of deemed employment payment on dividend received from an MSC

Jose works as a project consultancy manager providing his services through Roman Ltd.

Roman Ltd provides all the relevant administration relating to Jose's work and a number of others. It arranges for all work to be invoiced, collects payment and arranges payment of Jose's salary and dividends through the use of a special class of shares. Roman Ltd falls to be treated as an MSC within *ITEPA 2003, s 61B*.

During the year to 31 March 2018, Jose receives a salary of £6,000 and two dividend payments (in August 2017 and March 2018) totalling £80,000 (after providing for the relevant corporation tax).

During the year, Jose incurred expenses of £8,000 (which would have been deductible 'employment expenses' if he had been directly employed by his clients).

Jose's deemed employment payment for 2017/18 would be calculated as follows:

	£
Dividend payments	80,000
Less: Allowable expenses	(8,000)
Net amount	72,000
Therefore:	
Employer's NIC – £72,000 × 13.8/113.8	8,731
Deemed employment payment (subject to PAYE and NIC)	63,269

Restriction for travelling and subsistence expenses

6.49 *ITEPA 2003, s 61G(3)* places 'tainted' MSCs at a further disadvantage by blocking tax relief for travelling and subsistence expenses (including statutory mileage allowance relief) for its workers.

Transfer of debt provisions

6.50 In the past, HMRC attempted to challenge MSCs under the previous IR35 legislation. However, once HMRC had successfully established unpaid PAYE and NIC, one of the key practical problems was collecting it.

Many unscrupulous providers side-stepped HMRC's 'clutches' by engaging in 'phoenixism' – they were able to cease trading with few if any assets (so HMRC did not collect the outstanding tax) and the business would be transferred to a new company.

Consequently, under *SI 2007/2069*, HMRC was given fairly wide-spread powers to collect the relevant unpaid tax from other 'related' parties. If the MSC fails to settle its PAYE/NIC debt and the PAYE debt is incurred after 6 January 2008 this may be collected from these other parties in the following order:

(1) the MSC director (or other office holder or associate of the MSC);

(2) the MSC provider (or other office holder or associate of the MSC provider);

(3) other persons actively involved in the provision of the MSC.

HMRC may not serve a transfer notice on those persons listed under (3) above if the relevant PAYE debt is incurred prior to 6 January 2008.

If HMRC decides that the Exchequer is at risk due to PAYE and NICs debts which have not been recovered within a reasonable period, HMRC can transfer the debt to any of the parties listed above. HMRC has confirmed that it will not approach those in category 3 unless it had attempted to collect the debt from the MSC and those in categories 1 and 2 and those attempts had failed. To ensure consistency of treatment, HMRC will use a central team to decide how these provisions will be enforced. See guidance note on HMRC's website for further interpretation of the 'transfer of debt' provisions

6.51   In HMRC's view, an MSC provider would not get a tax deduction for settling the PAYE debt on behalf of the MSC. HMRC has indicated that those who encourage or are actively involved in operating MSCs from outside the UK have a higher risk of having the MSC's PAYE and NIC debt transferred to them!

PLANNING CHECKLIST – PERSONAL SERVICE COMPANIES AND MANAGED SERVICE COMPANIES

Company

- Review all contracts performed by the company to check if the work provided would be treated as an employment.

- Consider indemnities for PAYE and NIC in contracts. Ensure accounting system can produce timely information to calculate any deemed employment income.

- Consider changing company year end to 31 March to minimise accounting work.

- General company expenses can be covered by the 5% allowance for IR35 purposes (the 5% allowance helps to cover such items as accountants' fees).

- Check if the company meets all the relevant conditions to be an MSC. However, if the company provides legal or accounting services in a professional capacity, this would take it outside the MSC rules.

- In the case of an MSC, consider indemnities for PAYE and NIC so that the debts are not transferred to third parties.

Working shareholders (PSCs) operating in the private sector

- Wherever possible, ensure legal contracts and actual substance of arrangements support 'self-employment' status. This is particularly important following the *Autoclenz* decision.

- Directorship services provided after 5 April 2013 fall within the IR35 regime and thus will be treated as deemed earnings. Many non-executive directors who provide their services through personal service companies are affected by this change.

- Review pricing of contracts which may fall within IR35 to cover additional tax due.

- Review travel and subsistence expenses to determine whether they would fall to be allowed under the relevant *ITEPA 2003* provisions if incurred in connection with a relevant engagement. Since 6 April 2016, 'home to work' expenses may often be disallowed.

- Deduct any expenses that would have been allowable if the worker had been an employee of the end client eg pension contributions.

- Consider transferring ownership of expensive equipment to the individual to avoid disallowance of capital allowances.

- Use pension funding to mitigate income tax liability on deemed IR35 earnings, subject to the annual allowance/tapered annual allowance (subject to any unused relief brought forward from the three previous years).

- Ensure PSC makes a claim to reduce the taxable value of dividends by any amounts already taxed as deemed employment income payments.

Working shareholders (PSCs) operating in the public sector

- Wherever possible, ensure legal contracts and actual substance of arrangements support the fact that the PSC is 'working' without supervision, direction and control so that the 'off-payroll rules do not apply to the engagement.

- Review pricing of contracts which may fall within the 'off-payroll' rules to cover the additional tax and NI that will be deducted.

- Ensure that the public sector body 'engager' provides details of its invoicing deadlines and their subsequent payment date. This is because the public sector body's finance team will invariably have to wait for fees to be processed by its payroll team.

- A statement should be requested from the public sector body showing the split of net fees, VAT and qualifying expenses.

- All invoices provided to the relevant public sector 'engager' should provide sufficient personal information for the public sector body to set up an appropriate payroll record.

- Care should be taken to ensure that all invoices only contain *qualifying* business expenses. This will assist the public sector engager to deduct them so that only the net fees are subjected to tax and NICs

- When processing payments *from* the PSC that have already been taxed and 'NIC'd' by the engager, these should be taken free of tax and NICs (with an appropriate report being made on the full payment submission).

Chapter 7

Benefits and Expenses

STRATEGY FOR WORKING SHAREHOLDERS

7.1 Most working shareholders will want the company to meet the cost of all expenses which could be said to have a business connection or relationship, no matter how remote that connection may be.

Although the director can claim tax relief under the general rule in *ITEPA 2003, s 336* for those expenses that are 'wholly, exclusively and necessarily incurred in the performance of the duties of the employment', this is notoriously restrictive terminology. From a strategic point of view, it is generally sensible to arrange that the company meets all expenses (directly or by reimbursement) which would not have been incurred but for the existence of the employment in question.

Many working shareholders also want the company to provide them with as many 'fringe' benefits as is possible, provided their personal income tax liability is not of such a magnitude that it would be cheaper for them to purchase the item in question.

This chapter reviews the more important types of benefits and expense payments, including the following:

Use of assets generally	7.8–7.10
Company cars and private fuel	7.11–7.42
Personal ownership of car, including authorised mileage payments	7.43–7.47
Company vans, motorbikes and cycles, and subsidised travel	7.48–7.55
Travel and subsistence costs	7.55–7.61
Beneficial loans	7.62–7.63
Living accommodation	7.64–7.75
Relocation expenses and removal expenses	7.74–7.78
Other common employee benefits	7.79–7.86

This chapter also covers various issues relating to structuring remuneration packages, typical transactions with working and non-working shareholders, the relevant P11D compliance obligations/payrolling obligations and PAYE Settlement Agreements.

Leaving aside the company car and private fuel, there can be advantages in a whole host of goods and services being provided by the company for the employee. There will be an income tax charge on the employee to cover the 'private' element of the benefit, but this is often less than the real value to them of having the benefit. This is especially the case when one considers that (ignoring NICs) a 40% tax-paying employee who wants to purchase goods costing say £900 would need to use £1,500 of gross salary, whereas he would be charged to income tax on £900 (tax = £360) if the company provided the item. Care needs to be taken with this philosophy, however, as there could be no end to the 'private' goods which the employer provides. Instead, the employing company should concentrate on buying those goods which are connected with the 'employment' and which the working shareholder would purchase personally if the company did not do so.

Since 6 April 2016 employers have the option to avoid the completion of P11D forms after the tax year end in favour of the majority of benefits-in-kind now being able to be taxed on the employee via the payroll (see 7.100A).

TAX RELIEF FOR THE COMPANY

7.2   The deductibility of the benefit for corporation tax purposes must always be considered. This is something that HMRC will sometimes question.

If the provision of a benefit constitutes revenue expenditure there should be no problem in obtaining corporate tax relief. This is because it is simply part of the cost of obtaining the director's/employee's services within a 'total' remuneration package and the expense is, therefore, incurred wholly and exclusively for the purposes of the company's trade.

Where the benefit is provided through capital expenditure, however, the position can be more difficult. For the employer to obtain capital allowances on the expenditure it has to be on the provision of machinery or plant for the purposes of the trade. Taking the example of a boat, it is likely that only restricted capital allowances would be claimable to reflect the business aspect. Restricted tax relief for the company (or possibly no relief at all) would *not* necessarily avoid an income tax charge on the director or employee.

POTENTIAL IMPACT OF THE DISGUISED REMUNERATION RULES

7.3   Following *FA 2011's* introduction of *ITEPA 2003, Part 7A* ('Employment Income provided through Third Parties' – often referred to as the 'disguised remuneration' rules'), care must be taken to determine whether any benefits provided by a *third party* (which is an essential component of the regime) are subject to tax under these rules (see 5.18). However, in the vast majority of cases, *ITEPA 2003, s 554G* provides a fairly wide exclusion from the disguised remuneration rules for most employee benefit packages. Benefits provided by the employing (or fellow group) company are not within the scope of the disguised remuneration rules.

'HOBBY' ASSETS

7.4   Experience suggests that HMRC are particularly vigilant to the use of yachts, helicopters, racing cars, race horses and other similar 'toys' purchased by owner-managed companies. Indeed, if an HMRC Inspector picks up the presence of such assets within a company, a full investigation will inevitably follow. Although such assets are often 'dressed-up' or structured in a way to make them look like a sponsorship, advertising or a separate leasing business activity, HMRC suspect that they are really 'hobby' assets and are frequently successful in demonstrating that they are available for private use and are therefore taxable on the owner-manager and will seek to restrict capital allowance claims on them.

Owner-managers who wish to use their company to finance their personal and family pursuits generally regret it after they have been subject to a full-blown HMRC investigation!

STRATEGY FOR OTHER EMPLOYEES

7.5   The strategy is generally likely to be rather different for employees who are not shareholders. Fringe benefits will often be provided as an incentive device, with particular emphasis on those where the income tax charge on the employee is less than the real value to him.

A structured remuneration package could be introduced using the 'cafeteria' system whereby the employing company determines the fixed gross annual cost or 'benefit fund', with the executive then choosing the components within specified limits. The 'cafeteria' system is illustrated later in this chapter by a comprehensive example (see 7.90).

NATIONAL INSURANCE CONTRIBUTIONS ON EXPENSE AND BENEFITS

Class 1A NICs

7.6   Class 1A National Insurance Contributions (NICs) are now charged on most benefits in kind and expense payments. This would include payments for the employee's benefit (irrespective of whether the liability is the employee's or the company's).

This is generally based on the same amount as the employment income tax charge, although there are a few exceptions.

Class 1A NICs will generally apply unless the benefit is:

- exempt from income tax;

- wholly covered by a deduction under *ITEPA 2003, s 336*;

- covered by an exemption as a qualifying business expense (exemptions replaced most items included in dispensations when these were abolished on 6 April 2016);

- part of a PAYE Settlement Agreement (PSA); or

- subject to Class 1 NICs on the employee and employer

The Class 1A NIC liability is based on the cash equivalent of the benefit in the same way as the income tax charge and is reported on the form P11D and P11D(b), where the overall NIC liability is calculated.

The P11D form is colour-coded to assist with the calculation of the Class 1A liability – the expenses and 'cash equivalents' attracting Class 1A NICs are those entered in the brown boxes with the '1A' indicator (see 7.102). The employer's overall Class 1A liability is submitted on form P11D(b) (Return of Class 1A National Insurance Contributions due) – this calculation is made at the 'employer level' rather than for each employee. This form also contains the employer's declaration that all the required forms have been submitted and the relevant details on those forms have been fully and truly stated.

Since 6 April 2016, the Class 1A NIC liability is also incurred on benefits that have been taxed through the payroll – so called 'payrolling of benefits' – which is now on a statutory footing. Where benefits are taxed in this way, the Class 1A needs to be accrued each pay period and paid over annually along with any liability arising from benefits that are still reported on the P11D.

Class 1A NICs are payable at the current employer's rate of 13.8%. On the other hand, no employee contributions are due on benefits that are subject to a Class 1A NIC charge. The payment is due by 19 July 2018 (for 2017/18).

Class 1 NIC charge on earnings

7.7   Transactions made on a company credit card for the supply of goods, money or services for the employee's private use are treated as earnings for NIC purposes. This imposes a Class 1 NIC liability on the value of such transactions and will potentially generate a director's/employee's liability at either 12% or 2% (depending on the level of earnings).

Since 6 April 2016 any taxable expenses in respect of travel, for example home to work travel, must be reimbursed through the payroll subject to PAYE and Class 1 NICs. Only fully deductible expenses can be ignored for P11D reporting.

Qualifying employers can claim a NIC employment allowance offering a reduction of up to £3,000 (£2,000 before 6 April 2016) in their secondary (*employer's*) Class 1 NICs. See 5.5A for detailed coverage.

USE OF ASSETS

Calculation of taxable benefit

General rules

7.8   Directors and employees are charged to income tax annually for the *use* of an asset (other than a car, van or living accommodation). The taxable benefit is 20% of the market value of the asset when it is first provided (to anyone in the business, not just the current employee who is enjoying its use) or on the rental paid for the asset if that gives a greater taxable benefit [*ITEPA 2003, s 205(1)–(3)*].

Therefore, a fast-depreciating asset could be provided and the tax charge on the employee could be kept to a minimum in relation to the value enjoyed by them. There would also be a separate income tax charge on any expenses incurred by the employer in providing the asset, for example insurance to allow an asset to leave the company's premises.

A taxable benefit also arises where an employer provides a 'personalised' number plate for a director's/employee's *private* car. The annual charge would be 20% of the market value of the asset when it was first made available.

Where the asset is used for a mixture of business and private purposes, the taxable benefit is only calculated on the private use element.

Since 6 April 2017, a new *ITEPA 2003, s 205A* provides for a reduction in the calculated tax charge. This supersedes HMRC's prior practice and now provides for a statutory basis for adjusting the charge so that the taxable benefit is only based on the days the asset is available for private use and so on. Where an asset has shared use *ITEPA 2003, s 205B* provides for the tax charge to be calculated on a 'just and reasonable' basis.

However, Class 1A NICs arise on the *full* annual value of mixed-use assets, except where the private use is insubstantial.

The combined taxable benefit and NIC charge on exotic 'hobby' assets over a number of years can be substantial, particularly where there are interest and penalties 'on-top'! Such assets are prime targets for HMRC investigations (see 7.4). It is also worth noting that VAT is not recoverable to the extent that an asset has a non-business purpose. Whilst 'business purpose' is not defined in the legislation, it would include assets used for sporting and leisure oriented activities, for the personal benefit of director, proprietors and partners and in connection with non-business activities (HMRC VIT10200).

Subsequent transfer of asset

7.9   Where the ownership of the asset 'used' by the employee is subsequently transferred to them, *ITEPA 2003, s 206* states that an income tax charge then arises based on the *greater* of:

● the market value of the asset at the *time of transfer*; and

● the market value when it is first provided by the company to this employee *less* the amounts already charged for the use of the asset.

The transfer of previously 'loaned or hired' computers and bicycles is simply based on the market value of the transferred asset at the time of transfer [*ITEPA 2003, s 206(6)*]. HMRC provide a matrix of residual value for bicycles previous hired to employees (see 7.52).

The transfer of ownership charge can possibly be avoided as follows:

(*a*)   for (say) clothing or computer equipment, by donating it to charity;

(*b*)   the employee continuing to pay rent equivalent to the annual value so that no charge to income tax arises on the use of the asset (ie with no transfer of ownership).

Fast-depreciating assets could be furniture or consumer durables for the director's/employee's home, but the advantage to the company would be less than for business clothing which helps to promote its image. The company may well be able to make special arrangements so that it purchases the clothing at a discount.

Taxable benefit on computers

7.10   Employers should be aware that computers and related IT equipment made available to employees may, in certain circumstances, attract a taxable benefit.

HMRC states:

> 'Section 316 of the Income Tax (Earnings & Pensions) Act 2003 provides that no income tax will arise on accommodation, supplies or services used in employment duties. This includes computer equipment provided for business purposes where any private use made is not significant. Consequently, where employers provide computer equipment to employees solely for them to carry out the duties of the employment at home, HM Revenue and Customs accepts that it is unlikely that private use of the computer will be significant, when compared with the primary business purpose of providing the computer equipment'.

If significant private use is made of a computer provided for business purposes a tax charge will arise on the private use element based on the value of the computer and the extent of the business and private use. Employers will also be liable to Class 1A National Insurance contributions.

COMPANY CARS AND PRIVATE FUEL

Company cars – basic rules

7.11   The calculation of the taxable benefit on a 'company car' is based on *the appropriate percentage for the year* applied to the *price of the car.* This *appropriate percentage* is generally based on the CO_2 emission levels of the relevant car (for post-31 December 1997 registrations), otherwise it depends on the engine size of the car. There is no discount for (high) business mileage or for older cars [*ITEPA 2003, ss 120–148*]. (See 7.15 below.)

For the purposes of the company car benefit rules, a car is a mechanically propelled road vehicle *other than* a goods vehicle (for example, commercial vehicles such as lorries, trucks or vans), a vehicle not commonly used as a private vehicle (for example, buses and coaches), a motor cycle or an invalid carriage (*ITEPA 2003, s 115*). In applying this definition, the legislation looks at the predominant purpose for which the vehicle was constructed rather than its actual use. For the tax treatment of vans provided to employees, see 7.48.

From 6 April 2010 to 5 April 2015, electric cars were completely exempt from the taxable benefit and Class 1A NIC charge (see 7.18). From 6 April 2015 until 5 April 2018 there will be a differential of four percentage points between the 0–50 and 51–75 g/km CO^2 bands and between the 51–75 and 76–94g/km bands. As electricity is not regarded as fuel by HMRC, there is no fuel benefit charge!

A special exemption also applies for cars with 'pool car' status – see 7.34.

The price of the car is the sum of the following:

(*a*)   the published list price of the car when it was first registered (including the price of any optional extras or accessories supplied with the car) [*ITEPA 2003, ss 122–131*];

(*b*)   VAT (plus any other tax which may be charged on a car, but not the cost of the road fund licence) [*ITEPA 2003, s 123(2)*];

(*c*)   delivery charges [*ITEPA 2003, s 123(2)*];

(*d*)   the published price of accessories or optional extras provided subsequently, unless these amount to less than £100, in which case they can be ignored [*ITEPA 2003, s 126(3)*].

Security features are not regarded as accessories. These include expenditure on armour designed to protect the car's occupants from explosions or gunfire and bullet resistant glass.

Note that the 'price' of a car is no longer capped (the previous £80,000 'cap' was abolished on 6 April 2011). Thus, taxable benefits for very expensive cars are now based on their true full 'value' (*ITEPA 2003, s 121*).

All the relevant details (including, for each car, the make and model, date of first registration, CO_2 emission level, dates the car was made available, list price, etc) must be reported on the P11D (section F).

Where the employer has registered for payrolling of benefits these details are not reported on the P11D for 2016/17 onwards. In such cases, the cash equivalent value is taxed via the payroll by virtue of a notional addition to taxable pay (see 7.100A). From 2018/19, the additional section F information *must* be included in the Full Payment Submission (FPS) – the fields are optional for 2017/18.

'Made available by reason of employment'

7.12   A taxable benefit only arises if the car is made available by reason by reason of employment and must be available for the director's/employee's private use [*ITEPA 2003, s 118*].

The First-Tier Tribunal reached an interesting decision in a case involving a Ferrari owned by an antiques company [*Michael Golding v HMRC* [2011] UKFTT 232. In this case, the judge was persuaded that there had been no private use of the car since, during the relevant period, the car was either being used as a marketing tool or was up for sale. Mr Golding also lived approximately 50 miles from the company's garage where the car was stored. The judge concluded that:

'it would be artificial to regard the car, in those circumstances, as "made available" to the appellant in his capacity as an employee for his use and benefit (whether or not he chose to use it)'. Thus, 'even if a director or employee does drive or use a vehicle owned by a company, that is not determinative of whether or not that vehicle has been "made available" to him by reason of his employment or directorship'.

In *A Whitby v HMRC (and related appeal)* FTT [2009] UKFTT 311, it was confirmed that a taxable benefit charge arose on various cars, even though the company provided them on commercial lease terms to certain directors. A taxable benefit was also held to apply where the directors' cars were leased from a third party, with the cost of the lease being charged to the directors' loan accounts (*Stanford Management Services Ltd v HMRC (and related appeals)* FTT [2010] UKFTT 98. In both these cases, the taxable benefit was reduced by payments made by the directors (see 7.13 below).

The case of *Victor Baldorino v HMRC* [2012] UKFTT 70 (TC) involved similar facts. The company leased three cars and they were available for Mr Baldorino's use.

Mr Baldorino, a director of Atmosphere Management Ltd (AML), disputed seven years' worth of assessments, which included the benefit of these cars. The cars were available for his use and there appeared to be no restriction for private use. Although the company paid the leasing payments, they were charged to Mr Baldorino's director's loan account. (Incidentally, HMRC had allowed a deduction for the amounts charged to the director's loan accounts, which the Tribunal noted as a 'generous interpretation' of the legislation.) Mr Baldorino effectively repaid the lease charges by way of mileage charges and dividends.

The key issue was whether the cars were made available to Mr Baldorino by reason of his employment and for his private use. The FTT concluded that the company had *not* acted as an agent in providing the cars. It had treated the lease payments as its own liability. There was no right of recourse to Mr. Baldorino (which would have indicated that the company was acting as his agent).

The FTT therefore held that the lease agreement was between AML and the lessor. This meant that the cars were made available to Mr. Baldorino by reason of his directorship.

7.12A The concept of 'by reason of employment' is wider than 'from the employment'. This was made clear in *Southern Aerial (Communications) v HMRC* [2015] UKFTT 538. The First Tier Tribunal decided there was a taxable benefit on cars taken out on hire purchase by a company. This was despite the fact that the HP payments were paid for by the husband and wife 'partnership' which supplied services to the connected company.

The couple claimed the cars were not provided to them by the company but by the partnership. They contended that the partnership had been set up for business reasons but the FTT commented that, on the balance of probabilities, it was set up primarily to hold cars outside the company to avoid the benefit charges. The partnership had incurred the full cost of the agreement even though the company had taken out the HP agreement and recharged the partnership.

The cars were provided by 'reason of their employment' with the connected company

The FTT concluded that the cars were made available to the couple by reason of their employment with the company, and hence they were subject to a car benefit charge.

'Private use' payments by directors/employees

7.13   The company car 'taxable benefit' can be reduced if the director/employee is required to make a payment as a condition of the car being made available for private use and the payment is only for that purpose.

The 'deduction' rules in *ITEPA 2003, s 144(1)* were carefully considered by the First-Tier Tribunal in *Peter Marshall v HMRC* [2013] UKFTT 046 (TC). However, *FA 2014, s 25* now specifically requires the 'making good' payment to be made within the relevant tax year. HMRC has indicated that, by concession, it will allow employees to 'make good' up to the P11D deadline instead (see 7.100). From 6 April 2017, new sections were added (where relevant) to *ITEPA 2003* to set the 'making good' deadline as 6 July (from the end of the relevant tax year) for *all* benefits in kind (since, the law was silent on the deadline in respect of certain benefits).

These requirements of *ITEPA 2003, s 144* were interpreted strictly in *Brown v Ware (HMIT)* [1995] SSCD 155. It was held in this case that no relief was available for a 'contribution' made by employee so that he could drive a better car since this was not a payment for private use. It is therefore sensible that where any agreement is made for a deduction from net pay in respect of a company car, it explicitly states this relates to a 'contribution for private use'

For treatment of 'one-off' capital contributions, see 7.30.

Other related car benefits

7.14   It is worth noting the additional benefit for the cost of providing a cherished or private number plate for a company car.

HMRC's view is that most of the cost relates to the right to use the relevant numbers or letters and it is not therefore treated as an 'accessory'. However, the car benefit does not cover the provision of a chauffeur/driver, so the private cost proportion of the cost of providing a chauffeur/driver must be included as a separate taxable benefit. Company car (and van) drivers who incur a congestion zone/toll charge and have this amount reimbursed by the company will not suffer tax on this amount, even where this is part of their ordinary commuting costs. (The congestion charge effectively attaches to the car as opposed to the driver.) Thus, the 'exemption' in *ITEPA 2003, s 239(4), (5)* applies. This broadly states that any benefit in connection with a company car or company van does not give rise to any further taxable benefits under *ITEPA 2003, s 203(1)* other than on the provision of any 'driver'. As the charge is an employer liability (it is the company's car), no NIC liability arises as it is a payment in kind.

However, congestion/toll charges reimbursed on *'employee-owned'* cars will attract tax and NIC *unless* they are in respect of business journeys when they are allowable.

CO_2 emissions tables

7.15 For 2017/18, the taxable benefit for cars with petrol engines emitting CO_2 starts at 17% (for cars emitting more than 75 g/km). If exceptionally the emissions are below 75 g/km the benefit will be at 13% for cars with petrol engines with emissions in the range 51-75g/km and 9% for those in the range 0-50g/km.

An 18% rate applies to cars emitting between 95 g/km and 99g/km. This means that a car emitting CO_2 of 97 g/km is subject to a car benefit equivalent to 18% of the car's list price. Each additional 5g/km then increases the appropriate percentage by one point, subject to a maximum of 37% of the list price. Class 1A NICs also apply to the taxable benefit, increasing the overall 'cost' of running company cars (see 7.6).

The Vehicle Certification Agency produces a free indicative guide to the CO_2 emissions figures for all new cars (registered from 1 March 2001) – this can also be found at http://carfueldata.direct.gov.uk/search-new-or-used-cars.aspx.

For cars registered before 1 January 1998, see 7.20.

For all cars registered from (at least) March 2001, the relevant CO_2 emissions figure is stated on the Vehicle Registration Document (V5) (employers supply emissions details on the Form P46 (Car) when a car is changed or first supplied). Thus, the CO_2 emissions figure applying at the date of the first registration is set for the life of the car.

The CO_2 emission's ceiling for claiming 100% capital allowances on such cars is currently 75 g/km (from 1 April 2015) and will fall to 50 g/km from April 2018.

The relevant amounts for 2016/17 are set out in the 2016/17 edition of this book.

Car benefit calculator – 2017/18

CO$_2$ emissions rating (g/km) NOT EXCEEDING (note 1)	% of list price	
	Petrol	**Diesel**
0–50	9	12
51–75	13	16
76–94	17	20
95–99	18	21
100–104	19	22
105–109	20	23
110–114	21	24
115–119	22	25
120–124	23	26
125–129	24	27
130–134	25	28
135–139	26	29
140–144	27	30
145–149	28	31
150–154	29	32
155–159	30	33
160–164	31	34
165–169	32	35
170–174	33	36
175–179	34	37 (max)
180–184	35	37 (max)
185–189	36	37 (max)
190 and above	37	37 (max)

Notes:

1   Under the tax legislation, the CO$_2$ emissions figures for a car are rounded down to the nearest five grams per kilometre for the purposes of the statutory table (g/km) [*ITEPA 2003, s 139*]. However, to qualify for the 9%/12% rate, the emissions must be no more than 50 g/km. To qualify for the 13%/15% rate, the emissions must not exceed 75 g/km.

The 'simplified' table above works with the actual CO$_2$ emissions.

2   Where the car is 'not available for part of the year', the relevant scale charge is reduced on a pro-rata basis, subject to the rules mentioned in 7.26 below.

3   The taxable benefit for *diesel* cars is 3% higher in every case than for petrol engines, up to a maximum of 37% of the list price and is likely to remain so until 2020/21. Diesel cars generally have lower CO_2 emissions than petrol cars, but the particulates from diesel engines have contributed to increases in respiratory illnesses – the 'simple' flat 3% increase recognises this. Since April 2011, the 3% supplement also applies to diesel cars meeting the Euro IV emission standard

4   Employees of motor dealers often have access to number of different cars. Historically, they have calculated their car benefit using a locally agreed 'average' car. HMRC permit the representative 'average' car to be calculated on a national or regional basis for the dealership (see *EIM 23380*).

Worked examples of taxable car benefits

7.16

Example 1

Calculation of car benefit

Mr David is the sales director of Specialist Kicks Ltd. He drives around 40,000 business miles a year in a company-provided BMW 318i Manual ES142 that uses petrol.

The BMW 318i has a CO_2 emissions rating of 142 g/km and cost £21,145 in June 2009.

Thus, Mr David's taxable benefit for 2017/18 is £5,709 , being 27% × £21,145. (There are no discounts for the high business mileage.)

Example 2

Calculation of company car benefits

The 2017/18 tax and the company's NIC Class 1A charges relating to the cars and fuel provided to the directors of Foxes Ltd are calculated (assuming their marginal tax rate is 40%) as follows:

Director	Car	Fuel	List price	CO_2 g/km	Relevant %	Taxable benefit	Tax at 40%	Class 1A NIC @13.8%
Mr J Vardy	Vauxhall Corsa	Diesel	£20,045	94	20%	£4,009	£1,603	£553
Mr C Ranieri	Landrover Discovery V8I ESDR 7 seat	Petrol	£34,735	397	37%	£12,851	£5,140	1,773

Alternative fuel vehicles

7.17   Alternative fuel vehicles are generally more environmentally friendly but cost more than 'normal' petrol cars. For diesel hybrid powered cars, the 3% diesel surcharge is reflected in the 'discounted' scale charges for 2017/18. (Equivalent figures for 2016/17 are shown in the previous year's edition of this book.)

	2017/18
Electric car (see 7.11)	9%
Hybrid electric and petrol car	Normal scale charge based on emissions
Bi-fuel gas and petrol cars	Bi-fuel cars are typically capable of running on road fuel gas and petrol and will therefore have two separate fuel tanks. If such a car has more than one official CO_2 emissions figure the lower figure should be used when determining the appropriate percentage and calculating the car benefit charge

Tax breaks for electric cars

7.18   The Government wishes to embrace the development of the electric car, which now carries a plethora of tax breaks and other benefits.

Electric cars were completely exempt from any taxable benefit for five years from 2010/11, providing valuable tax and NIC savings for employers and employees. From 6 April 2015 to 5 April 2020 the taxable benefit charge will move up progressively from 5% as shown below:

2015/16	2016/17	2017/18	2018/19	2019/20
5%	7%	9%	13%	16%

They also attract 100% capital allowances, exemption from car tax, and do not incur any congestion charges. Furthermore, electric cars carry free parking and no expensive fuel bills – there is no taxable fuel scale charge! The electricity cost is typically 2p per mile.

These cars also qualify for a government grant of up to 35% of the cost of a new car, up to a maximum of either £2,500 or £4,500 depending on the model/ its emissions (as the grant is also available to low emission cars). The 'cost' is the full purchase price paid for the basic vehicle – including number plates, vehicle excise duty and VAT. It excludes delivery charges, the first registration fee, or any optional extras. The dealer applies the discount for the grant at the time of purchase.

Employees who drive a large number of business miles during the year may find it cost-effective to 'convert' their company cars to run on LPG instead of petrol or diesel or even consider an electric car.

For company cars, which are fuel-electric hybrids or all-electric and have a rechargeable battery, the list price of the vehicle must always include the cost of the battery, whether or not it is leased separately. If an employer leases a battery for an employee's company car, there is a taxable benefit, which would normally be based on the cost to the employer.

In relation to electric car charging stations, the provision by an employer of a charging station for an employee to charge a private electric car gives rise to a benefit-in-kind. However, if the private use is trivial HMRC may be approached to consider excluding the benefit under the trivial benefit rules.

Automatic cars for disabled employees

7.19   If an employee who holds a disabled badge at any time during a tax year can only drive a car with an automatic transmission for which the emissions figure is greater than it would have been for an equivalent manual car, the appropriate percentage is calculated using the approved CO_2 emissions figure of the closest manual equivalent car first registered at or about the same time as the automatic car.

Pre-1 January 1998 cars and cars with no CO_2 emissions rating

7.20   The taxable benefit scales do not apply to:

- vehicles with no approved CO_2 emissions rating (for example, cars which have been imported from outside the EU); or

- older vehicles registered before January 1998 for which the CO_2 emissions rating is unknown [*ITEPA 2003, ss 140* and *142*].

The 2017/18 taxable benefit in such cases is based on a percentage of the list price as follows:

Engine size	No emissions figure Petrol	No emissions figure Diesel	Pre-January 1998 car
Up to 1,400 cc	18%	19%	18%
1,401–2,000 cc	29%	32%	29%
Over 2,000 cc	37%	37%	37%

Classic Cars

7.21   A classic car is one that is more than 15 years old at the end of the tax year and has a market value greater than £15,000. On the last day of the tax year, if the market value of the car and any qualifying accessories exceeds the original list price the car benefit charge must be calculated using the market value. The market value must be recalculated and agreed with HMRC every tax year. For classic cars registered before 1 January 1998, the car benefit charge will depend on engine size and not CO_2 emissions as noted in the table above.

VAT recovery on purchase/lease of car

7.22   As a rule, a company cannot recover the input VAT on the purchase cost of a car. Where the car is leased, 50% of the input VAT on lease payments is recoverable (where the car is used partly for business and private purposes by the director/employee).

Where it can be demonstrated that a purchased or leased car is genuinely planned to be used *exclusively* for business purposes, all the VAT may be recovered (subject to any partial exemption restriction). The test is restrictive since it means that 'it is *not* intended to make the car available for the private use of anyone, save where it is done in the course of a commercial leasing or rental operation'.

Home to work use is regarded as private, unless the employee works from home. In the case of *C&E Comrs v Elm Milk Ltd* [2006] STC 792, the Tribunal, the High Court and the Court of Appeal accepted that a Mercedes E320 provided to the only director of a company was solely intended for business use. A board minute provided that the car was not available for private use and that any such use would represent a breach of the employee's employment contract. The director travelled some 50,000 miles on business each year and the car was garaged overnight near the company's premises (where the keys were kept!), although this was also nearby the director's home. The fact that the director used his wife's Rover for private use probably clinched the decision!

The 'motor car' definition for VAT purposes is similar, but not identical, to that which applies for the employee benefits legislation (see 7.11). Taxis, minicabs, self-drive hire cars and cars used for driving tuition will normally qualify for full input recovery.

Where the input VAT has been blocked, no VAT is chargeable on any contributions made by the employee for private use of the car. Where VAT has been fully recovered on a car, output VAT must be charged on a subsequent sale. Similarly, if a 'business' car begins to be used for private purposes, this triggers a 'self-supply' for VAT purposes. Output VAT must then be accounted for on the current price of the car with no recovery of the related input VAT.

Car fuel benefit

7.23   The system for calculating the car fuel scale charge on a *company car* is based on the relevant car's CO_2 percentage. A director's/employee's fuel scale charge for 2017/18 is computed by reference to a base figure of £22,600 (£22,200 for 2016/17), against which the relevant CO_2 percentage (the same as their company car benefit percentage – see table in 7.15) is applied [*ITEPA 2003, s 150*].

The recent increases to the appropriate percentages for company cars have had an adverse 'knock-on' effect for those paying the fuel scale charge.

The (practical) minimum and maximum charge for 2017/18 is therefore normally £2,034 (£22,600 × 9%) and £8,362 (£22,600 × 37%) respectively (see CO_2 emissions table in 7.15). Where the director or employee starts or stops receiving private fuel during the tax year, the relevant taxable fuel benefit is apportioned.

Based on the prevailing figures (and given the lower cost of fuel), it is difficult to see any circumstances in which it makes sense for the employing company to provide *private* fuel since the tax charge on the benefit is likely to exceed the true cost of the fuel. From the company's point of view, these amounts also attract a significant Class 1A NIC cost. Employers should consider whether they should withdraw free (private) fuel as a benefit in kind or insist that it is all reimbursed where a fuel card is provided.

Taxable benefits for private fuel are not adjusted for any particular level of business mileage. To avoid the fuel scale charge, the employee must reimburse the company with the *full* cost of all the fuel used on 'non-business' journeys during the tax year. A partial reimbursement does not reduce the scale charge [*ITEPA 2003, s 151(2)*].

By concession, HMRC permits reimbursements to be made after the end of the year provided they are made within a reasonable period after the tax year-end (giving companies time to process their final mileage claims and repayments) or within 30 days of discovering an unintentional error (*HMRC EIM para 23782*).

However, this treatment is not the law and the Special Commissioner refused to apply it in *Impact Foiling Ltd and others v HMRC* [2006] STC (SCD) 764. In this case, the company had invoiced the directors the full cost of their 2002 to 2004 fuel in January 2005, which was a substantial delay. However, since 2017/18 *ITEPA 2003, s 151(2)* now makes it clear that the deadline for making good private fuel payments is 6 July following the end of the relevant tax year.

Probably the safest way to avoid the fuel scale charge is for the directors and employers to pay for all their fuel initially and then to reclaim genuine business mileage from the company using the advisory fuel rates (see 7.26).

Where fuel is provided for an employee's *own car*, the fuel scale charges above do *not* apply. Instead an income tax and NIC charge will arise on the cost to the employer of providing the fuel.

VAT recovery on fuel

7.24   Where a company provides free or cheap fuel for private use, the input VAT on the fuel is recoverable in full. However, the company must then account for VAT, based on the fixed scale charge (which varies according to the car's CO_2 emissions rating).

Recent *quarterly* VAT fuel scale rates are shown below. The VAT scale charge figures are *VAT inclusive* and thus, with a current 20% rate, the charge must be multiplied by 20/120 (or 1/6th):

CO_2 g/km emissions rating	Quarterly VAT scale charge From 1 May 2017 £
120 or less	140
125	211
130	224
135	238
140	252
145	267
150	281
155	295
160	309
165	323
170	337
175	351
180	365

CO_2 g/km emissions rating	Quarterly VAT scale charge From 1 May 2017 £
185	379
190	393
195	408
200	422
205	436
210	449
215	463
220	478
225 or more	492

Where the CO_2 emissions figure of a vehicle is not a multiple of 5, the figure is rounded down to the next multiple of 5 to determine the level of charge.

Thus, the VAT due on fuel provided on a car with CO_2 emissions of 200 g/km for the VAT quarter ended September 2017 would be calculated as £422 (scale charge) × 20%/120% = £70.33 .

Opting out of the VAT scale charge and claiming VAT on business fuel

7.25 The VAT fuel scale charges are likely to be beneficial where cars build up high levels of private motoring. However, the fuel scale charges are not compulsory. As an alternative, companies can opt out of the scale charge process by only claiming back the VAT element on fuel that has been used for *business travel*. In such cases, the company can recover VAT on the purchased fuel by reference to the business mileage (as a proportion of the total mileage) for each car.

Detailed mileage records must be kept and in this context, it is often incorrectly assumed that 'home to work' travel is business (which will only be in exceptional cases where 'home base' status has been agreed with HMRC). For example, assume that that an owner-manager's total mileage is 4,290 of which 3,780 can be identified as relating to business journeys, and the total cost of the fuel is £428.

This would enable input VAT to be reclaimed on the fuel of £62.85, calculated as follows:

Business mileage cost – £428 × 3,780/4,290 = £377.12.

Input tax reclaimed on fuel – £377.12 × 20/120 (or 1/6) = £62.85.

Companies also have the option of not reclaiming any VAT on their fuel spend. This might be helpful where the total mileage is very low so that the VAT on the scale charge gives rise to an excessive VAT cost. However, if the company wishes to opt-out completely, this applies to all their fuel, including that used for vans and lorries etc.

Reimbursement of private fuel for company cars ('Advisory fuel rates')

7.26 HMRC regularly publish 'advisory rates' to be used for the reimbursement of private fuel from directors/employees driving *company cars*, which aim to save time and costs. These advisory rates can be used where the company initially pays for all the fuel and then recovers the 'private' element from the director/employee driver. Where these rates are used to 'recover' the cost of private fuel, no income tax or Class 1 NIC arises.

These rates may also be used to reimburse employees for the cost of fuel on 'business' journeys, thus avoiding the need to keep details of the actual costs. The rates are reviewed quarterly or when there is a material change in petrol prices.

HMRC private mileage advisory fuel rates are now reviewed and amended in late March, June, September and December each year and can be found at www.gov.uk/government/publications/advisory-fuel-rates.

Recent rates are shown below:

Advisory fuel rates for company cars

From 1 September 2017

	Petrol	Diesel*	LPG
Up to 1400 cc	11p	9p	7p
1401cc–2000 cc	13p	11p	8p
Over 2000 cc	21p	12p	13p
*up to 1600cc 1601cc–2000cc and Over 2000cc			

From 1 June 2017 to 31 August 2017

	Petrol	Diesel*	LPG
Up to 1400 cc	11p	9p	7p
1401cc–2000 cc	14p	11p	9p
Over 2000 cc	21p	13p	14p
*up to 1600cc 1601cc–2000cc and Over 2000cc			

From 1 March 2017 to 31 May 2017

	Petrol	Diesel*	LPG
Up to 1400 cc	11p	9p	7p
1401cc–2000 cc	14p	11p	9p
Over 2000 cc	22p	13p	13p
*up to 1600cc 1601cc–2000cc and Over 2000cc			

From 1 December 2016 to 28 February 2017

	Petrol	Diesel*	LPG
Up to 1400 cc	11p	9p	7p
1401cc–2000 cc	14p	11p	9p
Over 2000 cc *thresholds as above	21p	13p	13p

Companies can pay at the current or previous rates in the month following the date the rates changed, and may wish to make supplementary payments.

The above rates are also accepted for VAT purposes. The amount reimbursed by the director/employee is chargeable to VAT at 20%. The company may use other 'reimbursement rates' if they are justifiable. However, if a higher rate is paid that cannot be justified by reference to the actual costs incurred, then the 'excess' amount is subject to income tax and Class 1 NICs through the payroll

COMPANY CAR – PLANNING POINTS

Car not always used

7.27   The car benefit charge is reduced, on a time basis, when the car is incapable of being used at all for at least 30 consecutive days or it is not actually provided throughout the relevant tax year. The car fuel benefit is reduced on the same basis.

Consequently, where employees do not need the car for a certain period, it is recommended that they hand in their keys. The company should prepare a memo confirming the non-availability of the car until the keys are returned to the employee. Provided the period of 'non-availability' is at least 30 consecutive days, there should be a pro-rata reduction in the tax charge [*ITEPA 2003, s 143(2)*].

However, for company cars driven by directors of a family company there may be difficulties in establishing that the car is unavailable for a period, as illustrated in *Taxation*, 15 November 2001. A 'Feedback' contribution referred to a case of a director who had a heart attack and did not use the car for 12 months. He had changed the insurance to 'third party, fire and theft' only and surrendered his driving licence. Somewhat surprisingly on the facts, this case had to be taken to the General Commissioners, who resolved it in the director's favour!

Which cars to buy

7.28 Given that taxable car benefits are based on CO_2 emissions, any decision to purchase a new company car should include consideration of the vehicle's emission rating. Looking at matters from a pure tax perspective, the best way to keep the company car tax bill down will be to choose a cheaper, more fuel-efficient car.

Drivers of automatic cars should be wary of the fact that they tend to have an emission's rating typically three or four tax bands worse than their manual counterparts.

High-mileage company cars do not receive any special discount and will generally suffer a relatively high scale charge. In some cases, they would probably benefit by switching to a cash alternative, having their own car and being compensated for their business mileage under the approved mileage allowance payments (AMAPs) system (discussed in 7.44).

Tax-favoured 'low emission' cars

7.29 A number of very respectable eco-efficient cars can now be purchased and many more companies and their car users are seeking to take advantage of the generous tax breaks and government grants (see 7.18 above) which are available on these cars.

Ultra-low emission cars qualify for 100% first year capital allowances (and will do so until 2018), thus enabling the car to be fully written-off for corporate tax purposes in the year of purchase (see 4.25). Similarly, if low-emission cars are leased (rather than purchased outright), their lease rental payments are fully deductible (see 7.40).

Low-emission cars attract low taxable benefits for the director/employee. For example, a car costing £10,000 would only have suffered a monthly tax charge during 2017/18of £28.33 in the hands of an employee (assuming a 17% scale percentage and employee paying tax at the basic rate) (see 7.15).

A number of cars qualify for this favourable tax treatment, including the following models:

Model	CO₂ emissions (g/km)	Fuel	List Price
Fiat 500 0.9 TwinAir	90	Petrol	£13,940
Lexus CT200h	94	Hybrid	£21,714
Skoda Greenline Fabia 1.2TDI	89	Hybrid	£13,120

All of these cars would produce a car benefit of 17% of their list price. Some of these cars may be attractive to employees and will assist in minimising their tax costs.

The company also benefits from first year allowances against its corporate tax liability, lower Class 1A NICs and lower road fund licence costs (and, currently, exemption from congestion charges!).

When making a 'eco-car' purchasing decision, it should be noted that the company can only claim 100% capital allowances if the rating is below 75 g/km (from 6 April 2016 (see 7.15).

As 'high-performance' *electric* cars are fast becoming a reality, some 'adventurous' owner-managers may wish to consider the tremendous tax breaks available on these cars.

Salary sacrifice arrangements (known as optional remuneration arrangements from April 2017)

7.29A A number of companies have implemented salary sacrifice arrangements with eco-efficient cars being provided to employees. However, these have become less attractive as the tax rates rise for low-emission cars and the changes to optional remuneration arrangements (OpRAs) from 6 April 2017.

Typically, the employee 'sacrifices' some of their salary for a 'new' leased car (see 7.85). This has the benefit of reducing the employer's NIC costs (ie NIC on lower salary and 'lower' Class 1A NIC liability on car benefit). There is also scope for tax savings, depending on the facts of each case.

7.29B   The changes to the taxation of company cars provided via an OpRA also include arrangements where an employee has the choice of a cash allowance rather than a company car (known as a type B arrangement) (see also 7.87A).

Where the cash allowance is chosen, this is simply taxed as earnings.

However, where the car is selected in preference or the employee sacrifices salary for a company car, a new 'car benefit' calculation applies for new OpRA arrangements taken out (or where existing contracts were amended within the employee's control) after 5 April 2017.

The new car benefit is referred to as the 'modified cash equivalent', and involves a 'two-step' calculation:

Step 1 – Take the *higher* of – Salary/cash allowance *or* 'Normal' company car benefit using 2017/18 emission tables

Step 2 – Reduce the taxable amount at Step 1 by any capital contribution or contribution for private use. The *P11D 2017/18* has been redesigned to accommodate this new value.

Since the current PAYE regulations do not provide for the 'modified cash equivalent' to be payrolled employers who have continued or begun to 'payroll' company cars from 6 April 2017, are effectively operating *ultra vires*. However, HMRC will amend the PAYE regulations from April 2018. By concession, HMRC will not require a P11D to be submitted for OpRA benefits that have been payrolled (using the correct taxable benefit).

7.29C Any OpRAs taken out before 6 April 2017 continue to attract a company car benefit calculated on the previous rules but using the 2017/18 emissions' values until 6 April 2020/21, unless any relevant contract change takes place before that date (within the employee's control).

Director/employee capital contributions

7.30 Many family or owner-managed companies have a policy on company cars, which allows a group of employees to have the use of a car up to an allotted price level. If an employee then wishes to have a more expensive car, the company may be happy to arrange this provided the employee meets the difference out of their own pocket. There is a reduction in the tax charge where the employee contributes a capital sum to the cost of the car or accessories when the car is first made available to them.

The deductible capital contribution up to a fixed level of £5,000 reduces the list price, on which the taxable benefit is computed [*ITEPA 2003, s 132*]. However, if the employee is entitled to a *full* reimbursement of the contribution when the car is subsequently sold, HMRC considers that no capital contribution has been made – probably because the refundable contribution is really a loan.

On the other hand, if the employee is only entitled to a proportionate reimbursement (usually based on the sale value), the employee can retain the 'deduction' for the full capital contribution and is not subject to any tax on the reimbursed amount (see HMRC leaflet IR 172). Based on this reasoning, it appears possible still to secure a full reduction in list price (up to £5,000) by providing that only a 'small' amount should be refunded to the company (as it would remain *partly-refundable*). In certain cases, the initial contribution towards the cost of the company car may be funded by a non-taxable interest-free loan from the company (using the £10,000 *de minimis* exemption – see 7.62).

Under the 'capital contribution' rules, the director/employee only gets the benefit of a reduction at the relevant CO_2 percentage (applied to the reduced list price). The reduction in the taxable benefit will apply for every year 'their' company car is used for private purpose. However, it may be better to arrange for the director's/employee's proposed contribution to be paid over a period rather than as an initial lump-sum. It could then be expressed as a payment made as a condition of the car being made available for their private use. In that way, the legislation allows the annual contribution to be deducted from the actual taxable benefit.

Taking a lower-value car

7.31   Looking at the other extreme, an employee could choose to take a car below the price range allotted to them by the company. In that case, the company could make a payment of the difference to a pension plan for the employee's benefit. This is tax-neutral where the company structures the payment as an additional voluntary contribution.

Car for spouses and adult children

7.32   Perk cars, such as those provided to spouses or a child at university, fare relatively well under the company car regime. This is because discounts are no longer offered for heavy or average business mileage. The normal taxable benefit arises even where the car is used not by the owner-manager (director) but by a member of their family or household [*ITEPA 2003, ss 114(1)(a) and 721(5)*]. Without this rule, it would, of course, be easy to avoid the tax charge.

Example 3

Calculation of car benefit (for spouse)

Mrs Becks is married to Mr Becks, who is managing director of Galaxy Footballs Ltd. Mrs Becks does some administrative work for the company, which provides her with a BMW 7 Series 735i. The list price of her BMW when it was first registered was £28,240. The car has a CO_2 emissions rating of 235 g/km and Mrs Becks has minimal business mileage.

Mrs Becks' taxable benefit for 2017/18 is:

£28,240 × 37% = £10,448.

7.33   Before 6 April 2016 it was possible for the owner-manager's spouse (or civil partner) to be provided with (say) a suitable 'eco-friendly' car with no tax charge arising by ensuring that he or she did not exceed the £8,500 earnings and benefits limit rule for taxing company car benefits.

However, the £8,500 threshold was abolished on 6 April 2016. Thus, if the spouse is either a director or employee there would be a company car scale charge under the normal rules.

There may also be financial benefits in providing 'environmentally-friendly' cars to other family members, such as children at university, since the car does not have to be used in the business.

This means, for example, that a 'student-child' could be provided with a 'green' car (in the environmental sense!) costing (say) £15,000. In such cases, the car would generally be treated as being provided by reason of the owner-manager's directorship. This would result in a maximum annual tax charge for them (in 2017/18) of only £1,020 (17% × £15,000 × (say) 40%), provided the car's CO_2 emissions rating does not exceed 94 grams per kilometre. Furthermore, the company should be able to obtain capital allowances on the car and be able to reclaim the VAT on the car's servicing costs.

The 'pool car'

7.34 Instead of having the exclusive use of a car, the employee could be entitled to use a 'pool car'. If this is the case, there would be no income tax charge on them (*ITEPA 2003, s 167*).

For a car to form part of a 'car pool', various conditions have to be satisfied. In broad terms:

- the car must actually be used by *more than one* employee and not ordinarily be used by any one of them to the exclusion of the others;
- any private use must be merely incidental to business use;
- the car must not normally be kept overnight at or near the residence of the director or employee unless that person happens to live in the vicinity of the employer's premises where the car is garaged [*ITEPA 2003, s 167*].

In HMRC's view, the requirement for private use to be 'merely incidental' to business use imposes a qualitative test rather than a quantitative test. A typical example would be where an employee who is required to undertake a long business journey is allowed to take a pool car home the previous night in readiness for an early morning start. The journey from office to home is, of course, private use, but in this particular context it is subordinate to the lengthy business trip the following day and is undertaken to further the business trip. In such cases, HMRC would regard the private use as being merely incidental to the business use, unless it happened too often.

7.35 Leaflet IR 480 states that a car is treated as not normally kept overnight at or near the homes of employees where the occasions on which it is taken to the employees' homes does not exceed 60% of the year. Where a car is garaged at employees' homes on a large number of occasions (albeit within the 60% limit), HMRC suggests that the private use from home to work would *not* be merely incidental to business use. These are stringent conditions and room

326

for manoeuvre is limited. However, a prestige car kept at the forecourt of the company's premises could fit the bill and help promote the company's image.

Where there is insufficient evidence to demonstrate that the 'pool car' conditions have been met, the tribunal will not allow the 'exemption' to be claimed.

In *Vinyl Design Limited and related appeals v HMRC* [2014] UKFTT 205 (TC), it was argued that the cars were pool cars.

There were no written records kept to document the use of the cars and all fuel for the cars was purchased by the company. The cars were kept at the two directors' homes overnight, which, they argued, was to protect them from a high risk of vandalism at the company workshop and to enable the directors to visit clients directly from their homes in the morning. They also contended that they were 'on call' 24 hours a day but no evidence was provided to support this.

The directors contended that these cars were only available for business use. There was a written agreement that prohibited their private use of the 'purported' pool cars. Their personally-owned cars were used for their 'private' journeys.

The FTT held that company cars were not pool cars. This ruling was reached since the directors failed to provide any evidence relating to the use of the cars by staff and there were no written logs or any procedures in place to show the use of the cars. Other factors that supporting the FTT's decision were the fact that:

- the cars were kept at the directors' homes (although the reasons given for this were acknowledged): and.

- although the taxpayers had their own 'private' cars, the company 'pool' cars were also available for their private use.

Similarly, in *Derek Munden v HMRC* [2013] UKFTT 427 (TC), the FTT dismissed an appeal for a Porsche 911 to be treated as a 'pool' car. Mr Munden, his wife and former company employees used the car and the FTT were informed that the car was only used for business purposes. However, once again, the appeal failed because of the failure to provide concrete evidence showing how the car had been used.

The FTT's findings in these cases reiterate the importance of keeping full and accurate documentation in relation to 'pool' cars. See also *Yum Yum Ltd v HMRC* [2010] UKFTT 331 and *McKenna Demolition Ltd v HMRC* [2011] UK FTT 344 and *Alexander Jubb v HMRC* [2015] UKFTT TC04760.)

HMRC REPORTING REQUIREMENTS

7.36 Where a company car is provided for the first time or where any other changes occur concerning the provision of a company car, the company must report the details on form P46 (Car) to HMRC within 28 days of the end of the quarter (to 5 July, 5 October, 5 January or 5 April) in which the change occurred. The relevant CO_2 emissions' data is also provided on form P46 (Car). Form P46(car) must *not* be submitted if the car is 'payrolled', with the appropriate tax charge being added to taxable pay each pay period (see 7.100A).

Directors or employees who are provided with a car for the first time should be informed of the benefit on which they will be taxed. (Where fuel is provided, they should keep accurate records of the private business miles driven). The penalties for not submitting form P46 (Car) or submitting inaccurate forms are the same as for late submission of forms P11D (see 7.100).

COMPANY CAR VERSUS OWN CAR

7.37 One way to judge whether or not a company car (plus fuel) is worthwhile for any tax year is to ascertain the cost per private mile in terms of the tax charge, and then compare that with the actual cost. Examples 4 and 5 below compare the tax cost for 2017/18 with the estimated running costs of the car.

Example 4

Tax cost per private mile versus actual running cost per mile (1)

	Car	
	Subaru WRX STi	
(a)	List price	£31,995
(b)	CO$_2$ emissions rating	242g/km
(c)	Relevant percentage	37%
(d)	Car benefit	£11,838
(e)	Fuel benefit base	£22,600
(f)	Relevant fuel percentage	37%
(g)	Fuel benefit	£8,362
(h)	Add (d) and (g)	£20,200
(i)	Tax at 20% on (h)	£4,040

Tax per private mile	
Miles	Tax (pence)
2,000	202p
4,000	101p
6,000	67p
8,000	51p
10,000	40p
12,000	34p

Note: Estimated running costs (including fixed costs) per mile (based on petrol at 137p per litre) for 10,000 and 15,000 miles would range between (say) 60p to 48p respectively. Hence, if the private mileage is high, the tax cost should be acceptable.

Example 5

Tax cost per private mile versus actual running cost per mile (2)

	Car	
	Volvo v90 Series	
(*a*)	List price	£35,260
(*b*)	CO_2 emissions rating	116g/km
(*c*)	Relevant percentage	25% (Diesel)
(*d*)	Car benefit	£8,815
(*e*)	Fuel benefit base	£22,600
(*f*)	Relevant fuel percentage	25%
(*g*)	Fuel benefit	£5,650
(*h*)	Add (d) and (g)	£14,465
(*i*)	Tax at 40% on (h)	£5,786

Tax per private mile	
Miles	*Tax (pence)*
2,000	289p
4,000	145p
6,000	96p
8,000	72p
10,000	58p
12,000	48p
14,000	41p

Note: Estimated running costs (including fixed costs) per mile (based on petrol at 120p per litre) for 10,000 and 15,000 miles would range between (say) 65p to 55p respectively. Where the annual private mileage is likely to be more than (say) 10,000, the provision of a company car and fuel will probably be beneficial tax wise.

TAX ISSUES FOR COMPANY

Class 1A NIC charge on company car benefits

7.38   There is an extra burden on a company when it provides a car for private use by an employee. This is the Class 1A NIC at a flat rate of 13.8% levied on the same taxable benefit figure for the private use of a car and also for any private fuel.

This Class 1A NIC is often a substantial cost for many family or owner-managed companies. Clearly, a company should be able to secure a reduction in its NIC costs by encouraging its employees to drive low CO_2 emission cars and to opt out of free fuel.

No Class 1A NIC liability applies where:

(*a*)   the car is not available for private use (and this can be demonstrated by an audit trail); or

(*b*)   the employee fully reimburses the cost of private motoring.

Car leasing versus purchasing

Capital allowances on outright purchase

7.39   The employment benefit tax charge on the employee is unaffected by the method the employer uses to provide the car. The employing company can claim capital allowances when a car is acquired via:

● outright purchase;

● hire purchase (or any lease contract that provides an option to purchase at the end of the primary lease term).

For the most eco-efficient cars (emissions of 75 g/km or less from 1 April 2015 and less than 95 g/km between 1 April 2013 – 31 March 2015), the entire cost of the car can be written-off for tax purposes by claiming 100% first year capital allowances (see 4.27).

Capital allowances on cars are now entirely emission-based with new or unused cars currently attracting writing down allowances (WDAs) as follows:

- Over 75g/km to 130g/km: 18% annual WDA (ie they fall within the main pool);

- Over 130g/km: the lower WDA rate of 8% always applies.

Thus, all cars *acquired from April 2009* (including those costing more than £12,000) either enter the main '18% WDA' pool or a lower special 8% rate pool (see 4.25).

Tax treatment of lease rental costs

7.40   For leased cars, tax relief as revenue expenditure is claimable on the lease rental costs when a car is acquired via:

- contract hire;
- finance leasing.

For finance leasing, the tax deductibility of rental payments follows the amount charged under FRS 102 (or the predecessor standard SSAP 21 as outlined in SP 3/91), although there may be a restriction in the deductible amount for certain cars (see 7.41 below).

Under UK GAAP part of the capital repayment element is deductible as revenue expenditure through the depreciation charge to the profit and loss account. The finance charge is also deductible. This normally means that no adjustment is necessary for corporation tax purposes with relief being given for the depreciation and finance charge. See 4.5A for further discussion of FRS102.

For contract hire under a with-maintenance contract, it should be arranged for the maintenance element to be the subject of a separate contract and amount. In that way, the cost of the maintenance element is segregated and fully tax deductible, whereas ordinarily the full amount might be subject to the potential restriction as part of the rental cost (see 7.39 below).

Restriction on deductible leasing costs

7.41   The tax deductible leasing costs on contract hire and finance leasing may be subject to a restriction.

For lease contracts entered into after 31 March 2009, there is a 15% disallowance where the leased car's emission rating exceeds 130 g/km (from 1 April 2013), ie only 85% of the cost is tax deductible.

More eco-friendly cars with emissions of 130 g/km (from 1 April 2013) or less are not subject to any restriction (irrespective of whether their original retail price exceeds £12,000). (Where there is a chain of leases, any disallowance will only apply to one lessee in that 'chain'.)

For cars leased before April 2013 the 15% disallowance is applied to cars with CO_2 emissions exceeding 160 g/km.

However, the lease rental payment disallowance for *existing* (pre-1 April 2009) leases is still based on the 'expensive car' rules (although there is no restriction for qualifying low emission cars). This disallowance applies where the car's retail price when new exceeds £12,000. In such cases, the *deductible* rental payment is calculated using the fraction:

$$\frac{12,000 + \text{retail price}}{2 \times \text{retail price}}$$

Example 6

Allowable hire costs

In July 2016, Drinkwater Ltd leases a Land Rover Discovery Sport SE car for its managing director under a normal contract hire deal. The Sport 2.0 Litre TD4 Diesel has an emissions rating of 139 g/km

The car has a retail price, when new, of £28,140 . The annual lease cost is £11,500.

There is a 15% disallowance of the annual lease rental payments since the emissions rating of the Freelander exceeds 130 g/km.

Thus, the annual tax-deductible lease cost is

£11,500 × 85% (being 100% − 15%) = £9,775

CHOICE OF COMPANY CAR OR SALARY

7.42   The company could offer an increased salary to those employees who decide not to accept a company car. The question for the company is how much of a cash alternative to offer. A neutral position for the company would be to offer exactly the same amount as the cost for providing the car. However, the employee may be better or worse off depending on his level of private mileage. Sophisticated modelling techniques can be used to calculate how much employees should receive to allow them to personally own exactly the same car at no additional cost.

PERSONAL OWNERSHIP OF CAR – KEY POINTS

Purchase of own car

7.43   The alternative to the company car is for the director or employee to purchase a car of their own. In the right circumstances, it may be possible for an employee to purchase a company-owned car at market value after the company has suffered the 'heavy' first year's depreciation. A reliable indicator of market value can be found from Glass's Motoring Guide, available at *www.glass.co.uk.* If the car is transferred to the director/employee at an under-value, the consequent benefit is taxable and also subject to Class 1A NICs (or if the car is a readily convertible asset, Class 1 NICs).

Where the director or employee personally owns the car, the company could pay a mileage allowance for their business use.

Approved mileage allowance payments (AMAPs)

7.44   There is a statutory system of mileage rates that can be paid free from income tax and NICs. Where a director or employee uses their own car or van for business travel, the company can pay them a tax/NIC-free mileage allowance up to the approved mileage allowance payments (AMAPs) rates. Payments made in excess of the statutory AMAPs rates are liable to income tax and NICs in the normal way.

Employers can pay employees up to 5p a mile tax-free for each 'fellow employee' passenger carried in their vehicle. It is not possible for employees to claim this tax relief where employers do *not* actually make this payment.

The Budget 2011 (by *SI 2011/896*) increased the main AMAP rate to 45p per mile to recognise the substantial increases in fuel costs – it had previously remained at 40p per mile since 2002 (*ITEPA 2003, s 230*).

7.45   HMRC's approved mileage allowance payments (AMAPs) for business journeys (ie the amounts which may be paid free of income tax and NICs), are as follows:

Approved mileage allowance payments for 2017/18

	Rate per mile
Annual business mileage	
Up to 10,000 miles	45p
Over 10,000 miles	25p
Note: The rate used for NIC purposes is 45p, regardless of business mileage	
For each passenger making same business trip	5p

Rules for claiming business mileage payments

7.46   Where employers pay less than the statutory rate, employees may claim tax relief on the difference. This is done most easily through their SA return or personal tax account.

Claims for tax relief based on the actual 'allowable' expenditure incurred by the director/employee are no longer allowed. This is the case even where the 'actual' basis would result in tax relief greater than that offered by the AMAPs rates.

7.47 In the past, companies could reclaim a pre-agreed VAT element to recover the estimated VAT input tax relating to business fuel. However, since 1 January 2006, HMRC requires the company to hold appropriate VAT invoices to (at least) cover the (pre-agreed) input tax on the business fuel part of the reimbursed mileage allowance.

In practice, companies will only be able to recover the agreed fuel input tax where employees have provided VAT invoices (at least) covering their fuel purchases (made on the employer's behalf). Normally, such VAT invoices will not exceed £250 and can therefore be less detailed – eg they do not need to show the employer's name. Where a reimbursement agreement is in place, HMRC generally accepts that the purchases are being made in the employer's name.

TAXATION OF COMPANY VANS

Definition of van

7.48 Instead of having a car provided by their employer for private use, an employee may be given the use of a van.

Broadly, a van is a *goods* vehicle (ie primarily designed to carry goods, etc) with a 'normal' design weight not exceeding 3,500kg [*ITEPA 2003, s 115(1), (2)*]. (If the design weight of the vehicle exceeds 3,500kg, then it is a 'heavy goods vehicle'.) For some vehicles, it might not always be easy to determine whether they constitute a 'van' or a 'car' (as to which, see 7.11) for employment benefits purposes. In such cases, HMRC will normally look at the pre-dominant purpose for which the vehicle was built (as opposed to its actual use). Clearly, where HMRC accepts that the vehicle can be treated as a van, the employee's tax charge is likely to be reduced significantly or may be avoided completely under the work/commuting exemption (see 7.49).

VAT incurred on the purchase of vans can normally be recovered in full.

Double cab pick-ups can be an especially difficult area – for these purposes, HMRC treat a double cab pick-up with a payload carrying capacity of one tonne (1,000kg) as a van. Where the payload area is fitted with a hard cover, the weight of the cover must be deducted from the payload weight. The 'one tonne' test applies to the net weight. (See HMRC Employment Income Manual EIM 23150.)

Given the recent blurring of the distinction between cars and vans, (the then) HM Customs & Excise issued a list of 'car-derived' vans in its Business

Brief 16/2004 (the list was issued for VAT purposes but this could apply for income tax purposes). This lists the vehicles produced or converted by the manufacturers/sole concessionaires that have been notified to Customs and meet the relevant criteria for a 'van'. These include, for example, a Land Rover Freelander (1.8 Petrol and 2.0 Diesel) and Discovery (2.5 Diesel), Rover Commerce (CDV 1.4 and CDV 2.0 TD), and Vauxhall Corsa (Corsavan and Combo) and Astra (Astravan).

Tax exemption on vans provided for work/commuter journeys

7.49   Many employees are now able to take their company vans home without suffering any taxable benefit. No taxable benefit arises where an employee only uses the van for work journeys (for example, delivering goods and calling on customers) and ordinary commuting between home and their workplace (which is normally regarded as 'private use'). Insignificant private use is also allowed (like HMRC's examples of taking rubbish to the tip once or twice a year or regularly making a slight detour to drop off a child at school!) However, see 6.24 for restrictions relating to personal service companies etc under IR 35.

Detailed mileage records should be kept to demonstrate that no taxable benefit arises on the employee-user ie private use is restricted to travel between home and work. Further protection should be obtained if the private use of the van is restricted to 'commuting' by formal agreement/under an employment contract.

Tax charge on vans

7.50   Some directors and employees may be happy to have a company van (particularly the more ergonomic type!) for their extensive private use (ie falling outside the 'work/commuter' use exemption above). They may also take the view that any disadvantage is largely outweighed by the significant reduction in the income tax charge.

Where a van is made available for the private use of a director/employee (or member of their family or household) which falls outside the 'work/commuting' exemption in 7.49:

- the taxable 'cash equivalent' of the van for 2017/18 is £3,230. (£3,170 in 2016/17). An additional charge of £610 (£598 in 2016/17) is made for the provision of private fuel. The 'cash equivalent' also attracts Class 1A NICs.

- The taxable benefit on a van with 'zero' CO_2 emissions is reduced to just £646 ie 20% of the 2017/18 van charge. Zero emission vans attracted no benefit charge until 6 April 2016.

- Where the van is unavailable to the employee for at least 30 consecutive days or it is a 'shared/pool' van for part of the year (see 7.51), the basic cash equivalent is reduced on a pro-rata basis on the same basis as a company car – see 7.28 [*ITEPA 2003, ss 156, 157*]. Where a van is made unavailable for a 'shorter period' (ie less than 30 days), but it is replaced by another van for that period, *ITEPA 2003, s 159* effectively treats the 'replacement van' as taking the place of the normal van, thus avoiding any additional tax charge.

Any cash contribution made by the employee for the private use of the van (as a condition of it being made available for private use) is then deducted to arrive at the final taxable benefit. The contribution must be made within the relevant tax year (or by concession by the P11D submission deadline).

New *electric* vans attract a 100% first year allowance on post-31 March 2010 expenditure (second-hand vans are not eligible for this FYA) *(CAA 2001, s 45DA)*;

Tax charge on shared vans

7.51　A van is treated as a 'shared van' if it is made available for the *private* use of more than one employee concurrently [*ITEPA 2003, s 157*]. Where a van is part of a 'van pool' (broadly defined in the same way as 'pool' cars), it will not be treated as being available for private use and is therefore exempt from tax [*ITEPA 2003, s 168*].

The cash equivalent of a 'shared van' is first calculated as set out in 7.50. Thus, if the van was unavailable for at least 30 consecutive days, there would be a pro-rata reduction in the benefit (based on the number of days that the van was unavailable). Where an employee's private use of a 'shared' van is restricted to ordinary commuting between home and work (as in 7.49), they would not suffer any taxable benefit in respect of that van.

The tax charge is apportioned between the relevant employees on a 'just and reasonable' basis.

Example 7

Taxable benefits for a shared company van

Zola's Electricals Ltd has three company vans, which are available for the employees' private use and are shared between its three service engineers during the year ended 5 April 2018.

The service engineers' shared use of the vans during the year has been calculated as follows:

Van		Service engineer		
	Mr Collins	*Mr Konchesky*		*Mr Gabbidon*
WHU 100	75%	25%		–
WHU 101	25%	50%		25% (but only used for work/commuting)
WHU 102	–	25%		75% (but only used for work/commuting)

The company requires Mr Collins to contribute £1,000 towards his private use of the shared vans during the year.

	Mr Collins		*Mr Konchesky*		*Mr Gabbidon*
	£	£	£	£	£
WHU 100					
Charge	3,230		3,230		N/A as only used for work/ commuting
Reduction 25%	(808)	2,422	75% (2,422)	808	
for sharing			—	—	
WHU 101					
Charge	3,230		3,230		N/A as only used for work/ commuting
Reduction 75%	(2,422)	808	50% (1,615)	1,615	
for sharing	—		—		
WHU 102					
Charge	–		3,230		Commuting Exemption
Reduction			75% (2,422)	808	
for sharing		—	—	—	
		3,230		3,231	
Less: Cash		(1,000)		–	
Taxable benefit		2,230		3,231	

Other travel-related benefits

Bicycles and motorcycles

7.52   Often derided, the 'tax-free' company bicycle can be attractive in the right circumstances (Oxford and Cambridge notably, where bicycles rule!)

The tax and NIC exemption applies to the benefit of a bicycle or related safety equipment lent by an employer to an employee for travel to and from home and work [*ITEPA 2003, s 244*]. Similarly, no tax or NIC arises on workplace parking for bicycles and motorcycles

The bicycle exemption does not apply unless the benefit is available generally to all employees (although there is no 'generally available' condition for the provision of workplace parking), but clearly common sense has to be used to see which employees could possibly have use for a company bicycle! Where the bicycle is subsequently purchased by the employee, no tax charge arises provided the amount paid is at least its current market value. HMRC provide a residual market value matrix at www.gov.uk/hmrc-internal-manuals/employment-income-manual/eim21667a.

A number of companies (for example, Cyclescheme) offer a comprehensive scheme to loan bicycles to employees (in conjunction with a large number of independent bike shops). The bicycles are typically provided through a salary sacrifice (OpRA) arrangement (see 7.87A). Since gross salary is sacrificed for a non-taxable benefit, the employee saves income tax and NIC. The arrangement also reduces the company's Class 1 NIC. The employee normally has the option to purchase the bike at the end of the 'loan' period. The provision of the bicycle through an OpRA scheme is unaffected by the tax charges that are levied on most benefits in kind provided via an OpRA from 6 April 2017 (see 7.87A).

For business use of an employee's *own* bicycle, tax relief at 20p per mile can be claimed tax-free from the employer (or at any lower rate per mile! This only covers business use, so excludes travel to and from home and work. Again, if the circumstances fit, this could be a useful tax relief claim. Similarly, tax relief can be claimed for the business use of an employee's own motorbike at 24p per mile (if the employer reimburses business mileage at less than 24p per mile).

Car parking and parking fines

7.53   There is no tax charge on a director or employee where the company provides a free parking space for a car, van or motorcycle at or near the workplace. Facilities for parking bicycles are also tax-exempt [*ITEPA 2003, s 237*].

However, where the parking space is provided via an OpRA arrangement after 5 April 2017, this will be taxed (see 7.87A). A 'transitional' exemption applies to OpRA arrangements for a workplace parking space agreed before 6 April 2017, which will normally continue to be tax-free until 6 April 2018.

Where a company pays a parking fine as the registered owner of a car etc, no taxable benefit should arise on the employee/director as the company car benefit charge covers all costs associated with the car.

However, the fine should be disallowed for corporation tax purposes on the authority of *CIR v Alexander von Glehn Ltd* [1920] 19 TC 232 as HMRC do not consider it to be incurred wholly and exclusively for the trade (see HMRC BIM 42515). This view was confirmed in *G4S Cash Solutions (UK) Ltd v HMRC* [2016] UKFTT 0239 (TC). G4S contended that the £580,000 it incurred on fines for various parking violations were legitimate trading expenses. They had been incurred in order to deliver cash to their customers. However, the FTT concurred with HMRC's longstanding view that statutory fines for breaking the law were not tax-deductible. It was noted that after the relevant period covered by the case, G4S had managed to reduce its parking fines by 50% by reviewing its processes!

Most tax practitioners would contend that, in many cases, such fines are a normal cost of doing business and hence should be allowed (in much the same way as a newspaper may claim relief for costs relating to defamation actions!).

In contrast, if the fine is the *employee's* liability (as the owner of the car), this is a taxable benefit for the employee, but the company should be able to claim a trading deduction for it.

Free or subsidised works buses

7.54 With the general aim of reducing the amount of commuting by car, no employment income tax or NIC charge arises on the 'benefit' of free or subsidised works buses (and on subsidies paid to local bus companies where the employees are carried free or at a reduced rate). Details of the conditions for the exemption can be found at EIM 21850.

Taxis and mini-cabs for late night working

7.55 Following a recommendation by the Office of Tax Simplification, Budget 2011 intended to abolish the 'benefit in kind' exemption for the provision of infrequent taxis and mini cabs from work to home as a result of 'late working'. However, after consultation, this proposal was scrapped. This means that employees who are occasionally (less than 60 times a year) required to work late (after 9pm) will not be subject to a benefit-in-kind on their taxi fare (*ITEPA 2003, s 248*)

TRAVEL AND SUBSISTENCE COSTS

Allowable business travel

7.56 Family or owner-managed companies will generally meet all (reasonable) 'business' travel costs incurred by directors and employees. The rules relating to admissible 'business travel' were revised by the *Finance Act 1998* to bring the system into line with modern working practices.

The current legislation is in *ITEPA 2003, ss 337–340.*

Travelling expenses are allowed where they cover the full cost of necessary travel in the performance of the duties, and the full cost of travel to/from a place where necessary duties are performed. For this purpose, 'in the performance of the duties' covers travel:

(*a*)   to/from a place the employee has to attend; or

(*b*)   to carry out duties at a 'temporary workplace'; or

(*c*)   after duties have commenced (necessary 'on-the-job' travel).

A 'temporary workplace' is a workplace where the employee goes only to perform a task of limited duration or other temporary purpose. This includes attendance for a continuous period likely to last not more than 24 months or where less than 40% of working time is spent. It does not include a permanent workplace under a fixed term appointment of less than 24 months.

A journey which is really 'ordinary commuting' (see 7.49) cannot be made a business journey just by arranging a business appointment on route. The test is, necessity to attend the particular place rather than the personal convenience of attending.

Subsistence costs

7.57 The cost of business travel includes subsistence costs related to the journey.

Overnight subsistence expenses (such as accommodation and costs) will normally be exempt provided they are accompanied by receipts, such as a hotel bill. Where a company rents accommodation to save long term hotel costs, HMRC will generally treat the property rent as part of the exempt subsistence payment [see EIM31836].

Any 'personal expenses', such as Sky TV and newspapers etc. will be taxable as a benefit in kind, subject to the £5 (UK) or £10 (overseas) per night exemption for 'Incidental Overnight Expenses' (IOEs), which might cover an employee's telephone calls, dry-cleaning and so on (*ITEPA 2003, s 240*).

This useful exemption is granted to cover expenses that would not normally be allowable (on the basis they are 'private' in nature) but are incurred as a result of the 'inconvenience' of working away from home.

Disallowable costs

7.58   On the other hand, costs are disallowed where they represent 'ordinary commuting' travel or travel between employments. 'Ordinary commuting' means any travel between a 'permanent workplace' and home, or any other place that is not a workplace.

A 'permanent workplace' is a workplace (other than a temporary workplace) attended regularly in the performance of the duties of the employment – this is the base from which the director or employee:

- performs their duties; or
- is allocated the tasks to be carried out by them in the performance of their duties.

There is, however, an exception to this rule and travel costs are admissible where there are two employers and both employers are members of the same group (51% subsidiaries). Travel is 'on-the-job' travel between employers for a joint project, or where duties are performed wholly or partly overseas.

The only exception to the prohibition in respect to paying mileage for home to work travel is where the work begins at the moment the employee is called out and continues throughout the journey. Typically, this would apply to life-saving advice being given by a medic en-route to a hospital setting.

'IR 35' cases

7.59   From 6 April 2016, the 'travel and subsistence' rules for personal service companies caught by IR35 have been aligned with those for employees. Broadly, home to work travel and subsistence expenses are *not* eligible for tax relief (see 6.24).

Worked examples

Example 8

Necessary 'business' travel – 1

Mr Clough lives in Derby. He has no normal place of work as a computer consultant, although he occasionally visits HQ in London. He spends a few days or weeks at the offices, etc, of various clients of his employing company. His travel expenses are reimbursed.

Mr Clough has no tax liability on his reimbursed travel expenses as his journeys are to/from a place where necessary duties are performed and are not ordinary commuting travel.

Example 9

Necessary 'business' travel – 2

Nobby lives in Hartlepool and works in Nottingham. He commutes by car every day.

He visits a client's office in Leeds by car, driving there directly and returning home. The cost is reimbursed by his employer.

Mr Stiles does not suffer any tax on the reimbursed cost, as the journey is to/from a place where necessary duties are performed and is not ordinary commuting travel.

Triangular travel

7.60   Where triangular travel is involved, the company may feel it is inappropriate to reimburse more than the additional cost of the trip. In such situations, the employee can claim tax relief on the difference between the actual cost and the amount reimbursed.

Example 10

Triangular travel

Nigel normally travels 14 miles to his workplace. To avoid travelling an extra 18 miles to visit a customer, he travels direct to/from home to the customer. This involves a 24-mile trip as shown below:

Nigel could receive tax-free reimbursement for 48 miles. If the employer only reimbursed 20 miles, being only the additional distance travelled (48 miles *less* 28 miles saved by not going to the normal workplace), Nigel could claim tax relief on the cost for 28 miles.

NICs on business travel

7.61   There are no NICs payable on reasonable business travel and subsistence allowances paid to employees. NICs are charged on payments which more than reimburse the employee for the cost of business travel.

For car mileage allowances, there is no NIC liability if they do not exceed HMRC's approved 45p per mile AMAPs rate (see 7.44). (It is impracticable to use the two-tier rates as NICs are calculated in each earnings period during the tax year).

BENEFICIAL LOANS

Calculation of taxable benefit

7.62   A taxable benefit arises on the provision of a beneficial loan which is made available by reason of employment. Such loans are typically interest-free or are 'cheap', carrying less than a market rate of interest.

Broadly, the taxable benefit is equivalent to:

●   the amount of interest that would have been paid if the director/employee had paid interest at the 'official rate of interest' (which approximates to a commercial rate); *less*

●   any interest actually paid by them.

The benefit is normally calculated using the 'average method'. This calculates the average loan for the tax year by averaging the balances on the loan accounts at the beginning and at the end of the tax year. The official interest rate is then applied to this average balance. (If the loan was first made or repaid during the year, the balance is taken on the relevant date of the loan/repayment, as appropriate). It is also possible to elect for the benefit to be calculated precisely on a daily basis.

The official rate of interest for 2017/18 is 2.5% and the published (average) rates for past tax years are:

	Official rate
2016/17	3.00%
2015/16	3.00%
2014/15	3.25%

There is no taxable benefit or Class 1A NICs charge on loans made to employees where the total of all loans (at any time in the relevant tax year) to the same employee does not exceed £10,000 (prior to 6 April 2014 the limit was £5,000). This should exempt the majority of interest-free season ticket-loans.

There is also no taxable benefit on *qualifying* loans (ie where assuming interest had been paid on the loan it would have been deductible for tax purposes). This would include a loan made to a shareholder to buy shares in a close (unlisted) trading company, such as the company for which they work [*ITEPA 2003, ss 173–187*]. Such qualifying loans do not need to be reported on the form P11D.

Where a loan is made to a director/shareholder, a corporate tax charge may arise under *CTA 2010, s 455* (see 2.58).

Loans to purchase a main residence

7.63   It should be noted that interest paid on a loan to purchase the employee's main residence is *not* tax deductible (although many will remember when it used to be!)

Consequently, any cheap loan facility to purchase a main residence attracts a taxable benefit. However, the company might provide alternative assistance towards the purchase of a house by an employee by making temporary deposits with building societies for preferential mortgage treatment.

The granting of a loan to an employee at a reduced rate of interest for the purchase of a house is a traditional benefit offered by banks and insurance companies. There is no real reason why a family or owner-managed company should not offer the same benefit, but it may not be wise in view of the substantial funds likely to be needed and the level of control required over the use of the loan proceeds.

Example 11

Beneficial loans to employees

Venables Ltd, trading as a sugar refiner, provides house purchase loans of £30,000 to employees to help them purchase their main residence.

The interest rate charged on the employee loans is 2% per annum.

The official rate of interest is 2.5% for 2017/18, so the income tax liability on each employee is based on a benefit of £150 , ie £30,000 × 0.5% (2.5%–2%).

Tax rate	Income tax liability
20%	£150 @ 20% = £30
40%	£150 @ 40% = £60

Note: Venables Ltd would also be liable for Class 1A NICs on the taxable benefit figure of £150 .

LIVING ACCOMMODATION

Overview of tax rules

7.64   An employment tax charge arises where living accommodation is provided for an employee/director (or members of their family), subject to certain 'narrow' exemptions (see 7.65 and 7.66).

The provision of living accommodation for an employee/director is subject to two charging provisions which depend on the cost incurred by the company (for these purposes, 'cost' represents the cost of acquiring the property plus any improvements to it) (see 7.675 and 7.68).

The same rules apply to both UK and overseas property, although there is an important exemption for individuals who purchase *overseas* property through a company (see 7.73).

Where accommodation is provided, it is probably sensible to make sure that the director/employee does not obtain a protected tenancy. This can be avoided by:

(*a*)   providing a 'service tenancy', linked to the employment and enabling the company to terminate the tenancy on termination of the employment if it can be shown that the accommodation is provided for the better fulfilment (not necessary fulfilment) of the duties of the employment; or

(*b*)   the company showing it requires the accommodation for another employee; or

(*c*)   the tenancy being outside the scope of the protected tenancy legislation.

Accommodation provided for proper performance of duties

7.65   There is no income tax charge where the accommodation is provided for a director or employee in certain circumstances (often referred to as the 'representative occupation' exemption). However, the restrictive nature of this exemption means that it is generally of little use to the vast majority of working shareholders. The exemption in *ITEPA 2003, s 99* applies where either:

(*a*)   it is necessary for the proper performance of the employee's duties that they should reside in the accommodation; or

(*b*)   the accommodation is provided for the better performance of the duties of the employment, and it is customary for employers to provide living accommodation for those engaged in such employment.

Furthermore, these exemptions do *not* apply to *directors* unless they work full-time and hold 5% *or less* of the company's shares. If the 'full time' test is not satisfied, the director may still qualify for the exemption where the company is 'non-profit' making (ie it does not carry on a trade and its functions do not consist wholly or mainly in holding investments or other property) *or* it is established for charitable purposes only [*ITEPA 2003, s 99(3)*].

Employees may face difficulty in obtaining exemption following the case of *Vertigan v Brady* [1988] STC 91. The exemption in (*a*) above was held to be directed to a necessity based on the relationship between the proper performance of the employee's duties and the accommodation provided, and not on the personal demands of the employee.

The exemption in (*b*) is generally thought to cover the 'flat over the shop' situation for a shop manager or a caretaker's on-site residence. This was held to require identification of three constituent factors in identifying where the employment was 'one of the kinds of employment in the case of which it is customary for employers to provide living accommodation', which are:

- the statistical evidence as to how common the practice was;

- how long the practice has continued; and

- whether it had achieved acceptance generally by the relevant employers.

In practice, these are likely to be relatively restrictive exemptions – common 'permissible' examples would include landlords of country pubs, agricultural workers living on farms, caretakers living on premises, and wardens living within sheltered housing accommodation.

Accommodation provided as a result of a security threat

7.66   Similarly, the provision of accommodation is also exempt if there is a special threat to the employee's security, so that special security arrangements are in force and the employee resides in the accommodation as part of those arrangements [*ITEPA 2003, s 100*].

Where cost of accommodation does not exceed £75,000

7.67   Where the purchase price paid by the employer for the accommodation does not exceed £75,000 (*ITEPA 2003, s 105*), the taxable benefit is:

	£
Rental value of the property	A
Less: Actual rent paid by the employee	(B)
Taxable benefit	C

The rental value is the amount that would have been payable if the employee had paid an annual rent equal to the annual value. For these purposes, the gross rateable value is taken as an indication of the commercial rent that the tenant might pay.

The following gross rating values are used:

– England & Wales	– 1972 gross rating value
– Northern Ireland	– 1976 gross rating value
– Scotland	– 1985 gross rating value × 100/270

In all other cases, the value can be determined by the District Valuer.

In most cases, the annual value will be very much lower than the actual commercial rent as rateable values have not changed in England and Wales since 1973.

The gross rateable value can only be used where the provider of the accommodation, usually the employer, owns the property. Sometimes there will be no rateable value (for example the property may be recently built), in which case an estimate is made. If there is a dispute on the amount of the 'annual value', this can be appealed to the First-Tier Tribunal.

If the company rents the premises the tax charge is generally based on the rent payable by the company less any rent paid by the employee. (In such cases, the company's rent is likely to be greater than the gross rateable value) [*ITEPA 2003, s 105*].

Any lease premium paid by the company is also taxed as rent (except where the property is being leased for more than ten years). The taxable lease premium is spread over the period of the lease and added to any annual rent charge in calculating the benefit (subject to any deduction for amounts made good by the employee).

Where cost of accommodation exceeds £75,000

7.68   *ITEPA 2003, s 106* levies a tax charge on such accommodation, which is made up of two elements:

- the basic 'annual rental/value' charge calculated under (a) above; plus

- an 'additional yearly rental' charge calculated as follows:

    $ORI \times (C - £75,000)$

Where:

(i)   ORI is the official rate of interest in force on 6 April in the tax year – 2.5% for 2017/18 (see 7.62);

(ii)   C is the cost of the property together with any improvements (less any amount reimbursed by the director/employee or paid by them for the grant of the tenancy).

This is subject to the 'market value' rule, which generally applies where the company acquired their interest in the property more than six years before it was provided to the director/employee. In such cases, C becomes the *open market value* of the property when it was first occupied by the director/employee (as opposed to the original cost) plus the cost of any subsequent improvements. However, since all the conditions for the 'market value' method will rarely apply, the 'cost' basis will often be used.

If the accommodation is only made available for less than a year, the chargeable amount is appropriately reduced. Similarly, if the property is shared by more than one employee, the charge will be scaled down having regard to all the relevant facts (and the total amount charged *cannot* exceed the amount that would be charged on sole occupation) [*ITEPA 2003, s 108*].

Accommodation expenses and assets

7.69 There is a separate tax charge on directors and employees in respect of ancillary benefits, such as expenditure incurred or reimbursed by the employer on heating, lighting, cleaning, repairs, furnishings, etc. *Before* 6 April 2016, there was no tax charge for employees earning less than £8,500 per year.

This charge applies regardless of whether the provision of the accommodation is tax-exempt. However, if the accommodation itself is exempt as being necessary for the performance of the employee's duties, etc (see 7.66), then this tax charge is restricted to 10% of the employee's net emoluments [*ITEPA 2003, s 315*]. Furthermore, in such cases, there is no tax charge on council tax or water rates/charges.

Where the accommodation is not tax-exempt the provision of assets in the property (such as furniture, television and video, hi-fi equipment, etc) is subject to a special 'annual value' tax charge. This is computed as 20% of the market value of the relevant assets when they were first provided [*ITEPA 2003, ss 201 and 205*] reported in section L of the P11D (assets used).

There is no tax charge on alterations and additions to the premises of a structural nature or repairs which would be the lessor's obligation if the premises were let under a lease to which *s 11* of the *Landlord and Tenant Act 1985* applied. However, such expenditure must be borne by the employer and not by the employee who is then reimbursed [*ITEPA 2003, s 313*].

Example 12

Beneficial occupation of accommodation

Wright Ltd purchases a house for £185,000. An employee occupies the property throughout the tax year 2017/18 and pays rent of £200 per annum. The gross rateable value is £2,000. The employee meets the lighting and heating costs and other normal tenant's running expenses. The accommodation was furnished by Wright Ltd at a total cost of £5,000.

Income tax for 2017/18 on:			£
Accommodation charge – s 104	Step 1	Gross rateable value	2,000
	Step 2/3	2.5% of (£185,000 – £75,000)	2,750
			4,750
	Step 4	Less: rent paid	(200)
		Accommodation charge	4,550
Provision of assets – charge under s 205		20% of cost of furnishings of £5,000	1,000
			£5,550

The total income tax charge on this £5,550 deemed income should then be compared with the annual market rent that would otherwise have been paid by the employee. The potential rent might well exceed £2,220 (£5,550 × (say) 40% – say £185 per month, depending on the house value and location.

Main planning points

Restricting availability of the property

7.70   If an employee uses living accommodation provided by their employer for (say) 30 days in a tax year, it is necessary to consider whether the charge is based on the annual value for the complete tax year. The legislation refers to the accommodation provided in any period. Hence, to restrict the tax charge to the actual period of occupation by the employee or member of their family or household, it might be necessary to show that the accommodation could only be occupied by them for that period. Appropriate documentation would need to be in place to demonstrate that this was because of conditions imposed by the employer (rather than through the employee's choice).

If the employer provides living accommodation by acquiring a right to 'time-share' a holiday home for a specific period, this would restrict the tax charge on the employees by reference to the period for which the home is available for occupation.

Furnished letting

7.71   With the annual value (gross rateable value) being the measure of the tax charge where the provider of the accommodation owns the property, the tax charge on the employee is invariably less than the commercial rent that would otherwise have been paid. Tax-efficient arrangements include the employer acquiring the freehold or long leasehold of premises and repairing and fitting them up to the standard requirement for furnished lettings.

The employee is then granted a lease (after the repair work has been carried out so that no tax charge is levied thereon). The lease would be on the normal basis of the employer/lessor meeting the cost of exterior repairs, ground rent, etc and the employee/tenant paying the rates, lighting and heating costs, etc.

7.72 For overseas property owned by the employer, the tax charge would normally be based on the market rent obtainable on a letting in the absence of any rateable value. (HMRC have been known to accept using the rateable value of a similar size property in a coastal part of England as a convenience measure.) In such cases, ESC A91 provides that no tax charge will arise under standard tax charging rule in *ITEPA 2003, s 105* (see 7.67).

Certain cases, such as where an individual has structured their purchase of overseas property through a company, may be eligible for exemption (see 7.74).

As a general rule, the annual tax charge on the furniture and fittings is 20% of the market value when they were first provided (as in 7.70). However, where the provision of the living accommodation is exempt from the tax charge on the basis of representative occupation, maximum advantage can be taken of the limitation of the tax charge on ancillary benefits to 10% of net emoluments. The furnishings and fittings can be of the highest quality without any additional tax charge arising, provided they are held to be 'normal for domestic occupation' as required by *ITEPA 2003, s 315(3)(c)*.

Example 13

Exempt accommodation necessary for employment duties – fixtures and fittings

N'Golo Ltd purchases antique furniture, household appliances, television, hi-fi equipment, etc for £20,000, which are placed in 'exempt' accommodation. This would normally give an annual income tax charge on the director/employee on the annual benefit of £4,000 (20% of £20,000). The employee's net emoluments are, say:

	£	£
Salary, benefits and expenses		28,600
Less Allowable expenses	(400)	
Pension contributions	(2,200)	(2,600)
Net emoluments		26,000

The tax charge is therefore based on 10% of £26,000 = £2,600, instead of the standard £4,000 benefit charge.

Exemption for overseas property held through an overseas company

7.73 Ownership of overseas property by UK citizens has grown dramatically in recent years. In a substantial number of cases, the properties are acquired through an offshore company. There are a number of reasons for this, including the desire to avoid local rules restricting foreign ownership or forced heirship regimes which require that a significant part of the property must pass on death to the owner's children.

Even though such property-owning structures have not been motivated by UK tax planning considerations, HMRC originally took the strict view that a benefit charge arose on the 'individual' owner, which was strengthened by the ruling in *R v Allen* [2001] STC 1537. This was generally because the individual shareholder of the company would fall to be treated as a 'shadow director' – ie someone who provides instructions or directions which are normally followed by the actual directors (see *ITEPA 2003, s 67*).

Because of these potential tax issues, many individuals have used an overseas company to acquire the property as a nominee on their behalf. Provided the legal documents are drawn-up correctly, the individual would be treated as beneficially owning the property for UK tax purposes and therefore no UK benefit charge can be sustained.

In the Budget 2007, HMRC effectively acknowledged that it was inequitable to impose a benefits charge in such cases (after some excellent 'behind the scenes' work by The Chartered Institute of Taxation). Accordingly, legislation enacted in the *Finance Act 2008. ITEPA 2003, s 100A* provides an exemption in respect of non-UK living accommodation provided by a company for a director (including any member of his family) or any other officer of the company. However, the exemption is framed in such a way to cover only those cases where a company has been used (only) to hold the overseas property. The relevant conditions are:

- The property is held by a company that is *wholly owned* by individuals (therefore trustee ownership would not count). This condition can also be satisfied where individuals own a holding company, with the property being held in a subsidiary.

- The property is the company's only or main asset and its only activities are those that are incidental to its ownership of the property.

- The property is not funded either directly or indirectly by a 'connected company'. However, this condition is met if any borrowing is made at a commercial rate or results in a taxable benefit for the 'owner'.

Where these conditions are satisfied for the relevant tax year, the exemption (which only applies to income tax) will apply retrospectively without any time limit. However, this is a fairly narrow exemption and is therefore unlikely to apply to the vast majority of overseas holiday homes owned or property investments held by owner-managed companies.

Tax-efficient investment

7.74 The provision of holiday accommodation by a family or owner-managed company is not only tax efficient, it can also have the following advantages:

(i) the prospect of capital growth as a purchased investment;

(ii) an incentive to employees if the accommodation is situated in a desirable location – the employer could award varying periods of stay based on predetermined performance targets;

(iii) it can force working shareholders to take a necessary and meaningful break from their work positions, which they might otherwise avoid;

(iv) it may provide an attractive venue for working conventions for salesmen or senior executives.

The tax charge on the provision of a 'holiday' in a company-owned property (not costing over £75,000) is illustrated in Example 14.

While the provision of holiday accommodation can often be tax efficient, it is important to ensure that it does not impact upon the trading status of the company for CGT entrepreneurs' relief or IHT Business Property Relief purposes.

Example 14

Holiday accommodation

Ranieri (Leicester) Ltd owns the following two 'holiday' premises, each of which can be used by its employees for holidays once a year (for a maximum stay of two weeks). During the year ended 5 April 2018, Mr Claudio takes up his full allocation and his consequent tax liability is calculated as follows:

	UK property	Overseas property (not eligible for FA 2008 exemption)
Gross rateable value	£520	not applicable
Market rent	£3,120	£8,320
Period of stay	2 weeks	2 weeks
Tax charge on:	2/52 × £520	2/52 × £8,320
	= £20	= £320
Marginal tax rate	40%	40%
Income tax payable	£8	£128

Deductible expenses

7.75   The amount of the charge as a benefit for the provision of living accommodation can be reduced by an expense claim under *ITEPA 2003, s 336*. This enables the director or employee to claim expenses that would have been deductible had the accommodation been paid for out of their employment earnings. Some guidance as to the scope for this reduction in the tax charge is provided by HMRC's booklet IR 480 at sections 21.22 and 21.23:

'If accommodation is provided for an employee, for example in a flat or hotel, while the employee is on business duties away from his or her home and normal place of work, the cost of this may be allowable as a deduction under the expenses rule. For example, a company in Yorkshire may rent a London flat for an employee who has to make frequent business trips to London. The extent of any tax allowance will depend upon the circumstances. If the accommodation is no more than an alternative to hotel accommodation and is not available for private occupation the whole cost of renting and running the flat may be allowed as a deduction. On the other hand, if the employee or his or her family also had the use of the flat as a private residence any allowance would be restricted.

If, however, a London flat is provided for an employee whose job is in London and the flat is used by the employee as a *pied à terre* no allowance would be due. Equally if the flat is used by the employee or the employee's family as their only or second home, no deduction for tax purposes would be due.'

RELOCATION PACKAGES AND REMOVAL EXPENSES

Basic rules

7.76 There is an income tax and NIC exemption for directors and employees for qualifying removal benefits and expenses reasonably incurred or provided in connection with a change in the employee's residence [*ITEPA 2003, ss 271– 289*]. The exemption is restricted to a maximum of £8,000 [*ITEPA 2003, s 287*] of qualifying benefits provided and expenses incurred (see 7.69). To qualify these must be provided or incurred *before* the end of the tax year following that in which the job change takes place or a later time if reasonable [*ITEPA 2003, s 274*].

The change in residence must be made wholly or mainly to allow the employee to reside within a reasonable daily travelling distance of his employment base. Furthermore, the change must result from:

(*a*) the employee becoming employed by a new employer; or

(*b*) an alteration of the duties of an existing employment; or

(*c*) the place of performance of the duties of an existing employment being changed.

Furthermore, the employee's old residence must not be within a reasonable daily travelling distance of the new workplace, but it does not need to be disposed of for the tax exemption to apply. The requirement is to cease to use the old residence as the main residence and instead use the new residence as such [*ITEPA 2003, s 273*].

The £8,000 relocation exemption prevents the removal benefits and expenses being taxed as earnings. They are therefore ignored for all purposes, including the form P11D. Any excess amount over the £8,000 attracts income tax and Class 1A NICs and is returned on the form P11D. Control is largely via a PAYE audit.

Qualifying removal benefits and expenses

7.77 The qualifying removal benefits and expenses are summarised below:

* *acquisition benefits and expenses* – this covers legal expenses on acquisition, legal expenses on loan raised, loan procurement fees, survey fees, Land Registration fees, stamp duty and public utilities connection charges – the interest acquired by a member of the employee's family or household is included [*ITEPA 2003, s 277*];

* *abortive acquisition benefits and expenses* – this is as for buying/ renting a new home above, provided the interest in the residence fails to be acquired because of circumstances outside the employee's control or because he reasonably declines to proceed [*ITEPA 2003, s 278*];

- ***disposal benefits and expenses*** – this covers legal expenses of selling the old home, legal expenses on loan redemption, loan redemption penalty, estate agent/auctioneer fees, advertising, public utilities disconnection charges, security, maintenance and insurance costs when unoccupied and rent payable when unoccupied [*ITEPA 2003, s 279*].

Again, the interest disposed of by a member of the employee's family or household is included. HMRC accepts this also covers the interest owned by a co-habitee;

- ***transporting belongings*** – this covers the removal costs of transporting domestic belongings, insurance cover, temporary storage and detaching/attaching/adapting domestic fittings from the old residence to the new residence [*ITEPA 2003, s 280*];

- ***travelling and subsistence*** – this covers a wide range of expenditure:

  - (*a*)   travel and subsistence (ie food, drink and temporary living accommodation) of the employee and family/household members on temporary visits to a new area in connection with the residence change;

  - (*b*)   employee's travel to/from the former residence and new employment base;

  - (*c*)   costs of temporary living accommodation for the *employee* (but not family/household);

  - (*d*)   employee's travel to/from the old residence and any temporary accommodation;

  - (*e*)   travel of employee and family/household from the old residence in connection with the change in residence;

  - (*f*)   subsistence of a child under the age of 19 being a member of employee's family/household, while remaining in living accommodation in the old area for educational continuity after the change or in the new area for educational continuity before the change;

  - (*g*)   travel of the child between their living accommodation and the employee's new or old residence as appropriate [*ITEPA 2003, s 281*];

- ***replacement of domestic goods*** – this covers the cost of replacement of domestic goods used at the old residence but unsuitable for use at the new residence, *less* any sale proceeds of the goods replaced [*ITEPA 2003, s 285*];

- ***bridging loan expenses*** – this covers interest on a bridging loan where a period elapses between incurring expenditure on acquiring a new residence and receiving the proceeds of sale of the old residence – the loan limit is the market value of the old residence and no account is taken of that part of the loan used to purchase the new residence or to redeem a loan on the old residence [*ITEPA 2003, ss 272(2)(b)* and *284*].

If the bridging loan is a cheap loan provided by the employer, this is excluded from relief under this head. However, if the rest of the relocation package does not exceed £8,000, the balance can be included in this way [*ITEPA 2003, s 288*].

Other issues

7.78   A flat rate allowance may be paid rather than reimbursing specific expenditure, in which case the allowance can be paid gross, provided HMRC are satisfied that it does no more than reimburse eligible costs. The allowance should be included on the form P11D, if not exempt under the specific relief.

The £8,000 limit is unlikely to be reasonable for many UK moves, and is certainly unreasonable for international relocations. Example 15 illustrates a typical case that exceeds the £8,000 limit even where some eligible heads have nil entries.

Example 15

Relocation package

Gary was a senior production manager with Crispgoals Ltd. In September 2017, the company relocated him from its Leicester production plant to its head office based in London.

The following costs were incurred in connection with Gary's relocation:

	£
Expenses on sale (house sold for £100,000)	1,500
Expenses on purchase (house bought for £100,000)	2,000
Abortive acquisition costs	Nil
Removal costs	2,500
Temporary accommodation	3,500
Bridging loan expenses	Nil
Replacement of domestic goods	2,500
	£12,000

PAYE is not applied to the excess of eligible costs over £8,000. Instead, the excess over £8,000 is included on the form P11D (see 7.100).

OTHER COMMON EMPLOYEE BENEFITS

Workplace nurseries and employer-supported childcare

7.79   Many working parents rely on childcare arrangements and so this can be a very attractive benefit to provide for employees. Employer-supported childcare generally gives rise to a taxable benefit under normal principles, based on the cost to the employer of providing such assistance. However, employee supported childcare arrangements will attract a valuable income tax and Class 1/Class 1A NIC exemption provided they meet certain conditions. These arrangements broadly cover all children of the employee up to the 1 September after their 15th birthday.

Given the valuable tax exemption, employer supported childcare schemes are often incorporated into salary sacrifice arrangements. Fortunately, the tax exemption offered by child care arrangements is not affected by the post-5 April 2017 taxation of salary sacrifice (OpRA) rules (see 7.87A).

See also 7.79A for the 'new' tax-free child-care scheme.

There are three separate forms of eligible child-care relief:

- *Employer-provided childcare or workplace nurseries* – This is where the childcare is provided on the company's premises, such as in the form of a nursery or crèche. To qualify as a 'tax-free' benefit (regardless of the cost of the place), the care must be provided on premises controlled by the company, or the company must play a significant role in managing and financing the care facilities [*ITEPA 2003, s 318*]. This requirement has generally prevented many smaller family companies from providing tax-free childcare for their employees. However, it is possible for the company to enter into 'partnership arrangements' with commercial nursery providers, provided the company is still 'wholly or partly responsible for the financing and managing' the child care facility. (The exemption for Class 1A NICs is wider and extends to employers contracting for places in commercial nurseries or for the services of a childminder, as well as to childcare vouchers).

- *Childcare voucher scheme* – This involves the employees receiving 'childcare' vouchers from their employer. Up to a limit of £55 per week per employee, these tax and NIC-free vouchers form a valuable contribution towards the provision of childcare. Payment must be made in vouchers – it is possible for the company to establish its own voucher scheme, rather than outsourcing it. No employees may newly join a childcare voucher scheme from 6 April 2018. A new government scheme, tax-free childcare is now open to qualifying parents (see 7.79A).

Payments will *not* be eligible for the 'childcare' exemption where the employee contracts privately for the childcare, which is then settled by the company [*ITEPA 2003, ss 270A and 318A–318D*].

- *Third-party contracted child-care* – A company can provide childcare through a third party. In this case, the first £55 per week of childcare costs per employee is exempt from tax and NICs.

The childcare under the *childcare voucher* and *'third-party' contract* schemes, must be:

- open to all the employees (or, where appropriate, to all the employees working at the location where the scheme operates); and

- provided by a registered child-carer or an approved home child-carer.

The *FA 2011* introduced a concession for companies operating a 'salary sacrifice' scheme for childcare provision, employees. In such cases, employees could not take part in the childcare scheme if it would reduce their remaining earnings below the national minimum wage. Consequently, such employees can be excluded without affecting the availability of tax relief for the other employees.

Employees are only entitled to one weekly £55 exemption, even if the care is provided to more than one child. The *FA 2011* introduced an important restriction for higher-rate taxpayers. For those joining schemes *after 5 April 2011*, the income tax exemption is only given at the basic rate of tax.

Thus, the relief available to higher rate taxpayers is restricted to the basic income tax rate (20%) by reducing the weekly exempt amount (*ITEPA 2003, s 270A(6ZA)*). The overall effect is to give all employees tax relief of £11 per week. This means that the relevant weekly exempt amounts would be as follows:

Taxpayer	Weekly exemption
20%	£55
40%	£28
45%	£24

To decide which exempt amount to apply, the employer is responsible for making an assessment of each employee's earnings at the start of the year. Any failure to carry out this 'basic earnings assessment' will prevent tax relief being available for the employer's scheme. (Although Scottish tax thresholds have diverged from the rest of the UK for 2017/18, 'the rest of UK rates' are used for the basic earnings assessment for Scottish parents in receipt of childcare vouchers so they are not disadvantaged.)

There is no reason why the proprietorial directors of a family or owner-managed company cannot enjoy the tax-free childcare arrangements. It is worth noting that a husband and wife can each claim a separate exemption in respect of the same child. (Clearly they would both have to be directors/ genuine employees.),

New tax-free childcare scheme

7.79A   In March 2013, the Government announced that it would be introducing a new 'tax-free' childcare scheme for UK resident parents who are both in paid work (employment or self-employment). The scheme is available for children up to the age of 12 (17 for disabled children) but initially from early 2017 it will be for children aged up to five. However, the age restriction for children up to 12 years once the scheme is fully rolled-out, means that childcare vouchers are still the most attractive option for parents with teenagers requiring care (see 7.79).

The scheme is not open to households who are entitled to universal credit or in receipt of support from an employer-supported childcare scheme. Each parent's income must not exceed £100,000 per annum with a minimum requirement that each has 'earnings' (or income from self-employment) of at least 16 hours per week at the national living wage/national minimum wage.

Broadly, the scheme will provide *working* parents with a benefit for *each child* equal to the *lower* of

- £2,000 (£4,000 if the child is disabled): or

- 20% of childcare costs.

Parents using the scheme will pay money into a digital account managed by National Savings and Investments. A separate account must be used for each child. The funds will be used to pay the registered childcare provider of their choice. The government will pay its contribution into this account on a quarterly basis up to a maximum of £500 (£1,000 per quarter for a disabled child).

After the new scheme is launched, employer-supported childcare schemes will be closed to new entrants from *6 April 2018* . Current participants in existing employer-supported childcare schemes will have the option of remaining in their current scheme or opting into the new scheme. However, if they leave an employer who offers a voucher scheme or simply opt to take tax-free childcare they will not be able to take vouchers in future. Workplace childcare provision will be unaffected.

Corporate clothing

7.80   Nowadays, HMRC tends to accept that no income tax charge should arise on employee 'uniforms'. This can be extended to more attractive corporate clothing, including a suit, provided there is a prominent company name or logo sewn into the garment. Many companies send samples of the relevant clothing to obtain 'informal clearance' that it meets the necessary criteria for the 'corporate clothing' exemption. The employer's policy should be consistent so that, say, all employees meeting customers/clients or on view to them are able to wear the corporate clothing.

Within a family or owner-managed company, corporate identity through clothing certainly has its place.

Where employees are required to 'wash' their uniforms, it is possible for them to obtain tax relief of around £60 per year. On request (most easily actioned through the employee's personal tax account), HMRC will add this allowance to their PAYE tax code.

Life cover and permanent health insurance

7.81   Life cover for death in service, and sickness and disability insurance, often forms part of a pension scheme and, as such, is tax efficient since this is not a taxable benefit in kind as long as the sickness or disability policy pays out to the employer who then uses it to fund any continuing salary provision.

However, from 6 April 2017, any (additional) life cover provided through a salary sacrifice (OpRA) arrangement would be taxable (see 7.87A) and the amount of salary given up is the reportable amount on the P11D.

If the policy pays out tax-free to the employee, then the insurance premium is a taxable benefit in kind. The attractiveness of permanent health insurance as part of a benefits programme lies in its ability to provide an income of 75% of salary on disability right up to the normal retirement date. Thus, this ensures the employees' continued participation in the pension scheme instead of having to rely on benefit levels applicable at the enforced early retirement date.

Home telephone

7.82   Many employees regularly or permanently work at home to reduce the costs of office premises. In such cases, the reimbursement of telephone costs is normally expected. However, a number of potential tax and NIC pitfalls need to be managed.

Where an employer arranges for a phone line to be installed in the employee's home and personal use is *not* permitted, it does not matter whether the 'phone' contract is with the employer or employee. So long as it is *paid by the employer*, there are no tax or NI implications/reporting.

On the other hand, where the employee pays and then claims it on their expenses, the *line rental element* should be paid through payroll on a 'grossed-up' basis. The business calls are ignored for reporting purposes.

Where private use is permitted, there is obviously 'mixed-use' and so the position is as follows:

Contract with	Private use permitted	Who pays supplier	Reporting
Employer	Yes	Employer	Section M Class 1A NIC line if private calls covered Section M (not Class 1A) if employee reimburses private calls
Employee	Yes	Employer	Section B rental and all calls (counter claim for business calls) Class 1 NIC payable through payroll for rental and private calls
Employee	Yes	Employee then reimbursed	Tax and NIC via payroll for rental & private calls Do not report business calls if these can be substantiated, if not, gross up the payroll and the employee must counterclaim for tax relief

Mobile phones

7.82A   The benefit of private use of a mobile phone/smartphone is exempt from tax [*ITEPA 2003, s 319* (except where the mobile phone/smartphone) is provided under a post-5 April 2007 salary sacrifice/OpRA arrangement – see below).

The provision of a mobile phone must be regarded as attractive, given their increasing importance to business communications. The employer needs to exercise some control over the amount of private use, given the potential costs involved. The exemption is restricted to one mobile phone per employee. However, a 'second phone' could be supplied under the exemption for office supplies (desks, chairs, computers etc) as long as private use was insignificant.

Provided the mobile phone contract is in the company's name (which is often the case), no Class 1A NIC liability arises. However, if the employing company reimburses the employee's own mobile phone bill, this will be treated as 'NICable' earnings under general principles, except where business calls can be identified. Phones cannot be supplied to family members who are *not* employees.

The provision of mobile phones under salary sacrifice/OPRA arrangements entered into after 5 April 2017 is subject to a tax and Class 1A NIC charge.

The charge is based on the amount of salary given-up and becomes reportable on the employee's P11D (see 7.87A for detailed coverage of salary sacrifice/OpRA rules).

If the phone is in a company vehicle, hands-free facilities can be provided tax-free and are not counted as car accessories.

Top-up cards are 'non-cash vouchers' but are exempt from tax and NIC under *ITEPA 2003, s 266(2)* where they are used to facilitate the loan of a mobile phone to an employee for private use. However, this exemption only applies where the benefit in kind arising on the loan of the mobile phone would have been exempt if a voucher had not been used.

Laptops and tablets that can connect to Facetime or Skype are not classed as mobile phones but are treated as computers.

HMRC's published guidance (*Revenue & Customs Brief 02/12*) states that smartphones (such as BlackBerries, iPhones (and similar PDA devices) are regarded as mobile phones rather than treated as computer equipment. This means that smartphones provided to employees for their personal use (without a transfer of ownership) do not give rise to a taxable benefit.

Broadband

7.82B   Many employers provide broadband access to their employees as part of the employees' homeworking arrangements. The employee's tax treatment depends on a number of factors, including who contracts with the broadband provider, who pays for it, and the employee's business/private use of the broadband service.

Since most employees will have internet access, there is also the difficulty of proving there is no cost 'differential' in using this for business as well as personal use. If the broadband was in place before the employee began to work at home, HMRC will argue there is no additional cost incurred.

Where this is the case, if the employer still wishes to reimburse broadband costs, £4 per week/£18 per month can be paid free of tax and NIC as a 'homeworking allowance'. This can be paid unreceipted but not via salary sacrifice (OpRA). Alternatively, the broadband costs can be included in a PAYE Settlement Agreement.

The main tax treatments are summarised in the table below:

	Employer provides broadband and pays for it	Employee contracts with broadband provider
Used for business purposes	Exempt under *ITEPA 2003, s 316* provided there is no *significant* private use. No tax reporting necessary	Fully reimbursed by employer for business use (with no significant private use) HMRC accepts that payment can be exempt under *ITEPA 2003, s 316A* (if there are additional costs incurred as a result of employee working at home) Where not reimbursed Employee can claim tax relief for (identifiable) business element of costs
Mixed business and private use	If there is significant private use Full amount taxed as benefit in section M of the P11D (may be able to deduct business use element if it can be identified). Class 1A NIC on the P11D benefit	Employer pays the provider Since the employer is paying for an amount due under employee's contractual arrangement, this is a taxable benefit (reported on the P11D in section B, as appropriate (see 7.100). Class 1 NIC applied to the cost of the benefit and deducted through payroll
		Costs reimbursed by employer Treated as salary and subject to PAYE/NIC
		Employer reimburses identifiable business expenses only These can be ignored for P11D reporting

Private health insurance and medical check-ups

7.83   Private health insurance cover is a valuable benefit to provide, as it can be a cost-effective way for the working and non-working shareholder, and other employees, to obtain access to private medical treatment.

The director or employee is charged to income tax on the cost to the company. However, where the company generally has at least six members within a group scheme, it will be able to obtain a larger 'group' discount than the individual director/employee would have done on a 'personal' basis. The director/employee is, therefore, charged to income tax on a lower amount (than the cost would be to an individual). From the company's viewpoint, it is an attractive proposition to arrange for its senior personnel to have access to private healthcare where the service is normally quicker than under the NHS.

The company also has to pay Class 1A NICs on the cash equivalent of the benefit provided via Section I of the P11D regardless of the level of earnings of the employee.

In contrast, where the company reimburses the cost of medical insurance premiums that have been taken out personally by the director/employee, such amounts are counted as general earnings and subject to tax and Class 1 NICs.

Medical treatment given outside the UK whilst on business and insurance against such treatment is still free from tax and NICs.

Since January 2015, medical treatment funded by the employer and recommended by a medical professional is tax free. This may, for example, be under a Return to Work plan provided by the Fit for Work service, to facilitate a return to work after a period of four weeks' absence.

Employer-provided health screening and medical check-ups are exempt from tax provided they are generally available to all employees on similar terms [*Income Tax (Exemptions of Minor Benefits) (Amendment) Regulations 2007, SI 2007/2090*]. The provision of eye-tests and specialist glasses for VDU users are also tax-exempt by virtue of the *Health and Safety (Display Screen Equipment) Regulations 1992*.

Scholarship and apprenticeship schemes

7.84   From time to time, companies send employees on full time/'sandwich' training courses at Universities or technical colleges. Broadly, the employee must be enrolled on a full-time course for at least one academic year and attend for at least 20 weeks in that year.

The HMRC Statement of Practice, SP4/86, enables 'tax exempt' support to be given to employees for their lodgings, travel and subsistence expenses up to a maximum of £15,480 for each academic year. However, university and other tuition fees paid by the employee are *not* covered by the exemption. If the annual limit is exceeded, the full amount becomes taxable. Such payments are also exempt from NICs (provided they are made under an employment contract). Courses that are run at the company's own training centre cannot benefit from this concessionary exemption.

Subsidised canteens

7.85 Meals provided in a company canteen on a free or subsidised basis will generally be exempt from any benefits charge. However, this facility must be available to all employees (and, if the company operates a hotel or restaurant business, the staff must eat in a designated area).

However, *FA 2010* prevented this exemption from being abused in salary sacrifice arrangements where employees are given a 'structured contractual entitlement' to the benefit of canteen meals instead of cash salary – often achieved by the offer of a swipe card with the sacrificed cash put on it. In such cases, the normal taxable benefits rules will apply to meals that become taxable under these arrangements.

Minor and trivial benefits

7.86 For many years HMRC has been prepared to treat certain benefits as being exempt from tax, on request from the employer, on the grounds that the cash equivalent of the benefit taxable on the employee would be so trivial as to be not worth pursuing. However, these so-called 'trivial benefit' rules were not well understood by employers or consistently applied by HMRC.

Consequently, on 6 April 2016 these tax exemptions were fully legislated (*ITEPA 2003, s 323A*). Minor and trivial benefits would include flowers on the occasion of an employee's marriage, or Christmas presents such as a bottle of wine or a box of chocolates and so on.

For *close companies* (ie most family and owner managed companies), trivial benefits of up to £300 per year for each director can be provided free of tax and NIC.

Other (non-close) companies can provide trivial benefits as many times as they wish to during the tax year tax and NIC-free (even to the same employee) provided:

- the value of each gift does not exceed £50 including VAT;
- the gift must not be cash or a cash voucher – although store gift vouchers are acceptable;
- it is *not* given in recognition of past or future performance (ie the gift relates to a 'non-work'/personal event); and

- it not given as part of any contractual obligation.

- it is not provided via salary sacrifice (OpRA) (see 8.87A)

The statutory 'trivial benefits' exemption is relatively generous and is likely to cover many items that would have previously been taxed under a PAYE settlement agreement.

The exemption is likely to cover a celebratory meal for a retirement or a wedding, since it should enable the £150 per head tax exemption for an annual party (see below) to go a lot further. It is also possible for a trivial benefit to be given in the form of up to £50 worth of gift vouchers each time with no tax or NIC implications.

Some other minor benefits are specifically exempted by statute. For example, an employer may currently spend up to £150 per person on an annual function for employees, such as a Christmas party, without the employee incurring a taxable benefit [*ITEPA 2003, s 264*].

A long service gift may be given after at least 20 years' service as long as it is valued at no more than £50 per year of service, ie £1,000 for 20 years' service.

£150 per year per employee (rising to £500 from 6 April 2017,) of pension advice costs can be provided by the employer tax-free for each employee

SALARY SACRIFICE ARRANGEMENTS OR OpRAs (OPTIONAL REMUNERATION ARRANGEMENTS)

Principles of salary sacrifice/OpRA arrangements

7.87 In the past, salary sacrifice arrangements have often proved to be a useful way of reducing the employer's Class 1 NIC costs, particularly when spread across the workforce. In some cases, a salary sacrifice could also be quite beneficial for the employees. However, from 6 April 2017 most salary sacrifice arrangements will lose their favourable tax treatment, with special transitional rules applying to existing arrangements (see 7.87A).

A salary sacrifice/OpRA arrangement involves an employee agreeing to forgo part of their salary (possibly by not taking up part of a proposed salary increase) in return for receiving one or more additional non-cash benefits from the employer.

HMRC accepts that employer and employees have the right to 'arrange the terms and conditions of their employment and to enjoy the statutory tax and NIC treatment that applies to each element in the remuneration package' (see *HMRC Employment Income Manual at EIM 42752*).

Up until 6 April 2017 (see 7.87A), a salary sacrifice arrangement has been treated as effective for tax purposes where:

- the employee gives up an appropriate part of their contractual pay entitlement before it is treated as received for income tax and NIC; and

- the revised employment contract provides for lower cash remuneration and (normally) a benefit in kind. Broadly, this means that an employee must give up their right to future pay (before it becomes taxable/'NIC-able').

If the relevant earnings have been 'received' for tax purposes, they are taxed even if they are not actually subsequently paid. In practice, HMRC often wish to see the relevant documentation to ensure that an employee's 'cash' pay has been reduced and a benefit in kind has been provided by the employer. The reduction must be reasonably permanent and HMRC expect to see an employment contract varied for at least a 12-month period. Provided the contract is varied for at least 12 months, HMRC are likely to accept that the conversion of the benefit has no money's worth. However, this minimum period does not apply to childcare vouchers, workplace parking, auto-enrolment pension contributions and bicycles since they are specifically exempted from tax under any provision (including the general earnings rule in *ITEPA 2003, s 62*).

The implementation of the arrangements must be handled carefully to ensure they produce the desired tax (and NIC) savings.

Under the general principle established in *Heaton v Bell* (1969) 46 TC 11, where an employee could receive an additional amount by surrendering the right to a benefit (such the use of a car, etc), this was 'money's worth' and thus taxable as earnings under what is now *ITEPA 2003, s 62* (special provisions prevent this rule applying to cars and living accommodation). Thus, offering complete flexibility to swap between cash salary and benefits is likely to be vulnerable to the tax charges under the *Heaton v Bell* principle (as well as being an administrative nightmare!). It is therefore important that employees do not have the right to revert back to a higher salary at will.

Salary sacrifice arrangements frequently produce tax savings and cost reductions arising from the bulk purchase of the benefits made available.

Other issues also need to be considered when implementing salary sacrifice arrangements, such as the impact on employees' mortgage applications, the effect on any tax credit claims, the effect on future salary rises (where calculated on a percentage basis) and the National Minimum Wage (see 2.10). ,

Tax rules for OpRAs (from 6 April 2017)

7.87A HMRC has 'clamped' down on the use of salary sacrifice arrangements – now referred to as Optional Remuneration Arrangements OpRAs. Consequently, *from 6 April 2017*, the general rule is that where a benefit-in-kind is provided through a salary sacrifice/OpRA it will be charged to income tax and Class 1A NICs (subject to certain transitional rules and some exceptions) – see 7.87B.

As part of a 'clampdown' on the use of salary sacrifice/OpRA arragements, the Finance Act 2017 introduced new legislation *from 6 April 2017*. The broad thrust of the new rules is that where most benefits-in-kind are provided through a salary sacrifice/OpRA they will be taxed and charged to Class 1A NICs under special charging rules. There are certain transitional rules that defer the starting date for the tax charge in various cases (see 7.87B below).

Under the new regime, even where the benefit provided by the salary sacrifice is exempt, it will be subject to a tax charge/Class 1A NICs. Broadly, the tax charge is based on the *greater* of the amount of salary sacrificed and the taxable value of the benefit (if any) (but see 7.79B. Not all 'salary-sacrificed' benefits are caught by these rules – the notable exceptions are employer pension contributions, employer-supported childcare/workplace nurseries (see 7.79), and cycles (see 7.52)

However, employers can continue to provide benefits on top of salary or through a 'cafeteria' system (ie where benefits are selected from a 'fund'). The key trigger for the *FA 2017* OpRA regime is that salary is being sacrificed for a benefit *or* benefits

FA 2017 defines two type of arrangements:

- *salary sacrifice arrangements are termed 'type A arrangements'* – these are where an employee gives up cash earnings in exchange for a benefit in kind (ie what employers have traditionally regarded as salary sacrifices); and *Optional Remuneration Arrangements (OpRAs's) are known as type B arrangements* – these are where employees choose a benefit (such as a car or living accommodation) rather than a cash allowance).

Charging rules and starting dates for taxing OpRAs

7.87B   OpRAs taken out from 6 April 2017 onwards (apart from the 'protected group' of benefits (see 7.87A) will be taxed according to the new charging rules.

The new *FA 2017* charging rules are summarised as follows:

- For any previously tax-exempt benefits such as mobile phones, workplace parking, life-assurance, permanent health insurance, the taxable benefit is the amount of salary given up

- For loans, cars, vans, living accommodation, non-cash vouchers, credit cards, and school fees, the taxable benefit is the modified cash equivalent two-step calculation outlined in 7.29B

- For all other benefits, the taxable benefit is the greater of the salary 'given up' and the cash equivalent value calculated under the normal rules.

However, the *FA 2017* OpRA charging rules do not apply to certain 'protected' benefits, which are pension contributions and advice, childcare vouchers, workplace nurseries, annual leave purchases, bicycles, outplacement training and counselling and company cars with less than 75 g/km emissions.

Furthermore, there are various transitional rules which prevent the new basis of tax/Class 1A NIC charge for OpRAs taken out *before 6 April 2017* applying until a later date. These are summarised as follows:

Relevant benefit	*Date when FA 2017 charging rules apply*
Living accommodation or cars over 75 g/km emissions.	6 April 2021 or the date of any earlier change in the contract.*
School fees	6 April 2021 provided the OpRA remains in place for the same child, school, and employer.
All other benefits	6 April 2018 (or the date of any earlier 'contract change'*).
* For these purposes, the effective date of change is when the underlying contract with the provider is renegotiated, unless the change is outside the control of the employee, eg such as where the employee's car or mobile phone is damaged or where the employee goes on statutory leave.	

Once the transitional protection period has ended, the benefit in kind that is provided in place of the salary is taxed under the *FA 2017* OpRA rules, either through the P11D form or via the payroll (if the employee has opted to payroll benefits).

VAT considerations

7.88   Following the European Court of Justice decision in *Astra Zeneca v HMRC* [2010] STC 2298 (C-40/09), HMRC now consider that the provision of benefits in return for a salary sacrifice represents a supply for VAT (see *Revenue & Customs Brief 28/11*). Consequently, where a company provides employees with benefits under a salary sacrifice arrangement, they will (where appropriate) be subject to VAT on the amount of the salary sacrificed (ie the consideration for the benefit). This VAT treatment has applied since 1 January 2012.

In practice, the *Astra Zeneca* ruling will affect those benefits that are typically made available by way of salary sacrifice arrangements, such as bicycles, cars and mobile telephones. In such cases, companies will account for VAT on the relevant salary forgone (or, if higher, the cost of the benefit), although they will be entitled to reclaim any VAT incurred in supplying the goods or services in question. However, pension contributions and childcare vouchers provided under salary sacrifice arrangements will not be affected since they are exempt from VAT.

THE REMUNERATION PACKAGE AND FLEXIBLE BENEFITS

Basic approach

7.89   For senior employees who are not shareholders, or who only have a non-influential minority holding, a structured remuneration package could be provided. This is generally easier to provide for a new employee.

However, there is no taxable employment income in certain circumstances where there is an offer of cash or benefits. With care, there should be no problem where an existing employee takes fringe benefits at the time of a salary review or on promotion.

Membership of a contribution-free pension scheme is part of the package. The subject of pension schemes is covered in Chapter 10.

Flexible benefits programme

7.90   This is a slightly different way of providing a remuneration package. It offers employees a choice in receiving benefits using the cafeteria or menu system, involving somewhere between 10 and 15 options, although of course this must be dependent upon the particular requirements and mode of operation of the employer concerned.

The aims of a flexible benefits programme include the following:

(*a*)   improving staff motivation;

(*b*)   presenting the employer as a caring employer;

(*c*)   meeting the employee's own preferences via the cafeteria system;

(*d*)   reducing the income tax liability of the employee by selecting some non-taxable benefits (for example, extra holiday, pension contributions, death in service life cover);

(*e*)   reducing the income tax liability of the employee by selecting some benefits which are taxable at cost rather than value (for example, retail vouchers where major retailers give a discount of up to 5%, or private health insurance where a group discount of 30% or more is available, but the employee is taxed on the actual cost to the employer);

(*f*)   reducing the cost to the employee of an item which they would in any event either require or like to have (for example, employer's bulk purchase at a substantial discount of items such as critical illness cover); and

(*g*)   potential savings in NICs.

The annual allowance

7.91   The employer gives the employee an 'annual flexible allowance' with details of the benefit options available. The employee then indicates their preference for the desired levels of benefits and it is made clear exactly what the cost is from the pre-determined annual flexible allowance.

The cost from the allowance will of course vary depending on many circumstances, but as an illustration could involve the following:

- private medical insurance for employee only – £600;
- company car (no private fuel) – £9,000;
- financial counselling – £700;

- personal tax service – £700;
- increasing holiday entitlement by five days – £1,200.

7.92   The options available within a family or owner-managed company are likely to concentrate on those where there is a clear benefit to the company and where the administrative aspects of providing a flexible benefits programme are carefully contained.

Example 16

Structuring a remuneration package

Lancaster Gate Events Ltd is to spend around £54,000 per annum on a new executive, Mr Southgate, who is offered the cafeteria system of choosing a remuneration package.

Mr Southgate decides upon the following:

	Gross cost to Lancaster Gate Events Ltd (ignoring corporate tax relief)		Gross 'benefit' to Mr Southgate	Taxable on Mr Southgate (2017/18)	
	£		£	£	
Salary cost	38,703	(a)	35,000	35,000	
Pension contribution	2,500		2,500	Nil	
Volvo 70 series 2.3 car	5,400	(b)	6,000	6,703	(g)
Price £31,920					
Emissions 113 g/km = 21%					
Petrol	3,060	(c)	2,040	4,746	(h)
Mobile phone	1,000		1,000	Nil	(i)
Private health insurance	350	(d)	500	350	
Clothing	1,080	(e)	1,200	216	
Class 1A NICs	1,658	(f)	Nil	Nil	
	53,751		48,240	47,015	

Notes:

(a)   Salary £35,000 and employer's Class 1 NIC of £3,703 (13.8% on excess over £8,164).

(*b*)   Contract hire at £450 per month (net of 10% company discount).

(*c*)   18,000 total miles including 12,000 private miles @ 17p per mile based on petrol at 130p per litre.

(*d*)   30% discount on group scheme for health insurance.

(*e*)   10% discount on clothing, but as it is not corporate clothing, taxable benefit: 20% × £1,080.

(*f*)   13.8% × £12,015 (£6,703 + £4,746 + £350 + £216).

(*g*)   Original list price of £31,920 and CO_2 emissions rating of 113 g/km. Taxable benefit is 21% × £31,920 = £6,703

(*h*)   Fuel scale benefit – £22,600 × 21% = £4,746.

(*i*)   Not subject to tax or Class 1A NICs.

Tax efficiency of benefits

7.93   The tax efficiency of employee benefits depends on a number of factors, including the calculation of the tax charge and the amount the employee would have to spend personally (out of their post-tax income) of providing that benefit personally.

A broad 'benefit efficiency' percentage calculation for the relevant benefit might be calculated as follows:

$$\frac{\text{Cost to employee} \times 100\%}{\text{Cost to company}}$$

Using this calculation, the greater the 'benefit-efficiency' percentage, the more tax efficient would be the benefit. The *cost to the employee* would be the amount the employee would have to incur personally to provide the relevant benefit. The 'taxable benefit' would be the amount of the benefit that is subject to tax in the employee's hands.

OTHER TRANSACTIONS BETWEEN THE COMPANY AND ITS SHAREHOLDERS

Working and non-working shareholders

7.94   Where a close company's business involves the provision of goods or services, and the company provides them to a director (or indeed to any employee) at a discounted price there can be an income tax charge.

Where the same arrangement is made for a *non-working* shareholder, this gives rise to a taxable distribution (based on the cash equivalent under employment benefit rules) made by the company under *CTA 2010, s 1064)*.

Calculation of taxable benefits

7.95   The income tax charge is based on the cost to the company of providing the goods or service *less* so much as is paid by the director [*ITEPA 2003, ss 203, 204*]. For goods, this should mean that the director/employee has no tax liability if they pay at least the wholesale price.

For services, there may be a negligible additional cost of providing them to a specific individual given that further expenditure may not be incurred. Indeed, following the case of *Pepper v Hart* [1992] STC 898, in-house benefits are taxed by reference to their 'marginal cost' only.

7.96   From an *IR Press Release* dated 21 January 1993, the position for a family or owner-managed company and its directors or employees can be summarised as follows:

(*a*)   goods sold at a discount to a director or employee which results in them paying at least the wholesale price involve no or negligible net benefit;

(*b*)   if the company is running a private school, teachers paying at least 15% of the normal school fees for their children have no tax charge;

(*c*)   professional services not requiring any additional personnel can be provided free of tax to directors or employees; this covers, for example, legal or financial services provided by in-house personnel (any disbursements would involve a tax charge on the users, if they do not pay for them);

(*d*)   if an asset is used both for business and private purposes, fixed costs relating thereto are not included in determining the tax charge where the private use is incidental to the business use as they are not *additional* costs (this does not apply to cars or vans where a fixed scale charge applies).

Assets acquired at under-value

7.97   Where a working shareholder or owner manager acquires or buys an asset, such as a property, from the company, it is advisable to obtain a professional valuation. This will reduce the risk of HMRC seeking to tax it as an unintended distribution or taxable benefit. For example, property may be transferred to the owner manager at a competent value of (say) £400,000 but the company may ultimately agree a figure of £480,000 with HMRC's District Valuer. Assuming a professional valuation was obtained prior to the transaction,

HMRC will not seek to tax the 'under-value' element of £80,000 (ie £480,000 less £400,000) as a distribution received by the working-shareholder/owner manager provided they 'repay' the £80,000 to the company.

In such cases, it is recommended that the market value is promptly agreed with HMRC's District Valuer. (Form CG34 can be used (downloaded from the .Gov website) to obtain a post-transaction pre-return 'valuation check'. This will reduce the risk of HMRC seeking to argue that the 'under-value' amount is in effect a loan, which would incur a *CTA 2010, s 455* liability (see 2.59) and potential beneficial loan charge (see 7.68).

In such cases, if the *working* shareholder/owner manager does not pay full market value for the transferred asset or receives it for no consideration, they could be taxed on any 'under-value' element under the distribution [*CTA 2010, s 1000*] *or* as earnings (HMRC generally consider the land to be 'money's worth' for *ITEPA 2003, s 62* purposes – see also HMRC EIM 08001). Under *ITEPA 2003, s 62* (employment income generally takes precedence over the benefits in kind rules (subject to the items listed at EIM 00530).

A distribution-in-specie (see 9.8) would clearly arise where the company has declared it as a legal distribution, with the appropriate minutes to support that view.

On the other hand, if the company votes the amount as a bonus to the owner-manager/director and states that the property is being transferred in satisfaction of their bonus entitlement, then it will be taxed as an employment benefit. (Provided the property is not a readily convertible asset (see 5.13 and 8.39), the transaction should not be subject to PAYE but would still need to be reported on the P11D. If the property is received as earnings, PAYE and Class 1 NICs would be due in the normal way.

In the absence of any paperwork, board minutes or other evidence indicating the reason for the transfer of the property, HMRC will examine the relevant circumstances. However, if the recipient is a director/employee who actively works for the company, HMRC are likely to treat it as earnings rather than a distribution.

Company's tax treatment

7.98   For chargeable assets, the company would have to substitute market value in calculating its chargeable gain on the disposal, and the shareholder would be treated as acquiring the asset at market value (provided the transaction is between connected persons). This applies under *TCGA 1992, s 18*, where the shareholder has control of the company or the shareholder and connected persons have control of it [*TCGA 1992, s 286(6)* and *(7)*].

7.99   The market value rule also applies where an asset is transferred in consideration for services rendered as an employee (as would often be the case) or where it is *not* an arm's length transaction [*TCGA 1992, s 17(1)*].

THE P11D FORM AND PAYROLLING BENEFITS

Introduction

7.100   The P11D form is an extremely important form, being the return of expense payments and benefits. HMRC encourage online filing of P11Ds, although they can be submitted in paper form. However, where employers have voluntarily registered to tax *all* expense payments and benefits, they will not have to file a P11D (see 7.100A). If they have registered to payroll only certain benefits in kind, then these can be omitted from form P11D and only the non-payrolled benefits need to be reported.

The deadline for submission is 6 July after the relevant tax year and covers all employees who have received taxable benefits and expenses during the tax year, although HMRC may not charge penalties if the return is filed by 19 July. There is no automatic penalty for a 'late' P11D submission. If HMRC seek a penalty, the company would be notified of HMRC's application to a tax tribunal to charge a penalty of up to £300 per late P11D. If the forms are filed before the tribunal hearing, the penalty is avoided. However, any further delay could mean an additional penalty charge of up to £60 per late P11D per day of continuing failure [*TMA 1970, s 98(1)*].

HMRC now applies the normal penalty rules for incorrect P11Ds (see 4.59–4.63 for further details). This means that the percentage penalty loading (applied to the potential tax lost) varies according to taxpayer behaviour, and the degree of culpability or guilt, as summarised below:

	Penalty loading %
Genuine mistake after taking reasonable care	0%
Careless action	30%
Deliberate but not concealed action	70%
Deliberate and concealed action	100%

Forms P11D must be prepared for all company directors (if they receive benefits and expenses), even if they draw only a very small or no salary from the company and *all* other employees. A common error when preparing P11Ds is to assume that all expenses are tax deductible.

Before 6 April 2016 only employees who earned (including benefits, etc) at a rate of at least £8,500 per year had all their benefits and expenses reported, unless these were covered by a P11D dispensation.

HMRC provide employers with various options to file P11Ds and the overarching return P11D(b):

- PAYE Online

- The online End of Year Expenses and benefits Service

- Paper forms that can be download from www.gov.uk

Under the self-assessment provisions, employers must provide each employee with a copy of the completed form P11D or a statement of their benefits, by 6 July following the tax year to which it applies, otherwise the penalties listed above can apply.

Employees whose benefits are payrolled (see 7.100A) will already have been provided with information about the 'benefit' amounts that have been included in taxable pay in respect of the benefit. These details will either appear on the employee's payslip or in a year-end statement provided to them (by the same deadline as their P60 ie 31 May). Clearly, care must be taken to ensure that these amounts are not taxed again via the employee's self-assessment return.

HMRC produce a number of P11D working sheets to help with the calculation of 'cash equivalents' for various benefits. The following sheets can be downloaded from *www.gov.uk/government/collections/paye-forms#expenses-and-benefits-working-sheets*:

- living accommodation (P11DWS1);

- cars and fuel benefits (P11DWS2);

- vans for private use (P11DWS3);

- interest-free and low interest loans (P11DWS4);

- relocation expenses (P11DWS5); and

- mileage allowance and 'passenger' payments (P11DWS6).

Payrolling benefits

7.100A   Since 6 April 2016, HMRC has provided a statutory reporting option for expenses and benefits, known as 'payrolling benefits'.

Under this regime, employers will tax expenses and the cash equivalent of benefits through the payroll. Employers must register with HMRC to 'payroll' benefits before the start of the relevant tax year. On receipt of the registration, HMRC remove the chosen benefit(s) from the affected employees' tax codes.

Not all employees in a PAYE scheme need be moved on to payrolling – the system is entirely voluntary. For example, those with complex reward packages such as expatriate employees can remain with a P11D submission. Equally an employer may decide to payroll (say) medical insurance benefits but report company cars via the P11D.

For the chosen benefits (all P11D sections apart from beneficial loans, and living accommodation can be payrolled for 2017/18), the employer divides the estimated cash equivalent value (the P11D figure) by the pay frequency and adds that amount as a notional addition to taxable pay. Thus, by the end of the tax year, the tax that would have been collected by a subsequent coding adjustment has been collected in-year. However, the cash equivalent value is *not* subject to Class 1 NICs (ie no addition to pay subject to NICs is made) since the benefits are charged under Class 1A on the employer only and paid after tax year-end).

It is not clear whether this system will entirely replace P11Ds but it is a very attractive proposition for the Treasury to receive the tax up-front and not have to process over 4 million P11Ds each year. Many employers will not be as keen since many of them currently outsource P11D production to an agent as they have limited expertise in this area.

Exempt benefits and expenses and dispensations

7.101 HMRC's P11D/P9D dispensation process ceased on 6 April 2016. However, items that are exempt or fully deductible for tax purposes are now *exempt* from P11D reporting. This would include the following:

- Annual parties and similar functions (see 7.86);

- Reasonable travel and subsistence expenses (see 7.56 and 7.57);

- Certain allowable expenses, such as professional subscriptions, uniforms, business telephone calls on employee's personal phones;

- Non-taxable benefit of parking at or near the employee's work place;

- Exempt payments of incidental overnight expenses;

- Exempt periodic medical check-ups and eye tests for employees who use computers etc;

- Trivial benefits provided to employees (see 7.86).

Until 5 April 2016 expenses payments and benefits covered by a dispensation agreed by HMRC did not have to be included on the form P11D/P9D. This avoided the employer having to report such items and the director/employee then having to claim exemption or making a claim for tax relief for qualifying business expenses.

The P11D reporting exemption does, of course, mean that HMRC no longer provides the 'safety net' of signing off that an employer's expense and benefits policy is compliant. There is therefore a potential risk that HMRC may not agree with the employer's view that certain items are exempt from tax.

Scale rate payments within HMRC guidance, which are often used by employers for 'travel and subsistence' expenses (rather than using 'receipted' amounts) are now subsumed into regulations. This practice can therefore still be relied upon not to generate any tax charge. Higher amounts paid as a 'scale rate' must still be agreed with HMRC, with the agreement being in place for five years at a time.

Completing the form

7.102   The HMRC P11D Guide and the accompanying work sheets (which are tax year specific) provide a good deal of information to help the employer through the minefield of benefits and expenses reporting requirements. In the case of any uncertainty, reference should also be made to the relevant chapter of the IR 480 and 490 booklets which covers various benefits and expenses.

Care should be taken to ensure all P11Ds and P11D worksheets are prepared correctly. HMRC has issued a P11D quality standard for forms, which must include:

- employer reference;

- employee's name and National Insurance number (or their date of birth and gender);

- the list price of any company car provided;

- if box 10 in section F is completed (total cash equivalent of car fuel provided), so must box 9 (total cash equivalent of cars provided) be completed;

- if a beneficial loan is provided and is reported in section H, box 15 (cash equivalent of loans) must be completed.

PAYROLL AND BENEFITS COMPLIANCE

Key filing dates for 2017/18

7.103   A timetable showing the main PAYE and NIC obligations for 2017/18 is set out below:

19 April 2018 (22 if paying electronically)	Last date for paying PAYE and NIC for 2017/18*. Final year end declaration due via FPS or EPS
	*Interest is charged after this date.
31 May 2018	Employees should have been provided with a P60 by this date.
6 July 2018	Last date for submission of P11D and P11D(b).
	– Late submission of P11Ds may attract discretionary penalties of up to £300 per return (plus a further £60 per day for continuing failure).
	– Late submission of P11D(b) attracts automatic penalties of £100 for every 50 employees for each month (or part month) the returns are outstanding.
	Employees should be supplied with copies of P11D information.

	Any PAYE Settlement Agreements must be in place for the relevant tax year.
19 July 2018	Last date for payment of Class 1A NICs on benefits and expenses – this may be a combined figure from benefits and expenses that have been payrolled as well as from the P11Ds).
	Interest is charged on late payments.
19 October 2018	Tax and NICs on PAYE Settlement Agreements are due to be paid.
	Interest is charged on late payments.

Online filing of RTI returns

7.104   Employers are required to file their RTI returns online on or before an employee's contractual payment date. For full details of the RTI regime, see 5.11A.

PAYE tax and NIC payments are subject to a penalty where they have been underpaid or paid late (see 5.12 for detailed coverage).

If an adjustment is made after the end of the tax-year under special IR 35 arrangements, HMRC will not charge any late payment penalties made under the terms of those arrangements.

For Class 1A and 1B NIC payments, HMRC determinations, or corrections to returns, the 'penalty date' is 30 days after the due date. A 5% penalty is levied if the full amount remains unpaid 30 days after the due date (increasing by an additional 5% or 10% if the full amount is unpaid after 6 months or 12 months of the due date respectively).

The standard penalty regime applies for all employee PAYE and Form P11D returns. HMRC has indicated that provided 'reasonable care' is taken *no* penalties will be charged on mistakes in returns. For these purposes, 'reasonable care' would include keeping accurate records, seeking advice when unsure about the correct tax treatment and informing HMRC about any errors that are discovered on returns that have already been submitted. On the other hand, errors arising from failing to take reasonable care are likely to have substantial penalty loadings (see 4.59–4.63).

BENEFITS OF PAYE SETTLEMENT AGREEMENTS

7.105   Many companies provide a range of minor or irregular benefits (for example, motivational awards, taxable costs of providing staff parties (where the cost exceeds the £150 per head limit), etc – see 7.86). In such cases, the company is usually willing to settle the director's/employee's tax liability.

This can be done under a PAYE Settlement Agreement (PSA) under which the company undertakes to pay the relevant tax and Class 1B NICs on behalf of the appropriate directors and employees (*ITEPA 2003, ss 703–707*). The tax and NICs must be calculated on a 'grossed-up' basis as settlement of the directors'/ employees' personal tax liability would itself give rise to a taxable benefit. The PSA effectively excludes the relevant benefits from the employees' taxable income and there is no need for them to be reported on the forms P11D.

ALLOWABLE EXPENSES

7.106 When an item appears on a form P11D it does not automatically mean that the employee concerned will suffer income tax on it. Technically what happens is that all items are brought into charge to income tax and some of them can then be covered by an expenses claim.

Such claims can only succeed if the relevant expenditure comes within any one of the following restrictive heads:

(*a*)   travel in the performance of the duties of the employment or travel to/from a place where necessary duties are performed (see 7.55) [*ITEPA 2003, ss 337–342*];

(*b*)   fees and subscriptions to professional bodies or learned societies which are listed in *ITEPA 2003, s 343(2)* whose activities are relevant to the employment [*ITEPA 2003, s 343*];

(*c*)   any other item of expenditure which is incurred wholly, exclusively and necessarily in the performance of the duties of the employment [*ITEPA 2003, s 336*].

PLANNING CHECKLIST – BENEFITS AND EXPENSES

Company

- As a general rule, the company should generally meet all expenses with a business element.

- Consider the corporation tax deductibility of expenses and benefits, but in the majority of cases relief should be available as an employment cost.

- Do not provide unnecessary goods for private use of directors.

- Consider finance lease or contract hire of company cars.

- Significant tax savings are available on the provision of eco-friendly or 'electric' company cars and in most cases the company will also benefit from 100% capital allowances on them.

- It is possible to claim 50% of the input VAT on lease payments for company cars.

- In many cases, it is not economic for companies to provide their employees with private fuel. It is generally more efficient for employees to meet their own private fuel costs and reclaim the fuel costs incurred by them for business motoring.

- Obtain HMRC 'approval' for proposed salary sacrifice (OpRA) arrangements after implementing them. In light of the changes from 6 April 2017, companies should review whether OpRAs are still a suitable method of providing employee benefits.

- Make full use of PAYE Settlement Agreements.

- To avoid expensive penalties, ensure compliance with stringent year-end PAYE/NIC filing deadlines, check returns, and keep accurate underlying records.

- Ensure PAYE and NIC liabilities are reported on time under the RTI system.

Working shareholders

- Maximise claims for income tax relief on business element of expenses and benefits.

- Arrange for company to meet all expenses and benefits that have a justifiable business purpose.

- Consider the CO_2 emissions rate when purchasing or leasing new company cars.

- Compare tax cost of company car against costs of running the same vehicle privately and claiming AMAPs.

Other employees

- Look to fringe benefits as an incentive, where income tax liability is less than the real economic value.

- In appropriate cases, consider 'salary sacrifice' arrangements and tax-free/efficient benefits.

Non-working shareholders

- Attempt to achieve a balance between commercial acceptability and tax advantages to the recipient of benefits.

Chapter 8

Providing shares to employees

USES AND STRATEGIES FOR EMPLOYEE SHARES

Key practical and tax issues

8.1 Many enlightened owner-managed companies now provide shares to their managers and employees, despite the natural reluctance of the owner-manager(s) to concede part of their equity share capital. Empirical studies have shown that providing managers and employees with valuable shares or share option rights can be a very powerful incentive and motivator. The employing company invariably benefits from increased commitment and productivity and the retention of its key managers; the interests of senior managers are now far more closely aligned with the shareholders.

However, HMRC are keen to ensure that any profit or reward element on *unapproved* shares/share options is taxed as employment income. The law in this area has become increasingly complex following the introduction of the employment-related securities and restricted securities legislation in 2003.

In contrast, if an employer has self-certified that the share plan meets the relevant legislative conditions to qualify as an HMRC's tax-advantaged share plan, the tax consequences for the director/employee should generally be the same (or indeed more favourable) as for shares held in any other company.

Although the process and mechanism for 'approval' changed in 2014, these schemes are still commonly referred to as *'approved'* schemes and are referred to as such throughout this chapter (unless otherwise stated). Typically, under an *approved* scheme, there should be no employment-related income tax liability on acquisition and the full gain on a subsequent sale of the shares should be subject to capital gains tax (CGT).

However, when issuing or granting options over employee shares, owner managers should always consider the dilutive impact on them and the other existing shareholders.

The employee being offered a small number of shares in a family or owner-managed company might not consider them to be of any real or meaningful value, with future capital growth only being capable of realisation in the event of flotation on the stock market or a take-over. Nevertheless, employees are still able to 'cash-in' their shares by selling them to an employee benefit trust or the company (under a purchase of own shares transaction).

The normal CGT rate is 20% for many employee shareholders and option holders (unless they can benefit from the 10% entrepreneurs' relief rate). Thus, employee share arrangements designed to maximise the amount of profit falling within the CGT regime remain attractive when compared with the penal income tax/NIC charges that arise on most other forms of employee rewards and bonuses.

EMI and unapproved schemes

8.2   Where an Enterprise Management Incentives (EMI) scheme is available, this will very often be the preferred route since it achieves a highly desirable tax position for the employee and employer. For options granted at full value, there are no income tax or NIC costs yet the company can obtain a corporate tax deduction for (broadly) the value of the EMI shares on exercise.

Following the *Finance Act 2013*, the beneficial 10% ER CGT rate will normally be available on the sale of EMI shares, even where the options are exercised shortly before the sale of the company (see 8.50).

The benefits of holding EMI options/shares are clear. In contrast, where shares are given under an *unapproved* scheme the tax charge can be expensive because the shares are received by reason of the office or employment.

Employee shareholder shares legislation contained an important capital gains exemption and proved to be popular for short period of time but this exemption is no longer available from 1 December 2016 (see 8.86A–8.86C).

Under an unapproved scheme an income tax liability and, possibly, an NIC charge may arise before the shares are actually sold (which may make it difficult to fund the tax and NIC payments). However, if *unapproved* shares can be provided when they are at a relatively low value (with the benefit of a substantial 'minority' valuation discount), this can be much simpler and often works relatively well.

For 'unapproved' arrangements, the main employment income tax charge occurs when a director/employee receives free or cheap shares, whether from a direct share award or on the exercise of a share option. This tax charge is based on the 'benefit' received, which is broadly calculated by reference to the market value of the shares less any consideration paid by the employee.

The *FA 2003* made substantial changes to the tax treatment of shares that are issued subject to restrictions or conditions. In the past, it was often possible to minimise income tax charges on employee shares by making the acquisition conditional or by restricting their rights in some way, thus depressing the value that would be subject to income tax (under the 'money's worth' principle in *Weight v Salmon* (1935) 19 TC 174 (see 8.10)). The *FA 2003* provisions (contained in *ITEPA 2003, Pt 7, Ch 2*) now ensure that employment income tax charges are levied on any 'artificial' increase in value created by the removal or alteration of such restrictions, etc. This legislation is widely drawn and could potentially apply to many types of shares issued to directors and employees.

Special vigilance is therefore required to avoid creating any unnecessary income tax charges under these rules. In the vast majority of cases, the income tax exposure can be substantially or completely eliminated by making an appropriate election (see 8.32). Although EMI shares can also potentially fall within the 'restricted securities' regime, no tax problems should arise where the share options have been granted at full value at the date of grant (see 8.62).

The Supreme Court's decision in *Grays Timber Products Ltd v CIR* [2010] UKSC 4 underlines the need to introduce enhanced 'exit' rights with care. Based on the rather special facts of the case (and in particular the close link between the terms of a share subscription agreement and the taxpayer's employment rights), the court ruled that the 'excess' consideration received on a share sale (over the statute-based 'market value' of the shares) fell to be taxed as employment income (rather than subject to CGT) (see 8.37).

HMRC are now taking a more stringent line on the reporting of employee share awards and options and other related chargeable events. All HMRC share scheme reporting has now moved online and the deadline for registration is 6 July following the tax year in which the shares were awarded (see 8.69 and 8.87).

Potential impact of disguised remuneration rules in *ITEPA 2003, Pt 7A*

8.3 The 'employment income provided through third parties' legislation (often called the 'disguised remuneration' rules) in *ITEPA 2003, Pt 7A* can impose an immediate PAYE and NIC charge on the transfer of assets (for example, shares) by a 'third party' (such as a trust) to an employee (see 5.18).

This legislation has the potential to catch 'commercial' employee share schemes and, in some cases, could impose a tax charge even if the employee does not ultimately receive the relevant shares.

However, *ITEPA 2003, ss 554J–554M* provides various 'prescriptive' exemptions from the *ITEPA 2003, Pt 7A* tax/NIC charges for various share scheme transactions. These legislative exclusions should provide protection in most cases although, of course, 'normal' tax charges can still arise under the employment related securities and other rules. Furthermore, HMRC guidance also confirms that no *ITEPA 2003, Pt 7A* charges will be sought in relation to commercially-based employee share arrangements.

Corporate tax deductions for employee shares

8.4   Companies can claim a statutory tax deduction for employee/director share awards or option exercises. The relief is broadly based on the amount that would have been charged to income tax in the recipient's hands. Relief is also available for shares transferred under approved shares on a similar basis, which makes EMI schemes even more attractive (see 8.89–8.92).

EMPLOYEE SHARE SCHEMES – PRACTICAL DESIGN ISSUES

Legal and commercial considerations

8.5   The company will have to consider a number of practical issues in determining the detailed legal and commercial considerations for the provision of shares or share options for its employees. The key issues include the following:

- Does the company want the employee to hold shares from the start?

- Which director or employees will participate in the share scheme and are their holdings viewed as quasi-proprietorial in nature or simply a 'stake' to obtain some capital value on 'exit'?

- The potential dilutive effect of any share options or share award: will the increased employee engagement be of greater benefit than the dilution of the share capital? Can an approved scheme be used? If the company's scheme qualifies for EMI, this will normally be the preferred choice.

- What price should be paid for the shares or on the exercise of the share options? Is the option a reward for past service or an incentive for future performance? Minority discounts typically given in valuing such shares enables a company to support a valuation that can give the employee a favourable share price.

- Where share options are used, when will the employees be allowed to exercise their options? This may only be on a subsequent flotation, when the company is sold, or some other 'exit' event.

- What rights would attach to the employee shares? Will they carry the same rights as the existing shares (such as on voting and dividend rights) or will the employee shares be a separate class of shares with perhaps more restricted rights (for example, as to capital and dividends)? This will mainly be driven by the overall objectives for the share scheme.

- Is it appropriate for the employees just to share in the capital growth of the company from the date the shares acquired? If it is, consider using 'growth' shares since this will often involve lower tax valuations/charges.

- Can the employees sell their shares, and if so to whom can they be sold? Is there a need to set up an employee trust to create a 'market' for the employees' shares?

- On what basis are the shares to be valued? For 'unlisted' family and owner-managed companies, a clear valuation model can be helpful to determine the value when the employee sells their shares to an employee share trust or back to the company (on a purchase of own shares).

- If the company is sold (ie there is a 'change of control'), what mechanism should be in place to deal with the employee shares?

- What happens to an individual employee's shares if they leave the company? Should they be treated more favourably if the employee leaves due to disability, death or redundancy? Should they be treated less favourably if they leave voluntarily?

- If the shares are being offered to a number of employees, how should the terms and benefits of the scheme be communicated to them? If an employee's expectations of the future value of the options/shares are set too high, the incentive impact can be severely reduced.

There are also a number of other factors that must be considered within a family or owner-managed company environment.

Approved versus unapproved share schemes

8.6   The Enterprise Management Incentives (EMI) scheme has, in recent years, been the most popular vehicle for providing share options to directors and employees of owner-managed companies. This position is likely to continue following the beneficial changes introduced by *FA 2013*, which enable the vast majority of option holders to benefit from ER on the sale of their EMI shares (see 8.50 and 8.71).

The EMI rules contain various restrictions that prevent them being used by very large or 'controlled' companies and in relation to certain 'prohibited' trading activities (see 8.64–8.66).

In some cases, an approved company share option plan (CSOP) (see 8.74–8.77) may provide a suitable alternative. However, the £30,000 limit (based on the market value of the shares at grant) under a CSOP often proves to be unduly restrictive in many cases.

There will be many cases where, for a variety of reasons, a company will only be able to provide shares under an *unapproved* arrangement. Under an unapproved scheme, an employee may be asked to pay market value for their shares or suffer an income tax charge by reference to market value. Where a reasonably low 'market value' can be agreed with HMRC for the very small minority shareholding, the tax can probably be managed. On the other hand, if the share value is relatively high, the payment of income tax without any concurrent sale proceeds can be a practical problem.

An unapproved share option scheme enables an option to be granted at a lower price than the share price at that time. This gives an immediate value to the option rights as a 'golden hello' to a new executive or as 'golden handcuffs' to a key existing executive. As a general rule, the *'benefit' of the option* cannot be taxed at the date the option is granted, irrespective of the period over which the option can be exercised. (This exemption is also available under the EMI scheme (see 8.51).

An exit-based *unapproved* share option does not offer any real tax benefits, since virtually the entire 'value' would attract income tax and NIC. This means that (almost all) the sale value is likely to be taxed at a combined 47% income tax/NIC rate with additional 13.8% employers' NIC rate on top. On the other hand, an exit-based EMI option generally enables an employee to realise the sale value of their shares at 10% (with the benefit of entrepreneurs' relief (ER)).

Material interest

8.7   HMRC approved share plans are not available to an individual who holds a material interest in the company. Interests of associates must be included in the test, which means that approved plans may be limited to unrelated employees or those with minority holdings.

The size of holding which will constitute a material interest varies as shown below by reference to the ordinary share capital and, for a close company, to the assets which would be distributed in the event of the company being wound-up.

Scheme	Current test for material interest
Enterprise management incentive (EMI) share options	Over 30%
Company share option plans (CSOP)	Over 30%*
SAYE share options	N/A*
SIPs	N/A*
Employee shareholder shares	Over 25%

* A restriction for shareholdings of over 25% applied before 17 July 2013

Dilution of share capital

8.8   Awarding shares to employees often results in the company making a new issue of shares, thereby diluting the value of the existing shareholdings. This may be objected to by non-working shareholders who are less likely than working shareholders to appreciate the overall benefits of allowing certain employees to acquire shares. The existing shareholders (both working and non-working) may also be loath to see a fragmented share ownership with several people owning very small holdings.

The potential impact on dilutive employee options on shareholder's EMI entitlements needs to be monitored and planned for. For example, management shareholders with (say) a 5% stake in the company are likely to be very dissatisfied if the exercise of employee share options before a sale dilutes their holding below the crucial 5% required for ER!

Investor protection committees publish guidelines designed to prevent dilution of shareholders' equity for *quoted* companies. These provide a useful starting point for non-working shareholders' involvement in developing a strategy, albeit that an unquoted company would probably wish to have greater flexibility.

A simple strategy is to limit the issued share capital for all employee share schemes to (say) a limit of between 5% and 10% of the ordinary share capital. These percentages are in line with various investor groups, such as pension funds and the British Venture Capital Association guidelines.

Phantom share options

8.9   Phantom share options are essentially a cash-based bonus arrangement. They usually involve a cash bonus being paid where the company's share price increases by a specified amount, or where shares are issued by reference to pre-determined profit targets being met.

For most family or owner-managed companies, such plans are likely to be of limited use. The company's share price will not be readily available (unless, for example, the company is listed on the Alternative Investment Market). Share values are not, therefore, going to be an appropriate measure of performance and a cash bonus scheme linked to profits or sales, etc will generally be preferred.

SIMPLE ISSUE OR GIFT OF SHARES

Employment income tax issues

8.10   Many family or owner-managed companies may not wish to use share options or other means of deferred share ownership, preferring a simple issue or gift of shares to selected employees instead. This will invariably trigger an income tax charge on the employee, with the 'profit' element being taxed as earnings under *ITEPA 2003, s 62* under the principles laid down in *Weight v Salmon* (1935) 19 TC 174. In certain cases, this amount may also be treated as earnings for NIC purposes (see 13.36). However, as the market value is based on a 'money's worth' principle, the tax charge may be reduced to a palatable amount if a 'lowish' discounted minority valuation can be agreed for the shares. This can be a very simple and effective method of giving an employee an interest in shares, particularly if it is a reward for past services. For basis of share valuation, see 14.40–14.43.

Where the shares are gifted or transferred from another shareholder, this will have potential CGT implications (see 13.39).

The use of 'growth' shares may also be beneficial in restricting the initial tax cost (see 8.24).

Where shares are issued to an employee, *CA 2006, s 588* provides that they are taken to be allotted where the employee acquires the unconditional right to be included in the company's share register (this would be when the beneficial interest in the shares is acquired – see *ITEPA 2003, s 477(4)*). If a private company has only one class of share capital the directors may allot shares without shareholder approval (unless the company's articles expressly prohibit this). In any case, there is no need to obtain shareholder approval for share awards granted under an employee share scheme (as defined in *CA 2006, s 1166*).

The standard pre-emption rights for share allotments do *not* apply to employee share schemes [*CA 2006, s 566*].

Special tax rules apply for shares received by a director/employee where the shares are 'restricted securities' within *ITEPA 2003, s 423* (see 8.16–8.38). Clearly, where shares are subject to 'employee-specific' restrictions or conditions, etc that are sufficiently material so as to reduce their value, they will fall to be treated as 'restricted'. Typical restrictions include the forfeiture of shares if the employee subsequently leaves the company or fails to meet performance targets.

8.11   Where restricted shares are acquired, the tax charge is based on the 'money's worth' principle (the under-value element being treated as earnings under *ITEPA 2003, s 62*). Consequently, the taxable amount would be calculated by reference to the actual value of the shares *taking the inherent restrictions into account*. However, immediate attention must be given to making an election under (normally) *ITEPA 2003, s 431* (see 8.32). The *ITEPA 2003, s 431* election is a rather odd arrangement in that it is signed by employer and employee and merely retained by the company and not forwarded to HMRC.

Where the election is made, *ITEPA 2003, s 431(1)(a)* alters the basis of the tax charge to one which is based on the market value of the shares ignoring the various restrictions. Special rules apply to shares that are subject to the risk of forfeiture that fall away within five years (see 8.28).

Failure to make the election will mean that part of the value passing to the director/employee on a subsequent chargeable event (such as a future sale of the shares) will also be subject to income tax (and possibly NIC) (see 8.31 and 8.35). By making the election, the director/employee ensures that any income tax exposure at the date of acquisition is limited to the *unrestricted value* of the shares (ie the value of the shares ignoring the relevant restrictions). This ensures that any future growth in value is entirely within the beneficial CGT regime (see 8.32).

8.12 In practice, it may not always be easy to determine whether the restrictions attaching to certain shares are sufficiently substantive to render them 'restricted' within *ITEPA 2003, s 423*. One of the key requirements is that the relevant restrictions have the effect of reducing the value of the shares, which can often be a subjective matter.

Depending on the precise nature of any restrictions, it may be possible to agree with the HMRC – Shares & Asset Valuation Office that there is no discernible difference between the unrestricted and restricted value of the relevant shares – this effectively makes the shares 'unrestricted' (see *ITEPA 2003, s 423(1) (b)*). However, anecdotal evidence suggests that HMRC may still seek to treat the shares as 'restricted' where the shares are simply subject to the usual transfer restrictions and pre-emption rights. However, it is possible to argue that where directors have the usual right to refuse to register shareholders, this may not always be enforceable as a matter of general law. Nevertheless, given the lack of complete certainty in this area, many would argue that a protective *ITEPA 2003, s 431* election should always be made. Indeed, in practice such elections are invariably made, even where the risk of the relevant shares being treated as 'restricted' is remote (see also 8.17 and 8.32).

See 8.87 for HMRC's new reporting requirements on employee share acquisitions.

As part of the arrangements for providing shares to employees/directors, the company may pay the income tax on the employee's behalf (obviously incurring a further 'grossed-up' tax charge for settling the employee's pecuniary liability).

CGT treatment of employee shares

8.13 When offered shares in their employing company, many directors and employees generally tend to focus on the potential capital gains benefits. Although the shares may incur an income tax charge on acquisition (unless they are offered under an HMRC approved scheme) many employees anticipate the prospect of realising a substantial capital gain on 'exit' (at favourable CGT rates).

Employees will normally pay CGT at 20% (or 10% to the extent they have sufficient 'income tax' basic rate band capacity) on their 'exit' gains. However, some employees' gains will be covered by the annual exemption and would be tax-free.

Some senior management/director-shareholders may be able to benefit from entrepreneurs' relief (ER), giving access to a 10% CGT rate on sale. In such cases, they will need to hold at least 5% of the ordinary (voting) shares at least one year before the sale (see 15.33 for detailed conditions), unless they are obtaining their shares from the exercise of EMI share options (see 8.2 and 8.50).

For CGT treatment on the sale of EMI shares, see 8.50.

CHECKLIST OF KEY PRACTICAL POINTS

8.14   In establishing any share scheme, each party should consider the following main practical issues:

(*a*)   the identification of the key personnel and shares to be offered;

(*b*)   the planned revision of the company's share capital structure to provide shares subject to options;

(*c*)   the future share capital structure, with the implications of any dilution for existing shareholders;

(*d*)   draft scheme rules;

(*e*)   how the directors/employees will finance the exercise of their options;

(*f*)   determination of the current market value of the relevant shares;

(*g*)   plans for future flotation or sale;

(*h*)   the possibility of the company purchasing its own shares from a scheme member;

(i)   the likelihood of any future business restructuring or re-organisations, which may, for example, invalidate an EMI or CSOP option.

UNAPPROVED SHARE SCHEMES – SUMMARY OF KEY TAX CHARGES ON EMPLOYEE SHARES

Main employment income and NIC charging provisions

8.15   An employee/director is subject to an employment income tax charge in the main circumstances summarised below. Clearly, the various income tax charging rules generally only apply where the shares are acquired by reason of the directorship or employment, and the legislation extends this to cover a past or prospective office/employment (see also 13.31).

This will normally be the case where shares are awarded or share options are granted to a director or employee. The main exception to this rule is where shares are transferred to a family member, since this would be a personal gift to a family member etc (see 8.17).

Where shares fall outside the restricted securities regime or where no *ITEPA 2003, s 431* election is made (see 8.32), the employee is taxed on the 'benefit' of receiving the shares at an under-value under the 'earnings' rule in *ITEPA 2003, s 62*.

In such cases, the value of the shares is based on their 'money's worth' under *ITEPA 2003, s 62(3)* (*Weight v Salmon* (1935) 19 TC 174 and *Tennant v Smith* (1892) 3 TC 138). This means that the value of the shares would take account of their personal rights and restrictions and information known to the actual employee. Thus, for example, if the directors of the relevant company were engaged in confidential talks for a potential sale, arguably almost all its employees would not be aware of this and hence the shares would be valued on a much lower amount (ie ignoring the potential offer/sale price).

Restricted securities regime for share issues or transfers

Background

8.16   The 'restricted securities' regime was introduced by the *FA 2003* to provide a comprehensive framework for taxing employee shares, particularly dealing with shares that were issued subject to restrictions or conditions or were artificially depressed in value. For these purposes, 'securities' are widely defined and includes loan notes, government gilts, warrants, units in a collective investment scheme, and futures, etc as well as shares. In the context of family and owner managed companies we will, of course, invariably be concerned with shares or securities (and these terms are generally used here).

Due to their pervasive nature, the introduction of the 'restricted securities' legislation attracted widespread criticism. On a strict statutory interpretation, these provisions appear to potentially catch many 'innocent cases' even where there has been no intention to manipulate the value of the shares by changing or lifting restrictions, etc.

Since the legislation was issued, some boundaries have been placed on its practical application, largely through:

- the answers to Frequently Answered Questions (FAQs) on HMRC's website; and

- a series of joint statements, such as 'The Memorandum of Understanding between the BVCA (British Venture Capital Association) and the (then) Inland Revenue on the income tax treatment of managers' equity investments in venture capital and private equity backed companies', issued on 25 July 2003 (see 8.25 and 8.26).

The potential application of the restricted securities legislation to earn-out deals satisfied in shares/loan notes is reviewed at 15.74.

Scope of 'restricted securities' regime

8.17 Broadly speaking, the 'restricted securities' provisions apply to any shares:

- acquired by a current, prospective or past director (*ITEPA 2003, s 5*) or employee by reason of their office or employment [*ITEPA 2003, s 421B*];

- which, at the time of acquisition:

    (i) are subject to compulsory transfer or forfeiture for less than their market value (for example, when an employee ceases to work for the company). (HMRC's view is that if there is a chance that the employee would receive less than market value, then he is not entitled to at least market value within *ITEPA 2003, s 423(2)(c)*); or

    (ii) carry restrictions on disposing or retaining or restrictions on any other rights attaching to the shares; or

    (iii) contain other restrictions that make retaining the shares or exercising the rights attaching to them disadvantageous; and

- as a result of which the market value of the shares is less than they would be, but for these restrictions [*ITEPA 2003, s 423*].

HMRC treat restricted shares/securities as if they had two values – an actual market value taking into account all the restrictions (the AMV or 'restricted value') and an 'unrestricted market value' (UMV), assuming all the restrictions and similar provisions were taken out. The difference between the unrestricted and restricted market value of the shares will drive their tax treatment.

The legislation only applies where the shares are acquired *by reason of the individual's office or employment*. This also extends to cases where some other person (such as a family member) acquires the shares by reason of someone else's employment or office. However, shares that are given in the 'normal course of domestic family or personal relationships' are exempted (*ITEPA 2003, s 431B (3)(b)*). Thus, in a family company, shares transferred to spouses, adult children or other close family members should not be subject to any employment income tax charges (see also 13.31).

Under the precise wording of the legislation, this exemption did not apply where a company issued shares, but HMRC seemed to allow the exemption in such cases. However, in August 2012 HMRC appeared to change its practice when it updated the Employment-Related Securities Manual (at ERSM20220). Consequently, where the owner manager procures the *issue* of shares to a close family member, HMRC may not accept that this qualifies for the *ITEPA 2003, s 431B(3)(b)* 'close family or personal relationship' exemption. Therefore, it seems prudent for owner managers to transfer/gift their shares to close family members!

There is a very important rule that deems a director or founder shareholder receiving shares through a subsequent bonus or rights issue as being within the scope of these provisions, even where their original shareholding was acquired before 16 April 2003. However, there would normally be no tax charge on the bonus share issue, etc, since any reduction in value of their existing shareholding is treated as consideration for the new shares (*ITEPA 2003, s 421D*).

Shares are not restricted simply because they do not carry the full range of benefits – for example, if they are non-voting or do not carry any dividend rights – provided these limited rights apply to all the shares of the same class indefinitely. However, where the shares are only subject to temporary limitations (for example, they are non-voting for a prescribed period and then become voting), they will be restricted (HMRC Employment Related Securities Manual, para 30310).

If the shares fall within the 'restricted securities' regime, special tax considerations apply when they are originally acquired (see 8.10–8.12, 8.25 and 8.32). Unless an *ITEPA 2003, s 431* election is made, the director/employee would be 'exposed' to an income tax charge where subsequent 'chargeable events' (as defined in *ITEPA 2003, s 426*) occur, being where:

- the shares cease to be 'restricted' as a result of a removal of the restrictions or effluxion of time (see 8.31 and 8.35); or

- the restrictions attaching to the shares are varied; or

- the shares are sold whilst they are still restricted.

In those cases where the shares are readily convertible assets (see 8.39), the income tax becomes payable under PAYE and NICs become payable by the employee and employer.

Clearly, if it can be demonstrated that the shares are not 'restricted' within the meaning of *ITEPA 2003, s 423* (see above), then any tax charge on acquisition would normally be calculated under general principles. Thus, where free or cheap (non-restricted) shares are awarded, the 'benefit' received is treated as a general earnings, based on *Weight v Salmon* (1935) 19 TC 174 (see 13.29).

For coverage of the special exemption for shares etc provided to employees in research institution 'spin-out' companies, see 8.24 of 2013/14 and earlier editions of this book.

Founders' shares

8.18 A much stricter stance appears to be taken with 'founders' shares' as HMRC has indicated that such shares would normally be taken to be employment-related securities. However, this does not necessarily mean that an income tax charge will arise. Some value has to pass to the employee on the acquisition of the shares. HMRC have confirmed that it is not the intention to tax normal commercial growth as employment income (*HMRC Employment Related Securities Manual, para 20240*).

As a general rule, it is no longer possible to argue that shares acquired by managers on a management buy-out are 'founders' shares' (see 8.25).

Shares subject to transfer restrictions and pre-emption rights

8.19   There has been considerable debate as to whether most shareholdings in private companies would be restricted on the grounds they are subject to the standard transfer restrictions and pre-emption rights. There have been suggestions that such conditions may not necessarily make them fall within the restricted securities regime. The standard 'restriction' contained in most articles is that the directors may refuse to register a transfer to any person that they disapprove of. Some have pointed out that the existence of these pre-emption rights can be considered as favourable to the existing shareholders, since it removes the risk of 'undesirable' shareholders etc.

Furthermore, given that compulsory 'fair valuation' is applied to a pre-emption transfer of shares, there is a strongly held view that the shares would not be restricted (since this value is likely to exceed a discounted fiscal valuation of a minority shareholding). In any event, shares with (only) *standard* pre-emption rights are likely to be treated as having the same value with or without those rights. Consequently, in such cases, only the basic 'excess over market value' charge under *Weight v Salmon* would need to be considered (see 13.29).

However, even where it is very unlikely that the shares would be regarded as 'restricted securities' under a legalistic analysis, many advisers assume that HMRC might subsequently treat them as 'restricted'. They therefore adopt a practical 'belt and braces' approach by ensuring that protective *ITEPA 2003, s 431* elections are always made (see 8.32). This approach seems to be justified because there have been a number of reported cases where HMRC now seem to be taking the view that private company shares are 'restricted' because of the presence of pre-emption rights or some other restrictions on shareholders' abilities to sell their shares freely!

Many contend that this point is debatable since 'restrictions' which are inherent characteristics of the shares affecting all the shareholders, as opposed to being specific to the employees or directors, should be ignored for this purpose. Furthermore, as explained above, the existence of pre-emption rights also has a potential upside for shareholders. Whilst HMRC may not be readily sympathetic to such arguments, they might be worth pursuing in a 'defensive' situation.

Leaver clauses

8.20   Shares issued to directors/employees typically require the shares to be sold if the employee leaves. Different exit rules apply for 'good' and 'bad' leavers:

- 'good leavers' are usually those employees who die in service, retire at normal retirement age or are made redundant. Good leavers are usually given the capital growth on their shares up to the point when they leave. Thus, the pre-emption price would generally be the higher of the original price paid for their shares or market value/fair value;

- 'bad leavers' would include employees who are fired or leave to join a competitor. A bad leaver would be required to give up their shares at the lower of market value and the amount originally paid for their shares.

Under *ITEPA 2003, s 424(1)(b)*, a 'bad leaver' clause requiring an employee to give up their shares if they leave on the ground of misconduct does not count as a 'restriction' under the restricted securities regime (misconduct typically involves breaking the company's rules and may also include 'termination for cause' (see Employment Procedures Manual, para 30240)).

Where a 'bad leaver' receives the 'bad leaver price', invariably resist attempting to apply the *TCGA 1992, s 17* 'market value' rule for CGT purposes. This is on the basis that the departing employee has received their legal entitlement under the articles.

It is always important to remember that (in contrast to an actual award of shares) options do not give rise to any employee 'leaver' issues. Options generally lapse on cessation of employment and a well-drafted option will exclude any potential 'value' from the employees' entitlement to compensation.

Valuation issues

8.21   Valuations under the *ITEPA 2003* employee shares regime follow the capital gains methodology. This means that the relative size of the shareholding (and its overall cost) will determine the appropriate information standard. These principles are fully explained in 14.34–14.39. It is perhaps worth noting here that most employee holdings will represent small minority interests. Consequently, the details that would be deemed to be available for the purpose of the valuation would be restricted to signed accounts, press information, company website news, and general industry knowledge (see 14.36).

The statutory CGT basis of valuation requires a willing hypothetical vendor and a prudent hypothetical purchaser, who could be anyone. Where there is a restriction on sale (either in the articles, shareholders' agreement, or employment contract), HMRC's view is that the shares must be valued as if that restriction remains relevant in the purchaser's hands.

On this basis, the hypothetical purchaser looks very much like an employee(!), but this interpretation is not readily supported by share valuation jurisprudence or indeed HMRC – Shares & Asset Valuation (SAV) office! The existence of a 'bad leaver' price in the articles could therefore influence the restricted value of the shares, depending on whether the (hypothetical) employee shareholder was more likely to leave before any sale of the company. In practice, such an assessment is likely to be ignored by the SAV office, especially since the CGT basis clearly contemplates a hypothetical purchaser who could be anyone at all.

However, it might be possible to argue successfully that the existence of a 'bad leaver' price should not restrict the value of the shares. Where the preemption right extends to the same class, the other shareholder(s) stand to gain by acquiring the shares at a favourable 'par' value. So since it is not known which shareholder would leave first (all shareholders being 'hypothetical'), the overall effect would be relatively neutral. On the other hand, where the pre-emption right first extends to a different class, the existence of a bad leaver price would restrict the share value.

There is some practical evidence to suggest that there is little consistency in HMRC's approach to valuations. For example, some HMRC valuers have agreed Actual Market value (AMV) and the Unrestricted Market value (UMV) (see 8.17) at the same figure while others have insisted on a 10% to 20% difference between the two figures (without any particular reason).

A common approach is to assume that the 'traditional' share valuation is the AMV, which should be increased by an appropriate fixed percentage to give the UMV. However, many argue that this is incorrect since it would produce dissimilar UMVs for identical shares subject to different restrictions. It therefore follows that the correct approach would be to treat the share value as the UMV with a suitable reduction being applied to reflect the relevant restrictions.

Impact on approved share schemes

8.22   'Restricted' shares acquired under Enterprise Management Incentives (EMI) options fall within the scope of 'restricted securities' legislation. However, an *ITEPA 2003, s 431* election is *deemed* to be made when the EMI option is exercised for (at least) their market value at the date of grant (*ITEPA 2003, s 431A*). However, for 'discounted' EMI options (ie where an income tax charge arises on exercise), an *ITEPA 2003, s 431* election is generally recommended (see 8.62).

'Post-acquisition' taxable events (see 8.31) arising on 'restricted' shares issued under HMRC approved schemes, such as company share ownership plans (CSOPs), SAYE schemes and share incentive plans (SIPs), are subject to the 'restricted securities' rules. However, no tax charge arises on the *acquisition or award* of shares under these approved schemes.

'Narrow' employee-controlled company exemption

8.22A   There is a 'narrow' exemption from the relevant income charges under *ITEPA 2003, s 426* for 'employee-controlled' companies under *ITEPA 2003, s 429*. Broadly, in relation to a *particular class of shares*, an 'employee-controlled' company is one where the majority of the shares of that class are held by or for the benefit of employees who are able to control the company [*ITEPA 2003, s 421H*].

Since 2 December 2004, the exemption is also circumscribed by the requirement to ensure that the avoidance of tax or NICs was not one of the main purposes of the arrangements under which the shares were acquired.

It is important to appreciate that this exemption is fairly limited in scope, since it only applies if *all* the shares are affected by the same relevant chargeable *event*. This exemption would *not* therefore apply where, for example, an employee (not protected by an *ITEPA 2003, s 431* election – see 8.32) subsequently sells their shares without the company being 'sold'.

Use of 'nil or partly paid' shares

8.23   The use of 'nil or partly paid' shares can be an attractive solution where tax-favoured option schemes are not available or are impractical to implement. The rights attaching to the nil/partly paid shares must be set out in the company's articles.

Under a nil/partly paid share arrangement, the company agrees to issue shares to an employee at the current market value of the shares. However, the employee does not actually pay the full subscription price at that point. Nevertheless, an employee is potentially liable for the price of the shares should the company decide to 'call' for payment (which would certainly exercised by a liquidator should the company be wound-up).

The basic tax analysis of a nil/partly-paid share arrangement:

- The employee agrees to pay the full market value for the shareholding, so there is no taxable benefit. (However, a full tax charge will arise where the shares have mainly been issued for a tax/NIC avoidance purpose – as distinct from tax efficiency or commercial necessity – for example, the shares may be too expensive for the employee to purchase now (*ITEPA 2003, s 446UA*). It is always prudent to make an *ITEPA 2003, s 431* election.

- The nil/partly paid shares would be treated as a readily convertible asset. Thus any income tax charge arising on them would be subject to PAYE and NICs – this is because they would not qualify for any corporation tax deduction (see below and 8.40).

- The unpaid subscription monies are treated as a notional loan. However, the taxable benefit of the notional 'interest-free' loan is normally exempt since the 'notional interest' would qualify for tax relief under *ITA 2007, s 383 (ITA 2007, s 392)*, since it would be incurred on a loan to purchase shares in a close trading company (*ITEPA 2003, ss 178(a)* and *446S(3)*).

A departing employee who is not a 'good leaver' (for example, leaving for reasons of disability, ill health or redundancy) should be required to sell back his shares at cost.

Although the point is not free from doubt, the better view is that unpaid calls on the shares are outside the scope of the loan to participator rules (*CTA 2010, s 455*) (see 2.56). This is on the basis that the unpaid calls do not constitute 'a debt' until they are legally called by the company. The company cannot sue the employee for the debt until it becomes due. In this context, it is unwise for the articles to include any timetable or provisions for making calls.

There are a number of technical obstacles that prevent nil/partly paid shares from qualifying for the statutory corporation tax deduction for employee shares – for example, the relief is only given on shares that are fully paid up (see 8.89).

On a sale, the shares would benefit from CGT treatment (potentially with the benefit of ER if the holding is more than 5%). The 'notional loan' would be treated as being repaid (*ITEPA 2003, s 446U*).

'Nil or partly paid' share arrangements are reasonably well established and are usually accepted by HMRC but could be open to challenge if they are 'misused'.

Use of growth shares

8.24   In recent years, growth share arrangements have emerged as a useful mechanism for key employees to benefit from an equity stake with increasing value if the business grows.

The growth share is issued to the employee immediately but the capital rights typically vary depending on an actual value of the company at the point of sale. The rights can be layered to be consistent with the employer's (or investor's) objectives. Thus, for example, an employee's shares might participate in the capital value of the company as follows:

Capital value on sale or liquidation	Entitlement
Up to £1 million	1%
Between £1 million and £10 million	5%
Above £10 million	7%

Growth shares involve the actual issue of shares in the company with all the rights and obligations of a shareholder.

The concept works well in early stage businesses where the value in the shares is entirely prospective, giving those shares a low value at the point of purchase with the potential for substantial growth. This therefore minimises the required purchase price or the value of any taxable benefit on acquiring the shares at undervalue.

A subsequent sale of the shares will be subject to CGT in the normal way, and ER may be available if the relevant conditions (including the enjoyment of at least 5% of the voting rights) are satisfied.

The use of growth shares is a well-established arrangement and a properly structured arrangement should be accepted by HMRC without too much difficulty.

Management buy-outs and employment-related securities

Implications of shares being treated as restricted securities

8.25   Before the *FA 2003*, it was generally believed that where a management team set up a new company (Newco) to acquire the target company, their Newco shares would *not* be treated as acquired by reason of employment.

Under the current legislation, the management team's Newco shares would be 'employment-related securities' (see 8.17) since the shares are treated as made available by virtue of their previous employment with the target company.

Furthermore, the shares issued to managers on the 'majority' of buy-outs are likely to be 'restricted securities'. This is because many managers' shares will be subject to the usual 'good leaver/bad leaver' provisions that require the compulsory transfer of their shares at less than market value if they leave the company within a specified period other than by reason of ill health or disability, etc.

The full implications of *ITEPA 2003, Pt 7* must therefore be considered when issuing shares to a manager on a Management Buy-Out (MBO) or Management Buy-in (MBI). In such cases, the shares are likely to be restricted securities and may be acquired at an 'under-value' as compared to the price paid for shares issued to others, such as by a private equity provider.

The same tax issues can arise where managers receive shares in the buy-out company vehicle (Newco) in exchange for their previous shares in their 'old' company ('Oldco'). *ITEPA 2003, s 421D* effectively operates to deem both the old shares and therefore the new 'consideration' shares to be received 'by reason of employment', even where the 'old' shares were acquired before 16 April 2003 (see 8.16).

Although the normal 'share for share' exchange rules should apply for CGT purposes (see 15.44), the consideration given for the Newco shares by the managers for the purposes of the 'employment-related' securities regime is the (relevant proportion) of the deal value placed on Oldco's shares. Given that the value of Oldco's shares would reflect any (material) relevant restrictions in Oldco's articles, the unrestricted market value of the managers' Newco shares could exceed the actual market value of their Oldco's shares. The tax outcome will clearly depend on the relevant valuations in each particular case and it may be possible to argue that there is no real difference between the restricted and unrestricted values of the shares. It may also be possible to argue that the 'consideration' given by the managers for their Newco shares is the same as the amount given by the institutional investors. However, if there is a material difference in values, it is possible for an employment income tax charge to arise on the share exchange.

As a general rule, the managers will elect under *ITEPA 2003, s 431* to be taxed by reference to the 'unrestricted market value' of the Newco shares. (Indeed, this will invariably be a requirement of the private equity provider to ensure that the company is not exposed to additional PAYE/NIC liabilities on an 'exit'!)

Memorandum of understanding ('MOU') with BVCA

8.26 The British Venture Capital Association (BVCA) sought to clarify with the (then) Inland Revenue the extent to which shares issued to managers in venture capital and private equity backed companies would be caught under the 'employment-related securities' regime in *ITEPA 2003, Pt 7*. Typically, this applies to shares issued to the management team in MBO and MBI transactions.

Some helpful guidance on the issues raised is contained in the 'Memorandum of Understanding' (MOU) that was issued on 25 July 2003, which can be found at: www.bvca.co.uk/Portals/0/library/Files/StandardIndustryDocuments/PDF_1. pdf.

The BVCA Memorandum follows a 'safe harbour' approach for shares issued to managers (provided there are no inherent tax-avoidance arrangements). However, it is still open for taxpayers to argue each case on its own particular circumstances. Where there is uncertainty about the application of the MOU guidelines to a particular 'buy-out', this may be resolved by applying to HMRC for an informal clearance or ruling (see 15.40).

Where there are no 'ratchet' arrangements (see 8.27), HMRC will accept that the price paid for the managers' shares is equivalent to:

- the initial unrestricted market value (IUMV), where the shares are 'restricted securities'; or

- the market value, if the shares are *not* restricted;

provided the following conditions are met:

(*a*)   the managers' shares are ordinary share capital;

(*b*)   any preferred debt or equity capital provided by the private equity provider is on normal commercial terms;

(*c*)   the price paid for the managers' shares is *not less* than the price the private equity provider pays for its 'equivalent' ordinary shares;

(*d*)   the managers acquire their shares at the same time as the private equity provider acquires its ordinary shares (in practice, HMRC generally appear to accept cases where the shares are acquired within up to 90 days of each other);

(*e*)   the managers' shares have no features that give them (or allow them to acquire) rights not available to other holders of ordinary share capital;

(*f*)   the managers are fully remunerated through salary and bonuses (where appropriate) under a separate employment/service contract (see paras 3.1 and 4.1 of the Memorandum).

Managers' shares often carry restrictions of the type laid down in *ITEPA 2003, s 423(2)*. For example, the typical requirement in a 'leaver' clause is to transfer the managers' shares for less than market value. The managers will be treated as paying a price that is *not* discounted as a result of these restrictions, provided the price paid is the same as that paid by the venture capitalist (see (*c*) above). Thus, in such cases, the price paid would (at least) be equivalent to the IUMV of the shares.

Similarly, the (initial) value of shares would not be depressed where they are subject to the commonly used 'drag-along' and 'tag-along' provisions – 'drag-along' rights force the minority shareholders to sell their shares in cases where the majority wish to sell the company; 'tag-along' rights give the minority shareholders the right to sell their shares where an offer has been made to the controlling shareholders. These provisions are unlikely to reduce the value of the shares since they enable the minority shareholders to obtain market value for their shares on an 'exit'.

Potential impact of ratchet arrangements

8.27   In many MBO and MBI deals the ordinary shares issued to managers are subject to a 'ratchet' mechanism, so that the managers' shares obtain additional rights and value when target rates of return are achieved by the private equity provider or when pre-determined performance targets are met by the company.

Ratchets are generally designed to achieve a private equity provider's commercial objectives. The 'ratchet' mechanism laid down in the Articles or Shareholders' Agreement can either increase the interest of the managers' shares or reduce the interests attaching to the other shares (typically held by the private equity investor).

403

For example, the private equity investor may start off with (say) 80% of the ordinary shares with management having the other 20%. If the company's performance (normally measured by the investors 'internal rate of return') exceeds the relevant target(s) or 'hurdles', then part of the private equity investor's holding will convert into worthless deferred shares. This would then reduce the investor's economic stake to (say) 75% with management's holding rising to 25%. Such mechanisms are frequently referred to as 'positive' or 'upward' ratchets.

On the other hand, 'negative' or 'downward' ratchets work by reducing management's equity stake – with their initial stake being set at the maximum possible assuming all relevant performance targets were achieved. Thus, if the target internal rate of return is not achieved, then management's shares convert into worthless deferred shares with a consequent reduction in their equity stake.

There remains a risk, albeit a debatable one, that ratchets may be subject to an income tax charge under *ITEPA 2003, s 447*.

These 'ratchet' mechanisms also provide an incentive for the managers. If the company prospers, the ratchet will increase their shares of the exit proceeds.

The BVCA MOU (July 2003) states that a ratchet should *not* produce any income tax charge under the *ITEPA 2003, Pt 7, Ch 4* 'post-acquisition benefits' regime, provided certain conditions are met:

(*a*)   there are no personal performance conditions attached to the ratchet;

(*b*)   the ratchet arrangements are in existence when the private equity provider acquired its shares; and

(c)   the managers paid a price for shares reflecting their maximum economic entitlement.

Following the MOU, many ratchet arrangements were structured as a 'negative' ratchet to give the managers the maximum equity interest on 'day one'.

Under perhaps the more common route of a 'positive ratchet', where managers' shareholding interests can appreciate (as a result of the other (private equity provider's) shares being diluted), it was argued that managers must effectively pay a 'premium' for the 'upside' element.

In June 2004, the (then) Inland Revenue indicated that an income tax charge would arise where the initial price paid by the managers did *not* reflect their full economic entitlement under the ratchet. The increase in value may result from the lifting of restrictions because new rights are acquired or simply as a consequence of the equity holding being increased. In such cases, any additional 'value' passing to the managers under an incremental ratchet based on performance would be taxed as a post-acquisition benefit derived from the shares under *ITEPA 2003, Pt 7, Ch 4*. The (then) Revenue's view was that the increase in the value of the managers' holding should be taxed by reference to the valuation of the shareholding at the time of the 'ratcheted' increase in the managers' shareholding. Any such charge would be subject to PAYE and NIC as the shares are deemed to be RCAs for this purpose under *ITEPA 2003, s 698(3)*.

HMRC have subsequently revised their view (following legal advice), which is reflected in revised guidance issued on 21 August 2006. In summary, HMRC accepted that a charge under *ITEPA 2003, Pt 7, Ch 4*, was not sustainable where the benefit to the manager reflected 'ratchet' rights that already existed in their shares when they were first acquired.

HMRC confirm that where shares are acquired under arrangements consistent with those described in the MOU (see 8.26 (*a*) to (*f*) above) then no *ITEPA 2003, Pt 7, Ch 4* 'post-acquisition benefit' charge will arise on the disposal of the shares or (if earlier) on the operation of the ratchet. Furthermore, where the ratchet also meets conditions (*a*) and (*b*) above, any gains realised on exit will only be subject to CGT.

This seems to suggest that condition (c) (the managers must pay a price that reflects their maximum economic entitlement under the 'ratchet' arrangement) no longer applies, and hence a 'positive ratchet' would not, in itself, give rise to a *Pt 7, Ch 4* charge. However, it does appear that the price paid for the shares should reflect the future value of the ratchet, albeit with a discount for the risk that the ratchet may not operate. It therefore is prudent to structure ratchet deals with managers paying a price that reflects the 'maximum' amount they may end up with (with appropriate discounts for uncertainty etc). Furthermore, protective *ITEPA 2003, s 431* elections should also be made in case HMRC do not accept that the full unrestricted value has been paid.

Shares subject to conditions or forfeitable shares

8.28   Shares that are issued on a 'conditional' basis are now taxed as a 'restricted security' and therefore a tax charge would generally arise under *ITEPA 2003, s 426* when the conditions are lifted and the director/employee enjoys the full benefit of the shares (see 8.35).

Such shares are commonly used under long-term incentive plans (LTIPs), where shares are usually given to employees or directors at nil or nominal cost, but subject to pre-determined performance conditions being met.

However, the basic rule is that no *initial* income tax (or, where relevant, NIC) charge on forfeitable shares is made where the terms of the award are such that the forfeiture restriction will cease within five years of acquisition (*ITEPA 2003, s 425(1), (2)*).

In such cases, a full income tax charge arises when the restriction is lifted within five years. This tax treatment can be avoided by the employer and employee making an *ITEPA 2003, s 425(3)* election.

By making this election, the employee will suffer an income tax charge at the time of the initial award (with a corresponding corporate tax deduction being claimed – see 8.89). *ITEPA 2003, s 425(3)* elections are irrevocable and must be made within 14 days of the share acquisition. Approved *ITEPA 2003, s 425* election forms can be found on the HMRC website at www.hmrc.gov.uk/manuals/ersmmanual/ERSM30370.htm.

An *ITEPA 2003, s 425* election differs from the (more frequent) *ITEPA 2003, s 431* election, the latter being used to being taxed on the full unrestricted value of the shares (rather than the discount relating to forfeiture restrictions).

The elections do not have to be submitted to HMRC, but must be retained since they may be requested for inspection as part of an HMRC enquiry.

Where the election is made, the tax charge is based on the full market value of the shares *ignoring the depreciatory effect of the forfeiture risk [ITEPA 2003, s 425(3)]*.

When the forfeiture or any other restriction is lifted, this will constitute a chargeable event under *ITEPA 2003, s 426* (see 8.31). In calculating the tax charge on this subsequent event, the initial income tax charge is deducted to arrive at the final taxable amount *(ITEPA 2003, s 428(7)(b))* (see 8.35).

Even where there is no immediate charge, an 'acquisition-based' charge could still arise under certain other provisions, such as where shares are acquired 'partly paid' or under a securities option *[ITEPA 2003, s 425(2)]*.

Example 1

Tax treatment of forfeitable shares

On 31 January 2017, the trustees of the Toffees Ltd employee trust awarded Mr Valencia 1,000 shares in Enner Ltd. The restricted value of the shares was £1 each, recognising that the shares would be forfeited within three years if certain performance targets were not achieved during that period. The value of the shares, ignoring the forfeiture restriction, is £2.50 per share.

Because the 1,000 shares are forfeitable within three years, no tax charge arises in January 2017 under *ITEPA 2003, s 425(1)*.

If the shares are retained after three years (because the performance targets are satisfied), there will be a charge when the forfeiture restriction is lifted. Thus, if the shares were worth (say) £5 per share in January 2020, Mr Valencia will suffer a tax charge of £5,000 (being £1,000 × £5 × 100%) (see 8.35).

However, if a joint *ITEPA 2003, s 425* election were made by 14 February 2017, Mr Valencia would have an initial employment income charge on £1,000 (ie £1,000 × £1 (restricted value)).

The percentage of the initial unrestricted market value charged on acquisition is therefore 40% (being £1,000/£2,500 × 100%).

A further income tax charge would arise when the restricted is lifted in January 2020 on £3,000 (being 1,000 × £5 × 60%)

The election has reduced the amount taxed as employment income by £1,000 (being £5,000 less £4,000 (£1,000 + £3,000)).

Note – if the market value of the shares when the restrictions are lifted is lower than when they were first acquired, there is no mechanism for relief and no tax refunds are possible.

Tax charges on exercise of unapproved share option

8.29   The exercise of an option to acquire employment-related shares or securities is taxed under *ITEPA 2003, s 476*. The income tax charge is based on the excess of the market value of the shares when the option is exercised *over* the amount given for the shares (ie the exercise price) – see 8.35 (Example 2).

In an era of very high income tax rates, directors and employees must consider the timing of any option exercises so as to minimise their income tax liabilities. For example, if may be preferable to exercise an option in a period when the taxable element will only be charged at 40%.

See 8.87 for HMRC's on-line reporting requirements in respect of share options.

No tax charge arises on the exercise of 'approved' CSOP options [*ITEPA 2003, s 524*] or EMI options (to acquire shares for a price equivalent to their market value when the option is granted) [*ITEPA 2003, s 530*] (see 8.60 and 8.61). Note that the general *CA 2006* rules for share allotments (see 8.10) also apply to the grant of share options.

A UK-resident employee does not have any tax charge on the grant of the option itself, irrespective of the option's exercise period [*ITEPA 2003, s 475*].

Where the shares are transferred by an existing shareholder, an employment income charge still arises on the director/employee. However, for CGT purposes, *TCGA 1992, s 144ZA* states that the deemed CGT consideration for the transfer (ie both for the transferor and recipient) is the actual proceeds (rather than the shares' market value as would normally be the case under *TCGA 1992, s 17* – see 13.9 and 13.39). Any amount subject to an income tax charge on the exercise of the option would then be added to the director's/ employee's CGT base cost [*TCGA 1992, s 119A*].

The determination of the base cost for share options exercised before 10 April 2003 is complex due to the decision arising in the *Mansworth v Jelley* [2003] STC 53 case and HMRC's subsequent (changing) analysis of that decision.

Amount received on assignment or release of option

8.30   An employment income tax charge under *ITEPA 2003, s 476* also occurs where the director/employee (see *ITEPA 2003, s 472*) waives their right to acquire shares under the option or where they assign that right to someone else. The charge is based on the benefit in money or money's worth received in consideration.

The tax charge on any *cash* received for the assignment or release of an option is collected under the PAYE regime. Otherwise, the application of PAYE depends on whether the relevant shares are a 'readily convertible asset' (see 8.39).

Income tax charges on subsequent chargeable events

Chargeable events

8.31   In broad terms, shares, etc within the 'restricted securities' regime are vulnerable to an income tax charge in the tax year when a subsequent chargeable event occurs, such as where:

- the shares are sold; or

- the restrictions on those shares are lifted or varied [*ITEPA 2003, ss 426, 427*].

This income tax charge only bites if the shares were originally acquired by the director/employee for less than their 'unrestricted' market value. Thus, when the shares were first acquired, the income tax charge would be based on the value of the shares ignoring any restrictions attaching to them or, where a valid *ITEPA 2003, s 431* election is in place, by reference to that 'unrestricted' value (see 8.32).

If (at least) the unrestricted 'market value' is paid for the shares, then they should just be subject to CGT on their ultimate sale in the usual way.

Such chargeable events must now be reported on-line to HMRC on Form 42 (see 8.87).

Section 431 election for initial acquisition to be taxed on unrestricted value

8.32   Where the shares were acquired at less than their 'market value', an election can be made to pay income tax on the difference between unrestricted market value of the shares and the amount actually paid for them (see also 8.17 and 8.35 – Example 2). By taking the unrestricted market value of the shares, any restrictions are ignored for the purposes of assessing their value, which may produce a higher value than it otherwise would be. This means that the director/employee must either pay:

- an appropriate higher value for their shares; or

- income tax on the 'benefit' received by obtaining the shares for less than that 'unrestricted' amount.

In short, the director/employee must be satisfied that they are either paying the 'unrestricted' market value or incurring the tax on the relevant amount. If the valuation is unsound, HMRC could argue that the subsequent 'chargeable event' rules do, in fact, apply.

8.33 Clearly, the valuation of a minority shareholding in an unquoted company is a subjective matter, and it is not unusual for the employee/company and HMRC to determine different valuations. The employee may therefore believe that they have paid the proper market price for the shares but HMRC may subsequently succeed in arguing that a higher amount should have been paid for the shares. Provided an *ITEPA 2003, s 431* election has been made, the employee's maximum income tax exposure would be limited to the unrestricted market value of the shares at the date of acquisition (less any amount paid by then). Without an election, the employee could subsequently be exposed to a sizeable income tax liability if a 'chargeable event' occurs, such as a sale (see 8.35).

For example, if the value of the shares on an unrestricted basis is £1 and the employee pays the restricted value of 70p, then in the absence of an election, 30% of all future growth in those shares would be taxed to income tax and not CGT. However, by making a joint election for the director/employee to pay income tax on 30p per share, no further income tax is payable and the entire future growth in the shares would be liable to a lower CGT charge. The election also covers any NIC liability (if the shares are readily convertible assets).

In the majority of cases an election would therefore be beneficial as it removes any future increase in the value of the shares from the (higher) income tax net and into the more favourable CGT regime on their subsequent sale. In turn, this effectively ensures that the normal commercial growth in value of the shares is taxed at the lower effective CGT tax rate. The 'downside' of making the election is that income tax could potentially be paid on acquisition on a value that may never be realised, if the shares subsequently dropped in value.

Companies normally insist (especially where an 'exit' is envisaged, such as in private-equity backed buy-outs) that an election is always made to avoid any risk of incurring PAYE and NIC liabilities on part of the employees' sale proceeds on a sale of the company (since the shares would become Readily Convertible Assets at that point – see 8.39).

The *ITEPA 2003, s 431* election needs to be made jointly between the employer and employee and must be made within 14 days of the acquisition of shares.

The *ITEPA 2003, s 431* election does not have to be sent to HMRC, but must be carefully retained by the employer in the event of a subsequent HMRC enquiry into the employing company's records. The safe retention by the employer is particularly important given that *ITEPA 2003, s 431* elections may need to be produced at a later date as evidence to resist a potentially large income tax bill.

Pro-forma *ITEPA 2003, s 431* election

8.34   Pro-forma elections are available on HMRC's website at www.gov.
uk/hmrc-internal-manuals/employment-related-securities/ersm30450   (for
both a one-part election and a two-part election).

A copy of HMRC's prescribed joint election under *ITEPA 2003, s 431* is
reproduced below.

Joint Election under s 431 ITEPA 2003 for full or partial disapplication of
Chapter 2 Income Tax (Earnings and Pensions) Act 2003

Two Part Election   (For this joint election to be valid both Parts A and
B must be signed and dated)

Part A – To be completed by the Employee

1. Between

the Employee ... ... *[insert name of employee]*

whose National Insurance Number is ... ... *[insert NINO]*

and

the Company (who is the Employee's employer) ... ...
[insert name of company]

of Company Registration Number ... ... *[insert CRN]*

2. Purpose of Election

This joint election is made pursuant to section 431(1) or 431(2) Income
Tax (Earnings and Pensions) Act 2003 (ITEPA) and applies where
employment-related securities, which are restricted securities by reason of
section 423 ITEPA, are acquired.

The effect of an election under section 431(1) is that, for the relevant
Income Tax and NIC purposes, the employment-related securities and
their market value will be treated as if they were not restricted securities
and that sections 425 to 430 ITEPA do not apply. An election under section
431(2) will ignore one or more of the restrictions in computing the charge
on acquisition. Additional Income Tax will be payable (with PAYE and
NIC where the securities are Readily Convertible Assets).

Should the value of the securities fall following the acquisition, it is
possible that Income Tax/NIC that would have arisen because of any future
chargeable event (in the absence of an election) would have been less than
the Income Tax/NIC due by reason of this election. Should this be the case,
there is no Income Tax/NIC relief available under Part 7 of ITEPA 2003;
nor is it available if the securities acquired are subsequently transferred,
forfeited or revert to the original owner.

---

3. Application

This joint election is made not later than 14 days after the date of acquisition of the securities by the employee and applies to:

Number of securities … … … … … … … … … … .. *[insert number]*

Description of securities … … … … … … … … … *[insert description]*

Name of issuer of securities … … … … … … … *[insert name of issuer]*

* acquired by the Employee on … … … … … … … .. *[insert date]*

* to be acquired by the Employee between *[dd/mm/yyyy]* and *[dd/mm/yyyy]*

* to be acquired by the Employee after *[dd/mm/yyyy]* under the terms of *[insert scheme/plan name]*

(* delete as appropriate)

4. Extent of Application

This election disapplies (* *delete as appropriate*):

* S.431(1) ITEPA: All restrictions attaching to the securities, or

* S431(2) ITEPA: The following specified restriction : *[details of specified restriction]*

5. Declaration

This election will become irrevocable upon the later of its signing or the acquisition (* and each subsequent acquisition) of employment-related securities to which this election applies.

(* delete as appropriate)

In signing this joint election, I agree to be bound by its terms as stated above.

…………………………………………….. …../…../………

Signature of employee Date

Note: Where the election is in respect of multiple acquisitions, prior to the date of any subsequent acquisition of a security it may be revoked by agreement between the employee and employer in respect of that and any later acquisition.

Joint Election under s 431 for full or partial disapplication of Chapter 2 Income Tax (Earnings and Pensions) Act 2003.

Two Part Election   (For this joint election to be valid both Parts A and B must be signed and dated)

Part B – To be completed by the Employer

1.   Between

the Employees, listed on the attached schedule, who have completed **Part A** to this joint election.

and

the Company (who is the Employees' employer) … … … … … … … . . *[insert name of company]*

of Company Registration Number … … … … … … … … *[insert CRN]*

2.   Purpose of Election

This joint election is made pursuant to section 431(1) or 431(2) Income Tax (Earnings and Pensions) Act 2003 (ITEPA) and applies where employment-related securities, which are restricted securities by reason of section 423 ITEPA, are acquired.

The effect of an election under section 431(1) is that, for the relevant Income Tax and NIC purposes, the employment-related securities and their market value will be treated as if they were not restricted securities and that sections 425 to 430 ITEPA do not apply. An election under section 431(2) will ignore one or more of the restrictions in computing the charge on acquisition. Additional Income Tax will be payable (with PAYE and NIC where the securities are Readily Convertible Assets).

Should the value of the securities fall following the acquisition, it is possible that Income Tax/NIC that would have arisen because of any future chargeable event (in the absence of an election) would have been less than the Income Tax/NIC due by reason of this election. Should this be the case, there is no Income Tax/NIC relief available under Part 7 of ITEPA 2003; nor is it available if the securities acquired are subsequently transferred, forfeited or revert to the original owner.

3.   Application

This joint election is made not later than 14 days after the date of acquisition of the securities by the employee and applies to:

Number of securities … … … … … … … … … … … . . *[insert number]*

Description of securities … … … … … … … … … … *[insert description]*

Name of issuer of securities … … … … … … … … *[insert name of issuer]*

* acquired by the Employee on ... ... *[insert date]*

* to be acquired by the Employee between *[dd/mm/yyyy]* and *[dd/mm/yyyy]*

* to be acquired by the Employee after *[dd/mm/yyyy]* under the terms of *[insert scheme/plan name]*

(* delete as appropriate)

4. Extent of Application

This election disapplies *(* delete as appropriate)*:

* S.431(1) ITEPA: All restrictions attaching to the securities, or

* S431(2) ITEPA: The following specified restriction: *[details of specified restriction]*

5. Declaration

This election will become irrevocable upon the later of its signing or the acquisition (* and each subsequent acquisition) of employment-related securities to which this election applies.

(* delete as appropriate)

In signing this joint election, we agree to be bound by its terms as stated above.

..../...../............

Signed for and on behalf of the company ... ... Date

....

Position in company

Note: Where the election is in respect of multiple acquisitions, prior to the date of any subsequent acquisition of a security it may be revoked by agreement between the employee and employer in respect of that and any later acquisition.

Calculation of income tax on chargeable event

8.35 If no *ITEPA 2003, s 431* election is made, an income tax charge would be imposed on the chargeable event under *ITEPA 2003, ss 426–428*, by reference to the following formula:

UMV × (IUP – PCP – OP) – CE
Where:

UMV = Unrestricted Market Value at time of chargeable event.

IUP = Initial Uncharged Proportion, which is broadly the proportion of the unrestricted market value at the date of acquisition that was *not* charged to income tax.

PCP = Previously Charged Proportion, being amounts that have been charged to income tax on a previous chargeable event or events.

OP = Outstanding Proportion, being

$$\frac{\text{UMV less AMV}}{\text{UMV}}$$

Where:

UMV is as above and AMV is Actual Market Value *immediately after the chargeable event* taking account of restrictions.

CE = Consideration paid by the employee for varying rights, etc and any other expenses.

In the vast majority of cases, the formula will simplify to UMV × IUP. Broadly speaking, this would represent the fractional part of the unrestricted market value that was not charged to income tax (on acquisition) multiplied by the market value of the shares at the time of the event (eg sale proceeds on share sale).

Consequently, the amount of sale proceeds, etc that would be subject to income tax would grow in line with any increase in the amount by which the *initial* unrestricted value of the shares exceeded their restricted value.

A simplified calculation of the tax that would be levied on a chargeable event is given in Example 2 below.

COMPREHENSIVE EXAMPLE OF OPTION TO ACQUIRE RESTRICTED SHARES

Example 2

Tax treatment of restricted shares

On 1 October 2016, Mr Jussi exercises an option to purchase 10,000 £1 B ordinary shares in his employer company, Goalies Ltd, at their par value of £1 each, which represented a 3% equity holding in the company. The B ordinary shares were subject to various restrictions, including the fact that the shares had to be sold back to the company at par on cessation of employment.

Goalies Ltd draws up accounts to 31 December each year.

The value of each B share at 1 October 2016 was as follows:

	Per share
Restricted value	£2
Unrestricted value	£3

No election

Without an *ITEPA 2003, s 431* election, Mr Jussi would have taxable income of £10,000 under *ITEPA 2003, s 476*, being the difference between the restricted market value and the amount actually paid by him, as follows:

	£
Restricted market value – (10,000 × £2)	20,000
Less: Amount paid – (10,000 × £1)	(10,000)
Taxable on exercise of option	10,000

This would mean that Mr Jussi would also suffer an income tax charge based on around a third of the value of the shares on a future 'chargeable event'. Thus, based on the above facts, the amount subject to income tax on a subsequent sale of the shares in (say) December 2017 for £70,000 (when the company was sold and hence the shares become RCAs) would be calculated as follows:

UMV × (IUP – PCP – OP) – CE

Where:

UMV	=	£ 70,000 (being the sale price)	
IUP	=	$\dfrac{£30,000 \text{ less } £20,000}{£30,000}$	= 0.333
PCP and OP and CE	=	0	

Therefore, *ITEPA 2003, s 426* income tax charge:

£70,000 × (0.333 – 0 – 0) = £23,334

Thus, assuming Mr Jussi's marginal rate for 2017/18 is 45%, his income tax liability (collected under PAYE) would be £10,500 (being £23,334 × 45%).

He would also incur additional 2% NIC of £467 and the company would suffer NIC of £3,220 (ie £23,334 × 13.8%).

Goalies Ltd would be able to claim a corporate tax deduction of £10,000 (during the year ended 31 December 2016) and £23,334 (during the year ended 31 December 2017) (see 8.92).

Mr Jussi's CGT liability on the sale of the shares would be computed as follows:

		£	£
Sale proceeds			70,000
Less:	Cost (October 2016)	(10,000)	
	Amount taxed as income (October 2016)	(10,000)	
	Amount taxed as income (see above)*	(23,334)	(43,334)
Chargeable gain (subject to annual exemption)			26,666

*To prevent 'double taxation', the amount charged as employment income is treated as additional expenditure on the shares for CGT purposes (*TCGA 1992, s 119A*).

With election

Mr Jussi could jointly elect with Goalies Ltd (his employer) under *ITEPA 2003, s 431(1)* to be taxed at acquisition on the *unrestricted* value of the shares, as follows:

	£
Unrestricted market value – (10,000 × £3)	30,000
Less: Amount paid – (10,000 × £1)	(10,000)
Taxable on exercise of option	20,000

In this case, Goalies Ltd would be able to claim a corporate tax deduction of £20,000 (during the year ended 31 December 2016).

Although Mr Jussi suffers a higher income tax charge by making the election, any further growth in value of the shares falls completely within the favourable CGT regime. Thus, if the shares were sold for (say) £70,000 in December 2017, his taxable gain would be:

		£	£
Sale proceeds			70,000
Less:	Cost (October 2016)	(10,000)	
	Amount taxed as income (October 2016)	(20,000)	(30,000)
Chargeable gain (subject to annual exemption)			40,000

Sale of shares at more than market value

8.36   Where a director/employee sells their (employment-related) shares, *for more* than market value, *ITEPA 2003, s 446Y (ITEPA 2003, Pt 7, Ch 3D,)* imposes an employment income tax charge on the 'excess' amount.

For these purposes, the 'market value' concept in *TCGA 1992, s 272* is used – broadly this means the price that the shares might reasonably be expected to fetch on a sale in the open market. Amounts taxed under *ITEPA 2003, s 446X* are treated as a payment of employment income by the company and therefore *subject to PAYE and NIC.*

Implications of the 'Grays Timber Products' case

8.37   The ambit of these rules has now been considered by the Supreme Court in *Grays Timber Products v HMRC* [2010] UKSC 4.

The main facts were as follows:

- In 1999, Mr Gibson (the managing director of Grays Timber Products Ltd (Timber)) acquired about 6.5% of the ordinary share capital of Grays Group Ltd (Group) – Timber's parent company. Group's Articles conferred equal rights on all its ordinary shares.

- At the same time, there was a shareholders agreement (agreed by 83.3% of Company Groups' shareholders) which prevailed over any conflicting provision in its articles of association. Clause 4 of the agreement governed Mr Gibson's share of sale proceeds on any 'sale' of Group. The agreement also specified that Mr Gibson would enter into a service agreement with Group and that he would be appointed director of Timber and Group.

- The agreement provided that, should Group be sold, Mr Gibson's entitlement to the sale consideration would be calculated according to a formula. After two years, Mr Gibson would be entitled to one third of the increase in Group's value since Mr Gibson acquired his shares.

In 2003, Group was sold to a third party with Mr Gibson receiving £1,451,172 (as calculated under the shareholders agreement).

HMRC considered that Mr Gibson was only entitled to a pro-rata share under Group's articles. It followed that he had disposed of his shares for more than their 'market value' (being the (lower) price which the shares would have fetched on a hypothetical sale (under *TCGA 1992, s 272*) as determined under the pro-rata basis laid down in the articles). Consequently, HMRC pressed for income tax under *ITEPA 2003, Pt 7, Ch 3D (ITEPA 2003, s 446X)* on the excess of the sale proceeds of £1,059,687, being the amount by which his actual enhanced proceeds exceeded his pro-rata entitlement of £391,485. (The shares still fell within the employment-related securities regime, even though they were acquired in 1999.)

8.37 *Providing shares to employees*

The Scottish Appeal Court refused to accept the taxpayer's argument that the market value of the shares was the consideration actually paid by the purchaser. However, there was no evidence for this – for example, the transaction had not attributed any market value to Mr Gibson's shares in particular – and the only evidence was that the entire share capital of Group had been sold for about £6 million. The court therefore concluded that Mr Gibson had sold his shares for more than market value and the excess was taxable as employment income under *ITEPA 2003, s 446X*.

It seems that the court placed much weight on the link between the terms of the subscription agreement and Mr Gibson's service contract. Nevertheless, the case shows there may be a potential income tax exposure where shareholders receive sale consideration on a disproportionate basis (ie not in proportion to their shareholding ratios).

The Supreme Court upheld the Scottish Civil Appeal Court's decision. Mr Gibson's extra consideration on a sale of their shares, did not increase the 'market value" of their holding. These rights were personal to Mr Gibson and had been granted to him in relation to his service contract. Consequently, the 'personal rights' would not affect the price that a hypothetical purchaser would be willing to pay. They would not be valuable to the 'notional' purchaser and hence those shares were worth the same as the other shares.

Although these rights were contained in a shareholders agreement, the Supreme Court Justices indicated that this would also be the case where these 'personal' rights were enshrined in the Articles. Such rights were 'intrinsic' to the shares and thus income tax was payable on the excess of the (enhanced) sale proceeds over the market value of the shares. The decisive factor was that the rights could not be assigned to the hypothetical purchaser so as to give the enhanced value in their hands. (It was not therefore relevant that the rights were simply contained in a shareholders agreement, as had been concluded by the Special Commissioners and Scottish Civil Appeal Court.)

Arrangements for providing directors with shares giving an enhanced 'exit' value must now be implemented with care. Following the Supreme Court's decision, such enhanced rights must attach to the (class of) shares themselves and should not be personal to the holder of the shares. If the rights attach to the shares then they should be capable of being assigned to a (notional) buyer.

The ruling in the *Grays Timber Products Ltd* case gives a clear warning that any subsequent amendments to incorporate changes to a pro-rata apportionment of the sale consideration potentially gives rise to an income tax charge under *ITEPA 2003, Pt 7, Ch 3D*.

Clearly the treatment of 'excessive' sale consideration will depend on the precise facts of each case. For example, if the excess is a reward for services provided this should be subject to employment income tax via PAYE (with NIC) as a bonus. On the other hand, where the 'excess' is a payment for management taking on any potential claims that could arise from the warranties or indemnities, there might be an argument that this should not be subject to employment income tax.

In *Grays Timber Products Ltd*, the Supreme Court Justices expressed some concern that they were interpreting the 'market value' for *ITEPA 2003, s 446X* purposes in a different manner to the other *ITEPA 2003* provisions relating to restricted securities and shares with artificially depressed values. In such cases personal rights and restrictions are factored into the valuation of the shares which leads to some inconsistency in applying the 'market value' provisions for different charging provisions. Lord Walker hoped that 'that Parliament may find time to review the complex and obscure provisions of *Pt 7* of *ITEPA 2003*'(!).

Artificial enhancement of shares

8.38   A special income tax charge arises (under *ITEPA 2003, ss 446K–446P*) where there is a non-commercial increase in the value of 'employment-related' shares. A 'non-commercial' increase includes arrangements motivated by tax or NIC avoidance and non-arm's length transactions between (51%) group members (except a payment for corporate tax group relief).

The employment income tax charge only arises when the market value of the shares at the end of a relevant period (ie the first relevant period being from the date the shares are acquired to the following 5 April and subsequent relevant periods being based on the tax year to 5 April) is at least 10% greater than it would have been but for the 'non-commercial' arrangement. The following formula is used to calculate the tax charge for the relevant tax year.

IMV – MV		
Where:		
IMV	=	Market value of the shares at the end of the tax year
MV	=	Market value of the shares at the end of the tax year assuming any non-commercial increase in value of the shares is disregarded

APPLICATION OF PAYE/NIC ON SHARE SCHEME TAX CHARGES

Readily convertible assets (RCAs)

8.39   Most of the tax charges arising on 'unapproved' share and share option arrangements (as outlined in 8.15–8.35) are based on 'unrealised' gains and the director/employee does not receive any cash to finance the tax liability which often creates difficulties.

8.40 *Providing shares to employees*

This can be particularly harsh where the tax has to be paid under the PAYE system (together with National Insurance contributions (NICs)). Indeed, since employer's NIC would currently be payable on the chargeable amount, the potential NIC liabilities arising from employee share incentives can be substantial. However, the legislation enables the employing company to pass on the 'employer's NIC' liability on an exercise of a share option (and on other certain chargeable events relating to the shares) – see 8.42–8.45. In most cases, any *employee's* personal NIC liability should be the relatively modest marginal 2% (given that their other earnings will already have attracted 12% up to the 'upper earnings limit').

A PAYE and NICs charge arises where the relevant shares or restricted shares are subject to an income tax charge and constitute *readily convertible assets or RCAs (*see 8.40 below*)*. The legislation also states that where the shares themselves are not RCAs, but the consideration received for the shares is in the form of an RCA, then the underlying shares will also qualify as RCAs [*ITEPA 2003, s 698*].

8.40   There are two separate tests for RCA status, only *one* of which needs to be met for the relevant shares to be treated as an RCA. The RCA tests should be reviewed on a regular basis. For example, shares may not be RCAs at the time of an option grant, but circumstances may have changed so that they become RCAs when the shares are acquired on the exercise of the option.

Shares will be treated as RCAs where either:

• Test 1: Trading arrangements exist (or are likely to come into existence) which can be used to turn the shares into cash. This would include, for example, where an employer has set up a facility to enable employees to sell their unlisted shares to an employee trust or particular individual or where the employee has the benefit of a put option to sell their shares (see also 13.36); *or*

• Test 2: The company cannot claim a statutory corporation tax deduction for the shares or the relevant chargeable event in relation to the shares (see 8.89–8.92). For unlisted owner-managed companies, PAYE and NIC would therefore apply where the director/employee holds shares in a subsidiary company (see 8.91).

8.41   In most cases, PAYE and NIC should not therefore have to be accounted for on unlisted shareholdings in private companies. One of the main traps here would be to award employees shares in a subsidiary company, which would cause the shares to be RCAs. In such cases, consideration should be given to providing shares (with special rights only relating to the relevant subsidiary) in the parent company.

Transfer of NIC liability to director/employee

8.42   To avoid a potentially open-ended NIC liability (which must be provided in the accounts under GAAP – see UITF 25), employers and employees can jointly elect to transfer the employer's NIC liability to the employee (see 8.44). In such cases, no NIC liability provision would need to be made in the accounts.

Alternatively, the company can enter into a voluntary agreement under which the director/employee agrees to fund all or part of the employer's NICs liability arising on shares. This is less 'clean' from an accounting perspective since a full provision for the liability must still be made in the company's statutory accounts, with the expected NIC reimbursement being included as a separate asset (if the receipt is fairly certain). Only the 'net' charge is shown in the profit and loss account.

Clearly, the company must decide the method of 'passing-on' the employer's NIC before it grants a share option. The transfer of the company's NIC liability to the employee does not affect its corporate tax relief for its share awards and option exercises etc, which can be claimed in the usual way.

8.43   Under the *National Insurance Contributions and Statutory Payments Act 2004 (NICSPA 2004)*, the company can pass under the voluntary agreement any NICs liability on chargeable events arising in relation to share options or on chargeable events arising after the director's/employee's acquisition of restricted or convertible securities – for example, on the lifting of a restriction. Principally, these are the charges under *ITEPA 2003, ss 426* and *438*. Model elections can be obtained from HMRC's website.

The company's ability to transfer its NICs does not extend to the charges in *ITEPA 2003, Chs 3A–4*. Prior to the passing of the *NICSPA 2004* on 13 May 2004, only NIC charges in relation to share options could be covered by a voluntary agreement.

8.44   Alternatively, both parties may elect (with prior HMRC approval) for part or all of the NIC liability to be transferred to the director/employee. As with a 'voluntary agreement', the election covers any NIC liability arising from post-acquisition chargeable events in relation to restricted or convertible securities (including the exercise of share options). A model NIC election is available from HMRC.

In a 2016 consultation document, HMRC sought views and evidence about whether there is a need for the continued availability of the NIC election. Based on the responses received, it was clear to HMRC that there was still a need to retain the NIC election facility as it provides a protection that is not provided by an NIC agreement.

8.45 In all such cases, the individual will be able to set off any additional NICs they pay under such arrangements in calculating the income tax charge arising on the share option gains.

The NIC burden is thus passed on to the director/employee who may need to sell a larger proportion of shares to pay the tax and NIC due. The company may also grant options over a greater number of shares to compensate for the additional NIC charge. The cost of the employer's NIC effectively often moves to the shareholders who suffer an additional dilution of the share capital.

Example 3

Tax effect of employer's NIC liability passing to employee

In November 2017, Matt realised a gain of £250,000 on the exercise of his unapproved share option to acquire 5,000 shares in Jarvis Ltd. Matt had worked for the company for many years as a sales director.

As the option was exercised immediately before the company was sold to Wingers plc, the shares became RCAs. Thus, the income tax on the share option gain was payable under the PAYE system and also attracted employee's NIC of 2% and employer's NIC of 13.8%.

Matt had entered into an election with the company to pay the *employer's NIC*. His marginal tax rate for 2017/18 is 45%.

His total tax and NIC liability was calculated as follows:

	£		£
Employer's NIC liability – £250,000 × 13.8%			34,500
Income tax liability (taxed under PAYE)			
Share option gain	250,000		
Less: Employer's NIC	(34,500)		
	215,500	× 45%	96,975
Employee's NIC	250,000	× 2%	5,000
Total PAYE and NIC			136,475

This equates to a combined income tax and NIC charge of 54% (£136,475/£250,000) and illustrates why unapproved share options that are exercised on the sale of a company are not particularly tax efficient, particularly compared with EMI share options (see Example 6 at 8.73).

Reimbursement of PAYE

8.46   A particular tax trap can arise with share options if the amount of PAYE due on the option exercise is high, but the employee's salary is relatively low. There simply may not be enough monthly salary from which to deduct all the PAYE due, in which case the employer will have to account for the tax due.

If the *employee* fails to reimburse the employer with the tax due within 90 days *from the end of the relevant tax year*, a further tax charge arises under *ITEPA 2003, s 222* when the PAYE tax (not NIC) is treated as additional remuneration (see also 13.36). Before 6 April 2014, the tax had to be reimbursed within 90 days of the employee's acquisition of the shares.

Tax would become due on the 'non-reimbursed' PAYE and interest may also accrue if the tax due under *ITEPA 2003, s 222* is not paid within the deadline. The employee may be forced to sell at least part of his shareholding to avoid this problem.

The rules of an unapproved share scheme should always provide the employer with the authority to collect tax from participating employees. Indeed, many companies tend to deal with this problem by incorporating a 'sell to cover' authority in the share plan rules. This enables a company to withhold a suitable number of shares, which are then sold to realise sufficient monies to fund the PAYE due. The net balance is released to the employee. HMRC accept this set-off procedure as an acceptable reimbursement by the employee assuming this is made before the 90-day time limit after tax year-end.

The employers' NICs arising on the exercise of share options can be passed to the employee by agreement and deducted against their taxable employment income (see 8.42–8.45 above).

APPROVED SHARE SCHEMES AND PLANS

Overview

8.47   The income tax and NIC charges applied to unapproved share awards and options are generally avoided where employees acquire shares under one of HMRC's approved schemes.

Since 6 April 2014, HMRC no longer provides formal approval for share schemes. Instead, employers are required to 'self-certify' to qualify for the HMRC tax advantaged share plans. Self-certification requires the company to make an annual on-line declaration that the requirements of the applicable legislation are being met. This applies to all new and existing plans, and is completed through the new online system.

The main benefit of acquiring shares under a CSOP or EMI option (as compared with an unapproved share option/award) is that the tax on the gain between the grant and exercise is deferred until the shares are sold, and is then subject to beneficial (post-5 April 2016) CGT rates, typically 10% or 20%. Although EMI options are generally restricted to the more risky type of trading companies, EMI share options can be created for significantly higher values (up to the £250,000 market value restriction as compared with £30,000 for a CSOP).

Parent companies

8.48   In the context of a group, it is normal to use the parent company's shares to reward group employees. The legislation only permits shares in a subsidiary to be used where the parent company is *listed*. EMI options can only be granted by a parent company of a qualifying group – no EMI options can be granted in a 51% subsidiary.

Providing employees of subsidiaries with shares in the parent company can cause a conflict, especially where employee relations and involvement are, in the main, the responsibility of the subsidiary company's management. In such a case a 'non-equity' based profit-sharing scheme is likely to be more appropriate as a performance-linked motivation tool.

A group scheme can extend to all companies controlled by the grantor company under an approved share scheme. The legislation also provides that this can include a jointly owned company and any companies controlled by it (see, for example, *ITEPA 2003, Sch 4, para 4* re CSOPs).

ENTERPRISE MANAGEMENT INCENTIVES (EMI) SCHEMES

Background

8.49   The EMI scheme is structured as an option based scheme and is specifically aimed at the smaller 'higher risk' company. It provides greater benefits and is more flexible than a CSOP. In most cases, where directors or employees exercise their EMI options at the market value (on grant), their entire profit on sale will be taxed under the capital gains regime.

In a survey commissioned by HMRC (reported in 2008), 92% of the employers questioned mentioned that employee retention was the key reason for adopting an EMI scheme. Staff motivation and engendering a feeling of ownership were also cited as important benefits. EMI's associated tax advantages were also seen as attractive for employers. EMI options are by far the most popular type of tax-advantaged share scheme.

The detailed rules for EMI options are contained in *ITEPA 2003, ss 527–541* and *Sch 5*. The *FA 2008* introduced a very important 'total employee restriction, which prevents (further) qualifying EMI options being granted after 20 July 2008 where a company/group has 250 or more employees. However, existing EMI options granted by such companies remain unaffected.

A large number of EMI schemes are 'exit-based' with the share options being exercisable on a sale or flotation of the company. Most owner managers prefer this type of arrangement, since the option holders do not become shareholders until shortly before the sale of the company. This 'rewards' the employee option holders with a share of the sale proceeds (taxed at beneficial CGT rates).

Furthermore, payment for the exercise of the share option can be 'funded' from the employee's share of the sale proceeds with the option holder.

CGT treatment of EMI shares

8.50   The sale of EMI shares will typically be 'very small' minority holdings (ie individually often less than a 5% equity stake).

The *FA 2013* significantly improved the treatment of the sale of the vast majority of EMI shares. Provided they were acquired (ie the option was exercised after 5 April 2012), a *post-5 April 2013 disposal* of the shares will normally qualify for the beneficial 10% ER CGT rate (irrespective of the size of the holding).

Under the *FA 2013* amendments for the sale of EMI option shares (inserted into *TCGA 1992, s 169I(7A)–(7R)*):

- EMI shareholders do *not* have to satisfy any minimum shareholding or voting rights test (see 15.34).

- Furthermore, the 12-month shareholding period before the sale can now include (where appropriate) the period following the option grant.

- All the other ER conditions must be met, namely the company must be a qualifying trading company or holding company of a trading group and the seller must work for the company (which would be the case for an EMI option holder).

These requirements must be satisfied in the 12 months before the sale, which (as noted above) can include the post-option grant period.

The combined effect of these changes enables ER to be claimed on EMI shares where the option grant date falls before the 'beginning of the period of one year ending with the date of disposal' provided the other ER 'trading' and 'employment/officer' tests are met throughout this period.

The *FA 2013* changes benefit a vast number of exit-based EMI schemes. Before the *FA 2013* changes, EMI option holders would not have qualified for ER since (even if they met the 5% test), since they would not have held the shares for the required 12 month period. For post-5 April 2013 disposals, the EMI option holder can now count the period since the option was granted towards the 12-month holding period before sale.

8.50A For identification purposes, EMI shares are treated separately from the general share pool. When shares are disposed of:

- they are identified with EMI shares qualifying for ER, rather than with other shares; and

- with those acquired earlier rather than those acquired later.

8.50B Very small gains will fall within employees' annual CGT exemptions (possibly 'doubled' by arranging for some shares to be transferred through a spouse/civil partner, provided the scheme rules permit this). Otherwise, post-5 April 2016 gains will attract CGT at 20% or, to the extent that the seller has 'basic rate income tax band' capacity, 10%.

Key advantages of EMI schemes

8.51 Options granted under an EMI scheme contain many tax and commercial benefits. Thus, where it is available, EMI generally remains the scheme of choice. In most cases, where directors or employees exercise their EMI options at the market value (at the grant date), their entire profit on sale will be taxed under the capital gains regime and generally at the beneficial 10% ER CGT rate.

The ability to acquire shares at a later date based on the market value at the earlier grant date without any income tax/NIC charge still remains a key attraction of EMI (especially since the market value at grant will typically be subject to a significant valuation discount).

Technically, *ITEPA 2003, s 530* exempts from the normal income tax charging rules the excess of the market value of the shares at the time of exercise over market value at the 'grant' date (sometimes this is referred to as 'EMI relief').

The other key advantages of an EMI scheme for a family or owner-managed company are that:

- the company can obtain a statutory corporation tax deduction on the market value (less any amount paid on exercise) of the shares issued or transferred to satisfy EMI options (even though there is no income tax charge on the employee!). This is a very attractive proposition!

- employees will generally able to realise capital gains on the option shares taxed at 10% (with ER)

- the company can choose exactly who receives the options, subject to the 30% 'material interest' barrier;

- the options can be granted conditionally subject to performance criteria;

- the company can decide the exercise price and the option period;

426

- the market value of the shares can be agreed *in advance* of the option grant with HMRC's SAV;

- voting restrictions can be placed over the shares subject to EMI options to protect the owner-managers' position;

- the scheme does not need prior approval from HMRC, but notice of each option grant must be given to HMRC within 92 days of the grant.

A survey on EMI schemes conducted by FDS International Ltd on HMRC's behalf, found that at senior levels and among staff crucial to the company's success, options were considered to be an important commitment valued by the recipient. The potential for a future float or 'exit' was also felt to be an important element in the strategy for implementing an EMI scheme, which reflects my own practical experience. The survey also found that private equity providers were keen on EMI schemes since they viewed them as aligning the interests of employees and directors with their own financial ambitions.

According to the survey, implementing an EMI scheme generally involves professional fees of between £5,000 and £10,000. As a general rule, the cost tends to be less economic, the fewer the number of participants.

The majority of EMI schemes tend to be 'exit-based', with the EMI options becoming exercisable shortly before a sale or offer for the company. One of the key-attractions of 'exit-based' options is that the employee/director option-holders do not become shareholders until immediately before the company is sold. Consequently, the company does not have to consider the complications (and bear the costs) of changing its Articles or creating a shareholders' agreement to include various protective provisions for the owner managers, such as 'good and bad leaver' rules and 'drag along' rights.

Example 4

Comparison of EMI share gains under different employee CGT profiles

In January 2011, Red Devils (1958) Ltd (a qualifying company for EMI and ER purposes) granted the following EMI options to three of its key employees:

Employee	Number of Red Devils Ltd shares	Fully diluted % holding
D Edwards	12,000	3%
E Colman	10,000	2.5%
R Byrne	1,000	0.25%

All EMI options were to be exercised on a future sale/flotation of the company at their agreed market value of £8 per share (in January 2011)

In September 2017, Red Devils (1958) Ltd was acquired by Matt plc. Immediately before the sale was completed, all three employees exercised their 'January 2011' options.

The agreed sale consideration paid to all the shareholders of Red Devils (1958) Ltd was £15 per share.

The capital gains of the EMI shareholders (assuming they are higher-rate taxpayers) are computed as follows:

	D	E	R
	Edwards	Colman	Byrne
	£	£	£
Sale proceeds – £15 × 12,000/10,000 / 1,000	180,000	150,000	15,000
Less: Cost – £8 × 12,000/10,000 / 1,000	(96,000)	(80,000)	(8,000)
Chargeable gain	84,000	70,000	7,000
Less: Annual exemption	(11,300)	(11,300)	(7,000)
Taxable gain	72,700	58,700	–
CGT @ 10%	£7,270	£5,870	

The employees have exercised their EMI options, paying the market value as at the date of grant. This means that the entire growth in the value of the shares from grant date falls within the CGT regime and the share disposal qualifies for ER relief.

Contrast this with the position if the options had been unapproved. See Example 2 above where virtually all the value of the shares at the date of sale is subject to (significantly higher) income tax and NIC.

EMI schemes – summary of main conditions

Purpose and basis of EMI options

8.52 A qualifying option for EMI purposes is one which meets all the requirements of *ITEPA 2003, Sch 5*.

Options under an EMI scheme will normally be granted by the employing company or its parent company, but existing individual or employee trust shareholders may also offer their shares. No tax charge arises on the grant.

It is possible to build individual performance conditions into each EMI option, which can provide an important incentive tool.

Options can be granted on a conditional basis. Some companies tend to stipulate a period of two or three years before the options can be exercised (under a so-called 'vesting period'), although there is no statutory minimum period.

Individual limit for value of EMI shares under option

8.53 One of the most important requirements is that the value of unexercised EMI option shares (at the date of the option grant) held by any employee cannot exceed £250,000 (from 16 June 2012). (The previous limits were £120,000 between 6 April 2008 and 15 June 2012 and £100,000 before 6 April 2008.) EMI options can be granted over shares that are 'restricted'.

There is no statutory requirement to agree share valuations with HMRC's SAV office. However, it is generally advisable to establish and agree with the SAV two values at the date of grant – the Actual Market Value (AMV) and the Unrestricted Market Value (UMV).

The AMV will be the lower value since this reflects the market value of the shares after taking into account any restrictions (which may include restrictions on transfer) or the risk of forfeiture as laid out in the company's articles of association. UMV is the market value of a share ignoring any restrictions or the risk of forfeiture (see 8.62).

Provided that the price to acquire the EMI shares is at least equal to the AMV at the date of grant, the options are not regarded as being discounted options. Provided the options are 'full value' options, the legislation deems an *ITEPA 2003, s 431* election to be made in respect of the shares when they are acquired. They therefore can be exercised without incurring any income tax charge(s).

As a general rule, it is in the interests of the EMI option-holders to agree the lowest possible market value so that they can benefit from the maximum growth within the 'favourable' capital gains regime. However, the 'hidden' cost may be unacceptable dilution for the existing shareholders. Thus, many companies often require the EMI option holders to pay a realistic value for their shares (based on the value at the date of grant), which still be an attractive price because of the allowable minority discount.

The UMV at the date of grant is only used for the purpose of the individual £250,000 and company £3 million (see 8.54) limits and not for the purpose of establishing a charge to tax.

Where EMI options are *granted at a discount* to the current market value (see 8.60), and are over shares that are restricted or carry the risk of forfeiture, an income tax charge may arise after the options have been exercised when a chargeable event occurs (see 8.31 and 8.62). Directors and employees can avoid this by entering into an *ITEPA 2003, s 431* election (see 8.32). This issue does not arise where options are granted at full current market value (see 8.63).

It should be noted that where an employee has been granted EMI options worth £250,000, it is not possible to grant any further EMI options to them within the next three years (even where the initial EMI options have been exercised). Furthermore, the values of any existing CSOP options are also taken into account for the purpose of the £250,000 limitation [*ITEPA 2003, Sch 5, para 5*].

However, each director/employee may be awarded a different amount within the £250,000 financial limit. Many EMI option agreements provide that if (following negotiations) the market value of the relevant option shares exceeds the valuation limit (currently £250,000), then it will deem £250,000 worth of option shares as being granted under the EMI regime with the 'excess' amount being *unapproved* share options.

Global £3 million limit for EMI shares under option

8.54   The maximum value of 'unexercised' options over the company's shares must not exceed £3 million. Any option that exceeds this limit when it is granted will not qualify for EMI treatment. However, in practice given the £30 million 'gross asset' limitation (see 8.65) and the likely proportion of shares earmarked for EMI, very few companies seem to get close to breaching the £3 million aggregate EMI option value threshold.

Qualifying ordinary shares and EMI options

8.55   An EMI option must be over (fully paid and irredeemable) ordinary share capital giving a right to a share of profits and must be non-assignable.

The 'EMI' shares can be of any class and it is possible to place restrictions over the shares, for example, limited voting rights to protect the owner-managers' position. It is therefore possible for the EMI shares to be of a separate class, but care must be taken not to make the rights too limited or restricted, given that they must satisfy the 'commercial purpose' test (see 8.59).

Once the EMI options have been granted, *ITEPA 2003, s 536(1)(a)* provides there must be no alteration to the terms of the option which would cause

- the option to fail one or more of the qualifying EMI conditions in *ITEPA 2003, Sch 5* – fairly minor alterations to options would still be caught by this rule (see also 8.50) (see *CIR v Eurocopy plc* [1991] STC 707); or

- an increase in the market value of the EMI shares under option.

Such alterations would 'trigger' a disqualifying event (see 8.70). Furthermore, where the terms of an option are subsequently altered, there is a risk that this may result in a rescission of the original option with a new 'replacement' one being granted.

Employing companies are completely free to set their own exercise period, but the options must be exercisable (and any relevant conditions must be capable of being satisfied) within ten years to obtain the tax benefits. EMI options are, therefore, more flexible than CSOP options which have a mandatory three-year 'waiting period'.

The EMI option agreement must be in writing and specify:

- The date of grant

- A statement that the option qualifies under the EMI rules in *ITEPA 2003, Sch 5.*

- The number or maximum number of shares that may be acquired under the option

- The price payable or method for determining price

- When and how the option may be exercised

- Any conditions affecting the exercise of the option (such as performance conditions)

- Details of any restrictions that apply to the shares

HMRC accept that the details of restrictions, performance conditions or forfeiture conditions may be contained in another document (such as the articles, share scheme rules, or a shareholders' agreement) attached to the option agreement and incorporated into it by reference to the document.

An agreement cannot be legally binding unless it is entered into for a consideration (even if this is purely nominal). In practice, this issue is overcome by granting the option as a deed which recites all the relevant terms. The option does not qualify as an EMI option unless it is signed and executed.

Employee conditions and material interest test

8.56   Broadly, the employee's 'committed time' (ie spent on the employment) must be at least 25 hours per week or, if less, 75% of their available working time including self-employment. In some business 'start-ups', some EMI option holders will need to be paid at least the national minimum wage to ensure that they are accepted as an employee.

Companies are now required to confirm under HMRC's online process (see 8.69) that the EMI option holders have met the working time requirements (and that the employees have signed a declaration to that effect). Companies will therefore be required to obtain declarations from all the EMI option holders, although they are not submitted to HMRC. However, the company must retain the relevant declarations in case they are subsequently requested by HMRC.

EMI options cannot be granted to employees or directors if they have (together with associates) at least a 30% equity interest in the company, including unexercised options *other* than EMI options. Note, that for these purposes, the trustees of most employee benefit trusts are not counted as an associate.

Employee headcount restriction

8.57   The *Finance Act 2008* introduced an unpopular restriction which prevented EMI options being granted by a company/group with 250 (equivalent full-time) employees or more. This means that from 21 July 2008, companies that breach the 250-employee limitation test can no longer grant EMI options. However, any EMI options granted before that date still remain (irrespective of the employee headcount).

Replacement options

8.58   A replacement option granted on a takeover by a qualifying EMI company retains the EMI benefits of the original one (see special rules in *ITEPA 2003, Sch 5, paras 39–43*).

It should be noted that certain types of corporate reconstructions (such as an Insolvency Act 1986 s110 arrangement (see 13.61–13.82) may terminate EMI option contracts. Careful consideration should be given to employee share options in such circumstances.

Commercial purpose requirement

8.59   The EMI legislation contains a specific 'commercial purpose' test stating that an option only qualifies if it is granted '… to recruit or retain an employee in a company' and not for tax avoidance [*ITEPA 2003, Sch 5, para 4*]. It appears that, in practice, HMRC accept that almost all EMI schemes have been initiated because of the company's commercial requirements to have some type of equity incentive scheme in place.

Market value versus discounted options

8.60   The company has complete flexibility over the option price set for the EMI option shares. Many companies grant options to acquire the shares at their actual market value (AMV) *at the date of the grant* (which would reflect the impact of any substantive restrictions). In such cases, there should be no income tax (or NIC) charge when the option is exercised.

It is of course possible for 'discounted options' to be granted under an EMI scheme. The exercise price can therefore be set at a lower amount than market value at the grant date (although it is illegal to issue shares for less than their nominal value) without affecting the qualifying status and tax advantages of the scheme.

8.61 The basic thrust of the EMI regime is to tax the growth in value of the shares from the grant as a capital gain.

However, if the option has been granted at a *discount* to the initial market value of the shares, this is taxed as employment income *on exercise*. If the shares are RCAs, the PAYE and NIC rules outlined above will apply (see 8.39–8.41). The income tax charge on discounted EMI options is based on the amount of the discount, or, if lower, the excess of the market value of the shares at the date of *exercise* over the amount paid for them. This contrasts with the treatment of unapproved share option exercises where the charge is based on the market value at the exercise date. See 8.62 and 8.63 below where shares are 'restricted'.

Restricted EMI shares

8.62 It is possible that the EMI shares may fall within the 'restricted securities' regime (see 8.16). Therefore, the possibility of making a (protective) *ITEPA 2003, s 431* election must be considered. This would usually avoid any income tax charge arising on the option exercise (and on any disqualifying event) as a result of any restrictions attaching to the shares and ensure that their future growth in value is entirely within the CGT regime [*ITEPA 2003, ss 476, 530* and *541(2)*].

8.63 However, for EMI options exercised after 18 June 2004, the legislation *deems* that an *ITEPA 2003, s 431* election has been made provided no income tax liability arises on the *exercise of the option*. However, this can only be determined where the value of the shares at the date of grant has been agreed with the HMRC – Shares & Asset Valuation Office and the employee pays that amount on exercise. However, where the valuation has not been agreed, it would be prudent to make an actual *ITEPA 2003, 431* election when the option is exercised.

Qualifying company – independence requirement

8.64 A company will only be a qualifying 'EMI company' if it satisfies certain conditions which are designed to ensure that only small independent 'higher risk' companies qualify.

A company will meet the 'independence requirement' provided it is not a '51% subsidiary' of another company *or* under the control of another company *and* persons connected with that company within *ITEPA 2003, s 719* and hence *ITA 2007, ss 995* and *1124*.

For these purposes,

- a company is a 51% subsidiary if more than 50% of its share capital is owned directly or indirectly by another company [*CTA 2010, s 1154*];

- control is defined in terms of being able to conduct the affairs of the company through the holding of share capital, voting rights, or other powers contained in the company's articles of association or other document (such as a shareholders' agreement). Connected persons are defined in *ITA 2007, s 993*.

This rule is extended to cases which prevent valid EMI option grants where there are arrangements in existence for the company to become under the control of another. This can be problematic where a company is seeking to implement an EMI scheme and, at around the same time, the directors are about to enter into negotiations for a sale of the company. While it is not always possible to control the timing of these events, the company should ensure its EMI options are granted (well) before it enters into 'heads of agreement' for a sale transaction. Of course, if there is an impending sale, HMRC SAV office will argue for a considerably higher value on the EMI shares.

Care should also be taken if a limited partnership controls the company (which is often the case with a 'private equity' structure). In such cases, there is likely to be a corporate partner of the limited partnership (often the general partner) and all partners of a partnership are connected. This means that the independence requirement is frequently failed since the relevant company would normally be under the control of a company (the corporate partner) and other partners (persons connected with that company).

Where the shares in a company are held equally by (say) two joint venture shareholders (on a 50%:50% basis), HMRC will often contend that it fails the 'independence test'. The argument would run that the company's corporate shareholders are 'acting together' and thus the company is under the control of a company and persons connected with the company.

Qualifying company – gross assets and 'subsidiary company' tests

8.65   For a singleton company seeking to use the EMI scheme, the gross asset value shown in its balance sheet (according to UK GAAP) must not exceed £30 million when the options are granted (£15 million for options granted before 1 January 2002). The tax-favoured status of existing EMI options are not affected if the company's gross assets value subsequently increases above £30 million.

In the case of a (51%) corporate group, the £30 million gross asset test is based on the aggregate gross assets for the entire group. This calculation would include purchased goodwill by the group members but would exclude any goodwill arising on consolidation [*ITEPA 2003, Sch 5, paras 9–12*].

An 'EMI company' may have 'qualifying' subsidiary companies. All qualifying subsidiaries must be at least 51% (directly or indirectly) owned by the grantor company, subject to an exception for a property management subsidiary which must be 90% owned. (For these purposes, a property management subsidiary is one whose business consists wholly or mainly in the holding of land or property) [*ITEPA 2003, Sch 5, paras 11–11B*].

The 51% qualifying subsidiary requirement may prevent EMI options being available where the issuing company holds shares in a joint venture company which it controls, either on its own or with a connected person (applying the *CTA 2010, s 450* definition of control) but does not own more than 50% of its shares.

Qualifying trades

8.66   The grantor company must also carry on a 'qualifying trade'. Most trades should qualify but the definition is defined negatively so as to prevent prohibited 'low-risk' activities (as is the case for Seed Enterprise Investment Scheme, Enterprise Investment Scheme and Venture Capital Trust companies (see 11.43)).

Thus, the company's activities must not consist substantially (ie more than 20%) in the carrying on of 'excluded activities' such as dealing in land or shares, banking, leasing, receiving licence fees or royalties, legal and accountancy, property development, farming, and operating and managing hotels and nursing homes. Shipbuilding, producing coal and producing steel were also excluded by the *FA 2008* (to comply with EU State Aid directives).

High tech and E-commerce companies should be assisted by the special 'let-out' rule that enables a company to be an EMI company where it receives royalties and licence fees from the exploitation of 'internally created' intellectual property.

The *F (No 2) A 2010* also introduced a requirement for companies to have a permanent establishment in the UK – this broadly means that they must be carrying on a UK trade in the UK. This change was made to bring the EMI legislation in line with EU state aid guidelines. Previously a company had to be carrying on its trade wholly or mainly in the UK. It is therefore possible for an overseas company to grant EMI options where it has a permanent establishment in the UK (although most of its trade is carried on abroad).

Groups of companies

8.67   Where the company is a parent company of a group, all its subsidiaries must be at least 50% owned (as to shares, votes, assets and beneficial entitlement to profits). The £30 million gross asset limit is based on the combined balance sheet value of the group's assets (ie ignoring shares in group companies).

Furthermore, the group's business, taken as a whole, must not substantially consist of non-qualifying activities and at least one member of the group must satisfy the 'qualifying trade' test in its own right.

Valuation and notification procedure

8.68   The (unquoted) owner-managed company will clearly need to value the relevant shares at the date of grant to determine whether the £250,000 limit has been met. This valuation limit is based on the *unrestricted* value of the relevant EMI shares. An unquoted company is often valued on an appropriate multiple of its maintainable (post-tax) earnings with the pro-rata amount attributed to the shares being discounted for their minority status and any inherent restrictions (see Chapter 14).

The share value must be agreed with HMRC – Shares & Asset Valuation office (SAV), which will normally give such cases priority for agreement. (These valuations are not affected by the February 2016 withdrawal of the *ITEPA 2003* Post Transaction Valuation Checks.)

8.69   The EMI option has always been subject to a 'self-assessment' style notification and declaration process but this now has to be completed on-line via the 'self-certification' process.

A notice of each option grant must now be submitted on-line to HMRC within 92 days of the grant for each employee.

The notification contains a declaration from a director/secretary of the employing company confirming that the EMI rules are satisfied and employees have 'signed off' on the 'working time' commitment condition. Companies will now have to obtain a declaration from their relevant employees that the working time requirements have been satisfied but this is not submitted to HMRC. However, companies should retain the relevant declarations in case they are subsequently requested by HMRC.

The notification process is very important since failure to give the relevant notice within the 92-day period, will invalidate the relevant EMI options, which is likely to have disastrous tax consequences for the employees!

Individual option agreements should contain details of any restrictions attaching to the option – where there is doubt as to whether any particular provision constitutes a restriction it is prudent to include it as HMRC have been known to challenge the validity of options where they do not contain full details of all terms attaching to them.

Where the exercisable option shares are subject to a formula (often linked to the value realised for the company/business on an 'exit' event), the option agreement must specify the maximum number of EMI option shares [*ITEPA 2003, Sch 5, para 37(1), (2)*].

HMRC are entitled to make an enquiry into the employer EMI notification submission within 12 months of the end of the 92-day notice period. If no enquiry notice is issued, it can be assumed that the scheme has met the relevant EMI scheme requirements.

Where HMRC wishes to enquire into the eligibility of the EMI scheme, this will be concluded by a closure notice, which will give HMRC's decision as to whether the relevant EMI requirements have been met. Any 'negative' HMRC notice can be appealed within 30 days.

It is worthwhile devising a standard set of scheme rules governing its operation to demonstrate a level 'playing field' between employees.

It is possible for companies to seek an informal clearance in advance to obtain comfort that their proposed options satisfy the relevant legislative requirements by writing to:

H M Revenue & Customs Local Compliance Small Company Enterprise Centre Admin Team
SO777
Newcastle
NE98 1ZZ

The annual EMI reporting on Form EMI 40, which is due by 6 July following the end of the relevant tax year, must be filed online.

Impact of disqualifying events

8.70 If one of the relevant EMI conditions is broken (referred to as a 'disqualifying event') during the life of the option, the employee must exercise it within 90 days (40 days before 17 July 2013) to retain their EMI benefits (ie no tax charge on the increase over grant value).

A disqualifying event will be triggered, for example, if the company ceases to be independent or meet the 'qualifying trade' test or the employee ceases to work for the company, etc.

Many EMI schemes permit employees to exercise their EMI option within the 90-day period. However, some schemes do not, which will normally be disadvantageous to the employee.

Failing to exercise the option within the 90-day period will render the employee liable to an (additional) income tax charge on the growth in value of the shares between the disqualifying event and option exercise [*ITEPA 2003, ss 532–536*].

Example 5

Tax treatment of disqualifying event (on a 'discounted' EMI option)

In December 2007, Eggbertsson Ltd granted a discounted EMI option for 20,000 £1 shares (representing a 4% holding in the company) to one of its key employees, Mr Tevez. The option exercise price was 10p per share and the market value of the option shares at that time was £4 per share. The EMI option could only be exercised on a future sale of Eggbertson Ltd and there were no provisions enabling the option to be exercised as a result of a 'disqualifying event'.

Mr Tevez decided to leave the company in June 2009 (when the option shares were worth £12 each) and the company was sold in December 2010 for £19 per share.

Under the terms of the EMI scheme, Mr Tevez could only exercise his option when the company was sold in December 2010.

His tax position would be as follows:

- Employment income tax on the 'discount' element of the option (*ITEPA 2003 s 476*) – £78,000 (being the excess of the market value of his shares in December 2007 (£80,000 less £2,000 (10p × 20,000))

- Employment income tax on £140,000 – £380,000 (£19 × 20,000) less £240,000 (£12 × 20,000). This represents the increase in the value of the shares after the disqualifying event in June 2009 (when he left the company) up to the 'exercise' date in December 2010 (*ITEPA 2003, s 476*).

Mr Tevez's capital gain is £160,000 – this reflects the uplift in the value of his shares between the grant date and time of the disqualifying event, being based on the excess of £240,000 (£12 × 20,000) over £80,000 (£4 × 20,000). The capital gain on sale does *not* qualify for ER.

A graphical summary of the amount subject to income tax and CGT *for each share* is illustrated below.

Discounted EMI option – rising share price

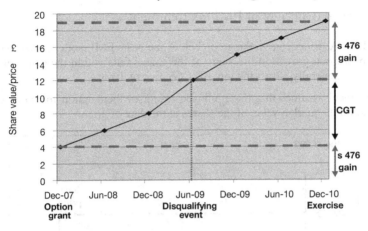

Other issues on sale of EMI shares

8.71   Employees are only likely to exercise their options if the value of their 'employing' company or group has increased and they can realise some of that value by exercising their option. Clearly, the employees of a family or owner-managed company would hope to realise substantial value on a sale or flotation. Other available exit routes would be a sale to another shareholder, employee trust, or sale back to the company, but these may be at discounted minority values.

Many EMI options are 'exit-based', which broadly means that they are only exercisable in the event of a company sale or float. Given that the 'value' of the EMI option shares attracts a statutory corporate tax deduction under *CTA 2009, Pt 12, Ch 2* (see 8.89–8.91), it is important to recognise that this will enhance the company's net asset value on sale.

Before the *FA 2014*, there was potentially nasty trap where the company was about to be sold to an *unlisted* company since the valuable corporate deduction for the exercise of the EMI options could be completely lost. This would be the case where the company came under the control of an unlisted company (see 8.91). However, the *FA 2014* introduced a welcome relaxation, which enables a corporate tax deduction to be claimed where the EMI options are exercised within 90 days of the sale transaction (ie the change of control).

The detailed tax implications for employees are dealt with in 8.50. Following the *FA 2013* relaxation in the ER conditions for EMI shares the majority of employees will now be subject to the beneficial 10% CGT rate on sale.

Graphical overview of EMI tax treatment

8.72 As illustrated in the graph below, the basic EMI model shows that all the post-grant growth in the value of the shares falls within the CGT regime and will generally attract the low ER CGT rate of 10%.

The model assumes that the employee exercises their option for an amount based on the market value of the shares at the date of grant.

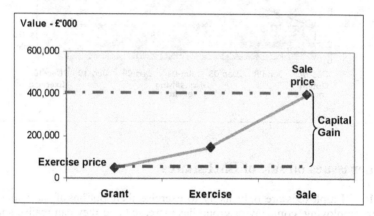

Comprehensive example of 'exit-based' discounted EMI options

8.73 A worked example showing the EMI tax treatment of a 'discounted' exercise and subsequent sale of the shares is given in Example 6 below.

Example 6

EMI share option granted at a discount and sale of company

Adrian is the financial director of Goalkeepers Ltd (a trading company). On 18 August 2009, he was granted an EMI option to acquire 1,000 £1 ordinary shares (representing a 2% stake) in the company at £3.80 per share exercisable at any time within ten years. The actual market value of the shares at that time was agreed at £7 per share.

In December 2017, assume an offer is made to acquire the entire share capital of Goalkeepers Ltd and Adrian exercises his option. (Since this is a 'discounted' option, Adrian enters into a joint *ITEPA 2003, 431* election when he exercises his option to ensure that all subsequent gains are subject to capital gains tax.)

The company is subsequently sold in January 2018 with Adrian receiving £200,000 for his shares.

Exercise of option

Adrian will have an employment income tax liability when he exercises his EMI option in December 2017 as he acquired the shares at a discount on their grant value, as follows:

	£
Unrestricted market value at date of grant (1,000 × £7)	7,000
Less: Exercise price – (1,000 × £3.80)	(3,800)
Employment income	3,200

As the company is about to be sold, the shares would be RCAs and thus PAYE and NIC would be payable on the £3,200 profit.

Sale of shares

Adrian's capital gain arising on the sale in January 2018 is likely to be calculated as follows:

	£	£
Sale proceeds		200,000
Less: Base cost	(3,800)	
Taxable 'discount' element	(3,200)	(7,000)
Capital gain		193,000
Less: Annual exemption		(11,300)
Taxable gain		181,700
CGT @ 10% (with claim for ER – see 8.50)		18,170

Note: If Adrian had been granted an *unapproved* option (and assuming that an *ITEPA 2003, s 431* election was made), he would have been subject to an income tax charge on the *current unrestricted value* of his shares (less £3,800 exercise price) on the December 2017 exercise. Only the small increase to the full January 2018 sale value of £200,000 would be taxed as a capital gain.

COMPANY SHARE OPTION PLANS (CSOPs)

Benefits of CSOPs

8.74　This is commonly known as the company share option plan (CSOP). CSOPs are available for use by all companies regardless of type of trade or size. The relevant CSOP legislation is contained in *ITEPA 2003, ss 521–526* and *Sch 4*. Since 6 April 2014, a tax advantaged CSOP scheme is known as a 'Schedule 4' CSOP scheme.

The main requirement for an (unlisted) owner-managed company is that it is independent (ie is not under the control of another company). Furthermore, it is not possible to grant CSOP options over shares in a subsidiary company.

CSOPs may be a useful method of providing equity for employees (up to the maximum value of £30,000 per employee) where the circumstances do not permit a valid EMI scheme. However, CSOP options can only be exercised after three years from the date of grant. CSOPs that are currently in place may continue alongside an EMI scheme, although the monetary limits of share options per employee will apply across both schemes (see 8.53).

A properly structured CSOP brings a number of benefits to an owner-managed company (particularly if its share ownership is already widely dispersed). Key advantages include:

- enabling employees to enjoy a share of the 'exit' value on sale or flotation;

- attracting key personnel with options granted on a selective basis, where the £30,000 monetary limit is not a problem;

- providing golden-handcuffs on existing key personnel with options granted on a selective basis;

- ensuring flexibility, with participants not being locked in;

- increasing productivity and efficiency;

- creating an awareness that the company's success is closely linked to an employee's personal wealth.

Eligible CSOP shares

8.74A　The CSOP option shares must be fully-paid ordinary shares, not-redeemable, and generally not subject to any restrictions. However, restrictions that attach to all the shares of the same class are permitted. Similarly, the legislation allows restrictions requiring the shares to be offered for sale on leaving provided they apply to all shares of that class (including 'non-CSOP' shares acquired by an employee).

Any discretion given to directors under the company's articles to refuse to accept the transfer of the shares is permitted provided the directors give an undertaking to HMRC that they would not exercise that power in such a way as to discriminate against the participant employees. The directors are also required to give notice to the CSOP option holders about this undertaking.

If the company has more than one class of shares, the majority of the issued shares of the same class as the 'CSOP' shares, must be employee-controlled.

Alternatively, the majority of the issued shares of the same class as the 'CSOP' shares must be people *other than* those who had acquired their shares by reason of employment/directorship and employee trusts.

Basic mechanics of a CSOP

8.75   Selected employees are granted an option to purchase shares at a later date, but with the price fixed at the outset – typically at their market value when the option was granted.

The requirement for a specific HMRC agreement to the share valuation method was removed by *FA 2016*. Instead, the law enables HMRC guidance to specify acceptable methods of valuation.

Any director/employee owning not more than 30% (25% prior to 17 July 2013) of the ordinary share capital and voting rights (counting shares held by associates) can be granted a CSOP option. The 'grant' value of shares under option to each director/employee cannot exceed £30,000.

To claim CGT treatment on selling the shares (with no income tax liability on exercising the option), the options must be exercised between three and ten years after the grant. Furthermore, neither the grant nor the exercise of the CSOP option must have mainly been motivated by tax or NIC avoidance arrangements [*ITEPA 2003, s 524(1), (2)*].

Unapproved CSOP options exercised within three years of their grant date give rise to an income tax liability, based on the *excess* of the market value of the shares less their exercise price. Where the shares constitute a 'readily convertible asset' (see 8.39), income tax would be paid under the PAYE regime along with NICs.

Under current rules, CSOP options can still be exercised on an 'approved' basis (ie without triggering an income tax charge) within three years of an earlier 'approved' exercise, provided this is between the third and tenth anniversary of the original grant date. This means that all CSOP options gain 'approved' status after three years.

8.75A   However, *FA 2013* permits the early exercise of CSOP options (on an 'income tax' free basis) provided they are exercised within six months after the employee ceases to be in 'qualifying employment' by reason of a transfer of the employment under the *TUPE Regulations* (see 12.21) or the employer company leaving the group.

The *FA 2013* changes also enable an income-tax free early exercise where the company is subject to a takeover (subject to conditions) and the CSOP scheme rules so permit [*ITEPA 2003, s 524(2E)*]. Existing CSOP schemes are deemed to include the necessary permissive provisions.

In other cases, 'good leavers' can exercise their CSOP options on an approved basis within three years of the *original grant date* provided they exercise them within six months of leaving their employment [*ITEPA 2003, s 524(2B)*].

Income tax charge on discounted CSOP options

8.76   An income tax and NIC charge can also arise on *discounted* options, ie where the option price (often fixed at a nominal amount) plus the exercise price are less than the market value on the date the option is granted. This employment income charge arises in the tax year of grant [*ITEPA 2003, s 526*]. Approved CSOPs are now caught by the 'restricted securities' rules (see 8.22).

For example, an income tax charge would arise where a CSOP option is granted for £1 per share with the right to exercise at £5 per share and a market value on grant of £8 per share. In this case, an income tax charge arises on £2 per share (ie £8 per share less £1 per share plus £5 per share). However, if the option exercise price of £5 per share is regarded as manifestly less than £8, the scheme would not, in any event, be an approved CSOP.

Performance conditions

8.77   The options can be performance related in that they are not able to be exercised unless the company and/or executive has met specified targets (see *CIR v Burton Group plc* [1990] STC 242). Measuring this by reference to the share price is clearly a problem with a private company and, in general terms, a performance related trigger may not be appropriate.

HMRC notification of CSOPs

8.77A   All CSOPs are now subject to self-certification (in the same way as EMI schemes – see 8.69). This means that companies must self-certify that their CSOP schemes meet the legislative requirements even where HMRC had previously granted approval.

The relevant CSOP notification must be submitted online to HMRC by 6 July following the end of the tax year in which the CSOP options are granted (*ITEPA 2003, Sch 4, para 28A(5)*). The notice contains a declaration by the company confirming that the Schedule 4 CSOP scheme meets the requirements of Parts 2–6 of Schedule 4.

Pre-6 April 2014 options granted under an HMRC approved CSOP scheme are deemed to be granted under a Schedule 4 CSOP scheme (see 8.74).

Importantly, where a CSOP scheme was approved by HMRC before 6 April 2014, the company must have notified and self-certified the scheme online before 6 July 2015 if it wished the scheme to continue to attract tax advantages in 2014/15 and following years. Failure to register the scheme will result in it losing its tax advantages!

CSOPs are now subject to the normal HMRC 'enquiry' process. HMRC may initiate an enquiry into the company's CSOP declaration no later than 6 July in the tax year *following the tax year* in which the notification deadline falls. For example, the notification deadline is 6 July 2017 for CSOP options granted in the year ended 5 April 2017. HMRC can open an enquiry at any time up to 6 July 2018 and at any time if it has 'reasonable grounds' for believing that the statutory CSOP requirements have not been met.

Sale of CSOP shares

8.77B   Provided an employee acquires the shares under a Schedule 4 CSOP scheme, their capital gain would be based on the sale price less the option exercise price (as with a qualifying EMI option – see 8.50).

However, unless the shares meet the strict conditions for ER relief (see 15.34), they will not qualify for the 10% CGT rate. The beneficial *FA 2013* relaxation of the ER conditions for EMI shares did *not* extend to the CSOP shares. Thus, unless the gains are small enough to be covered by the employee's annual CGT exemption, the gain is likely to be subject to CGT at the main rate of 20%.

While the exercise of the CSOP option will not normally be subject to any income tax charge, the company is able to claim a corporation tax deduction for the tax-free 'profit' made by the employee. Thus, the company will be able to claim relief on the amount by which the market value of the shares (at the time of exercise) exceeds the option exercise price.

SAYE SHARE OPTION SCHEMES

Background

8.78   Sometimes known as 'sharesave', the scheme uses SAYE contracts and is open to all employees. The scheme can be used in conjunction with an EMI scheme (see 8.49–8.73) or share incentive plan (see 8.84). Since 6 April 2014, a tax advantaged SAYE option scheme is known as a 'Schedule 3 SAYE Option Scheme'.

SAYE schemes tend to involve a considerable amount of 'costly' administrative supervision. However, a number of banks and building societies are in the 'SAYE market' and offer to provide companies with the necessary administrative support.

Key aspects of SAYE schemes

Open to all employees

8.79   A Schedule 3 SAYE Option Scheme provides beneficial tax treatment on shares options granted to employees. However, all the company's (UK resident) employees and full time directors must be entitled to participate in the scheme. (Prior to *FA 2013*, SAYE schemes were not available to employees and directors with an existing equity stake of more than 25%).

Since 6 April 2014, all Schedule 3 SAYE Option Schemes are subject to the same 'self-certification' process as other tax advantaged share schemes, with an online notification to HMRC (see 8.69 and 8.77A).

Main conditions attaching to SAYE options

8.80   The company can set a qualifying period of up to five years' service for eligibility. Employees/directors must participate on 'similar terms', so there can be variations by reference to levels of remuneration, length of service, and so on.

SAYE options are only exercisable within a six-month period after the third, fifth, or seventh anniversary from the date of the first SAYE subscription. The choice between three, five, or seven-year option periods is made at the outset by the company (or, if the company permits, by the relevant employee).

The SAYE option exercise price per share must be determined at the outset for all employees and may be set at a discount of up to 20% of the current market value of the shares.

Key tax benefits

8.81   The key benefits of SAYE schemes are:

- Interest (and any bonus) under SAYE contracts is exempt from tax.

- Exercise of approved option is also exempt from tax.

- Share option gains (ie difference between market value at date of exercise and exercise price) will be deductible for corporation tax purposes (see 8.89).

Note that prior to *FA 2013*, the exercise of SAYE option was *not* tax exempt where it was exercised within three years of grant (under any circumstances, eg a sale of the company), although it was possible for it to be 'rolled-over' on a sale under an option-for-option exchange.

The *FA 2013* made amendments to ensure that (from 17 July 2013) there is no income tax charge if SAYE options are exercised early as a result of a company takeover. This relaxation applies where the scheme rules allow for the early exercise of the options on a takeover (subject to certain prescribed criteria) [*ITEPA 2003, s 519(3A)*].

Existing schemes, which allow for early exercise (subject to tax), are deemed to have the necessary modifications to reflect the new rules. HMRC approval is not required for appropriate amendments made to other existing plans to satisfy the *FA 2013* changes.

SAYE contracts

8.82   The share options are linked to SAYE contracts entered into by employees. These must be certified SAYE contracts. Employees are obliged to make 36 or 60 monthly contributions, not exceeding £500 per month (before 6 April 2014, £250 per month) – minimum £5 per month. Contributions are normally deducted from the employee's salary.

Under (say) a three year SAYE contract, the maximum possible 'savings' (ignoring interest) would be £18,000 (36 × £500). Assuming full 20% discount is taken (see 8.80 above), the maximum initial market value of shares over which an SAYE contract can be granted is £22,500 (ie £18,000 × 100/80). However, over the relevant three year period, the actual value of the shares could have doubled to (say) £45,000.

Note that the increased *FA 2014* limits do not automatically override plan limits in existing SAYE rules, unless they refer to the maximums 'as specified in *ITEPA 2003, Sch 3*' or similar.

The 'market value' exercise price must be agreed with the HMRC's SAV office and specified at the time of grant.

SAYE scheme rules

8.83   A company's SAYE scheme must comply with various legislative requirements and cannot contain any features that might discourage employees from participating.

The rules of the scheme must be approved by directors/shareholders before submitting them for formal HMRC approval. HMRC have published a 'model' set of rules for such schemes.

SHARE INCENTIVE PLANS (SIPs)

Basic workings of an SIP

8.84 Share incentive plans (SIPs) have not enjoyed the same level of success as EMI schemes – this is probably because they are quite complex to understand. The amount of free shares that can be given to individual employees is relatively low and they would involve considerable administration for a reasonably sized workforce. SIPs have, therefore, mainly been used by quoted companies.

An SIP must be open to all employees on the same basis, but the company can impose a qualifying service period of up to 18 months. An SIP would involve the creation of a trust from which shares are appropriated to employees [*ITEPA 2003, ss 488–515* and *Sch 2*]. Prior to 17 July 2013, shareholders with an equity interest of 25% or more in the company were prohibited from participating in a SIP.

SIPs tend to involve a considerable level of administration for the comparatively small tax benefits offered. The tax advantaged SIP is now known as the 'Schedule 2 SIP'.

Many family and owner-managed companies have found that it is easier to use EMI (8.49 to 8.73) or CSOP-based schemes (8.74–8.77) instead.

Schedule 2 SIP schemes must now self-certify using HMRC's online procedure (see 8.69 and 8.77A).

8.85 The maximum value of shares that can currently be appropriated to one employee *in a tax year* is £9,000, split across the following categories:

(*a*) free shares gifted by the company: £3,600 (£3,000 before 6 April 2014);

(*b*) partnership shares purchased by employees: £1,800 (£1,500 before 6 April 2014) or, if lower, 10% of annual salary; and

(*c*) matching shares allocated in proportion to partnership shares: £3,600 (or £3,000 before 6 April 2014).

The increased *FA 2014* limits do not automatically prevail over the existing limits provided for in a company's SIP rules, unless the provisions expressly refer to the 'maximum amounts specified in *ITEPA 2003, Sch 2*' or something along those lines.

If the shares are held in the trust for five years after appropriation, there is no income tax charge on withdrawal. Withdrawals made within three years of appropriation generate an employment income tax charge based on the market value of the shares at that time. Withdrawals made between three and five years after appropriation create an income tax charge on the lower of the share value at appropriation and the value at the date of withdrawal.

However, *FA 2013* removed the income tax charge where shares were subject to withdrawal as a result of the company being taken over (subject to conditions).

Corporation tax relief is available for the cost of free or matching 'SIP-shares' under *CTA 2009, ss 983–998*. However, the *FA 2010* introduced special anti-avoidance provisions to prevent SIP schemes being created largely with the view to generating large corporation tax deductions (here the value of the shares is then artificially reduced rather than being passed to employees). Broadly, HMRC can deny relief will be denied where the SIP contribution is mainly motivated by tax avoidance arrangements. Companies are expressly prohibited from providing a cash alternative to shares.

Advantages of an SIP

8.86   The potential advantages for a family or owner-managed company of an SIP may include:

- allocation of free shares on the basis of employee performance;

- tax and NIC saving on salary paid as free shares or used to purchase partnership shares;

- golden handcuffs for employees as shares may be forfeited on termination of employment;

- corporation tax deduction for all set-up and operating costs of the scheme plus the market value of all free and matching shares allocated;

- promoting the employees' interest in the company and generating a feeling of involvement in the business.

From 15 September 2016, a SIP will cease to be a qualifying Schedule 2 SIP if a 'disqualifying event' occurs – see *ITEPA 2003, Sch 2, para 85A* for detailed circumstances giving rise to a disqualifying event.

EMPLOYEE SHAREHOLDER STATUS (ESS) REGIME

Background

8.86A   It has been recognised that the Employment Shareholder Status (ESS) rules have been exploited for tax avoidance purposes rather than being used for their intended purposes. This exploitation has led to the complete withdrawal of the ESS income tax reliefs and CGT exemption on shares acquired after 30 November 2016. Although, the availability of the ESS status is not affected by the changes, the government intends to close the status to new users at the earliest opportunity. This seems sensible as it is unlikely that such arrangements will continue to be used after November 2016 especially where the employees are still required to give up certain employment rights with no associated tax benefits.

The income tax and CGT tax benefits remain available in respect of ESS shares issued *before 1 December 2016* (see 8.86B and 8.86C).

The employee must *not* provide any consideration for the ESS shares apart from entering into the 'employee shareholder' agreement and giving up certain key employment rights. The employee cannot make any cash payment or give any other form of consideration. (Given that the shares must be issued as fully paid and cannot be issued at a discount, this becomes problematic where shares are issued. The DTI accepts that the 'par' subscription price can be paid by the owner manager or an EBT.)

The key employment rights surrendered by the employee include the right to unfair dismissal, redundancy, certain statutory rights to request flexible working and time off for training, and changing the maternity/adoption notification periods. However, employees will still be protected from 'automatic' unfair dismissals, such as those stemming from discrimination.

The ESS legislation requires the employees to be provided with specified 'written particulars' of the arrangement and independent legal advice (paid for by the employer). There is also a seven-day 'cooling-off' period before the ESS contract is finalised.

Under the 'pre-1 December 2016' ESS regime, only the first £2,000 worth of shares are exempt from income tax and NIC charges (see 8.86B). ESS may also provide useful capital gains exemptions in respect of 'pre-1 December 2016' arrangements (see 8.86C).

There is complete flexibility on the number/value of shares that can be awarded. The ESS shares may also be of a different class and can contain restrictions. ESS shares can also be structured as growth shares (see 8.24). In contrast to EMI, there are no restrictions in the activities that are carried on by the relevant company or group.

The terms under which the ESS shares are acquired and are ultimately disposed of are a matter for agreement between the parties. Thus, good and bad leaver provisions and 'drag along and 'tag along' clauses can still be imposed.

Income tax exemption of provision of pre-1 December 2016 ESS shares

8.86B Where an employee (together with any connected person) did not have a 25% material interest in the company, they were deemed to have given consideration for the ESS shares granted. However, the initial unrestricted market value (IUMV) of the shares, at the date of grant, must have been at least £2,000.

If an employee acquired ESS shares with a value greater than £2,000, they were only charged to tax on the difference between the tax-free £2,000 and the IUMV of the shares (assuming an *ITEPA 2003, s 431* election is made) [*ITEPA 2003, ss 226A–226D*].

Corporation tax relief was also available to the value of the ESS shares acquired, ignoring the deemed £2,000 consideration.

CGT treatment on subsequent sale of pre-1 December 2016 ESS shares

8.86C   For ESS shares issued before 17 March 2016, the shares awarded under the ESS contract (up to the initial value of £50,000 at the time of the award) are completely exempt from CGT (see 8.86C)

Where the IUMV on acquisition exceeds £50,000, the relief only applies to the appropriate portion of the shares [*TCGA 1992, s 263C(6)*]. Broadly, this is calculated at the relevant date when the £50,000 limit is exceeded, as follows:

$$\text{Total number of shares} \quad \times \quad \frac{£50,000 \text{ less IUMV of ESS shares already held at relevant date}}{\text{Total IUMV of ESS shares held on relevant date}}$$

However, following perceived abuse of this capital gains exemption, *FA 2016* introduced a lifetime capital gains limit of £100,000 (*TCGA 1992, s 236B(1A)*). This restriction only applies to shares issued under ESS arrangements after 16 March 2016 but the eligible exempt gain is still subject to the £50,000 'initial' IUMV restriction noted above. Any gains on disposals of ESS shares issued before 17 March 2016 do not count towards the £100,000 limit.

Where an ESS shareholding satisfies the normal rules for entrepreneurs' relief (see 15.34) – including having at least a 5% the ordinary share capital and votes for 12 months before the sale – the first £100,000 is CGT exempt with the remainder being taxed at 10%. If ER is not available, the excess is taxed at 20%.

If an employee breaches the 25% material interest condition (see above), the CGT exemption will not apply and the gain will be subject to CGT as normal.

The employee will normally be obliged to sell the ESS shares back to the company on leaving employment. In such cases, where the shares were issued before 1 December 2016, there is a useful income tax exemption so that only CGT would apply to the sale (without having to satisfy the normal 'five-year' requirements) (see 13.46 – Table 2). However, this 'exemption' does not apply for shares issued after 1 December 2016. Any consideration received for these shares would be taxed as an income distribution.

Example 7

Sale of ESS shares

On 1 October 2016, Alex enters into an ESS agreement with Gold & Sullivan Ltd under which he receives 3,000 shares (representing a 3% equity stake in the company) in consideration for entering into the contract. An *ITEPA 2003, s 431* election is also made.

HMRC's SAV office agree that the market value of Alex's 3,000 shares on 1 October 2016 is £4,500.

Alex is therefore subject to income tax on £2,500, being market value of £4,500 less £2,000 exemption.

Assume that, in (say) October 2018, the company is sold to a listed company and Alex realises net proceeds of £200,000 for his shares.

Since Alex acquired the ESS shares after 16 March 2016 (and before 1 December 2016), only the first £100,000 of his gain of £197,500 would be exempt from CGT. Alex's taxable gain (subject to any annual exemption) is therefore £97,500, which would be taxed at 20%, as shown below:

	£	£
Sale proceeds		200,000
Less: Base cost (amount subject to income tax)		(2,500)
Capital gain		197,500
Less: ESS CGT exemption		(100,000)
Capital gain (subject to annual exemption)		97,500

EMPLOYEE SHARE REPORTING TO HMRC

Form 42/other ERS return

8.87 HMRC is now stringently enforcing the annual reporting requirements for unapproved share arrangements for directors and employees.

All relevant events must be reported, regardless of whether any tax charge arises. Form 42 (other ERS return) and all other share scheme returns must now be filed using HMRC's Employment Related Securities (ERS) Online Service.

Clearly, HMRC will use this information to ensure that directors/employees report and pay the correct amount of tax under self-assessment. HMRC place significant importance on having a robust reporting procedure for reporting value passing to directors/employees through share-related benefits.

The main events required to be reported on Form 42 (other ERS return) include:

- the acquisition of shares or securities, including shares/securities acquired on the exercise of an option;

- the grant of an option (including EMI options granted over shares worth more than £250,000);

- chargeable events under the 'restricted securities' regime;

- artificial enhancement of value of shares/securities; and

- assignment or release of an option.

The 'employer' company normally reports the relevant events on the other ERS return/Form 42. However, this obligation also extends to any issuer or provider of the shares (such as an employee share trust).

The acquisition of initial subscriber shares or 'founder shares' in new UK incorporated companies does not need to be reported provided the following conditions are met:

- all the initial subscriber shares are acquired at their nominal value;

- the shares are not acquired by reason of another employment; and

- the shares are acquired by a person who is a director or prospective director of the company (or someone who has a personal family relationship with the director and the right is made available in the normal course of the domestic, family or personal relationship with that director).

There are separate online reporting requirements for shares acquired under HMRC approved schemes, such as a Schedule 4 CSOP Scheme (see 8.77A) or a Schedule 3 SAYE Option Scheme (see 8.79). Shares acquired on the exercise of a qualifying EMI option are reported online (see 8.69).

Reporting deadlines and penalties

8.88   The Form 42 (or ERS return) must be filed online by 6 July following the end of the relevant tax year. Thus, for the year ended 5 April 2017, the form should have been submitted by 6 July 2017 and annually thereafter. (HMRC extended the submission deadline for 2016/17 only to 24 August 2017 since there were difficulties with the online submission service.)

Companies need to ensure that they are registered to file using HMRC's Employment Related Securities (ERS) Online Service. They will submit the required details online with supporting information being provided in a specified format (HMRC provide templates). For further details, see www. hmrc.gov.uk/shareschemes/annualreturns

To ensure prompt compliance to the ERS online system, penalties for late or incorrect filing of annual returns will apply as follows:

Lateness	Penalty
After annual filing deadline	£100
3 months late	£300
6 months late	£300
9 months late	£10 per day

A fine of up to £5,000 may be levied by HMRC for failure to file a return electronically or where an annual share scheme return contains a material inaccuracy that is:

- careless or deliberate, or

- not corrected after the person becomes aware that it contains a material inaccuracy.

However, it is not all 'doom and gloom' since the introduction of the 'reasonable excuse' relaxations in *FA 2016*. Companies can now argue that their 'tax-approved' share schemes should not fail to qualify for the relevant tax reliefs if there was a 'reasonable excuse' for the failure to notify HMRC of the plan by 6 July following the end of the relevant tax year

CORPORATE TAX DEDUCTION FOR 'DIRECTOR/ EMPLOYEE' SHARE AWARDS OR OPTIONS

Basic rules

8.89 Companies can claim a corporate tax deduction for shares provided to their directors and employees. Broadly speaking, the company obtains relief on the amount charged to income tax in the hands of the recipient director/ employee.

A tax deduction is still available where the legislation specifically exempts the shares from an income tax charge, such as in the case of options exercised under an EMI scheme. In such cases, the relief equates to the amount that would otherwise have attracted income tax. Once the shares or options are relieved under these rules, relief cannot be claimed under any other provision.

Under IFRS 2 and FRS 102, unlisted companies will recognise the 'economic cost' of share awards and share options granted to employees (and others) as an expense through the profit and loss account. For ''micro-entities' adopting

FRS 105 (see 4.5A), there is no requirement to account for share awards and options, until the share are actually issued.

Where the company charges the profit and loss account with the value of shares/options provided to employees, the relevant 'accounting' charge will need to be adjusted for and replaced by the relevant statutory tax relief under *CTA 2009, Pt 12, Ch 2*.

Before the statutory deduction rules were introduced in *FA 2003*, companies could only obtain relief by making contributions to Employee Benefit Trusts (EBTs) under so-called 'tax symmetry' arrangements. This was because up until recently a 'share option' gain or a share issue did not produce a profit and loss account charge under normal accounting principles. The EBT then subscribed for the relevant shares, which were subsequently awarded to the employees.

Corporate tax relief can be obtained for expenses involved in running the share scheme under normal 'trading deduction' principles.

However, since 20 March 2013, *FA 2013* prevents relief for certain corporation tax deductions for employee share acquisitions outside the statutory relief mechanism. Thus, deductions for accounting charges and transfer pricing adjustments are denied. Similarly, there is no relief for share options that are not exercised (whether by lapse or surrender). On the other hand, relief is available where the company makes a cash payment to the employee for the cancellation of a share option (which, of course, will be subject to PAYE and NIC in the employees' hands).

Corporation tax relief is available for the costs of setting up the scheme, interest on borrowing for the purposes of the scheme and the costs of administering the scheme.

Main conditions for corporate tax relief

8.90   Corporate tax relief is given where an individual, by reason of their (or another person's) office or employment:

- is awarded (fully paid-up) shares or an interest in such shares (for example, as a gift or purchase at under-value); or

- acquires shares by exercising a share option; and

- suffers a charge to income tax charge on the shares [*CTA 2009, s 1007*].

Similarly, relief is given on the amount of any income tax charges that arise under the 'restricted securities' or convertible shares regimes [*CTA 2009, ss 1018, 1019, 1025* and *1030*]. It is possible to obtain HMRC SAV's agreement to the market value of the relevant shares before the corporate tax return is submitted.

Tax relief can still be claimed where directors/employees do not suffer an income tax charge because either:

- their shares are protected by a statutory exemption from income tax, such as share options granted under a Schedule 4 CSOP Scheme, an EMI scheme and Schedule 3 SAYE Option Scheme; or

- they are not resident in the UK.

In the case of an EMI scheme, the corporate tax deduction is given on the full amount of any discount (which would be taxed on the employee) and the amount of tax 'relief' given under the EMI scheme (being the increase in the value of the option shares from the date of the option grant to the date of exercise) [*CTA 2009, s 1019(2)(b), (3)(b)*]. For CSOP options, the deductible amount is the amount by which the market value of the shares (at the date of exercise) exceeds the option exercise price paid by the employee.

Relief is only available where the shares are awarded or options are granted for the purposes of the employing company's business (which must be within the charge to corporation tax). As long as this 'business purpose' test is satisfied it should be possible for relief to be claimed where an employee acquires shares after they have left the employment.

Qualifying shares

8.91   Relief is only available for 'qualifying shares', which must be non-redeemable and fully-paid. For *unlisted* companies, such as owner-managed companies, the shares must be in either:

- an independent company (ie one which is not under the control of another company) (see 8.71 for potential problems with 'exit-based' EMI options); or

- a 'non-close' company that is under the control of a listed company [*CTA 2009, s 1008*].

An important practical effect of this restriction is that relief is denied on employee share awards/exercises in a subsidiary of a *private company*. However, where a private company acquires control of a company which has unexercised employee share options, the *FA 2014* enables the relevant corporate tax deduction to be claimed provided the options are exercised within 90 days of the private company's acquisition (or the 'change in control').

There are no restrictions where shares or options are held in a subsidiary of a listed company.

The shares must be issued by the:

(*a*)   employing company; or

(*b*)   its parent company; or

(c)   a consortium member that owns either (a) or (b); or

(d)   a fellow 'consortium member' of (a) or (b) that is part of the same commercial association of companies of the consortium-owned company [*CTA 2009, ss 1008(1), (2)* and *1016(1), (2)*].

Mechanics of relief

8.92   The relief is broadly calculated as follows:

Market value of shares at time shares are transferred or option exercised	x
Less: Consideration paid by employee	(x)
Corporate tax deduction	x

Clearly, the total tax deduction will be the aggregate of all the above calculations for each employee. The way in which the relief is computed does not require that shares must come from the company – relief can still be claimed, for example, on shares transferred from a controlling shareholder, EBT or an employee share ownership trust.

Example 8

Statutory corporate tax relief for employee shares

Using the figures set out in Example 2 at 8.35, Goalies Ltd can claim corporate tax deductions as shown below.

		Corporate tax relief	
Accounting period – year ended	Event	With no *ITEPA 2003, s 431* election	With *ITEPA 2003, s 431* election
		£	£
31 December 2016	Exercise of option	10,000	20,000
31 December 2017	Sale	23,334	–

Special rules apply to reduce the company's relief for any amount that has been claimed under the previous system, such as where shares have been transferred from an EBT to which tax-deductible contributions had been made.

In most cases, relief will be claimed as a trading deduction where the shares were awarded or options granted for the purpose of the relevant business. Relief is generally given in the accounting period in which the recipient beneficially acquires the shares or exercises their share option.

The legislation allows the relief to be apportioned on a 'just and reasonable' basis between various businesses where the shares are awarded or options granted for the purposes of those businesses. This rule may apply where, for example, a parent company of a large group of companies grants options over its shares to employees of a subsidiary company with the primary aim of providing incentives to increase shareholder value as well as developing its subsidiary's trade.

Where, on a takeover, a company's share options are 'rolled-over' into options over the acquiring company's shares, tax relief can still be claimed in the original company for whose business the options were previously granted [*CTA 2009, s 1022*].

PLANNING CHECKLIST – EMPLOYEE SHARE SCHEMES AND PLANS

Company

- Consider limiting shares in employee share schemes to, say, 10% of ordinary share capital.

- Watch out for potential share option exercises diluting existing shareholders below critical tax shareholding requirements, such as the 5% ordinary shares voting shares requirement for ER which is tested throughout the 12 months before a sale.

- Ensure that statutory corporation tax relief is claimed on all shares awarded or share options exercised. Such relief can be claimed on *both unapproved and approved* (for example, EMI) share schemes.

- In the context of a 'private' corporate group, ensure that employee shares are issued in the parent company to avoid 'loss' of corporate tax relief (and prevent shares being liable to PAYE and NIC as readily convertible assets).

- Consider using an EBT, employee trust or a company purchase of own shares where an 'internal' exit route is required for outgoing employee shareholders.

- Where employee shares are to be provided by an EBT or employee trust, carefully check whether the arrangements are exempted under the 'disguised remuneration' legislation.

- An EMI scheme is likely to be most attractive for key or, in some cases, all employees. A CSOP may prove useful where the company does not have qualifying status for EMI.

- On 'exit-based' EMI options, consider the impact of the enhancement in the company's net asset value as a result of corporate tax relief being claimed on the value of the relevant EMI share option exercises.

- Ensure all share schemes are registered online to enable all employee share and share scheme reporting to be filed online.

  For 'unapproved' share awards and options, relevant share acquisitions and other relevant 'chargeable events' must be reported to HMRC online on Form 42/other ERS return.

- Don't leave employee share issues until a sale is imminent as this may severely limit the available planning choices.

Working shareholders

- Conventional shareholdings in private companies may or may not be restricted securities, although HMRC appear to take the view that standard pre-emption rights are sufficient to taint the shares as 'restricted'. However, given the uncertainty and the potential income tax exposure that exists with restricted shares, it is normally worth making a protective *ITEPA 2003, s 431* election to ensure that the shares only attract CGT on a future sale.

- Provided there are valid commercial reasons, it may be beneficial to sell some shares to an EBT (subject to the possibility of an *ITA 2007, s 684* challenge).

- Consider advantages offered by EMI share option scheme for favourable capital gains treatment (ensure that 30% 'material interest' test is not breached). The *FA 2013* relaxation of the entrepreneurs relief rules make EMI shares much more attractive, and especially so for 'exit-based' EMI schemes.

- Where directors/employees hold at least 5% of the (voting) ordinary shares, they should be able to benefit from the lower ER CGT rate of 10% on their gains. However, where they have unapproved or CSOP share options, the options would need to be exercised at least one year before any sale to meet the 'one year' minimum 5% shareholding period required by the ER legislation. Some employees may find it difficult to fund the purchase consideration far in advance of a sale. In such cases, unless gains are sheltered by the annual exemption, the employees are likely to be taxed at 20%.

- Take advice on whether to enter into an agreement or election to bear the employer's NIC liability arising on a share option.

Other employees

- Other employees generally have the same issues as working shareholders.

- Look upon a share option scheme as a possible means of obtaining a lump sum on flotation or take-over as a 'bonus' that may or may not occur.

Non-working shareholders

- Balance the advantages of share schemes used as incentive device for employees with the dilution of shareholders' funds.

Chapter 9

Distribution of profits and dividend planning

INTRODUCTION

9.1 Owner-managed companies may need to pay dividends for a number of reasons. In the vast majority of cases, dividends are likely to provide a tax-efficient way of extracting profits for the working shareholders, as illustrated at 2.12–2.16. Following the post-5 April 2016 increase in dividend taxation, the tax savings obtained from paying dividends have reduced. Despite this, paying dividends remains beneficial (see 9.11–9.12).

Companies that fall within the 'IR35' regime will generally have limited scope for paying dividends (see Chapter 6).

Many owner managers prefer to extract cash which is clearly surplus to the current and future requirements of the business, removing it from future exposure to business risk by way of dividend. Surplus cash *might* also prejudice a company's trading status for ER purposes but provided the cash has been derived from trading activities and is not actively managed as an investment asset, this should not be the case (see 15.37).

Dividends may need to be paid to those shareholders who have invested in the company to provide a regular income. For example, where the company was acquired by means of a management buy-out, venture capitalists may hold a significant part of the equity investment, often a preferential class of shares, upon which a dividend must be paid. (Dividends are not taxed in the hands of a corporate shareholder.)

On the other hand, certain shareholders may have invested for capital growth and do not require dividends. In practice, any conflicting requirements of the shareholders can often be satisfied by the use of separate classes of shares, with different rights as to dividends, votes and return of capital.

Where an Enterprise Investment Scheme (EIS) or Seed Enterprise Investment Scheme (SEIS) is in operation, care must be taken to ensure that the relevant shares do not provide a preferential right to dividends. Furthermore, dividends on the EIS/SEIS shares must be paid at a commercial rate (see 11.40 and 11.66). This rule also applies to shares subscribed for under the Investors' Relief regime (see 15.46).

PROCEDURE FOR PAYING A DIVIDEND AND CONCEPT OF 'DISTRIBUTABLE PROFITS'

Companies Act formalities

9.2 A dividend represents a payment made from a company's distributable profits in respect of a share in a company. A dividend can either be fixed in amount (for example, on a preference share) or a variable amount on an ordinary (equity) share.

For private companies incorporated after 30 September 2009, the method of paying dividends is likely to be regulated by the 'Model Articles for Private Companies Limited by Shares (contained in the *Companies (Model Articles) Regulations 2008, SI 2008/3229)*. Otherwise, the procedure is often governed by the company's Articles of Association – companies that were registered before 1 October 2009 will have adopted the standard Table A Articles. In such cases, Articles 102–108 of Table A will apply in the absence of any contrary rules [*Companies (Tables A to F) Regulations 1985, SI 1985/805*]. A final dividend must be recommended by the directors and approved by the shareholders in a general meeting.

Article 30 of the Model Articles (Article 103 of Table A) authorises the directors (under a Board resolution) to pay interim dividends. A resolution of the Board to pay an interim dividend does not create a debt and may, therefore, be revoked before it is paid (*Potel v CIR* (1970) 46 TC 658). Reliable up-to-date management accounts should be available to show there are sufficient distributable profits to support the intended interim dividend.

The normal procedure for paying dividends is to calculate the total dividend and then the dividend per share. Unless the articles state otherwise, dividends are payable to those shareholders registered at the time of the declaration. Each 'recipient' shareholder should receive a dividend voucher stating the amount of the dividend etc. Dividends paid after 5 April 2016 no longer carry a 10% tax credit and the shareholder is taxed on the amount received without any grossing-up (see 9.11–9.12).

In the case of an interim dividend, directors' Board minutes must be drawn up approving the payment. In the case of the final dividend, documentation must be prepared for the annual general meeting (AGM) to approve the dividend recommended by the directors. Where elective resolutions have been passed, the dividend payments should be validated by a written resolution of the Board of directors.

In some cases, HMRC may seek to argue that a dividend paid to a director shareholder should be treated as remuneration. However, any such challenge should easily be rebutted where the dividend has been properly declared in accordance with the Companies Act formalities and the company's Articles.

Dividends paid should be reflected as a debit against equity and hence should appear as a movement on reserves within the notes to the financial statements (and not on the face of the profit and loss account). Proposed dividends are not proper liabilities of the company (since there is no legal obligation to pay them until they have been formally ratified by the shareholders). Consequently, proposed dividends are simply shown as a note to the accounts, except where they represent a genuine liability of the company at the balance sheet date.

Dividends declared after the balance sheet date, but before the accounts have been authorised, should not be recognised as a liability since the company did not have an obligation to pay them at the reporting date. If they are material, post-balance sheet declared dividends should be reported as part of the notes to the accounts.

Preference shares

9.3 Preference shareholders normally have a fixed dividend entitlement (as a percentage of the amount paid up on their shares). Preference dividends are paid in priority to dividends to ordinary shareholders. There is, however, no automatic right to a payment of a preference dividend, since any dividend can only be declared out of distributable profits. Where preference dividends cannot be paid in a particular period (for whatever reason), they are assumed to be cumulative (in the absence of any express provision in the company's Memorandum or Articles of Association). Such dividends accumulate until they can be paid.

Redeemable preference shares are classified as a liability as a company has an obligation to redeem the shares on a specific date. Dividends on these shares would be recognised as expenses and classified as interest. Despite this presentation in the accounts, the dividends would still not be deductible for corporation tax purposes.

Determination of distributable profits and directors' duties

Dividends and distributions

9.4 The *Companies Act 2006* defines a distribution as any distribution of a company's assets to its shareholders, whether or not it is made in cash, excluding certain 'capital' payments in *CA 2006, s 829(1), (2)* (eg a redemption or purchase of own shares out of capital or a distribution to shareholders in a winding-up). We must remember that this is the legal definition, and may not always be the same as the prescriptive definitions for tax purposes in *CTA 2010, Part 23*.

Although the legal definition contemplates a transfer to a company's shareholders/members, the courts are prepared to extend this concept to appropriate parties connected with the shareholders. This was illustrated in *Aveling Barford v Perion* [1989] BCLC 626, where the court held that an asset transferred (at an undervalue) to a company controlled by the shareholder was a distribution under company law. Justice Hoffmann (at 631) confirmed:

> "Whether or not the transaction is a distribution to shareholders does not depend exclusively on what the parties choose to call it. The court looks at the substance rather than the outward appearance."

This principle is also confirmed in *ICAEW's Technical Release: TECH 02/17BL – Guidance on Realised Profits and Distributable Profits under the Companies Act 2017*. The guidance (at paragraph 2.3A) states that it is the purpose and substance of a transaction that is important rather than the label given to it. In particular, an undervalue transaction with a shareholder or sister company is capable of being a distribution since it involves an element of gift to the transferee company. The intentions and mindset of the parties may also be relevant here.

Distributions can arise where liabilities are assumed (if the assigning company does not receive consideration of the same amount). This is because the liability commits the company to transfer assets at a future date and its assets are therefore reduced when entering into the commitment.

A waiver of an amount receivable from a parent company would also be a distribution.

For further discussion of the legal treatment of demerger distributions and other distributions in specie, see 13.99–13.101.

Calculation of distributable profits

9.4A   A company cannot legally pay a dividend or make any other form of distribution unless it has sufficient distributable profits to cover the dividend/distribution [*CA 2006, s 830*].

For these purposes, distributable profits represent the company's accumulated *realised* profits less its accumulated realised losses (and any other amount written off in a reduction or reorganisation of capital). Realised profits and losses are determined in accordance with generally accepted accounting principles prevailing when the accounts are prepared [*CA 2006, s 853(4)*].

The *ICAEW Technical Release TECH 02/17BL* stresses the need to look at the substance of the relevant arrangements, especially in relation to intra-group transactions. For example, paragraph 9.34A of the guidance discusses the case where a group company transfers an asset to a fellow group company for consideration, which is left outstanding on inter-company loan account. Subsequently, the inter-company loan is waived, with the transferee company crediting the waived amount to its profit and loss account. If these transactions were part of a series of transactions, it is very likely that the 'credit' to the transferee's profit and loss accounts would not be a 'realised' profit, since it effectively represents a revaluation of the asset acquired for no cost.

Any reserve arising from a 'permissible' reduction of capital (ie share capital, share premium account, and capital redemption reserve) is treated as a realised profit [*Companies (Reduction of Share Capital) Order 2008, SI 2008/191*]. For example, a private company can reduce its share capital provided a solvency statement from its directors supports the reduction (see 13.98). On the other hand, these rules do not apply where (and to the extent that) a reduction of capital relates to a direct payment to the shareholders, since no reserve arises (see *ICAEW Technical Release TECH 02/17BL – para 2.8B*).

The relevant profits for determining the position are those reported in the company's last statutory accounts circulated to its members. If the statutory accounts contain a qualified auditors report, the auditor must indicate (in writing) whether the matters leading to that 'qualification' are material for determining whether the company has sufficient distributable profits.

Based on the above statutory rules, it is not necessary for a company to make a profit for the year in which the dividend is paid. However, there must be sufficient retained profits from prior years to cover it.

Where the statutory accounts show insufficient profits, interim accounts must be prepared for the period in which the distribution is intended to be made to enable a proper judgement to be made by the directors. In practice, reliable up-to-date management accounts, which make proper provision for all liabilities (including tax) should be adequate in most cases (see *CA 2006, ss 837–839*).

Where assets are distributed in specie, the Companies Act provisions stipulate the measure the amount of any legal 'distribution' (see 13.96).

Realised profits

9.5   Profits must be realised and for this purpose, profits are treated as realised in accordance with generally accepted accounting principles ('GAAP'). Companies do not have any legal or accounting obligation to disclose their realised profits and unrealised profits, but they must obtain sufficient records to enable them to identify the profits that are available for distribution.

Under UK GAAP/FRS 102, it is not possible to pay a dividend from an unrealised profit, such as a revaluation surplus. Similarly, it is not possible to pay a dividend from a share premium account or any capital redemption reserve. (Public companies and listed investment companies are subject to additional restrictions – see *CA 2006, ss 831* and *832*.)

9.5A   Profits are treated as realised in accordance with International Financial Reporting Standards (IFRSs) and UK GAAP/FRS 102. These standards generally require accounts to be prepared on a prudent basis, with appropriate prudent accounting policies being adopted. For example FRS 102 (at section 2.9) requires that where there are uncertainties around events and circumstances, appropriate disclosure is made and prudence is exercised relating to those uncertainties when preparing the accounts.

This concept is developed further in the *ICAEW TECH 02/17BL* (see 9.4 above). This technical guidance note indicates that a profit will be realised on a particular transaction where the company receives 'qualifying consideration', which is any of the following:

* Cash;

* An asset that is readily convertible into cash (see below);

* The release, or the settlement or assumption by another party, of all or part of a liability of the company;

* An amount receivable in any of the above forms, where the debt is reasonably certain to be collected; or

* An amount receivable from a shareholder where the company intends to make a distribution to them, equal to the actual 'offset' amount provided the two transactions are 'linked'.

Broadly speaking, an asset is considered to be 'readily convertible into cash' for these purposes when:

* the value at which it can be readily 'converted' into cash can be determined at the relevant date; and

* this value is observable by reference to price/rates by market participants; and

* the company must be able to immediately convert the asset into cash without any material adverse consequences.

Areas that would require special consideration would include, for example, profits on the sale of assets between group companies where no actual payment is received, share for share exchanges, transactions between related parties particularly where they do not appear to be on an arm's length or involving circular cash movements, and the inclusion of unrealised exchange gains on long-term monetary items (such as long term foreign currency loans).

As a general rule, accounting provisions (including depreciation provisions, goodwill amortisation, provisions for liabilities and deferred tax) are treated as realised losses. Reductions in asset revaluations would normally be treated as unrealised losses.

9.5B   It is also accepted that where a company uses 'fair value' accounting ('mark-to-market') basis for investment assets, then the profits computed on this basis are treated as 'realised' and therefore distributable.

It is important to appreciate that, in a group context, the profits available for distribution in each individual company are those stated in the accounts of the relevant company (as distinct from the consolidated group accounts). Where a subsidiary distributes an asset in specie, this will represent an *unrealised* profit in the (recipient) parent company's hands, unless the 'distributed' asset meets the definition of qualifying consideration (see above).

However, where the 'non-cash' asset is distributed by the parent company to its shareholder(s), *CA 2006, s 846* will apply to treat that 'unrealised profit' as a realised profit for the parent for the purpose of the onward distribution, provided the profit is recorded in the parent's accounts.

The directors must also have the appropriate provisions in the company's Memorandum or Articles of Association. This may require a dividend to be paid to certain classes of preferred shares in preference to the ordinary shares. The Articles may also carry some other restrictions, for example, as to whether capital profits are distributable. In some cases, dividends are paid by reference to a pre-determined formula prescribed in a shareholders' agreement.

Example 1

Determination of distributable profits

The directors of Boyce Ltd are considering the level of dividend that should be paid out to its shareholders in October 2017.

The statutory accounts for the year ended 30 June 2017 showed the retained earnings (ie the balance on its accumulated profit and loss account) of £1,725,000, which was made up as follows:

	£
Balance at 30 June 2016	1,500,000
Add: Total recognised income and expense for the period	660,000
Less: Currency translation differences on foreign currency net investment	(35,000)
Dividend paid during the year	(400,000)
Balance at 30 June 2017	1,725,000

The company also had a revaluation surplus on its trading property of £1,200,000, which was not reflected in the above figures (and does not form part of its distributable profits).

As the directors wished to pay a dividend of around £500,000, this should be well within the limits of its distributable profits of around £1,725,000 (subject to any significant realised losses in the period between 30 June 2017 and October 2017). The directors would also need to take the company's cash flow requirements into account.

DIRECTORS' FIDUCIARY AND STATUTORY DUTIES

9.6   In making a distribution, the directors have a fiduciary/legal duty to think about the company's best interests generally. Although this common law jurisprudence is maintained, this is reinforced by the *CA 2006,* which lays down a statutory statement of directors' duties. These statutory duties include acting within the company's powers, promoting the success of the company, exercising independent judgement, and applying reasonable care, skill and diligence.

When deciding whether to pay a dividend and, where appropriate, the relevant amount, the directors would need to consider the company's solvency. This would require them to look at the company's cash-flow profile and the ability to repay its debts as they fall due. The directors must therefore conduct a full and proper investigation into the accounts. Furthermore, the expectation of future trading losses should also be taken into account. See also paragraphs 2.3 and 2.3A of *ICAEW's Technical Release: TECH 02/17BL.*

Where a dividend is paid unlawfully (such as where there are insufficient distributable profits), the directors may be personally liable to make good the loss caused to the company and they may also be in breach of their common law duties. This would also be the analysis where the director is not a shareholder.

In the leading case of *Bairstow v Queens Moat Houses plc and Others* [2000] 1 BCLC 549, it was held that a director who authorised the payment of an unlawful dividend, which he knew was unlawful, would be liable to repay it.

Similarly, *CIR v Richmond (Re Loquitur Ltd)* [2003] STC 1394 demonstrates the serious consequences for directors who fail to exercise proper judgement in carrying out their fiduciary duties with regard to the payment of a dividend. In this case, the directors authorised and procured a dividend that was subsequently shown to be unlawful. This was because the company failed to provide for the corporation tax liability (around £2.3 million) on the sale of its 'Ronson' product range for £10 million. Although a claim had been made to roll over the gain, it was held that this claim failed. As the directors were in breach of their duties under (what was) *CA 1985, s 270,* they were personally liable to make good the money misapplied as an unlawful dividend (being limited to the full tax liability on the capital gain).

Where the *CA 2006* requirements governing the payment of dividends have been breached, the directors may be granted relief under *CA 2006, s 1157* where it can be shown that they acted honestly and reasonably. That said, the law imposes a high standards for directors. Consequently, in most cases they may find it difficult to persuade a court that they took all reasonable steps to satisfy themselves that the dividend was a legally competent one (even though it turned out to be unlawful).

The directors may also plead relief under the Statute of Limitations for dividends paid more than six years ago.

LEGAL AND TAX CONSEQUENCES OF AN UNLAWFUL DIVIDEND

9.7   If a company's dividend exceeds its distributable reserves, this will be an unlawful distribution and the company may be able to obtain repayment from the shareholder recipient. Where a shareholder knows or has reasonable grounds for believing that a particular dividend is illegal (due to the lack of sufficient distributable profits), *CA 2006, s 847* provides that they are liable to pay it back to the company.

The Court of Appeal held that an unlawful distribution received by the company's holding company (which knew the facts) was liable to be repaid (*Precision Dippings Ltd v Precision Dipping Marketing Ltd* [1986] Ch 447). Consequently, where a shareholder knowingly receives an illegal dividend, it is certainly arguable that they hold the cash received as a 'constructive trustee' for the company since they are liable to repay it (or such part of it that is unlawful). Similar issues can arise where assets are transferred to a 'related' company at an under-value – see 13.100.

The legal analysis of an unlawful distribution is usually followed for tax purposes. HMRC often argues that an 'unlawful dividend' represents a loan to the relevant shareholder(s), which may be subject to a *CTA 2010, s 455* charge (see 2.56). This is likely to be the case for the majority of unlawful distributions made by family and owner-managed companies.

In *It's a Wrap (UK) Ltd v Gula* [2006] EWCA Civ 544, unlawful dividends paid to members as 'quasi-salaries' (on the advice of their accountant to save tax!) were found on appeal to be repayable by the shareholders. Although they were unaware of the illegality, it was held that a shareholder was liable to return a distribution if they knew or *should have been aware* that it had been paid in circumstances which amounted to a contravention of the restrictions on distributions (irrespective of whether or not they knew of those restrictions) (see 9.5).

The company's director(s) may also be personally liable for any improper distributions as this may amount to a breach of their common law fiduciary duty and/or their statutory duties imposed by the *CA 2006* (see 9.6).

Cash and *in specie* dividends

9.8   A dividend can either be paid in cash or *in specie*. Generally, dividends can only be paid in cash whereas an *in specie* dividend (which involves the transfer of a specific asset) requires express authority in the Articles (this is given in Article 105 of Table A). It is, of course, possible for the Articles to be amended by a special resolution where the relevant authority is not available (note that the pre-1948 versions of Table A do not contain this power).

9.9   Before making an in-specie distribution, it is important to ensure that the company's articles contain the necessary power for it do so. It is normally preferable for in-specie distributions to be made as interim 'dividends'.

Unless the company is being made as part of a winding-up, the distributing company must sufficient distributable reserves to distribute the 'accounts' carrying cost of the properties/other assets. In such cases, *CA 2006, s 846* enables any revaluation surplus actually 'booked' in the accounts in respect of the distributed asset to be treated as distributable. Where no revaluation surplus is 'credited' in the accounts, only the 'carrying cost' (or value) of the asset recorded in the accounts would have to be met from the company's reserves. This principle is particularly important in determining whether the company has sufficient reserves to be able to facilitate a statutory demerger, which involves an in-specie distribution of shares in a 75% subsidiary or trade and assets (see 9.5 and 13.101).

It may be necessary to prepare management accounts to enable the directors to be satisfied that the distribution can be validly made.

An *in specie* distribution of an asset to a shareholder would involve a 'market value' disposal by the company for capital gains purposes [*TCGA 1992, s 17(1)*].

As a general rule, land and property distributed in specie should not attract any SDLT since it is being made for *no* consideration [*FA 2003, Sch 3, para 1* – note the override to the 'market value' rule in *FA 2003, s 54(4)*].

It is often desirable to transfer properties to the parent company as a distribution in specie, since this avoids the need to rely on the SDLT group relief provisions and its associated anti-avoidance and clawback provisions [*FA 2003, Sch 7, paras 1–6*]. However, an SDLT charge based on the market value of the land/property will apply where the company making the distribution had previously received the relevant land/property under the SDLT group relief provisions in the past three years [*FA 2003, s 54(4)(b)*].

In contrast, an SDLT charge would arise where the property is distributed in specie to a shareholder who also assumes (third party) debt/mortgage attaching to the property. In such cases, the SDLT charged is based on the value of the debt/mortgage assumed (as opposed to the market value of the property).

If the novated debt is owed to the recipient shareholder and the distribution is being made to them as part of a winding up, HMRC agree that there is no effective consideration and hence no SDLT is charged (see HMRC's SDLT Manual at SDLTM04043). On the other hand, HMRC might use the general SDLT anti-avoidance rule in *FA 2003, s 75A* to levy SDLT where the shareholder injects cash into the company (via shares/loan account) to repay third party debt before the liquidation.

DISTRIBUTIONS FOR TAX PURPOSES

9.10   A distribution may arise under the tax legislation, for example:

- where a company pays a cash dividend or distributes an asset in specie (see 9.8) to its shareholder(s);

- on a company purchase of its own shares (see 13.44);

- where assets are transferred to a shareholder for less than full consideration (ie at an undervalue) or where a *shareholder* transfers an asset to the company for more than its market value (ie at an overvalue) [*CTA 2010, s 1000(1B)*]; or

- where a *non-working* shareholder obtains a benefit or has personal expenses paid by the company [*CTA 2010, s 1064*] (see 2.66).

9.11   A distribution may arise where a shareholder sells an asset to the company at an over-value. This might occur, for example, when goodwill is sold to a company by a sole trader on incorporation. Let's assume the goodwill is sold at a market value of £500,000 (backed up by a professional market valuation report), which is credited to the shareholders' loan account. If HMRC – Shares and Assets Valuation Office – were to successfully challenge the goodwill value and it is ultimately agreed at (say) £350,000, there would be a prima-facie distribution of £150,000 (being the excess of the consideration received for the goodwill (£500,000) over its agreed market value of £350,000).

However, provided the goodwill was professionally valued (as in this case), HMRC are prepared for the distribution to be unwound by adjusting the shareholder's loan account. It is usually recommended for the 'consideration' clause in the sale contract to provide sufficient flexibility for it to be adjusted – for example, '£500,000 or such other amount as may ultimately be agreed by

HMRC – Shares and Assets Valuation Office'. If the valuation of the asset has not been backed-up by a professional valuation, then HMRC would treat the £150,000 'excess' as a distribution.

DIVIDEND TAXATION (FROM 6 APRIL 2016)

Summary of new dividend tax regime

9.12 Dividend taxation was radically revamped from 6 April 2016. The former dividend tax regime was modelled on the imputation system but, as stressed by the Treasury, was 'designed more than 40 years ago when corporation tax was 50 per cent and the total bill on dividends for some was over 80 per cent'.

The key features of the post-5 April 2016 regime are summarised below.

- Dividends do *not* carry any form of tax credit. The cash dividend or value of the distribution received is reported on the tax return (there is no grossing-up). Under the previous system, dividends carried a 10% tax credit and shareholders were taxed on the grossed-up amount (ie the cash dividend plus the 10% tax credit), receiving a 10% credit against their dividend tax liability (see 2015/16 and earlier editions of this book for coverage of pre-6 April 2016 dividend regime).

- All individuals receive a £5,000 'nil-rate' band for their dividend income (which reduces to £2,000 from 6 April 2018). This is sometimes referred to misleadingly as the £5,000 dividend allowance, but it does not strictly reduce the taxable dividend income. Dividend income is treated as the highest slice of income and is allocated to the various tax rate bands before taking the £5,000 dividend nil-rate band into account (see 9.12B). Dividend income cannot benefit from the £5,000 savings allowance.

- Subject to personal allowances and the £5,000 dividend nil-rate band, dividends are then taxed at the following rates in 2017/18:

Dividend tax rates – 2017/18	
Taxable dividend income received	*Tax rate*
Up to £33,500	7.5%
Between £33,500 and £150,000	32.5%
Above £150,000	38.1%

The above dividend tax rates represent sizeable increases on the comparable rates for 2015/16. Since 6 April 2016, the effective dividend tax rate within each tax band has increased by 7.5%. For example, in 2015/16 cash dividends within the top-rate band were effectively taxed at 30.6%, compared with 38.1% in 2017/18 and 2016/17.

Although 'Scottish' residents are subject to Scottish tax rates on their earnings, pension income and property income etc, they still pay tax on dividend income at the normal UK tax rates.

The increase in dividend taxation impacts on the 'bonus' v 'dividend' extraction model – see 2.14 for detailed worked examples.

9.12A   Following these changes, some owner managers will seek to retain more profits within the company at low rates of corporation tax and only extract the amount required for personal use. There may also be a tendency to take out these reserves on 'retirement' via a 'capital' company purchase of own shares transaction (see 13.46–13.47).

Those owner managers seeking to 'live' off their overdrawn loan accounts should be aware post-5 April 2016 loans/advances remaining outstanding more than nine months after the company's year-end will be subject to a *CTA 2010, s 455* tax liability of 32.5% (see 2.51). There may also be a beneficial loan charge based on the currently interest rate of 3% (see 7.60). For tax treatment of dividends received by UK companies, see 9.16. (See 17.73, 17.86 and 17.90 for the treatment of dividends received by trusts.)

Applying the £5,000 dividend nil-rate band

9.12B   The dividend nil-rate band taxes the first £5,000 (£2,000 from 6 April 2018) of taxable dividend income at 0%. Thus, from a computational perspective, the £5,000 nil-rate band is ignored when allocating the dividend income between the shareholder's basic or higher tax rate bands – see Example 2 below.

Example 2

Calculation of tax on dividend income in 2017/18 (with £5,000 dividend 'nil rate' band)

Adrian's taxable income for the year ended 5 April 2018 is as follows:

Property rental income (net of expenses)	£27,000
Dividend from San Miguel Ltd	£58,000

Adrian's tax bands are allocated as follows:

	Total	Personal allowance	Basic rate band	Higher rate
	£	£	£	£
Net property income	27,000	11,500	15,500*	
Dividend income	58,000		18,000*	40,000
Dividend nil-rate band	(5,000)		(5,000)	–
Taxable dividend	53,000		13,000	40,000
* 2017/18 basic rate band of £33,500				

Adrian's 2017/18 income tax liability is calculated below:

		Rate	Tax
	£		£
Net property income	15,500	20.0%	3,100
Dividend income (1)	13,000	7.5%	975
Dividend income (2)	40,000	32.5%	13,000
Total	68,500		17,075

The *PA Holdings* case – a challenge to dividend payments?

9.13   The *PA Holdings* case examined the tax treatment of dividends that had the 'character' of employment income. The taxpayer company (PA) attempted to deliver bonuses to employees by way of dividends on restricted preference shares, with the advantage of lower income tax for the employees, no PAYE/NIC and a corporate tax deduction for PA. The arrangements included the use of a Jersey company and an employee benefit trust (EBT) (see 5.14).

HMRC argued that the dividends were in fact earnings. Both the Lower and Upper Tier Tribunals ruled that they should be taxed as dividends as the 'dividend' priority rules in what was *ICTA 1988, s 20* applied. They did, however, find that they were to be treated as earnings for NIC purposes. HMRC appealed to the Court of Appeal on the 'dividend' point.

The key facts were:

- The employees had no contractual entitlement to the bonuses, but they had a valid expectation of receipt.

- The employees' 'bonus' entitlements were based on a long-standing formula, which were previously subject to PAYE and NIC under PA's pre-1999 EBT arrangements.

- The 1999 EBT's stated purpose was to 'motivate and encourage employees in the performance of their duties by the provision of bonus incentives and other awards at the discretion of the trustees'.

- PA also informed its staff about 'exciting proposed changes to the delivery of current bonus awards'.

Based on these underlying facts, the Court of Appeal determined that, in substance, the preference dividends represented earnings in the hands of the employees (*PA Holdings Ltd v HMRC* [2011] EWCA Civ 1414).

We should remember that the *PA Holdings* arrangements were pretty aggressive. They sought to re-characterise what had historically been bonus payments to its very large pool of consultancy staff.

The vast majority of tax advisers consider that the facts of the *PA Holdings* case are entirely different from those of typical owner-managed companies.

In April 2013, PA Holdings withdrew its appeal to the Supreme Court. Consequently, the judgement in the Court of Appeal is now final, although many consider that this leaves the law in this area in a confusing state. However, the general consensus seems to be that taxpayers can rely on earlier Treasury/HMRC assurances that genuine dividends for owner-managers will continue to be taxed as dividends (but see also 9.14 below).

Dividends on 'Alphabet' share arrangements

9.14   HMRC have always contended that the 'post-acquisition' benefits legislation in *ITEPA 2003, Pt 7, Ch 4* enables it to challenge dividends paid under so-called 'alphabet share' arrangements which are mainly driven by tax or NIC avoidance.

However, the Ministerial statement made by Dawn Primarolo on 21 June 2005 provided some comfort that HMRC would not generally seek to apply the special 'post-acquisition benefits' legislation to dividends paid to shareholders of owner-managed companies. It confirmed that these rules were only intended to deal with 'contrived schemes to disguise remuneration so as to avoid PAYE and NIC'.

HMRC's Employment Related Securities at ERSM90060 confirms that:

'Where an owner-managed company run as a genuine business, pays dividends out of profits and there is no contrived scheme to avoid income tax or NIC on remuneration or to avoid the IR35 rules, HMRC will not seek to argue that a Chapter 4 benefit had been received by the directors because of the exclusion provided by *ITEPA 2003, s 447(4)'* (ie there is no main tax/ NIC avoidance motive).

The *PA Holdings* case (in 9.13) above is a rather good example of the type of 'contrived' tax avoidance scheme that HMRC has in mind when looking at such arrangements!

There is a potential argument that a share that simply carries a right to a dividend and no other rights may not be a legal share at all. Depending on the exact circumstances involved, this might be construed as a sham or 'contrived' arrangement. For example, this may be the case where many different classes of shares are issued to employees – say A, B, C and D ordinary shares – that simply carried a right to a dividend and had no other meaningful rights in the company. In the author's view, such an arrangement would be particularly vulnerable to a challenge by HMRC under *ITEPA 2003, Pt 7, Ch 4*, especially where the salary levels of the employees were materially below commercial rates. The frequency of dividend payments may also be a factor. If HMRC succeeded in establishing that the arrangements fell within *ITEPA 2003, Pt 7, Ch 4*, the dividends would be taxed as employment income subject to PAYE and NIC. The use of 'alphabet share' schemes is likely to be less prevalent after the post-5 April 2016 increase in dividend tax rates (see 9.12).

Dividends paid on 'fully-fledged' ordinary shares provided to employees should be relatively robust from any HMRC attack (see also 5.3 for additional commentary). This should also be the case where the ordinary shares are of a different class, provided they carry a full bundle of legal rights (see 9.29).

The use of separate classes of *ordinary* shares in 'husband and wife' companies should also be safe from any HMRC challenge (see 9.40) since these shares would *usually* be protected by the 'shares made available in the normal course of domestic [and] family…relationships' exemption in *ITEPA 2003, s 421B*.

Overseas dividends received by individuals

9.15   Some owner-managers may be able to successfully establish a non-resident company in order to expand their trade in an overseas country. However, unless sufficient care is taken, HMRC will often be able to show that all the (highest-level) decisions affecting the company are taken in the UK, and hence 'central management and control' abides in the UK. This would make the company resident in the UK (under the rule in *De Beers Consolidated Mines Ltd v Howe* 5 TC 198) and therefore any dividends paid will be 'UK-source' and taxed as in 9.12 and 9.12A above.

Overseas dividends are taxed in the same way as dividends from UK resident companies (see 9.14) with the UK tax being reduced by any available double tax relief (ie relief for any overseas tax already suffered on them). Since 6 April 2016, overseas dividends are only grossed-up for any overseas withholding tax – there is no 'added' 10% tax credit.

Taxation of dividends/distributions received by UK companies

9.16   The corporation tax treatment of dividends received by UK companies changed in July 2009. Under the previous regime, dividends/distributions from UK resident companies were exempt from corporation tax under *CTA 2009 s 1285*. *Dividends* from non-resident companies were taxable, subject to double tax relief for foreign withholding tax and (for 10% plus shareholdings) underlying foreign tax.

The taxation of overseas dividends had been challenged under the rules of the EC Treaty in Test Claimants in the *FII Group Litigation v HMRC* [2010] STC 1251. The European Court of Justice (ECJ) referred the matter to the UK courts, which broadly concluded that, for the most part, the UK taxation of foreign dividends was in contravention of the EU treaty. The UK Government therefore had to do something about it!

The *FA 2009* therefore introduced rules to put the corporate tax treatment of UK and non-resident company dividends on to a level-footing. Unfortunately, the rules are fairly complex.

Broadly, *CTA 2009, s 931A* taxes all dividends/distributions (irrespective of their source) and then grants various widespread exemptions. Different rules apply for dividends received by a small company (under EU rules) (see 9.17) and 'medium/large' sized companies (see 19.18).

For these purposes, a recipient company is treated as 'small' if it is a 'micro or small' enterprise as defined in the Annex to the Commission Recommendation 2003/361/EC which broadly means that

●   it must have fewer than 50 employees; *and*

●   both its annual turnover and balance sheet value must not exceed €10 million.

Where a company is part of larger group, it will need to include staff headcount/turnover/balance sheet data from its fellow group companies in making this assessment

Small companies

9.17   Small companies are exempt on their dividend/distribution received provided all the *CTA 2009, s 931B* conditions are satisfied:

●   The paying company is UK resident or resident in a 'qualifying territory' (ie one which has a double tax treaty with the UK containing a non-discrimination provision).

- No tax deduction must have been given for the dividend/distribution in the hands of the paying/distributing company.

- The distribution must not be made 'as part of a tax advantage scheme', where one of the main purposes of the distribution is to obtain a tax advantage.

However, for technical reasons, distributions which represent an 'excessive' commercial return on securities (*CTA 2010, s 1000(1), para E*) *or* interest relating to certain types of securities which fall within *CTA 2010, s 1000(1),* paragraph F are *not* covered by the exemption. This is because

- 'Excessive' interest will generally fall to be dealt with under the transfer pricing rules;

- Other types of interest return on securities will generally already be exempted under the rule in *CTA 2010.*

Other companies

9.18   Dividends/distributions received by other (ie non-small) companies are exempt provided they fall within *one* of the five exempt classes listed in *CTA 2009, ss 931F–931I* (and do not contravene any of the specific anti-avoidance rules):

1   Dividends/distributions made in respect of *non-redeemable* ordinary shares.

For these purposes, an ordinary share is one that does not carry any present or future preferential right to dividends or to a company's assets on a winding-up. The underlying logic for excluding redeemable shares is probably due to the fact that HMRC regards them more in the nature of debt than equity.

2   Dividends/distributions from a 'controlled company' – which will often be invoked to exempt dividends from UK and overseas group companies.

3   'Portfolio-type' dividends/distributions received from a company in which the recipient holds less than 10% of the share capital.

4   Dividends (but not distributions) paid from 'good' profits (ie profits that do not include the results of transactions designed to achieve a UK tax reduction).

5   Dividends (but not distributions) from shares classified as loans under the loan relationship rules.

In complex cases, reference should be made to the anti-avoidance rules in *CTA 2009, ss 931J–931Q.*

Dividend reporting from 2017/18

9.19   From 6 April 2016, dividends no longer carry a 10% tax credit. Therefore, dividend certificates will simply need to show the cash dividend paid and other relevant details.

A sample shareholder dividend certificate is shown below.

DIVIDEND TAX VOUCHER
Company name – CAPUTO GARDENING SUPPLIES LTD
Final dividend for the period ended 31 December 2017
Shareholder
Mrs Ruth Black 19 Esther Avenue Luton LU3 3OK
Shareholding   2,000 £1 Ordinary Shares   Date paid: 11 June 2017
Dividend   £90,000
Sebastian Black
Company Secretary
You have a legal obligation to keep records of dividends for tax purposes

TIMING PAYMENTS OF DIVIDENDS

Rules for determining when a dividend is paid

9.20   It is well established in company law that the declaration of a dividend creates an immediate debt unless the company specifies a future date for payment. The legal position for a final and interim dividend differs slightly.

A final dividend is due and payable on the date it is declared and approved by shareholders at the AGM, unless the resolution declaring it specifies some later date (*Hurll v IRC* (1922) 8 TC 292). Thus, a debt is created when a final dividend is declared, which can be discharged by a cash payment, a cheque sent to the shareholder, or the company crediting the shareholder's account with the company or third party.

An interim dividend could be rescinded by the directors at any time until it is actually paid out to the shareholders. Consequently, an interim dividend only becomes due when it is *paid*. Thus, under company law, an interim dividend cannot be paid by 'crediting' an account.

However, HMRC's *Company Tax Manual* (CTM 20095) treats dividends as being paid when 'a right to draw on the dividend exists', such as when they are credited to an account (*Potel v IRC* (1970) 46 TC 658). Of course, it may be that the relevant credit is not made until a later accounting period, such as when the company's statutory accounts are prepared. For these reasons, it may be desirable to ensure physical payment of the dividend with the subsequent loan-back of those funds to the company (with an appropriate credit to the owner-manager's/shareholder's loan account).

Planning issues

9.21   The directors of the family company will normally have complete flexibility as to the timing and amount of dividend payments (assuming the company has Model Articles or the former Articles of Association follow article 70 in Table A or similar).

The directors/shareholders should therefore try to regulate the timing of dividends to ensure they make best use of their personal allowances, dividend lower rate bands and other reliefs. For example, it would not be efficient to pay substantial dividends in one tax year, if the directors/shareholders have little or no other income in an earlier and/or later year. Delaying a dividend until after 5 April can also provide a valuable deferral of the higher rate or top tax liability (depending on the individual's prior year income/self-assessment tax payment position, etc).

It is not possible to 'backdate' a dividend – this is likely to be regarded as deliberate false accounting. Any backdated dividend (if recognised at all) will be treated as being made on the actual date of payment for tax purposes.

DIVIDEND WAIVERS

Tax effect of dividend waivers

9.22   Dividend waivers are often used for planning purposes. Broadly, a dividend waiver involves a shareholder waiving their entitlement to the dividend before the right to the dividend has accrued. A dividend waiver can therefore be seen as a method of reducing the income the shareholder receives from the company.

A dividend waiver will be effective for income tax purposes if it is made before the right to the dividend has accrued. An interim dividend will not be counted as the shareholder's income provided the waiver is executed before the specified date of payment. Similarly, a waiver of a final dividend must be made before the relevant Board resolution is passed – in practice, it is normal to execute the waiver before the company's AGM (as a final dividend requires the shareholders' approval) (see 9.2).

In order for it to be legally effective, a dividend waiver must be made by a Deed. A Deed must be signed by the shareholder waiving the dividend and formally witnessed. The author has seen a number of cases where shareholders have simply written a letter to confirm their dividend waivers, which is not sufficient. In one particular case, the executors of a deceased shareholder sought to claim the purported waived dividends for the past six years from the company. Even though the deceased shareholder had clearly intended to fully waive his dividends, the executors were pressing for the unpaid dividends (some £600,000), which gave rise to a difficult legal dispute!

To prevent a dividend waiver from being treated as a transfer of value for IHT purposes, the shareholder must waive his right to the dividend (every time) by deed within the 12 months before it becomes payable [*IHTA 1984, s 15*].

Application of settlement legislation to dividend waivers

9.23   A dividend waiver could also be used to divert income to one or more of the other shareholders. HMRC may challenge such dividend waivers on the basis that the waiver constitutes a 'settlement' for income tax purposes. *ITTOIA 2005, s 620(1)* defines a settlement as including 'any disposition, trust, covenant, agreement or arrangement' – this wide definition would clearly catch a dividend waiver.

Any income arising from a settlement will be deemed to be the settlor's income where they or their spouse/civil partner has an interest in the settled property [*ITTOIA 2005, ss 624* and *625*]. Similarly, the settlements legislation also deems income paid to an unmarried (under 18) child of the settlor to be the settlor's for income tax purposes, unless the total does not exceed £100 per tax year for each child [*ITTOIA 2005, s 629*]. (See also 9.43 for detailed analysis of parental settlements for 'minor' children.)

Vulnerable situations

9.24   Case law demonstrates that an element of 'bounty' is necessary for the settlement provisions to apply (see, for example, *Bulmer v CIR* (1966) 44 TC 1; *CIR v Plummer* [1979] STC 793).

The requirement for the relevant arrangement to be bounteous was reaffirmed by the House of Lords in *Jones v Garnett* [2007] UKHL 35, although Lord Hoffmann preferred to say that the transaction must involve a benefit that would *not* have been provided at arm's length!

In the context of a dividend waiver, HMRC takes the view that 'bounty' is present where the waiver enables one or more of the shareholders (legally) to receive a larger dividend than would have been possible had no waiver been made.

9.25   Numerous cases have confirmed that dividend waivers can fall within the settlement rules. HMRC's Trusts Settlements & Estates Manual (at para TSEM4225) provides an indication of the factors that HMRC will consider when determining whether to apply the settlements legislation. These are summarised as follows:

- The level of retained profits, including the retained profits of subsidiary companies, is insufficient to allow the same rate of dividend to be paid on all issued share capital.

- Although there are sufficient retained profits to pay the same rate of dividend per share for the year in question, there has been a succession of waivers over several years where the total dividends payable in the absence of the waivers exceed accumulated realised profits.

- The non-waiving shareholders are persons whom the waiving shareholder can reasonably be regarded as wishing to benefit by the waiver.

- The non-waiving shareholder would pay less tax on the dividend than the waiving shareholder

In practice, HMRC is therefore only likely to take the 'settlement' point where the dividend waiver is considered to create a tax advantage.

Dividend waivers are often attacked where they have been used to increase the dividends paid to the proprietor's spouse or children or to the trustees of an accumulation and maintenance trust for his children.

Donovan and McLaren v HMRC

9.26   These principles were illustrated in the recent First-Tier Tribunal decision in *Donovan and McLaren v HMRC* [2014] UKFTT 048 (TC). The facts of the case were briefly as follows:

- Mr Donovan (Mr D) and Mr McLaren (Mr M) each had a 50% shareholding in Victory Fire Ltd (VFL). In 2001, they agreed to issue a 10% shareholding in VFL to each of their wives.

- In subsequent tax years, dividends were paid to the four shareholders. However, Mr D and Mr M made annual dividend waivers, enabling their wives to receive a larger share of the total dividend than would have been due by reference to their 10% holdings.

- A comparison between the dividend entitlements and the actual dividend payments over the relevant years showed the following:

Year ended 31 March	Dividends paid	Mr D's and Mr M's dividend entitlement (based on shareholding) Each	Dividends actually received by Mr D and Mr M Each	Mrs D's and Mrs M's dividend entitlement (based on shareholding) Each	Dividends actually received by Mrs D and Mrs M
	£	£	£	£	£
2006	111,240	44,496	27,000	11,124	28,620
2007	117,240	46,896	28,200	11,724	30,420
2008	128,964	51,586	30,200	12,896	34,282
2009	112,500	45,000	30,200	11,250	26,050
2010	130,000	52,000	33,000	13,000	32,000

Thus, for example, in the year ended 31 March 2010, the wives each received £32,000 (24.6% of the total dividend) whereas they would only have received £13,000 (10% of the total dividend) on a normal dividend payout.

HMRC argued that the settlements legislation applied to the dividend waivers, so that the arrangements were ineffective. Thus, as settlors, Mr D and Mr M would also be taxed on the dividend income 'diverted' to their wives.

The taxpayers appealed against HMRC's additional assessments, but their appeals were rejected on the following grounds:

- Mr D's and Mr M's contention that the waivers were motivated by commercial reasons was not convincing. The dividend waivers were clearly intended to take advantage of the wives' lower income tax rate bands so as to make an overall saving.

- The settlement rules can apply where there were arrangements, which used a company's shares to divert income – there did not necessarily have to be a tax avoidance motive (per *Jones v Garnett* [2007] UKHL at para 48 – see 9.29). A key question was whether Mr D and Mr M would have entered into the relevant arrangements with a third party at arm's length.

- Based on the facts, the waivers would not have been made when dealing at arm's length with a third party. This therefore involved the necessary element of bounty, which is sufficient to create a settlement within *ITTOIA 2005, s 620*.

- The wives had clearly benefited from the dividend waivers. The dividend income was property in which Mr D and Mr M had an interest within the terms of *ITTOIA 2005, s 625*, since the income was payable to their wives.

Importantly, dividend waivers cannot fall within the spousal 'outright gifts' exemption since they are simply a right to income. This was distinguished from the *Jones v Garnett (Arctic Systems)* ruling (see 9.29 and 9.31) because the essential arrangement here was *not* the allotment of the shares to Mr D's/ Mr M's wives but the waiver of the dividends.

It seems surprising that this case was taken since this is a classic case of how *not* to structure payment of the spousal dividends. The taxpayer was always going to lose since dividend waivers that give spouses more than they would be entitled to on a pro-rata distribution of the reserves will always be a settlement involving a transfer of income. And since this involved a transfer of income, the 'inter-spousal' outright gifts exemption was never going to be available.

Buck v HMRC

9.26A In the earlier case of *Buck v HMRC* [2008] SpC 716, the Special Commissioner, Sir Stephen Oliver QC, gave a similar ruling. In this case, Mr Buck (sole director) owned 9,999 out of the issued 10,000 ordinary shares.

His then wife owed the other share. Mr Buck had waived his dividend entitlement for the years ended 31 March 1999 and 31 March 2000, which enabled the company to pay a £35,000 dividend to his wife for each year.

The distributable profits at 31 March 1999 and 31 March 2000 were £46,287 and £46,694 respectively. Hence, the dividends paid to Mrs Buck would have been impossible without the dividend waivers. (In fact, without Mr Buck's dividend waiver, the company would have required around £300 million of reserves to provide his wife with a dividend of £35,000 on her pro-rata share!)

It was held that these arrangements were a settlement since they would not have been entered into had the individuals been acting at arm's length. The inference drawn from the facts was that Mr Buck waived his entitlements so that his wife could receive the dividend income. Furthermore, Sir Stephen Oliver also held that the outright gifts exemption did *not* apply in the case of a dividend waiver. There was no outright gift – merely a waiver of dividends (ie a right to income).

Provided above mentioned problems are avoided, there is no reason why dividend waivers should not be made in commercially justifiable cases. It is still important to follow the relevant legal and practical requirements for a valid dividend waiver, such as the need to draw up a formal deed of waiver that is signed, dated, witnessed and lodged with the company. To be effective for income tax purposes, the dividend waiver must be executed before the right to the dividend arises. Briefly, interim dividends must be waived before payment. A waiver of a final dividend should take place before the shareholders – often at the AGM – approve the final dividend.

It is generally preferable to avoid repetitive dividend waivers each year. HMRC often look at the pattern of dividend waivers made on a regular basis to determine whether there is a diversion of income as demonstrated by the *Donovan and McLaren* case. The use of different classes of shares to pay separate levels of dividend may be a more elegant solution (see 9.28).

Preventing a potential HMRC settlement challenge

9.27   Based on HMRC practice and the ruling in *Buck* above, it should be possible to resist an HMRC attack under the 'settlement' provisions if it can be demonstrated that the dividend declared per share (see 9.2) multiplied by the number of shares in issue does not exceed the amount of the company's distributable reserves.

HMRC could only argue that 'bounty' had occurred where the dividend declared could not be satisfied out of the current distributable profits unless the relevant waiver was made ie the waiver would enable the other shareholder(s) to receive a greater dividend than would otherwise have been possible. Under the settlement legislation, this element would be deemed to be the income of the shareholder executing the waiver (ie the settlor) and therefore taxed in their hands.

Example 3

Effect of dividend waiver

Cresswell Ltd has an issued share capital of 100 £1 ordinary shares, owned as to 20% by Mr Aaron and 80% by The Cresswell Children's Trust (which is a discretionary trust for Mr Aaron's minor children).

At 31 March 2014, it has distributable profits of £200,000.

If a dividend of £1,000 per share is declared and Mr Aaron waives his entitlement before the right to the dividend accrues, there is no 'bounty'.

On the other hand, if the company declares a dividend of £2,400 per share in the knowledge that Mr Aaron is going to waive his dividend, HMRC would argue that 'bounty' had occurred and under the parental settlement provisions, Mr Aaron would be taxed on the 'dividend' diverted.

The relevant figures are summarised below:

Dividend declared	£1,000 per share		£2,400 per share	
	£	£	£	£
Distributable profits		200,000		200,000
Less Dividend declared	100,000		240,000	
Amount waived (20%)	(20,000)		(48,000)	
Dividend paid		(80,000)		(192,000)
Retained profits		120,000		8,000

USING SEPARATE CLASSES OF SHARES

9.28   Dividend waivers are frequently used to avoid all or part of the declared dividends going to non-passive or 'non-working' shareholders. To avoid the perennial problem of entering into dividend waivers, a more elegant solution would be to sub-divide the company's ordinary share capital into two (or more) classes of shares.

However, this does not automatically by-pass the settlement rules. HMRC considers that it may be able to challenge certain arrangements involving the use of different classes of shares. For example, HMRC may seek to apply the settlement rules where the level of dividend paid on a particular class of share could *not* have been paid (by reference to the available reserves) without a bounteous arrangement to pay no or minimal dividends on the other class of shares (see HMRC para TSEM4225 – example 2).

However, *provided they are used sensibly*, the use of separate classes of shares would give the required flexibility to declare (different) dividends on each separate class. .

In most cases, each class of shares would simply have the right to enjoy dividends on their shares, but would be reliant on the directors to declare dividends on an annual basis. Of course, if one class of shares always benefits to the detriment of the other class, the shareholders of that class may be able to bring a competent claim for unfair prejudice (see also 9.40). If properly structured, the creation of separate classes of shares would qualify as a reorganisation of share capital within *TCGA 1992, ss 126* and *127*. It is important to ensure that the participating shareholders must retain the same economic rights.

A share reorganisation should normally be a 'tax neutral' event for the shareholder, with the 'new' shares stepping into the shoes' of their old shares.

If there is a material variation in a shareholder's rights after the 'reorganisation', HMRC may consider a value shifting charge under *TCGA 1992, s 29(2)*. However, in practice, provided the company is an unquoted trading company or holding company of a trading group, it should normally be possible to make a business asset 'hold-over' election under *TCGA 1992, s 165* (see 13.14–13.23).

PROVIDING DIVIDEND INCOME FOR THE SPOUSE

Income-shifting/income splitting – an overview

9.29   Since independent taxation, many married couples (or civil partners) have made useful tax savings by structuring their affairs so as to ensure that both spouses use up their personal allowances and basic rate tax bands. In more recent times, this practice has become known as income splitting or income-shifting.

For owner-managers, this strategy is a relatively easy one to implement. Typically, the owner manager could arrange to gift or issue an appropriate amount of shares to their spouse. The company could then pay sufficient dividends that would result in little or no tax in the hands of that spouse.

For example, in 2017/18, it should be possible for a spouse (with no other taxable income) to receive a dividend of (say) £45,000, which would attract tax of only £2,137 (see 2.36).

The landmark *Arctic Systems* case (*Jones v Garnett* [2007] UKHL 35) taught us that it was not so easy after all. Although Mr Jones eventually won his long running battle with HMRC, the case had to go all the way to the (then) House of Lords for a definitive ruling. The *Arctic Systems* case received considerable media attention, perhaps due to the fact that it was widely perceived to be a 'David v Goliath' battle – the small owner managed business pitted against the might of HMRC.

The *Arctic Systems* case involved an important principle of tax law. It asked whether HMRC could overturn the payment of dividends to a spouse and treat them as her husband's income for tax purposes (thus negating the tax savings). Since *Arctic Systems*, we have seen further cases coming before the Tribunals posing more or less the same questions.

Potential HMRC challenge under settlements legislation

9.30   In the mid-1990s, the Inland Revenue (as it was then) started to attack arrangements that provided dividend income to spouses in owner-managed companies. It employed the settlements legislation as its fiscal weapon, even though this law dated back to the 1930s.

The settlement legislation has been around in various guises since 1938 and is primarily aimed at situations where income has been diverted from the taxpayer to another party who pays little or no tax on that income. (Anyone who makes a settlement is called a 'settlor' and a settlement may be created directly or through an indirect provision of funds.) These rules apply where, amongst other things, the settlor *or their spouse (or civil partner)* retains an interest in the property transferred.

In common with most other anti-avoidance legislation, the tentacles of the settlement definition are widely spread. An individual 'settlor' will be treated as creating a 'settlement' for income tax purposes if they make any disposition, trust, covenant, agreement or arrangement or transfer of assets [*ITTOIA 2005, s 620(1)*]. It has been left to the courts to determine the ambit of this definition and there are a reasonable body of precedents dating back to times when personal income tax rates were exorbitant (at least by today's standards!).

It will be appreciated that the payment of dividends to the wife would normally be facilitated by the creation of a new class of shares or by the husband transferring some of his existing shareholding.

A settlement may be created without any formal (trust) documentation and may therefore potentially apply to many income-splitting arrangements, such as where a 'principal' shareholder has diverted 'income' that they have effectively 'earned' within a corporate structure to their spouse.

If an arrangement is caught by the settlement rules, the relevant income would be treated as the settlor's income under *ITTOIA 2005, s 625*. Thus, if HMRC is successful, the hoped for tax advantage would be completely negated, since the husband ('the settlor') would have been taxed on the dividend instead (at their highest tax rate). However, in the case of spouses (and civil partners), there is an important exemption for outright gifts between spouses (and civil partners), which was held to apply in the *Arctic Systems* case (see 9.38).

The landmark *Arctic Systems* case

9.31   The tax arguments surrounding spousal dividends in owner-managed companies came to a head in the *Arctic Systems* case.

By the time it reached the House of Lords, HMRC had spent some seven years embroiled in a legal battle with a small 'husband and wife' owned IT company called Arctic Systems. The husband (Mr Jones) was responsible for earning all the company's profits on computer consultancy contracts but drew only a minimal salary. Mr Jones was the sole director and chairman of the company, which enabled him to control both the day-to-day and the strategic management of the company. However, the 50:50 share-owning structure gave him the ability to pay large (tax-efficient) dividends to his wife (Mrs Jones).

9.32   To determine whether a settlement had been created in the *Arctic Systems* case, the Law Lords focused on construing the meaning of an 'arrangement' (see 9.30). They reviewed most of the leading case law authorities.

- An arrangement only constitutes a settlement if there is an 'element of bounty' (*CIR v Leiner* (1964) 41 TC 589 and *CIR v Plummer* [1979] STC 793). Lord Hoffmann preferred to put it another way – 'the settlor must provide a benefit that would not have been provided in an arm's length transaction'

- Lord Hoffmann found support in *Crossland v Hawkins* [1961] 39 TC 493 which (on similar legislation dealing with parental settlements in favour of their minor children) took a broad and realistic view of the taxpayer's arrangements.

- Further assistance was provided by *Butler v Wildin* [1989] STC 22 which involved an arrangement to benefit the infant children of two brothers. In this case, the children had subscribed for shares in a company set up by their parents (the brothers) using money provided by grandparents. Lord Hoffmann found authority here for saying that the relevant time for determining whether there was an arrangement was when the company was acquired and the shares allotted to the children. However, he would have found it difficult to say that the subsequent events (such as entering into third-party agreements and property development) were *not* part of the arrangements. It was the expectation of such events and the hope of profit that gave the 'element of bounty' to the arrangement.

9.33   Based on the existing jurisprudence, their Lordships found that the 'reward' structure set up by the Joneses did in fact create a settlement. Lord Hoffmann concurred with much of HMRC's arguments:

'… It was not a transaction at arms' length because Mr Jones would never have agreed to the transfer of half the issued share capital, carrying with it the expectation of substantial dividends, to a stranger who merely undertook to provide the paid services which Mrs Jones provided. That provided the necessary "element of bounty". The object of the arrangement was to keep the entire income within the family but to gain the benefit of Mrs Jones's lower rates. The dividends paid to Mrs Jones arose under the arrangement. Mr Jones, by working for the company, provided it with the funds, which enabled the dividends to be paid. He was therefore a settlor within the meaning of section 660G (2). As Mrs Jones was the spouse of Mr Jones, he was to be treated as having an interest in the income derived from her share and that income was therefore treated as his income'.

In giving his judgment, Lord Neuberger made a notable observation –

'If the parties intended an element of bounty to accrue, and that intended element of bounty does indeed eventuate, then, absent any other good reason to the contrary, there is indeed an "arrangement"'.

9.34   The House of Lords therefore had little difficulty in finding that Mr Jones *had* created a settlement in which his wife had an interest. The settlement therefore fell within (what is now) *ITTOIA 2005, s 624*. This provides that where a person creates a settlement but either they *or their spouse* (or civil partner) retains an interest in it, the income of that settlement is treated as belonging to them for income tax purposes.

Since the dividends were funded by Mr Jones' work, he was the settlor of the settlement. Mr Jones was treated as having a requisite interest in the dividend income since it was payable to his spouse.

9.35 Mr Jones did *not* therefore win on the 'settlement' point. *Arctic Systems* confirmed that any *gratuitous* transfer or issue of shares to a spouse is likely to be treated as a settlement; despite the fact there is no formal agreement or trust document. There will, of course, be cases where shares are provided on a sufficiently commercially defensible basis so as not to constitute a settlement, as illustrated by *Patmore v HMRC* [2010] TC 00619 (see 9.36).

Contrast with the *Patmore* case – looking at the totality of arrangements

9.36 Mr and Mrs Patmore had purchased the shares of an engineering company for £320,000, with the first instalment of £100,000 being funded by a second mortgage on their home. Their accountant advised them to reorganise the company's shares into separate A ordinary voting shares and B 'non-voting' shares.

Mrs Patmore ended up with only 2% of the A shares and 10% of the B shares with the remaining shares of each class being owned by her husband.

For a number of years, large dividends were paid to Mrs Patmore on her B 'non-voting' shares, which she then passed to her husband to repay the outstanding debt for the original purchase of the company.

In HMRC's eyes, this very much looked like a settlement. It argued that Mr Patmore used his control of the company to pay these dividends to enable his wife to benefit from a lower tax charge. HMRC therefore sought to tax Mr Patmore (as the settlor) on the B share dividends received by his wife.

However, the couple's adviser indicated that the A and B share structure simply gave the required flexibility to pay dividends to Mrs Patmore without necessarily paying dividends to her husband. Further, it was stressed this reflected Mrs Patmore's higher risk on the mortgage liability since she had no daily involvement in the company.

9.37 The tribunal judge, Barbara Mosedale, considered that the tax efficiency of the share structure was not a significant factor since the legislation did not impose a 'motive' test. Following Lord Hoffmann's approach in the *Arctic Systems* case, she concluded that the courts should take 'a broad and realistic view of all the arrangements ... in settlements-related cases'. She concluded that HMRC had not done so in this particular case.

Although HMRC agreed that Mrs Patmore had a joint and equal responsibility for the debt incurred on the purchase of the company, Judge Mosedale found that this analysis was not followed to its logical conclusion; this being that Mrs Patmore was entitled to half of the acquired shares and an 'appropriate share of the dividends'.

Somewhat helpfully, the judge concluded that there had been an inequitable division of the A ordinary shares between the couple. Mrs Patmore should have had 50% of the A shares but ended up with a very small shareholding, which meant there was a constructive trust in her favour. The shares allocated to Mrs Patmore did not reflect the amount of her original investment in acquiring the company. Thus, there was no bounty from Mr Patmore and hence no settlement had been created for tax purposes. Interestingly, the judge resolved matters by allocating the dividends declared on all classes of shares between the couple on an 'equal' basis!

Arctic Systems – HMRC loses on the 'outright gift' exemption

9.38   Back to the Joneses in the *Arctic Systems* case – the Law Lords found in their favour because they held that the important 'outright gifts' exemption (in what is now *ITTOIA 2005, s 626*) for inter-spousal settlements applied.

This exemption had been introduced as part of the independent taxation reforms in 1990, specifically to enable spouses to make outright gifts to each other without fear of the settlement rules being applied.

This valuable 'escape clause' applies where there is an outright gift of assets that does *not* represent an entire or substantial right to income. In *Arctic Systems*, the Law Lords held that the *ordinary shares* provided to Mrs Jones were more than a pure right to income – they had a bundle of rights, including the right to attend and vote at general meetings, rights to capital growth on a sale, and to obtain a return of capital on a winding-up.

HMRC contended that since Mrs Jones subscribed for her share there was no *gift,* but this point was quickly rejected by both Lord Hoffmann and Lord Neuberger. HMRC's analysis was too narrow. If there was sufficient bounty to create a settlement then there must be a gift on any normal interpretation of the word. It did not therefore matter that Mrs Jones's share was purchased from the company formation agents rather than being gifted to her by her husband.

9.39   Thus, the key conclusions emanating from the *Arctic Systems* judgement was that whilst the shareholding arrangements constituted a settlement, they were exempted under the outright gifts 'escape clause'.

Thus, provided a spouse (or civil partner) is provided with fully-fledged ordinary shares (carrying the normal full range of rights), any dividends paid on the shares should be treated as their income – the settlements legislation would not apply because the 'outright gifts' exemption would be available.

Many advisers prudently recommend that dividends paid to a spouse should be paid into their own separate bank account (as opposed to the couples' joint account).

It is perhaps worth noting that HMRC did not take its loss in the House of Lords very well. In fact, almost before the ink was dry on the judgment, the Treasury told us that such arrangements were 'unacceptable and unfair' and it was therefore going to introduce legislation to counter such income splitting or income-shifting practices. However, attempts to introduce anti-avoidance legislation were quickly derailed in the face of a massive 'thumbs-down' by the professional bodies and industry groups. Probably as a result of this collective resistance, the last Labour Government moved 'income-splitting' onto the 'back-burner'.

USE OF JOINTLY-HELD SHARES FOR MARRIED COUPLES

9.40 Since 6 April 2004, the use of jointly-held *shares in close companies* (see 1.3) no longer achieves any worthwhile tax advantages.

The *FA 2004* amended the legislation so that dividends paid on jointly-held shares by married couples are taxed in accordance with their underlying beneficial interests. Thus, if the underlying beneficial ownership in the jointly-held shares was split (say) 95% husband: 5% wife, the husband and wife would be taxed on 95% and 5% of the dividend respectively.

The same tax treatment applies to shares jointly held by civil partners.

PRACTICAL ISSUES WITH SPOUSE SHAREHOLDINGS AND DISCLOSURE ON TAX RETURNS

9.41 The House of Lords ruling in the *Arctic Systems* case demonstrates that the 'settlement' legislation can only be used to attack income-splitting arrangements in very small 'personal-service' type companies where the company's income stream solely arises from the efforts of one of the spouses but large dividends are paid to the other. In such cases, there is likely to be a settlement. This means that shareholding structures used to benefit minor children could also be vulnerable (since there is no equivalent *ITTOIA 2005, s 626* exemption).

The question is: where should the 'dividing' line be drawn? Even before the *Arctic Systems* case was first heard, the then Inland Revenue had expressed the view that larger businesses which had a number of employees, trading premises, capital equipment, and so on, would *not* be caught by these rules (see April 2003 *Tax Bulletin*). Presumably this is on the basis that the profit earning capacity of the company was a 'team effort' and not down to the work of just one person.

Furthermore, where a wife pays full market value for her shares (out of her own resources), it is reasonably clear that the dividends subsequently paid out on those shares would represent a normal commercial return on a proper business transaction with no element of bounty (see 9.33). HMRC also generally accepts that the issue of founder shares at par is also a commercial arrangement where the couple are both *fully involved* in the company. Similarly, there should be no difficulties where the main earner is paid a proper market rate for their services or where the couple's contributions to the company were more or less equal.

9.42   Even where the structure of the arrangements fall to be treated as a settlement, the House of Lords decision in the *Arctic Systems* case now confirms that the inter-spousal gifts exemption provides a valuable fall-back position (see 9.38). However, this will only be the case if ordinary shares with the full range of rights are used, including the right to vote and to receive a surplus on a winding up. (Company law also provides rights for members who are unfairly prejudiced and matrimonial law would also recognise the capital value of a wife's share.) Since the settlement rules affect civil partnerships in the same way as married couples, shares transferred between civil partners also attract the 'outright gifts' exemption.

9.43   Taxpayers (and/or their advisors) are required to self-assess any tax liability under the settlement legislation. In practice, there are likely to be shareholding structures and business arrangements that cover the full length of the 'acceptable/unacceptable' tax spectrum. Each case should therefore be considered carefully to determine whether it falls on the 'right side of the line'. Clearly, where cases are on 'all fours' with the circumstances in *Arctic Systems*, the taxpayer will be entitled to the 'outright gifts' exemption (see 9.38). In borderline or uncertain cases, taxpayers would generally give themselves the benefit of any doubt as to whether or not they report any income tax liability under the settlement provisions.

Following the Court of Appeal decision in *Langham v Veltema* [2004] STC 544 (see 4.57–4.58), a later discovery assessment can only be avoided where the precise point on which protection from discovery is required is brought to the attention of the Inspector who deals with the taxpayer's affairs; ie it is not sufficient to rely on information that may be held elsewhere within HMRC.

9.44   Some comfort can perhaps be gleaned from the judgement of Sir Stephen Oliver QC in *Mr & Mrs Bird v HMRC* [2008] Spc 720. Apart from ruling that the relevant arrangements by Mr & Mrs Bird constituted a parental settlement (see also 9.46 for details), he had to decide whether or not the Birds' failure to report the daughters' dividends on their own tax returns (under the settlement provisions) constituted fraudulent or negligent conduct (as contended by HMRC). If it was, HMRC was entitled to raise discovery assessments outside the five-year and ten-month time limit (as the rule was then) in *TMA 1970, s 34*. However, Sir Stephen Oliver rejected the charge of 'fraudulent or negligent conduct' primarily on the grounds that this 'would require a high level of constructive reasoning ... [and] demand a sophistication that is beyond what is expected of the assumed reasonable taxpayer'.

Indeed, the only relevant box in the 1995 tax return was headed 'Income and Capital from settlements for which you have provided funds'. It was also found that HMRC had failed to adduce any positive evidence that the daughters' funds came from the Birds. Thus, the Birds succeeded in escaping from three out of the five years under review.

USING SEPARATE CLASSES OF SHARES TO 'STREAM' DIVIDEND PAYMENTS

9.45   Many companies owned by married couples use different classes of ordinary shares to provide flexibility with dividend payments – see 9.28. (If a single class of ordinary shares were used, dividends would have to be paid on a pro-rata basis to the number of shares held. Although some adjustment could be made by dividend waivers, this can be cumbersome and may trigger the settlement legislation – see 9.22–9.27)

Where a husband and wife each own a separate class of ordinary shares, the director(s) can decide the level of dividend to be declared on each class of shares. The strict legal position is that each shareholder is reliant on the board of directors declaring appropriate dividends from the available profits and would not have any right over the retained reserves (unless this is specifically provided for in the company's articles).

SHARES PROVIDED TO CHILDREN, OTHER FAMILY MEMBERS AND FRIENDS

Application of the settlement rules

9.46   It is perhaps worth emphasising that the 'outright gifts' exemption in 9.36 only applies to inter-spousal settlements (and those made between registered civil partners). Such protection is *not* available where shares are transferred to a settlor's unmarried minor child/children or a trust set up for their benefit. The House of Lords ruling in *Arctic Systems* is therefore likely to strengthen arguments by HMRC that shareholdings structures set up in small service-type companies constitute a settlement. Consequently, dividends paid out to (or for the benefit of) the settlor's children are very likely to be taxed on the settlor [*ITTOIA 2005, s 629*].

HMRC appears to take the view that the settlement legislation is capable of applying to cases where the dividend income goes to a 'co-habiting partner', another family member, or a friend, although it has not seemed to press this point in practice. The Revenue certainly considered this to be a possibility in example 2 in its April 2003 *Tax Bulletin* (RI 268), which dealt with a case with 'Aunt Jane' holding shares. This is based on the notion that the settlor's earning power is the property being transferred. Thus, the settlor's ability to withhold their services represents a retention of their interest in the settlement and is caught by the basic 'settlor-interested' settlement rule in *ITTOIA 2005, s 625* (previously *ICTA 1988, s 660A*). However, this line of thinking was firmly rejected by Mr Justice Park *in Jones v Garnett* [2005] STC 1667. He concluded that if Mr Jones's co-shareholder had been his sister, the settlement rules could *not* have applied.

Providing dividend income for children

9.47 From a legal viewpoint, it is perfectly possible for minor children to receive a transfer of shares in a company and be a full member and shareholder of the company (although the company has the power to refuse to register the transfer). A minor can at any time before reaching their 18th birthday repudiate the shares.

Children have their own personal allowances and lower/basic income tax rate bands. However, it is notoriously difficult for parents to exploit these advantages. The 'parental-settlement' provisions in *ITTOIA 2005, s 629* will nullify any transfer of income by a parent to their children (including step-children and adopted children) if they are under 18 and unmarried, subject to the *de minimis* rule allowing £100 for each child every year .

For example, if a parent transfers some shares to their son or daughter, any dividend paid on these shares whilst they are an unmarried minor is taxed in the transferor-parent's hands. On the other hand, it is possible for another member of a family to make a tax-effective transfer of shares to a minor child (provided it is not part of a wider arrangement which would cause the parent to be identified as the 'real' or indirect settlor). These issues do not arise where shares are held by the owner-manager's adult children (see 9.45).

Adult children

9.48 Once a child reaches their 18th birthday (or marries), the income is taxed on them (ie the parental-settlement rule ceases to bite). A gift of shares to provide dividend income after their 18th birthday therefore offers considerable tax advantages. (It will normally be possible for any capital gain arising on the deemed market value of the gifted shares to be held over under *TCGA 1992, s 165*, or it may fall within the parent's annual CGT exemption – see 13.14–13.23.)

Notwithstanding the post-5 April 2016 increases in dividend tax, it is still possible to pay reasonable levels of dividend at a relatively low tax cost to 'adult' children (who have little or no other taxable income) (see 2.36).

Parents may find this strategy a less painful way of financing the increasing costs of their children's further education. The dividend income can, of course, be applied by the child for any purpose or simply saved.

Minor children

9.49   The parental settlement rules ensure that parents cannot provide a tax-effective transfer of income to their minor children (see 9.23), even if the arrangements made to 'divert' the income are fairly subtle. This is well illustrated by the recent Special Commissioner's decision in *Mr & Mrs Bird v HMRC* [2008] Spc 720. This was a fairly complex case involving a family company which was initially run by Mr and Mrs Bird, who each held one share in C Ltd. In December 1994, Mr Bird's father died and his estate was left equally to each of the Birds' three daughters upon them reaching the age of 18. When Mr Bird's father died, the oldest daughter was 15 and the other twin daughters were ten.

In 1995 C Ltd wished to expand but had difficulty in raising funds. Consequently, in March 1995, Mr Bird (acting as sole executor of his father's estate) made unsecured (interest-bearing) loans from the estate to C Ltd – £7,000 (March 1995) and £54,364 (May 1995).

In April 1995, C Ltd issued further shares which resulted in each daughter having a 20% shareholding in the company (60% of the company was therefore then held by the daughters). C Ltd remained profitable and in each year paid dividends to all the shareholders (including the daughters) until it ceased trading in 2002.

Based on the evidence presented, the Special Commissioner, Sir Stephen Oliver QC concluded that the dividends paid to the daughters (until they reached the age of 18) constituted income under a parental settlement within *ICTA 1988, s 660B* (now *ITTOIA 2005, s 629*). Consequently the daughters' dividends were taxable on Mr and Mrs Bird (see also 9.41 for additional point in relation to discovery assessments).

There is, however, nothing to stop another member of the family, for example a grandparent, from transferring income to their grandchildren. In principle, the parental-settlement legislation should not apply, provided that the transfer of shares cannot in any way be linked to a wider arrangement with the parent (so that the parent is identified as the 'settlor'). For example, a transfer of shares by a parent to a grandparent as part of an arrangement to transfer them on to a grandchild is particularly vulnerable to challenge. In such cases, HMRC are likely to be able to sustain the argument that the parent was the 'real' settlor (see *Butler v Wildin* [1989] STC 22 (see 9.35)). It is also important to remember that HMRC can counteract any pre-ordained series of transactions under the *Furniss v Dawson* doctrine (see 1.11).

Furthermore, any reciprocal arrangements are specifically caught as a 'settlement' by *ITTOIA 2005, s 620(3)*. As a general rule, shares transferred to children by other family members or friends (on their own volition) should not be vulnerable to attack under the 'settlement' rules. It clearly helps if the transferors have previously held the shares for a lengthy period. This will enable the dividends paid on those shares to be treated as the child's own income (invariably with no further tax liability). However, as a child cannot give a valid receipt, the dividend income will be received by the parents as 'bare trustees', which could be used to pay school fees!

Some owner-managers may wish to consider placing some shares in a discretionary trust for the benefit of their children. Dividend income paid to such trusts is not caught by the parental-settlement rules *provided that the income is accumulated within the trust*. On the other hand, the parent-settlor would be taxed on any income paid out from the trust for their children's benefit (subject to the £100 per child *de minimis* limit).

It is not possible to avoid this rule by making capital payments from the trust as they would be matched with any undistributed income and taxed on the settlor under *ITTOIA 2005, s 633*. See Chapter 17 for a full discussion on trusts.

PLANNING CHECKLIST – DISTRIBUTION OF PROFITS AND DIVIDEND PLANNING

Company

- Directors must consider the legal requirements, the company's cash flow and working capital requirements when determining the amount and timing of dividend payments.

- Consider extraction of funds that are clearly surplus to the current/ future trading requirements to remove them from commercial risk, but this is subject to the tax costs of extracting them. Surplus cash arising from trading activities should not jeopardise a company's trading company status for entrepreneurs' relief purposes provided it is not actively managed as an investment.

- The company can time its dividend payments to suit the income tax position of the shareholder(s).

Working shareholders

- Despite the increase in dividend tax rates from 2016/17, it is still likely to be beneficial to use dividends (as opposed to bonuses) as a mechanism for extracting surplus profits.

- Shareholders may obtain longer credit period for payment of higher rate tax where additional dividends are paid early in tax year (subject to self-assessment interim payment position).

- Consider using of separate classes of shares to provide flexibility with the level of dividends paid to different (groups of) shareholders (but be sensible!).

- Dividends paid to spouses who undertake significant work for the business should not be caught by the settlement rules (provided the spouse has fully-fledged ordinary shares with substantive rights). Consider making use of spousal dividends to mitigate the effect of the owner managers' higher dividend tax rates. Spouses' dividend income should be 'freely' retained by them

- HMRC are likely to successfully challenge any contrived or aggressive schemes that purport to provide tax efficient dividends on what are essentially employment rewards or bonuses.

Other employees

- Not affected by dividend strategies.

Non-working shareholders

- Dividend waivers must be made in writing (by Deed) before the right to dividend vests.

- Those waiving dividends may be taxed on them if the waiver is made late.

- Following the landmark ruling by the House of Lords in the *Arctic Systems* case, tax-efficient dividends paid to a spouse (or civil partner) should be safe from any HMRC challenge, provided these emanate from ordinary shares (and not non-voting preference shares). Government plans to legislate in this area have been put on hold indefinitely!

- Consider potential advantages of paying dividends to adult children (for example, while they are in higher education, etc).

- Non-working shareholders may be invited to waive their dividends by working shareholders, but they cannot be compelled to do so.

Chapter 10

Pension Scheme Strategies

THE OWNER-MANAGER'S PERSPECTIVE

10.1   Owner-managers have generally used conventional methods of pension provision. Their fairly special position enables them to take, and 'their' company to obtain, full advantage of the various tax breaks on offer.

However, experience has shown that many owner-managers have become increasingly sceptical of traditional methods of providing for a future pension. The frequent changes and increasing complications to the approved pension rules have not helped matters.

However, following the radical 'shake-up' to pensions in *FA 2014*, individuals now have greater flexibility in accessing their pension savings from age 55 (see 10.41). This considerable relaxation to some extent is tainted by the introduction of a tapered annual allowance in *the F (No 2) A 2015* which limits tax relief on pension contributions paid by high-earners from 6 April 2016 (see 10.23).

Nevertheless, the ability to drawn pensions without any restrictions may be more appealing than some of the other ways owner-managers can provide for their future (such as Individual Savings Accounts (ISAs), property investment, etc).

Various investment projection models suggest that ISAs may prove more attractive for *high earners* wishing to *top up* their retirement funds. ISAs are likely to become even more beneficial given the introduction of the tapered annual allowance since April 2016. Furthermore, the *FA 2016* changes also increase the attraction of ISAs, including the potential 25% tax-free 'top-up' for lifetime ISAs (LISA) and the ability to pass on the ISA benefits to a spouse/ civil partner, which pension industry experts say will encourage young savers to opt out of 'auto enrolment' in favour of the LISA which can be accessed earlier.

Although ISAs do not receive any tax relief on funds paid in (currently £20,000 in 2017/18), they will grow within a tax-free vehicle and do not attract any tax when withdrawn. Contrastingly, pension 'savings' receive tax relief (albeit restricted in some cases) but are largely taxed when the pensions are received in retirement.

499

Other potential opportunities for tax-efficient investment include Enterprise Investment Schemes, Seed Enterprise Investment Schemes, Venture Capital Trusts, and Offshore Investments. It may also be worth considering investing for capital gains, which are currently taxed at a maximum rate of 20% (28% for residential property) when realised.

RESTRICTIONS IN PENSIONS TAX RELIEF

10.2   The tendency to look for other forms of retirement saving beyond pension funds has also been driven by the restrictions that have been placed on tax relief for pension contributions over the past few years. The combination of various new complications and the substantial reduction in the annual pension input allowance, has dissuaded many individuals from making significant contributions to their pension 'pots'. However, with the tapered reduction in the annual allowance for those with an 'adjusted income' of over £150,000, the attraction of traditional pensions for moderately wealthy owner managers could be short-lived notwithstanding the *FA 2014* relaxations.

OVERVIEW OF THE CURRENT PENSIONS REGIME

10.3   The current rules are based on the major 'simplification' to the pensions legislation that was introduced on 6 April 2006 (known as 'A-day'), based on legislation introduced in the *FA 2004* (with many subsequent amendments!). From A-day the previous tax provisions relating to all types of pension schemes were replaced by a single scheme for all tax-privileged pension schemes. All existing approved pension schemes at A-day automatically became registered schemes under the A-day legislation.

The aim was to establish a single 'unified' regime for pensions, sweeping away the complexities and distinctions between the diverse pension systems that were previously in operation. However, whilst the pensions regime as a whole might be considered simpler, many would argue that the constant Government 'tinkering' with the rules in recent years has introduced many other complexities, leaving many to question whether the pensions code is really that much simpler!

In broad terms, UK resident individuals may concurrently belong to more than one pension scheme without any restriction (provided they are under 75 and that when added together their payments do not exceed the annual or lifetime limit). To secure tax relief, individuals must have a commensurate level of taxable earnings (although annual contributions of up to £3,600 gross are permitted regardless of any earnings). Pension funds have always enjoyed many tax benefits, including the ability to generally receive investment income and enjoy capital growth in a tax-free environment.

Personal tax reliefs for contributions are generally geared to the amounts paid and the maximum £40,000 annual allowance, subject to any carry forward of unused 'relief' from the previous three years).

Since 6 April 2016, tax relief for pension contributions made by high earners is subject to additional restrictions. This takes the form of a tapered reduction in the annual allowance where:

- an individual's 'adjusted income' (ie income including the value of any pension contributions) exceeds £150,000; and

- their income excluding pension contributions is greater than £110,000.

The rate of reduction in the annual allowance is £1 for every £2 the 'adjusted income' exceeds £150,000, up to a maximum reduction of £30,000. See 10.23A for further details.

Many owner-managers continue to make use of the ability to pay a gross amount of £3,600 each year into a pension scheme for members of their family who have little or no relevant earnings. Thus, for example, up to £3,600 (£2,880 net of basic rate tax relief) can be contributed to a pension scheme each year for 'non-working' spouses, children and grandchildren (see 10.30). Such arrangements are not caught by the settlement provisions (see 9.30).

10.4   Planning with 'registered pension schemes' involves three main phases:

Funding – Individuals/companies have various rules that regulate the amount that can be contributed to an 'approved' registered pension fund on a 'tax-privileged' basis.

This is mainly governed by the Annual Allowance (AA) provisions (see 10.23), which restrict the tax relief on 'pension inputs' to Defined Contribution (DC) or Defined Benefit (DB or 'final salary') schemes.

A further limit on the total amount that can be placed in a tax-exempt pension fund is the Lifetime Allowance (currently £1,000,000 (see 10.35), but which will become index-linked from 2018).

Investment – Although the original *FA 2004* simplification proposals removed many of the pre-existing restrictions placed on the choice of pension fund investments, the Chancellor subsequently felt that this freedom might be abused. Thus, certain restrictions were placed on those pension funds where the members have control or influence over the scheme's investment choices – known as 'investment regulated' pensions (see 10.12, 10.13 and 10.36).

Benefits – There have been various relaxations to the benefits which members can take from their pension funds on 'retirement' and to their dependants in the event of their death and the consequential tax liabilities on them (see 10.40 and 10.41).

Pension members (aged at least 55 years old) can now enjoy total freedom over how they take their pension income. For example, it will be possible for them to take the entire pension fund as a lump sum if they wished. Alternatively, they may choose to take their pension in 'chunks'. Twenty-five per cent of the cash taken will be tax-free, with the remaining 75% being taxed at the member's marginal income tax rate. Thus, members will be able to manage their income tax liability by taking their pension out in stages.

Until 6 April 2016, lump sum death benefits payable (where an individual dies age 75 or over) were taxed at 45%. However, lump sum death benefits are now taxed at the nominated beneficiary's marginal income tax rate. They are not subject to inheritance tax. The 45% charge continues to apply where a lump sum death benefit is paid to a 'non-qualifying' person (see 10.43), which includes a By-Pass Trust (see 10.44).

For detailed commentary on the pre-6 April 2011 pension rules, see 2009/10 and earlier editions of this book.

OVERVIEW OF PENSION SCHEMES

10.5   Apart from the state scheme, pensions are provided through a personal pension scheme and/or a company (occupational) pension scheme. The pensions legislation and supplementary regulations apply equally to both types of pension scheme. It is not necessary to seek HMRC 'approval' for a pension scheme – instead, the scheme merely has to be registered with a written declaration that all statutory requirements have been met. (All existing 'approved' schemes at A-day were deemed to be 'registered' on A-day.)

All existing pension schemes at A-day retained their existing nomenclatures even though the relevant tax conditions applying to that particular scheme ceased then. It is still useful to summarise the main features of the arrangements that have traditionally been used by family/owner-managed companies and their directors, which are:

(*a*)   occupational pension schemes ('OPSs') for all employees (see 10.6–10.9);

(*b*)   'top-up' executive schemes for working shareholders and other senior executives (see 10.10);

(*c*)   self-administered schemes for working shareholders (see 10.11–10.15);

(*d*)   personal pension plans ('PPPs') and group personal pension (GPP) schemes (see 10.16);

(*e*)   self-invested pension plans ('SIPPs') (see 10.17);

(*f*)   Auto-enrolment pensions for all employees (see 10.18–10.22).

The rules for operating company pension schemes are generally set out in guidance provided by HMRC Audit and Pension Schemes Services (APSS). The relevant practice notes can be found on HMRC's website at www.hmrc. gov.uk/pensionschemes/updates.htm.

Pension scheme members receive regular illustrations of their anticipated pension benefits (in present-day values), which provide a realistic assessment of the value of their pension funds and the extent of any further provision required.

The most attractive pension proposition is where higher rate tax relief is obtained on contributions paid in but only basic rate tax is paid when the pensions are subsequently taken.

OCCUPATIONAL PENSION SCHEMES

Final salary versus money purchase

10.6   The occupational pension scheme (OPS) traditionally provided benefits based on final salary. In the medium to long term, real investment returns had to cover both inflation and salary growth. Funding in this way, by reference to future liabilities of the pension fund, can create problems in policing the funds. Furthermore, under a final salary (or defined benefit (DB)) scheme, members will not always know the value of their pension benefits at any given time before retirement.

In recent years, 'final salary' schemes are fast becoming a dying species, primarily as a result of weak investment markets. As a result, many companies are being required to make substantial contributions to 'make good' the resulting pension fund deficits. Consequently, very few owner managed companies operate final salary schemes. The lack of consistency with defined benefit schemes has resulted in money purchase schemes (defined contribution schemes) becoming the standard choice. With defined contribution schemes, the value of the pension fund for each member is based on the contributions made to it and the investment return achieved.

Some companies have made payments to employees in final salary schemes to compensate them for a reduction in benefits or to transfer to a money purchase scheme. HMRC considers such payments to be taxable and 'NIC-able' as employment income.

Many employers offer access to a group personal pension scheme giving the employees a high degree of portability for their pension fund (see 10.16).

Relief for employer contributions

10.7   Employers' contributions to employees' registered pension schemes do not count as earnings or taxable benefits under *ITEPA 2003, s 308*. Similarly,

503

they do not attract employers' NICs (*SI 2001/1004, Sch 3*). However, the *FA 2013* blocked a loophole that previously enabled employers to make contributions to the pension schemes of their employees' other family members' pensions. These were often known as 'family pension plans' and enabled companies to make contributions to the schemes of other family members (even though they were not employed by the company!)

Following the *FA 2013* amendment, the *ITEPA 2003, s 308* exemption is now only given for contributions made by an employer to an employee's registered pension scheme, which must be made 'in respect of the employee'. Contributions made to other family members' schemes will give rise to income tax and NIC charges.

Pension benefits

10.8   The benefits that can be taken from an OPS now follow the standardised post-A-day rules (see 10.40). The previous complex formulae that applied to benefits taken under defined benefit and defined contribution schemes no longer apply.

Loans and pension mortgages to individual members of an OPS

10.9   Under an insured scheme, insurance companies can offer loans to individual members although this could result in payment charges. Security is required and using the loan to purchase a private residence can be an attractive proposition.

There are no longer any company law restrictions on 'loans' to directors (of private companies) (see 2.57). The personal loans/mortgages available vary considerably.

EXECUTIVE PENSION PLANS

10.10   Usually, executive pension plans ('EPPs') are insured defined contribution occupational schemes, which are taken out to provide benefits to a *single* member (although it is possible to have more than one member). The policies are therefore 'earmarked' for the individual member. This differs from other money purchase occupational schemes where typically an individual member's benefits relate to their share of assets held in a common pool of funds.

Since A-day, the previous actuarial funding limits cease to apply and the amounts that may be contributed to, and held by, an EPP are simply subject to the annual and lifetime allowances (see 10.23 and 10.35).

SELF-ADMINISTERED PENSION SCHEMES (SSASs)

Overview

10.11   In a large number of cases, working shareholders of a family or owner-managed company have tended to look upon a pension scheme as a tax-saving vehicle during their working lives, rather than as a means of providing income on retirement. Not surprisingly, HMRC have always been keen to remind everyone that a pension scheme is intended to provide benefits on retirement with the tax provisions providing appropriate encouragement.

Small self-administered schemes ('SSASs') have traditionally provided a tax-efficient pension fund vehicle for many owner-managers. SSASs are akin to a SSIP for a group of business owners etc. They are particularly appropriate where the working directors wholly own the company. Typically, membership of such schemes is restricted to just a few owner-managers and possibly their close relatives. There is no longer a maximum amount of members for a SSAS and it is even possible to have 'one-man' SSAS's.

As trustees of the pension fund, members are able to enjoy some control over the investments made by the pension fund (as opposed to leaving it to the pension scheme fund managers or insurance company concerned). This means that the relevant company can (subject to certain restrictions) retain the use of the sums paid into the fund.

However, provided all the members are trustees, a SSAS with fewer than 12 members (where the members make all decisions unanimously or where there is an independent trustee) does not have to comply with the member-nominated trustee requirements of the *Pensions Act 2004*. In practice, the trustees will often include an independent professional trustee to comply with the *Pensions Act 2004*. However, it is no longer an HMRC requirement to have a 'pensioner' trustee and tax reliefs are not conditional on the appointment or continued presence of such a trustee.

All SSASs existing at A-Day were subsumed into the current pensions regime and are deemed to be registered with HMRC. New schemes must be registered with HMRC, but are no longer subject to approval.

Where substantial funds are transferred to a SSAS, the share value of the company is reduced for CGT and IHT purposes, with the funds still effectively being available to the company to a certain extent.

Provided the company's contributions have been validly made into the SSAS, the funds held by the SSAS are beyond the reach of the sponsoring company's creditors.

Any contribution paid in respect of an individual member exceeding the £40,000 AA (or lower if the new tapered annual allowance for high earners applies (see 10.23A)), plus any unused relief brought forward, will result in an income tax charge for the relevant individual (see 10.23–10.26).

Eligible investments

10.12   A SSAS is able to invest in a fairly wide range of investments, including holding/purchasing the company's trading property (see 10.13) and making loans to the company (see 10.14).

Company pension schemes (previously formed under the 'old' Self Administered Pension Scheme (SSAS) rules) can be used to meet the owner-managers' personal pension requirements whilst also providing useful financial benefits for 'their' companies.

It was originally proposed that the types of investments made by a pension fund would be liberalised to include almost any asset. Many individuals were therefore planning to introduce residential property and other exotic assets, such as works of art, vintage cars, fine wines, etc (see 10.36 and 10.37). However, in the pre-Budget report delivered on 5 December 2005, there was a dramatic U-turn which heavily penalised the use of such assets. Those who were advanced in their planning understandably felt resentful to the turnaround in policy. However, the government clearly felt that retaining complete freedom over the choice of 'tax-relievable' investments would have led too many people to make too many imprudent decisions about building for their long term security.

A SSAS may buy shares in its sponsoring company/companies, provided:

- the amount invested in the shares in the sponsoring companies is less than 20% of the net value of the pension scheme funds; and

- the amount invested in the shares of any sponsoring company must be less than 5% of net value of the pension scheme funds.

In theory, there is no restriction on the proportion of the company's share capital that can be owned by the SSAS. The above shareholding 'limits' only apply to occupational pension schemes as defined in the *FA 2004*. Therefore, they do not apply to SSIPs (see 10.17).

The purchase price for the shares must be backed-up by an independent valuation. If the amount invested exceeds the above limits, the *excess* will be treated as an unauthorised payment, which will trigger a penal tax charge (see 10.34).

Pre-A-day, the holding of shares in an unlisted company was generally restricted to a more generous 30% of share capital. Existing (pre-A-day) company shareholdings can continue to be held under the post-A-day regime. See 10.37 for further details about eligible pension fund investments.

Property investments

10.13   Many SSAS's own property which they let to the employer company. The company obtains corporate tax relief on the rent paid and the SSAS receives it tax-free. Any capital growth on the property accrues tax-free within the SSAS.

A SSAS can purchase property from individuals connected with the company (which could *not* be done before A-day). Thus, where an owner-manager personally owns property, this can now be sold to 'their' pension fund at market value (enabling cash to be released to them). It is also possible for the sponsoring company to transfer its existing trading property to the SSAS to benefit from future tax-free growth, with the SSAS then renting the property to the company.

In strictness, it is not possible for the property to be transferred to the fund as an *in specie* contribution. However, with careful implementation, it might be possible, based on HMRC guidance, to transfer a property in specie if a debt had been created prior to the specie contribution being made (see 10.32A). Nevertheless, many providers are unwilling or cautious about administering such transactions, especially following the recent challenges by HMRC.

The transfer of the property will have capital gains implications and is likely to result in an SDLT charge (see 12.23–12.24). The effective CGT rate on the transfer is likely to be 20% – only commercial property can be transferred into the SSAS. Entrepreneurs' relief (ER) would not normally be available in such cases. The future capital growth in the property would be exempt from tax within the fund.

A SSAS can also invest in commercial property *for third party letting*.

Loans to company

10.14   Pension fund loans to the company must be secured, not exceed five years in duration (but can be rolled over once) and must be on commercial terms (with equal annual repayments and interest of *at least* a composite bank base rate plus 1%). Furthermore, such loans must not exceed 50% of the value of the pension fund.

As a general rule, the company no longer has to deduct and withhold 20% income tax on interest paid to pension funds, irrespective of whether the loan is intended to last for more than a year (see *ITA 2007, ss 930(1)* and *936(2)(g)*).

SSAS borrowing limits

10.15   Pension fund borrowings are restricted to 50% of the fund's assets and must be secured. Furthermore, the term of such borrowings must not exceed five years (see 10.38 for further details).

Borrowings for prospective property investment that took place before A-day could be carried through into the post-A-day regime. Before 6 April 2006, a SSAS could borrow up to 45% of the fund value plus three times the (prior) annual contributions made to the fund by the company and its members. It is still not possible for the fund to make loans to members.

Example 1

Advantages of SSAS owning company's trading premises

An SSAS was established for the three shareholder-directors of Gerrard Ltd in 1996. During 2017, the trustees of the SSAS (which included all three directors) decided to acquire new business premises for the company costing £1,200,000, partly using bank borrowing.

Gerrard Ltd pays a commercial rent of £85,000 per year, which is deductible for corporation tax purposes, but received tax-free in the hands of the SSAS. The rental payments and regular annual contributions are used by the SSAS to repay the bank borrowings. The capital appreciation in the property takes place in a tax-exempt vehicle.

PERSONAL PENSION PLANS (PPPs) AND GROUP PERSONAL PENSION (GPP) SCHEMES

10.16   Personal pension plans can be taken out by directors and employees, which effectively go with them from job to job or indeed from job to self-employment. The benefits are always based on the level of contributions (and not the level of final income on retirement).

Members can obtain tax relief on their personal contributions at their highest marginal tax rate up to the £40,000 AA (plus any unused relief brought forward) (see 10.23–10.24 for further details)).

Currently, contributions by members are paid net of basic rate tax (currently 20%) under the relief at source rules, with any higher rate relief being given through the self-assessment return. The pension provider reclaims the 20% basic rate tax deducted at source from HMRC, which effectively forms part of the member's contributions.

Some employers run group personal pension (GPP) schemes. Broadly speaking, GPP schemes are a collection of individual personal pension schemes operated by one administrator (normally the pension provider). However, the employer's involvement can be relatively limited as many of the duties imposed on trustees are avoided. The main responsibility of the employing company is to ensure that contributions are paid over to the pension provider within 19 days of the end of the relevant 'contribution' period.

SELF-INVESTED PERSONAL PENSION PLANS (SIPPs)

10.17 A self-invested pension plan or SIPP is effectively a personal pension 'wrapper' into which eligible investments are placed without any capital gains tax charge on profits. Consequently, there is no employer or pension fund involvement.

With a SIPP, the individual decides how the funds are invested. They can therefore choose their underlying pension fund investments. Traditionally, these have included quoted stocks and shares (including AIM shares), unit and investment trusts, insurance company managed funds and unit linked funds and commercial property. It cannot invest in residential property or tangible moveable property (see 10.12)

In contrast to managed funds, SIPPs will give much greater control over the choice of investments within the fund. Provided the fund is of a reasonable size, the SIPP can choose a fund manager (agreeing the charging basis) and draw up a suitable asset allocation model. Care should also be taken to agree investment performance criteria and the monitoring of results.

SIPPs are subject to the (post-A-day) unified rules that apply to all pension funds. However, since a SSIP does not have a sponsoring employer, there is more flexibility on the amount of the fund that can be invested either by way of share capital or loan investment in an unlisted company (see 10.37)). However, any share investment must be acceptable to the SIPP provider and should fall within the 20% 'controlling director' rules with an acceptable diversification of shareholders. Thus, where an individual (or their 'associate', eg spouse) already holds (say) 9% of the equity of a company, 'their' SIPP could make a 10% equity investment in the company (since this would be below 20% in total).

As noted above, a SIPP can own commercial property. It is possible for a SIPP to acquire the property from the SIPP member or 'their' company. The SIPP would have to charge a commercial rent, which would be tax deductible in the SIPP member's business/company.

It is relatively rare for companies to set up a SIPP for their directors or employees (although it may be possible for a company to form a group SIPP for its directors and employees).

In the past, SIPPs have generally required a minimum annual contribution of around £4,000 to make them viable. The arrival of online SIPPs (which have far lower charging structures) has made them more suitable for a far wider range of people.

Mortgages against SIPPs are available from third parties such as building societies and banks up to a factor of the annual pension contributions and with a minimum annual pension contribution being required. Such a facility is simply another source of finance (albeit of a greater amount than might be obtainable from traditional sources) with no benefit passing to the SIPP itself. To that extent, for a house purchase, it should be compared to a mortgage on the capital repayment basis or to a mortgage linked with an endowment policy.

THE AUTO-ENROLMENT SCHEME

Background

10.18   It is clear that many people currently make little or no provision for their future pension. Furthermore, there is a lack of employer-supported pension provision, particularly in smaller firms. Whilst the stakeholder pension scheme (introduced in April 2001) was intended to address this problem, there was little take-up by low earners.

The Government addressed the lack of pension saving, mainly by low/medium earners, in the *Pensions Act 2008* reform. The solution was to introduce a good quality pension schemes for those who were not already in a workplace pension scheme via the auto-enrolment scheme.

Thus, in appropriate cases, employers will be able to set up pension schemes with appropriate pension providers. These include the National Employment Savings Trust (or NEST), Welplan Pensions, Now: Pensions, and AutoEnrolment.co.uk ('auto-enrolment providers'). An auto enrolment scheme can be the only scheme operated by a company or it may run alongside its existing pension schemes.

All auto-enrolment pension providers are within the existing tax regime for registered pensions. The scheme is principally designed to help low-to-medium earners who do not currently have access to a suitable employer pension scheme or pensions product.

10.19   Once an employee has their pension, it will be completely 'portable' and will remain with them throughout their working life. Their personal pension accounts will provide a pension on retirement (and will benefit from the April 2015 changes – see 10.41). Companies with an existing good quality pension scheme can apply for exemption from the auto-enrolment scheme.

Companies that do not currently offer pension provision for their workforce (especially many smaller companies) will need to think about the type of pension scheme they wish to introduce and clearly communicate the details to their employees. Many small owner-managed companies are incurring additional payroll costs on full implementation of the 'auto-enrolment'.

10.20   It is no longer possible to set up a new stakeholder pension, although existing stakeholder pensions continue until the employee leaves or retires. (Please see 2012/13 and earlier editions of this book for detailed coverage of stakeholder pension schemes.)

Auto-enrolment

10.21 The Government recognises that the implementation of the auto-enrolment scheme will be complex and costly for many employers. Consequently, auto-enrolment is taking place on a staggered basis, between October 2012 (for companies with 120,000 plus employees) and April 2017/February 2018 (for those with less than 30 employees and new employers respectively).

If a company does not have an existing pension scheme, it must automatically enrol all their employees in an appropriate scheme if they are *aged 22 or more* (but below State Pension age), who *earn more than £10,000 per year* (2017/18 threshold). There are special rules for employees aged at least 16 who earn more than £5,876 in a year. If they ask to be enrolled, the employee must pay at least minimum contributions.

New employees must be registered from commencement of employment. It is possible for employees to opt out (but this 'opt-out' must be renewed every three years). The launch of Lifetime Individual Savings Accounts (LISAs) has encouraged young savers to 'opt-out' of auto-enrolment in favour of the LISAs which can be accessed earlier.

Companies have a duty to notify employees about their pension rights under the auto-enrolment scheme. Specimen templates can be found at www.nestpensions.org.uk

Minimum contributions into auto-enrolment pension schemes

10.22 Both employers and employees will be obliged to pay a minimum level of contributions based on all the employee's earnings (falling within their basic rate income tax band). Employees will receive an additional 1% through tax relief. Since April 2017, there is no maximum annual contribution

It is likely that the required minimum contribution levels will be phased in as follows:

	Total minimum contribution (see note 1)	Employer must pay at least (see note 2)
Oct 2012 (or from the employer's 'later' staging date) to 5 April 2018	2%	1%
6 April 2018 to 5 April 2019	5%	2%
6 April 2019 onwards	8%	3%

Notes

1   The contribution % is applied to an employee's qualifying earnings (the band between £5,876 and £45,000 for 2017/18.

511

2   This is the employer's minimum contribution – it can pay more if it wishes.

TAX TREATMENT OF PENSION CONTRIBUTIONS

Individual's tax relief and the annual allowance (AA)

10.23   Only cash contributions are eligible for relief – it is not generally possible to make contributions in the form of assets (but see 10.32A for treatment when seeking to contribute an asset in-specie). Exceptionally, shares acquired through an SAYE share option scheme (see 8.78) or share incentive plan (see 8.80) can be contributed *in specie* as a tax-deductible contribution.

Income tax relief for contributions to registered pension schemes is given on the *greater* of £3,600 (gross) or 100% of the individual's taxable *earnings*. An owner-manager's taxable earnings broadly include their employment income and benefits – dividends and investment income are *not* included.

Under the post-A-day rules, pension contributions tax relief was subject to an overall financial limit, in the form of an annual allowance (AA). The AA was originally very generous – in 2006/07 it was £215,000 and was increased every year with the 2010/11 AA reaching £255,000 (for details of pre-6 April 2011 AAs – see previous editions of this book).

There are carry forward provisions that enable any unused AA in the previous three years to be used in the current year (see 10.27).

These rules should also be considered in the context of the lifetime limit of £1 million as it provides a further restriction on the total value of pension savings that can benefit from tax relief when the contributions were made. When an individual's pension fund 'crystallises', the value of all their pension funds are totalled and tested against the prevailing lifetime allowance. Any excess will be subject to a penal income tax charge (see 10.35 for details).

Pension input periods (PIPs) are now aligned with the tax year (subject to transitional rules) (see 10.25A and 10.25B).

In the current fiscal climate, successive governments have viewed pension tax relief as imposing a massive 'cost' to the Exchequer and sought to restrict it. The (pre-2010) Labour government planned to limit tax relief for individuals with an annual income of over £130,000. However, at the time, the incoming coalition government rejected this basis, and simply restricted pension contribution relief by reducing the annual allowance to £50,000 from 2011/12 onwards which was further reduced to £40,000 from 2014/15. However, as part of the 'transition' towards tax-year-based pension input periods (PIPs), some may have had a special £80,000 AA for 2015/16 – see 10.25 and 10.25A for further details.

Further restrictions also apply for high-earners from 2016/17 onwards (see 10.23A).

High-earners 'annual allowance' restriction

10.23A   Since 6 April 2016, high earners have a further 'tapered' restriction in their AA. Because of the way the rules work, it will affect individuals whose *adjusted income* exceeds £150,000 (after adding back all pension contributions).

For these purposes, 'adjusted income' is income plus any pension contributions, including employer contributions. The inclusion of pension contributions in the definition prevents the use of salary sacrifice arrangements to bring the individual's income below the £150,000 limit.

However, those with 'threshold income' of less than £110,000 can effectively enjoy their full £40,000 AA and are not subject to any tapered reduction. For these purposes, 'threshold income' represents total income from all sources plus the amount of employment income given up for pension provision via a post-8 July 2015 salary sacrifice less the gross pension contributions paid into a pension scheme.

Thus, an owner manager could arrange for the company to make a pension contribution (for his benefit). The pension contribution would be added back in computing the owner manager's adjusted income but would not reduce his threshold income. The pension contribution is not treated as a salary sacrifice since the owner manager has no contractual entitlement to the pension contribution. Provided the threshold income was reduced below £110,000, the tapering rules would *not* apply.

Under the tapering provisions, the £40,000 AA is reduced by £1 for every £2 (ie by 50%) the adjusted income exceeds £150,000, up to a maximum reduction of £30,000. The effect of this restriction for various levels of adjusted income is shown below:

Adjusted income £	Available annual allowance £
150,000	40,000
160,000	35,000
170,000	30,000
180,000	25,000
190,000	20,000
210,000	10,000

High earners will therefore always have a minimum AA of £10,000.

Example 2

Calculation of AA for high earner

For 2017/18, Mr Byram's annual salary (including benefits) will be £110,000. He has no unused AA from previous years.

Mr Byram plans to make a gross pension contribution of £40,000.

Since his earnings would not exceed £110,000, he would be entitled to full tax relief of £16,000 (£40,000 × 40%) on his contribution.

On the other hand, if his employers also paid him a bonus of (say) £30,000, this would take his annual earnings to £140,000. His adjusted income (including his pension contribution of £40,000) would be £180,000.

This would mean that his tax relief on the same £40,000 contribution would reduce to £11,250, calculated as follows:

	£
Maximum AA	40,000
Less; Tapered reduction	
Excess income £30,000 (£180,000 less £150,000) × 1/2	(15,000)
Tapered AA	25,000
Pension contribution tax relief	£11,250
£25,000 × 45%	

The carry forward of unused AA continues to be available (see 10.23 and 10.27) but, where appropriate, the amount available is based on the unused tapered AA. This may have provided some additional scope for contributions for some high-earners in the initial years following the changes but is unlikely to be the case going forward.

Excess AA charge

10.24   If an individual's annual pension contribution exceeds the AA – currently £40,000 since 2014/15 onwards (£50,000 for 2011/12 to 2013/14 inclusive), *plus* any unused relief brought forward (see 10.27), they are liable to excess AA tax charge.

The taxable excess is treated as though it was the 'top slice' of an individual's taxable income, and will therefore be taxed at their marginal rate(s) (as appropriate, having regard to the relevant slice/slices of income. (Note – the higher rate and additional rate thresholds are extended by 'grossed-up' gift aid donations and personal pension contributions.)

The excess AA charge is therefore taxed at the marginal tax rate on which the individual claimed tax relief *(FA 2004, s 227(4), (4A))*. Although the excess is taxed, it is *not* regarded as taxable income (and cannot therefore be reduced by losses or other reliefs) *(FA 2004, s 227(5))*. If the excess AA charge for a year is £2,000 or less, it must be paid via self-assessment. Where it exceeds £2,000, it may be possible to pass this to the scheme administrator (see 10.28).

Pension fund administrators are required to send 'pension statements' (showing details for the current year and three previous years) to those members whose inputs have exceeded the annual allowance – see www.gov.uk/guidance/ pension-administrators-annual-and-lifetime-allowance-statements.

AA, PENSION INPUTS AND TRANSITIONAL RULES

Background to pension input periods (PIPs)

10.25 Pensions tax relief is based on the contributions *made in the tax year* *(FA 2004, s 188)*. However, the £40,000 (£50,000 before 6 April 2014) AA is tested against the 'pension input' made in the individual's pension input period (or PIP) *ending in the relevant tax year* for the purposes of calculating the 'excess' AA tax charge.

The concept of PIPs was introduced on A-day, but given the lower AA limit, it is important to understand how PIPs worked before 6 April 2016 since they were not necessarily aligned with the tax year. Subject to dealing with the transitional rules, PIPs are fully aligned to tax years in 2016/17, which makes life much easier.

When testing the PIPs against the 'pension input', it is necessary to look at all relevant pension contributions – ie personal contributions (the input is grossed-up at the basic rate tax added by HMRC), company contributions, and (for those in 'final salary' schemes) the increase in their pension 'promise (see 10.28).

The rationale for including *company contributions* is that the individual enjoys effective income tax relief on them, since they are not counted as a taxable benefit in kind!

Defined contribution pension schemes

10.25A Historically, the first PIP *started* when the first contribution was paid after 6 April 2011 (ie A-day) and ended on the first anniversary of its start date *(FA 2004, s 238)*. Subsequent PIPs last one year.

For those joining a new pension schemes after 6 April 2011, the *FA 2011* aligns the PIP with the tax year. This means that the first PIP of a new joiner will end on 5 April each year, unless another date is nominated (*FA 2004, s 238,* as amended by *FA 2011, Sch 17, para 16*).

However, under the *F (No 2) A 2015*, *all* PIPs are aligned to tax years from 6 April 2016. Consequently, there are transitional rules to deal with this changeover.

All PIP's open on 8 July 2015 (Summer Budget 2015 day) were closed on that date, with the next input period running from 9 July 2015 to 5 April 2016. From 2016/17 onwards, all subsequent PIP's are aligned with the tax year.

In the transitional period, all existing arrangements on 8 July 2015 could have two or three PIPs ending in the tax year 2015/16, depending on the start date of the PIP (see example 3 below). All PIPs ending between 6 April 2015 and 8 July 2015 fall into the 'pre-alignment tax year'. PIPs ending between 9 July 2015 and 5 April 2016 are in the 'post-alignment tax year'.

For example, if someone's PIP ends on (say) 30 September, their 'open' PIP to 30 September 2015 would end on 8 July 2015. Therefore they will have two PIPs for the transitional 2015/16 year:

- 1 October 2014 to 8 July 2015 ('pre-budget' PIP falling in the 'pre-alignment tax year'), and

- 9 July 2015 to 5 April 2016 ('post-budget' PIP falling within the 'post-alignment tax year').

Under these transitional PIP rules, it was possible that some individuals (at the 8 July 2015) were already making contributions against their 2016/17 AA. In such cases, they would have two years' worth of pension savings only matched against a single year's AA.

To deal with this possible unfairness, a special £80,000 AA limit applies for 2015/16 *only* (which potentially provides an extra AA of £40,000 to use before 6 April 2016). The 2015/16 £80,000 AA is given as follows:

- First, the £80,000 AA is used in the pre-alignment tax year against 'pre-budget' PIPs, and other 2015/16 PIPs that ended before 9 July 2015. Any unused annual AA from the previous three years is added to these amounts in the normal way (see 10.27).

- Any unused part of the 'pre-budget' AA s carried forward for use against the post-budget PIP, *but only up to a maximum amount of £40,000.*

It was possible for someone in a number of pension schemes to have different PIPs but with the *F (No 2) A 2015* changes to PIP's, all PIP's will be aligned to the tax year from 6 April 2016.

There is no pension input *amount* for a PIP that ends in the tax year in which a member dies or satisfies the 'severe ill health condition' (within *FA 2004, s 229(3)(a), (4)*). However, payments into a pension scheme where someone takes early retirement for less serious conditions are still counted as pension inputs. (This alters the previous pre-*FA 2011* rule which ignored contributions made in the year benefits were taken – *FA 2004, s 229(3)(a)*).

Defined benefit/final salary pension schemes

10.26 For those in *final salary* schemes (on A-day), pension rights are deemed to accrue on a daily basis (*FA 2004, s 238(2)*). This means that their first PIP will have begun on 6 April 2006 and ended 6 April 2007, so that their pension accrual during 2006/07 will be tested against the AA for 2007/08, with all future PIPS also being effectively one year out of sync! (see *HMRC Registered Pension Schemes Manual 06100060*). If a final salary scheme member joins after A-day, their PIP will start on a different day from existing (pre-A-day) members and they will therefore have different PIPs.

The calculation is modified for 2015/16. It is based on the total of the increase in the value of the individual's pension rights across the combined PIP's in the period to 5 April 2016, which is then apportioned to the 'pre-alignment' and 'post-alignment' tax years.

The calculation of the PIP for the 2015/16 tax year is modified but does not materially change the basis.

Example 3

PIPs for defined contribution scheme

Mr Milner has been a member of defined contribution scheme for many years, making quarterly contributions.

His first (post-5 April 2006) pension contribution was made on 30 June 2006.

Consequently, Mr Milner's first PIP would start on 30 June 2006 and end on 30 June 2007 (for the tax year ended 2007/08). His subsequent PIPs would start on 1 July and end on 30 June each year until 2015/16.

In the transitional year – 2015/16 – Mr Milner has the following PIPs:

- PIP 1 – 1 July 2014 to 30 June 2015 (the original PIP.

- PIP 2 – 1 July 2015 to 8 July 2015 (part of the original 2016/17 PIP, which becomes a second pre-budget PIP for 2015/16).

- PIP 3 – 9 July 2015 to 5 April 2016 (the new 'post-budget' 2015/16 PIP).

From 2016/17, Mr Milner's PIP's will be aligned with the tax year. Therefore his 2016/17 and 2017/18 PIP's will reflect pension contributions made in the year ended 5 April 2017 and 5 April 2018 respectively.

Carry forward of unused relief

10.27   In calculating the AA charge, taxpayers can bring forward any unused relief from the *three* previous years (*FA 2004, s 228A*). Put another way, unused relief for a year can only be used for the next three years.

It is only possible for taxpayers to bring forward unused relief from a year provided they were a member of a pension scheme in that year (although they did not necessarily have to make a contribution (*FA 2004, s 227A(4)*).

The facility to carry forward unused relief is particularly helpful to those wishing to make contributions from large bonuses and redundancy payments.

Usefully, the carry forward provisions include 'transitional' rules to carry forward unused relief for pre-6 April 2011 periods but for these purposes the AA for 2008/09, 2009/10 and 2010/11 is only deemed to be £50,000 (as opposed to the actual AA for these years).

In calculating whether an excess AA charge is appropriate on pension contributions, the 'available relief' is used as follows:

- The AA for the relevant tax year (used first – *FA 2004, s 228A(3)*); then

- The unused relief from the three previous years (taken on a FIFO basis) is taken.

On 28 November 2011, HMRC confirmed that, due to a defect in the drafting of the 'transitional' unused relief legislation, there will be no clawback of the carried-forward relief where any pre-6 April 2011 'transitional' year has pension contributions exceeding the deemed £50,000 AA.

There is no requirement to show the calculation on unused relief on the SA return, but workings should be retained in the event of an enquiry. It may be useful to record the unused relief on the 'white space'.

Example 4

Pension contributions and the AA

Mr Sakho, owns the entire share capital of 'his' company, Opportunist Strikers Ltd.

He made a single substantial pension contribution of £100,000 on 2 July 2017 and his taxable income (after deducting all reliefs but including the pension contribution) is £200,000. Mr Sakho's threshold income is £100,000 (£200,000 less £100,000) and therefore his 2017/18 AA is not restricted (see 10.23A).

Given that the £120,000 contribution exceeds the AA of £40,000 for 2017/18, it is necessary to calculate whether any excess AA charge is due.

Mr Sakho's pension contribution history is as follows:

PIP	Contributions in PIP	Tax Year	Annual Allowance
	£		£
2 Dec 2013 to 1 Dec 2014	30,000	2014/15	40,000
2 Dec 2014 to 8 July 2015	80,000	2015/16	80,000
9 July 2015 to 5 April 2016	0	2015/16	
6 April 2016 to 5 April 2017	20,000	2016/17	40,000
6 April 2017 to 5 April 2018	100,000	2017/18	40,000

His unused relief brought forward at 6 April 2017 is calculated as follows:

Tax Year	Contributions	(Deemed) Maximum AA	Unused relief
	£	£	£
2014/15	30,000	40,000	10,000
2015/16	80,000	80,000	–
2016/17	20,000	40,000	20,000

Mr Sakho therefore has unused relief of £30,000 (£10,000 + £20,000) to carry forward to 2017/18.

Although Mr Sakho would have originally claimed full tax relief on his £100,000 pension contribution in 2017/18, an appropriate part will be 'clawed-back' via an excess AA charge.

This is calculated as follows:

		£	£
2017/18 Pension contribution			100,000
Less: AA	2017/18	40,000	
Unused relief b/fwd		30,000	
Available relief			(70,000)
Excess			30,000
AA charge @ 45% (marginal rate)			£13,500

Additional pension contribution restriction

10.27A   Since April 2015, if a member makes a withdrawal from a *defined contribution pension* (in addition to any tax-free cash), their maximum annual pension contribution is restricted to £10,000 (see 10.41). However, this rule will not apply where one of the 'exception' conditions are met – these include very small pension funds (worth less than £10,000) and where a pension is currently taken as an annuity or scheme pension.

Excess charge for 'defined scheme benefit' members

10.28   Measuring the 'pension input' for a *defined benefit* (or 'final salary' scheme) is more complex. The pension scheme member accrues their rights by virtue of continued service. The funding of the scheme has no direct relationship with the increase in their pension rights. This could be done by obtaining full actuarial valuations each year but this would be a costly exercise. Consequently, the legislation provides that the increase in input value is simply based on a flat rate multiplier.

From 6 April 2011, the increase in the value of the 'pension promise' is multiplied by a flat rate of 16. Also, to eliminate the effect of inflation, the value of the opening 'pension promise' is indexed by the Consumer Prices Index over the PIP. See Example 5 below for illustrative 'pension input' calculation for a defined benefit scheme.

In some cases, a high salary increase (say on a promotion) combined with long service may give rise to a substantial input (which might still be protected from an AA charge due to the availability of unused relief from earlier years).

Example 5

Pension input for defined benefit scheme member

Mr Fonte is a member of a defined benefit scheme, which provides for a retirement pension of 1/60th of his final salary for each year of service.

On 6 April 2017, Mr Fonte's annual salary was £100,000 and he had been a member of the scheme for 15 years.

On 5 April 2018, his annual salary had risen to £120,000 with 16 years' service.

The increase in Mr Fonte's pension promise (ie his 'pension input' for 2017/18) is measured as follows (assuming no CPI increase):

5/4/18 – £120,000 ×16/60	32,000
6/4/17 – £100,000 × 15/60 × 0%	(25,000)
Increase	7,000
Pension input (× 16)	£112,000

Mr Fonte will have an excess AA charge in 2017/18 on £72,000 (£112,000 less £40,000) unless he has sufficient unused relief carried forward to 'shelter' the £72,000 excess.

'Scheme to settle liability' for an AA charge

10.29   An 'excess' AA charge which exceeds £2,000 can be met out of pension scheme funds. *FA 2004, s 237A* (as amended by *FA 2011, Sch 17, para 15*) provides that an individual can elect that the scheme administrator be jointly and severally liable with them for the AA charge.

This election is made by giving notice to the scheme by 31 July in the tax year following the tax year in which the AA charge arises. The 31 July following the tax year in which the charge arose is after the 31 January self-assessment deadline, which gives the individual time to determine their marginal tax rate and thus the tax payable by their pension fund.

Where such an election is made, this will lead to a 'reasonable' commensurate reduction in the individual's pension fund (*FA 2004, ss 237B* and *237E*). HMRC has confirmed that pension schemes are not permitted to make an administration charge for dealing with the AA charge and adjusting the pension benefits.

Planning using the £3,600 tax-deductible contribution

10.30   Contributions of up to £3,600 per year can be paid without reference to the level of the individual's earnings. This useful feature enables proprietors of family and owner-managed companies to provide pensions for their 'non-working' spouses, children and grandchildren. Contributions can be made using the 'normal expenditure out of income' exemption for IHT (see 17.9).

Making contributions in this way to a pension scheme could well be a useful method for wealthy grandparents to extract money from their estates for inheritance tax purposes. Provided the payments are regular (for example, are paid by monthly or quarterly direct debit), are paid out of income, and do not diminish the normal standard of living of the grandparents, they should fall within the 'gifts out of normal expenditure' exemption [*IHTA 1984, s 21*].

Using this planning arrangement, grandparents could invest £300 gross monthly (£3,600 a year) for each grandchild from birth up until the age of 18 (and then make no further contributions). Contributions are made net of basic rate income tax, so that the actual amount paid by the grandparents is £2,880 a year, to which HMRC would add £720 (£3,600 at the basic rate of 20%). (Where appropriate, the grandchild could claim the higher rate tax relief on the grandparents' contributions.)

Assuming investment growth of 4% a year (net of charges), about £95,000 in today's money would be accumulated by the time the child is 18. If this were then left to grow until the grandchild reached the pensionable age, the pension fund would be about £500,000. The actual return would of course depend on the performance of the fund and the level of annuity rates at the time the pension was drawn. Although the flexibility of this planning is significantly limited by the fact that the pension cannot be drawn until the age of 55, this may not matter – a substantial sum invested on behalf of the grandchildren could well free up their own savings to be invested in more flexible ways. In addition, planning of this kind may be particularly helpful where there is concern over an impetuous child and the grandparent wishes to fund an investment for later life.

The £3,600 contribution rule can also be used by UK employees who are seconded overseas. Provided they were a member of a pension scheme before leaving the UK and pay no UK tax, it is possible for them to pay a net amount of up to £2,880 a year to the scheme. They can do this for a maximum period of five years while overseas with the benefit of a tax credit from HMRC, thus enabling them to gross-up the payment to £3,600.

Migrant workers who come to the UK on secondment will be able to receive tax relief on contributions paid to overseas pension schemes that are recognised as such by HMRC. The relief will be restricted up to the level of their UK earnings.

Company contributions to registered schemes

10.31 Company contributions to a registered pension scheme can be deducted as a trading expense in the period in which they are paid, provided they are made wholly and exclusively for the purposes of the trade (*FA 2004, s 196*). Similar 'management expense' relief can be claimed by investment companies (see 4.43).

The pension rules provide that contributions must be made in cash – *in specie* contributions are not allowed (but see 10.32A).

The director/employee does not have any income tax charge on the company contribution by reason of *ITEPA 2003, s 308*. However, under the *FA 2011* regime, it must be remembered that any *company contribution* for an employee/

director is added to an individual's total pension inputs for the purposes of determining any excess AA charge (see 10.24–10.27). However, a company contribution is *not restricted by reference to the relevant individual's earnings,* which provides considerable flexibility for owner managers.

It appears that HMRC applies the 'wholly and exclusively' test against the individual's *total* remuneration package. Inspectors must first clear any proposed company contribution 'disallowance' with HMRC's Audit and Pension Schemes Services (APSS), which should ensure a degree of consistency.

Many controlling directors (and members of their family) tend to pay themselves substantial dividends and a small salary, which potentially creates difficulties in securing corporate tax relief for pension contributions made for their benefit. HMRC has indicated that the 'wholly and exclusively' test would be judged against the contribution that would have been required to fund the pension provision for a third party employee in comparable circumstances, and that the salary and other benefits including pension contributions should be commensurate with the duties undertaken by the director. It is difficult to determine such a 'market rate' for an owner-managed company director/participator. In practice, companies should be able to claim relief for fairly substantial contributions (up to the annual allowance), given that owner-managers invariably carry on considerably more onerous and responsible work than ordinary employees. In appropriate cases, the payment should be documented or verified by external supporting evidence (such as from an actuary's report).

It used to be beneficial to make a large company pension contribution where an owner-manager was over 55 years old (and started drawing benefits), since this was not treated as a pension input. However, the *FA 2011* now requires such contributions to be restricted by the AA (see 10.23).

The 'wholly and exclusively' requirement is, however, unlikely to be satisfied where the company wishes to pay contributions for those members of the owner-manager's family who do not actively work for the company or only provide limited duties.

In practice, there should be no problems in obtaining tax relief for company pension contributions for the workforce. If the company has an OPS, an employee may be eligible to become a member. However, he may choose to take out his own person pension plan (PPP) instead. Whether or not that is the better option depends partly on the company's policy on contributing to the employee's PPPs. If the employer is prepared to contribute, it is better for it to pay directly to the PPP rather than increase the employee's salary, so as to save employer NICs that are not chargeable on the former arrangement.

In Example 6, the employee gets tax relief on his contribution of £10,000 which cancels his tax liability on the extra salary.

Example 6

Company pension contribution to director's personal pension scheme

Best Ltd agrees to contribute £10,000 to a director's PPP in 2017/18. It is willing to do this either directly to the PPP or indirectly by increasing the employee's salary to allow him to make the contribution.

Best Ltd pays corporation tax at the rate of 19%.

Contribution by Best Ltd	£
Gross	10,000
Corporation tax relief @ 19%	(1,900)
Net cost	8,100
Extra salary to employee	£
Gross	10,000
NIC (13.8%)	1,380
	11,380
Corporation tax relief @ 19%	(2,162)
Net cost	9,218
The saving is £1,118 (or about 11% of the contribution)	

10.32 Corporate tax relief for very large 'one-off' contributions will be spread over a maximum of four accounting periods (see below). Spreading only applies under *FA 2004, s 197* where:

● there are contributions in two consecutive years; and

● the second year's contribution is more than 210% of the first year's; and

● the relevant excess contributions (RECs) *exceed* £500,000 (RECs are the difference between the second year's contribution and 110% of the first year's contribution).

REC	Number of accounting periods
£500,000 to £999,999	2
£1,000,000 to £1,999,999	3
£2,000,000 or more	4

Planning should enable a gradual step up of the contributions to maximise the 110% allowance and reduce the need for spreading.

Where spreading is applied, this is based on the company contributions actually paid in the period. These should exclude contributions made in respect of funding cost of living increases for current pensioners and funding future service benefits for employees who join the scheme this year – which are fully deductible. Furthermore, where the company has not paid any contributions in an accounting period (eg where a contribution holiday was taken), contributions for the next period are not subject to spreading.

To get around the 'spreading' rules companies sought to route their payments through another group company. However, the *FA 2008* introduced anti-avoidance rules (effective from 10 October 2007) to counter this type of planning.

Contributing assets to pension funds

10.32A The legislation expresses pension contributions in terms of cash sums, which strictly prevents in-specie contributions. However, according to HMRC guidance, it was considered possible (or at least it was until the recent challenges by HMRC – see below) to arrange to pay a monetary contribution, with the consequent debt being settled via a transfer of an asset or assets. Under these arrangements, an irrevocable legal debt must be created in relation to the transfer. The pension contribution does not take place until the legal ownership of the asset passes to the pension fund, thus settling the original debt.

The transfer of assets represents a disposal for CGT purposes and may also trigger an SDLT liability. The relevant assets must be valued for the purposes of the transfer so that the quantum of debt/contribution can be established. If the asset falls in value between the creation of the debt and its subsequent transfer, the shortfall must be made good by a cash pension contribution. On the other hand, if the asset increases in value, the 'excess' could be refunded or the cash could be applied as an additional contribution. Most pension providers prefer to avoid facilitating in specie contributions because of a fear of triggering an HMRC enquiry into the value of the relevant asset.

HMRC has challenged tax relief on a number of 'in specie' contributions made to 34 pension providers (mainly SIPPs) in 2016.

HMRC's latest newsletter (Issue 86 – April 2017) confirms that its position has not changed, which is that tax relief can only be claimed for *cash* contributions. Many have suggested that the reason for HMRC's stance arises from concerns that its guidelines were not being followed (eg valuing the assets and the nature of the assets being transferred into schemes). A legal challenge is currently being made and until the correct legal position has been determined, pension providers are unlikely to accept 'in specie' contributions.

Pensions surpluses repaid to employers

10.33 Authorised pension scheme surpluses (based on an actuarial valuation), which are normally only likely to arise in defined benefit schemes, can be repaid to the employing company provided certain conditions have been satisfied (see *Registered Pension Schemes (Authorised Surplus Payments) Regulations 2006, SI 2006/574*).

Where a registered scheme is subject to the 'surplus payments' provisions under the *Pensions Act 1995*, these must also be complied with to ensure the payment can be authorised. In the case of a continuing scheme, the trustees must obtain an actuarial certificate before exercising their power to repay a surplus.

Where an (authorised) surplus payment is made, the employer is liable to an 'income tax' charge (see 10.34 below). However, this tax must be deducted at source. Under the rules, the scheme administrator is required to withhold tax at 35% from the payment and account for it to HMRC (*FA 2004, ss 177* and *207*). This is effectively a free-standing tax charge and the company cannot mitigate it by the offset of tax losses etc.

Unauthorised payment charge

10.34 Where a pension scheme makes *unauthorised* payment, there is a tax charge of up to 55% on the scheme member. (The basic charge is 40% of the payment, with a 15% surcharge applying if certain limits are exceeded.)

A number of recent cases on unauthorised payment charges demonstrate the complexity of these rules.

In *O'Mara and another v HMRC* (2017) UKFTT 91 (TC), the taxpayers transferred their pension savings into a bespoke pension trust, which then lent the funds to 'their' company for business purposes. The loan to the company was treated as a payment to them personally as beneficiaries of the pension fund, as they jointly controlled the company. The FTT upheld HMRC's unauthorised payment charge on these amounts.

In *Administrators of Wren Press Pension Scheme v HMRC* [2017] UKFTT 131 (TC), the sponsoring company, Wren Press Ltd sold its printing presses to the SSAS and leased them back. The directors of Wren Press believed the printing presses were fixed assets and not 'tangible moveable property' (which was a prohibited investment – see 10.36). The FTT held that the printing presses were 'tangible moveable property' as it was possible to move them, and therefore agreed that this triggered an unauthorised payment surcharge.

HMRC sought to levy an unauthorised payments charge in relation to a 'botched' transfer between pension funds in the case of *Brown v HMRC* (2016) UKFTT 595 (TC), The transfer resulted in funds being 'banked' by the member and held for three years before they were paid into their SIPP. Given that the funds had come under the control of the member, the tribunal accepted that HMRC was justified in applying the unauthorised payments charge. However, the tribunal felt that it necessary to consider the rationale for surcharge, which was 'to penalise unauthorised payments where they are made to frustrate the purposes of the pension scheme tax regime and abuse its tax reliefs and exemptions.' This was not the case here – the taxpayer had simply been foolish! Consequently, the tribunal concluded it would not be just and reasonable for the surcharge to be applied.

The case of *Thorpe v HMRC* [2009] EWHC 611 (Ch) looked at the position where 'unauthorised payments' were returned to the scheme. Mr Thorpe was the sole beneficiary of the scheme and thought he could bring the scheme to an end under the rule in *Saunders v Vautier* [1835] 42 All ER Rep 58. However, although he was the only beneficiary at the time, it was possible that other beneficiaries could arise (he might marry or 'acquire' dependants within the meaning of the scheme rules). It was decided that Mr Thorpe was not entitled to the entire beneficial interest of the fund and the payment to him was a *taxable* unauthorised payment. However, the High Court ruled that Mr Thorpe, (acting as trustee) had committed a breach of trust when he sanctioned the unauthorised payment. Thus, he held it as a constructive trustee for the fund. He was willing and able to transfer the funds back and therefore no tax charge arose on the payment. A tax liability would have arisen on payments that he could not return.

As well as the 55% charge, there is also a scheme sanction charge of 40% (but generally reduced to 15%) on the scheme administrator (*FA 2004, ss 208–213*).

LIFETIME ALLOWANCE RELATING TO REGISTERED SCHEMES

10.35   The lifetime allowance for 2017/18 is £1,000,000 (to be indexed annually in line with the CPI from 2018/19). It previously stood at £1,250,000 for 2014/15 and 2015/16.

The rationale for the decreases over time is that, with the reduction in the AA to £40,000 (see 10.23), the lifetime allowance need not be so high. Until these recent reductions, the lifetime allowance generally increased each year!

The lifetime allowance represents the eligible amount of pension value that attracts tax relief.

Individuals who had built up substantial benefits in their pension funds were affected by the reductions in the lifetime allowance. Provided certain conditions were satisfied, the legislation generally enabled them to protect their pre-existing pension rights and benefits by locking in the value of the pension fund at 5 April 2016 (individual protection) or the 2015/16 lifetime allowance

£1,250,000 (fixed protection) respectively. No further pension benefits can accrue after April 2016.

Broadly speaking, the lifetime allowance is tested on drawing benefits, on reaching the age of 75 with unvested funds, or on death. The value of the fund can be easily measured in the case of a defined contribution scheme. However, in the case of a defined benefits scheme, the value is determined by reference to various formulae. These include the conversion of pension income into a capital equivalent.

Where a member's total capitalised pension wealth exceeds the lifetime allowance, the excess amount is subject to a Lifetime Allowance Charge (LTAC) or 'recovery' charge. The LTAC tax rate charged depends on whether the 'excess capital' is taken as a pension or cash withdrawal (25%) or a lump sum (55%). The scheme rules may lay down how any 'excess' should be taken and HMRC expects the LTAC to be deducted at source, with the net amount being applied towards the lump sum/pension benefit.

Although pension income only attracts a LATC of 25%, the residual amount is then taxed at the relevant marginal income tax rate in the member's hands, thus generally resulting in a penal total effective tax. The registered scheme administrator and the member are jointly and severally liable for paying the tax charge.

PENSION FUND INVESTMENTS

10.36 Tax relief is now only available where the pension funds invest in traditional investments and commercial property. It is also possible for commercial property transactions to take place with connected parties on arm's length terms (see also 10.13).

Where property is acquired which is to be developed as commercial property, this may be vulnerable to a tax charge. Whilst capital gains are exempt within a pension fund, trading profits are not. Profits from a property development activity may therefore be taxed.

Pension funds cannot invest in residential properties (such as buy-to-let and second homes), tangible moveable property and 'collectable' items (such as vintage cars and works of art). The Treasury justified these restrictions on the grounds that the pension fund tax breaks were only intended for those who were genuinely using the fund to provide themselves with a pension. It clearly wished to avoid leisure pursuits being sheltered from tax as a result of them being channelled through pension funds. The regulations also prohibit 'indirect' investment in residential property, etc – this would include, for example, the purchase of residential property by a company in which a SIPP holds 100% of the shares.

FA 2004, ss 174A, 185A–185I and *273ZA* and *Sch 29A* make provision for tax charges where an investment regulated pension scheme holds investments that are taxable property. Taxable property consists of residential property and most tangible moveable assets.

The provisions apply to taxable property that is held directly and also to indirect holdings of property. Pension funds are, however, able to invest indirectly in such 'prohibited' assets by investing in commercially diverse vehicles that hold residential properties. This would include investing in Real Estate Investment Trusts ('REITs') which hold residential properties.

Where a pension fund invests in a company, any 'chattels' owned by the company (worth less than £6,000 per asset) used for the purposes of its trade, management, or administration are exempt from the 'private property' charge rules. This would normally cover such items as desks, computers, plant and machinery.

10.37 Furthermore, where a trading vehicle (such as a company) meets certain conditions, and the pension scheme and associates (broadly, members of the pension scheme and their families) own no more than 10% of the vehicle and have no right to private use of any taxable property, there is no tax charge.

'Arm's length' trading vehicles also qualify as 'commercially diverse', provided that they meet *four* conditions:

- The vehicle's main activity is the carrying on of a trade, profession or vocation;

- The pension scheme either alone or together with associated persons does not have control of the vehicle;

- The pension scheme *member* or a 'connected person' [*CTA 2010, s 1122*] is not a controlling director of the vehicle; and

- The pension scheme does not hold an interest in the vehicle for the purposes of enabling a member (or connected person) to occupy or use the property.

It will be appreciated that this 'let out' will *not* be available to the majority of owner-managed companies.

Income and gains from the 'taxable' property would be taxed at the normal trust rates (see 17.86 and 17.92). Furthermore, the property would be subject to various unauthorised payment charges on the amount invested (40%) and possibly payment surcharges (15%), as well as a scheme sanction charge of (normally) 15% (see 10.34). It would therefore be sensible to hold such assets personally.

Pension funds can lend money to the employing company. However, loans made after 5 April 2006 must be secured, not exceed five years in duration (but can be rolled over once), and must be on commercial terms (with equal annual repayments and an interest charge at least equal to a composite bank base rate plus 1%). Furthermore, such loans must not exceed 50% of the fund. There is no requirement to re-negotiate existing borrowings to comply with the post-A-day limits. It is not possible for the fund to make loans to members.

Shares can be purchased in the sponsoring 'employer' company, but only up to a maximum amount of 5% of the pension funds assets. Helpfully, all investments currently held by an existing pension scheme may be maintained after A-day.

PENSION FUND BORROWINGS

10.38   Pension fund borrowings are limited to 50% of the value of the pension fund immediately before the borrowing takes place. This will therefore take into account any existing borrowings.

If the total borrowing exceeds the 50% limit, the scheme is treated as making an unauthorised payment, with the scheme administrator being liable to a scheme sanction charge (see 10.34). The scheme administrator must report to HMRC details of borrowings that exceeds the 50% limit.

Given that it is only possible to 'gear-up' by 50%, if the value of the existing fund is relatively low, fairly large contributions are likely to be needed to make sizeable commercial property investments. However, in some cases it may be possible for the owner-manager's company to make the required contributions (within the rules set out in 10.23–10.27).

VESTING OF PENSION FUNDS

Retirement age

10.39   The minimum age for taking retirement benefits is now 55. From 2028, it will rise to 57 and then increase in line with the rise in the state pension age.

Those with existing entitlements to lower retirement ages retain the right to retire at that age (provided this right was in force before 10 December 2003), although the member's lifetime allowance is proportionately restricted.

Benefits from the registered scheme may be taken before age 55 if the member is prevented from continuing their current occupation because of ill health (as confirmed by a registered medical practitioner).

The scheme rules may allow benefits to be taken while the member continues to work. Many owner-managers will clearly wish to take advantage of the fact that they can draw pension benefits while continuing to work in the company!

Pre-April 2015 rules for taking pension benefits

10.40   The tax-privileged pension benefits that can be paid out are purely dependent on the prevailing lifetime allowance (see 10.35).

The 2014 Budget announced radical changes to the way in which pension are drawn, which applied from April 2015 (see 10.41). The various restrictions imposed by the 'old' (pre-April 2015) regime were scrapped.

Broadly, under the 'old' (pre-April 2015) regime, investors could take their pension in a number of ways:

- *scheme pension* – the pension is provided from the registered scheme or appropriate insurance company (see 10.42). For occupational scheme members, this is the only option available although the scheme can offer unsecured income if the rules are amended to allow the scheme to do so;

- *lifetime annuity* – the annuity is secured through an insurance company;

- *drawdown* – Under income drawdown, members can choose how much they wish to draw down annually from their pension fund (subject to the limits imposed by the Government Actuary's Department (GAD)). Alternatively, if they satisfied the annual £20,000 'minimum income requirement', they could choose 'flexible drawdown', provided their pension funds were not depleted by 'excessive' income payments.

A detailed commentary of the pre-April 2015 regime is provided in the 2013/14 and earlier editions of this book.

Flexible pensions from April 2015

10.41   Since April 2015, pension investors (aged 55 increasing to 57 from 2028) have been able to enjoy complete flexibility over the amount of income they can draw from 'their' pension fund. Investors already in income drawdown before 6 April 2015 can switch to the new regime (ie enabling them to drawdown more than the GAD maximum – see 10.40).

These new pension rules are not without risk, since the increased flexibility may cause a member to completely deplete their pension fund – thus potentially 'running out of income' in retirement.

Under the post-5 April 2015 rules, members can take flexible amounts of income, in stages of different amounts, enabling them to manage their income tax liability.

They can choose to:

- take the entire fund as a single lump sum – 25% tax free and the rest taxed as income;

- take smaller lump sums as and when they like with 25% of each withdrawal being tax-free and the rest taxed as income;

- take up to 25% tax-free and a regular taxable income from the rest (via a drawdown arrangement – where they draw directly from the pension fund, which remains invested, or via an annuity).

Any withdrawals in excess of the 25% tax-free amount are subject to income tax at the member's marginal tax rate(s). It should also be possible to take the tax-free cash straightaway and the taxable income via drawdown at a later date.

Despite the increased flexibility offered by the new regime, annuities are still likely to remain a reliable choice for many, particularly cautious investors with modest funds, since their objective will be to ensure they have a regular fixed income for life.

As a general rule, pension contributions are subject to a £40,000 annual allowance (AA) (see 10.23, 10.23A and 10.27). However, a £4,000 (10,000 pre-6 April 2017) AA (also referred to as a 'money purchase annual allowance' (MPAA)) applies to those who have already flexibly accessed their pensions and wish to make additional contributions (see 10.27A). This restriction only applies where their defined contribution pension 'pot' is *worth more than £10,000*. In many cases, those with combined 'pension pots' of less than £10,000, can make further contributions within the normal AA rules.

For individuals in capped drawdown, the £10,000 AA only operates on personal pension contributions if they withdraw more than their capped amount.

Pension investors are offered free guidance called 'Pension Wise' (through a range of channels such as phone and face-to-face meetings) to help them make sense of their pension options, which are provided by impartial organisations such as, Citizens Advice Bureau, The Pensions Advisory Service (TPAS) or the Money Advice Service (MAS).

Recycling rules

10.42 The *FA 2006* introduced anti-avoidance rules to prevent the 're-cycling' of tax-free cash sums, whereby a scheme member aged 50 or over draws a lump sum tax-free and reinvests it into the scheme (obtaining tax relief) then withdraws 25% of the newly-invested sum (again tax-free), reinvests it (obtaining tax relief), withdraws 25% of this reinvested sum, etc.

Without the *FA 2006* restrictions, the value of the fund could be significantly increased by this method. Post-*FA 2006*, subject to certain conditions, the re-investment will now be treated as an unauthorised payment, with a resulting 40% income tax charge on the member. There is, however, still scope for limited re-cycling to increase the value of the fund, as it will only be caught if the lump sum is more than 1% of the lifetime allowance.

Death benefits

10.43   Pension payments normally stop on death. However, in some cases, the pension can be guaranteed for a fixed period, which does not stop on death.

However, under the pre-April 2015 regime, a pension could only be passed on as a tax-free lump sum provided the member died before age 75 having not taken any tax-free amount from the fund. In all other cases, the fund was subject to a 55% tax charge (except where a spouse, civil partner or dependent child under 23 take an income from it). The 55% tax charge was abolished from April 2015.

Under the new regime, there are basically three forms of death benefits. They can be paid in the form of a lump sum, by designating the plan into flexi-drawdown or in the form of an annuity (or a mixture of all three) – see 10.41.

A lump sum benefit can be paid to anyone who is a member of the discretionary trust under the scheme rules, typically family members or trustees of a trust created by the member during their life.

Following provisions introduced in the *Taxation of Pension Act 2014*, flexi-access drawdown benefits can be paid to:

- any dependants (such as the deceased member's spouse/civil partner, children under the age of 18 or 23 (if in full time education), children over the age of 23 who depended on the member because of their physical or mental impairment, or someone who was financially dependent on the deceased);

- a nominee (someone other than a dependent); and/or

- a successor (someone nominated by either a dependant/nominee who becomes entitled to the pension fund on the dependant's/nominee's death.

These rules make it possible to have a 'perpetual pension fund', since the process of passing on the benefits to other members can continue until the pension fund has been depleted.

The tax treatment of death benefits depends on whether they are taken before the member dies before their 75th birthday or on/ after that date – see 10.43A and 10.43B. Given the disparities between these tax treatments, members should review their arrangements as they approach 75 years of age.

Member dies before 75th birthday

10.43A   Where the member dies before reaching 75, the beneficiaries can take a tax-free lump sum death benefit providing that the lifetime allowance has not been breached and the lump sum is paid out within two years of the member's death. A special lump sum death benefit charge ('SLSDBC') of 45% applies to lump sums paid out *more than* two years after the member's death.

Alternatively, if death benefits are paid out through flexi-access income drawdown and the funds are designated into drawdown within two years of the member's death, no income tax arises on future withdrawals made by the beneficiaries. If more than two years elapse, the withdrawals will be subject to income tax at the beneficiary's marginal income tax rate.

Member dies aged 75 or over

10.43B   Since 6 April 2016, where the member dies aged 75 or more, death benefits paid either as a lump sum or flexi-access drawdown income are, taxed at the recipient's marginal rate of income tax. There is no UK inheritance tax charge.

However, a 45% SLSDBC income tax charge is still payable where a taxable lump sum death benefit is paid to a 'non-qualifying' person, such as a trust (other than a bare trustee) or a company. This charge will therefore arise with most 'bypass' trusts (see 10.44).

Under the pre-6 April 2016 system, all amounts withdrawn from the fund were subject to a flat 45% tax rate.

Bypass trusts for pension benefits

10.44   Traditionally, it has been fairly common to pass pension benefits through a discretionary trust. A trust will ensure that the fund is preserved for future generations, providing protection from the claims of creditors, ex-spouses and so on. These are often known as 'bypass' trusts

Furthermore, since the pension fund 'by-passes' the member's estate, it is not subject to IHT. The trustees of the registered pension scheme must have unfettered discretion in paying death benefits.

This would apply where the deceased has prepared a standard letter of wishes in favour of their spouse, children etc (without containing any binding instructions). If the deceased retains the right to have the death benefits paid into their estate or to nominate who the benefits are payable to, the relevant amount is chargeable to IHT under *IHTA 1984, s 152*.

However, since 6 April 2016, any lump sum death benefits paid to a bypass trust suffer the penal 45% SLSDBC paid by the trust (see 10.43A).

Subsequent payments made to beneficiaries suffer income tax at their marginal income tax rate. However, HMRC has confirmed that the recipient beneficiaries can claim a credit for the 45% SLSDBC paid by the trust in calculating their own income tax liability.

Example 7

Lump sum death benefits paid to a bypass trust

Mr Miller dies aged 79 in October 2017 with a money purchase pension fund valued at £100,000.

The full £100,000 is paid into a bypass trust. The scheme administrator therefore pays the SLSDBC to HMRC of £45,000 (£100,000 x45%) and the balance of £55,000 to the trustees of the bypass trust.

In February 2018, the trustees distribute £20,000 to Mr Miller's son, Sean. This is 'grossed-up' as a payment of £36,363 (£20,000 × 100%/55%), with a tax credit of £16,363 (45% × £36,363).

Sean's pays income tax of £14,545 – 40% on the gross trust payment of £36,363. He therefore has a residual tax credit of £1,818 (£16,363 less £14,545), which can be offset against his other tax liabilities.

Inheritance tax charges

10.44A HMRC's practice is treat any contributions made to a pension scheme as giving rise to a transfer of value for IHT where the member dies within two years of the transfer and was seriously ill at that time.

Bypass trusts fall within the relevant property regime for inheritance tax (IHT) purposes and are therefore subject to periodic 'ten-year' and exit charges (see 17.97 and 17.98).

The post-6 April 2016 tax rules are likely to reduce the attraction of bypass trusts (see 10.44). However, there will be cases where personal family considerations, such as control and asset protection, outweigh the higher tax costs.

EMPLOYER FINANCED RETIREMENT BENEFIT SCHEMES (EFRBS)

Background

10.45 Broadly, speaking an Employer Financed Retirement Benefit Schemes (EFRBS) is a flexible discretionary trust which enables benefits to be provided after retirement to the 'employee' members of the scheme.

Before 5 April 2006, such schemes were known as FURBS (Funded Unapproved Retirement Benefits Schemes and were originally designed to provide pension benefits for employees (over and above the limits applying to 'registered' pension schemes).

EFRBS can provide benefits in the form of a lump sum, a pension, or an annuity. After an employee's death, the trustees have the power to provide a pension or other benefits to the employees' dependents.

EFRBS do not enjoy any special tax advantages under the pension regime. However, they are very flexible since they are not restricted by the various constraints imposed on 'registered' pension schemes. For example, there is complete flexibility on the investment of funds and there is no need to take an annuity. The EFRBS funds can be applied for retirement income and the residual funds can be left for the next generation.

EFRBS may provide loans to member of the scheme, but pre-retirement loans must carry interest. HMRC requires a commercial rate of interest to be paid (for an unsecured loan). A lower rate should be possible if the loan can be secured in some way. It is apparent that HMRC does not accept the 'official rate of interest' (used for beneficial loan purposes) as an appropriate rate.

Tax treatment of company contributions to EFRBS

10.46   Before the *FA 2011* disguised remuneration regime, no income tax liability arose on the 'benefit' to the relevant employee (*ITEPA 2003, s 307*) and there was no NIC liability.

In recent years, EFRBS were promoted and used as a successor to Employee Benefit Trusts in aggressive tax planning schemes. Broadly, such arrangements sought to claim a corporation tax deduction for contributions made to an EFRBS. The trustees of the EFRBS then 'ear-marked' the contributed funds for the benefit of the owner manager(s) and possibly senior management. Typically, the funds were then lent to the owner managers/senior management on a commercial basis with the aim of avoiding any tax charge on their receipt.

However, since 6 April 2011, the 'disguised remuneration' regime applies where the amount contributed to an EFRBS is 'earmarked' for the benefit of a particular employee/member (as will frequently be the case). In such cases, a 'relevant step' will now be triggered under *ITEPA 2003, Pt 7A* (see 5.19). Consequently, the contribution will be treated as the individual's employment income with PAYE/NIC being applied at that time. However, any 'relevant step' relating to pre-6 April 2006 contributions is not subject to tax under these rules (since they would already have taxed on the employee) (see 10.49 and 5.19). The trustees of the EFRBS have the primary liability to account for PAYE/NIC, but if they do not satisfy this obligation, HMRC can recover the PAYE/NIC from the sponsoring company.

Based on HMRC guidance, where contributions are made to an EFRBS on a 'pooled' basis (ie so they cannot be attributed to a single member), they would not be caught by fall the disguised remuneration rules. This means that wholly unfunded EFRBS arrangements should be safe and may be attractive to some employers looking to provide a general 'top-up' pensions facility, although they lack security from the employee's perspective.

Where the amount is treated as 'earnings' under *ITEPA 2003, Pt 7A*, the company is able to claim an immediate corporation tax deduction. However, if the contribution is *not* taxed as earnings under the *ITEPA 2003, Pt 7A* regime or as employment income under the normal rules, the company cannot claim an immediate corporation tax relief. (Note – the 'employee benefit contribution' rules in *CTA 2009, s 1290* only provide relief where the payment has been charged to employment tax or is an 'excluded benefit' in the relevant accounting period or within nine months of the period end.)

As with EBTs, contributions made by a close company to an EFRBS may be vulnerable to an IHT charge under *IHTA 1984, s 94*, with the relevant value transferred to the trust being apportioned amongst the shareholders. However, some comfort can be obtained from the Special Commissioners decision in *Postlethwaite's Executors v CIR* [2007] STC (SCD) 83 (see 5.17 for further analysis).

Taxation of EFRBS

10.47   A UK resident EFRBS pays income tax at the relevant trust rate and 20% CGT on trust gains (with the exception of residential property which is taxed at 28%). Offshore EFRBS (which are very common) are only taxed on their UK source income. Also any interest on loans payable by UK members must be paid under deduction of tax at source.

Unless the trust falls within the *IHTA 1984, s 86* 'benefit of employees' exemption, it is liable to IHT ten-year charges (*IHTA 1984, s 58*) (see 17.93).

Taxation of benefits

10.48   Broadly, any lump sum, gratuity or other benefit is taxed on the recipient under *ITEPA 2003, ss 393–400* as employment income. Common types of benefit are those provided:

- on or in anticipation of the retirement of an employee/former employee;

- on the death of an employee/former employee;

in connection with the past service of an employee/former employee. As far as NIC is concerned, if benefits are drawn in the same way as for a registered scheme (eg 25% maximum lump sum and the balance as pension), they may be exempt from NIC.

However, post-5 April 2011, a prior employment tax and NIC will, in many cases, already have been triggered under the *ITEPA 2003, Pt 7A* disguised remuneration rules and hence this tax charge will be credited against the later tax charge. However, amounts relating to pre-6 April 2006 contributions are not subject to tax (see 10.49).

Funds accumulated within a FURBS are not included within an individual's lifetime allowance (see 10.35). Similarly, post-5 April 2006 contributions are not included in computing the individual's annual allowance (see 10.23).

Special treatment of pre-6 April 2006 FURBS/EFRBS funds

10.49 *Lump sum benefits* from pre-6 April 2006 FURBS (EFRBS)can continue to be taken tax-free provided the employer company has made no further contributions to the scheme after 5 April 2006.

Where such payments have been made, the amount of lump sum that may be taken without a tax charge is restricted to the market value of the scheme's assets at 5 April 2006, as increased by the amount of the RPI at the date of payment (plus any post-5 April 2006 *employee* contributions).

Similarly, the EFRBS will enjoy pre-A-day IHT treatment on its pre-6 April 2006 funds, including exemption from the ten-year periodic charge If further contributions have been made after 5 April 2006, beneficial IHT treatment is only given to the 'protected portion' of the fund (ie the pre-A-day fund).

PLANNING CHECKLIST – PENSION SCHEME STRATEGIES

Company

- 'Substantial' company pension contributions in respect of owner-managers must be capable of justification (based on the entire reward package, including the contribution).

- Watch the potential annual allowance (AA) charge where total pension inputs (including company contributions) exceed the AA, plus any unused relief brought forward.

- High-earners are subject to a reduced AA (subject to a minimum allowance of £10,000). Owner managers could mitigate the impact of these restrictions by carefully planning their income extraction from the company.

- Consider company pension (self-administered) scheme for working shareholders to be used as tax saving vehicle.

- Those companies that do not offer any form of pension provision for their workforce must think about the impact of the compulsory

---

auto-enrolment scheme which will require them to contribute to a pension for all their employees (aged over 22). The regime is being introduced on a staggered basis from late 2012 to 2018.

Working shareholders

- Owner-managers can only hold up to £1 million (lifetime allowance) in their pension fund on a tax- privileged basis (unless they have elected for fixed or individual protection).

- Where owner-managers personally own the company's trading property, they can realise cash at a favourable CGT rate by selling the property at market value to 'their' pension fund. This may attract an SDLT charge for the pension fund.

- Owner managers making personal pension contributions exceeding £40,000 in a tax year may have to pay an excess AA charge if the total contributions in their pension input period (PIP) *ending in the tax year* exceeds their available AA (plus any unused relief brought forward).

- The excess AA charge rules reduce the attraction of a company paying special contributions as part of a pre-sale tax planning arrangement for the owner manager.

- It will be helpful to keep a summary of unused 'AA' relief which can be carried forward for up to three years and can be used to avoid paying an excess AA charge. Unused relief can only be brought forward if the 'worker' was an enrolled member of a pension scheme in that year.

- Since April 2015, owner managers (at least 55 years old) enjoy complete flexibility in how they drawn their pension benefits. It is possible to take income in stages (of varying amounts) and/or a lump sum. Generally, the first 25% of *any payment* can be taken tax-free with the balance being subject to income tax at the marginal tax rate.

- Owner managers can now pass on their pension funds to their 'beneficiaries' *without any tax charge* (provided they die before age 75). On the other hand, where an owner manager dies on or after their 75th birthday, beneficiaries are subject to tax on the amount they receive at their marginal income tax rate.

- Since 6 April 2016, death benefits paid to a bypass trust are subject to a flat 45% tax charge. However, payments subsequently paid out to beneficiaries are subject to income tax in their hands on the 'grossed-up' amount. However, beneficiaries obtain a 45% tax credit against their income tax bill for the tax charge suffered by the trust.

- Owner-managers have the ability to draw their pension benefits whilst continuing to work in 'their' company.

- Amounts contributed to an Employee Financed Retirement Benefits Scheme will now frequently be taxed under the 'earmarking' provisions of the 'disguised remuneration' legislation.

Other employees

- Those earning below £10,000 per year may be better off staying in the state pension scheme, but many in the pensions industry think this is true for the vast majority regardless of their earnings.

- Consider the use of 'salary sacrifice' arrangements as a means of securing additional pension contributions.

Non-working shareholders

- Contributions of up to £3,600 per year may be made by an individual to a pension scheme for non-working shareholders, including spouses, children and grandchildren.

Chapter 11

Share Issues and Financing the Company's activities

INTRODUCTION

11.1   Typical 'investment' stages would include: 'seed', start-up, early stage, expansion, management buy-in, MBO and rescue/turnaround situations.

There are many ways in which a company can improve its finances. These can be internally generated by retaining profits or improving cash flow without any immediate tax consequences. This could include such areas as tighter credit control procedures, careful planning of payments to suppliers, controlling overheads, and managing stock levels.

As a result of difficult economic conditions in recent years, some companies have struggled to pay their tax bills (including corporation tax, PAYE and VAT). Provided HMRC is satisfied that the company is genuinely unable to pay its tax liabilities on time, it may agree to the relevant tax being paid on deferred payment terms under its 'Time to Pay' arrangements (see 4.54).

Externally generated funds may arise from the shareholders or from third parties, such as friends, business associates and so on. Other options would include bank overdrafts and loans, factoring and invoice discounting, regional grants and special loans. Recent economic conditions have significantly tightened the availability of bank lending. The Enterprise Finance Guarantee Scheme should enable viable businesses to access working capital facilities (backed by Government guarantee) (see 11.3).

Where additional equity investment is needed, the owner-manager may seek finance from a private equity firm/venture capitalist (see 11.4) or a business angel (see 11.5). Some owner managers are also looking to 'crowd funding' as an innovative means of securing equity investment – see www.crowdcube.com for further details.

The commercial impact and tax consequences can vary tremendously. The best method of raising finance from a tax viewpoint is often not apparent until the trading results have been established over a few years. Tax planning with the benefit of hindsight is of course impossible, but in this particular area there are often other factors which dictate the method of raising funds. The issue should be considered from all angles, with a combination of methods sometimes giving the optimum position.

In some cases, it may be possible to structure equity investments under the Enterprise Investment Scheme (EIS), which gives valuable income tax and CGT reliefs (see 11.27–11.55). Great care is required when the EIS is being used to attract investment from outside investors. In such cases, any 'promise' of relief by the company should be carefully explained and given appropriate 'caveats' and disclaimers. EIS relief in not affected by the *FA 2013* 'capping' rules.

For smaller 'start-up' companies, the Seed Enterprise Investment Scheme (SEIS) – a 'sister' relief to the EIS – may also be attractive, although there is a vast array of anti-avoidance rules that will need to be side-stepped (see 11.56– 11.67). SEIS relief is also not subject to the *FA 2013* 'capping' restriction.

The *FA 2016* introduced Investors' Relief (IR), which provides a significant CGT incentive for business angels and other investors. Provide they inject new funds into the company by subscribing for shares, which are then held for at least three years, gains arising on the sale of the shares are taxed at 10%. IR does not attract any form of income tax relief (see 11.68–11.68A and 15.45– 15.46)

Venture capital trust investments are briefly considered at 11.69–11.76.

Legal and other specialist input is also vital to ensure adherence with the *Financial Services Act* rules concerning 'investment advertisements' (especially *Financial Services and Markets Act 2000, s 21*). It is a criminal offence to make or assist in the promotion of a share issue unless the communications have been made (or have been approved) by an authorised person (unless one of the exemptions applies). Similarly, a prospectus may be required under the *Public Offer Securities Regulations 1995, SI 1995/1537.*

LONG-VERSUS SHORT-TERM FUNDING

11.2   Long-term funding will be in the form of share capital (equity) or long term loans. The owner-managers will inject equity or share capital finance and often provide 'shareholder loans'.

Short-term funding is generally required to finance the company's varying working capital requirements. Although this will frequently be in the form of a bank overdraft, recent years have seen a growth in invoice financing with many 'competitive' products now being available. Provided the company can satisfy certain criteria, invoice discounting can provide more flexibility giving the business the money it needs without having to provide the 'belt and braces' security required by banks. Importantly, it overcomes the problem of the lead time between invoice issue and the payment by the customer.

Many companies make the mistake of funding long-term objectives with short-term borrowings. If funding is required for in excess of 12 months, it may be well to discuss a term loan with the company's bankers and to agree favourable rates and conditions.

GOVERNMENT-BACKED FINANCE SCHEMES

11.3   In the difficult economic climate of recent years, 'small' businesses have generally found it difficult to obtain access to finance as banks have tightened their lending programmes. To support small businesses experiencing such difficulties the Government introduced the Enterprise Finance Guarantee Scheme (EFGS) in 2009.

The EFGS will generally support bank lending (between three months and ten years maturity), to UK businesses with a turnover of up to £41 million who are currently having difficulties obtaining the finance they need. There are certain restrictions to businesses operating in agriculture, financial, education, forestry, insurance, and transport sectors.

The scheme is fully managed by the participating lenders, including the decision as to whether it should be provided in connection with any specific lending transaction. Under the scheme, 'small' businesses are able to obtain loans of between £1,000 and £1.2 million backed by the Government guarantee, payable over up to ten years. (The maximum term is three years for overdrafts and three years for invoice finance facilities.) In return for a 2% annual premium the Government guarantees 75% of the relevant scheme loan. The 75% guarantee to the lender does not mean that the borrower is only liable for 25% of the debt. The scheme can also be used to refinance existing loans, convert overdrafts into loans, as well as providing overdraft facilities.

In May 2016, the initial phase of the 'Help to Grow' scheme, which was announced in February 2015, was launched. The scheme aims to generate £200 million (increased from £100 million in the Chancellor's Budget in March 2016) of new lending in its first two years. The lending under the 'Help to Grow' scheme will be available to businesses across all sectors.

Information on the EFGS and Help to Grow can be found at www.british-business-bank.co.uk .

VENTURE CAPITAL/PRIVATE EQUITY

11.4   In some cases, venture capitalists/private fund managers or so-called 'business angels' may also contribute a 'slice' of equity capital and/or loan finance. Most private equity firms 'target' companies requiring investment of over £100,000, mainly in the early and expansion stages of growth. According

543

to the British Venture Capital Association ('BVCA') (www.bvca.co.uk), most of the companies 'backed' receive amounts of less than £1 million.

Private equity is not suitable for every company, especially for those owner-managers who are independently minded and do not wish to concede any part of their equity to an outsider. Similarly, private equity is unlikely to be suitable for so-called 'life-style' businesses which enable their owners to enjoy a good standard of living and job satisfaction. Private equity firms generally look for entrepreneurial businesses that have potential for realistic growth, backed up by a credible business plan and an experienced and ambitious management team. Companies are also likely to benefit from the experienced input and commitment of the private equity executives.

Under a typical private equity transaction, the selling shareholders will often have some retained interest in the business (through equity share capital and/or loan notes). Management will also hold some of the equity interest. The percentage of share capital held by the private equity fund can vary from a large controlling equity stake (for a highly-leveraged buy-out) to less than 50% for 'growth' funding. The funds generated from the private equity deal will generally be used to buy the outgoing shareholders' shares and to provide growth capital.

Where a business is in its 'growth stage' the selling shareholders will be expected to remain heavily involved in the running of the business, which can sometimes lead to tax issues under the 'Transactions in Securities' (TiS) rules. Helpfully, under the TiS regime, a 'fundamental change of ownership' exemption applies where, after the 'partial sale', each seller does not hold more than 25% of the company's ordinary share capital and other 'economic' right. Where the seller is unable to satisfy the conditions for this exemption, HMRC would have to consider whether the transactions was driven by obtaining an 'income tax advantage' test (see 15.82).

Where venture capital/private equity funding is provided, there will normally be a shareholders' agreement, which regulates the shareholder 'relationship' between the 'management' team and venture capitalist(s) etc, specifying their respective powers and obligations to the company and between themselves.

In some ways, venture capital is a partnership between the investor and owner-manager which focuses almost exclusively on building the capital value of the business for future realisation. A private equity investor will always ensure that there is a mechanism for achieving their 'exit' at an appropriate stage, such as by a company purchase of own shares, selling the shares to another private equity firm, a 'trade' sale of the shares or flotation.

Private equity has come under the spotlight in recent years, with criticism from Trade Unions, amongst others, that private equity firms are acting as 'asset strippers', and that private equity companies tend to be run for short-term gain rather than adopting a long-term approach which would benefit employees and customers.

Although the private equity sector has come under increasing scrutiny, its highly positive contribution to the UK economy must also be recognised – for example:

- Private equity backed companies grow sales, profits, and employment faster than other companies.

- Because of this, returns of private-equity backed companies have consistently outstripped the returns of listed entities

- The private equity industry attracts significant investment into the UK (over 70% of its investors are based overseas).

BUSINESS ANGELS

11.5   Business angels are wealthy individuals (often successful entrepreneurs or senior managers) who wish to invest their own money in return for an equity stake. They typically invest between £10,000 and £100,000 in start-up and other early stage financing in return for a share of the rewards if the company succeeds. They can also bring management expertise to the company.

CROWDFUNDING AND PEER TO PEER LENDING (P2P)

11.5A   An alternative to business angels is crowdfunding (or crowd financing or crowd-sourced capital) and/or peer to peer (P2P) lending which essentially involves a number of individuals each investing, lending or contributing smaller amounts of money to a company. The company's business is usually showcased through a web-based platform and the money raised is pooled when the funding target has been reached.

Typically crowdfunding is used for start-ups and early staged businesses where the return is usually an equity stake in the company.

P2P is usually used where more established businesses need additional funding and the reward is simply interest on their investment.

FA 2016 introduced a new income tax relief on irrecoverable P2P loans. The relief allows P2P loans that become irrecoverable to be relieved against interest received from other P2P loans in the tax year the amount becomes irrecoverable (*ITA 2007, s 412A*).

For companies seeking funding using equity based platforms, the availability of relief for investors under the Enterprise Investment Scheme (EIS) and/or Seed Enterprise Investment Scheme (SEIS) would usually be an important 'selling point'. The company should obtain confirmation from HMRC under its advance assurance schemes before creating its online pitch to investors.

Investors' relief may also be available to investors where the conditions are met. See 11.27 (EIS), 11.56 (SEIS) and 15.46 (Investors' relief) for further discussion.

COMPANY BORROWINGS

Interest

11.6   The tax treatment of interest on company borrowings is governed by the 'loan relationship' rules. The loan giving rise to the interest is a loan relationship, and the interest, usually calculated on an accruals basis, is a 'debit' of that relationship. The relief given for the interest depends on whether or not the loan was taken out for the purposes of the company's trade.

Amounts borrowed to buy fixed assets for use in the trade, for working capital, or an 'asset purchase' of a trade will be treated as trading loan relationships. Borrowing to finance an investment or to purchase shares in a trading company will be non-trading (see also 4.4(*h*) and 4.45(*d*)).

Highly-leveraged private equity deals can often make the borrowing company 'thinly capitalised' and this may lead to a disallowance of some or all of the interest cost (under the 'transfer pricing' rules (see 4.11)). Withholding taxes may also apply where overseas private equity funds are involved or where interest is allocated or paid to individuals, for example the private equity fund executives.

Late interest rules

11.6A   The 'late interest' rules may also apply to defer tax relief for allowable loan interest where the lender is an *individual* shareholder. The rules apply where interest remains unpaid more than 12 months after the end of the relevant accounting period. It is fairly common for interest on private equity deals to be 'rolled up' and not payable until exit. Where the 'late interest' rules are triggered, corporation tax relief for the interest is available when it is eventually paid, rather than when it is accrued in the accounts.

Trading loan relationships

11.7   Interest on loans taken out for the purposes of the trade is treated as an expense of the trade and is an allowable deduction in arriving at the profits of the trade.

If the interest augments or creates a trade loss for corporation tax purposes, the trading loss can be carried forward to set against future profits of the same trade [*CTA 2010, s 45*]. However, since 1 April 2017, companies with profits below £5 million may carry forward their (post-31 March 2017) losses for offset against future profits from different types of income and profits of other group companies. For more profitable companies and groups, the offset of these losses are restricted where they have profits in excess of £5 million (see 4.40 for detailed rules).

Alternatively, the trading loss can be offset against any profits of the same accounting period [*CTA 2010, s 37(3)(a)*] and if required then against any profits of the previous 12 months [*CTA 2010, s 37(3)(b)*].

Non-trading loan relationships

11.8   Interest payable on non-trading loan relationships (ie loan relationships entered into other than for the purposes of the trade) is aggregated with any other non-trading relationship debits and credits (for example, interest receivable, discounts, etc).

If the resultant figure is a net credit (ie total non-trading credits exceed non-trading debits), then this is taxed as a non-trading profit. Similarly, if a net debit arises, this is relieved as a non-trading deficit (see 4.4(*h*)) [*CTA 2009, s 301*].

Under current rules, a non-trading loan relationship (LR) deficit can be relieved in various ways. First, it is possible to surrender all or part of the LR deficit by way of group relief (without having to offset it against the surrendering company's profits first) [*CTA 2009, s 457(2)(a)*].

Up to 31 March 2017, relief for any non-trading LR deficit is also available under *CTA 2009, s 459*:

● by set-off against the total profits of the same accounting period (which is referred to in the statute as the deficit period); and

● by carry-back and set-off against *non-trading loan relationship* profits arising in the previous 12 months.

Failing that, pre-1 April 2017 LR deficits must broadly be carried forward and offset against the company's future non-trading profits (ie *all profits except trading profits*) [*CTA 2009, s 457*]. The same offset rules apply where these pre-1 April 2017 LR deficits are carried forward against post-31 March 2017 non-trading profits (except that they will be subject to the £5 million annual allowance restriction (see 4.40 and 4.40A for further details).

However, post-31 March 2017 non-trading deficits can be offset against its future total profits (including trading profits, rental income, investment income, capital gains and so on) and the total profits of fellow group companies.

This offset is subject to the £5 million 'annual allowance' restriction rules. See 4.40A for detailed coverage.

Companies have the ability to use their post-31 March 2007 non-trade LR deficits in favour of any pre-1 April 2007 deficits.

Example 1

Loan relationship – 'accruals' basis of recognition for tax purposes

Brooking Plastics Ltd borrowed £50,000 on 1 January 2017 for a four-year period with a fixed interest rate of 10% per annum. The amount was borrowed to purchase a new plastic moulding machine. Interest is payable every six months from 1 July 2017.

The company's accounting year end is 31 March. The company's accounts have always been drawn up on the accruals basis. The accounts for the year ended 31 March 2017 would include accrued interest for three months of £1,250 (£50,000 @ 10% × 3/12). This amount is deductible as a trading expense in the corporation tax computation for the accounting period to 31 March 2017.

The interest relieved as a trading expense for later periods would be as follows:

Year to	£
31/3/18	5,000
31/3/19	5,000
31/3/20	5,000
31/3/21	3,750

Example 2

Relief for non-trading loan relationship deficit

Sturridge Ltd is a member of the Kop (Holdings) Ltd group. In the year ended 31 March 2018, it had a non-trading loan relationship deficit of £100,000.

Its corporation tax computations for the three years ended 31 March 2019 show the following profits:

Year ended 31 March	Trading profits
2017	–
2018	52,000
2019	60,000

Its fellow group member, Sterling Ltd, made profits of £10,000 in the year ended 31 March 2018.

Sturridge Ltd's non-trading loan relationship deficit is offset as follows in the year ended 31 March 2018:

	£
Total non-trading deficit	100,000
Offset against current year-total profits of the deficit period (y/e 31/3/18)	(52,000)
Group relief surrender (Sterling Ltd)	(10,000)
Non-trade LR deficit c/fwd	38,000

Sturridge Ltd's unused non-trading loan LR deficit would be relieved in the year ended 31 March 2019 as follows :

	£
Trading profits	60,000
Less: B/fwd non-trade LR deficit offset *	(38,000)
Total taxable profits	22,000
*As this deficit arose after 31 March 2017, it can be carried forward against future trading profits.	

SHAREHOLDER LOANS TO COMPANY

Tax relief for interest on loans taken out to lend to company

11.9 It is possible for shareholders to borrow the funds themselves and then to lend these to the company. Relief for personal borrowings can generally be obtained at much higher tax rates than corporate borrowings.

The shareholder can only obtain interest relief where the borrowing company is a qualifying close company within *CTA 2010, s 34* – broadly, a company that is mainly trading or property letting (to third parties).

The company must apply the funds wholly and exclusively for the purposes of its business or that of an associated company [*ITA 2007, s 392*]. Relief from income tax will be available to the shareholder in respect of loan interest paid (but *not* in respect of bank overdraft interest) provided certain conditions are satisfied (see 11.10–11.12).

Allowable interest payments are deducted against total taxable income. For relief to be obtained the borrower must, therefore, have sufficient taxable income to offset it. It is not possible to carry excess interest payments forward or back to set against total income of future or prior years.

From 6 April 2013 onwards, there is a 'cap' on the amount of interest relief that can be deducted against the borrower's income. Broadly, the relief is limited to the higher of £50,000 or 25% of income. In such cases, any relief not used in the year would be lost since there are no provisions for carrying it forward (see 11.14A). The detailed 'capping' rules, which also affect other income tax relief, are explained at 11.14 and 11.14A.

This cap also applies to a number of other income tax reliefs. See 11.14–11.14B below for further discussion of these rules.

If the shareholder has a high level of taxable income it might be considered preferable for them to borrow personally, subject to the impact of the *FA 2013* 'cap' on available relief, as the tax rates are higher for an individual than for a company. This is, of course, unlikely where the individual needs to extract income from the company to repay their borrowings, as this will create an additional personal tax liability.

The 'material interest' and 'full time working' conditions

11.10   A shareholder will qualify for interest relief where they possess a 'material interest' in the relevant company, ie the shareholder must control either directly (or indirectly through intermediate companies) over 5% of the ordinary share capital of the company. This ownership can be alone or through associates. Alternatively, a right to acquire more than 5% of the assets on a winding up would also satisfy the 'material interest' test [*ITA 2007, ss 393(4)* and *394*].

Ordinary shareholders who do *not* meet the 'material interest' test would also be entitled to relief provided that they have worked for the greater part of their time in the actual management or conduct of the company (or 'associated company') [*ITA 2007, s 393(3)*].

IR Tax Bulletin November 1993 sets out the Revenue's views on the meaning of working 'for the greater part of their time in the actual management or conduct of the company', which is strictly construed.

A distinction is drawn between directors and other individuals. Clearly, a director would satisfy this test. Failing that, the individual must possess significant managerial or technical responsibilities and must be concerned in the overall running and policy making of the company as a whole. Managerial or technical responsibility for just one particular area will not be sufficient. However, it is accepted that whether an individual satisfies the 'actual management or conduct' test is a question that can only be answered by consideration of the full facts of the particular case. (HMRC interprets 'the greater part of the individual's time' as meaning more than half the working day throughout the period in question.)

Members of family or owner-managed companies whose management is divided between several individuals may therefore have difficulty in claiming relief for interest if they do not have a shareholding over 5%.

The 'qualifying close company' condition

11.11   The company concerned must be a 'qualifying close company' within the meaning of *ITA 2007, s 393A*. The company must therefore satisfy the following conditions.

- It must be a *close* company, which broadly means that it is controlled by five or fewer shareholders *or* by shareholders (of any number) who are directors of the company (see also 3.12) [*CTA 2010, s 439*].

- The company must *not* be a close investment holding company (CIC). This 'negative' statutory definition effectively means that it must wholly or mainly exist for one or more of the purposes listed below:

  - carrying on a trade or trades on a commercial basis – this will include land dealing and share dealing companies;

  - making investments in land, such as the letting of property to non-connected persons (a company would therefore be a CIC if it mainly lets property to a person/persons connected with the company (see *CTA 2010, s 1122* for the wide nature of the 'connected' party definition for these purposes, which includes counting 'associates');

  - the holding of shares in or making loans to companies which are qualifying companies (ie non-CICs) or whose business is mainly managing 'qualifying' subsidiaries;

  - coordinating the activities of two or more qualifying companies – many holding companies would fall into this category.

The definition of 'close company' in *ITA 2007, s 393A* was extended by *Finance Act 2014* to include companies resident in other EEA states that would meet the definition but for the UK residence test.

Conditions to be satisfied when interest is paid

11.12 At the time *when the interest is paid* by the individual, the requirements set out both in 11.10 and 11.11 above must still be met. However, if the company has lost its close company status, for example due to additional equity having been issued to a private equity provider, relief will still be available provided that the company continues to trade (see SP 3/78).

Recovery of capital

11.13 The individual must also be able to demonstrate that, in the period from the application of the proceeds of the loan to the payment of the interest, they have not recovered any capital from the company [*ITA 2007, s 406*].

The events giving rise to a 'recovery of capital' include a sale, gift, or repayment of share capital or the repayment of a loan made to them by the company [*ITA 2007, s 407(1)*], regardless of whether any of the monies have been applied in reducing the actual original loan.

Thus, where a company repays part of the shareholder's loan, the – 'repayment' will represent a 'recovery of capital' and is treated as reducing the qualifying loan. The allowable interest would then be based on the deemed *reduced* qualifying loan. If the loan is repaid regularly during the year, HMRC may accept an average of the opening and closing balances as approximating to the deemed qualifying loan for interest relief purposes.

Security issues

11.13A Where an individual makes the borrowing the bank or lending institution will normally insist upon security, for example, the applicant's house or insurance policy. Sometimes shareholders are of the opinion that this can be avoided if the company takes out the loan. Often this is not the case and the lending institution will again insist upon personal security being provided by the director shareholders.

Cap on income tax relief

11.14 Since 6 April 2013, *ITA 2007, s 24A* has applied a 'cap' on the amount of income tax relief claimed against total income in respect of certain tax reliefs. This 'capping' restriction applies to loan interest relief for loans to invest in close companies and partnerships under *ITA 2007, Pt 8, Ch 1*.

The capping rules also apply to a number of other reliefs, including the offset of trading losses against general income (*ITA 2007, s 64*) and *ITA 2007, s 131* loss relief for capital losses on non-EIS and non-SEIS qualifying shares against income (*ITA 2007, Pt 4, Ch 6*). For full details of the tax reliefs affected by the 'capping' rules see *ITA 2007, s 24A(6)*. All these reliefs are deducted against the individual's total income before their personal allowances.

Calculation of income tax relief limit

11.14A The limit is the *greater* of £50,000 or 25 per cent of an individual's 'adjusted total income' for the relevant tax year. It applies to the aggregate of all the relevant reliefs claimed for a tax year.

An individual's 'adjusted total income' is calculated as follows:

Taxable income before reliefs (*ITA 2007, s 23*)	X
Add: Payroll giving deductions	X
Less: Pension contributions (where relief given at source) (gross)	(X)
Adjusted total income	X

Where an individual has several available reliefs that are subject to 'capping', they will need to carefully consider which offset should take priority. For example, the allowable interest offset would be lost if it is not used in the relevant year. In most cases, it would therefore make sense to deduct the interest relief in priority to other reliefs that can be carried forward if they are not used.

HMRC has confirmed that reliefs can be offset in the most favourable manner for these purposes.

Example 3

Income tax capping rule – interest relief

Bobby's relevant tax information for 2017/18 is set out below:

	£
Salary	100,000
Dividend from Zamora Ltd (gross)	400,000
Pension contributions (gross)	10,000
Trading losses arising in sole trade (retailer of football merchandise)	150,000
Qualifying interest (on loan borrowed to finance Zamora Ltd, a close trading company)	50,000

The tax offset for Bobby's sole trade losses and qualifying loan interest would both be potentially restricted under the 'capping' rules.

Bobby's adjusted total income is £490,000, calculated as follows:

	£
Salary	100,000
Dividend	400,000
Total income	500,000
Less: Pension contribution	(10,000)
Adjusted total income	490,000

Bobby's maximum tax relief limit for 2017/18 is therefore £122,500 (25% of £490,000). The amount of tax relief Bobby can claim in 2017/18 for the trading losses and the qualifying loan interest is capped at this amount.

Bobby decides to claim the loan interest relief of £50,000 in full, and the balance of his maximum relief is made up of £72,500 of the trading losses.

The remaining trading losses of £77,500 (£150,000 less £72,500) can be carried forward to offset against his total income in 2018/19.

Irrecoverable shareholder loans

11.15   In some cases, the shareholder may be unfortunate enough to find that the loan becomes irrecoverable. Provided that the company has used the funds only for the purposes of its trade, the individual can claim an allowable loss for CGT purposes on the amount of the loan which is proved to be irrecoverable.

The relief also applies where the loan involves a guarantor who is called on to pay the debt, such as where the individual shareholder personally guarantees the company's bank borrowings. The guarantor then qualifies for the loss for capital gains purposes [*TCGA 1992, s 253*].

Normally, losses in respect of irrecoverable loans are deemed to arise when claimed, but the claim can be backdated to an earlier period within the previous two years [*TCGA 1992, s 253(3A)*]. A similar situation applies to shares that have become worthless [*TCGA 1992, s 24(2)*]. (The detailed treatment of shares which become of 'negligible value' and irrecoverable loans is examined in 16.47–16.55.)

FINANCING WITH SHARE CAPITAL

Basic legal aspects of share issues

11.16   FRS 102 defines ordinary shares as an equity instrument that is subordinate to all other classes of equity instrument, including preference shares. The *tax* definition of an ordinary share may not necessarily be the same and depends on the precise characteristics of the shares (see 11.24B).

Holders of ordinary shares are entitled to vote in matters put before shareholders in general meetings (normally in proportion to their percentage ownership of the company).

The 'ordinary' shareholders are also be entitled to dividends (generally paid at the company's discretion and provided there are sufficient distributable profits (see 9.4 and 9.4A) and after allowing for any preference share dividends). They will also be entitled to receive their share of the company's economic value, whether on a winding-up or via a sale. Ordinary shares can be structured to carry specific rights and restrictions – for example see 8.24 and 13.65.

Private companies are not permitted to offer or allot their shares to the 'public'. The directors have the power to issue shares, but it is only possible to issue shares up to the amount of the company's authorised share capital.

Companies are not required to specify an authorised share capital on incorporation – instead an initial statement of capital will be required, which must be subsequently updated when required – for example, when a new issue of shares takes place.

If further shares are 'required', then the authorised share capital can be increased by an ordinary resolution of the members. It is always necessary to check the company's articles before a new share issue is made. (Existing companies can amend their articles to remove any reference to authorised share capital.)

Shares are often issued at a premium, where the price paid to the company exceeds the nominal value of the share(s) issued. The nominal value is the minimum price for which the shares can be issued. Thus, if shares with a nominal value of £1 are issued at a price of (say) £2.50, there is a premium of £1.50 (ie £2.50 less £1).

A share premium often arises where shareholders contribute assets etc to a company in consideration for an issue of a pre-determined amount of shares (in nominal value terms). The excess of the 'contributed' assets over the total nominal value of the consideration shares represents a share premium. Further, in some company buy-out transactions, lenders often require the shareholders to subscribe for additional shares at a premium to demonstrate their confidence in the company's future.

Where the consideration for the share issue exceeds its nominal value, the excess amount must be credited to a share premium account in the company's books [*CA 2006, s 610*]. Historically, the use of the share premium account was restricted. It could only be used to write off expenses incurred in connection with the share issue giving rise to that premium or issuing fully-paid bonus shares. However, it is now possible for a share premium account to be used in a 'capital reduction' exercise under the *Companies Act 2006* (see 13.60).

Companies cannot issue shares at a discount, ie for a consideration that is less than their nominal value. Consequently, any issue of shares at a discount to their nominal value will be invalid. Care must be taken to avoid breaching this rule where, for example, when setting the exercise price on employee or other share options or where a company issues shares for a 'non-cash' consideration. It is therefore often wise to 'play safe' and issue shares with a relatively low nominal value. This creates a 'margin for error' since any balance is allocated to share premium account.

The directors have a duty to act in the best interests of the company when issuing shares. Thus, if a £1 nominal value share is worth (say) £2.50, they would need to have a good reason for issuing it at a price below £2.50.

A company's shares are deemed to be paid-up where the consideration received is a cash consideration. This is widely defined in *CA 2006, s 583* and includes a release of a liability of the company for a liquidated sum – *CA 2006, s 583(3) (c)*.

A private company can accept virtually any form of valuable consideration, including the provision of services, goodwill and know how [*CA 2006, s 582(1)*]. There is no statutory obligation on the directors to obtain a formal valuation of the relevant assets. However, they will need to ensure that the value of the assets is at least equal to the nominal value of the shares being issued as consideration (see above).

Private companies with PLC status

11.17   Some 'private' owner managed companies are keen to have 'PLC' or 'plc' (Public Limited Company) status, which they feel will provide them with greater prestige and 'kudos' in the market place. Companies can use 'PLC' as opposed to 'LIMITED', even where they have no intention of listing their shares on a recognised stock exchange.

However, PLC status carries a number of important requirements and restrictions. A key prerequisite is that they will need to have a minimum allotted share capital of £50,000 of which 25% must be paid up, and have obtained a trading certificate from Companies' House. Furthermore, a PLC must have at least two shareholders, two directors and a minimum of one 'appropriately qualified' company secretary.

PLC's cannot take advantage of many of the exemptions for private companies and must file their accounts within six months of their year-end.

Issue of shares and pre-emption rights

11.18   Where shares are being issued for cash, *CA 2006, s 561* requires that they must first be offered to the existing shareholders in proportion to their existing shareholdings – generally referred to as 'pre-emption rights'. The offer to existing shareholders remains open for 21 days and the shares can only be presented elsewhere if a member declines to take up their offer (*CA 2006, s 562*).

It is possible to override these statutory pre-emption rights by special resolution (which must be passed by 75% of the company's members) [*CA 2006, s 569*]. Some private companies' articles *exclude* the statutory pre-emption rights in *CA 2006, s 561*, but will usually contain further pre-emption restrictions.

SH01 (which includes a statement of share capital) must be filed (in paper or online) with the Registrar of Companies within one month of the date on which the shares are allotted. Where the shares are being issued for a non-cash consideration, the form will generally show the proportion that each share is to be taken as being 'paid-up' and a description of the consideration. (If there is no written contract specifying the consideration, then a form 88(3) must be completed.)

Once the board of directors has agreed to issue the shares, the register of members must be written-up and new share certificates issued. The shares are not issued and a person does not become a shareholder until their name has been entered in the register of members (see also 11.39).

It is now quite common for shareholder agreements to contain 'drag-along' rights. Where the controlling shareholders wish to sell the company to a third party, the 'drag-along' provisions will enable them to force the other (minority) shareholders to sell their shares to the third party at the same price and terms. This enables the buyer to secure the purchase of 100% of the target company's issued share capital.

Register of persons with significant control (PSCs)

11.18A Since April 2016, companies must identify and record people who have significant control (PSCs) over them. These details must be kept on a PSC register, which must be filed at Companies House. The PSCs are confirmed as part of the annual Confirmation Statement. Any changes in the company's PSCs must be recorded on its PSC register and updated on the following annual confirmation statement.

In many cases, PSCs are those (including trusts) who hold more than 25% of the relevant company's issued share capital and/or voting rights or those who have the ability to appoint or remove the majority of the board of directors.

Different rules apply where a company is under the control of another company, such as a holding company. In a typical group structure, the immediate 'holding' company is normally regarded as a 'registerable' relevant legal entity (RLE). This means that, in a group of UK companies, each wholly owned subsidiary simply records its immediate 'holding' company in its PSC register.

Companies must take 'reasonable steps' to determine and identify their PSC/ registerable RLE. They are required to confirm the relevant details with each PSC and enter these on the PSC register. The PSC will disclose the PSC's name, address, country of residence and nationality together with the nature of their control. If a company has no PSCs, this should be disclosed on the PSC register.

The PSC register provides greater transparency over who owns and controls a company and will assist with money laundering investigations.

Income tax relief for interest on loans to acquire shares

11.19   The rules for income tax relief on loan interest to buy *ordinary shares* are basically the same as where borrowings are used to pass funds to a qualifying *close* company (see 11.9–11.13). Importantly, the *FA 2013* capping rules may affect the amount available for offset. The detailed 'capping' rules are explained at 11.14–11.14A.

In contrast to the relief for shareholder loans, the legislation does *not* specifically require the subscription monies received *on a share issue* to be applied for the purposes of the company's trade. It is important to note that interest relief is available where the shares are acquired by subscription or purchased from a third party [*ITA 2007, s 392*].

Some couples may take out a joint loan to acquire shares. In such cases, if only one of the spouses meets the conditions for interest relief, that spouse can still claim their share of the interest as a tax deduction (*Tax Bulletin, February 1992*).

In start-up situations the company may not have commenced trading at the time the loan is applied to acquire shares in the company. The ICAEW raised this matter with the (then) Inland Revenue in 1992 since in many cases the company could not start trading until the relevant funds had been invested in the company. The Revenue recognised this and confirmed that interest relief would be allowed provided the trade starts within a 'reasonable period' of time after the loan has been applied to acquire the shares and the company remains close when trading starts (see ICAEW TAX 15/92 – dated 16 November 1992).

Vigilance is also required in the case of MBO transactions, where the management team invariably borrow money to fund the purchase of shares in a new company (Newco). Newco is used to coordinate the various sources of financing, including bank and venture capitalist debt, and then acquires the target company or business. However, following the decision in *Lord v Tustain* (1993) STC 755, HMRC accepts a wider interpretation of the qualifying close 'trading' company condition for interest relief purposes (see 11.11).

However, if the company *ceases to be close* (because the original managers' shares are diluted by private equity investment) before trading commences, HMRC will deny relief.

Although the relevant conditions for relief must also be satisfied when each interest payment is made, HMRC does not insist that the company retains its 'close company' status at that time *(SP3/78)*.

An important bar to obtaining 'loan interest' tax relief is where the ordinary shares qualified for relief under the Enterprise Investment Scheme (EIS)

[*ITA 2007, s 392(3)*] or Seed Enterprise Investment Scheme (SEIS) relief. The EIS is discussed at 11.27–11.55 and the SEIS is dealt with in 11.56–11.68.

The 'recovery of capital' conditions in *ITA 2007, s 392* also apply (see 11.13). This means that the shareholder's interest relief will be restricted where there has been a 'recovery of capital' – such as on a sale or gift of the shares. In these cases, the qualifying loan for interest relief purposes is deemed to be reduced by the sale proceeds or the market value of the shares, as appropriate.

This restriction could also strictly apply where shares are sold in exchange for shares, within *TCGA 1992, s 135*. However, *ITA 2007, s 410* confirms relief will not be restricted. However, this treatment only applies to those cases where interest relief would have been available had the borrowing been taken out to acquire the 'consideration' shares received. Effectively, this normally means that the acquiring company must be a qualifying close company (see 11.11).

Capital loss on shares

11.20 Where a shareholder suffers a loss on selling the shares, the allowable loss established for CGT purposes may qualify for income tax relief. This relief can also be claimed on a capital distribution received on a liquidation or for shares claimed to be of negligible value under *TCGA 1992, s 24(2)* (see 16.47).

Income tax relief for capital losses on shares (share loss relief)

Key requirements for *ITA 2007, s 131* relief

11.21 Income tax relief can be claimed for capital losses arising on shares under *ITA 2007, ss 25(3)* and *131*, provided:

(*a*) the individual originally *subscribed* for the shares (ie relief is not available where the shares are acquired 'second-hand'); and *either*

(*b*) the shares were the subject of a qualifying EIS relief claim and the EIS relief has not been withdrawn (see 11.27–11.51); *or*

(*c*) the shares were held in a *qualifying trading company* or holding company of a trading group (see 11.21A below).

Broadly, there is no *s 131* relief for shares in an 'investment' company or group.

Where this relief is claimed on shares, *which have not been subject to an EIS or SEIS income tax relief claim*, the deductible amount may be 'capped' under *ITA 2007, s 24A* (see 11.14–11.14A). (The reason why EIS and SEIS-based reliefs are not subject to 'capping' is because they effectively have their own statutory limits.)

The increased risk of injecting funds by way of shares being issued must be compared with the likely extra tax relief as a deduction from income rather than against chargeable gains. With a new family or owner-managed company, where prospects are encouraging, a balance between share capital and loans is likely to be the solution, particularly as loans can easily be repaid.

Qualifying trading company for non-EIS shares

11.21A   Where the shares have not been subject to an EIS claim, the company must be a qualifying trading company or holding company of a trading group. SEIS shares must fulfil these conditions since the 'EIS relief claim' condition does not include SEIS shares. These conditions vary depending on whether the shares were issued before or after 6 April 1998.

For shares issued after 6 April 1998, this means that the company:

(*a*)   must have carried on its business wholly or mainly in the UK throughout the relevant period until the shares are disposed of (HMRC generally accepts that this condition is met where more than one half of the company's trade has been carried on in the UK.); and

(*b*)   at the time the shares were issued, the company

- must *not* be engaged to a substantial (more than 20%) extent in carrying on one or more non-qualifying trades (see 11.44);

- must *not* have any shares listed on a qualifying stock exchange or arrangements for the shares to be listed;

- satisfied the gross assets test (eg since 6 April 2006, its gross assets must *not* exceed £7 million immediately before, and £8 million immediately after). (Although the 'gross asset' limits increased for EIS shares on 6 April 2012, they remained unchanged for non-EIS ones)

Where the company is trading when the shares are disposed of, it must have been trading throughout the six years to the disposal date. Failing that, it must have been trading throughout its active existence.

If the company or trading group ceased to trade, relief is still available provided the cessation is within three years of the share disposal date and the company/group did not then start a 'non-qualifying' trade (see 1.44) or an investment business.

Slightly different rules apply to the qualifying trading company conditions for shares issued before and after 6 April 2007, 6 March 2001, and 6 April 1998. Although these changes are relatively small, reference should be made to the prevailing legislation at the time the shares were issued.

VAT treatment of share issue costs

11.22   The case of *Kretztechnik AG* (Case C-465/03) marked an important change in the VAT status of share issues. Before the European Court of Justice (ECJ) ruling, share issues were treated as an exempt supply. However, the ECJ held that share issues were not a supply at all for VAT purposes.

This means that the VAT on the related professional costs became 'residual' overhead VAT and can be recovered (to the extent that the company makes taxable supplies).

UK companies should therefore normally be able to reclaim their VAT on share issues, subject to any partial exemption restrictions.

Even where the company makes other exempt supplies for VAT as part of its business, it may still be able to recover any attributable 'exempt' input tax under the *de minimis* partial exemption rules.

DEBT-FOR-EQUITY SWAPS

Commercial rationale for debt-for-equity swaps

11.23   Where a company is in financial difficulties or is suffering from high gearing, its major lender(s) may be prepared to swap its debt for increased equity participation. Furthermore, as loan repayment maturity dates get closer, the existing shareholders may also be prepared to consider re-structuring the company's balance sheet, especially if the chances of re-financing appear slim.

In such cases, some lenders take the view that the company still has the potential of producing a worthwhile return in the future. They may therefore be prepared to discharge some or all of their debt in exchange for an issue of new shares – often known as a debt-for-equity swap. The consequent increase in the company's issued shares will inevitably dilute the stake held by the existing shareholders, sometimes quite substantially.

Using new shares to replace debt will lead to savings in interest payments and give a business a much better chance of returning to profit! Debt-for-equity swaps are therefore driven by the mutual interest of the borrowing company and its lender to ensure the company does not go into insolvency.

The treatment of debt-for-equity swaps (involving funding debt/loans) is largely dealt with under the corporate loan relationship regime, which gives a number of tax breaks for such transactions provided that they are correctly structured within the legislation. If the debt is a trading debt, this may also come within these rules by virtue of the 'relevant non-lending loan relationship rules' in *CTA 2009, s 481* (see *CTA 2009, s 481(3)(f)*). However, it should be possible to bring a trading debt within the clear protection of the loan relationship rules by ensuring that a loan note is issued to evidence the debt.

Corporate tax treatment for borrower

11.24 In *distressed* debt cases, a debt-for-equity swap is likely to involve part of the relevant debt/loan being discharged in consideration of new shares being issued.

Tax issues arise where part of the debt is released. Where the parties are 'unconnected', any profit element arising in the borrower's accounts (where part of the debt is actually released) would normally be taxable under the loan relationship legislation. However, where all or part of the debt is cancelled as part of a debt-for-equity swap, the 'borrowing' company will often 'credit' the relevant amount to its share premium account.

In this context, *CTA 2009, s 321* would enable any credit recognised within shareholders' funds to be taxed in the same way as amounts passing directly to the profit and loss account. Thus, although any debt 'release' comprised in the debt-for-equity swap would be potentially taxable, no taxable credit will arise provided the debt/equity swap satisfies the relevant conditions in *CTA 2009, s 322* (see 11.24B).

Related legal and accounting issues

11.24A FRS 102 states that:

- any difference between the carrying value of the liability that is extinguished and the 'consideration' that is paid must be recognised in profit or loss (FRS 102, section 11); and

- equity instruments must be recognised on issue at the fair value of the cash or other 'consideration' received (FRS 102, section 22).

However, apart from this FRS 102 offers no specific guidance on accounting for debt for equity swaps. The accounting treatment will depend on the precise facts of each case (see also UITF Abstract 17). For example, where 'distressed debt' is involved, the company may recognise the 'discount' element in the value of the shares through share premium account (see Example 4).

Where a company does not remove the entire debt through the debt-for-equity swap, the issue of shares may reflect the consideration for both the cancellation of the relevant debt and the modification of the terms of part of the debt that remains outstanding. Many debt-for-equity swaps will entail the debt being reduced to an appropriate level.

Consequently, if the accounting treatment allocates the consequential 'release credit' between the fair value of the remaining debt and the new shares, it is uncertain whether the entire amount is protected by the *CTA 2009, s 322* exemption (particular as the equity value is likely to be relatively low). In practice, this potential problem is usually avoided by separating the debt and equity elements. The part of the debt which is being extinguished is novated to the holding company which enables a 'clean' debt-for-equity swap to be implemented. The residual debt is left in the 'borrowing' subsidiary company. On this basis, no part of the 'release credit' can be attributed to the residual debt since this is not in the holding company's books.

Conditions for loan relationship 'debt-for-equity' swap relief

11.24B The release credit *comprised in a debt-for-equity swap* is exempt under *CTA 2009, s 322* provided the following conditions are satisfied:

- The 'amortised cost' basis must have been used in the period in which the loan relationship debt is released [*CTA 2009, s 322(1)*]. Under the amortised cost basis, a loan relationship is reflected in the accounts at cost less any repayment, release, etc [*CTA 2009, s 313(4)*]. The vast majority of companies are required to use this basis for their loan relationships, so this condition should generally be satisfied.

- The release must be made in consideration of, or any entitlement to, *ordinary* shares in the borrowing company [*CTA 2009, s 322(4)*]. For these purposes, 'ordinary shares' broadly includes all shares *except* those paying a fixed dividend coupon. This means that the shares must contain a variable dividend right. Fixed or zero rate preference shares will not therefore qualify for the beneficial tax treatment. (Note – under the loan relationship rules, a share in a company must have an entitlement to receive distributions – *CTA 2009, s 476(1)*.)

The requirement for the release to be made 'in consideration' of ordinary shares appears to be construed purposively by HMRC. In HMRC's *Corporate Finance Manual* at CFM 33202, this condition would not be satisfied where, almost immediately after the debt-for-equity swap, the (bank) lender sold its newly-acquired shares to the existing shareholders who did not wish to have their equity holdings diluted.

In substance, HMRC would argue that the bank's debt had effectively been realised for shares. HMRC would therefore look at the timing of any subsequent sale of the lender's shares, although a commercial decision to sell them (after (say) six months) is likely to be acceptable. If there is any uncertainty about whether a proposed debt-for-equity swap would qualify for the tax-free 'release' of debt, it is recommended that a non-statutory clearance is sought.

It is important to ensure that the terms of the debt-for-equity swap agreement reflect that the entire release is comprised in the swap. If, for example, it shows that part of the debt is released for no consideration, the borrower will be taxed on this amount under the general principles discussed above. It is often suggested that where any amount is released separately through the profit and loss account, there is a risk that HMRC may regard this as being a separate release which is *not* 'in consideration' for the new ordinary shares.

The mechanics of a typical debt-for-equity swap are illustrated in the worked example below.

Example 4

Debt-for-equity swap – tax treatment for borrower

Radio Zola (Radio) Ltd is a commercial radio operator. Its current ordinary share ownership and debt structure is as follows:

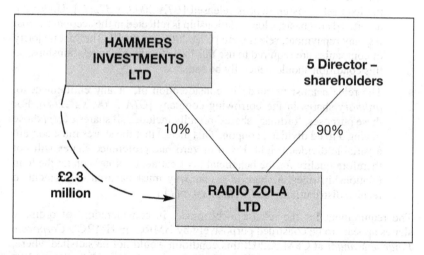

In recent years, Hammers Investments Ltd (Hammers) has also injected interest-bearing loans of £2.3 million to Radio. (Radio accounts for these on an amortised cost basis.) Over the last two years or so, Radio has experienced a substantial decline in its advertising revenues. This fall in revenue, together with the substantial interest payments on the Hammers loan, has generated sizeable trading losses.

Radio's directors have approved with Hammers their plans to re-brand the business which they hope will enable it to return to profit in the medium term. As part of this strategy, Hammers has agreed to cancel £2 million of its interest-bearing loan in return for new ordinary shares in Radio, which would then give it a 49% stake in the company.

To ensure that Radio avoids any tax charge on the debt-for-equity swap, Hammers will therefore enter into an agreement where £2 million of its existing debt of £2.3 million is discharged in consideration for a fresh issue of ordinary shares by Radio.

The following entries would be made in Radio's accounts:

	Dr	Cr
Hammers loan account	£2,000,000	
Ordinary share capital		£20,000
Share premium		£1,980,000

No tax charge arises on any part of the release reflected in the share premium account credit.

Other tax issues

11.25   In some cases, the issue of new shares on a 'distressed' debt-for-equity swap will result in the lending company acquiring 'control' of the borrower. The borrowing company may therefore need to consider the impact on such areas as:

- *Tax group reliefs* – If the borrower is part of a tax group, the debt-for-equity swap may dilute the existing group shareholding below critical tax (50% and 75%) thresholds (see 3.47 and 4.41). Thus, for example, if the group's shareholding falls below 75%, the borrowing company will lose its ability to surrender tax losses to its fellow group companies.

  The borrowing company may also become de-grouped for 'capital gains' purposes and stamp duty land tax (SDLT) purposes, which may trigger a capital gains charge (under *TCGA 1992, s 179*), an intangibles charge (under *CTA 2009, ss 780* and *781*) or an SDLT clawback (under *FA 2003, Sch 7, para 9*) (see 13.71).

- *Unused trading losses* – under *CTA 2010, ss 673* and *674*, if HMRC can demonstrate there has been a *major change* in the nature or conduct of the (borrowing) company's trade in the 'relevant period' it can prevent unused trading tax losses being carried forward beyond the date of the debt-for-equity swap (ie the 'change of ownership' (see 12.59). Broadly, for post-31 March 2017 trade losses, where there is a change in control after 31 March 2017, the relevant period begins three years before and ends five years after that change. For earlier periods, the relevant period is three years either side of a change in 'control'. Similar rules apply to companies carrying on investment businesses [*CTA 2010, ss 677–686*] but these are much wider in scope since they can be triggered simply by a 'significant increase in the amount of the company's [share] capital'.

Tax position of the lender

11.26   A 'distressed' debt-for-equity swap may make the lender connected with the borrower for the accounting period (for loan relationship purposes) in which the swap occurs [*CTA 2009, ss 348* and *466*]. This is because the lender will often acquire 'control' of the borrowing company [*ICTA 2007, s 472*].

As a general rule, a connected lender cannot obtain any tax relief for impairment losses or amounts written off on a release of a 'connected' company debt. However, *CTA 2009, s 356* permits the lending company to obtain a tax deduction for any amount written-off where the borrower treats that part of the relevant loan as discharged and this is done in consideration of the issue of *ordinary* shares to it. Broadly speaking, the lender's CGT base cost will be the market value of the shares at the time of the swap (which in such cases is likely to be below the amount treated as subscribed for the shares – see 16.56).

ENTERPRISE INVESTMENT SCHEME (EIS)

Introduction

11.27   The aim of the EIS is to provide a targeted incentive for new equity investment in unquoted trading companies and of course nearly all family or owner-managed companies are just that. It is possible to invest under the EIS scheme as a direct share subscription in a single company or through a managed EIS fund run by a venture capitalist. Only 'direct' EIS investments are considered here.

Business angels should be attracted to the EIS as they can be employed by the company and draw reasonable remuneration. This naturally allows them to have a degree of 'hands on' involvement in the company which, in turn, usually gives them greater security over their investment. There are, however, several restrictions which may mean that investors may be difficult to find.

Potentially, the EIS has a major role to play when a family or owner-managed company requires funds. The fact that well over £22 billion of equity has been invested under the EIS (and VCT) schemes provides an indication of its success, and the *FA 2012* relaxations of the EIS financial and business size limits has opened them up to larger owner managed companies.

FA 2012 introduced a 'sister' relief – the Seed Enterprise Investment Scheme (SEIS), which is aimed at attracting equity investment into very small 'start-up' companies (see 11.56–11.68). All *ITA 2007* references to the EIS legislation in this chapter only apply to shares issued after 5 April 2007 (and before 6 April 2025).

The *F (No 2) A 2015* introduced some targeted refinements to the tax-favoured venture capital relief rules, with the emphasis now being placed on share issues intended to finance organic growth taking place in the earlier trading life of a company (see, for example, 11.32, 11.34 and 11.34C). Knowledge intensive companies also now enjoy preferential treatment (see 11.32A).

With the introduction of further rules and changes to the already highly prescriptive conditions each year, it now becomes an increasingly complex task to determine whether a competent EIS claim can be made!

How EIS works

Basic EIS rules and limits

11.28 The EIS investment must be:

- made by a qualifying investor (see 11.33);

- subscribing wholly in cash (see 11.39);

- for fully paid-up eligible shares (see 11.39); and

- issued to raise money for the purposes of a qualifying business activity (see 11.44) and (following *F (No 2) A 2015*) to promote business growth and development.

The investor must also retain the relevant EIS shares for *at least three years* after the share issue (although they can be transferred to a spouse) otherwise the EIS relief is clawed-back (see 11.51).

Furthermore, the investor must *not* be connected with the company at any time in the designated period (see 11.33 and 11.35).

This is done to ensure that companies continue their hiring and growth through the scheme. Job creation and the associated improvement in citizens living standards is, after all, the underlying reason for the government supporting these schemes.

Income tax relief is available at 30% on subscription monies of up to £1,000,000 (since 6 April 2012) in each tax year or (if less) the amount that would reduce the taxpayer's liability to nil. Where shares are subscribed for in excess of the £1,000,000 limit, the maximum EIS relief is apportioned to each share acquired.

The 30% EIS income tax relief is still given to 20% basic-rate taxpayers. Note that EIS relief is *not* subject to the *FA 2013* 'capping' rules (see 11.14 and 11.14A).

It is also possible to obtain EIS relief by carrying-back qualifying investments made from the next tax year (in the period to 5 October).

Before 6 April 2012, the EIS share subscription limit was £500,000 and for pre-6 April 2011 EIS share issues, income tax relief was given at 20%.

FA 2012 abolished the EIS minimum annual investment amount of £500 [*ITA 2007, s 157(1), (2)*]. Thus, from 6 April 2012, there is no minimum limit for EIS subscriptions.

For a 'start up' company, EIS relief is not obtained unless and until the company has carried on the qualifying trade for four months.

EIS eligible shares also attract an outright CGT exemption (see 11.30) and can be used to defer capital gains on other disposals (see 11.31).

Provided that the EIS investment qualified for income tax relief, it can subsequently be realised free of CGT after three years (five years for shares issued before 6 April 2000). Note that the three-year holding period runs from the date that the trade commenced if this was after the issue of the EIS shares.

After two years, EIS shareholdings invariably qualify for 100% business property relief for IHT purposes (see 17.19).

Example 5

Calculation of EIS relief for 2017/18

On 1 January 2018, Mr Carragher subscribes £800,000 for 20% of the ordinary share capital in Jamie Limited, which is a qualifying company for EIS purposes.

His income tax liability *before EIS relief* in 2017/18 is £400,000. The effect of his EIS claim is as follows:

	£
Income tax liability (pre-EIS relief)	400,000
Less: EIS relief – £800,000 × 30%	(240,000)
Income tax liability	160,000

If the relevant EIS conditions are breached at any time before 1 January 2021, the income tax relief received in 2017/18 will be clawed back (see 11.51).

Mr Carragher will be able to sell the shares in Jamie Ltd free from CGT provided both he and Jamie Ltd continue to meet the EIS income tax relief qualifying conditions until 1 January 2021 (see 11.30 and 11.52).

Carry-back election

11.29   If an EIS investment is made in the first half of a tax year (ie 6 April to 5 October inclusive) an election can be made to relate back the *entire EIS investment* (ie up to the £1,000,000 limit) for offset against the investors taxable income of the preceding tax year.

EIS CGT exemption

11.30 Gains made on the sale of EIS-relieved shares are exempt provided that they are disposed of after the relevant 'three-year' period – normally three years from the date on which the shares are issued (or if the shares were issued before 6 April 2000, five years from the issue date) [*TCGA 1992, s 150A(2)* and *ITA 2007, ss 159(2)* and *256*] (see 11.51).

EIS investors who are mainly seeking the CGT exemption must ensure that they still make a claim for the EIS income tax relief. This point was confirmed in *Robert Ames v HMRC* [2015] UKFTT 337. Mr Ames had subscribed for shares meeting all the relevant EIS conditions. However, he did not claim EIS on his tax return (since there was little income). He subsequently sold the shares at a significant gain and claimed the EIS CGT exemption. However, the FTT agreed that the CGT exemption should be denied on the basis that no EIS relief was claimed and hence there was no EIS relief attributable to the shares (*TCGA 1992, s 150A*).

If the EIS shares are disposed of within the relevant 'three-year' period, the EIS relief is restricted/withdrawn and a taxable gain arises in the normal way (see 11.51).

EIS CGT deferral relief

11.31 Individuals can also defer their chargeable gains on any disposal where they reinvest them in a qualifying company under the CGT EIS deferral relief regime. The *FA 2015* gave an important boost to the EIS CGT deferral rules by enabling the deferred gain to qualify for entrepreneurs' relief (ER) when it subsequently crystallises (provided the relevant ER conditions were satisfied on the original gain) – see 11.31A and 15.100A.

Given that EIS CGT deferral relief can be claimed by existing shareholders (irrespective of whether they are 'connected' with the relevant company), this often proves to be a popular way for owner-managers to relieve their capital gains. This was clearly illustrated in the case of *Blackburn (t/a Alan Blackburn Sports Ltd v HMRC* [2008] EWHC 266 (Ch) where Mr Blackburn, who controlled the company with his wife, subscribed £1.19 million for shares to defer his capital gains – see 11.39.

The detailed rules for EIS CGT deferral relief are discussed extensively at 15.92–15.102.

Obtaining ER on deferred gains

11.31A Under the pre-*FA 2015* regime, where an 'ER-eligible' gain was postponed under the EIS CGT deferral rules, it was not possible to enjoy ER on *that* gain. This tended to reduce the attraction of opting for EIS CGT deferral, since the deferred gain invariably crystallised at the main CGT rate. On the other hand, if no EIS CGT deferral was claimed, the 10% ER CGT rate could be claimed.

However, the *FA 2015* now enables EIS CGT *deferred gains* to obtain ER under the 'deferred entrepreneurs' relief' rules in *TCGA 1992, ss 169U* and *169V*. Therefore, provided the original gain qualifies for ER (and arose after 2 December 2014), this can be postponed under the EIS CGT deferral rules with the benefit of ER. Provided the relevant election is made under *TCGA 1992, s 169V(5)* (by the 31 January following the end of the tax year in which the deferred gain crystallises), the gain will be taxed at the 10% ER CGT rate.

Maximum overall limit on amounts raised through risk capital schemes

11.32 The *FA 2007* introduced overriding rules on the total amount that can be raised by an investee company under any of the tax-privileged 'risk capital' schemes (being EIS, SEIS, SITR, and a qualifying holding of a VCT scheme) – this is known as the 'risk capital schemes requirement' (*ITA 2007, s 173A*).

Under this rule, an equity investment will only qualify for EIS relief provided the total amount raised by the company under 'risk-capital' schemes within the 12 months ending with the relevant share issue does not exceed £5 million (£2 million before 6 April 2012).

This 12-month 'risk capital schemes' limitation is applied on a 'rolling-basis. If the £5 million limit is exceeded, EIS relief is denied on the *whole* of that investment. For example, if a company raises £4,000,000 under a qualifying EIS share issue on 1 December 2016 and then intends to raise a further £1,200,000 under EIS in May 2017, relief will be denied on the entire £1,200,000. On the other hand, if it restricted the May 2017 EIS issue to (say) £950,000, this would qualify.

From 18 November 2015, the issuing company is subject to a lifetime limit for the amount it can raise under the risk capital schemes (see above). Most companies have a maximum lifetime limit of £12 million. However, 'knowledge intensive' companies (see 11.32A) enjoy a £20 million lifetime limit.

Knowledge intensive companies

11.32A 'Knowledge intensive' companies are given preferential treatment in relation to some of the qualifying 'venture capital' relief tests – for example, see 11.32, 11.34C, and 11.42E).

To qualify as a 'knowledge intensive' company under *ITA 2007, s 252A*, the company must meet all the conditions listed below. In the case of a parent company, these tests are applied to the (51%) group.

- One or both of the operating cost conditions in *ITA 2007, s 252A(2), (3)*.

  Condition 1 – In at least *one* of the three previous years, research and development or innovation expenditure represented at least 15% of the company's (group's) operating costs

  Condition 2 – In *all of the three previous years*, research and development or innovation expenditure represented at least 10% of the company's (group's) operating costs

- One or both of the innovation and skilled employee conditions

  The innovation condition – when the relevant (EIS) shares are issued, the company must be engaged in creating intellectual property (IP) – see *ITA 2007, s 252A(6)* for further explanation. A company will also qualify if it reasonable to assume that (within ten years of the relevant share issue), the exploitation of its IP and/or new products, services or processes using its IP will form the greater part of its business (or the group activities) (*ITA 2007, s 252A(5)–(7)*).

  The skilled employee condition – throughout the three-year period following the relevant share issue, at least 20% of the company's (or group's) full time equivalent employees are skilled employees (*ITA 2007, s 252A(8)*).

Main EIS conditions

Qualifying investor

11.33   A qualifying investor is an individual liable to UK income tax who is *not connected with the company* (see 11.35) at any time in the designated period. The designated period broadly:

- begins two years *before* the issue of the shares; and

- ends immediately before the third anniversary of the share issue (or if the company was not trading when the shares were issued, the third anniversary of the date trading commenced) [*ITA 2007, ss 157(1)* and *163(1), (2)*].

The *F (No 2) A 2015* prevents *existing* shareholders from obtaining EIS relief unless *all* of their existing shares were issued under EIS, SEIS (see 11.56) or SITR (see 11.77) *or* are subscriber shares (*ITA 2007, s 164A*).

'The use of the money raised' requirement

11.34   The 'EIS' shares must be issued for the purposes of raising money for a qualifying business activity – see 11.42B (*ITA 2007, s174*).

For shares issued after 21 April 2009, all of the money raised by the EIS share issue must be wholly employed for the purposes of a qualifying trade *or* research and development (R&D) (see 11.44) within *two years* of the share issue (or, if later, within two years of the company commencing to trade). See 11.34A for review of cases that have considered whether a valid employment of 'EIS' subscription monies has been made.

As a practical measure, it is often helpful to place all EIS subscriptions in a separate bank account – this will make it easier to demonstrate that they have been applied for qualifying purposes.

The *F (No 2) A 2015* stipulates that share subscription monies that are directly/indirectly employed in acquiring any of the following assets will *not* qualify for EIS relief:

- acquiring an interest (or further interest) in a 51% subsidiary of the issuing company;

- a trade; or

- intangible assets (as defined in the corporate intangibles legislation – see 12.50A to 12.50C); or

- goodwill employed for the purposes of the trade.

This amendment (found in *ITA 2007, s 175(1ZA)*) applies from 18 November 2015 and marks a significant restriction on the use of EIS subscription monies. This rule effectively prevents EIS monies being used to 'finance' a business acquisition (whether via a share purchase or a trade and asset purchase). The policy intention being that EIS is now only intended to finance organic growth.

The use of the money raised' requirement

11.34A A number of cases have confirmed the importance of clearly demonstrating how EIS subscriptions have been applied.

In *Richards & Skye Inns Ltd v HMRC* [2011] UKUT 440 (TCC), [2012] All ER(D) 198 (Jan), Mr Richards had claimed EIS CGT deferral relief for share subscriptions in Skye Inns Ltd that were made in three separate tranches. HMRC rejected the claim for relief on the third tranche as it had not fulfilled the 'employment of subscription monies' requirement in *TCGA 1992, Sch 5B, para 1(2)(g)*. At that time, the legislation required that 80% of the money raised must be employed in the company's qualifying activity within the 12-month qualifying period. The taxpayer's appeal to the Upper Tribunal was subsequently rejected.

The subscription monies had been intended to be used for an acquisition, but this did not go ahead. Instead, the funds were held in an instant access savings account, with the company subsequently using the cash to fund its operating expenditure when the business was running at a loss.

The Upper Tribunal held that the subscription monies had not been 'employed' within the required period. The Tribunal explained that share subscriptions are considered to be properly 'employed' where they were:

- 'actually spent on realistic net increases to the net trading assets';

- 'reserved to supplement the current receipts of the trade, either in funding losses or meeting expenses that can be ranked as current business requirements;' or

- 'earmarked ... in the relevant period for some specific purpose (which does not necessarily have to be a purpose calling for expenditure in that period)'.

In the Richards & Skye Inns Ltd case, whilst the monies had originally been intended for an acquisition, they could not be said to be 'earmarked' for use in a later period, because the acquisition never proceeded.

The question of whether monies were 'earmarked' for the required purpose was also considered in *Benson Partnership Ltd v HMRC* [2012] UKFTT 63 (TCC). In that case, it was held that monies could not be earmarked for use for the required purpose earlier than the time when a stage payment of the amount was due in respect of an ongoing contract for capital works.

In *Harvey's Jersey Cream Ltd v HMRC* [2013] UKFTT 663 (TC), a company had been a partner in a trading partnership, with the other four partners (father and his three children) being the company's shareholders.

The company had applied to HMRC to issue EIS certificates for the company's purported EIS share issue. The key facts were as follows:

- each partner took drawings from the partnership;

- each partner subscribed for shares in the company in amounts corresponding to those drawings

- the company paid the circa £1.25 million raised by the share issue to the partnership.

HMRC refused to issue EIS certificates on the basis that the money raised by the share issue had not been 'employed wholly for the purposes' of a qualifying business activity.

The First-tier Tribunal agreed, ruling that that 'the monies raised were not employed in the activities of the qualifying trade', since the EIS monies went used in a circular manner to increase the company's share in the partnership – they were not therefore employed for the purposes of the trade.

11.34B The relevant qualifying trade/R&D activity can be carried on by the company issuing the EIS shares *or* its 90% qualifying subsidiary, thus giving groups flexibility in arranging the company or companies that carry on the relevant activity without prejudicing the investors' EIS reliefs [*ITA 2007, s 175*].

Other shares can be issued contemporaneously without prejudicing the investors' tax relief on valid EIS share issues. An issuing company can make:

- a bonus issue to its existing shareholders, or

- an issue of shares to 'non-EIS' investors for a 'non-cash' consideration

without affecting the eligibility of an *EIS* share issue made on the *same day*. There is no restriction on the use of money raised by the issue of non-EIS shares.

Company age requirement

11.34C The *F (No 2) A 2015* imposes a time limit on the availability of issuing EIS eligible shares (*ITA 2007, s 175A*) – referred to in the statute as 'the permitted maximum age condition'. EIS has always been intended to support early stage companies and hence this rule enables the benefits of EIS goes to companies that need it the most.

For most companies, EIS-eligible share issues can only be made within *seven years* of the commencement of trade (the legislation calls this the date of the 'first relevant commercial sale'). This time limit is extended to ten years for 'knowledge intensive' companies (see 11.32A).

However, this restriction does *not* apply if the company has:

- previously issued shares under the SEIS, EIS, or VCT regimes; or

- undergone a fundamental change in the nature of its business.

FA 2016 clarified the method for determining whether a company meets the maximum age limit.

'No connection with the issuing company' requirement

11.35   The term 'connected with the company' basically means that the 'investor' (together with their associates) must *not* directly or indirectly possess (or be entitled to possess) *over 30%* of:

(*a*)   the issued ordinary share capital of the company or any subsidiary; or

(*b*)   the issued share capital of the company or any subsidiary; or

(*c*)   the voting power in the company or any subsidiary [*ITA 2007, ss 163* and *170*].

Test (*b*) above was modified by the *FA 2012* to exclude 'loan capital' and hence now only looks at the issued share capital of the company. For pre-6 April 2012 share issues, test (*b*) included 'loan capital' which often created difficulties since some potential EIS investors had already advanced loans to the investee company.

A further economic test for connection is provided in *ITA 2007, s 170(2)*. This provides that an investor will be connected with the investee company if they would be entitled to more than 30% of the company's (or relevant subsidiary's) assets on a winding-up that would be available for distribution to the equity holders (ie ignoring loan creditors).

Where the size of an individual's investment is likely to breach the 30% connection test, it is worth considering issuing the shares at a premium. This reduces the number of ordinary shares required to be issued to the potential investor(s) and the voting rights they would hold. This may also be a commercial requirement of the existing shareholder(s), who would generally wish to avoid any unnecessary dilution of their interest.

For the purposes of the 'connection' test, the EIS definition of 'associate' is narrower than the one which normally applies for most other tax purposes – notably, brothers and sisters cannot be treated as associates [*ITA 2007, s 253*].

An investor would be 'associated' with any trust that they created. One particular trap applies to business partners – these are 'associated'. Thus, in establishing whether the 30% 'connection' test is breached, all the holdings held by the partners must be aggregated. This normally prevents any qualifying EIS investment being made by the partners of a partnership or members of an LLP.

Employees and directors of the issuing company would normally be denied EIS relief since they are deemed to be connected with it under *ITA 2007, s 167*. (Certain reciprocal arrangements are also caught under *ITA 2007, s 171*.) However, a special provision still enables 'incoming' directors to obtain relief (see 11.36).

Exceptionally, the 30% connection test does *not* apply to the period between the incorporation of the company and the earlier of when the company started to prepare for trading or its first share issue (ie *after* the original subscriber shares).

If the investor held one or more of the subscriber shares of the company before it began trading and before any other shares had been issued, they would not be regarded as connected with the company at that time simply by reason of this [*ITA 2007, s 170(5)*].

Potential investors should appreciate the risk element in view of the fact that they cannot hold over 30% of the issued ordinary share capital, nor be entitled to acquire more than 30% of the assets on a winding up [*ITA 2007, s 170(1)*] during their designated period. However, they are likely to obtain greater comfort by working for the company as a director and there is a special exception from the normal 'employee/director' connection test which enables 'incoming' directors to obtain EIS relief (see 11.36 below).

EIS consequences of being a director or employee

11.36 As a general rule, the investor (or any of their associates) must *not* be:

- an employee (for this purpose, a director is not an employee);
- a partner; or
- a paid director or director previously involved in carrying on the trade (but see exception below for incoming directors)

of the investee company or any of its 51% subsidiaries in the five-year period beginning two years *before* the share issue [*ITA 2007, ss 163* and *170*].

Relaxation for 'incoming' directors

11.36A Investors would ordinarily be connected with the company if they are directors and would therefore be debarred from EIS relief. However, if that is the *only* reason for connection, *ITA 2007, ss 168* and *169* provide that EIS relief is still available to an 'incoming' director (under the 'business angel' rules) provided that the following conditions are satisfied:

(*a*)   the director's remuneration is reasonable for the services performed;

(*b*)   when issued with the eligible shares, the director-investor was not and had not previously been:

(i)   connected with the investee company (see 11.35); or

(ii)   involved in carrying on the trade (or any part of it) now being carried on by the investee company or its subsidiary (this is widely drafted to catch 'involvement' in the capacity as a sole trader, partner, (unpaid) director, or employee).

In summary, an investor who was previously *unconnected* with the company may become a *paid* director and still qualify for EIS relief, provided that the remuneration is 'reasonable' in relation to their duties (and it must not be 'linked' to the amount of their investment). The ability to become a 'paid' director will often be an attractive feature to a new investor. It is recommended that an existing director does not draw any salary until after their EIS share subscription. Once a director qualifies for an EIS share issue under the 'business angel' rules, they can qualify under subsequent EIS issues during the next three years.

However, where the investor is an *existing* paid director or employee of the investee company or any of its 51% subsidiaries (*before* the share issue), they will not qualify.

Key anti-avoidance rules

11.37 The share issue must be made for genuine commercial reasons and not part of a tax avoidance scheme [*ITA 2007, s 178*].

For shares issued after 6 April 2012, the relevant EIS shares must not be issued in connection with, or as a consequence of, particular 'disqualifying arrangements'. Disqualifying arrangements are those that generate access to the tax reliefs but where the benefit of the investment is passed onto another party or, where the business activity would otherwise be carried on by another party [*ITA 2007, s 178A*].

There is no EIS relief if arrangements already exist at the time the shares are issued for the disposal of the shares, a disposal of the company's assets, the cessation of its trade, or the guaranteeing of the EIS investment [*ITA 2007, s 177*].

Note that income tax relief cannot be claimed on interest paid on borrowings taken out to subscribe for a qualifying EIS share issue [*ITA 2007, s 392(3)*] (see 11.19).

Investor warranties

11.38   The investor's EIS relief can subsequently be restricted or withdrawn by the investee company's actions. Consequently, where a material amount is being invested, it would often be reasonable for the investor(s) to obtain an appropriate set of EIS-specific warranties and indemnities from the company. These might include the investee company warranting that it will:

- not change the rights attaching to the investor's EIS shares (see 11.39);

- use all reasonable endeavours to carry out a qualifying trade (see 11.44);

- not purchase any non-qualifying subsidiaries or enter into any joint ventures (see 11.47 and 11.48).

Eligible shares

11.39   The legislation normally gives EIS relief in the tax year in which the shares are *issued* (ie when the shares are entered in the company's Register of Members (*National Westminster Bank plc v CIR (1994) STC 580*)), although the relief may be claimed in the previous year by making a carry back claim (see 11.29).

The Court Of Appeal decision in *Blackburn (t/a Alan Blackburn Sports Ltd v HMRC* [2008] EWHC 266 (Ch) shows the potential dangers of advancing monies to the company before the shares are formally issued. There should be a proper share subscription agreement, supported by appropriate Board resolutions and minutes. These should make it clear that the monies are being paid into the company by way of a subscription for the 'EIS' share issue.

To be eligible for relief the shares must be subscribed for entirely in cash and must be fully-paid up at the time of issue. In *Blackburn*, HMRC contended that certain share issues had not been 'fully paid-up' at the time of issue and therefore failed this test. However, the Special Commissioners firmly rejected this. They found that the shares were not *unconditionally* issued and therefore were issued when subsequent payment was made (a few days later) and HMRC did not appeal on this point (see also 11.41).

The EIS legislation also requires that the shares are new ordinary shares which do not carry any *preferential right* as to dividends, asset distributions on a winding up or redemption for three years from issue.

The decision in *Flix Innovations Ltd v HMRC* [2016] UKUT 301 confirms that if the shares contain *any* preferential right to assets on winding up, they will not qualify for EIS relief. The taxpayer tried to argue that there was a deminimis rule for these purposes, but this was firmly rejected by the Upper Tribunal since the legislation was 'closely articulated' and *ITA 2007, s 173(2)(aa)* used the word 'any'!.

For share issued after 5 April 2012, shares that carry a preferential right to dividends may qualify, provided the dividend amount and the date dividends are payable is not dependent on a decision of the company, the shareholder, or anyone else and provided the dividends are not cumulative.

In some cases, it may be considered desirable for EIS shares to carry certain restrictions and this can be done without breaking their EIS status.

'Value received' rules

11.40 The purpose of the EIS is to encourage fresh equity investment and therefore there are 'receipt of value' rules that deny or restrict relief where there are arrangements that do not result in 'new money' being available to the company.

Thus, the investor's original EIS relief is restricted or withdrawn completely where they are deemed to 'receive value' from the investee company (or any connected person) during the so-called 'period of restriction' – Period C in *ITA 2007, s 159(4)* – normally, the one year before and the three-year period following the EIS share issue).

Where the investor receives value from the company (*ignoring any 'insignificant amount'*), their original EIS relief is reduced on a pro-rata basis. Thus, the reduction in relief is calculated as the 'value received' multiplied by 30%. Where this exceeds the EIS relief (after taking into account any prior reductions), the original EIS relief is completely withdrawn.

Insignificant receipts of value are ignored (broadly, amounts up to £1,000, although greater amounts may qualify where they are insignificant in relation to the total EIS investment). These clawback rules will also be disregarded where the investor returns the amount received without unreasonable delay.

The legislation effectively looks at direct and indirect returns of value. The relevant circumstances identified in *ITA 2007, s 216(2)* in which value is deemed to be 'received' *include* the investee company:

- repaying, redeeming or repurchasing any of the investor's shares;

- repaying a debt owed to the investor in connection with the arrangements for the EIS share issue (excluding loans made after the shares were issued) (see 11.41);

- providing any benefit or facility to the investor;

- disposing of an asset to the investor for no consideration or at an undervalue; or

- making any payment *other than* such qualifying payments as reasonable remuneration, permissible reimbursement of expenses, commercial interest, rents or dividends, etc (see *ITA 2007, ss 168(2)(3), 216(2)(h)).*

The *investor's EIS relief* is restricted in a similar way where any company (or any subsidiary) redeems or repays the share capital of *any other shareholder* in the 'period of restriction' [*ITA 2007, s 224*].

Value received by repayment of debt

11.41 Only repayments of loans *in the course of arrangements for the EIS issue* are treated as a 'return of value'. An investor's EIS relief should not therefore be prejudiced, provided that any prior repayment of a loan is *not* made in connection with any arrangements for the acquisition of the shares [*ITA 2007, s 216 (2)(b)*]. This means that where individuals make short-term loans to the company the repayment of such loans should not jeopardise their EIS tax relief on qualifying share investments made within the following 12 months.

The Court of Appeal in *Blackburn (t/a Alan Blackburn Sports Ltd v HMRC* [2008] EWHC 266 (Ch) adopted a pragmatic approach on the similar 'debt repayment' rule relating to an EIS CGT deferral relief claim under *TCGA 1992, Sch 5B*. HMRC had originally rejected Mr Blackburn's claim for EIS capital gains deferral relief on some £1.19 million which was 'injected' into the company through six separate share issues between September 2008 and January 2001. The Court of Appeal had to consider share issues 1, 5 and 6 where part of the payments were made before the shares were issued. HMRC's contention was that, in the absence of proper applications and allotments, the advance payments were a 'debt' and hence the EIS relief was denied under the 'return of value' rules in *TCGA 1992, Sch 5B, para 13*. The Court of Appeal rejected this argument (as regards issues 5 and 6) on the basis that the advance payments were not 'debts' in the normal sense of the word. However, perhaps surprisingly, relief on the first issue was rejected (on the basis that the company had not established any course of dealings at that point and it was therefore possible to treat the monies as a loan!). (The treatment of issues 2, 3 and 4 is considered in 11.39.)

Arrangements made for the repayment of an investor's debt in the 12 months before an EIS issue will also be denied under the 'receipt of value' rules, as illustrated in *Segesta Ltd v HMRC* [2012] UKUT 176. Segasta Ltd was the parent company of Blackpool Football Club Ltd (BFC), and Mr Oyston was the principal shareholder of Segasta Ltd.

There were a complex series of transactions designed to provide EIS CGT deferral relief.

- BFC already owed a substantial amount to Mr Oyston.

- My Oyston's loan account was repaid by BFC with monies advanced from Segate Ltd, which had been borrowed from the group's bank.

- My Oyston used these monies to subscribe just over £4 million for further shares in Segasta Ltd.

- The circa £4 million share subscription proceeds were then used to repay the bank borrowings.

In effect, the above transactions were of a circular nature.

HMRC denied Mr Oyson's claim for EIS CGT deferral relief on the basis that he has received value from the company within the meaning of *TCGA 1992, Sch 5B, para 13(2)(b)*.

The Upper Tribunal (UT) agreed indicating that part of the share monies were effectively used to repay My Oyston's loan account and this was a return of value, so all his EIS shares ceased to be eligible shares.

The UT also observed that:

'Parliament should be taken to have wished to legislate such a strict set of conditions to be satisfied in order to claim EIS reinvestment relief. Use of such conditions greatly simplifies and facilitates the policing by the revenue authorities of the proper use of the relief and operates as a clear safeguard against the possibility of abuse.'

Qualifying company

11.42 A company is a qualifying company for EIS purposes provided:

(*a*) it is unquoted when the shares are issued – no arrangements must exist for the company to be listed or to become a wholly owned subsidiary of a new holding company if arrangements exist for that company to be listed [*ITA 2007, s 184*];

(*b*) it is a trading company or parent company of a trading group (see 11.47) carrying on a qualifying business activity – ie *qualifying trade/ trades or research and development* (see 11.44) – for at least three years after the share issue [*ITA 2007, s 181*];

(*c*)   it has total gross assets (based on the balance sheet) of not more than £15 million before the relevant EIS issue and no more than £16 million afterwards [*ITA 2007, s 186*].

The company's total 'gross assets' (ie before deducting any liabilities) are measured according to their balance sheet value (at that point) based on generally accepted accounting principles (and on the same basis as prior accounts) [see *IR Statement of Practice SP 2/00*]. Where the company is a parent company of a trading group, the aggregate of the group's assets (ignoring shareholdings in its subsidiaries) is taken;

(*d*)   the company must have a permanent establishment in the UK – which would generally be met simply by having a trading activity in the UK [*ITA 2007, s 179(1)–(5)*]. Before the law was changed in 2010, a company had to be trading '*wholly or mainly*' within the UK; and

(*e*)   it has fewer than 250 full time employees (or their equivalents) at the date on which the relevant shares are issued. However, under the *F (No 2) A 2015*, 'knowledge intensive' companies (see 11.32A) enjoy a more favourable limit of having 500 full time employees.

The employees test applies to a company or group of companies. The test is only applied at the point the shares are issued. It does not matter if the company/group employee 'headcount' exceeds 250 (or 500 for 'knowledge intensive' companies) after the EIS issue, since there are no clawback provisions.

If the issuing company ceases to qualify within the relevant three-year period, the investor's EIS relief is completely withdrawn.

Similarly, if the company is wound up during the relevant three-year period, it would cease to be a qualifying company. However, it can retain its qualifying status, provided the winding up or dissolution is for genuine commercial reasons and not tax avoidance. A similar rule applies where a company appoints a receiver or administrator [*ITA 2007, s 182)*].

The 'independence' requirement

11.43   A company is only able to issue eligible EIS shares provided that it satisfies the so called 'independence' requirement throughout the 'three year' period following the EIS share issue. This means that the issuing company must *neither be;*

(*a*)   a 51% subsidiary of another company; *nor*

(*b*)   under the 'control' of another company

Furthermore, it must not be subject to any arrangements to cause it to be within (a) or (b) above [*ITA 2007, s 185(2)*]. The *CTA 2010, s 1124 (ICTA 1988, s 840*) definition applies for these purposes, which broadly looks at the ability of the other 'investor' company to control the EIS company's affairs, through voting power, a shareholders agreement and so on *Steele v EVC International* NV69 TC88.

It is very easy for EIS investors to 'trip-up' under this rule, as demonstrated in *Gregory Finn, Averil Finn, Andrew Cornish and Robin Morris v HMRC* [2014] UKFTT 426(TC). Their company (ProtonStar LED Ltd – 'ProtonStar') sought an AIM listing via a 'reverse takeover' of another company (as this was cheaper than a direct AIM application!). Consequently, ProtonStar, came under the control of another AIM company (Enfis Limited) within the relevant three year period following the issue of the EIS investor's ProtonStar's shares. ProtonStar had therefore breached the 'independence' rule within *ITA 2007, s 185*. (*ITA 2007, s 209* also withdraws EIS relief where the shareholders sell their shares within the relevant 'three-year' period – see 11.51.) The Tribunal had little difficulty in confirming that the ProtonStar EIS investors had lost their EIS relief under this rule (see also 11.55)

Qualifying trade

11.44 As a general rule, the broad policy aim of the EIS regime is to prevent 'lower risk'/asset-backed activities from attracting EIS relief.

All trades (and research and development activities) qualify, with the exception of those activities falling within the special exclusions (mentioned below, using the *ITA 2007, s 192* references), carried on at *any time in the three years from the share issue* (or, if later, the three years from commencement of the trade):

(*a*) dealing in land, commodities, futures, shares, securities or other financial instruments;

(*b*) dealing in goods otherwise than as wholesale or retail distributors;

(*c*) banking, insurance, money lending, debt factoring, hire-purchase financing, etc;

(*d*), (*e*) leasing (this includes letting pleasure craft ships and letting other assets on hire – see 11.45) or receiving royalties or licence fees (although the exploitation of the company's 'internally' generated intellectual property is permitted – see 11.46);

(*f*) providing legal or accountancy services;

(*g*) property development (but this 'exclusion' only operates where the company has an interest in the land being developed (see *ITA 2007, s196*);

(*h*) farming or market gardening;

(*i*)   forestry activities, woodlands, or timber production;

(*ia*)   shipbuilding;

(*ib*)   coal production;

(*ic*)   steel production;

(*j*)   operating or managing hotels or guest houses, etc, but only where the hotel/guest house has an interest in or occupies the relevant property (see *ITA 2007, s 197*);

(*k*)   operating or managing nursing or residential care homes, provided the business has an interest in or occupies the relevant property (see *ITA 2007, s 197*);

(*l*)   the subsidised generation or export of electricity (other than certain community interest or cooperative schemes), although it has been announced that this category is to be abolished [*ITA 2007, s 198A*];

(*m*)   the subsidised generation of heat or subsidised production of gas and fuel;

(*n*)   From 18 November 2015, wholly or substantially making reserve electricity generating capacity available;

(*o*)   the provision of services or facilities to another business that is 'substantially' carrying on any of the activities falling within (*a*) to (*ka*) above where there is a common controlling interest [*ITA 2007, s 199*].

FA 2016 changes exclude energy generating activities including the production of gas or other fuel for EIS investments made after 5 April 2016.

Full details of the 'excluded activities' are contained in *ITA 2007, ss 192–199*.

Where the company engages in carrying on one or more excluded activities on a very small scale, this may not necessarily be fatal to the shareholder's EIS relief although the position must be carefully monitored. *ITA 2007, s 189(1)* effectively enables the investee company to carry on the above excluded activities to an 'insubstantial' (less than 20%) extent without prejudicing its qualifying EIS status (see 15.41 for further discussion about the '20% test') [*ITA 2007, s 189(1)*].

Furthermore, it is unlikely that EIS relief will be available if significant 'personal' activities are run through the business, as illustrated in *East Allenheads Estate Ltd v HMRC* [2015] UKFTT 0328 (TC)). In this case the company ran a grouse shooting estate with associated luxury accommodation. However, it spent significant amounts of the purported 'EIS' share subscription monies on various improvements to the property used by it (but owned by its main investor) and on art and antiques! This expenditure benefited the owner of the property. The FTT concluded that this was not an integral part of a qualifying trade and hence EIS relief was refused.

Reference must always be made to the detailed legislation to determine whether a particular company will qualify for relief. The investee company's trade must also be conducted on a commercial basis with the view to realising profits [*ITA 2007, s 189(1)(a)*]. In practice, it is always advisable to first seek advance clearance from HMRC that the trade qualifies for EIS purposes (see 11.49).

EIS relief will be denied where the company is in 'financial difficulty' – for example, subject to insolvency proceedings. This change was required to bring the EIS legislation into line with the EC State Aid Risk Capital Guidelines.

Leasing activities

11.45 HMRC interprets 'leasing' as covering any trading activity that allows the customer (lessee/hirer) the use of the company's property and such arrangements would normally prevent EIS relief being claimed (subject to the 20% *de minimis* test) [*ITA 2007, s 192(1)(d)*]. This would include many cases where assets are 'hired' out and the customer is free to use the asset as their own. Common examples would include car hire, television and video rentals, and warehousing facilities.

On the other hand, arrangements where the customer cannot use the asset freely are effectively regarded as the provision of a service and would be treated as an allowable activity. This would include the chauffeured car hire (for example, 'wedding car' hire) and certain storage activities where the customer is denied free access (see *IR Tax Bulletin,* August 1995).

There would seem to be a fine line drawn between (say) a *self storage* warehouse where the customer has reasonable access and (say) a storage facility that is primarily operated by the investee company. In the former case, EIS is unlikely to be available, whereas in the latter case, the customer is paying for a service or facility and therefore EIS should be given. In such cases, it is recommended that an advance EIS ruling is obtained from HMRC (see 11.49).

Royalties and licence fees

11.46 The general EIS prohibition on the receipt of royalties and licence fees (by the investee company) (see 11.44) is relaxed where the income:

• derives from the company's *own* research or development activities – these must be intended to result in a new (innovative) patentable invention or computer program; *or*

• is mainly from the exploitation of intangible assets created by the company. The definition of intangible assets is that used in normal accounting practice and would include intellectual property and industrial know-how. The investee company can, therefore, create and exploit its own intellectual property (for example, patents, copyrights, designs, computer software, etc). Where some of the royalties or licence fee income relates to 'third-party' intellectual property rights, these can be ignored provided they do not represent a substantial (20%) part of the total income.

HMRC would regard the receipt of licence fees as a 'non-qualifying' activity for EIS purposes. Thus, a car park trade would not attract EIS relief because its income would largely be in the form of licence fees for car parking. On the other hand, where the grant of a right over land is merely incidental to the main 'service' (such as in the case of a cinema provider), then it would be ignored (see *IR Tax Bulletin*, August 1995).

Group situations – parent company of a trading group

11.47   A company can also be a qualifying EIS company if it is a parent company of a trading group that has at least *one* subsidiary. For these purposes:

- *each* of its subsidiaries must be a qualifying 51% subsidiary with the important exception that any subsidiary 'benefiting' from the proceeds of an EIS issue (or whose qualifying activity is being counted in relation to an EIS issue – see 11.34) must be a 90% subsidiary (see 11.48). Furthermore, any property management subsidiary must also be a 90% subsidiary of the investee company [*ITA 2007, ss 190* and *191*]; and

- taking all the group's activities together, the qualifying trade requirements in 11.44 are satisfied, with any non-qualifying activities being below the 20% *de minimis* limit. For the purpose of the 'activities' test, group shareholdings and intra-group lending/property letting are effectively ignored, ie the group is effectively looked at on a 'consolidated accounts' basis [*ITA 2007, ss 190* and *191*].

A qualifying trade can be also be carried on by:

- a 90% subsidiary of a wholly-owned subsidiary of the issuing company; or.

- a 100% subsidiary of a directly-held 90% subsidiary of the issuing company.

Relevant 'subsidiary' requirements

11.48   The relevant subsidiary shareholding requirements (ie 51%, 75% or 90%, as appropriate) must be tested against the normal type of economic ownership measures, such as shares, voting power, entitlement to dividends and assets on a winding-up. Thus, if the investee company subsequently acquires a shareholding in another company, the investment must broadly be at least 51% of its share capital.

Similarly, non-controlling shareholdings (ie less than 51% investments) are treated as investments. Consequently, unless their total value is insubstantial (under the 20% *de minimis* rule) compared to the group's total value, the investee company will be a non-qualifying company for EIS purposes.

Thus, if a parent company subsequently acquires investments (which are not qualifying subsidiaries), it may cease to qualify for EIS purposes. The EIS legislation does not have any 'joint venture' provisions that treat investments in certain *trading* joint ventures as effectively being transparent (as is the case with the substantial shareholdings exemption (see 3.34)).

HMRC EIS clearance application

11.49   HMRC operates a formal Advance Assurance Application procedure to confirm whether a potential investee company satisfies the relevant conditions for being a qualifying company and whether the rules for the share issue are met. Informal advice can also be sought about queries relating to whether the trade qualifies, the application of the 'connection rules', and so on.

These points can be confirmed by completing the online form EIS-SEIS (AA), which can be found at www.gov.uk/government/publications/enterprise-investment-scheme-advance-assurance-application-eisseisaa

It is important to remember that advance EIS clearances are given on the basis of the information provided and hence failure to disclose material facts may invalidate the clearance given.

Once the company has traded for a period of four months (or longer if involved in certain activities such as R&D), it can then provide the required information relating to the EIS share issue(s) on an EIS 1 form, available on request from the SCEC or from the HMRC website or online at www.gov.uk/government/publications/enterprise-investment-scheme-compliance-statement-eis1 .

In some cases, it will be important to determine when the relevant trade started. The ruling in *Birmingham and District Cattle By-Products Co Ltd v IRC* (1919) 12 TC 92 draws a distinction between preparing to trade and starting to trade. Thus, in this case, it was held that the trade started when it the manufacturing process commenced. The date when a trade commences is invariably a question of fact. of As a general 'rule of thumb', a trade will normally start when the company is in a positon to sell its goods or services to customers/clients.

After is has 'approved' the form EIS 1, HMRC will then issue the authorisation (on form EIS 2) to enable the company partly to complete and issue the form EIS 3 certificate(s) to the relevant investor(s). Each investor must submit their form EIS 3 with the relevant tax returns to their own tax offices in order to claim the EIS relief.

The investor's tax relief

11.50   The EIS relief (currently 30% of the share subscription) reduces the investor's income tax liability rather than their income – it is therefore akin to a 'tax credit' style relief. The investor's tax liability for the purposes of determining the EIS relief is calculated ignoring the following:

(*a*) personal allowances and maintenance payments which attract relief at a reduced rate;

(*b*) double taxation relief or unilateral relief;

(*c*) basic rate tax relief deducted at source from certain payments.

Disposal of EIS shares – withdrawal/restriction of EIS relief

11.51 If the EIS shares are disposed of by way of a non-arm's length bargain *within three years*, the EIS relief is completely withdrawn, based on the rate at which it was originally given (ie 30% for EIS shares issued after 5 April 2011) [*ITA 2009, s 209(2)*]. However, relief is not withdrawn where the shares are transferred to a spouse/civil partner [*ITA 2007, s 209(4)*].

For *arm's length disposals* within the relevant three-year period, the relief is withdrawn or reduced on a pro-rata basis.

The restriction of the EIS relief is the *lower* of:

(*a*) the EIS relief originally claimed on the shares

(*b*) the original EIS rate claimed multiplied by the sale proceeds received on the disposal

This broadly means that where the shares are sold at a profit, the original EIS relief is completely withdrawn. Where the shares are sold at a loss, the EIS relief will generally be reduced by the amount in (*b*) above.

In those cases where the original EIS relief was restricted – because the amount subscribed exceeded the relevant EIS limit, the amount at (b) is multiplied by: *reduced relief* EIS at 30%.

Any disposal of 'EIS-relieved' shares made within the relevant 'three-year' period must be reported to HMRC within 60 days (*ITA 2007, s 240*). Failure to give a notice will attract a penalty.

Example 6

Disposal of eligible shares – EIS relief position

2015/16	Moore claims EIS relief due on £150,000 @ 30% = £45,000
2017/18	Moore sells all the shares (at arm's length) for £90,000

Reduction in EIS relief for 2015/16 = £90,000 × 30% = £27,000

Disposal of EIS shares – CGT exemption

11.52   Where the sale of 'EIS-relieved' shares after the three-year holding period results in a capital gain, this is exempt from CGT. (The original EIS relief is also retained.) However, if the shares are sold within the relevant three-year period, the original EIS relief is restricted/withdrawn completely (see 11.51).)

However, an allowable capital loss would arise where the shares are sold at a loss (irrespective of whether the disposal is before or after the three-year holding period (see 11.28). In such cases, the loss calculation is adjusted so that the deductible CGT base cost of the shares is reduced by the amount of EIS income tax relief given.

Any capital loss can normally be set against income under the 'share loss relief' rules in the same and/or the previous tax year under *ITA 2007, s 131*. Note that the *FA 2013* income tax relief 'cap' (see 11.14-11.14A) does *not* apply to amounts of share loss relief on qualifying EIS (or SEIS) shares (provided the income tax relief has been retained).

On the other hand, share loss relief on investments that have only been subject to an EIS CGT deferral claim (see 11.31), would be subject to 'capping' (see 11.14 and 11.14A).

Example 7

Disposal of eligible shares – income tax and CGT position

Mr Hargreaves subscribed for shares in June 2016 for £100,000. EIS relief of £30,000 (£100,000 × 30%) was obtained in 2016/17.

Subsequently, assume that in (say) January 2018, Mr Hargreaves sells the shares for £60,000.

EIS relief position – 2016/17

Withdrawal of relief in 2016/17 = £60,000 @ 30% = £18,000

CGT position – 2017/18

The EIS shares are sold at a loss and therefore the CGT base cost must be reduced by the amount of EIS relief retained – £12,000 (being the original relief of £30,000 less the withdrawn amount of £18,000).

	£	£
Proceeds		60,000
Cost	100,000	
Less EIS relief retained		
(£30,000 – £18,000)	(12,000)	(88,000)
Allowable loss		(28,000)

If the conditions in *ITA 2007, s 131* are met, the loss can be set against Mr Hargreaves' taxable income for 2017/18 and/or 2016/17. Since EIS relief has been retained, there should be no 'capping'.

Disposal of EIS shares for share consideration – income tax and CGT treatment

Basic rule for share consideration

11.53   When an EIS company is sold, part of the consideration for the EIS shares may be in the form of shares issued by the acquiring company.

Where the sale takes place *after* the relevant three-year period, *TCGA 1992, s 150A* treats this as a normal CGT disposal (ie the normal CGT share exchange reorganisation rule does not apply). In summary, the tax analysis is as follows:

- Any deferred gains against the EIS shares are brought into charge (see 11.31).

- The capital gain on the EIS shares will be exempt under the normal EIS rules, regardless of whether consideration is received in the form of cash or shares (subject to the normal CGT rules on EIS disposals (see 11.30 and 11.52)).

- The base cost of the new consideration shares will be their market value at the time of the exchange.

- Any gains on the subsequent disposal of the new consideration shares will not be exempt under the EIS provisions (as they will not be EIS qualifying shares).

There are some important exceptions to these rules – see 11.54 and 11.55.

Takeover by EIS company

11.54   Where 'EIS' shares are sold (after the requisite holding period) for a consideration consisting of EIS eligible shares in another qualifying EIS company, there is no disposal. In such cases, the new EIS shares stand in the place of the old EIS shares in all respects and attract the same relief. However, this treatment only applies where HMRC has issued a certificate in relation to the new shares.

Furthermore, the normal advance clearance should be obtained from HMRC to confirm that they are satisfied that the share exchange is being made for bona fide commercial reasons and does not form part of a tax-avoidance scheme (*TCGA 1992, s 138*).

Acquisition by a new company

11.55 A special rule applies where a new company (which only has subscriber shares) acquires 100% of an existing EIS company wholly for shares (of the same class) in the new company (*ITA 2007, s 247*). The 'narrow' ambit of this rule was discussed in *Gregory Finn, Averil Finn, Andrew Cornish and Robin Morris v HMRC* [2014] UKFTT 426 (TC). The Tribunal found that the EIS investors in this case (see 11.43) could not benefit from the 'relieving' provision in *ITA 2007, s 247(1)(a)*, since this enables EIS relief to continue where the 'acquiring' company's only issued shares are subscriber shares'. It concluded that 'subscriber shares' could only be interpreted to mean 'shares that are to be issued to those who subscribe to the Memorandum of Association' of a company on its initial formation. Since the acquiring company had subsequently issued shares on different occasions, the shares issued by it were not 'all subscriber shares'.

However, where the precise conditions of *ITA 2007, s 247* are satisfied (including obtaining HMRC approval), the new company will acquire the existing EIS company without triggering any disposal for its EIS sharholders. The EIS relief relating to the old shares in the existing company is transferred across to the new shares issued by the 'new' acquiring company. The existing EIS shareholders' holdings are treated as continuing for EIS purposes [*TCGA 1992, s 150A(8D)*]

Clearly, the old company must have issued EIS eligible shares and issued an EIS 3. This means that the old company must have been trading for at least four months (see 11.49)

SEED ENTERPRISE INVESTMENT SCHEME (SEIS)

Introduction

11.56 Owner managers often face difficulties in obtaining external funding, especially where businesses are in the 'start-up' phase. From a potential investor's point of view, such investments would be regarded as high-risk. The Government recognises that investments in fledgling companies should therefore be given greater tax incentives.

Consequently, from 6 April 2012, *FA 2012* introduced the Seed Enterprise Investment Scheme (SEIS) to provide attractive tax breaks for equity investment in start-up companies. The relief was originally set to run only until 5 April 2017, but was subsequently made permanent.

The SEIS contains three key tax reliefs:

- Income tax relief of 50% on the amount subscribed (up to a maximum of £100,000 per tax year) for new ordinary shares in qualifying companies. The 50% relief is given irrespective of the investor's marginal tax rate (see 11.57);

- After three years, the qualifying SEIS shares can be sold completely free of CGT (see 11.67); and

- For SEIS investments made in 2012/13 only, investors could 'exempt' their capital gains made in 2012/13 and 2013/14 (on any type of asset) against their qualifying SEIS investment (up to the maximum £100,000 subscription).

  Finance Act 2013 extended this rule to enable a *50%* CGT exemption to be claimed for gains arising in 2013/14 and subsequent years that are 'invested' under SEIS in the year of the gain or the following year (see 11.67A).

Where a claim is made for SEIS CGT relief, the capital gain is no longer chargeable, unlike the 'equivalent' relief under EIS that enables deferral of gains until the EIS shares are disposed of (see 11.31).

After two years, investments in SEIS companies will normally be eligible for 100% business property relief for IHT purposes (see 17.19).

The SEIS is closely modelled on the EIS regime (see 11.27 to-11.51) but there are some notable differences.

The Government's policy intent behind SEIS is clearly laudable. However, given that the SEIS relief is relatively small compared to EIS and VCT, it is perhaps disappointing that it is cloaked with numerous complex restrictions. This is largely due to HMRC's paranoia that the relief could be subject to abuse, such as through arrangements designed to seek SEIS by recycling existing trades!

SEIS income tax relief on shares

11.57 Since 6 April 2012, individual investors can claim *50%* SEIS income tax on the amount subscribed (wholly for cash) for ordinary shares in a qualifying company in a tax year, with the maximum subscription being 'capped' at £100,000. The 50% SEIS relief is given irrespective of the investor's marginal tax rate.

The £100,000 SEIS investment limit is much lower than the current EIS subscription limit of £1,000,000, which may encourage some 'would-be' investors to seek relief under EIS instead (see 11.27).

Note that the new income tax relief cap introduced in *FA 2013* (see 11.14-11.14A) does not apply to income tax or share loss relief relating to EIS or SEIS qualifying shares.

11.58 The investor's tax relief is given as a reduction in computing their income tax liability (and therefore they must have sufficient tax in charge for offset).

Investors can *carry-back* all or part of their SEIS subscription to the previous tax year and obtain relief at the relevant SEIS rate for that year (but no carry back is permitted *before 2012/13*).

Example 8

SEIS investment – income tax relief

Jack has persuaded his brother, Bobby, to invest £80,000 into 'his' new company (Charlton's Bikes Ltd). The company incorporated in June 2017 and is about to commence a trade of designing and building specialised custom-made bikes.

Jack will procure an issue of 200 £1 ordinary shares in the company to Bobby, giving him a 25% interest (with the remaining 75% being held by Jack). Bobby's £80,000 investment will therefore reflect a 'share premium' of £79,200. Jack has also promised to give Bobby a seat on the board.

Assuming all the relevant SEIS conditions are met, Bobby will be able to claim SEIS income tax relief of £40,000 (50% × £80,000) in 2017/18 provided he has sufficient taxable income.

There are no SEIS obstacles with Bobby being a director (see 11.61). Further, although they are brothers, Jack and Bobby are not 'associated' for SEIS purposes and hence Bobby does not breach the substantial (30%) interest condition (11.62).

11.59 Investors can only claim SEIS relief if they have a compliance certificate from the investee company. The SEIS relief must be claimed within five years from 31 January following the tax year in which the shares are issued.

11.60 The SEIS shares must be retained for at least *three* years with relief being withdrawn if the investor disposes of their shares during that period.

However, investors can transfer SEIS shares to their spouse/civil partner without jeopardising their SEIS tax reliefs.

Similarly, if the company or investor breaches one of the relevant SEIS qualifying conditions (see below) during the relevant three year period, the income tax relief is withdrawn (as are the appropriate CGT exemptions).

There are a number of anti-avoidance rules preventing reciprocal arrangements and those mainly designed to secure a tax advantage.

Employees and directors

11.61 Current employees of the investee company (and any qualifying subsidiary) are *not* eligible for SEIS relief although past employees may qualify. Similarly, relief is denied to any *associates* of the investor who are employed by the relevant company (*ITA 2007, s 257BA*).

The 'employee' prohibition test runs from the date of incorporation up to the third anniversary of the relevant share issue (known as 'Period A').

However, it is possible for *directors* to make a qualifying SEIS investment and *ITA 2007, s 257BA(2)* provides that directors are *not* treated as employees for these purposes.

SEIS significant interest test

11.62 SEIS relief is *not* available to investors who hold a 'significant interest' in the investee company at any time during Period A (see 11.61 above), although 'pre-trading' subscriber shares are excluded.

The 'significant interest' test (in *ITA 2007, s 257BF*) prevents investors qualifying for SEIS relief where they, together with their associates, have more than a 30% interest in the investee company's:

• ordinary share capital;

• issued share capital; or

• voting power

For these purposes, the 'associates' test is narrower than the one that normally applies for other tax purposes – notably brothers and sisters are not treated as associates (as with EIS – see 11.35).

The 30% 'significant interest' test means that it is feasible for as few as four directors to qualify for SEIS relief up to the maximum SEIS company limit of £150,000 (for example, £37,500 each).

11.63　Importantly, *loan capital* is excluded from the 'significant interest' test. This means that investors can provide some loan funding to the company without prejudicing their SEIS relief, although care must be exercised to ensure any repayment of such loans falls outside the 'receipt of value' rules (see 11.66 below).

The 30% substantial interest rule is augmented by an economic ownership test. This also treats investors as having a significant interest if they would be entitled to more than 30% of the net assets available to the company's equity holders on a (notional) winding-up.

Requirements relating to SEIS shares

11.64　There are various requirements relating to SEIS shares, which are summarised below:

- Shares must be fully paid-up ordinary shares, which must not contain any preferential right to dividend, assets on a winding-up or redemption (*ITA 2007, s 257CA*). Furthermore the company cannot raise funds under EIS or VCT investment before any SEIS shares are issued.

- The shares must be issued for the purposes of qualifying business activities carried on by the company or a 90% qualifying subsidiary – see 11.65 (*ITA 2007, s 257CB*).

- All the share subscription monies must be spent on the qualifying activities within *three years* of the share issue (known as 'Period B'), although 'insubstantial' amounts not spent by the end of year three can be ignored (*ITA 2007, s 257CC*). Money invested in purchasing shares in another company does not count.

- There must be no pre-existing arrangements to secure an exit for the investor (*ITA 2007, s 257DD*).

Qualifying company conditions

11.65　The SEIS places numerous highly prescriptive restrictions on the qualifying company to ensure that the relief is targeted towards very small 'fledgling' businesses.

The key conditions are summarised below.

Trading	Throughout 'Period B' (ie the three years following the share issue), the issuing company must exist wholly for the purpose of carrying on one or more new qualifying trades or research and development (ignoring any incidental purposes).
	Importantly the trade must be a 'new' trade. This means that it must have been carried on for *less than two years* before the relevant SEIS share issue *and* the company must *not* have carried on any other trade.
	Broadly, if the issuing company is a parent company, the group (taken as a whole) must carry on qualifying activities throughout Period B (see 11.64 above), although any non-qualifying activities are ignored provided they are *not* substantial.
	For these purposes, qualifying activities follow the normal EIS provisions (see 11.44–11.46)
	If the company goes into administration (for genuine commercial reasons) this does not affect its trading status.
Qualifying business	Only the issuing company or any 90% qualifying subsidiary must carry on the new qualifying activity (including any preparatory work or research and development) during Period B (see 11.64).
UK permanent establishment	Throughout Period B the issuing company must carry on its trade in the UK through a permanent establishment. (This means that an overseas company could qualify if it is carrying on a UK-based trade.)
Financial health	The issuing company must not be in financial difficulty when the 'SEIS' shares are issued (as determined under EU regulation (2004/C 244/02).
Unquoted company status	When the shares are issued, the company must be unquoted (ie none of its shares must be listed on a recognised stock exchange) and no arrangements must be in existence for it to become listed.

Control and independence	Throughout Period A, the issuing company must be independent (ie not under the control of any other company) and there must be no arrangements for it to become so (see 11.43).
	During Period A, the issuing company must not control any subsidiary that is not a qualifying subsidiary.
	Since 6 April 2013, companies that are initially controlled by another company will not fail the independence condition provided two conditions are satisfied during the 'initial' period:
	– the company has only issued subscriber shares; and
	– preparations for trading have not yet begun.
	This change, introduced by *FA 2013*, ensures that companies should not fail the 'independence condition' where they are set-up by a formation agent (since they would normally have been under the control of another company).
No partnership connection	During Period A, the issuing company and any 90% qualifying subsidiary must not be a member of a partnership or limited liability partnership.
Gross assets test	Immediately before the shares are issued, the company's gross assets (per its balance sheet) must not exceed £200,000.
	Where a parent company makes the SEIS share issue, the £200,000 'gross assets' test is based on the 'consolidated' group assets.
Employee count	When the shares are issued, the company/group must have less than 25 full-time equivalent employees (including directors and calculated on a 'just and reasonable' basis).
No prior EIS/ VCT share issues	The company must not have had made any EIS or VCT share issues before (and on the day of) any SEIS issue.

SEIS receipt of value rules

11.66   As with EIS relief, the SEIS legislation contains similar provisions, which completely withdraws or reduces the original SEIS relief where investors (or connected persons) receive value from the investee company at any time in Period A. (See 11.61 for definition of Period A.)

This will also lead to a cancellation of any CGT exemption or CGT reinvestment relief claimed on the shares (see 11.67 and 11.68). The transactions which constitute a 'receipt of value' are widely defined in *ITA 2007, s 275FF* (see 11.40 and 11.41). In practice, this means that an SEIS shareholder can only receive 'ordinary commercial payments' from the company, such as salary, dividends or expenses. However, insignificant receipts are ignored (see 11.42).

As far as director investors are concerned, they will need to ensure that their remuneration packages are 'reasonable' and that any dividends taken represent a normal commercial return on the investment.

SEIS CGT reliefs

CGT exemption

11.67 After three years from share issue date, capital gains arising on the sale of SEIS-relieved shares are completely exempt from CGT (provided the SEIS income tax relief has not been withdrawn). The exemption is only given where SEIS income tax relief was originally claimed. If the SEIS shares are sold at a loss, the capital loss is reduced by the SEIS income tax relief (see 11.52).

CGT exemptions on SEIS investment

11.67A As an additional fiscal 'carrot', SEIS investment (up to the maximum £100,000 limit) can be 'reinvested' in gains to secure permanent relief from CGT.

For gains arising in 2013/14 and subsequent years will secure 50% exemption from CGT provided they are reinvested under SEIS in the year in which the gains arise or the following year. (See 2015/16 edition of this book for treatment of 2012/13 gains.)

Unlike the 'equivalent' relief under the EIS scheme, claims for SEIS CGT relief result in the gains permanently ceasing to be chargeable, which make this relief particularly valuable.

Example 9

SEIS investment – 50% CGT exemption

Mr Gerrard sold an investment property on 1 September 2017 realising a gain of £150,000.

On 1 January 2018 he invests £100,000 for 2,000 ordinary shares (giving a 20% holding) in Stevie Ltd. Stevie Ltd is a start up trading company and qualifies for SEIS purposes.

Mr Gerrard's marginal income tax rate is 45% in 2017/18.

Mr Gerrard makes a claim for SEIS relief on his investment in Stevie Ltd, which secures:

	£
SEIS income tax relief – £100,000 × 50%	50,000
CGT exemption – £100,000 × 50% × 20% CGT saving	10,000
Total effective SEIS relief in 2017/18	60,000

Furthermore, provided Mr Gerrard and Stevie Ltd continue to meet the SEIS qualifying conditions through the three years to 1 January 2021, a subsequent sale of his Stevie Ltd shares after that date will be CGT-free.

INVESTOR'S RELIEF (IR)

11.68 The *FA 2016* introduced Investor's Relief (IR), which enables investors to obtain a 10% CGT rate on a sale of shares in a qualifying trading company. Broadly, the 10% IR CGT rate is only available where the investor subscribes for shares (thus injecting new funds into the company) and retains those shares for at least three years.

As a general rule, directors and employees cannot qualify for IR. However, there are some limited relaxations to this rule enabling investors to become 'unpaid' directors following their qualifying IR share subscription. Similarly, employees may also obtain relief if there was no reasonable prospect of them taking up employment with the investee company when they acquired their 'IR' shares. In this case, IR relief can still be claimed where they subsequently became employed at least 180 days after their IR share subscription. These relaxations were introduced at late stage in the passage of the *Finance Bill 2016*, to enable business angels allow to become more closely involved with the company's development.

11.68A IR simply provides a 10% CGT rate of disposal (subject to a lifetime IR gains limit of £10 million. This limit is entirely separate from the £10 million ER lifetime gains limit (see 15.24). Provided the relevant qualifying conditions are met, it is possible to for a shareholder to enjoy £10 million gains taxed at the 10% ER CGT rate and a separate £10 million of gains at the 10% IR CGT rate.

Although IR has some similarities with the EIS conditions, it only provides a lower CGT rate of 10% – there is no income tax relief on the original share subscription.

The detailed IR rules are covered in 15.45–15.46.

VENTURE CAPITAL TRUSTS

Introduction

11.69   VCT investments are targeted incentives for investing in a range of small to medium-sized unquoted companies carrying on qualifying trades in the UK. They represent a combination of an EIS company and an authorised investment trust company, with the VCT's shares being quoted on the stock market. As part of obtaining EU approval under the 'State Aid' guidelines, VCTs may also be listed on an approved EU/EEA exchange.

Although VCTs are inherently risky, the potential 30% income tax saving currently available on the amount invested can make them relatively attractive investments. In essence, they enable an individual to invest in unquoted (including AIM) companies by buying shares in a (*non-close*) quoted VCT company. In contrast to direct investment in unquoted shares, the VCT shares can be sold in the market.

To deal with the Government's concern about aggressive VCT schemes using VCTs, *FA 2014* introduced various new anti-avoidance rules. Broadly, these rules prevent recycling arrangements that involve VCTs buying back tranches of shares, then investors reinvesting the proceeds in new shares, then the VCT buying back more shares and so on. From 6 April 2014, such 'recycling' transactions will effectively lead to a loss in the fund's qualifying VCT status.

Additionally, VCT tax relief is not available on VCT investments that are either conditionally linked to a share buy-back, or which have been made within six months of a disposal of shares in the same VCT.

The VCT structure

11.70   HMRC approval for a VCT is required under *ITA 2007, s 259*. Many of the provisions of *ITA 2007, s 259* applying to authorised investment trust companies also apply to an authorised VCT, but one of the exceptions is that there is no requirement that the VCT is resident in the UK. The VCT managers will be responsible for ensuring that the VCT continues to comply with the requirements of *ITA 2007, Pt 5, Chs 3 and 4*.

Currently, at least 70% (by value) of the VCT's investments must be in *shares and securities* which are qualifying 'unquoted' holdings (which do not include 'enterprises in difficulty'). Where a VCT sells a qualifying investment that has been held for at least six months, the disposal proceeds will be ignored for the purpose of the 70% test for the next six months, allowing the VCT time to reinvest or distribute the sale proceeds.)

At least 70% (by value) of the qualifying holdings must comprise eligible shares which are ordinary share capital in qualifying investee companies (see 11.39). These shares must not carry any present or future preferential rights as to dividends or assets on a winding up or redemption.

No holding in any single company may exceed 15% of the VCT's total investments, but that restriction does not apply to investments in unit trusts, government or local authority securities, or investments in other VCTs. At least 10% of the VCT's total investment in any single company must be in non-preferential ordinary shares.

The VCT must also ensure that it retains no more than 15% of its income from investments in shares and securities. 'Investments' includes money that the VCT holds (or that is held on its behalf).

11.71   VCTs are subject to the 'risk capital schemes requirement' (see 11.32). Thus, for an 'investment' to be treated as a qualifying holding of a VCT, the investee company (or group of companies) must have raised no more than £5 million (£2 million before 6 April 2012) under any or all of the tax-favoured schemes (EIS, SEIS, SITR, and VCT) in the past 12 months. From 18 November 2015, a new *lifetime* limit of £12 million applies to each investee company. However 'knowledge intensive' companies enjoy a 320 million lifetime limit (see 11.32A).

If the VCT breaks any of the qualifying conditions, the investors lose all their tax benefits (see 11.72–11.73).

Qualifying investee companies

11.72   The unquoted companies in which the VCT invests must carry on a qualifying trade (see 11.44–11.46).

The VCT legislation effectively applies the similar tests and rules as those that operate for the EIS. For example, the 'employees' test (see 11.21(*e*)) and 90% subsidiaries rules (11.47) also apply to qualifying companies acquired by VCTs. Furthermore, under the *F (No 2) A 2015*, companies in which the VCT invests must comply with the 'company age' condition (see 11.34C) and the prohibition on using VCT subscription monies to acquire businesses or shares in companies (see 11.34). The beneficial modifications for knowledge intensive companies also apply (see 11.32A).

11.73   A VCT can only invest in 'non-controlling' holdings in investee companies. Each investee company's gross assets must *not* exceed £15 million before the VCT investment and £16 million immediately after the investment is made.

Although an investee company can have 51% subsidiaries, any subsidiary company using funds raised through the VCT must be a 90% subsidiary. Similarly, any property management subsidiary of the investee company must be a 90% subsidiary.

VCT investor's tax reliefs

11.74   Income tax relief is now given at a *fixed rate* of 30% on new ordinary shares *subscribed* for in a VCT up to an overall investment limit of £200,000 in any tax year. Although investors will typically be higher rate taxpayers, VCT investments made by basic rate taxpayers also benefit from a 30% tax 'rebate'.

Spouses enjoy their own £200,000 VCT relief, thus enabling married couples to increase their overall VCT investment to £400,000.

The claim(s) must be made within five years of the 31 January following the end of the relevant tax year – in practice, the claim will normally be made by completing the relevant box on the tax return.

The income tax relief is retained provided the VCT shares are held for at least *five* years. After that period, the market quote should help the investor to dispose of their shares if they wish to do so.

Tax relief on a VCT investment is offset against the individual's tax liability in priority to other deductions and reliefs which are given by way of tax offset. This order of priority means that VCT relief is given before EIS relief.

11.75   Provided the VCT investments fall within the £200,000 limit:

- any dividends paid by the VCT are exempt from tax in the investor's hands, which is especially beneficial for higher rate taxpayers (non-taxpayers cannot reclaim the dividend tax credits) [*ITTOIA 2005, Ch 5*]; and

- there is no CGT on a subsequent sale of the VCT shares (and, similarly, any capital losses are not allowable) [*TCGA 1992, s 151A*].

11.76   Given that VCTs primarily invest for capital growth, investors also indirectly benefit from the VCT's own 'tax-free' capital gains on the realisation of its underlying investments. The 'five-year' rule does not apply to transfers between spouses (or civil couples) but is binding on the 'successor' spouse/civil partner.

The dividend and capital gains exemptions are also available on the purchase of *existing* VCT shares, but these do not attract any 'up-front' income tax relief on the purchase cost (the lower market prices of existing VCT shares reflect this!).

It is not possible to 'hold-over' or defer *capital gains* against VCT investments

SOCIAL INVESTMENT TAX RELIEF (SITR)

11.77   Since 6 April 2014, individuals can claim social investment tax relief (SITR). The aim of the SITR is to encourage private investment in social enterprises (SE). It has many similarities to the EIS and SEIS. Please see 2015/16 edition of this book for detailed rules.

PLANNING CHECKLIST – SHARE ISSUES AND FINANCING THE COMPANY'S ACTIVITIES

Company

- Borrowing arrangements should ensure corporate tax relief is secured on a prompt basis.

- In appropriate cases, companies in financial distress should consider a debt-for-equity swap to improve their balance sheet.

- Start-up or fledgling companies could consider first raising equity finance under the Seed Enterprise Investment Scheme (SEIS).

- Eligible companies should look to VCTs, EIS and SEIS investors to obtain equity funds. Investors' relief also provides a significant 'investment' incentive, giving 10% CGT rate on exit after three years (subject to a lifetime cap of £10 million).

- It is not possible to secure EIS equity investment if the company/ group has more than 249 full time equivalent employees. The threshold is 499 employees for knowledge intensive companies.

- Companies *cannot* use EIS share subscription monies to acquire businesses via direct trade/asset or share purchases. The key principle now is that EIS monies must be used to generate organic growth.

- Before making an EIS share issue the company must ensure that the anticipated subscription monies do not breach the 'risk capital schemes' overall investment limit of £5 million (for EIS, SEIS, and VCT investments made during the past 12 months). This £5 million limit is tested on a rolling basis over the past 12 months and includes the proposed EIS share issue.

- Companies are now subject to a £12 million *lifetime* limit for monies raised through EIS, SEIS, SITR and VCT share subscriptions. The limit is £20 million for knowledge intensive companies.

- The directors should monitor the company's business activities on a regular basis to avoid prejudicing EIS and other 'risk venture capital' reliefs.

- The company should always obtain advance clearance from HMRC before making an EIS issue on form EIS-SEIS(AA).

- 'Social Enterprise' companies can raise funds under the Social Investment Tax Relief (SITR) scheme from 2014/15 onwards.

Working shareholders

- Consider the advantages of using company borrowings (with perhaps a personal guarantee) to acquire assets, etc given the additional tax costs that normally arise on extracting funds from the company to repay personal borrowing.

- Use capital or borrowings to subscribe for further shares, striking a commercial balance between debt and equity. Shareholders should be aware of the increased financial risk that is involved in subscribing for shares rather than loaning funds. Loan accounts can be repaid more easily and are therefore more flexible.

- Incoming directors can make qualifying SEIS and EIS investments provided care is taken to ensure compliance with the relevant conditions.

- Owner managers with significant CGT liabilities can shelter their gains by subscribing for new equity shares in their company under the EIS CGT deferral relief rules (which do not contain any restriction regarding 'connected' investors). If the original gain qualified for entrepreneurs' relief (ER), this relief can now be enjoyed where the gain is subject to EIS CGT deferral. A claim for ER on the deferred gain is made when the gain subsequently crystallises.

- For SEIS investments made in 2013/14 and in subsequent years, a 50% exemption is available for capital gains arising in the same year (or the following year).

- EIS investors should try to obtain appropriate warranties and indemnities from the company to reduce the financial risk of subsequently losing their EIS relief.

- Income tax relievable interest cannot be claimed on monies borrowed to finance EIS or SEIS shares.

- In appropriate cases, consider VCT investments (up to £200,000 per tax year) for saving income tax at 30%.

Non-working shareholders

- The strategy for non-working shareholders is broadly the same as for working shareholders.

- Existing shareholders are unable to claim EIS relief unless their shareholdings were acquired under EIS or SEIS or as subscriber shares on incorporation.

- Interest relief is available on their personal borrowings (to inject (non-EIS) share capital or loan finance) provided they have over 5% of the ordinary share capital.

- Since 6 April 2014, qualifying SITR investments offer 30% income tax relief and the opportunity to defer gains against SITR investments.

Chapter 12

Expanding the Company's Activities and Structuring Business Acquisitions

MAKING A BUSINESS ACQUISITION

12.1   Companies can expand organically or by acquiring established businesses. The decision to make an acquisition should be based on a definite strategy. The company must have a clear idea of what it needs to achieve from the acquisition, for example, increased capacity and economies of scale, additional market share, new technology or diversification into new products or services. Sensible business acquisitions usually enable a company to grow at a faster rate.

The business may also be expanded by the use of franchising (see 12.83–12.85).

The acquiring company must do a considerable amount of homework in identifying suitable targets and approaching selected prospects to draw up a shortlist. A considerable amount of valuable management time can be devoted to this exercise, which may be detrimental to the running of the existing business. Management should therefore consider obtaining professional assistance from a reputable corporate finance department or firm.

Typical acquisition process

12.2   For the vast majority of deals where the acquirer has identified and approached a potential Target company/business, the typical acquisition process can be outlined as follows:

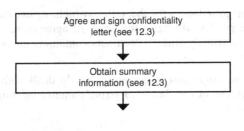

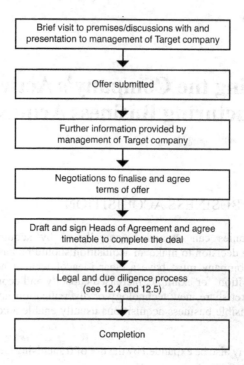

A preliminary review of the Target company/business should be made to enable the buyer to confirm its rationale for making the acquisition, assess likely consideration price, and consider any other commercial issues.

An early review of the Target will also enable the buyer to identify potentially major issues that would impact on the acquisition, such as: major tax irregularities; the recent loss of a large customer; cost rationalisation opportunities; management structure; and potential liabilities. The buyer will also want to understand the asset and the working capital requirements of the Target and the impact of those factors on the funding of the deal. This early review may well shape the buyer's approach to due diligence (see 12.4 and 12.5).

Agreeing outline terms

12.3   After negotiations with the seller (which, again, can be very time consuming), the parties will agree the heads of agreement, which is a fairly detailed non-contractually binding document containing the principal terms of the deal.

To ensure that the important issues are correctly dealt with from the start, the heads of agreement (or 'heads of terms') should be drafted by legal or accounting advisers.

As the buyer is about to start incurring considerable expense in undertaking the due diligence exercise, it should obtain a legally binding 'exclusivity agreement'. This is a commitment by the seller not to engage with any other interested parties for an agreed period of time and not to provide any information to any third parties relating to the target company. As part of this process, the buyer would be required to enter into a 'confidentiality/non-disclosure agreement. This ensures the buyer maintains confidentiality about the potential sale and the information provided about the target company (for example, relating to IP, customers, financials, and so on).

A well-prepared heads of agreement will enable the lawyers to prepare the first draft share or asset purchase agreement (SPA).

The heads of agreement would normally cover the following areas:

(*a*)   the subject matter of the purchase (ie is it a purchase of shares or assets?);

(*b*)   the consideration for acquisition and the payment terms and often the basis on which the sale price is arrived at – eg earnings multiples/balance sheet values etc (see 12.57 for discussion on valuation issues);

(*c*)   whether the price is to be satisfied by cash or shares/loan notes issued by the buyer;

(*d*)   conditions which may be applicable to either buyer or seller;

(*e*)   the basic terms of warranties and indemnities to be included in the SPA (a warranty is basically a promise that information provided is true (see 12.73–12.76) and an indemnity is a promise to financially compensate the seller if a specific financial cost materialises, normally for unforeseen tax liabilities – see 12.77–12.79);

(*f*)   the terms on which key management will continue working (consultancy and service agreements are often involved).

(*g*)   any other specific terms of importance perhaps relating to due diligence, such as details of key customers,, property issues (the seller may be retaining property), or other deal specific items.

(*h*)   the timing of the deal.

Agreement should be obtained as to the approach that will be taken on potentially contentious issues at this stage.

Due diligence investigation

12.4   The buyer will often require a due diligence investigation before it makes the acquisition. Since a *share purchase* entails significantly more commercial and tax risks, a correspondingly higher level of due diligence would normally be required compared to a trade and asset purchase.

The buyer will obtain full details of the financial performance and commercial operations of the target business, including details of its product range, position in the market, management team, customer base, intellectual property, properties, etc. A well-advised seller will require the buyer to enter into a binding confidentiality agreement in relation to information disclosed during the negotiations.

The buyer (and/or its lenders) will usually instruct accountants and possibly other experts to undertake a 'due diligence' investigation into the target company (or, where an asset purchase is contemplated, the target company's business). A comprehensive due diligence exercise will review the commercial, financial, tax, legal and environmental aspects of the target company and its business.

The *accountants'* due diligence report would typically cover the target's:

(*a*)   corporate structure;

(*b*)   management and personnel;

(*c*)   trading operations;

(*d*)   accounting and management information systems;

(*e*)   sales, marketing and distribution;

(*f*)   purchasing and raw material supplies;

(*g*)   research and development;

(*h*)   accounting policies; and

(*i*)   financial, tax and trading position (the scope of a tax 'due diligence' investigation is detailed in 12.5).

The review would typically examine past performance, current trading and future prospects of the business. The review of future prospects can be a particularly onerous forecasting exercise, particularly if the buyer is paying a premium price for a growing business.

A surveyor may also report on the properties owned by the target company and, if there is an 'old-fashioned' defined benefit scheme in place, an actuary's report may be required on the target's company pension scheme. An environmental audit may be appropriate if there are potential risks inherent in the nature of the target's business or the business's location.

The scope of due diligence may vary from deal to deal: a buyer will be given limited opportunities in a sale by an administrator and a large corporate may undertake a disproportionately rigorous due diligence process.

Data rooms

12.4A   The use of 'data rooms' is becomingly increasingly common. Data rooms are usually set up by the seller's lawyers as a special room to assemble all the due diligence information about the target company or business. They will contain various items, such the business's key documents/contracts, details of the business operations, commercial licences, tax returns/computations, and so on.

In some cases, data rooms are 'virtual' online collections of documents that can be accessed and reviewed by the buyer's solicitors.

Tax due diligence

12.5   The tax due diligence will provide the buyer with a full picture of the target's tax affairs and liabilities and those relating to the proposed transaction.

The tax due diligence would be primarily aimed at those areas that are considered to pose the greatest 'tax risk'. Tax issues can often be an important area since it may throw up significant actual or potential tax exposures. This may lead to the buyer insisting on extensive indemnities, a retention of part of the sale proceeds, or a downward adjustment in the purchase price to cover the relevant tax liabilities.

The scope and coverage of a tax due diligence exercise will inevitably depend on the precise nature of the target's company's/group's trade and the industry or business sector in which it operates.

12.5A   The tax work is likely to cover (to a greater or lesser extent):

- corporate taxes;

- payroll and social security taxes (such as PAYE and NIC);

- employee share reporting and related issues;

- sales taxes (such as VAT and Customs duties); and

- transfer taxes (stamp duty land tax ('SDLT') and stamp duty).

A detailed and properly targeted review should identify historical tax risks and issues. Once the scope of the due diligence exercise has been agreed, the buyer's advisers will determine the relevant documentation they require for review. This is likely to include copies of relevant tax returns, tax computations, correspondence with HMRC and other tax authorities and so on).

On the corporate tax side, part of this work usually involves a review of the target's effective corporate tax rates on its accounting profits for recent periods with explanations being sought for material variances from the normal 'expected' tax charge. This would also include an examination of the target's deferred tax accounting. The acquirer will need to be satisfied that the company/group has submitted its tax returns and paid its tax on time and the computations have been prepared with reasonable skill and care. This review would also assess whether the company/group has any open HMRC enquiries and the outcome of those enquiries etc.

12.5B   Some key tax issues that frequently arise in relation to acquisitions of owner-managed companies are:

- Potential *CTA 2010, s 455* liabilities on shareholders' overdrawn loan accounts (see 2.49–2.60).

- Availability of any tax losses, in particular to ensure their validity and whether the purchase is likely to give rise to any risk of forfeiture under the 'major change in the nature of the trade' rules (see 12.60).

- Transfer pricing exposures – SMEs are generally exempt from the UK transfer pricing legislation (see 4.11–4.12). However, for medium-sized companies, HMRC do have the power to require adjustments through the issue of a transfer pricing notice (see 4.12) and small companies must apply transfer pricing on all transactions with connected companies in (broadly) 'tax-haven' jurisdictions. HMRC also has the ability to deny 'excessive' tax deductions for management charges etc, since they would not have been incurred wholly and exclusively for the purposes of the trade (see 4.8).

- Inter-company balances will often be waived shortly before a sale. It should be established that the balances can validly be waived on a 'tax-neutral' basis (see 4.9 and 4.9A) and that no unlawful distribution issues arise under company law (see 13.99–13.101).

- Overseas permanent establishments – It is becoming increasingly common for employees to work overseas, with the risk of creating taxable permanent establishments in other jurisdictions. The nature of such employees' activities may therefore need to be carefully assessed.

- Potential corporate gains, intangibles and stamp duty land tax (SDLT) degrouping charges. Where a company/'sub-group' is being purchased out of a group, this may crystallise degrouping tax charges. The potential degrouping charge exposures should be quantified by checking for assets acquired from fellow group companies in the past six years (corporate capital gains and intangibles (see 3.38)) – three years for SDLT purposes (see 3.39). Only *capital gains* degrouping charges will normally be exempted under the SSE regime (see 3.39).

- Historic R&D claims – The acquirer will wish to ensure that all enhanced R&D relief has been validly claimed (see 4.10 to 4.10D).

- Withholding tax often arises on annual interest and royalties paid overseas, which should be accounted for under the CT61 procedure. Many treaties/

610

the EU Interest & Royalties directive provide for a reduced or nil rate of withholding, with HMRC consent being required for interest payments. The due diligence exercise may require the target company to rectify its failure to account to HMRC for any unpaid withholding tax etc.

• Payments made to contractors can give rise to potential employment tax exposure, especially where they are retained on a long-term basis or work on the company's premises (see 6.9 to 6.21). Where contractors etc. work through a personal service company, the current IR 35 regime means that the companies operating in the *private sector* should not be exposed to any PAYE/NIC risks (see 6.1C). HMRC also seem to carefully scrutinise consultancy payments made to non-executive directors for PAYE/NIC compliance.

• Many companies now have some form of employee share scheme, often in the form of an employee management incentives (EMI) scheme. The due diligence exercise should check to ensure that the relevant EMI rules have been satisfied. This will include, for example, ensuring the 'retention and motivation' purpose has been satisfied (see 8.59), the options were notified within the 92 day period, and the employees have made the relevant working time declarations (see 8.69).

• Benefits-in-kind reporting and compliance should be reviewed for potential risk areas, such as directors loan accounts (see 2.53–2.55 and 7.62), the application of the £150 staff entertainment exemption (see 7.86), and whether PAYE settlement agreements are in place to cover minor or trivial benefits (see 7.105).

• VAT reviews will generally focus on the correct and prompt filing of VAT returns and payments, the correct application of the 'option to tax' rules, historic claims for irrecoverable input tax, and where appropriate, suitable partial exemption calculations.

The due diligence report should also analyse the tax consequences of the proposed deal structure together with any potential tax charges that would be triggered by a change in the ownership of the target company and how these may be mitigated.

Post-acquisition integration of target business

12.6   An area often underestimated is the integration of the new business within the purchasing company. In some cases, the seller shareholders may have been the key drivers of the business and need to be kept on in managerial or technical positions. Planned economies arising from the integration may be difficult to achieve in practice without upsetting the dynamics of the business acquired.

FINAL SALE CONTRACT

Sale and purchase agreement

12.7   The sale and purchase agreement will build on the principles and terms agreed at the heads of agreement stage, the main areas being:

(*a*)   the detailed agreement for the sale;

(*b*)   the price payable, detailing any specific adjustments to it (see 12.57); the process for the preparation of any completion accounts (see 12.57A); and how the consideration is to be satisfied;

(*c*)   conditions relating to the completion of the agreement and the completion procedure; and

(*d*)   warranties and the deed of indemnity (or tax covenant) (see 12.69–12.80).

Non-compete covenants

12.8   The acquiring company should also obtain a 'non-compete' or restrictive covenant prohibiting the seller company/shareholder from:

- carrying on the same or similar business;

- within a reasonable geographical area; and

- for a certain number of years.

The purchasing company is entitled to a statutory trading deduction (under *CTA 2009, s 69*) for payments to obtain a 'non-compete' undertaking (where the seller shareholder/director is liable to an employment tax charge on the receipt under *ITEPA 2003, s 225*).

Restrictive covenant payments are only liable to NICs if they are paid to an employee of the paying company. Thus, where an acquiring company makes the payment, this would not incur any NIC charge as no employer/employee relationship exists.

However, sellers will now generally be reluctant to agree to allocating part of their share sale consideration to a non-competition covenant, given that (even without the availability of ER) they will enjoy a much lower tax rate on their capital gain than on the 'employment income' receipt for the non-competition covenant. Thus, it very rare to see any apportionment of the price in this way.

STRUCTURING AN ACQUISITION – ASSETS OR SHARES?

Overview

12.9   A business acquisition can basically be structured either as a purchase of the trade and assets of the target company as a going concern, or the shares of the target company carrying on the business.

The acquiring company may be able to benefit from the tax relief available on certain intellectual property (IP) purchases. Although tax amortisation relief was effectively 'blocked' on goodwill/customer-related intangibles purchased after 7 July 2015, relief continues to be available on IP assets, such as patents, know-how, and registered design rights.

This gives rise to an important planning consideration. If the proposed business acquisition includes valuable IP assets, these should be clearly specified in the sale and purchase agreement, together with the related consideration allocated to them. Valuable tax relief would be lost if these assets were included within the amount paid for the goodwill.

Goodwill and debts are exempt from stamp duty. However, any *commercial* land and property acquired on a business purchase can attract a significant SDLT cost at rates of up to 5% (see 12.25).

One of the key advantages of an asset-based deal, is that the buyer is generally not at 'risk' in relation to any latent historic tax liabilities within the selling company. One of the key disadvantages is the loss of continuity of the trading entity. This may adversely impact relationships with customers and suppliers. The operation of TUPE makes employee matters potentially complicated (see 12.21).

On balance, buyers now generally find asset-based acquisitions increasingly attractive. This is likely to create a tension with sellers who usually obtain the best tax treatment by selling their shares. However, many 'distress' sales (where sellers are desperate to sell to enable their businesses to survive) will often be structured as an asset deal (or a share sale of a new 'hive-down' company) (see 12.66–12.68). This enables the buyer to leave unwanted historic liabilities behind, although the operation of TUPE makes it practically impossible to 'insulate' the new 'transferee' company against potential employee issues.

When negotiating the deal, each party will have their own preferred route in mind. For example, the buyer may perceive that there are considerable pre-acquisition risks with the target's business and will not want to be hit with any latent liabilities. In such cases, the buyer may insist on the deal being structured as an asset purchase. The relative bargaining strength of the parties normally dictates the ultimate deal structure. However, in tightly negotiated deals, a 'price adjustment' may be struck where one party requires a particular route (say) to benefit from a particular tax relief.

Summary of tax effects – share versus asset purchase

12.10

	Assets	Shares
1. Tax relief on assets purchased, for example, *IP-related intangible* fixed assets, capital allowance assets and trading stock.	Relief generally based on price paid for individual assets. *(No amortisation relief for goodwill/ customer-related intangibles purchased after 7 July 2015.)*	Relief continues to be claimed on historic cost in target company.
2. Tax losses.	Not transferred with the trade and thus normally forfeited.	Transferred for use against post-acquisition profits (subject to anti-avoidance rules).
3. Degrouping charges	None.	Potential charges arising from prior intra-group transfers include: – capital gains (although these will often be exempted under the SSE rules – see 3.38) – intangibles (no SSE protection is available here – see 3.39) – stamp duty land tax.
4. Stamp duty land tax/ stamp duty	Up to 5% on *commercial* land and property.	½% on amount paid for shares.
5. Contingent liabilities.	Not transferred (except employee liabilities (TUPE))	Transferred (subject to warranties/indemnities).

OUTLINE OF TRADE AND ASSET PURCHASE

Tax reliefs on acquired assets

12.11   As a general rule, the buyer will often prefer to acquire the assets on which tax relief can be claimed such as trading stock (which is normally deductible in the first period) and plant and machinery.

A further benefit is the ability to obtain trading deductions on IP-related intangible fixed assets, such as know-how, patents and other IP rights. Corporate tax relief is given on such acquisitions under the rules in *CTA 2009, Pt 8*. The tax relief is broadly based on the amount that is written off or amortised in the buyer's accounts for the relevant period.

However, for post-7 July 2015 transactions, tax amortisation relief is no longer available for purchased goodwill and 'customer-related' intangibles, such as customer lists (see 12.49–12.51). Where the proposed acquisition includes 'material' intellectual property assets, they must be clearly show in the schedule of assets (see 12.19(d)) acquired together with the relevant purchase consideration (see 12.9).

The buyer may also benefit from an uplift in base values for capital allowances and capital gains purposes (ie exceeding the amount that would have been available to the target company).

Forfeiture of target company's tax losses

12.12   On an asset deal, the buyer would not be entitled to benefit from the target company's unused tax losses. Such losses are effectively lost since the seller company can only offset its trading losses provided the same trade continues (see 4.40).

Exceptionally, *CTA 2010, s 944(3)* allows trading losses to be transferred to the acquirer (on a trade and asset purchase) where the trade effectively remains under the *same* (at least 75%) beneficial ownership, provided certain other conditions are satisfied (see 12.66A).

Reduced commercial risk

12.13   An asset-based deal is invariably more advantageous for the buyer. By buying the assets, the buyer avoids responsibility for past actions of the company and the contingent liabilities such as tax, litigation etc which remain with the seller. Although the buyer can minimise these risks by a careful due diligence exercise, warranties and tax indemnities, it is better not to assume any liabilities in the first place rather than be embroiled in pursuing a warranty claim etc against the seller post-acquisition.

An asset purchase can often be quite complex from a legal and administrative viewpoint (see 12.19), although this also gives the buyer the ability to 'cherry pick' the desirable assets. There can also be difficulties relating to the transfer of licences and approvals which the business depends upon.

However, responsibilities for the employees' contracts of employment (and hence the accrued entitlements to redundancy pay etc) are invariably transferred to the buyer under the *Transfer of Undertakings (Protection of Employment)*

Regulations 1981 (TUPE). The rules surrounding TUPE make it difficult to carry out any post-deal rationalisation of the work force (see 12.21).

Roll over of existing capital gains

12.14 An asset purchase is particularly useful where the acquiring company or group has generated capital gains on the sale of existing 'chargeable' trading assets. However, capital gains on qualifying assets (such as property) cannot be rolled over against the acquisition of goodwill (which is included in a separate intangibles roll-over regime (see 12.53)). Consequently, the main categories of reinvestment expenditure that currently qualifies for *capital gains* roll over relief are:

- property occupied and used for trading purposes; and

- fixed plant and equipment.

Stamp duty land tax versus stamp duty on shares

12.15 Where the trade and asset purchase includes UK land and property, there is likely to be a stamp duty land tax (SDLT) cost. Where a substantial amount is being paid for property, the SDLT costs can be quite significant and often attract higher rates than the ½% stamp duty charge that is levied on the purchase of shares. Thus, for example, SDLT is charged where the total consideration paid for 'commercial' land and property exceeds £150,000 (but see 12.18).

Since 17 March 2016, the maximum SDLT rate on commercial property is 5% (which is payable on purchase consideration exceeding £250,000 (see 12.26 for SDLT rates).

No stamp tax is payable on intellectual property, goodwill or the transfer of book debts – see 12.20.

BASIC OVERVIEW OF SHARE PURCHASE

Increased commercial exposure

12.16 In contrast to an asset-based acquisition, a purchase of shares carries the risk of taking over the target company's undiscovered or contingent liabilities. Carefully drafted warranties and indemnities are therefore required to reduce the purchaser's potential financial exposure.

Clearly, it is often preferable to identify and quantify the potential risk by conducting an appropriate due diligence investigation beforehand (see 12.4–12.5). A buyer should be prepared to adjust the warranties and, particularly, indemnities if the due diligence investigation throws up any unexpected issues. The due diligence work, 'data room' information, warranties, and disclosure letter should be regarded as a joint exercise in information gathering.

Tax benefits

12.17 Although no immediate tax relief can be claimed for the cost of the shares purchased, in many cases the shares are now likely to qualify as a 'substantial shareholding' under *TCGA 1992, Sch 7AC*. Consequently, a subsequent disposal of the shares may benefit from the valuable Substantial Shareholdings Exemption (SSE), enabling them to be sold completely free of tax (see 3.42).

If the company has unrelieved tax losses they will remain within the company for the indirect benefit of the purchaser, subject to the potential application of certain anti-avoidance rules (see 12.63).

Potentially lower stamp duty costs

12.18 A share acquisition often attracts a lower stamp duty liability due to the lower rate of ½% payable on the purchase price of shares (the ½% charge arises irrespective of the amount paid for the shares).

The extent of any saving would depend on the 'make-up' of the target company's underlying assets (including any value referable to goodwill) and the amount of its debts and liabilities. This is because the ½% stamp duty charge on shares is, in effect, based on the *net* value of the company (ie its *total* assets (including goodwill) *less* debts/liabilities). There may be cases where the stamp duty charge would be greater than the 'comparable' SDLT charge (which is confined to the *full* value of the *property*), bearing in mind that goodwill and debts are not subject to stamp taxes.

Thus, for example, consider a company that is being sold for £10 million that has various trading properties worth around £1 million. In this case, the stamp duty cost to the purchaser would be £50,000 (ie ½% of £10 million). However, if the company's trade and assets were purchased instead, the SDLT payable on the properties would be £39,500 (0% on the first £150,000; 2% on the next £100,000; and 5% on the remaining £750,000).

TRADE AND ASSET PURCHASE – DETAILED ASPECTS

Sale and purchase agreement

12.19 The agreement for an asset purchase should identify precisely the assets and liabilities which will be taken over. This could comprise:

(*a*)   freehold/leasehold premises;

(*b*)   plant, machinery and vehicles;

(*c*)   leasing, hire purchase and other agreements;

(*d*)   intellectual property, trademarks, designs and know-how;

(*e*)   goodwill;

(*f*)   stock and work-in-progress;

(*g*)   debtors and creditors;

(*h*)   benefit of contracts;

(*i*)   employees (particularly key personnel); and

(*j*)   business accounts and records;

(*k*)   together with details of any assets/liabilities to be excluded from the sale (which may be more appropriate if the deal is everything *except* certain specified assets or liabilities).

12.20   Trade debtors, etc can be assigned without any stamp tax implications.

Depending on the nature of the business, there may be a need to assign contracts and leases which may create practical difficulties, for example, the target company may have non-assignable contracts and third-party consents may not be readily obtainable. Many modern businesses also hold licences and approvals to carry on their business, which may be difficult to transfer to a new entity. In some cases, the key concern is the lead time that would be involved to secure an effective transfer.

Also there are often commercial issues in alerting customers and suppliers to a change in the identity of a trading partner.

Fewer warranties tend to be required on an asset sale, which will normally cover such areas as the particular assets (and liabilities) transferred, the previous conduct of the company's trade, key customers and suppliers, etc, assignment of trade debts and exemption from stamp duty.

Transfer of undertakings rule for employees

12.21   Employees will normally be transferred automatically on an asset and trade sale under the *TUPE* provisions. Broadly, the sale will be treated as a 'relevant transfer' under the *TUPE* rules since it will fall to be treated as the 'transfer of an economic entity which retains its identity' in the buyer's hands.

The *TUPE* rules mean that the buyer acquires all the employees' previous employment history and obligations. The selling company must provide the buyer with 'relevant employee information' in relation to all the employees – which will include (for each employee):

- Identity and age;

- Details of employment that the employer is obliged to give the employee (under *ERA 1996, s 1*);

- Information of any disciplinary procedures taken against an employee or any grievance procedure taken by an employee taking place within the previous two years.

- Industrial Injury claims can also migrate across making insurance due diligence essential.

Where there is a large workforce, the gathering of this information is likely to prove a fairly onerous process. There are significant penalties for non-compliance with these rules.

The selling company is also obliged to inform its employees about the proposed sale of the business and 'consult' with them (through appropriate employee representatives) with a view to seeking agreement.

It is also worth remembering that a dismissal associated with a TUPE transfer is automatically deemed to be unfair *unless* it is for economic, technical or organisational reasons. This can add a significant administrative burden in relation to planned redundancies etc.

Allocation of purchase consideration

12.22   The buyer's primary objectives will be to maximise any 'immediate' tax deductions and minimise SDLT. For both corporate tax and SDLT purposes it is important to include the 'breakdown' of the total purchase price against the various assets in the purchase contract. (An apportionment of the consideration must be made for SDLT/stamp duty purposes – see 12.29). If the apportionment of the price is stipulated in the purchase agreement, the parties cannot argue about it after the contract has been signed. As a general rule, HMRC are unlikely to interfere with any arm's length transaction between unconnected parties, unless it is clearly artificial (for example, see *EV Booth (Holdings) Ltd v Buckwell* [1980] STC 578). In any deal, there is usually a parameter of values of each asset which can be substantiated commercially.

However, it is important to note that HMRC have the statutory power to re-allocate or apportion the consideration on a just and reasonable basis. For example, see: *CAA 2001, s 562* (capital allowances); *TCGA 1992, s 52(4)* (capital gains); and *CTA 2009, s 165(3)* (unconnected purchase of trading stock). Where there is a large disparity between the contract values and the subsequent fair values attributed to assets in the statutory accounts (under FRS 102 – see below), it appears that HMRC are seeking to apply the accounting fair values as a 'just and reasonable' amount.

The purchase of goodwill and other intangible assets is dealt with under *CTA 2009, Pt 8*, which is generally based on the amounts amortised in the accounts in accordance with GAAP. In practice, this means that these amounts will generally be derived from the fair values adopted in the accounts under FRS 102, FRS 105 or IFRS 3 which may not necessarily reflect the amounts stipulated in the sale and purchase agreement. Indeed, *CTA 2009, s 856(3)* states that where assets are acquired together, then any amount allocated to goodwill and intangibles in accordance with GAAP must be used for tax purposes. If there is no such apportionment, *CTA 2009, s 856(4)* imposes a 'just and reasonable' allocation.

Although tax amortisation relief was abolished for goodwill and *customer-related* intangibles acquired after 7 July 2015 (see 12.49), the 'fair value' accounting principles still apply to determine the acquisition values of these assets under the intangibles regime – for example, the 'allocated' acquisition amount would be used to determine the profit/loss made on a subsequent disposal.

Stamp duty land tax (SDLT) on property included in trade and asset purchases

Overview of SDLT

12.23   The purchaser is liable to pay:

- stamp duty land tax (SDLT) on the purchase of UK land and property [*FA 2003, s 121*]; and

- stamp duty on any purchase of shares.

SDLT is charged on all UK land and property transactions. However, since 1 April 2015, land transactions in Scotland are subject to the Scottish Land and Buildings Transaction Tax (LBTT). LBTT is subject to very similar rules as SDLT but has different tax rates.

SDLT is effectively a mandatory tax since it does not rely on the existence of a legal document or the legal completion of a land transaction [*FA 2003, s 42*]. Non-UK property is not within the charge to SDLT, although it may be subject to a similar tax in the overseas jurisdiction.

Basic charge to SDLT

12.24   Under the SDLT legislation, a 'land transaction' represents an 'acquisition' of a 'chargeable interest' (*FA 2003, s 43*). This means that tax is payable not only on a normal land purchase but also on the creation, release, surrender, or variation of a chargeable land interest. This clearly includes the grant of a lease, which is subject to special rules (see 12.33 below). SDLT is also charged on the value of any fixtures substantially attached to the land under land law. Items that retain their character as chattels and moveable property will not be charged to SDLT.

Penal SDLT charges can apply where a *company* acquires expensive 'residential' property (see 12.31).

Broadly, SDLT is payable on the 'completion' of a land transaction by the purchaser (*FA 2003, s 42*). However, the SDLT charge is brought forward where a land transaction is 'substantially performed', such as where a substantial (90%) amount of the consideration is paid (which includes the first 'rent' payment on a lease) or where the purchaser takes possession (for example, occupation).

The purchaser (broadly the person acquiring the relevant land interest) (*FA 2003, s 43(4), (5)*) must submit their 'self-assessed' land transaction return (SDLT 1) and pay the relevant SDLT within 30 days from the 'effective date', ie normally when the contract is completed or substantially performed [*FA 2003, ss 77 and 86*]. (An acquisition of a freehold interest does not have to be notified where the consideration is less than £40,000).

Care is clearly required to ensure that the SDLT return contains accurate figures for chargeable consideration or where relevant, market value and so on. Such returns are subject to SDLT enquiry with the normal tax-related penalties for 'careless' errors (see 4.59–4.64). Many SDLT avoidance schemes, which previously needed to be disclosed to HMRC, were blocked by *Finance Act 2012*. Furthermore, HMRC has won nearly all the aggressive SDLT avoidance cases brought before the courts. SDLT is subject to the GAAR regime (see 1.19).

SDLT rates

12.25   SDLT (at the appropriate rates) is applied to the chargeable consideration for the relevant land transaction. Different tax rate scales apply to residential property and non-residential or 'mixed-use' property. For each category of property, the SDLT is now charged under the 'slice principle', with the relevant SDLT rate being applied to the amount of the consideration falling within each band.

In the context of a trade and asset acquisition, the property will normally be of a 'commercial' (non-residential) nature. However, for completeness, residential property is defined in *FA 2003, s 116* and includes buildings that are used or suitable for use as dwellings, their accompanying gardens and grounds, and residential accommodation for school pupils and students (other than those in higher education).

Certain buildings, such as hospitals, hotels or 'care' homes, are effectively deemed to be non-residential. The transfer of six or more dwellings in a *single* transaction is also regarded as 'non-residential' for all SDLT purposes, except for the 15% SDLT charge on 'high value' dwellings acquired by companies (see 12.31) [*FA 2003, s 116(7)*].

Commercial property

12.26 Since 17 March 2016, the following SDLT rates apply for non-residential or mixed-use property:

Consideration band	Rate
Up to £150,000	0%
£150,001 – £250,000	2%
Above £250,000	5%

The amount of the purchase price falling within each band is taxed at the relevant rate to arrive at the SDLT payable.

The application of a nil or lower rate of SDLT depends on the relevant land transaction *not* being part of a linked transaction. Broadly, linked transactions are those made as part of a single scheme or arrangement between the *same* seller and purchaser (or their 'connected' parties). If the transaction is linked (such as on a trade acquisition), the rate of SDLT is fixed by reference to the *total* consideration for all the linked chargeable land transactions [*FA 2003, s 55(4)*].

Residential property

12.27 Since 1 April 2016, the *normal* SDLT rates for *corporate* purchases of residential property (but see also 12.31) are as follows:

	Rate
If total consideration less than £40,000	0%
If consideration is £40,000 or more	
Up to £125,000	3%
£125,001 – £250,000	5%
£250,001 – £925,000	8%
£925,001 – £1,500,000	13%
Above £1,500,000	15%

SDLT is charged on the amount of the purchase price that falls within each band.

Residential dwellings purchased by a company for more than £500,000 may be charged SDLT at a penal 15% rate (unless one of the 'business-related' exemptions is available) (see 12.31 and 12.31A).

Dwellings chargeable at the 15% SDLT rate are also likely to be subject to the Annual Tax on Enveloped Dwellings (ATED) charge each year (see 12.32).

12.27A *FA 2011* introduced relief for transfers involving multiple dwellings (*FA 2003, Sch 6B*). This relief can be claimed on acquisitions of two or more dwellings in one land transaction, In such cases, the SDLT is calculated on the *average* consideration paid for all the dwellings (but this calculation will be based on the additional 3% SDLT (as in the table above). The SDLT figure (on the average 'price') is then multiplied by the total number of dwellings to find the total SDLT payable.

Chargeable consideration

12.28   SDLT is levied on the 'chargeable consideration', which includes money or money's worth. Importantly, where the purchaser assumes an existing liability of the seller/transferor (such as an existing property mortgage), this forms part of the chargeable consideration for these purposes.

The chargeable consideration will include any VAT that is payable on the property, although in many cases VAT 'transfer of going concern' relief should enable the property to be transferred on a 'VAT-free' basis. However, this is not the case where VAT becomes chargeable following an option to tax being made *after* the 'effective date' of the transaction for SDLT.

On a trade and asset purchase, the properties purchased will be 'linked', and therefore the rate of SDLT will be based on the *total* 'chargeable consideration' (ie the amount paid for all the UK properties).

The SDLT treatment of deferred consideration depends on whether it is:

- contingent; or

- uncertain or unascertained.

Contingent consideration (ie a fixed amount that is payable or ceases to be payable if some future event occurs) is initially brought into account for SDLT purposes on the basis that it will be payable – the contingency is therefore disregarded. Where the deferred consideration is uncertain or unascertainable, the SDLT return (and hence the SDLT payable) is initially based on a 'reasonable estimate' of that future consideration. The buyer can elect to defer the payment of the SDLT where at least one tranche of any contingent or uncertain consideration is payable six months after the effective transaction date (*FA 2003, s 90*).

The original SDLT liability is subsequently adjusted when the circumstances surrounding the contingency are resolved or where the (initial) unascertainable consideration becomes determined. This is done by making a further SDLT return within the normal 30-day period.

Allocation of asset values and valuation issues

12.29   The seller's and buyer's agreed allocation of the total consideration between the various assets must be specified on the Stamp Taxes form – the apportionment must be made on a 'just and reasonable' basis. (Professional advisers should note the Court of Appeal decision in *Saunders v Edwards* [1987] 1 WLR 1116 which held that a solicitor involved in making a blatantly 'artificial' allocation was guilty of professional misconduct.)

The total consideration for the assets must agree to the various constituent elements (broadly) between cash, the issue of shares or loan notes, and the assumption of liabilities.

Goodwill and trade-related purposes

12.30   In September 2013, HMRC confirmed its practice with regard to goodwill valuations relating to trade-related properties (such as public houses, residential care homes, hotels, restaurants and so on). Where a business is sold as a going concern the sale price generally reflects the combined value of the tangible assets and goodwill. HMRC argue that the combination of both tangible and intangible assets often enables substantial value to be realised and that in the past inadequate value has been attributed to property assets.

HMRC and the Valuation Office Agency (VOA) adopt the accounting approach when valuing goodwill. Broadly, this involves valuing the assets of the business, including the property (but excluding goodwill), at their fair values. The goodwill value is the 'balancing figure' when the total fair value of the (net) assets has been deducted from the sale consideration (see 12.51).

When valuing trade-related properties, HMRC and the VOA seek to value the property on an existing use basis (since such properties are not normally sold as separate assets on the open market). Adopting the approach taken by the Royal Institution of Chartered Surveyors (RICS), this involves valuing the property on the basis of the profits that a 'reasonably efficient operator' can generate from the property in its existing use.

For tax purposes (especially SDLT), HMRC concludes that property-related businesses are invariably sold with property rights and it is necessary to recognise the contribution that each asset makes to the combined value of the business. It therefore follows (according to HMRC), that a property from which a successful business trades must have some goodwill of its own. Many tax advisers do not agree with this proposition – they take the view that goodwill attaches to the business and that the property value is independent of this.

Property values are largely determined by their location. Property values can generally be reliably estimated by expert valuers based on local property valuation databases, and these are normally derived from the inherent characteristics of the property and its location. However, just because a business trades successfully from a particular location, it does not necessarily follow that the successful trading increases the value of the property. If a hotel or pub is situated in a place where a profitable trade can be expected, that particular 'location' will influence its value and will be reflected in the property valuation.

Many would argue that HMRC's/VOA's approach places too much emphasis on RICS guidance, which specifically states that apportionments for tax purpose fall outside its scope. It is reasonably clear that HMRC's approach attributes a greater value to trade-related properties in the sale and purchase of a business than was the case previously.

Goodwill is often difficult to value. However, where there is a third party sale, the value of goodwill should be ascertainable under GAAP since it has an agreed basis of calculation being the *excess* of the consideration paid for a business over the fair value of its net tangible assets (see 12.51). HMRC's current practice is arguably flawed, since it does not consider the separate commercial returns that can be earned from the property (eg net present value of market rental income) and the return from the trading activity. Gathering such information is not likely to be difficult and would enable a sensible 'goodwill' value being attributed to the property element.

HMRC has met considerable reluctance to accept its stance in relation to trade-related property valuations and we may see a challenge in the tribunal at some stage!

Example 1

SDLT payable on a trade and asset purchase

On 30 June 2017, Bonds plc purchased the trade and assets (including goodwill) of Billy Ltd's successful computer game software design and development business for a total consideration of £4,100,550.

The sale and purchase agreement allocated the consideration as follows:

	£
Freehold property (including immovable fittings and fixtures)	1,200,000
Goodwill	2,500,000
Computer and office equipment	580,000
Debtors	270,670
Creditors	(450,120)
Cash consideration	4,100,550

An SDLT liability of £49,500 arises on the freehold property (including the immovable fixtures), calculated as follows:

		£
First £150,000	0%	–
Next £100,000	2%	2,000
Next £950,000	5%	47,500
Total		49,500

No stamp tax arises on the other assets.

Since the acquisition was made *after 8 July 2015*, Bonds plc cannot obtain corporate tax relief on the amount paid for goodwill based on the amount amortised in its accounts each year (see 12.49–12.51). However, capital allowances would be claimed on the computer and office equipment.

15% SDLT on purchase of 'expensive' residential dwellings by companies

Basic charging provisions

12.31   A penal 15% SDLT rate applies to *new* purchases of *UK residential* property worth over £500,000 by UK or non-UK *companies* (*FA 2003, Sch 4A, paras 1–3*). The £500,000 limit has applied since 20 March 2014.

These rules only apply where the purchase consideration attributable to a single dwelling exceeds £500,000, which is referred to in the legislation as a 'higher threshold interest' or HTI. Various exemptions are available which considerably reduce the scope of the 15% charge (see 12.31A).

This penal SDLT charge combined with the annual tax on 'enveloped' dwellings (ATED) (see 12.32) therefore imposes a heavy burden on UK companies acquiring high value 'residential' properties that are not used for commercial purposes or developed in the course of a trade.

The aim of these penal charges is to deter structuring acquisitions of *residential* property via companies – a practice known as 'enveloping' – so that a subsequent sale of the property can be structured as a share sale (which only attracts stamp duty of 0.5%).

Property purchased by or on behalf of a partnership, which includes a corporate partner, is also subject to the 15% SDLT charging regime. However, these rules do not apply to residential property acquired by trusts (and corporate trustees are also exempt).

Each dwelling is valued independently to determine whether it exceeds the £500,000 threshold. If the relevant transaction includes one or more HTI's and other properties, it will be treated as two separate chargeable transactions. The legislation provides that the total consideration given in the single bargain (referred to as the 'primary transaction' must be apportioned between the two elements on a just and reasonable basis (see *FA 2003, Sch 4A, paras 2(3), (4) and 9*). In such cases, the 15% SDLT charge would apply to the HTI(s) and the relevant SDLT rate would apply to the remaining property or properties. The company must complete two separate SDLT returns for the HTI(s) and the other properties respectively.

For example, on the purchase of a block of flats in June 2016, the 15% rate would only apply to the extent that more than £500,000 of the purchase price is attributable to any single flat within the building and would only apply to that part of the price attributable to those £500,000 plus flats. Where there is a 'mixed-use' property acquisition, such as a shop with a residence above, they are treated as separate chargeable transactions and the total consideration is apportioned between the various elements.

Where more than six dwellings are acquired at the same time, the deemed 'non-residential' SDLT treatment outlined in 12.25 does *not* apply for the purposes of the 15% charge.

Example 2

Apportionment of consideration for purposes of 15% SDLT charge

In June 2017, Byram Ltd (a UK company) paid £1,350,000 for a luxury residential property in Kensington, London. The property consisted of two self-contained flats with flat 1 and flat 2 valued at £1,100,000 and £250,000 respectively. Flat 1 was to be occupied by the 100% shareholder – Mr Sam and Flat 2 was let out to a third party at a commercial rent.

Since the properties are acquired through a company, the total SDLT charge is £175,000, calculated as follows:

Property	Chargeable consideration £'000	SDLT rate	SDLT £'000	£'000
Flat 1	1,100	15%		165
Flat 2	125	3%	3.75	
	125	5%	6.25	
	250			10
Total SDLT				175

FA 2013 **business-related exemptions from 15% SDLT charge**

12.31A The *FA 2013* considerably widened the scope of the exemptions from the 15% SDLT charge.

The current 'business' exemptions are contained in *FA 2003, Sch 4A, paras 5–5F*. These exemptions broadly cover HTIs, which are being acquired exclusively for business and other 'allowable' purposes (see 12.31). The exemptions likely to be relevant to an owner-managed company are:

- Rental investment to unconnected parties;

- Property development or dealing trades;

- Properties enjoyed by the public on a commercial basis for at least 28 days a year, such as stately homes;

- Employee accommodation (provided the employee does not have more than a 10% stake in the business);

- Farmhouses of an appropriate character occupied by full-time farm workers on a commercially run farm.

The property letting, development, and dealing exemptions will not apply if a non-qualifying individual occupies the property (even on a commercial basis). Non-qualifying individuals are widely defined in *FA 2003, Sch 4A, para 5A*. In the context of the relevant acquisition, they would include the company buyer and those connected with the company, such as its shareholders, their spouses and relatives, spouses of those relatives, business partners and relevant settlors.

The exemptions, *which must be claimed*, are all subject to withdrawal if the relevant conditions for the exemptions are not satisfied throughout the three years following the acquisition of the property. This is to ensure that the relevant conditions for the relief would be satisfied on a reasonably permanent basis.

Annual Tax on Enveloped Dwellings (ATED)

Basic ATED charging rules

12.32   Since 1 April 2013, high value dwellings are subject to the ATED, unless any of the 'business-related' exemptions are available. The scope of the ATED regime is similar to that governing the 15% SDLT charge (see 12.31) and has identical 'business-related' exemptions (see 12.31A and 12.32B), although there are some differences in the valuation thresholds (see below)

The ATED legislation is contained in *FA 2013, Pt 3 (ss 94–174), Schs 33–35*. The ATED applies to:

- Dwellings situated in the UK;

- Which are valued at over a specified amount (see below); and

- Owned completely or partly by a company, a collective investment scheme (CIS) or by a partnership that includes at least one corporate partner or CIS (collectively known as a 'non-natural person' (NNP)

The specified amounts are:

Date*	Amount
1 April 2013	£2,000,000
1 April 2015	£1,000,000
1 April 2016	£500,000

* Valuation date or, if later, date of purchase.

Ownership by trusts, partnerships, or limited liability partnerships will *not* be subject to the ATED. The ATED is subject to the GAAR regime.

ATED charges

12.32A   The ATED charge is based on various valuation bandings, as follows:

Rate bands for ATED		
Property Value	*2016/17*	*2017/18*
£500,001–£1,000,000 (Note 1)	£3,500	£3,500
£1,000,001–£2,000,000 (Note 2)	£7,000	£7,000
£2,000,001–£5,000,000	£23,350	£23,550
£5,000,001–£10,000,000	£54,450	£54,950
£10,000,001–£20,000,000	£109,050	£110,100
£20,000,001 plus	£218,200	£220,350

Note

(1)   Only applicable from 1 April 2016.

(2)   Only applicable from 1 April 2015.

It is the company's responsibility to obtain the appropriate property valuations, which must be made on a 'willing seller and willing buyer' basis. To demonstrate to HMRC that 'reasonable care' has been taken, this would involve seeking at least one professional valuation. Where a property consists of entirely separate multiple dwellings, such as a block of flats, each one will need to be valued separately for these purposes.

If the property valuation falls within 10% of one of the banding thresholds, the company can request a 'pre-return banding check' confirmation from HMRC to ensure the correct banding is used.

The ATED is levied for each 'chargeable period' (which is the 12 months to 31 March each year). Where the relevant dwelling is acquired or changes its use part way through a chargeable period, the ATED is calculated on a pro-rata basis.

For future years, the legislation provides that the ATED liability will be indexed according to increases in the CPI to September in the previous year.

ATED reliefs and exemptions

12.32B   The ATED exemptions are virtually identical to those available for the 15% SDLT charge, although ATED is an annual tax as opposed to the SDLT transaction-based tax. Consequently, the ATED exemptions effectively operate on a daily basis with the amount of relief being based on the number of days the relevant 'exemption' conditions have been met during the chargeable period to 31 March (see 12.32A). Clearly, if the exemptions have been satisfied throughout the relevant chargeable period, there would be no ATED charge.

The main ATED exemptions are the same as those listed for the 15% SDLT charge in 12.31A above.

ATED returns and compliance

12.32C Where the relevant ATED-chargeable dwelling is held at the start of the chargeable period, the return and payment must be made by 30 April in that period. Thus, for the period beginning 1 April 2017, the return must be submitted, and the tax paid, by 30 April 2017. Unfortunately, companies within the scope of ATED are still required to make a 'nil' ATED return.

A company only has 30 days from the first day it is subject to the ATED to submit its ATED return. For a new-build property, this is extended to 90 days.

Penalties for late submission could potentially amount up to £1,600 for being a year late. In *Lucas Properties Ltd* (TC4374), the tribunal upheld penalties of £1,300 on a 'late-filed' nil ATED returns in respect of 'exempt' properties!

If an exemption gives rise to no ATED liability (see 12.31A), the claim for the ATED must be made on an appropriate ATED 'Relief Declaration Return'. On the other hand, an ATED return is still required where the exemption does not fully extinguish the ATED liability, so that some tax is payable.

SDLT on leases

Basic principles

12.33   Some 'trade and asset' deals involve the seller leasing the business property to the buyer (as opposed to an outright sale). The SDLT legislation defines a 'lease' as:

- an interest or right in or over land for a term of years (whether fixed or periodic); or

- a tenancy at will or other interest or right in or over land terminable by notice at any time.

[*FA 2003, Sch 17A, para 1* (as introduced by the *Stamp Duty and Stamp Duty Land Tax (Variation of the Finance Act 2003) (No 2) Regulations 2003, SI 2003/2816.*]

A lease does not include a 'licence to use or occupy land'. Such licences do not attract SDLT (*FA 2003, s 48(2)(b)*). However, a licence only provides a 'non-exclusive' right of occupation, which only gives the occupier a mere contractual right rather than a property right with the additional protection that gives. A legal document may be 'drawn up' as a 'licence', but if it effectively grants an exclusive right of possession to the occupier, it will be treated as a lease (*Street v Mountford* [1985] 2 All ER 289, HL).

Put simply, the SDLT charge on the grant of a lease is calculated on the net present value (NPV) of the total rent payable under the terms of the lease (known as 'the relevant rental value'). The methodology here is to discount each separate rent payment back to its present day value, using a discount rate of 3.5% per year. The total of these discounted rent payments are then found to give the relevant rental value for the lease transaction.

The SDLT calculation follows the 'slice' system so that SDLT is only levied on the amount falling within the relevant band.

No SDLT liability arises on *commercial* property where the relevant rental value does not exceed £150,000. Since 17 March 2016, SDLT is charged at 1% on the relevant rental value exceeding £150,000 up to £5,000,000 (see Example 3 below). Any excess over £5,000,000 is charged at 2%.

Residential properties are exempt where the relevant rental value is no more than £125,000. However, a 1% SDLT charge applies to any excess over £125,000.

HMRC must be notified about the grant of all leases (that exceed seven years or more) or lease assignments on the land transaction return SDLT1. Notification is required for leases of less than seven years' duration, where they carry an SDLT liability.

HMRC's Stamp Taxes website provides a simple 'lease calculator' which automatically computes the SDLT on lease rentals.

Example 3

SDLT payable on lease

In January 2017, The Zola Trading Co Ltd granted a four-year lease of an industrial unit to Upson Ltd. The lease provided for a yearly rent of £160,000 over the four-year lease term. The SDLT would be calculated as follows:

Year	Rent (£)	Discount factor @ 3.5%	NPV £
2017	160,000	0.9661835	154,589
2018	160,000	0.9335107	149,362
2019	160,000	0.9019427	144,311
2020	160,000	0.8714423	139,431
NPV of rent payable under the lease			£587,693

The SDLT payable by Upson Ltd on the grant of the lease is £4,376 calculated as follows:

			£
First	£150,000	@ 0%	–
Next	£437,693	@ 1%	4,376
	£587,693		4,376

Special lease provisions

12.33A In practice, property leases can be structured in a variety of ways. The NPV calculation for fairly 'simple' leases with a specified rent for a fixed period should be relatively straightforward.

If it is possible for a lease to end before its fixed term (for example, under a 'break' or 'forfeiture' clause), this is disregarded in ascertaining the lease period. Such provisions cannot therefore be used as a device to shorten the lease period for the purposes of the NPV calculation. Any option to renew the lease is also ignored (*FA 2003, Sch 17A, para 2*). Thus, where a ten-year lease gives the lessee the option to extend the term for a further four years, it is still treated as a ten-year lease for working out the NPV of the lease rents.

Other lease agreements may be more difficult to interpret in terms of calculating the NPV of the rents. For example, a lease may contain a formula for calculating the rent (which may be based on the turnover of the lessee's business or increased annually in line with the retail prices index (RPI)). *FA 2003, Schs 5* and *17A* lay down the detailed rules for determining the 'rent' payable over the lease (including rent reviews) and the term of the lease in special situations.

Lease premiums

12.33B A separate SDLT charge arises on lease premiums received on the grant of the lease, which is calculated under the normal SDLT rules (*FA 2003, Sch 5, para 9(1), (4)*) (see 12.24). The lease premium would be treated as 'chargeable consideration' and taxed at the relevant rates (as shown in 12.26 and 12.27).

The special anti-avoidance rules that applied to leases granted for both a premium *and* an annual rent ceased on 16 March 2016.

VAT and the transfer of going concern (TOGC) provisions

Basic TOGC conditions

12.34   The transfer of the trade should not be subject to VAT, as the transfer of going concern (TOGC) provisions in *art 5* of the *VAT (Special Provisions) Order 1995 (SI 1995/1268)* should apply.

One of the key requirements is that the assets are part of the transfer of a business as a going concern. Given the relatively subjective nature of this test, it is perhaps not surprising that TOGC relief cases regularly appear before VAT Tribunals!

Where the buyer acquires the goodwill and all the assets of an existing trade (together with its workforce), these requirements will normally be satisfied. In the ECJ case, *Zita Modes Sárl v Administration de l'enregistrement et des domains* C-497/01 [2003] All ER (D) 411, it was held that the buyer does not need to have pursued the same kind of business as the seller before the transfer, but must intend to carry that business on after the transfer (as opposed to liquidating the assets).

The VAT treatment of some deals may be less clear-cut. In these cases, TOGC relief would only be justified where, in substance and taking all relevant factors into account, the buyer acquires the activities of a 'going concern' that can be continued. While statements made in the sale and purchase contract to the effect that the parties regard the transaction as a TOGC may be helpful, they are not conclusive. The transfer of goodwill and business name would be good 'indicators' of a TOGC. Other persuasive indicators would include the transfer of customer lists, transfer of contracts, business premises, transfer of plant and equipment, substantial stock, staff and the provision of a restrictive covenant.

However, in *Associated Fleet Services 17255*, it was held that a business was capable of being transferred as a going concern even where no employees were being transferred across.

In *Amor Interiors Ltd* [TC4542], Old Mill Furniture Ltd ('Old Mill') transferred stock and fixed assets to an associated company, Amor Interiors Ltd ('Amor') in 16 transactions over a two-month period. Amor continued to use the same staff and premises. The Tribunal took a broad view of the facts and found that Old Mill's business (or at least part of it) had been transferred to Amor as a TOGC within the meaning of *Value Added Tax (Special Provisions) Order 1995, SI 1995/1268, art 5(1)(b)*.

HMRC indicate that there should not be any significant break in the trading pattern before or immediately after the transfer.

Following the ruling in *Intelligent Managed Services v HMRC* [2015] UKUT 0341 (TCC) HMRC will normally adopt a 'sensible' approach to TOGC transfers involving a VAT group. In particular, while VAT grouping treats the representative member as carrying on the business of each group member, it does not change the nature of the businesses carried on by the individual group members. Their activities remain separate as a matter of fact. Similarly, where there is a transfer of a business out of a VAT group, the normal TOGC rules will apply (*Revenue and Customs Brief II (2016)*).

It is important to identify any property falling within the Capital Goods Scheme (CGS) that is transferred under a TOGC – typically property (including refurbishments) that have been acquired in the past ten years costing more than £250,000 (excluding VAT) where VAT was suffered on the purchase price. In such cases, the CGS history will pass to the buyer.

Unfortunately, HMRC are no longer prepared to give 'informal' TOGC rulings in the vast majority of 'routine' cases (but a ruling may be sought for complex cases in accordance with VAT Notice 700/6).

VAT status of buyer

12.35   The fact that a 'new company' buyer does not have a VAT registration number (or has not taken steps to register for VAT) at the time of the purchase does not prevent it from being a TOGC. Assuming the other conditions are met, a trade purchase will qualify as a TOGC where the taxable turnover exceeds the VAT registration threshold. A business is currently obliged to register for VAT if its taxable turnover in the previous 12 months exceeds £85,000 (*and the seller's 'historic' turnover is counted for this purpose*), or is expected to exceed £85,000 in the next month alone.

Property rental businesses

12.36   The default VAT provisions treat sales of land and property as exempt from VAT, but there are numerous exceptions to this rule which treat the supply as standard or zero-rated. Many property letting businesses will be subject to an option to tax election, so that the sale of the property would be standard rated.

However, on a sale of the property letting business, the TOGC rules should operate so that the supply is not subject to VAT provided the buyer notifies HMRC that it elects to opt to tax the property before the transfer (or any earlier tax point for VAT, for example, the receipt of cash consideration). These rules also apply to property that has been occupied by the seller for trading purposes in the relatively rare cases where an option to tax has previously been made. The TOGC rule would not apply where the property letting business ceases after the transfer – for example, where the tenant acquires the property so that it becomes owner-occupied.

The purchaser also has a statutory obligation to tell the seller that they have made the option and that it will not be disapplied (under the rules in *VATA 1983, Sch 10, para 2*). If the seller does not receive this notification from the purchaser, the TOGC treatment may be invalidated. Since the onus is on the seller to apply the correct VAT treatment, a prudent seller will generally ask for written evidence that the purchaser's option to tax has been made by the relevant date (such as a copy of the notification letter) and confirmation that the purchaser's option to tax will not be disapplied.

While it is possible for the purchaser to retain the seller's VAT registration number (by completing Form VAT 68), this is not usually recommended as the purchaser would then inherit any potential VAT liabilities of the previous owner.

Incorrectly charged VAT

12.37   Where seller has incorrectly charged VAT (because it has subsequently been found that the transaction should have been treated as a TOGC), the seller should cancel any VAT invoice by issuing an appropriate credit note (refunding the VAT). If this is not done, HMRC can still collect the relevant VAT from the seller, but the purchaser will not be able to reclaim it (as a TOGC is not a taxable supply). However, HMRC may permit the purported 'input VAT' should be recovered if HMRC is satisfied that the seller has accounted for and *paid* it over to HMRC (*VAT Notice 700/9/02, para 2.2* and *Internal Guidance V1-10, Chapter 2, para 3.2*).

VAT recovery on legal and professional costs

12.38   Where the TOGC rules apply, VAT will still be payable on legal and professional costs relating to the transaction. Assuming the purchaser is 'fully taxable' for VAT purposes (for example, where the assets being purchased are subsequently used for the purposes of making taxable supplies), such VAT can be reclaimed in full.

The same VAT treatment applies to costs relating to advice sought by the company when raising finance for any proposed business purchase. These are a general business expense for VAT and recoverable in line with the purchaser's VAT recovery rate.

Similar treatment applies to share issue costs (since the share issue is *not* an exempt supply for VAT purposes) following the ruling in *Kretztechnic AG v Finanzamt Linz* (C-465/03). The ECJ held that an issue of new shares does not constitute a transaction within the scope of the Sixth Council Directive (77/388/EEC), Art 2(1). The issuing company therefore has the right to deduct the VAT on expenses relating to the share issue (provided all the company's supplies are taxable for VAT).

If the transfer of assets does not fall within the TOGC rules, the seller should account for VAT on the purchase price. The buyer's recovery of this VAT as well as VAT incurred on other acquisition costs (such as professional costs) would depend on the VAT status of the underlying business. Thus, for example, the VAT would be fully recoverable if the transferred business is fully taxable but only partly recoverable on the transfer of a partly exempt business.

Corporate tax relief on borrowing costs

12.39 In many cases, the purchasing company will need to borrow from a bank or other lending institution to finance the purchase of the trade and assets. In such cases, the interest incurred on the borrowing would normally be deductible as a trading expense under the loan relationship rules [*CTA 2009, s 297(3)*]. If the interest is 'substantial', immediate relief will only be given provided the purchasing company has sufficient tax 'capacity' (ie taxable profits) to absorb the interest costs, although any excess interest 'loss' could be surrendered under the group relief provisions.

Any related borrowing costs, such as loan arrangement or guarantee fees, would also qualify for relief as a trading expense. The tax relief is based on the amount charged in the accounts. In such cases, the borrowing costs are normally 'capitalised' (and shown as a reduction against the loan) in the accounts – with the amounts being 'expensed' over the life of the loan.

From 1 April 2017, the corporate tax deduction for interest and other finance costs will be restricted to 30% of EBITDA (see 14.19), with the first £2 million being fully deductible. These rules do *not* apply where the company/group's interest/finance annual expense does not exceed £2 million and therefore they should not affect the majority of owner-managed companies.

New trade or expansion of existing trade

12.40 The integration of the acquired trade with the purchaser's existing business may be treated as merely expanding its own trade or the commencement of a new trade (for example, see *Cannon Industries Ltd v Edwards* (1965) 42 TC 625 and *George Humphries & Co v Cook* (1934) 19 TC 121). If the acquisition is treated as an extension of the purchaser's existing trade, there are no adverse consequences and any unused trading losses of the purchaser's existing trade may effectively be offset against the profits of the 'enlarged' trade.

On the other hand, if HMRC successfully argued that a new trade had commenced, any unused trading losses of the existing business could not be offset against future profits of the merged business (see 4.40 for further details).

It may be possible to avoid this problem by treating the acquisition as a separate trade and preparing tax computations for the two trades.

The increased profits arising from the trade acquisition may cause the company to be liable to pay its corporation tax in instalments (subject to the 'one year' period of grace where the profits are less than £10 million (reduced for associated companies) (see 4.50)).

CORPORATE TAX TREATMENT OF ASSETS PURCHASED

Buildings

12.41   Industrial, hotel and agricultural buildings allowances were abolished from 31 March 2011 and no relief will normally be available for expenditure incurred on buildings. However, purchasers must not overlook the opportunity to identify the 'plant and machinery' element in the relevant buildings and agree an amount that could justifiably be allocated to it (see also 12.44–12.48).

For tax treatment of fixtures and integral features attached to buildings, see 4.20 and 12.44.

In certain cases, relief can be claimed on commercial buildings situated in a 'qualifying' enterprise zone. 100% enterprise zone initial allowances can be claimed on industrial/commercial buildings purchased unused or within two years of first use. (The expenditure must be incurred within ten years of the site being designated within an enterprise zone.) Almost all the original enterprise zones are now time-expired, but new zones were announced in the Autumn Statement in 2015 and the Budget in 2016, giving a total of 48 zones by 2017.

If the purchasing company or group has made capital gains on qualifying assets, either within one year before or three years after the date of acquisition, the expenditure on the freehold/leasehold property can be used to roll over these gains [*TCGA 1992, s 152*]. (Goodwill gains can no longer be rolled over against property acquisitions – see 12.53.)

Plant and machinery

Overview

12.42   Currently, expenditure on plant and machinery may attract plant and machinery capital allowances. However (since 1 January 2016) the first £200,000 should be eligible for the 100% annual investment allowance (AIA), giving an immediate write-off of the expenditure (although the amount of relief depends on other qualifying expenditure already incurred by the company). See 4.2 for AIA limits before 1 January 2016.

If the acquiring company is a member of a group, this will depend on how much of the AIA annual limit has been 'used-up' by other group members. Certain assets do not qualify for AIAs including cars and integral features [*CAA 2001, s 38B*] (see 4.20–4.22).

The definition of 'plant' extends beyond industrial plant and can include central heating, moveable office partitions, computers, special electrical installations and so on (see 4.16–4.17). Specific types of plant and equipment, which meet certain energy or water-saving performance criteria, rank for special 100% FYAs – see 4.23)

12.43   The balance of plant and machinery expenditure not attracting AIAs (or FYAs) generally qualifies for the 'default' 18% WDA, which is calculated on a reducing balance basis [*CAA 2001, ss 11(4)* and *15(1)(a)*].

The qualifying expenditure is added to the purchaser's existing pool, with 18% being claimed on the total balance (see 4.29).

Certain types of plant (notably integral features (see 12.45), long life plant, and thermal insulation) must be taken to a separate 'special rate' pool, which is subject to an annual WDA of 8% (reducing balance basis).

For a detailed discussion of plant and machinery capital allowances generally see 4.15–4.34.

In certain limited areas, where there is a strong element of manufacturing, enhanced capital allowances are available.

Example 4

Calculation of plant and machinery allowances on asset purchase

Curbishley Ltd (a singleton company) is a manufacturer of specialised car components and draws up accounts to 31 December 2017. On 20 July 2017, it acquired the trade and assets of a competitor business for £1,925,000 (excluding cars). No other plant was purchased during the year.

For the year ended 31 December 2017, it will be able to claim:

- AIAs of £200,000 (which attract a 100% allowance)

- 18% WDAs on the balance of £1,725,000 (£1,925,000 less £200,000) = £1,725,000 × 18% = £310,500

This leaves £1,414,500 (£1,725,000 less £310,500) to be carried forward in the pool to be claimed as WDAs in future years.

In the year ended 31 December 2018, WDAs of £254,610 (£1,414,500 × 18%) would be claimed, leaving a balance of £1,159,890 to qualify for WDAs of 18% in the following year and so on.

With a WDA of 18% (computed on a reducing balance basis), it will take 12 years to obtain tax relief for around 90% of the expenditure.

Fixtures and integral features

Identifying 'fixtures' within buildings

12.44   Fixtures can often represent a significant part of an industrial or commercial building. Special rules are required because (in law) any fixture attached to a building becomes the property of the freeholder. The capital allowances legislation therefore contains a number of special provisions that treat the fixtures as belonging to the company, etc that incurred the expenditure.

Determining whether an item is a fixture essentially depends on its degree of annexation to the land and the purpose of its attachment – the greater the degree of attachment, the more likely it will be that the item is a fixture. A fixture is defined in *CAA 2001, s 173(1)* as 'plant and machinery that is so installed or otherwise fixed in or to, a building ... to become in law, part of that building or land'.

As a general rule, the court will generally consider the item to be a fixture where it is placed on or attached to the land with the intention of becoming an integral part of, or a permanent and substantial improvement to, the land's architectural design and structure. More obvious items include alarm systems, air-conditioning, lifts, escalators, and 'deeply embedded' heavy plant and machinery.

Integral features

12.45   WDAs on fixtures that are 'integral' to a building – known as integral features – can be claimed and go into a separate 8% pool and do not attract WDAs via the main pool. Integral features covers lifts, heating systems, external solar shading, electrical systems (including lighting systems) and cold water systems.

Agreeing consideration paid for fixtures and integral features

12.46   When a building is purchased or a leasehold interest is assigned, it is likely to contain various fixtures/integral features upon which plant and machinery allowances can be claimed (see 4.14–4.19 and 12.44). There can often be difficulties in determining the part of the total purchase consideration that relates to the fixtures and integral features.

Typical fixtures (and integral features) include

- Air conditioning
- Boilers
- Cabling
- Ducting
- Demountable partitions
- Fire alarm systems

- General lighting
- Piping
- Plumbing
- Sanitary ware and showers
- Smoke detectors
- Switches and sockets

Based on data collected by specialist capital allowances boutique firms, average capital allowance claims, based on a percentage of purchase price for various types of property are:

Offices	20%
Care/Nursing homes	25%
Medical centres	25%
Distribution centres	15%
Hotels	25%
Restaurants	20%
Retails shops	12%
Theatres	20%
Pubs	18%

Following the *FA 2012*, special rules will normally apply where a property containing fixtures/integral features is bought from a seller who has previously claimed capital allowances on them (see 12.47).

Requirements for a valid fixtures/integral features claim

12.47   HMRC tightened the capital allowances rules on the acquisition of fixtures in response to concerns that buyers of property were claiming excessive capital allowances. Because buyers often delayed 'pooling' the relevant fixtures, HMRC were often unable to establish whether or not a previous owner had claimed allowances on the same fixture, which would limit the amount claimable by the buyer to original cost (*CAA 2001, s 185*).

A buyer can now only claim capital allowances on fixtures/integral features acquired in a commercial property provided:

- The seller has 'pooled' all the relevant fixtures before the sale (or has claimed a 100% allowance) ('the mandatory pooling' requirement) (see 12.47A); and
- The seller and the buyer agree the 'consideration' value of those fixtures/integral features under a *CAA 2001, s 198* (or *s 199*) election (or, if they

cannot agree the value, the amount that is determined by the First Tier Tribunal ('the fixed value requirement). Note that (for a post-23 July 1996 building), the amount allocated as fixtures can never exceed the seller's or the last owner's original cost (see 12.48);

● The *CAA 2001, s 198* election must be made (or the matter referred to the First Tier Tribunal) within two years of the purchase being completed (see 12.48).

Under this process, the buyer's purchase consideration for the fixtures/integral features would mirror the seller's disposal value for capital allowance purposes.

Agreement of the above capital allowance points should take place as part of the standard pre-contract enquiries for the purchase of commercial properties.

The 'mandatory pooling' rule only applies where the seller is entitled to claim capital allowances on the fixtures/integral features (see 12.47A). The underlying purpose is to make sellers bring the fixtures/integral features expenditure into the capital allowances system and to provide a 'traceable' audit-trail of disposal and acquisition values made by successive owners.

The seller can satisfy the mandatory pooling requirement by allocating the relevant expenditure on fixtures/integral features to a 'pool' in a tax period before it ceases to own them (*CAA 2001, s 187A*). The seller can therefore meet this condition, for example, by pooling the expenditure in the period the sale takes place.

Practical issues with mandatory pooling requirement

12.47A To satisfy the 'mandatory pooling requirement' the seller must have included the expenditure on the fixtures in their pool of expenditure qualifying for capital allowances (although the seller does not necessarily need to have claimed the relevant capital allowances).

It is therefore important for buyers to find out about the seller's capital allowance position at an early stage in the transaction. If the seller is entitled to claim capital allowances but has not done so, the buyer will need to take action to preserve its claim to the allowances. It is also recommended that the sale agreement requires the seller to pool its 'fixtures' expenditure. The ability to claim capital allowances can clearly be used as a factor in negotiating the sale price.

The pooling requirement only applies where a seller is entitled to claim capital allowances. Thus, it is not required where the seller is exempt from tax (such as a charity or pension fund) or where the seller holds the relevant property as trading stock (eg a developer). In such cases, the buyer must provide written documentation to support its claim and should be able to demonstrate that a 'just and reasonable' amount has been attributed to the fixtures/integral features (see *Fitton v Gilders & Heaton* [1955] 36 TC 233 and *CAA 2001, s 562*).

Care is required where the current seller is exempt from tax but acquired the property after 1 April 2014 from a 'tax-paying' business. In such cases, the 'pooling requirement' would need to have been satisfied on the *previous* sale in order for the subsequent purchaser to claim the allowances on the property fixtures.

Section 198 elections

12.48   Sellers and buyers must make a *CAA 2001, s 198* election for a buyer to claim allowances on 'second-hand' fixtures (unless an application is made to the Tax Tribunal to agree the value). This is known as the 'fixed value requirement'. The election must be submitted to HMRC within two years of completion and, once accepted by HMRC, it becomes irrevocable. It is recommended that the *CAA 2001, s 198* election be agreed before the property purchase is completed!

Failure to make a valid *CAA 2001, s 198* election is likely to have serious tax consequences. Unless the Tribunal are asked to determine the 'consideration' value (see 12.47), if an election is not made, the buyer cannot claim any capital allowances on the fixtures and integral features acquired with the property. Furthermore, subsequent buyers will be prevented from obtaining allowances on the property's fixtures.

Where an election is made, the seller brings the value agreed in the election into account as a disposal value in its capital allowance computation. The buyer claims allowances on the same amount. *CAA 2001, s 198* elections should specify amounts for both integral features (see below and 4.24) and other fixtures. The election only applies to fixtures and does not extend to chattels, and is not required where the seller cannot claim capital allowances (see 12.47A).

The value(s) specified in the election effectively allocate the allowances between seller and buyer. A seller will retain all the allowances if the elected amount is (say) £1. On the other hand, the buyer will take over the allowances if the elected value is equal to the original cost of the fixtures/integral features acquired with the property. The seller would suffer a recapture of the allowances by bringing in the original cost of these items as a disposal value in its pool(s) of qualifying expenditure.

In limited circumstances, such as where the seller has ceased trading, the 'fixed value requirement' does not need to be satisfied. In such cases, the seller must make a written statement specifying the disposal value of the fixtures within two years of the disposal.

Where the Tribunal is *not* requested to agree the 'consideration' value, a failure to make a valid *CAA 2001, s 198* election will adversely affect future buyers of the relevant property. They will be prevented from making any 'fixtures-related' capital allowances claims (see 12.47).

Some buyers may take advantage of the situation where a seller has not been well advised. Since *CAA 2001, s 198* elections often work against buyers, they may simply ignore the *CAA 2001, s 198* process (and hope the seller does!). Then, at a late stage, they will apply to the Tribunal to determine the value (on a 'just and reasonable' basis).

The *CAA 2001, s 198* election must be completed correctly to be valid for capital allowance purposes. Strictly, the relevant fixtures must be identified on an 'asset by asset' basis in detail. However, HMRC do accept some level of amalgamation at 'elemental' level with meaningful descriptions (eg hot water system, sanitary appliances and so on). It is good practice to include the 'agreed form' of the *CAA 2001, s 198* election within the property's sale and purchase agreement.

A pro-forma specimen *CAA 2001, s 198* election is provided below:

Election under s 198 of the Capital Allowances Act 2001

We the Seller and the Buyer wish to elect (under the Sale and Purchase Agreement) and Section 198 of the Capital Allowances Act 2001, as follows:

Seller's Name and address		Hurst Retail Ltd Sirs Road Chadwell Heath RM 66 1GH
Seller's UTR	:	19571 97210
Buyer's name and address	:	Moore Properties 6 Wembley Way Wembley NW 108 6BM
Buyer's UTR	:	19641 96706
Property	:	Irons Warehouse, Irons Trading Estate, 11 Green Street, Upton Park, E13 9AZ
Title number	:	WH 194158
Interest	:	Freehold
Date of exchange	:	12 April 2017
Date of completion	:	12 April 2017
Total price	:	Five hundred and sixty thousand pounds only (£1,560,000) (exclusive of VAT)
Plant and machinery in respect of which election is made	:	See attached schedule for details of individual items of fixtures and integral features
Part of total price to be attributed to plant and machinery fixtures	:	Two Hundred Thousand Pounds (£400,000) (exclusive of VAT)

Part of total price to be attributed to integral features	One Hundred Thousand Pounds (200,000) (exclusive of VAT)
Signed	Signed
Name	Name
For and on behalf of the Seller	For and on behalf of the Buyer

---

Example 5

Fixtures claim on property purchase

On 6 August 2017, Wright Hotels Ltd purchased a hotel from Sissons Inns Ltd for £2.5 million. Sissons Inns Ltd had previously claimed capital allowances on fixtures costed at £700,000

Both parties agreed that the consideration for the fixtures was £250,000 and the integral features were £150,000, which was reflected in a valid *CAA 2001, s 198* election.

Since the hotel was purchased after 1 April 2014, there is a mandatory pooling requirement (which is satisfied since Sissons Ltd has made a previous capital allowances claim).

The parties have met the 'fixed value requirement' since they have agreed the value allocated to the fixtures and integral features in a valid *s 198* election, which must be submitted before 6 August 2019.

Wright Hotels Ltd will able to claim capital allowances on the £250,000 and the £150,000 it has 'paid' for the fixtures and integral features respectively.

Goodwill and intangibles

Scope of corporate intangibles regime

12.49   Since 1 April 2002, companies have generally been able to deduct the amortisation charge for goodwill/intangibles acquired (from an unrelated third party) under *CTA 2009, Pt 8*. However, the *Finance (No 2) Act 2015* has now abolished this tax relief for goodwill/*customer-related* intangibles *purchased after 7 July 2015*, which has major implications for companies structuring business acquisitions.

Goodwill is generally defined as the difference between the purchase price and the fair value of the identifiable assets and liabilities acquired. It will therefore be the balancing figure out of the purchase consideration after accounting for the revised 'fair value' of the assets acquired.

Broadly speaking, there are now *three* main types of goodwill/intangible assets for corporate tax purposes:

- Goodwill purchased or internally created before 1 April 2002 (see 12.50).

- Goodwill/intangibles acquired/created between 1 April 2002 and 7 July 2015 (see 12.50A and 12.50B).

- Goodwill/intangibles acquired/created after 7 July 2015 (see 12.50C and 12.50D).

Sometimes there can be arguments about when internally generated goodwill was acquired. The legislation resolves this arbitrarily by stipulating that goodwill is created when the relevant trade starts (which would be based on established tax principles) *CTA 2009, s 884*.

Pre-1 April 2002 goodwill

12.50 Goodwill acquired or created by a company *before 1 April 2002* remains firmly within the corporate 'capital gains' regime. Consequently, despite the accounting treatment, there is no tax amortisation relief for such goodwill. The tax is dealt with on a realisation basis when the company sells or transfers goodwill. Only at this point will the company deduct its acquisition cost from the sale proceeds in calculating its capital gain.

However, if the goodwill is organically grown, the company may not have any base cost unless it can benefit from March 1982 rebasing. For example, if a company was trading successfully in March 1982 it can often establish a significant base cost for its trading goodwill held at 31 March 1982 (see 15.13).

Goodwill/intangibles purchased between 1 April 2002 and 7 July 2015

12.50A Goodwill and other intangible assets acquired *between 31 March 2002 and 7 July 2015* fall within the corporate intangibles regime (now dealt with in *CTA 2009, Pt 9*). In such cases, tax relief is given on the goodwill amortisation charged in the company's accounts. As an alternative to the accounts amortisation, companies could elect to claim tax relief at the rate of 4% (straight line) of the original intangible asset cost per year. The election must be made within two years of the end of the accounting period in which the asset is acquired [*CTA 2009, ss 730–731*].

On its introduction in April 2002, the intangible regime was seen as giving companies a valuable tax-break for business acquisitions. Therefore, when this benefit was taken away for goodwill/certain intangibles acquired after 7 July 2015, it is perhaps not surprising this was viewed as an 'unfriendly' business measure.

However, tax-deductible amortisation for goodwill acquired/created between 1 April 2002 and 7 July 2015 is retained (but see 12.50B for abolition of tax relief on 'connected' incorporation transfers after 3 December 2014). Thus, the *F (No 2) A 2015* restriction (see 12.50C) has no effect on companies that were already claiming goodwill tax relief before 7 July 2015. The amortisation relief generally forms part of the company's tax-adjusted trading profits/loss.

Since the tax relief is generally based on the amortisation charged to profit and loss account in accordance with FRS 102/FRS 105, the 'write-off' period drives the timing of the tax relief. Under FRS 102, goodwill is considered to have a finite *useful life*, and is required to be amortised on a systematic basis over its life. This means that an annual amortisation charge is written off against a company's profits. In exceptional cases, if it is not possible to make a reliable estimate of the useful life, FRS 102/FRS 105 stipulates that the 'default' amortization period cannot exceed ten years.

FRS 102 does not specifically require any regular impairment review. However, FRS 102 does require that a 'recoverable' amount be established for each asset (or groups of assets), which means that an impairment loss may still arise in relation to goodwill (although this should be relatively rare). Broadly, if the 'recoverable amount' of the goodwill is less than its carrying value, the reduction in value is charged against profits as an impairment write-off.

Any increase recognised in the accounts value of goodwill (created or acquired before 8 July 2015), as a result of the transition to FRS 102 would be a taxable credit (albeit restricted to the relief already given) under the intangibles regime (*CTA 2009, ss 871–873*). Similarly, any additional impairment will be tax deductible.

Where pre-1 April 2002 goodwill is being sold by the seller, it is possible for the disposal to be taxed by reference to the 'contract' value (in the seller's hands) with the buyer obtaining intangibles tax relief based on the goodwill reported in the accounts after applying the 'fair value' process. HMRC accept that this is the correct analysis for goodwill and other intangibles.

Example 6

Tax-deductible amortisation of goodwill/intangibles under asset and trade purchase (before 8 July 2015)

On 5 January 2015, David Holdings Ltd concluded its negotiations for the purchase of the trade and assets of Helen & Anna Sports Ltd's high-tech sports equipment business.

David Holdings Ltd draws up accounts to 31 December each year.

The allocation of the purchase consideration is as follows:

	£
Freehold property	1,500,000
Plant and equipment	1,100,000
Goodwill	500,000
Patent rights	800,000
Know-how	500,000
Trade debtors (net of trade creditors and other liabilities)	200,000
Net consideration, satisfied in cash	£4,600,000

The above amounts were also reflected in the company's accounts (since they approximated to the fair values of the assets).

David Holdings Ltd will amortise its intangible fixed assets over the following periods:

	Years
Goodwill	5
Patent rights	10
Know-how	4

Since this was a pre-8 July 2015 acquisition, the company will be able to claim a tax deduction for the goodwill purchase (and can continue to claim the relief for periods after 7 July 2015).

Thus, the total goodwill/intangibles tax deductible amortisation charge for the year ended 31 December 2015 is £305,000, calculated as follows:

	P&L charge
Goodwill (£500,000/5 years)	100,000
Patent rights (£800,000/10 years)	80,000
Know-how (£500,000/4 years)	125,000
Total amortisation	305,000

If the (post-31 March 2002) goodwill/intangibles were subsequently sold, the accounting profit would often equate to the taxable 'trading' profit (unless, for example, any intangibles roll-over relief has been claimed against the goodwill acquired).

The profit/loss would represent the excess of the sale proceeds over the tax written down value of the asset but without any indexation allowance. Profits arising on the sale of goodwill could be rolled-over under the intangibles regime by purchasing new goodwill/intangible assets only.

Restriction for goodwill acquired on 'connected' incorporation

12.50B As part of a general 'clampdown' on tax efficient incorporation planning, the *FA 2015* blocked tax amortisation relief for goodwill and 'customer-related' intangibles purchased by a 'connected' close company between 3 December 2014 and 7 July 2015 (*CTA 2009, ss 849B–849D*). However, these provisions were short-lived since they were abolished on 8 July 2015. Following the wider abolition of tax relief for goodwill on *all* post-7 July 2015 transactions (see 12.50C below), they simply were no longer required.

Goodwill/intangibles acquired/created after 7 July 2015

12.50C No tax amortisation relief is available for goodwill and customer-related intangibles acquired after 7 July 2015. *CTA 2009, s 816A* provides that 'no debits' are tax-deductible for these 'relevant assets', which are defined as:

- Goodwill.

- Information relating to customers or potential customers.

- Contractual or non-contractual relationships with customers.

- Unregistered trademarks or other signs used in the business.

- A licence or right relating to any of the above assets.

This means that the goodwill/intangible amortisation (or impairment) for these assets would be added-back as an adjustment to profit in a company's tax computations.

Any taxable profit or tax loss would crystallise when a 'relevant asset' was subsequently sold (which would inevitably be different from the profit/loss reported in the accounts due to the accounting amortisation). The 'credit' (profit) would invariably be treated as a trading receipt under *CTA 2009, s 747*.

However, any loss arising on the sale of a (post-7 July 2015) relevant asset is treated as a non-trading debit (*CTA 2009, s 816A(4)*). Non-trading debits arising on intangible assets can be set-off against the company's total profits of the same period (*CTA 2009, s 753(1)*) or group relieved (*CTA 2010, s 99(1)*). *Since 1 April 2017*, any remaining non-trading debits are carried forward and set-off against future total profits and/or group relieved subject to the loss offset cap rules (see 4.40A). *Before 1 April 2017*, it was not possible to carry forward 'intangible' non-trading debits against future trading profits.

Tax-deductible post-7 July 2015 goodwill/intangibles

12.50D Intangible fixed assets that do not fall within the 'relevant asset' definition in 12.50C are not subject to any 'tax amortisation' restriction. Intangibles amortisation relief is therefore still available for intellectual property assets such as patents, know-how, registered designs, registered brands, copyright or design rights, and so on.

Therefore, when structuring any trade and asset acquisitions that include these intellectual property assets, these items should be 'carved-out' out separately in the sale and purchase agreement with a commercial price being allocated to each of them.

Example 7

Tax-deductible amortisation of goodwill/intangibles under asset and trade purchase (after 7 July 2015)

Assume the same facts as in Example 6 above, except that the acquisition of Helen & Anna Sports Ltd's sports equipment business took place on 1 October 2017.

David Holdings Ltd therefore only charges a pro-rata amortisation of the purchased goodwill and other intangibles to its profit and loss account for the year ended 31 December 2017, as shown below:

	P&L charge
Goodwill (£100,000 × 3/12)	25,000
Patent rights (£80,000 × 3/12))	20,000
Know-how (£125,000 × 3/12)	31,250
Total amortisation	76,250

Since the goodwill was acquired after 7 July 2015, David Holdings Ltd cannot claim any tax relief for the goodwill amortisation charge of £25,000.

However, because the patent rights and know-how are *not* 'relevant assets' within *CTA 2009, s 816A*, tax relief is still available for the £51,250 amortisation relating to these assets in 2017 and on future amortisation charges relating to them.

Negative goodwill

12.51 The economic climate of recent years saw an increasing number of 'distressed' business sales. In many cases, such transactions gave rise to 'negative goodwill' in the hands of the buyer. This is because, when the acquired assets are 'fair valued' under FRS 102 in the acquiring company's books, the aggregate fair value of the acquired assets *exceeds* the consideration paid for the business. The balancing excess amount is treated as *negative goodwill,* which is akin to a discount on the fair value of the assets acquired.

12.52 Under GAAP, the acquiring company matches the negative goodwill with the fair value of the non-monetary assets (such as trading stock and fixed assets) purchased. The negative goodwill credit is then released to profit and loss account over the period in which these assets are recovered through use (depreciation) or sale – so it would often be on a weighted pro-rata basis to the periods in which stock and plant depreciated.

From a tax viewpoint, any negative goodwill credit is only taxable under the intangibles regime where it relates to a relevant (identifiable) intangible asset within *CTA 2009, Pt 8* (which is relatively rare).

Profits on sale of post-March 2002 goodwill and IP

12.53 Any profits on the *sale* of (post-31 March 2002) goodwill and intangibles is treated as income rather than capital gains [*CTA 2009, ss 735– 736*].

However, the taxable (trading) profit can be deferred under an 'intangibles' style roll-over relief, provided the proceeds are reinvested into other goodwill/ intangible assets, within the normal roll-over 'reinvestment window' starting one year before and ending three years after the gain arises [*CTA 2009, ss 754– 763*]. Qualifying reinvestment in goodwill and intangibles by a 75% fellow-group company can also be counted for these purposes (*CTA 2009, ss 777– 779*).

12.54 Where tax amortisation relief is available on the 'reinvestment' purchase of goodwill and intangibles, the 'intangibles' roll-over regime effectively brings back into charge an appropriate part of the 'rolled-over' profit over the life of the new asset. This is because the tax base cost of the new 'replacement' asset(s) is effectively reduced by the gain/profit that has been rolled-over against it, as illustrated in Example 8 below. Thus, in such cases, where intangibles regime roll-over relief is claimed there will be a difference between the accounts cost and tax cost of the goodwill/intangible assets.

Example 8

Effect of intangibles roll-over relief

On 2 January 2017, Carroll Ltd purchased the trade and assets of Claret & Blue Ltd. This included the purchase of know-how for £1,000,000, which was to be amortised over ten years.

Carroll Ltd elected to roll-over a previous gain of £400,000 which arose on the sale of goodwill in August 2015 against the purchase of the above know-how. The goodwill was in respect of its 'London' trading division.

Carroll Ltd draws up its accounts to 31 December each year.

The tax effects of the roll-over claim for 2017 to 2019 are illustrated below:

		Tax deduction		
		2017	2018	2019
	£	£	£	£
No roll-over claim				
Know-how – cost	1,000,000	100,000	100,000	100,000
With roll-over claim				
Know-how – cost	1,000,000			
Less: Goodwill gain rolled-over	(400,000)			
Adjusted tax cost	600,000	60,000	60,000	60,000

The effect of the roll-over relief claim is to reduce the annual tax write-off in respect of the know-how by £40,000 (effectively this part of the goodwill 'gain' is being taxed each year).

Trading stock

12.55   *Unconnected seller* – The purchase of trading stock is relieved as a trading expense, as and when the stock is realised. Where the stock is acquired on from an unconnected seller, the buyer generally brings in the amount paid for the stock. HMRC would only be able to challenge the amount allocated to the purchase of stock if it is so artificial as to fall outside the protection of *CTA 2009, s 165(3)* (*Moore v R J Mackenzie & Sons* (1972) 48 TC 196).

In 'distress' sale cases, the amount paid for stock (as allocated in the split of the consideration under the sale and purchase agreement) is often below the fair value amount that is debited to trading stock in the accounts.. For example, as part of a trade and asset purchase, the amount allocated to stock in the sale and purchase agreement might be (say) £520,000 but the FRS 102/FRS 7 fair value booked in the acquirer's accounts is £750,000. The accounting profit would therefore be determined after deducting the £750,000 when the trading stock is realised whereas the amount agreed with the seller for the purchase of the stock was £520,000 under the sale and purchase agreement. The better view, based on the decided cases such as *Stanton v Drayton Commercial Investment Co Ltd* [1982] STC 585, is that the profit should be based on the amount allocated to trading stock in the sale and purchase agreement and therefore an adjustment is required. (Note – while *CTA 2009, s 46* says GAAP applies when determining accounts profits, this is subject to any adjustment required by *law* (which can be interpreted to include common law established by judges).)

12.56 *Connected seller – CTA 2009, s 166(1)(a)* applies in all cases to treat the stock as being sold at its market value. However, this is subject to the special *CTA 2009 s 167* election which enables both parties to substitute the *higher* of the actual sale price or book value. In practice, the election normally enables the buyer to acquire the stock at its actual transfer value for tax purposes. The election must be made within two years of the end of the seller's CTAP.

Before the *Finance (No 2) Act 2015* changed the treatment on 8 July 2015, the transfer pricing rules took priority over the 'automatic' market value rule imposed by *CTA 2009, s 166(1)(a)*, which could produce a tax saving opportunity.

SHARE PURCHASE – DETAILED ANALYSIS

Purchase price and valuation issues

12.57 A purchase of shares does not produce any cessation of trade problems for the company – the business continues in its existing form albeit under new ownership.

The buyer, however, will inherit the target's previous history and any previous tax problems. Normally, the risk can be minimised by obtaining appropriate warranties and indemnities from the seller (see 12.70–12.80).

The 'headline' enterprise valuation of a company will typically be based on the trading performance of the underlying business, irrespective of its funding structure and working capital cycle. Consequently, the buyer's headline purchase price will assume the target company is acquired on a 'debt-free and cash-free' basis, with its normal level of working capital.

However, these working assumptions will often trigger various adjustments to the final purchase price for the shares (see 12.58). In many cases, these adjustments can be material and subjective, and can result in protracted negotiations to arrive at the final agreed price – see Example 9 below.

Seller and buyers often disagree about the treatment of deferred income. Buyers generally take the stance that the deferred income is akin to debt, since the relevant services will need to be delivered after it acquires the company. On the other hand, sellers tend to argue that this is simply part of the company's normal working capital. The treatment adopted for deferred income will depend on the individual circumstances of each transaction. It is recommended that the parties agree the principles of dealing with deferred income at an early stage in the deal negotiation process.

Example 9

Typical adjustments in arriving at purchase price for company

Reds UK Ltd purchased 100% of the issued share capital of Lukaku Ltd. Reds UK Ltd valued Lukaku Ltd on the basis of eight times its (adjusted) maintainable EBITDA of £850,000.

Following various negotiations leading up to the completion of the purchase, various adjustments were made to the enterprise value to arrive at the share value/price ('equity value') as shown below:

		£'000
Enterprise value *(8 × maintainable EBITDA of £850,000)*		6,800
Loan term loan		(500)
Actual working capital at completion	950	
Normalised working capital requirement	(850)	100
Share value/purchase price		6,400

Completion accounts

12.58 The final sale price is often subject to a 'completion accounts' adjustment. Frequently, this will involve an amendment for working capital. The deal value assumes that the buyer will acquire the company with its normal level of working capital. However, if the actual working capital at 'completion' is more than the calculated normal level, the seller would be compensated for the 'excess'. This might be factored into the purchase price or the seller may be required to extract the amount as a dividend (which is normally less tax efficient) (see 15.105). The sale and purchase agreement would need to lay down the agreed principles on which the 'completion accounts' are prepared, taking into account the basis of the commercial deal, the target's accounting policies, and GAAP etc.

However, some deals are now struck using the so-called 'locked-box' mechanism. Under this method, the sale price for the shares is based on a historical 'balance sheet' and no value is allowed to leave the business between the locked-box date and the completion – hence the 'locked box' terminology. In such cases, the seller is required to 'warrant' the accuracy of the locked-box balance sheet. The buyer would therefore be able to claim for any loss suffered as a result of the relevant balance sheet being 'overstated'.

Stamp duty on share purchase

12.58A   Stamp duty at ½% is payable on the purchase consideration given for the shares (rounded up to the nearest £5).

The stamp duty liability is declared on the stock transfer form completed in respect of the transfer of shares to the buyer, which is sent to HMRC's stamp office in Birmingham or Edinburgh.

This purchase of the shares will invariably trigger a new notification under the Register of persons with significant control (PSCs) rules (see 11.18A).

Base cost of shares

12.59   The consideration given for the shares, together with other allowable costs of acquisition (including stamp duty (see 12.58A), will establish the buyer's base cost for future capital gains purposes.

However, in future, this will often be a relatively unimportant issue as the ultimate gain on the sale of the shares is likely to be completely exempt under the SSE.

If the purchaser issues shares or loan notes, the market value of the shares/loan notes will be treated as the consideration given. This will normally be the value attributed to the transaction where the parties are at arm's length (*Stanton v Drayton Commercial Investment Co Ltd* [1982] STC 585).

As a general rule, all legal and professional fees relating to the acquisition of shares will be disallowed as a capital cost (although relief is given for the related costs of borrowing to finance the acquisition – see 12.39).

Future use of trading losses

12.60   A share purchase may be particularly desirable if the target company has accumulated (tax-adjusted) trading losses which may be available for offset against future trading profits of the target company (and, for losses arising after 31 March 2017, against other profits/income streams – see 4.40).

However, special anti-avoidance rules apply to prevent the future offset of trading losses against 'post-acquisition' trading profits. The revised rules (from 1 April 2017), deny the losses being offset where a major change in the nature or conduct of the 'target' company's trade occurs within five years of the purchase of target [*CTA 2010, ss 673* and *674*]. There are similar restrictions for carried forward group relief losses (see 4.40).

Before 1 April 2017, these rules would be triggered on any such major change which occurs three years either side of the sale.

Given the vulnerability of unused tax losses under *CTA 2010, ss 673* and *674*, it is best to ensure that any payment for them as part of the purchase consideration is deferred until such time as the offset of the losses is effectively 'agreed' by HMRC – for example, when the enquiry period for the CT600 return has passed assuming appropriate disclosure is made in the return (see 4.57A–4.57D).

The 'acquisition' of unused tax losses can be a very valuable asset, in many cases sheltering a number of years of future trading profits from corporation tax. Thus, where the acquired company has substantial trading losses it is essential that the operation of the target company is carefully managed to avoid any forfeiture of the losses.

After the acquisition, the buyer has control and must ensure that any (sometimes inevitable) changes to the acquired company's trading activities of the company are carefully kept outside the range of the *CTA 2010, ss 673* and *674* 'radar'. SP 10/91 indicates that, when determining whether a 'major change' had occurred, HMRC would look at the extent of changes in a company's business premises, the identity of its suppliers, management or staff, its methods of manufacture or the pricing or purchase policies. A major change in one factor would be decisive. (It has been held that 'major' means something more than 'significant' but less than 'fundamental' (*Purchase (Insp of Taxes) v Tesco Stores Ltd* [1984] STC 304).)

Helpfully, HMRC would not generally seek to argue major changes had occurred simply to increase operating efficiency and to keep pace with developing technology. Further, it would not seek to apply *CTA 2010, ss 673* and *674* where a company seeks to rationalise its product range or changes its products provide this does not constitute a 'major change' in the type of products etc dealt with.

Some of the examples that SP 10/91 puts forward as triggering a 'major change in the nature of the trade' include a saloon car dealership switching to tractors and a public house converting to a discotheque!

In *Willis v Peeters Picture Frames Ltd* [1983] STC 453, a group which manufactured and sold picture frame mouldings acquired a loss-making company operating in the same field. Although the acquired loss-company continued manufacturing it changed its selling methods from mainly wholesale on the open market to wholesale among group distribution companies. However, the Court of Appeal held these changes were not sufficient to constitute a major change in the company's trade.

Subject to the potential application of the above anti-avoidance rules, it may also be possible to transfer losses where an asset-purchase is restructured as a hive-down, followed by the purchase of a new 'clean' company (see 12.66). However, the carry-over of tax losses into the new subsidiary can be restricted where the transferor company is technically insolvent after the hive-down (see 12.66A)). (Since the new subsidiary would have not have any existing trade, there is no need to consider the 'loss streaming' rules in *CTA 2010, ss 951* and *952*.)

Capital losses and pre-entry loss rules

12.61　Any unused capital losses in the target company would effectively be 'ring-fenced' under the pre-entry loss rules in *TCGA 1992, Sch 7A*, and are also subject to further anti-avoidance rules introduced by *FA 2006* [*TCGA 1992, s 184A*]. These rules were introduced to prevent 'capital loss' buying, ie where the acquiring company sheltered its own capital gains by routing the disposal of assets through the purchased 'capital loss' company. Such pre-entry capital losses can only be deducted against gains arising on assets owned by the target company at the date of acquisition or on gains realised on assets subsequently acquired from third parties.

Similar restrictions apply to the pre-acquisition element of a capital loss realised on a subsequent disposal of any assets held by the target company on acquisition.

Tax relief for borrowing costs

12.62　Interest incurred on borrowing to finance the acquisition of shares will normally be treated as a non-trading debit under the loan relationship rules. As a non-trading debit, it will initially be offset against any loan relationship income (such as interest receivable) of the same accounting period. A claim can be made to offset any net non-trading *debit* for the period in a number of ways, for example, against the company's current taxable profits, or by surrender to fellow group companies under the group relief rules (see 4.4(*d*) for further details).

Other costs incurred in relation to debt financing (such as loan arrangement fees) would generally be accounted for in accordance with FRS 102/FRS 4), thus, such costs will be 'debited' to the balance sheet as a deduction from the relevant debt/loan and then written off in the accounts over the life of the debt. Under the loan relationship regime, relief will therefore only be given for the amount written-off against the company's profit and loss account for the relevant period.

From 1 April 2017, corporate tax deductions for finance costs (and interest) exceeding £2 million per year are generally restricted to 30% of the relevant company's EBITDA (see 12.39).

VAT recovery on acquisition costs

12.63 An acquisition of shares is treated as a business activity for VAT purposes. The recovery of input tax on costs associated with the acquisition is based on the buyer's VAT status and is regarded as a business overhead. If the purchasing company is fully taxable for VAT purposes, then all the input tax is recoverable. If the company is partially exempt, the input tax would be restricted in accordance with the partial exemption rules.

If shares are issued as part of the consideration, the input VAT on the related professional costs may now be recoverable. This follows HMRC's acceptance of the ECJ ruling in *Kretztechnic AG v Finanzamt Linz* (C-465/03) which applies to the VAT treatment of all types of share and debt issues. In *Kretztechnic AG*, the ECJ held that an issue of shares was *not* a supply for VAT purposes. Therefore, the VAT input on all costs associated with the issue of shares can be recovered in the same way as general overhead expenses. Thus, a fully taxable business would be able to recover all the input VAT.

It is not uncommon for the purchasing company to 'pick-up' costs incurred by the bank or venture capital provider. In such cases, the related VAT would not be recoverable since the services have not been provided to the buyer.

Integration with buyer's existing activities

12.64 Once acquired, the buyer will need to decide how the company will be integrated with its existing operations. The acquired company may be left as a separate subsidiary company, in which case the various reliefs available to groups will apply (see 3.47).

Since 1 April 2015, the creation of an additional 'active' company has no impact on the 'group's corporation tax rate (since all companies now pay tax at 20%). However, it may mean that one or more companies will have to pay their tax in quarterly instalments (see 4.50A).

Alternatively, the trade of the target company may be hived-up and integrated with the buyer's existing trade or kept separate on a divisionalised basis (see 3.31).

Payment of interest and dividends within the group

12.65 Payments of annual interest, patent royalties and so on are now made on a 'gross' basis (ie without deducting tax) where the recipient is a

UK resident company (or UK branch) (although this rule is vulnerable to a challenge as being discriminatory under EU law). Thus, such payments can be made between group companies without any tax being withheld.

The interest will generally be deductible for tax purposes under the loan relationship (LR) provisions based on the amount charged in the accounts. Since 1 April 2017, broadly speaking groups with an annual interest/finance cost charge exceeding £2 million are restricted to a tax-allowable interest deduction on the 'excess' amount equal to 30% of EBITDA (see 12.39).

Interest costs are relieved as a trading deduction where the loan was borrowed to finance trading activity or capital investment within the trade. In other cases, for example where a shares in a new subsidiary are purchased, the related interest is deducted as a non-trading debit for LR purposes.

The recipient group company is normally taxed on the interest receivable (as a non-trade credit, assuming the loan was not made in the course of a lending trade).

Dividends can flow up the group without any material tax consequences. The dividend income is generally 'tax-free' in the hands of the recipient group company. There are certain limited exceptions to the exemptions in *CTA 2009, Pt 9A, Chs 2* and *3*, which mainly apply to dividends from companies resident in overseas tax-havens or where tax avoidance arrangements have been entered into (see 9.14–9.16).

USE OF HIVE-DOWNS

Succession of trade rules for capital allowances and tax losses

12.66 If there is considerable risk, for example, a large contingent liability, the buyer may require the seller to hive the trade down first into a newly formed subsidiary. The subsidiary would then be acquired as a clean company with the unwanted liabilities remaining behind in the transferor company.

It is recommended that the trade and assets are transferred under a hive-down agreement. This will detail the relevant assets (and liabilities) that are being transferred to the subsidiary and the allocation of the agreed purchase consideration between the assets. The purchase consideration is often left outstanding on inter-company loan account, with the buyer subsequently injecting sufficient cash into the company (typically on loan) for it to be repaid.

12.66A A hive-down of the trade and assets to the 'new' subsidiary should fall within the mandatory 'succession of trade' conditions of *CTA 2010, ss 940A–948*. This broadly requires the trade to have been carried on under the same (at least) 75% common ownership both before *and* after the hive-down – the post-hive down ownership test would be met by ownership of the subsidiary's shares.

The succession of trade rules enables:

- The transferor company's capital allowance assets (such as plant and machinery) to be transferred to the subsidiary at their tax written down value (thus, avoiding any balancing adjustment for the transferor), irrespective of the actual transfer price placed on the assets in the hive-down agreement.

- Any unused tax losses relating to the trade to be transferred to the subsidiary for offset against its future profits. The detailed loss offset rules are explained in 4.40 and 4.40A. However, in the context of a 'hive-down', the tax losses can only be transferred in full provided the *transferor* company broadly remains solvent immediately after the hive-down. The losses transferred are restricted, if the transferor's balance sheet is left with net 'relevant liabilities' (ie an excess of relevant liabilities over relevant assets (including the purchase consideration for the trade and assets hived-down)). In such cases, the amount of trading tax losses transferred is reduced by the 'net relevant liabilities'.

To ensure the beneficial provisions of *CTA 2010, ss 940A–948* apply, care must be taken that no binding contract or similar arrangement to sell the subsidiary company is made *before* the hive-down takes place. This would cause the holding company (ie the transferor) to lose beneficial ownership of the subsidiary *before* the hive-down, thus breaking the post-hive-down '75% ownership condition' (see *Wood Preservation Ltd v Prior* [1969] 45 TC 112).

A further requirement is that the subsidiary must be carrying on the trade for a suitable period *after* the hive-down, whilst it is still under (at least) the 75% ownership of the 'transferor' holding company. The Special Commissioners decision in *Barkers of Malton v HMRC* [2008] UKSPC 689 demonstrates the risks of failing to satisfy this test (see 13.64).

The transfer of the trade would normally take place under the transfer of going concern rules for VAT purposes (see 12.34).

Trading stock

12.66B Care should be taken with the tax treatment of trading stock sold to the new subsidiary. This will be a connected party transfer within *CTA 2009, s 166*. Although it is normal to place a 'sale value' on the stock in the hive-down agreement, the deemed 'market value' rule applies for tax purposes (see 12.66).

However, the transferor and subsidiary can make a joint election (within two years of the hive-down date) for (broadly) the stock to be treated as sold at its actual sale value.

Intra-group transfers for chargeable assets, intangibles and degrouping charges

12.67 Protection is initially available for 'capital gains' chargeable assets, which are transferred across for tax purposes on a no gain/no loss basis under *TCGA 1992, s 171*.

Similar 'tax-neutral' treatment is also available for (post-31 March 2002) intangibles (*CTA 2009, ss 775* and *776*).

However, a degrouping gain will be triggered if the transferee 'group' company is sold outside the group within six years of the intra-group transfer. Since *FA 2011*, the degrouping gain is added to the seller's sale consideration for the shares in the subsidiary. Thus, where the share sale is exempted under the SSE, the degrouping capital gain is also effectively covered by the exemption (see 3.38 and 12.67A).

On the other hand, this beneficial rule does *not* apply to degrouping charges under the intangibles regime (see 12.67A).

SSE on sale of subsidiary and degrouping charges

12.67A *TCGA 1992, Sch 7AC, para 15A* ensures that a competent claim for SSE should be available where the subsidiary is sold shortly after a hive-down.

This is because the seller (transferor) company is deemed to satisfy the minimum 12-month SSE 'substantial shareholding' period while the 'hived-down' assets were used for trading purposes by the *group*. Furthermore, the new subsidiary is deemed to have been a trading company for the minimum 12-month 'SSE' period before the sale (see 3.32 and 3.33).

On a strict reading of the legislation, the transferor must be part of a capital gains group' while the relevant asset is being used (see *TCGA 1992, Sch 7AC, para 15A*. It appears that HMRC also apply this strict interpretation of these rules (see HMRC CG manual at CG53080C). It is not therefore recommended to rely on the 'degrouping' protection in 12.67 if a *singleton company* exists before the new subsidiary is created (ie where the transferor was not part of an existing capital gains group).

Subject to the above technical difficulty, the combined effect of the these 'deeming' provisions means that hive-downs should not give rise to any capital gains degrouping charges, since the capital gains degrouping charge will be added to the SSE exempt sale consideration/gain of the new subsidiary. This assumes that HMRC would not try to invoke the anti-avoidance rule in *TCGA 1992, Sch 7AC, para 5* on the ground that the 'sole or main benefit' of the arrangements was to secure a tax-free gain under the SSE regime!

Unfortunately, the favourable degrouping SSE treatment for capital gains does *not* extend to *intangibles* degrouping charges. Thus, whilst any post-March

2002 goodwill (or other intangibles) included in the hive-down would be hived-down on a tax-neutral basis (under *CTA 2009, ss 775* and *776*), they will be subject to an intangibles degrouping charge under *CTA 2009, s 780*.

In the case of a distressed business, the value of the goodwill is likely to be negligible or very small, so no material tax charge should arise. If a significant intangibles degrouping profit arises, then it may be possible to reallocate it to a fellow group company and/or roll it over against new (group) acquisitions of goodwill and other intangible assets [*CTA 2009, ss 791* and *792*].

Where the hive-down transfers included UK property and SDLT group relief was claimed, an SDLT degrouping clawback charge is likely to arise (see 12.61).

SDLT issues

12.68 Any land and property (or shares) transferred as part of the 'hive-down' may not be available for SDLT (or stamp duty) intra-group transfer relief.

Broadly speaking, intra-group relief is denied where there are arrangements for the subsidiary to leave the group, as will invariably be the case when the hive down takes place. [*FA 2003, Sch 7, para 2; FA 1927, s 27(3)(c)*]. However, in the case of SDLT, even if the 'arrangements' rule can be side-stepped, any SDLT relief would be clawed-back under *FA 2003, Sch 7, para 4* where the subsidiary leaves the group (within three years).

PROTECTING THE BUYER

'Caveat emptor' principle and due diligence

12.69 The legal principle of *caveat emptor* (let the buyer beware) is predominant in the context of a 'share' purchase of a company. The company retains responsibility for all liabilities and actions and therefore the purchasing company will inherit all these problems, subject to any express agreement with the seller in the contract.

The buyer should therefore ensure that its inherited liabilities are limited to those which were known at the time of acquisition and hence were fully reflected in the price paid for the company. In many cases, a full due diligence investigation will be conducted by their accountants. This should give the buyer the necessary assurances about the operation of the business, the value of its assets, its tax position and particularly the full extent of its liabilities. If a limited due diligence investigation is considered appropriate, this should concentrate on those areas where the buyer perceives the greatest potential problems. For example, in the case of a manufacturing company, this may be the condition, age and realisable value of the stock, potential future costs of cleaning 'contaminated' industrial land, warranty claims in respect of defective products, and so on.

Warranties and indemnities

12.70   In some cases, a full investigation by the buyer's accountants may not be justifiable or practicable, particularly if there is time pressure to complete the deal. The prospective buyer must therefore seek protection under the sale agreement, by means of obtaining adequate warranties and indemnities. The buyer will normally do the first draft of the sale and purchase agreement (SPA) to place the full burden on the seller. The seller will aim to make the buyer aware of all relevant facts through the disclosure letter.

12.71   A *warranty* is a contractual representation made by the seller(s) (or warrantor(s)). It is a factual statement about any relevant aspect of the target company, such as the conduct of its trade, its assets, its financial position, tax matters and so on. The warranties effectively provide a 'snapshot' in time of the company at the point of acquisition – they are not forward looking. If the warranty is subsequently shown to be incorrect, the seller(s) will be in breach of contract and would therefore be liable to pay contractual damages to the buyer. Contractual damages can be substantially more difficult to establish than an indemnity based warranty claim: a buyer should not rely on the ability to bring a warranty claim as a substitute for thorough due diligence.

On the other hand, an indemnity refers to an agreement to compensate (normally) the buyer on a pound for pound basis for the loss caused by a particular event. In practice, indemnities are often confined to giving protection against historic tax liabilities (in the tax indemnity or tax covenant). However, they can in some cases be extended to commercial matters. Indemnities tend to provide a simpler and more effective mechanism of recovery than warranties. A buyer will often add indemnities to get protection against issues revealed by due diligence. Examples of non-tax indemnities would be in respect of prospective litigation or employee claims.

Principal functions of warranties and tax indemnity

12.72   The basic aim of warranties and the tax deed of indemnity (or tax covenant) should be to allocate the financial risks between the buyer and seller. However, warranties and, to a lesser extent, indemnities play a vital role in forcing the seller to think and make disclosure about relevant items and events. Such draft 'information seeking' warranties can then be used to draw up specific warranties applicable to the precise circumstances.

The warranties will appear in the sale and purchase agreement (SPA) between the sellers and buyers (often accounting for about two-thirds of the agreement!).

A separate tax deed of indemnity (or tax covenant) should be given in favour of the buyer, thus enabling any indemnity payments to be treated as adjusting the purchase consideration (see 12.81 – ESC D33).

WARRANTIES

The use of warranties to obtain information

12.73 One of the main purposes of drafting comprehensive warranties is to flush out all relevant information about the target company (or group) through disclosure by the seller in a disclosure letter. The buyer normally prepares the first draft of the SPA with comprehensive tax and commercial warranties. The seller must carefully consider the full implications of each warranty statement and provide all relevant facts and qualifications on the warranties through the disclosure letter (any warranty considered irrelevant may be deleted from the SPA).

The disclosure letter

12.74 The disclosure letter will qualify or modify various warranties. The production of a clear and comprehensive disclosure letter is a vital exercise for the seller. The buyer will not be able to make any claim for an incorrect or breached warranty where the seller has restricted or qualified it by providing full details in the disclosure letter.

The enquiries and analysis involved in the preparation of the disclosure letter will concentrate the seller's mind on any potential problems within the target company or group. The danger for the seller is the possibility of innocent non-disclosure. It is reasonable for a seller to require that any information obtained in the buyer's due diligence investigation is deemed to be disclosed.

Buyers can suffer a deluge of very late disclosures involving mountains of paperwork, which could put them at a disadvantage. They should therefore insist that draft disclosures and supporting documentation are produced at an early stage to allow time to consider their significance. Buyers can also refuse to accept disclosures which are too vague or which attempt to inappropriately shift risk. However, they cannot turn a 'blind eye' to matters they know about which are not formally disclosed.

Obviously, any disclosure of a significant liability or problem of which the buyer was previously unaware is likely to lead to the terms of the transaction being renegotiated. The buyer may request a reduction in price or require a specific indemnity or retention (see 12.82 below).

The increasing use of data rooms for disclosure of relevant information relating to the target company generally makes the 'disclosure' process more efficient and transparent (see 12.4A)

Damages for breach of warranties

12.75   The warranties also enable the buyer to claim damages for misrepresentation or breach of contract to compensate for the loss. If a warranty is breached or proved to be untrue, the buyer can be compensated for the 'loss' suffered in consequence. The measure of damages is the amount that could reasonably have been expected to arise at the date of the contract (ie to place the buyer in the same position had the warranty been true). The difficulty here is that the loss is probably suffered by the Target company and the key question is 'is the Target now worth less? And how much less would the buyer have paid if they had known about the issue or breach?

A court may decide the amount of damages after hearing expert evidence which can be a costly and time-consuming exercise. In such cases, the buyer is often encouraged to compromise even where there is a strong case. However, the use of a 'liquidated damages' clause in the sale agreement provides a practical formula for calculating the 'loss' and avoids court involvement, but is very rare. Warranty claims are notoriously difficult to successfully make.

Normal limitations on warranty claims

12.76   It is normal for warranty claims to be limited to a specific figure. This will often be the total sale consideration but the amount will depend on the circumstances of each case, such as where a substantial part of the consideration is to be satisfied by shares in the acquiring company.

Where a 'distressed company' is being acquired, typically for £1, setting the warranty/indemnity liability 'cap' on the sale consideration will rarely be appropriate and a higher figure closer to the 'economic value' of the deal may be used. Where a higher limit is agreed but the purchase consideration is (say) a nominal £1, the tax treatment of a warranty (or indeed indemnity) payment is unlikely to benefit from the 'adjustment of sale price' mechanism in ESC D33 (see 12.81).

De minimis limits will be established to avoid trivial claims. Where there are multiple sellers there will often be individual limits for each individual limiting their liability to the amount they have actually received. Sellers may even have a behind the scenes 'deed of contribution' where they agree to share liabilities.

Seller will also impose other appropriate restrictions, such as limiting the period within which a warranty claim can be made, for example, one to two years from the date of completion for commercial warranties and six to seven years for tax warranties.

In *Idemitsu Kosan Co Ltd v Sumitomo Co Corp* [2016] EWHC 1909, the buyer was time-barred under the SPA from pursuing a claim for contractual breach of warranty. Consequently, the buyer attempted to bring a claim for misrepresentation against the seller, contending that the warranties amounted to representations and hence the seller had made pre-contractual representations. The High Court dismissed the buyer's claims since the giving of a contractual warranty did not amount to a representation. Discussions etc made during the drafting of the SPA could amount to pre-contractual representations actionable under the *Misrepresentation Act 1967*. However this argument could not be used here since the SPA contained 'an entire agreement and non-reliance' clause. This clause specifically stated that the buyer had not relied on nor had been induced to enter into the SPA by any representations or warranties *other than the contractual warranties.*

THE TAX INDEMNITY/TAX COVENANT

Role of the tax indemnity

12.77 The current legal practice is to have a tax deed of indemnity or tax covenant supplementing the warranties. A tax indemnity is given by the covenanter(s) (the seller(s) – generally jointly and severally if more than one) to the buyer under which they will indemnify the *full* amount of any *relevant tax liability* which subsequently arises in the target company or group.

The tax indemnity is more direct and provides the buyer with a convenient method of recovering money from the seller. In contrast with warranties, buyers do not have to prove their loss only that the target company has an unsatisfied or unprovided pre-completion tax liability. Furthermore, buyers have no inherent duty to mitigate their losses under common law. Sellers are therefore exposed to a potentially greater liability under the indemnity.

Tax liabilities covered by indemnity

12.78 The tax indemnity would cover all relevant taxes, such as corporation tax, PAYE, NICs, VAT, stamp duty, overseas taxes and so on. Broadly, the tax indemnity would cover any tax on profits or events arising on or before the last statutory accounts date and tax on disposals, dividends, etc since then up to the date of completion. The indemnity invariably 'picks-up' taxable events arising on completion, enabling it to cover such tax liabilities as the intangibles degrouping charge (under *CTA 2009, s 780*) and the stamp duty land tax degrouping charge (under *FA 2003, Sch 7, para 9*).

The primary objective of the tax indemnity is to protect the buyer against any unprovided *pre-acquisition* tax liabilities. The cancellation or forfeiture of any tax relief or losses will often be counted as a 'deemed' tax liability for the purposes of a claim under the indemnity. Where the withdrawal of any tax relief, etc gives rise to a tax liability, the claim would be the amount of that liability. The loss of *future* tax reliefs (against a pre-sale tax charge or event) is a more difficult area. The extent to which it should be indemnified is a matter for negotiation, particularly if the price paid by the buyer does not reflect such reliefs.

Generally, the buyer will also seek to be indemnified against all costs, interest on overdue tax and tax penalties which may arise on the tax liabilities covered by the indemnity.

Typical 'seller protection' provisions

12.79   The seller(s) should seek to limit their liability under the tax indemnity by inserting appropriate 'exclusions' or 'carve-outs' from it. From the seller's perspective it would be reasonable to *exclude* from the indemnity any tax liability which:

- is covered by a provision or reserve in the last accounts or (where relevant) completion accounts – the buyer should only be covered for unanticipated tax liabilities;

- arises from transactions carried out in the ordinary course of the business after the date of the last accounts;

- would not have arisen but for a voluntary act or omission by the buyer or the target company post-completion;

- arises as a result of a retrospective increase in tax rates or a change in legislation;

- can be recovered or reclaimed by the buyer or the target company from someone else (including insurance); and

- has been 'compensated' by an over-provision' that has been determined on other tax items in the last accounts or completion accounts.

If the target company pays its tax in instalments, certain adjustments may be required to the tax indemnity. For example, the seller may not wish to pay the additional tax and interest which arises due to an event taking place after completion, even if it arises in the normal course of trade.

The seller's liability under the tax indemnity is also usually covered by the same restrictions on claims as used for warranties (see above). However, buyers generally resist accepting disclosures, etc against the indemnity.

Control of target's tax affairs

12.80   The 'buyer' would normally deal with the target company's tax affairs after completion. However, the seller(s) will seek to have some control over the tax affairs for the pre-sale periods to limit their liability under the warranties and/or tax indemnity.

The seller(s) therefore normally require appropriate terms in the tax indemnity giving them the ability to handle and negotiate with HMRC in relation to any pre-sale tax liability. This should ensure that any such liabilities are vigorously contested and defended. On the other hand, the buyer will not want the previous owner to have the ability to dictate the target's tax affairs after the take-over. Thus, a reasonable position to take in the tax indemnity would require the seller to be properly advised in the event of any potential tax appeal case, for example, by using tax counsel of appropriate experience.

CGT TREATMENT OF INDEMNITY PAYMENTS

12.81 Until the introduction of ESC D33 (on 19 December 1988, revised in November 2001) the target company itself was often a party to the deed. It is now best practice to avoid the target company being treated as a party to the deed.

Under ESC D33, any payment made under a tax deed by the seller to the *buyer* is regarded as an adjustment of the purchase price under *TCGA 1992, s 49*. Consequently, the payment does not give rise to a taxable receipt in the buyer's hands. The concession also requires that the indemnity payment is made under the terms of the contract for sale. The indemnity should preferably be in the form of a schedule attached to the sale agreement. However, HMRC are prepared to accept the use of a separate tax deed (as still used by some lawyers) provided the covenant is part of the overall terms of the sale agreement (see *Capital Gains Manual*, CG13042). HMRC accepts that the buyer can direct a damages payment to the Target company without affecting this treatment.

On the other hand, where an indemnity payment is made to the target company, this would normally be treated as a capital sum derived from an asset – ie the contractual right or the right to bring a legal action – following the doctrine laid down in *Zim Properties Ltd v Procter* [1985] STC 90. This means that because no consideration has been given for the indemnity, the entire damages payment would be taxable in the buyer's hands. Under the ESC D33 analysis, there is an underlying asset, and hence the payment would be taxable in full (ie it would not qualify for the £500,000 exemption for damages that do *not* relate to any underlying asset – ESC D33 (as amended from 27 January 2014).

Despite the protection given in ESC D33 for warranty and indemnity payments made directly to buyers, the deed/tax covenant usually requires all payments to be 'grossed up' so as to give buyers the same post-tax receipt (in the unlikely event of the payments being taxed). As the tax indemnity aims *fully* to reimburse the buyer for the unprovided tax liability, this is a difficult argument to resist. In practice, the seller generally agrees to the 'gross-up' clause provided the buyer does everything possible to mitigate the risk that the 'gross up' will apply. Thus, the seller will insist that the tax indemnity is only given to the buyer and that all payments are made to the buyer (and *not* the target company) , so as to fall within the terms of ESC D33.

Where a 'distressed company' is purchased for a nominal amount, it is likely that the beneficial tax treatment offered by ESC D33 for warranty/

indemnity payments may not be available (see 12.76). This would therefore mean that the seller's payment would normally be taxed as a capital gain in the company's hands under the principles established in the *Zim Properties* case (see above). In such cases, the buyer will often seek a 'gross-up' clause so that the seller has to pay an amount to cover both the warranty/indemnity claim and the tax on it. If a competent claim is made, this would prove very expensive for the seller. Consequently, the parties might consider an alternative approach involving the use of deferred shares. Under this method, if a warranty/indemnity claim is made, the seller must agree subscribing for economically worthless shares equal to the value of the claim. This should avoid a tax charge in the company's hands, but the downside is that it requires complex legal drafting.

RETENTION AGAINST WARRANTY/INDEMNITY CLAIMS AND TRANSACTION INSURANCE

12.82   It is not inconceivable that the seller may become insolvent, be liquidated or simply vanish; for example if an individual shareholder is intending to be based outside the UK after completion or the vendor company is a 'mere shell'. The seller or warrantor may therefore not be easy to pursue or may have no financial resources. In such cases, the warranties would effectively be unenforceable.

It may therefore be appropriate for the buyer to negotiate for a certain portion of the sale consideration to be 'retained' (as security for the payment of funds due on a breach of warranty). The retention monies will usually be held by one or both parties' solicitors in an 'escrow' account. An overseas buyer (US in particular) will often require a retention as a matter of course.

In some cases, the seller or the buyer may be prepared to take out 'warranty and indemnity insurance' to cover their financial risk. Sellers can take out insurance to insure against any future warranty /indemnity claims. This enables them to retain as much of the deal value as possible and avoids locking-up proceeds in an 'escrow' account. This insurance is however expensive and complex to obtain.

Buyers can also take out appropriate insurance to cover their warranty/ indemnity claims without having to pursue the sellers or worry about their ability to pay.

Tax liability insurance is generally tailored to the specific circumstances of each case, with appropriate exclusions and limitations (eg inaccurate representations given by the insured, fraudulent acts). The premium payable would reflect the relevant risks involved and might be considered costly. However, in some cases, insurance may offer a practical solution to difficult deal negotiations.

FRANCHISING

Advantages of franchising

12.83   There is no reason why a family or owner-managed company should not expand its business by offering a franchise. This involves franchisees running 'clones' of the franchisor's established business, under licence and in return for an initial fee and ongoing fees. A brand name is used and this is the main difference as compared with networking. Franchising is particularly useful if the product or service is capable of being delivered in a standardised manner and reduced to a documented process.

The advantage of using franchising as a means of expansion is that this expansion is achieved through someone else's funds. Furthermore, the franchisees do the managing and are likely to show more commitment than an employee who is used to expand the company's own business.

Faster growth should be achieved by the franchisor, with a higher return on capital, and indeed there are few disadvantages as far as a franchisor is concerned in the early years.

At a later stage, successful franchisees could create problems as they might well need convincing that they would not be better off withdrawing from the franchise agreement and starting up on their own in the same line of business. Furthermore, at some point, the franchisor might well feel that more money could be made by opening 'company-owned' sites under an established name and reputation.

Choosing a franchisee

12.84   Great care is needed when choosing a franchisee. There is a potential risk factor as far as confidentiality is concerned and, all things considered, choosing a franchisee is more important than choosing an employee. Franchisees will have their own ideas about how to run the business but nevertheless they are using the company's name so control is needed. A properly drafted franchise agreement with a prescribed adherence to the franchisor's model is essential.

Tax treatment

12.85   When looking at tax considerations for a franchisor, it is important to determine the legal nature of all receipts under the terms of the franchise agreement. The fee the company receives for granting the franchise is capital expenditure by the franchisee, but is likely to be a revenue receipt of the franchisor. The franchisee would be able to obtain tax relief on the 'amortised' capital payment under the corporate 'intangibles' regime (see 12.49–12.51).

The franchisee will obtain a trading deduction on their management service fees in the normal way. These are 'revenue' costs and are not 'customer-related', so this expenditure would not be affected by the 'goodwill' restrictions covered in 12.50C.

PLANNING CHECKLIST – EXPANDING THE COMPANY'S ACTIVITIES AND STRUCTURING BUSINESS ACQUISITIONS

Company

- On a trade and asset deal, it is particularly important to agree the individual amounts paid for each type of asset.

- Where commercial property is acquired as part of an asset and trade purchase, it is essential that the amount agreed for the fixtures (and integral features) should be agreed with by both parties and reflected in a *CAA 2001, s 198* election (or an application should be made to the Tribunal to determine the relevant value).

- Companies can claim tax amortisation relief (as a trading expense) for goodwill and intangibles purchased between 1 April 2002 and 7 July 2015. This would normally be based on the amortisation charged to the profit and loss account.

- For goodwill and 'customer-related' intangibles acquired after 7 July 2015, there is a total ban on all amortisation relief. Companies that acquired goodwill/customer-related intangibles before 8 July 2015 can continue to claim a trading deduction for the amortised goodwill/customer-related intangibles.

- Intellectual property related intangibles still qualify for tax amortisation relief.

- The purchase of commercial property frequently entails a considerable stamp duty land tax cost.

- Beware of the penal 15% SDLT charge that is levied on an 'expensive' residential dwelling (costing more than £500,000) acquired by a company. Important business-related exemptions from this charge are provided to property letting, property dealing or redevelopment companies etc.

- The annual tax on enveloped dwellings (ATED) may apply to 'high value' (£500k from 1 April 2016) residential dwellings acquired by a company. Similar business exemptions apply for property letting, property dealing, and redevelopment companies etc.

- Share purchases are often seen as beneficial as they provide 'succession of trade' in the target company and retention of any unused tax losses. Careful management of the target company's trade is generally required to avoid the 'major change in the nature of trade' anti-avoidance rules in *CTA 2010, ss 673* and *674*, which can deny the availability of the tax losses against the target's post-acquisition profits.

- In some cases, a hive-down may be a desirable way of the buyer acquiring a 'clean' company with the benefit of the trade's accumulated tax losses (provided the original 'transferor' company is solvent at the hive-down date). Furthermore, provided the transferor company is part of a 'capital gains' group, any de-grouping charges will often be exempted under the special 'extended' SSE rules. However, such protection is not available to (post-March 2002) goodwill and intangibles.

- Integration of the 'target' trade with the acquirers should be structured to avoid prejudicing any unrelieved tax losses.

Working shareholders

- The shareholders of the acquiring company need to limit their commercial exposure on a corporate acquisition by obtaining carefully structured warranties and tax indemnities. Full disclosure can generally be obtained on all material items affecting the target company. These commercial risks can also be reduced by a 'risk-based' due diligence exercise before the deal proceeds.

- Obtain non-competition covenants from sellers.

Other employees

- Rationalisation of workforce can lead to high redundancy and compensation costs (employment contracts are automatically transferred on asset purchases).

Non-working shareholders

- Require controlling/working shareholders to protect their position. May need a shareholder's agreement to protect their interests.

Chapter 13

Share Transfers, Share Buy-Backs and Company Reorganisations/Demergers

INTRODUCTION

13.1 Developments in the life of a family or owner-managed company may make it necessary for the company to change its structure by including new shareholders or to increase or decrease the number of shares in existence. An existing shareholder may wish to give shares to the next generation as part of succession or capital tax planning. The directors or shareholders may decide to provide a valuable 'key' manager or new manager with shares as an incentive and to foster a sense of proprietorship.

13.2 The mechanics of providing shares, whether through a new issue or by a transfer from an existing shareholder, may involve a CGT liability. However, in most cases, business asset hold-over gift relief should be available (see 13.14 and 13.27) to 'defer' the tax liability (provided the fairly stringent 'trading' company requirement can be satisfied).

If shares are made available to an existing or new employee or director for less than full consideration, the employee will suffer an 'employment income' tax charge on the 'profit' element, unless it can be demonstrated that the shares do not derive from their employment or prospective employment. This can normally be demonstrated if the employee is a member of the family or close friend (see 13.31).

Where employees or directors receive shares carrying 'restricted rights', these may also be vulnerable to certain income tax charges. However, it is possible to minimise their impact by making a joint *ITEPA 2003, s 431* election with the employing company within 14 days of the share issue/award (see Chapter 8 (especially 8.17 and 8.32) and 13.33 and 13.34).

13.3 The ability of a company to buy in its own shares means that the shareholders can look to the company itself as a willing buyer for their shares. This provides a useful 'exit' route in a number of situations. For example, where the controlling shareholder wishes to realise the value of his shares and, at the same time, make way for the next line of management. A buy-in can also be used to buy out a dissident or uninterested shareholder. The company law and tax aspects of an own share purchase are covered at 13.41–13.59.

Some companies are also taking advantage of the *Companies Act 2006* provisions enabling them to lawfully reduce their share capital – these provisions are explained at 13.60–13.60B.

13.4   Some family businesses eventually develop to the stage where different members of the family run various activities or trades. If the shareholders each have different aspirations and requirements regarding the running of their divisions this may lead to a need to separate out the various trades. The trades could be transferred to new companies so that the relevant shareholders can run them independently. This can be achieved by a reconstruction or demerger – the mechanics and tax implications are discussed at 13.61–13.98B below.

GIFT OF SHARES – MARRIED COUPLES (AND CIVIL PARTNERS)

Inter-spousal transfers

13.5   Where shares are transferred between a married couple (or between civil partners – see 13.8) who are living together during the tax year in which the disposal takes place, no CGT liability arises. A married couple (or civil partners) are not considered to be living together if they are separated by court order or by deed of separation or they are separated in circumstances that are likely to prove to be permanent [*ITA 2007, s 1011*].

The inter-spousal transfer is treated as a disposal, for such a consideration as will result in no gain/no loss to the transferor spouse [*TCGA 1992, s 58*]. For a post-5 April 2008 transfer, this means that the transferee spouse will acquire the transferred shares at the transferor's original CGT base cost. Since indexation ceased to be available for all disposals after 5 April 2008, this cannot be carried across as part of the transferee's deemed base cost (see 13.6). The transferred shares would be treated as an acquisition of shares by the transferee spouse (and will form part of their share pool). On a subsequent disposal, the transferee spouse is treated as acquiring the shares at the same time as the transferor.

Pre-6 April 2008 inter-spousal transfers

13.6   When taper relief was introduced on 6 April 1998, the previous indexation regime for individuals and trusts was retained but was frozen at April 1998. This meant that for intra-spousal transfers, the transferee spouse automatically inherited the transferor spouse's indexed base cost (ie the transferor's base cost plus the accrued indexation thereon).

Some individuals decided to 'bank' their CGT indexation before it disappeared on 6 April 2008. One popular way of doing this was for married couples to transfer the relevant asset between themselves, which HMRC confirmed was acceptable tax planning ahead of the new CGT regime. This would have triggered a deemed 'no gain/no loss' consideration for the transfer, enabling the recipient spouse to carry forward the accrued indexation as part of the asset's base cost. The *Finance Act 2008* confirms that, where the transferor held the asset at March 1982, the recipient spouse's future base cost (on a pre-6 April 2008 intra-spouse transfer) would equate to March 1982 value of the asset plus the related indexation (being 104.7% of that value) [*TCGA 1992, s 35A*].

A special 'indexation' restriction applies where the transferee spouse subsequently realises a capital loss on an asset acquired on a (post-29 November 1993) inter-spousal transfer. In such cases, any indexation built into the transferee's capital loss (including that 'inherited' from the transferor spouse), will be deducted to give a no gain/no loss result [*TCGA 1992, s 56(2)*]. No such restriction arises where the transferee's disposal gives rise to a capital gain.

Shares held in joint names

13.7 It is helpful to note that where close company shares are held in joint names by a married couple, the joint holding is treated as held individually by the husband and wife. For CGT purposes, the joint shareholding would be taxed in accordance with its beneficial ownership. This would normally be a 50:50 split, although it is possible for the couple's beneficial interests in the shares to be held in different proportions as tenants in common.

Transfers between civil partners

13.8 Same-sex couples registered as civil partners are able to enjoy the same tax breaks as married couples. Consequently, the transfer of shares between members of a civil partnership is treated as a no gain/no loss disposal. The CGT mechanics of the transfer are dealt with in the same way as explained in 13.5 and 13.6.

GIFTS OF SHARES – FAMILY MEMBERS, EMPLOYEES, ETC

Basic CGT treatment

13.9 A straightforward gift or 'undervalue' transfer of shares from an existing shareholder to another family member or close friend, etc will invariably represent a disposal at market value for CGT purposes. This will apply whether the parties to the transaction are connected or not [*TCGA 1992*, *ss 17 and 18*]. In such cases, it is often possible for the parties to hold-over the gain under *TCGA 1992, s 165* (see 13.14).

A deemed 'market value' disposal also arises where shares are gifted or transferred at an undervalue to a director or an employee in recognition of their services provided to the company [*TCGA 1992, s 17(1)*] (see 13.31). This rule applies where the shares are simply transferred without an option (and for share options exercised before 10 April 2003). If the disposal is to a connected person, and a loss results, that loss is only available for set-off against future gains from a disposal to the same person [*TCGA 1992, s 18(3)*].

However, where existing shares are acquired on the *exercise of an option*, *TCGA 1992, s 144ZA* disapplies the 'market value' rule to the acquisition of the shares. In practical terms, this means that the transferor (for example, the owner-manager or an employee benefit trust) has disposal proceeds equal to the amount actually received on the exercise of the share option (plus any amount received for the grant of the option). Similarly, the transferee employee's/director's base cost is the actual consideration paid for the shares, increased by any amount charged as 'employment income' under *TCGA 1992, s 119A* (see 13.40). (Note that the 'actual consideration' rule imposed on option shares is not affected by *TCGA 1992, ss 144ZB–144ZD*. These provisions are broadly aimed at most 'non-commercial options', but specifically exclude share options [*TCGA 1992, s 144ZB(2)(a)*].)

13.10 Where the director/employee acquires 'new' shares under an option through a share issue, *TCGA 1992, ss 17(2)* and *149A* collectively treat the shares as being acquired for the actual amount paid (once again, subject to any increase under *TCGA 1992, ss 119A* and *120* for any 'employment income' charges).

Special CGT valuation rules for consecutive disposals to connected persons

13.11 Where the gift/transfer is part of a series of disposals made to the same person or a connected person (within *TCGA 1992, s 286*) over a six-year period, the CGT anti-avoidance rules in *TCGA 1992, s 19* may apply. These provisions seek to circumvent the potential 'valuation' advantage that may be gained by fragmenting the disposal of a significant shareholding into a number of smaller minority holdings. Because of the sizeable valuation discounts often applied to small minority shareholdings, the aggregate CGT valuations would often be much less than the valuation that would have applied to a disposal of an equivalent larger holding. (For a detailed discussion on relevant share valuation principles, see 14.49–14.62.)

Although the application of *TCGA 1992, s 19* is often overlooked in practice, HMRC can seek to apply it where the above conditions are satisfied. In such cases, HMRC will aggregate the various disposals to the same person/

connected persons and calculate the value of the aggregated shareholding (as if it were a single holding). The CGT valuation of each previous relevant disposal will then be increased as a pro-rata proportion of the 'aggregate' valuation (ie replacing the original 'discounted' disposal value).

Clearly, HMRC are unlikely to invoke these rules where the previous transfers were subject to CGT hold-over claims.

Example 1

Application of *TCGA 1992, s 19* to series of prior transfers to connected persons

Mr Busby formed Babes Ltd in May 1969 holding all the 1,000 shares in the company.

In recent years, Mr Busby has transferred some of his shareholding to his children as follows:

Date	Transferee	Relationship to Mr Busby	No of shares
May 2015	Georgie	Daughter	300 shares
August 2013	Nobby	Son	250 shares

In June 2017, Mr Busby transferred 200 shares out his remaining holding in Babes Ltd to Bobby (his youngest son).

The current share valuations of holdings in Busby Ltd are as follows:

Holding	Value per share
75%	£250
50%	£200
20%	£40

Mr Busby's CGT consideration on the shareholding gifted to Bobby (who is connected with him) would be based on its market value.

However, this is part of a series of transactions with connected persons within the previous six years under *TCGA 1992, s 19*. Thus, the value of the shares used for this purpose would be that applicable to a 75% holding. (75% represents 750 shares made up of 300 shares to Georgie, 250 shares to Nobby and the current gift of 200 shares to Bobby.) The deemed market value consideration for the transfer to Bobby would therefore be £50,000 (ie 200 shares × £250 per share). Because *TCGA 1992, s 19* applies, the 200 shares are not valued in isolation (ie at £40 per share).

The gift to Bobby also triggers a revision of the prior share valuations under *TCGA 1992 s 19*. Thus, the 300 shares to Georgie and 250 shares to Nobby should be based on a 75% value in May 2015 and August 2013 respectively.

However, provided the company is a qualifying trading company, it should be possible to make a *TCGA 1992, s 165* hold-over relief election for those transfers (see 13.4–13.18).

Inheritance tax treatment – potentially exempt transfers

13.12   The gift or transfer at undervalue of shares by an existing shareholder to an individual qualifies as a potentially exempt transfer for IHT purposes [*IHTA 1984, s 3A*].

Where the recipient of the shares is an (unrelated) employee/director, it is usually possible to demonstrate that the relevant shares are being transferred to them for valid commercial reasons (without any intention 'to confer a gratuitous benefit'). Thus, where the recipient is considered vital to the company's future, there should be a strong argument for exempting the transaction under *IHTA 1984, s 18* (see 17.6), although of course the employee would still suffer an employment income charge if the shares were gifted or acquired at under-value.

In cases where the transaction is treated as a potentially exempt transfer (PET) (for example, where there is a familial connection), any IHT liability should often be avoided. The transferor would either survive the 'seven-year' period or, if the PET crystallises, business property relief (BPR) should be available (provided the recipient still retains the shares and the company continues to be a qualifying company) (see 17.10 and 17.23).

Gifts or transfers at an undervalue to an interest in possession or discretionary trust constitute chargeable transfers for IHT purposes. However, since most owner-managed trading companies will qualify for IHT BPR, it should still be possible to transfer their shares into a trust without any immediate IHT charge. Shares that do not attract BPR will, however, incur a 20% IHT 'entry' charge on any value transferred in excess of the available IHT nil rate band (see 17.64).

Legal formalities

13.13   The transfer of shares by way of gift would be valid when the transferor has executed a share (stock) transfer form and the transfer and certificate is delivered to the transferee (*Re Rose* [1952] Ch 499). However, in *Pennington v Crampton* [2004] EWCA Civ 819, a gift was also held to be valid where the transferor had clearly intended to make an immediate gift of the shares, but (due to her death) the share transfer form/share certificate had not been delivered. In such cases, the use of the share transfer form was sufficient to transfer the beneficial interest in the shares.

BUSINESS ASSET HOLD-OVER RELIEF

Basic conditions for hold-over relief

13.14   A non-arm's length transfer of unquoted shares in a trading company will normally be eligible for business asset hold-over gift relief under *TCGA 1992, s 165*. However, hold-over relief is *not* available in the following two cases:

- where *shares* are transferred to a *company* [*TCGA 1992, s 165(3)*]; and

- where an individual transfers shares to a 'settlor-interested trust' (ie where the transferor, their spouse/civil partner or dependent (minor) child is an actual or discretionary beneficiary of the relevant trust) [*TCGA 1992, s 169B*] (see also 17.66).

13.15   To qualify, the shares in question must be *unquoted shares* in a trading company or holding company of a trading group.

In broad terms, *s 165* hold-over relief will therefore only be available provided at least 80% of the company's/group's activities are trading. This is because the legislation only permits up to 20% of the total activities to be of a 'non-trading' nature without prejudicing the relief [*TCGA 1992, s 165(8)*]. When determining whether a 'trading group' exists, any intra-group transactions are effectively ignored.

For full details of the 'trading company' and 'holding company of a trading group' definitions, see 15.40–15.43. However, for business asset hold-over relief purposes, the normal joint venture rules outlined in 15.43 still apply (*TCGA 1992, s 165A(7), (12)*).

Hold-over relief can also be claimed for *quoted* shares in a personal trading company/holding company of a trading group [*TCGA 1992, s 165(2)*]. A personal company is one in which the individual transferor exercises at least 5% of the voting rights [*TCGA 1992, Sch 6, para 1(2)*].

As a general rule, where shares in a 'non-trading' or investment company are gifted or transferred at an undervalue, hold-over relief cannot be claimed and therefore the transferor will suffer a CGT liability based on their market value [*TCGA 1992, s 165(2)(b)*].

Procedure for making hold-over election

13.16   The transferor and transferee must jointly elect for hold-over relief, except where the transfer is made to trustees, in which case only the transferor makes the claim [*TCGA 1992, s 165(1)(b)*]. Under self-assessment, the hold-over election must be made on the prescribed form on help sheet HS 295 which should preferably be submitted with the transferor's tax return.

A claim for hold-over relief must be made within four years from the end of the relevant tax year in which the disposal took place [*TMA 1970, s 43(1)*].

Since the claim is not irrevocable, HMRC has confirmed that where the claim is made with the self-assessment return, it can only be amended or withdrawn within 12 months from the statutory filing date [*TMA 1970, s 9ZA*]. If the claim is made outside the return, *TMA 1970, Sch 1A (3)(1)(b)* provides that any amendment must be made within 12 months from the date of the original claim.

Mechanics of hold-over relief

13.17   Where the shares are gifted such that they are transferred for no consideration or are transferred at an undervalue, hold-over relief for gifts of business assets will be available [*TCGA 1992, s 165*]. This will have the effect of eliminating the transferor's chargeable gain – see Example 2 below.

The gain will in turn be deducted from the transferee's deemed market value acquisition cost [*TCGA 1992, s 17*]. The held-over gain will therefore become chargeable if and when the transferee subsequently makes a disposal of the gifted shares. In effect, the transferee will inherit the transferor's original base cost.

Example 2

Business asset hold-over relief on pure gift

On 1 June 2017, Brian Clough gave his son, Nigel, 30% of the shares in the family company, Cloughies Breakfast Foods Ltd, which he incorporated in August 1989.

The value of the shares transferred on 1 June 2017 has been agreed by the HMRC – Shares & Asset Valuation Office at £60,000. Brian wishes to eliminate his gain by claiming *s 165* hold-over relief.

	£
Consideration = MV	60,000
Less: Part disposal cost (say)	(2,500)
Capital gain	57,500
Less: TCGA 1992, s 165 relief	(57,500)
Chargeable gain	£Nil

Nigel's CGT base cost will be £2,500 (ie MV of £60,000 less gain held over of £57,500). This is effectively the 'cost' of the shares transferred.

Dispensation from formal share valuation

13.18   It will be appreciated that the computational effect of a full hold-over claim can be computed without reference to the market value of the shares (see 13.17)). Consequently, HMRC will (in most cases) permit a hold-over claim to be made without the need to prepare a formal computation of the chargeable gain or to agree a formal valuation of the gifted shares. This helpful concessionary treatment (provided by SP 8/92), must be claimed in writing on form HS 295 (see 13.16), by both the transferor and the transferee.

Both parties must confirm they are satisfied that the (estimated) value of the shares exceeds the original base cost and also provide full relevant details of the shares transferred, including the date of their acquisition and the allowable expenditure.

HMRC will generally require proper valuations to be prepared where the hold-over relief is restricted in some way (see 13.20).

Shares sold at an under-value

13.19   If the shares are sold at an under-value for an amount exceeding the transferor's base cost or deemed March 1982 base value, the gain eligible for hold-over relief will be restricted by the amount of the excess consideration (and the concessionary treatment under SP 8/92 (see 13.18 above) is not available) [*TCGA 1992, s165(7)*]. This restriction effectively ensures that the realised element of the gain (ie actual consideration in excess of cost) becomes taxable.

If the relevant ER conditions are satisfied (see 15.33), the resultant taxable gain can be charged at the 10% ER CGT rate.

Since the hold-over restriction only applies where shares are sold for more than their base cost, it is therefore possible for shares to be sold at their original base cost or rebased March 1982 value without incurring a capital gain, provided a hold-over election is made.

Example 3

Hold-over relief where actual consideration received

In Example 2, if Nigel had provided some actual consideration, of say £20,000, Brian's held-over gain would be restricted by £17,500 which is the amount by which the actual cash received £20,000 exceeds the base cost of £2,500:

	£	£
Indexed gain (as Example 2 above)		57,500
Less: TCGA 1992, s 165 relief:		
Gain	57,500	
Less: Amount restricted	(17,500)	(40,000)
Chargeable gain		17,500
Less: Annual exemption		(11,300)
Taxable gain		6,200
Assuming Brian makes an ER claim –		
ER – CGT @ 10%		£620

Nigel's CGT base cost would then be £20,000 (i.e. £60,000 less held-over gain of £40,000), which represents the amount he paid.

Restriction in hold-over gain for company's non-business assets

13.20   There are a number of potential traps which may restrict the amount of hold-over relief and therefore create unexpected tax liabilities. It should perhaps be reiterated first that, given the stringent 'trading company' definition, the shares would only be eligible for *s 165* hold-over relief in the first place provided the relevant company's non-trading assets/activities did not breach the 20% test (see 13.15).

13.21   The most important restriction is where a personal company (i.e. broadly one in which the individual transferor has at least 5% of the voting rights) holds chargeable non-trading/investment assets when the shares are transferred. It is therefore necessary to examine the company's balance sheet before any transfer of shares is made. In such cases, the held-over gain is limited by reference to the following formula:

$$\text{Relevant gain} \times \frac{\text{Market value of chargeable business assets}}{\text{Market value of chargeable assets}}$$

Consequently, a chargeable gain will arise to the extent that the value of the company's chargeable assets (*for capital gains purposes*) reflects non-trading or investment assets. Any surplus cash funds held by the company do not enter this calculation since they are not a chargeable asset for CGT purposes [*TCGA 1992, Sch 7, para 7*].

13.22 The current market value of the company's goodwill does not appear on its balance sheet, but must still be counted as a chargeable (business) asset. Goodwill represents the difference between the value of a business as a whole and the aggregate of the fair value of its identifiable net assets (see FRS102 and 12.51). The goodwill value can, therefore, normally be derived by valuing the company/business first – this will usually be based on a 'multiple of earnings' – and then deducting the value of the company's tangible net assets.

Clearly, where a restriction is required due to the presence of chargeable 'investment' assets, the inclusion of goodwill will have a beneficial effect on the chargeable business asset/chargeable asset calculation. However, note that post-31 March 2002 goodwill is dealt with under the corporate intangibles regime (and hence, unfortunately, does not count as a chargeable asset for these purposes).

A similar 'consolidated' chargeable assets calculation is required for shares in a holding company of a trading group. Broadly, this would bring in the chargeable business assets and chargeable assets for each group member (ignoring the investments in its 51% subsidiaries). If a subsidiary is not wholly owned, only the relevant percentage of the chargeable assets/chargeable business assets is included.

ISSUE OF NEW SHARES

Value shifting charge

13.23 A controlling shareholder might be tempted to procure an issue of shares to a prospective shareholder in order to avoid a direct disposal out of their holding. However, where new shares are issued for less than full consideration, a deemed CGT charge may arise under the value shifting legislation in *TCGA 1992, s 29*. Broadly speaking, a deemed disposal will arise where:

(*a*)   a controlling shareholder exercises control; and

(*b*)   as a result, value passes out of shares owned (or rights over the company exercisable) by them (and/or someone connected with them under *TCGA 1992, s 286*); and

(*c*)   this value passes into other shares in or rights over the company [*TCGA 1992, s 29(2)*].

13.24 A deemed CGT charge can also occur where a group of shareholders exercise control in concert to cause value to be shifted out of their shares into other shares (see *W Floor v Davis* [1979] STC 379). These rules apply even if there is no intention of tax avoidance.

13.25   Controlling shareholders may therefore be subject to a value-shifting charge where they procure an issue of shares to others, which causes their own shares to depreciate in value. In such cases, the shares acquired by the allottees are likely to be worth more than the cash subscription price they paid for them.

A deemed CGT charge also catches any value flowing out of the controlling shareholder's holding when there is a variation in the rights that attach to their shareholding or other shares. It is now fairly well settled that *TCGA 1992, s 29* cannot apply where a person transfers value from one class of shares into another class of shares owned by them. This means that individuals cannot make a disposal or a shift of value to themselves – see article in *British Tax Review* 1977 by Sir Andrew Park (at page 113) and *Taxation* (14 January 1999, page 347).

Where rights are altered or restrictions are removed over employment-related shares and their value is increased, this rise in value may be taxed under the wide-ranging provisions of *ITEPA 2003*. Typically, the increase in value could be taxed as a post-acquisition chargeable event under *ITEPA 2003, ss 426* and *427*.

Employee shares – tax issues

13.26   Clearly, where shares are issued to an employee/director at an undervalue, they will be subject to an employment income tax charge in accordance with the general principles established in *Weight v Salmon* 19 TC 174 (see 8.10 and 13.29–13.35). It should not be forgotten that the company would normally be able to claim a corporate tax deduction for the amount taxed as employment income (see 8.86).

Although the issue is not clear-cut, HMRC have tended to take the view that shares in private companies are often 'restricted securities' under the 'employment-related' securities regime. The reasoning for this is that the shares are 'restricted' because they are subject to the standard pre-emption provisions normally found in a private company's Articles. Consequently, given the potential tax risks in this area, advisers generally take the view that it is best to assume they are 'restricted' and ensure that protective *ITEPA 2003, s 431* elections are made in all cases (see below).

Where shares issued to employees/directors are subject to more substantive restrictions, they will invariably be 'restricted securities'. The employee/director will still suffer an employment income tax charge to the extent they pay less than market value for their shares. However, 'restricted securities' are particularly vulnerable to further income tax charges on subsequent future events (such as on a sale of the shareholding or lifting of restrictions, etc).

It is usually possible to completely or partially eliminate these potential income tax charges provided a joint *ITEPA 2003, s 431* election is made between the employee and the company. It is generally recommended that such elections are always made, since there is always a risk that HMRC may (retrospectively) contend that the relevant shares were restricted (see 8.13–8.34 for further commentary).

Availability of hold-over election

13.27 *TCGA 1992, s 29* creates a deemed disposal by the controlling shareholder and deems a corresponding acquisition of an interest in the shares by the 'benefiting' shareholder

In the writer's experience, HMRC have been prepared to accept business asset hold-over relief claims under *TCGA 1992, s 165* for 'value shifting' disposals. Thus, in many cases, it should be possible to avoid a value-shifting charge if both parties enter into a *TCGA 1992, s 165* hold-over election.

Example 4

Effect of value shift on issue of shares

Alan owned the entire 1,000 £1 issued ordinary shares in Mullery Ltd. His shareholding was worth some £150,000 in March 1982 and is currently worth £600,000 – the company has authorised share capital of 5,000 £1 ordinary shares.

In August 2017, Alan arranged for the company to issue 800 £1 shares at par to a valued manager, Alf. This depreciated the value of Alan's holding to £250,000.

Since Alan has control of the company and had exercised it so that value shifted out of his shares into those held by Alf, Alan would be treated as making a part disposal of his shares at market value under *TCGA 1992, s 29(1)*.

It is assumed that £100,000 would be paid for the shares if the parties had been dealing at arm's length (given the relatively minor restrictions in the company's Articles, this would also equate to the unrestricted value).

Alan makes a *TCGA 1992, s 165* hold-over election on the gain arising:

2017/18 – August 2017 disposal	£
Deemed consideration (MV):	100,000
Less: March 1982 base value (part disposal)	
£150,000 × $\dfrac{£100,000}{£100,000 + £250,000}$	(42,000)
Chargeable gain	58,000
Less: TCGA 1992, s 165 relief	(58,000)
Taxable gain	–

Inheritance tax issues

13.28 The IHT legislation contains similar provisions for value passing out of someone's estate as a result of the alteration of share rights in an unquoted *close company*. The IHT provisions examine the diminution in value to the donor's estate. Thus, where the alteration reduces the value of the donor's shareholding, this will be treated as a transfer of value by the relevant shareholders, subject to the exemption for non-gratuitous transfers and business property relief (if the various conditions are met at the relevant time), etc (see 17.6 and 17.19) [*IHTA 1984, ss 10, 103*].

It is important to note that the IHT value shifting transfer is a *chargeable transfer* for IHT purposes and does not qualify as a potentially exempt transfer [*IHTA 1984, s 98(3)*].

EMPLOYMENT INCOME TAX CHARGES FOR DIRECTORS AND EMPLOYEES

Income tax charge under 'Weight v Salmon' principle

13.29 An income tax charge will arise on the director or employee where they have received shares either as a gift or at a reduced price. This employment income charge arises on the amount of the undervalue element (based on the money's worth of the shares – see 14.40) in accordance with the general principles established in *Weight v Salmon* [1935] 19 TC 174, since this amount represents earnings within *ITEPA 2003, s 62*.

In practice, it is normally very difficult to refute an employment income tax charge where shares are being transferred to a director or employee. The best 'litmus' test is to ask the question 'would the shares have been made available on these terms to the individual if they were not a director or employee of the company?' If the answer is 'no', the shares will be treated as a benefit derived from the employment. Usually, the only realistic chance of avoiding the 'benefit' of shares being taxed as earnings is where shares are gifted to a member of the family, as this would characterise the transfer of the shares as a personal gift in the context of a family relationship or close friendship (see also 13.31).

Companies should ensure that they 'pick-up' and claim the appropriate tax relief on all employee share awards, options and other taxable events (see 8.86).

HMRC withdrew their informal Post-Transaction Valuation Check (PTVC) facility on 31 March 2016 for valuations required for the purposes of (unapproved) employee share valuations under *ITEPA 2003*. PTVCs remain available for other types of valuations, such as EMI, employee shareholder status shares, and capital gains valuations using form CG34.

Thus, employees will normally have to prepare a share valuation for the purposes of their SA tax returns. HMRC would be able to check the share valuation by opening an enquiry into the employee's return.

It is recommended the relevant share valuation should be prepared in conjunction with, or agreed by, the company to ensure consistency with any corporation tax deduction claimed for the employee shares (see 8.89).

Restricted or unrestricted shares

13.30   In practice, HMRC often regard all private company shares as restricted (see 13.26 and further below). Thus, as a general rule, tax advisers recommend that an *ITEPA 2003, s 431* election is made (see 8.17, 8.32 and 13.34).

Where a *ITEPA 2003, s 431* election is made, the income tax charge is based on the open market value of the shares (ignoring 'intrinsic' restrictions attaching to the shares). *Personal* restrictions, such as those specifically relating to the director/employee are ignored (eg the forfeiture of the shares if personal performance targets are not met. A *ITEPA 2003, s 431* election may have the effect of increasing the employment income tax charge on acquisition, but this ensures that all future capital growth in the shares is within the CGT regime (see 13.34).

Thus, by making a *ITEPA 2003, s 431* election the employment income tax charge would be based on the open market value of the shares (as defined in *TCGA 1992, s 272* – see 8.31). This assumes a hypothetical sale between unidentifiable sellers and purchasers. Therefore it is not possible to assume that the hypothetical purchaser is a director or employee. However, in many cases, there is unlikely to be a material difference between the money's worth of the shares (see 14.41) and their open market value.

Where a director/employee is provided with shares that do not impose any further special restrictions, they may not be 'restricted securities' under *ITEPA 2003, Pt 7, Ch 2*. However, there are some uncertainties about whether the standard restrictions imposed by the Articles of Association of most private companies are sufficient to make the shares 'restricted' (see also 13.26). These provisions would normally include the usual pre-emption provisions on share transfers, the board veto on share transfers, compulsory fair valuation, etc. Such rights are treated as an inherent characteristic of the shares (rather than employee specific provisions).

HMRC generally take the view that these conditions are likely to be sufficient to make the share 'restricted'. However, it is debatable whether they create the necessary reduction in the value of the shares to bring them within the 'restricted security' definition in *ITEPA 2003, s 423(1)(b)*.

Example 5

Calculation of employment income charge under *Weight v Salmon* principle

Alf subscribed for 800 £1 ordinary shares in Mullery Ltd at par when those shares were worth £100,000 (see Example 4). As Alf is an employee of the company, he is subject to an employment income tax charge on the 'undervalue' element, as follows:

	£
Market value of shares	100,000
Less: Actual price paid 800 × £1	(800)
Taxable amount	99,200

Although it is considered that the standard Table A restrictions should not cause the shares issued to Alf to be treated as 'restricted securities' (since the unrestricted and restricted value would virtually be the same), a protective *ITEPA 2003, s 431* election should still be made (see 13.34).

Alf's CGT base cost should be £100,000 (see 13.39).

Employment-related and restricted securities regimes

Scope of restricted securities legislation

13.31 Shares issued or transferred to directors or employees may be subject to various employment income tax charges under *ITEPA 2003, Pt 7 (ss 417–484)*.

The most important aspect of this legislation is probably the 'restricted securities' regime.

In the context of a family or owner-managed company, shares issued to a director or employee are caught where:

(a) they constitute 'restricted securities'; and

(b) the shares are acquired by reason of the individual's current, former or prospective directorship or employment; and

(c) the shares are acquired for less than their market value ignoring the relevant personal/employee specific restrictions.

Restricted securities are widely defined for these purposes, but include shares and interests in shares carrying restrictions. In essence, the market value of such shares must be less as a result of the relevant restrictions (see 8.15 and 13.32). See Chapter 8 for a detailed analysis of the 'employment-related securities' regime.

Shares, etc are not caught by the 'employment-related securities' regime where the right or opportunity is made in the normal course of the domestic, family or personal relationships of that person (*ITEPA 2003, s 421B(1)–(3)*). Owner-managers should therefore normally be able to 'safely' gift or transfer shares to their spouse or children without the shares attracting any 'restricted securities' tax charge in the recipient's hands. HMRC has confirmed that where shares are provided in a company controlled by an individual or their family, and the shares or option has been procured by them, this will normally meet the *ITEPA 2003, s 421B* 'exemption'. In such cases, it is necessary to show that there is a demonstrable relationship between the individual/family and the employee and no element of 'remuneration' reward is intended. Please see more detailed coverage of this exemption at 8.17.

Where a private company is not 'family-controlled' with perhaps a wide spread of shareholders, there might be cases where shares are (for example) treated as being awarded to a wife by reason of her husband's employment rather than because of a close family relationship.

The 'restricted securities' regime potentially applies to shares issued under the Enterprise Management Incentives (EMI) scheme, but it does not generally apply to shares issued under the other types of Approved Share Scheme (subject to certain exceptions – see 8.22).

Relevant restrictions

13.32 Director/employee shareholdings are frequently subject to 'restrictions'. These would include requirements for the director/employee to sell their shares back to the company at their nominal or par value on leaving or certain events giving rise to a forfeiture of the shares.

HMRC seems to take the view that shares issued subject to the standard pre-emption conditions might be sufficient to make them 'restricted', although the point is debateable (see 13.30). The legislation is really aimed at employee specific restrictions. However, in practice, advisers still recommend that *ITEPA 2003, s 431* elections are generally made to avoid any risk (see 8.32 and 13.30).

Employment income tax charges

13.33 Any income tax charge arising on the acquisition of shares is based on the general 'earnings' rule in *ITEPA 2003, s 62* (see 8.15 and 13.29). It does *not* arise under the employment related securities rules in *ITEPA 2003, Pt 7*.

Broadly speaking, an employment tax charge occurs where a director/employee acquires the shares for less than their market value (money's worth) (see 13.29).

To prevent any avoidance of tax by manipulation of share rights or restrictions etc, the employment related securities legislation imposes further additional income tax charges on certain events etc.

These additional charges can be avoided ensuring that amount paid on acquisition is based on the unrestricted market value of the shares, normally by making an *ITEPA 2003, s 431* election (see 13.34).

Provided the director/employee pays the unrestricted value amount, any future growth in the shares normally falls within the CGT regime.

It is therefore generally advisable to make a protective *ITEPA 2003, s 431* election to avoid any risk of incurring an income tax liability on a subsequent chargeable event, for example, when the shares are sold. This ensures that if there is any subsequent valuation challenge from HMRC, any income tax risk is isolated to the difference between the unrestricted value and the amount paid when the shares were acquired.

Election to be taxed on initial unrestricted value of shares

13.34 There is a valuable 'escape' provision in *ITEPA 2003, s 431(1), (2)* which enables the director or employee to enter into an election with the 'employer' effectively to be taxed 'up-front' by reference to the (unrestricted) market value of the shares. An election is likely to be beneficial in the vast majority of cases and particularly where the shares are expected to increase in value. For 'standard' ordinary shares, there is unlikely to be any material difference between their unrestricted and restricted value. (Importantly, *ITEPA 2003, s 431(1)* elections are now deemed to have been made for 'full value' EMI options, thus obviating the need to make actual elections where the EMI shares are acquired at their 'date of grant' market value (see 8.62–8.63).)

Pro-forma elections can be obtained from the HMRC website at www.gov.uk/ hmrc-internal-manuals/employment-related-securities/ersm30450. The main *ITEPA 2003, s 431* elections are reproduced at 8.34.

The election must be made within 14 days of the receipt of the shares (which fits in with the PAYE timetable).

Reporting obligations

13.35 HMRC require details of (unapproved scheme) shares or securities acquired by directors or employees to be reported on the (wide ranging) Form 42 (see 8.84). These online reporting requirements apply to share awards, the grant and exercise of share options, as well as any chargeable events under *ITEPA 2003, Pt 7* (see 8.15–8.38). Details must be given even where no income tax arises, for example, where an employee acquires shares at their market value.

The required information can be uploaded via the employment related securities option in the company's PAYE online area. The company will need to register before it can use this service. The deadline for submission of this information is 6 July after the end of the relevant tax year. Thus, for the year ended 5 April 2017, the form should have been submitted by 6 July 2017, although for this year the deadline was extended to 24 August 2017 (see 8.87–8.88).

PAYE and NIC on share benefits – readily convertible assets (RCAs)

13.36 Employment-related income tax liabilities must be accounted for under PAYE if the shares are 'readily convertible assets' within *ITEPA 2003, s 702*. Class 1 NICs are also levied on the 'taxable' benefit of shares and unapproved share option exercises where the relevant shares are 'readily convertible assets' or RCAs (see also 8.39).

Any employment income liability arising on shares in a (private) family or owner-managed company would often be dealt with in the recipient's self-assessment return. However, private company shares may fall within the PAYE (and NIC) regime if 'arrangements exist' now or at some future date which enable the recipient director/employee to realise an amount similar to the cost of the shares. This would include situations where there is an impending sale of the company or where employees are able to sell their shares to an employee trust. A formal or informal understanding that employees will be able to realise the value of their shares in due course may also be caught.

The RCAs definition also extends to include shares or share option exercises that do *not* qualify for a corporation tax deduction under *CTA 2009, Pt 12* (see 8.86)). Notably, this would include shares in a *subsidiary* of an *unlisted* company – (see 8.87) (*CTA 2009, s 1008(1), condition 2(b)*).

Where shares are RCAs, the company is liable to account for PAYE and NIC on the 22nd of the tax month following that in which the shares, etc were received. For example, the PAYE and NIC on shares (that constitute RCAs) acquired by an employee on (say) 10 September 2017 would be due on 22 October 2017.

If the PAYE tax is not recovered from the employee/director within 90 days *after the end of the tax year* in which the shares are provided, a further income tax charge will arise on the director or employee under *ITEPA 2003, s 222* (see also 8.46).

The director/employee would generally make a cash reimbursement of the tax. The company could also recover the PAYE from any other cash payment made to the director/employee in the remainder of the tax month after conversion. The *ITEPA 2003, s 222* charge can also be avoided if the company makes a beneficial interest-free loan (properly documented at that time) to the employee/director to enable them to reimburse the PAYE tax.

Where the shares are subject to PAYE, the employing company will need to estimate their value. It is no longer possible to obtain a PTVC from HMRC for such cases (see 13.29).

Shares which are not RCAs

13.37 Where the shares do not constitute RCAs, any taxable benefit arising on the shares must be returned as a benefit on the employee's personal tax return at a proper valuation, which may have to be agreed with HMRC – Shares and Asset Valuation – by way of an enquiry into the employee's SA tax return. It is no longer possible to agree the share valuation with HMRC after the shares are acquired under the PTVC procedure (see 13.29 and 14.46).

The employing company will have filed online the relevant share award/option details on the Form 42 (which provides HMRC with a useful cross-check!).

Use of Enterprise Management Incentives schemes and approved Company Share Option Plans

13.38 The potential tax charges under the 'restricted securities' legislation can be avoided by granting 'full value' share options under the Enterprise Management Incentives (EMI) scheme (see 8.49–8.73 for full coverage of the EMI regime). However, EMI options cannot be granted by companies with more than 250 employees, and hence an EMI scheme may not always be possible (see 8.57).

For *post-18 June 2004* EMI options, the legislation automatically deems an *ITEPA 2003, s 431* election as having been made when the shares are acquired (provided the options are not 'discounted' – ie they are being acquired for at least their market value at the date of grant) (see 8.53) .

Similarly, shares acquired on the exercise of an approved Company Share Option Plan (CSOP) do not generally create any employment tax charge. In such cases, the employee/director is required to pay the market value of the shares (based on when the option is granted) when they exercise their CSOP option (see 8.74–8.77B).

CGT treatment for transferor/transferee employee

Direct acquisition of shares

13.39 Where shares have been gifted (or sold at an undervalue) by an existing shareholder to a director/employee, it is likely that they will be required to enter into a hold-over election under *TCGA 1992, s 165*.

This means that the recipient's deemed CGT market value base cost will be reduced by the transferor shareholder's 'held-over' gain.

The director/employee recipient would be liable to an earnings based charge under *ITEPA 2003, s 62* on their acquisition of the shares (see 13.29 and 13.33). The CGT provisions that prevent a 'double charge' to tax do *not* apply to cases where the employee/director suffers a general earnings charge (see *TCGA 1992, s 120*). Consequently, the employee does not receive any addition to their CGT base cost to reflect their earlier employment income tax charge under *ITEPA 2003, s 62*. Consequently, the employee's (post-hold-over) reduced CGT base cost means that a double tax charge would appear to arise in such cases.

Where the shares are 'restricted', *TCGA 1992, s 149AA* provides that the base cost is the amount paid (if any) paid by the employee/director plus the amount taxed on them under the general earnings rules. However, HMRC is now of the view that the deemed 'market value' rule in *TCGA 1992, s 17* overrides this analysis (following the logic expressed at CG56321C). Once again, the market value base cost would be reduced by the held-over gain (with the employee having suffered an earnings charge).

The 'above' double charge problems do not arise where the shares are acquired on the exercise of an option (see 13.40), since the 'actual consideration' rule in *TCGA 1992, s 144ZA* overrides the market value rule. Any employment tax charge arising on the exercise of an option falls within *ITEPA 2007 s 476* (which is in, Part 7). Thus, this charge can be added to the employee's CGT base cost (see 13.40)

Where an employee/director acquires new shares on subscription, HMRC will normally treat them as having been acquired at market value. Although the shares have been acquired without a corresponding disposal, the view appears to be that full market value has been given by reference to the employee's/ director's duties (so that the potential restriction in *TCGA 1992, s 17(2)* to the 'actual consideration' given does not apply). This understanding is confirmed in the Capital Gains Manual, para CGT56356. The 'market value' CGT base cost will therefore generally equate to the amount taxed as employment income plus the subscription price.

A 'market value' base cost may also be obtained if the share issue is subject to a 'value shifting' charge under *TCGA 1992, s 29*, subject to the impact of any *TCGA 1992, s 165* hold-over election – see 13.23–13.27.

The resultant CGT base cost is broadly the same where a director/employee acquires restricted securities (see 13.31) or convertible securities. *TCGA 1992, s 149AA* prescribes that the transferee's base cost of the restricted securities is made up of the actual consideration given by the employee and the amount which is treated as employment income.

Where a qualifying *employee benefit trust* (within *IHTA 1984, s 86* – see 5.16) transfers shares to directors or employees, *TCGA 1992, s 239ZA* will often apply to limit the trust's taxable proceeds to the actual amount received by the trust provided the recipient employees are subject to a full employment income tax charge on the shares. The deemed 'market value' rule is therefore dis-applied. However, this beneficial treatment does *not* apply where the recipient employees already hold at least 5% of the company's shares.

Shares acquired on exercise of options

13.40   Where shares are acquired under a share option *TCGA 1992, s 144ZA* prescribes that the recipient director/employee is treated as acquiring their option shares for an amount equal to:

(*a*)   the actual amount received on the exercise of the share option; and

(*b*)   any amount paid for the option itself.

TCGA 1992, s 149A prevents the 'market value' rule from applying to the actual grant of the option.

On the exercise of an unapproved share option, the 'recipient' director/employee is subject to an income tax charge under *ITEPA 2003, ss 476 and 477(3)(a)*. Similar tax charges arise on discounted EMI or non-qualifying CSOP options. In those special cases where the relevant shares constitute 'readily convertible assets' (see 8.39 and 13.36), PAYE and NIC liabilities will apply to the gain arising on the exercise of the option.

The director/employee's CGT base cost would be increased by any amount which has been taxed as employment income under *TCGA 1992, ss 119A* and *149AA*.

Where relevant, the transferee would be treated as disposing of the shares for the combined amounts in (a) and (b) above.

PURCHASE OF OWN SHARES (POS)

Advantages of a share buy-back

13.41   The use of the company as a willing buyer for the purchase of its own shares (POS) can provide a useful and tax-efficient exit route for its shareholders. Such arrangements have played an invaluable role in owner-managed business succession planning. A typical scenario would be where the controlling shareholder wishes to retire from the business and hand over the reins of control to the incumbent management team. The team may represent the next generation of the proprietor's family and/or an established group of respected key managers. A direct purchase of the proprietor's shares by the family members/management team is unlikely to be practical since they are unlikely to have sufficient funds. Furthermore, any borrowing they made to finance the share purchase would have to be repaid from additional taxed income extracted from the company (for example, by way of bonuses or dividends), which is likely to be an expensive option.

A more efficient solution would be for the company to buy-back the proprietor's shares. The purchase consideration is satisfied by the company – any additional borrowing required would be within the company and repaid out of its trading cash flows. Since the proprietor's shares can be cancelled on the buy-back the remaining shareholders (ie the management team) will then have control of the company.

Broadly speaking, in the circumstances detailed above, under a POS, cash leaves the company to pay for the purchased shares with the remaining shareholders owning a larger slice of the smaller 'cake'. The immediate cancellation of the shares bought back, increases the relative percentage ownership for the remaining shareholders since they would then have a 'larger' share of the company 'cake'.

In the vast majority of cases, the purchase price agreed for the POS will have been freely negotiated. If HMRC consider that the POS is not an arm's length bargain (see 14.33), it can seek to substitute market value for the actual consideration (*TCGA 1992, s 17*). Furthermore, if HMRC can demonstrate that the seller shareholder has sold their shares for more than their market value, the excess can be treated as employment income, which would be taxed under PAYE and subject to NIC charges (see 8.37).

A buy-back can also be used on the death of a shareholder where his personal representatives or beneficiaries do not wish to keep the shares. A typical arrangement in most owner-managed companies is for all shareholdings to be subject to put and call options, which become exercisable on the shareholder's death. Appropriate life or 'key-man' insurance is put in place by the company to provide the necessary funds for it to purchase the shares. This has a number of benefits. The existing shareholders avoid losing control to a 'disinterested' widow/widower and it provides a mechanism for the estate to receive cash for the deceased's shareholding – particularly helpful where the estate is illiquid and the main asset is the shares.

The Companies Act 2006 (Amendment of Part 18) Regulations 2013, SI 2013/999, which came into force on 30 April 2013, has made some beneficial changes to POS rules for private companies (see, for example, 13.42).

Furthermore, a private company no longer has to cancel the shares purchased from the shareholder. It may now, if it wishes, decide to hold them as 'treasury shares', which may be used for future employee share awards or share options. Companies wishing to use the 'repurchased' shares as treasury shares must ensure that they are permitted to do so by their articles.

Key legal requirements

13.42 It is vital that the POS arrangements follow the legal requirements laid down in *Companies Act 2006, Pt 18*.

Under the *Companies Act 2006*, companies have to pay for the repurchased shares immediately upon their acquisition (see 13.43).

However, from 30 April 2013, this requirement is relaxed where the company is purchasing the shares for *the purposes of an employee share scheme.* (For these purposes, an employee share scheme is widely defined (see *CA 2006, s 1166* and would include all the employee share schemes dealt with in Chapter 8.)

Thus, where the shares are effectively being acquired for the purposes of an employee share scheme, companies may now pay for the 'repurchased' shares on a deferred consideration basis, thus easing their cash flow burden.

In all other cases, immediate payment for the shares is still required.

As a general rule, a POS transaction must be made from distributable reserves (*CA 2006, s 691(1)*), out of the proceeds of a fresh issue (but see 13.43, Table 1, note 8), or provided certain conditions are met, out of capital.

However, since 30 April 2013, companies have been able to make 'low value' purchases regardless of whether they have sufficient distributable reserves (effectively out of 'capital'). This facility is limited to £15,000 (or if less, 5% of the value of its share capital) in any financial year. Companies must amend their articles to enable them to take advantage of this exception.

Further relaxations have also been made to the rules concerning shareholders' resolutions and procedures for purchasing shares out of 'capital' (see 13.43 and Table 1 below).

Failure to comply with all the relevant rules would mean that the purported acquisition of the shares by the company is void and therefore legally unenforceable [*CA 2006, s 658(2)*]. Where a POS share cancellation was intended, this would mean that the relevant shares would not be cancelled and would, therefore, still be retained by the seller (*HMRC Company Taxation Manual*, para CTM17505). In such cases, the company's payment to the purported 'seller' shareholder is likely to be treated as a loan, which might produce a liability under *CTA 2010, s 455* (see 2.56).

HMRC have stated that they will only consider a clearance application for a transaction that appears to be a valid POS (*Tax Bulletin*, Issue 21). Consequently, such arrangements must be carefully planned in advance.

In particular, the company will need to have built up a sufficient level of retained profits (subject to the 'limited' exception noted above) to satisfy the intended buy-back consideration. Under company law, the purchase price must be met out of distributable profits. Although it is also possible to use the proceeds of a fresh issue of shares, the 'premium' or profit element paid on the buy-back (which will often be a substantial part of the proceeds) must be from the distributable reserves [*CA 2006, s 692(2)*].

It may be possible for the seller-shareholders to retain a 'special share' to enable them to share in any 'uplift' in value if the company is subsequently sold in the medium term. Such 'variable' rights cannot be structured as deferred consideration for the shares, since the relevant consideration on repurchased shares has to be paid in full on completion. Thus, the special shares retained by the seller would contain rights similar to an 'anti-embarrassment' clause on a normal company sale, although care would need to be taken to ensure the widely drawn '30% post-buy-back' connection test is not broken (see 'Table 2' conditions for shareholder – (4)).

Stamp duty

13.42A The *Finance Act 1986, s 66* provides that ½% stamp duty is payable on the 'purchase' consideration paid by the company (charged on the return (form SH03) which must be delivered to the Registrar of Companies within 28 days of the purchase).

Summary of legal conditions and accounting treatment

13.43 The main legal requirements for a POS by a private company are summarised in Table 1 below. A Board meeting would be held to report on the proposed POS and to pass the necessary *ordinary* resolution (a special resolution for all POSs was required before 30 April 2013).

The contract for the purchase must be approved in advance, although the company may enter into the contract provided the shareholders authorise the contract terms by an ordinary resolution [*CA 2006, ss 693, 693A* and (for employee share schemes) *694(2)*].

Although a POS can be approved by an ordinary resolution, companies should first check their articles to ensure that they do not specifically require a special resolution. If the contract is not approved, the company cannot purchase the relevant shares and the contract lapses.

For private companies, each purchase of its own shares has to be authorised by a shareholder resolution, which might prove cumbersome. The *2013 regulations* (see 13.41) therefore allow shareholders to give the board a general authority to make a POS for the purposes of an *employee share scheme*, subject to limits on the number of shares purchased and the price paid.

The company must make a return to the Registrar of Companies within 28 days of the POS [*CA 2006, s 707*], stating the following details for each POS:

- the number, type, nominal value of shares purchased and cancelled, and date of the transaction

- the number, type, nominal value of shares purchased and held in treasury (see 13.42), and date of the transaction.

The POS contract(s) must be retained for ten years.

Details of the POS must be disclosed in the director's report in the company's accounts.

Note that failure to satisfy the relevant legal conditions will invariably make the transaction void and legally unenforceable, as a number of cases demonstrate:

- In *Stuart & Kinlan v Crimmin* [2006] EWHC 779 (Ch) a liquidator pursued a retiring director, Mr Crimmin. The liquidator claimed that Mr Crimmin had not acted in the company's best interests when negotiating for it to repurchase his shares and that the proper legal procedures for the POS had not been followed. One of the main issues was that Mr Crimmin had agreed to sell all his shares for a total consideration of £130,000 payable in two instalments, which therefore did not comply with the requirement that full payment must be made when the company purchased the shares.

  This proved to be a lucky escape for Mr Crimmin! Whilst the court agreed with the liquidator that the POS was void – which meant that the company should reclaim the sale proceeds – the court used its powers to grant relief. It found that Mr Crimmin had acted honestly and reasonably, and should therefore be excused from repaying the money received from POS.

- In *Baker v HMRC* [2013] UKFTT 394 (TC), there was a falling out between two director shareholders. This resulted in the company buying back Mr Baker's shares for a total amount (in cash and in kind) of £120,000. Mr Baker also resigned as a director and employment was terminated. The POS took place in January 2006, with various cash payments and asset transfers being made in 2005/06.

When the POS was made, the latest company for the year ended 31 October 2004 showed distributable reserves of around £47,000. HMRC initiated an enquiry into Mr Baker's 2005/06 return and decided to treat the entire £120,000 as an income distribution.

Mr Baker's accountants appealed on the basis that the POS breached company law and was therefore void. The case proceeded to the First-tier Tribunal.

The FTT concluded that the POS breached company law because it involved:

- payments of deferred consideration (see 13.42); and

- the company had insufficient distributable profits for the transaction.

The Tribunal concluded that the POS and the company's obligation to pay for Mr Baker's shares, were void due to the breaches in company law. Thus, Mr Baker was under an obligation to return the cash and assets he received for his shares to the company. Consequently, there was no taxable 'income distribution' for tax purposes.

13.43A The accounting entries for a POS out of the company's distributable reserves are as follows:

	Dr	Cr	Notes
Profit and loss account	X		With the total POS consideration
Cash		X	With the total POS consideration
Share capital	X		Nominal value of the shares being repurchased
Capital redemption reserve		X	Nominal value of the shares being repurchased

Table 1

Company law requirements for POS by a private company

1   The relevant shares must be fully paid up.

2   The consideration for the shares must be paid for'on purchase [*CA 2006, s 691(2)*] (unless the shares are being purchased for the purposes of an employee share scheme – see 13.42 (*CA 2006, s 691(3)*).

   Unless the employee share scheme exemption applies (see 13.42) rules, payment must be made on completion of the transaction and it is not possible for payment(s) to be made on a deferred basis (but see 13.58 and 13.59 below for possible alternative structures).

3   *CA 2006* does not require a company to have express power in its Articles of Association to make a POS although its articles may restrict or prohibit a POS [*CA 2006, s 690*].

4   The contract for the ('off-market') share repurchase must be available at the board meeting and approved by an *ordinary resolution* of the company's shareholders, unless a general authority has been given (see 13.43 above). (From a practical viewpoint, it is sensible for the shareholders whose shares are being repurchased not to vote as this avoids any possibility of the approval being rendered invalid under *CA 2006, s 695(2)*.)

   The company must give notice of the cancellation of shares to the Registrar of Companies within 28 days of receipt of the shares, specifying which ones are to be cancelled.

5   It would appear that the 'share repurchase' resolution could be passed by a written resolution (but not signed by the shareholder whose shares are being repurchased). In such cases, the contract must be produced to each shareholder at or before the time the resolution is produced for their signature.

6   There is no limit to the number of shares which may be purchased back, although at least one irredeemable share must be held after the purchase.

7   The purchased shares are immediately cancelled on redemption/ repurchase [*CA 2006, s 706(b)*] or may be held as treasury shares for future sale or transfer to employees under employee share scheme arrangements.

8   The shares to be purchased can be bought by the company:

    (*a*)   out of its distributable profits; or

    (*b*)   out of the proceeds of a fresh issue of shares; or

    (*c*)   out of capital, provided all distributable profits are used first.

However, any payment made out of the proceeds of a fresh issue cannot 'frank' any premium (effectively the seller's 'profit' element) made on the 'repurchased' shares.

Since 30 April 2013, provided the company has authority in its articles, the above rules can be ignored for certain 'low-value' POS transactions. This 'exemption' applies where the purchase consideration is £15,000 (or if less, 5% of the value of its share capital). These limits apply for each financial year (see 13.42).

9   A capital redemption reserve (which is non-distributable) must be set up to the extent that shares are purchased from distributable reserves – the amount transferred being equal to the nominal value of the shares purchased. This facilitates the maintenance of the company's capital base.

10   Where the shares are purchased out of *capital* this requires, inter alia, a *special resolution*, a statutory declaration of solvency by the directors (accompanied by a 'concurring' auditor's report), and publicity in the *London Gazette* and a national newspaper.

However, where shares are being repurchased for the purposes of an employees' share scheme, a payment out of capital only requires approval by a special resolution and a solvency statement by the directors.

11   The share repurchase contract must be retained at the registered office for ten years.

DISTRIBUTION TREATMENT

Calculation of distribution

13.44   Under basic principles, a POS is treated as an income distribution under *CTA 2010, s 1000*. The income distribution is the amount by which the sale consideration exceeds the original subscription price of the repurchased shares (including any premium paid) (see *CTA 2010, ss 1024–1026* and Company Taxation Manual CT 17510). Thus, if the seller originally acquired the shares 'second-hand', it is necessary to look back to the price paid by the original subscriber.

Since 6 April 2016, no tax credit attaches to distributions and the taxable amount is simply the amount of the POS distribution (without any 'grossing up'). See 2015/16 and earlier editions of this book for pre-6 April 2016 treatment of POS distributions.

For 2017/18, tax is chargeable at the seller's 'dividend' tax rate(s), depending on the level of their total income (with the distribution treated as the top slice of their income), as follows:

Total taxable income (including buy-back distribution)	Tax rate applied to distribution
Below basic rate income threshold – £33,500	7.5%
Between basic rate threshold and £150,000	32.5%
Above £150,000	38.1%

Sellers generally wish to avoid paying the 'penal' dividends tax rates and will seek to consider ways of structuring their POS within the CGT regime (see 13.46).

However, there will be cases where the consideration for the POS is sufficiently low with the selling shareholder only being a 'basic-rate' taxpayer. Here it will generally be beneficial for the seller to receive their proceeds as an 'income' distribution since it will only be taxed at 7.5%.

If the shares being purchased were originally acquired in exchange for shares on a prior takeover, the original subscription price (the new consideration given) would be the full market value of the shares 'sold' on the prior share exchange. (It is not the nominal value of the shares issued in exchange.) However, since the shares will have a lower base value (for CGT purposes under the 'new for old' reorganisation rules), this means that part of the POS proceeds will be charged to CGT.

Example 6

Buy-back taxed as distribution

In July 2017, Mr Slaven sold his 200 £1 ordinary shares in Bilić Ltd back to the company for £200,000. He originally subscribed for the 200 £1 shares at par on the incorporation of the company in December 2014. Since Mr Slaven enjoys a considerable salary and bonus package, his marginal 'dividend' tax rate is 38.1%

As Mr Slaven has held his shares for less than five years, the transaction cannot benefit from the CGT treatment (see 13.46 below and Table 2 – 'seller shareholder' condition 1). The share 'buy-back' transaction would therefore be taxed as a distribution, at Mr Slaven's marginal dividend tax rate, as follows:

	£
Amount received	200,000
Less: Subscription price	(200)
Distribution	199,800
Tax liability (£199,800 less dividend nil rate band £5,000) × 38.1%	74,219

CGT treatment of 'income' distribution buy-back

13.45   Although the POS 'distribution' is subject to income tax, the seller also makes a disposal for CGT purposes. However, *TCGA 1992, s 37(1)* excludes from the taxable consideration any amount which has been charged to income tax (thus avoiding any 'double tax' problem).

The POS distribution is therefore eliminated from the CGT consideration which would then equate to the original amount paid for the shares. In most cases, this will give a neutral CGT result, but if the seller-shareholder has a higher base cost, for example, 31 March 1982 rebasing value or actual 'second-hand' purchase consideration, they would establish an allowable capital loss. This loss would be freely available as it is not restricted by the 'connected party' loss rules in *TCGA 1992, s 18*. This is because the company does not acquire the shares on a buy-back transaction, which is a prerequisite for *TCGA 1992, s 18* to apply.

FA 2003, s 195(2) confirms that shares bought back by the company are *not* treated as 'acquired' for tax purposes. This rule also operates for shares that are acquired as treasury shares (see 13.43, Table 1(5)). This means that there is deemed to be *no* acquisition for tax purposes where a company takes the shares into 'treasury'.

If the seller was the original subscriber, it might be possible to make a claim for share loss relief, which would provide an income tax offset for the capital loss under *ITA 2007, s 131* (see 16.49–16.52). One potential stumbling block is the requirement for an arm's length disposal in *ITA 2007, s 131(3)(a)*, which may be more difficult to sustain on a 'buy-back' sale by a controlling shareholder. However, if successful, a *s 131* claim could be used to reduce the income tax charge on the distribution itself!

CAPITAL GAINS TREATMENT

Requirements for CGT treatment

13.46 CTA *2010, ss 1033 et seq* effectively imposes mandatory CGT treatment for the POS if the relevant conditions are satisfied. Strictly, the legislation prevents the 'income' element from being treated as a distribution for tax purposes. This means that the shareholder's entire return is a capital gains receipt.

For CGT treatment to apply, the purchasing company must be a trading company, which in this context means wholly or mainly trading (*CTA 2010, s 1048(1)*). This is less stringent than the 'trading' test used for Entrepreneurs' Relief (ER). It may therefore be possible for the company to pass the 'trading' hurdle for *CTA 2010 s 1033* with the shareholder's gain not being eligible for ER (where, for example, the company's non-trading activities exceed HMRC's 20% de minimis rule). The 'trading company' requirement means that any POS by an investment company will always be taxed as an income distribution.

The POS must be for the benefit of the company's or group's trade; this often means that the shareholder must sell his shares, although he may retain a small sentimental stake (of no more than 5%) [*CTA 2010, s 1033(2)* and SP 2/82].

Many share buy-backs are sensibly used to arrange for the current owner-manager to retire and make way for new management, which is normally acceptable as satisfying the 'trade benefit' test (see SP 2/82, para 2). However, where the funding of the share repurchase is prejudicial to the trade, this test is unlikely to be satisfied, as demonstrated by the Special Commissioner's decision in *Allum & Allum v Marsh* [2005] (SSCD) 191. In this case, all the company's shares were owned by a married couple except one, which was owned by their son. They wished to retire from the business and leave their son in control. This was achieved by the company purchasing their entire shareholding. However, the share re-purchase was funded by the sale of the company's trading premises. The sale proceeds also funded the repayment of the directors' loan and voluntary 'ex-gratia' payments of £30,000 each(!). The company's operations were reduced considerably following the sale of the premises and the loss of the directors' financial support and services, all of which were linked to the share buy-back. Consequently, it was held that the shares had not been purchased wholly or mainly for the benefit of the trade, but to facilitate the directors' retirement.

13.46A It is always advisable to take advantage of the clearance procedure in *CTA 2010, s 1044*. If no prior clearance is obtained and insufficient facts are given on the seller's tax return, HMRC can always make a 'discovery assessment' (see 4.55) to treat a purported capital gain as an income distribution instead (see *Brown and Brown v HMRC* [2012] UKFTT 425 (TC)).

The main conditions for CGT treatment are summarised in Table 2 below:

Table 2

Main conditions for *CTA 2010 s 1033* capital treatment

Conditions for company	*Statutory references (all to CTA 2010)*
1 The company must be an unquoted trading company or an unquoted holding company of a trading group (shares quoted on the AIM are treated as unquoted for this purpose).	*s 1033(1)*
2 The purchase must be made wholly or mainly for the purpose of benefiting the company's trade (or the trade of any of its 75% subsidiaries).	
'For the purpose of benefiting a trade' is sensibly interpreted in IR SP 2/82. HMRC would normally wish to see the seller giving up his entire interest in the company, although the retention of a minimal 'sentimental' stake may be allowed. Furthermore, to ensure the 'trade benefit' test is satisfied, any existing directorship with the company must be severed and a director should not normally continue to act for the company in a consultancy capacity (see SP 2/82).	*s 1033(2)*
3 The POS must not form part of a scheme or arrangement to enable the owner to participate in the profits of the company without receiving a dividend or to avoid tax.	*s 1033(2)(b)*
4 Conditions 2 and 3 above do not apply to certain cases involving personal representatives of a deceased shareholder. This is where 'all or almost all' (see IR SP 2/82, para 6) the payment (excluding the CGT paid thereon) is applied by them in discharging the IHT liability of the deceased shareholder within two years of death. However, they must also show that the IHT liability could not otherwise have been satisfied without causing undue hardship.	
Also, in such cases, the conditions required to be satisfied by the seller shareholder (see below) are ignored.	*s 1033(3)*

Conditions for shareholder	*Statutory references (all to CTA 2010)*
1 The seller must be resident in the UK in the tax year of purchase.	*s 1034*
2 The shares must have been owned by the seller for at least five years before the date of sale. (Periods of prior ownership by a spouse/civil partner can also be included.)	
If the seller inherited the shares, the period of ownership of the deceased shareholder/personal representatives can also be counted and the ownership requirement is reduced to three years.	*ss 1035 and 1036*
3 The seller must dispose of all their shares. If they do not, their proportionate shareholding (including associates – see below) must be substantially reduced, although HMRC would not normally accept that this benefits the trade (see condition 2 for company above).	*s 1037*
4 The seller must *not* be 'connected' with the company immediately after the purchase (and there must be no scheme or arrangements in place that would enable them or their associates to have disqualifying interests in the company).	*s 1042*
For these purposes, the seller would be connected with the company if they (together with their associates (see below)) possess or are entitled to acquire more than 30% of:	
(*a*) the issued ordinary share capital; (or) (*b*) the loan capital and issued share capital; (or) (*c*) the voting power of the company.	*s 1062(2)*
For this purpose, loan capital includes any money borrowed by the company and any debt for capital assets acquired by the company [*CTA 2010, s 1063*].	
The interests of associates must therefore be added to the seller's for the purposes of the 'connection test'. In the context of a POS, the 'associate' test is narrower. It will include an individual's spouse (or civil partner), any trust created by them (or in which they may benefit); and their minor children. However, the definition excludes, for example, adult children, brothers and parents. In this context, shares held by other family members must be beneficially held by them (see *Preston Meats Ltd v Hammond* [2005] (SSCD) 90).	*ss 1063(4),1059 and 1060*

Optimising the seller's tax position

13.47 In many cases, the seller should effectively be able to choose the tax treatment of the sale of the shares back to the company. Assuming the relevant *CTA 2010, s 1033* conditions for CGT treatment can be satisfied (see above), the seller can either 'opt' for income distribution (see 13.54) or capital gains treatment. Unfortunately, this cannot be done by simple election.

In the majority of cases, ER should be available on the seller's capital gain, which should enable them to benefit from a CGT rate of 10% on up to the current ER lifetime threshold of £10 million (or, if less, their unrelieved ER gains allowance). In due course, some shareholders may also be able to obtain the investors relief (IR) CGT rate of 10%.

In these cases, the seller will invariably prefer CGT treatment since their tax charge will be just 10% (and well below the effective dividend tax rates that would operate on most 'income' buy-back distributions).

If the seller does *not* qualify for ER/IR, CGT treatment is still likely to be beneficial, given the rate is 20%, if they would otherwise suffer the 'higher' dividend tax rates of 32.5%/38.1%.

The detailed qualifying conditions for ER and the relevant computational rules are reviewed in 15.33–15.39. However, even though ER only requires the seller to satisfy the 'personal company' and 'employee/director' requirements throughout the one year before the buy-back disposal, the seller must have held the shares for a minimum of *five years* (three years, if inherited) to secure the necessary capital gains treatment on a share buy-back (see Table 2 at 13.46 – conditions for shareholder (2)).

13.48 If the seller has built up their shareholding over a period of years, the 'five year' holding requirement is tested by taking the earlier share acquisitions before the later ones (ie on an FIFO basis), which is preferential to the seller. If the 'five year' test is satisfied (and CGT treatment is available), the normal CGT rules will apply for the purpose of computing allowable base costs etc (see 14.64).

13.49 A 'capital gains' buy-back has become the standard 'route' given the lower tax charge that will often be available to the 'outgoing' shareholder. An example of the comparatively low tax cost which may be available on a share repurchase from a retiring shareholder in 2017/18 is shown in Example 7 below:

Example 7

CGT structured POS exit in 2017/18

Michael wishes to retire as a full-time working director of Owen Ltd in January 2018 and has ensured that the company has built up sufficient reserves and funds to enable his 75% shareholding to be sold back to the company for £600,000. (Michael started the company in 1975 and his shareholding was worth £75,000 in March 1982.)

After the buy-in, the company will be controlled by his two adult sons, who have effectively managed the business in recent years and currently hold the remaining 25% of its shares.

Michael qualifies for ER and wishes to claim it on his capital gain on the share buy-back in 2017/18, which is projected as follows:

	£
Sale proceeds	600,000
Less: March 1982 value of shareholding	(75,000)
Chargeable gain	525,000
Less: Annual exemption	(11,300)
Taxable gain	513,700
ER CGT @ 10%	£51,370

POS from trustee sellers

Where POS proceeds are 'capital' in the hands of the trust

13.50 Under established trust law principles, the sale proceeds received on a POS transaction by trustees will generally be on 'capital' account. However, where the normal 'distribution' treatment applies, the 'distribution' element would fall to be taxed as income in the trustee's hands (despite its capital nature).

Since the amount is capital under trust law, the proceeds of the POS are not normally payable to income beneficiaries (under an interest in possession trust). However, *ITTOIA 2005, s 383* makes it clear that 'dividends and other distributions are to be treated as income', even though they might be regarded as capital in law.

Under the normal rules, the trustees would be liable to 'basic-rate' dividend tax. However, *ITA 2007, s 481(3)* provides that the amount of the POS 'distribution' is subject to the 'dividend trust rate' (38.1% from 6 April 2016) of the distribution) in the trustees' hands. (The dividend 'nil rate' band is not available to trustees.)

This special charging provision is needed since otherwise the POS distribution would not be caught by the normal 'additional rate' charging provisions in *ITA 2007, s 479* which only apply to (broadly) accumulated income or income payable at the discretion of the trustees. The trustees also make a disposal for CGT purposes, but the CGT consequences will normally be 'neutral' (see 13.45).

On the other hand, if the *CTA 2010, s 1033* 'no-distribution' treatment applies, *the POS proceeds received by the trustees are taxed as a capital gain in the normal way* – see 13.46 and Table 2 above. HMRC have also confirmed (see HMRC Trusts Settlements and Estates Manual 3205) that where the conditions in *CTA 2010, s 1033* apply, then *ITA 2007, s 482* (the special rates for trustees) will not apply.

Settlor interested trusts

13.51　A potential difficulty arises with shares sold by the trustees of a settlor-interested trust (see 17.44). Where the POS is treated as an income distribution, this would be taxed in the settlor's hands (the dividend 'nil rate' band may be available). However, there would be no *TCGA 1992, s 37* reduction against the capital gain since this is only given to 'the person making the disposal' (ie the trustees).

Consequently, the trustees would also suffer a capital gain (based on the same sale proceeds). (The 'settlor-interested' UK trust gain rules were abolished on 6 April 2008 so that the gain would now be taxed on the trustees.) HMRC have confirmed (albeit under the pre-6 April 2008 regime) that they would apply *TMA 1970, s 32* to eliminate the capital gain in such cases. (*TMA 1970, s 32* broadly enables HMRC to reduce all or part of a tax charge if it is satisfied the taxpayer has suffered tax more than once for the same transaction.)

POS from corporate sellers

13.52　Because of the many limitations in the capital gains POS rules in *CTA 2010, ss 1033–1048*, a POS from a corporate seller will often be treated as a distribution. The net taxable distribution is (broadly) calculated as the excess of the POS consideration less the 'repayment of capital (broadly, the amount that was subscribed for the shares when they were first issued).

Where the POS is from a corporate seller, HMRC have long held the view (see SP4/89 and *Strand Options and Futures Ltd v Vojak* 76 TC 220 (CA) that the *TCGA 1992, s 37(1)* exclusion of 'income' distributions from CGT proceeds does not apply. Thus, there will still be a capital gains calculation based on the full sale proceeds. HMRC's view under SP4/89 was that distributions were *not* charged to corporation tax.

Since 1 July 2009, most distributions are still not 'charged' to corporation tax under the modified rules in *CTA 2009, Pt 9A* and *s 931RA* makes it clear they would still be included within the sale proceeds when calculating a POS gain. However, in most cases, the POS gain should be exempt under the SSE rules (see 3.42).

HMRC clearance for CGT-based treatment

13.53 Typically, the seller is likely to seek CGT treatment for their 'buy-back' transaction. They (or more likely their advisers) must ensure that all the detailed 'CGT' conditions will be satisfied and that they are considered when arranging the financing of the purchase consideration.

Advantage should always be taken of the advance clearance procedure in *CTA 2010, s 1044* under which the company can obtain assurance from HMRC that the contemplated transaction qualifies for desired tax treatment.

A 'capital gain' share repurchase by a close company could potentially be subject to an income tax charge under the 'Transaction in Securities' (TiS) provisions in *ITA 2007, s 698*.

The TiS rules were radically changed from 6 April 2010, becoming more targeted in scope. A key element was the introduction of a 'fundamental change of ownership' exemption, which broadly prevents a 'full exit' from the company from being caught. This exemption applies where, after the relevant share sale, at least 75% of the company's ordinary share capital (and other economic rights) is held by 'unconnected' persons (see 15.84 for further commentary). Consequently, there should *strictly* be no need to seek an *ITA 2007, s 701* clearance in such cases.

In any event, as with all buy-back transactions, it must be ensured that the seller (together with their associates) does not remain connected under the 30% rule (see Table 2 – conditions for shareholder (4)) as well as the relevant TiS exemption.

In difficult or uncertain cases, advance clearance should be obtained under *ITA 2007, s 701*) on the basis that the buy-back is being undertaken for 'non-tax avoidance' reasons to remove any doubt. A single clearance application should be made under both *CTA 2010, s 1044* and *ITA 2007, s 701* (see 15.84). The clearance should be sent to

H M Revenue & Customs CTIS Clearance
S0483
Newcastle
NE98 1ZZ

The company must also submit details of the buy-back transaction to HMRC within 60 days of the buy-back transaction where *s 1033* 'capital' treatment applies. In practice, only a short letter is usually necessary with a copy of the prior clearance application and HMRC's *s 1044* clearance letter.

Breaking the CGT conditions to obtain distribution treatment

13.54   There may be situations where the seller will obtain more advantageous tax treatment by having their buy-back treated as a distribution (although these situations are likely to be relatively rare). For example, they may have substantial 'income' losses which can be relieved against the income distribution or their buy-back proceeds may be small enough to be taxed entirely within their basic-rate band. It is important to remember that in such cases, CGT treatment will be automatically applied where the relevant conditions in *CTA 2010, s 1033* are satisfied – ie the CGT treatment is not optional.

If distribution treatment is required, then one of the CGT conditions must be deliberately broken to disapply the automatic CGT treatment. It may therefore be necessary to engineer a deliberate breach of (at least) one of these conditions. Some comments on the main methods used are given below:

(*a*)   *CTA 2010, s 1034(2)* states that if the shares are held through a nominee, the nominee must be a UK resident. Transferring the shares to a non-resident nominee could therefore break this rule. The transfer to a nominee would not involve any disposal for CGT purposes (see *TCGA 1992, s 60*). This route might be vulnerable to a challenge by HMRC under the dicta in *Furniss v Dawson* [1984] STC 153 (see 1.12);

(*b*)   it may be possible for the seller to immediately lend back some of his proceeds to the company to break the 'connected with company' test in *CTA 2010, s 1042(1)*. The aim here is to ensure that the buy-back proceeds are immediately lent back to the company as a loan exceeding 30% of the combined share and loan capital (HMRC treat an ordinary loan as loan capital). This is probably the most 'popular' route for ensuring distribution treatment. In many cases, an immediate loan back to the company of only a small amount would break this condition;

(*c*)   a transfer of shares to/from a spouse (or civil partner) prior to the share purchase or a termination payment to the seller will usually be regarded as an arrangement to avoid tax. It has been reported that clearance for capital treatment is invariably refused in such cases (see, for example, *Taxation*, 23 July 1998, page 456);

(*d*) it might be possible to put forward the argument to HMRC that the buy-in was not for the purposes of the trade, but to provide cash for the shareholder.

13.55 Sufficient certainty can be obtained in advance about the efficiency of the arrangements to provide a distribution treatment by invoking the 'negative clearance' procedure in *CTA 2010 s 1044(3)*. This requires HMRC to confirm within 30 days they are satisfied that the purchase falls outside *CTA 2010, s 1044(3)*.

Tax comparison between CGT and income distribution treatment

13.56 A comprehensive example illustrating the tax effects of a proposed buy-in under *CTA 2010, s 1033* and as a distribution is provided below.

Example 8

Capital gains v distribution treatment for POS

Mr Ferguson is the controlling shareholder of Govan Ltd, a company which he formed in 1986. Mr Ferguson is 72 years old and would like to retire from the company in December 2017. He owns 700 of the issued £1 ordinary shares. His two sons, Ryan and Paul own the remaining 300 shares between them.

Mr Ferguson needs to realise the value of his shares as he has no other major assets. He has agreed with his sons that control of the company should remain in the hands of his family and outside shareholders should not be brought in. However, his sons cannot personally afford to buy him out. Mr Ferguson has been advised that all these objectives can be satisfied by Govan Ltd purchasing his shares. His shares will then be immediately cancelled, leaving the company under the control of Ryan and Paul, without any direct personal cost to them. The company's auditors have determined that Mr Ferguson's shares should be sold at their fair value of £700,000. Mr Ferguson pays tax at the top income tax rates.

Mr Ferguson subscribed for his 700 £1 ordinary shares at par in July 1966 and they were worth around £60,000 in March 1982. Prima facie, Mr Ferguson and Govan Ltd would be able to satisfy the conditions for capital treatment in *CTA 2010, s 1033* (see Table 2 at 13.46).

Tax implications for Mr Ferguson

CGT treatment can be expected to apply to the proposed POS of Mr Ferguson's shares and he would make an ER claim to reduce his CGT liability. If the POS takes place in December 2017, Mr Ferguson's expected CGT liability would be calculated as follows:

December 2017 – CGT disposal	£
Sale proceeds	700,000
Less March 1982 value	(60,000)
Chargeable gain	640,000
Less Annual exemption	(11,300)
Taxable gain	628,700
ER CGT @ 10%	£62,870

However, if Mr Ferguson's POS was treated as a distribution, a tax liability of £266,433 would arise (ignoring the dividend 'nil rate' band), calculated as follows:

December 2017 – Distribution	£
Amount received	700,000
Less: Amount subscribed on issue	(700)
Distribution	699,300
Income tax thereon £699,300 × 38.1%	£266,433

The CGT route reduces Mr Ferguson's tax liability by a considerable £203,563 (£266,433 less £62,870) and undoubtedly this would be more favourable.

If the POS is treated as a distribution for tax purposes, this does not prevent a disposal arising for CGT purposes. However, *TCGA 1992, s 31* prevents double taxation by eliminating the element of the consideration taxed as distribution 'income' from the charge to CGT. This means that the seller is normally treated as selling his shares for an amount equal to the subscription price and therefore no gain arises. However, a loss may arise if March 1982 rebasing applies (see below) or where shares were purchased for an amount exceeding the subscription price.

As March 1982 rebasing applies, Mr Ferguson will also have a capital loss under the distribution route, as demonstrated below:

	£
Sale proceeds	700,000
Less Taxed as 'distribution' income	(699,300)
CGT proceeds	700
Less March 1982 value	(60,000)
Capital loss	(£59,300)

HMRC accept that where a company buys in its own shares there is no acquisition by the company as those shares are immediately cancelled under *CA 2006, s 706*. (Even though companies are now able to acquire and hold repurchased shares in 'treasury', the tax rules still treat such shares as having been cancelled.)

Consequently, the capital loss restriction on disposals to connected persons in *TCGA 1992, s 18(3)* does not apply so the capital loss is freely available. It may be possible to relieve the capital loss against the individual's income (including the distribution) under the share loss relief rules *ITA 2007, s 131*. The relief under *ITA 2007, s 131* can only be used where, inter alia, the loss was incurred 'by way of a bargain at arm's length'. Relief may therefore be claimed by a minority shareholder, but HMRC might be difficult where the POS is from a controlling shareholder.

Tax consequences for Govan Ltd

If the POS is treated as 'capital' under *CTA 2010, s 1033*, Govan Ltd would be treated as having made a capital payment on which no tax relief is available – it would not be a distribution.

If the CGT rules are not brought into play, Govan Ltd would be treated as having made a distribution.

Conclusion

It would clearly be beneficial for Mr Ferguson's POS to be treated as a capital gain as it gives him a much lower tax liability. Care must therefore be taken to ensure that the necessary pre-conditions for CGT treatment (see 13.46) are fully satisfied.

BUY-BACKS – FINANCING ISSUES AND PROBLEMS

Company law requirements

13.57   Company law requires that payment for the purchased shares be made on completion [*CA 2006, s 691*]. The company will therefore need sufficient cash or borrowing resources (bank or venture capital) to finance the purchase price. There must also be sufficient distributable reserves at the time of the buy-back (unless the repurchase is of low value (see 13.42).

The company may not be able to satisfy the repurchase price immediately out of its financial resources and/or retained reserves, particularly as commercial prudence would dictate having a buffer of cash and reserves to meet contingencies, etc.

Phased buy-back of shares

13.58   In such cases, the company could agree to buy back the relevant shares in successive stages, conditional upon future distributable profits and cash being available.

However, if the shareholder requires CGT treatment, a phased share buy-back programme must pass the 'substantial reduction' test (and also satisfy the 30% 'connection' test in relation to the shares held after each buy-back 'tranche'). This means that after each tranche of shares is bought back, the seller's fractional interest must not exceed 75% of his pre buy-in fractional interest (taking into account repurchased shares that are immediately cancelled). This test must be satisfied after each share repurchase (*CTA 2010, s 1037*).

The minimum number of shares that need to be repurchased to satisfy the test can be computed as follows:

$$\text{Minimum number} = \frac{nx}{4x - 3n}$$

Where: n = the number of shares comprised in the seller's holding (including associates)

x = company's issued share capital

HMRC will expect to see an agreed programme for buying out (all) the shares so that the shares buy-back satisfies the 'benefit of trade' test.

Care is required with the legal mechanics of the phased buy-back – an unconditional contract to buy back all the shares (albeit over a period of time), creates a CGT disposal at the date of the contract [*TCGA 1992, s 28*], which would mean paying all the CGT 'up-front'. In such cases, it may be better to use put and call options to defer the CGT liabilities for each subsequent buy-back. This puts beyond any doubt that the CGT only becomes payable as and when each option is exercised.

In the exceptional cases where the shareholder requires distribution treatment, a conditional contract to buy the shares in separate tranches works well (there is no need, for example, to satisfy the 'substantial reduction' test). As an alternative, it may be appropriate for the seller to lend part of the 'buy-back' consideration back to the company on interest bearing loan account to be drawn down as the company's cash flow permits. This may cause the seller to fail the 'connection' test (where the loan-back exceeds 30% of the company's combined share and loan capital) – see 13.46, Table 2 – conditions for shareholder (4). Thus, the scope for using a seller 'loan-back' is usually limited where CGT treatment is required.

Example 9

Phased share buy-back programme

Mr Sam holds 20,000 of the 100,000 £1 ordinary shares in Big Ltd. He has agreed that the company will buy back all 20,000 of his ordinary shares over two years, in two equal tranches, for a total consideration of £400,000, starting from 31 December 2016, conditional on there being sufficient reserves and cash.

Mr Sam has substantial capital losses and therefore requires CGT treatment. Therefore, amongst other things, the 'substantial reduction' test must be satisfied after the first 10,000 £1 ordinary shares are purchased.

The POS programme is as follows:

	Share Capital					
	Mr Sam	*Others*	*Total*	*CRR*	*P&L a/c*	*Cash*
	£'000	*£'000*	*£'000*	*£'000*	*£'000*	*£'000*
Balances at 1 Jan 2016	20	80	100	–	470	300
Cash flow						70
Post tax profit					80	
Dec 2016 buy-in	(10)	–	(10)	10	(200)	(200)
Balances at 31 Dec 2016	10	80	90	10	350	170
Cash flow						
Post-tax profit					120	100
Dec 2017 buy-in	(10)	–	(10)	10	(200)	(200)
Balances at 31 Dec 2017	–	80	80	20	270	70

Notes:

1   An amount equal to the nominal value of the shares bought back must be transferred (from the profit and loss account) to a non-distributable capital redemption reserve (CRR).

2   The shares are cancelled when repurchased.

3   The 'substantial reduction' test for the December 2016 buy-in is satisfied as Mr Sam's holding is reduced by at least 25%.

	Before	*After*
Mr Sam's holding	20/100 = 20%	10/90 = 11.1%
Proportionate shareholding is reduced by 44.5% ((20% – 11.1%)/20%)		

4   Mr Sam would be eligible to claim ER on his CGT disposals.

Implementing a multiple completion POS

Mechanics of a multiple completion POS

13.59   In practice, HMRC is also prepared to allow CGT treatment (assuming all the other conditions are met) on an unconditional multiple completion contract to buy back the shares. This was also confirmed in the *ICEAW Technical Release 745*. Broadly, this involves the seller contracting to sell their shares back to the company, but with the legal completion of the buy-back subsequently taking place in tranches, as illustrated below:

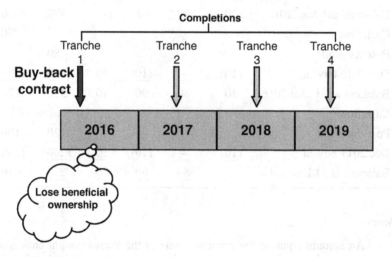

Multiple completion share buy-back

Under the multiple completion route, the selling-shareholder must give up their *beneficial* interest in the repurchased shares on entering into the contract and therefore the 'substantial reduction' test does not apply. Thus, the seller cannot subsequently take dividends or exercise voting rights over the shares.

It is generally accepted that, for CGT purposes, the disposal of the entire beneficial interest in the shareholding takes place at the date of the contract

[*TCGA 1992, s 28*]. (However, see below for a possible alternative analysis from HMRC!)

The seller therefore needs to ensure that they have sufficient cash resources to be able to pay the full CGT liability by the 31 January following the tax year in which the buy-back contract is made.

The writer has successfully obtained tax clearance from HMRC for a number of multiple completion share buy-backs. However, sometimes, the HMRC clearance team may not readily appreciate the legal effect of the POS and may ask certain questions before granting clearance.

HMRC appear to take the view that company law still entitles the selling shareholder to vote on their shares, despite the fact that they have contracted to sell them and have lost beneficial ownership. HMRC has indicated that the voting rights cannot be removed by contract. Assuming this view is correct, this could make the selling shareholder 'connected' with the company under *CTA 2010, s 1062(2)(c)* if the voting rights on the 'non-completed' POS shares exceed the 30% limit. However, if this is likely to be a potential issue, HMRC accept that the problem can be corrected by converting the relevant shares into a separate class of non-voting shares.

The multiple completion POS contract needs to be carefully worded and contain appropriate protection for the seller.

Entrepreneurs' relief issues

13.59A At the CIOT 2016 Autumn Conference, a leading tax barrister indicated that he was working on a case that involved HMRC seeking to deny ER on the subsequent 'multiple completion' payments POS.

It appears that HMRC were seeking to assert a different CGT analysis by applying a very literal reading of *TCGA 1992, s 28* which fixes the CGT disposal date. *TCGA 1992, s 28* applies where 'an asset is disposed of and acquired under a contract'. HMRC argued that since there is strictly no acquisition under a POS (see 13.45) the timing rule in *TCGA 1992, s 28* does not apply here. If this is correct, the timing of the disposals would fall within 'capital sums derived from assets' legislation in *TCGA 1992, s 22*. This would mean that, under a multiple completion POS, a CGT disposal would arise each time part of the POS proceeds is received.

Under this analysis, the seller should be able to obtain entrepreneurs'' relief (ER) when the initial tranche is paid (since this will normally be received at the date of the POS contract). However, for various technical reasons, the seller would not be able to make a competent ER claim on the subsequent tranches of consideration received (for example, he would have resigned as a director on 'day one').

Obtaining a competent POS clearance under *CTA 2010, s 1044* in such cases does not assist (see 13.53) – this simply confirms that the amount payable to the shareholder under the POS transaction is not treated as a distribution (and is therefore subject to CGT). The clearance does not provide any confirmation that ER is available.

However, it appears that HMRC have decided not to take the case mentioned above – there were certain procedural defects. Tax advisors are therefore taking a view that a future challenge in this area is unlikely which at least gives some comfort when structuring multiple completion POS transactions!

The barrister involved and many other leading tax advisers, firmly believe that HMRC's technical case was relatively weak (see, for example, Sarah Cohen's article in *Tax Journal*, 28 July 2017 (page 23)). Under a multiple completion POS, the seller makes a disposal of their entire beneficial interest in the shares at the date of the contract – this represents a disposal for CGT purposes. An appellate tribunal is likely to take a purposive view on the application of *TCGA 1992, s 28* and would not seek to deny ER on a literal construction of the legislation.

Multiple completion POS deals do not involve any form of tax avoidance. The arrangements simply enable the company to 'defer' part of the purchase consideration in a 'Companies Act' compliant manner. In fact, under the conventional analysis, all the CGT is paid up-front on the basis of the contract date under *TCGA 1992, s 28*.

REDUCTION OF SHARE CAPITAL UNDER THE *COMPANIES ACT 2006*

Background

13.60 Owner-managed companies can now reduce their share capital with relative ease. Following *Companies Act 2006, Pt 1, Ch 10* the legal process for a reduction of share capital is fairly simple and no longer requires the expense of seeking court approval.

These capital reduction rules can be used to assist owner-managed companies in various ways, including:

- To create distributable reserves (often by removing a deficit on reserves) to enable a legally valid dividend to be paid.

- To remove so-called 'dividend blocks' within a corporate group, where dividends cannot be paid up to the parent company because an intermediate group company has a substantial deficit on its reserves.

- To effect a corporate reconstruction or demerger of an investment business without having to liquidate a company under an *Insolvency Act 1986, s 110* scheme (see 13.98).

Many companies have relatively small amounts of issued share capital and may feel that these capital reduction techniques may not apply to them. However, the ability to reduce capital goes beyond the nominal value of issued share capital to include share premium account and capital redemption reserves. While it is not permissible to apply a property revaluation reserve as part of a capital reduction exercise, the same result can be achieved by first using the revaluation reserve to issue fully paid-up bonus shares equal to the capitalised amount. Having created additional share capital, this can then be reduced in accordance with the *CA 2006* provisions.

Substantial share capital invariably arises on company reorganisations. For example, a considerable amount of share capital may arise on a share-for-share exchange. In such cases, the tax and legal analysis is that the value of the shares issued equates to the market value of the acquired company; this is useful for implementing capital reduction demergers (see 13.98).

Legal procedure

13.60A A share capital reduction requires a special resolution made by the shareholders.

Briefly, within the 15-day period *before* the resolution, the directors must support the capital reduction by providing a solvency statement complying with *CA 2006, s 643*. The solvency statement, which must be approved by each director, confirms that

- there are no grounds for the company being unable to pay its debts; and

- that any winding-up of the company within 12 months would be a solvent liquidation (see 16.3).

There is *no* requirement for a supporting statement from the company's auditors.

After the special resolution is passed, the company must within 15 days send the Registrar of Companies:

- a copy of the special resolution;

- the solvency statement; and

- a statement of capital.

The statement of capital reflects the company's share capital after the reduction has taken place.

Share capital reduction to create reserves

13.60B In practice, the capital reduction process is mainly used to eliminate a profit and loss account deficit. The company will simply reduce its share capital (with each shareholder's holding being reduced on a pro rata basis) with a corresponding credit being made to the profit and loss account.

The amount transferred to the profit and loss account will then form part of the company's distributable profits, as confirmed by the *Companies (Reduction of Share Capital) Order 2008, SI 2008/1915*.

HMRC considers that dividends/distributions paid out of profits created in this way will be treated as a normal income distribution for tax purposes (see CTM 15440). This is the case despite the fact that it originally arose from a reduction on share capital.

HMRC could use the 'transaction in securities' (TiS) legislation to treat the distribution as subject to income tax at dividend tax rates. This is because the recipient shareholder(s) will generally retain their equity stake in the company and HMRC may consider that the repayment of share capital has been used to avoid income tax (see 15.82–15.91).

Before the *FA 2016*, it was generally felt that this risk was small, since there were a number of respectable counter-arguments to a TiS challenge. For example, since the amount essentially represents a return of the shareholder's original capital, the exemption in *ITA 2007, s 685(6)* should apply. Unfortunately, this sub-section was repealed by *FA 2016, s 33(4)* from 6 April 2016, which inevitably increases the risk of a TiS challenge (see 15.83)

Where share capital is reduced in this way, the shareholders' equity interest should not alter. Furthermore, since no payment is involved, the reduction of the share capital will fall within the capital gains share reorganisation rules in *TCGA 1992, s 126*. The elimination of part of the shares will not therefore involve any disposal (*TCGA 1992, s 127*). The shareholder's CGT base cost will simply be represented by fewer shares, ie the base cost of the retained shares will increase.

Example 10

Using a capital reduction to create reserves

An extract from Hurst & Peters Ltd's balance sheet at 31 October 2017 shows the following:

		£
Share capital	10,000 Ordinary shares of £1 each	10,000
Share premium		200,000
Profit and loss account		(80,000)
		130,000

Geoff and Martin own the company equally and are also its directors.

The company was affected by a substantial loss on a major contract last year, but the shareholders require dividends of £40,000 *each* this year and the company has no distributable reserves.

Acting on professional advice, the directors are comfortable that they can create the necessary reserves by reducing the company's share capital under the *Companies Act 2006* procedure.

They wish to create £100,000 of reserves, and thus a special resolution is passed to eliminate £180,000 of the share premium account

After the reduction, the shareholders' funds shown in the balance sheet were made up as follows:

		£
Share capital	10,000 Ordinary shares of 50p each	10,000
Share premium		20,000
Profit and loss account		100,000*
		130,000

* The company now has sufficient reserves to declare a dividend of £80,000 (£40,000 for both Geoff and Martin). Since the reserves were created by a transfer to the profit and loss account, the dividends would be subject to income tax in the normal way.

Direct repayment of share capital to shareholders

13.60C On the other hand, the company may simply repay its share capital directly to the shareholders, which avoids any 'intermediate' credit to the profit and loss account. The accounts entries will simply be: debit share capital, credit cash (or if assets are being distributed in specie, credit the relevant asset accounts).

Depending on the precise facts, where the amount repaid represents a return of the original share capital, this should not give rise to a taxable distribution (*CTA 2010, s 1000(1B)(a)*). The arguments surrounding the potential application of the TiS rules are discussed in 15.60B above.

Since there is no income distribution, the amount repaid may well be a capital distribution under *TCGA 1992, s 122*. However, if the shareholder subscribed for their shares, the receipt should be covered by their base cost, so no gain arises. This analysis may be different if the shareholder *acquired* the shares from a third party.

The 'return of capital' provisions are also used to facilitate a demerger without triggering a 'distribution' income tax charge (see 13.98).

INSERTING A NEW HOLDING COMPANY

13.60D   Company reconstruction exercises are often best effected through an intermediate step of inserting a new holding company above the existing company.

A new company is incorporated, which then acquires the original company by means of a 'tax-free' share for share exchange under *TCGA 1992, s 135* (see 15.48). This would allow the shareholders to swap their shares in the old company for shares in the new holding company without triggering a CGT disposal.

The old company will become a 100% subsidiary of the new holding company, with the shareholders 'at the top' holding shares in the new company in the same numbers and proportions as they had held in the old company.

HMRC should accept that the share exchange is being undertaken for commercial purposes, although it is recommended that confirmation from HMRC is obtained using the advance clearance procedure in *TCGA 1992, s 138*. Generally one combined clearance application would be drafted to cover all of the steps in the proposed restructuring (see 13.82).

13.60E   To ensure the new holding company does not incur a stamp duty liability on its acquisition of the old company, the share exchange must satisfy the detailed conditions in *FA 1986, s 77*. As the share swap should involve a 'mirror-image' exchange of shares, *FA 1986, s 77* should normally apply to the acquisition of the original company by the new holding company.

However, *FA 2016* introduced a new anti-avoidance rule in *FA 1986, s 77A*, which applies for share exchanges taking place after 28 June 2016. *FA 1986, s 77A* prevents the *FA 1986, s 77* stamp duty exemption applying where, at the time of the share exchange, there are 'disqualifying arrangements' in place for a change of control of the acquiring company.

The 'control' definition in *CTA 2010, s 1124* applies for these purposes. In broad terms, this looks at the shareholder's ability to secure that the affairs of the relevant company are conducted in accordance with their wishes. The exercise of control could be secured through the holding of shares, voting power, or powers in the articles/shareholders agreement. The case of *Irving v Tesco Stores (Holdings)* [1982] STC 881 reviewed the application of the identical predecessor provision in *ICTA 1988, s 840*, which found (by way of *obiter*) that control of the board of directors would also be sufficient.

Most advisers agree that *FA 1986, s 77A* would deny the stamp duty exemption for a share exchange that takes place before a 'capital reduction' demerger, which involves a subsequent change of control of the new holding company (see 13.98A).

Relief under *FA 1986, s 77* must be applied for in writing to the Stamp Taxes Office in Birmingham. The application must contain sufficient information for HMRC to consider whether the conditions for relief have been met.

Where *FA 1986, s 77* relief is not available, stamp duty will be payable at 0.5% on the market value of the shares.

COMPANY PARTITIONS AND DEMERGERS

Partitioning company between shareholders

13.61 Many owner-managed or family businesses develop to the stage where different members of the owner-managers/family team become responsible for separate parts of the business. Sometimes, the owner-managers may subsequently have a fundamental disagreement about the direction of the business or simply find that they 'cannot work together'. In such cases, they may decide to 'partition' the company so that each shareholder takes over the relevant part of the business.

A 'split' of a company's or group's businesses may also be driven by a number of other reasons, such as:

- commercial risk management – because of the different levels of business risk inherent in various types of trade, the shareholders may decide to retain the 'higher' risk ones in separate legal entities;

- differing financing requirements of each trade – only certain businesses may have the ability to attract wider forms of financial support (such as venture capital) or it may be that it would be easier to raise finance for one of the businesses if it were not so closely associated with the other; and

- plans to sell off defined parts of the business – a demerger may be used where there is an intention to sell one or more of the businesses carried on by a company/group but retain the others. In such cases, it is likely that a 'non-statutory' type of demerger would be needed to separate the relevant businesses before the sale.

It may also be attractive to separate the trading and investment businesses to optimise the tax reliefs obtainable under Entrepreneurs' Relief (ER) (see 15.33) or the Substantial Shareholdings Exemption (SSE) (see 3.42).

A company or group partition exercise would broadly entail the relevant company transferring the trade and assets of the relevant businesses (or shareholdings in its trading subsidiaries) to separate shareholder groups. Without special relieving provisions, this could trigger significant tax liabilities for both the company and the shareholders.

However, it should normally be possible to split or demerge the relevant business units on a 'tax-neutral' basis, apart from perhaps a stamp duty or stamp duty land tax (SDLT) cost (see 13.62), by 'partitioning' the company under a 'non-statutory' type of demerger (see 13.63) or one of the permitted statutory demerger schemes.

For company partitions, a demerged business engaged in property letting or property investment is likely to attract a full SDLT charge (since 'acquisition' relief is not given is such cases) (see 13.74).

The legal and other costs of advising on company demergers would usually be disallowed on the basis that the expenditure is of a 'capital' nature or is not incurred wholly and exclusively for the purposes of the company's trade (the demerger transaction being incidental to a change of ownership of a trade, etc) (*Kealy v O'Mara (Limerick) Ltd* [1942] 2 ITC 265).

Non-statutory v statutory demergers

13.62   In essence a demerger involves the division of a company or group into two or more companies or groups, with the ultimate share ownership being maintained or separated:

- a non-statutory demerger necessitates winding up the company and distributing the relevant 'business' and assets or subsidiaries to new companies owned by some or all of the shareholders, using the procedure laid down in the *Insolvency Act 1986, s 110*. This is covered at 13.63–13.83;

- a statutory demerger entails distributing one or more trading subsidiaries directly to all or some of the shareholders, or one or more trades or trading subsidiaries to new companies owned by some or all of the shareholders under the statutory code in *CTA 2010, Ch 5*. A statutory demerger avoids winding the company up, subject to numerous restrictions, such as, that there is no 'intention' to sell the demerged company. Statutory demergers are dealt with at 13.84–13.98.

The *Companies Act 2006* now enables a company to reduce its share capital with relative ease (see 13.60 and 13.60A). Consequently, many more companies are now using these provisions to implement demergers, especially non-statutory ones. Under a 'reduction of capital' demerger, a new holding company will typically be inserted above the existing company via a share exchange (see 13.60D, 13.60E and 13.98). A typical capital reduction demerger is covered in Example 12.

Non-statutory demerger under *IA 1986, s 110*

13.63   In many cases, a non-statutory form of demerger is normally used as it is difficult to satisfy all of the various tax and legal conditions for a statutory demerger. Non-statutory demergers are commonly used in the following cases:

- Where an investment business (such as property letting) is being demerged (the statutory demerger legislation only allows the splitting of trades).

- If there is an intention to sell off one or more of the demerged businesses (this is not permitted under the statutory demerger legislation).

- Where the company has insufficient distributable reserves to declare a dividend in specie equal to the underlying book value of the assets/or subsidiary transferred [*CA 2006, s 846*] enables any unrealised profit, recognised in the accounts ie, the difference between the market value and book value of the asset, to be treated as realised for this purpose (see 13.99)).

Under a non-statutory demerger, the company is wound-up and the relevant 'business' and assets or subsidiaries are distributed to new companies owned by the shareholders, using the procedure laid down in *IA 1986, s 110*.

The detailed procedure and tax consequences of a company partition under an *IA 1986, s 110* scheme will be explained through the use of a comprehensive case study example (see Example 11).

Example 11

Company partition scheme under *Insolvency Act 1986, s 110*

Background

Barnes (Transport & Haulage) Ltd carries on two separate businesses which are considered to be of similar value. The shares in Barnes (Transport & Haulage) Ltd have always been owned equally by John Barnes and Paul Barnes, two brothers, since the company was incorporated in 1975. John runs the transport and warehouse business and the haulage business is managed by Paul.

It has now been decided that the two businesses would be better operated if John and Paul owned their respective businesses, to develop as they wish. The company's tax advisers have recommended that (for a number of reasons, including the lack of sufficient distributable profits) the demerger should be effected by a reconstruction under *IA 1986, s 110*.

Key steps in *IA 1986, s 110* reconstruction

The various steps would be as follows:

(*a*) Barnes (Transport & Haulage) Ltd is formally liquidated by the shareholders passing a special resolution – it is not possible to use the 'informal' dissolution procedure in *CA 2006, s 1000* to carry out this type of reconstruction;

(*b*) the share capital of Barnes (Transport & Haulage) Ltd would be converted into two classes of ordinary shares – 'A' and 'B' shares split according to the respective values of each trade – in this case of similar value. If the businesses were of unequal value, they could be equalised through the apportionment of liabilities and/or an equalisation payment – although any payment would be chargeable to CGT on the recipient shareholder;

(*c*) John will form 'Barnes Transport Ltd' to take over the transport and warehouse business and Paul will form 'Barnes Haulage Ltd' to take over the haulage business;

(*d*) under *IA 1986, s 110*, a scheme of reconstruction takes place under which the liquidator:

  (i) transfers the transport and warehouse business to Barnes Transport Ltd which, in turn, issues shares to John as consideration;

  (ii) transfers the haulage trade to Barnes Haulage Ltd which, in turn, issues shares to Paul as consideration.

Inserting a new holding company as a special purpose liquidation vehicle

13.64 It may well be that the original company or holding company of a group would have problems in transferring contracts, licences or leases. The shareholders may also feel that the legal announcement of the liquidation (which is completely tax driven) may be misinterpreted by its customers and other business contacts, etc. If the liquidation of the original company is likely to involve such commercial difficulties, then it normally is possible to use a 'special purpose' holding company. This 'new' company can acquire the original company by means of a 'tax-free' share for share exchange under *TCGA 1992, s 135*. (This transaction would be included as part of the combined *TCGA 1992, s 138* clearance application (see 13.82).)

As this should involve a 'mirror-image' exchange of shares, the stamp duty exemption in *FA 1986, s 77* should normally apply to the acquisition of the original company by the new holding company. Given that the holding company will eventually be liquidated, the *FA 1986, s 77A* anti-avoidance rule (introduced by *FA 2016*, which applies from 29 June 2016) should not apply here (see 13.60E and 13.98A).

The 'clean' holding company is then liquidated but the liquidation transfers must be made from this company. This may include 'hiving-up' one or more businesses from the original company and the new 'interposed' holding company distributing these businesses and the original company's shares to the new companies.

In such cases, it is vital for the newly formed holding company to carry on the relevant businesses for an appropriate period before their onward distribution, to ensure that the requirements of the relevant tax 'reconstruction' reliefs (including *CTA 2010, Pt 2, Ch 1*), and any VAT transfer of going concern relief (see 12.32)) can be fully satisfied. The holding company should actually carry on the business(es) for an appropriate 'short' period (with the transactions being booked in its accounts).

The importance of ensuring that the trade is actually carried on for a meaningful period was underlined by the recent decision in *Barkers of Malton v HMRC* [2008] UKSPC 689. In this case a trade was hived down to a subsidiary at 9am (with the trade being carried on by the holding company as undisclosed agent for its subsidiary). The subsidiary then sold the hived-down trade an hour and a half later! The Tribunal found that the requirements of the 'succession of trade' rules in (what was) *ICTA 1988, s 343* had not been satisfied. Simply owning the trade for one hour and a half was not enough. No transactions had been recorded during that period and the reliance on agency was insufficient. This decision gives a clear warning to those who adopt a casual approach in this area!

Basis of split and valuations

13.65 Each separate shareholder group will want to ensure that they get their 'fair' share of the partitioned businesses/companies. This will generally involve obtaining professional valuations and negotiations being conducted on an arm's length basis. HMRC will also wish to ensure that the division of the businesses/companies gives each shareholder/shareholder grouping their appropriate share of the distributing company and that no value shift occurs between the shareholders.

The value of the businesses/companies allocated to each shareholder is typically based on the value of their proportionate shareholding in the distributing company (based as a percentage of the total share capital with no minority discount (since it is effectively a sale!)).

Provided the partition has been negotiated on an arm's length basis, HMRC will not insist on a precise split of value. For these purposes, assets and liabilities should be valued and divided at the time the partition takes place, with some form of 'completion accounts' being drawn up.

In many cases, the allocation of the net asset values between each business/company may not reflect the value fairly attributable to the relevant 'post-partition' shareholder groups. The allocation will therefore require adjusting to bring the values into line with the underlying shareholder entitlements. For example, creditors/loans of one business can be allocated to another or cash balances may be allocated to one of the businesses and a bank overdraft to another. HMRC generally accept that such arrangements may be required to arrive at the proper allocation of values, but these should be disclosed in the advance clearance application (see 13.82).

In more extreme cases, one group of shareholders may need to pay some form of compensatory 'equality' payment to another. This will generally be treated as a capital sum derived from the shares under *TCGA 1992, s 22*, and will thus be subject to CGT in the hands of the recipient shareholders.

Barnes (Transport & Haulage) Ltd – diagram of transactions

13.66   The various transactions are illustrated diagrammatically.

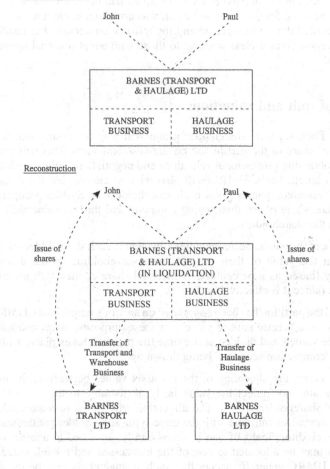

The corporate structure will therefore end up as follows:

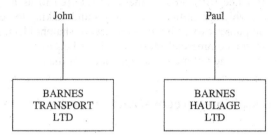

The distributing company (Barnes (Transport & Haulage) Ltd) and *TCGA 1992, s 139* reconstruction relief

13.67   Without any special relieving provisions, a corporate reconstruction/ demerger would invariably give rise to a 'double tax' charge. The distribution of the business to the shareholders would result in the transferor company being charged to tax on gains attributable to goodwill and properties, etc (deemed to be disposed of at their market value). The recipient shareholders would also be taxed on the market value of the assets received by them.

Provided the corporate gains reconstruction relief in *TCGA 1992, s 139* applies, Barnes (Transport & Haulage) Ltd (being the transferor company) will be treated as disposing of its chargeable assets (included in the transfers to the two new companies) on a no gain/no loss basis. The transferee companies will be deemed therefore to have acquired the assets at their original cost (rebased to March 1982, where relevant) together with the accrued indexation allowance [*TCGA 1992, s 139(1)* and *Sch 3, para 1*].

The *s 139* corporate gains 'reconstruction' relief can only apply if there is a scheme of reconstruction (see 13.68). Before *FA 2002*, the definition of a 'reconstruction' was based on a number of old stamp duty cases. Perhaps the most important definition is found in *Re South African Supply and Cold Storage* [1904] 2 Ch 268 (see 13.73), which was previously paraphrased in HMRC's Capital Gains Manual (before the *FA 2002* statutory definition) as follows:

> 'A reconstruction involves the transfer of a company's business … to another company consisting of substantially the same shareholders.'

Many types of demerger satisfied this condition since the shareholders of the new 'transferee' company (which takes over the business) were substantially the same as the shareholders of the transferor company. However, some demergers were designed to split the businesses between different shareholders/ shareholder groups – sometimes referred to as 'partitions'. In such cases, each demerged business would be carried on by a different shareholder or group of shareholders and would not therefore meet the requirement that (substantially) the same shareholders should carry it on.

However, the Inland Revenue used to operate a generous concession in Statement of Practice (SP) 5/85 (sometimes referred to as a 'press release reconstruction'), which permitted a company's undertaking to be divided into two or more companies owned by different sets of shareholders, provided this was carried out for commercial reasons. (There had to be a segregation of trades or businesses and not merely a segregation of the company's assets.)

Statutory definition of reconstruction under *TCGA 1992, Sch 5AA*

13.68   SP 5/85 had no statutory basis and was successfully challenged by the taxpayer in *Kersley (Morgan's Executors) v Fellows* [2001] STC 1409. Somewhat unusually the taxpayer did not want the CGT reorganisation treatment applied by *TCGA 1992, s 136* since this gave a lower base cost for the transferred assets.

The then Revenue responded in *FA 2002* by introducing a statutory definition of a 'scheme of reconstruction' (within *TCGA 1992, Sch 5AA*) which applies from 17 April 2002. This effectively codified the Revenue's existing practice (hitherto applied by SP 5/85) on a statutory basis, so that there was no opting out. Among other things, the new statutory definition encompassed a pure reconstruction with the relevant businesses continuing to be owned by the same shareholders and a partition of a business between *different* shareholders, as in the case of *Barnes (Transport & Haulage) Ltd*.

SP 5/85 and the old case law definitions of reconstruction are now replaced by the statutory regime in *TCGA 1992, Sch 5AA* for the various capital gains reliefs. However, the old case law precedents (see 13.73) still apply for stamp duty and stamp duty land tax.

Under the *TCGA 1992, Sch 5AA* statutory definition, a 'scheme of reconstruction' must satisfy the following key elements:

- only the ordinary shareholders of the relevant business must receive ordinary shares under the scheme (via a new issue of shares), ie no one else must be entitled to the new share issue [*TCGA 1992, Sch 5AA, para 2*];

- the proportionate interests of the shareholders both before and after the reconstruction must remain the same [*TCGA 1992, Sch 5AA, para 3*]. (It is generally necessary to carry out a preparatory reorganisation of the distributing company's share capital to create separate classes of share. In such cases, the 'equality of entitlement' condition is tested after the completion of the share reorganisation [*TCGA 1992, Sch 5AA, para 6*]; and

- the business previously carried on by the 'original' company or companies must subsequently be carried on by one or more successor companies [*TCGA 1992, Sch 5AA, para 4*].

Alternatively, the scheme must be carried out under a compromise or arrangement under *CA 2006, s 895* (or equivalent provision) [*TCGA 1992, Sch 5AA, para 5*].

The statutory reconstruction rules still enable a partition of the business between different groups of shareholders to qualify as a reconstruction for capital gains purposes. As far as Barnes (Transport & Haulage) Ltd is concerned (Example 11), the proposed partition scheme should satisfy these conditions:

- both John and Paul receive shares in their Barnes Transport Ltd and Barnes Haulage Ltd respectively;

- their proportionate interests in the business remain the same after the reconstruction (ie there is no value shift), even though they have each taken over a separate part of the original business;

- the two successor companies (Barnes Transport Ltd and Barnes Haulage Ltd) will carry on the business previously carried on by Barnes (Transport & Haulage) Ltd.

Other key conditions for *TCGA 1992, s 139* relief

13.69   The operation of the 'no gain/no loss' rule in *TCGA 1992, s 139* for the transfer of chargeable assets on a reconstruction requires a number of other conditions to be satisfied:

(*a*)   the scheme must involve the transfer of the whole or part of one company's business to another company;

(*b*)   the scheme must be effected for bona fide commercial purposes and not for the avoidance of corporation tax, CGT or income tax – advance clearance can be obtained from HMRC to confirm that this condition is satisfied [*TCGA 1992, s 139(5)*] (Note that HMRC may refuse granting a *s 139(5)* clearance where the distributing company has begun to market one or more of the businesses (new companies) for onward sale!)

(*c*)   both the transferor and transferee companies must be UK resident (or within the charge to UK corporation tax) at the time of transfer [*TCGA 1992, s 139(1)*]; and

(*d*)   the transferor must not receive any part of the consideration for the transfer other than the assumption of its liabilities by the transferee companies [*TCGA 1992, s 139(1)(c)*].

The 'reconstruction' transactions contemplated by Barnes (Transport & Haulage) Ltd and its shareholders should therefore enable capital gains to be deferred at the company level.

Reconstruction relief for post-31 March 2002 intangibles

13.70   Any (post-31 March 2002) intangible fixed assets included in a reconstruction would also be transferred on a tax neutral basis – thus effectively being transferred at their original cost [*CTA 2009*, s 818]. The conditions for intangibles reconstruction relief are virtually the same as those for *TCGA 1992, s 139* relief in 13.68 and 13.69 above, which includes satisfying the genuine commercial purpose test in *CTA 2009, s 831*). Certainty can be obtained by the transferee by obtaining an appropriate tax clearance from HMRC under *CTA 2009, ss 831(2)* and *832*.

Practical aspects of reconstruction relief

13.71   HMRC will accept that shares in a 75% subsidiary constitute a 'business' for the purposes of *TCGA 1992, s 139* reconstruction relief. The position is less clear for 51% subsidiaries (despite the wording in *TCGA 1992, Sch 5AA, para 4(3)*)

On the other hand, minority shareholdings (even if they trade in the same industry) will not be treated as part of the business of the transferor company (see *Baytrust Holdings Ltd v CIR* [1971] 1 WLR 1333).

Where TCGA 1992, s139 corporate reconstruction relief is available, this will always take precedence over any entitlement to the corporate Substantial Shareholdings Exemption (see 3.40 and 3.43) (*TCGA 1992, Sch 7AC, para 6(1) (a)*).

Any *TCGA 1992*, s 179 degrouping gains (on chargeable gains) are now added to the sale proceeds of the disposing company for capital gains purposes (*TCGA 1992, s 179(3D)*). HMRC has confirmed that where a degrouping gain is attributed to the disposing company's proceeds on a *TCGA 1992, s 139* transfer it is effectively 'exempted' under the no gain/no loss 'deemed consideration' rule.

This analysis come from the wording in *TCGA 1992, s 139(1B)* –'*Nothing in s 179(3D) prevents the companies being treated as mentioned in subsection 1 [of TCGA 1992, s 139]*'. Whilst the degrouping gain is 'exempted' under the 'no gain/no loss' rule, it does *not* get added to the transferee company's deemed 'no gain/no loss' consideration.

The effective 'degrouping' exemption under a *TCGA 1992, s 139* no gain/ no loss transfer is only available for chargeable 'capital gains' assets. It will not therefore apply where a degrouping charge arises under the corporate intangibles relief (*CTA 2009, ss 775* and *776*). In such cases, a taxable intangibles degrouping profit (loss) will still be deemed to arise in the 'degrouped' subsidiary (see 3.49).

Interaction of Substantial Shareholdings Exemption rules with post-demerger companies

13.72   Where, as a result of a group reorganisation, a company acquires a subsidiary which is subsequently to be sold, the deemed period of ownership is extended where those shares were acquired under a no gain/no loss transfer, typically under *TCGA 1992, s 139* (see 13.69) *[TCGA 1992, Sch 7AC, para 10]*.

Under the post-31 March 2017 SSE regime, this should mean that as long as the distributing company and transferee company have held (and/or deemed to have held) the (qualifying trading) subsidiary for at least 12 months, SSE should be available (see 3.32 and 3.33).

Key stamp duty land tax (SDLT) and stamp duty reliefs

13.73   In the case of a 'partition', stamp duty land tax (SDLT) is charged on the value of land and property transferred (see 12.23–12.31), while stamp duty would be levied on the value of shares in companies that are transferred to the new companies as part of the reconstruction exercise. It is worth noting that the transfer of goodwill and debts do not attract any stamp duty costs, which is beneficial for many partition exercises.

It should be noted that where there is a 'pure reconstruction' with 'mirror image' shareholdings before and after the transfer, it may be possible to satisfy the strict conditions of *FA 2003, Sch 7, Pt 2* and *FA 1986, s 75* to secure complete exemption from SDLT and stamp duty respectively. The *FA 2003, Sch 7, para 7* reconstruction relief applies to all 'chargeable transactions' including property sales and the grant, surrender or assignment of leases. As will often be the case, the consideration for the acquisition must consist of the issue of (non-redeemable) shares in the acquiring company or the assumption/ discharge of the transferor's liabilities. Both the stamp duty and SDLT reliefs require the transaction to be carried out for genuine commercial reasons and not mainly for tax avoidance.

The complete exemption from SDLT is only given where post-transfer each shareholder holds the same shareholding interest (or as nearly as may be the same proportion) as they did previously in the transferor.

For stamp duty and SDLT purposes, there is no statutory definition of a 'reconstruction'. (The *TCGA 1992, Sch 5AA* definition (see 13.68) only applies for the purpose of the various capital gains 'reconstruction' reliefs – it does not apply to stamp taxes).

For both stamp duty and SDLT, special conditions must be satisfied and guidance must also be sought from case law. Probably the most authoritative definition of a 'reconstruction' comes from Buckley J in an old stamp duty case (*Re South African Supply and Cold Storage Co Ltd* (1904) 2 Ch 268):

'What does 'reconstruction' mean? To my mind it means this. An undertaking of some definite kind is being carried on, and the conclusion is arrived at that it is not desirable to kill that undertaking, but that it is desirable to preserve it in some form, and to do so, not by selling it to an outsider who shall carry it on – that would be a mere sale – but in some altered form to continue the undertaking in such a manner as that the persons now carrying it on will substantially continue to carry it on. It involves, I think, that substantially the same business shall be carried on and substantially the same persons shall carry it on. But it does not involve that all the assets shall pass to the new company or resuscitated company, or that all the shareholders of the old company shall be shareholders in the new company or resuscitated company. Substantially, the business and the persons interested must be the same.'

The proposed split of the business carried on by Barnes (Transport & Haulage) Ltd, with its two trades being transferred to different shareholders, would not meet the specific 'mirror image' shareholding requirements in the stamp taxes legislation. (The SDLT exemption will not therefore apply to the property transfers included in the reconstruction undertaken by Barnes (Transport & Haulage) Ltd in Example 11 at 13.63). It will therefore be appreciated that such company partitions will often involve an SDLT and/or stamp duty cost.

Where SDLT 'reconstruction' relief is not available, it will sometimes be possible to claim a reduced SDLT rate of ½% under the 'transfer of undertakings' or 'acquisition' relief in *FA 2003, Sch 7 para 8*. SDLT acquisition relief is only given where the consideration for the acquisition is satisfied by the issue of non-redeemable shares to the transferor company or all/any of its shareholders, provided the transaction is undertaken for genuine commercial reasons and not mainly for tax avoidance.

In such cases, the acquiring company is permitted to satisfy part of the consideration by assuming or discharging the transferor company's liabilities. (Although a limited amount of cash consideration may also be given, this would prevent the corporate capital gains reconstruction relief being given (see 13.69 (*d*)).) However, see 13.74 for the important exclusion for property dealing or property investment businesses.

Where shares are transferred on a partition, they would normally carry a normal stamp duty liability of 0.5% (without the need to invoke the relieving provisions 'transfer of undertakings' reduced rate relief in *FA 1986, s 76*).

SDLT problems for property investment/dealing businesses

13.74 There is likely to be a significant SDLT liability where the partition includes a (mainly) property letting or property dealing business. However, HMRC appear to take the view that this restriction does *not* apply to property development trades, which may therefore qualify for acquisition relief.

In broad terms, the (½%) acquisition relief is only available if the business being acquired is *wholly or mainly* a trade (but *not* a property dealing trade). It should be emphasised that this restriction does not apply to the SDLT reconstruction relief, which may still exempt property-related investment businesses.

FA 2003, Sch 7, para 8(5A) now effectively blocks acquisition relief for properties comprised in a property investment business (not a trade) or property dealing business, thus exposing them to the full SDLT rates. This means that, in practice, the acquiring company would only obtain the benefit of such relief for properties used in a trade or possibly where the trade being transferred has a 'small' property letting activity.

SDLT clawback charges

13.75 SDLT reconstruction or acquisition relief claimed on properties (see 13.73) would be 'clawed-back' where control of the acquiring company changes hands within three years after the relevant reconstruction/acquisition transfer. The claw-back only operates if the acquiring company still retains the relevant properties when it changes ownership. The primary purpose of the claw-back charge is to prevent the relevant SDLT reliefs being exploited to transfer property to third parties through the use of special company vehicles.

For these purposes, control of the acquirer would change where it becomes controlled by a different person or group of persons (using the wide 'control' test in *CTA 2010, ss 450* and *451* (see 3.23)).

Specific exemptions prevent the claw-back charge being triggered where control of the company changes in certain specific cases. This would include, for example, where control alters as a result of court-ordered divorce, changes in loan creditors, or where the company comes under the control of a new holding company by virtue of a stamp duty free transfer under *FA 1986, s 77* (*FA 2003, Sch 7, para 10*).

Where the SDLT relief is clawed-back, the SDLT liability is effectively computed based on the market value of the retained property/properties using the prevailing SDLT rates at the date of the original reconstruction/acquisition transfer, ie the SDLT that would have been paid if no relief had been given (less any actual SDLT paid under the acquisition relief).

'Capital allowance' assets and tax losses

13.76 The reconstruction provisions do not prevent the normal corporation tax consequences of a cessation of trade unless the 'succession of trade' provisions of *CTA 2010, s 948* can be brought into play (see 12.66). If the succession provisions apply, this will enable any trading losses and the tax written-down value of plant to be carried over into the transferee company.

In Example 11 (at 13.63), the common 75% beneficial ownership test required for a succession of trade transfer within *CTA 2010, Pt 22, Ch 1*, may not be satisfied after the reconstruction. Before the transfer, each trade is owned equally by John and Paul whereas after the transfer, each trade is owned separately by John and Paul. However, there is a fairly strong argument for saying that as 'associates' (brothers), John and Paul are regarded as one person [*CTA 2010, s 941(7), (8)*] which would then enable the succession of trade rules to apply, but HMRC might contest this approach.

Where it is important to obtain *CTA 2010, Pt 22, Ch 1* relief, for example, where one of the transferred trades has substantial tax losses, consideration should be given to hiving down the relevant trades to new wholly-owned subsidiaries under *CTA 2010, Pt 22, Ch 1* first. The liquidator would then distribute these subsidiaries in specie to the new companies under the protection of *TCGA 1992, s 139* (the subsidiaries would be regarded as businesses).

However, any *TCGA 1992, s 179* de-grouping charge in respect of the *chargeable assets* previously transferred under *TCGA 1992, s 171* on the hive-down will effectively be exempted under the deemed 'no gain/no loss' corporate gains reconstruction rule in *TCGA 1992, s 139* (see 13.71). This useful relief does not apply to *CTA 2009, s 780*-type de-grouping charges arising under the intangibles regime (ie on goodwill and other IP assets created or acquired after 31 March 2002). Consequently, a taxable intangibles profit will crystallise within the distributed subsidiary.

The statutory demerger code offers a specific exemption for all types of de-grouping charge (see 13.84). The possibility of implementing a statutory demerger should therefore be considered where an *Insolvency Act 1986, s 110* reconstruction is likely to involve a material de-grouping tax charge. The tax costs of the various demerger routes must therefore be compared to determine the best way of structuring the transactions.

If the trade succession provisions in *CTA 2010, Pt 22, Ch 1* do not apply (see 12.66), it may still be possible for plant to be transferred at tax written-down values (thus avoiding a balancing charge) provided there is common 51% control at shareholder level by electing under *CAA 2001, s 266*.

Transfer of trading stock

13.77 Where trading stock is 'sold' on a reconstruction, the consideration is reflected in the shares issued by the 'new' successor company. Since full consideration has been given, this would strictly mean that the trading stock passes at its market value and it is not therefore possible to make an election for it to be transferred at original cost/book value under *CTA 2009, s 167*. However, in practice, since no consideration actually passes directly to the transferor company (the stock is distributed in *specie*), HMRC generally accept a transfer at book value provided the same amount is used by both companies (and a competent *CTA 2009, s 167* election is made to disapply the deemed market value rule, which would invariably be the case).

However, where the 'UK to UK' transfer pricing rules apply to the distributing company, the stock is treated as being transferred at its market value (since the transfer pricing rules take precedence under *CTA 2009, s 161*).

VAT – transfer of going concern relief

13.78   The transfer of the trade and assets transferred would normally qualify as a 'transfer of a going concern' (TOGC) for VAT purposes and hence the value of the transferred assets (such as plant, trading stock, etc) would not be subject to VAT [*VAT (Special Provisions) Order 1995, art 5*].

Where land and property is transferred (which has been subject to an option to tax election), the transferee company will also need to elect before the transfer is made to enable the property to be transferred 'VAT-free' under the TOGC rules. The transferor must therefore be satisfied that the transferee company has opted to tax (see also 12.34).

Position of shareholders (John and Paul)

13.79   Potentially, where shareholders of an existing company receive shares in another company on a reconstruction, this would be regarded as an income distribution, being an indirect transfer by the company to its members. This is why it is essential for the disposing company in Example 11 (at 13.63) – Barnes (Transport & Haulage) Ltd in this case – to be liquidated before the reconstruction exercise. Amounts received during the course of a winding up do not constitute an income distribution (see 16.18) [*CTA 2010, s 1030*]. Furthermore, (post-5 April 2016) liquidation distributions of (irredeemable) shares are not affected by the *FA 2016* 'anti-phoenixing' legislation (*ITTOIA 2005, s 396B(7)(b)*) (see 16.28).

The value of the shares acquired by John and Paul would therefore fall to be treated as a capital distribution [*TCGA 1992, s 122(1), (5)*]. However, John and Paul will be protected from any CGT liabilities under *TCGA 1992, s 136* provided the shares are issued as part of the arrangements for a scheme of 'reconstruction'. Here again, this scheme would satisfy the various requirements of *TCGA 1992, Sch 5AA* (see 13.68).

Under *TCGA 1992, ss 136* and *127*, John and Paul will be treated as making no disposal for CGT purposes as regards their shares in Barnes (Transport & Haulage) Ltd with the result that the shares they acquire in their respective new companies – Barnes Transport Ltd and Barnes Haulage Ltd – will be treated as the same asset acquired at the same time as their old shares. If the original shares are retained, they will be regarded as having been cancelled and replaced by a new issue – the original base cost will then have to be apportioned between the various shareholdings.

HMRC will normally accept the 'pre-reconstruction' shareholding period as counting towards the 'one year' ER qualifying period where *TCGA 1992, s 127* applies, although this treatment is not strictly available under the CGT legislation (see *CGT entrepreneurs' relief and share for share exchange* note issued by CIOT Technical Department – 26 May 2010). This would be beneficial where a new recipient/successor company is sold within one year of the reconstruction. However, the relevant shareholder would also have to satisfy the ER conditions in the transferor/distributing company for the appropriate (pre-reconstruction) period.

Main requirements for *TCGA 1992, s 136* relief

13.80   *TCGA 1992, s 136* requires the following conditions to be satisfied:

(*a*)   there must be an arrangement between the disposing company and its shareholders;

(*b*)   the shareholders must receive shares (and/or debentures) in the 'new' company in respect of and in proportion to their shares in the disposing company – these shares must either be retained or cancelled [*TCGA 1992, s 136(1)(b)*];

(*c*)   the reconstruction must be effected for bona fide commercial reasons and not for the avoidance of tax. The advance clearance procedure in *TCGA 1992, s 138* is used to confirm that HMRC are satisfied that this is the case [*TCGA 1992, s 137(1)*].

Position of recipient companies (Barnes Transport Ltd and Barnes Haulage Ltd)

13.81   The new companies will acquire the relevant chargeable assets at the transferor's base cost (rebased to March 1982, if appropriate) with accrued indexation allowance [*TCGA 1992, s 139*].

It should be noted that de-grouping charges cannot apply in this situation as the chargeable assets are not transferred to a 'group' company.

Planning a company partition and relevant tax clearances

13.82   Each partition exercise will be underpinned by various generic tax principles and reliefs. In practice, each tends to have its own unique issues and challenges. It is not always possible to implement a corporate reconstruction without any tax cost, for example, a partition may involve SDLT or stamp duty liabilities. There will also be a whole panoply of legal, accounting, and commercial issues, which may have a direct bearing on the structure of the reconstruction exercise.

13.83 To obtain certainty in advance that HMRC is satisfied that transaction(s) are being made for genuine commercial reasons (rather than mainly for tax avoidance), a 'combined' tax clearance application should be submitted under the various sections mentioned below (see 15.89 for relevant details).

- *TCGA 1992, s 138* for the shareholders' CGT reconstruction relief (see 13.79 and 13.80), and any prior share exchange (see 13.64).

- *TCGA 1992, s 139(5)* for the corporate gains reconstruction relief (see 13.67–13.69) and/or *CTA 2009, ss 831(2)* and *832* for intangibles reconstruction relief (see 13.70).

- *ITA 2007, s 701* – Transaction in Securities (TiS) legislation – (see 15.89).

PERMITTED TYPES OF STATUTORY DEMERGER

13.84 A 'non-statutory' demerger scheme requires the transferor company to be liquidated to avoid the shareholders being subject to tax on an income distribution. This may not always be feasible or desirable.

As will be seen, it is not necessary for all the existing shareholders to take shares in the demerged businesses or companies. Each business carried on by a company or group can be passed to a different shareholder or different shareholder 'groupings'.

Thus, if the various tax and legal conditions had been achievable, it would have been possible to demerge the two businesses carried on by Barnes (Transport & Haulage) Ltd (see Example 11 at 13.63) by way of a statutory demerger. This could be achieved without having to liquidate Barnes (Transport & Haulage) Ltd, with a simple demerger distribution of one of the trades.

The statutory demerger rules in *CTA 2010, Ch 5* permit three types of demerger, without the need for a liquidation.

It achieves this by treating a qualifying demerger distribution as an 'exempt' distribution and therefore there is no income tax charge in the shareholder's hands. Each statutory demerger takes the form of a distribution in specie of one or more trades or shares in one or more 75% subsidiaries:

Type 1 (Direct demerger)	— The direct distribution by a company of shares in a 75% subsidiary (or subsidiaries) to all or any of its members (*CTA 2010, s 1076*).

Type 2 (Indirect demerger)	— The transfer of a company's trade or trades to one or more 'transferee' companies in consideration for the issue of shares in those companies to all or any of the members of the distributing company (*CTA 2010, s 1077(1)(a)(i)*). This is known as an 'indirect' distribution.

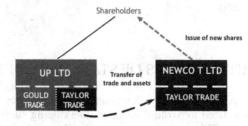

Type 3 (Indirect demerger)	— The transfer of shares in a 75% subsidiary (or subsidiaries) to one or more 'transferee' companies in consideration for the issue of shares in the companies to all or any of the members of the distributing company (*CTA 2010, s 1077(1)(a)(ii)*). This is known as an 'indirect' distribution.

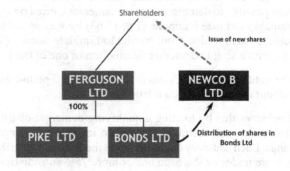

However, many contemplated demergers will be unable to satisfy the numerous pre-conditions, commonly the prohibition on demergers in contemplation of a sale and the use of a demerger to separate trades from investment businesses. In such cases, a non-statutory 'liquidation' demerger will normally have to be used instead (see 13.63).

STATUTORY DEMERGER RELIEFS FOR SHAREHOLDERS

Exempt distribution rule

13.85 Provided the various qualifying conditions are met, the shares received direct or the 'consideration' shares received for the transfer will not rank as an income distribution in the shareholders' hands. The distribution is termed an 'exempt distribution' and does not, therefore, give rise to an income tax liability in the (individual/ trustee) shareholder's hands [*CTA 2010, s 1075*].

Although this exemption does not prevent the 'distribution' falling within the capital gains regime, the CGT reconstruction reliefs will invariably be available to prevent any tax charge arising (see 13.86 and 13.87 below).

Type 1 – Direct demerger

13.86 On a Type 1 'direct' demerger, the distribution is not treated as a capital distribution, which would have created a part disposal for CGT purposes.

SSE may potentially apply to exempt the distributing company from the gain for corporation tax purposes (see 13.71 and 13.89) (*TCGA 1992, s 139* will not normally apply here since the distribution will usually be to *individual* shareholders).

However, this does *not* mean that the shareholders will acquire the shares at their market value under general principles. This is because there is a specific rule in *TCGA 1992, s 192(2)* which treats the shares in the distributed subsidiary as being received in a 'new for old' reorganisation for CGT purposes. Thus, the shares in the subsidiary are related back to their shareholding in the distributing company under the deemed application of *TCGA 1992, s 127*. (The shares in the distributed subsidiary would therefore be deemed to be acquired by the recipient shareholders at the time of the 'original' shareholding at their pro-rata base cost of the original shares (based on the respective market values of the distributing and subsidiary company/companies).

Type 2 and 3 – Indirect demergers

13.87 A Type 2 or 3 demerger should usually qualify as a scheme of reconstruction within *TCGA 1992, Sch 5AA* (see 13.68). (Because of the restrictions imposed by the statutory demerger rules, shares in a 75% (as opposed to a 51%) subsidiary must be transferred under a Type 3 demerger – this is treated as a transfer of a business under the 'reconstruction' rules.)

The issue of shares in the new recipient companies as part of the demerger should fall within *TCGA 1992, s 136* (see 13.79 and 13.80). This means the 'new for old' reorganisation relief rules would apply) [*TCGA 1992, s 127*].

STATUTORY DEMERGER RELIEFS FOR DISTRIBUTING COMPANY

Exempt distribution

13.88 The distributing company is treated as having made an 'exempt distribution' [*CTA 2010, s 1075*].

Treatment of disposal under a Type 1 direct demerger and application of SSE

13.89 A Type 1 demerger does not normally qualify for *TCGA 1992, s 139* relief (as the assets are not generally transferred to a company's shareholders). However, many Type 1 demergers should be exempt under the Substantial Shareholding Exemption (SSE) (see 3.40), assuming the relevant conditions are satisfied.

Of course, if for some technical reason the demerger disposal does not qualify for the SSE, a chargeable gain will be triggered on the disposal of the demerged subsidiary's shares, based on their market value. In such cases, it may be possible to mitigate the gain, for example, by paying a pre-sale dividend or transferring assets out at an undervalue (subject to avoiding any value shifting charges under *TCGA 1992, ss 30–33*).

13.90 A Type 1 demerger is likely to be particularly attractive if it qualifies for the SSE as (being an in-specie distribution – see 9.8) it is also normally exempt from stamp duty.

The shares must actually be distributed 'in specie'. This avoids the pre-existing 'debt' stamp duty trap. Any prior declaration of a dividend equal to the value of the subsidiary creates a debt (within *SA 1891, s 57*) and thus gives rise to stamp duty (at 0.5%) when it is then satisfied by the transfer of the shares.

Section 139 reconstruction relief for corporate gains on indirect demergers

13.91 Under general principles, capital gains would normally arise by reference to the market value of the assets being transferred [*TCGA 1992,* *s 17*]. However, Type 2 and 3 (indirect-type) demergers will usually qualify for 'reconstruction' relief under *TCGA 1992, s 139* to prevent capital gains being generated on the transfer of the relevant assets. Such distributions will generally meet all the relevant conditions for *s 139* relief – for example, the trade/shares in a 75% subsidiary will be transferred to another UK company for no consideration (except for the assumption of liabilities).

Although shares in a (51%) subsidiary are treated as a business for the general 'reconstruction' rule in *TCGA 1992, Sch 5AA, para 4(3)* (see 13.71), the actual demerger conditions are more restrictive. The relevant provisions require the demerger to consist of shares in a 75% subsidiary.

The SSE (see 3.42) could potentially apply to the disposal of a qualifying shareholding, such as on a Type 3 demerger. However, where the disposal falls within the *TCGA 1992, s 139* corporate reconstruction provisions (providing 'no gain/no loss' disposal treatment), these will take precedence over the SSE [*TCGA 1992, Sch 7AC, para 6(1)(a)*].

De-grouping charge exemption

13.92   In a Type 1 and Type 3 demerger, a de-grouping charge could arise under *TCGA 1992, s 179* in consequence of assets transferred intra-group to the demerging company within the previous six years. However, a specific exemption is given for any de-grouping charge [*TCGA 1992, s 192(3)*]. Similar protection is given from the de-grouping charge under the intangibles regime under *CTA 2010, s 787*.

No protection is available for SDLT de-grouping charges. An SDLT clawback charge may arise where property has previously been transferred to a subsidiary (under the SDLT intra-group transfer exemption) which subsequently leaves the group via a demerger within three years of the original transfer (provided it still retains the property) (*FA 2003, Sch 7, para 3*).

Other relieving provisions

13.93   The statutory demerger provisions do not offer a complete 'tax-free' regime for demergers. They mainly prevent the demerger distribution from being taxed in the shareholders' hands. Reliance must, therefore, be placed on the other corporate 'succession' or reorganisation legislation to obtain exemption or carry-over of various tax reliefs.

Any unused trading tax losses may be vulnerable under *CTA 2010, ss 673* and *674* (see 12.59) where the demerger of the shares to a group of shareholders triggers a 'change of ownership', although such cases are looked at sympathetically (see SP 13/80).

STATUTORY DEMERGER CONDITIONS

Summary of main conditions

13.94 A demerger will only qualify for the 'exempt distribution' treatment and the special reliefs mentioned above if it satisfies all the relevant conditions. These conditions are more onerous than for a non-statutory demerger by liquidation and reference must always be made to the detailed legislation in each case.

The main conditions for a qualifying demerger are summarised below:

(*a*) all companies participating in the demerger transaction (the 'relevant companies') must be resident in the UK or an EU member state [*CTA 2010, s 1081(1)*];

(*b*) the distributing company must be a trading company or member of a trading group [*CTA 2010, s 1081(2)*]. After the demerger, the distributing company must remain a trading company or member of a trading group [*CTA 2010, s 1082 (2) or 1083(2)*]. For these purposes, the 'trading company' and 'trading group' requirements are based on the less stringent 'wholly or mainly' trading test.

However, this condition need *not* be met where the distributing company is a 75% subsidiary of another company or where it is wound up after the demerger of two or more 75% subsidiaries without there being any net assets available for distribution (other than to cover liquidation costs, etc) [*CTA 2010, s 1082 (3), (4)*];

(*c*) at the time of its distribution, a demerged 75% subsidiary must be a trading company or member of a trading group [*CTA 2010, s 1081(2) (b)*];

(*d*) the distribution must be made wholly or mainly for the benefit of some or all of the trading activities formerly carried on by the company/group [*CTA 2010, s 1081(3)*];

(*e*) the distribution must not form part of a scheme or arrangement for:

   (i) the avoidance of tax, stamp duty or SDLT [*CTA 2010, s 1081(5))*];

   (ii) the making of a 'chargeable payment' (see 13.96 and 13.97 below) [*CTA 2010, s 1081(5)*];

   (iii) the transfer of control of the demerged company to persons other than members of the distributing company (such as on a subsequent sale of the company) [*CTA 2010, s 1081(5)(d)*].

   (iv) the cessation or sale of a trade after the demerger distribution [*CTA 2010, s 1081(5)(e), (f)*].

There are further pre-conditions for each type of demerger [*CTA 2010, ss 1082 and 1083*].

Statutory demerger tax clearances

13.95   Advance clearance can be obtained from HMRC to confirm that they are satisfied that the demerger has been carried out for bona fide commercial reasons and not for the avoidance of tax [*CTA 2010, s 1091)*]. Indeed, tax clearances under *TCGA 1992, s 138* for the shareholders' CGT reconstruction relief; *TCGA 1992, s 139(5)* for the corporate gains reconstruction relief and *ITA 2007, s 701* (transaction in securities legislation) will also be necessary (see 13.89).

A single combined tax clearance application covering all the above sections should be made – see 15.83 for details.

Example 12

Statutory demerger of trade and assets to a new company

Background

Winston is the 100% shareholder of Reid Hotels & Spas Ltd (RHS) and is its Chief Executive. RHS prepares accounts to 31 October each year.

The business first started in 1980 – when RHS acquired a hotel and spa complex in Green Street – and a further hotel at Chadwell Heath was acquired in 2002. The company then diversified in 2008 by purchasing a number of 'up-market' residential care homes for about £10 million.

Winston feels that RHS has now developed to a stage where it has two quite separate and distinct businesses. He feels that the current structure makes it difficult to brand each business separately, especially through the company website, and it has created some confusion for its potential customers. Furthermore, RHS has also had a few 'scary' claims in the care homes business, which thankfully were resolved at little cost, but this served as a timely reminder to Winston about the future potential risk of having both businesses within the same company.

Winston would also like to award some shares to the dedicated management team that runs RHS's care homes business but without giving them any interest in the hotel and spa side of the business.

Following a series of lengthy meetings with his professional advisers, which discussed a number of options, Winston has agreed to implement a statutory demerger of the care homes business.

Before implementing the demerger, it was confirmed that there were adequate distributable reserves to make a distribution equal to the carrying value of the assets of the care homes business (less certain liabilities) (see 13.101).

Appropriate permission has been obtained from the relevant local authorities to transfer the business to a new company and the relevant statutory tax clearances were obtained (see 13.95 above).

Main tax implications of statutory demerger

The proposed statutory demerger takes place on 31 October 2017 in the form of a distribution under *CTA 2010, s 1077 (1)(a)(i)* – ie a 'type 2' demerger (see 13.84, 13.87 and 13.91 above). Thus, the 'care homes' assets and trade will be transferred to a new company (Winston's Quality Care Homes Ltd (WQCH) in consideration of a fresh issue of shares in WQCH, as illustrated below:

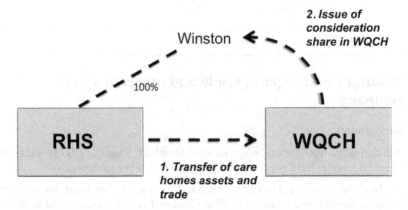

Since the transaction satisfies the statutory demerger rules, the distribution made by RHS would be exempt from income tax in Winston's hands (see 13.85).

Since the demerger has been motivated by commercial reasons (see above), *TCGA 1992, s 139* would enable the chargeable assets (such as property and goodwill) to be transferred on a no gain/no loss basis. Thus, no tax liability would arise in RHS relating to these assets (see 13.87).

Part of Winston's original base cost of his RHS shareholding will be attributed to his new WQCH shares under *TCGA 1992, s 136* under the CGT share reorganisation rule. *TCGA 1992, ss 136* and *127* effectively ensure that Winston would not have any taxable capital distribution on the receipt of his 'consideration' shares in WQCH.

Importantly, there should be no SDLT liability on the properties transferred since the SDLT reconstruction provisions in FA *2003, Sch 7, para 7*, should apply (the shareholdings in both RHS and WQCH will 'mirror' each other) (see 13.73).

Chargeable payments

13.96 Any 'non-commercial' payment (broadly representing the value of the demerged assets/shares) made to shareholders within five years of the demerger is taxed as income. The payment is not an allowable deduction for corporation tax purposes.

A chargeable payment would also lead to a withdrawal of the de-grouping charges exemption (but not the other 'demerger' and 'reconstruction' reliefs).

The chargeable payments rules are very widely drawn in *CTA 2010, ss 1086–1090* and it is normally advisable to seek advance clearance from HMRC under *CTA 2010, s 1092* that any contemplated 'payment' would not be caught.

Practical case involving chargeable payments and subsequent sale

13.96A In practice, probably the most important restriction is the one that denies statutory demerger treatment where it is intended to sell the demerged company. In some cases, it may be necessary to demonstrate to HMRC that at the time the demerger was executed there was no intention to sell the demerged company.

The author advised on a transaction where HMRC were sceptical about the directors' plans following the demerger of a subsidiary. Shortly after the demerger, the directors received an 'unsolicited' offer from a large corporate group to acquire 100% of the recently demerged company. This potential purchaser had demonstrated sound strategic reasons for seeking the acquisition. The offer was received just a few months after the demerger had been completed. A satisfactory demerger clearance had been obtained from HMRC, following an application which cited genuine commercial reasons for the demerger (which included the need to cater for different management styles and responsibilities over two distinct trades as well as key issues surrounding finance, risk and ease of administration).

After considerable discussions, the shareholders agreed to sell the company for a substantial amount payable over a period of three years, dependent upon achievement of certain targets.

Because of the earlier 'statutory demerger', the purchaser had obvious concerns that the payment of the purchase consideration could be regarded as a chargeable payment given the relatively wide scope of *CTA 2010, ss 1088* and *1089*. This included any payment motivated by tax avoidance reasons which is made to a shareholder of the demerged company. If the amount was considered a 'chargeable payment', it would be taxed as income and would also nullify any de-grouping charge protection (see 13.92), although the other demerger reliefs remain undisturbed.

For various reasons, the purchaser insisted that confirmation from HMRC was sought under *CTA 2010, s 1092* that the sale consideration (including the deferred payments) was being paid for genuine commercial reasons and would not be treated as a chargeable payment. After making considerable enquires into the offer letter and negotiations surrounding the sale, HMRC were satisfied that there was no intention to sell the demerged company at the time of the demerger. HMRC accepted that the sale proceeds were not chargeable payments, and therefore fell to be treated as a normal capital gain.

Key VAT issues on demergers

13.97 If there is a direct 'statutory' demerger distribution of shares in a 75% subsidiary (see 13.86), there is no consideration, so there should be no supply for VAT purposes.

Contrastingly, on an 'indirect' type of demerger, the transferee company issues its shares in consideration for the transfer of the business or shares in a subsidiary company, thus creating a supply for VAT purposes.

In the context of a demerger, HMRC are likely to contend that the vast majority of the legal, professional and other relevant costs relate to exempt supplies of the transfer of the demerged companies. Thus, the input tax directly related to these costs will fall to be irrecoverable (subject to the possible application of the VAT grouping and partial exemption *de minimis* rules). See also HMRC's VAT input tax manual – VIT40100 to VIT64050.

To the extent that the costs can be allocated to the issue of shares, it may be possible to reclaim the related input VAT. The ECJ in *Kretztechnic AG v Finanzamt Linz* (C-465/03) ruled that the issue of shares did not create any supply for VAT purposes (see 12.62). Consequently, provided the issuing company only makes taxable supplies, the 'share issue' input tax can be fully deducted as a general business overhead.

If the demerger involves the transfer of a business/assets as a going concern (see 13.78), the input VAT on the related legal and professional costs should be recoverable under the 'general business overheads' rules. Thus, if the company is 'fully taxable' for VAT, this will enable it to recover all the VAT.

RETURN OF CAPITAL DEMERGERS

Inserting a new holding company

13.98 The *Companies Act 2006* enables private companies to reduce their share capital without having to seek 'court permission', provided certain statutory safeguards are complied with (see 13.60).

A demerger can therefore be structured as a return of capital, which means that the shareholders do not suffer any income tax charge under the distribution legislation. This is achieved by ensuring that the demerged companies represent a 'repayment of capital' on their shares.

It is therefore usually necessary to 'interpose' a new holding company under a share for share exchange so that it can reflect the market value of the group. Since the legal analysis is that the shareholders have 'subscribed' for the new shares in the holding company at a full 'market value' consideration, this should provide sufficient 'capital' to 'frank' the demerger distribution under company law principles.

From a tax perspective, the demerged company/companies will not create a taxable distribution since the amount received will represent a repayment of capital (*CTA 2010, s 1000(1B)(a)*).

From a CGT perspective, the share exchange should fall within the relieving provisions of *TCGA 1992, s 135*. Thus, the shareholders would swap their shares in the original company for shares in the holding company without triggering a CGT disposal (see 15.48). HMRC should accept that the share exchange is being undertaken for legitimate reasons, but it is recommended that confirmation from HMRC be obtained using the advance clearance procedure in *TCGA 1992, s138*. Generally one combined clearance application would be made (see 13.83).

Stamp duty exemption and the *FA 1986, s 77A* 'disqualifying arrangements' rule

13.98A 'Mirror-image' share for share exchanges where the 'selling' shareholders proportionate holdings and share classes etc are maintained in the new holding company should qualify for the stamp duty exemption in *FA 1986, s 77*. Thus, the new holding company would not incur any stamp duty on its acquisition of the shares in the original (target) company.

Relief under *FA 1986, s 77* is claimed after the share exchange has taken place by making a written application to the Stamp Taxes Office in Birmingham. HMRC has set out a suggested draft *s 77* claim letter (indicating the information that must be provided) at www.gov.uk/hmrc-internal-manuals/stamp-taxes-shares-manual/stsm042430.

However, many 'capital reduction' demergers are likely to involve a subsequent 'change in the control' in the holding company, typically when the demerged company is transferred out. From 29 June 2016, the *FA 2016* introduced a new anti-avoidance rule – *FA 1986, s 77A* – which denies the *FA 1986* stamp duty exemption where, at the time of the share exchange, there are 'disqualifying arrangements'. Broadly, this would be the case where it is reasonable to assume that the main or one of the main purposes of the arrangements is to secure that a particular person or persons will obtain control of the acquiring company (ie the new holding company).

For these purposes, the *CTA 2010, s 1124* definition of 'control' applies for this purpose. This stipulates that someone has the requisite control where they have *the* majority shareholder voting rights (under the articles or a shareholders agreement) or where they have the power to appoint the majority of directors. The key point is that through such means someone has the power to conduct the company's affairs in accordance with their wishes. *Irving v Tesco Stores (Holdings)* [1982] STC 881 contains a useful commentary on *ICTA 1988, s 840*, which was the identical predecessor provision.

The steps required for a typical capital reduction demerger are pre-planned before the individual steps are set in motion (see 13.98D). Consequently, *FA 1986, s 77A* will often deny the *FA 1986, s 77* stamp duty exemption for the acquisition of the original company's shares by the new holding company, where the effect of the demerger is to split different trades/businesses between different shareholder(s), even if they are family members. This means that the acquiring company will generally be subject to stamp duty at 0.5% on the consideration given for the shares in the target company.

Many advisers consider that *FA 1986, s 77A* should not be applied to genuine 'capital reduction' demerger arrangements, particularly since a further stamp duty charge will often arise on the subsequent transfer of the target company's shares to the recipient shareholders new company (in consideration for an issue of shares to them).

In contrast, where the demerger simply splits the company's/group's trades/ businesses between the *same* shareholders through different entities, *FA 1986, s 77A* is unlikely to bite.

Merger relief and accounting for share exchange in Newco

13.98B   Where a new holding company (Newco) is 'inserted' above an existing company under the share exchange rules in *TCGA 1992, s 135* (see 13.98) – for example prior to a capital reduction demerger – the legal requirements for 'merger relief' in *Companies Act 2006, s 612* are likely to be satisfied.

Under normal legal principles, the difference between the nominal value of the shares issued by Newco and the market value of the acquired company (Target) would be transferred to a share premium account (*CA 2006, s 610* and *Shearer v Bercain* [1980] 3 All ER 295).

However, merger relief under *CA 2006, s 612* relieves Newco from the requirement to create a share premium account in these cases. To put it another way, it relieves Newco from the requirement to record the issue of the shares at fair value.

Broadly speaking, merger relief applies where Newco issues equity shares and, as a result, it becomes the holder of at least 90% of the equity shares in the target company (Target). Many learned authorities consider the application of merger relief to be compulsory based on the wording of *CA 2006, s 612(2)*. For example, see *Deloitte GAAP 2017 – Volume A* at 2.15.2 (Wolters Kluwer), *PWC's Manual of Accounting – New UK GAAP* (3rd edn) at 22.56, and *Sale of Shares and Businesses by Andrew Stilton* – (2015, Sweet & Maxwell) at 16.15.4. Probably the most important advantage given by merger relief is that Target's pre-acquisition profits would be available for distribution. However, in the context of a 'capital reduction' demerger, this may not be so important, since Target will subsequently be transferred, this is not so important in the context of a 'capital reduction' demerger.

However, there also appears to be a respectable view that merger relief is optional, as expressed in *Ernst & Young New UK GAAP* (2014 edn, at 25.49) and Bill Telford and Lynne Oats *Accounting Principles For Tax Purposes* (2014 edn) at Example 25.1. Some also consider that using merger relief on a share exchange that is taking place before a 'demerger' by capital reduction does not reflect commercial reality.

Where merger relief is taken, Newco can effectively choose to state its investment in Target at:

- the nominal value of the issued shares (by virtue of the relief given in *CA 2006, s 615*); or

- fair market value, taking the difference to a 'merger reserve' (as opposed to a share premium).

Perhaps more confusingly, the author has seen many companies account for the cost of investment at fair market value and record the difference as a 'share premium' account. Many accountants would recognise this as 'acquisition accounting' or purchase accounting.

From a cosmetic viewpoint, many would argue that acquisition accounting is more transparent and in accordance with the economic reality of the demerger transaction. If Newco applies merger relief and accounts and records the investment at nominal value, HMRC might seek to ask questions about the tax analysis!

As far as capital reduction arrangements are concerned, it is important to note that a 'merger reserve' does *not* form part of share capital (see 13.60). Therefore, it is *not* possible to use a merger reserve to facilitate a capital reduction demerger. In cases where Newco has recorded a 'merger reserve', it should be possible for it to be used to create a fully paid up bonus issue of shares. Subsequently, this could be used as share capital (which could then be used as part of the capital reduction demerger)

The reader will appreciate that the applicability of merger relief is not clear-cut. However, where the parties have carried out a 'capital reduction' demerger in good faith, it is possible that a court may seek to uphold those intentions.

However, as a matter of tax law, the shareholders of Target who sell their shares to Newco would be treated as having given full market value consideration for their Newco shares for 'distribution' purposes (although the tax 'new for old' fiction still applies for CGT purposes – see 15.48).

It should be mentioned that merger relief is not the same as merger accounting. Merger accounting is used when preparing *consolidated* accounts and avoids having to fair value the assets/liabilities at the date of the 'combination' and enables the results of the combined businesses to be reported as though they were a continuing business. With merger accounting, the consideration shares are recorded at nominal value and there is no need to recognise any pre-acquisition profits. FRS 102 permits merger accounting for group re-organisations where there is no change in the ultimate share ownership, but acquisition or 'purchase' accounting may be used if preferred

For the reasons given above, the author's preferred approach now is to arrange for Newco to obtain a robust valuation of Target (which would be important for 'distribution' purposes) and issue a suitable amount of shares equal to this value. Thus, for example, if Target were valued at (say) £4 million, Newco would issue four million of ordinary shares at £1 each. This avoids having to deal with any share premium or merger reserve issues!

From a company law viewpoint, as long as the directors have obtained a robust independent valuation, they would be considered to have acted reasonably.

Example 13

Accounting for a share exchange

The shareholder of Boyce (1965) Ltd is about to undertake a 'capital reduction' demerger. Boyce (1965) Ltd currently has 1,000 £1 ordinary shares and it carries on two trades, which have been professionally valued at £5 million.

As part of this process, they arrange for a new holding company, Greenwood Holdco Ltd, to acquire 100% of Boyce (1965) Ltd in consideration for a new issue of five million £1 ordinary shares.

Greenwood Holding Ltd's summarised balance sheet immediately after its acquisition of 100% of Boyce (1965) Ltd would be as follows:

	£'000
Investment in Boyce (1965) Ltd	5,000
Share capital	
5,000,001* £1 ordinary shares	5,000

*Includes one subscriber share

Structure of a typical capital reduction demerger

13.98D In many ways, a demerger by capital reduction involves using many of the principles and tax reliefs already discussed in this Chapter.

One of the key considerations in any form of demerger/reorganisation is to avoid a distribution tax charge arising in the shareholders' hands in respect of the demerged business(es). A capital reduction demerger avoids a distribution since it is based on the analysis that the shareholders are 'receiving' a return of capital (see 13.98).

The design and implementation of a typical capital reduction demerger is illustrated in Example 14 below.

Example 14

Capital reduction demerger involving separation of trading and property investment activities

Background

Arnautović Coaches Ltd (ACL) was incorporated in April 1989 and over the last ten years it has established two separate divisions:

- The coach operating business, which is based at premises the company owns at Potters Industrial Estate, Stoke.

- The property rental business consists of the letting of various business units situated at The Twente Business Centre (TBC), Stratford, which the company owns.

For many years, the shares in ACL have been owned as follows:

	£1 Ord shares
Marko Arnau	60
Emilia Wein	30
Sarah Bremen	10

ACL's directors Marko, Emilia and Sarah are siblings

Marko runs the coach operating business and Emilia and Jennie operate the property letting business.

The directors have discussed the possibility of 'partitioning' the company's business activities for many months. This has largely been driven by their desire to manage the activities they run on a day-to-day business within separate business entities free from the personal interference of their 'other' directors!

However, to avoid the commercial upheaval of transferring coach operating licences etc, ACL must retain the coach operating business at all costs.

After the demerger, Marko would have sole ownership and management of the coach operating trade. His sisters wish to own and look after the property letting business.

Tentative valuations have been prepared for the purposes of the demerger. After appropriate allocation of the bank and shareholder debt, the coach operating and property letting business has been valued at £4.5 million and £3 million respectively. These values have been arrived at to ensure they reflect the underlying shareholdings.

Main consideration for structuring demerger

It is not possible for ACL to use a statutory demerger since the property letting division would be an investment business (which is not permitted (*CTA 2010, s 1081(2)*) (see 13.94).

Although a liquidation 'demerger' using *Insolvency Act 1986, s 110* is possible, this would involve liquidation costs etc (see 13.63). Also, both divisions and the relevant assets may have to be transferred out of ACL, which is undesirable and will increase the stamp tax costs.

The parties agree that the most tax and commercially efficient form of demerger would be via a reduction of share capital under the *Companies Act 2006, s 641* (see 13.98). The demerger would be structured on the basis that the coach operating business must remain in ACL.

Possible demerger structure and tax analysis

A suitable demerger arrangement might be as follows:

- Step 1 – Insertion of a new company (Newco) over ACL by way of a share for share exchange.

- Step 2 – Transfer of the property letting business to Newco via a distribution in specie.

- Step 3 – Reorganisation of Newco's share capital to reflect the proposed equity interests in the two business divisions following the reconstruction.

- Step 4 – Transfer of the shares in ACL to another new company (Marko Ltd), via a reduction of Newco's capital.

The various steps and the tax analysis are considered below:

Step 1 – Under the share exchange, the ACL shareholders will receive shares in Newco in exact proportion to their holdings in ACL. This share exchange should therefore fall within the CGT reorganisation rules in *TCGA 1992, ss 127 and 135* (see 15.48 and 13.98).

The consideration given by the ACL shareholders for their subscription for the shares in Newco will equal the value of their existing shares in ACL, totalling some £7.5 million (£4.5 million + £3 million) (see *Step 4*).

Since there would be a change in the control of Newco (under *Step 4*), stamp duty relief under *FA 1986, s 77* is unlikely to be available.

FA 1986, s 77A (see 13.98A). The stamp duty cost would be around £37,500 (£7.5 million × 0.5%).

Step 2 – The property letting business (ie The Twente Business Centre Units and related assets) would be distributed in specie to Newco (due to the requirement to retain the coach operating business in ACL).

On the basis that Newco assumes no debt, there should be no SDLT on the transfer of the property assets to Newco via a distribution in specie (see 9.9). It will be necessary to ensure that ACL has sufficient distributable reserves/revaluation reserves to 'frank' the in-specie distribution (see 13.101). This avoids the need to rely on the SDLT group transfer relief rules, which contain clawback and degrouping rules (see 3.37).

The transfer will be deemed to take place on a 'no gain/no loss' basis for corporate gains purposes under *TCGA 1992, s 171*.

Step 3 – To facilitate a distribution of the coach operating business (in the form of the shares in ACL), there will be a prior reorganisation of Newco's share capital. The existing 'Newco' ordinary shares would be reclassified into:

- C shares, which would be entitled to the profits, assets, and voting rights relating to the coach operating business.

- R shares, which would be entitled to the profits, assets, and voting rights relating to the property letting business.

The alteration of the shares and their re-categorisation should fall within the CGT reorganisation rules in *TCGA 1992, s 126*. Thus, for the shareholders, their new C and R shares would 'step into the shoes' of their previous shareholdings.

At this stage, the corporate structure would be as follows:

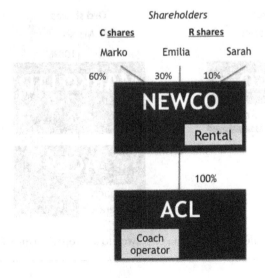

Step 4 – Newco will distribute the shares in ACL to another new company, Marko Ltd by way of a reduction of its share capital. Newco would transfer its ACL shares to Marko Ltd in consideration of a fresh issue of 'Marko Ltd' shares to Marko (ie the 'C' shareholder).

After this transfer, the C shares in Newco (being of no economic value) would be cancelled.

Full control of Newco would then vest in the R shareholders. This is why *FA 1986, s 77A* would deny stamp duty share exchange relief being claimed in *Step 1*.

The capital reduction would be carried out under the procedure outlined in *Companies Act 2006, Pt 17, Ch 10*. The transfer of the ACL shares effectively constitutes a repayment of the capital the shareholders had given for the shares issued by Newco – therefore no distribution arises for tax purposes (see 13.98).

Newco's transfer of the shares in ACL fall within the corporate gains reconstruction rules in *TCGA 1992, s 139*, and hence a no gain/no loss disposal treatment would apply.

Marko would obtain shareholder gains reconstruction relief under *TCGA 1992, s 136* on the receipt of his new shares in Marko Ltd.

Newco leaves the 'Newco group' (as a result of the distribution of ACL) but no degrouping charge should arise in respect of the property transferred to it under *Step 2* due to HMRC's 'two-company group practice' (see HMRC CG45410 – Special rule 5).

The final corporate structure will be:

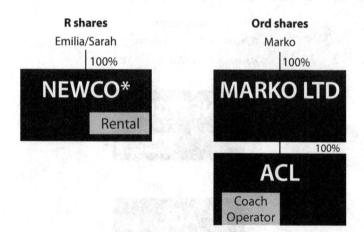

*Emilia and Sarah would alter the name of Newco to a 'proper' business name.

COMPANIES ACT REQUIREMENTS – DEMERGER DISTRIBUTIONS AND OTHER INTRA-GROUP TRANSFERS

Legality of demerger and other reorganisation transfers

13.99 The company law implications must always be considered when structuring a statutory demerger. The *Companies Act 2006* seeks to provide certainty on the treatment of demerger distributions and other 'pre-reorganisation' asset transfers to fellow group companies. Such demergers and other transfers must satisfy certain legal requirements; otherwise the transaction may be set-aside and negate all or part of the intended demerger or reorganisation.

The 'Aveling Barford' case

13.100 The case of *Aveling Barford Ltd v Perion Ltd* [1989] BCLC 677 created a number of uncertainties in relation to the commercial price at which assets should be transferred, and still remains good law for companies that have negative reserves.

Broadly, Aveling Barford (which was in financial difficulties and had negative reserves of around £18m) sold a large site (its employees' sports field!) to Perion (which was effectively a commonly controlled company). The sale was completed in February 1987 at an agreed price of £350,000, although the property was worth considerably more. Later, in August 1987, the site was sold for some £1,560,000.

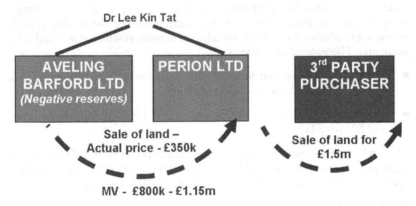

Mr Justice Hoffmann held that the sale at undervalue to Perion was a breach of the director's fiduciary duty. Furthermore, the grossly undervalued sale enabled Perion to realise a profit. Perion was controlled and 'introduced' by its sole beneficial shareholder. It therefore followed that the transaction was a 'dressed-up' distribution. Since Aveling Barford had a deficit on its reserves, this meant there was an unauthorised return of capital, which was ultra vires (and the transaction was incapable of being ratified by shareholders).

The *Aveling Barford* decision made clear that where a company has negative reserves, a transfer at below book value is an unlawful distribution. Its implication where a company has positive reserves is less clear. Before the *CA 2006*, it was generally thought that where transfer took place at book value, there should be no legal distribution, although there was some doubt since there was often an 'undervalue' element in the transfer. Some thought that a company required sufficient reserves to cover any excess of market value over sale price. However, a transfer at market value could never create an unlawful return of capital.

For further detailed discussion on the legal issues surrounding distributions and dividends, see 9.2–9.7.

It should be appreciated that the *CA 2006* concepts of a distribution are different from those that apply for tax purposes. Broadly, the main tax distribution rules are set out in *CTA 2010, s 1000*. As a general rule, tax law determines that a (taxable) distribution arises on the transfer of assets to a shareholder to the extent that the *market value* of the assets transferred exceeds any consideration paid/given by the shareholder.

Companies Act 2006 requirements

13.101 The *CA 2006* now makes clear the measure of any distribution for assets for *company law* purposes. *CA 2006, s 845* provides that, where a company has distributable reserves, the measure of any distribution is based on the book value of the asset (ie broadly the amount at which it is stated in the accounts). The general principles are:

- where the transfer consideration (TC) of an asset is at least equal to its book value (BV), there is no distribution;

- where the TC of an asset is less than its BV, the distribution is the excess of BV over TC.

Thus, where a company has realised profits, assets can be transferred at their book value without creating a distribution (although, of course, this is likely to create a distribution for tax purposes under *CTA 2010, s 1000*).

Similarly, where a company is about to undertake a statutory demerger distribution, it must have sufficient distributable profits to cover the carrying book value of the subsidiary/assets being 'demerged'. In such cases there is no TC and therefore the distribution amount under company law (but not for tax purposes) is simply the BV of the net assets or the shares in the 75% subsidiaries.

For these purposes, revaluation surpluses that have been booked in the accounts can be treated as realised profits under *CA 2006, s 846*. This will typically apply where properties have been subject to a prior revaluation. In such cases, the revaluation surplus can effectively be applied as part of the 'distributable profits' for the purpose of the in-specie distribution of the property.

The principles in *Aveling Barford* (see 13.100) remain relevant for companies that have no distributable profits. In such cases, where assets are transferred at an undervaluation, this will be an unlawful distribution.

Directors should also be mindful of their fiduciary duties. In some cases, it may therefore be prudent to transfer the assets at their full market value. If the transferring company went into liquidation or administration, transfers at 'market value' would not be vulnerable to being overturned under 'two-year' rule in *Insolvency Act 1986, s 238*.

Accounting for demerger transactions

13.102   Section 5 of FRS 102 is likely to apply to the treatment of the demerged business in the distributing company's profit and loss account – for example, if the demerged business meets the criteria for a 'discontinued operation', the results of the demerged business may need to be separately disclosed on the statutory profit and loss account.

The key accounting issue will generally be the measure of the distribution in the accounts. This will follow the *CA 2006* principles outlined in 13.101 above. Consequently, the demerger distribution would be recorded in the *accounts of the distributing company* at the *carrying cost* of the relevant net assets or shares that are being demerged. The fair or market value of the assets is irrelevant for these purposes.

The company must have sufficient distributable reserves to make a distribution of this amount. However, *CA 2006, s 841(5)* provides that any revaluation reserve arising on the relevant properties being transferred (or any merger reserve created when a demerged subsidiary was originally acquired) can be treated as distributable for these purposes (only).

Demerger costs would normally be charged to the profit and loss account as exceptional reorganisation costs (see 13.61 for tax treatment).

However, if the distributing company produces consolidated accounts, a demerger distribution of a subsidiary will show the distribution at the group's share of the demerged subsidiary's assets (including goodwill) at the date of the demerger.

Example 15

Accounting for statutory demerger of trade and assets

Based on the 'statutory demerger' in Example 12 above, assume that the carrying value of the relevant care home assets to be demerged were as follows:

	£ million
Care home properties	13.5
Net current assets re Care homes (ie consumables, debtors less creditors)	0.7
	14.2

RHS's accounts at 31 October 2017 show retained reserves of around £20 million and a revaluation reserve of £6 million, £2 million of which relates to the care homes properties.

RHS can therefore record the demerger distribution in its accounts at £14.2 million, with £2 million coming from the revaluation reserve and the balance of £12.2 million being deducted from the retained (distributable) reserves.

PLANNING CHECKLIST – SHARE TRANSFERS, SHARE BUY-BACKS AND COMPANY REORGANISATIONS/DEMERGERS

Company

- Several businesses can normally be partitioned amongst different shareholders on a broadly tax-neutral basis under a non-statutory 'liquidation'/capital reduction demerger or a statutory demerger.

- A 'partition' arrangement may be helpful where a company or group has a mixture of both trading and investment businesses. The partition of a property letting or property dealing business is likely to be charged at full SDLT rates, but pure reconstructions remain unaffected. A pure reconstruction (where the shareholdings remain the same) may also be driven by the desire to reduce the business risk attaching to certain trades within the existing company or group.

- A *TCGA 1992, s 139* reconstruction transfer of shares in a (75%) subsidiary enables any de-grouping gains to be exempted under the deemed 'no gain/no loss' consideration rule. However, intangibles degrouping charges are not protected on a reconstruction

- The Substantial Shareholdings Exemption may apply to direct demerger distributions of '75%' trading subsidiaries (which should also be exempt from stamp duty).

- Statutory demergers avoid a liquidation but can only be carried out where the distributing company has sufficient distributable reserves to execute a demerger distribution equivalent to the 'carrying cost' (per the accounts) of the assets/shares transferred. Such demergers cannot be implemented where there are plans to sell the demerged company. In such cases, it *may* be possible to use a liquidation-based or 'capital reduction' 'non-statutory demerger' under *Insolvency Act, s 110* (provided this is done well ahead of any prospective sale and certainly before the potential purchaser is identified).

- It is frequently possible to structure a (non-statutory) demerger under the *CA 2006* reduction of capital rules. This avoids the complications and costs that arise with a liquidation-based demerger. However, since 29 June 2016, *FA 1986, s 77A* may deny the normal *FA 1986, s 77* stamp duty exemption on the preparatory share exchange. This should only be the case where there is a split of the relevant trades/business amongst different shareholders.

- Where a company is unable to pay dividends due to a shortage of distributable reserves, it may be possible to create additional reserves by using the *CA 2006* procedures to reduce share capital.

- Employee share schemes will generally 'cease' on a demerger and consideration will need to be given to 'replacement' share schemes etc.

Working shareholders

- In many cases, shares awarded or option shares exercised in private companies are only subject to the standard Companies Act model articles or old Table A conditions. There still remains some uncertainty about whether such shares would be regarded as 'restricted securities'. However, even where the relevant shares are unlikely to be 'restricted', it is still generally prudent to make a 'defence' *ITEPA 2003, s 431* election.

- Where shares are subject to substantive restrictions on transfer or forfeiture, etc (that reduce their value), they are likely to constitute 'restricted securities'. In such cases, the recipient director/employee would suffer an employment income tax charge on the restricted value of the shares (less any amount paid for them). However, it will normally be beneficial for them to make an election under *ITEPA 2003, s 431* to be taxed on the 'unrestricted value' of the shares up-front (and/or pay that amount for the shares).

- Funds can be extracted from the company on the shareholder's retirement in a capital gains-efficient manner by arranging for the company to buy back the shares. To obtain CGT treatment, it is important to demonstrate that any buy-back motivated by retirement will benefit the ongoing trade of the company.

- Capital gains tax treatment on a share buy-back is generally only available where the shares have been held for at least five years. In many cases, the outgoing shareholder will be able to reduce their CGT liability by claiming the lower ER 10% rate.

Other employees

- Shares awarded or shares acquired under an option (at less than their money's worth) may constitute 'restricted securities'. In such cases, it will normally be advisable to make an election under *ITEPA 2003, s 431* to be taxed on the initial 'unrestricted value' of the shares.

- They can look to the company to buy their shares where they wish to cease their involvement with the company. The value paid for their shares often depends on whether they are classed as a 'good' leaver (for example, ill-health or have reached retirement age) or a 'bad' leaver.

Non-working shareholders

- Non-working shareholders may not be able to benefit from ER on a share buy-back unless they hold an office with the company (such as being a non-executive director).

- Non-working shareholders must participate in a corporate reconstruction.

Chapter 14

Valuing a Family or Owner-Managed Company

INTRODUCTION

14.1 Share valuations are required in a variety of situations. Commercial valuations fix the price at which shares in unquoted companies should change hands in actual transactions, or where a valuation is sought for the purposes of a divorce settlement, financing arrangement, or unfair prejudice action by a minority shareholder.

Tax legislation also requires shares to be valued in various circumstances, giving rise to the need for fiscal or tax-based valuations. This chapter discusses commercial and tax based valuations. It will be seen that, although similar concepts apply to both these types of valuation, there are marked differences in approach.

COMMERCIAL VALUATIONS

14.2 Commercial share valuations determine the price to be paid for the shares where, for example:

(*a*) the shareholders wish to sell the company or a prospective purchaser wishes to make an offer for the company;

(*b*) a shareholder is retiring and is required to sell his shares to the other shareholders or back to the company under an own share purchase (see 13.41–13.59).

The price will essentially be negotiated, based on all the relevant circumstances at that time.

A commercial value inevitably reflects the circumstances of both the vendor and the purchaser in that it seeks to arrive at a negotiated value reflecting that which the vendor is giving up and that which the purchaser acquires as a result of the acquisition.

VALUATIONS REQUIRED UNDER THE COMPANY'S ARTICLES OF ASSOCIATION

14.3   The Articles of Association for the vast majority of private companies will contain pre-emption provisions restricting the shareholder's ability to transfer their shares. Typically, any shareholder proposing to transfer their shares (other than to a member of their family or family trust) is obliged to offer them first to the other shareholders, or the directors, or to someone nominated by the directors. These provisions will need to be examined carefully where the shareholder wishes to dispose of their shares on 'retirement', etc.

The Articles will also provide a mechanism for fixing the price (value) and often require the amount to be determined by the company's auditors. The Articles may, for example, require the auditors to value the shares on a discounted minority basis or on a full pro-rata one (usually adopting a 'quasi-partnership' approach – see 14.27). A full pro-rata value would normally be such proportion of the (full 'control') value of the entire equity shares as the relevant shares (being valued) bear to the total number of issued equity shares.

Alternatively, the transferor may be required to state the price required for their shares and this will be used, provided that the directors agree it. In some cases, the Articles may provide a formula to be used by the auditor or other professional 'valuer'. A requirement to value the shares at their 'fair' value differs from the 'market value' basis insofar as it is presumed to be *fair to both parties* to the transaction.

Such share valuations are often based on a straight pro-rata proportion of the company's value. The Law Commission report on *'Shareholder Remedies'* (Law Com No 246) proposed that the company's shareholders should be able to elect for the valuation to be discounted for minority shareholdings. A 'fair value' basis may also be relevant where a company purchases its own shares. The value placed on the vendor's shares may need to reflect some of the increase in value accruing to the other shareholders (resulting from the increase in their proportionate holdings following the 'buy-in').

UNFAIR PREJUDICE ACTIONS

14.4   A court has a general power to make any order it sees fit under *Companies Act 2006, s 994*. However, in most cases involving disputes between shareholders, the court will order the purchase of the minority shares at a 'fair value' either by the other shareholders or by the company itself. Although courts also have the power to grant a winding-up order, they are unlikely to use it where petitioners have another available remedy and they are acting unreasonably in pursuing a winding-up instead (*Re a Company (No 003028 of 1987)* [1988] BCLC 282. A winding-up order is generally used as a last resort.

Thus, an independent 'fair valuation' is frequently required for the purposes of making an offer to buy the shares of a minority shareholder (petitioner). Minority shareholdings are generally sold at a discount to reflect the fact the shares do not confer control of the company (see 14.37–14.39). However, the position of the shareholder who may be regarded as a quasi-partner is less clear (see 14.27). It is often argued that no discount should be applied to the value of the share of a 'quasi-partner' shareholder but the case of *Irvine v Irvine* [2006] EWHC 1875 (Ch) shows that this may not always be appropriate.

VALUE OF COMPANY

Gathering empirical data of similar deals, etc

14.5   Where the shareholders are seeking to sell the entire company, they will require an indication of how much the company is worth. The capitalised earnings basis (ie applying an appropriate multiple to the sustainable profits of the business) is the principal determinant of value. Empirical evidence of prices at which similar/comparable businesses have recently changed hands will provide a very important guide. Details of recent disposals can be obtained from a wide variety of sources, including:

- The Financial Times (historical statistics);

- Reuters Investor (www.reuters.co.uk);

- Acquisitions Monthly;

- Investors Chronicle

- BDO Private Company Price Index (see 15.19) ;

- CORPFIN and similar databases; and

- Industry trade press.

The general economic climate, the state of the particular industry in which the company trades and its particular position within it will also influence the valuation.

In many ways, a company is worth what somebody is prepared to pay for it. Consequently, the 'price' can also reflect the prospective purchaser's rationale for acquiring the business, for example, to achieve increased market share, economies of scale and so on. An attempt should be made to quantify the financial benefits (such as post-acquisition synergies, etc) accruing to the purchaser.

Capitalised earnings model

14.6   The commercial valuation of a company or business is essentially a matter for negotiation between the vendor and the purchaser. The basic approach is to determine what the company or business can earn or realise. The majority of company and business valuations are based on earnings. A capitalised earnings valuation requires an estimate of the business's future maintainable earnings and the application of an appropriate rate of return or price/earnings (P/E) multiple.

Standard industry methods

14.7 It should be noted that certain industries have well established 'benchmark' valuation methods. For example hotels (price per room), advertising agencies (multiple of billings), professional firms (multiple of fee income), radio stations (multiple of hours listened), etc. These valuations are geared to the fact that the purchaser is willing to pay for turnover or market share and that profitability and margins are relatively similar within a given industry sector.

This practice has recently been highlighted in the case of *Wildin v HMRC* [2014] UKFTT 459 (TC), which involved the valuation of goodwill for tax purposes on the incorporation of an accountancy firm (as well as the March 1982 value of the goodwill).

The First-Tier Tribunal (FTT) acknowledged that valuation is an art not a science and that its job was 'to ascertain the best method for valuing goodwill for this taxpayer on these facts and on the basis that no method will provide a perfect answer'. The FTT therefore felt able to place great reliance on the empirical evidence and concluded that the firm's goodwill should simply be calculated by reference to a multiple of its gross recurring fees, since many accountancy practices change hands on this basis. HMRC's argument (based on many accepted authorities) that the firm's net assets should reduce the fee multiple-valuation was rejected.

Discounted cash flow basis

14.8 Some would argue that the value of a controlling interest should be based on discounted cash flow (DCF) as the purchaser/investor is ultimately only interested in cash generation (which is not affected by accounting policies). This approach would require details of the forecast cash flows over a substantial period of time, which would then be discounted at an appropriate interest rate – the interest rate would reflect the time value of money and the investor's perception of the risk inherent in the investment. The sum of the discounted cash flows would give the net present value of the investment.

A DCF valuation may be used for new business ventures where there is no track record or trading history – such as e-commerce business applications, or where the business has an erratic cash flow profile.

Although this is a theoretically defensible approach, in practice the purchaser/investor often has insufficient details to perform this type of calculation.

MAINTAINABLE EARNINGS

14.9

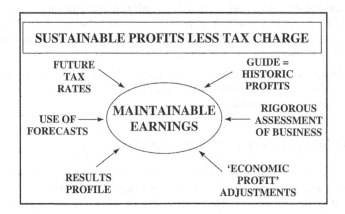

Determining the sustainable profits

14.10   The principal determinant of business valuations is usually the capitalised earnings basis. Historic profits are generally taken as a starting point for determining a company's *maintainable or sustainable profits* as they are based on actual trading results and provide readily ascertainable (and audited) figures.

Maintainable earnings represent the maintainable profits after deducting the appropriate future tax charge (and any preference dividend). A useful working definition of 'maintainable profits' would be 'the level below which, in the absence of unforeseen and exceptional circumstances, the profits would not be likely to fall in an average year'.

Historical profits will only provide a guide to the business's future maintainable earnings. A rigorous assessment of the company's reported accounting profits will be required to quantify the adjustments needed to arrive at the true sustainable economic profit of the business.

Potential items that may require adjustment are:

● any exceptional or non-recurring items – such as the loss of a major customer or substantial bad debt write off, profits or/and losses on the sale of fixed assets, investments, etc;

● income and expenses relating to discontinued or new operations and products;

● departures from generally accepted accounting principles (GAAP);

- excessive directors' remuneration and benefits, pension contributions and so on, which reflect returns to the directors in their capacity as owner-shareholders – this 'excess' element is effectively a 'quasi-dividend', as this would not be paid to an arm's length management team (conversely, if the directors extract 'their' profits wholly or substantially as dividends the profits will need to be adjusted to reflect the commercial costs for their management or other roles in the business);

- business transactions that are not conducted on arm's length terms, such as the benefit of an interest-free loan from a controlling shareholder or fellow group company.

Indicators of future sustainable profits

14.11 It is important to remember that the historical profits are being used as a guide to the business's *future* profit levels. As a general rule, if the adjusted profits reflect a stable position, it will often be appropriate to use the last reported results as a basis for the future maintainable profits. Where the trading history is volatile, a 'judgemental' average may be used. Weighted averages should not always be applied as a matter of course, as their theoretical justification is weak. The valuer may be required to exercise a commercial judgement to evaluate the business's prospective profits.

Forecasts or projections may be used as a guide, provided that it is recognised that they are based on certain assumptions and are potentially unreliable (vendors clearly have a 'vested' interest in suggesting high future profits!). Future trading plans (such as the impact of new products) and market conditions must also be 'factored' into the estimate of future maintainable profits. The performance of the general economy also tends to have a significant bearing on the company's future profitability.

Clearly, an assessment of future earnings is likely to be made when valuing a company with potential high growth but with no historic track record, such as an online gambling business – the current volatility in this sector should, however, dictate a degree of cautious prudence in estimating earnings and prospective/exit multiples.

Dealing with surplus assets

14.12 As the earnings basis values a company's ability to generate earnings, income from 'surplus' assets and investments that are not required for generating the operating trading profits must be excluded from the maintainable 'earnings' figure. The vendor may often be required, or wish, to extract 'surplus' assets (often of a 'private' nature) before the company is sold. In appropriate cases, the market value of surplus assets is then added to the earnings-based figure to arrive at the total valuation of the company.

Future tax rate

14.13   Once the maintainable profits have been determined an appropriate future tax rate is applied to arrive at the maintainable earnings. From 1 April 2017, a 19% corporate tax rate should normally be used.

PRICE/EARNINGS (P/E) MULTIPLE OR RATE OF RETURN

14.14

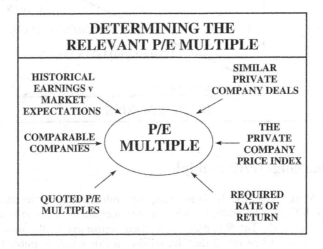

The investor's required rate of return

14.15   The amount that an investor is willing to pay for an investment is based on their required rate of return. If the investor's rate of return is not known, then it can be determined from comparable recent deals in the market.

The rate of return comprises the 'risk-free' rate (such as that earned on gilts) plus the 'risk premium' (based on the risk inherent in the investment, for example, the uncertainty of whether future earnings will be achieved; uncertain trading conditions). This is invariably difficult to quantify and largely depends upon the individual investor's attitude to risk. The conceptual relationship between the rate of return required and the varying degrees of investment risk is illustrated graphically below.

The primary company/business valuation model (ignoring future growth in earnings) is as follows:

$$\text{Value} = \frac{\text{Maintainable earnings}}{\text{Required rate of return}}$$

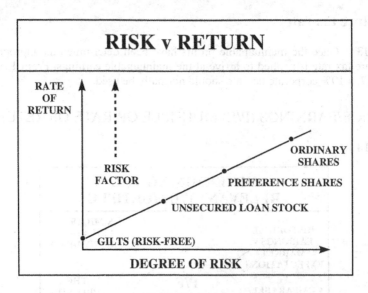

Price/earnings (P/E) multiples

14.16 More typically, business/company valuations are determined by using the P/E ratio or multiple *(which is the reciprocal of the rate of return or earnings yield)*. The P/E multiple is then *multiplied* by the maintainable earnings. It should be noted that the published P/E ratios of publicly traded companies are generally derived from the prices obtained from transactions in very small holdings, although at times the market price may be heavily influenced by institutional investors, speculators and potential takeover bids.

The P/E multiple is calculated as:

$$\frac{\text{Price per share}}{\text{Net earnings per share}}$$

Companies with publicly traded shares must use International Accounting Standard (IAS) 33 (as adopted by the EU) to determine the 'earnings per share' calculation.

IAS 33 stipulates that the basic earnings per share is calculated by taking the (consolidated) net profit/loss for the period attributable to the ordinary shareholders and dividing this by the weighted average number of ordinary shares outstanding during the period (the denominator).

The profits attributable to the ordinary shareholders will therefore be struck after deducting taxation and, where appropriate, minority interests and preference dividends. The full amount of dividends for cumulative preference shares should be included, irrespective of whether the dividends have been declared.

Where the profit or loss from continuing operations is reported, the basic EPS is reported using the post-tax profit from the continuing operations attributable to the ordinary shareholders.

If there has been a change in the number of ordinary shares during the relevant period, the number of shares outstanding is calculating by a time-weighted factor (taking the days each relevant tranche of shares has been in issue).

The P/E ratio can be thought of as the number of years' earnings per share represented by the share price.

Selecting an appropriate P/E multiple

14.17   Considerable judgement is required when selecting an appropriate P/E ratio or multiple. Clearly, empirical evidence of prices at which similar or comparable businesses have changed hands will provide a very important guide. Details of recent disposals can be obtained from a wide variety of sources – see 14.5 for details.

If such details are not readily available, published P/Es for comparable quoted companies can be used – select a limited number of companies that are closest to the company being valued. Since published P/Es are based on transactions involving very small minority stakes, they may need to be increased to reflect the value of the entire company.

On the other hand, P/E ratios are often based on historical earnings figures while share prices generally anticipate market expectations. The effect of this lag between (low) historical earnings and share prices based on future expectations can be quite pronounced and the P/E ratio would need to be discounted for this.

If a comparable company cannot be found, the average P/E ratio for the industrial/business sector in which the company operates may be used as a guide. This can be found in the FT Actuaries Share Indices (FTASI) published in the Financial Times. (The industry sector P/E index is a weighted average of the P/E multiples of the major companies in the sector and thus reflects the market's rating of the larger quoted companies.)

Quoted P/E multiples are normally appropriately discounted in arriving at a suitable multiple for an unquoted company (bearing in mind that unquoted companies are often smaller and their shares are not readily marketable). The discount factor can be up to 50% and sometimes more (see 14.43 – Example 3).

Another factor that needs to be recognised is that the prices (and hence P/E multiples) of quoted companies are invariably determined from market transactions of small minority shareholders. Thus, in a takeover scenario, the price would be substantially increased to reflect a 'bid' premium.

EBITDA valuations

14.18 Valuations based on capitalised EBITDA multiples are becoming increasingly common in the UK, having been firmly established in the USA and later Europe. Although EBITDA measures are not recognised by UK GAAP, the vast majority of private equity firms and corporate finance advisers have now adopted EBITDA valuations.

EBITDA is the acronym for *earnings before interest, tax, depreciation and amortisation*. This measure therefore looks at the operating profits of a business before tax charges, ignoring subjective accounting depreciation and goodwill amortisation charges. Furthermore, it does not take into account the company's finance structure. Arguably, this enables more meaningful comparisons to be made between companies

By excluding the effects of tax, depreciation, and financing, the EBITDA become an approximate measure of operating cash flows. Applying the relevant multiple to a company's sustainable EBITDA produces the company's 'enterprise value'. The value of the company's equity shares can be found by deducting the amount of any debt from the enterprise value. If the company has 'surplus' cash instead, this is added to the enterprise value to determine the equity valuation

14.18A The calculation of EBITDA valuations is based on similar principles to P/E based valuations. Thus, it is first necessary to arrive at a 'normalised' figure for 'operating profits' (ie EBITDA). Therefore, as with the determination of maintainable profits, adjustments may be necessary to reflect a commercial charge for owner-manager's/directors' salaries/bonuses, non-recurring expenditure and so on (see 14.10).

The EBITDA multiple used is often based on an industry sector average (typically based on a sample of similar or 'comparable' businesses sold). As with all multiples, care is required to ensure that it 'suitable for purpose'. It is understood that in recent times, the range of EBITDA multiples for private company transactions has averaged somewhere between 4 and 8 (based on cases where relevant data is available).

Many argue that it may not be appropriate to use EBITDA valuation methodology when valuing small companies, since it does not take into account the level of capital expenditure, which is often a key determinant of profit generation. The level of capital expenditure required to maintain a company's business is generally reflected through its depreciation charges. However, where small companies are valued under EBITDA principles, anecdotal evidence suggests that an EBITDA multiple of between 3 and 5 is often used. Adjustments may be made to the multiple to reflect such factors as the turnover growth rate, gross profit margins, over reliance on a few customers and any inherent business risks.

Many valuers will still value companies using the traditional P/E multiples (see 14.16–14.17) as a 'sanity-check'!

Example 1

EBITDA valuation

Marko Music Promotions Ltd has traded successfully as a music concert promoter for many years.

Based on recent accounts and its future budgets, its maintainable earnings have been calculated as follows:

	£'000
Sales	14,850
Cost of sales	(13,100)
Gross profit	1,750
Administrative expenses	(1,080)
Depreciation	(240)
Interest payable	(50)
Profit on ordinary activities before taxation	380
Tax on profit on ordinary activities	(76)
Earnings	304

The company's current level of debt is £500,000.

Based on these figures, the 'normalised' EBITDA is as follows:

	£'000
Profit on ordinary activities before taxation	380
Add:	
Excess directors' remuneration	100
Depreciation	240
Interest payable	50
EBITDA	770

Based on research, an appropriate 'current' EBITDA multiple for music promotions and similar businesses is 6.2.

Therefore the enterprise value for Marko Music Promotions Ltd is

£770,000 × 6.2 = £4,774,000

After deducting its debt of £500,000, the value of its ordinary share capital (equity) is around £4.274,000

The BDO Private Company Price Index (PCPI)

14.19   The BDO Private Company Price Index (PCPI) is especially useful when valuing private companies. Until 2013, the PCPI was based on the arithmetical mean of the P/E ratios achieved on actual private company sales completed in the relevant quarter period where sufficient information has been disclosed. BDO also tracks the average P/E ratios of deals involving a private equity buyer – known as the Private Equity Price Index (PEPI).

The calculation of these indices changed in 2013, so they are now calculated as an EBITDA to enterprise value multiple (see 14.18 and 14.18A). These changes were made to reflect the level of debt in deals and to use EBITDA, which is considered to be a less subjective measure of profitability.

It should be noted that, as private companies are often owner-managed, their reported or published profits may be understated. This means that it might sometimes give misleading information, since it may not take into account the 'inside information' on which the actual sale price is based.

For example, the owner-managers may have remunerated themselves generously. Very often, private companies also tend to incur expenses that would not continue to be paid post-sale. On this basis, the *PCPI* may be slightly over-stated. On the other hand, some companies' profits may be overstated because the owner-managers may have rewarded themselves via large dividends (rather than bonuses).

All these differences would have been adjusted in arriving at the amount paid for the company but may not be apparent from the publicly available profit data used to calculate the sale price. In fact in *Elliott v Planet Organic Ltd* [2000] BCC 610 (at p 615), the PCPI was referred to as a 'flimsy guide' but it was still followed by the court!

The PCPI is often regarded as the most authoritative source on private company valuations by leading accountancy firms and HMRC's Shares & Asset Valuation team.

The tables below provide a useful quarterly comparison between the PCPI and PEPI.

Table – PCPI and PEPI multiples from Q1 2015 to Q1 2017

Quarter ended	PCPI (using EBITDA multiples)	PEPI (using EBITDA multiples)
March 2015	9.2	10.9
June 2015	10.0	10.8
September 2015	9.5	10.7

Quarter ended	PCPI (using EBITDA multiples)	PEPI (using EBITDA multiples)
December 2015	9.3	10.9
March 2016	10.3	11.5
June 2016	10.2	11.5
September 2016	10.0	11.3
December 2016	10.5	11.3
March 2017	10.1	13.2

For the quarter to 31 March 2017, the PCPI shows that private companies were sold to trade buyers for an average of 10.1 times historic EBITDA (see 14.19 below). The PEPI indicates that for the same period, on average, private companies were sold to private equity buyers for 13.2 times historic EBITDA.

The PCPI and PEPI are both average measures and should be used in that context. Many other factors will also influence the particular valuation. Over the last four years to 31 March 2017, the included deals for the PCPI had a mean enterprise value of £81.6 million and a median enterprise value of £16 million. The included deals for the PEPI had a mean enterprise value of £117 million and median enterprise value of £40 million. Since these represent fairly large companies, a further discount will generally be required when valuing smaller-sized companies.

During the three months ended 30 June 2017, the UK economy seems to be performing better than anticipated after the Brexit vote. Consumer spending is buoyant, the business confidence index is healthy, and strong output data is reported for the manufacturing sector. However, business investment remains inhibited by political uncertainty and the impending Brexit negotiations.

For the quarter ended 31 March 2017, BDO reported that:

'Many trade buyers and private equity investors complain that there aren't enough good quality businesses coming to market. So, when a good company does come to market, the competition is driving prices. It is a good time to be selling'.

NET ASSET VALUATIONS

Basic net asset valuation principles

14.20 A valuation based on 'net assets' is not a true method of determining a going concern value for a trading company. A net asset based valuation will involve calculating the total *current* value of assets less current and long-term liabilities (properties, etc, may therefore need to be revalued). Net asset valuations are inherently subjective; for example estimating the value of used plant and equipment can be difficult. Such valuations also ignore goodwill, unless purchased goodwill is recorded in accordance with GAAP.

Use of net asset valuations

14.21 A net asset value can be viewed as a prudent method of valuation, as it ignores the risks inherent with future earnings, etc. Companies with poor profits or large losses may have a going concern ('earnings') valuation which is less than their net asset backing.

In certain situations, the company may only have a 'value' on a liquidation. Winding-up valuations should recognise the 'break-up' value of the assets and the closure costs.

A more common situation is one where the going concern value is less than the 'net asset' value, but where it is still worthwhile for the business to continue. This shortfall in net asset value is known as 'negative goodwill'.

Net asset values are really only directly applicable:

- for companies with quality assets, such as property investment and hotel businesses;

- where the company's assets are being 'under-utilised' (ie the profits do not provide an adequate return on the assets);

- where the business is making substantial losses and there is a strong likelihood of liquidation/'break-up'.

Validation check on 'goodwill'

14.22 After computing an earnings based valuation, further comfort is usually obtained by computing a net asset valuation. A net asset valuation is based on the company's balance sheet values, adjusted to reflect the current market value of properties, intellectual property and possible stock write-downs, etc.

The difference between the earnings based valuation and the net asset value of the company represents the goodwill valuation. The purchaser will then ask whether the amount effectively being paid for goodwill is appropriate, given the nature of the business and the current economic climate.

Special considerations

14.23 The basis of valuation will primarily depend on the vendor's reason for selling and the purchaser's rationale for making the acquisition. In practice, the skill is to determine the correct basis of valuation. In certain cases, the valuation would also need to reflect the benefits of synergy with the purchaser's existing business, the costs of merging with the purchaser's existing business, etc (see 14.28–14.30).

If a company is loss making, the value will be based on the future perception of the business and its prospects for recovery (ie, is it only a temporary downturn or will the company cease to exist?). In the latter case, a break-up value of the assets would be appropriate with adjustments to reflect the forced sale value of assets, irrecoverable debts and termination costs, etc.

14.24   There is likely to be difficulty in assessing the maintainable earnings of companies with little or no track record. Forecast profits are likely to be used as a basis for valuation, but a purchaser would need to be comfortable with the underlying assumptions. In practice, a purchaser is likely to make part of the sale price contingent on profit warranties, or value the business in 'hindsight' by using an earn-out (see 15.57).

Example 2

Valuation of company – case study

Collins Ltd operates a chain of retail outlets selling high quality hi-fi and multi-media equipment. The retail outlets are situated in a number of 'affluent' towns in the south east of England. The company also provides a complete sound and media support facility for conferences and corporate events, which contributes healthy margins to the company's overall results.

It is necessary to value the company in July 2017 to gauge the price that could be expected on a future sale of the company. The most appropriate basis of valuing the company is by reference to its earning capacity.

Recent trading history

The recent results of Collins Ltd (all audited) are summarised as follows:

	Year ended 30 June		
	2015	*2016*	*2017*
	£'000	*£'000*	*£'000*
Turnover	840	760	802
Profits before directors' remuneration	320	266	303
Directors' remuneration	(90)	(95)	(139)
Trading profit before interest	230	171	164
Interest	(10)	(8)	(7)

	Year ended 30 June		
Profit before taxation	220	163	157
Taxation	(46)	(34)	(31)
Profit after taxation	174	129	126
Effective tax rate	21%	21%	20%

Maintainable earnings

14.25   Based on discussions with the company's management, the year ended 30 June 2017 showed a small improvement in trading conditions. However, this took place in the first six months of the accounting period and sales have declined over the last three months.

Based on these factors, it would be prudent to estimate maintainable (pre-tax) profits at around £150,000.

The accounts would then be analysed for any unusual items, etc and for adherence to standard accounting policies, which give rise to the following adjustments:

Example 2

Maintainable earnings computation

	£'000	£'000
Maintainable profits		
Estimated to be		150
Adjustments		
Reduction in depreciation charge (company's rates more prudent than the norm)		25
Excessive directors' remuneration (based on prevailing industry rates for two directors) (£139,000 – £100,000)		39
Adjusted maintainable profits		214
Less Taxation (£214,000 × 19%)		(41)
Maintainable earnings		173

Selecting an appropriate P/E ratio

14.26   The assessment of an appropriate P/E ratio is obviously a subjective exercise, and there are many factors that need to be considered.

A survey of recent comparable transactions revealed that a small hi-fi discount stores chain retailer had sold out in March 2017 on a multiple of 4.

The 'exit' multiples for the majority of smaller unquoted companies have historically stood at a 30% to 40% discount to (non-financial) quoted companies.

On 27 July 2017, the majority of the quoted P/Es in the general retailers section fell within the range of 10 to 20 based on historic results. The FTSE Actuaries All Shares P/E index for the general retailers sector was 14.85. The FTSE SmallCap (excluding investment companies) index stood at 29.26.

When valuing smaller owner-managed companies, it is accepted that a discount should be applied against comparable publicly quoted companies (see comments in 14.17). In July 2017, the outlook for the UK economy was relatively uncertain.

All these factors should be taken into account in the valuation judgment.

Collins Ltd is a relatively small company and, based on all the above data, a P/E ratio of 5 is considered appropriate.

Value of Collins Ltd

Maintainable earnings (per 14.25):	£173,000
P/E (per 14.26):	5
Value of 100% of the issued share capital of Collins Ltd £173,000 × 5 =	£865,000

Given the limited information available, on 27 July 2017, the entire share capital of Collins Ltd could be valued in the range of £850,000 to £880,000.

Quasi-partnership valuations

14.27   Many companies are incorporated on the principle of a 'quasi-partnership', which can often have a significant impact on their share valuations. In such cases, the articles or shareholding agreement will usually provide that the shares are subject to pre-emption transfers at the pro-rata value (of the company) without any minority discount being applied.

This principle was affirmed (by the Privy Council) in *CVC/Opportunity Equity Partners Ltd v Demarco Almeida* [2002] 2 BCLC 108, which involved an 'unfair prejudice' action brought by a minority shareholder. Applying the dicta in the important case of *Ebrahimi v Westbourne Galleries* [1973] AC 360, Lord Millett highlighted the main characteristics of a 'quasi-partnership' company, which include:

- a business association formed or continued on the basis of a personal relationship of mutual trust and confidence;

- an understanding or agreement that all or some of the shareholders should participate in the management of the business; and

- restrictions on the transfer of shares so that a member cannot realise their stake if they were excluded from the business.

In essence, the shareholders have used a corporate vehicle to carry on a business that could easily have been run by them as a partnership. A quasi-partnership valuation may be appropriate where a member has been unfairly prejudiced and brings a successful action under *CA 2006, s 994*. Where the courts find that a quasi-partnership exists, it may require the relevant member's shares to be purchased at a pro-rata value of the company (ie based on a notional sale) without being reduced by any minority discount (see also *Re Bird Precision Bellows Ltd* [1984] 3 All ER 444).

Shares in 'husband and wife' companies are often dealt with in a similar way in divorce cases.

However, the case of *Irvine v Irvine* [2006] EWHC 1875 (Ch) demonstrates that, in appropriate cases, the courts are still prepared to discount the value of a minority shareholding for the purposes of an unfair prejudice action. In this case, a 30% discount was applied to a 'non-controlling' 49.96% holding. This 30% discount was also applied to the 'excessive remuneration' drawn by the majority shareholder, which was also successfully claimed by the minority shareholder as part of the action.

PURCHASER VALUATION ISSUES

Purchaser 'pricing' issues

14.28 A prospective purchaser will normally seek an assessment of the target business's future earnings stream. This will entail a detailed assessment of the post-acquisition earnings of the target business after adjusting for the financial impact of proposed changes. For example, the earnings could reflect the anticipated cost savings of fewer directors/ managers being required after the acquisition and certain other economies of scale. Further adjustments may be necessary to reflect different financing structures and judgment about future trading conditions, etc (see 14.29–14.30). As a general rule, the purchaser should not pay more than the acquisition is worth to *them*.

The purchase price – the amount that is required for the deal to be accepted by the vendor(s) – should be less than the 'synergy value' to the purchaser. Synergy value represents the net present value of cash flows that will flow from the synergy and improvements that are made post-acquisition.

Synergy value

14.29   Synergy value will reflect:

- cost savings, such as job cuts, economies of scale, reducing duplication of facilities, etc;

- reduced funding costs (resulting from the pooling of working capital finance resources and cash surpluses);

- tax benefits.

Earnings multiple valuation

14.30   In practice, many purchasers will use the normal earnings multiple approach to evaluate whether or not the price they are being asked to pay for the business is sensible. The purchaser's view of prospective earnings will be adjusted to reflect the structure and operations of the company/business post-acquisition. Thus, the earnings could reflect the anticipated cost savings of fewer directors/managers being required and certain other economies of scale. Further adjustments may be necessary to reflect different financing structures and the purchaser's judgment about future trading conditions, etc.

Using an earn-out to resolve the 'price-gap'

14.31   Negotiations for the sale of a company often reveal a gap between the vendor's asking price (often based on 'next years' profits!') and the purchaser's view of its value, which is generally based on the company's most recent audited accounts and often a cynical view of its projected profits.

The 'earn-out' type deal evolved to reconcile this 'price gap', enabling the company to be sold for an amount which depended on its future results and enabling both parties to strike a deal which they might otherwise have been unable to achieve.

A typical earn-out scenario is where the target business has been built up and still relies upon the technical ability or creative flair of its few owner-managers. The purchaser can ensure that the value of the business is preserved and enhanced by retaining the vendor's services during the earn-out period, secured by an appropriate service agreement. During this period, the vendor will concentrate on enhancing the company's profitability.

Earn-out deals are commonly used on the sale of 'service' type businesses. In such cases, there is typically no strong 'asset-backed' balance sheet and the purchaser will also have concerns about the business retaining its key personnel post-completion.

If the vendor is successful, they will obtain large 'earn-out' payments, thus increasing the total consideration for the sale of their shares. However, 'earn-outs' often pose particular tax problems for the vendor which must be addressed (see 15.59–15.60).

FISCAL OR TAX-BASED VALUATIONS

Why fiscal valuations are required

14.32 Fiscal or tax-based valuations are required by the tax legislation in various situations, for example:

(*a*)   shares held at 31 March 1982 must be valued at that date for CGT rebasing purposes;

(*b*)   shares transferred otherwise than at arm's length must be valued (although if hold-over relief can be claimed both parties can elect to dispense with the valuation (see (13.18));

(*c*)   determining the value of shares chargeable to inheritance tax on death or by reason of a lifetime transfer becoming chargeable on a death within seven years;

(*d*)   determining the taxable employment income arising on shares (including restricted securities) made available to employees (see Chapter 8 and 13.29–13.36), or to ensure that no such benefit arises when shares are made available under a formal approved employee share scheme;

(*e*)   determining the value of shares which are the subject of options granted under an Enterprise Management Incentive (EMI) scheme, an approved Company Share Option Plan (CSOP) or an unapproved share plan (see Chapter 8).

Arm's length and connected party share transfers

14.33 Shares transferred otherwise than at arm's length are deemed to be transferred at their open market value. This will always be the case where shares are sold or gifted to a connected person (*TCGA 1992, s 18*). Shares passing between unconnected persons are treated as being by way of a bargain at arm's length, unless, exceptionally, there is donative intent. This was considered in *Bullivant Holdings Ltd v CIR* [1998] STC 905. The High Court upheld the Special Commissioner's decision that the amount paid for two

25% shareholdings acquired from two unconnected individuals was a full and fair price, even though it appeared to be very low based on the relevant facts. Nevertheless, the evidence supported that the deal was struck by the parties at arm's length.

It is possible that the commercial price agreed on a sale of shares between unconnected parties may differ from the open market value arrived at for tax purposes. The actual conditions and information on which the sale is based will be different from the hypothetical assumptions and case law which govern the determination of market value for tax purposes.

If the actual consideration for a sale of shares appears to be considerably different from their market value, it is important that sufficient evidence is retained, such as documentary evidence of real negotiations between the parties showing that they each took separate legal and commercial advice. This can then be used to demonstrate to HMRC (if a challenge is made) that the transaction was freely negotiated and no gratuitous benefit was intended.

BASIC VALUATION CONCEPTS

Open market value

14.34 The statutory rules for determining market value are deceptively simple. In *TCGA 1992, s 272(1)* and *IHTA 1984, s 160(1)*, the market value is the price which those assets/the property might reasonably be expected to fetch if sold in the open market. There is of course no open market for unquoted shares. A considerable body of case law and practice has therefore been built up over the last hundred or so years to provide the conceptual framework for valuing unquoted shares. Although valuations are carried out on an academic basis, it must always be remembered that share valuation is an art, not a science; or 'intelligent guesswork' as Mr Justice Dankwerts called it in *Holt v CIR* [1953] 1 WLR 1488.

The value of a share is therefore what the valuer can successfully argue it to be. The tax or taxes on which the valuation turns will have a bearing on the situation. For example, if the shares are being valued for March 1982 rebasing purposes, as high a value as possible will be negotiated. If the same shares were being valued on death for IHT, a (much) lower value is likely to be argued for.

Hypothetical sale

14.35 The main principles were succinctly summarised by Mr Plowman J in *Re Lynall (deceased)* (1971) 47 TC 375. Unquoted shares are to be valued on the basis of a hypothetical sale, based on a price that could be reasonably expected to be paid:

(*a*)   by a hypothetical willing purchaser;

(*b*)   to a hypothetical willing seller ;

(*c*)   in the open market.

In this context, it is assumed that all sale preparations have been made and the parties are hypothetical and anonymous. The hypothetical sale is deemed to take place in a real open market where the entire world can make bids. The market value is the best price the purchaser could reasonably pay – the price which the seller would expect to sell the shares for is irrelevant.

A fiscal valuation always refers to a specific date. It effectively assumes that the consideration is taken in the form of an outright cash purchase on a given date without conditions – thus potential earn-out deals (see 14.31) or other forms of consideration (such as shares or loan notes) are ignored. Furthermore, issues covered by warranties and indemnities are assumed to be factored into the hypothetical price (see 12.70). Such factors mean that fiscal share valuations tend to be lower than any actual sales that have taken place around the fiscal valuation date.

The value has to be the best price that could be obtained by the vendor (whose actual identity is irrelevant) in an arm's length bargain in the open market. To put it another way, we have to imagine that the shares are being offered for sale to the whole world and that the value is the best price obtainable from the competing bids. For this purpose, the restrictions on the transfer of shares normally found in most Articles of Association are disregarded in the hypothetical open market, although the purchaser is deemed to take the shares subject to those restrictions.

This concept of the hypothetical purchaser was addressed in *Grays Timber Products Ltd v CIR* [2010] UKSC4, which considered whether shares with enhanced rights on a sale should be taken into account when arriving at their market value. (Although this was for determining whether the shares were sold for more than their market value under *ITEPA 2003, s 446X*, the same CGT valuation principles applied.) A key finding in the judgement was that if these rights are *personal* to a shareholder they would be of no value to the 'hypothetical purchaser'. This is because such rights would be extinguished on sale and thus cannot be transmitted to the purchaser. Thus, it followed that no purchaser would ever pay for them.

This followed the principle established in *CIR v Crossman* [1937] AC 26 which requires the hypothetical purchaser to 'step into the seller's shoes' in the sense that he acquires the same property but does not take on the seller's personal characteristics (see also 8.37).

Grays Timber Products was decided on its own special facts. The problems created by the ruling can be overcome by providing the enhanced rights in the articles to a particular class of shares (since they would be transferable to a (hypothetical) purchaser (see also 8.37).

Although the same valuation rules generally apply for both CGT and IHT, there is a fundamental difference between the computational approaches. For CGT purposes, the valuation normally relates to the shares that are being disposed of (subject to the special rules in *TCGA 1992, s 19* – see 13.11).

IHT valuations will normally seek to establish the loss to the transferor's estate and will therefore involve valuing the transferor's shareholding both before and after the transfer (as opposed to the actual holding being transferred) (see 17.5). In most cases, this will mean that the value of the shares transferred for CGT and IHT purposes will differ. Where CGT hold-over relief is claimed under either *TCGA 1992, s 165* or *260*, an election can be made to avoid a formal valuation of the shares (see 13.18).

Deemed information standards

14.36 The hypothetical willing purchaser is assumed to be reasonably prudent and will therefore obtain all information that would be reasonably required (see *TCGA 1992, s 273(3)* and *IHTA 1984, s 168*). According to HMRC's Share Valuation Manual (Chapter II), regard must be had to the 'information that is reasonably available to the purchaser of the particular shareholding being acquired'. This would depend on such things as:

- the physical availability of the information (it must actually be available although may not be published); and

- the influence of the potential purchaser (either in terms of voting power or the cost/size of the investment.

The relevant details required would largely depend on the size of the shareholding and the amount of capital invested. For example, a prudent hypothetical purchaser acquiring a controlling interest would certainly require detailed knowledge about the relevant company. Thus, when valuing a 'controlling' holding, all the information that would be available to the directors is assumed to be available to the prudent purchaser, including confidential information.

This would include the company's historic and current year financial accounts, budgets and forecasts, details of remuneration paid to directors, arrangements with major customers and suppliers and so on.

On the other hand, less information would be available to a purchaser of a minority stake. As a *general* rule, for a holding of 25% or less, only audited accounts and published information are assumed to be available. Where a more substantial minority holding is involved (ie more than 25%), the purchaser may also expect to have an indication of the company's financial results since the last accounting date. However, the extent of information deemed to be available may also depend on the 'weight of money' involved.

For example, in *Administrators of the Estate of Caton (deceased) v Couch* [1995] STC (SCD) 34, [1997] STC 970, it was accepted that a hypothetical purchaser considering an investment of £1,000,000, representing only a minority holding of 14.02%, would have required access to confidential management information. Consequently, the purchaser would have reasonably required details as well as up-to-date information from management accounts and budget forecasts. Relevant details about the sale prospects were taken into account in the valuation process and the potential sale value was discounted by 50% (reflecting the fact that no formal offer had been made).

HMRC Shares & Asset Valuation Office (SAV) takes the view that, if the shareholding is small (ie less than 5%) and large sums of money are not involved, a prospective purchaser would only have access to published information. In *Clark (executor of Clark, deceased) v Green* [1995] STC (SCD) 99, a small minority holding of 3% (agreed to be worth over £168,000) was held to be of insufficient size or outlay for a prospective purchaser to have reasonably required information about a possible sale, but did reasonably require unpublished management accounts regarding the recently completed financial year.

Despite the principles explained above, in practice, SAV seem to be requesting more recent financial results and budget data etc and even information subject to a non-disclosure agreement. For example, in the context of EMI share option valuations, such information is requested on the EMI Form 23. This states that the 'valuation agreement is subject to the proviso that SAV must be notified of any changes in circumstances (whether considered available under section 273 or not) or the market position before the options are granted'.

Where *very* small companies are concerned, SAV may not be too strict on the application of the information standard, unless it would make a material difference to the valuation.

Shareholder rights and voting power

14.37 The valuation will primarily be influenced by the relative size of the shareholding. Majority/controlling shareholdings confer greater rights and power than minority/non-controlling shareholdings and are therefore worth more per share. It is usually helpful to allocate the shares being valued into one of the following categories.

Voting power	Rights of shareholder
90% or more	Can accept offer to sell shares in company and can give purchaser compulsory power to acquire remaining shares. Enjoys total control of company.
75%–89.9%	Has effective control of the company. Has requisite votes to pass a special resolution and can put the company into liquidation or sell it as a going concern.
50.1%–74.9%	Enjoys day to day control (but cannot pass special resolution).

Voting power	Rights of shareholder
50%	May have shared control or a deadlock situation. Can block an ordinary resolution regarding normal business requirements. Value would depend on spread of other shareholdings.
25.1%–49.9%	Influential minority – has right to block a special resolution (which requires 25% of the votes). Value would depend on spread of other shareholdings.
10.1%–25%	Small minority, but cannot be bought out by majority.
Up to 10%	Small minority liable to forced sale on a takeover under compulsory purchase legislation.

When undertaking a fiscal share valuation it is clearly important to be aware of the relevant rights attaching to the shares, especially where there are different classes of shares.

Comparison between majority and minority shareholders

14.38 Majority shareholders (having more than 50% of votes) can pass an ordinary resolution. They therefore enjoy practical command of the company, being able to decide the company's dividend policy, level of directors' remuneration and can often determine whether the company should be sold, floated, or wound up. A control holding will therefore be based on the value of the entire company. In the case of a going concern, the value will be based on the company's underlying profitability and hence the earnings basis of valuation is normally used for trading companies (see 14.9–14.17).

By contrast, minority shareholders are relatively impotent. They do not have control and the value of their holding would be primarily determined by the rights in the company's Articles of Association, the size of their own holding and the spread of other shareholdings. Frequently, the Articles will impose a restriction on the right to transfer shares, subject to the Board's discretion. The minority shareholder will therefore be locked in and would not usually have any effective sanction against the Board of Directors. The restricted rights of a minority shareholder therefore produce a much lower valuation.

As dividends generally constitute the return for the minority shareholder, such holdings may be valued on a dividend yield basis, particularly where the taxpayer wishes to establish a low valuation. However, many unquoted companies do not pay dividends, even though there are sufficient earnings to do so, or their dividend payment record may be erratic. In such cases, the preferred approach would be to value the holdings on an earnings yield basis, although a lower (ie discounted) P/E ratio would be applied than for a control holding. The level of discount varies according to the size of the holding and the spread of the other shareholdings (for example, a 40% shareholding may give practical control if the remaining shares are spread amongst ten shareholders).

Valuation discounts

14.39   There are no published formulae for discounts and HMRC – (Share and Assets Valuation (SAV)) usually succeeds if the negotiations turn on the level of discount to be applied. Generally, discounts of between 45%–75% are sought by HMRC for small minority holdings.

For example, in *Administrators of the Estate of Caton (deceased) v Couch* [1995] STC (SCD) 34, [1997] STC 970, discounts of 60% to 70% were considered appropriate for a 14.02% holding in an unquoted trading company. However, in *Foulser v HMRC* [2015] TC 4413, the First-Tier Tribunal (FTT) took the view that a discount of just 50% should be given when valuing a 9% holding. Although each case is dependent on its own facts, this seems very low when discounts of around 75% are often agreed in practice.

Where a shareholder holds 50% of the shares, but also has a casting vote as chairman, this does not give control in the context of a fiscal valuation of shares. A sale of the shares only is being placed in the hypothetical open market, and these do not carry control without the chairman's contract that gives the vital casting vote. A 50% shareholding is therefore treated as a 'dead-lock' holding and would often be subject to a 25% discount (subject to the size of the other holdings).

Lower discounts of 30% to 40% are normally applied for larger minority holdings of up to 49% (see SAV Manual). However, the level of discount will vary according to the circumstances of each case, such as the spread of the other shareholdings – it is generally a matter of negotiation. Use of the earnings basis avoids calculating notional dividends, which are less easy to support in negotiations with HMRC. Earnings based valuations have become popular when valuing minority shareholdings for March 1982 rebasing purposes as this generally enables higher values to be negotiated with HMRC.

In the *Foulser* case, the FTT applied a 20% valuation discount to a 'controlling' 51% holding. The FTT also concluded that a 'bid-premium' of 35% should be added to the 'typical' quoted company P/E multiple of 15 to give an adjusted P/E multiple of 20.25, although this was a substantial-sized company with post-tax profits of some £2.6 million.

EMPLOYEE SHARE VALUATIONS FOR EMPLOYMENT INCOME PURPOSES

Unrestricted shares (or where no *s 431* election is made)

14.40   The valuation of shares that are unrestricted or not subject to an *ITEPA 2003, s 431* election falls outside the restricted securities regime.

Consequently, where such shares are awarded to a director or employee at an undervalue, they are taxable as earnings under the *Weight v Salmon* (1935) 19 TC 174 principle (ie the so-called 'earnings' rule in *ITEPA 2003, s 62*).

The value is based on the money or 'money's worth' that could be realised in the open market by the recipient employee. This focuses on the subjective benefit to the employee, the value being based on the employee's 'own' information or knowledge about the company's affairs – there is no 'deemed' information standard (see also 8.15). (This may mean that employees with holdings of the same size may each have a different valuation, according to their 'personal' knowledge.) The inherent rights and restrictions attaching to the individual's shares such as under the Articles of Association would also be taken into account.

Unrestricted and restricted valuation bases

14.41   Where the shares are restricted (for example, they are subject to certain employee-specific restrictions, such as the requirement to sell the shares at a reduced price on leaving) and subject to an *ITEPA 2013, s 431* election (see 8.32), the CGT 'market value' rule in *TCGA 1992, s 272* must be used – see 14.34–14.36 (*ITEPA 2003, s 421(1)*). Inside information available to a director/employee purchaser is ignored for CGT (and IHT) based valuations – remember, it is an *imaginary purchaser*. Of course, this is where the (academic) assumptions upon which fiscal valuations are based differ from transactions in the real world.

In the vast majority of cases, an *ITEPA 2003, s 431* election will be made to base the tax charge on the 'unrestricted' market value of the shares (or UMV) (see 8.32). This will ensure that any subsequent growth in the value of the shares falls within the CGT regime.

Consequently, the shares would be valued using normal CGT criteria, but would ignore the effect of any personal or employee specific restrictions relating to the shares. Furthermore, the provisions in any shareholders' agreements or similar arrangements outside the company's articles would be ignored. CGT valuation principles reflect the normal 'pre-emption' restrictions imposed on all shareholders by the articles (since the hypothetical purchaser takes the shares subject to those provisions). Based on recent experience with Shares Valuation, this may represent about 25% to 30% of the normal discount for a small minority holding. Much of that discount is likely to reflect the lack of marketability of the shares.

Where a 'restricted value' of the shares is required, this would necessarily reflect the detrimental impact of employee specific restrictions.

- *Specific restrictions on transfer* – A typical discount of between 2% to 4% per each year (of restriction) would be applied to the unrestricted market value, subject to an overriding total limit of 10% to 15%.

- *Forfeiture conditions* – These generally require the employee to sell their shares on 'leaving' for an amount that is less than their market value and may have a material impact on the fiscal share value in the case of a (increasingly) profitable company. The discount applied to the unrestricted value would be influenced by such factors as the length of the forfeiture period and the difference between the transfer price given on leaving and initial unrestricted value. Likely discounts would range between 10% and 20% of the unrestricted value.

- *Non-voting restrictions* – Traditionally, a discount of up to about 10% is often applied when valuing small holdings of non-voting shares (as compared to the equivalent voting shareholding). The unrestricted value of shares carrying temporary restrictions on voting would probably be discounted by 1% of every year of restriction (up to an overall limit of 10%).

- *Dividend restrictions* – This usually requires looking at the dividends likely to be paid by the company over the period of restriction. The total potential dividends are then discounted to their net present value, with a further discount being applied for the 'risk' element (recognising the financial and 'dividend-paying' prospects of the company and the period of restriction).

The 'risk discounted' net present value of the likely dividends forgone would then be deducted from the unrestricted value of the shares (and may also be expressed as a discount percentage of that unrestricted value).

Despite the above analysis, in recent years SAV seem to have adopted a more pragmatic approach with regard to the determination of the unrestricted market value in most straightforward cases. Thus, having arrived at the actual market value or AMV (according to the rules in *TCGA 1992, s 272* (see 14.35 and 14.36), SAV then add on a premium (typically between 10% and 15% of the AMV) to arrive at the unrestricted market value (UMV).

HMRC now appears to contend that the standard pre-emption restrictions that invariably apply to private company shares would be sufficient to make them 'restricted'. However, it is debatable whether such 'restrictions' cause the share to have a lower valuation (as required by *ITEPA 2003, s 421*). In such cases, *ITEPA 2003, s 431* elections are usually made on a protective basis to cover any 'valuation' risk.

Other employee share tax charges

14.42 For the purposes of computing the other various tax charges under the 'employment-related' securities legislation (in *ITEPA 2003, Pt 7, Chs 2–5*), such as on the award of employee shareholder status (ESS) shares (see 8.86A) and exercise of unapproved share options (see 8.29), all relevant share valuations are subject to the statutory 'open market' basis of valuation that applies for CGT [*TCGA 1992, ss 272–273*] (see 14.34). The application of the 'market value' rules was tested in *Grays Timber Products Ltd v CIR* [2010] UKSC4 (see 14.35).

EMI and other approved share schemes

14.43 Valuations prepared to determine the market value of shares at the date of an EMI option grant have always followed the CGT valuation basis [*ITEPA 2003, Sch 5, para 55*].

Given that EMI valuations are typically 'minority-based', the hypothetical purchaser would only have access to publicly available information, such as the last published accounts, information on the company's website, press comments and so on (see 14.36). Such valuations should therefore ignore employee 'insider information'. However, in practice, SAV often requests this information (such as the latest management accounts and budgets) and seeks to take this data into account in agreeing share valuations at the grant date (see 8.19).

If the EMI option shares are 'restricted', the £250,000 limit on the market value over shares under EMI options will be based on the *unrestricted* market value of the shares (UMV), which is their value ignoring the effect of restrictions. However, under the EMI rules, employees will need to pay an option exercise price at least equal to the actual market value of the shares at the date of grant (ie the value taking into account the restrictions). Provided this is done, then an *ITEPA 2003 s 431(1)* election is deemed to have been made, thus ensuring that no part of any subsequent gain is subject to income tax (see 8.63).

However, where the option exercise price is 'discounted' (ie it is below the actual market value of the shares at the 'grant date', then an actual *s 431(1)* election will be needed.

In theory, the CGT based value gives the UMV (which must then be discounted to reflect any restrictions).

The same valuation concepts also apply for determining the market value of shares under an approved company share option and share incentive plans.

Although a valuation can be agreed before, or up to, 15 months from the date of grant, best practice is to agree the valuation with SAV when the company is ready to grant the relevant EMI options. The agreed valuation generally remains valid for 60 days from the date of SAV's agreement (unless there are material changes in circumstances during this period).

When putting forward an EMI share valuation for agreement by HMRC Shares and Assets valuation it is important to complete and submit HMRC form VAL231 and provide all the relevant background information. This will include providing:

- articles of association and any shareholders' agreement;
- accounts for up to three years before the valuation date;
- details of recent share transactions and any dividends paid;
- outline of any prospects for a sale or flotation.

HMRC's guidance for EMI share valuations is particularly useful and can be found at www.hmrc.gov.uk/svd/val-land-prop.htm#2 (see section 2 – Unquoted shares).

Example 3

HMRC example of EMI valuation for established trading company

(This is reproduced from HMRC guidance but cross-references have been made to appropriate sections in this book)

A company has been trading for around ten years and wishes to incentivise its employees by granting them a pool of up to 5% of the company's enlarged share capital. The company is not currently in the process of a sale or flotation.

The company's most recent performance is:

	Full audited accounts to Nov 2010	Full audited accounts to Nov 2011	Management accounts to Nov 2012
Turnover	£6.5m	7m	7.5m
Post tax profit	£525k	£600k	£600k
Dividends paid	£1 per share	£1 per share	£1 per share
Dividend cover	2.62	3	3

The fully diluted share capital would be 200,000 £1 ordinary shares.

The management accounts for 2012 have been utilised as it is considered that the last published accounts (to Nov 2011) are now stale at the valuation and it is reasonable to take into account more up to date information.

Based on this record of profits, maintainable earnings are taken as £600k per annum, which equates to earnings per share (EPS) of £3, on the basis of the fully diluted share capital.

Dividends are maintainable at £1 per share and are well covered.

A quoted company (on full London Stock Exchange) that operates in the same market as this company, shows a price earnings (P/E) ratio of 12.03. Applying a discount of around 60% to 65% to the quoted P/E – to reflect the differences between a minority holding in this company and the quoted company (see also 14.17) – indicates a final P/E ratio of 4.5*.

Applying a P/E of 4.5 to EPS of £3 then indicates an AMV of £13.50 per share for a minority holding in this company (see also 8.53 and 14.43).

Looking at the dividends, the same quoted company had a dividend yield of 3.40%. Increasing this by a multiple of say 2 – once again to reflect the differences between the quoted company and this company – indicates a revised yield % of 7.4%.

Applying this yield to the maintainable dividend of £1 per share (equal to 100%) then indicates an AMV of £13.50 per share, ie the same as the valuation on an earnings basis.

The UMV can then be taken at around a 20% premium to the AMV, ie at £16.20 per share, to reflect the fact that the Articles of Association for the company give the Board full veto on any share transfers and this and other restrictions are to be ignored when considering the UMV.

* A suitable multiple (of profits) may also be arrived at by reference to data on the sales of companies – both private and quoted – in similar markets to the company under consideration. Careful research of the terms of such company sales should be undertaken by the valuer before such transactional multiples are utilised, to ensure that the implied multiples are, so far as possible, reliable and comparable.

If the company has a high level of debt on its balance sheet, which reduces any post-tax profits substantially, the value of its shares can be arrived at by reference to an Enterprise Valuation (EV) looking at its maintainable Earnings Before Interest Depreciation and Amortisation (EBITDA) (see 14.18 and 14.18A). It is then possible to apply an EBITDA multiple from a comparable quoted company. Deducting the company's debt from the resulting EV will then leave the Equity Value, from which the minority share value can then be assessed, utilising appropriate discounts.

Whilst EBITDA multiples for quoted companies are not available in publications such as the Financial Times, these can be calculated by the valuer, usually by adding a particular quoted company's Market Capitalisation to its long term debt, to arrive at its EV. The EBITDA for the quoted company can then be calculated by reference to its accounts and dividing the EV by the EBITDA, to give the multiple. It can then be appropriate to discount the quoted company's EBITDA multiple to reflect the differences between the quoted company and the unquoted company which is being valued (see also 14.18A).

DEALING WITH HMRC – SHARES AND ASSETS VALUATION TEAM

Referral of valuations to HMRC – Shares and Asset Valuation Office (SAV)

14.44   HMRC Share and Asset Valuation Office (referred to as 'SAV') values all assets for tax purposes, apart from UK land and property. Thus, its valuation remit extends beyond unquoted shares to intangible assets, foreign property bloodstock, boats, wines, and other chattels.

It is important to appreciate that Inspectors of Taxes and Examiners at the Capital Taxes Office are generally required to make a 'tax risk' assessment on valuations and will generally refer all 'risk-rated' share valuations and goodwill valuations to the SAV.

Where a share valuation is included on the tax return, the taxpayer must tick the CGT schedule on the self-assessment tax return to indicate that an 'estimated value' has been used. Any tax return incorporating a share valuation will be referred to SAV, unless the Inspector is able to resolve the matter by reference to a file held locally or there is little or no tax at stake.

The HMRC Enquiry Handbook indicates that SA tax returns including CGT valuations, estimates, etc may be taken up for review and these cases may lead to 'aspect' enquiries (where the Inspector only enquires into one or two specific aspects of the tax return).

Dealing with SAV

14.45   In an article in the CIOT's *Tax Adviser* (June 2014), Mike Fowler (Assistant Director of the SAV) indicated that about 80% of values are accepted by the SAV without challenge. About 45% of referrals are accepted within a few days of receipt in SAV, with the remaining referrals being referred to SAV's valuers for a more detailed assessment – of these a further 35% are accepted without challenge. The remaining cases are then subject to negotiation with most being settled on an 'acceptable compromise' basis.

Remember that SAV is largely reliant on the information provided by the taxpayer/agent and they will have a more detailed knowledge of the company than SAV.

Valuation 'aspect' enquiries

14.45A   Where SAV wishes to challenge a valuation, it instructs the local Inspector to issue a notice of enquiry under *TMA 1970, s 9A*. The matter is then taken out of the local Inspector's hands. The SAV Examiner would send their individually tailored enquiries to the taxpayer or taxpayer's agent. While the share valuation is being negotiated, the taxpayer's tax return remains open, but HMRC will not enquire into unrelated matters once the normal enquiry period (of 12 months from the filing date) has passed (Statement of Practice 1/99).

Following the decision in *Langham v Veltema* [2004] STC 544, it is important to ensure that HMRC cannot subsequently raise 'discovery' assessments due to insufficient details being shown about the use of an 'un-agreed' share valuation. It is therefore recommended that tax returns should provide a note to the effect that the valuation may be incorrect. Clearly, this would not be necessary where the valuation has already been agreed by (SAV) under the post-transaction valuation check system (see 14.46).

Post-transaction valuation check procedure

14.46   A head start can be made in agreeing valuations by making use of SAV's 'Post Transaction Valuation Check Procedure'. This enables valuations to be sent to the tax office (soon) after the relevant transaction on form CG34, before the filing date for the SA return. If submitted early enough, this should considerably accelerate the negotiation and agreement of share valuations. SAV have indicated that it will give such cases priority attention (to avoid the need to issue *TMA 1970, s 9A* notices). A further benefit is that the maximum additional tax exposure (on the basis of SAV's alternate value) would be highlighted at an early stage.

Under the 'fast-track' system, the form CG34 is sent to SAV which should either accept the value or put forward an acceptable alternative within 56 days. If SAV are unable to agree the valuation, they will enter into negotiations with the view to agreeing a value before the SA return filing deadline.

There will be cases where the value is submitted too late, or where the valuation is complex, which cannot realistically be settled before the SA return is submitted. In such cases, the SA tax return must still be submitted before the deadline with the taxpayer's proposed share valuation. If the share valuation is not agreed by nine months *after* the filing date for the tax return, HMRC will be asked to issue a (protective) *TMA 1970, s 9A* notice. Where the final agreed valuation differs from the taxpayer's (estimated) valuation incorporated in the tax return, the taxpayer is invited to make an amendment to his self-assessment liability under *TMA 1970, s 28A*.

From 31 March 2016, SAV ceased to provide a Post-Transaction Valuation Check service for unapproved employee share awards or options due to resource constraints (see 13.29).

Share valuation reports

14.47   The author's preferred approach is to submit a realistic share valuation report to SAV at the outset. The report would clearly set out all the relevant background information and the principles upon which the share valuation is based. To avoid having to deal with avoidable time-consuming questions later on, it is much better to provide all relevant information in the report up-front.

The main items covered in the report would be:

(*a*)   the purpose of valuation indicating which tax or taxes are involved;

(*b*)   the date on which the shares are being valued (this is critical as information which cannot be established at that date is not admissible);

(*c*)   the statutory principles upon which the value is based;

(*d*)   financial and trading background, this would include a summary of past results, trends, profit forecasts, shape of the company's order book, state of the industry in which the company operates, economic background and other factors affecting the valuation;

(*e*)   a clearly reasoned valuation, showing detailed calculations and the reasons for the various steps.

14.48   According to Mike Fowler's article in *Tax Adviser* (see 14.45 above), the main reason why valuations are 'rejected' at SAV's initial 'sift' is because 'insufficient information has been provided for a robust valuation judgement to be made'. He suggests that the 'best way to increase the likelihood of a proposed valuation being accepted is to supply a (normally) short, well focused valuation report'.

HMRC's Share Valuation examiners should not be under-estimated – they have considerable experience and expertise and are armed with an extensive database. Examiners will always consider realistic valuation submissions carefully. It is unwise to submit an unrealistic valuation in anticipation of SAV starting from the opposite side, with a view to meeting somewhere in the middle. This approach usually signals a weakness to SAV, which makes it easier for them to commence negotiations on very strong ground and the taxpayer will often find it very difficult to recover from this position.

In his *Tax Adviser* article, Mike Fowler (see above) suggests that improved communication between taxpayers/agents and SAV can assist with resolving problems and help to build a good working relationship. In prolonged cases, a meeting (at which the taxpayer is present) with SAV is often recommended.

SAV wants to resolve cases quickly and promptly identify those cases where agreement is not possible. SAV are now more willing to take 'disputed' cases to the First-tier Tribunal (and no longer need to refer such cases to HMRC's Solicitors' Office).

The case of *Denekamp v Pearce* [1998] STC 1120 provides a useful reminder that all the relevant valuations and points must be presented in any appeal before the Special Commissioner. In this case, the taxpayer's attempt to persuade the High Court to include goodwill in his 31 March 1982 valuation was doomed to fail. This was not presented in his evidence before the Special Commissioner who gave a proper conclusion in the light of the evidence placed before him and the court could not subsequently intervene.

Fiscal share valuation techniques

14.49 Share valuations are normally based on one of the following methods (or sometimes a *weighted* combination of two or all three of them):

(i) *Earnings (capitalised earnings) basis*

Maintainable earnings per share × P/E ratio.

(ii) *Net assets basis*

Balance sheet value of net assets (after deducting liabilities), adjusted to reflect current open market value of assets (divided by number of shares in issue).

(iii) *Dividend yield basis*

$$\frac{\text{Gross dividend \%}}{\text{Required gross dividend yield}} \times \text{Nominal value per share}$$

HMRC Shares and Assets Valuation has provided some useful guidance on unquoted share valuations at www.hmrc.gov.uk/svd/val-land-prop.htm#2 (see section 2 – Unquoted shares). This also indicates the various details that are normally required to support a share valuation.

Earnings basis – majority shareholdings

14.50 On the basis that a company's profits provide an acceptable return from the assets employed, SAV will invariably value majority shareholdings by reference to the company's future maintainable earnings.

The earnings basis was discussed in 14.9–14.17 and the same considerations apply where shares are valued for fiscal reasons.

14.51 The general approach is to look at the company's profit record for the last three years although a longer period may be necessary if the trade is cyclical. The profit record is used to give a guide to the company's future performance and various adjustments may therefore be required to reflect reasonable directors' remuneration and pension contributions. The SAV manual indicates that 'evidence suggests that a pension of up to 20% of the total directors' remuneration package is reasonable' (see also 14.10). A 'notional' tax charge is then applied to arrive at the maintainable or sustainable earnings.

The information assumed to be available to a prospective purchaser would be based on the size of the shareholding and the value of the transaction. For a controlling interest (of 50% or more) the purchaser would be deemed to have access to all the available financial information, including the possibility of a future sale, management accounts and the order book, etc (*Administrators of the Estate of Caton (deceased) v Couch SpC* [1995] SSCD 34; [1997] STC 970).

Hindsight information which becomes available after the date on which the value is being determined cannot be used to influence the valuation.

P/E multiples

14.52   The P/E multiple applied to the maintainable earnings is *best* assessed by looking at the ratios of comparable *unquoted* companies, ideally based on recent known company sales/takeovers.

If comparable reported transactions cannot be found, the P/E multiple for an appropriate comparable quoted company or industry sector is normally used (see 14.17) – HMRC's (SAV) manual discourages the use of *quoted* P/E multiples for valuing majority shareholdings.

The P/E multiple for the quoted company/sector will usually need to be discounted to reflect the differences in prospects, size of company, geographical coverage, profitability, quality of management, as compared with the unquoted company being valued. In practice, quoted company multiples are often discounted by around 60% to 50% to arrive at a suitable multiple for a 'comparable' private company (see also 14.39).

Valuation discounts – majority holdings

14.53   Unless the company is wholly-owned, the value would be discounted to reflect the size of the controlling interest, which would normally be in the following regions:

Voting power	Discount %
99%–75%	5%–10%
51% – 75%	15%–20%

Earnings basis – minority holdings

14.54   Non-controlling shareholdings may also be valued on an earnings basis. A purchaser of an influential minority stake would be expected to have similar information but in less detail. The details provided for a small minority (5%–25%) would be dictated by the transaction value, ranging from full disclosure to the basic information contained in the published accounts, etc. For small minority holdings, 'excess' director's remuneration and pension contributions should *not* be added back to profits as such shareholders would not be able to influence the level of director's remuneration, etc. In the case of non-influential minority holdings, published accounts are only assumed to be available when signed. Valuation discounts normally sought for minority holdings by SAV are set out in 14.39.

Example 4

Valuation of controlling interest on earnings basis

Standen's Bakers Ltd has carried on a long established family bakery business, with various retail bakers' shops in Sussex. Mr Jim, who owns 80 of the company's 100 £1 ordinary shares, has received an offer for the company. He acquired his shareholding in 1971 on the death of his father and wishes to estimate the March 1982 value of the holding to compute his likely CGT liability.

The company's pre-tax profits for the three years to 31 December 1981 (adjusted for excessive director's remuneration) were as follows:

	£'000
y/e 31/12/79	238
y/e 31/12/80	207
y/e 31/12/81	382

Prospects for the business were good in March 1982 and management accounts showed increased monthly profits to that date. A supportable figure of maintainable profits would be £400,000.

The company's tax charge between 1979 and 1981 ranged between 25% and 30%, as a result of capital allowances and stock relief claims. It would therefore be appropriate to apply a tax charge of 30%.

Maintainable earnings:	£'000
Maintainable pre-tax profits	400
Less Tax at 30%	(120)
Maintainable earnings	280
Relevant P/E's for the food sector at 31 March 1982 were:	
Food manufacturing (average)	7.85
Food retailing (average)	13.77

Given that a 'control' holding is being valued, a P/E of 10 could prudently be taken.

Valuation of company:

= Maintainable earnings × P/E ratio

= £280,000 × 10

= £2,800,000

Value per share:

£2,800,000 × 100 = £28,000 per share

Value of Mr Jim's 80 shares at 31 March 1982:

Discounted by 10%

£28,000 × 90% = £25,200 per share.

£25,200 × 80 shares = £2,016,000

NET ASSETS BASIS

When net asset valuations may be appropriate

14.55   Asset based valuations are adopted where:

- the company has substantial asset backing (such as property and investment companies);

- the company is about to go into liquidation; or

- a purchaser is likely to strip the assets out of the company and wind it up (usually if the assets are underutilised).

For example, in *Cash & Carry v Inspector* [1998] STC (SCD) 46 the trading results of a cash and carry business deteriorated steadily from 1978 to a loss making position in 1982. In this case, the company's shares were valued on a net assets basis, uplifted to reflect the market value of its property.

Furthermore, although a going concern value will normally be calculated by reference to earnings, it is always worthwhile valuing the business on an asset basis as a cross check. Material differences may need to be explained or investigated. Normally, the capitalised earnings basis should exceed the value of the tangible net assets with the difference being the goodwill element – is the goodwill figure reasonable in the circumstances? However, if the asset value exceeds the earnings basis, this could indicate that the earnings have been under-capitalised.

Going concern valuation

14.56 There are various types of asset based valuations. If the company is being valued as a going concern, then the open market value of its assets at the valuation date would be taken. The book value of the assets may therefore require adjustment. Although the balance sheet may fairly reflect the value of stock, debtors and possibly plant, a revaluation adjustment may be required in the case of land and buildings.

Break-up basis

14.57 If a 'break-up' basis of valuation is applicable (ie the value that would be realised on a liquidation), then the realisable value of the assets will be taken. HMRC's Share Valuation manual suggests that a further reduction of between 10% and 30% of the net asset value may not be unreasonable for the asset stripper's profit.

14.58 The closure would also involve redundancy payments and other termination costs (for example, cancellation of lease agreements, etc), costs of liquidation and tax charges arising on the disposal of assets. For these reasons, the break-up value of the business is much lower than either a going concern or 'balance sheet' value.

Example 5

Net asset valuation

An extract from the balance sheet of Standen's Bakers Ltd at 31 March 1982 (see Example 4 at 14.54), together with estimated market value, shows:

	Net book value £'000	Market value £'000
Freehold shop premises	430	700
Leasehold shop premises	210	250
Processing Unit and Warehouse	100	450
Net current assets	980	
	1,720	

Current value of net assets

	£'000
Current market values of	
Freehold shops	700
Leasehold shops	250
Processing Unit and Warehouse	450
Net current assets	980
	£2,380

Value per share

$$= \frac{\text{Net asset value}}{\text{Number of shares}}$$

= £2,380,000/100 shares

= £23,800 per share (before discount applicable to relevant shareholding).

SAV may seek a discount against this value to take account of the contingent CGT in the asset values. *At 31 March 1982*, this would be a *maximum* of 28% of the gain inherent in the shops and warehouse, reduced to reflect the remote probability of the tax becoming payable.

DIVIDEND YIELD BASIS

When a dividend yield basis should be used

14.59   A small minority shareholder's return will be based on the company's dividend policy. If the company has a reliable track record of dividends which are either constant, or show a steady increase or decrease, a dividend yield basis may be used. If the company is about to go into liquidation, a break up asset basis would be used with a significant discount for lack of control, etc.

An earnings based value can be used for an influential minority shareholder, particularly where the other shares are thinly spread and he is able to exert some degree of influence. It is important to remember that a fiscal valuation can take no account of the personal qualities or actual influence of the individual shareholder on dividend policy, etc. The transaction is assumed to be an imaginary one in the assumed open market between a hypothetical willing vendor and hypothetical willing purchaser.

An earnings valuation may also be more appropriate if the company's dividends widely fluctuate, or it does not pay dividends. Although it is possible to assume a notional dividend (based on an appropriate 'dividend cover', etc), this is very subjective.

In the author's view, it is better to adopt an earnings valuation which can be argued with greater certainty (particularly if a March 1982 rebasing value is sought), although a greater discount would be required to reflect the impotence of a small minority holding.

Dividend yield formulae

14.60 A dividend yield is calculated as follows:

$$\frac{\text{Nominal value of shares} \times \text{Dividend (as \% of nominal value)}}{\text{Value of share}} = \text{Dividend yield}$$

Thus, to calculate the value of the shares, the formula becomes:

$$\frac{\text{Nominal value of shares} \times \text{Dividend (as \% of nominal value)}}{\text{Dividend yield}} = \text{Value per share}$$

Required dividend yield

14.61 The starting point is to determine the required dividend yield. In practice, SAV will normally start by applying the dividend yield from a comparable quoted company. It is usually difficult to find a true comparison particularly for small family businesses who typically carry on a limited range of activities (quoted companies often have a diverse spread).

Consequently, the average dividend yield from the most comparable sector of the Financial Times Actuaries Shares Indices is normally taken. This average yield would then be increased to recognise the increased risk associated with investment in unquoted companies, such as the lack of marketability of the shares, smaller size, and limited activities. SAV suggests that the yield on quoted shares should be uplifted by between 10% and 30% for the lack of quotation and normal restrictions on transfer. However, in *Administrators of the Estate of Caton (deceased) v Couch SpC* [1995] SSCD 34, a yield of three times that of quoted shares was accepted, even though it was considered to be on the high side. However, if the unquoted company has features which reduce risk to an investor, such as high asset backing, quality products, enjoys a niche market, a high level of dividend cover, etc, then the required yield should be adjusted downwards.

14.62 An alternative approach which is sometimes taken in practice is to take a risk free rate of return (for example, the yield on medium term gilts) and then add a premium for the degree of risk associated with the investment.

This would give the investor's required rate of return. Some valuers *double* the relevant income yield on medium-term gilts, which is then adjusted to reflect a normal 'dividend-cover' of between three and four times and the reliability of dividend payments.

Example 6

Value of shares on a dividend yield basis

Frank owns 50 £1 shares (representing a 5% holding) in Lampard's Electricals Ltd, which trades as a retailer of electrical goods.

SAV has agreed that the 5% holding can be valued on a dividend yield basis as follows:

Net dividend per share	=	£2.00
Dividend percentage	=	$\dfrac{£2}{£1} \times 100 = 200\%$
Comparable quoted dividend yield	=	6%
Adjustment for:		
Non-marketability, reduced size of company, etc		4%
High asset backing		(2%)
Dividend yield		8%
Value per share		
$\dfrac{\text{Dividend percentage} \times \text{Nominal value per share}}{\text{Dividend yield}}$	=	Value per share
$\dfrac{200\% \times £1}{8\%}$	=	£25 per share

MARCH 1982 REBASING VALUATIONS

Basic approach

14.63   The valuation of shares at 31 March 1982 is often required for the purposes of CGT rebasing. The March 1982 rebasing legislation assumes that the shareholder has notionally sold and reacquired their shareholding at its market value at 31 March 1982. Each shareholder is looked at separately for rebasing purposes, which often gives an unfair result for minority shareholders (see below).

Individual or trustee shareholders selling shares that they held at March 1982 can only deduct the March 1982 value of those shares (without any indexation allowance).

The value of a controlling interest held at March 1982 will be based on the value of the company at March 1982, with a small discount if the company is not wholly owned (see 14.53). The notional acquisition at March 1982 is based on the proportion of the shares held at that date.

Share pooling rules

14.64   Since 6 April 2008, individual/trustee shareholders must pool all the shares (of the same class) that they hold in each company for CGT purposes. This means that all shares acquired at different times in the same company are now treated as a single asset, regardless of when they were actually acquired. It should be noted that for all CGT purposes, any rights or bonus issues are strictly allocated to the original share acquisition (as opposed to the actual date of the rights or bonus issue).

Under these rules, share sales are first identified with any shares purchased on the 'same day' and within the next 30 days (designed to counter 'bed and breakfasting' arrangements). After that, they will then be identified with the single share pool (which will frequently be the case for owner-managed companies).

For summary of pre-6 April 2008 share identification rules, see 2010/11 and earlier editions of this book.

14.65   The market value of any shares held at 31 March 1982 will form part of this pooled holding. Where shares of the same class in a company have been acquired at different times (before 1 April 1982), ESC D44 provides they are treated as a 'single holding' for the purposes of a rebasing valuation at 31 March 1982.

Following the introduction of share pooling, the March 1982 rebasing value will only be fully accessed when the vendor sells all their shares. Where the vendor only sells/transfers part of their holding, the March 1982 value will simply be a component of the average base cost of the part-disposal.

Example 7

Part disposal of mixed share pool

In June 2017, Alan sold 400 out of the 2,000 ordinary shares he held in Toon Scorers Ltd.

Alan held 1,250 shares at 31 March 1982, which have an agreed value of £60 per share.

The other 750 shares were acquired in October 2010 by way of a gift from his brother, Kevin, under the protection of a *TCGA 1992, s 165* hold-over relief claim – which gave Alan a 'net' base value of £67,500.

Holding	Number	Base cost/value
		£
March 1982 holding	1,250	75,000
October 2010 – Gift from Kevin (with *s 165* relief)	750	67,500
Balance at June 2017	2,000	142,500
June 2017 – Disposal (400/2,000 × £142,500)	(400)	(28,500)

Alan will be able to deduct £28,500 as his part-disposal base cost against his disposal proceeds.

Part disposal valuations

14.66 Where there is a part disposal of shares from a majority holding, the deductible March 1982 base value would be a pro-rata proportion of the value of the shares held in March 1982 (not the March 1982 value of the shares being sold), as illustrated in the example below.

Example 8

Part disposal of (March 1982) majority holding

In October 2017, Malcolm sold 200 out of the 700 shares he held in Macdonald's Foods Limited, a successful foods company. Malcolm's sale consideration was £600,000 (net of disposal costs).

The company had an issued share capital of 1,000 £1 shares. Malcolm's 700 shares were acquired by him at par in 1975.

Malcolm has been managing director of the company since it started trading in 1979.

The relevant share valuations at March 1982 were:

Holding %	Value per share £
100	300
70	250
25	100

As Malcolm held a 70% interest at 31 March 1982, he would be entitled to value his March 1982 holding at £250 per share for all CGT disposals. He would also be entitled to claim the 10% entrepreneurs' relief CGT rate on his chargeable gain (see 15.34–15.35).

His 2017/18 CGT would be calculated as follows:

	£
Sale proceeds	600,000
Less Part disposal – March 1982 base value	
200 shares × £250 per share (70% majority value)	(50,000)
Chargeable gain	550,000
Less: Annual exemption	(11,300)
Taxable gain at ER rate	538,700
ER CGT rate @ 10%	53,870

Fragmented March 1982 shareholdings

14.67 Each shareholding is looked at separately when valuing shares at March 1982 – there is no aggregation principle. This rule works rather unfairly in the context of a family company where shareholdings are fragmented amongst different members of the family.

A minority holding at March 1982 would be discounted to reflect the shareholders' inability to control, restrictions on transfer, and reliance on the directors for his dividend income. This means, for example, that a minority (discounted) 25% holding would be worth substantially less than 25% of the value of the entire company.

On a sale of the entire company, each shareholder will have a pro-rata share of the proceeds (which will generally reflect the value of the whole company). However, the March 1982 value of a minority shareholding would not be a pro-rata share of the March 1982 value of the company. Thus, a minority shareholder is bound to have a disproportionately large gain, even if the value of the company has kept pace with inflation since March 1982.

14.68 Some comfort can be derived from *Hawkings-Byass v Sassen* [1996] STC (SCD) 319. Here, the Special Commissioners considered that multinationals and the two existing rival family 'shareholder' groups would be prepared to pay a premium to acquire certain minority holdings (18.16%, 11.09%, and 9.09%) in a trading company. They therefore fell to be regarded as 'special purchasers' in determining the 31 March 1982 value of these shareholdings. It was accepted that the shares could be valued as a pro-rata value of the entire company (based on its assets and turnover), but with a one-third reduction to reflect the inherent uncertainties of such bids, such as the ability of the rival family groups to raise the finance. However, a 20% premium uplift was given on this value to arrive at the value of the 18.16% holding.

In some cases, it may be possible to argue that the shareholdings should be valued on a (higher) 'quasi-partnership' basis which would mean taking a simple 'pro-rata' valuation of the entire company (see 14.27). This basis is only likely to apply where it can be demonstrated that one or more of the other shareholders would be 'special purchasers' prepared to pay a pro-rata basis.

Example 9

Valuing minority shareholding at 31 March 1982

In September 2017, Lineker Sports Clothes Ltd was sold for £1,000,000. The company had an issued share capital of 1,000 shares, which had always been held equally by five shareholders (each holding 200 shares).

Based on the sale price, the following statistics can be derived:

Net earnings (ie post tax)	£80,000
Net earnings per share	£80
P/E ratio	12.5

The value of each individual's shareholding at 31 March 1982 is computed along the following lines:

Maintainable net earnings at March 1982 (say)	£20,000
Net earnings per share	£20

The FT Actuaries Textiles Sector P/E at 31 March 1982 was 13.42. After adjusting for non-marketability, minority holding, etc, a P/E ratio of 6.0 is taken for a 20% holding. The value per share is therefore £120 (ie £20 × 6).

Each shareholder receives proceeds of £200,000, but will only have a deductible March 1982 base value of £24,000, ie £120 per share × 200 shares.

Husband and wife shareholdings at 31 March 1982

14.69 Special rules apply where a company is controlled jointly by a husband and wife. Although each separately has a minority holding, their shares must still be valued in isolation (there is no equivalent of the 'related property' rule which applies for IHT (see 17.8)). However, if the couple own shares in the same company (of the same class) at 31 March 1982 and the wife subsequently transfers her shares to her husband, those shares can be treated as held by him at 31 March 1982 for the purposes of the rebasing valuation. The same rule applies if the husband transfers shares to his wife (see *TCGA 1992, Sch 3, para 1* and SP5/89).

The mandatory 31 March 1982 share valuation will automatically apply to the entire March 1982 holding (ie including those originally held by the transferee spouse and those subsequently transferred). This concession provides a valuable tax saving opportunity where the sale of a 'husband and wife' company is contemplated. By arranging a transfer of shares from one spouse to the other, the recipient spouse may be able to substantially increase their March 1982 valuation by switching it on to a controlling basis. The transfer of shares should be executed before a purchaser is found to avoid the risk of HMRC countering the advantage under the *Furniss v Dawson* principle (*Furniss v Dawson* [1984] 1 All ER 530). (See the decision in *R v CIR, ex p Kaye* [1992] STC 581.) However, the impact on the shareholders' ER entitlement would also have to be considered.

Example 10

Valuation at March 1982 – aggregation of spouse's holding

The March 1982 valuations for the shares in Hughes Builders Ltd were as follows:

	Shares	*March 1982 value per share*	*March 1982 Valuation*
		£	£
Mr Hughes	40	120	4,800
Mrs Hughes	40	120	4,800
Mr Emilyn	20	30	600
	100		

However, if prior to a sale of the company, Mr Hughes transferred, say, 36 shares to Mrs Hughes, she would then have 76% holding. This holding (valued on an earnings basis) might be worth, say, £700 per share. Mrs Hughes' total base value would then be increased to £53,200 (76 × £700 per share).

Mr Hughes will be entitled to keep the original March 1982 valuation for the four shares he retains.

Valuing shares by reference to size of transferor's March 1982 holding

14.70 Where shares held at 31 March 1982 are subsequently transferred between husband and wife, ESC D44 enables the *transferee* spouse to elect for their valuation to be calculated by reference to the size of the *transferor's* holding. This will often enable a higher March 1982 valuation to be obtained (due to the lower 'valuation' discounts applied to larger shareholdings) (see Example 10 below). The election must be made within 12 months of the 31 January in the tax year following that in which the shares are sold, or such later time as permitted by HMRC.

Example 11

Application of ESC D44

Mariner's (Boats and Leisure) Ltd was incorporated in 1976 with 100 £1 ordinary shares, which were held as follows:

Mr Mariner	80
Mrs Mariner	20

Mr Mariner transferred a further ten shares to his wife in May 2015.

On a subsequent sale, Mrs Mariner can elect under ESC D44 to compute her March 1982 valuation as 30/80ths of the value of an 80% shareholding in the company at that date (rather than a 30% holding in isolation at 31 March 1982).

KEY MARCH 1982 REBASING ISSUES

Main basic principles

14.71 It is useful to highlight some of the main principles affecting March 1982 share valuations:

(*a*) It is not possible to index back to March 1982 from the ultimate sale price. On the other hand, the use of foresight is permissible and should be used to demonstrate that the trading prospects and future growth, etc were rosy before March 1982.

(*b*) If there are any arm's length transfers of any shares within a year of March 1982, these may provide very persuasive evidence of a high March 1982 valuation.

If, on the other hand, low valuations have previously been established with SAV for CGT or capital transfer tax purposes close to March 1982, they should be distinguished, by reference to the size of the shareholding and other circumstances. This stance is clearly easier to sustain if the original value was agreed with SAV reserving its position on a 'without prejudice' basis.

(c)   The size of the shareholding will influence the level of financial and other information deemed to be available to a prospective purchaser at 31 March 1982. Controlling shareholders have full access to in-house information, such as management accounts, forecasts, etc leading up to March 1982. On the other hand, minority holdings of 'low value' shares may only be entitled to those published accounts which are signed before 31 March 1982. This may mean, for example, that if the accounts to 31 December 1981 were not available at 31 March 1982, only the 31 December 1980 and previous year's accounts could be taken.

(d)   The maintainable profits are normally determined from the last three years audited accounts, adjusted for excessive director's remuneration, etc. The general recession in the early 1980s meant that most companies experienced a decline in profits between 1979 and 1982. This trend may work to the advantage of a minority shareholder, bearing in mind the information standards mentioned in (c) above. On the other hand, this may be detrimental to controlling valuations which are based on up-to-date information.

(e)   Many companies did not pay the headline corporation tax rate in the early 1980s, due to the availability of 100% capital allowances and stock relief. This can be used to substantiate a lower or even a nil tax charge, thus increasing the maintainable earnings. (Note, however that P/E ratios (at 31 March 1982) published in the *Investors' Chronicle* reflect a full corporation tax charge and are higher than the FTASI. A consistent approach must therefore be taken.)

(f)   The SAV's 'Post Transaction Valuation Checks' system (see 14.46) should be used to obtain early comfort and agreement on 31 March 1982 share valuations. This is done by completing HMRC's prescribed form CG34 *after* the relevant share transaction. In many cases, provided the form is submitted promptly, the 31 March 1982 valuation should be agreed before the 31 January deadline for the self-assessment return (IR press release 4 February 1997).

(g)   There is also an alternative SAV procedure for early agreement of 31 March 1982 share values (only) where this is required by a number of shareholders of the same company. The 31 March 1982 valuations for each shareholder can be submitted to SAV *after* the disposal. All shareholders with similar holdings to be valued at March 1982 must be prepared to be bound by the value agreed. For these purposes, the

SAV must be provided with a full list of the shareholders, giving the size of their holdings at both 31 March 1982 and the date of disposal, and supplying details of their individual tax offices (*IR Press Release –* 18 November 1991). However, many shareholders are likely to prefer the 'fast track' system using form CG34 which enables them to agree their 31 March 1982 values on an *individual* basis.

Practical points from the *Marks v Sherred* case

14.72   The Special Commissioners' case of *Marks v Sherred SpC* [2004] SSCD 362 gives an interesting practical insight into the contrasting arguments surrounding a 31 March 1982 valuation of shares. The relevant shareholding being valued was a 66% holding in Ross Marks Ltd, a domestic electronics import and sale business. Both sides agreed that the correct basis of valuation was to use the capitalised earnings basis (see 14.50–14.54).

The taxpayer's expert witness based her calculation on the last available accounts to *31 March 1981* (which showed turnover of around £1.5 million and pre-tax profits of £160,000). However, in the next year (US$/£) exchange rate movements and increased overheads had adversely affected profits. Consequently, she recalculated the figures to smooth out the effects of the exchange fluctuations by reference to the average for the previous three years, which gave net maintainable earnings of £190,000. Using a P/E multiple of 11, this valued the shares at £1,050,000.

The Revenue expert decided that a hypothetical purchaser would be more heavily influenced by the current trading and adverse exchange position at the time as the company paid for almost all its stock in US dollars (and it did not hedge its dollar position). He also considered that a purchaser would require sight of the 1982 books. On the other hand, he thought that a purchaser would seek to make savings on the existing high levels of directors' remuneration and entertaining. These findings produced maintainable earnings of £85,000, and based on a multiple of 10, gave a valuation of £561,000.

14.73   Following *Caton v Couch SpC* [1995] SSCD 34 (see 14.51), the Commissioner agreed with the Revenue's expert that a purchaser would insist on seeing even confidential information, and so would look at all possible current trading data leading up to the purchase. At March 1982, the exchange rate was $1.82 to the £ (which was considerably less than the 'smoothed' rate of $2.13 to the £ used by the taxpayer's expert). The company would have to acquire products based on current conditions although a purchaser would seek to cut costs. Another relevant factor was that the company was contemplating moving part of its manufacturing to the UK to reduce its exchange risk. Furthermore, if the business was basically sound, a prudent purchaser would not be unduly influenced by one bad year (1982).

Having weighed up all these factors, the Commissioner valued the shares at £633,000 (by applying a multiple of 10 to net maintainable earnings of £95,510).

PLANNING CHECKLIST – VALUING A FAMILY OR OWNER-MANAGED COMPANY

Company

- Maintainable earnings are normally used to value a business as a going concern – the maintainable earnings must reflect the likely future circumstances of the business and therefore historic results may need to be adjusted.

- EBITDA valuations are becoming increasing popular particularly where the relevant company has material levels of debt. However, care must be taken to ensure a suitable EBITDA-based multiple is used. Based on reported deals over the past 20 years, EBITDA multiples have 'averaged' between 4 and 8.

Working shareholders

- Commercial valuations of the entire company/business are based on a full knowledge of its prospects, trading results, conditions, etc.

- Minority share valuations required under the Articles are frequently discounted (unless a 'quasi-partnership' basis is appropriate).

- Fiscal valuations are only based on details that would reasonably be relevant to the size of the relevant 'stake' in the company (other gleaned information is ignored).

- It is often possible to support a robust 'favourable' 31 March 1982 share valuation with a carefully structured business case.

Other employees

- 'Unrestricted' shares are valued on a 'money's worth' principle which reflects the employee's personal knowledge about the company's affairs.

- Restricted shares (that are subject to employee-specific conditions) are valued on a CGT 'open market' basis, therefore taking into account only details that would be relevant to a hypothetical purchaser. However, somewhat incongruously, HMRC – SAV often seeks to take interim management accounts and budgets into account.

- Shares in an approved share option or EMI scheme are valued according to CGT 'open market' principles.

Non-working shareholders

- 'Minority' share values are heavily discounted – this is good news where tax is payable, but bad news for March 1982 rebasing deduction purposes.

- Consider transferring shares to/from spouse to increase size of holding for March 1982 rebasing valuation retrospectively.

Chapter 15

Selling the Owner-Managed Business or Company

PREPARING A BUSINESS FOR SALE

15.1   As economic activity increases there is plenty of evidence to demonstrate that buyers are keen to purchase 'smaller' owner-managed businesses that have survived the economic downturn and are well positioned to take advantage of opportunities over the next few years. Indeed, many buyers and investors with readily available cash or access to relatively cheap finance have been quick to make acquisitions whilst sale prices still remain relatively attractive.

Owner-managers must plan for the sale of their company well in advance. To obtain the best possible price, the owner-manager should seek to maximise the company's earnings. For example, they might need to consider whether it is possible to lift margins or postpone expenditure with a long-term payback (for example, an advertising campaign). The timing of any planned exit will depend on a number of factors. These would include market trends (there are likely to be more potential buyers in a market expected to grow), the general level of mergers and acquisitions activity within the relevant market/industry sector and the future prospects within it.

To stand a realistic chance of obtaining the best price, the owner-manager will need to demonstrate that the underlying performance of the business is strong, preferably showing an improving trend. Many prospective purchasers will also wish to ensure that the business has a dedicated and committed management team. Other important factors would include a tightly controlled business, strong brand image and market profile, proven ability to attract a wide range of 'desirable' customers, and a clean 'tax profile'. The identification of these (and other key issues) should take place well in advance (in some cases up to two years) to enable the required improvements to take place in the business well before it is put up for sale. In some cases, it may be necessary to 'clean-up' the company by eliminating shareholder loans and personal use of company assets.

Recent empirical evidence suggests that the majority of owner-managers who have built up successful companies expect to sell them on and start again, indicating the emergence of the so-called serial entrepreneur. A large majority of owners hope and expect that they would be able to sell their business on to trade or financial acquirers in the next two to three years, after which they intend to repeat the exercise. Obtaining the 'right' price is regarded as the biggest priority when selling, with job security for staff also being considered a principal concern.

POSSIBLE SALE ROUTES AND STRUCTURES

15.2   Many company sales are made to 'trade' buyers – which can be a competitor, an overseas buyer wishing to obtain a 'foothold' in the relevant sector in the UK, or a company seeking to enter into a new market via acquisition. Depending on the relevant factors, the purchaser may be willing to pay a premium to enter into the owner-manager's market. One important area will be to ensure that the seller's management team remain committed to the deal. If key managers hold shares, this will provide a degree of incentive. In some cases, it may be desirable to award one-off bonuses as a 'sweetener'

The owner-manager may wish to sell to their existing senior management team under a management buy-out (MBO). Some owner-managers look on an MBO as a reward for loyalty and support to management for their role in developing the business. In many cases the management team may not be able to assemble sufficient financial resources to buy the business. Private equity funding will often be used to help to bridge the gap. For these reasons, the price obtained under an MBO deal is generally lower than the owner-manager can expect to receive under a trade sale. Furthermore, many trade buyers will often be prepared to pay a premium (see 14.28).

There are two main sale structures. Owner-managers may either secure the sale of the trade and assets out of the company or they can sell their shares in the company. Each method gives rise to different commercial, tax and legal consequences, which therefore influences the way in which the transaction is structured.

Generally, the sellers prefer to sell their shares, whereas the purchaser will often prefer to buy assets (unless the stamp duty land tax cost is prohibitive – see 12.24), but there will be situations where one party requires the opposite route to the one the other party is seeking. In the writer's experience, there are often one or two key factors, which will dictate the manner in which the business is to be sold. Although this is a matter of negotiation between the two parties, in some cases one of them will have the 'upper hand' in imposing the structure of the deal.

This chapter focuses on the tax implications and strategies for the seller. The purchaser's position is considered in detail in Chapter 12.

BASIC CGT RULES

Date of disposal

15.3   The sale of the company's assets or shares will involve a disposal for CGT purposes. A disposal is recognised for CGT at the time an unconditional contract is entered into, and not the date of completion. In *Jerome v Kelly* [2004] STC 887, the House of Lords reinforced the view that this provision only dealt with the timing of the disposal. It does not go as far as saying that this is when the disposal is made (ie when an asset is transferred on completion). The date of disposal under a conditional contract arises when the relevant condition precedent is satisfied or waived [*TCGA 1992, s 28*].

On an asset sale, the company's corporation tax accounting period (CTAP) ends on the date the trade and assets are sold, normally representing the cessation of trade for the seller company (see 15.7 for illustration on an asset sale).

Asset sale – payment of corporation tax

15.3A   Many owner managed companies will pay their corporation tax nine months after the end of the relevant CTAP.

However, 'large' companies (ie broadly those with annual taxable profits exceeding £1.5 million) must pay their corporation tax (electronically) in instalments, starting six months and 13 days from the start of the accounting period with the final instalment ending on a date which is three months and 14 days after the end of the accounting period (see 4.40–4.51). Interim instalments are payable every three months, as the length of the company's accounting period allows. In most cases, instalments are paid in the seventh, tenth, twelfth and fifteenth months after the start of the CTAP. (Note that the £1.5 million profit limit is divided by the number of 'related 51% group companies' (see 3.18.)

For CTAPs starting after 31 March 2017, companies with taxable profits exceeding £20 million will have accelerated quarterly instalment payment dates, with their tax being paid in the third, sixth, ninth and twelfth months of their CTAP. If company has related 51% group companies, the £20 million threshold is divided by the number of these companies plus one.

Share sale – payment of CGT

15.3B   Under self-assessment, individuals are liable to pay their CGT on 31 January following the year of assessment. Thus, if someone sells their shares in (say) October 2017, they will pay their CGT on 31 January 2019. Where they anticipate selling their shares shortly before the end of the tax year, consideration should be given to deferring the date of disposal until after 5 April, as this will delay the payment of the tax by one year.

Different tax payments dates may apply where an earn-out forms part of the sale consideration (see 15.68).

Consideration

15.4 In most cases, it will be reasonably straightforward to ascertain the consideration received for the disposal of the shares or other business assets. However, in some situations, the precise legal drafting of the obligations placed on the purchaser might be construed as additional 'consideration' received by the seller.

For example, in the recent case of *Cooling v HMRC* (2015) UK FTT 223 (TC), the First-tier Tribunal (FTT) held that the consideration for a share sale included the assumption by the purchaser of a debt owed by the seller to the target company, even though the consideration clause provided that the value of the debt assumed by the purchaser was assumed to be nil. The FTT agreed with HMRC that the consideration should be increased for CGT purposes by the amount of the debt assumed by the purchaser.

The FTT referred to the earlier decision of the High Court in *Spectros International Plc v Madden* [1997] STC 114. In the *Spectros* case, the sale agreement required the purchaser to pay $20,001,000, of which $20,000,000 should be used to clear the target company's bank overdraft (which had been used to pay a pre-sale dividend) and $1,000 for the target company's common stock (ie shares). The court had little difficulty in rejecting the seller's contention that the company's common stock had been sold for $1,000. Justice Lightman held that, on a true construction of the agreement, the 'consideration' paid for the common stock was $20,001,000 since the seller could direct how the amount should be applied. He added that if the parties had intended to sell the common stock for $1,000, the sale agreement could easily have been worded to achieve this. It is therefore important to ensure that any obligation to clear a company's indebtedness is dealt with as a 'subsidiary' term of the contract rather than forming part of the main 'consideration' clause.

In *Collins v Revenue and Customs Commissioners* [2009] EWHC 284 (Ch), part of the stated consideration for the purchase of shares consisted of making a payment to the target company to fund a contribution to the seller's pension scheme. This was treated as part of the seller's sale consideration for CGT. Once again, the precise legal wording of the sale contract was unhelpful to the seller. However, the courts follow the clear wording of the specific agreement and will not attempt to redraft it to obtain a better tax result. In the *Collins* case, the target company could have made the pension contribution before the shares were sold, with an appropriate reduction being made in the consideration for the shares to reflect this.

Deferred consideration

15.5 If a fixed part of the consideration is deferred, this must initially be included in the CGT consideration, without any discount for the delay in receipt or the fact that it may not be paid (see 15.64–15.68 for the treatment of variable 'earn-out' consideration). The same rule applies even if the deferred element of the consideration is conditional upon a specified event. The original CGT liability will only be revised if the taxpayer can satisfy the Inspector that part of the consideration has proved irrecoverable [*TCGA 1992, s 48*].

The requirement to bring the full amount of the deferred consideration into the original CGT computation and pay tax on it can often give rise to cash-flow difficulties. Thus, provided the sale consideration is payable over a period exceeding 18 months, HMRC may allow the seller to pay the tax in instalments. This instalment relief must be claimed by the seller [*TCGA 1992, s 280*]. HMRC's practice is to look for CGT instalments equivalent to 50% of each deferred tranche of sale proceeds until the CGT is fully paid. The instalment period cannot exceed eight years.

In *Collins v Revenue and Customs Commissioners* [2009] EWHC 284 (Ch) the deferred consideration included further payments based on future turnover, which was therefore variable in nature. The actual amount received was lower than expected and the taxpayer sought a partial refund of the original CGT. However, it was held that the (unascertainable) deferred consideration fell to be taxed in accordance with the principles in *Marren v Ingles* (1980) STC 500 (see 15.65), and thus the *TCGA 1992, s 48* refund mechanism was not available.

On a share sale, it is often preferable to obtain a tax deferral by securing the issue of a loan note from the acquiring company for the deferred consideration (see 15.54–15.58).

SALE OF ASSETS AND TRADE

Legal overview

15.6 The starting point in framing any agreement for the sale of the trade and assets is to identify precisely the assets and liabilities which will be taken over. This may also involve the assignment of leases and novation of trading contracts. Employees will be transferred under the *Transfer of Undertakings (Protection of Employment) Regulations 2006, SI 2006/246* (see further coverage in 12.21).

The legal documentation for an asset sale is likely to contain fewer warranties than under a share sale. Most sale agreements will require the seller to covenant that he will not compete with the business being sold within a reasonable time scale and/or defined geographical limits (although unreasonable 'non-compete' covenants are unlikely to be upheld by the courts).

General tax consequences

15.7   Under this method, the company will sell the trade, together with its various trading assets. This will inevitably create a cessation of the trade for tax purposes, which will bring an end to the accounting period for corporation tax purposes, unless the company is continuing another trade [*CTA 2009, s 10(1)(d), (e)*]. The termination of the accounting period will accelerate the payment of tax liabilities. For example, take a company that does not pay tax at the main rate and normally produces accounts to 31 December each year. It sells its trade and assets on 31 August 2017 thus creating a corporation tax accounting period (CTAP) of eight months to 31 August 2017. The tax for this period would, therefore, fall due on 1 June 2018 (ie nine months following 31 August 2017).

Any unrelieved trading losses will effectively be lost when the seller company ceases to trade [*CTA 2010, s 45(4)*]. Where there are substantial trading losses that would otherwise go unrelieved, the company should seek to allocate more of the sale consideration (on a commercially justifiable basis) to those assets giving rise to a trading receipt, such as trading stock, plant and intangibles falling within the *CTA 2009, Pt 8* regime. If the seller company is part of a group, it may be possible to shelter the taxable profits on sale by way of group relief (see 4.39).

Capital gains may arise on the disposal of property and goodwill (provided this was held by the company on 1 April 2002) (see 15.13). Under the corporate capital gains regime, indexation relief continues to be given in full.

Disposals of industrial buildings (and hotels/agricultural buildings) no longer trigger any balancing adjustment (see 15.12).

The sale of 'new' goodwill and any other intangible fixed assets (acquired or created by the seller company after 31 March 2002) generally give rise to a taxable trading receipt.

Potential double tax charge

15.8   Probably the main disadvantage of an asset sale is the potential double charge to tax. This is further exacerbated by the lower CGT rates that are often secured on share sales (where entrepreneurs' relief (ER) is available).

The proceeds for the sale of the business will be subject to corporation tax. If the seller needs the cash from the sale of the business, a further tax liability will be suffered on the extraction of the net proceeds from the company. The manner in which the cash is extracted will influence the tax liability (see Chapter 2).

Apportionment of sale consideration

15.9   The tax payable by the company would depend upon the nature of each asset and the consideration that has been attributed to each one. In this context, it is important to achieve a sensible allocation of the total price paid for the business amongst the various individual assets and this should be specified in the sale agreement. For example, if the company has unused trading losses which would be lost on cessation, it may be possible to absorb them by allocating higher values to assets that would produce additional trading receipts, such as trading stock or plant and machinery which would produce a balancing charge.

In some cases, it may be possible to save tax by placing a realistic value on the business' books and records, with the tenable argument that the value of each valuable individual file, book, etc is below the £6,000 chattel exemption in *TCGA 1992, s 262*. Given the wide range of the underlying books, files and computer records, it would be difficult for HMRC to argue that the books and records are a 'set of articles'. (If they were treated as a 'set', this would negate the 'capital gains' benefit of each individual item being below £6,000.)

Provided the seller and purchaser have negotiated the price at arm's length and the allocation has been specified in the sale agreement, HMRC are unlikely to challenge the apportionment of the total price. However, it should be noted that HMRC have a statutory power to re-apportion the consideration on a 'just and reasonable' basis for virtually all types of asset. This authority is given for the purposes of computing chargeable gains; capital allowances and corresponding balancing adjustments; and the tax on the sale of trading stock (on cessation). For relevant legislation, see *TCGA 1992, s 52(4)*, *CAA 2001, s 562*, and *CTA 2009, s 165(3)* respectively. In *EV Booth (Holdings) Ltd v Buckwell* [1980] STC 578, it was held that a *party* to a sale could not resile from the apportionment in the contract for CGT purposes. Justice Browne-Wilkinson also went on to say, by way of obiter, that the Inland Revenue might be able to look through the apportionment in some cases. In practice, HMRC is only likely to challenge the split of the consideration in arm's length deals where the allocated prices are blatantly unrealistic. HMRC (Stamp Taxes) will also generally accept any 'sensible' allocation for SDLT purposes (see 12.29).

A slightly different approach is taken for goodwill and other intangible fixed assets under *CTA 2009, Pt 8*. Since this is an accounts-based regime, *CTA 2009, s 856(3)* states that the amounts allocated in the accounts under GAAP must be used for the intangibles legislation in *CTA 2009, Pt 8* (see 12.49), although no relief is now given for goodwill acquired after 8 July 2015.

The detailed considerations that might apply in relation to the main categories of asset are set out in 15.10–15.18 below. Many of these factors will also influence the manner in which the price is apportioned.

Optimising seller's indexation allowance(s)

15.10 On a corporate trade and asset sale, it is particularly important to recognise that the indexation allowance (which is still available to companies) cannot create or increase a capital loss. If the intended apportionment of the sale price gives rise to a restriction of indexation allowance on one or more assets (thus giving a 'nil' gain), yet one or more of the other assets show capital gains, the allocation should be adjusted. If the price of each 'indexation-restricted' asset is increased, this will reduce or eliminate the wasted indexation allowance. As far as possible, the broad rule of thumb must be to ensure that each asset is sold for an amount at least equal to its CGT base cost and the accrued indexation thereon (see Example 1 below).

Example 1

Minimising loss of indexation relief on asset sale

Noble Ltd is negotiating the sale of its hi-fi retail business as a going concern, involving the sale of its trade and assets. The company purchased the business in March 1997.

Both parties have agreed a price of £500,000 for the retail premises and goodwill (with stock being purchased at book value). The draft sale agreement has apportioned the price as follows:

	£
Retail premises	350,000
Goodwill	150,000

The net capital gain based on the above apportionment would be:

	Sale Price	Cost	Indexation @ (say) 80%	Capital Gain
	£	£	£	£
Goodwill	150,000	(20,000)	(16,000)	114,000
Retail premises	350,000	(250,000)	(100,000)*	0
	500,000			115,000

* £250,000 × 80% = £200,000 but restricted to £100,000 to produce no gain. Indexation relief of £100,000 is therefore 'wasted'.

A more sensible apportionment (assuming the figures could be justified) would be:

	£
Retail premises	460,000
Goodwill	40,000

This would reduce the chargeable gain to £14,000 as shown below:

	Sale Price	Cost	Indexation at 80%	Capital Gain
	£	£	£	£
Goodwill	40,000	(20,000)	(16,000)	4,000
Retail premises	460,000	(250,000)	(200,000)	10,000
	500,000			14,000

Property

15.11 The disposal of freehold or leasehold property may give rise to a capital gain or loss. The seller may wish to retain the property and grant a lease to the purchaser instead. Any premium received on the grant will represent a 'part-disposal' for capital gains purposes, with an appropriate apportionment of base cost using the standard formula:

$$\frac{A}{A + B}$$

Where   A = sale proceeds

B = market value of the property (subject to the lease)

If a 'short' lease is granted, part of the premium will be taxed as property business *income* [*CTA 2009, s 217*]. The amount taxed is computed by reference to the following formula:

$$P \times \frac{(50 - Y)}{50}$$

Where   P = the amount of the premium; and

Y = the number of complete years of the lease (except the first year).

If the property was owned at 31 March 1982, its value at that date can be deducted as the base cost in arriving at the capital gain. With indexation based thereon currently running at about 240% (for a corporate seller), the capital gain may be small or nil, given the trend in property values over the period. Stamp duty land tax will be payable by the purchaser on the acquisition of the freehold/leasehold interest or the grant of a lease (see 12.24).

Where a leasehold interest, which has less than 50 years to run, is being sold, the deductible base cost is restricted by a 'depreciation' adjustment, *TCGA 1992, Sch 8* and a disposal at book value may therefore produce a taxable gain.

Where the property has been occupied and used for the purposes of the trade, it may be possible to roll-over any capital gain against the acquisition of qualifying re-investment expenditure. This may be useful if the company or group has other trading activities or is likely to begin a new trading venture in the near future [*TCGA 1992, ss 152* and *175*]. It is not possible to roll over 'property' capital gains against acquisitions of goodwill and other intangibles [*TCGA 1992, s 156ZA*].

Gains on assets owned *personally* by a shareholder may also be rolled over in this way provided the old and the new assets are used in the shareholder's *same* 'personal company' [*TCGA 1992, s 157*]. For these purposes, a personal company is one in which the individual holds at least 5% of the voting rights. A claim for roll-over relief was denied by the Special Commissioners in *Boparan v HMRC* [2007] (SpC 587), where 'personally-owned' chicken breeding farms and feed mills were let to a 100% *subsidiary* company. Since Mr Boparan (the shareholder) did not directly exercise the voting rights of the subsidiary, it was not his 'personal company'. It was not sufficient that control of the subsidiary could effectively be achieved on a 'look-through' basis by virtue of Mr Boparan's ownership of the holding company's shares. Had the assets been let to the holding company instead or had Mr Boparan had a minimum 5% direct equity voting stake in the subsidiary, his roll-over relief claim would have been successful.

Industrial buildings or hotels

15.12   The seller may have claimed industrial buildings allowances (IBAs) or hotel buildings allowances ('HBAs'). However, these allowances were completely abolished on 1 April 2011, and thus there is no clawback of previous allowances.

Goodwill

Tax treatment of pre- and post-1 April 2002 goodwill and intangibles

15.13   Goodwill or other intangible fixed assets are subject to two distinct tax regimes depending on whether the relevant asset was acquired or originated before 1 April 2002 or from this date onwards.

If the seller held the goodwill or intangible asset on 31 March 2002, it falls within the capital gains regime. In many cases, the goodwill will be created internally by the seller over the period of its trading. There is no question of any apportionment being made since *CTA 2009, s 884* states that if the company was in business before April 2002, then its entire goodwill will be taxed under the capital gains rules. The same treatment applies if the selling company had acquired the trading goodwill from a related party that owned it before 1 April 2002. This would apply, for example, on a prior intra-group transfer where the transferor group company carried out the relevant trade before April 2002.

Where goodwill is taxed as a *capital gain* and the selling company was trading in *March 1982*, the March 1982 value of the goodwill can be deducted as the base cost, plus a significant indexation uplift (see 15.11). If the company can show that it was generating substantial profits prior to March 1982, this will be particularly beneficial.

The goodwill valuation for March 1982 may be derived from the March 1982 rebasing value of the 'company' – ie it would be based on an appropriate earnings multiple after deducting the value of the company's tangible net assets at 31 March 1982 – see 14.6, 14.9–14.18 and 14.22.)

Where the selling company only commenced trading (or purchased the goodwill/intangible asset from an 'unrelated' party) after 31 March 2002, the profit or loss on disposal falls within the 'income' regime in the *CTA 2009, Pt 8*. The taxable profit or allowable loss will usually be the amount reported in the accounts, which would be based on the sales proceeds less the amortised cost per the accounts (there is no indexation relief).

The *F (No 2) A 2015* blocked tax amortisation relief for goodwill purchased after 7 July 2015. Thus, where goodwill is acquired after 7 July 2015, the taxable profit will generally be the excess of the sale proceeds over the original purchase cost (with no indexation).

These key principles are illustrated below:

Sale of goodwill/ intangibles

Trade A was carried on before April 2002 and therefore the sale would be taxed as a capital gain.

Trade B started in October 2004 and therefore the profit on sale would be taxed as (trading) income under *CTA 2009, Pt 8.*

Know-how

15.14   On a sale of goodwill under the 'old' *capital gains* regime (see 15.13), there may still be advantages in allocating part of its disposal value to know-how owned by the company – for example to offset against unused trading losses brought forward.

Know-how is defined in *CTA 2009, s 176(1)* and *CAA 2001, s 452(2)* and includes industrial information about manufacturing and processing goods or materials. However, the sale of know-how on a disposal of the trade is treated as a sale of *goodwill unless* a joint election is made between the seller and purchaser within two years following the sale [*CTA 2009, s 178*]. It is therefore vital to ensure that a joint election is made where the transaction is to be treated as a sale of know-how and this should ideally be signed before the sale contract or be a binding condition of the contract.

Provided that the appropriate election is made, the seller company can treat the know-how profit as a trading receipt.

The *purchaser* will generally be able to obtain tax relief on the know-how (based on the amount written off each year under GAAP) under *CTA 2009, Pt 8.*

Roll-over relief for capital gain/income profit

15.15   The sale of goodwill will either produce a capital gain or income profit (as discussed in 15.13 above). However, in both cases, the capital gain/income profit can only be rolled-over against reinvestment in goodwill and intangibles under *CTA 2009, Pt 8, Ch 7.*

The reinvestment period starts one year before and ends three years after the gain/income profit arose. Under the intangibles roll-over relief regime, the gain/income profit is deducted against the reinvestment expenditure for the intangibles regime.

For goodwill purchased/acquired before 8 July 2015, the rolled-over gain/income profit therefore reduces the future tax amortisation of the acquired goodwill or other intangible fixed asset. (In such cases, the intangibles amortisation is based on the tax written down value of the new asset rather than the carrying value debited in the accounts) (see also 12.47 and 12.50) [*CTA 2009, s 758*].

For goodwill acquired after 7 July 2015, the rolled-over gain/income profit is effectively deferred until the 'replacement' goodwill/intangible asset is subsequently sold.

It is important to recognise that (since April 2002) it is not possible to roll-over capital gains on goodwill under the *TCGA 1992* capital gains business asset roll-over regime. These gains can now only be rolled-over against new qualifying expenditure on goodwill, intellectual property, brands and so on [*TCGA 1992, s 156ZA*].

For these purposes, the gain/income profit is deemed to be reinvested as the last component of the reinvestment expenditure. Thus, if the qualifying expenditure on the acquired goodwill/other intangible asset is less than the proceeds arising on the sale, it is only possible to roll-over the amount by which the reinvestment expenditure exceeds the original cost of the old asset, as shown in Example 2 below.

Example 2

Roll-over of capital gain on goodwill purchased after 7 July 2015

The Moore Group Ltd has operated a number of different leisure-based businesses for many years.

In December 2016, it sold its chain of night clubs. As part of this deal, it received £2,000,000 for the related goodwill which generated a capital gain of £2,000,000. (Since the company started the trade, there was no base cost for goodwill.)

In October 2017, it decided to purchase a small advertising business paying £1,500,000 for the goodwill (including the client lists).

The company will only be able to claim partial roll-over relief on the capital gain of £2,000,000 because it has only spent £1,500,000 of the December 2016 sale proceeds.

	£
Expenditure on goodwill/client lists (October 2017)	1,500,000
Less: Base cost of Night Club business goodwill	(–)
Amount available for roll-over relief	1,500,000

Following the claim for roll-over, the tax written-down value of the new goodwill/client lists is reduced to nil as follows:

	£
Goodwill/client lists – cost	1,500,000
Less: Intangibles roll-over relief	(1,500,000)
Tax written down value	–

If the company had paid £2,500,000 for the small advertising business, it would have been able to claim full roll-over relief on the capital gain of £2,000,000 since the £2,000,000 proceeds from the sale of the Night Club business would have been fully reinvested. In this case, following the roll-over relief claim, the tax written down value of the new goodwill/client lists is £500,000, would be calculated as follows:

	£
Goodwill/client lists – cost	2,500,000
Less: Intangibles roll-over relief	(2,000,000)
Tax written down value	500,000

No tax amortisation' of the £500,000 would be allowed since the goodwill/client lists were acquired after 7 July 2015.

Plant and machinery

Balancing adjustments on sale

15.16 In practice, plant often tends to be sold at its net book value. As the company is ceasing to trade, this will give rise to a taxable balancing charge, where the proceeds exceed the tax written down value (TWDV) of the plant. (A balancing allowance arises if the TWDV exceeds the sale proceeds.) If the company wishes to minimise the balancing charge, it may prefer to sell the plant at TWDV. Provided that the purchaser can claim capital allowances on the plant, HMRC cannot substitute market value [*CAA 2001, s 61(2) Table* (Disposal event 1)].

Many buildings contain fixtures (eg some parts of the electrical system, lifts, etc), upon which plant and machinery allowances would normally have been claimed. Where the building is sold, part of the sale proceeds should be ascribed to the 'fixtures'. The amount allocated to the capital allowances 'pool' by the seller will be governed by the joint election under *CAA 2001, s 198* between the seller and purchaser (although the amount cannot exceed the original cost of the fixtures) (see 12.43A).

(The *s 198* election must contain various details, including the agreed amount, the parties to the election and their tax district references and details of the relevant fixtures and property – see 12.44 and 12.45.)

Capital gains treatment and chattels exemption

15.17 It should not be forgotten that plant (used for trading purposes) will qualify as a chargeable asset for CGT purposes. Thus, if the plant is sold for an amount in excess of its indexed base cost, a capital gain will arise, although where the consideration for an individual item of plant is less than £6,000, the gain is not taxable [*TCGA 1992, s 262*]. Where the seller company is disposing of a large number of individual items of plant, which qualify for the £6,000 chattel exemption, it will often be advantageous to specify the consideration allocated to each item in the sale agreement. This documentary evidence would be used to support the claim for the chattels exemption in the event of an HMRC enquiry (see also 15.9 – sale of books and records).

Capital gains arising on the sale of *fixed* plant and machinery would be eligible for capital gains roll-over relief in the normal way.

Loss restriction for capital allowances claimed

15.18 Plant is usually sold below its original cost (for example, at net book value), producing a capital loss. However, because of a special rule, the base cost for CGT purposes must be restricted by the net capital allowances claimed on the asset, being the difference between cost and proceeds [*TCGA 1992, s 41(1), (2)*]. This will invariably produce no gain or loss. If the other assets cannot take full advantage of indexation (for example, if there is no base cost), the seller's overall tax position may be enhanced by selling plant for an amount at least equal to the cost plus accrued indexation. In such cases, the sale proceeds would be restricted to cost when computing the balancing adjustment for capital allowance purposes.

Trading stock and work in progress

15.19 Any profit arising on the sale of trading stock and work in progress will be treated as a trading receipt. Where the trading stock and work in progress is sold to another UK trader, HMRC generally accepts the price agreed between the two parties [*CTA 2009, ss 162 and 165 (and CTA 2009, s 163)*].

However, *CTA 2009, s 165(3)* requires the amount allocated to stock on a *'cessation'* sale to be computed on a just and reasonable basis. Nevertheless, in most cases, there should still be some scope for flexing the price at which the stock is sold in order to achieve the desired tax position.

If trading stock is sold to a *connected person* on cessation, the transfer is deemed to be at market value. This deemed 'market-value' treatment could be displaced by a joint election to treat the transfer as being made at the higher of the actual sales price or book value. (The election can only be made if both these amounts are less than market value.) [*CTA 2009, ss 166 and 167.*]

However, before 8 July 2015, if the *transfer pricing regime* applied to the sale (see 4.11–4.12), the arm's length 'transfer price' would apply to the seller (and no election was possible) [*CTA 2009, s 162(2)*]. The purchaser should of course be able to make a compensating adjustment under *TIOPA 2010, s 174*. This rule was effectively removed from 8 July 2015, so that a 'deemed' market value rule now automatically applies, subject to the ability to make an election to transfer at the greater of the actual sales price or book value.

VAT – transfer of going concern relief

15.20   In the vast majority of asset and trade sales, VAT will not be chargeable on the sale of the assets, as the transaction will be treated as a non-supply under the transfer of a going concern (TOGC) provisions in *Value Added Tax (Special Provisions) Order 1995, SI 1995/1268, art 5* (see also 12.32 for detailed commentary of the TOGC rules).

HMRC is no longer prepared to give an informal ruling as to whether a particular trade and asset sale constitutes a TOGC (in relation to straightforward deals). The onus will therefore be on the seller company to satisfy itself that no VAT should be charged. Where the seller treats the sale as a TOGC for VAT purposes, it should obtain protection by ensuring that the sale price in the contract is exclusive of VAT. Furthermore, the seller should have a contractual right to raise a VAT invoice if HMRC subsequently considers that VAT should have been charged on the sale.

Pre-liquidation dividends versus capital distributions

15.21   Once the trade has been sold, the individual shareholders will often wish to extract the proceeds from the company.

If the proceeds are extracted by way of dividend before the company is liquidated [see *CTA 2010, s 1030*]; the cash received is taxed at the shareholder's marginal tax rate(s).

Since 6 April 2016, dividends are taxed under a completely different regime (without any 10% tax credit being added to the cash dividend). Dividend income remains taxable as the highest slice of income, and the first £5,000 of dividend income is taxed at 0% (see 9.12A).

Subject to these rules, dividends are taxed at the following rates in 2017/18.

Dividend income (cash received)	Dividend tax rate
Within dividend basic rate band – £33,500	7.5%
Within dividend higher-rate band – £33,501 to £150,000	32.5%
Within dividend additional-rate band – £150,001 and above	38.1%

It will therefore be more efficient to distribute the net proceeds as a capital distribution (after the company has been placed into liquidation). In many cases, shareholders should be able to qualify for Entrepreneurs' Relief (ER) on such capital distributions (up to their current £10 million, or lower unused ER gains, limit). Any excess gains above the ER limit will be taxed at the top (post-5 April 2016) CGT rate of 20%.

A more detailed discussion on determining the best method of extracting surpluses prior to or on a winding-up or dissolution is given in 16.15–16.27.

Example 3

Sale of trade and assets

In January 2017, Mr Silva was approached by City plc to acquire the assets and undertaking of his profitable haulage business, The D Silva Transport Ltd (TDST Ltd). He incorporated the company in 1978 with £100 share capital and his shares were worth £1 million at 31 March 1982.

City plc has offered a total consideration of £4.45 million for the business.

TDST Ltd normally makes up accounts to 31 March each year. Its current summarised balance sheet (together with the relevant tax written down values (TWDV)) is as follows:

	£'000	
Warehouse property	410	
Lorry fleet	550	(TWDV = £385,000)
Debtors	390	
Bank overdraft	(200)	
Creditors	(400)	
	750	

The trading 'goodwill' was worth £480,000 at 31 March 1982. The warehouse was purchased in August 2003 at a cost of £410,000.

The prospective purchaser's accountants have performed a brief acquisition review and have supplied the following tentative valuations for the assets to be taken over:

	£'000
Warehouse property	1,200
Lorry fleet	550
Goodwill (balance)	2,700
	4,450

Mr Silva draws an annual salary of £200,000 from the company. He has not previously used any part of his ER. After the disposal, Mr Silva wishes to retire from business.

The net amount that could be paid to Mr Silva on the basis of the above deal is computed below.

Tax liabilities on sale of TDST Ltd's assets

TDST Ltd's tax liability on the sale of the relevant assets in (say) April 2017 is computed as follows:

Chargeable gains			
	Warehouse	*Goodwill*	*Total*
	£'000	*£'000*	*£'000*
Sale proceeds (net of disposal costs)	1,200	2,700	
Less: Cost/March 1982 value	(410)	(480)	
Indexation at (say) 48%/238%	(197)	(1,142)*	
Gain	593	1,078	1,671
Balancing charge on lorry fleet	*Lorry Fleet*		
Eligible cost/proceeds	550		
Less: TWDV	(385)		
Balancing charge			165
Taxable profit on sale of assets			1,836
Tax thereon @ 19%			349

** *There is no clawback of IBAs on the warehouse.*

Capital gains arising on capital distribution

TDST Ltd's distributable reserves upon completion would be as follows:

	£'000	£'000
Per current balance sheet		750
Book profit on disposal:		
Warehouse (£1,200,000 – £410,000)	790	
Goodwill	2,700	3,490
Liquidation and other realisation costs (say)		(72)
Tax on disposal		(349)
Available to distribute		£3,819

Assume all the reserves were distributed as a capital distribution on liquidation in (say) August 2017. Mr Silva would qualify for ER (on the capital distribution *TCGA 1992, s 169(5)* (condition B)) since:

- he has satisfied the relevant employee/shareholding tests (for at least 12 months) before the trade ceased (ie when the trade was sold in April 2017);

- the capital distribution was made within three years of the April 2017 'cessation' date.

Furthermore, since Mr Silva is permanently retiring, he will not be affected by the 'anti-phoenix' TAAR in *ITTOIA 2005, s 396B* (see 16.28).

With ER, the 'net proceeds' available to Mr Silva would be around £3,538,000, computed thus:

	£'000
Capital distribution	3,819
Less March 1982 value	(1,000)
Chargeable gain	2,819
Less Annual exemption	(11)
Taxable gain	2,808
ER CGT @ 10%	281
Post-tax proceeds	£3,538

A pre-liquidation dividend in 2017/18 (on which tax would probably have been payable at 38.1%) would have been clearly disadvantageous.

SALE OF SHARES

Main advantages of share sale

15.22 Some of the key tax advantages of selling shares are summarised below:

(*a*) the avoidance of the double tax charge, as the seller receives the proceeds directly (see 15.7);

(*b*) most owner managers should be able to secure an ER CGT rate of 10% on (up to) their first £10 million of eligible gains, with the balance being taxed in 2017/18 (and 2016/17) at 20% (previously the main CGT rate was 28%). The ER regime is covered in detail in 15.34 to 15.45.

Investors' relief (IR) also enables gains on qualifying disposals to benefit from a 10% rate. IR is available for qualifying investors who subscribe for shares after 16 March 2016 and hold them for three years. The lifetime limit for IR is £10 million, which is in addition to the ER lifetime limit. The IR rules are dealt with in 15.46 to 15.46B

(*c*) the ability to defer the capital gain on disposal where the acquiring company is able to satisfy the sale consideration through the issue of shares or loan stock;

(*d*) the seller could avoid CGT by emigrating for the requisite five-year period (see 15.113);

(*e*) the seller may be in a position to obtain EIS CGT deferral relief (by reinvesting the proceeds in shares of a qualifying EIS company) (see 15.92);

(*f*) a share sale may enable some value to be received for the company's tax losses (which could not be transferred to purchaser on an asset sale) (see 15.7).

15.23 As a sale of shares constitutes a 'transaction in securities' or TiS, the anti-avoidance rules in *ITA 2007, s 684* are potentially applicable (see 15.82–15.91). However, if there is a 'fundamental change in ownership of the company' (see 15.84) within *ITA 2007, s 686*, the seller will be exempt from the TiS rules. The fundamental change in ownership rule is tested in relation to each seller of the company. In broad terms, the exemption would generally operate where the company is being sold to a third party (ie where there is no connection with any of the sellers)

HMRC introduced this important 'let-out' to avoid the need to seek advance clearance on 'clean' straightforward sales. Although the exemption is certainly useful, some sellers may still wish to seek the comfort of a clearance where they are nervous about the application of the TiS rules to some aspect of the transaction. Furthermore, advance tax clearances may still be required for other purposes – for example, where part of the sale consideration is being satisfied in the form of shares or loan notes (see 15.47).

Where the 'fundamental change in ownership' exemption is not available, sellers will need to gain HMRC's acceptance that the transaction is being undertaken for genuine commercial purposes and not tax avoidance by seeking clearance under *ITA 2007, s 701* (see 15.89–15.91).

Selling shares under the entrepreneurs' relief (ER) and investors' relief regimes

15.24 Most owner-managers are likely to qualify for entrepreneurs' relief (ER) on selling their companies, which effectively delivers a 10% CGT rate on their 'exit' gains up to overall 'lifetime' ER gains limit of £10 million. Any gains in excess of the £10 million ER threshold are taxed at the main CGT rate of 20% (28% prior to 6 April 2016).

The £10 million ER threshold has applied since 6 April 2011 (for details of earlier CGT rates and ER limits – see 15.37). The reduction in the 'main' CGT rate to 20% (in April 2016) does, of course, reduce the effective value of ER.

If the owner-manager's share sale gain is likely to exceed £10 million, it may be possible to increase the ER capacity by transferring part of their shareholding to other 'suitable' family members. ER is discussed extensively in 15.34–15.45C.

For 'very small' share sales, some sellers may pay CGT at the lower 10% CGT rate in any case, (this being the post-5 April 2016 rate applicable to gains falling within the basic rate' band for income tax purposes). The 10% CGT rate is unlikely to apply very often!

The *FA 2016* introduced an investors' relief (IR), which broadly enables business angels and other passive investors to obtain a 10% CGT rate on a disposal of shares after *three years*. IR requires an injection of new cash into the company via a subscription for ordinary shares. The IR provisions are summarised in 15.46–15.46B.

Sales by trustees and personal representatives will always be liable to CGT at the 20% rate (except in the rare cases where trustees are able to claim the 10% ER CGT rate (see 15.39).

Legal and commercial aspects

15.25 As a purchaser of shares will effectively inherit all the company's liabilities and problems, a share sale agreement usually includes extensive warranties and indemnities given by the seller, except perhaps in the case of a management buy-out. The function of warranties and indemnities is discussed in 12.66–12.76.

Company law can also impinge heavily on share sales. A careful check should be made to ensure that all pre-sale and related transactions fall within the company's articles and objects clause in its Memorandum of Association.

A well-advised purchaser may seek to negotiate a reduction in the 'consideration' price for the company's shares to allow for the contingent tax inherent in the value of the company's assets (the amount of the discount would depend on the likelihood and timing of the assets being sold). In practice, this point is often taken in connection with property development companies where the properties are likely to be sold in the short to medium term. On the other hand, the seller shareholders of a trading company would normally resist this stance.

Apportionment of the sale consideration

15.26 The sale consideration, the form in which it is taken (for example, cash and/or loan notes and/or shares in the acquirer), and the apportionment between the seller shareholders will invariably be laid down in the sale and purchase agreement. In many cases, sellers may be given a free choice as to the form in which they receive their sale consideration and there is no tax rule which requires them all to take the same proportion in (say) cash and shares in the acquiring company.

In some cases, each seller's sale consideration entitlement may not reflect their proportionate shareholding. Some sellers may receive an amount that is more than their pro-rata entitlement based on their shareholding. This may be in accordance with special rights laid down in the Articles of Association or shareholders' agreement. It may also be possible that different shareholders manage to secure different amounts from the purchaser.

However, HMRC is beginning to look more closely at such situations and may seek to impose an employment income tax charge on shareholders who receive more than their entitlement based on a straight pro-rata split of their shareholdings. The argument is that they have disposed of their shares for more than their market value and hence the excess falls to be taxed under *ITEPA 2003, Pt 7, Ch 3D* – see 8.35 for further discussion.

The impact of 'financial assistance'

15.27 The *Companies Act 2006* abolished the statutory prohibition on the provision of financial assistance for the purchase of shares in a private company from 1 October 2008.

However, directors entering into a transaction that involves providing 'assistance' for the purchase of 'their' company's shares must still consider the interests of its creditors and minority shareholders. They must also check to ensure that the company has the relevant legal capacity to provide financial assistance under its articles – many lenders now insist on a specific provision empowering the company to provide financial assistance.

Any financial assistance provided must be consistent with the directors' duty to act in good faith and must be likely to promote the success of the company for the general benefit of its shareholders. The directors should provide detailed board minutes to reflect their reasoning for giving the assistance. They would also need to examine the effect on the company's cash flow and net asset position and ensure that the assistance would not create any financial problems.

Clearly, if the company is struggling financially and there is a risk of insolvency, the provision of assistance is unlikely to be in the best interests of the company's creditors. Furthermore, the directors may liable for wrongful or fraudulent trading or the assistance might be set aside under the *Insolvency Act 1986* provisions dealing with transactions at undervalue or 'preferences'.

15.28   The common law restrictions evolving from the ruling in *Trevor v Whitworth* [1887] cannot generally be invoked following the removal of the statutory restriction (see *Fifth Commencement Order of the Companies Act 2006, Sch 4, para 54*. However, the common law principles can still apply to unlawful reductions in capital. Thus, where the company has insufficient distributable reserves, these rules can still be invoked to set aside loans or gifts made by the company to facilitate the purchase of its shares (see 13.100).

A private company cannot give assistance for the purpose of the acquisition of shares in its *public* parent company.

MAIN CGT RULES FOR SHARE SALES

Date of disposal

15.29   The seller will normally generate a capital gain when they sell their shares. A disposal of an asset will be recognised for CGT purposes when an unconditional contract is executed for its sale (*TCGA 1992, s 28(1)*).

The case of *Thompson v Salah* (1971) 47 TC 559 provides authority for the proposition that a (prior) oral contract can create a disposal for CGT purposes (except in relation to land) even though it may be unenforceable.

In the case of a conditional contract, the date of disposal is deferred until the relevant condition precedent is satisfied (or waived) (*TCGA 1992, s 28(2)*). A condition precedent refers to an event, which is outside the control of the contracting parties – for example obtaining satisfactory tax clearances or relevant regulatory approval etc.

On the other hand, a 'condition subsequent' is merely a term of the contract required to be fulfilled by one of the parties and does not create a conditional contract for CGT. For example, in *Eastham v Leigh London & Provincial Properties* (1971) 46 TC 687, one party to the contract covenanted to build an office block and the other party agreed to grant a lease if the office block was completed. It was held that the requirement to build the office block was a condition subsequent being a term of the contract that had to be fulfilled to carry out the contract.

Cash consideration is immediately chargeable to CGT in the tax year of disposal (*TCGA 1992, s 28*). Tax must be paid on any fixed (ie ascertainable) deferred consideration, even it if is conditional, although HMRC will refund the tax when it is satisfied that the conditional amount will not be paid. Instalment relief may be available for the tax payments; given the difficulty of paying the tax before the full cash proceeds are received (*TCGA 1992, ss 48 and 280*).

Historically, fixed deferred consideration has been structured through the use of loan notes as this enabled the relevant CGT to be deferred. However, sellers will now (usually) have to make an election to tax the 'loan note' consideration 'up-front' to benefit from the 10% ER CGT rate on this part of the consideration (see 15.57).

Calculation of capital gain

15.30 In broad terms, an *individual's/trustee's* capital gain is calculated simply as the amount by which the sale proceeds (net of allowable incidental costs of disposal) exceed the amount that they originally paid for the shares – often referred to as the 'base cost'.

For individuals/trustees, March 1982 rebasing is compulsory for shares held at 31 March 1982.

Example 4

CGT computation for sale of shares

On 13 July 2017 Alan sold his 100% shareholding in Taylor Ltd for a cash consideration of £4 million (net of legal and professional costs).

Alan originally acquired his shareholding in June 1995 for £100,000. Taylor Ltd has always been a trading company.

Assuming that he claims ER, his CGT liability will be computed as follows:

	£
Net sale proceeds	4,000,000
Less: Acquisition cost (June 1995)	(100,000)
Chargeable gain	3,900,000
Less: Annual exemption (2017/18)	(11,300)
Taxable gain	3,888,700
ER CGT @ 10%	£388,870

Pooling of shares

15.31   Since 6 April 2008, all shares in a particular company (of the same class) are generally treated as a single 'pooled' asset, regardless of when they were actually acquired.

This means that where a part disposal of shares occurs, the base cost for each share sold will be based at the average cost of the pooled shares.

Example 5

CGT computation for part disposal of shares

In August 2017 George sold 400 of his 2,000 shares in Best Winger Ltd for £1,500,000 (net of transaction costs).

George previously acquired his shares as follows:

	Number of shares	£
May 1996 – Purchase	1,500	150,000
June 2007 – On death of founder shareholder – MV	500	1,200,000

George's capital gain would be calculated as follows:

Share Pool

	Number	CGT cost £
May 1996 – Purchase	1,500	150,000
June 2007 – Inherited on death of founder (MV)	500	1,200,000
	2,000	1,350,000
August 2017 – Disposal (£1,350,000 × 400/2,000)	(400)	(270,000)
Balances c/fwd	1,600	1,080,000

CGT computation

	£
Net sale proceeds	1,500,000
Less: Part-disposal cost (from pool)	(270,000)
Capital gain (subject to annual exemption)	1,230,000

Capital losses and the annual exemption

15.32 Sellers will generate a capital loss where their deductible base cost/value exceeds the related sale proceeds. Capital losses arising from 'unacceptable' tax planning (in HMRC's view) may be challenged under the general capital loss anti-avoidance rule (in *TCGA 1992, s 16A*) introduced from 6 December 2006 by the *FA 2007*. Broadly, these provisions prevent losses being allowed for CGT purposes where they arise from arrangements (mainly) designed to secure a tax advantage.

The GAAR may also be applied to nullify particularly abusive arrangements to create capital losses (see 1.19).

15.33 Special rules prevent the annual exemption being wasted by the use of brought forward losses. For these purposes, the legislation applies the concept of 'adjusted net gains', being the total chargeable gains for the year less the capital losses for the *same* tax year. Provided that the adjusted net gains for the year do not exceed the annual exemption, any allowable losses brought forward are ignored and can be carried forward in full. If the adjusted net gains for the year exceed the annual exemption, the amount of brought forward capital losses, which may be deducted, is restricted to the 'excess' amount only. Capital losses brought forward are, therefore, only used to reduce the adjusted net gains down to the annual exempt amount.

ENTREPRENEURS' RELIEF (ER)

Main qualifying ER conditions

15.34 For normal share sales the following ER conditions must be satisfied throughout the 12 months before the disposal (*TCGA 1992, s 169I(1), (2)(c), (5), (6)*). The seller shareholder must:

- hold shares in a trading company or holding company of a trading group (see 15.40–15.44); and

- be a director or employee of that company (or fellow group company) (see 15.34A) *and* it must be their 'personal company' – ie they must own at least 5% of the *ordinary* share capital (carrying at least 5% of the voting rights) (see also 15.35 and 15.35A).

Most owner-managers should have little difficulty in satisfying the relevant tests. The 'director/employee' requirement should not be that onerous, since there is no requirement to work on a 'full time' basis – part-time working would therefore suffice. A review of some key cases involving the 'employment' test in relation to ER is dealt with in 13.34A. Special beneficial rules apply to EMI option shares (see 15.36 below).

A large number of minority and employee shareholders will be unable to meet the conditions necessary to secure ER. They will therefore typically suffer a higher CGT rate of 20% (28% before 6 April 2016).

The ruling in *J K Moore v HMRC* [2016] UKFTT 115 (TC) shows that HMRC interpret the '12-month' rule strictly. John Moore (JM) owned 30% of the shares in Alpha Micro Components Ltd and 'fell-out' with his fellow shareholders. This resulted in JM leaving the company by way of a compromise agreement. Consequently, JM was required to sell his shares back to the company.

According to the forms filed at Companies House he resigned on 28 February 2009 but the company's resolution to repurchase his shares was made on 29 May 2009. HMRC challenged Mr Moore's claim for ER since he had not been a director of the company throughout the period of one year ending with the disposal of his shares – he had resigned three months before the resolution for the share buyback. The First-tier Tribunal concluded that a purchase of own shares could only take place when the resolution is passed (see 13.43A) and this could not have been earlier than 29 May 2009. JM therefore did *not* meet the '12-month' test and his claim for ER was denied.

ER and the 'employment' test

15.34A The case of *Corbett* [2014] TC 3435 shows that, in certain circumstances it might be even possible to claim ER when an employment had 'officially' ceased. In this case, the taxpayer (Mrs Corbett) worked as an assistant (and was the wife) of a senior executive. Mrs Corbett also held shares in the vendor company.

A potential purchaser, an AIM listed company, stated that it was against their policy for the spouses of senior executives to be working in the company. Mrs Corbett left the company and HMRC argued she was not entitled to ER on the eventual sale. Mrs Corbett successfully countered that the change was cosmetic and her husband received extra remuneration to compensate for her carrying on her pre-existing employment. The First Tier Tribunal found that the employment substantively continued, and the potential technical breaches of the minimum wage regulations were irrelevant.

In determining whether the seller has the required 'employment' status, HMRC may enquire whether the seller has a contract of service (see *TCGA 1992, s 169S* and *ITEPA 2003, s 4*). If HMRC seeks to test the 'employment' condition, it will usually refer to the case of *Ready Mixed Concrete (South East) Ltd v Minister of Pensions & National Insurance* [1968] 1 All ER 433. The key extract from that case shows that a 'contract of service' must meet three conditions, which are:

'(i)   The servant agrees that in consideration of a wage or other remuneration he will provide his own work and skill in the performance of some service for his master.

(ii)   He agrees, expressly or impliedly, that in the performance of that service he will be subject to the other's control in a sufficient degree to make that other master.

(iii)   The other provisions of the contract are consistent with its being a contract of service.'

This would appear to carry an implied rule that the relevant individual must be paid.

The courts have sometimes taken a more relaxed view. For example, in *Richard Hirst v HMRC* [2014] (TC04038), the First-tier Tribunal held that the 'employment' condition had been satisfied for ER purposes in unusual circumstances. To control costs during difficult trading conditions, Mr Hirst resigned from his position as managing director in December 2007. In December 2008, Mr Hirst was found guilty of assault and the criminal prosecution meant that he could not retain his directorship. However, he retained a company laptop and phone and the cost of his home internet access continued to be met by the company.

While the Tribunal did *not* accept Mr Hirst was a 'shadow director', it concluded that the work undertaken by Mr Hirst between December 2007 (when he resigned his directorship) and the sale of his shares in July 2009 was significant. Consequently, on the facts and applying the principles in *Ready Mixed Concrete* (see above), it held that an employment relationship existed between the company and Mr Hirst.

ER and the 'ordinary share capital'/'voting rights' test

15.35   The 5% 'shareholding/votes' test must be satisfied by the individual seller alone (for example, there is no attribution of spouse's or relatives' shares). Individual sellers are required to own at least 5% of the *ordinary shares* throughout the relevant period (but see 15.49 for treatment where there has been a recent share exchange).

For shares held in joint names (for example by a married couple), each joint owner is treated as holding shares (and votes) equivalent to the value of their share of the holding. For married couples or civil partners, this will normally be 50% each.

Ordinary shares are widely defined in *TCGA 1992, s 169S(5)*, which refers to the definition in *ITA 2007, s 989*), which states that ordinary shares comprise

'all the company's issued share capital (however described), other than capital the holders of which have a right to a dividend at a fixed rate but no other right to share in the company's profits'

Thus, for example, *fixed rate* preference shares might be excluded from the definition of 'ordinary share capital', although each case must be examined on its own facts.

HMRC's view is that the issued share capital test is measured in terms of the nominal value of the shares (based on the Justice Megarry's analysis in *Canada Safeway Ltd v IRC* [1973] CH 374, which was also approved more recently in *HMRC v 1) Taylor and 2) Haimendorf* [2010] UKUT 417 (TCC).

HMRC has confirmed in its Employee Share Schemes User Manual [*ESSUM43230*] that shares with no dividend rights may be accepted as ordinary shares (ie HMRC do not contend that they carry the right to a fixed dividend of 0%). However, practical problems have arisen with ER claims involving the existence of shares that have *no* right to a dividend.

In *A Castledine v HMRC* [2016] UKFTT 145 (TC), Mr Castledine claimed ER against the gain arising on the disposal of his loan notes. The company had two classes of shares – ordinary shares and deferred shares. The deferred shares had been created for commercial reasons. They carried *no* entitlement to dividends or votes, and had no realistic expectation of a distribution on winding up.

Mr Castledine held 5% of the shares designated as 'ordinary share' capital (which also carried the voting rights). However, when the deferred shares were taken into account, he only held 4.99% of the total issued share capital. HMRC refused Mr Castledine's ER claim on the basis that the deferred shares were 'ordinary share capital'. Since they had *no* right to a dividend, they could *not* fall within the 'carve-out' in *ITA 2007, s 989* (see above). On the other hand, the taxpayer argued that the deferred shares had none of the characteristics of ordinary share capital and it could not have been Parliament's intention for them to be included when calculating the relevant percentages for ER.

However, whilst the FTT was sympathetic, it found that the wording of *ITA 2007, s 989* was unambiguous. Since the deferred shares had *no* dividend rights, they had to be counted as part of the ordinary share capital. The FTT concluded that Mr Castledine held less than 5% of the ordinary share capital and therefore his claim for ER failed.

The same reasoning was reached by the Upper Tribunal (UT) in *HMRC v Michael and Elizabeth McQuillan* [2017] UKUT 0344 (TCC).

Mr and Mrs McQuillan claimed ER on the sale of their shares in January 2010. For most of the 12 months before the sale, the company's issued share capital was as follows:

	Ordinary shares of £1 each	Non-voting redeemable shares of £1 each
Mr McQuillan	33	–
Mrs McQuillan	33	–
Mr and Mrs Pennick	34	30,000
Total	100	30,000

Mr and Mrs Pennick's £30,000 £1 redeemable shares carried no dividend or voting rights; their only entitlement was to be redeemed at par.

HMRC refused Mr and Mrs McQuillan's ER claim on the basis that each of them did *not* hold more than 5% of the issued ordinary share capital, as defined within *ITA 2007, s 989*. The 'non-voting' redeemable shares did *not* carry any dividend rights and therefore carried no *right* to a dividend (at a fixed rate). Therefore, the redeemable shares were 'ordinary share capital' for ER purposes. The UT (reversing the FTT ruling) therefore found that Mr and Mrs McQuillan each held 0.11% of the issued ordinary share capital (ie 33 shares/30,100 × 100) and did not qualify for ER. (Although the UT sympathised with the McQuillans, it felt bound to follow the unambiguous definition of ordinary share capital.)

Following the *Castledine* and *McQuillan* decisions, if it is intended that 'non-dividend' paying shares should fall outside the 'ordinary share capital' definition, they should be given a *very small* fixed dividend entitlement.

Care is also required with companies that have private-equity investment or other classes of shares. The existence of different classes of shares is likely to substantially increase the 'ordinary share' capital and hence may dilute many small minority holdings below the required 5%.

Potential pre-sale dilution issue

15.35A The exercise of employee share options shortly before a sale will also dilute existing shareholdings and must be factored into the potential ER availability for 'minority' shareholders. This will typically occur with exit-based EMI share options, which are generally exercised shortly before or on the day of sale.

There has always been a concern that ER could be denied to an existing shareholder whose holding is diluted below 5% as a result of the exercise of an employee share option *on the day of sale*. HMRC were asked for their view on the following practical situation (see *ICAEW Tax Faculty – TAX GUIDE 1/12 – Entrepreneurs' Relief – Practical Points – Example A7*).

Shareholder X holds 5% of the ordinary share capital in a company and has done so throughout the period of at least one year up to the date of the sale of the entire share capital of the company.

There are holders of share options who intend to exercise their rights and acquire shares on the date of sale shortly before taking part in and signing the contract for sale.

The contract for sale is entered into on, say, 12 noon on the day of sale.

By virtue of the exercise of the options earlier in the day, at the time of disposal (ie signing of the contract) X will hold less than 5% of the ordinary share capital of the company.

HMRC responded as follows:

> 'The direct application of the statute, without need for interpretation of the words of that statute, provides the answer to the query.
>
> We do not consider that the legislation for ER can be read as making any division of a day on a minute by minute (or second by second?) basis. In particular it does not require an interpretation that the statute must read as "throughout the period ending with the date of disposal" ends on midnight the day before the sale.
>
> Assuming that X satisfies all the other conditions for the relief, it is clear that X would not be ineligible from claiming ER on the disposal of his shareholding solely by virtue of the exercise of options earlier in the day on which he disposes of his shares and the exercise of options results in his ownership and voting rights dropping below the critical 5% threshold.'

However, based on the above analysis, where an existing shareholder's interest is diluted below the 5% voting share capital requirement, 5% for example, during the week before the sale they will lose their ER entitlement. This is because the 5% holding will not have been held throughout the 12 months before the disposal.

Special *FA 2013* relaxation for EMI option shares

15.36   Under the *FA 2013* provisions, EMI option holders can enjoy the 10% (ER) entrepreneurs' relief CGT rate on sale *without having to meet the 5% shareholding condition* (see 15.34 and 8.71).

These beneficial ER provisions apply to shares *acquired after 5 April 2013* on the exercise of an EMI option, provided the following conditions are satisfied:

- The shares are sold more than 12 months after the grant of the relevant EMI option (ie the option period counts towards the 12-month ER qualifying period);

- The company is a trading company or holding company of a trading group throughout this '12-month' period; and

- The option holder is an employee or director of the company (or any fellow group member) throughout this 12-month period (which should be the case for an EMI option holder!).

Shares will not qualify for ER if the relevant option is exercised more than 90 days after a disqualifying event.

Given that the 'option period' counts towards the 12-month holding period for ER, these rules will be especially helpful to 'exit-based' EMI schemes, where the options are typically exercised shortly before the company is sold (see 8.51). Thus, provided employees sell the relevant EMI shares more than 12 months after the date their options are granted, they will qualify for the 10% ER CGT rate.

Where relevant EMI shares are subject to a share exchange within *TCGA 1992, s 135* (see 15.48), the new shareholding will count as 'relevant EMI shares' provided it is a 'qualifying exchange of shares for EMI purposes (see *ITEPA 2003, Sch 5, para 40*). This means, for example, that the acquiring company would have to meet the qualifying trade and independence tests (see 8.64 and 8.66).

If the relevant conditions for ER were not satisfied, the 'EMI shares' would be subject to a 20% CGT charge on sale.

Example 6

Beneficial ER treatment on sale of EMI shares

Bale Madrid Ltd is a UK resident company, specialising in the promotion of pop and sporting events in the UK and worldwide, and is a qualifying EMI company.

In October 2010, Gareth was granted an EMI option to acquire 1,000 shares in Bale Madrid Ltd at £2.60 each (which was the then market value agreed with HMRC – Shares and Assets Valuation). Gareth's 1,000 shares under option represent 1% of the *fully diluted* share capital of the company.

Under the terms of the Bale Madrid Ltd EMI scheme, the options could be exercised only when an offer had been accepted for the sale of the company.

On 2 September 2017, the directors of Bale Madrid Ltd agreed to accept an offer by Real M plc to purchase 100% of the company's shares for £50 million (ie at £500 per share).

The EMI option holders, including Gareth, were permitted to exercise their options on 10 October 2017 and the sale of Bale Madrid Ltd was completed on 20 October 2017.

Gareth would be able to claim ER on the sale of his 1,000 EMI shares since they were acquired after 5 April 2013 and all the relevant conditions are satisfied. In particular, it does not matter that his holding represents just 1% of Bale Madrid Ltd's share capital and that he has only owned the shares for some 10 days. It is sufficient that his 'EMI' shares have either been under option or held by him for at least one year before they are sold.

Gareth's CGT liability on the sale of his 1,000 shares would be £48,630, calculated as follows:

	£
Net sale proceeds (1,000 × £500)	500,000
Less: Acquisition cost – October 2017 (1,000 × £2.60)	(2,600)
Chargeable gain	497,400
Less: Annual exemption (2017/18)	(11,300)
Taxable gain	486,100
ER CGT @ 10%	£48,610

Basic mechanics of ER

15.37   ER is modelled on the old 'retirement relief' regime, although there is no minimum age requirement (and there is no need to retire!). The shares only need to be held on a qualifying basis for at least one year to obtain ER.

The *F (No 2) A 2010* radically changed the way in which ER is given. For qualifying disposals after 22 June 2010, the gain is simply taxed at an ER CGT rate of 10%. ER is subject to a £10 million lifetime gains limit per individual. Gains in excess of this £10 million limit are taxed at the top CGT rate of 20%.

Before 23 June 2010, ER chargeable gains were reduced by 4/9ths. Since all gains (including ER gains) were taxed at a flat rate of 18%, the 4/9ths ER reduction resulted in a chargeable balance of 5/9ths taxed at 18%, which produced an effective CGT rate of 10% (ie 5/9 × 18%). (See 2010/11 and earlier editions of this book for detailed coverage of pre-23 June 2010 ER regime.)

The previous ER gains limits were:

6 April 2008 to 5 April 2010	£1 million
6 April 2010 to 22 June 2010	£2 million
23 June 2010 to 5 April 2011	£5 million

The ER gains allowance is given to both husband and wife, separately, which may be an important consideration when structuring shareholdings.

Claiming ER

15.38   ER must be claimed by first anniversary of the 31 January following the tax year of the share sale – ie within (just less than) 22 months after the end of the relevant tax year in which the share sale is made. Thus, for example, an ER claim on a qualifying gain in 2017/18 must be made by 31 January 2020.

Once claimed, ER is applied to the complete eligible gain (up to the maximum £10 million cumulative threshold) – it cannot be restricted in any way. However, selling shares in separate tranches could provide some flexibility, with an ER election being made against specific disposals.

Trustees can also claim ER in certain special cases where their trust has one or more beneficiaries holding an 'interest in possession' (see 15.39).

ER disposals by trustees

15.39   Trustees can also claim ER in certain special cases where their trust has one or more 'qualifying' beneficiaries holding an *interest in possession* over the entire trust fund or part of the trust (eg a 'sub-fund') which contains the relevant shares (*TCGA 1992, s 169J*).

Thus, this relief only applies to those trusts where the beneficiary/beneficiaries enjoy(s) an immediate entitlement to the trust income as it arises (see 17.55). However, the trustees do *not* have their own separate ER gains allowance. They merely have the opportunity to benefit from the beneficiary's unused ER allowance (who must give their consent to the 'surrender'). There are special rules to deal with cases where there is more than one qualifying beneficiary (see *TCGA 1992, s 169O*).

The main trust conditions are directed at the 'qualifying beneficiary' rather than the trustees. Thus, the trustees can make a claim for ER provided the *qualifying beneficiary*

- is a director or employee of the company (or any fellow-group company), and

- holds at least 5% of the ordinary shares in the company (carrying at least 5% of the voting rights) in their own right.

There is no shareholding 'percentage' requirement for the trustees. These 'trust' conditions must be satisfied throughout a period of *12 months* ending within the *three years* before the sale (which is different from the normal 12 months before the sale test for individual ER claims (see 15.34)). The company must also be a trading company or a holding company of a trading group (see 15.40–15.42) throughout this period.

Although the legislation is not entirely clear, there is a prudent view that the trust must be in existence for at least 12 months. Arguably, it cannot be the *beneficiary's* personal company if the trust is not in existence – since there cannot be a beneficiary without a trust.

There is a view that the legislature cannot have intended for trustees to benefit without having 'clocked-up' 12 months ownership with a qualifying beneficiary (as otherwise trusts would be treated much more beneficially than an individual seller).

The conditions mean that to facilitate a potential ER claim by a trust, the (qualifying) beneficiary must have a personal holding of at least 5% of the shares (carrying at least 5% of the votes). The qualifying beneficiary effectively assigns to the trustees all or part of their unused ER allowance (by entering into a joint election). Therefore, if the beneficiary has used all their £10 million allowance, this will preclude any ER claim by the trustees. (*TCGA 1992, s169N(8)* makes clear that where the trust sells the relevant shares on the same day as the beneficiary (in their own right), the beneficiary is deemed to sell their's first.)

Any decision for a beneficiary to surrender part of their ER allowance to the trust is not straightforward. For example, if they expect to use their unused ER allowance in the future, they are unlikely to consent. Furthermore, if the beneficiary is not entitled to receive a capital appointment/advancement from the trust, they may not be willing to give up their unused relief (unless perhaps the trustees agreed to make a compensatory payment!).

Example 7

ER claim by trustees

Scott and Bobby have been beneficiaries of a family trust that was created in June 1999. The trust holds 15% of the voting ordinary shares of Green Street Ltd (a qualifying trading company for ER purposes).

Since 2003, Scott has also been a director of Green Street Ltd owning 10% of the company's (voting) ordinary shares in his own right.

Under the terms of the trust, Scott and Bobby are entitled to an equal share of the trust's income.

In June 2017, the trustees sell their 15% in Green Street Ltd for £275,000.

The following considerations apply to determine whether the trustees are able to make a competent claim for ER:

- The sale of the shares is a disposal of 'settlement business assets' within *TCGA 1992, s 169J(1)(a)*.

- Scott is a qualifying beneficiary (*TCGA 1992, s 169J(1)(b)*) since he is entitled to an interest in possession of part of the trust property that comprises the shares in Green Street Ltd.

- The relevant condition in *TCGA 1992, s 169J(4)* is met since throughout a period of one year, ending within three years of the share sale:

- Green Street Ltd is Scott's personal company (since he holds at least 5% of the voting ordinary shares in his own right) and is a qualifying trading company: and

- Scott is a director of the company.

- Bobby is also entitled to a share of the income of the settled property including the Green Street Ltd shares. Thus, *TCGA 1992, s 169O* applies to apportion the gain eligible for ER on a 50%:50% basis. However, no ER claim can be made in respect of Bobby's share.

- Assuming Scott elects with the trustees to claim ER on 'his' proportion of the gain:

    - £137,500 (50% × £275,000) will be eligible for the 10% ER CGT rate.

    - £137,000 relating to Bobby's share will be chargeable to the 20% trust CGT rate (subject to any available annual exemption).

Trading company/group test

15.40   The ER 'trading company/group' test is virtually the same as the one that previously applied for business asset taper relief and is therefore relatively stringent (*TCGA 1992, s 165A*). One of the key requirements for ER on a straightforward company share sale is that the seller must hold their shares in a trading company or a holding company of a trading group throughout the 12 months before the disposal date.

For ER purposes, a trading company qualifies if it carries on trading activities and its activities do *not* include 'substantial' non-trading activities (see 15.41). The trade must be conducted on a 'commercial basis' with the view to the realisation of profits.

A company will qualify for ER where it carries on activities:

- in the course of, or for the purposes of, its trade;

- for the purposes of a trade it is preparing to carry on;

- with a view to its:

    (i)   acquiring or starting to carry on a trade;

    (ii)   acquiring a significant (ie 51%) interest in the share capital of

        - another trading company; or

        - a holding company of a trading group company (see 15.42); or

        - a qualifying shareholding in a joint-venture company (see 15.43).

provided that this is actually done as soon as 'reasonably practicable in the circumstances' [*TCGA 1992, s 165A(4), (5), (6)*].

A property letting business of furnished holiday lettings (within *CTA 2010, s 65*) counts as a trade [*TCGA 1992, s 241(3)*].

Since the ER 'trading company' test is virtually the same as the one that applied for (pre-6 April 2008) 'business taper', previous HMRC statements and practices for business taper should also be followed for ER. For example, HMRC indicated that where a company sets aside funds and receives investment income, this would not prevent it from being engaged 'wholly' in trading. However, in such cases, the investment must be closely related or integral to the trading business or represent a 'short-term' deposit of funds to meet known future trading liabilities. Furthermore, where a company temporarily holds funds pending their onward distribution to its shareholders, these can normally be counted as a trading activity (*IR Tax Bulletin*, Issue 62, December 2002).

Potential risk areas that are likely to be regarded as 'non-trading' include investment property let to third parties; 'portfolio shareholdings; loans to directors/shareholders and 'non-group' companies and possibly 'excessive' cash balances (but see also 15.41). Investments in 'joint ventures' may qualify as trading provided the relevant conditions are satisfied (see 15.43A).

To ensure the availability of ER, a prudent approach should be adopted. This would require, for example, any potentially 'tainted' non-trading activities being transferred to a separate company or being retained in the (proprietor) shareholder's personal ownership.

De minimis test for non-trading activities

15.41 A company is permitted to have non-trading activities for ER provided they do not have any *substantial* effect on the company's activities. HMRC interpret 'substantial' as more than 20%. Thus a 20% benchmark is effectively applied to a range of potential measures to determine whether a company's 'non-trading' activities represent more than 20% of its business. Under self-assessment, it is up to the taxpayer to decide whether the *de minimis* threshold is satisfied (see *Taxline*, March 1999).

All or some of the measures mentioned below would be considered, depending on the facts of the particular case:

● turnover;

● the asset-base, including the value of non-trade assets, such as investments;

● expenses;

● time spent by management and employees.

Thus, for example, the turnover/sales income from non-trading activities would be compared with the total turnover generated by the company and so on. It may be necessary to build up the correct picture over time and this may involve striking a balance between all these factors (*IR Tax Bulletin*, Issue 62, December 2002). There is also a view that the profit and loss account provides a better measure of 'activity' than a balance sheet, and therefore more weight should be given to a company's turnover, income and employee costs.

Although the 20% *de minimis* rule has been adopted by HMRC as their interpretation of 'substantial', it should not be taken as a definitive statutory test. Although HMRC invariably analyses the most difficult cases in practice by applying this methodology, it should not unduly restrict the meaning of 'substantial', which was intended to be an absolute test rather than a relative one (see 3.44). If any appeal were taken to the Commissioners on this point it is likely that they would form a qualitative assessment on whether any non-trading activities were 'substantial'.

In less 'clear-cut' cases, the principles established in *Farmer (executors of Farmer dec'd) v CIR* [1999] STC (SCD) 321 (an IHT case on Business Property Relief (BPR) may also be usefully applied to support a company's 'trading' status. In *Farmer*, the Special Commissioner required the whole business to be looked at 'in the round' and all relevant factors had to be considered in determining its qualifying status for BPR. The fact that the property lettings were more profitable than the farming business was not considered to be conclusive – 'the overall context of the business, the capital employed, the time spent by the employees and consultants, and the levels of turnover' all supported the finding that the business mainly consisted of farming.

The judgment in *Farmer* was recently approved of and followed by the Upper Tier Tax Tribunal in *CIR v Andrew Michael Bandler (As executor of the will of the late fourth Earl of Balfour)* [2010] UKUT 200 (TCC) (see 17.27A for a detailed review of this case).

Areas where there may be difficulties include companies carrying large cash balances. In the author's experience, such cash balances would have to be shown to be required for working capital or the future requirements of the trade. Clearly, it would be helpful if the company prepared contemporaneous evidence to substantiate this, such as board minutes or formal business plans. Furthermore, funds retained for distribution to shareholders should *not* count as being held for non-trading purposes.

In one particular case in which the author was involved, the Inspector was satisfied that a substantial cash balance was required to enable the business to strike profitable deals (as it was able to pay cash 'on the nail!'). Similarly, large cash deposits that are required to carry on the trade would be accepted as being for trading purposes; for example travel agents normally need to keep a fixed level of cash on deposit for bonding requirements. A payment received from a large contract may be held on deposit, etc to meet a future trading requirement (such as the payment of a trade liability or investment for future expansion of the trade (see *ICAEW Tax Faculty, Taxline*, November 2004)).

On the other hand, if the cash is clearly surplus to the current or future needs of the business, it may be prudent for it to be 'extracted' by the shareholders to avoid the potential loss of ER. However, there is a strong view that any surplus cash would have to be actively 'managed' before it was considered to be a 'non-trading' activity of the business. This follows the thinking in *Jowett v O'Neill and Brennan Construction Ltd* [1998] STC 482 (see 3.29) which ruled that the mere holding of surplus funds in a bank account does not amount to an activity in any case. Applying that principle, the holding of 'non-managed' surplus cash would be completely ignored.

In summary, HMRC tends to accept that cash generated from trading activities should not necessarily prejudice a company's 'trading' status. However, if cash balances are applied and managed as 'investment' assets then HMRC will treat them as 'non-trading' items.

Holding company of a trading group

15.42 To qualify as a holding company of a trading group, a two-stage test must be satisfied:

(*a*)   the company must be a holding company – ie a company that has one or more 51% subsidiaries (*TCGA 1992, s 165A(2)*);

(*b*)   the group must be a trading group, ie, when looking at all its activities together, it must carry on trading activities (as defined in 15.36), although 'insubstantial' non-trading activities within the 20% *de minimis* rule noted in 15.41 are permitted (*TCGA 1992, s 165A(7)*).

The statutory definition looks at 'all the activities of the group' *taken together*. This means that all intra-group activities are ignored – thus the letting of property by one (51%) group member to another would be disregarded when looking at the level of non-trading activities. However, this 'netting-off' does not apply to transactions with qualifying joint venture companies (see 15.43).

Investments in joint ventures

Background to original joint-venture rules

15.43 Substantial investments in 'joint-venture' (JV) companies could potentially prejudice a company's/group's 'trading' status for ER purposes (unless they fall within the 20% *de minimis* rule for 'non-trading activities' (see 15.41). Of course, there should be no difficulty where a company/group holds a 'controlling interest' in a JV company since this would count as part of the group's activities under the deemed 'single entity' rule (see 15.42).

Different rules operate where a company/group has a 'non-controlling' interest in a 'trading' JV. This would be regarded as an investment activity under first principles. However, it was recognised that this would prejudice genuine JV trading relationships. Consequently, under the 'original' (pre-18 March 2015) rules, a shareholding in a JV company was effectively treated as 'transparent' provided the 'investing' company/group held at least 10% of its ordinary share capital and:

(a) the joint-venture company was itself a trading company or holding company of a trading group (see 15.40–15.42); and

(b) at least 75% of the joint-venture company's equity share capital was held by five or fewer participating shareholders (irrespective of their tax residence status).

(These JV rules still apply for SSE purposes (see 3.34).)

In many cases, the beneficial JV rules enabled the investing company/group to be treated as carrying on the (relevant share) of the JV trade, thus enabling shareholders to benefit from ER on most share disposals. Unfortunately, in recent years, HMRC perceived that these useful JV rules were being abused to access ER in certain 'unintended' cases. This was particularly prevalent in secondary buy-out transactions, where there was insufficient equity available for senior management to satisfy the 5% 'ordinary share capital/voting rights test requirement, as illustrated in *Example 8* below.

In response to the perceived abuse of the JV rules, the *FA 2015* completely abolished the 'look-through' provisions. Regrettably, depending on the precise facts, this meant that the ER 'trading' status of many commercial JV structures were adversely affected.

Fortunately, in the face of considerable criticism, HMRC 'backtracked' and introduced a more-targeted approach to JV's in the *FA 2016*. HMRC had recognised that the original *FA 2015* changes were ill conceived so the *FA 2016* JV provisions were backdated to apply to disposals made after 17 March 2015 (see 15.43A).

Example 8

Exploitation of original joint venture rules before *FA 2015*

In December 2013, ECWC (1965) Ltd acquired 100% of Sealey Ltd as part of a secondary buy-out transaction, with new equity funding being introduced by M1860 VC Ltd and the senior management team.

There was insufficient residual equity for the senior management team to have '5% shareholdings' in ECWC (1965) Ltd. The five members of the senior management team were therefore advised to form Irons Ltd to hold 'their' ECWC (1965) Ltd 'shares', with each member acquiring 20% of the equity and the voting rights of Irons Ltd.

The resultant corporate structure is shown below:

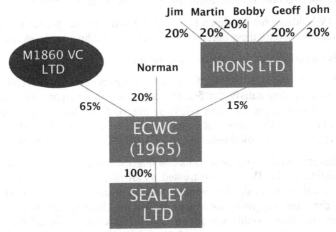

Under the *original* JV rules, 15% of the trading activities of ECWC (1965) Ltd/Sealey Ltd (treated as one trading entity) would be attributed to Irons Ltd for the purposes of the ER 'trading company' test.

This meant that the senior management team would be in a position to claim ER when Irons Ltd was liquidated after a subsequent sale of ECWC (1965) Ltd. (Irons Ltd's sale of its 15% interest in ECWC (1965) Ltd would qualify for the SSE exemption, using similar JV attribution rules (see 16.6A and 3.34).

Treatment of joint venture companies (disposals post-17 March 2015)

15.43A The *FA 2016* introduces a more carefully targeted JV rule, which is backdated to apply to share disposals made after 17 March 2015. This legislation only applies for ER purposes.

Under these rules, a company's investment in a JV company can be treated as 'transparent' provided the shareholder claiming ER satisfies the 5% 'shareholding' and 'voting rights' condition in relation to the underlying JV company (*TCGA 1992, Sch 7ZA, Pt 3*). The shareholder's holding/voting rights in the underlying JV is found by adding their direct *and* indirect shareholdings in the JV company. In many cases, the shareholder is likely to have just an indirect shareholding in the JV company through the investing company. The effective shareholding is calculated using the following formula:

R × S × 100, where:

R = The fraction of investing company's ordinary share capital rights (as appropriate)

S = Investing company's fractional direct/indirect interest in the JV

Note – JV holdings held within a (51%) group structure are 'traced' through the group holdings and for these purposes all 51% group holdings are treated as 100%.

There is an equivalent formula for calculating voting rights.

Thus, the 'look-through' ER rule for JV companies is personal to each claimant shareholder. If they satisfy the 5% shareholding/voting rights rule, they can treat the JV as transparent when assessing the 'trading' status of the company/group. The shareholder must, of course, meet all the other ER conditions (see 15.34–15.36). The detailed rules are in *TCGA 1992, Sch 7ZA, paras 2–12*.

If the shareholder does not meet both 5% interest tests, the relevant company's shareholding in the JV must be treated as an investment (and any dividend income received from the JV would count as investment income). This *may* lead to the company/group failing to satisfy the 'trading' status test for ER purposes, but this would depend on the full assessment of all the various 'activity' measures as discussed at 15.40 and 15.41 above.

Example 8 above shows how the JV rules were exploited to obtain ER in circumstances that were not intended by HMRC. Under the post-*FA 2016* regime, the senior management shareholders would not be able to benefit from ER since their 'indirect' shareholding and voting power in the underlying JV is only 3% (being 20% equity interest in Irons Ltd × 15% interest in ECWC (1965) Ltd).

Example 9

ER – Application of JV rules (post-17 March 2015 disposal)

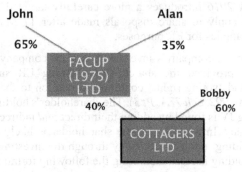

FACUP (1975) Ltd does not carry on any business in its own right, apart from its JV shareholding in Cottagers Ltd, which operates as a musical promoter and publisher. The shareholdings specified below carry commensurate voting rights.

In December 2016, John sells his 65% shareholding in FACUP (1975) Ltd to an unconnected third party.

John has an effective 26% (indirect) shareholding/voting interest in Cottagers Ltd (calculated as 65% (interest in FACUP (1975) Ltd) × 40% (FACUP (1975) Ltd's interest in Cottagers Ltd). Therefore, John would be entitled to attribute 40% of Cottagers Ltd's activities to FACUP (1975) Ltd for the purposes of determining whether it is a trading company for the purposes of *his* ER claim.

Consequently, 40% of the gross assets, sales, profits, expenses and employee/management time of Cottagers Ltd's business would effectively be allocated to FACUP (1975) Ltd (see 15.41). Based on these facts, FACUP (1975) Ltd would be a trading company for the purposes of John's ER claim.

ER treatment of corporate partners

15.43B Before the *FA 2015* changes, where companies held interests in partnerships (including Limited Liability Partnerships), those interests were treated as 'transparent' for the purposes of the ER 'trading' conditions. In essence, this meant that the corporate partner was treated as carrying on an appropriate portion of the partnerships's trade.

The *FA 2015* amendment abolished the transparency treatment for partnerships since HMRC felt this was being abused. However, as with the initial JV changes (see 15.43) this 'blanket' abolition went too far since it prejudiced the ER 'trading' treatment for commercially structured corporate partnerships. Thankfully, HMRC responded to the criticism and engaged with the professional bodies to make these changes more targeted.

The *FA 2016, s 86* and *Sch 13* introduced the final changes which were backdated to 18 March 2015 (recognising that the intial *FA 2015* changes were flawed!). These revised rules provide that a company's activities as a member of a partnership are treated as transparent and hence part of its trading activities (where certain conditions are satisfied).

As with the JV rules, the 'trading' test for corporate interests in partnerships is dealt with on a shareholder by shareholder basis. Thus, in relation to an individual shareholder (referred to as 'P' in the legislation), a company's interest in a partnership is treated as part of its trading activities where P is effectively entitled to at least 5% of:

- the underlying partnership's profits and assets; and
- the partnership voting rights.

The amount of P's effective interest is determined by taking the aggregate of their direct partnership stake and the effective indirect interest held by the relevant corporate partner (as well as via other direct interest companies).

The detailed provisions are in *TCGA 1992, Sch 7ZA, paras 13–23*. It is worth making the point that these rules apply only for the purposes of the ER 'trading' test – they do not apply for other trading test purposes, such as for gifts of business assets relief (see 13.15).

Example 10

ER – treatment of shares held by corporate partner

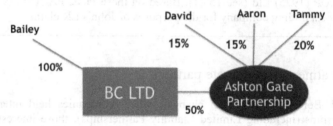

The above percentages reflect entitlement to partnership profits, assets and voting rights. The Ashton Gate Partnership carries on a sports fitness and consultancy trade.

Bailey's effective interest in Ashton Gate partnership is 50% (being 100% × 50%). BC Ltd does not carry on any other acitivity apart from holding its interest in the Ashton Gate partnership.

Thus, on any future 'disposal' of his 100% shareholding in BC Ltd, Bailey should be able to treat BC Ltd as a trading company for ER purposes as it would be deemed to carry on 50% of the partnership's trading activities.

Dealing with risk and informal HMRC clearances

15.44   In certain cases, shareholders may have doubts as to whether their company satisfies the relatively stringent criteria to be a qualifying 'trading company or holding company of a trading group' for the purposes of ER. For example, a company or group may hold substantial cash investments giving rise to a real concern as to whether any 'excess' element falls within HMRC's 20% *de minimis* rule (see 15.41).

Some degree of certainty can be obtained from HMRC under the 'non-statutory' business clearance procedure (introduced from April 2008). HMRC has indicated that it is willing to accept applications in cases of genuine uncertainty on issues affecting shareholders' ER entitlement (provided that this is commercially significant). It is therefore possible, for example, to obtain a ruling from HMRC as to whether a company qualifies as a 'trading company' or 'trading group' for ER purposes. HMRC has indicated a target date of 28 days for replying.

HMRC has confirmed that it would continue to accept clearance applications for confirmation of a company's trading status, even though this would be used by the shareholder rather than the company itself (see *ICAEW Tax Faculty – TAX GUIDE 1/12 – Entrepreneurs' Relief – Practical Points – Example G1*).

ER on associated disposals of personally held property

15.45 Where an individual qualifies for the relief on the disposal of shares, they can also obtain relief on an associated disposal of an asset that has been used by the company (*TCGA 1992, s 169K*). This would typically be a property that is personally owned by a shareholder/director, which has been used by the company for its business, but it might also cover the sale of intellectual property that is personally held (outside the company) by the seller shareholder.

For post-17 March 2015 disposals, *TCGA 1992, s 169K* requires the following conditions to be satisfied for a qualifying 'associated disposal' (in the context of an ER-related share sale within *TCGA 1992, s 169K(2)(b)*):

- The asset must have been held by the seller-shareholder for at least three years (*TCGA 1992, s 169K(1ZA)*);

- The seller-shareholder must dispose of their shares in the company, all or some of which are ordinary shares, with a *minimum* disposal of a 5% shareholding *in the company* (both in terms of ordinary share capital and voting rights) (*TCGA 1992, s 169K(1B)*).

  Furthermore, there must be no arrangements for the shareholder or someone 'connected' with them to repurchase the shares (as defined in *TCGA 1992, s 169K(1D)*);

- The seller's disposal is made as part of their 'withdrawal from participation' in the company's business and there must not be any arrangements in place to repurchase the shares (*TCGA 1992, s 169K(4)*). Arguably, following the *FA 2015* '5% disposal' requirement this requirement now appears to be superfluous; and

- Throughout the *12-month* period prior to the sale of the shares, the relevant property has been used for the purposes of the company's trade (*TCGA 1992, s 169K(4)*).

The last condition may be quite restrictive in terms of timing. For example, the sale of the property some time before the share sale would not qualify (since it would not have been used for the purposes of the company's trade up to the date of the disposal of the shares).

In practice, HMRC may be prepared to accept a claim for 'associated disposal' relief where the property disposal was genuinely linked to a share sale (despite the fact that the strict CGT disposal date of the property occurred before the sale of shares). HMRC confirmed this point, although it was made in the context of the 'cessation of trade' associated disposal rules in *TCGA 1992, s 169K(4)(b)* (*see ICAEW Tax Faculty – TAX GUIDE 1/12 – Entrepreneurs' Relief – Practical Points – Example A3*). In such cases, HMRC indicated that it may still accept a claim for 'associated disposal' relief where there is a 'genuine business disposal linked to a genuine business cessation'; associated disposal relief can still be claimed (even though the strict CGT disposal date occurs before the trade ceases).

15.45A The ER on an associated disposal can be also scaled down on a 'just and reasonable' basis (under *TCGA 1992, s 169P*) to reflect cases where (amongst other things):

- the property has only been *partly* used for the purposes of the company's trade throughout the seller's period of ownership;

- a rent has been charged (*after 5 April 2008*) by the 'seller' to the company for its use of the property.

The restriction is generally calibrated from the date that the property was first acquired, with an important exception being made for the receipt of rent. In this context, rent is defined as 'any form of consideration given for the use of the asset'.

In making the 'just and reasonable' restriction for rent, any period before 6 April 2008 is ignored (*TCGA 1992, s 169S*). This makes sense since, under the pre-6 April 2008 taper regime, the payment of rent did not affect the availability of business taper on personally held property let to trading companies. Thus, where the owner-manager had previously charged a commercial rental for the property before 6 April 2008, this would not restrict their 'associated disposal' ER. However, continuing to charge a rent after 5 April 2008 will lead to a 'just and reasonable' restriction in the gain (potentially) qualifying for ER. Thus, where a full market rent has been charged throughout the (post-5 April 2008) period of ownership, the gain would not qualify for associated disposal relief. HMRC would effectively regard the asset as a non-eligible *investment* one.

INVESTORS' RELIEF (IR)

10% IR CGT charge

15.46 Investors' relief' (IR) was introduced in the *FA 2016*, and is contained in *TCGA 1992, Pt 5, Ch 5*. IR enables gains on qualifying disposal to be taxed at 10%. This is a 'capital gains' only relief (there is no 'upfront' income tax relief). The 10% IR CGT rate is only available after the shares have been held for at least three years (*TCGA 1992, s 169VC*). *TCGA 1992, s 169VK* stipulates that an individual's IR is subject to a £10 million lifetime gains 'cap' (which is separate from the ER £10 million limit (see 15.37).

A claim can be made to tax gains on IR-eligible shares (net of any allowable capital losses) at the 10% IR CGT rate.

Where the investor disposes of a 'mixed' holding of IR-eligible shares and non-IR shares, the gain eligible for IR is based is calculated on a pro-rata basis. Thus, the qualifying IR gain is multiplied by applying the fraction Q/T, where:

Q = Total number of IR-eligible shares included in the disposal; and

T = Total number of all shares comprised in the disposal

IR must be claimed by first anniversary of 31 January following the tax year in which the shares are sold (*TCGA 1992, s 169VM*).

Main IR conditions

15.46A

- The 'investor' must have *subscribed* for ordinary shares (after 16 March 2016) in an unlisted company. IR relief is not therefore available for shares purchased 'second-hand'. However (in contrast to ER) there is no minimum shareholding requirement. Trustees can also qualify for IR (*TCGA 1992, ss 169VC(1), (7)(b)* and *169VI*).

- The shares must be fully paid-up in cash and issued on arm's length terms. Furthermore, the share issue must be made for genuine commercial reasons (and not mainly for a tax avoidance purpose) (*TCGA 1992, s 169VB*).

- The investor must hold the relevant ordinary shares for at least three years (this is known as the 'share-holding' period). The three-year share-holding period cannot begin until 6 April 2016 at the earliest (*TCGA 1992, s 169VB(2)*).

- IR is not *normally* available to directors or employees of the investee company or any 'related' company at any time in 'three-year' share-holding period (*TCGA 1992, ss 169VB(2)(g)* and *169VM*).

  However, there are two important exceptions to this general rule, which enables investors to qualify for IR where:

  – they *subsequently* become an unpaid director after the relevant 'IR' share issue (*TCGA 1992, s 169VM(3), (4)*); or

  – they did not intend to be employed by the company at the time of the 'IR' share subscription but started (paid) employment more than 180 days after the relevant share issue (*TCGA 1992, s 169VM(5)*).

These exceptions are intended to help 'business angels' become more closely involved with the investee company's development.

There are no other 'connection' conditions, so it would be possible (for example) for the investor to hold more than 30% of the issued share capital/voting rights.

- The investee company must qualify as a trading company or holding company of a trading group throughout the 'three-year' share-holding period. These definitions adopt the 'trading' tests used in *TCGA 1992, s 165A* (see 15.40–15.43B).

- The IR legislation contains special rules to 'look-through' any share exchange or company reorganisation for the purposes of applying the three-year 'holding' test, although investors can elect to pay the 10% IR CGT charge on the market value of the shares received on the relevant share exchange or company reorganisation (*TCGA 1992, ss 169VN–169VT*).

Return of value rules

15.46B   IR is denied where the investor 'receives value' from the investee company (other than insignificant value). The IR 'value received' rules are modelled on the ones used for the EIS – see 11.40 and 11.41 (*TCGA 1992, Sch 7ZB*).

In practice, this means any dividends paid out to the investor must not exceed a 'normal return' on an equity investment in the company and any loans made by the investor to the company cannot exceed a 'reasonable commercial return.

Example 11

IR CGT computation

In December 2017, Ronald subscribed for £200,000 £1 ordinary shares at par in The Toffeemen Ltd. This gave him a 20% equity stake. He was not previously connected with the company and was subsequently appointed as an unpaid non-executive director.

Assume the entire issued capital of the company was sold in (say) June 2021 for £5,000,000.

Since Ronald had held his shares for at least three years, he would be able to claim IR on his capital gain, as follows:

	£
Sale proceeds (ignoring incidental costs of disposal)	1,000,000
Less: Acquisition cost (Dec 2017)	(200,000)
Chargeable gain	800,000

Less: Annual exemption (2021/22) (say)	(14,000)
Taxable gain	786,000
ER CGT @ 10%	£78,600

STRUCTURING THE CONSIDERATION FOR A SHARE SALE

Types of consideration

15.47 Sellers may sell their shares for:

(*a*) a cash consideration;

(*b*) shares in the acquiring company;

(*c*) loan notes issued by the acquiring company;

(*d*) a mixture of the above.

The consideration may be paid immediately on completion or on a deferred basis. Deferred consideration can either be structured as fixed (see 15.4) or variable, for example, depending on the future profits under a so-called earn-out arrangement (see 15.64). There is much to be said for receiving all the consideration up-front as a guaranteed amount, despite the fact that it will attract an immediate tax liability.

Consideration satisfied in shares

Basic share exchange rules

15.48 Where sellers of a private company receive shares in the acquiring company in exchange for their shares, the CGT liability on the disposal can usually be deferred under *TCGA 1992, s 135* provided:

(*a*) the acquiring company ends up with more than 25% of the target company's ordinary shares (or the greater part of the voting power in the target company); and

(*b*) HMRC is satisfied that the transaction was undertaken for commercial reasons and not for tax avoidance (see 15.50) [*TCGA 1992, s 137*].

It is usually advisable to obtain advance clearance on this point from HMRC under *TCGA 1992, s 138*. If only part of the consideration is satisfied in shares, then only a pro-rata portion of the gain can be 'rolled-over'. Thus, if the consideration consists of a mixture of cash and shares in the acquiring company, *TCGA 1992, s 128(3)* will come into play to treat the cash received as a disposal of an interest in the shares. In computing the capital gain on the cash 'element', the base cost of the original shareholding would be apportioned on a pro-rata basis (ie cost multiplied by cash consideration/total consideration (being cash plus the market value of the new consideration shares). The balance of the original base cost would be attributed to the new shares in the acquiring company.

Strictly, the CGT reorganisation rules provide that the 'new' shares received by the seller in the acquiring company are treated as having been acquired at the same time and for the same amount as his old shareholding [*TCGA 1992, s 127*]. Thus, if the original shares were held at 31 March 1982, the base cost of the new 'consideration' shares will be the 31 March 1982 value of the old shares.

Where the seller receives both shares and cash (as discussed above), the new shares would only carry part of the original base cost (deemed to be acquired at the same time as the original shares).

Where ER is potentially available on the sale, it is possible to make a special election to disapply the 'no disposal' rule. This enables ER to be claimed against the consideration received as shares in the acquirer (see 15.52).

For other tax implications of a share exchange, see 13.64, 13.98 and 13.98A.

Example 12

Sale consideration satisfied in shares

In July 2017 Mr Beckham sold all his 51% shareholding in Galaxy Ltd to Freekicks plc for £5,000,000, which was satisfied in the form of 500,000 new ordinary £1 shares (worth £10 each) in Freekicks plc.

Mr Beckham originally acquired his Galaxy Ltd shares for £100,000 in May 1993. Going forward, his new shareholding in Freekicks plc represented about 20% of its share capital (carrying commensurate voting rights). Mr Beckham will also continue to act as Operations Director for Galaxy Ltd.

Assuming that the necessary *TCGA 1992, s 138* clearance is obtained, Mr Beckham's share exchange will not give rise to any disposal for CGT purposes. He will be treated as having acquired his 500,000 £1 Freekicks plc shares in May 1993 for £100,000, ie 20p each.

He probably will not wish to make an election under *TCGA 1992, s 169Q* (see 15.52), since he is likely to benefit from ER on a subsequent sale of his Freekicks plc shares.

Based on current facts, he should qualify for ER since he now holds around 20% of the ordinary shares in Freekicks plc and is a director of Galaxy Ltd (a fellow-group company of Freekicks plc).

Share exchanges and the ER 'personal company' test

15.49   On a close reading of the ER 'personal company' definition in *TCGA 1992, s 169S(3)* and *TCGA 1992, s 135* share exchange legislation, it is difficult to come to the conclusion that the 'look through' CGT reorganisation provisions can treat the pre-share exchange period as counting towards the minimum one year 'personal company' condition for ER purposes. Thus, where a sale of the 'new' shares takes place within one year of a share exchange, it would appear that the sale could not qualify for ER.

The CIOT Technical department put this problem to HMRC in 2010 and obtained confirmation from HMRC's Capital Gains Technical Group that (provided no *TCGA 1992, s 169Q* election has been made – see 15.52 below), the pre-share exchange period would count towards the one year personal company test, provided that the relevant ER conditions were satisfied in relation to the previous shareholding. This practice would appear to be in the nature of an HMRC concession since the legislation does not strictly provide for it.

The genuine commercial purpose/no tax avoidance test

15.50   The seller only receives their CGT deferral under *TCGA 1992, s 135* where they take shares and/or loan notes wholly/partly as consideration for their original shares provided that the transaction has been structured for genuine commercial purposes and not mainly driven by tax avoidance motives [*TCGA 1992, s 137*].

The seller can obtain certainty on this point by applying for advance clearance under *TCGA 1992, s 138* to confirm that HMRC is satisfied that the 'commercial purpose/no tax avoidance' test has been met. It should be noted that a clearance under *TCGA 1992, s 138* would not necessarily guarantee that the other preconditions for *s 135* relief have been met, as HMRC invariably points out by way of caveat in their clearance letter.

However, the 'commercial purpose/tax avoidance' test in *TCGA 1992, s 137* does not apply to 'minority' shareholders who hold no more than 5% of the target company's shares. The rationale for this useful rule is that such shareholders are unlikely to have any say in how the transaction is structured – they are effectively deemed to be acting commercially.

Issues arising from the *Snell* case

15.51   HMRC will almost certainly deny clearance where they consider that the taxpayer has taken shares/loan notes with the view to becoming non-resident (to avoid a UK CGT charge on their sale consideration). This was demonstrated in the case of *Snell v HMRC* [2007] STC 1279. In December 1996, Mr Snell agreed to sell his shares for a total consideration of around £7.3 million, of which approximately £6.6 million was taken in the form of loan notes. Mr Snell left the UK on 2 April 1997 and subsequently became non-UK resident. HMRC sought to deny the deferral of the gain attributable to the loan notes on the grounds that *TCGA 1992, s 137* applied since one of the main purposes of Mr Snell taking loan notes was to avoid CGT. Mr Snell did not make a *s138* clearance application!

The High Court concurred and concluded that the main purpose of the arrangements (ie the taking of the loan notes with the view to their redemption whilst non-resident) was for the avoidance of CGT. Thus, *TCGA 1992, s 137* applied to prevent the operation of *TCGA 1992, s 135* and Mr Snell had a CGT disposal when he received the loan notes. In reaching their decision, the High Court placed particular significance on the Special Commissioners' findings of fact. It was very important to consider what was in Mr Snell's mind at the time he agreed to take loan notes. This was largely based on contemporaneous documentary evidence, which looked at such things as information memorandums and reports by the taxpayer's advisers. Although there were obvious difficulties in considering Mr Snell's 'purpose' (given that this took place a long time ago), the Special Commissioners concluded that, on the balance of probability, Mr Snell was much more likely to have dictated that he wanted a loan note 'in the expectation that it would be redeemed when he was non-resident'.

Special election to obtain ER on share exchange

Effect of election

15.52 Because the 'reorganisation' rule provides there is no CGT disposal, the seller would normally be unable to claim ER on the value of the acquirer's shares received as part of their sale consideration. This would be unfortunate if the seller was unable to claim ER on a later sale of their 'consideration' shares – for example, because they did not possess the requisite 5% shareholding in the acquiring company.

The ER legislation recognises this problem and provides that the seller can make a special election (under *TCGA 1992, s 169Q*) to opt out of the normal share-for-share exchange treatment. By making an *s 169Q* election the seller is treated as having made a normal CGT disposal with the value of the acquirer's shares being reflected as all/part of their overall sale consideration. In such cases, the benefit of the ER would be reflected in the (higher) market value base cost of the shares in the acquiring company.

Example 13

Effect of special ER election on share exchanges

Martin has been a 'management' shareholder since June 2000 and holds 10% of the equity share capital of Peters Ltd (a successful music publishing and recording company). He acquired his 10,000 £1 shares at par but was subject to an employment income tax charge on their full market value of £20,000 (which was therefore his base cost).

In July 2017, Peters Ltd was taken over by Boleyn plc. As part of this transaction, Martin received sale consideration of £600,000, which was satisfied as follows:

	£
Cash	200,000
Shares in Boleyn plc, valued at	400,000

Martin's shares in Boleyn plc would represent a 3% shareholding (with commensurate voting rights). He is therefore unlikely to qualify for ER on a subsequent sale of these shares. However, by making a *TCGA 1992, s 169Q* election, he could benefit from ER on the *total* consideration received on the July 2017 sale, as shown below:

		£
Sale consideration	Cash	200,000
	Boleyn plc shares	400,000
		600,000
Less: Base cost		(20,000)
		580,000
Less: Annual exemption		(11,300)
Taxable gain		568,700
ER CGT @ 10%		£56,870

Martin's base cost of his Boleyn plc shares would be their full market value of £400,000 (as opposed to £13,333 (4/6 × £20,000), being the pro-rata original cost of his Peters Ltd shares if the reorganisation rules had applied).

Deciding whether to make a *s 169Q* election

15.53   The *TCGA 1992, s 169Q* election is made on an 'all or nothing' basis. Thus, for example, it is not possible to restrict its application to gains of up to the (current) £10 million ER limit. Such elections must be made within (just less than) 22 months after the end of the tax year in which the sale occurs.

The potential consequences of making a *TCGA 1992, s 169Q* election should always be considered when structuring any deal, which should include some assessment about the investment prospects of the 'consideration' shares.

Because the reorganisation rule is disapplied, the seller would generally incur a CGT liability on the 'ER-relieved' gain. The seller would therefore need to ensure that they had sufficient cash consideration to fund the tax liability. Furthermore, the timing of any future tax liability (when the higher base cost comes into play) must also be considered.

Clearly, such an election would not be appropriate where the 'cash' element of a company share sale produced chargeable gains exceeding the ER limit of £10 million.

LOAN NOTE CONSIDERATION – QCBs VERSUS NON-QCBs

QCB v non-QCBs

15.54   In many deals, the seller may agree to accept deferred payment for part of the sale consideration by taking loan notes in the acquiring company. As a general rule, where the purchaser satisfies part of the consideration by issuing loan notes, an appropriate part of the seller's gain is deferred until the loan note is redeemed for payment. The precise mechanics of the deferral depends on the tax status of the loan note, as this varies between Qualifying Corporate Bonds (QCBs) (see 15.55–15.57) and non-QCBs (see 15.62). In the GAAR guidance (April 2013), HMRC has confirmed that the structuring of loan notes to fall within the non-QCB regime is an acceptable form of tax planning (see 1.19A).

These CGT deferral rules are subject to HMRC being satisfied that the loan note has been issued for genuine commercial reasons and not mainly to avoid tax (*TCGA 1992, s 137*) (see 15.50). The seller would normally apply for a *TCGA 1992, s 138* clearance to seek advance confirmation of this point from HMRC.

QCBs

15.55   Most non-convertible loan notes will represent Qualifying Corporate Bonds (QCBs). Where the acquiring company satisfies the consideration by the issue of QCB loan notes, no immediate CGT liability arises. A *TCGA 1992, s 138* clearance should be obtained to ensure that HMRC is satisfied that the loan note has been issued for a bona fide commercial purpose and not for tax avoidance (see 15.4 and for 'combined' tax clearance procedure see 15.89).

However, the capital gain (or loss) based on the *deemed* disposal of the shares at the time of the exchange is held-over and will become payable (or allowable) when the QCB is either paid or redeemed. Effectively, the seller's tax position is frozen at the date of the exchange with the payment of the CGT being postponed on an interest-free basis [*TCGA 1992, s 116(10), (11)*].

15.56 For *post-5 April 2008* redemptions, any taper relief that would have accrued on the held-over gain is lost. *TCGA 1992, s 116(10)* only holds over the chargeable gain, which is before taper relief [*TCGA 1992, s 2A(2)*]. Thus, where the gain becomes charged on a (post-5 April 2008) redemption no taper relief will be applied. However, in certain cases, it may be possible to claim transitional ER against the pre-6 April 2008 gain (see 15.59).

For special 'transitional' treatment of QCB loan notes that were acquired as consideration on a *pre-5 April 2008 share sale*, please see 2013/14 and earlier editions of this book. Similarly, for treatment of QCB gains acquired as consideration for sales taking place between 6 April 2008 and 22 June 2010, please see 2016/17 and earlier editions of this book.

QCB gains and *TCGA 1992, s 169R* elections to 'bank' ER

15.57 The *Finance (No 2) Act 2010* made an unwelcome change to the way ER is dealt with on QCB gains held-over from 23 June 2010. This follows the change in ER to a straight 10% CGT charge. In such cases, any available ER is no longer factored into the held-over gain, so that the 'gross' gain is postponed.

If the seller wishes to claim ER on their QCB gain, they must make a special election under *TCGA 1992, s 169R*. This treats the QCB gain as being a chargeable disposal at the time of the share sale (ie the original shares are treated as sold for the QCB consideration), against which the ER CGT 10% rate can be claimed. By making an election, the normal QCB hold-over rules in *TCGA 1992, s 116(10)* do not apply. The *TCGA 1992, s 169R* election must be made by the first anniversary of the 31 January following the tax year of the share sale.

This change therefore gives rise to a dilemma for sellers – should they elect under *TCGA 1992, s 169R* and pay 10% ER CGT 'up-front' on the share gain or defer their share gain under *TCGA 1992 s 116(10)* and (probably) pay CGT at 20% on the full held-over gain on redemption (with no ER)?

If a seller opts to tax the QCB gain up-front to obtain a low ER CGT 10% rate, they would need to ensure that the deal structure provides sufficient cash funds to pay the CGT liability on the 31 January following the tax year of the sale.

Where the *TCGA 1992, s 169R* election is made, there is no QCB hold-over and thus the redemption does not trigger any taxable gain. See Example 14 below.

Example 14

Treatment of QCB gains and ER

In May 2017, Joe sold his 40% shareholding in Magic Cole Ltd to Claret plc for £4,000,000 of which:

- £500,000 was paid in cash on completion: and

- £3,500,000 was satisfied by the issue of a Claret plc QCB loan note (bearing interest at 9%, bank guaranteed and redeemable after 12 months)

Joe subscribed for his 40,000 £1 shares in Claret Ltd at par in May 2003.

Joe's CGT position is as follows:

2017/18 – CGT on cash consideration

Cash		£
Sale consideration — Cash		500,000
Less: Base cost $£40,000 \times \dfrac{£500,000}{(£500,000 + £3,500,000)}$		(5,000)
Capital gain		495,000
Less: Annual exemption		(11,300)
Taxable gain		483,700
ER CGT @ 10%		£48,370

If Joe does *not* make an election under *TCGA 1992, s 169R*, all the QCB gain is held-over (without the benefit of ER).

Postponed QCB gain

		£
QCB consideration		3,500,000
Less: Base cost £40,000 less £5,000		(35,000)
Postponed gain		3,465,000

The postponed gain is likely to become taxable on redemption at 20%, being £693,000 (ignoring the annual exemption).

2017/18 – Taxable QCB gain at ER CGT rate

If Joe makes an election under *TCGA 1992, s 169R* for the QCB consideration to be taxable in 2017/18, he can obtain a 10% ER CGT rate on the QCB gain.

	£
QCB consideration	3,500,000
Less: Base cost	(35,000)
Capital gain	3,465,000
ER CGT @ 10%	346,500

An election to benefit from ER would give Joe a substantial tax saving provided he can manage the acceleration of his tax liability.

Potential issues with *TCGA 1992, s 169R* elections

15.58   One of the potential difficulties with the *TCGA 1992, s 169R* election is that there is no statutory mechanism for unwinding the CGT disposal treatment if all or part of the QCB consideration becomes irrecoverable.

The 'up-front' CGT charge still remains but this is due to the *s 169R* election. (For the avoidance of doubt, this is *not* the latent tax charge under *TCGA 1992, s 116(10)(b)* that has always been a problem with QCBs, which (by concession) HMRC does not seek, provided the 'worthless' QCB is donated to charity – (see 15.60).

15.59   Consequently, if a seller anticipates making a *TCGA 1992, s 169R* election, important consideration should be given to seeking bank guarantees on the QCB loan notes. This removes the 'bad debt' risk. Although some purchasers will resist providing bank guarantees (the amount guaranteed generally forms part of their borrowing facility), sellers are often advised to push for it and accept the inherent cost.

If the loan notes are short-dated ones, then it may be possible to keep the election open so that a 'wait and see' approach can be taken. The decision to make a *TCGA 1992, s 169R* election would have to be made by the *first anniversary* of the 31 January following the tax year of sale (ie just less than 22 months following the tax year of sale).

Bad debt relief issues with QCBs

15.60   A serious disadvantage with QCB loan notes is that no bad debt relief is available if the acquiring company is unable to pay (since a QCB is not a chargeable asset for CGT purposes).

However, when the loan note is redeemed for little or no value (for example, by the liquidator), the original gain would still be taxed in full. In these dire circumstances, HMRC (by concession) permit the worthless loan note to be 'gifted' to a charity under *TCGA 1992, s 257* without triggering any held over gain (see Revenue Interpretation RI 23). Where the loan note has been subject to a *TCGA 1992, s 169R* election, this remedy will not be appropriate since the gain will already have crystallised (see 15.57 and 15.58).

However, it would be prudent not to rely on this concession and there may sometimes be practical problems in 'finding' a charity to participate. It is therefore always advisable to seek commercial bank guarantees for the loan notes, which means the seller will always get their money and so the lack of 'bad debt' relief with QCBs ceases to be a problem.

Non-QCBs

Common non-QCB terms

15.61 Different rules apply where the purchaser issues non-QCBs.

The terms of such loan notes are designed to fall outside the definition of a QCB in *TCGA 1992, s 117*. Thus, common types of non-QCBs would include loan notes which:

- are convertible into shares in the acquiring company;

- carry the right to subscribe for further shares or loan notes (see, for example, *Businessman v Inspector of Taxes* [2003] STC (SCD) 403); and

- contain the right of repayment in a foreign currency at a spot rate prior to redemption.

In such cases, the possibility of the loan note generating an exchange gain which might be a 'deep gain' (when viewed at the outset), was considered sufficient for it to be treated as a Relevant Discounted Security (RDS) (within what is now *CTA 2010, Pt 5, Ch 8*). Unless the holder's potential gain was appropriately 'capped', this could cause the (purported non-QCB) loan note to be a QCB. However, HMRC confirmed that they would not seek to apply the RDS rules in this way.

Some useful commentary on the use of 'foreign currency conversion' clauses to create non-QCB loan notes was provided in *Harding v HMRC* [2008] EWCA Civ 1164. In this case, the taxpayer's loan notes contained an option for redemption in various foreign currencies so that they fell outside the QCB definition in *TCGA 1992, s 117(1)(b)* (which requires a *QCB loan note* to be 'expressed in sterling and in respect of which no provision is made for conversion into, or redemption in, a currency other than sterling'.

Although the main tax issue arising in *Harding* has now been dealt with by amending legislation, HMRC did accept that a right to redeem a loan note in a foreign currency would be sufficient to make it a non-QCB, even where there was a 'cap and collar' mechanism to reduce the foreign currency risk (in this case, the potential foreign currency exposure on redemption was limited to two per cent). Until recently, it had been assumed that a (sterling) loan note that carried a clause enabling it to be converted into a euro (at the relevant conversion rate on the adoption of the euro) was treated as a non-QCB (based on HMRC's stated view).

However, the Upper Tribunal held that the disposal of a sterling-denominated loan note that contained a 'euro conversion clause' should not be treated as a

QCB (*Nicholas MF Trigg v HMRC* [2016] UKUT 0165 (TCC)). This decision, which was contrary to the 'purposive construction' based ruling of the First-tier Tribunal decision, was made on the basis that 'sterling' could only mean 'pounds sterling'.

Basic CGT treatment for non-QCBs

15.62   Where a debenture (ie any written acknowledgement of a debt) is received in exchange for shares/debentures under the CGT reorganisation rules, this is automatically deemed to be a security for CGT purposes under *TCGA 1992, s 251(6)*. It is not, therefore, necessary for the debenture to constitute a (debt on a) security under normal principles (ie it does not necessarily have to be 'marketable', readily transferable and so on).

Non-QCB loan notes represent a security. Consequently, where they are received in exchange for shares, this is treated as a share reorganisation under *TCGA 1992, s 127* (by virtue of the share exchange rules in *TCGA 1992, s 135*) (see 15.48). The appropriate part of the seller's original base cost in the target company's shares is therefore treated as being given for the non-QCB security at the original acquisition date(s).

Since the CGT deferral for non-QCBs is governed by the CGT reorganisation rules in *TCGA 1992, s 127*, ER may potentially be claimed on the value of the sale consideration received as a non-QCB (assuming that the relevant ER conditions are satisfied) by making a *TCGA 1992, s 169Q* election (*TCGA 1992, s 169Q(1)*). By making this special election, the value of the non-QCB consideration is brought into the seller's CGT computation at the date of the sale (in the same way as explained in 15.52 for share exchanges). (Following the change in the treatment of ER on QCB gains, the corresponding QCB election now operates in a similar way to non-QCBs.)

Before structuring any deal or deciding whether a *TCGA 1992, s 169Q* election would be beneficial, the relevant factors in 15.52 and 15.53 should be considered.

15.63   In the past, where the seller was unable to obtain a commercial bank guarantee for the loan note, many considered that a non-QCB offered a more prudent alternative to a QCB. This was because a non-QCB avoided the QCB-type risk of triggering a CGT charge on the cancellation of the loan note (for example, where the acquiring company becomes insolvent – see 15.60). The CGT reorganisation treatment also means that automatic 'bad debt' relief is obtained, as any gain or loss on the ultimate redemption of the non-QCB loan note is calculated by reference to the amount actually repaid (rather than the original sale value). Therefore, little or no gain would arise where the holder is forced to accept minimal redemption proceeds (because, for example, the acquiring company has become insolvent).

The above treatment does *not* apply where a seller has 'banked' their ER entitlement 'up-front' by making a *TCGA 1992, s 169Q* election. In such cases, they would have crystallised their 'loan note' gain at the date of sale and are likely to have generated a 'substantial' capital loss when the loan note is cancelled/redeemed for little or no consideration (see 15.62). Since the seller cannot carry back their loss, this unfavourable tax position will not be that different to a QCB loan note holder who had elected to be taxed at the date of the share sale under *TCGA 1992, s 169R*.

EARN-OUT DEALS

Background to earn-outs

15.64 Earn-outs fulfil a useful function by reconciling the so-called 'price gap' that often exists between a seller and purchaser. Many sellers believe that they are selling their business ahead of its maximum profit potential. Consequently, they will want to negotiate a price for the business that reflects its future earnings potential. On the other hand, most prudent purchasers will only be willing to agree a deal based on future (increased) profits when they are actually 'delivered' by the business. Thus, by incorporating an 'earn-out' arrangement as part of the pricing mechanism for the purchase of the shares, the seller's and purchaser's objectives can be satisfied.

An earn-out deal typically involves the seller receiving a fixed sum on completion, with further sums being paid over the next two or three years, calculated on a formula based on the actual results of the business over this period. The seller usually continues to be employed in the business during the earn-out period in a key management, technical or sales position. Thus, through their efforts during the 'earn-out' period, sellers have the incentive to increase their disposal consideration, thereby ensuring that the purchaser's acquisition is successful.

However, a number of tax issues should carefully be thought through before the earn-out consideration clauses are agreed, otherwise the seller may have some undesirable, or, indeed, unintended tax charges – these are discussed in 15.65 to 15.70. Furthermore, care must also be taken to avoid the risk of HMRC characterising all, or some, of the earn-out payments as an 'employment' bonus, since this would trigger PAYE and NIC charges (see 15.79).

The *Marren v Ingles* dicta

15.65 The tax treatment of an earn-out transaction is largely based on the decision in *Marren v Ingles* [1980] STC 500. Consequently, where a taxpayer sells an asset (the original or main asset) with a right to receive a future unquantifiable sum (for example, a formula based earn-out), the value of that right is included as part of the CGT consideration received for the original asset. Thus, to the extent that ER is available, the gain enhanced by the value of that right (included as consideration) would qualify for ER in the usual way.

It was further held that the taxpayer acquires, as an entirely separate asset, a 'right' or 'chose in action'. Thus, as and when the earn-out payments are received, further (deemed) CGT disposals arise in respect of the earn-out right itself under *TCGA 1992, s 22* (representing capital sums derived from the right to receive the earn-out and not the disposal of shares).

Even where the seller has ER available after the original share sale, 'earn-out' gains can never qualify for the relief. As they effectively relate to a (part) disposal of the *earn-out right*, they do not meet the 'disposal of shares' requirement for ER (see 15.34). Thus, gains arising on earn-out payments made after 5 April 2016 would invariably be taxed at 20% (28% prior to 6 April 2016).

If the deferred consideration can be readily ascertained at the date of the sale, this is taxed under *TCGA 1992, s 48* (and the *'Marren v Ingles'* principles do *not* apply) (see 15.5).

Election to carry back capital loss on earn-out payments

15.66 One of the main potential problems arising from the *Marren v Ingles* treatment is the risk of being taxed on an unrealised gain, ie the seller would suffer tax on the value of the right (when their shares are sold). In an extreme case, if the earn-out falls (well) below expectation, this could result in a capital loss arising on the disposal of the right in a subsequent tax year. Before the *FA 2003* introduced a special relief, any such capital loss could not be carried back to reduce the seller's original capital gain. This meant that the seller would suffer tax on an amount that exceeded his overall economic gain from the earn-out transaction.

Under *TCGA 1992, ss 279A–279D* capital losses arising on *earn-out rights* can be carried back against the gain on the original sale of the shares (which includes the original value of the earn-out right). This special capital loss carry back rule is only available to individual and trustee sellers (companies do not benefit from this facility).

An individual or trustee seller can make an election under *TCGA 1992, s 279A,* provided broadly:

- the right was acquired as full/partial consideration for the sale of another asset;

- the right is a *Marren v Ingles* right to 'unascertainable' consideration (such as in the case of an 'earn-out');

- when the right was acquired, there was no corresponding disposal of it (for example, where it arose from the contract for the sale of shares); and

- the disposal of the original asset (such as shares) was made in an earlier tax year.

Where an election is made under *TCGA 1992, s 279A*, any allowable capital loss arising on the disposal of the (earn-out) right can be 'carried back' and set-off against the gain arising on the sale of the original asset (for example, the shares).

A *TCGA 1992, s 279A* election is irrevocable and must specify:

- the relevant capital loss;
- the right disposed of;
- the tax year in which the right was disposed of;
- the tax year in which the right was acquired; and
- the original asset(s).

The election must be made by the first anniversary of the 31 January next following the tax year of loss. Each loss must be the subject of a separate election.

Structuring as a bonus arrangement

15.67 Occasionally some cash earn-out transactions have been structured as a 'bonus' arrangement to avoid the undesirable tax effects of the *Marren v Ingles* dicta. This broadly involves providing for a 'profit-based' bonus under the seller's director's service agreement which replaces the earn-out in the sale agreement. The bonus would only be taxable as earnings when *received*. This may also suit the purchaser as the bonus would be deductible against the target company's trading profits (which may outweigh the inherent employer's NIC cost). However, since CGT rates are still much lower than income tax rates, most sellers are likely to prefer the traditional 'earn-out' route.

Even though a significant part of the earn-out may be taxed 'up-front', it is likely to be taxed at a much lower rate than the PAYE income tax on a bonus. However, HMRC might seek to challenge certain 'earn-out' deals (with the view to taxing them as employment income). This is likely to be the case where it considers that the substance of the 'earn out' arrangement is to provide a reward for services as an employee/director as opposed to consideration for the sale of shares (see also 15.79).

Quoted company purchasers also tend to prefer the earn-out route to avoid potentially substantial bonuses having a detrimental impact on their earnings.

Worked example of cash-based earn-out

15.68 The CGT treatment of a (cash) earn-out transaction is explained in Example 15 below.

Example 15

CGT treatment of share sale on a 'cash' earn-out basis

Tony formed Cottee Ltd in July 1986 subscribing for the entire share capital of 50,000 £1 ordinary shares at par.

On 5 January 2018, Tony sold all his shares in Cottee Ltd on an earn-out basis. The sale contract provided for:

- initial cash consideration of £500,000 (net of disposal costs) to be paid on completion; and

- a deferred earn-out consideration based on the 'defined earn-out' profits for the three years ending 31 December 2020, payable in cash six months following the end of each relevant accounting period.

Tony also entered into a three-year director's service agreement, under which he would continue as managing director of the business during the three year earn-out period.

Technical overview

Tony's earn-out consideration is 'unascertainable' at the date of disposal (5 January 2018). Under the rules established in *Marren v Ingles,* he is treated as selling his shares for an initial cash consideration (£500,000), plus the value at that date of the right to receive the earn-out consideration (which is agreed by HMRC – Shares Valuation at £1,120,000). Tony is eligible for ER and therefore is able to claim relief on the share sale.

When the earn-out payments are made on 30 June 2019 and 2020 (relating to the years ended 31 December 2018 and 2019), they will trigger a part-disposal of the right /chose in action. In each case, the actual earn-out payment is taxed after deducting the part disposal cost of the right [*TCGA 1992, s 22(1)*]. ER cannot be claimed on these 'earn-out' gains – since they do not relate to a sale of shares. Based on current legislation, the gains (after deducting any annual exemption) are likely to be taxed at the top CGT rate of 20%.

The base value of the right is apportioned between each part disposal by applying the A/A+B formula in *TCGA 1992, s 42*. It is necessary to compute the residual value of the right (ie B) at the date of each part disposal – the value of the residual right at 30 June 2019 and 30 June 2020 is agreed at £1,100,000 and £900,000 respectively.

The earn-out (for the final year ended 31 December 2020) payable on 30 June 2021 will represent the final disposal of the right under *TCGA 1992, s 22(1)* with the residual base value of the right being applied against the earn-out consideration.

877

CGT computations: 2017/18–2021/22

The relevant capital gains, which arise on the 'earn-out' sale, are calculated as follows:

2017/18

	£
Consideration (Sale of shares – Jan 2018)	
(£500,000 + value of right £1,120,000)	1,620,000
Less: Base cost (July 1986)	(50,000)
Chargeable gain	1,570,000
Less: Annual exemption	(11,300)
Taxable gain	1,558,700
ER CGT @ 10%	155,870

2019/20

Assuming the earn-out consideration for the year ended 31 December 2018 is £650,000, a part disposal of the right will arise on its receipt on 30 June 2019.

	£
Consideration	650,000
Less: Part disposal of right	
£1,120,000 × $\dfrac{£650,000}{(£650,000 + £1,100,000)}$	(416,000)
Chargeable gain (before annual exemption)	234,000

2020/21

Let's assume that the earn-out consideration for the year ended 31 December 2019 is £936,000. A part disposal of the right will arise on its receipt on 30 June 2020.

		£
Consideration		936,000
Less: Part disposal cost of right		
Initial value of right	1,120,000	
Used in 2019/20	(416,000)	
Balance available	704,000	

$£704,000 \times \dfrac{£936,000}{(£936,000 + £900,000)}$	(358,902)
Chargeable gain (before annual exemption)	577,098

2021/22

On the basis that the earn-out consideration for the year ended 31 December 2020 is £980,000, the final disposal of the right will arise when it is received on 30 June 2021.

		£
Earn-out consideration		980,000
Less: Base cost of residual right		
Initial value of right	1,120,000	
Used in 2019/20	(416,000)	
Used in 2020/21	(358,902)	
		(345,098)
Chargeable gain (before annual exemption)		634,902

Optimising ER on earn-outs

Valuing the earn-out right

15.69 Until relatively recently, sellers often preferred to avoid incurring the initial CGT charge on the value of the right, since this was an *unrealised* gain. This is relatively easy to achieve in practice since the seller can negotiate with the purchaser to structure the earn-out so that it can only be satisfied by the issue of actual loan notes in the purchasing company. This would bring the earn-out consideration within the automatic deferral rule in *TCGA 1992, s 138A* (see 15.71 below).

In essence, the *Marren v Ingles* treatment fragments the share sale into (at least) two different CGT disposals, being:

- The share sale itself; and

- The part-disposals/disposal of the earn-out rights (which are triggered when the earn-out payments are received).

Under the current CGT regime, this means that:

- With an ER gains limit of £10 million, there is far more ER 'headroom' now on the amount of the earn-out right attracting the 10% ER CGT rate as part of the share sale consideration.

- Currently, there is a 10% differential between the 10% ER CGT rate on the initial value of the earn-out right (taxed as part of the share sale consideration) and the 20% CGT rate that applies to gains on the actual earn-out payments (although this could be more if CGT rates were to rise in later years!).

Thus, assuming that there is sufficient scope within the seller's overall 'deal' value, there is perhaps some sense in placing a more realistic(!) initial value on the earn-out right. This valuation now becomes an important factor in 'splitting' the overall CGT charge on the deal between the ER CGT 10% rate (on the share sale) and the 20% rate on earn-out gains. Thus, provided it can be substantiated under valuation principles, the higher the value of the earn-out right that can be agreed with HMRC, the greater the amount of tax that can be saved.

Some will point to the fact that this will lead to a higher *up-front* CGT charge. However, given the prevailing level of interest rates, the 10% tax saving should outweigh the 'interest cost' of accelerating part of the tax charge.

Using a 'profit warranty' approach

15.70 In some cases, it might be possible to maximise the value of the 'earn-out' consideration taxed at the ER CGT rate of 10% by structuring the share sale for the maximum possible deferred consideration value.

In such cases, the deferred consideration should be ascertainable, and should not therefore be subject to the *Marren v Ingles* computation basis. Instead the full deal value will be taxable under the 'fixed' deferred consideration rule in *TCGA 1992, s 48* (see 15.5). This has the benefit of bringing in the full deferred amount without any discount for risk and contingency, which often substantially reduces the value of the earn-out right under the *Marren v Ingles* rules.

Under the *ascertainable* deferred consideration route, effect is given to the 'earn-out' arrangement by providing that any under-performance against the maximum profit/earnings etc. is 'clawed-back' by a series of 'profit-warranties'. Since such deals are typically based on a multiple of earnings, it should be possible to define the warranty damages in terms of an appropriate multiple of the profit 'shortfall'. Careful drafting of the profit warranty clauses is clearly required to ensure that this route is effective.

The subsequent warranty payments would therefore *reduce* the original maximum deferred consideration under *TCGA 1992, s 49(2)*. In this way, the seller should pay the 10% ER CGT rate on the entire deal value (up to the available ER gains limit).

Earn-outs satisfied in shares or loan notes

TCGA 1992, s 138A treatment

15.71   Many earn-outs are structured so that all or part of the seller's earn-out can only be satisfied by shares or loan notes in the purchasing company. In such cases, a corresponding part of the capital gain on the future earn-out right (which would otherwise be taxed under the principles in *Marren v Ingles* – see 15.65) can effectively be deferred under *TCGA 1992, s 138A*. However, a larger number of sellers are now likely to 'opt-out' of the *TCGA 1992, s 138A* deferral route to maximise their ER (see 15.69 below).

Where shares are sold on an earn-out basis (that can only be satisfied by shares and/or loan notes), this right is automatically deemed to be a security. This has two consequences:

- the seller avoids the 'up-front' tax charge based on the value of the right;
- the seller is treated as exchanging their original shares (normally partly) in exchange for a deemed (non-QCB) security (representing the earn-out right).

This effectively provides 'paper-for-paper' treatment for the subsequent earn-out right.

15.72   If the seller has any option to take part of the earn-out in cash, the deferral relief offered by *TCGA 1992, s 138A* will not be available. However, it is possible to have an earn-out agreement, which is structured so that an identifiable part is satisfied in shares/debentures and the remainder is satisfied in cash. In such cases, *TCGA 1992, s 138A* relief would be available on the 'shares/debentures' earn-out element but an initial tax charge would arise on the cash element.

The deferral relief in *TCGA 1992, s 138A* can only operate if the share exchange rules in *TCGA 1992, s 135* would apply but for the intermediate earn-out right, ie assuming the earn-out right is shares or debentures issued by the acquiring company [*TCGA 1992, s 138A(2)*]. Consequently, the detailed requirements of *TCGA 1992, s 135* must be fulfilled (see 15.48).

Deemed non-QCB treatment under *TCGA 1992, s 138A*

15.73   *TCGA 1992, s 138A(3)(a)* provides that the earn-out right is deemed to be a security issued by the acquiring company and is *not* to be treated as a qualifying corporate bond ('QCB'). By treating the earn-out right as a deemed security, this enables the gain attributable to the earn-out right to be deferred until the shares or loan notes received under the earn-out are subsequently sold or redeemed (see 15.75–15.76 below).

An illustrative diagram showing the mechanics of a typical earn-out transaction satisfied in shares and/or in loan notes is shown below.

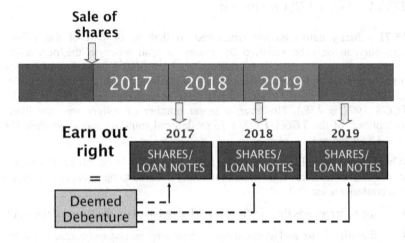

Apportionment of base costs

15.74   The base cost of the seller's deemed security is derived from the base value of their old shares in the target company. Typically, the seller will receive some initial consideration (received on completion), which may be cash or actual shares/loan notes or a combination of both, in addition to the earn-out consideration to be satisfied in the form of shares or loan notes.

The initial cash consideration is subject to an immediate CGT charge as a 'part disposal' in respect of the seller's shares in the target company under *TCGA 1992, s 128(3)*. The base cost of the seller's old shares may need to be apportioned in three ways:

(*a*)   initial cash consideration – to be used in the part disposal calculation under *TCGA 1992, s 128(3), (4)*;

(*b*)   initial shares/loan notes – to form the base cost of those new shares or, in the case of QCBs, to be used to calculate the gain/loss at the date of the exchange under *TCGA 1992, s 116(10)*;

(*c*)   deemed *TCGA 1992, s 138A* security – subsequently to form the base cost for the future shares/loan notes.

Dealing with actual QCBs/shares issued as earn-out consideration

15.75   Where the earn-out consideration is satisfied in the form of a QCB loan note, this will be dealt with under the 'corporate security' conversion/exchange rules in *TCGA 1992, s 132*. This treats the event as a CGT reorganisation and hence brings the special QCB rules in *TCGA 1992, s 116(10)* into play. Broadly, the gain held-over against the QCB would be the amount of the relevant earn-out consideration, less the pro-rata base cost. (The pro-rata base cost is derived from the original cost of the shares that was carried into the deemed security when the seller sold their original shares.)

The postponed gain would generally be taxed at the prevailing 20% CGT rate when the QCB is finally encashed – HMRC permits a minimum redemption period of six months from issue.

In some cases, the acquiring company satisfies the earn-out in the form of a fresh issue of its shares (or a non-QCB). The number of shares issued would generally depend on the earn-out consideration and the (agreed) prevailing market price/value of the acquirer's shares.

In such cases, a combination of the *TCGA 1992, s 132* exchange and *TCGA 1992, s 127* CGT reorganisation rules will apply to treat the new shares/security as having been acquired at the same time (and pro-rata) base cost as the seller's original shares. Any subsequent gain on sale/encashment would generally attract CGT at 20%. However, if all the relevant ER conditions were satisfied at the time, the lower ER CGT rate would be available on a disposal of the 'consideration' (see 15.34)).

The deemed 'earn-out' security and ER

15.76 The ER legislation does not contain any special rules to assist with earn-out transactions. However, ER is capable of applying to securities, since *TCGA 1992, s 169I(2)(c)* states that a 'disposal … consisting of … shares in or *securities* of a company' is a qualifying disposal for ER. As the deemed non-QCB treatment prescribed by *TCGA 1992, s 138A* applies for all the purposes of the *TCGA 1992*, the deemed non-QCBs could potentially attract ER.

In many cases, the deemed non-QCB will be 'exchanged' for actual QCB loan notes within *TCGA 1992, s 132*, with the relevant earn-out gain being captured and held-over under *TCGA 1992, s 116(10)*.

Where the 'earn-out' QCBs are issued after 22 June 2010, this will follow the rules in 15.55 and 15.57. Where (exceptionally) ER is available (see below), the benefit of the 10% ER CGT rate can only be obtained by making a *TCGA 1992, s 169R* election to tax the QCB at the date of its issue (following the determination of the relevant earn-out payment).

In the absence of a *TCGA 1992, s 169R* election, the 'earn-out' gain will be deferred in the normal way until the QCB is redeemed, which would then generally be subject to the 20% main CGT rate (see 15.57).

ER will only be available in those (relatively rare) cases where, throughout the 12 months prior to the 'disposal' event, the seller:

- holds shares in a *trading company* or *holding company of a trading group* which is their 'personal company'; and

- is a director or employee of that company/fellow group company.

In most cases, the seller is unlikely to be able to meet the 'personal company' requirement since this requires them to hold at least 5% of the ordinary share capital (carrying at least 5% of the voting rights) of the 'acquiring company'. This means that, unless the seller also holds at least 5% of the *voting ordinary shares* in the purchasing company post-sale, they would not be able to apply ER to their 'earn-out' loan notes.

Opting out of deemed *TCGA 1992, s 138A* deferral treatment

15.77 By making an election under *TCGA 1992, s 138A(2A)*, the seller effectively opts to tax the earn-out on a *Marren v Ingles* basis (see 15.65 and 15.68). The right would then be taxed at 10% (if and to the extent there is unused ER) and the excess of the actual earn-out consideration over the initial value of the right would usually be taxed at 20% (from 6 April 2016). Many sellers may therefore opt to make the election to achieve a potential 10% tax saving, although this would have to be weighed-up against the opportunity cost of the 'interest' by paying the CGT early.

Broadly, *TCGA 1992, s 138A(2A)* 'opt-out' elections must be made within (just under) 22 months from the end of the tax year in which the original share sale is made.

Worked example of earn-out satisfied in loan notes (under *TCGA 1992, s 138A*)

15.78 The CGT treatment of an earn-out transaction satisfied by QCB loan notes is illustrated in Example 16 below.

Example 16

CGT treatment of earn-out satisfied in (QCB) loan notes

Harry formed Hammers Ltd in September 1988 subscribing for the entire share capital of 40,000 £1 ordinary shares at par. On 7 July 2017, he sold all his Hammers Ltd shares to Rangers plc. The sale contract provided for:

- an initial cash consideration of £5.5 million (net of disposal costs) to be paid on completion; and

- a deferred earn-out consideration based on the 'defined earn-out' profits for the two years ending 30 June 2019, which was to be satisfied in the form of 'short-dated' Rangers plc loan notes (that would be issued when the accounts for the relevant years (and the earn-out profits) were approved). The maximum earn-out consideration for the year ending 30 June 2018 and 30 June 2019 is £2.4 million and £3.6 million respectively.

The earn-out right has been valued at £3 million (in July 2017).

Harry would also continue as managing director of Hammers Ltd during the earn-out period.

Assume the *actual* earn-out consideration is (say) £1.8 million and £2.5 million for the year ended 30 June 2018 and 30 June 2019 respectively. The actual Rangers plc 'earn-out' loan notes are received in October after the relevant year-end and redeemed in the following May. (The CGT on the earn-out consideration would be taxed when the loan notes are encashed.)

CGT computations: 2017/18–2020/21

Harry's earn-out transaction automatically qualifies for *TCGA 1992, s 138A* relief, since the right to the earn-out can only be satisfied in the form of Rangers plc loan notes. His capital gain on the share sale (for 2017/18) would therefore only be computed by reference to the initial cash consideration.

The right to the 'earn-out' loan notes would be treated as a 'deemed non-QCB security' under *TCGA 1992, s 138A* and therefore qualifies for 'paper-for-paper' relief under *TCGA 1992, s 135*. (The deductible base cost is apportioned between the cash and earn-out elements of the consideration.)

The relevant CGT computations are as follows:

2017/18

Sale – July 2017	£
Consideration –	5,500,000
Less Apportioned base cost	
£40,000 × $\dfrac{£5,500,000}{(£5,500,000 + £3,000,000*)}$	(25,882)
Chargeable gain	5,474,118
Less: Annual exemption	(11,300)
Taxable gain	5,462,818
CGT liability	
ER CGT @ 10% – £5,462,818 @ 10%	£546,282
* Value of earn-out right	

TCGA 1992, s 138A treats the earn-out right as a deemed non-QCB. When the earn-out figures are determined and the actual QCBs are issued for these amounts, the relevant gains are computed and held-over under *TCGA 1992, s 110(16)*. These gains crystallise when the QCBs are encashed in the following May.

2019/20

Earn-out – May 2019	£
Earn-out proceeds	1,800,000
Less Apportioned base cost	
$£14,118 * \times \dfrac{£1,800,000}{(£1,800,000 + £2,000,000**)}$	(6,688)
QCB chargeable gain crystallising	1,793,312
* Residual base cost = £40,000 less £25,882 (used in 2017/18) ** Value of residual earn-out right	

2020/21

Earn-out – May 2020	£
Earn-out proceeds	2,500,000
Less: Residual base cost (£14,118 less £6,688 used in 2019/20)	(7,430)
QCB chargeable gain crystallising	2,492,570

Note: QCB gains would be taxed at the prevailing CGT rate in the year of redemption (likely to be around 20%). However, if Harry makes an election under *TCGA 1992, s 138A(2A)*, a much larger part of the overall deal value would be taxed 'up-front' at the beneficial ER CGT rate of 10%.

Potential income tax and NIC charge on earn-outs satisfied by loan notes/shares

15.79 The introduction of the complex 'employment-related' securities regime in *FA 2003* created some uncertainties in relation to the tax treatment of earn-outs satisfied by loan notes and/or shares in the acquirer. HMRC considers that such a right effectively falls within the definition of a 'securities option' within *ITEPA 2003, s 420(8)*. Interestingly, where the purchaser has the choice of satisfying the earn-out in cash *or* shares/loan notes, this will *not* be a 'securities option'. However, the *TCGA 1992, s 138A* deferral will not be available here and so the strict *Marren v Ingles* basis will apply (*TCGA 1992, s 138A(1)(d)*).

Where the 'right' is obtained *by reason of employment or prospective employment* (as defined in *ITEPA 2003, s 47*), the receipt of the 'earn-out' loan notes or shares would be subject to both income tax and National Insurance Contributions (NICs). However, HMRC has confirmed that where an earn-out fully represents consideration for the sale of the target company's shares (as it will normally do), then the income tax/NIC charges under *ITEPA 2003, Pt 7, Ch 5* would *not* apply.

15.80   On the other hand, where all or part of an earn-out relates to value provided to an employee as a reward for services over a performance period, this 'earnings' element would suffer an income tax and NIC charge under *ITEPA 2003, Pt 7, Ch 5*.

The following key factors would generally determine whether an earn-out is further sale consideration rather than earnings:

- the sale agreement shows that the earn-out is part of the valuable consideration given for the target company's shares and the value received from the earn-out reflects the value actually received for those shares;

- it would be helpful to demonstrate the genuine commercial nature of the earn-out as consideration for the target's shares in any advance clearance made under *ITA 2007, s 701* and *TCGA 1992, s 138* (see 15.50 and 15.89);

- where the seller continues to be employed in the business, the earn-out does not reflect 'compensation' for receiving less than the full remuneration for their continuing employment;

- clearly, there should not be any *personal* performance targets incorporated in the earn-out;

- furthermore, the earn-out must not be conditional on future employment beyond a reasonable 'hand-over' period to protect the value of the business being sold.

In appropriate cases, HMRC are normally prepared to give confirmation that an 'earn-out' will not be treated as employment income.

15.81   Clearly, the above points should be considered when drafting the sale documentation. Any evidence that future bonuses were reclassified or 'commuted' into purchase consideration would indicate that the earn-out was, at least partly, earnings rather than consideration for the disposal of securities.

Where the earn-out is partly deferred consideration for the target's shares and partly a reward for services or an inducement to continue working for the business, then a 'just and reasonable' apportionment of the value would be made.

POTENTIAL APPLICATION OF THE TRANSACTIONS IN SECURITIES (TIS) LEGISLATION

15.82 It is important to appreciate that the 'Transactions in Securities' (TiS) anti-avoidance rules in *ITA 2007, s 684* can potentially apply to counter the tax advantage obtained by selling family or owner-managed (ie 'close') companies in such a way as not to suffer income tax. A TiS is widely defined in *ITA 2007, s 684(2)* and includes the sale of shares. (The definition was widened on 6 April 2016 to include repayments of share capital/share premium, and liquidation distributions.) .

Most owner-managed and family company sales potentially fall within the TiS provisions by virtue of *ITA 2007, s 685*. The TiS legislation broadly applies (amongst other things) where a seller receives 'relevant consideration' in connection with the distribution of assets of a close company as defined in *CTA 2010, s 439* [*ITA 2007, s 989*] (see 3.12). In other words, the seller has received consideration on a sale of a company that could have been taken as a dividend.

Given the ability to enjoy capital gains at lower tax rates, HMRC can use *ITA 2007, s 684* as a weapon to counter any deals which appear to be structured to give the shareholder(s) an 'income tax advantage' rather than being (mainly) commercially driven.

Whilst all owner-managed company sales fall within the ambit of TiS, the vast majority should be effectively exempted under the 'fundamental change of ownership' rules (see 15.84 below). The revised TiS provisions now focus on the intended target, which is to catch cases where the seller purports to enjoy sale proceeds as a lowly taxed capital gain yet retains a sizeable interest in the business after the sale, such as on a sale to a 'connected' company.

The operation of the TiS rules relating to liquidations is covered in 16.30. The 'anti-phoenix' TAAR on phoenixism is discussed in 16.27–16.31. Details of the pre-6 April 2016 TiS rules can be found in the 2015/16 or earlier editions of this book.

The current TiS regime

15.83 The TiS legislation will apply where *all* the following conditions are met

- The shareholder must be a party to a TiS (or two or more TiSs);
- Broadly, they must receive relevant (*non-income* taxable) consideration in connection with the distribution, transfer or realisation of assets of a close company;

- The shareholder cannot take advantage of the 'fundamental change of ownership' exclusion (see 15.84);

- The shareholder's main purpose (or one of their main purposes) of the TiS/TiSs is for them to obtain an income tax advantage *and* an income tax advantage must actually be obtained. The 'commercial purpose' motive test was abolished in March 2010. However, despite this, HMRC's view is that the presence of significant commercial drivers for the proposed transaction indicate that that obtaining an income tax advantage was unlikely to be one of the main advantages.

  The 'income tax advantage' condition was widened on 6 April 2016 to include *any* person seeking to obtain an income tax advantage (ie not just the 'selling shareholder (see 15.86).

However, the TiS regime includes a very important 'fundamental change in ownership' exclusion rule. Share sales which meet the relevant conditions, are completely exempt from the TiS legislation.

The 'fundamental change of ownership' exemption

15.84 In the context of a company sale, the application of the TiS legislation is applied to each seller. However, *ITA 2007, s 686* provides a valuable exemption to the seller where the 'fundamental change of ownership' test is met.

Since 6 April 2016, the exemption applies where, as a result of the TiS/TiSs, the seller *does not own, directly or indirectly, more than 25% of the close company's*:

- ordinary share capital;

- share capital carrying the distributions; and

- voting rights.

The test therefore looks at the shareholding interests retained by the selling shareholders in the original company. ,

The sellers' 'associates' are also included when determining whether the seller's/sellers' economic equity interests in the company exceed 25%. The 'associates' definition in *ITA 2007, s 681DL* applies for these purposes, which includes spouses/civil partners, brothers, sisters, parents and children as well as the trustees of any settlement created by a seller.

In the majority of cases, the entire share capital of the company will be sold to another company. In such cases, the 'deeming' rule in *ITA 2007, s 686(5)* applies. Under this rule, where the selling shareholder (a controlling interest in) holds more than 25% of the shares in the company that acquires the original

(Target) company, they will *not* be able to rely on the fundamental change of ownership exemption.

The 'fundamental change of ownership' exemption should easily be satisfied on a 'clean' exit where the seller is completely unconnected with the purchaser, as will invariably be the case for commercial 'trade' sales.

There will, of course, be cases where, for example, the seller retains an equity interest in the business going forward that does not meet the 'fundamental change of ownership' test. However, in such cases, the application of the TiS provisions will be tested against the 'income-tax advantage' test (see 15.83 and 15.86) and HMRC would decide each case on its own merits.

Vulnerable cases

15.85 Despite the introduction of the 'fundamental change of ownership' exemption in March 2010, many advisers still tend to apply for advance *ITA 2007, s 701* clearances (see 15.89) where the exemption applies, since there is often a mistaken belief that this confirms that HMRC is satisfied with the commerciality of the transaction. However, an *s 701* clearance simply confirms that HMRC is satisfied that obtaining an income tax advantage is not a main driver behind the sale transaction.

In practice, cases are likely to be vulnerable to an HMRC challenge under the TiS where there is a 'continuing' shareholder connection, for example, where a company is being sold to a 'connected' or related company or in certain secondary MBO transactions. Where the seller effectively retains a material interest in the business (and fails 'the fundamental change of ownership' test), HMRC will often suspect that the sale is being engineered to extract cash at low CGT rates. Determining whether the relevant transactions are carried out for tax avoidance reasons is a subjective matter, which looks at the overall intention and motives of the directors and shareholders.

In recent years, HMRC has taken particular interest in the potential application of the TiS rules to secondary buy-outs. Typically, in such cases, an existing venture capitalist wishes to realise their investment and a new 'replacement' investor is found. The new investor will form a new company (Newco), funded by a mixture of debt and shares. Newco will then purchase the target company, buying-out its existing venture capitalist and management shareholders. In many deals, the management shareholders receive Newco shares, as well as cash and loan notes. These deal structures are often viewed by HMRC as falling within *CIR v Cleary* 44 TC 399 (see 15.86).

In such cases, the seller should use the clearance procedure to obtain certainty before proceeding with the transaction to confirm that HMRC does not consider 'income tax' avoidance to be one of the main drivers (see 15.86).

HMRC generally have no issue where the sale to the 'related' purchaser is structured as a share for share exchange (without any material cash consideration).

For a review of recent judicial rulings on the TiS provisions, see 15.88.

Example 17

TiS 'fundamental change of ownership' exemption

Mr Sam sells his 100% holding in shares in Three Lions Ltd to FA Ltd on 27 September 2017

The share capital of FA Ltd is owned entirely by unconnected third parties (and does not include Mr Sam or any of his associates). Under the rule in *ITA 2007, s 686(5)*, Mr Sam is not therefore deemed to hold any shares in Three Lions Ltd post-sale. He would therefore qualify for the fundamental change of ownership exemption from the TiS provisions.

Obtaining an income tax advantage

15.86 *ITA 2007, s 687* provides a revised definition of an 'income tax advantage' for these purposes. In broad terms, an 'income tax advantage' is obtained where the income tax that would arise if the relevant 'sale proceeds' were a qualifying distribution *exceeds* the CGT liability on the same amount. Given the large differential between income tax and CGT rates (especially with ER), an income tax advantage would be enjoyed by the vast majority of sellers.

The comparative calculation looks at the available profits that could have been distributed to the relevant shareholder. Thus, any sale proceeds in excess of the maximum dividend that could have been paid to the seller (based on the company's distributable profits), are ignored. However, since 6 April 2016, the amount of profits deemed to be available for distribution also includes the distributable reserves of any 51% subsidiary company. Thus, in the case of a group holding company, the reserves of all its subsidiaries are now (definitively) included in the profits available for distribution companies as well, and counteraction will be possible to the extent that those companies have reserves (*ITA 2007, s 685(7)*).

Where a 'continuing' seller shareholder takes loan notes, this is generally regarded as deferred cash consideration.

Where a *ITA 2007, s 701* clearance has been refused, HMRC has generally applied a 'wait and see' test to look at the distributable reserves of the issuing company when the loan notes are redeemed. However, in some cases, the author has seen HMRC seeking to levy *ITA 2007, s 684* tax on loan notes at the time of issue. In such cases, HMRC may be prepared to give clearance if the loan notes cannot be repaid until the management shareholder 'exits' (or the acquiring company is sold) or if *non-redeemable* preference shares are taken instead.

The 'Cleary' case

15.87 It is helpful to look at the leading *Cleary* case since this demonstrates the main principles used by HMRC in their application of the TiS legislation. The case involved two sisters who needed some cash and one of 'their' companies, Gleeson Development Co Ltd (Development) had substantial cash funds. Consequently, they sold M J Gleesson Ltd (Gleeson) (in which they each held 50% of the shares) to Development. The shares in Gleeson were sold for their true market value of £121,000.

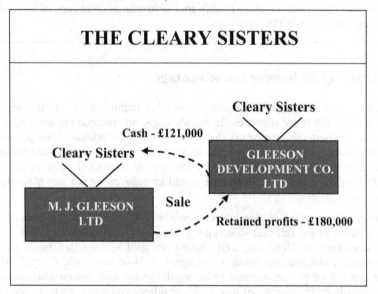

However, the then Inland Revenue issued a counteraction notice (under what is now *ITA 2007, s 684*) charging the entire £121,000 proceeds to income tax. The Revenue considered that the three preconditions for the legislation to apply were satisfied, namely:

- The sale of the shares was a TIS.

- The sale fell within the prescribed condition in what was *ITA 2007, s 689* (under the predecessor TiS legislation). The company was under the control of five persons or less and the sisters had received consideration that would have been available for distribution by way of dividend (had it not been applied in acquiring the shares in Gleeson).

- There was a tax advantage – income tax had been avoided.

The House of Lords agreed with the Revenue – the sale of the shares had come within the strict wording of (what is now) *ITA 2007, s 701*. The Cleary sisters lost their case on the basis that the capital sum represented amounts that could otherwise have been paid out as (taxable) dividends.

It is perhaps worth observing that the *Cleary* case would still be caught by the TiS rules today. In particular, the sisters would not have satisfied the 'fundamental change of ownership' rules since they remained connected with Gleeson through their control of Development.

Recent TiS decisions

15.88   In recent years, the TiS rules have been also held to apply in the following cases:

Lloyd v HMRC [2008] SpC 672

HMRC succeeded in applying (what is now) *ITA 2007, s 684* to 'internal' share sales before the Special Commissioners in the *Lloyd* case. As part of a management succession programme, Mr Lloyd sold his 38.2% holding in a company (Prosaw Ltd) for £275,000 to another company (Prosaw Holdings Ltd – 'Holdings'), which was controlled by him. The sale consideration was funded by a dividend paid to Holdings by Prosaw. There was evidence to suggest that this was being done before the abolition of CGT retirement relief in 6 April 2003. Although the Special Commissioner accepted that there were commercial reasons for the transaction, he also found that one of the main objects of the sale was to enable a tax advantage to be obtained. (The £275,000 could have been paid directly by Prosaw but this would have resulted in an income tax liability of £62,357 – as compared with the £6,392 CGT on the share sale.)

Snell & Snell v HMRC [2008] SpC 699

In *Snell*, the Special Commissioner found for HMRC in a similar (apparently) 'retirement relief' motivated sale. This case demonstrates that any attempt to escape the income tax charge under (what is now) *ITA 2007, s 684* on de minimis grounds, on the basis that the relevant tax is too small to be one of the main objects, may well fail. In this case, the relevant tax was only 7% of the current value of the transaction. This was held to be large enough to be one of the main objects of the deal.

Grogan v HMRC [2011] STC 1

Mr Grogan was a director and majority shareholder in Nigel Grogan Ltd (NGL), which operated three car dealerships. In February 2003, NGL sold two of its dealerships and was in negotiations to sell the other one. Subsequently, NGL contributed £633,000 to a qualifying employee share ownership trust (QUEST) and obtained a corporation tax deduction under *FA 1989, s 67*. In December 2003, the QUEST acquired 15,750 NGL shares from Mr Grogan for £630,000.

HMRC contended that these transactions were caught by the TiS rules on the grounds that the company's contribution to the QUEST and its subsequent acquisition of Mr Grogan's NGL shares was motivated by tax avoidance. It was contended that the QUEST had no real commercial purpose since, as at December 2003, NGL's only employees were Mr Grogan and his secretary. Furthermore, Mr Grogan's advisers' promotional material had emphasised the tax advantages and their fees for setting up the QUEST was calculated by reference to the total tax savings.

Although the tax deduction for the QUEST was based on specific statute, the Upper Tribunal agreed that the 'wider scheme' of the arrangements had to be considered. It was held that they were motivated by tax avoidance and thus the TiS rules applied.

Example 18

Application of *ITA 2007, s 684* on partial 'exit'/MBO

Goran City (Plastics) Ltd has traded for many years as a plastics injection moulder. Mr Sven (the founding shareholder) has 80% of the ordinary share capital, having passed 20% to the company's management team in 1998.

In June 2017, Mr Sven entered into an MBO transaction with his management team under which they acquired a substantial interest in the company, but with Mr Sven retaining a (controlling) 51% stake in the business going forward.

Goran City (Plastics) Ltd has distributable reserves of some £7 million at the time of the deal.

The management team therefore set up a Newco to acquire the entire share capital of Goran City (Plastics) Ltd for a total consideration of £10 million, which is satisfied as follows:

	Sven	Management Team	Total
Shares in Goran City (Plastics) Ltd	80%	20%	100%
Consideration	£'m	£'m	£'m
– Cash	5.92	–	5.92
– Shares in Newco Ltd	2.08	2.00	4.08
	8.00	2.00	10.00

The shares received by Mr Sven and the management team in Newco should be treated as a share for share exchange within *TCGA 1992, s 135* (see 15.48).

HMRC will take the view that the cash of £5.92 million is being taken by Mr Sven to obtain an 'income tax advantage' since the income tax payable on a deemed dividend of that amount would (considerably) exceed the corresponding CGT on the same amount.

It is almost certain that HMRC would refuse an *ITA 2007, s 701* clearance for Mr Sven since it falls within the TiS rules above. He is clearly connected with Goran City (Plastics) Ltd after the sale since he is deemed under *ITA 2007, s 686(5)* to have a controlling interest in it. Thus he would *not* be exempted under the 'fundamental change of ownership' rule. HMRC would probably enquire why he did not take all his sale consideration in the form of shares in Newco!

Ultimately, unless Mr Sven changed the terms of the MBO before proceeding – for example, by agreeing to take £8 million in the form of Newco shares – he is very likely to be subject to a *s 698* counteraction notice, which would tax the £5.92 million as a 'dividend'. (Goran City (Plastics) Ltd has sufficient reserves to be able to pay a dividend of £5.92 million to Sven so no restriction in the counteraction assessment would be given.) The assessment on the £5.92 million would be at the quasi-dividend rate of 38.1%.

Clearance applications under *ITA 2007, s 701*

15.89   *ITA 2007, s 684* is broadly designed to prevent shareholders from effectively receiving the value of the company's reserves (which could otherwise have been paid out as dividends) in an income tax-free form. The sellers' equity interest in the target company (before the sale) and, where appropriate, any 'continuing' interest held through the purchasing company should be set out in the application.

Experience suggests that clearance is likely to be refused where the potential seller is effectively retaining a 'substantial' economic interest in the business post-sale (either personally and/or through 'related parties'). Problems in obtaining *ITA 2007, s 701* clearance have typically been encountered on share sales to 'connected' companies, employee benefit trusts, and pension funds and so on.

The clearance application should clearly explain the commercial reasons for the sale and why the transaction is *not* being carried out for tax reasons. HMRC normally prefer to see a step plan indicating all the relevant material transactions, and any recent transactions that may have a bearing on the proposed deal. (A *single* advance clearance application should be made to cover all relevant 'tax clearance' requirements (for example, covering both *ITA 2007, s 684* and *TCGA 1992, s 138* (see 15.50).) HMRC has a statutory obligation to respond within 30 days. If their reply contains queries or a request for further information, this must be dealt with within 30 days (or, at HMRC's discretion, a longer period) [*ITA 2007, s 701(2), (3)*].

The relevant contact and address details for *non-market* sensitive clearance applications are:

HM Revenue and Customs
CTIS Clearance S0483
Newcastle
NE98 1ZZ

Market sensitive clearances should be sent to the Team Leader at the same address.

It is possible to send clearance applications by email to reconstructions@hmrc. gsi.gov.uk (although information about market/price sensitive matters or well-known individuals should not be sent by email).

At the *CIOT London Branch Corporate Tax Conference* (22 September 2015), Martin Roberts (Head of HMRC's Clearance and Counteraction Team) indicated that common 'errors' made in clearance applications were failure to provide details of all parties involved in the relevant transactions (and their tax reference numbers), not providing the commercial rationale or case for the transaction(s), and failing to indicate the relevant statute for which clearance was being sought. Furthermore, he indicated that HMRC's 'task' is made easier if the appropriate statutory reference is always given for each step in the relevant series of transactions. The clearance application team may be telephoned on 020 7438 7474 (but they do not generally like constant chasing!).

Deciding *not* to apply for clearance exposes the taxpayer to a lengthy 'waiting' period. The *FA 2016* confirms that HMRC has six years following the end of the relevant tax year to open an enquiry under the TiS legislation.

Processing of clearance applications and dealing with 'refusals'

15.90   The clearance team generally aim to divide clearance applications according to their perceived tax risk:

- 'low-risk' cases, which should be turned around within seven days; and

- 'high-risk' cases, which would require a review by at least one other Inspector and may take up to the full 'statutory' 30 days to reply.

Clearances are often refused where the commercial rationale for a transaction has not been clearly stated. In practice, the majority of clearance refusals given by HMRC tend to be given on the basis that the transaction falls within the *Cleary* principles (see 15.87).

It should also be noted that the refusal to grant an *ITA 2007, s 701* clearance does not necessarily mean that HMRC will raise an *ITA 2007, s 684* counter-action assessment. In practice, the sellers have a choice. Either they must go through with the transaction (and the worrying uncertainty of an *ITA 2007, s 684* liability) or they may try to discuss the situation with the clearance Inspector. In the vast majority of cases, the clearance team may reserve their position until the transaction proceeds.

ITA 2007, s 698 counteraction assessments

15.91   *FA 2016* changed the mechanism for the counteraction of income tax advantages under the TiS provisions, bringing it more closely into line with the self-assessment enquiry process. These changes operate from 6 April 2016.

Where HMRC considers the TiS rules apply, it will issue a notice of its intention to make an enquiry into the taxpayer's return relating to the application of the TiS. HMRC must issue the 'TiS' enquiry notice within six years from the end of the tax year in which the relevant TiS (typically a share sale) took place.

Where HMRC's enquiry concludes that the TiS rules should apply to the sale transaction, HMRC will counter the tax advantage by issuing a counteraction notice and adjusting the tax return. If HMRC finds there is *no* TiS adjustment, it will issue a 'no-counteraction' notice. Unhelpfully there is no time limit specified for HMRC to reach its conclusion. However, an application can be made to the Tribunal to force HMRC to issue a 'counteraction' or a 'no-counteraction' notice.

The *s 698* notice counters the 'income tax advantage' obtained by the seller and thus will look at the amount of the sale proceeds that could have been extracted as a distribution from the relevant company (and, where appropriate, subsidiary companies (see 15.86). HMRC will look at the level of the target company's/group's (and the purchaser's) reserves at the relevant point (see Examples 18 above and Example 19 below). For these purposes, the reserves would not always be measured at the date of sale. HMRC could, for example, take the level of reserves when 'consideration' loan notes are redeemed.

The assessed amount is then taxed at the seller's effective dividend tax rate. For 2017/18 (and 2016/17), this will typically be 32.5% and/or 38.1% (for amounts above £150,000).

Example 19

Computation of *ITA 2007, s 698* counteraction assessment

Mr O'Neil was involved in a management buy-out in April 2017. He sold his shareholding in the original 'Target' company for a cash consideration of

£800,000 and shares in the acquiring company (Newco). These consideration shares in Newco gave him an effective 51% equity stake in the business going forward.

HMRC refused the company's *ITA 2007, s 701* clearance in respect of Mr O'Neil, although he did obtain *TCGA 1992, s 135* share exchange relief for the shares issued by Newco.

Mr O'Neill's tax return for 2017/18 was filed on time. HMRC opens an enquiry into the tax return in April 2019 requesting details of the transaction. After receiving the information requested and negotiations with Mr O'Neil's advisers, an *ITA 2007, s 698* counteraction notice (based on a qualifying distribution) of £600,000 was agreed. This produces the following tax liability:

	£
Deemed qualifying distribution	600,000
Income tax @ 38.1%	228,600

Mr O'Neil's April 2017 capital gain would be adjusted to be based on sale proceeds of £200,000 (£800,000 less net amount taxed under *s698* of £600,000).

ENTERPRISE INVESTMENT SCHEME – CGT DEFERRAL RELIEF (IN RELATION TO SHARE SALES)

Basic rules and qualifying conditions

15.92 Sellers planning to purchase shares in other 'qualifying' non-quoted trading companies may be able to defer all or part of their 'share sale' gain under the Enterprise Investment Scheme (EIS) CGT deferral regime. It is worth noting that the shares do not necessarily have to attract EIS income tax relief to be eligible for EIS CGT deferral relief. The *F (No 2) A 2015* restrictions for existing shareholders (see 11.33) do *not* apply for EIS CGT deferral purposes.

The relief is available to both individuals and trustees. Although gains on any type of asset (including gains crystallising on the redemption of a QCB – see 15.55) are capable of being deferred under the EIS deferral rules, the comments here are confined to its use in relation to OMB share sales.

Sellers may also be able to exempt their share sale (and other) gains under the special Seed Investment Enterprise Scheme (SEIS) rules (see 11.68 and 15.103).

Sellers cannot defer their gains by investing in a Venture Capital Trust (VCT).

15.93 The EIS CGT deferral rules in *TCGA 1992, Sch 5B* provide that all or part of the gain (for example on a share sale) can be deferred by investing in one or more qualifying EIS companies within one year before, or up to three years after, the gain arises. This reinvestment period may be extended at HMRC's discretion (see HMRC VCM 23030).

The seller must subscribe *wholly in cash* for eligible shares in a qualifying company and be UK resident at that time. Note that there is no requirement for the investor to make a competent EIS income tax claim. It is now possible to obtain entrepreneurs' relief on the deferred gain by making a claim for deferred entrepreneurs' relief (see 15.100 and 15.100A).

Broadly, eligible shares must be fully paid-up ordinary shares, and not contain any *preferential* right to assets on a winding-up or redemption. Since 6 April 2012, shares may carry certain preferential rights to dividends, but such dividend rights cannot be dependent on a decision of the company etc (*TCGA 1992, Sch 5B, paras 1* and *19; ITA 2007, s 173(2)*).

If the investment is made within the year before, the seller must retain the shares when the gain is made.

Key EIS CGT deferral conditions

15.94   EIS CGT deferral relief is only given if:

- the individual's share subscription is used to finance a 'qualifying business activity' (broadly a qualifying trade, or research and development activity) by the company *or* its qualifying 90% subsidiary as defined for EIS purposes – (see 11.44 and 11.45) [*TCGA 1992, Sch 5B, para 1; TA 2007, ss 179* and *189–199*];

- the entire share issue proceeds are employed by the qualifying trade within the two-year period required by *ITA 2007, s 175*, which starts from when the shares were issued (or, if later, when the trade began). – (see also 11.34);

- the investee company is a qualifying company (see 11.42 and 15.97), which must not be in 'financial difficulty' (see 11.44);

- the share issue is made for bona fide commercial purposes and not for tax avoidance.

The relevant EIS share issue must not be connected with any disqualifying arrangement. Broadly, this prevents relief being given where the main purpose of the share issue was to access relief but where the benefit of the investment is effectively passed to another party or where the trade would otherwise have been carried on by another party) (*TCGA 1992, Sch 5B*).

No EIS CGT deferral relief is available, and if relief has been claimed may be withdrawn, if the shares become subject to a put or call option arrangement (*TCGA 1992, Sch 5B, para 12(1)*). For example, where the investor has a put option giving them the right to sell the relevant shares.

Although the *F (No 2) A 2015* made numerous changes to the EIS income tax conditions (see 11.28, 11.32 and 11.32A) it did not affect EIS CGT deferral relief. Furthermore, it would appear that the restrictions in *ITA 2007, s 175* that apply for EIS income tax relief regarding the company's use of the share subscriptions monies (see 11.34) do *not* apply to EIS CGT deferral relief. This means that it should be possible for the company to use the share subscription monies, for example, to acquire a trade or business.

Relief will be 'clawed-back' where various subsequent chargeable events occur. The most common of these is where the relevant EIS-CGT deferral shares are sold or where the individual 'investor' receives value from the company within three years (see 15.101)

Investors can only claim EIS CGT deferral relief provided the total amount invested in the company under the various tax-favoured 'venture capital' schemes during the previous 12 months, ending on the day of the relevant EIS issue, does not exceed £5 million (£2 million before 6 April 2012)).

The £5 million limit is tested on a 'rolling basis' and any 'EIS' investment breaching the limit is disallowed in full (*TCGA 1992, Sch 5B, para 1(2)(da), (7)*). The tax-favoured venture capital schemes comprise EIS, SEIS and VCT investment in the relevant company (see 11.32 for further details) (*ITA 2007, s 173A*).

Reinvestment in 'own' company

15.95 It is possible for sellers to reinvest in their 'own' company, as there is no 'connection' test for the *CGT deferral relief*. (However, EIS income tax relief and CGT exemption on disposals carry further restrictions, for example, the investor's equity interest cannot exceed 30% – see 11.51.)

The seller can be a passive shareholder of the 'investee company' if they wish. However, many investors will want a directorship to monitor and control their investment risk. In such cases, the level of their remuneration should be kept to a reasonable level (ie consistent with their commercial duties) in the first three years to ensure that this does not jeopardise their relief.

Reinvestment in original company (or group company)

15.96 No CGT deferral relief is given for a share subscription in the company where the gain arose from a disposal of shares in the same company (or in a fellow group company) (*TCGA 1992, Sch 5B, para 10*).

It might, however, be possible (with appropriate planning) for an individual to 'reinvest' in the same trade through a *new company*, which is used to acquire the trade of the original company (see 15.94).

Qualifying company

15.97   The investee company must be a qualifying company within *ITA 2007, Pt 5, Ch 4*.Thus, for example, the share issue will only qualify if its *gross* assets (per its balance sheet under GAAP):

●   do not exceed £15 million *before* the relevant shares are issued; and

●   do not exceed £16 million *after* the relevant shares are issued.

If the investee company has qualifying subsidiaries, the 'gross assets' test is computed on an aggregate 'group' basis (see 11.41(c)).

The monies raised by the EIS share issue must be employed for the purposes of the qualifying trading or research and development activities within two years of the share issue (see 11.34) (see also 15.94).

The investee company can never raise more than £5 million in the 12 months ending with the relevant 'EIS' share issue *(TCGA 1992, Sch 5B, para 2(da))*.

The company must have *less than 250* (equivalent) full time employees when the shares are issued. However, the company's workforce can subsequently exceed 249 full time employees without triggering any clawback of the relief. The *F (No 2) A 2015* increased the employee limit to 499 full-time employees for 'knowledge intensive' companies (see 11.32A and 11.42 (e)).

Qualifying trade

15.98   The 'qualifying company' and 'qualifying trade' rules follow the EIS income tax relief provisions. These are set out in 11.42–11.48.

The company must also meet the relevant qualifying company and qualifying trade conditions when the share investment is made and throughout the relevant three year period (otherwise the relief will be clawed back).

The general aim of the 'qualifying trade' rules is to prevent perceived 'lower risk' activities attracting relief. However, most wholesale and manufacturing trades will qualify for relief.

The qualifying company conditions for EIS CGT deferral relief are largely based on the EIS rules – see further commentary in 11.33–11.48). Reference must always be made to the detailed legislation to determine whether a particular company will qualify.

Advance clearance procedure

15.99   HMRC operates a formal advance clearance procedure to confirm whether a potential investee company satisfies the relevant conditions for being a qualifying company and whether the rules for the share issue are met. The clearance application is now made online at www.gov.uk/government/publications/enterprise-investment-scheme-advance-assurance-application-eisseisaa.

The company completes form EIS 1 after the relevant EIS share issue (giving details of the shares issued etc). EIS1 is also completed online, at www.gov.uk/government/publications/enterprise-investment-scheme-compliance-statement-eis1. HMRC will then authorise the company to issue the EIS 3 (1998) certificates to the investors (which incorporates a claim for the CGT deferral relief).

Operation of EIS CGT deferral relief

15.100   Sellers must make a claim to defer a specified amount of their gain by matching it against the investment expenditure on the relevant qualfying shares. The amount specified for deferral may be all or part of the gain, thus giving complete flexibility in the amount of relief taken. For example, where at least the full amount of the gain is reinvested in relevant qualifying EIS shares, the deferral relief may be restricted so as to leave sufficient gain in charge to absorb the annual exemption.

The maximum amount of EIS CGT deferral relief is the *lower* of:

- the chargeable gain on the shares; or

- the amount subscribed for shares in the qualifying EIS company.

If there has been a previous EIS deferral claim against the shares, the gain is matched against the 'unmatched' part of the relevant EIS share subscription.

Gain realised after 2 December 2014 may be eligible for deferred ER where they are subject to an EIS CGT deferral relief claim (see 15.100A). Please see 2016/17 and earlier editions of this book for treatment of EIS deferral relief on gains made between 23 June 2010 and 2 December 2014.

EIS CGT deferral and deferred entrepreneurs' relief

15.100A Under the deferred ER rules in *TCGA 1992, ss 169U* and *169V*, ER-eligible gains can be deferred against qualifying EIS investments and still attract ER when the deferred gain is realised (for instance on the disposal of the qualifying 'EIS-CGT deferral' shares). Where a gain has been deferred more than once, for example, by serial reinvestment in more than one holding of 'EIS (CGT deferral) share', the 'underlying disposal' associated with the first deferral must to meet the relevant ER conditions.

To qualify for the deferred ER, the original gain must qualify for ER in the normal way. In such cases, the ER claim must be made within (just less than)

22 months following the end of the tax year in which the deferred gain becomes chargeable (strictly, by the first anniversary of the 31 January following the tax year in which the deferred gain becomes taxable (*TCGA 1992, s 169U(5)*).

The deferred ER rules also apply to gains deferred under the social investment enterprise CGT deferral rules (see *11.78*).

Clawback of relief

15.101   The (EIS CGT) deferred gain is effectively 'held-over', but does not reduce the base cost of the 'reinvestment' EIS shares.

However, *TCGA 1992, Sch 5B, paras 3* and *13* provide that the deferred gain will crystallise (and be taxed at the prevailing CGT rate in the year of clawback):

- On the sale or transfer of the relevant EIS shares at any time (except on the transfer to a spouse or civil partner).

- Where the individual (or their spouse who has acquired the EIS shares) becomes non-resident within *three years* (except in certain cases where 'full time' employment is taken abroad). (A period of five years applies to pre-6 April 2000 share issues.)

- Where the relevant EIS shares cease to be 'eligible shares' (for example, as a result of the company ceasing to be a qualifying company) within the relevant period of three years following the share issue (or, if later, the commencement of trade) (see *Taxation*, 18 February 1999, page 486).

- If the individual (or, in some cases, another person) 'receives value' (see 15.102) from the investee company within the period of restriction, ie the one year before and three years following the share issue (or, if later, when the trade started). (For shares issued before 5 April 2001, different relevant periods applied.)

Key 'receipt of value' concepts

15.102   The 'receipt of value' rules *exclude* the receipt of reasonable director's remuneration and dividends representing a normal return on *those* shares.

A more liberal regime also applies on loans repaid to investors. Before *FA 2004*, the EIS CGT deferral relief was often denied on shares issued within the 12 months following the repayment of a loan account. This generally prevented relief being given where an individual's loan account was wholly or partly capitalised for shares (presumably on the basis that it did not represent 'new' money) [*TCGA 1992, Sch 5B, para 13(2)(b)(i), (7)(i)*].

Where a loan account is wholly or partly repaid in these circumstances, this will not prevent a CGT deferral relief claim provided the repayment is not linked to the subsequent share issue. This welcome change recognises the commercial reality of many situations where a company seeks emergency funding (see also 11.41).

Any company share buy-back within the period of restriction after the share subscription will also result in the shares ceasing to be eligible shares, since a share buy-back is treated as 'value received by other persons' under *TCGA 1992, Sch 5B, para 14.*

The detailed 'receipt of value' legislation is contained in *TCGA 1992, Sch 5B, paras 13–14.*

Insignificant receipts of value are ignored for this purpose. See 11.40 for detailed coverage.

Example 20

EIS CGT deferral relief claim on share sale

In May 2017, Mr Gerrard received £650,000 from the sale of his controlling interest in Kop Ltd, upon which he realised a chargeable gain of £550,000.

In December 2017, Mr Gerrard set up his own retail company, LAG Ltd, subscribing for 500,000 £1 ordinary shares (representing the entire share capital).

LAG Ltd is a qualifying company for EIS purposes (and all the other relevant conditions are satisfied). However, Mr Gerrard cannot claim any EIS income tax relief on the acquisition of his LAG Ltd shares since he is clearly 'connected' with the company for EIS purposes. Thus, he would *not* be entitled to the EIS capital gains exemption on a subsequent sale of his shares in LAG Ltd after the relevant three year period (see 11.52).

Following his investment in LAG Ltd, Mr Gerrard makes an EIS CGT deferral claim for £500,000 under *TCGA 1992, Sch 5B* for his Kop Ltd gain (being restricted to his share subscription in LAG Ltd). Mr Gerrard's CGT base cost of his LAG Ltd shares is £500,000 – the deferred gain of £500,000 does not reduce the base cost.

The balance of the Kop Ltd gain – £38,700 (£50,000 balance of chargeable gain less £11,300 annual allowance) would be subject to the 10% ER CGT rate in 2017/18.

If Mr Gerrard sold his *LAG Ltd* shares in, say, June 2019, the crystallised gain of £500,000 on the shares in Kop Ltd would (subject to any annual exemption) be taxed at the 10% ER CGT rate (by making a claim for deferred ER (see 15.100A)). This is in addition to any actual gain that arises on sale of the LAG Ltd shares.

SEED ENTERPRISE INVESTMENT SCHEME CGT EXEMPTION

15.103 The Seed Enterprise Investment Scheme (SEIS) was introduced in *Finance Act 2012* and is aimed at helping small, early-stage companies to raise equity finance by offering a range of tax reliefs to investors who purchase new shares in those companies. SEIS complements the long established EIS scheme.

SEIS applies to qualifying shares issued after 5 April 2012 and offers a range of valuable tax reliefs. The rules have been designed to mirror those of EIS as it is anticipated that companies may want to use EIS after an initial investment under SEIS.

Since 2013/14, an SEIS investor can obtain a 50% SEIS exemption for gains arising on any asset in the year of the SEIS share subscription (limited to a maximum amount of £100,000) (*TCGA 1992, Sch 5BB, para 1*).

It is possible for all or part of an SEIS investment to be treated as made in the previous tax year under *ITA 2007, s 257AB(5)*. It is understood that HMRC enables this rule to be used for the SEIS 'reinvestment' CGT exemption. Thus, if a gain arises in 2017/18, it is possible to treat an SEIS investment in 2016/17 as having been made in 2017/18, thus enabling 50% of the gain to be exempt under the SEIS provisions.

TCGA 1992, Sch 5BB, paras 5 and *5A* prescribe that the amount qualifying for 50% exemption is based on the *lower* of 50% of

- the relevant SEIS subscription (subject to a *maximum of £100,000*);
- the relevant (unmatched) gain; or
- such lower amount as specified in the claim.

Advance clearance procedure

15.103A As for the EIS, HMRC operates a formal SEIS advance clearance procedure to confirm whether a potential investee company satisfies the relevant conditions for being a qualifying company and whether the rules for the share issue are met. HMRC recommends using the online clearance application facility (which is the same as is described above for EIS at 15.99) at www.gov.uk/government/publications/enterprise-investment-scheme-advance-assurance-application-eisseisaa.

The company completes form SEIS 1 after the relevant SEIS share issue (giving details of the shares issued etc). SEIS1 is also completed online, at https://www.gov.uk/government/publications/seed-enterprise-investment-scheme-compliance-statement-seis1. HMRC will then authorise the company to issue the SEIS 3 certificates to the investors (which incorporates a claim for the CGT exemption).

For detailed commentary on this and the other SEIS tax reliefs, see 11.56–11.68.

Example 21

50% exemption on 2017/18 gain matched with SEIS investment

In May 2017, Andy sold his 3% holding in Anfield Ltd, realising a capital gain of £75,000, which would be taxable at 20%.

However, Andy wishes to invest in his friend's new merchandising company, Over Land & Sea Ltd. Thus, in August 2017, he subscribes for £80,000 of its ordinary shares, on which he claims SEIS relief.

Andy can also claim to exempt £37,500 of his 2017/18 gain, against the SEIS investment, being the lower of

- £37,500 (50% × gain of £75,000)

- £40,000 (50% × investment of £80,000)

The remaining gain of £37,500 (subject to the deduction of any available CGT exemption) is taxed at 20%.

CGT EXEMPTION FOR SALE OF A CONTROLLING SHAREHOLDING TO EMPLOYEE OWNERSHIP TRUST (EOT)

15.103B The *FA 2014* introduced a special CGT exemption for those owner managers who wished to sell a 51% holding in 'their' company to an employee ownership trust (EOT) (*TCGA 1992, ss 236H–263T*).

The CGT exemption is dependent on various fairly restrictive conditions being satisfied. The main ones are:

- The EOT must acquire a *controlling* ('51% plus) interest in the company's ordinary shares and broadly retain it on an on-going basis;

- The company must satisfy the trading requirement (this follows the definition in 15.40 to 15.43);

- The EOT must be for the benefit of all eligible employees (broadly excluding shareholders who have held 5% or more of the company's equity shares).

- The eligible employees must generally benefit from the trust on the same terms (although benefits can be allocated by reference to salary, hours worked, length of service).

An EOT may not be practicable if there are relatively few employees. This is because the number of directors of the company (and/or persons connected with them) must not exceed 40% of the total number of employees and directors.

It is recommended that the sellers seek an advance *ITA 2007, s 701* clearance under the Transaction in Securities legislation to confirm HMRC will accept that the sale to the EOT should be taxed as a capital gain (rather than being subject to an income tax charge at 'distribution rates) (see 15.82–15.91, especially 15.88).

If the owner manager wishes to sell their controlling interest at full market value, the EOT would need to consider how the purchase consideration should be funded. The company would be exposed to a *CTA 2010, s 455* at 32.5% (25% before 1 April 2016) on any loans provided to the EOT (see 2.56A). Further, the trust may find it difficult to secure bank funding (without recourse to the company itself).

However, it may be possible to sell the shares to the EOT on a deferred consideration basis (using *TCGA 1992, s 48*) (see 15.5). The deferred consideration payments could be funded from contributions made by the company (although they would not be tax-deductible for corporation tax purposes since they would not be taxed as 'benefits' in the employees hands (*CTA 2010, s 1290*)).

A secondary benefit of using an EOT is the potential ability to provide the employees with income tax-free bonuses of £3,600 per year.

There is no need to use a designated EOT but it does contain a number of attractive tax advantages. A 'non-qualifying' employee trust could also be used to acquire a controlling (or non-controlling) stake in the company, but it would not carry the tax benefits of an EOT. However, the owner manager may be content to simply incur the 10% entrepreneurs' relief CGT rate! (see 15.34).

PRE-SALE TAX PLANNING STRATEGIES

Application of the *Furniss v Dawson* doctrine & GAAR

15.104 In addition to the various tax structuring principles already outlined in this chapter in connection with company share sales, there are a number of other pre-sale strategies that may provide a useful reduction in the seller's tax liability.

Certain tax planning techniques may be vulnerable to challenge by HMRC under the '*Furniss v Dawson*' doctrine (see 1.10–1.17). The key 'tax avoidance' cases have established that the '*Furniss v Dawson*' principle can only apply where an intermediate tax planning step has been inserted at a time when the ultimate transaction has reached 'the point of no return'. As a general rule, this would be when there is no practical likelihood that the subsequent (sale) transaction would not happen.

Negotiations for the sale of shares in an unquoted company can often be prolonged and it is not unknown for a transaction to be aborted shortly before a sale was to take place. The implementation of a pre-sale tax mitigation strategy should therefore normally be effective, even if it takes place (say) only two to three weeks before the sale agreement is executed.

Furthermore, HMRC can also use the GAAR to cancel any tax saved by abusive tax schemes (see 1.19).

Pre-sale dividends and 'surplus cash'

15.105 Individual/trustee sellers now generally pay CGT at rates varying between 10% and 20%. As a general rule, it will not, therefore, be efficient to extract a pre-sale dividend for tax mitigation purposes. (For similar reasons, pre-sale stock (or scrip) dividend alternatives are no longer recommended.)

Many 'deals' require the shareholders of the 'target' company to compute a 'normalised' working capital amount at completion. Any cash held above these requirements would be treated as 'surplus' as not being required for use in the business. A purchaser will therefore require the seller shareholder(s) to extract any 'surplus' cash balances held by the company before completion., In many cases, the most practicable method of doing this would be for the seller to declare an appropriate cash dividend (although it would be subject to the relevant dividend tax rate).

Alternatively, it may be possible for the purchaser to pay a 'grossed-up' amount for the shares to reflect the cash. A corporate purchaser should be able to access the cash after the acquisition without any additional tax cost (apart from the increase in stamp duty on the purchase of the shares). This would usually be preferable for the seller as they would maximise their tax-efficient capital gains. However, not all purchasers will be amenable to 'grossing-up' the sale consideration and may insist on any surplus cash being extracted as a pre-sale dividend.

HMRC are aware that such 'grossing-up' arrangements are occurring in practice, as highlighted in its consultation document of 9 December 2015. In this document, HMRC expresses some concern that profits are being 'money-boxed' rather than being distributed to shareholders. While no change in the law has been proposed yet, 'money-boxing' of cash is on HMRC's radar!

Ex-gratia/termination payments

15.106 Many shareholder-directors are strongly tempted by the prospect of a £30,000 tax-free ex-gratia/termination payment prior to the sale. By arranging for a corresponding deduction in the share price, this would save them CGT at their effective rate. However, where such payments coincide with the sale of shares in a family or owner-managed company, the Inspector's almost automatic reaction is to disallow the payment. This is normally on the basis that the payment is either a distribution or part of the consideration for the sale of the shares, which would deny the benefit of the £30,000 tax-free exemption in the individual's hands (*James Snook & Co Ltd v Blasdale* (1952) 33 TC 244) (see also 5.27).

In special circumstances, it might be possible to argue that the termination payment was made for valid commercial reasons unconnected with the sale. However, it will be necessary to demonstrate that all shareholders received full market value for the shares and that the termination payment was an independent transaction.

15.107 It is vital that the making of any ex-gratia payment should not be in the agreement for the sale of the shares and a Board resolution should be passed indicating that the payment is considered to be in the interests of the company.

Further dangers arise when the recipient of a termination payment is at or approaching retirement age. HMRC's view is that such payments normally represent an 'unapproved pension benefit' which should be taxed as employment income (see 5.36).

Pension contributions

15.108 The scope for making 'one-off' company pension contributions has now been considerably restricted and incurring a penal excess annual allowance (AA) tax charge can become a trap for the unwary! Company contributions are subject to the *FA 2011* £40,000 AA 'input' rules which is further restricted for high-earners from 6 April 2016 (see 10.23A).

Pension contributions made as part of a 'termination package' are not counted as a termination payment provided the amount is paid to an approved pension scheme [*ITEPA 2003, s 408*].

Inter-spousal transfers and ER

15.109 Proprietors' spouses often hold shares in owner-managed companies to benefit from the spreading of dividends for income tax purposes.

Although the ER lifetime gains limit is now at a very generous £10 million, some owner-managers (particularly those anticipating extremely large gains) may still wish to transfer a suitable shareholding to their spouse to enable them to benefit from ER in their own right.

Care must be taken to ensure that the recipient spouse is able to meet the necessary ER conditions in their own right. Thus, they will need to be a (genuine) director/employee (although not necessarily working full-time), and hold at least 5% of the ordinary shares/voting rights (see 15.34). The recipient spouse would need to meet these conditions for a minimum of one year before the relevant share sale. The spouse's ER holding period runs from when they actually acquired the shares from the transferor spouse.

Maximising CGT base value at March 1982

15.110 Where the seller held the shares at March 1982, they will be able to deduct the March 1982 value of the shares, together with indexation relief from the sale proceeds. While this may provide a significant relief for a controlling shareholder of a company, which was profitable in 1982, a minority shareholder will typically have a low March 1982 base value (as the shares will be discounted for lack of control, etc (see 14.38, 14.39 and 14.68)).

15.111 This can be a problem in 'husband and wife' owned companies, if neither have control. However, by concession, it is possible to boost the March 1982 value by arranging for one spouse to transfer sufficient shares to give the other control before the onward sale of the company (see 14.70).

BECOMING NON-UK RESIDENT

Overview

15.112 Perhaps the most radical step contemplated by many sellers (and achieved by few!) is to establish non-resident status in order to avoid paying UK capital gains tax on the sale of their company. While this has always been possible with careful planning (and a certain willingness to give up the often overlooked pleasantries of living in the UK!), the *Finance Act 1998* added further difficulties by imposing a 'five year' absence rule.

Prospective sellers will often pay ER CGT at 10% with owners of investment companies attracting a 20% tax rate on exit. At these relatively reasonable rates, many will seriously question whether they are willing to endure the inevitable personal and economic upheaval of emigrating for five years to avoid this tax, although, of course, their decision may ultimately depend on the *absolute* amount of tax potentially payable.

Before the *FA 2013* introduced the Statutory Residence Test (SRT) on 6 April 2013, an individual's residence status was largely determined by HMRC practice and some pretty out-dated case law. Many would argue that the SRT provides greater certainty about an individual's residence position, but it is very prescriptive and therefore complex.

This section focuses on the 'temporary non resident rules', which levy UK CGT on gains made whilst non-resident (see 15.113–15.115) and the post-5 April 2013 SRT (see 15.116–15.122).

The *FA 2013* also introduced a statutory 'split-year' treatment, which typically applies where an individual leaves the UK during the tax year to take up full time employment abroad or where they cease to have a UK home (see 15.122C and 15.122D for detailed coverage).

For detailed coverage of the pre-6 April 2013 residence rules, please refer to the 2012/13 and earlier editions of this book.

Certain types of *income* received from an owner-managed company (close company) during an intervening period of temporary non-residence are also subject to an UK income tax charge in the year of return (see 15.121).

Temporary non-resident rule

15.113 Broadly speaking, most long-term UK resident sellers who leave the UK, must be prepared to go abroad (as a non-resident) for at least five complete years (ie 60 months) from the day of departure. This is due to the temporary non-resident rules in *TCGA 1992, s 10A* that were amended in the *FA 2013* for departures made after 5 April 2013.

A seller is subject to UK CGT tax on gains made whilst they are 'temporarily non-resident' within the meaning of *FA 2013, Sch 45, Part 4*. For these purposes, individuals are considered to be temporarily non-resident where:

- They had sole UK residence for a residence period;

- Immediately following that period ('period A') one or more residence periods occur for which the individual does not have sole UK residence;

- They were UK tax resident for at least four out of the seven tax years immediately preceding the year of departure

- Their temporary period of *non-residence* is five years or less.

For these purposes, the individual's resident status would be tested under the SRT set out in *FA 2013, Sch 45* (see 15.116–15.122).

Each tax year is treated as a 'residence period'. However, the legislation provides for 'split year' treatment in certain circumstances (see 15.122C and 15.122D). Where the tax year is split, there are two residence periods: one period for the part of the year in which the individual is UK resident and the other being the 'non-UK resident' period.

An individual is treated as having *'sole UK residence'* for an entire tax year if they are UK tax resident for that year *without being treaty non-resident for any part of that year*. However, for split tax years, the individual would only be solely UK resident for the 'UK resident' part of the split year.

The five-year rule does *not* apply to assets acquired by the taxpayer after the date of departure or in any intervening year when the taxpayer was non-resident [*TCGA 1992, s 10A(3)(a)*].

Practical implications

15.113A Individuals should normally be able to avoid UK CGT on a sale of 'their' company *whilst they are non-resident* provided they remain non-resident for a period of five years (60 months), from the day they leave (assuming that the 'split year' treatment is available and subject to being treaty non-resident). On the other hand, if they are only treated as ceasing to be UK resident from the end of the relevant tax year, the five years will begin on the 6 April following the date of their departure (see 15.113).

In contrast to the pre-*FA 2013* regime, capital gains made after the date of departure in the tax year may initially be exempt from CGT where the split year treatment is available. However, great care must be taken to prevent a binding sale contract being created before the date of departure. Thus, any communications between the parties and heads of agreement, etc. must clearly be stated as being 'subject to contract'.

Sellers must also ensure that they can navigate through the 'five year' non-residence rule to avoid CGT charges on gains made during a 'temporary non-residence period' (see 15.113), whilst also avoiding potentially significant overseas tax liabilities (see 15.118).

Since 6 April 2013, the seller's residence status throughout this period will be tested against the SRT (see 15.116–15.122). Individuals will always be regarded as tax resident in the UK if they spend more than 183 days here, irrespective of any other consideration (see 15.119).

Some sellers maybe unsure about whether they are able to remain non-resident for the full five-year period. If there is a possibility (no matter how remote) of them returning to the UK within the five year period, it is recommended that they make a protective ER election (where appropriate) by the first anniversary of the 31 January following the tax year of disposal (see 15.38).

Under the temporary non-resident rules, the relevant gain(s) is/are calculated at the original disposal date but taxed when the seller returns to the UK (see 15.114). In many cases, this would mean that the seller would be 'out of time' to make an ER claim, thus incurring a 20% CGT charge on an ER-eligible shareholding. Consequently, HMRC accepts that it is possible to make a protective ER claim, which would be valid if it transpires that the gain would be taxed under the *TCGA 1992, s 10A* regime.

In practice, sellers should be able to succeed in shedding their UK residence status when they sell their company with a view to retiring abroad for the long term or where permanent emigration is contemplated!

CGT entry charge

15.114   Where an owner manager becomes UK resident during the 'five year' period, the capital gain on their previous share sale (realised whilst non-resident) will be taxed in the tax year of return to the UK. Similarly, relief will be given for any capital loss realised on the shares. These rules only apply to gains and losses arising on any chargeable assets held before departure, which are realised during a non-resident period of less than five years.

In computing the UK CGT on the entry charge, it may be possible to benefit from the beneficial 10% ER CGT rate, provided a competent (protective) election had been filed with HMRC (see 15.113A). Credit would also be given for any overseas tax incurred on the gain in the usual way. The legislation was amended in *F (No 2) A 2005* to ensure that the CGT entry charge cannot be prevented by the terms of any double tax treaty provision.

Overseas tax planning

15.115   As part of the overall tax planning exercise, the seller should take appropriate professional advice about the tax position overseas. There is no point in emigrating to avoid UK CGT if a substantial tax liability arises in the destination country. In some cases, it might be necessary to take a long holiday elsewhere to avoid being resident in the destination country for the year, especially if a material tax liability is likely to arise there. The most desirable destinations are tax-havens or those that do not tax capital gains.

Statutory residence test (SRT)

Background

15.116   The Government wanted to provide more clarity for taxpayers as the *Gaines-Cooper* case highlighted many grey areas in the interpretation of the UK's residence rules (which were largely based on HMRC practice and many 'old' tax cases). Accordingly, in June 2011, the Government announced its proposals for introducing a statutory residence test (SRT), which went through a detailed consultation process before the final rules were enacted in *FA 2013, Sch 45*.

The SRT legislation continues to treat those who retain close connections with the UK as UK resident. However, for those with more complicated affairs, the SRT takes into account both the amount of time they spend in the UK and certain key 'ties' they have with the UK ('sufficient ties' – see 15.123 below).

Once someone has become resident and built up various UK ties, they would have to scale these back significantly and/or spend far less time here before they can 'sever' their UK residence status.

Since 6 April 2013, individual sellers will need to self-assess their UK residence status in accordance with the SRT. However, since the SRT takes into account an individual's residence status over the previous three years, it may be necessary to seek a determination of their tax residence status under the pre-6 April 2013 regime (see 2012/13 and earlier editions of this book). Alternatively, it is possible to make an election for the pre-6 April 2013 tax years' residence position to be determined under the SRT legislation.

Basic SRT rule

15.117 Under the basic SRT, an individual is treated as UK resident for the relevant tax year if they meet:

(*a*)   the *automatic UK residence test* for that year (see 15.118–15.120); or

(*b*)   the *sufficient UK ties* test is met for that year (see 15.121 and 15.122A)

If *neither* of these tests are met, the individual will *not* be UK tax resident for the relevant year (*FA 2013, Sch 45, paras 3, 4*). As will be seen below, the relevant tests are applied in a hierarchical order.

Where an individual becomes UK resident under any of the above tests for a particular tax year, they will be regarded as UK tax resident for the entire tax year, unless the 'split year' treatment applies (see 15.122C and 15.122D).

It is possible for an individual to be 'dual resident' – ie resident in the UK under the SRT and resident in another country under its local law. In such cases, the relevant double tax treaty will generally decide where that individual is resident (see 15.122B).

Automatic overseas (*non-residence*) test

15.118 The legislation first applies an automatic overseas test, which takes priority over all the other tests (*FA 2013, Sch 45, para 5*). Thus, individuals will *not* be UK tax resident for the relevant tax year where they qualify under one of the automatic overseas rests in *FA 2013, Sch 45, paras 11–14*. These are summarised as follows (ignoring cases where the taxpayer dies in the tax year):

- *spending very little time in the UK* – ie they were UK resident in at least one of the previous three tax years and they spend fewer than *16 days* in the UK during the relevant year (this rule does not apply in the year of death); or

- *visitors* – ie they were not UK resident in the three previous tax years and they spent less than *46 days* in the UK that year; or

- *working full time overseas* – this test is met provided the individual works overseas on a full time basis (average of 35 hours or more per week) *and* in the relevant tax year they spend less than:

  - 31 days working more than three hours per day in the UK; and

  - 91 days in total in the UK.

For these purposes, 'work' include employment, self-employment and work-related travel. A day of presence in the UK is one where an individual is resident in the UK at midnight, unless they are in transit or there are exceptional circumstances beyond the individual's control (eg sudden or life-threating illness or local emergencies).

Automatic UK residence test

15.119 If the above automatic overseas residence test is failed, then an individual will be treated as *automatically resident* in the UK for a tax year (under *FA 2013, Sch 45, paras 6–10*) if:

- They spend more than 183 days in the UK in the tax year: or

- Their permanent home (or, if more than one, all their homes) is/are in the UK and they were present in that home for at least 30 days in the tax year. (The 'permanent home' status is generally measured over a 91-day period starting or ending in the relevant in the relevant tax year.) However, this will only be the case where they spent less than 30 days in an overseas home or there was a period of 91 consecutive days where they has no overseas home); or

- They work full time in the UK – ie they worked full time in the UK for at least 75% of the total number of days over a 365-day period with no significant breaks from work and all or part of that period falls within the relevant tax year. Furthermore, the individual must have worked for *more than three hours per day* for *more than 75% of the relevant tax year*; or

- They died in the tax year with their normal home being in the UK (provided they have been UK resident under one of the above automatic residence tests for the last three years).

15.120 The 'permanent UK home' test is aimed at 'wanderers' or those individuals who may not acquire a base abroad.

The concept of a home can be a difficult one. It is widely defined to include all or part of a building, a vehicle, a vessel or a structure of any kind. A place is counted as someone's home where, based on all the facts, there is a sufficient permanence or stability about their living arrangements. However, periodic use of a holiday home or temporary retreat would not count as a home (*FA 2013, Sch 45, para 25*).

The 'sufficient ties' test

15.121 Where the automatic UK residence test does *not* apply, the 'sufficient ties' test comes into play.

Under the 'sufficient ties' test, an individual's residence status depends on the relationship between the number of days spent in the UK and the number of 'UK ties'. Thus, the fewer 'UK' ties someone has, the greater the number of 'UK days' they are allowed to have before becoming UK resident.

The legislation specifies the relevant UK ties for these purposes

- *Family tie* – Where the relevant individual has a UK resident spouse or cohabitee (ie living together as husband and wife'), civil partner, or minor child who resides in the UK. Minor children are excluded if they are at a boarding school provided they spend less than 20 days in the UK outside term time.

- *Accommodation tie* – Individual has a place to live in the UK that is available to them during the tax year for a continuous period of 91 days and they spend at least one night there (or 16 nights if staying with relatives) in the tax year.

- *Work tie* – Where an individual works in the UK for at least 40 days (for more than three hours a day) in the tax year.

- *90-day tie* – Individual spends more than 90 days in the UK in either or both immediately preceding tax years.

- *Country tie* – Individual spends the greatest number of nights in the UK in the tax year.

Those arriving in the UK will not establish a UK 'country tie' if they have *not* been UK resident in any of the three previous tax years.

15.122 There are effectively two 'sufficient ties' tables that determine the number of days in the UK that are required to make an individual UK resident for the relevant tax year. As shown below, there is one for 'leavers' (ie those who have been UK resident in any of the last three tax years befor the relevant tax year being tested) and one for 'arrivers' (ie those who were not UK resident in any of the last three tax years before the relevant tax year):

Number of days spent in the UK that would trigger UK residence	*Number of UK ties to establish UK residence*	
	UK resident in any of the last three years (Leavers)	*Not resident in none of the last three years (Arrivers)*
16 to 45 days	All 4 ties	Automatically non-resident
46 to 90 days	3 ties	All 4 ties (excluding 'country tie')

Number of days spent in the UK that would trigger UK residence	Number of UK ties to establish UK residence	
	UK resident in any of the last three years (Leavers)	Not resident in none of the last three years (Arrivers)
91 to 120 days	2 ties	3 ties
121 to 182 days	1 tie	2 ties
More than 183 days	Always UK resident	

15.122A One of the main effects of the sufficient ties test is to make it much harder to shed UK residence than it is to become UK resident. Thus, for example, someone who comes to the UK to take up employment here might have only two ties (typically, a place to live (accommodation tie) and working here for more than 40 days (work tie)). Thus, provided they spend less than 120 days in the UK, they would avoid being resident here.

However, if they spent (say) 100 days working in the UK in the year of arrival, they are likely to have a third UK tie in the following tax year (since they will have been in the UK for more than 90 days in the previous tax year (90-day tie). Thus, to avoid UK residence in the second year, they must avoid being in the UK for more than 90 days.

Thus, as a broad rule of thumb, 'arrivers' to the UK should be prepared to limit their UK days to less than 90 in each tax year (although they could spend up to 120 days in the first year).

Example 22

Leaving the UK before selling 100% shareholding in trading company

At the end of January 2017, Alex left the UK to live in Switzerland for the foreseeable future, mainly due to health reasons. He managed to sell his sole home in March 2017.

Alex is divorced and has lived in the UK all his life. He has built up a successful trading company, Going For A Song Ltd, in which he owns 100% of the issued share capital.

Alex sells his 100% stake in Going For A Song Ltd to Cameroon plc on 20 April 2017 for £15 million, coming back to the UK on that date to sign the sale and purchase agreement.

Provided Alex spends no more than 16 days in the UK in the year ended 5 April 2018, he should be automatically non-UK resident in 2017/18 without any need to consider the 'sufficient ties' test (see 15.118).

Given that he is unlikely to spend any material amount of time in the UK in 2017/18, this is probably the safest way to ensure that he avoids any UK CGT on the sale of his company.

However, should he become UK resident in the next five years – say from 6 April 2017 – he will incur a CGT liability under the temporary non-resident rules (see 15.113). Alex may therefore wish to make a protective ER claim to ensure that he would have the benefit of the 10% ER CGT rate if he returns within the next five years.

Example 23

Leaving the UK

Simone is an Italian national. He is single and has worked full time in London for his Italian employer (Zaza Holdings Limitata) for the past five years.

On 1 June 2017, he 'left' the UK to work in the company's headquarters in Milan, but continued to spend about 20% of his time working in London. He resumed living in his 'Milan' home but retained his leasehold flat in Canary Wharf (London) to use for UK visits

Simone's plan is to spend about six days a month in the UK in 'one-week' blocks, arriving in the UK on Sunday night and returning to Milan on Friday night. Therefore, after allowing for holidays etc, he expects to spend about 58 'midnights' in the UK.

Simone would not automatically be non-resident for 2017/18 since he is not working overseas full time and his UK visits exceed 15 days. Furthermore, he would be in the UK for less than 183 days and would not be automatically UK resident, since he lives in his overseas home and no longer works full time in the UK.

Based on these facts, Simone is likely to remain UK resident in 2017/18 since he will be in the UK for more than 45 days in this year. This is because he was previously UK resident and he is likely to have three UK ties in 2017/18, being:

		Reason
•	Accommodation tie	Canary Wharf flat available for more than 91 days and occupied for at least one day
•	Work tie	Works more than 40 days in the UK
•	90 day tie	Spent more than 90 days in the UK in 2016/17

Dual residence and tax treaties

15.122B It is possible for an individual to be resident in more than one country due to the different rules that may apply to determine tax residence in each country. For example, someone may be UK resident but may also be tax resident in another country under its tax legislation.

Where there is dual residence, this is generally resolved by the tax treaty between the UK and the other country. Most treaties will follow the OECD model. This provides that an individual will be resident where they have their permanent home. However, if this is inconclusive, the treaty will determine the individual's residence by reference to their 'centre of vital interests' – taking in sequential order, their habitual abode and then their nationality. In rare cases, where this test cannot determine the individual's tax residence, the tax authorities of each country are required to settle this by mutual agreement.

Split year residence treatment

15.122C If the SRT makes an individual UK resident for a tax year, the normal rule treats them as UK resident for the entire tax year. This applies regardless of whether they become UK resident or ceased to be UK resident at some point during the tax year.

However, in eight specified circumstances, the 'split-year' treatment enables an individual to be treated as UK resident for part of the tax year and *non-resident* for the remaining part (*FA 2013, Sch 45, Part 3*). Since non-residents are not subject to UK tax on their foreign income and gains, the split year treatment can avoid double taxation. UK CGT would normally apply to the gains arising on the sale of shares in the UK resident part of the split year (subject to the temporary non-resident rules – see 15.113).

Three of the split year 'cases' (Cases 1 to 3), which are summarised in 15.122D below, relate to individuals who ceased to be UK resident during the year (leavers). The remaining five cases (Cases 4 to 8) relate to those who become UK resident during the year – these are defined in *FA 2013, Sch 45, para 48–51*.

15.122D

Split year cases for leavers – summary of Cases 1 to 3

In Cases 1 to 3, the relevant individual must be

– UK resident for the previous tax year;

– UK resident for the relevant tax year; and

– Non-UK tax resident for the following tax year

The date of the split may be the date of departure from the UK but this is not always the case.

The additional requirements for each case are summarised below.

Case 1	*Starting full time work overseas*

An Individual must have left UK to work full time overseas for more than 35 hours per week on average. From the date of departure, only a limited 'pro-rata' amount of days can be spent in the UK (whether working or on leave).

Case 2	*Partner of someone starting full time work overseas*

The partner of an individual who has left the UK to work full time overseas (under Case 1), who moves overseas to continue living with them.

However, the partner must not have a home in the UK during the overseas part of the year. Alternatively, the partner may have homes both in the UK and overseas, but must spend more time in the overseas home.

The partner must *not* spend more than the permitted limit of days in the UK (broadly based on a pro-rata of 90 days, depending on their UK departure date).

Case 3	*Ceasing to have a UK home*

An individual must have a UK home at the start of the relevant tax year and cease to have any UK home at some time in that tax year.

After the individual ceases to have a UK home, they must spend less than 16 days in the remainder of the year.

Furthermore, within the *following six month period*, they must

– become tax resident in another country; or

– be present at the end of each day in another country; or

– have their only home in another country.

Deferring UK tax charge prior to intended emigration

15.123 It is notoriously difficult to defer the tax charge where the acquiring company issues loan stock (or shares) in exchange for the seller's shares, where they intend to emigrate at some future date. Subsequently, when the seller becomes non-resident, the deferred gain would crystallise on the redemption of the loan note and would be realised without a UK tax charge, subject to the temporary non-resident rules in 15.113–15.114).

TCGA 1992, s 138 clearance applications are invariably refused where the issue of loan notes is purely designed to avoid tax as opposed to being dictated by the purchaser's commercial requirements – see the recent case of *Snell v HMRC* [2006] EWHC 3350 (Ch) which confirms HMRC's view on this point (see 15.51). It should be noted that if the seller has indicated an intention to emigrate after the sale, this must be fully disclosed in the *TCGA 1992, s 138* clearance application otherwise any tax clearance could not be relied on (see 15.50).

Close company income charged under temporary non-resident regime

15.124   Before the *FA 2013*, owner managers were able to side step the temporary non-resident rules by taking substantial income from their companies instead of generating capital gains. For example, provided the owner-manager's company had substantial reserves, they could emigrate for a (much) shorter period (covering at least one complete tax year) with a view to extracting a substantial dividend from the company whilst non-resident.

As a non-UK resident, UK dividend income was taxed (often with the benefit of the previous 10% tax credit) but *FA 1995, s 128* prevented any additional dividend tax liability.

15.125   However, the *FA 2013* blocked this type of 'non-resident' planning for income. Since 6 April 2013, the temporary non-residence rules (see 15.113 to 15.114) apply to specific type of 'close company' income received by its 5% shareholders whilst they are (temporarily non-resident).

The temporary non-resident regime imposes a full UK income tax charge on dividend income, waivers of loans to participators (see 2.65), and stock dividends. Only dividends paid from *pre-departure* profits are caught.

Non-domiciled sellers

15.126   Non-domiciled (and UK resident) individuals must make a special claim (under *ITTOIA 2005, s 809B*) if they wish to use the 'remittance basis' for taxing their foreign income and capital gains (unless their unremitted income/gains are less than £2,000). Where a 'remittance-basis' election is made, the individual cannot benefit from the normal personal allowances and the CGT annual exemption.

However, since 6 April 2017, non-domiciled individuals are deemed to be UK domiciled *for all UK tax purposes* if they have been UK resident in the UK for 15 out of the 20 tax years immediately preceding the relevant tax year. This means that such individuals are taxed on an arising basis on all their (worldwide) income and capital gains (ie like the vast majority of UK taxpayers). Importantly, they can no longer use the remittance basis under any circumstances!

There are certain transitional protections for those who become deemed UK domiciled under this rule on 6 April 2017. For example, they can rebase their foreign assets at 6 April 2017 so that only the post-5 April gain would be taxed. Such transitional reliefs are *not* available where someone becomes UK domiciled *after 6 April 2017!*

This deemed domicile status can only be lost provided the individual 'clocks-up' six years of non-resident status (although a 'shorter' period may apply for IHT purposes) (*ITA 2007, s 835BA* and *IHTA 2004, s 267*).

'Formerly domiciled resident' individuals are also subject to special 'UK deemed domicile' rules. This catches someone who has a UK domicile of origin, was born in the UK, and then acquires a foreign domicile of choice. If they become UK resident again, they are deemed to be UK domiciled immediately.

Subject to the above 'deemed domiciled' rules, 'long term' UK resident non-doms must pay a remittance basis charge (RBC) to benefit from the remittance basis rules. The amount of the RBC depends on the length of time they have been in the UK. Short-term residents – ie those that have been UK resident for less than seven out of the last nine years, do not have to pay any RBC. All those eligible for, and claiming, the remittance basis are often referred to as 'remittance basis users'.

The RBC charges *for 2017/18* are summarised as follows:

Previous UK tax residence status: *UK RESIDENT FOR*	*RBC*
Less than seven out of the last nine tax years	Exempt
More than seven out of the last nine tax years	£30,000
More than 12 out of the last 14 years	£60,000

Overseas income and gains are treated as remitted if the proceeds are remitted to the UK in any form (and the post-5 April 2008 regime widens the scope of remittances that are 'taxable').

The RBC of £60,000/£30,000 will offset the tax arising on the actual remittance of funds, provided it is paid directly to HMRC.

Notwithstanding the above constraints, it still may be possible for a non-domiciled seller, (depending on their UK residence 'history profile') to defer (and possibly avoid) tax altogether by setting up the 'right' structure when the company is first incorporated.

Typically, this would entail establishing a foreign incorporated company (which would be UK tax resident on the grounds of being centrally managed and controlled here). The foreign company's shares would be regarded as non-UK assets (and hence, when sold, CGT would only be payable on a remittance basis, subject to the payment of the RBC. Alternatively, if a UK company is used, some, or all of the shares can be placed in a non-resident trust while their value is relatively low.

However, since 6 April 2017, this type of planning would be ineffective where the individual had been UK tax resident for the past 15 years..

USE OF NON-RESIDENT TRUSTS AND STRUCTURES

Non-resident trusts

15.127 Penal anti-avoidance legislation now significantly negates any tax advantages of using non-resident trusts and underlying non-resident companies. One major problem is that a deemed 'market value' disposal would arise on the emigration of an existing UK trust or direct transfer of shares to a non-resident trust [*TCGA 1992, ss 17(1)* and *80*]. After 5 April 1999, pre-19 March 1991 non-resident trusts are also subject to the settlor-charge (in the same way as post-18 March 1991 trusts) where the settlor and immediate members of their family can benefit under the trust (see 17.58).

Non-domiciled settlors

15.128 Overseas trusts may still prove to be effective CGT shelters for individuals who are neither *domiciled nor deemed domiciled* (although since 6 April 2017 they do *not* shelter gains arising on UK residential property).

Overseas trusts created by non-domiciliaries are not subject to the settlor charge under *TCGA 1992, s 86* (see 17.57). However, gains arising in such trusts would be taxed when the trust makes a capital payment to its *UK resident and UK domiciled* beneficiaries (see 17.60). Capital payments to *non-domiciled* (and UK resident) beneficiaries became subject to the charging rules on 6 April 2008. Thus, non-domciliaries are taxed on capital payments that are 'matched' with gains arising after 6 April 2008. For these purposes, a rebasing election can be made to exclude the pre-6 April 2008 element of a gain from being taxed.

Non-domicilliaries who become deemed UK domiciled on 6 April 2017 (see 15.126) enjoy certain transitional trust protections. Thus, even though they become deemed UK domiciled, they will *not* be subject to the settlor charge provided there are no subsequent additions to the overseas trust. However, if further amounts are added to the trust (post-6 April 2017), the trust protection is lost forever and all the trust gains would be taxable on the settlor from that point onwards.

Furthermore, the beneficiary 'capital payments' regime in *TCGA 1992, s 87* ceases to apply where an individual becomes deemed domiciled under the rules outlined in 15.126. The 'sting in the tail' is that if they receive any capital payments from the trust, this would be a 'benefit', which would mean that all gains would then be taxed on them on an arising basis (since they would lose their protection).

Subject to the above restrictions, non-domiciled individuals can still retain gains in their overseas trust without them being taxed in the UK (and it might be possible for them to extract them on a subsequent emigration, whilst they are no longer UK resident).

Transferring shares into overseas structures

15.129 It is not possible to gift, or transfer at an undervalue, shares to a company (regardless of its residence status) under the protection of a *TCGA 1992, s 165* business asset hold-over election. Consequently, the transfer of shares into any form of overseas corporate structure will produce a tax liability on what is essentially an unrealised gain. This also thwarts a pre-sale transfer of shares into an 'offshore bond' structure (which used to be set up by a number of leading merchant banks and insurance companies).

Whilst the use of offshore corporate and offshore bond structures might still be used in 'start-up' situations, where there is no pregnant gain in the shares, their future role must surely be of very limited application in view of the GAAR etc and the reasonably palatable CGT rates. Very few are now likely to incur the costs and additional risks associated with overseas structures.

INHERITANCE TAX ISSUES POST-SALE

15.130 Sensible tax planning is a vital integral part of securing a successful sale of an owner managed company. For many owner managers this is their one big chance to get the maximum financial return for many years of hard work. However, an often overlooked area is the seller's inheritance tax profile post-sale.

Before the sale, the value of the company would normally have been outside the IHT net (due to the availability of 100% business property relief (BPR) (see 17.19). However, the after tax sale consideration will *not* be protected from IHT and is therefore potentially exposed to a 40% IHT charge on death. Given that many owner managers tend to sell their companies at or near retirement age, this potential IHT problem cannot be easily solved.

Some owners might wish to consider using discretionary trusts, using the protection of BPR/CGT hold-over. Provided this is done well in advance of a sale, this will ensure the sale proceeds would arise in the discretionary trust. Although the CGT on sale would be at 20% (no ER is available), this may be a price worth paying to shelter the sale proceeds from a 40% IHT charge.

Alternatively, the use of Discounted Gift Interest Trusts ('DGTs') may prove a helpful solution (see 17.44 and 17.45 for a detailed review).

PLANNING CHECKLIST – SELLING THE OWNER-MANAGED BUSINESS OR COMPANY

Company

- The corporate tax liability on asset sales may be reduced by sensible allocation of disposal proceeds – avoid creating 'wasted' indexation losses.

Working shareholders

- A share sale is generally preferred as this avoids a double tax charge.

- Where shareholders allocate their sale consideration on a basis which is *not* proportionate to their shareholdings, there is a risk that those receiving more than their pro-rata entitlement (who are directors/employees) may be exposed to an employment income tax charge on the 'excess' amount.

- Owner-managers should claim ER wherever possible (since it reduces their effective CGT rate to 10% on up to £10 million of share sale gains). In some cases, owner-managers might consider transferring sufficient shares to their spouse to increase the available ER (with the spouse being eligible for ER in their own right). However, the transferee spouse would have to meet the qualifying ER conditions in their own right (including having at least a 5% shareholding in the 12 months before the disposal).

- If there is a genuine uncertainty about whether the company/group meets the stringent 'trading' status test for ER, it may be desirable to seek a non-statutory business clearance from HMRC to remove any doubts on this point.

- Sellers who are receiving shares as part of their sale consideration (and have unused ER) should consider making the special *TCGA 1992, s 169Q* election to benefit from ER on the consideration satisfied in the form of shares in the acquirer.

- Where a seller is given QCB consideration on a share sale, they can only access the 10% ER CGT rate if they make an election under *TCGA 1992, s 169R* to tax the QCB consideration on the share sale date. If they wish to take advantage of the QCB deferral, it is not generally possible to claim ER and therefore the postponed CGT gain is likely to be taxed at 20% (without any ER).

- Earn-out transactions should be carefully analysed and planned for to ensure that the intended CGT position is obtained. With an ER gains limit of £10 million, there may be some CGT advantages in structuring a cash-based earn-out which will enable the seller to 'lock-in' some of the earn-out value at the 10% ER CGT rate. In contrast, any gains on the subsequent earn-out payments are likely to be taxed at 20%.

- Where the earn-out is to be satisfied in the form of shares/loan notes in the acquiring company, the value of the earn-out right is not taxed 'up-front'. This effectively means that the entire value of the earn-out is likely to be taxed at the main 20% CGT rate. In many cases, sellers are now likely to prefer to elect out of the automatic *TCGA 1992, s 138A* deferral to increase the amount taxable at the (much) lower 10% ER rate.

- Ensure that earn-out are structured to minimise any risk of them being subject to income tax under the *ITEPA 2003* 'employment-related' securities regime.

- Business angels (who have not been previously connected with the company) should consider subscribing for shares under the Investors' Relief (IR) regime. They can become an unpaid director and still obtain the 10% IR CGT rate on a sale of their shares after three years.

- Where the seller meets the 'fundamental change of ownership' requirements under the Transaction in Securities (TiS) rules, there is no legislative need to obtain clearance under *ITA 2007, s 701*. This exemption will often be satisfied on sales to 'unconnected' companies. However, many owner managers may still prefer to seek an *ITA 2007, s 701* clearance. Where sale consideration is taken in shares and/or loan notes, a *TCGA 1992 s 138* clearance would still be necessary.

- Sellers that do not clearly meet the 'fundamental change of ownership' TiS test should apply for advance clearance under *ITA 2007, s 701* (and, where appropriate, *TCGA 1992, s 138*). They should allow sufficient time to do so (allowing for the 'statutory' 30-day response period). HMRC will look at each case on its merits but often find that one of the motivating reasons for the sale is to generate tax-friendly capital gains on the proceeds. If this were the case the *ITA 2007, s 701* clearance would normally be denied.

- A pre-sale dividend is generally likely to increase the seller's overall tax liability and should usually be avoided (consider adding potential dividend to the sale price instead).

- Deferred ER is now available for gains postponed under the EIS CGT deferral rules. This enables the ER 10% rate to be claimed subsequently when the postponed gain becomes chargeable.

- If a seller wishes to avoid CGT by ceasing their UK 'residence status', this must be carefully implemented to avoid the temporary non-resident rules. In most cases, these provisions require an individual to leave the UK for *five complete years* to avoid incurring a CGT charge on gains made whilst they are non-resident. They should have greater certainty in establishing non-residence by adhering to the various requirements of the statutory residence test legislation.

- The seller shareholders can limit their exposure under the warranties and indemnities by disclosing all relevant details in the relevant disclosure letter.

- A post-liquidation capital distribution is likely to be a better method of extracting the post-tax profits arising from an asset sale (as opposed to a 'pre-liquidation' income dividend).

- Watch out for potential IHT exposure on the post-tax proceeds from a company sale. Consider the use of discretionary trusts and/ or Discounted Gift Trusts as a means of sheltering the future IHT liability.

Other employees

- A share sale provides them with the opportunity to realise a gain from an employee incentive scheme share.

- Employees holding at least 5% of the ordinary shares/votes should be able to enjoy the (lower) ER CGT 10% rate on sale.

- The sale of 'EMI shares' will generally qualify for ER without having to satisfy the 5% ordinary voting share capital requirement. Furthermore, the 12-month qualifying period for the other ER conditions now effectively includes the period from the date the option is granted, which is particularly useful for exit-based EMI schemes. .

- Employment contracts will continue to run on both asset or share sales.

Non-working shareholders

- They should resist giving warranties and indemnities (as the running of the company is outside their control).

- Their individual tax position may be prejudiced by structure of deal – must analyse early as changes can sometimes be made.

Chapter 16

Winding-Up, Administration of Companies and Disincorporation

BACKGROUND

16.1   The shareholders of a family or owner-managed company may decide to wind it up voluntarily, perhaps following a sale of the assets and trade or a planned closure of the business. In such cases, there will often be a surplus available for distribution to the shareholders after the interests of the creditors have been satisfied. It will be essential to ensure that the surplus funds are distributed in a tax-efficient manner (see 16.15–16.33). For liquidation distributions made after 5 April 2016, if 'tax-driven' phoenixism is involved, the shareholders are likely to be subject to 'penal' dividend income tax rates (see 16.28–16.31).

Where a company is wound-up voluntarily, there may be time to implement appropriate corporate tax planning measures to increase the amount ultimately available to the company's shareholders.

In some cases, the existing shareholder(s) may simply wish to 'disincorporate'. This would normally entail winding the company up and transferring its trade and assets to the shareholder(s). The shareholders would then continue to carry on the trade through a sole trader or partnership structure (see 16.34–16.50). For certain 'small' companies, it may be possible to claim the *FA 2013* disincorporation relief (see 16.50–16.50C).

16.2   An insolvent company may be put into administration. An administrator will often be appointed by a key creditor seeking to enforce its security under a floating charge. However, an administrator can also be appointed by the company, its directors or by the court. The process of administration often enables a company to be rescued, which might involve the trade being sold on as a going concern (see 16.52 and 16.53).

If a company is wound-up by a receiver or creditor, then its shareholders are likely to lose most, if not all, of their capital stake. It will then be necessary to consider what tax relief can be claimed in respect of their shares (see 16.54–16.59) and any irrecoverable shareholder loans (see 16.60–16.65).

Where the company is insolvent, the actions of the receiver/liquidator will be dictated by commercial requirements but, where possible, these should be conducted on the most tax efficient basis to enhance the amount available for both creditors and shareholders. However, there is no point in planning to reduce tax liabilities that are never going to be paid due to insufficiency of funds.

CONSEQUENCES FOR THE COMPANY

Pension provision

16.3 Before the company ceases trading the proprietors'/directors' pension provision should be considered. Unless full provision has already been made, there may be some scope for making 'top-up' payments to an approved pension scheme, subject to the relevant £40,000 annual allowance restriction (but see 10.23–10.24). Provided the pension contributions are paid in the final corporation tax accounting period (CTAP) (ie up to cessation of trade), a full trading deduction can normally be claimed with no spreading of contributions (see 10.32). This will also reduce the funds remaining for distribution and hence the shareholder's exposure to tax.

Where a company has not made any pension provision for its proprietors/directors, it may be possible for the company to enter into a Hancock Annuity arrangement. The company would purchase an annuity from an insurance company before the trade ceases. Following the case of *Hancock v General Reversionary & Investment Co Ltd* (1918) 7 TC 358, the purchase of an annuity to fund a future pension was held to be deductible against profits – it was not a capital payment. The insurance company would then be responsible for paying the pension.

HMRC has confirmed that 'Hancock' annuities can still be purchased post-A Day as long as they comply with the current pension rules (see Chapter 10). A specially purchased Hancock annuity for a retiring employee would normally be set up through a registered scheme in the same way as any other pension scheme, especially if a tax-free lump sum is to be provided. Tax relief for the employer contribution is subject to the 'wholly and exclusively' rule. (It is also possible for the company to purchase a Hancock annuity through a registered scheme.)

Under a Hancock-type arrangement, all benefits will have vested, so it does not have to satisfy the annual allowance rules (see 10.23). The lifetime allowance (see 10.30) does apply. If the retiring employee is over 75 or has exhausted their lifetime allowance, then benefits could be provided by an employer-financed retirement benefit scheme.

Termination of CTAP and closure costs

16.4 The company's trade will usually have ceased before it is wound-up and this will have a number of important tax consequences.

The cessation of the company's trade will bring about a termination of the company's current CTAP [*CTA 2009, s 10(d)–(f)*]. Generally, this will accelerate the date on which the company pays its tax liability. Companies which do not pay their tax in instalments, must pay the corporation tax for the final CTAP within nine months following the end of that period. For other companies, the final instalment date is effectively brought forward, being due three months and 14 days after the end of the CTAP (see also 15.6).

Any unprovided expenses incurred after the cessation of trade (known as 'post-cessation' expenses) can only be offset against post-cessation receipts (see 16.9), which reduces the prospect of obtaining relief [*CTA 2009, ss 196 and 197*].

In drawing up the tax computation to cessation, particular care must therefore be taken to ensure that specific provisions are made for all known trade expenses that have been incurred up to the date of cessation. This will include provisions for warranty claims and bad and 'impaired' trading and loan relationship debts.

HMRC will disallow any expenses incurred in connection with the cessation of trade. However, following the Privy Council's decision in *Commissioner of Inland Revenue v Cosmotron Manufacturing Co Ltd* [1997] STC 1134, HMRC will normally allow relief for contractual redundancy or severance payments made on cessation of trade. The rationale is that the payment is made under a pre-existing contractual or statutory obligation incurred as a consequence of the employees being employed for the purposes of the trade (*Tax Bulletin*, Issue 39, February 1999).

Termination payments that do not qualify under the above principle, such as ex-gratia payments, can be specifically relieved under the statutory trading deduction rules. Specific statutory relief is given for statutory redundancy payments and any additional redundancy payments (up to three times the amount of the statutory redundancy payments). Such payments are treated as paid on the date of cessation if they are paid after the trade ceases [*CTA 2009, s 74(4)*]. See 5.32–5.38 for income tax treatment of termination payments in the recipient employee's hands.

Sale of plant etc

16.5 The cessation of trade will give rise to a deemed disposal of plant and machinery for capital allowance purposes, resulting in a balancing adjustment [*CAA 2001, s 61(2), Table, item 6*]. If the plant is sold either before or shortly after the trade ceases, the disposal value will generally be the net disposal proceeds [*CAA 2001, s 61(2), Table, item 1*].

The sale of industrial and agricultural buildings or hotels no longer gives rise to any balancing charges/allowances (see 12.41).

Capital gains on property sale

16.6   The sale of the company's chargeable assets may also produce capital gains, giving rise to a significant tax liability. Broadly, the disposal of a property etc is recognised for capital gains purposes when an unconditional contract for the sale is made [*TCGA 1992, s 28*].

Since 1 April 2017, companies enjoy much greater flexibility in the offset of their (post-31 March 2017) trading losses. As a general rule, losses generated after 31 March 2017 can be carried forward and offset against total taxable profits (which includes capital gains), subject to the £5 million limit and 50% restriction rule (see 4.40 for further details). However, where the trade has ceased, it is not possible to offset the losses against capital gains arising on the sale of the trading property.

A similar problem arises for unused pre-31 March 2017 trading losses, which can only be carried forward for offset against future trading profits (again subject to the same £5 million/50% 'offset' restrictions).

Therefore, where the company has sufficient trading losses available, it should aim to enter into the sale contract for the property on or before it closes down the trade (although completion can take place afterwards). This would enable any gain on the property sale to be sheltered by the current trading losses that might otherwise be forfeited on cessation.

Where it is not possible to sell the property until some time after the trade has ceased, it might be beneficial to crystallise the gain before the trade ceases by arranging for the property to be sold to the owner-manager and then possibly licensed back to the company. The sale of the property would attract SDLT in the purchaser's hands (see 12.24).

In some cases the property will be distributed in specie to the owner-manager. If this is done before the winding-up, this would be treated as an income distribution, taxable at the current effective rates of 32.5% or 38.1%. The in-specie distribution would also give rise to a capital gains disposal, based on its market value (see 9.8).

An in-specie distribution of the property would generally be exempt from SDLT, although SDLT would be levied on any mortgage or loan assumed with the property (since this represents actual consideration).

Sale of subsidiary company

16.6A   There may be cases where a 'holding' company is selling its sole subsidiary company. Before 1 April 2017, where a holding ceased to be a member of a trading group, it would generally be unable to exempt the gain on the sale of the trading subsidiary under the Substantial Shareholding Exemption (SSE). This is because the holding company would not have satisfied the previous 'member of a trading group' requirement immediately after the sale of the subsidiary (as required under what was *TCGA 1992, Sch 7AC, para 18 (1)(b)*, see 3.43). In such cases, it was still possible to obtain SSE but only under the (very tortuous!) provisions of *TCGA 1992, Sch 7AC, para 3* ('the subsidiary exemption') – for a full discussion of this exemption, please refer to the 2016/17 edition of this book at 16.6A and 16.6B.

However, it is no longer necessary to rely on the 'subsidiary exemption' since the 1 April 2017 relaxations to the SSE regime. One of the key changes is that the status of the investing company is now irrelevant. Therefore, the investing company could become an investment company or dormant after the sale of the subsidiary, and still secure the SSE on the disposal (provided all the other relevant conditions for SSE were satisfied (see 3.32–3.35).

Sale of trading stock

16.7   Where the company's trading stock and work in progress is sold to an unconnected UK trader, the actual sale proceeds will be credited in the trading account for tax purposes. In such cases, HMRC would not normally be able to impute a market value for tax purposes (see 12.55) [*CTA 2009, ss 162–165*].

Relief for trading losses

16.8   The liquidator or administrator must consider how to make best use of any remaining tax adjusted trading losses, Any unrelieved 'trade' tax losses cannot normally be carried forward beyond the date of cessation except where they can be offset against post-cessation receipts (see 16.9).

In such cases, the main reliefs which are likely to be relevant for (tax adjusted) trading losses are as follows:

(*a*)   the offset of trading losses for the final CTAP to cessation against the company's total profits (before charitable donations relief) of that period [*CTA 2010, s 37(3)(a)*] (see 4.36);

(*b*)   the offset of any remaining trading losses by carrying them back against the total profits (before charitable donations relief) for the previous year [*CTA 2010, s 37(3)(b)*];

(*c*)   under the terminal loss rules, tax adjusted trading losses arising in the final 12 months before cessation of trade can be carried back against the company's total profits against the CTAPs falling within the three previous years on a LIFO basis (see 4.37) [*CTA 2010, ss 37(3)* and *39*]. See Example 1 for detailed terminal loss computation. A company's CTAP terminates on cessation of trade – if an earlier CTAP straddles and ends in the final 12-month period, any trading loss for that CTAP is time apportioned and added to the terminal trading loss claim.

Terminal loss relief must be claimed within two years of the end of the loss-making accounting period (either on the CT600, an amended tax return or by way of a separate claim).

(d) for trading losses arising after 31 March 2017, an additional form of terminal loss relief is available for trading losses carried forward to the period when a trade ceases – referred to as 'terminal loss carried forward relief). In such cases, any unrelieved losses may be set off against the total taxable profits of the three years ending with the date the trade ceases (*CTA 2010, s 45F*). However, no relief is available under these rules for periods before 1 April 2017.

None of the above trading loss offsets are subject to the (post-31 March 2017) 50% restriction rules.

Example 1

Terminal loss relief

Michail Ltd normally prepares accounts to 31 December each year. The company ceased trading on 30 April 2018, having sold its trade and assets under a distress sale to a competitor company. However, in the four months to 30 April 2018, it made a tax-adjusted trading loss of £78,500.

During the year ended 31 December 2017, Michail Ltd also suffered a trading loss (tax-adjusted) of £240,000.

Michail Ltd's terminal loss claim is computed as follows:

Computation of terminal loss – 12 months to 30 April 2018

	£
4 months to 30 April 2018	78,500
8 months to 31 December 2017	
8/12 × £240,000	160,000
Total loss	238,500

Relief for terminal loss

	2014	2015	2016
Trading profits	180,400	140,730	80,470
Non-trade LR interest	640	420	–
Total profits	181,040	141,150	80,470
Less: Terminal loss relief			
8 months to 31/12/17 – £160,000 loss		(79,530)	(80,470)
4 months to 30/04/18 – £78,500 loss		(61,620)	
TTP	181,040	Nil	Nil

* The loss for the eight months to 31 December 2017 can be carried back against the total profits of CTAPs covering the three years to 31 December 2016 (ie prior to the loss making CTAP). The loss is fully offset against 2016 and 2015.

The remaining loss of £80,000 (£240,000 less £160,000) for the 12 months to 31 December 2017 cannot be relieved. It cannot be relieved under the terminal loss carried forward relief rules since no offset is available for pre-31 March 2007 periods.

** The loss for the four months to 30 April 2018 can be carried back against the total profits of CTAPs covering the three years to 31 December 2017 (ie prior to the loss making CTAP). In this case only £61,620 of the £78,500 loss can be relieved against the 2015 profits, leaving unrelieved losses of £16,880.

Post-trading receipts and election to carry back to cessation date

16.9 Income receipts arising after a company has ceased to trade are assessable as 'non-trading' post-cessation receipts [*CTA 2009, ss 190–192*]. These would include the write-back of excessive provisions (upon which tax relief was originally claimed) and the unanticipated recovery of a bad debt that had been provided against or written-off [*CTA 2009, s 192*] and the release of trading liabilities after the trade has ceased [*CTA 2009, s 193*].

Post-cessation expenses can normally be deducted against post-cessation receipts. However, *CTA 2009, s 198* provides that a special election can be made for post-cessation receipts received within six years of the trade ceasing (ie the final trading CTAP) to be carried back to the cessation date. This election is likely to be beneficial if the company has unused trading losses (which may be forfeited on cessation). The election must be made within two years of the end of the CTAP in which the amount is received. By bringing the 'receipt' into account on the last day of trading, the company would often be able to shelter the tax on it by carried forward trading losses under *CTA 2010, s 45*) or current year losses under *CTA 2010, s 37(3)(a)* (see 16.8 (*a*) above).

Due to the carry forward restrictions on post-31 March 2017 trade losses where the trade has ceased (see *CTA 2010, s 45A*), it will generally remain desirable to elect to carry back post-cessation receipts to the last day of trading to obtain relief for them.

Dealing with overdrawn directors' loans

16.10 In some cases, there are likely to be overdrawn directors' loan accounts that need to be repaid or cleared.

Owner-managers may be tempted to write their overdrawn loan accounts off. This will invariably trigger an income tax charge in their hands under *ITTOIA 2005, s 415* (see 2.61). Many would argue that there has to be a formal deed of waiver for a legally competent release or waivor of a loan!

As part of the winding-up process, liquidators may seek to distribute the overdrawn loan account to the director-shareholder as an in-specie capital distribution (see 16.24). Although the tax treatment may not be clear-cut, a prudent view would be that the in-specie distribution' of the loan account (asset) is very likely to trigger an income tax liability in the owner manager's hands under *ITTOIA 2015, s 415*. In such cases, the distribution of the loan could give rise to an effective cancellation/forgiveness (release) of the debt, since by operation of law it is no longer repayable. Therefore, *ITTOIA 2015, s 415* may apply to produce an income tax charge on the amount released at the relevant dividend tax rate (see 2.61).

On the other hand, there would be no such release where the full capital distribution is paid out to the director-shareholder (upon which a 10% ER CGT charge would normally arise) (see 16.18 and 16.24). All or part of this cash could then be used to repay the overdrawn loan account. Any cash still remaining in the company can then be paid out as a subsequent capital distribution. It is important that 'cash' actually moves in carrying out these transactions.

Pre-liquidation tax liabilities

16.11 The liquidator will need to take account of pre-liquidation tax liabilities as either preferential or ordinary claims [*IA 1986, ss 175, 386*]. Broadly, preferential creditors have the right to repayment of their debts ahead of the unsecured creditors.

Preferential creditors are confined to liabilities broadly representing unpaid employee remuneration, etc for the four months before the winding-up. Notably, unpaid VAT, PAYE and NIC liabilities are no longer preferred creditors.

Furthermore, assessed taxes do *not* count as preferred debts, so any unpaid pre-liquidation corporation tax would rank as an unsecured creditor. Corporation tax arising during the liquidation is, however, normally treated as a liquidation expense (*Re Toshoku Finance UK plc, Kahn (liquidators of Toshoku Finance UK plc) v CIR* [2002] STC 368).

A practical approach will normally be required by the liquidator of the insolvent company when dealing with the company's tax affairs. He must inform HMRC of his appointment and determine the outstanding corporation tax position. Where the company is insolvent or has substantial brought forward tax losses, HMRC may be prepared to agree a 'nil liability' position without the need to submit detailed tax computations (but a CT600 must be submitted). However, if the liquidator wishes to agree an amount of trading losses for the purposes of a loss relief claim (see 16.8), HMRC will require sufficiently detailed computations and accounts to agree the amount of the loss.

Post-liquidation tax liabilities

16.12   The commencement of a winding-up terminates the company's current CTAP and a new accounting period will begin. (A winding-up normally starts when the resolution is passed or the petition is presented to place the company into liquidation [*CTA 2009, s 12(7)*].) Each successive CTAP will last for 12 months with the final CTAP ending on the date the winding-up is completed [*CTA 2009, s 12*]. Once a liquidator is in place, a cessation of trade will not end an accounting period. Similar rules apply where a company goes into administration (see 16.51).

Corporation tax liabilities which arise during the course of the winding-up are treated as an expense or disbursement of the liquidation (see *Re Beni-Felkai Mining Co Ltd* (1933) 18 TC 632). In most cases, the only taxable income received during the winding-up period is interest receivable on realised funds. However, interest received from HMRC on overpaid corporation tax (in the company's final 'winding-up' CTAP) is exempt from tax where the amount is less than £2,000 [*CTA 2010, s 633*].

As a necessary disbursement of the liquidation, the tax liabilities must (together with any overdue tax) be met in priority to the claims of all creditors and the liquidator's remuneration. However, where appropriate, the liquidator can apply to the court for an Order of Priority to be made to ensure that his remuneration and expenses can be dealt with equitably.

Legal formalities

Members' voluntary liquidation

16.13   The shareholders of a solvent company can proceed to wind-up the company voluntarily. Generally, a special resolution of the shareholders is required to place the company in voluntary liquidation. Before this is done, the directors need to make a statutory declaration of solvency. After having made a full inquiry, the directors must declare that the company will be able to pay its debts within 12 months following the commencement of the winding-up.

A member's voluntary liquidation must be dealt with by a licensed insolvency practitioner. Sometimes the costs of a formal voluntary liquidation may seem relatively high compared to the value of the company's assets.

Under a liquidation, a company can generally be restored to the Register within a period of six years after the winding-up has been completed (although claims for death or serious injury can be made at any time) [*CA 2006, s 1030*].

Such an order can be brought by a shareholder or creditor or any other interested person. Where a company has been subject to a formal liquidation, a 'restoration claim' (together with supporting documents) must be made to the court for it to be restored, with copies also being filed with Companies House and the Treasury solicitor.

A creditor who surfaces after the company has been liquidated has six years to put the company back on the register and even then can only overturn distributions made if the liquidator did not take proper steps to contact creditors.

Dissolution under *CA 2006, s 1000*

16.14   A solvent company may be dissolved as a result of the company's name being struck off the register by the Registrar of Companies under *CA 2006, s 1000*. Before 2012, this route was often preferred to liquidation since it generally cost less! However, since the abolition of ESC C16 on 29 February 2012, owner managers will now generally opt for the more beneficial 'capital gains' tax treatment under a formal liquidation. (The statutory 'replacement' for ESC C16 in *CA 2006, s 1030A* provides effective CGT treatment only where the amount(s) distributed is/are less than £25,000, which is very restrictive (see 16.16 for further details.)

CA 2006, s 1003 imposes additional stringent requirements on the directors, such as the need to notify all shareholders, employees, creditors, etc with tough penalties for non-compliance. Furthermore, it is necessary to wait at least three months after the trade has ceased before an application can be made.

In the past, the strict legal position was that a company could not repay its share capital (and other non-distributable reserves) to shareholders on a dissolution. This meant that any share capital, etc, would fall to be treated as 'ownerless goods' and would therefore pass to the Crown under the *bona vacantia* rule in *CA 2006, s 1012*.

However, by going through the relevant procedure a company can now effectively reduce or repay its share capital. The resolution for reducing/repaying share capital must be supported by a solvency statement (signed by each of the company's directors) indicating that the company is able to repay its debts as they fall due both at that time and for the next 12 months – this should not be a problem when a company is being dissolved after all its debts have been repaid.

It is therefore possible for owner managed companies to reduce their share capital to, say, £1 by special resolution. A share premium account or capital redemption reserve can also be reduced under the same rules. The company should directly reduce the share capital/share premium account to ensure that HMRC will accept that this is a return of the original share subscription. Although a company could reduce its share capital to create a 'corresponding' increase in its distributable reserves, this is not recommended. This is because any 'distribution' from the profit and loss account will lose its character as a capital repayment and will be taxed as an income distribution (see 13.60B).

A repayment of share capital /share premium should *not* be included as part of the £25,000 capital distribution 'cap' under *CTA 2010, s 1030A* (see 16.16).

As with liquidations, a dissolved company can generally be restored by a court order within six years from the publication of the striking off notice in the Gazette [*CA 2006, s 1030*]. Any member or creditor who 'feels aggrieved' can apply to the court for such an order. It would therefore be possible for a creditor to come forward at any time during the six-year period to overturn a transfer of assets to the members. Where there is a claim for damages against the company for personal injury, the 'restoration' period is unlimited.

DEALING WITH SURPLUS AVAILABLE TO INDIVIDUAL/ TRUSTEE SHAREHOLDERS

Capital distributions

16.15 Where a company has surplus funds (ie after its creditors have been paid), it is necessary to decide how these can be extracted for the shareholders' benefit in the most tax efficient manner.

A shareholder is treated as making a disposal of an interest in the relevant shares for CGT purposes when they become entitled to receive the capital distribution from the company [*TCGA 1992, s 122(1)*]. The commencement of the liquidation does not trigger any deemed disposal for the shareholder

Distributions made in the course of dissolving or winding-up the company are treated as 'capital distributions' and are therefore chargeable to CGT [*TCGA 1992, s 122*]. Where an in-specie capital distribution is made, the recipient is taxed on the market value of the asset (*TCGA 1992, s 122(5)(b)*) (see 16.24).

In the normal course of events, a distribution made to shareholders during the course of the winding-up does not count as an 'income' distribution for tax purposes [*CTA 2010, s 1030*].

However, if the winding-up arrangements involve 'unacceptable phoenixism', HMRC can apply the 'anti-phoenix' TAAR (Targeted Anti-Avoidance Rule) to tax (post-5 April 2016) liquidation distributions at 'dividend' tax rates (see 16.28–16.31)

HMRC can also use the Transactions in Securities (TiS) legislation to tax liquidation distributions at penal dividend tax rates. HMRC is likely to invoke the TiS provisions where it considers the winding-up to be (mainly) driven by the avoidance of income tax. Since *FA 2016*, HMRC is more likely to use the TAAR rather than the TiS rules to deal with unacceptable forms of 'phoenixism' (see 16.28).

Distributions prior to dissolution of a company

16.16 Following the abolition of ESC C16, distributions made in anticipation of a company's dissolution under the Companies Act 2006 (see 16.14) are normally taxed as income distributions (see 9.12). Therefore, such 'pre-dissolution' distributions will often be taxed at higher rates than if they had been within the CGT regime (see 9.12).

However, *CTA 2010, s 1030A* provides an important exception to this rule. This states that where a company's aggregate 'pre-dissolution' distributions are below £25,000, they can effectively be treated as capital distributions (see 16.15). There should be clear board minutes stating that the relevant distribution is being made 'in anticipation' of the dissolution of the company.

HMRC do not provide any advance assurance process under *CTA 2010, s 1030A* from HMRC. The shareholders will simply apply the 'capital gains' treatment under self-assessment. The 'anti-phoenix' TAAR does not apply to dissolutions under the *Companies Act 2006* (see 16.28).

However, *CTA 2010, s 1030B* removes this favourable capital treatment if the company:

- is not finally struck-off within two years from the making of the distribution; or
- has failed to collect its debts and/or satisfy its liabilities

This means that the distribution will then be subject to dividend tax rates as an income distribution.

Furthermore, should the distributions made in anticipation of a dissolution exceed £25,000, then *all* of the distributions will be taxed as income rather than capital. However, HMRC has confirmed that where share capital is repaid (following the *CA 2006* procedure), the £25,000 'cap' will not apply to this element since this is regarded as a return of share capital and does not therefore fall to be treated as a 'distribution' under *CTA 2010, s 1000B(a)*.

In practice, the imposition of an effective £25,000 'cap' on the amount eligible for CGT treatment prevents the vast majority of owner managers extinguishing 'their' companies under the dissolution route (remember the predecessor ESC C16 had no monetary limit).

Consequently, companies with net assets of (materially) more than £25,000 will now be forced down the formal liquidation route, and will have to bear the costs of a formal winding-up (see 16.13).

Example 2

Distribution made in anticipation of company dissolution

The directors of Randolph Investments Ltd applied to dissolve the company in June 2017. Before the dissolution, the company's residual reserves of £50,000 were paid out as a distribution to the sole shareholder, Mr Darren. His only other income for 2017/18 is net rental income of £180,000 (there are no financing costs).

Since the distribution exceeds £25,000, it will not benefit from the 'capital' treatment under *CTA 2010, s 1030A*.

Consequently, Mr Darren's tax liability on the distribution of £50,000 in 2017/18 is computed as follows:

	£
'Dissolution' distribution	50,000
Less: Dividend 'nil-rate' band	(5,000)
Taxable distribution	45,000
Income tax at 38.1%	£17,145

CGT on capital distributions

16.17 In many cases, capital distributions made should be entitled to entrepreneurs' relief (ER) (see 16.18). Such capital distributions no longer carry any indexation allowance.

ER enables the gain arising on the capital distribution to be taxed at 10% up to the current £10 million lifetime limit with the remaining gains being taxed at the 'higher' CGT rate of 20%. (This limit is calculated on a 'cumulative' lifetime basis for multiple ER claims.)

Following the *FA 2016*, some shareholders may be able to claim the 10% Investors' Relief CGT rate. Since IR has a three-year qualifying period, shareholders cannot claim the 10% IR CGT rate until 6 April 2019 at the earliest.

For 2017/18, where ER is not available, gains would invariably be taxed at 20% (and/or, to the extent there is unused basic rate band available, 10%).

Entrepreneurs' Relief on capital distributions

Qualifying conditions for ER

16.18   Capital distributions made during a winding-up (or distributions made under the provisions of *CTA 2010, s 1030A*) may be eligible for ER, since they are treated as a disposal of an interest in shares under *TCGA 1992, s 122 (TCGA 1992, s 169I(2)(c))*.

ER can be claimed in such cases provided the conditions in *TCGA 1992, s 169I(7)*, are satisfied:

1   The company must be a trading company (or holding company of a trading group) in the one year before it ceases to trade (or ceases its 'holding company of a trading group' status).

2   Throughout the one year before the company ceases to trade (or be a qualifying holding company), the recipient shareholder is required to have:

   –   held at least 5% of the ordinary share capital (carrying at least 5% of the voting rights), and

   –   served as a director or employee of the company (or fellow group company).

3   The relevant capital distribution must be made within three years after the date the trade ceases (or the company ceases to be a qualifying holding company). HMRC have no discretion to extend this 'three-year' period.

Sometimes there may be some concern about the company's trading status in the 12 months leading up to the cessation of trade. This is particularly the case where a service or consultancy business has retained surplus cash. While care still needs to be exercised with substantial cash balances, HMRC now appear to have adopted a more pragmatic approach. HMRC tends to accept that cash generated from a company's trading activities should not necessarily prejudice its 'trading' status. However, problems may arise where the surplus cash has been invested and is actively managed as an investment. It may therefore be advisable to obtain HMRC's acceptance that the company meets the trading status requirements by using the 'non-statutory' business clearance procedure. This would involve setting out the technical concerns 'putting all the cards on the table' and then (using the relevant arguments in 15.40 and 15.41) provide a reasoned basis for demonstrating that the company would satisfy the ER 'trading' company test in the 12 months to cessation.

The mechanics for claiming ER are covered in 15.34A.

Planning considerations

16.19 These special ER rules are based around the date the company ceases to trade (or loses its qualifying 'holding company' status without becoming a trading company).

Particular care must be taken to ensure that the company is in a position to pay a capital distribution within the three years after it has ceased to trade. The liquidator must therefore endeavour to realise the company's assets within this time-frame.

Example 3

Calculation of taxable gain on capital distribution

Ferdinand Ltd ceased trading on 30 May 2017 after selling its trade and assets. The company was then immediately wound up with a capital distribution of £850,000 being paid on completion of the winding up on December 2017.

Mr Rio incorporated Ferdinand Ltd in March 1975 with 100,000 £1 ordinary shares and his shareholding was worth £200,000 at 31 March 1982. (He is a higher rate taxpayer.)

Mr Rio's capital gain on the capital distribution would be calculated as follows:

	£
Capital distribution	850,000
Less: March 1982 value	(200,000)
Chargeable gain	650,000
Less: Annual exemption	(11,300)
Taxable gain	638,700
ER CGT @ 10%	63,870

* Mr Rio has been a director of Ferdinand Ltd holding 100% of the shares and voting rights in the 12 months before the *trade ceased* on 30 May 2017. He therefore qualifies and claims ER on the capital distribution which is made within three years of the company's trade ceasing.

Multiple capital distributions

16.20   If a shareholder receives more than one capital distribution, all but the last one will be treated as a part disposal in respect of the shares. The normal

$$\frac{A}{A + B}$$

part disposal formula in *TCGA 1992, s 42* will be used to apportion the base cost of the shares where:

A = the amount of the interim capital distribution

B = the residual share value at the date of the interim distribution.

16.21   In practice, a relatively relaxed approach is taken with regard to agreeing interim valuations of shares (for the purpose of calculating 'B') where the liquidation is expected to be completed within two years of the first distribution (SP/D3). For example, if all the distributions are made before the CGT is calculated, HMRC will normally agree that the residual share value at the date of any interim distribution equals the total amount of subsequent distributions, without any discount for the delay in the receipt of the subsequent payments.

16.22   Depending on the amounts involved it may be beneficial to phase the timing of the capital distributions over as many tax years as possible. This will enable the shareholders to benefit from more than one annual exemption.

Although all parties may be anxious to conclude the liquidation as quickly as possible, by timing the liquidation shortly before the start of the tax year, it may be possible to pay capital distributions over three separate tax years (but paid over a period of only (say) 18 months). Where there are a number of shareholders, the benefits from using multiple annual exemptions may be considerable.

Example 4

Tax treatment of multiple capital distributions

Brooking Ltd went into liquidation on 1 June 2017, having ceased trading on 6 April 2017. After the trade ceased, the company leased out its trading premises on a short lease until the property was sold during the liquidation.

Mr Brooking formed the company in September 1997, subscribing for all the 20,000 ordinary £1 shares at par.

The liquidator made the following distributions to Mr Brooking from the residual profits and initial capital.

6 July 2017	£45,000
31 March 2018 (final)	£24,000

Entrepreneurs' Relief is available and claimed by Mr Brooking on the capital distributions (which are made within three years of the company ceasing to trade).

Mr Brooking's CGT computation would be as follows:

	£	£
2017/18:		
6 July 2017		
Capital distribution	45,000	
Less: Part disposal cost		
$£20,000 \times \dfrac{£45,000}{(£45,000 + £24,000)}$	(13,044)	
Chargeable gain		31,956
31 March 2018		
Final capital distribution	24,000	
Less: Cost: £20,000 less £13,044 used in July 2017	(6,956)	
Chargeable gain		17,044
Total chargeable gains		49,000
Less: Annual exemption		(11,300)
Taxable gain		37,700
ER CGT @ 10%		£3,770

Small capital distributions

16.23 'Small' interim distributions are deducted against the shareholder's base cost, thus effectively postponing any gain [*TCGA 1992, s 122(2)*]. For these purposes, a distribution not exceeding £3,000 is always taken as small. In all other cases, the distribution is accepted as 'small' provided it does not exceed 5% of the value of the relevant shareholding at the relevant date. However, HMRC do not insist on deducting the small proceeds against the cost where it is beneficial for the shareholder to crystallise a capital gain, for example, if it can be covered by an otherwise unused annual CGT exemption (*IR Tax Bulletin*, Issue 27, February 1997).

Where the capital distribution exceeds the allowable CGT base cost, the 'small proceeds' rule does not apply. Instead, the shareholder can elect to offset the capital distribution against his base cost [*TCGA 1992, s 122(4)*]. Once the base cost has been fully used, the balance of proceeds and any subsequent distributions will be fully chargeable to CGT.

Distributions in specie

16.24   If a liquidator distributes assets to the shareholders in lieu of their entitlement to a cash distribution, this will still constitute a capital distribution for tax purposes [*TCGA 1992, s 122(5)*]. In specie capital distributions can still rank for ER in the usual way (see 16.18).

Capital distributions of assets are always treated as a transaction at market value because the shareholders are connected with the company [*TCGA 1992, s 17(1)(a)*].

In contrast to a capital distribution for cash, a distribution in specie involves two disposals – one by the company in respect of the asset disposed of (which would be relieved by indexation relief) and one by the shareholder in respect of his shares. The value of the capital distribution may qualify for ER (see 16.18). Some liquidators seek to distribute overdrawn directors' loan accounts in-specie to the (owner-manager) shareholders, but this could trigger an income tax charge in the shareholders hands under *ITTOIA 2005, s 415* (see 16.10).

In specie distributions of shares or property should be exempt from stamp duty/stamp duty land tax (see 9.8).

In-specie distributions of chargeable assets often give rise to an acute form of the 'double charge' effect, as shown in Example 5 below.

Example 5

Tax charges on an in-specie capital distribution

Johnny owned the entire share capital of Budgie Byrne Ltd, which went into voluntary liquidation on 1 October 2017 following a sale of its business in July 2017. The company still holds the freehold factory that is leased to the purchaser of the business, which is currently worth £1,200,000 (and was purchased in September 2002 for £600,000.)

In December 2017, the factory is distributed to Johnny. This triggers a capital gains disposal for the company and a capital distribution in Johnny's hands under *TCGA 1992, s 122*.

The part-disposal cost of the shares is calculated as £40,000 (since the company still has further amounts which it needs to distribute).

Disposal by company

	£
Market value of property	1,200,000
Less: Base cost	(600,000)
Less: Indexation relief £600,000 × (say) 0.5	(300,000)
Chargeable gain	300,000
CT @ 19%	57,000

CGT disposal for Johnny (2017/18)

	£
Capital distribution*	1,200,000
Less: Part disposal cost	(40,000)
Capital gain	1,160,000
Less: Annual exemption	(11,300)
Taxable gain	1,148,700
ER CGT @ 10%	114,870

* The in-specie distribution of the factory is not charged to SDLT (since there is no consideration – *FA 2003, Sch 3, para 1*).

PRE-LIQUIDATION DIVIDEND VERSUS CAPITAL DISTRIBUTION

Benefits of CGT treatment

16.25   Most capital distributions received by owner managers from genuine liquidations should be eligible for ER, although care is needed to ensure that the relevant conditions are satisfied in the 12 months before the trade ceases (see 16.18). There is an added advantage in that payments paid out up to three years after the cessation of trade will still qualify for ER.

Provided the shareholder has not previously used any ER relief, they will pay an ER CGT rate of 10% on gains (up to the ER limit of £10 million), with 20% CGT applying to any excess (see 16.17).

Certain groups of shareholders will not benefit from ER (such as 'non-working' passive shareholders or small minority shareholders holding less than 5% of the voting equity (unless the shares were acquired under an EMI scheme). They will frequently pay CGT at 20%.

In contrast, pre-liquidation dividends received by a higher rate taxpayer would be subject to income tax at much higher rates. Consequently, subject to the exception noted in 16.26 below, it will generally be preferable to wait until the company is wound-up before extracting its retained profits as a capital distribution (which is taxed at a lower rate).

It will now rarely be advantageous to make 'dissolution-related' distributions under the statutory rule in *CTA 2010, s 1030A* (see 16.14).

Dividends taxed at low income tax rates

16.26 There may be some cases where it would be advantageous to extract the company's reserves as a (pre-liquidation) income distribution. For example, if the amounts to be distributed (perhaps over a number of years) could be paid within the shareholders' 'basic rate' income tax bands the 7.5% tax charge should be quite acceptable (especially if the shareholder can also use their £5,000/£2,000 nil-rate band – see 9.12).

Such planning must be considered and implemented before the company is wound-up, since income dividends can only be paid before it is placed into liquidation.

HMRC AND 'UNACCEPTABLE' PHOENIX ARRANGEMENTS

Unacceptable 'phoenixism'

16.27 Where a company is liquidated for genuine commercial reasons, particularly where it was not motivated by tax considerations, shareholders should obtain 'capital gains' treatment on their liquidation distributions (see 16.15).

A genuine liquidation would typically follow the cessation of the trade or business, possibly due to the owner-manager's retirement or following the sale of the trade and assets to another entity that is under substantially different control. Way back in 1960, the (then) Revenue issued a statement that it would not seek to apply the Transactions in Securities (TiS) legislation to such 'ordinary' liquidations. This was in line with assurances given by the minister when the TiS legislation was enacted (Hansard, 25 May 1960, Col 5 11) (see 16.30).

In recent years, the beneficial CGT treatment of liquidation distributions has led to an increased use of tax-driven phoenix arrangements. Typically, this would involve the owner manager transferring the company's trade to a new company owned by them and/or their close family members. (There may of course be tax charges arising on the transfer of the assets to the new company.) The original company would then be wound-up in the expectation that the distributions received from the liquidator would be taxed at the 10% ER CGT rate. Sometimes this process would be repeated more than once!

HMRC have always taken a dim view of this type of tax-engineered 'phoenixism'. In HMRC's view, these are contrived arrangements by shareholders to extract the company's distributable profits without paying (much higher) dividend income tax rates. In 2017/18, the income tax rates for sizeable dividends are 32.5% (between £33,500 and £150,000) and 38.1% (above £150,000). On the other hand, if the same amounts were received as *capital distributions* with ER, they would be taxed at 10%.

It seems that a number of phoenix arrangements were not being picked-up by HMRC's fiscal radar. In most cases, this was probably down to a lack of proper disclosure on shareholders' tax returns or a failure to report such transactions altogether! HMRC clearly felt that it needed additional statutory weaponry to counter the growing use of 'unacceptable' phoenix practices.

In appropriate cases, HMRC may also be able to deny the application of ER to liquidation distributions on the basis that holding substantial cash and/or investment assets prevents the company meeting the qualifying 'trading status' condition (see 16.18).

For treatment of pre-6 April 2016 liquidations and winding-up distributions, see Chapter 16 in 2015/16 and earlier editions of this book.

THE 'ANTI-PHOENIX' TAAR

Scope of the TAAR

16.28 HMRC unveiled its new statutory weapon in *FA 2016, s 35* which introduces a new *ITTOIA 2005, s 396B* – often referred to as the 'anti-phoenix' TAAR (Targeted Anti-Avoidance Rule). The TAAR applies to relevant 'liquidation distributions' made after 5 April 2016 and seeks to counter 'unacceptable' phoenix arrangements by taxing them at dividend income tax rates.

The potential scope of the TAAR is very wide. The TAAR lays down four conditions, *all* of which must be satisfied to trigger the TAAR for the relevant shareholder. These conditions are summarised below:

- **Condition A** – Immediately before the company is wound-up, the individual shareholder must have held at least a 5% equity (and voting) interest in the company;

- **Condition B** – The distributing company must be a close company (or was a close company at some point within the two years before the winding-up);

- **Condition C** – Within two years from the receipt of the liquidation distribution, the recipient shareholder carries on, or is involved with, the same/similar trade or activity previously carried on by the distributing company.

  The required 'involvement' of the shareholder can be through any business format and is deliberately widely defined in *ITTOIA 2005, s 396B(4)* to include being in business:

  – as a sole trader; or

  – through a partnership/LLP in which they are a partner; or

  – via a company in which they (or a 'connected person') have a 5% equity and voting interest.

  Cases where a 'connected' company carries on the same/similar business are also caught.

  HMRC's guidance demonstrates that the 'involved with' requirement in *ITTOIA 2005, s 396B(4)* is intended to catch any form of arrangements between connected parties that seek to avoid the rules. For example, even an employment relationship with a connected company would be treated as being 'involved' with a same or similar trade or activity (see *HMRC CTM36325*). However, satisfying Condition C alone is not sufficient – Condition D must also be satisfied, which will often act as the main 'filter' (see below).

- **Condition D** – Having regard to *all the circumstances*, it is reasonable to assume that the main purpose or one of the main purposes of the liquidation or arrangements is the avoidance or reduction of income tax.

  Where conditions A to D are met, the TAAR applies to 'liquidation distributions' made within two years of the recipient shareholder carrying on the same trade/activity (as defined in Condition C). Therefore, in theory, it might be possible to side-step the 'income dividend' treatment if the shareholder is prepared to wait for more than two years before starting the same or a similar business activity through a company or partnership etc. However, in offensive cases, HMRC could still make a counteraction under the TiS regime (see 16.30).

  The practical application of Conditions C and D are particularly subjective. While they clearly catch 'tax-engineered' phoenix operations, they could also apply to a number of legitimate liquidations. *ITTOIA 2005, s 396B(5)* stipulates that the circumstances in Condition D particularly include the fact that condition C is met. HMRC has stressed that while Condition C may be widely drawn, its intention is that Condition D narrows the application of the TAAR to circumstances where, when considered as a whole, the arrangements appear to have a tax advantage as one of the main purposes. Thus, Condition D becomes the real 'crunch' test.

In its guidance (see *HMRC CTM36340*), HMRC has mentioned some of the relevant factors that are likely to be taken into account in considering whether there is an 'income tax' avoidance motive behind the arrangements. These are:

– Is there a tax advantage, and if so, is its size consistent with a decision to wind-up a company to obtain it?

– To what extent does the trade or activity carried on after the winding-up resemble the trade or activity carried on by the 'wound-up' company?

– What is the involvement in that trade or activity by the individual who received the distribution? To what extent have their working practices changed?

– Are there any special circumstances? For example, is the individual merely supplying short-term consultancy to the new owners of the trade?

– How much influence did the person that received the tax advantage have over the arrangements? Is it a reasonable inference that arrangements were entered into to secure this advantage?

– Is there a pattern, for instance, have previous companies with similar activities been wound-up?

– What other factors might be present to lead to a decision to wind-up? Are these commercial and independent of tax benefits?

– Are there any events apparently linked with the winding-up that might reasonably be taken into account? For example, was the only trade sold to a third party, leaving just the proceeds of the sale?

In each case, HMRC will seek to establish whether it is reasonable to view the liquidation and surrounding arrangements as being (mainly) motivated by income tax avoidance – ie where the individuals involved are seeking to 'convert' what would otherwise be (taxable) dividend income into beneficial capital gains.

Specific exemptions from the TAAR

16.28A The TAAR cannot apply where the 'liquidation distribution' does not produce a gain for CGT purposes (*ITTOIA 2005, s 396B(7)*). Thus, for example, shareholders would be protected from the TAAR if the amount of the capital distributions fell below their CGT base cost (see 16.15).

Similarly, in-specie distributions of irredeemable shares are not caught by the TAAR. These exemptions should ensure that genuine company reconstruction operations under *Insolvency Act 1986, s 110* do not fall within the TAAR, although it is difficult to see them being driven by tax-avoidance in the first place (see 13.63).

Practical issues with the TAAR

16.29 There are concerns that HMRC could seek to apply the TAAR to the legitimate commercial use of separate special purpose companies, which are frequently used by property developers, concert promoters and similar activities. Such companies are used to carry out a particular project or activity to ring-fence commercial risks and perhaps to allow for different investors. HMRC has indicated that the application of the TAAR here would depend on the precise circumstances of each case.

Tax advisers would argue that the use of special purpose companies is not mainly driven by the avoidance of income tax. However, given the subjective nature of the TAAR, there is now a degree of uncertainty. In response, many special purpose companies are now likely to be owned within a corporate group structure rather than as separately owned entities (see 3.21 and 3.27).

Unfortunately, HMRC do not provide an advance statutory clearance to confirm that it is satisfied that there is no 'main' income tax avoidance purpose. HMRC's view is that any advance tax clearance obtained under *ITA 2007, s 701* (see 16.30) does *not* cover the anti-phoenix TAAR legislation (see HMRC CTM36350). Furthermore, HMRC will normally refuse to accept 'non-statutory' clearance applications since they are not considered appropriate to deal with the 'subjective' motive test in Condition D!

HMRC has provided several examples to illustrate how it sees the TAAR being applied in practice. These are reproduced below.

HMRC guidance examples*

Example 1

Mr A has been the sole shareholder of a company, which carries on the trade of landscape gardening for ten years. Mr A decides to wind up the business and retire. Because he no longer needs a company he liquidates the company and receives a distribution in a winding up. To subsidise his pension, Mr A continues to do a small amount of gardening in his local village.

Conditions A to C are met, because gardening is a similar trade or activity to landscape gardening. However, when viewed as a whole, these arrangements do not appear to have tax as a main purpose. It is natural for Mr A to have wound up his company because it is no longer needed once the trade has ceased. Although Mr A continues to do some gardening, there

---

is no reason why he would need a company for this, and it does not seem that he set the company up, wound it up, and then continued a trade all with a view to receiving the profits as capital rather than income. In these circumstances, Mr A's distribution in the winding up will continue to be treated as capital.

Example 2

Mrs B is an IT contractor. Whenever she receives a new contract, she sets up a limited company to carry out that contract. When the work is completed and the client has paid, Mrs B winds up the company and receives the profits as capital.

Again, conditions A to C are met because Mrs B has a new company which carries on the same or a similar trade to the previously wound up company. Here, though, it looks like there is a main purpose of obtaining a tax advantage. All of the contracts could have been operated through the same company, and apart from the tax savings it would seem that would have been the most sensible option for Mrs B. Where the distribution from the winding up is made on or after 6 April 2016, in these circumstances the distribution will be treated as a dividend and subject to income tax.

Example 3

Mrs C is an accountant who has operated through a limited company for three years. She decides that the risk involved with running her own business is not worth her effort, and so decides to accept a job at her brother's accountancy firm as an employee. Her brother's firm has been operating for eight years. Mrs C winds up her company and begins life as an employee.

Conditions A to C are met because Mrs C is continuing a similar activity to the trade that was carried on by the company. She is continuing it as an employee of a connected party, triggering Condition C. But looking at the arrangements as a whole it is not reasonable to assume that they have tax advantage as a main purpose, so Condition D will not be met. Mrs C's company was incorporated and wound up for commercial, not tax, reasons; although she works for a connected party it is clear that the other business was not set up to facilitate a tax advantage because it has been operating for some time. In these circumstances, the distribution from the winding up will continue to be treated as capital, absent any other considerations.

* Extracted from HMRC's standard response letter to requests for non-statutory clearances under the TAAR, which can be found at www.ion. icaew.com/taxfaculty/b/weblog/posts/distributions-in-a-winding-up

These examples are pretty clear-cut and probably do not cover the wide spectrum of cases that are likely to apply in practice. These examples emphasise the approach of looking at the totality of the arrangements to determine whether they were (mainly) driven by the avoidance or reduction of income tax.

HMRC indicates that it expects the vast majority of distributions in a winding up will continue to be treated as capital receipts.

Potential application of the Transactions in Securities legislation

16.30   HMRC have always been able to invoke the Transaction in Securities (TiS) legislation to deal with unacceptable forms of 'phoenix' transactions (see 15.82–15.87). However, the *FA 2016* widened the scope of the TiS legislation to firmly include distributions made in the course of a winding-up. Liquidation distributions are now treated as a TiS under *ITA 2007, s 684(2)(f)*.

Thus, if HMRC believes that a winding-up is motivated by the avoidance of income tax, it could make a counteraction assessment to tax the liquidation distributions at (dividend) income tax rates (see 15.91).

Given the potential risk of liquidations being caught by the TiS provisions, many prudent advisers often seek an advance *ITA 2007, s 701* clearance before implementing a legitimate winding-up (see 15.89). This enables them to proceed with the comfort that HMRC would not seek to tax the liquidation proceeds at 'dividend' income tax rates under the TiS regime.

As a general rule, HMRC would first seek to apply the TAAR in *ITTOIA 2005, s 396B* to deal with 'phoenix' cases and are now only likely to use the TiS rules as a weapon of last resort.

It is worth noting that HMRC failed to sustain a TiS counteraction assessment in relation to a liquidation in *Ebsworth v HMRC* [2009] FTT 199 (TC). In this case, Mr and Mrs Ebsworth were separating and Judge Shipwright held that the liquidation and related transactions were carried out for genuine commercial reasons rather than the avoidance of income tax. However, this ruling depended on the precise facts of the case and, if the relevant arrangements took place after 5 April 2016, the Ebsworths might be taxed under the 'anti-phoenix' TAAR in *ITTOIA 2005, s 396B*. (See 16.31 of the 2015/16 edition of this book for full coverage of the *Ebsworth* case.)

Self-assessing the TAAR

16.31   Owner-managers must determine whether they should self-assess their liquidation distributions under the TAAR. Given the complexity of the provisions, they are likely to rely on the guidance provided by their accountants/ advisers. It is unfortunate that HMRC does not provide any advance statutory clearance procedure to obtain confirmation that the TAAR will not be invoked. HMRC's position is that it does not give clearances on the application of a 'main purpose' motive test. It would appear that requests to seek a ruling from HMRC using the 'non-statutory' clearance rules have been unsuccessful.

The *FA 2016* now provides that liquidation distributions firmly fall within the definition of a TiS. Consequently many advisers feel justified in seeking an *ITA 2007, s 701* clearance before implementing a winding-up. If HMRC provides a satisfactory clearance, this would imply that it accepts the transactions were not (mainly) motivated by the avoidance of income tax. However, it is HMRC's view that a satisfactory *ITA 2007, s 701* clearance does not cover the TAAR provisions (see 16.29). However, some take the view that if HMRC has agreed that a liquidation is not mainly motivated by the avoidance of income tax, this should be a pretty persuasive defence in the event of HMRC subsequently seeking to apply the TAAR.

Example 6

Application of the anti-phoenix TAAR and TiS rules to proposed liquidation

Alan has worked for over 20 years as a freelance radio presenter and 'disc jockey' (DJ).

For the past 15 or so years, Alan has run these activities through his 100% owned limited company, Big Al Ltd. Alan has 100 £1 ordinary shares in Big Al Ltd, which were issued at par. He regularly draws a salary of around £20,000 and an annual dividend of £50,000 from Big Al Ltd. He has no other income or major outgoings.

Alan is now approaching 66 and wishes to retire from his radio work by the end of 2017 and is contemplating winding-up his company. However, he wants to continue with his 'private' DJ work at parties and weddings, etc, albeit on a scaled-down basis, reducing to about two bookings per month.

Big Al Ltd has a bank balance of about £660,000 and distributable reserves of around £730,000.

Tax analysis

Since Alan plans to carry on some DJ work as a sole trader (and this activity has previously been carried on by Big Al Ltd) he might be vulnerable to an income tax dividend charge on his liquidation proceeds under the TAAR.

However, having regard to all the circumstances, it is reasonable to take the view that Alan has effectively retired from his mainstream work and that the liquidation of 'his' company is not mainly motivated by the avoidance or reduction of income tax (see 16.28). It would be sensible for him to liquidate his company and continue his interest in DJ work on a relatively small scale as a sole trader.

Alan would therefore have a robust case for reporting his liquidation distribution(s) received on the liquidation as capital gains, taxed at the ER CGT rate of 10%. It might be prudent for him to seek a non-statutory clearance from HMRC to confirm that Big Al Ltd qualifies as a trading company for ER purposes in the 12-month before the trade ceases, notwithstanding the company's substantial cash balance (see 16.18)

Since distributions made in the course of a winding-up are within the scope of the TiS legislation, Alan might consider applying for an advance *ITA 2007, s 701* clearance to obtain assurance that HMRC would *not* seek to counter the liquidation distributions under *ITA 2007, ss 684* and *689*. Provided HMRC gave clearance under *ITA 2007, s 701* this would suggest that the liquidation of Big Al Ltd was not driven by tax avoidance, which *might* strengthen Alan's defence against any subsequent attempt by HMRC to invoke the TAAR.

ER ON ASSOCIATED DISPOSALS OF PERSONALLY HELD PROPERTY

Conditions for associated disposal relief

16.32   Some owner-managers prefer to hold the company's trading premises personally (away from the clutches of the company's creditors!). In such cases, it is likely they may wish to sell the property to a third party at the same time or shortly after the company has ceased trading.

There are special rules which extend the availability of ER to mitigate the gain arising on such disposals (known as 'associated disposals') where the shareholder makes a qualifying disposal for ER [*TCGA 1992, s 169K(1), (2)*]. In the context of a disposal arising on a *capital distribution*, the seller-shareholder must meet the conditions summarised in 16.18.

Furthermore, to obtain ER under the 'associated disposal' rules, two additional conditions must be satisfied:

- The associated disposal must involve a disposal of at least 5% of the ordinary shares (carrying at least 5% of the voting rights). *FA 2015* introduced this rule for disposals (ie capital distributions) made after 17 March 2015 (for further details see 15.45).

  In the context of a winding-up, a capital distribution creates a disposal of an interest in the relevant company's shares, so the 'disposal' test *should* normally be met [*TCGA 1992, s 169K(3)*]. Broadly, HMRC would expect the associated disposal to be triggered by the liquidation/dissolution of the company (giving rise to the shareholder's exit).

● The property (or other personally owned asset) disposed of must have been used in the company's trade throughout the one year before it ceased trading [*TCGA 1992, s 169K(4)*]. It is therefore important to ensure that the property etc is used in the trade right up to the cessation of that trade.

Restrictions on gain qualifying for associated disposal ER

16.33 As a general rule, associated disposal relief only comes into play if the shareholder has unused ER remaining after calculating their taxable gains on the capital distributions. Associated disposal relief is relatively restrictive and the gain on the associated disposal qualifying for relief may be restricted under *TCGA 1992, s 169P*. The main areas in which relief may be restricted and the basis on which this is done is summarised:

Circumstances	*TCGA 1992* reference	Restriction to relief
Property only used for the purposes of the company's business for only part of the period of ownership.	*s 169(4)(a)*	Relief restricted to period of business use only.
Only part of the property is used for the purposes of the company's business.	*s 169(4)(b)*	Relief is given on a pro-rata basis for the time that it was used for business purposes.
Company pays rent to shareholder for using the asset.	*s 169(4)(d)*	No relief is available if a full market rent was received. Partial relief is available where the rent paid was less than the full market rent. For these purposes, *no* account is taken of rent relating to a pre-6 April 2008 period (*FA 2008, Sch 3, para 6*)

Any restriction of the gain qualifying for associated disposal relief is made on a 'just and reasonable basis' by reference to the full ownership period of the relevant asset (subject to the special 'transitional' rule noted above which prevents any pre-6 April 2008 rent payments restricting relief). However, where the shareholder continues to charge a full commercial rent to the company for its use of 'their' asset after 6 April 2008, HMRC will deny relief completely (since it is regarded as an investment asset as opposed to a trading one).

The restriction in respect of rental income is likely to cause particular difficulties to individuals who borrowed to acquire a commercial property and let it to their company. They will generally wish to charge a rent to the company to fund their personal loan interest payments.

Example 7

Capital distribution with associated disposal

On 8 July 2018, Roberto received a 'capital' distribution of £1,400,000 on the winding-up of his 100% owned company, Firmino Ltd. The company's trade ceased on 4 April 2018 and the liquidator was appointed shortly after.

Roberto personally acquired the freehold warehouse on 6 April 2002, which has been used by the company since then. He charged a market rent for the property until 5 April 2012, after which he decided to charge half the market rent.

The property was sold to a competitor company, Terry Ltd, on 7 April 2018 and realised a capital gain (net of disposal costs) of £476,000.

The company has used the property has been used for trading purposes throughout up to the cessation of trade on 4 April 2018.

However, because Roberto has charged rent for the use of the property, the gain qualifying for associated disposal relief is calculated on a 'just and reasonable' basis as follows:

Period	Ownership/ Trade Years	Apportioned Gain	Rent %	Gain qualifying for associated disposal relief
		£		£
6 April 2002 to 5 April 2008*	6	178,500	100%	178,500
6 April 2008 to 5 April 2010**	2	59,500	0%	–
6 April 2010 to 4 April 2018+	8	238,000	50%	119,000
	16	476,000		297,500

Therefore, in 2017/18, the gain eligible for ER associated disposal relief (taxed at the ER 10% CGT rate) is £297,500 and the balance of the gain £178,500 (£476,000 less £297,500) would be taxed at the normal 20% rate.

The capital distribution of £1,400,000 would be subject to CGT and should qualify for ER (see 16.18).

* Rent charged before 6 April 2008 is ignored for these purposes

** Where a full market rent is charged none of the gain for this period will qualify for associated disposal relief

+ 50% of the gain would qualify for the period during which half the market rental is charged. The three days between cessation of trade and the disposal are ignored.

DISINCORPORATION OF THE BUSINESS

Corporate v partnership/sole trader structure

16.34 The choice of trading medium invariably depends on a whole range of tax and commercial factors. The recent changes in both corporate and personal tax rates will have affected the relative tax costs between company and partnership/LLP/sole trader formats.

However, for those at the smaller end of the business spectrum, the fiscal 'scales' may now be tipping in favour of running very small businesses as a sole trader (or partnership/LLP). A number of proprietors will have found that trading through a company is 'not all it was cracked up to be' – for example, paying substantial amounts of tax on company cars, operating PAYE on their own 'drawings', additional accountancy fees, Companies Act compliance and reporting, and so on. A number of small businesses may therefore consider disentangling themselves from a company structure by 'disincorporation'. This envisages that the trade carried on by the company will be transferred to its shareholder(s), who would then continue to carry on the trade as a sole trader or partnership/LLP.

Disincorporation transactions would fall within the ambit of the anti-phoenix TAAR in *ITTOIA 2005, s 396B* since they would invariably entail a liquidation distribution to the shareholder's/shareholders' unincorporated business vehicle (see 16.28). However, provided the disincorporation was implemented for sound commercial reasons and/or the assets were entirely reinvested in the sole trader/partnership business, there should be little or no risk of any liquidation distributions being subject to income tax.

Similarly, the liquidation distribution(s) would also fall within the TiS regime (see 16.30). The shareholders may therefore wish to apply for advance clearance under *ITA 2007, s 701* to confirm that HMRC agrees the winding-up is not being made to avoid income tax.

Planning a disincorporation

16.35   Unfortunately, the process of 'disincorporating' a business does not have any mainstream CGT relieving provisions. Despite the continuity of ownership, the current tax rules do not facilitate the transfer of the company's assets (including goodwill) on a 'tax-neutral' basis.

Under the current tax regime, the potential tax charges and events which arise on a disincorporation would be similar to those which would occur on any 'third-party' sale of a company's business and assets (see 15.5–15.18). Consequently, there may be some tax to pay on getting the trade and assets out of the company into the shareholder's hands, enabling them to continue to carry on the business as a sole trader/partnership. It should normally be possible to avoid any clawback of capital allowances.

16.36   However,   for   the   smaller   'one-man-band'   type   business, disincorporation may be implemented with minimal tax costs, especially where there is little or no 'freely transferable' goodwill (see 16.49 below). The *TCGA 1992, s 162B* disincorporation relief (introduced by *FA 2013*) should assist such companies to defer any corporation tax charges on their goodwill gains (see 16.50–6.50D)

Legal mechanics and basic tax treatment

16.37   From a company law viewpoint, the disincorporation of a business can be implemented either as:

- a members' voluntary winding-up – this can only be used where the company being liquidated is solvent (see 16.13); or

- a simple dissolution (although relatively few companies are now likely to adopt this procedure – see 16.14).

Where a formal liquidation is used, the trade and assets will be transferred to the new unincorporated business, owned by the shareholder(s). The liquidator will pay off the creditors and distribute the surplus to the shareholder(s) – see 16.13.

The distribution to the shareholder(s) should be a capital one under *TCGA 1992, s 122* (see 16.15). However, HMRC would need to be satisfied that the disincorporation has *not* (mainly) been driven by an attempt to extract the company's reserves at beneficial capital gains rates. If HMRC successfully applies the anti-phoenix TAAR in s *ITTOIA 2005, s 396B* (see 16.28–16.29) or the TiS provisions (see 16.30), the distribution of the reserves would be subject to income tax at dividend rates (see 9.12).

Inevitably, a disincorporation will normally involve a classic 'double tax' charge, since the tax suffered by the shareholder on the capital distribution on the appreciation in the value of the company's chargeable assets has already been taxed in the company.

16.38   The various mechanics and tax consequences of a disincorporation are illustrated through the following case study example:

Example 8

Disincorporation case study

Mark has run his small bed and breakfast business since 1992 through his 100% owned company, Noble's Towers Ltd. He would now like to run the business as a sole trader, since this is more appropriate to its future scale of activities. The disincorporation takes place on 30 June 2017 when the company trade is transferred to Mark and Noble's Towers Ltd is wound up.

The balance sheet at 30 June 2017 (reflecting the trading profits to date) is as follows:

	Note	Book value £'000	£'000	Market value £'000
Freehold property	*1*		120	240
Goodwill	*2*		–	20
Fittings, plant and equipment	*3*			
Cost		20		15
Less: Depreciation	*4*	(8)	12	12
Stock	*4*		10	
Debtors			7	
Bank overdraft			(4)	
Creditors	*5*		(9)	
Represented by share capital (£100) and reserves			£136	

Notes:

1   The freehold property has not been subject to depreciation – and represents the cost of the premises when it was acquired in March 1995.

2   The goodwill value is considered to represent 'free' goodwill (and is not attributable to the premises or Mark personally!).

3   The tax written down value of the plant etc on 1 January 2017 was £9,000.

4   Stock and plant etc are transferred at their book values.

5   No tax provision has been made in the above figures.

In the six months to 30 June 2017, the tax adjusted trading profit (before making any cessation adjustments) was £40,000.

Main corporation tax consequences

Deemed consideration of trade

16.39   There is a deemed cessation of trade for corporation tax purposes on its transfer to Mark (even though the actual trade is continuing under different ownership) [*CTA 2009, s 41*].

Termination of corporation tax accounting period

16.40   The cessation of trade automatically brings to an end the current corporation tax accounting period (CTAP) of Noble's Towers Ltd. The company will therefore have a six-month CTAP to 30 June 2017 [*CTA 2009, s 10(1)(e)*].

Unused trading losses

16.41   If Noble's Towers Ltd had any unused trading losses, these would effectively be lost on the disincorporation since they cannot be carried forward beyond the deemed cessation of trade [*CTA 2010, s 45*]. There is no provision for their transfer to the unincorporated successor business.

If the company had a current year trading loss in the final CTAP, this could be offset against any other corporation tax profits, including chargeable gains of the current and preceding one year [*CTA 2010, s 37*]. However, any current trading loss arising before 1 April 2017 could not be matched against chargeable assets (see 16.8 for potential use of trading losses).

Transfer of closing trading stock

16.42   As Noble's Towers Ltd (the transferor company) is 'connected' with Mark (see *CTA 2009, s 168*), who will continue to carry on the trade, the deemed 'market value' rule in *CTA 2009, s 166* will apply to the transfer of closing stock. (Based on the facts of the case study, the amount of stock held by the company's 'bed and breakfast' trade is relatively small, so this is not a material issue here).

However, in most cases, it should be possible for the parties to make a joint election under *CTA 2009, s 167* to transfer the stock at its actual transfer value (or, if higher, the book value).

Capital allowances: plant and machinery

16.43 The normal 'capital allowance' cessation rules apply. No writing-down allowances are given in the final basis period and a balancing adjustment is calculated [*CAA 2001, s 61* and *Table, Item 6*]. The balancing adjustment will generally be computed by reference to the actual transfer value.

However, if both parties make an election under *CAA 2001, s 266* the cessation rules will not apply and the plant can be transferred at its tax written down value [*CAA 2001, s 267*]. In this context, an election to transfer the plant at its tax written down value may not be advantageous if the 'disincorporated' company is going to have unrelieved trading losses. In such cases, the balancing charge can be used to absorb the loss, thus increasing the tax value of the plant for the successor business.

VAT

16.44 Assuming the business is VAT registered, the general rule is that where a trade ceases, the 'registered person' is deemed to make a taxable supply of all the goods then held by the business. However, since the business will be transferred to the shareholder(s) who will continue to carry it on as a sole trader/partnership, there should be no VAT levied on the transfer (by virtue of the 'transfer of going concern' provisions in *VAT (Special Provisions) Order 1995, art 5* (see also 12.34). It may be considered appropriate to elect to continue to use the business's existing VAT registration number (on form VAT 68), particularly as the history of the business will be well-known to the shareholder(s).

Capital gains on transfer of assets to Mark

16.45 As the market value of chargeable assets in Noble Towers Ltd exceeds £100,000, disincorporation relief under *TCGA 1992, s 162B* is not available (see 16.50). Therefore the company is likely to trigger taxable gains where assets are transferred to the shareholder as part of the disincorporation process. The chargeable assets of the company (including goodwill) are deemed to be disposed of at market value for tax purposes [*TCGA 1992, s 17*].

The capital gains likely to arise in Noble's Towers Ltd are summarised as follows:

Goodwill (transferred with trade on 30 June 2017)	£'000
Market value	20
Less: Base cost/indexation	(–)
Chargeable gain	20

The property would (probably) be distributed in specie during the winding-up to avoid SDLT. However, this will still trigger a chargeable gain in the subsequent CTAP by reference to the property's market value (note – companies can still claim indexation relief):

Freehold Property – in-specie distribution:	£'000
Market value	240
Less: Base cost	(120)
Less: Indexation – £120,000 × (say) 80%	(96)
Chargeable gain	24

Corporation tax computations

16.46 The corporation tax computations covering the CTAP to 30 June 2017 (when the trade and assets (except property) are transferred to Mark) and the subsequent CTAP (say) to 31 October 2017 (when the winding up is completed) are set out below.

Provided the appropriate tax elections are made in relation to trading stock (under *CTA 2010, s 167*) and plant [*CAA 2001, s 266*], the corporation tax computation for the six months to 30 June 2017 would be as follows:

CTAP – six months to 30 June 2017

	£'000
Tax adjusted trading profit (no cessation adjustments)	£40
Chargeable gains on sale of Goodwill (see 16.45)	£20
Taxable profits	£60
Corporation tax liability @ 19%	£11.4

CTAP – four months to 31 October 2017

	£'000
Chargeable gain on property (see 16.45) = Taxable profits	24
Corporation tax liability @ 19%	£4.5

The additional corporation tax arising from the assets transferred as part of the disincorporation is relatively modest and is likely to be an acceptable cost of getting the business into Mark's hands for him to carry it on as a sole trader.

However, not all disincorporation exercises will be as simple or as inexpensive. Where property is held within the company and/or there is clearly significant business goodwill, the 'double-tax' costs may make it very costly, possibly persuading those involved to maintain the corporate 'status-quo' – see 16.48 and 16.49 for a further discussion of the relevant issues relating to property and goodwill respectively.

Tax liabilities arising on shareholders

16.47 The company will normally be wound-up as part of the disincorporation and the amounts/assets distributed will normally represent a capital distribution in the hands of the shareholder(s).

Since the main objective of the disincorporation is to reduce the administrative burdens of running a company, some corporation tax is being triggered on the assets, and only a relatively small amount of liquid assets are being extracted, there should be little risk of HMRC involving the anti-phoenix TAAR (see 16.27–16.29) or the TiS legislation (see 16.30).

Based on the case study, the computation of the likely capital distribution and estimated CGT thereon payable by Mark is set out below:

Estimated capital distribution

	£'000	£'000
Net reserves at 30 June 2017 (before disincorporation)		136
Realisations:		
Goodwill – surplus on transfer		20
Freehold property – surplus on distribution in specie –		
£240,000 less £120,000		120
		276
Less: Corporation tax liabilities – say £11,400 + £4,500 (say)	(16)	
Liquidator's fees and other costs (say)	(8)	(24)
Surplus available to distribute		£252
Satisfied by		
Distribution *in specie* – market value of property		240
Distribution in specie – other net assets		12
		£252

Estimated CGT

Based on the above capital distributions Mark's estimated CGT liability (ignoring his negligible base cost) with the benefit of the 10% ER CGT rate would be around £24,000 calculated as follows:

	£'000
Capital distributions	
Cash	12
Market value of property	<u>240</u>
Total amount	252
Less: Annual exemption	<u>(11)</u>
	<u>241</u>
CGT liability @ 10% ER CGT rate	£24

Dealing with property on disincorporation

16.48 In those cases where the shareholder personally holds the trading premises and has granted the company a (non-exclusive) licence to occupy it, no further action is normally required.

However, where the property is owned by the company, the CGT cost of 'disincorporating' may prove to be prohibitive, particularly if a substantial capital gain is likely to arise. If the decision to disincorporate has been made and the tax cost of transferring the property is manageable, then it may often be preferable to 'distribute' it to the shareholders in specie during the winding-up. This will normally avoid any SDLT charge (see *FA 2003, Sch 3, para 1*) and ranks as a capital distribution in the shareholder's hands. However, any assumption of a property loan/mortgage by the shareholders would represent 'consideration' for the transfer, with a consequent SDLT charge.

If the property is sold to the shareholders on or just before the trade ceases (this may be done, for example, to access trading losses that might otherwise remain unused), then SDLT will be payable at the relevant rate (see 12.25).

Treatment of goodwill

16.49 The business goodwill invariably follows the transfer of the trade on disincorporation and may therefore generate a significant capital gain, depending on the market value agreed with HMRC. (However, where the business was established after 31 March 2002, the gain will be treated as a taxable (trading) credit under the intangibles regime in *CTA 2009, Part 8*.)

For many small businesses, HMRC have typically contended that the value of transferable goodwill is low or insignificant. This is because, HMRC argue, that most, if not all, of the goodwill attaches to the proprietor personally and so is not capable of being transferred. (The over-analytical approach adopted by HMRC in relation to goodwill was questioned by the Special Commissioner in *Balloon Promotions v HMRC* (SpC 524)). It is, however, likely that many very small 'one-man-band' type businesses will have minimal goodwill which should facilitate a relatively easy disincorporation.

On the other hand, there will be a number of businesses which have built up significant 'free' goodwill attributable to the reputation built up by the business, its name, and trade connections and so on. Any potential uncertainty surrounding the value of goodwill in these cases must be carefully factored into the tax cost likely to arise on the disincorporation. Agreeing the value of goodwill with the HMRC – Shares and Asset Valuation Office could well turn out to be a protracted process and may be uncertain. In some cases the CGT involved may well make the disincorporation unacceptable.

DISINCORPORATION RELIEF UNDER *TCGA 1992, s 162B*

Background

16.50   A special tax 'deferral' relief is now available for smaller companies to ease the tax burden on 'disincorporation'. Following recommendations made by the Office of Tax Simplification (OTS) in 2012, the Government accepted the need for a special relief to assist those 'small' companies who would prefer to 'switch' to sole trader or partnership status for commercial and tax reasons.

The disincorporation relief (in *TCGA 1992, ss 162B* and *162C*) will only last for a 'five year' period (from 1 April 2013 *until 31 March 2018*) and *excludes* transfers to LLPs.

Where the conditions for relief are met, claims under *TCGA 1992, s 162B* provide relief from corporation tax on chargeable gains and/or profits on post 31 March 2002 intangibles that would otherwise arise on the transfer of goodwill and property.

The relief is perhaps not as generous as was recommended by the OTS. Shareholders do not obtain any income or capital gains tax relief on distributions of assets from the company. There is also no provision for the transfer of losses from the company to the new unincorporated business.

Conditions for disincorporation relief

16.50A *TCGA 1992, s 162B* enables a joint claim to be made for disincorporation relief where a company transfers its business to some or all of its shareholders provided it is a 'qualifying business transfer'.

A *qualifying business transfer* is one that satisfies *all* the following conditions:

- the business is transferred as a going concern;

- the business is transferred with all its assets (or all of them other than cash);

- the aggregate market value of the qualifying assets transferred (broadly, goodwill and 'chargeable' land and property assets) does not exceed £100,000;

- all the shareholders to whom the business is transferred are individuals (but not members of an LLP); and

- each of the shareholders has held their shares for at least 12 months prior to the business transfer date.

Claims for disincorporation relief

16.50B   The claim must be made jointly between the company and all the shareholders to whom the business is transferred. It must be made within two years of the transfer date and once made it is irrevocable.

Provided a *TCGA 1992, s 162B* claim is made, land and property and *pre-1 April 2002* goodwill is deemed to be transferred at the lower of:

- the original cost of the asset; and

- the market value of the asset.

If the transfer relates to *post-31 March 2002* goodwill, *CTA 2009, s 849A* treats it as being transferred at the lower of:

- its tax written down value (ie cost less 'tax allowable' amortisation); and

- its market value.

However, if the goodwill is not carried in the company's balance sheet, the transfer value is deemed to be 'nil'. In the rare cases where purchased goodwill has not been amortised, the lower of original cost or market value is taken instead.

Transfer of other assets

16.50C   *TCGA 1992, s 162B* only deals with relief from corporation tax on chargeable gains or profits on post 31 March 2002 intangibles.

Consequently, there are a number of other potential tax charges, which may arise on a disincorporation.

These may be able to be mitigated using other existing tax provisions, for example:

- Transfer of trading stock election under *CTA 2009, s 168* (see 16.42)

- Election to transfer plant and machinery at its tax written down value (see 16.43).

Tax charge on assets distributed to shareholders

16.51   In the vast majority of cases, the shareholder(s) will generally procure an in-specie distribution of assets by the company to them.

However, it is important to appreciate that the *s 162B* disincorporation relief does *not* extend to the normal tax charges that arise when assets are distributed to the shareholders (for no consideration) (see 16.24, 16.45 and 16.47).

Businesses wishing to 'disincorporate' will often seek to distribute the assets to the shareholders during a formal members winding-up (see 16.13 and 16.37), since the value of the assets would be treated as a capital distribution. In most cases, this would enable the recipient shareholder(s) to enjoy the beneficial 10% CGT ER rate on their capital distributions.

Striking off' the company under the *Companies Act 2006* process is unlikely to be tax efficient in the majority of cases – see 16.16.

Example 9

Disincorporation using *TCGA 1992, s 162B* relief

Hansen Ltd is 100% owned by Alan, who has decided that he now wishes to operate as a sole trader so that rival firms cannot see his business results.

Consequently, the company transfers its trade and assets to Alan on 30 June 2017. The last accounts were prepared to 31 March 2017 and the corporation tax on the profits for the year ended 31 March 2017 and period to 30 June 2017 has been paid early.

Relevant extracts from the company's accounts and records show the following:

	Balance sheet at 30 June 2017 (£)	
Goodwill	Nil	(Market value – £75,000)
Plant and machinery	20,000	(TWDV at 31/3/17 – £10,000)
Trading stock	30,000	
Debtors	5,000	
Creditors	(10,000)	
Net assets	45,000	

The company is liquidated and the market value of the assets distributed to Alan is £120,000 (net assets of £45,000 + goodwill of £75,000).

Since the value of the chargeable assets (goodwill) is £75,000, the transaction would qualify for *TCGA 1992, s 162B* relief.

Hansen Ltd and Alan make a joint *TCGA 1992, s 162B* election to defer the corporation tax that would otherwise arise on the goodwill of £75,000 'distributed to Alan. Alan is therefore treated as acquiring the goodwill at its original 'zero' base cost.

Appropriate tax elections are made for the trading stock and plant and machinery (see 16.50C above).

The aggregate market value of the assets (including goodwill) distributed to Alan of £120,000, would be taxed as a capital distribution (see 16.24), which should qualify for the 10% ER CGT rate (see 16.18).

COMPANIES IN ADMINISTRATION

Purpose of administration and role of administrator

16.52   Where a company is struggling and looks unlikely to be able to pay its creditors as they fall due, the directors have the option of petitioning for an administration order. The administration option is generally pursued to rescue the company's business and achieve a higher realisation of value than under a formal liquidation.

Once a company is in administration it is protected from any winding-up orders and creditors are prevented from taking any action to enforce their debt.

An insolvency practitioner is appointed to run the company and their role is to rescue the business wherever possible and achieve the best possible deal for the company's creditors.

The administrator's proposals must satisfy one of the three statutory purposes outlined in *Insolvency Act 1986, Sch B1, para 3*. These are to:

- rescue the company as a going concern;

- achieve a better result for the company's creditors as a whole (than would be achievable under an immediate 'winding-up'; or

- realise property in order to make a distribution to one or more of the secured or preferential creditors.

An application for an administration order is often subject to the bank's consent (since it will typically have a floating charge under its loan/debenture). The banks must be given five days' notice in which they may appoint their own administrative receiver.

An administrator acts as an officer of the court (irrespective of whether they have been appointed by the court) [*Insolvency Act 1986, Sch B1, para 5*]. The administrator is the proper officer of the company for tax purposes under *TMA 1970, s 108*.

The *Insolvency Act 1986* ranking of creditors determines the outcome for each separate class of creditor.

Tax implications of administration

16.52A For corporation tax purposes, a new CTAP starts on entering into administration and ends on the cessation of the administration. Subject to this the normal CTAP rules will apply – thus typically, once a CTAP starts on the commencement of the administration, the CTAPs will follow the normal 12-month statutory accounting periods whilst the company is in administration [*CTA 2009, s 10(1) and (2)*]. Companies will continue to trade during the administration period.

In contrast with formal liquidations, the appointment of an administrator does not generally disturb existing group or shareholder relationships for tax purposes, although HMRC appear to take the view that the ability to surrender losses to companies 'above' or in 'parallel with the company that is administration may be restricted – see below.

Related 51% group company test – This test determines whether the company is subject to the quarterly instalment payment rules (see 4.50).

Where a company is in administration, this does not affect the existing shareholder's or shareholders' control. Therefore a company in administration is still likely to be counted as a related 51% group company.

Group relief – HMRC contends that companies in administration fall within the 'arrangements' anti-avoidance rule in *CTA 2010, s 154*. The argument is that the administrator is able to 'control' the company's affairs within the meaning of *CTA 2010, s 1124*.

The main principles are best illustrated by looking at the following group structure. Geoff Ltd is 100% owned by Bobby Ltd, although it is currently in administration.

HMRC would contend that the affairs of Geoff Ltd (which is in administration) are conducted in accordance with the wishes of the administrator for *CTA 2010, s 1124* purposes when it enters into the insolvency procedure (even though its shares are still 100% beneficially owned by Bobby Ltd). This means that current trade losses generated by Geoff Ltd cannot be surrendered to Bobby Ltd (or indeed any other subsidiaries that are directly owned by Bobby Ltd).

This analysis has received judicial support in *Farnborough Airport Properties Ltd and others v HMRC* [2016] UKFTT 0431. The tribunal ruled that the receiver was able to take control of the company within the meaning of CTA 2010, s1124. The whole of the company's property was placed in the receiver's hands and the receiver had very extensive powers under the debenture deed, which included the specific power to carry on the company's business

On the other hand, the group relief relationships with companies below Geoff Ltd (such as Martin Ltd) remain unaffected since Geoff Ltd still controls them for group relief purposes.

PRE-PACKAGED ADMINISTRATIONS

16.53 In a large number of cases, a 'pre-pack' or pre-packaged insolvency sale will be negotiated to sell the business and its assets as it is placed into administration. A 'pre-pack' avoids the significant risks that arise where a company trades throughout the administration, such as the continued funding of the business and retaining customer confidence and key employees.

Typically, a pre-pack will entail the sale of the trade to a new company that includes the directors of the original company (in administration).

A pre-pack is used by the directors or shareholders of a distressed business to free the company from the burden of unmanageable debt.

Under a 'pre-pack', the purchaser is identified and the deal is agreed in advance, so that it can be completed almost immediately after the company enters administration.

The original company would then be wound-up or dissolved. This may mean that some or all of the company's unsecured debts remain unpaid.

Despite continued adverse comments in the press, pre-packs have been successful in achieving a rapid recovery of the underlying trade and preserving its value, whilst maximising the return to creditors. Pre-packs normally protect the workforce which transfers into the purchaser under TUPE. The administrator has to show that the pre-pack deal was in the best interests of the company's creditors and achieves proper value for its shareholders.

In many cases, the distressed business will have been 'marketed' for sale in the months leading up to the administration, with no buyers willing to pay a price sufficient to discharge all or a sufficient part of the bank debt. Furthermore, the proposed administrator will have carried out appropriate valuations of the business. Of course, the administrator must be satisfied that the deal strikes the right balance and is agreed on suitable terms. The terms of the deal and its rationale will have to be clearly explained and be acceptable to the creditors.

RELIEF FOR SHAREHOLDERS OF INSOLVENT COMPANIES

Negligible value claim

16.54   Where the shares are worthless, a shareholder can make a 'negligible value' claim. There is no specified form for making the claim, but it should clearly identify the shareholding which is being claimed as becoming of negligible value, the date on which the capital loss is deemed to arise (see below) and that the claim is being made under *TCGA 1992, s 24(2)*.

HMRC should accept a 'negligible value' claim where the shares are 'worth next to nothing' (see Capital Gains Manual CG 13124). This will enable the shareholder to be treated as disposing of their holding for no or virtually no consideration (and immediately reacquiring it at that same value)

The deemed disposal does not take place until the claim is [*TCGA 1992, s 24(2) (a)*]. However, some flexibility is given in establishing the tax year in which the capital loss arises since there is a limited 'retrospection' period. *TCGA 1992, s 24(2)(b)* permits a negligible value 'capital loss' claim to be backdated to an earlier date specified in the claim, which must be within two years before the start of the tax year in which the claim is made. Importantly, a 'backdated' claim can only be made if the shares were held by the claimant *and* were also worthless at that earlier date.

It is not necessary for a company to be struck off or to cease trading for its shares to become of negligible value. This was confirmed in *Brown v HMRC UKFTT* [2013] (TC03118). The FTT upheld the taxpayer's negligible value claim for shares he held in a loss-making research and development company that was being kept afloat by one of its key directors. Even though it was trading, the possibility of it making sufficient profits to pay dividends was very remote.

The tax rules do not specify any particular form for the claim. Claims for the current year could be made by letter to HMRC, possibly with a form CG34 for post transaction valuation checks enclosed if appropriate (see 14.46). Retrospective claims for the prior years could be made on the tax return, by an amendment to the return if possible, or by letter.

It is perhaps worth noting that the Inspector has the discretion to accept certain types of negligible value where the claim is free from any doubt or difficulty (such as the need to agree share valuations). These are for capital losses of under £100,000 on shares in UK unquoted companies that, at the date of the claim or any earlier specified date:

- were in an insolvent liquidation; or
- had ceased trading with no assets.

If a shareholder does not make a negligible value claim, their capital loss will then be deemed to arise when the company is finally dissolved. In practice, this would be when the liquidation is completed or when the company is finally dissolved – a disposal arises for CGT purposes when the shares are finally extinguished [*TCGA 1992, s 24(1)*].

Genuine capital loss claims should not be affected by the general Targeted Anti-Avoidance Rule (TAAR) in *TCGA 1992, s 16A*. These provisions are primarily aimed at arrangements that are intended to avoid tax – typically from marketed avoidance schemes.

The *FA 2013* relief 'capping' rules and negligible value claims

16.55   Where an *ITA 2003, s 131* claim is to be made for the capital loss arising on the negligible value claim, the impact of the *FA 2013* 'capping' rules may need to be considered (see 11.14 and 11.14A). Broadly, these rules restrict the amount of the *ITA 2003, s 131* relief (and any other relevant relief) to the *greater* of

- £50,000; or
- 25 per cent of an individual's 'adjusted total income' (see 11.14)

It is important to ensure that a negligible value claim is made in or 'backdated' to a tax year which enables the maximum possible loss offset. For further discussion of the income tax relief limit see 11.14–11.14C and 16.56.

Base cost issues with shares

16.55A Negligible value claims are sometimes refused because HMRC successfully demonstrates that the shareholder's base cost is substantially less than the amount paid for the shares.

This is often the case where the shares have been subscribed for shortly before the date of the negligible value claim and are deemed to have been acquired at a (low) market value. There are various anti-avoidance rules that effectively ascribe a (low) market value base cost to the shares acquired in such circumstances:

- the 'non arm's length bargain rule' in *TCGA 1992, s 17(2)*;

- 'shares acquired for debt' restriction in *TCGA 1992, s 251(3); or*

- share reorganisation base cost limitation rule in *TCGA 1992, s 128(2))* (see also 16.63).

In such cases, HMRC and the courts have often been able to establish that the shares had little or no value at the date they were acquired. For example, in *David Harper v HMRC* [2009] UKFTT 382 (TC), the First Tier Tribunal denied the taxpayer's negligible value claim because the relevant shares were worthless when he acquired them. Crucially, the taxpayer had not retained proper evidence of the value of the shares at the time of acquisition, and hence he could not prove that the shares had a positive value at that time.

Similarly, in *R & J Dyer v HMRC* [2016] UKUT 381, the Upper Tribunal concluded that the taxpayers' shares were already of negligible value when they acquired them in 2007. The taxpayers had acquired shares in their daughter's fashion company (by means of a partial capitalisation of an existing loan). When the shares were acquired, it was found that the company had no contractual rights over the daughter's services, her trademarks, or her designs. Furthermore, it had been making losses supported by substantial loans. Consequently, the company was worthless when the shares were acquired and the negligible value claim therefore failed.

In *Saund v HMRC* [2012] UKFTT 740 (TC), Dr Saund had lent funds in 2004 to a company that was to operate a language college. His wife was the sole shareholder and he was the sole director. In January 2007, Dr Saund became aware about the lack of financial controls at the company and its failure to pay its creditors. At a board meeting in January 2007, it was therefore proposed, that Dr Saund should 'capitalise' his loan by subscribing for 99 new shares in consideration for the discharge of his loan. However, the share issue was never entered in the company's share register and the company was wound up in February 2007.

Unsurprisingly, Dr Saund's attempt to make a negligible value claim failed and thus he could not secure his income tax loss relief claim for 2006/07.

The First Tier Tribunal agreed with HMRC that the relevant shares had never been issued in accordance with company law. No entry had been made in the company's register in respect of the share issue. Referring to *Halsbury's Laws of England*, the Tribunal found that:

> '...the term "issue" in relation to shares means something distinct from allotment and imports that some subsequent act has been done whereby the title of the allottee has been completed...The shares are issued when an application to the company has been followed by allotment and notification to the purchaser and completed by entry on the register of members'.

Whilst this was sufficient to dismiss the claim, the Tribunal also indicated that the shares were already of negligible value in January 2007, when the proposed capitalisation was agreed. Thus, even if the share issue had been valid, the relevant shares would not have any material base cost.

Example 10

Backdated negligible value claim

Mr Cohen's company, Craven Cottage Ltd, went into liquidation in November 2016. The liquidation was completed in July 2017 without Mr Cohen receiving any distributions from the liquidator.

Mr Cohen formed the company in June 1988 subscribing for 20,000 £1 ordinary shares.

A negligible value claim is made in January 2018, which backdated the deemed disposal of his shares to March 2017 (ie 2016/17).

The calculation of the allowable loss arising in 2016/17 is as follows:

	£
Capital distribution	–
Less: Cost	(20,000)
Allowable loss	(20,000)

Share loss relief (Income tax relief for capital losses on shares)

Application of *ITA 2007, s 131* relief to companies in liquidation

16.56 In certain circumstances, shareholders may be able to make a share loss relief claim under *ITA 2007, s 131* for a capital loss incurred on their ordinary shares. This will enable them to offset the capital loss against their other taxable income. Relief for the capital loss can be claimed against the shareholder's other income of the tax year of the loss and/or the previous tax year. Income tax relief is particularly valuable, as capital losses cannot be relieved unless and until the shareholder makes a capital gain.

ITA 2007, s 131 income tax relief is given before any deduction for sideways trading loss relief (*ITA 2007, s 64*) and start-up trading losses (*ITA 2007, s 72*) (*ITA 2007, s 133(4)*). If the capital loss cannot be fully relieved against income, then the balance is carried forward as a capital loss (*TCGA 1992, s 125A*).

However, since 6 April 2013, the benefit of this relief is likely to be diminished in many cases due to the *FA 2013* income tax 'capping' rules (see 11.14 and 11.14A). Thus, the *ITA 2007, s 131* offset (along with any other relevant reliefs) is restricted to the *greater* of

- £50,000; or

- 25 per cent of an individual's 'adjusted total income'. Adjusted total income is broadly the individual's total income *before* personal allowances, plus payroll giving deductions, less gross pension contributions.

In relation to liquidations, income tax relief can be claimed in respect of a capital loss arising on:

- a capital distribution during a winding-up;

- the cancellation (extinction) of the shares under *TCGA 1992, s 24(1)*; or

- a negligible value claim under *TCGA 1992, s 24(2)* [*ITA 2007, s 131(3)*].

In many cases, it may be beneficial to establish that a deemed capital loss has arisen by making a negligible value claim. This treats the shares as having been disposed of and immediately reacquired at their negligible value (see 16.54).

As far as timing is concerned, the deemed capital loss can be specified to arise at the date of the claim or at any time within the two years before the start of the tax year in which the claim was made (provided the shares were also 'negligible' at that time).

Where ITA 2007, s 131 relief is claimed for a deemed 'negligible value' loss, a clear claim must also be made under TCGA 1992, s 24(2). This was confirmed by the Special Commissioner's decision in *Marks v McNally* (2004) SSCD 503, where a share loss relief claim was denied because of the failure to show unambiguously that the capital loss was being claimed under *TCGA 1992, s 24(2)*. Where the *ITA 2007, s 131* relief is to be based on a negligible value 'capital loss', the timing of the negligible value claim should be arranged to give the maximum possible *ITA 2007, s 131* offset (see 16.55).

ITA 2007, s 131 relief is also available for a capital loss arising on the dissolution of the company where the shares are effectively extinguished normally without any capital distribution being received [*ITA 2007, s 131(3)(c)*] (see 16.56).

'Subscriber share' requirement

16.57   Shareholders can only obtain share loss relief (against their taxable income) if they originally subscribed for the shares. *ITA 2007, s 135(2)* provides that the term 'subscribed for' requires the shares to be issued to an individual in consideration of money or money's worth.

Shares acquired on a no gain/no loss basis from a spouse who originally subscribed for the shares also qualify (*ITA 2007, s 135(3)*). Similarly, relief is available for shares acquired by way of a normal bonus issue (*ITA 2007, s 135(4)*) and shares acquired in joint names (see *Revenue & Customs Brief 41/10*). However, it is *not* possible to claim relief for shares acquired 'second-hand', including shares acquired from a deceased's estate.

Special identification rules deal with cases where the claimant shareholder has a 'mixed' shareholding – ie where the shareholder has 'subscriber' shares qualifying for *ITA 2007, s 131* relief and other shares acquired by purchase, gift, etc. However, these are unlikely to be necessary on a liquidation since all the shares would generally be treated as disposed of at the same time.

Where the shareholding is made up of BES shares, EIS 'income tax' relief shares and EIS 'CGT deferral' shares, these 'subscription' shares are broadly identified on a FIFO basis.

Relevant conditions for share loss relief

16.58   The 'insolvent' company must also satisfy numerous conditions. The detailed conditions are provided in 11.21 and 11.21A.

In 'liquidation' cases, the company will not normally be trading at the date of the CGT disposal or deemed CGT disposal (such as on a negligible value claim). In such cases, relief under *ITA 2007, s 131* is only available provided the company ceased trading within the previous three years and had not started any non-qualifying activity (such as property investment) in the period afterwards.

Furthermore, before it ceased trading, the company must also have satisfied the requirement to trade for at least six years (or, if less, throughout any shorter period of its active existence).

Mechanics of *ITA 2007, s 131* share loss relief

16.59   Share loss relief for disposals (or deemed 'negligible value' disposals) is claimed against the shareholder's income for the tax year of the disposal and/ or the previous tax year (*ITA 2007, s 131*). Note that any offset in 2013/14 and future years is subject to the *FA 2013* capping rules (see 11.14, 11.14A and 16.56).

Where a claim is made for both years, the claim must specify the year against which the *ITA 2007, s 131* deduction is to be claimed first. Otherwise, the claim must specify the relevant year being claimed [*ITA 2007, s 132*].

Under self-assessment, any carry back claim is treated as a claim for the later year. The relief is calculated as the reduction in the previous year's tax liability as a result of the claim. The consequent reduction in the previous year's tax liability is treated as an additional 'payment on account' of the later year [*TMA 1970, Sch 1B, para 2*].

The claim must be made within 12 months after the 31 January following the tax year in which the loss is incurred [*ITA 2007, s 132(4)*].

Example 11

Share loss relief claim under *ITA 2007, s 131*

Kevin originally subscribed for 200,000 £1 ordinary shares at par in Nolan Ltd in 2003

After over 10 years' trading, Nolan Ltd started suffering losses when it failed to adopt new technologies and processes to keep up with its competitors.

The company's trade ceased altogether on 1 May 2017 and it was put into liquidation on 31 May 2017.

Kevin received a capital distribution of £18,000 on 1 October 2017

His adjusted total income for 2017/18 was £260,000 and for 2016/17 was £190,000.

Kevin makes a successful *TCGA 1992, s 24(2)* claim for his shares in Nolan Ltd to be treated as becoming of negligible value when the company ceased trading on 1 May 2017.

Following the negligible value claim, Kevin's capital loss in 2017/18 is £182,000, which was calculated as follows:

	£
Capital distribution	18,000
Less: Base cost	(200,000)
Capital loss	(182,000)

Kevin subsequently makes an *ITA 2007, s 131* claim for the capital loss to be claimed against his other income of the year of the deemed disposal and the previous year, ie 2017/18 and 2016/17. The deadline for the claim is 31 January 2020.

Kevin's maximum tax offset limits are as follows:

2016/17 – £50,000 (ie the greater of £50,000 and £47,500 (25% of £190,000))

2017/18 – £65,000 (ie 25% of £260,000 which is greater than £50,000)

The remaining loss of £67,000 (£182,000 less (£50,000 + £65,000) will be carried forward as a capital loss.

RELIEF FOR SHAREHOLDER LOANS

Capital loss relief for irrecoverable loans

Outline of *TCGA 1992, s 253* relief

16.60   Generally, a simple debt is outside the scope of CGT and therefore if it becomes irrecoverable, relief would not be available for the creditor's loss. However, an individual shareholder (or indeed any other individual lender) can make a claim under *TCGA 1992, s 253* to obtain a capital loss equal to the principal element of their irrecoverable loan (which can include credit balances on current accounts). Corporate lenders generally obtain relief under the loan relationship regime unless they are 'connected' with the borrowing company (see 4.9 and 4.9A).

The claimant will receive a capital loss equal to the amount that the Inspector has agreed is irrecoverable. The capital loss cannot be offset against income under *ITA 2007, s 131* (as it does not relate to shares).

The capital loss on an irrecoverable loan arises when the claim is made. However, it is also possible to establish the loss at an earlier time, being within the two previous tax years before the tax year in which the claim is made, provided the loan was also irrecoverable at that earlier date [*TCGA 1992, s 253(3), (3A)*].

Conditions for *TCGA 1992, s 253* relief

16.61   To make a competent claim under *TCGA 1992, s 253*, a number of conditions must be satisfied, the most important of which are:

(*a*)   the loan must be irrecoverable and the claimant must not have assigned their right of recovery;

(*b*)   the amount lent must have been used wholly for the purposes of a trade (which can include capital expenditure and trade setting-up costs) carried on by a UK resident company. This 'application for trading purposes' test is also satisfied where the borrowing company has lent the monies to another 'fellow' group company for use in its trade. The fellow group company must be a trading company (see 15.36–15.38) and be part of a 75% group relationship. Relief is also available where the borrowed amount is used to repay a loan that would have qualified. The relief is not therefore available for loans to investment companies or to purchase 'investment' assets;

(*c*)   the loan must *not* constitute a 'debt on security' (broadly, a debt on security represents a loan held as an investment which is both marketable and produces a return or profit to the holder) [*TCGA 1992, s 253(1), (3)*].

In judging whether a loan has become 'irrecoverable' at the date of the claim (or earlier date), HMRC are likely to examine the prospects of its recovery based on relevant balance sheets and other information. The Inspector would seek to determine whether there is a reasonable likelihood of the loan (or part of it) being repaid, having regard to the borrowing company's current and probable future financial position.

In practice, where the borrower is insolvent and has ceased trading and it is clear that the loan (or part of it) would not be repaid, a *s 253* claim would usually be accepted for the relevant amount. On the other hand, relief may be denied where the borrowing company is still trading (albeit making losses). Similarly, if the borrowing company was in a parlous state when the loan was made, the Inspector may refuse the claim on the grounds that the loan had not *become* irrecoverable as required by *TCGA 1992, s 253(3)(a)* – ie the loan would be treated as having been irrecoverable from the outset.

In *Crosby (Trustees) v Broadhurst* [2004] STC (SCD) 348, the Special Commissioners agreed that relief was available on an irrecoverable loan that had (as part of the terms of the borrowing company's sale) been waived before the formal claim was submitted to the Inspector. They did not accept the Inspector's view that the loan had to be in existence at the time the claim was made.

The courts also take a fairly strict line when determining whether the company had borrowed the money for the purposes of its trade (see (*b*) above), as demonstrated in *Robson v Mitchell (Inspector of Taxes)* [2005] STC 893.

This involved a builder who had personally guaranteed a loan to his property development company and had provided security in the form of a number of personally-held properties. The claim was therefore under the 'loan guarantee rules in *TCGA 1992, s 253(4)* (see 16.62). This loan was used to replace an earlier overdraft and some of the original overdraft appeared to have been used to fund work carried out on a non-commercial basis on the builder's personally owned properties. Consequently, it was found that the overdraft had not been used for the purposes of the company's trade and the builder's claim for *TCGA 1992, s 253* relief was thrown out. It was also confirmed that clear evidence is required from the taxpayer that the loan had been spent wholly for a qualifying purpose. Justice Neuberger confirmed that 'where money lent is used to repay an existing indebtedness, the purpose served by the use of the money is characterised by the existing indebtedness'.

Any subsequent recovery of part or all of the debt will be treated as a chargeable gain arising at the date of repayment. Capital loss relief cannot normally be claimed on intra-group loans under *TCGA 1992, s 253* (but see 16.65).

Guarantee payments

16.62   Where an individual shareholder has provided a personal guarantee which is called in by the lender, they will be able to claim capital loss relief on any payment made under the guarantee. Claims for guarantee payments made by an individual must be made before the fifth anniversary of the 31 January following the tax year in which the payment is made.

Capital loss relief may also be available where a group company makes a payment under a guarantee in relation to a borrowing by a fellow group company. (The rules specifically provide that relief is not denied because the guarantor and the borrower are in the same group.) The claim must be made within six years of the accounting period end in which the payment is made. The group guarantor company would become entitled to the rights of the original lender and can therefore claim capital loss relief if it is prevented from claiming a deduction under the loan relationship legislation [*TCGA 1992, s 253(3), (4)(c)*].

Example 12

Capital loss relief for irrecoverable loan

Wright Ltd has traded profitably for a number of years. However, the company has experienced a downturn in trading during the last three years. In May 2011, Mr Billy, the controlling shareholder, had to make a cash injection of £80,000 to the company to ease its ailing finances. However, in December 2017, the company's bankers called in the receiver and the company was subsequently wound-up. No part of Mr Billy's loan account was repaid.

Mr Billy can therefore claim under *TCGA 1992, s 253* for the £80,000 to be treated as an allowable loss for CGT purposes.

If Mr Billy realises a capital gain of, say, £50,000 in 2016/17, he should be able to relieve it with his capital loss on the loan, provided he makes the claim by 5 April 2020. To do this, Mr Billy must be able to satisfy the Inspector that the full amount of the loan (or substantially all of it) was irrecoverable by 5 April 2018.

CONVERTING LOANS INTO NEW SHARES

16.63   Given the potential advantages of income tax relief by making a claim under *ITA 2007, s 131*, shareholders may be tempted to 'capitalise' their loans by subscribing for further shares. However, if the company is insolvent, the amount subscribed for the new shares is unlikely to be (fully) reflected as part of the shareholder's CGT base cost.

Where the shares are issued in satisfaction of the debt, *TCGA 1992, s 251(3)* deems the shares not to be acquired at a greater amount than their market value. Where the company is distressed or insolvent, this will typically be a low or of negligible value. Under *TCGA 1992, s 17(1)* (which may also be in point) the shares will deemed to be acquired at their (negligible) market value where the amount subscribed is greater than market value.

Alternatively, the capitalisation of the loan for new shares may constitute a 'reorganisation' for CGT purposes. This would be the case where, for example, all the existing shareholders subscribe for additional shares in proportion to their existing holdings. (This test might be satisfied where a company is owned by a single shareholder who has also advanced a loan to the company, which they now wish to capitalise.) On a 'reorganisation', *TCGA 1992, s 128(2)* effectively provides where the amount subscribed was not by way of an arm's length bargain, that this amount will only be reflected in the shareholder's base cost to the extent that the relevant shareholding increases in value.

Debt conversions were examined by the Special Commissioner in *Fletcher v HMRC* [2008] SpC 711. In this case, the company capitalised a loan made to it by issuing new 'B' ordinary shares (which had minimal rights). The company subsequently went into liquidation and the B shareholder made a negligible value claim for the capital loss on the B shares.

HMRC argued that the shares had no base cost and thus no loss arose (since the B shares had no value when the loan was capitalised applying the market value rule in *TCGA 1992, s 251(3)*).

However, the Special Commissioner found that the CGT reorganisation rules in *TCGA 1992, s 126* must apply on the authority of *Dunstan v Young, Austen and Young Ltd* [1989] STC 69 (although this point had not been made by the taxpayer's representative!). Applying this case, the Commissioner concluded that an increase in share capital could be a 'reorganisation' even if it did not come within the precise wording of s 126(2), provided the existing shareholders acquired the new shares because they were existing shareholders and this was in proportion to their existing holdings.

The Special Commissioner held that the face value of the debt (£50,000) could be added to the shareholder's original base cost under *TCGA 1992, s 128*. He decided that the potential restriction in the *TCGA 1992, s 128(2)* proviso was not in point. (This restriction operates where the consideration was given by way of a non-arm's length bargain). Since the B shares were treated as acquired on a reorganisation, there was no acquisition for CGT purposes [*TCGA 1992, s 127*] and *TCGA 1992, s 251(3)* was not in point

Many consider the decision in *Fletcher* to be a lucky escape for the taxpayer. Where an owner-managed company is insolvent or distressed, there will normally be difficulties in securing a (full) CGT base cost, as shown in some of the judicial decisions covered in 16.55A. In such cases, it will normally be disadvantageous to substitute share capital for shareholder loans. Instead, the shareholder should seek to claim capital loss relief for his irrecoverable loan under *TCGA 1992, s 253* (see 16.60–16.61) since if it is 'converted' into shares there is unlikely to be any form of tax relief!

Example 13

Capitalising debt and 'market value' rule

In recent years, Mr Ivan has lent £240,000 to his friend's company, Mallorca Ltd, to assist it through a difficult period.

Unfortunately, it has now been decided that the company would cease trading and Mr Ivan has been invited to 'capitalise' his loan with the £240,000 being used to subscribe for new ordinary shares in Mallorca Ltd.

Mallorca Ltd's summary balance sheets (before and after the proposed capitalisation of Mr Ivan's debt) is shown below:

	Before proposed capitalisation of loan	*After proposed capitalisation of loan*
	£	£
Net assets	50,000	50,000
Mr Ivan loan	(240,000)	–
	(190,000)	50,000
Represented by		
Share capital	10,000	250,000
Profit and loss	(200,000)	(200,000)
	(190,000)	50,000

However, Mr Ivan will not obtain a full CGT base cost for his shares, since the value of the company has only increased by about £50,000 (due to its prior insolvent position). Although Mr Ivan 'paid' £240,000 for his shares, his base cost will only be about £50,000.

Losses incurred on Qualifying Corporate Bonds (QCBs)

16.64 In some cases, the shareholder may hold a loan note evidencing the debt. This will invariably constitute a Qualifying Corporate Bond (QCB) and represent a 'debt on security'.

No CGT loss relief is available for QCB loans made after 16 March 1998.

Loans made by companies

16.65 Capital loss relief under *TCGA 1992, s 253* is not available where the lender is able to claim a deduction under the loan relationship rules [*TCGA 1992, s 253(3)(a)*]. In many cases, a corporate lender should be able to claim a 'non-trading' loan relationship deduction for an impairment loss on a 'non-trading' loan (ie where the loan is effectively written off or provided against as an irrecoverable bad debt). A trading deduction would only be available where the loan was made in the course of a trade.

However, if the borrower is a connected person, such as a fellow group member or a 'parallel' company under common control, then it is not generally possible to claim a tax allowable impairment loss [*CTA 2009, s 354*].

In this context, *CTA 2009, s 355* provides a mechanism for a lending company to obtain relief *only on amounts arising after it ceases to be 'connected' with the borrower* which subsequently become subject to an impairment 'write-off'. This means that amounts remaining outstanding when the borrower goes into liquidation cannot be relieved (*CTA 2009, s 355(2)*). It should be noted that GAAP usually requires impairment of debts that are not expected to be recovered. Hence the lender is likely to have already impaired most, if not all, of the loan balance prior to the commencement of liquidation etc. when the companies were connected within *CAA 2009, s 354*. Relief will only be available on such amounts that remain 'unimpaired'.

The legislation works by preventing any tax deduction being taken for impairment losses that were denied relief whilst the companies were 'connected'.

It is helpful to understand why the 'connection' test in *CTA 2009, s 466* would be broken where the 'connected party' debtor goes into insolvent liquidation or administration. In broad terms, *CTA 2009, s 472* provides that a person has control of a company for this purpose if they are able to conduct the company's affairs in accordance with their wishes through holding the requisite shares, voting power or powers conferred by the Articles of Association or any other documents (such as a shareholders' agreement). Where the borrowing company goes into liquidation or administration, this 'control' nexus is likely to be broken since the liquidator/administrator would take over the management of the company's affairs. Thus, for example, a parent company would lose its ability to control the affairs of its insolvent subsidiary and hence would no longer 'control' the company within *CTA 2009, s 472*.

Exceptionally, where the lending company is able to deduct an impairment loss for amounts becoming impaired post-liquidation, it will normally be allowed as a non-trading deduction.

PLANNING CHECKLIST – WINDING-UP, ADMINISTRATION OF COMPANIES, AND DISINCORPORATION

Company

- Company should consider appropriate pension contributions *before* trade ceases.

- Specific provision should be made for all known costs and expenses in the tax computation for the period ending on the cessation of trade.

- It is possible to elect for post-cessation receipts to be carried-back as a 'trade receipt' to the last day of trading. This would be useful if the company has unused trading losses which can be used to shelter them.

- If an insolvent company wishes to claim relief for trading losses, it must produce appropriate accounts and tax computations to enable HMRC to agree the amount of the loss claimed.

- Where a distressed company goes into administration, it still remains the beneficial owner of its assets for tax purposes and should not affect key corporation tax group relationships. However, special 'anti-avoidance' rules may prevent group relief being obtained in certain cases.

Working shareholders

- It will normally be more tax efficient to extract surplus reserves by way of a capital distribution.

- In many cases, ER should be available to reduce the shareholder's CGT liability on their capital distributions (up to the £10 million threshold). The relevant ER shareholder and 'trading company' conditions must be satisfied in the year before the trade ceases. Where these tests are met, capital distributions only obtain ER where they are paid within three years of the trade ceasing.

- In certain situations, it may be appropriate to maximise use of the annual CGT exemptions by phasing capital distributions over more than one year.

- Genuine or 'clean' liquidations that arise as a result of the shareholder's retirement or following the sale of the trade and assets to an unconnected third-party would not be vulnerable to the 'anti-phoenix' TAAR. In these cases, shareholders will obtain capital gains treatment on their liquidation distributions.

- Liquidation arrangements that include the transfer of the trade/business to another company under the same or substantially the same ownership, which are driven by the desire to extract the company's reserves at beneficial 'CGT' rates are very likely to fall within the 'anti-phoenix' TAAR. This enables HMRC to tax the purported 'capital' distributions at penal 'dividend' income tax rates.

- The 'anti-phoenix' TAAR would potentially apply where companies are wound-up to facilitate the transfer of the trade to the shareholder's sole trade or a 'related' partnership/LLP. Where this is driven by the avoidance of income tax, HMRC can tax the liquidation distributions as 'income' dividends.

- Associated disposal ER relief may be available to reduce the shareholder's CGT liability on the sale of personally-held property used in the company's business. However, this must take place as part of the shareholder's liquidation exit. Only rent charged for the use of the property after 5 April 2008 would restrict the gain qualifying for ER.

- Where the shareholders wish to disincorporate and continue to carry the trade on through an unincorporated business, they should consider the potential CGT costs of doing so – particularly, if the company holds valuable property and/or has substantial 'transferable' goodwill.

- A 'one-man-band' type company may be disincorporated at an acceptable tax cost. Where the market value of the company's goodwill and property assets does not exceed £100,000, *TCGA 1992, s 162B* disincorporation relief could be used until 31 March 2018.

- If the company's trading property is to be acquired by the shareholder(s), consider transferring it by way of a distribution in specie rather than a sale – this is likely to save SDLT.

- Capital losses on 'worthless' shares can be triggered up to two years earlier by making a negligible value claim.

- It is possible to obtain income tax relief for capital losses on shares in 'eligible' trading companies but the 'capping' rules may restrict the loss offset).

- Capital loss relief can be claimed on shareholder-loans that become irrecoverable (no income tax relief is available for irrecoverable loans). If the company is insolvent, any capitalisation of loan accounts into shares often leads to a loss of capital loss relief.

Other employees

- The cessation of the trade may provide an opportunity to enjoy up to £30,000 in tax-free redundancy/termination payments.

Non-working shareholders

- May also benefit from capital distributions (possibly on a 'staggered' basis – see above).

- Negligible value claims can be used to trigger earlier relief for capital losses (as indicated above).

Chapter 17

Succession Planning and Passing on the Family or Owner-Managed Company

INTRODUCTION

17.1   Owners of most family or owner-managed companies either seek to pass the business on to the next generation or sell it to a third party, perhaps by means of a management buy-out or straight sale. This chapter examines the tax and commercial implications of passing the business down to the next generation. In some cases, the business will be passed on to the next generation for little or no consideration. Alternatively, the retiring shareholder may seek payment for their shares, perhaps by arranging a sale of their shareholding back to the company.

17.2   The current capital tax regime is probably as favourable as it is ever going to be in terms of providing for succession in the family or owner-managed company. When Capital Transfer Tax (the predecessor of IHT) was introduced in 1974, there was no relief for family or owner-managed businesses. Following the *Finance Act 1996* changes, all shareholdings in unquoted trading companies are completely exempt from IHT. On the other hand, shareholdings in family investment companies will be fully chargeable to IHT.

March 1982 rebasing and business asset hold-over relief for unquoted (trading company) shares (see 13.14) usually make CGT on lifetime transfers of shares a manageable problem, although the recipient will inherit the deferred CGT liability in the shares. However, the availability of a tax-free CGT uplift on death combined with the 100% IHT exemption often makes it attractive to retain the shares until death.

RELEVANT INHERITANCE TAX PRINCIPLES

Scope of IHT

17.3   It is helpful to begin with a brief review of the IHT system, particularly as it applies to gifts of unquoted shares. The IHT tax regime taxes certain lifetime transfers of capital and estates transferred on death and also on transfers into and out of trusts. Transfers to spouses and civil partners are exempt.

IHT is payable by UK domiciled (or UK deemed domiciled) individuals on their worldwide assets and is calculated on the cumulation principle.

Most lifetime gifts to individuals are treated as potentially exempt transfers (PETs), and will be exempt from IHT provided the donor survives seven years after the date of the gift (see 17.10). However, a PET will *not* be effective if the donor continues to enjoy or reserve a benefit over the gifted asset, since the asset will be deemed to remain in their estate under the 'gift with reservation of benefit' rules (see 17.10A).

In contrast, most lifetime transfers into a trust are immediately chargeable transfers for IHT (subject to the donor's nil rate band and any available reliefs). Each chargeable transfer is added to the total amount of prior chargeable transfers within the previous seven years to determine the rate of IHT (see 17.13).

Although IHT planning is within the scope of the GAAR legislation (see 1.19) only limited transactions currently fall within the DOTAS regime. However, HMRC is looking to extend the DOTA provisions to artificial and contrived forms of planning in the near future (see 1.31)

In recent years many more estates are being drawn into the IHT 'net'. HMRC's annual receipts from IHT are in excess of £4.9 billion based on the figures released for 2016/17, which is a 4% increase from 2015/16. However, the *FA 2008* changes which enable a surviving spouse to benefit from an additional nil rate band (unused by their deceased spouse) has helped to alleviate the IHT liability for many 'middle class' families. The introduction of the 'residential nil-rate band' (RNRB) from April 2017 should also alleviate the IHT burden for more families.

IHT deemed domicile rules

17.4   Non-UK domiciled individuals are only liable to IHT on UK-situs assets, subject to any double tax treaty provisions.

However, from 6 April 2017, 'non-domiciliaries' who have been UK resident for at least 15 of the 20 preceding tax years *and* for at least *one* of the four tax years ending with the relevant tax year will be deemed UK domiciled for IHT purposes in that year. A similar rule also applies for income tax and CGT purposes.

It is therefore possible for someone to become deemed domiciled for IHT purposes in a year when they are non-UK resident! An individual must therefore leave the UK in their 14th year of UK residence (and *not* their 15th year) to avoid becoming deemed domiciled here. (Before 6 April 2017, individuals only became deemed domiciled for IHT purposes, where they had been UK resident for 17 out of the last 20 tax years.)

Furthermore, those who had a domicile in the UK at the date of their birth will revert to having a UK domicile for tax purposes, including IHT, *whenever they return and resume their UK residence status*. This will be the case even if under general law they have acquired a domicile of choice in another country.

Another important 'non-dom' reform was introduced on 6 April 2017. IHT was extended to *all* UK residential property owned indirectly by *non-UK domiciled* individuals through any offshore structure (see 7.9B). This IHT charge applies irrespective of the non-domiciled individual's residence status for tax purposes.

IHT rates and nil rate bands

17.4A   For 2017/18, the IHT rates on chargeable *lifetime* transfers are as follows:

Chargeable transfers within previous 7 years	*Rate*
Up to £325,000 (the nil rate band)	Nil
£325,000 plus	20%

Notes:

(*a*)   The nil rate band has been 'frozen' at £325,000 since 2009/10 and will remain so until 2020/21. A new residential nil rate band (RNRB) applies from 6 April 2017 (see 17.15A–7.15C).

(*b*)   Since 22 March 2006, chargeable lifetime transfers mainly comprise transfers to companies and most types of trust (such as interest in possession trusts and discretionary trusts)

(*c*)   Where a surviving spouse or civil partner dies after 8 October 2007, a claim can be made to transfer the unused nil rate band of a pre-deceasing spouse/civil partner (see 17.15).

The nil rate bands for chargeable transfers made in earlier years (since March 1992) were as follows:

	Nil rate band £
6 April 2006 – 5 April 2007	285,000
6 April 2007 – 5 April 2008	300,000
6 April 2008 – 5 April 2009	312,000
6 April 2009 – 5 April 2021	325,000

The residential nil rate band (RNRB)

17.4B The residence nil-rate band ('RNRB') applies from 6 April 2017 when a residence is passed *on death* to direct lineal descendants, typically children.

The RNRBs are as follows:

2017/18	£100,000
2018/19	£125,000
2019/20	£150,000
2020/21	£175,000

It will then increase in line with CPI from 2021/22 onwards. There is a tapered withdrawal of the RNRB for estates with a net value of more than £2 million. This reduces the RNRB by 50% of the net estate value over the £2 million threshold.

The RNRB is also available where a person downsizes or ceases to own a home *after 8 July 2015* and assets of an equivalent value, up to the value of the RNRB, are passed on death to direct descendants.

Any unused RNRB band of a deceased spouse can be transferred to a surviving spouse or civil partner.

See 17.15A–17.15C for detailed coverage of the RNRB.

'Loss to donor' principle

17.5 IHT is based on the 'loss to donor' principle. The measure of the value transferred is the reduction in the value of the donor's estate [*IHTA 1984, s 3(1)*]. In relation to a transfer of shares, the transfer of value for IHT purposes would be computed as follows:

Value of shareholding before the gift	X
Less Value of shareholding after the gift	X
Transfer of value for IHT purposes	X

Since the donor is primarily liable for the IHT, the loss to their estate will also include the IHT on the chargeable transfer (see 17.7).

The 'diminution in value' principle can mean that the 'transfer of value' for IHT purposes may *exceed* the value of the shares actually transferred. This would certainly be the case where a controlling shareholder transfers a small minority stake out of his holding, but thereby loses control – the value of a controlling holding would be worth considerably more than the value of a non-controlling holding (discounted to reflect the lack of influence). This principle is illustrated in Example 1 at 17.7.

Despite the uncertainty created by the wording in *IHTA 1984, s 3A(2)(a)*, where the value of the shares etc in the donee's hands is less than the value of the reduction in the donor's estate, HMRC still treats the entire reduction in the donor's estate as the transfer of value.

Commercial and arm's length transactions

17.6 Commercial transactions are excluded from being a transfer of value under *IHTA 1984, s 10* where, broadly, they do not confer any gratuitous benefit and were made on an arm's length basis between unconnected persons. If the transfer is to a connected person, it must be shown that a similar deal would have been struck between unconnected parties. A sale of unquoted shares must also be at a freely negotiated price or at a price expected to result from free negotiations. Difficulties may arise where shares are sold for an amount which does not reflect the loss to the donor's estate.

For example, a controlling shareholder may sell some shares (out of his controlling holding) to various key employees of the company at what is considered to be a fair price – the actual minority value. This would be reasonable given their wish to retain key employees who are vital to the future success of the company and the fact that the employees are unlikely to pay more than the actual value of the shares purchased. If the shares gifted cause the transferor's shareholding to cross a critical valuation threshold (see 14.36–14.39 and Example 1 below), there would be a transfer of value but it would be contended that the transaction was not intended to confer any gratuitous benefit. HMRC might accept this argument based on the relevant supporting facts, but they would only need to consider this if the donor died within the relevant seven years and crystallised the tax (the transfers would be PETs).

Computing IHT on a lifetime chargeable transfer

17.7 Since the IHT on a lifetime chargeable transfer is the primary liability of the transferor, the loss to his estate will also include the tax. Consequently, unless the transferee agrees to bear the tax, the net transfer will have to be 'grossed up' by the tax.

Example 1

Computing transfer of value

Keegan (Investments) Ltd is an unquoted investment company.

The shareholdings in Keegan (Investments) Ltd, together with their respective values were as follows:

	Number of shares	Value per share
Mr Keegan	51	£14,000
Mr Macdonald	30	£5,000
Mr Waddle	19	£2,000

In May 2017, Mr Keegan transferred 21 of his shares to a discretionary trust for the benefit of his family, leaving him with 30 shares. It was agreed that the trustees would bear the IHT.

The transfer of value for IHT purposes would be:

	£
Value of Mr Keegan's shareholding before the transfer –	714,000
51 shares × £14,000 per share	
Less Value of Mr Keegan's shareholding after the transfer –	(150,000)
30 shares × £5,000 per share	
Transfer of value	564,000

Note: For CGT purposes, the value of the shares transferred would be £2,000 per share (being the value of a 21% holding). However, CGT hold-over relief would be available on a transfer to a discretionary trust under *TCGA 1992, s 260,* provided it is not a settlor-interested trust (*TCGA 1992, s 169B*). Broadly speaking, this means that neither Mr Keegan, nor his wife, nor his dependent children are discretionary beneficiaries of the trust – see 17.67.

Related property

17.8 The related property rules prevent an individual fragmenting their shareholding by transferring some of their shares to a spouse, civil partner, or certain 'exempt' trusts [*IHTA 1984, s 161*]. The related property provisions require the transferor's shares *and* those held by their spouse or civil partner, etc ('related property') to be valued as a single asset (based on the degree of control, etc).

Shares held by other members of the family and family trusts are not aggregated as related property and in some cases it may therefore be beneficial to spread the shareholdings along these lines.

The effect of the related property rules is illustrated below.

Example 2

Impact of related property on valuation

Assume that prior to Mr Keegan's transfer to a discretionary trust (in Example 1), the shareholdings were held as follows:

Mr Keegan	30
Mrs Keegan	21
Other shareholders	49
	100

In measuring the value of the 21 shares transferred, Mr Keegan would be deemed to hold 51 shares before and 30 shares after the transfer *for IHT valuation purposes*. Thus, the transfer of value would be computed as follows:

	£
Value of Mr Keegan's shareholding before the transfer:	420,000
30 shares × £14,000 per share (based on 51% valuation)	
Less Value of Mr Keegan's shareholding after the transfer:	(45,000)
9 shares × £5,000 per share (based on 30% valuation)	
Transfer of value	375,000

Main exemptions

17.9   Certain exemptions are available against the transfer of value in arriving at the chargeable transfer for IHT purposes. If, or to the extent that, a lifetime transfer to an individual is not covered by the relevant exemption(s), it will generally be treated as a potentially exempt transfer (PET) (see 17.10).

In practice, the most important exemptions are:

(a)   Spouse exemption

Lifetime and death transfers made to a (UK) domiciled spouse (or civil partner) are completely exempt from IHT. Note that the spouse exemption also applies where a spouse/civil partner is granted an interest in possession *on death*.

A special rule applies on a death of a *surviving* spouse. The surviving spouse's estate may claim the benefit of the proportion of the 'unused' nil rate band (and RNRB) on the first death [*IHTA 1984, s 8A*] (see 17.15 and 17.15A–17.15C).

Different rules apply where the donee spouse/civil partner is non-UK domiciled. In such cases, the 'spouse' exemption is limited to the level of the nil rate-band (£325,000 for 2017/18) [*IHTA 1984, s 18*]. The rationale for a 'cap' on transfers to *non-domiciled* spouses is reasonably clear. UK domiciled individuals are liable to IHT on their worldwide assets, whereas non-UK domiciliaries are taxed only on their *UK-situs* assets (see 17.9A). Thus, without the cap, it would be possible for a UK domiciliary to make unlimited transfers of their foreign-*situs* assets to their 'non-domiciled' spouse, thus taking them outside the UK IHT net.

Since 6 April 2013, non-domiciled spouses or civil partners can elect to be treated as UK domiciled for IHT purposes – this does not affect their domicile status for income tax or CGT [*IHTA 1984, s 267ZA*]. This enables couples to benefit from a total exemption from IHT on transfers between themselves during life and on death. The downside of making the 'deemed domiciled' election is that a foreign-domiciled spouse then becomes liable to IHT on their worldwide assets.

The election is irrevocable and continues to apply unless and until the non-domiciled spouse has been non-UK resident for five complete tax years. In other words, the election only ceases to have effect from the end of the fifth tax year of non-residence. This prevents foreign spouses from electing to be treated as UK-domiciled for IHT purposes to get the immediate benefit of an uncapped transfer from their spouse/civil partner while later reverting to non-UK domiciled status to regain beneficial IHT treatment on their overseas assets.

The election must be made in writing during lifetime or on death. Thus, a non-UK domiciliary can elect following the death of their UK domiciled spouse or civil partner, provided the election is made within two years of the death.

(b)   Annual exemption

An annual exemption of £3,000 per annum is available, although one year's unused exemption can be carried forward to the next year [*IHTA 1984, s 19*].

(c)   Small gifts exemption

Outright lifetime gifts of up to £250 per donee each year are exempt – this is often useful for small presents! [*IHTA 1984, s 20*.]

(d)   Normal expenditure out of income

This is a potentially generous exemption since it is not subject to any monetary limit and depends on the donor's circumstances. The gifts must form part of the donor's normal expenditure so that they are left with sufficient income to maintain their standard of living [*IHTA 1984, s 21*]. The expenditure must form part of a regular pattern of payments (for example, this might include life insurance premiums paid for the benefit of another, school fees for grandchildren, or Gift Aid payments). The relief is only available if the donor meets the expenditure from their surplus net income (after income tax).

Thus, expenditure made out of one-off receipts, such as inheritances or capital proceeds from the sale of investments are unlikely to qualify for the exemption.

In determining whether the expenditure is 'normal', each case is judged on its own facts, looking very closely at the transferor's standard of living and the pattern of giving. See, for example, *Bennett v CIR* [1995] STC 54, where it was stated that a pattern of gifts is intended to remain in place for more than a nominal period and for a sufficient period (barring unforeseen circumstances) fairly to be regarded as a regular feature of the transferor's annual expenditure.

The 'normal expenditure out of income' exemption is generally claimed by the deceased's executors. Hence, the donor should retain contemporaneous documentary evidence during their lifetime to support their reliance on this relief. Schedule IHT 403 (included in the IHT return account IHT 400) provides a helpful template for recording income and expenditure for the purposes of the exemption.

(e) Gifts in consideration of marriage or a civil partnership

IHTA 1984, s 22 provides specific exemptions for gifts made in consideration of a marriage or civil partnership, according to the relationship of the donor, as follows:

Parent of either party to the marriage	£5,000
Gift by one party to the marriage to the other	£2,500
Lineal ancestor	£2,500
Others	£1,000

(f) Business Property Relief

Business property relief (BPR) (now also referred to as Business relief) provides a very valuable relief for the majority of owner-managed or family companies and careful vigilance is required to ensure that it is not jeopardised or wasted. This book refers to the relief as BPR, which is covered extensively in 17.19–17.33.

(g) Agricultural Property Relief

Agricultural property relief (APR) normally provides a 100% exemption on the transfer of qualifying agricultural property but only up to the *agricultural value* of the property [*IHTA 1984, ss 115–124C*]. However, BPR will often be available on the non-agricultural value.

APR is also available on shares in a farming company that is controlled by the transferor. In such cases, agricultural property must form part of the company's assets and the APR is restricted to the value of shareholding that is represented by the agricultural value of the agricultural property. 100% APR is normally available where the company occupies the agricultural property or where the property is let after 31 August 1995. Where the relevant BPR conditions are satisfied, 100% BPR should be available on the value attributable to the non-agricultural holding.

(h) Charitable gifts or certain registered clubs –

Gifts to charities or certain registered clubs are exempt from IHT (whether made during the donor's lifetime or on their death) (*IHTA 1984, s 23*). The Court of Appeal has held that the charity must be UK registered (*Routier & Anor v HMRC* [2016] EWCA Civ 938).

A reduced IHT rate of 36% on death may also apply where (broadly) the deceased leaves at least 10% of their net estate to a charity or charities (see 17.14B).

Excluded property

17.9A Excluded property is perhaps one of the most important IHT exemptions. The most common category of excluded property is property situated outside the UK owned by non-domiciled individuals, for example overseas land, offshore bonds (with an overseas life company) or shares in an overseas registered company [*IHTA 1984, s 6*]. However, since 6 April 2017 special charging rules that apply for UK residential property held indirectly through overseas company/trust structures (see 17.9B).

Another important category is overseas property comprised in a non-UK resident trust that was created when the settlor was non-domiciled [*IHTA 1984, s 48(3)*]. Notably, the assets in the trust retain their 'excluded property' status, even if the settlor's domicile changes.

However, since 6 April 2017, individuals with a UK domicile at birth but who have established a domicile of choice outside the UK, can no longer take advantage of a trust with 'excluded property' status while they are UK tax resident.

UK residential property held indirectly via excluded property trusts

17.9B As part of an important package of reforms to the taxation of 'non-domiciliaries, special IHT charging rules were introduced on 6 April 2017.

In the past, non-domiciled individuals tended to shelter their UK property interests by holding them in an overseas company owned by an 'excluded property' trust. Since the trust held shares in an overseas company, this was treated as 'exempt' excluded property for IHT purposes.

However, since 6 April 2017, the IHT legislation now looks though such 'overseas trust/company' structures and taxes any 'indirectly-held' *UK residential property*. Consequently, non-domiciliaries that 'indirectly' hold

UK residential company through an *overseas* trust/company or other foreign 'opaque' entity are subject to IHT in the same way as any UK domiciled individual. Subject to special rules, the value of the underlying UK residential property is taxed as though it was held directly.

It should perhaps be emphasised that these special charging provisions only apply to UK *residential property*. They do *not* apply to other overseas-situs assets held in an overseas structure.

Potentially exempt transfers (PETs)

17.10   Following the *FA 2006* changes, only outright gifts of shares or other assets to *individuals* will qualify as potentially exempt transfers (PETs) [*IHTA 1984, s 3A(1A)*].

Where an individual transfers shares, cash or other property to *any trust* (subject to very narrow exceptions) this is treated as a *chargeable transfer* (and does not fall within the PET rules).

Before 22 March 2006, most lifetime transfers were treated as potentially exempt transfers (PETs). Thus, for example, the transfer of shares, etc to an individual, an interest in possession trust, or an accumulation and maintenance trust would have been a PET [*IHTA 1984, s 3A(1)*].

A PET becomes permanently exempt from IHT, provided the donor survives seven years from the date of the transfer. After seven years, the gifted shares would be excluded from the donor's estate (subject to the gift with reservation of benefit rules (see below) and cannot therefore be taken into account in computing the tax on the donor's subsequent 'chargeable' gifts and taxable estate held on death [*IHTA 1984, s 3A(4), (5)*].

However, if the donor dies within seven years of transferring the shares (under a PET), the value of those shares *at the date of the original gift* is included in their chargeable estate on death. However, any IHT crystallising on a PET made more than three years before the donor's death is eligible for a tapered reduction. This reduces the relevant IHT on a sliding scale between 20% and 80% (see 17.11 below).

When making a material PET, it may be considered appropriate to take out a (declining) term insurance policy to fund the IHT in the event of the PET failing within seven years. Such policies provide for a lump sum only if the insured dies within a specified period or before a specified age – no payment is therefore made if the insured survives the relevant period – and (the policies) are, therefore, one of the cheapest forms of insurance.

A PET has the beneficial effect of freezing the value of the gifted shares. Any subsequent appreciation in value would escape IHT. If the asset has reduced in value the taxpayer may claim that the reduced value be used for the purposes of the calculation of the tax payable [*IHTA 1984, s 131*].

BPR (see 17.18) may be available to eliminate or reduce the IHT liability on a PET of unquoted shares becoming chargeable. However, there would be no BPR if the transferee has disposed of the gifted shares before the transferor's death [*IHTA 1984, s 113A(1), (2)*]. This would mean that the tax on the crystallised PET on the original gift of the shares is calculated without regard to BPR.

Gifts with reservation of benefit (GROBs)

17.10A   The broad aim of the IHT regime is to restrict effective lifetime gifts to those cases where the donor is content to enjoy no further use or occupation of the property gifted and survives the 'seven year' period.

Special anti-avoidance rules in *FA 1986, s 102* therefore apply to gifts made where the donor reserves a benefit (known as a gift with reservation of benefit or GROB) (see also 17.46, 17.51 and 17.100). These prevent effective transfers being made for IHT purposes (after 17 March 1986) where the donor is still able to enjoy any benefit from the gifted property. Consequently, if the donor subsequently dies whilst still preserving some benefit or use from the property, it will be treated as part of their chargeable estate on death. However, if the donor ceases to benefit from the property during their lifetime, they will be treated as making a PET of the property at that time.

The GROB legislation contains detailed provisions that block planning arrangements designed to side-step the GROB rules (see *FA 1986, ss 102–102C*), which has been supplemented by the charge on pre-owned assets, which operates from 6 April 2005 (see 17.117–17.125).

The GROB provisions apply to PETs and lifetime chargeable transfers (see 17.12). This may therefore result in the same gift being taxed twice. In many cases, any 'double charge' should be mitigated under the *Inheritance Tax (Double Charges Relief) Regulations 1987, SI 1987/1130*.

IHT crystallising on a PET

17.11   The calculation of IHT on the PET becoming chargeable on the death of the donor involves adding the value of the PET to their total *chargeable* transfers made within the seven years before the PET.

The PET (after any available annual exemption, etc) is treated as the 'top slice' for the purpose of calculating the relevant IHT (which will be at the 'death rate' of 40% after the donor's nil rate band has been used).

IHT taper relief is available where the PET occurred more than three years before the donor's death, discounting the amount of IHT payable by the following rates:

Period before death	Reduction in IHT
3–4 years	20%
4–5 years	40%
5–6 years	60%
6–7 years	80%

This process is repeated for subsequent PETs. The tax on the PET crystallising on the donor's death would normally be borne by the donee (who can provide for the tax by taking out a decreasing term assurance policy – see 17.10). As the tax is payable by the donee, the tax is calculated on the value of the PET only – there is no 'grossing up'.

Types of lifetime chargeable transfers

17.12　Following the *FA 2006*, we now have a much wider range of lifetime transfers that are immediately chargeable to IHT (subject to the nil rate band, etc).

The main types of chargeable transfer will include transfers to:

- an interest in possession trust;

- a discretionary trust; or

- a company.

Such transfers are *not* PETs.

Treatment of lifetime chargeable transfers

17.13　Chargeable transfers are subject to a lifetime IHT charge of 20% if the value transferred (reduced by any IHT business property relief (BPR) etc)) exceeds the transferor's available nil rate band – this is the amount of the current nil rate band (see 17.4A) after allowing for any chargeable transfers made in the previous seven years.

Additional IHT may become payable if the donor does not survive seven years. The tax is calculated on a similar basis to a PET becoming chargeable (see 17.11). The IHT on the original transfer is re-calculated using the current death rates (ie 40% after the nil rate band has been used). If the chargeable transfer was made more than three years before the date of death, this may be eligible for a taper relief reduction (based on the sliding scale in 17.11).

Credit is then given for tax paid on the original transfer (however, no repayment can be made if the lifetime IHT is higher).

Example 3

Computing IHT on lifetime chargeable transfers

Following on from Example 1, the IHT payable on the transfer to the discretionary trust by Mr Keegan in May 2017 (assuming there were no prior chargeable transfers in the previous seven years and the trustees paid the tax) would be £46,600 calculated as follows:

	£
Transfer of value	564,000
Less: Annual exemption (2017/18)	(3,000)
Annual exemption (unused 2016/17 b/fwd.)	(3,000)
Chargeable transfer	558,000

Note: No BPR is available as the company is an investment company.

IHT thereon	£
on first £325,000 @ 0%	–
on next £233,000 @ 20%	46,600
	46,600

If Mr Keegan died in August 2020 (just over three years later), the additional tax payable by the trustees would be:

	£
On first £325,000 @ 0%	–
On next £233,000 @ 40%	93,200
	93,200
Less: Taper reduction @ 20%	(18,640)
	74,560
Less: Tax already paid re May 2017 transfer	(46,600)
Additional tax	27,960

TRANSFERS ON DEATH

Calculation of chargeable estate on death

17.14   On death, the total value of the individual's estate (after deducting allowable liabilities and funeral expenses) is chargeable to IHT [*IHTA 1984, ss 5(1)* and *172*]. See 17.14A for the treatment of liabilities.

The individual's estate also includes the value of any gifted assets over which they retained a benefit (under the so-called 'gift with reservation of benefit' or GROB rules – see 17.51 and 17.100).

Business property relief (BPR) and agricultural property relief may be available in respect of qualifying assets, and is given as a reduction against the value of the qualifying asset included in the chargeable estate on death (see 17.19).

Various exemptions may also be claimed for assets passing to a spouse, charity, etc.

The transfer on death is effectively treated as the individual's final transfer, which is equal to the value of their estate before death. The IHT payable must therefore take into account the total chargeable transfers (including PETs which crystallise on death – see 17.10 and 17.11) made within the previous seven years.

Once the deceased's available nil rate band (and, where relevant, the residential nil rate band – 'RNRB') (see 17.15A) has been used, IHT would be payable at the rate of 40%. However, the unused IHT nil rate band of a pre-deceased spouse/civil partner can also be claimed by the executors of the 'surviving' spouse/civil partner (effectively increasing the amount sheltered from IHT on the second death) (see 17.15 below). Where available, the pre-deceased spouse/civil partner's unused RNRB can also be applied (see 17.15A).

The IHT rate on the estate is reduced to 36% where (broadly) at least 10% of the 'net value' of the estate is left to charity/charities (see 17.14B).

The IHT return on death (and calculation of tax) is made by the personal representatives on form IHT 400. HMRC do not need precise asset valuations where the assets pass to an 'exempt' beneficiary, such as a surviving spouse. In most cases, a reduced IHT account can be made where the gross value of property passing to chargeable beneficiaries (together with the value of transfers made in the prior seven years) is below the nil rate band. Very small estates are exempt from making IHT returns.

Treatment of certain liabilities for IHT purposes

17.14A The taxable value of an estate, such as on death, is generally computed after deducting the individual's liabilities [*IHTA 1984, s 5(3)*]. The basic IHT rules permit liabilities to be deductible provided they are incurred for consideration in money or money's worth. Furthermore, where an asset has been used to secure a liability, the IHT rules require that the loan must be deducted against the value of the asset on which it is secured [*IHTA 1984, s 162(4)*].

However, *FA 2013* introduced various restrictions which limit the IHT deduction that can be taken for certain loans. The first two provisions state that loans financing the purchase of exempt 'excluded property' or relieved property are deducted from the value of the assets qualifying for relief. This means that, effectively, such loans would not be relievable since they would be deducted against exempt assets.

The relevant *FA 2013* restrictions are summarised below:

Liabilities attributable to financing excluded properties [*IHTA 1984, s 162A*]

Loans that have been used to finance the purchase of 'excluded property' (see 17.9A) are not deductible for IHT purposes. In effect, the loan is matched with the value of the exempt excluded property. Under this restriction, a non-domiciliary would not obtain any IHT advantage by charging UK property with a loan, and investing the loan monies overseas in acquiring non-UK situs assets (excluded property). This rule takes priority over the general provision that requires a secured loan to be deducted against the charged asset. Loans for 'the maintenance, or an enhancement, of' excluded property are also caught.

However, the rules do enable the relevant liability to be deducted against the estate where the excluded property has been disposed of (and the proceeds form part of the taxable estate) or to the extent that the loan exceeds the value of the excluded property (subject to certain conditions).

Liabilities attributable to financing certain relievable property [*IHTA 1984, s 162B*]

Restrictions apply to loans that have been used to finance the acquisition, maintenance or enhancement of property qualifying for BPR (see 17.9 (f), and 17.19), APR (see 17.9 (g) and Woodlands relief). This restriction applies to liabilities incurred after 5 April 2013.

Such liabilities must now be matched against the value of the property qualifying for BPR and APR, with the relief only being given on the 'net value' of the property. However, if the loan exceeds the value of the 'relievable' property, then the excess amount can be deducted against the value of the estate in the normal way (provided certain conditions are satisfied).

These rules will catch many innocent situations such as where a home loan has been used to finance the purchase of qualifying shares in a trading company. Such loans would now be deducted against the 'exempt' value of the shares rather than the home, and hence would not secure any reduction in the IHT liability.

The discharge of liabilities after death [*IHTA 1984, s 175A*]

As a general rule, liabilities that are not repaid on or shortly after death will not be deductible against the value of the estate. However, the legislation provides that such loans can be deducted if there is a real commercial reason for non-payment, which has not been mainly driven by obtaining a tax advantage (and assuming there are no other provisions that would apply to restrict the deduction).

HMRC has indicated that it will accept that the IHT 400 can be completed with a deduction for all liabilities. However, if a liability remains unpaid, then a corrective account must be submitted and the additional IHT paid. A key target of this rule is loans from EBTs to a deceased where an IHT deduction is claimed but there is no intention that the loan would ever be repaid.

Reduced IHT death rate to 36% for charitable bequests

17.14B The normal 40% IHT rate reduces to 36% if the net value of the estate passing to charities (including charitable trusts) is 10% or more.

For these purposes, the '10% test' for charitable legacies is computed against the 'baseline' amount [*IHTA 1984, Sch 1A*]. Broadly, this is the net estate less:

- all available reliefs and exemptions (eg spouse exemption, business property relief etc); and

- the available IHT nil rate band.

Charitable legacies etc are therefore excluded from the 'baseline' calculation.

If the total value of charitable legacies is 10% or more of the baseline amount (excluding any deduction for charitable legacies), the entire estate is taxed at 36%. In 2013/14, 9.3% of all deaths resulting in an IHT charge benefitted from the reduced 36% rate costing the exchequer some £28 million.

Where the estate consists of two or more components (ie free estate, settled property and jointly-owned property) the 10% test is calculated by reference to each component. Where the 10% test is passed for a particular component, the entire component is taxed at 36%. However, it is possible to make an election to merge these relevant components, which may be useful if a substantial amount is donated to charity from a particular component [*IHTA 1984, Sch 1A, para 7*].

Example 4

Calculation of reduced IHT liability with charitable bequests

Matt died on 20 January 2017, leaving 90% of his estate to his two daughters and the remaining 10% to Football Beyond Borders, a UK charity.

His wife died in 1988 and left all her estate to him.

His IHT-chargeable estate and the consequent IHT liability was as follows:

	£	£
Main residence (Cheadle)		2,800,000
Portfolio of listed shares		900,000
Chattels		56,000
Cash		25,000
Less: Sundry liabilities		(11,000)
Net estate		3,770,000
Less: Charity bequest – 10% × £3,770,000		(377,000)
Net taxable estate*		3,393,000
On £650,000** @ 0%		–
On £2,743,000 @ 36%		987,480
IHT liability		987,480

* Value of estate too large for residential nil rate band (see 17.15A)
** 100% of spouse's nil rate band is available since unused at her death in 1988 (see 17.15)

Therefore, Matt's two daughters would receive some £2,405,520 (£3,393,000 less IHT £987,480) and the charity would receive £377,000

Transferable nil rate band from a pre-deceased spouse

17.15   The *Finance Act 2008* enables the estate of a surviving spouse or civil partner to benefit from any unused nil rate band of their pre-deceasing spouse/civil partner [*IHTA 1984, s 8B*].

The survivor's personal representatives will normally make the formal claim for the unused nil rate band of their pre-deceasing spouse/civil partner (which is made using form IHT 402), and delivered with the form IHT 400 (see 17.14)). The claim for the unused nil rate band should be accompanied by:

- A copy of the pre-deceased's will (if any) and any deed of variation
- The death certificate
- The marriage/civil partnership certificate
- A copy of the grant of representation (or confirmation in Scotland)

HMRC appear to accept that complete information may not be available for deaths that occurred many years ago and give Inspectors some discretion in deciding whether the claim is valid (see *IHT Manual 43008*).

For deaths after 8 October 2007 (ie when the transferable nil rate band rules came into force), additional details are required to those above, including a copy of the pre-deceased's IHT 400 (previously IHT 200) or reduced account form IHT 205 (form C5 in Scotland) or full details of assets in the estate (including values) – HMRC have indicated that such information should be retained from the 'first death' and, as a practical measure, it would be sensible to keep all this information together with a copy of the survivor's will.

The date of the predeceased spouse's/civil partner's death is irrelevant, but it is necessary to calculate the amount of their nil rate band that remains unused. Thus, if all their estate previously went to the surviving spouse, then their entire nil rate band would remain unused. However, in other cases, the unused percentage of the pre-deceased's nil rate band must be determined.

The statutory calculation of the available (ie unused) nil-rate band claimable is summarised as follows:

1   The unused nil-rate band on first death

$$= M - VT$$

Where:

M = Maximum nil rate band available to pre-deceased's estate (including any additional amounts that might be claimable from any spouse/civil partner that the pre-deceased survived (on an earlier marriage or civil partnership))

VT = Value actually transferred on first death (as a chargeable transfer) or nil if no value transferred

2   Specified percentage

$$= (E\,/\,NRBMD) \times 100$$

Where:

$E = M - VT$ (ie the unused nil rate band on first death)

$NRBMD$ = Maximum nil rate band available on first death

3   Claimable nil rate band by survivor's personal representatives = Prevailing nil rate band at time of survivor's death × Specified Percentage (in 2)

The 'transferred' nil rate band of the predeceased can only be used against the IHT payable on the surviving spouse's/civil partner's death – it cannot be applied on a lifetime chargeable transfer. Thus, the transferred nil rate band may be used to shelter the IHT on the survivor's free estate (including any property treated as a gift with reservation of benefit (see 17.10) and a qualifying interest in possession held by them (ie on a pre-22 March 2006 trust – see 17.80). It can also be used against a failed PET (see 17.11), which takes priority over the IHT on the estate on death.

Example 5

Claim for pre-deceased spouse's unused nil rate band

Kathy died on 1 November 2017 leaving an estate of £1,500,000 (which did not include any residential property as she had lived in rented accommodation for many years). Her husband, Martin, had died in February 1997.

Under his will, Martin had left chargeable legacies of £30,000 to his children with the residue passing to Kathy.

Kathy's executors can claim to use Martin's unused nil rate band, which would be calculated as follows

1	*Martin's unused nil rate band*	
	M (Nil rate band at February 1997) =	£200,000
	VT (Value transferred) =	£30,000
	Therefore: M – VT =	£200,000 – £30,000
	Therefore: M – VT =	£170,000
2	*Specified percentage*	
	E = M – VT =	£170,000 (in 1 above)
	NRBMD (Maximum nil rate band in February 1997 =	£200,000
	(E/NRBMD) × 100 =	(£170,000 / £200,000) × 100
	(E/NRBMD) × 100 =	85%
3	*Claimable unused nil rate band*	
	Nil rate band in November 2017 =	£325,000
	Therefore – £325,000 × 85% =	£276,250

Kathy's executor's can therefore claim Martin's unused nil rate band of £276,250 to use against Kathy's chargeable estate (as well her own nil rate band).

Note: If Martin had not made any chargeable legacies, the executors would have been able to claim an additional £325,000 instead (ie 100% of the 'November 2017' nil rate band).

Residential nil rate band (RNRB)

Background

17.15A An individual's default residential nil-rate band (RNRB) consists of their personal RNRB (claimed on IHT form 435) plus any unused RNRB transferred from a pre-deceased spouse/civil partner (claimed on IHT form 436).

The RNRB applies when a residence is passed *on death* to an individual's lineal descendants after 5 April 2017 – the legislation refers to this as 'closely inherited'. The maximum amount available to each individual is being phased in as follows:

	RNRB
	£
6 April 2017 – 5 April 2018	100,000
6 April 2018 – 5 April 2019	125,000
6 April 2019 – 5 April 2020	150,000
6 April 2020 – 5 April 2021	175,000

Thereafter the relief will increase in accordance with the CPI.

The amount of the RNRB is limited by reference to the value of the residence (net of any mortgage charged on it) that is 'closely inherited'.

In addition, any unused RNRB can be transferred to the deceased's spouse or civil partner's estate. This can also be done where a surviving spouse/civil partner died before 6 April 2017, even though the additional threshold wasn't available at that time!

In the case of deaths before 6 April 2017, the 'transferable RNRB' available to the surviving spouse or civil partner is set at £100,000 (subject to any taper restriction). As with the transferable nil rate band, there may be practical difficulties in finding the relevant information where the death occurred many years ago. To ensure the RNRB relief is closely targeted, it is tapered where the net estate value (after deducting any liabilities but *before* any reliefs and exemptions such *as the spouse exemption and APR/BPR*) is above £2 million.

The RNRB is tapered at the rate of £1 for every £2 that the net estate exceeds £2 million *(IHTA 1984, s 8D(g))* – see 17.53.

Since the chargeable estate is a snapshot at death, it is possible for it to be reduced by lifetime gifts (including death bed gifts) to reduce or prevent the impact of the taper rules.

Example 6

Calculating the 'tapered' RNRB

Dylan (single) died on 18 April 2017 with a net estate (before IHT exemptions and reliefs) of £2,100,000, made up as follows:

	£
Main residence	850,000
38 shares in Tombides Ltd	1,200,000
50% share in farming partnership (land etc)	300,000
Total assets	2,350,000
Less: Mortgage	(250,000)
Net estate before reliefs	£2,100,000

	£
Maximum RNRB	100,000
Less: Taper reduction (1/2 × (£2,100,000 less £2,000,000)	(50,000)
Available RNRB	50,000

Key conditions

17.15B The RNRB can be claimed where:

- an individual's estate includes a qualifying residence (or a qualifying residential interest); and

- some or all of that property is 'closely' inherited (whether effected by will, under intestacy rules or otherwise).

A 'qualifying residential interest' represents an indivdual's interest in a dwelling-house that was their residence *at some point in time*. It is not therefore necessary for the house to be their residence throughout ownership! The value of the garden or grounds is also included as part of the residence without any area restriction.

The RNRB relief is limited to a single dwelling house. Where the estate includes more than one dwelling house, the personal representatives can elect to select which residential property is the deceased's qualifying residential interest.

Furthermore, the residence must be included in the estate immediately before death *(IHTA 1984, s 8H)*. However, in certain cases, the RNRB may be obtained under the 'downsizing' rules (see 17.15C).

For these purposes, residential property is treated as 'closely inherited' where it is passed on to a child, grandchild and other direct lineal descendant (including step children, adopted children (treated as children of both the natural parent and adoptive parent) and foster children etc) or spouses and civil partners *of the children*. It follows that taxpayers who have no children cannot benefit from a RNRB.

The RNRB may also be used against property that is included in the deceased's estate as a result of the gift with reservation of benefit rules (see 17.10A) provided the donee of the gift is a 'lineal descendant' of the donor.

Certain interest in possession trusts may also qualify but transfers to discretionary trusts will not meet this requirement (even where the only beneficiaries' are the settlor's children). Nevertheless, if an appointment is made from the trust to a qualifying beneficiary within two years under *IHTA 1984, s 144*, relief is available (see 17.48) (see *IHTA 1984, s 8K* for detailed definitions*)*.

Detailed rules are included at *IHTA 1984, s 8G* for calculating the amount of the RNRB which can be transferred to a person's estate from their deceased spouse's or civil partner's estate.

If the value of the residence exceeds the value of the chargeable net estate for IHT (typically, where there is substantial borrowing), the RNRB is restricted to the value of the net estate.

The RNRB is not set against the residence but is given in calculating the charge on the estate. These provisions clearly need to be considered when drafting wills and reviewing existing wills.

Example 7

Computing the RNRB

Karen's husband died in 2015 leaving his entire estate to her. Karen dies in January 2018 and the value of her estate was £1.5 million. This includes her residential property, which was valued at £1 million, which she leaves to her daughter. The residue passes to her sister,

Karen also made a PET to her sister of £650,000 in 2016.

On Karen's death in January 2018, her IHT position is as follows:

- Her nil rate band of £325,000 is first set-off against the failed PET, leaving £325,000 chargeable to IHT.

- Her husband's unused nil rate band can be claimed and used to offset the balance of the failed PET (see 17.15).

- Karen's total available RNRB in 2017/18 is £200,000 (being £100,000 for her and £100,000 from her deceased husband).

Based on the above, Karen's IHT liability is £520,000, calculated as follows:

	£
Total assets	1,500,000
Less: RNRB	(200,000)
Chargeable estate	1,300,000
IHT @ 40%	520,000

Downsizing relief

17.15C So as not to deter the sale of residential property in later years – for example, as a result of downsizing or selling the property to move into residential care, the *FA 2016* introduces an additional strand to the RNRB. Pre-death gifts of the residence will also qualify for the relief, with the value of the property being used at the date of the gift.

Broadly, the downsizing RNRB is available for deaths after 5 April 2017 but applies for property sales/gifts taking place after 7 July 2016.

However, the 'downsizing' RNRB is only available where the RNRB requirements would be met apart from the fact that the residence ceased to be owned before death. There is also the important requirement that the proceeds from the sale of the residence are 'closely inherited' as described in 17.5B above.

17.15D Conceptually, the amount of the 'downsizing RNRB' is intended to equate to the RNRB that would have been available had the former home remained in the estate. In straightforward cases (where there is no home in the estate on death), the calculation of the 'downsizing RNRB' is made as follows:

Step 1	Compute the maximum RNRB that would be available when the former home was sold = Max RNRB at disposal date (£100,000 if this was before 6 April 2017) plus any transferred RNRB at the date of death.
Step 2	Work out relevant percentage = Value of former home (when sold)/Maximum RNRB (at step 1) × 100 *However, the relevant percentage cannot exceed 100%.* If value of former home is less than maximum RNRB, the relevant percentage will be less than 100%
Step 3	Multiply the RNRB at the date of death by the relevant percentage

Although the principles are reasonably clear, the practicalities of the legislation and the calculations involved can be challenging! See the worked examples from HMRC's Guidance at www.gov.uk/government/case-studies/inheritance-tax-residence-nil-rate-band-case-studies.

The 'downsizing' legislation is very complex but the relief should be available in most straightforward cases. Taxpayers who have no children cannot benefit from a RNRB.

Example 8

Using 'downsizing' relief for RNRB

Arthur is 82 years old and was widowed in 2001. His wife left Arthur her entire estate, including a half-share of the marital home

Unfortunately, Arthur began to experience mobility problems. He therefore decides to sell his house in early October 2016 for £450,000 and moves into sheltered accommodation in time for Christmas.

Arthur dies in May 2017 and leaves his entire estate of £1.2 million to his two children.

Although Arthur did not own his residence when he died, his personal representatives can claim the 'downsizing' RNRB because

- he died after 5 April 2017;

- the residence was sold after 7 July 2016;

- the residence would have otherwise qualified for the RNRB were it not sold before Arthur's death; and the cash proceeds of the sale are in Arthur's estate on death and they will be gifted to his children.

Arthur's personal representatives will therefore be able to claim the RNRB of £100,000 plus a further RNRB of £100,000 that was not used by his deceased spouse. (Since the value of the Arthur's former home exceeded the maximum RNRB at the date of disposal, the relevant percentage is 100% (see 17.15D). The RNRB at the date of death is £100,000 × 100% = £100,000)

The personal representatives can also claim his wife's unused nil-rate band (see 17.5).

Business property relief (BPR)

17.16 If the shareholder retains all or some of their shareholding until death, the shares would normally be excluded from their chargeable estate due to the availability of 100% business property relief (BPR) (see 17.19 to 17.34 for detailed coverage). This relief is sometimes referred to as 'Business relief'. The shares should always be specifically transferred under the will (otherwise the benefit of the BPR reduction in IHT would effectively be spread across the entire estate).

The prospect of obtaining 100% BPR from IHT combined with a tax-free uplift in base value for CGT purposes will often discourage the controlling shareholder from transferring their shares before death. Given the controlling shareholder's natural reluctance to give up his shares, this stance is understandable. Clearly, it is not possible to 'guarantee' that the 100% BPR will be available and/or subject to the same conditions on the owner manager's death.

Valuation of shares

17.17 It is important to appreciate that, for CGT purposes, the shares will effectively be rebased to their market value at the date of death [*TCGA 1992, s 62*]. Consequently, any capital gain in the shares will be 'washed out' on death; similarly there will be no relief for any loss.

The value 'ascertained' for IHT purposes on death would usually be taken as the CGT base value [*TCGA 1992, s 274*]. However, the related property rules (see 17.8) may therefore apply to give a higher base value for IHT purposes. See Chapter 14 for detailed commentary on fiscal share valuations (especially 14.32–14.39 and 14.49–14.62).

In a large number of cases, the shares would be completely exempt from IHT due to the availability of 100% BPR or otherwise. In such cases, the valuation of the shares would not need to be 'ascertained' for IHT. This means that the value for the shares cannot be agreed until a subsequent disposal takes place. Furthermore, HMRC – Shares Valuation are then likely to take the view that the shares should be valued in isolation under the normal CGT rules in *TCGA 1992, s 272*, without regard to related property (*HMRC Interpretations, RI110 (April 1995) Inheritance Tax – valuation of assets at the date of death*).

Deeds of Variation

17.18   In broad terms, a Deed of Variation (DOV) is a formal written instruction from a beneficiary to the personal representatives, to redirect property passing to them under a will/intestacy to another. Jointly-owned assets passing by survivorship can also be redirected under a DOV.

A DOV is therefore a gift and under general IHT principles this would be treated as a 'transfer of value' by the original 'transferor' beneficiary (or beneficiaries). However, *IHTA 1984, s 142(1)* provides that the assets redirected under the DOV are instead treated as made by the deceased for all IHT purposes (as opposed to a transfer of value by the beneficiary or beneficiaries).

The parties to the DOV must include the original beneficiary (including anyone disadvantaged by the variation) and the personal representatives, where the variation leads to an IHT liability/increase in an IHT liability. Although there is no requirement for any new beneficiaries to be party to the DOV, it is usual to make them party to the DOV by confirming acceptance of the gift. Similarly, where a DOV is used to create a new trust, the trustees are normally invited to join in to confirm their acceptance of the trust.

The favourable IHT treatment of a DOV is only available where the conditions in *IHTA 1984, s 142(2)* are satisfied. The variation must be in writing and there must be no consideration given between the parties (other than the surrender of benefit by the original beneficiary/beneficiaries). It is therefore important to ensure that legal costs involved in the drafting and implementation must be borne by the original beneficiary/beneficiaries. Furthermore, there must be no 'reciprocal arrangements' between the parties so that any benefit flowing from the DOV subsequently passes back to the original beneficiary/beneficiaries under some other arrangements.

The DOV is only effective if it is made within two years of the date of death and it must contain an irrevocable statement by the parties whose interests are varied that they intend the variation to have that effect [*IHTA 1984, s 142(1)*]. The personal representatives' consent is also required where additional IHT is payable.

The importance of correctly drafting the DOV was evidenced in the recent case of *Vaughan-Jones & Anor v Vaughan-Jones & Ors* [2015] EWHC 1086. The claimants were seeking to rectify the original DOV as it did *not* include the relevant statements to take advantage of the IHT and CGT benefits and was therefore ineffective for tax purposes. The judge held that there was strong evidence to suggest that the omission of the statement for IHT purposes was a 'mistake' and granted the rectification. However, based on the available evidence, he was *not* convinced that there was any relevant intention to include a statement for CGT purposes. Consequently he denied the rectification for CGT purposes.

A DOV can be beneficial in a number of situations. For example, a DOV may be used to ensure that ensure that maximum benefit is taken of the deceased's nil rate band or perhaps enabling BPR to be claimed on shares that would otherwise have passed to the surviving spouse. In many cases, this might be achieved by redirecting the relevant assets to a discretionary trust.

Similar beneficial treatment applies for CGT purposes [*TCGA 1992, s 62*], although it is not necessary to invoke both relieving provisions. However, since 6 April 2006 special deeming rules operate for CGT (and income tax) purposes where property becomes held on trust as a result of a DOV. In such cases, the person 'giving-up' their entitlement as legatee, etc is treated as providing the property for the trust. However, where the property was already comprised in a trust under the will and the DOV redirects it into another trust, then the deceased is treated as the settlor [*TCGA 1992, s 68C*]. This follows the previous treatment that applied for CGT, based on the ruling in *Marshall v Kerr* [1994] STC 638.

BUSINESS PROPERTY RELIEF (BPR) FOR THE FAMILY OR OWNER-MANAGED COMPANY

Rationale for BPR

17.19 Business Property Relief (BPR) (sometimes now also referred to as Business relief) was introduced by the *FA 1976*. At that time, the primary aim of the relief was to ensure that, on the death of the owner-manager, the business could continue within the family without having to be sold or broken-up to fund the IHT liability. Since then, there is general acceptance that BPR encourages investment in risky trading businesses.

Over time, BPR has extended to a wider range of business assets, including minority shareholdings in trading companies.

However, there is a growing feeling that the generous BPR is being exploited, perhaps as a result of its relatively generous qualifying rules. HMRC is about to conduct a review of BPR and this should be factored into current planning considerations.

100% relief for qualifying shareholdings

17.19A 100% BPR applies to all unquoted shareholdings (including non-voting ordinary or preference shares) in trading companies. (Shares in AIM companies are 'unquoted' for this purpose and hence qualify for 100% BPR). Qualifying shareholdings are completely exempt from IHT, both on a lifetime transfer and on death. BPR operates by reducing the value transferred – in this case to nil [*IHTA 1984, s 104(1)*].

The relevant shareholding must be held for at least two years prior to the transfer/death to qualify for the relief [*IHTA 1984, ss 106, 107*]. Where shares are acquired on the death (as opposed to a lifetime transfer) of a spouse, their period of ownership also counts towards the two-year minimum ownership period [*IHTA 1984, s 108(b)*]. Where the two-year period is not satisfied, relief may still be available under the special rules for replacement business property [*IHTA 1984, s 107*], or successive transfers made within two years [*IHTA 1984, s 109*].

BPR is available to both working and passive shareholders – it is not necessary for the shareholder to be a director or work full time in the business (for further potential restrictions, see 17.25–17.34).

Securities in unquoted trading companies may also qualify for 100% relief, provided the special 'control' conditions in [*IHTA 1994, s 105(1)(b)*] are satisfied.

It may be possible to defer any IHT liability on shares that do not qualify for 100% BPR (for example, shares in a family investment company) and certain other assets by electing to pay it over ten years in equal instalments (see 17.98, Example 17). The IHT can be deferred on an interest-free basis for most business assets (see *IHTA 1984, ss 227, 228, 233* and *234* for detailed conditions).

50% relief for business property owned by a controlling shareholder

17.20   Where the owner-manager personally holds property or plant and machinery outside the company which are used in the company's trade, then BPR of 50% should be available on these assets on a chargeable lifetime transfer or on death (see also 17.106). However, the shareholder only qualifies for this relief if they control the company. For these purposes, related property, such as shares held by a spouse (see 17.8), is also taken into account in determining whether the transferor has the necessary control.

The Special Commissioners' decision in *Walkers Executors v CIR* [2001] STC (SCD) 86 may be helpful in cases where only 50% of the shares are held. In this case, the shareholder was chairman of the board of directors and beneficially owned only 50% of the company's ordinary shares. Under the company's Articles of Association, the chairman was entitled to a casting vote at a general meeting of the shareholders. The combination of the 50% shareholding and the casting vote was held to be sufficient to secure control and thus 50% BPR was given on property owned by the (deceased) shareholder which had been used in the company's business. The *Companies (Model Articles) Regulations 2008* (which apply to private and public companies incorporated on or after 1 October

2009) are likely to provide for a chairman to be appointed and for them to have a casting vote. However, relief may not be secured in those cases which provide for a 'rotation' of the casting vote, as the chairman may die at the 'wrong' time!

Loan accounts

17.21 Family and owner-managed companies are often financed by loans from shareholders (which can be repaid more readily). However, loans, debts, directors' current account balances, etc do not qualify for BPR. In appropriate circumstances, it may therefore be beneficial to 'capitalise' such loans as preference or ordinary shares, taking care that the rights, etc attaching to the new shares do not create any unintended shift in the balance between the company's existing shareholdings.

Planning with rights issues of shares

17.22 In appropriate cases, a rights issue of shares can be used to access BPR where an owner manager personally holds substantial cash but is unlikely to meet the two year BPR ownership period before death – ie they are in 'poor health' and unlikely to live very long.

Such planning relies on the special rules in *IHTA 1984, s 107(4)*, which provide that unlisted shares which are 'acquired' under a CGT reorganisation within *TCGA 1992, ss 126–136* (such as on a rights issue) are identified with shares already held by the owner manager. Thus, a right issue of shares would be treated as held for the same period as the owner-manager's existing shares. These 'new' shares would therefore invariably qualify for BPR immediately after they were issued (since they would be deemed to have satisfied the 'two year ownership' test).

An attempt to use this type of planning failed in *The Executors of Mrs Mary Dugan-Chapman & Anor v HMRC* [2008] SpC 666. However, this was only because of a failure to implement the rights issue correctly, which requires an offer to all the company's shareholders in proportion to their existing shareholdings.

In this case, Mrs Chapman, who was recently widowed and had failing health, was advised by Counsel to capitalise her £300,000 loan account by subscribing for further shares under a rights issue in the family trading company. HMRC accepted that BPR was available on these 300,000 £1 shares. However, documentation was prepared for a further share subscription of £1,000,000 by Mrs Chapman. She subscribed for the shares (through an attorney) but died two days later. However, because there was no offer to the other shareholders at the time of this subscription, it was *not* a rights issue. Consequently, since the shares did not fall within the special provisions in *IHTA 1984, s 107(4)*, the Special Commissioner held that BPR was not available on Mrs Chapman's subsequent £1,000,000 share subscription. Following this decision, the

'Chapman family' took a successful negligence claim against the lawyers on the grounds that, had the planning been executed properly, BPR would have been available (see *Vinton v Fladgate Fielder* [2010] EWHC 904 (Ch)).

BPR on a PET of shares becoming chargeable

17.23   Where a PET of shares (see 17.10) becomes chargeable on the donor's death (within seven years of the gift), BPR will only be available on the 'failed PET' if the *donee* has retained the shares until the donor's death and the shares still qualify for relief at that point [*IHTA 1984, s 113A*].

Binding contract for sale of shares

17.24   No BPR is available if a binding contract for the sale of the relevant business property has been entered into at the date of transfer (*IHTA 1984, s 113*).

The question of whether a 'binding contract for sale' exists at the date of the relevant transfer is a question of fact, which will be determined by the precise circumstances of each case. Private company shareholders should therefore be aware of agreements which require their executors to sell their shares to the remaining shareholders if they die before retirement. This is fatal as HMRC regard this as a binding contract for sale and therefore deny BPR (SP12/80).

The basic rationale behind this rule is to prevent the transferor from obtaining BPR where they enter into a binding agreement to sell their relevant business property and then make an immediate transfer of it. In effect, the transfer becomes one of all or part of the proceeds of sale.

HMRC will look very carefully at the availability of BPR in cases where an actual sale or flotation of a company takes place shortly after a transfer of the shares.

No BPR restriction applies where the business (or interest in a business) is sold to a company wholly or mainly in exchange for shares *or* the sale is part of a reconstruction or amalgamation transaction.

The 'binding contract for sale' restriction may (exceptionally) catch certain buy and sell agreements which are sometimes entered into by shareholder-directors of owner managed companies. Typically, these agreements are triggered where one of the shareholders dies before retirement and gives the surviving shareholders the right to purchase the deceased shareholder's shares (from funds provided by life assurance policies).

17.25   In most cases, if the company's articles simply require the personal representatives of the deceased shareholder to *offer* to sell the shares back to the company or other shareholders (without any legal obligation by them to purchase the shares), this will not constitute a binding contract for sale. On the other hand, such agreements will cause BPR to be denied where the deceased's shares pass to their personal representatives and

- the personal representatives are required to sell the shares to the other shareholders; and

- the other shareholders must buy them (SP12/80).

In practice, the potential denial of BPR is normally avoided by using 'put and call' options (see 17.37 and 17.51) which give the deceased's personal representatives an *option* to sell the deceased's shares and the remaining shareholders (or the company) the *option* to buy the same shares (out of the proceeds of an appropriate life insurance policy – see 17.37). Either party can, therefore, ensure that the shares are transferred without the risk of losing BPR (as there is no binding contract for sale). From a CGT perspective, it may be desirable to have successive (and different) exercise periods for the put and the call option.

BPR QUALIFICATION ISSUES AND TESTS

Qualifying and non-qualifying activities

17.26 BPR relief is primarily focused on trading companies and groups. However, the statutory qualification for BPR is framed in a 'negative' way.

Broadly, as far as companies are concerned, 100% BPR is available on any shareholding provided the company's business does not consist *wholly or mainly* of;

- dealing in shares and securities or land and buildings: or

- making or holding investments (subject to very limited exceptions) [*IHTA 1984, s 105(3)*].

For these purposes, 'mainly' is taken to mean more than 50% (see 17.27). Its worth noting that this is increasingly being seen by HMRC as being generous compared to the more stringent '80%' test that applies for entrepreneurs' relief (see 15.40 and 15.41).

However, shares do not rank for BPR where a company's business consists wholly or mainly of dealing in securities, stocks, shares, or land or buildings. On the other hand, property development should qualify as a trading activity (see 17.30).

BPR is therefore determined on an 'all or nothing' basis, which means that the relevant shares either fully qualify or they do not. Relief will therefore be completely denied if the company is an 'investment company', which wholly or mainly makes or holds investments, even if it carries on a 'small' trade

[*IHTA 1984, s 105(3)*]. Similarly, it is possible for shares to qualify for 100% BPR in full where the company is predominantly trading even though it also carries on (say) a modest property rental business (subject to any reduction for 'excepted assets' – see 17.33).

The exclusion for 'investment companies' does not apply to qualifying holding companies (see 17.29).

It is important to remember that BPR is available if the company carries on a qualifying business which has a wider meaning than trade. This point was applied successfully by the taxpayer in Phillips and others (*Executors of Rhoda Phillips Deceased) v HMRC* [2006] STC (SCD) 639 where HMRC had argued that the shares in a company that made loans to other family companies did not qualify for BPR. This was on the basis that the company's business was that of 'making or holding investments' under *IHTA 1984, s 105(3)*. However, the Special Commissioner took the view that the company did not make or hold investments. He decided that BPR was available since the company was '… in the business of making loans and not in the business of investing in loans'. The loans were therefore a finance facility (money lending) rather than investments.

Various problems can arise in practice, for instance, with companies which carry on qualifying and non-qualifying activities, for example, a company which builds houses and receives rental income from a number of properties. The various caravan park and other property letting cases heard by the Special Commissioners in recent years show that the question of determining whether a business consists mainly in the making of investments is not always an easy one to decide (see 17.31).

The BPR regime does not contain any territorial limitation. Thus, for example, where

- an owner managed company opens up a branch in an overseas location through which it carries on a business there, or

- sets-up an overseas 'trading' company (as a fellow-group company);

these will be treated as qualifying business activities for BPR purposes.

100% BPR can also be claimed on shares directly held in an overseas-registered and/or overseas resident company.

BPR will not be available if a company is in liquidation at the relevant time, except where the company is being wound-up for the purposes of a reconstruction under which the trade or businesses are continuing [*IHTA 1984, s 105(5)*] (see 13.63).

Applying the 'mainly' test to 'mixed businesses'

17.27 HMRC's Capital Tax Office (CTO) generally look at the relevant turnover, profit and underlying net asset values for each activity and 'mainly' is interpreted for this purpose as being over 50%. HMRC Shares and Assets Valuation Manual para 111150 indicates that the preponderant activities of the business, its assets and sources of income and gains, will be reviewed over a reasonable period before the relevant transfer. The fact that the business profits have been assessed as trading income is not determinative of, or even relevant to, this point (see *Furness v CIR* [1999] STC (SCD) 232).

The issue of whether an 'investment' business is carried on is a question of fact and degree, to be determined by reference to the specific features of each case. Although the activities of the business should be tested at the date of the transfer/death, the courts and HMRC tend to look at the position that has been established over the most recent years.

In this context, the important ruling in *Farmer (executors of Farmer deceased) v CIR* [1999] STC (SCD) 321 may be particularly helpful. In Farmer a large part of the business comprised lettings of farm buildings (22 tenancies) and static caravans. The capital employed in the letting business was £1.25 million compared to £2.25 million on the rest of the farm, although the rents received exceeded the farming profits. The Special Commissioner found that a wide variety of factors should be examined over a period of several years, including time employed on managing the various activities (divisions), turnover, expenditure, levels of staffing, and capital employed together with profits earned. Having regard to all the criteria, it was then 'necessary to stand back and consider in the round whether the business consisted mainly of making or holding investments'. Based on this, it was held that all the evidence supported the conclusion that the business consisted 'mainly of farming'. The fact that the letting activity was more profitable than the rest of the business was not conclusive.

The approach in *Farmer* was followed by the Court of Appeal in the leading case of *CIR v George* [2004] STC 147, which involved a caravan park operator. The main activities included providing pitches for 'residential caravans, utility services, the sale and storage of caravans, and the provision of a club/bar (open to all). However, it was concluded that the business should be viewed in 'in the round'- it was an active family business and the holding of investments was only one component of it. Thus, the business was not mainly that of making or holding investments.

Lessons from the *Brander* case

17.27A The principles in the *Farmer* case were followed in the subsequent case of *HMRC v Brander (Executor of the Will of the late Fourth Earl of Balfour)* [2010] All ER (D) 94 (also referred to as the *Balfour* case). This case involved a BPR claim for the 'mixed' business of a traditional Scottish landed estate. The estate's activities consisted of agricultural operations (both occupied and let farmland), woodland, forestry management, related sporting interests, and the letting of cottages and other estate properties to estate workers or others.

Having decided that the estate carried on one composite business, the main point at issue was whether the business was 'wholly or mainly the holding of investments', which would lead to a complete denial of the 100% BPR claim.

A summary of the key financial data considered by the Upper Tribunal in its assessment of the BPR status of the trade is shown below:

	Turnover		Net profit		Time spent	
Year	*Trading*	*Letting*	*Trading*	*Letting*	*Trading*	*Letting*
	£000	**£000**	**£000**	**£000**	*%*	*%*
1996	166	47	39	2		
1997	185	56	50	1		
1998	124	58	23	10		
1999	142	68	23	21		
2000	122	67	–16	31		
2001	120	82	11	8		
2002	102	95	26	–22	79%	21%
to Nov 2002	119	96	14	43	78%	22%

The Upper Tribunal helpfully summarised the relevant case law on determining whether a 'mixed' business activity was 'wholly or mainly involved in the making of or holding of investments'. The key points were as follows:

- The 'intelligent businessman test' should be applied to determine whether the business (mainly) consisted of the holding of investments, which looked at the uses to which the assets of the business were put and the way they were 'turned to account'.

- The question of whether the business was 'wholly or mainly the holding of investments' was entirely a 'question of fact'.

- It was necessary to look at the business 'in the round' (as decided in the earlier *Farmer* case – see 17.27 above). This entailed looking at the overall picture and the relative importance of investment and trading activities, which should be considered over a period of time.

Based on all the evidence and, despite the fact that the capital value of the let properties exceeded the value of the other properties (in the ratio of 1.88 to 1) at the date of death, Judge Reid concluded that the business was *not* mainly the holding of investments. Consequently, the entire estate was entitled to the BPR exemption.

If the *predominant* activity is qualifying, then BPR is given on the *entire value* of the company's shares, subject to any restriction for 'excepted assets' (see 17.33). Where the company predominantly carries on a non-qualifying activity (for example, property letting), no BPR is given, ie it is an 'all or nothing' test.

HMRC informal clearance procedure for BPR

17.28 HMRC operate a non-statutory clearance procedure which enables business owners to obtain confirmation that their shares will qualify for BPR before (or after) making a transfer of value. When applying for clearance, owner-managers must demonstrate the commercial significance of the transaction in relation to the business itself and the material uncertainty over the application of the BPR exemption. HMRC will not consider 'hypothetical cases' – ie a commercially significant transfer must be contemplated and there must be a potential IHT charge (in the absence of BPR). HMRC will endeavour to reply within 28 days. To assist in making a clearance application, HMRC provide a very helpful checklist (which is available on their website at www.gov.uk/government/uploads/system/uploads/attachment_data/file/377648/annex-c.pdf).

Informal clearances on a company's BPR status will generally remain valid for a limited period of six months. HMRC have given assurance that it will consider itself bound by the advice given where the taxpayer reasonably relies on the advice, having fully disclosed all relevant facts.

'Qualifying' holding companies

17.29 Group holding companies can often benefit from the protection of the 'holding company' exception in *IHTA 1984, s 105(4)(b)*. Holding companies and subsidiaries are as defined in the *Companies Act 2006* [*IHTA 1984, s 103(2)*].

Broadly speaking, a holding company would either be:

- a member of the subsidiary and be able to control its board of directors; or

- hold more than 50% of its equity share capital.

Whilst holding companies generally make and hold investments, the BPR prohibition does not apply where the relevant company's business is wholly or mainly acting as the holding company of one or more subsidiaries whose business is not an excluded one (broadly an investment business). In essence, the test is that the group must be mainly carrying on trading activities.

Thus, it is possible for shares in a holding company to qualify for BPR, even if it holds shares in some 'investment' subsidiaries. However, when calculating the amount of the transferor's BPR, the value of any 'investment' subsidiary must be excluded from the value of the holding company's shares – effectively reducing the value qualifying for relief. In such cases, it might be possible to improve the BPR position by transferring an investment business to another group company without disturbing the qualifying 'trading' or 'holding' company status of the recipient group company. For example, if it can be shown that a company is mainly a trading company, any 'secondary' investment business activity/assets will also effectively qualify for BPR.

17.29A A subsidiary will *not* be denied relief as an 'investment' subsidiary if its business consists 'wholly or mainly' in the holding of land or buildings wholly or mainly occupied by another group 'trading' company (*IHTA 1984, s 111(2)(b)*). However, on a strict reading of legislation, this exemption does not apply where the relevant property is held by the ultimate holding company (as opposed to a subsidiary). However, there is anecdotal evidence to suggest that HMRC do not take this point in practice, since it is generally accepted as an anomaly in the law. The counter argument would that the holding company holds the properties to facilitate the trade in other parts of the group. Furthermore, HMRC's confirmation with regard to the treatment of intra-group loans made by a holding company would appear to support this approach.

Furthermore, an asset held by one group company is not counted as an 'excepted asset' (see 17.33) if it is used or is required for the current *or* future purposes of a business carried on by another group 'trading' company (*IHTA 1984, s 112*)

As well as holding shares in its subsidiaries, a holding company's business may include the provision of loans and other finance to its subsidiaries. HMRC has confirmed that intra-group loans used by subsidiaries for trading purposes would generally be allowable (see correspondence between HMRC and CIOT in December 2010/January 2011).

Example 9

BPR on holding company structures

(a)   Structure 1

Shareholders

BONDS HOLDINGS LTD

100%

BILLY LTD
Trading company

100% BPR should be available to the individual shareholders of Bonds Holdings Ltd since it is a qualifying holding company within *IHTA 1984, s 105 (4)(b)* (ie its business is a holding company of (at least) one 'trading' subsidiary (Billy Ltd)).

(b) Structure 2

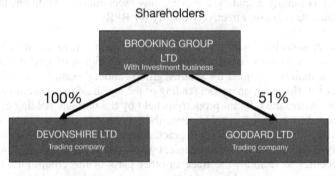

Brooking Group Ltd carries on an investment business and holds shares in two trading subsidiaries (Devonshire Ltd and Goddard Ltd).

The individual shareholders of Brooking Group Ltd should qualify for BPR since the company appears to be *mainly* a qualifying holding company within *IHTA 1984, s 105 (4)(b)*. This should be the case where the combined value of its trading subsidiaries effectively exceeds the value of the investment business operated within Brooking Group Ltd itself. The value of the investment business is effectively sheltered by BPR and there is no *IHTA 1984, s 111* restriction (since the investment business is *not* within a subsidiary).

(c) Structure 3

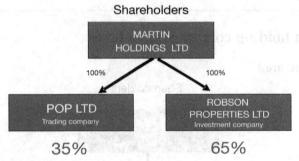

Based on the values of the underlying subsidiaries (Pop Ltd and Robson Properties Ltd), Martin Holdings Ltd is mainly carrying the business of holding shares in investment (as opposed to trading) subsidiaries. Thus, on the facts, Martin Holdings Ltd appears to be *mainly* an investment company (rather than a holding company of a 'trading group').

The shareholders of Martin Holdings Ltd would not qualify for any BPR (even on the 'trading' element within the group).

However, the BPR position for the shareholders might be improved by using a *IA 1986, s 110* reconstruction or 'capital reduction' demerger to separate the trading and investment activities so that they are held separately by the shareholders (through two new companies) (see 13.57A and 13.98). BPR would then be available on the 'trading' element within Pop Ltd).

Property development companies

17.30   Some BPR claims for 'property development' company shares may give rise to difficulties, largely due to the often blurred distinction between 'non-eligible' dealing (see 17.26) and 'eligible' development activities. As a general rule, development involves changing the character of the land or changing/improving a building – but sometimes it is difficult to determine how much work is required for it to be treated as 'development'. Sometimes land acquired with the object of development may have to be sold on due to planning difficulties, but this does not necessarily mean property dealing, especially if the business clearly carries on other development work/activities.

In the current economic climate many property development companies may have to temporarily let property that was originally intended for development. The existence of rental income does not necessarily point towards an 'investment' activity as demonstrated in *DWC Piercy's Executors v HMRC* (2008) SpC 687. The Special Commissioner had to determine whether a company qualified for BPR (or whether it was mainly holding or making investments). HMRC had denied BPR as the company received substantial amounts of rental income from its retained land bank and it was therefore considered to be carrying on the business of making or holding investments.

Historically the company had developed and sold 256 flats but then switched to small community shopping centre developments. One particular development ran into difficulty regarding planning permission due to uncertainties regarding a rail-link. It was therefore forced to build some short term industrial workshops with the intention of replacing these when residential development became feasible. It was held that the land still continued to be held as trading stock (even though it produced a rental income) and there was nothing to demonstrate that it had been appropriated as an investment. The company's shares therefore qualified for BPR.

Furnished holiday lettings

17.31   Until the recent Upper-Tier Tribunal ruling in *HMRC v Pawson* [2013] UKUT 050 (TCC), the general view was that where services such as cleaning, laundry and gardening were being provided, a furnished holiday letting business would qualify for BPR.

However, the ruling in *Pawson* means that furnished holiday lettings are unlikely to qualify for BPR especially where the business consists of a single property unless a comprehensive range of services are provided. In arriving at his decision in this case, Mr Justice Henderson held that:

- in any 'normal' case, even an actively managed property letting business would be considered as an 'investment' business, which should not qualify for BPR; and

- there is no reason to consider that a furnished holiday letting business should be given any peculiar treatment in this context.

Permission to appeal the decision was denied on paper by Lord Justice Lloyd on 23 May 2013.

HMRC has also reconsidered its approach to cases involving holiday lettings. In particular, HMRC will be looking more closely at the level and type of services, rather than who provided them, in order to determine whether the property qualifies for BPR. Inspectors are now likely to refer any BPR claim on a holiday let to the HMRC Appeals Team for consideration.

This approach is further evidenced in *Green v HMRC* [2015] UKFTT 334 (TC). Once again, 100% BPR was denied on the grounds that the holiday letting business consisted mainly of the making or holding of investments. The taxpayer argued that a significant amount of work was involved in running a furnished holiday lettings business and put forward some strong economic business arguments (relating to comparative yields from standard property lettings and furnished holiday lettings). However, the tribunal agreed with HMRC that the work mainly represented tasks that were associated with the maintenance and upkeep of the property. Consequently, apart from a few services (eg cleaning, the welcome pack, the provision of WiFi, linen, towels, and so on) the business was 'mainly' one of holding the property as an investment.

Decided cases on investment businesses

17.32 The following activities have *not* qualified for BPR on the grounds that they (mainly) constituted 'investment' businesses:

- letting of industrial units on three-year leases (*Martin (executors of Moore, deceased) v CIR* [1995] STC (SCD) 5);

- letting furnished flats on assured shorthold tenancies (*Burkinyoung (executor of Burkinyoung, deceased) v CIR* [1995] STC (SCD) 29);

- owning and managing a caravan park, including the receipt of pitch fees for caravans – from short and long-term residents – and letting of chalets

(*Hall (executors of Hall, deceased) v CIR* [1997] STC (SCD) 126; *Powell (personal representatives of Pearce, deceased) v CIR* [1997] STC (SCD) 181; and *Weston (executor of Weston, deceased) v CIR* [2000] STC (SCD) 30).

- An office block that was actively managed by the trustee landlord, which provided such services as a mail room, porter service, internet, cleaning and 24-hour security. BPR relief was denied for the purposes of computing the ten-year anniversary charge (*Trustees of David Zetland Settlement v HMRC* [2013] UK FTT 284 (TC)).

- A furnished holiday letting, that provided minimal services (cleaning between lettings, telephone, television, and regular inspection by the cleaner/caretaker), was denied BPR – (*HMRC v Pawson* [2013] UKUT 050 (TCC) (see 17.31).

- An eight-acre industrial estate owned and managed by a company was found to be predominantly an investment activity. Thus, the shares in the company did not qualify for BPR (*Best v HMRC* [2014] UKFTT 77 (TC))

However, in contrast, a caravan park operator successfully claimed BPR in *Furness v CIR* [1999] STC (SCD) 232 – based on the facts, particularly the net profit from caravan sales having consistently exceeded caravan pitch rentals, the business was not mainly the holding of investments (see also 17.27 and 17.27A).

BPR restriction for excepted assets

17.33   A close review of the company's activities and assets is necessary to ensure that the shareholder's BPR is not restricted by the 'excepted assets' rule. BPR is reduced to the extent that the value of the shares reflects any 'excepted assets' held by the company [*IHTA 1984, s 112*]. Broadly, this is an anti-avoidance provision aimed at preventing 'taxable' personal assets being 'sheltered' from IHT by being held within a BPR-eligible company – this might include holiday villas and other 'private' assets that are held within the company for the owner-manager's private use. The excepted assets restriction will also prevent BPR being given on 'excess' cash reserves being built up within a company.

An asset is an 'excepted asset' if it was not used wholly or mainly for business purposes in the previous two years unless it is required for future use in the business [*IHTA 1984, s 112(2)*]. HMRC will generally seek to examine the accounts and other relevant documentation to establish whether the company's assets were being used by the business at the time of death/ chargeable transfer. It is likely that large cash balances may be queried by HMRC on the grounds that they may not be required for future business use.

There will, of course, be seasonal trades which generate a large cash balance at particular times of the year. In such cases, it should be possible to show that the cash was required to meet significant expenditure on re-stocking etc after the date of death.

Other cases will be less clear-cut, such as the circumstances in *Barclays Bank Trust Co Ltd v CIR* [1998] STC (SCD) 125. Here, the Inland Revenue accepted that £150,000 of a cash balance of £450,000 was needed for future use in the business, so that the remaining £300,000 constituted an 'excepted asset'. On the relevant facts, the Special Commissioner ruled on the relevant facts that the £300,000 was not required for business purposes. The fact that an asset might be required for the business at any time in the future did not prevent it being counted as an 'excepted asset'. The *IHTA 1984, s 112(2) (b)* 'required' test did not extend to the possibility that the money might be required should a suitable opportunity present itself after 'two, three or seven years' time'. No clear evidence was presented which showed that the money would be used for a clear business purpose or project (such as here when the company invested £355,000 in an import 'venture' some seven years after the relevant death).

Where the company has passed the mainly 'trading' test but includes a combination of both trading and investment activities, investments which form part of an investment business will not be treated as excepted assets. As a result, where a trading company has over time accumulated a number of investments, the entire value of its shares will qualify for BPR provided it remains predominantly a trading company and the investments are managed as a business (see 17.26 and 17.34).

Other assets which are likely to be excluded from BPR as excepted assets include assets used personally by the shareholder, such as holiday homes, yachts, private jets, where there is little or no business use.

Assets used for investment business

17.34 Leading counsel, Kevin Prosser QC, considers that assets used in a 'secondary' investment business can be required for *business* purposes, as well as those used for trading purposes. It is therefore possible to present an argument that cash is required for the future use of an investment business. However, the mere holding of cash on deposit does not constitute an investment business (see *Taxation*, 25 June 1998, page 325).

The 'excepted assets' restriction works by excluding the part of the value of the shares transferred which is attributable to the excepted asset. This is very much a question of negotiation and would, for example, depend on whether the valuation of the shares was based on earnings or assets.

Brown's Executors v CIR – excess cash deposits – a helpful case on future intentions

17.34A Where a company holds excess 'cash deposits', it may still be possible to argue that its shares qualify for BPR on the grounds that the cash is required for future business purposes. This was demonstrated in *Brown's Executors v CIR* [1996] STC (SCD) 277, which involved a company that carried on a nightclub business. The club was sold in 1985 and the sale proceeds were invested on short-term bank deposits. The directors subsequently investigated the possibility of buying another nightclub and were still looking in November 1986 when Mr Brown died holding a significant shareholding. The Special Commissioners rejected the Inland Revenue's contention that the company was an investment company as it only held cash on deposit. They accepted the executor's argument that the company had not changed the nature of its business at the date of Mr Brown's death as it was actively seeking a new club and the funds on short term deposit were held for this purpose. Thus, BPR relief was given on Mr Brown's shares.

Worked example of BPR on chargeable estate on death

17.35

Example 10

Calculation of IHT on death and BPR

Mr Matthews dies on 26 October 2017, leaving an estate summarised as follows:

(*a*)   family home valued at £200,000;

(*b*)   personal chattels worth £50,000;

(*c*)   200 ordinary shares in Stanley Ltd (representing a 20% interest) valued by the HMRC – Share and Assets Valuation Office at £560,000. Stanley Ltd manufactures sportswear;

(*d*)   the entire share capital (1,000 ordinary shares) in Matthews Ltd valued by HMRC – Share Valuation at £800,000;

Matthews Ltd trades as a retailer of sports merchandise through a chain of shops – HMRC – Capital Taxes has successfully contended that £350,000 of the share value relates to substantial (permanent) cash deposits which are not required for working capital or the purposes of the business;

(*e*)   bank balances and a portfolio of investments valued for IHT purposes at £360,000.

Mr Matthews had made no gifts within the previous seven years.

Mrs Mathews died in 2010 leaving all her net estate (valued at £500,000) to Mr Matthews absolutely.

Under Mr Matthews' will, all his assets (including the shares in Stanley Ltd and Matthews Ltd) passed to his son, who is a managing director of Matthews Ltd.

Mr Matthews' chargeable estate for IHT purposes is as follows:

		£	£
(a)	Family home		200,000
(b)	Personal chattels		50,000
(c)	Shares in Stanley Ltd	560,000	
	Less: BPR (100%)	(560,000)	–
(d)	Shares in Matthews Ltd	800,000	
	Less: Excepted assets	(350,000)	350,000
		450,000	
	Less: BPR (100%)	(450,000)	–
(e)	Bank balances and investments		360,000
	Chargeable estate		960,000
	IHT payable		
	* NRB – £650,000 × 0%		–
	**RNRB – £200,000 × 0 %		–
	Balance of £110,000 @ 40%		44,000
			£44,000

* Can use deceased wife's unused nil rate band (NRB) – 100% × £325,000. Therefore total NRB = £650,000

** RNRB – Value of estate before reliefs is £1,970,000 (£960,000 + BPR claims £1,010,000 (£560,000 + £450,000). Therefore, RNRB = £200,000 (£100,000 full RNRB available plus wife's unused RNRB of £100,000).

SUCCESSION ISSUES FOR THE OWNER MANAGER

Importance of succession planning

17.36   The owner-manager must really consider their basic objectives for the future development and running of the business before embarking on any serious capital tax planning. Empirical evidence shows that the chances of the family business surviving beyond the first generation are not that great. The probability of a first generation of a family-owned business successfully passing to the second generation is about 30% and the odds of the second generation passing the business to the third are as little as 10%. However, there is a belief that these prospects improve by using a trust to hold shares in the company. Furthermore, a trust can protect the shares against potentially damaging events, such as divorce, insolvency, or incapacity of family members (see 17.54)

In the context of an owner-managed business, 'succession planning' can perhaps be best described as prudent and considered strategies which will help protect the business from *unnecessary* deterioration arising from future (possibly unexpected) events. Clearly, it is important to provide for the continuity of the business and its management in the event of the owner-manager's death, disability or pre-determined retirement plans.

However, most owner-managers tend to avoid confronting the 'succession planning' issue. For many, *their* business is *their* life – it often defines them as a 'successful person' – and they are reluctant to give up the control and the financial security that goes with it. Furthermore, they seldom wish to face the emotional issues that are likely to be involved in transferring the business to the next generation. But 'ducking the succession issue' will not be in the best long term interests of the business, and in some cases may lead to its sudden demise. Having a proper strategy in place for succession will help to maintain/build the value of the company and provides security for its employees.

The reasons why many owner-managers find it difficult to hand-over the 'reins of control' are varied, but typically entail such factors as the fear of retirement, the potential threat to their identity, or perhaps the inability to make a choice amongst their children. Although these are all understandable reasons, owner-managers have a real responsibility to have a mechanism in place for passing-over the management and/or ownership of their company over a period of time.

Every owner-manager should develop and produce a *written* succession plan, which should be reviewed and updated at regular intervals. Part of this exercise will entail assessing the skills and future potential of their successors. Where appropriate, training and development plans should also be put in place and the owner-manager should involve the family members and employees in their thinking.

In some cases, there will not be a natural 'family' successor willing to take over. It is important to reach this conclusion as early as possible. This will give the owner-manager the necessary time to realise their investment, possibly by selling their shares to a third party trade purchaser or an incumbent management buy-out team.

Key-man insurance

17.37 A key-man insurance policy may be taken out to provide a much needed cash sum for the company in the event of the owner-manager's or another 'key' shareholders' death. Care must be taken to evidence that the primary purpose of the key-man insurance is to provide the funds to enable the owner-manager's shares to be acquired on death.

In the unfortunate event of a pay-out, HMRC will invariably look at the reason why the key-man insurance policy was established. Based on the author's experience in several cases(!), provided it can be shown that the proceeds were intended to finance the purchase of the shares from the deceased's estate, they should be exempt from tax as a capital sum. (In *Greycon v Klaentschi* [2003] STC 370 it was held that where a key-man policy is taken out for a capital purpose, the proceeds are themselves capital).

It is not sufficient simply to state that none of the premiums were previously deducted for corporation tax. Evidence to the underlying purpose is the key. If it is lacking, this may lead HMRC to conclude that the proceeds were intended to cover a 'shortfall' in profits in the event of a death and should therefore be subject to corporation tax (see *Williams Executors v CIR* 26 TC 23).

Typically, on death, the company may use the relevant funds to buy-back the owner-manager's/key shareholder's shares on death, often providing much needed cash for their spouse and other dependants. For BPR reasons, the deceased's shares will often be subject to 'put and call' options, enabling the estate to sell (put) the shares or the company to buy (call for) them (this avoids creating a binding contract which would deny BPR – see 17.23).

In some cases, the remaining shareholders themselves will undertake to purchase the deceased's shares. Such arrangements are covered by a shareholders' 'protection insurance' policy. This would be taken out on the life of each shareholder written into trust for the benefit of the other shareholders.

Key-man policies may also be required by banks and other lenders to improve a company's borrowing potential.

Succession planning options

17.38 Once the commercial decisions have been taken, the relevant capital tax planning strategies can be implemented to meet those objectives.

The owner-manager will usually need to keep their options open (for example, their children may be too young to express any leanings or interest towards the business). The tax planning approach must be 'tailored' to the owner-manager's personal circumstances. It is usually unwise for proprietors to commit themselves to any particular course of action too early on.

For instance, the owner-manager will (naturally) be reluctant to transfer any shares until they have decided that the shares will pass to the next generation and a sale has been ruled out. The unexpected may happen, for example, premature ill-health or a fantastic offer to buy the company which cannot be turned down! All such eventualities must be catered for as far as it is practically possible. The main options available to the owner-manager are discussed below.

Allocation of shares between family members

17.39 Ideally, capital tax planning should be considered when the company is incorporated, as the shares will then be of minimal value.

Fragmenting the company's shareholdings amongst different members of the family, including family trusts, will have a beneficial effect on share value and perhaps more importantly will enable future appreciation in value to accrue outside the donor's estate. However, owner-managers will invariably want to be in control of their own destiny and be able to exercise leadership. Consequently, they (perhaps together with their spouse) will normally require at least a 51% shareholding.

If there is a possibility that the company may be sold in the future, the proprietor is likely to retain a substantial proportion of the shares. At this stage, the owner-manager's children are likely to be very young (or not even born) and the owner-manager will not know whether the children will be interested and sufficiently competent to work in the company.

Some owner managers appreciate that flexibility and effective control may be retained by placing some shares into a family discretionary trust (see 17.84).

Transfer of shares to next generation

17.40 For the existing family company, the passing of shares and ultimately control to the next generation clearly depends upon whether the proprietor's children (or other members of the family) are interested in developing the business. Perhaps more importantly, the proprietor's children should also demonstrate that they have the necessary commercial acumen and expertise to develop the business (entrepreneurial parents do not always have entrepreneurial children!).

Certain members of the family may not wish to play an active role in the business. If this is the case, the controlling shareholder could take out a life insurance policy (as early as possible) with a view to providing a cash sum on death for these 'non-active' members. This would enable the appropriate degree of balance to be struck with the shares passed on to the family members involved in the business. The proprietor may also need to take pre-emptive action to minimise the risk of losing key managers or employees who may feel that they were being 'passed-over' or neglected.

Obtaining financial independence

17.41   Most proprietors are financially dependent on their company and they are, therefore, likely to seek to maintain control of it to secure their future income in retirement. They may not trust their children to provide them with a consultancy fee or an 'unfunded' pension from the company.

This is why pension planning remains an important part of succession planning (pension planning is considered in Chapter 10). Owner-managers should aim to build up a healthy pension and adequate savings over their working life from dividends and remuneration from their companies. They can then be financially secure and independent in retirement, enabling them to surrender control.

The owner-manager may also be able to unlock capital from the company through a purchase of its own shares with their gain usually benefiting from the favourable CGT rates (see 13.41–13.43). The retention of trading property held outside the company might be used to provide rental income during retirement.

No succession route available

17.42   If the proprietor does not have a natural successor in the family, they may wish to sell their shares to a key employee, manager or management team. Soundings would need to be taken early on to see whether the employees/managers were interested in acquiring the company and if so, whether they could raise some personal finance and obtain the required bank/institutional borrowing. It is also possible to structure a management buy-out through a company purchase of its own shares (along the lines indicated in Examples 7 and 8 in Chapter 13).

Planning for a 'trade' sale

17.43   If the proprietor plans to realise his investment in the company via a 'trade' sale of his shares to a third party, this must be planned at an early stage. (The various implications of selling the owner-managed company were dealt with in Chapter 15.) In the writer's experience, the process of selling the family business can take several years before the 'right' deal is struck. Advance planning reduces the cost and disruption to the business and gives time to rectify any weaknesses in the business, thus enhancing its value.

It is often found that the value of the business is heavily dependent on its controlling shareholders. In such cases, the purchaser may (not unreasonably) require them to work in the business for the next two or three years to hand over their expertise and contacts, etc perhaps using an 'earn-out' arrangement (see 15.64).

17.44   Owner-managers are now likely to realise 'exit' gains at 10% (with the benefit of entrepreneurs' relief on the first £10 million), with any excess gains being taxed at the 'top' CGT rate of 20%. However, in some cases, it may be possible to increase the ER even further by fragmenting shareholdings to 'qualifying' family members (see 15.34).

It must be recognised that a sale of the company completely changes the owner-managers IHT profile. Before the sale, 100% BPR would normally be available to exempt the value of their 'qualifying' shareholding from IHT but after the sale, the entire post-CGT consideration would potentially be exposed to IHT at 40%. Given that many owner-managers tend to sell out when they approach retirement age, normal IHT solutions may not be effective. A number of owner managers are now opting to use Discounted Gift Trusts (DGT) to remove substantial post-sale cash from their chargeable estate whilst ensuring a future income stream (see 17.45).

Alternatively, the proceeds realised on the sale of the company could be reinvested in IHT exempt or favoured assets (for example, woodlands or investments on AIM), subject to the two year ownership test.

Use of Discounted Gift Trusts (DGTs)

17.45   Discounted Gift Trusts (DGTs) are essentially financial products which are available from a number of reputable providers. An outline of how a DGT works is given below.

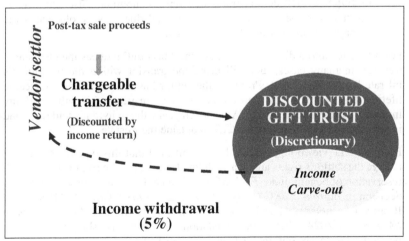

The use of a DGT and its related tax analysis (in relation to post-sale IHT planning) can briefly be summarised as follows:

- The owner-manager would acquire a bond, which would be written into trust – this can be either an absolute (bare) trust (see 17.54 and 17.66) or a discretionary trust (17.54 and 17.84), although discretionary trusts provide greater flexibility.

- A DGT will provide the individual with a future income stream – for the rest of their life (or until the fund is exhausted). The income is calculated using the annual 5% 'tax-free' withdrawal facility (A lower or higher percentage can be taken but, if higher, there would potentially be income tax payable on the excess. Income tax would also potentially be payable if the 5% withdrawals last for more than 20 years.)

- The 'carved-out' income stream is a return of capital and 'discounts' the value transferred into the trust. These retained rights are assumed to have been sold on the open market for IHT purposes and represents the value of property not being gifted.

- The fund required to produce the income stream is actuarially calculated and its value immediately falls outside the individual's estate liable to IHT. (However, if the individual does not spend their income stream, this will increase the value of their estate again.)

- HMRC have published tables (which can be found on HMRCs website) to ensure consistency of approach in calculating the income (annuity) stream – the value of the future income would be the reduction given in calculating the transfer of value for IHT purposes. HMRC have made it clear for many years that someone over 90 was not entitled to any discount. The ruling in *Bower & Anor v Revenue & Customs* [2009] STC 510 demonstrates that only a 'nominal' discount will be given where the taxpayer is 'uninsurable' due to very old age – the taxpayer in *Bower* was a 90 year-old lady.

For a transfer into a discretionary trust, the 'discount' reduces the chargeable transfer. In many cases, this will bring the transfer within the individual's nil rate band (see 17.4A). Provided the settlor has not made any chargeable lifetime transfers (CLT) within the previous seven years, this will avoid any immediate lifetime IHT charge. After seven years, the individual's nil rate band is refreshed and the value of the CLT is outside their estate.

From an IHT viewpoint, HMRC have confirmed that this type of 'carve-out' (where the settlor's rights are clearly defined) does not give rise to any gift with reservation of benefit under *FA 1986, s 102* since this is in accordance with the decision in *Ingram & IRC (Lady Ingram's Executors v CIR)* [1999] STC 37. It should be noted that DGTs are not affected by the post-*Ingram* rules in *FA 1986, ss 102A–102C*. This legislation only prevents 'shearing' schemes being used to 'carve out' interests *in land* (see 17.54).

Where a discretionary trust is used, the value of the DGT at the ten-year anniversary would not be liable to any ten-year charge provided it falls below the nil rate band (at that time). Amounts remaining in the DGT on the settlor's death pass to their beneficiaries under the terms of the trust.

Where a DGT is written as an absolute trust, the 'discount' reduces the value of the PET.

In summary, provided the taxpayer is 'insurable', a DGT can provide a beneficial shelter from IHT, with any investment growth occurring outside the taxpayer's estate. With care, it should be possible to create a DGT with no immediate IHT cost.

The use of DGT's is accepted by HMRC and its GAAR Guidance (see 1.19A) confirms that the use of DGTs is not considered abusive since they have been accepted by long established practice.

PASSING SHARES TO THE NEXT GENERATION

Lifetime transfers

17.46 If the owner-manager wishes to transfer shares to their children or other members of the family, this can basically be done in one of two ways. Shares could be transferred, perhaps on a phased basis, as they approach retirement. Such transfers to individuals will qualify as PETs for IHT purposes and CGT business asset hold-over relief should normally be available (see 13.14).

The effect of a hold-over election is to pass on the contingent CGT liability to the transferee shareholder(s). As the transfer is a PET, if the donor dies within seven years of gifting the shares, an IHT charge will arise (subject to the availability of BPR and taper relief).

When the transfer is made it is important that the controlling shareholder has not reserved any benefit (such as very favourable employment rights or benefits) in relation to the shares gifted as they would be regarded as remaining in their estate for IHT purposes [*FA 1986, s 102*].

Any continuing remuneration drawn as a director will be disregarded by HMRC as long as it is 'reasonable'. However, where the former owner-manager wishes to remain as a director it is desirable for him to enter into an appropriate service agreement, which would be binding on the company and viewed by the company as being in its interests. Ideally, this decision should be taken by an independent Board evidencing that the service contract is for the company's benefit. Any pension arrangements and benefits in kind should be written into the contract.

The IHT transfer of value (based on the 'diminution in value' principle) may differ from the value used for CGT purposes (see 17.5 and 17.7). For CGT, the value of the shareholding actually transferred is taken. Frequently, it will not be necessary to value the shares transferred if both parties agree to dispense with submitting a market value when making a hold-over election (see 13.18).

Value freezing schemes

17.47 As it is now relatively easy to transfer ownership of a family trading company, the use of value freezing or value shifting schemes has declined in popularity. Such schemes might be considered if the proprietor does not wish to transfer his shareholding or where the company's activities restrict the availability of business asset hold-over relief.

There are many scheme variations, all involving various tax and valuation complications, so specialist professional advice should always be obtained. Generally, they would involve a bonus issue of new shares (which only participate in future growth and profits), which would be placed in the children's hands or the use of a parallel company for placing genuine *new* business.

Passing shares on death

17.48 The owner-manager could retain their shares (or most of them) until death. Normally, the 'qualifying' shares would pass to the children, etc free of IHT due to the availability of 100% BPR. It may be considered inappropriate for the children to take the shares directly outright, for example, if they are too young. In such cases, a suitable trust vehicle could be used (see 17.54).

If the most desirable distribution of the estate is not clear at the time of the will, it is possible to use a discretionary will trust. Under *IHTA 1984, s 144*, capital distributions made from the trust within two years of death are treated as made under the will. For example, a discretionary will trust could be created for the benefit of the surviving spouse and the children. This would ensure that the income and capital would remain available to the spouse if required.

Where an appointment is made to a spouse within three months of death, it can be read back into the will under *IHTA 1984, s 144*.

It might be considered preferable for IHT exempt shares to be passed to the children, etc at this stage, for example, if they are managing the business or perhaps to protect against any adverse changes in capital tax. Furthermore, the surviving spouse (or civil partner) can take the chargeable assets free of IHT anyway under the spouse exemption.

17.49 The children will inherit the shares at their market value at the date of death for CGT purposes (and do not therefore take over any contingent CGT liability in the shares which would have occurred had the shares been transferred before death). The combination of absolute exemption from IHT and CGT rebasing to probate value is particularly beneficial. Indeed, this favourable tax treatment provides a persuasive argument for holding on to the shares until death.

This, of course, assumes that the 100% BPR exemption will remain intact (see 17.19). Consequently, if the family wish to sell the shares shortly after the death, there will be no clawback of BPR and there should be little or no CGT due to the deemed 'market value' base cost established on death. In such cases, where 100% BPR is available, it will normally be necessary to agree the probate value of the shares afterwards (see 17.17).

It should not be forgotten that the owner-manager may be under some moral pressure to pass at least some of the shares to their children before death to motivate them and maintain management morale.

There, will of course, be many cases where the owner-manager's shares have to be acquired by the company or the remaining shareholders, with appropriate key-man' or shareholder protection insurance being in place to fund the purchase (see 17.37 for detailed commentary).

DRAWING UP A WILL AND RELATED PLANNING ISSUES

The will

17.50 It is important to get the basic aspects right, such as ensuring that a will is properly drawn up and is regularly reviewed to take account of changing personal circumstances and changes in tax law (such as the recently introduced RNRB) (see 17.15A).

Where an individual has assets in an overseas country or countries (for example, a holiday villa in Portugal or Spain), it will normally be advisable to make concurrent 'overseas' wills to deal (only) with the relevant assets in those jurisdictions.

The main will would cover UK assets, and should exclude the overseas assets and make reference to the overseas will(s). It is important to avoid the trap of any subsequent overseas will accidentally revoking the main UK one!

Destination of shares and other assets

17.51 It is important to ensure business property relief (BPR) and agricultural property relief (APR) entitlements are maximised. For example, where possible the 'BPR eligible and other relievable assets' should not be left to the surviving spouse. In many cases, the shares, etc should be left directly to the children or possibly through an appropriate will trust (with the surviving spouse being included as one of the beneficiaries) (see 17.48). In such cases, the will should contain a specific 'gift' of the shares to the children/will trust. There will, of course, be situations where the shares are subject to 'put and call' options enabling the shares to be purchased by the company or the existing shareholders (see 17.24 and 17.37).

It is possible for the 'chargeable' part of the estate to be left to the surviving spouse (or civil partner) on a flexible interest in possession trust (see 17.55).

Wide powers would be given to trustees to terminate that interest to enable the surviving spouse to benefit in a different capacity. Provided the life interest trust is created under a will (or intestacy) *and* that interest in possession 'kicks-in' on the testator's death, the will trust – strictly known as an immediate post-death interest trust (IPDI) – ranks for special treatment under *IHTA 1984, s 49A*. In broad terms, the IPDI is treated as an 'old-style' life interest trust (see 17.82). Consequently, the property passing into an IPDI for the surviving spouse/civil partner will benefit from the spouse exemption (see 17.9).

An IPDI trust gives the surviving spouse access to income for life which may make them feel more comfortable with making PETs to reduce the value of their estate. Using an IPDI, the trustees (which may include the spouse) could subsequently decide to terminate the spouse's interest over part of the assets. Such assets could, for example, be appointed on a discretionary trust (for the children's/spouse's benefit) within the spouse's unused nil rate band (as this would be a chargeable transfer).

The surviving spouse is *deemed* to make a transfer of value within *IHTA 1984, s 52* on the termination of their interest in possession. However, where this occurs after 21 March 2006, this is also regarded as a 'gift' [*IHTA 1984, s 102ZA*]. This means that the GROB rules would apply where the surviving spouse continues to benefit from the trust property – this would be the case, for example, where the spouse is able to benefit from a discretionary trust (see 17.10 and 17.54). (The deemed disposal should not be caught by the pre-owned asset (POA) rules (see 17.116).)

IPDI trusts (see 17.82) can also be used to protect significant capital assets for the ultimate benefit of the deceased's children. For example, the surviving spouse could be given a life interest in the property that terminates on her death or remarriage. Such trusts are frequently used in 'second' marriages, since they enable the surviving spouse to enjoy the same quality of life. However, on the spouse's death, the underlying assets would pass to the deceased's own children rather than their step-children (unless that is desired as well). Furthermore, an IPDI trust can avoid assets being potentially diverted away from the 'bloodline' children in the event of the surviving spouse marrying again.

Married couples/civil partners with relatively simple affairs may feel that it is not necessary to equalise their estates, since they are generally able to transfer unused nil rate bands and unused residential nil rate bands to their surviving spouse/civil partner (see 17.15–17.15C).

However, in many cases a nil rate band will trust will offer greater flexibility – for example, where someone had remarried and has children from a prior marriage. A will trust would ensure that assets can be passed to the relevant children after their death (and avoid being transferred in accordance with the surviving spouse's wishes).

Furthermore, if the surviving spouse is in business, a will trust should offer some protection from creditors (as opposed to an outright transfer of assets).

Following the introduction of the RNRB, many couples may wish to take action to reduce the aggregated estate below £2 million to preserve the maximum RNRB (see 17.15A and 17.53).

Life policies and death-in-service pension payments

17.52 In some cases, it may be considered appropriate to nominate (at the discretion of the pension fund trustees) the tax-free 'death-in-service' amount of a pension policy in favour of a family discretionary trust (perhaps including the surviving spouse). This would ensure that the funds remain outside their estate on death but the trust could be given powers to lend money to them on an interest-free basis.

In certain cases, any tax-free death-in-service benefit could be used to purchase, from the deceased's surviving spouse, illiquid assets that have been left to her, such as shares in the family or owner-managed company.

Appropriate life insurance arrangements should also be in place to cover potential IHT liabilities which cannot be mitigated by planning. Life insurance premiums can normally be paid for the benefit of the other members of the family free of IHT, usually under the 'normal expenditure out of income' rule or annual exemption (see 17.9) – the benefits of the policy should be held in trust for the beneficiaries so that they do not form part of the individual's estate.

Some life policies are written in trust for the spouse/partner and/or children or are taken out to provide funds to pay off loans or mortgages.

Dealing with the family home and other properties

17.53 In many cases, the family home represents a significant part of the estate. If property, such as the home, is jointly owned, it is important to establish whether it is owned as a joint tenancy or as tenants in common.

Where property is held under a *joint tenancy*, each joint tenant owns the whole of the property and hence, on death, the entire asset will pass to the surviving owner. In such cases, the will or intestacy rules are irrelevant and there is no need to obtain a grant of probate since legal title passes automatically on the production of a death certificate. A joint tenancy is therefore likely to be appropriate for a married couple where they are confident that the survivor will provide for their children on the second death.

If property is held as tenants in common, each party owns their relevant interest – typically on a 50%–50% basis. Thus, when one of the owner's dies, their share of the property will pass according to their will (or under the rules of intestacy). (A joint tenancy can be 'converted' to ownership as tenants in common by a deed of severance (the Land Registry will also need to be informed)).

This would enable their share to be passed directly to the children. However, this stratagem requires complete trust in the children. Since they would own a share in the house, they could force a sale of the home or the value of their share could be taken into account if they got divorced. Such problems could be avoided by the will providing for the share in the home to be passed into a (nil-rate band) discretionary trust, with the children as beneficiaries but, say, a trusted friend or other family member acting as a trustee.

Where the family home is held as tenants in common, the will can still provide for the deceased's share of the home to be left to the surviving spouse (or co-habiting partner). This would clearly attract IHT on the survivor's death. Similarly, if the surviving spouse or partner is given a right to occupy the family home for life, this again would be treated as part of their chargeable estate for IHT purposes – since the right is given under a will, this would be an IPDI. Consequently, the underlying property would be treated as part of the survivor's estate on death. It is not possible for the surviving spouse/partner to gift the house to (say) their children, with the survivor continuing to occupy it. This would clearly be caught by the gift with reservation rules (see 17.10A) except where a commercial rent was paid.

In appropriate cases, it may be desirable to leave the home to the surviving spouse, leaving (say) cash to a 'nil rate' band discretionary trust for the surviving spouse/children, etc. If the surviving spouse requires the cash post-death, they may be able to arrange for the trustees to lend it to them with a proper charge being made on the house (thus reducing the value of their potential estate). Specialist advice must be taken before implementing this and similar arrangements and must avoid the potential traps highlighted in the case of *Phizackerley v R&CC* [2007] STC (SCD) 328.

The ability to pass on any unused NRB and RNRB on the death of the first spouse to be used in the estate of the survivor should now ease some of the problems in passing down the family home (see 17.4B, 17.4C and 17.15A–17.15C).

In some cases, couples with estates exceeding £2 million may wish to consider making suitable lifetime gifts to ensure the full available RNRB is available on death (see 17.15B). Similarly, spouses/civil partners may wish to reduce the assets passing to their survivor to ensure the aggregated estate is below £2 million. A discretionary will trust might be considered in these situations (see 17.55).

USE OF TRUSTS

Benefits of using trusts

17.54 Trusts can be used to shift value and future capital growth outside the proprietor's estate. Trusts can be a more flexible and helpful method of transferring shares or other assets than an outright absolute gift. Many proprietors are sceptical about the use of trusts and it will be necessary to dispel their fears. It is worth pointing out that trusts have been in existence for hundreds of years and are widely used (whatever HMRC might think!) to protect family assets (including shares in the family/owner-managed company). Understandably, many parents are nervous about their children marrying 'fortune hunters' or having direct control of family assets where they are considered too young to handle them responsibly or make decisions affecting them. Furthermore, trusts are particularly efficient vehicles for holding shares in family/owner managed companies to facilitate succession planning and control the destination of assets from beyond the grave.

It is helpful to begin with the leading definition of a trust provided by Sir Arthur Underhill:

> 'A trust is an equitable obligation, binding a person (who is called a Trustee) to deal with property over which he has control (which is called trust property) for the benefit of persons (who are called the Beneficiaries or the *cestuis que trust*) of whom he may himself be one and any one of whom may enforce the obligation.'

The trustees do not therefore personally own the trust property, just the legal interest in it in a fiduciary capacity. They hold the trust property on behalf of the beneficiaries, who may be named or ascertained by description in the trust deed. The trustees will generally make decisions over the trust assets acting in the best interests of the beneficiaries as a whole.

These beneficiaries have the beneficial ownership of the property, as prescribed by the terms of the trust deed. The individual creating the trust is usually referred to as the 'settlor'. In most cases, it will be necessary to register the trust deed with HMRC.

Trusts can either be created during the settlor's lifetime (by a formal trust deed) or by will (a 'Will Trust'), which is treated as written at the date of the settlor's death. In the case of lifetime trusts, settlors can appoint themselves and possibly their spouses as trustees. This enables them to retain the decision making and control over the trust. Although trustees have a duty to act in the interest of the beneficiaries, this should normally coincide with the proprietor's own wishes. The courts generally impose an onerous duty of care on trustees.

In some cases, the settlor may wish to appoint a 'protector' of the trust (for example, a close family friend) to 'watch over' the trustees. A protector would have certain powers, such as the ability to appoint and dismiss trustees.

The property transferred into the trust (such as the shares) will be set aside for either specified individuals or a nominated class of individuals until a given age or event.

Trusts also enable the underlying income and capital value of the settled shares to be protected where the children are too young to handle capital properly or if there are concerns about the children's spouses or partners. By transferring shares into trust, the owner-manager can defer his decision as to which children, grandchildren (or anyone else) should inherit and what stake they should have in the company. Such difficult decisions may not become clear until much later on and may often involve a degree of conflict – for example, family values which generally entail equality of treatment may be at odds with the need to reward those who are the top 'family' contributors to the success of the business. Furthermore, as the children grow up, the owner manager will often find that only some of the children will seek involvement and responsibility in the business.

If a trust entitles the settlor or their spouse/civil partner to potentially benefit from the trust, it will not be effective for income tax purposes and indeed would be treated as a gift with reservation of benefit for IHT (see 17.100). To avoid such problems, the trust deed must be drafted to irrevocably exclude the settlor or their spouse/civil partner from benefit (see 17.61–17.64).

Despite the best efforts of the courts, trusts continue to play a valuable role in protecting assets on divorce or marriage breakdown. Where this is a key consideration, owner-managers should exclude their spouse (or spouses of their children) from the class of beneficiaries at the outset. If the spouse is to be a beneficiary of a trust, it is possible to provide power to irrevocably remove them at a later date should this become necessary.

Main types of trust

17.55 The main types of trust can be summarised as follows:

Bare trusts (or simple trusts) – With such trusts, the beneficial owner of the property is fully entitled to both the income and capital of the property, although the property is held in the trustee's name. In such cases, the trustee effectively holds the property as a nominee. A bare trust can be created or arise in a number of different circumstances. For example, property may be held by parents as bare trustees for their minor children simply because the children cannot legally hold property or give valid receipt for money until they reach the age of majority. Similarly, where under the terms of a trust a beneficiary becomes 'absolutely entitled as against the trustee(s)', the trustee(s) will hold the property as a bare trustee pending the legal transfer of the trust property to that beneficiary (see 17.70 and 17.71).

Interest in possession (or life interest) trusts – These trusts give one or more beneficiaries the right to the income (or enjoyment of the trust property) for a defined period, often for life. (This is a concept of trust law – *FA 2006* has not changed the characteristics of such a trust – merely its IHT consequences.)

Such trusts are often referred to as life interest or fixed interest trusts (and are known as 'life renter' trusts in Scotland). An interest in possession trust is often used where the settlor wishes to give an immediate benefit of income to a beneficiary but intends the capital to be gifted to someone else (see 17.72 and 17.73). Such trusts might be used, for example, to give a child an income stream but deferring the entitlement to the actual capital until later on in life. The settlor must ensure that they do not retain any benefit from the trust property as the assets would be treated as remaining in their estate for IHT purposes and the trust would also be 'transparent' for income tax purposes (see 17.61).

Discretionary trusts – Under a discretionary trust, the income and capital is to be paid out at the trustees' discretion. The trustees may decide to retain the income and accumulate it for future use. Thus, the beneficiaries only have a hope or expectation of income or capital – they are not entitled to it as of right (see 17.79). (Employee benefit trusts are a specialised form of discretionary trust (see 5.14 and 5.15).)

Given their potential power, the choice of trustees for a discretionary trust is very important. Settlors (ie the individuals creating the trust) are normally advised to leave a 'letter of wishes' with the trustees, even where they start off by being one of the trustees.

The letter of wishes sets out the settlor's present and future intentions for the trust property. The letter is sent to the trustees on a 'private and confidential' basis, and records the settlor's reasons for the trust and their motives. It may give suggestions on how discretions might be exercised in the light of potential future circumstances. Although the letter of wishes should give some assistance to the trustees as to the settlor's insight, they are not bound by its contents. As such, the letter of wishes must not become a series of instructions.

Accumulation and maintenance trusts – A&M trusts used to be a very popular trust vehicle for holding assets for children and grandchildren (aged under 25). Such trusts were effectively a product of a specific beneficial IHT regime, which was abolished on 22 March 2006. There are many A&M trusts in existence where their terms were amended before 6 April 2008 to take advantage of special transitional IHT 'protection' (see 17.101–17.106). The remainder will be taxed under the discretionary trust regime (see 17.84–17.90).

Special types of FA 2006 trusts – As part of a radical 'shake up' of the IHT trust regime in *FA 2006*, the government introduced a number of specialised rules to alleviate the potentially disadvantageous IHT effects on many existing trusts.

These rules have effectively created a number of special trust regimes, which *include*:

- immediate post-death interests ('IPDIs') (see 17.82);

- transitional serial interest ('TSIs') (see 17.83);

- age 18 to 25 trusts (see 17.106–17.110); and

This book does not cover the special treatment of bereaved minor trusts.

NON-RESIDENT TRUSTS

Overview

17.56   Given the wide-ranging anti-avoidance legislation that applies to non-resident trusts, the vast majority of owner-managers are now likely to use *UK* *resident* trust vehicles as part of their estate/succession planning. It should be noted that the coverage of trusts in this chapter is mainly confined to *UK resident* trusts. However, given that a number of owner-managers will have previously set up *non-resident* trusts for CGT planning it is useful to briefly review their current CGT treatment.

A trust will *not* be resident in the UK for a tax year if either:

- *all* the trustees are non-UK resident; *or*

- the settlor was either non-UK resident *or* non-UK domiciled when they created the trust and there is at least one non-UK resident trustee.

The vast majority of tax planning opportunities and benefits that used to be provided by non-resident trusts have now been negated by stringent tax legislation. While *non-UK domiciled* individuals were initially safeguarded from these provisions, the *FA 2008* changes brought the beneficiaries of their trusts within the CGT charging rules.

The *FA 2008* changes considerably lessened the appeal of non-resident trusts for non-UK domiciled individuals, although they still have some attractions in appropriate cases.

More recent legislation largely negates the use of non-resident trusts for UK residential property. For example, since 6 April 2015, non-resident trusts will incur a 28% CGT charge on the sale of UK residential property (although only on gains arising post-6 April 2015) (see 17.58A). Similarly, since 6 April 2017, non-domiciled individuals are liable to *IHT* on UK residential property, even where it is *indirectly* held by them through non-resident structures (see 17.4 and 17.9B).

Exit charge on migration

17.57   Where a UK trust becomes non-resident (by switching entirely to non-resident trustees) it is subject to an 'exit' charge under *TCGA 1992, s 80*. (A number of European Union cases have questioned the validity of tax 'exit' charges imposed on migration but it is unsafe to rely on them in planning!)

The 'exit charge' is computed by reference to a deemed disposal (and reacquisition) of all the trust's assets (including any shares held in an owner-managed company) at their market value. Assets that remain within the charge to UK tax are not subject to the exit charge. The trustees are taxed on the resultant gain(s).

The UK settlor charge

17.58   A (UK resident and domiciled) *settlor* is taxed on capital gains made by a 'non-resident' trust in which they have an interest [*TCGA 1992, s 86*].

Trust gains attributed to a settlor for 2017/18 are taxed at the main 20% CGT rate. However, see 17.58A for the 28% CGT charging rules where the non-resident trust sells UK residential property after 5 April 2015.

A very wide 'settlor-interest' definition applies for non-resident trusts. Settlors are treated as having an interest in an overseas trust if any interest (even discretionary) is held by them, their spouse/civil partner, their children (and their spouses), or a company controlled by them and their spouses/children. For *post-16 March 1998* trusts, the inclusion of grandchildren as beneficiaries will also be caught by this rule.

Where the beneficiaries of the trust only consist of friends and other relatives (such as the settlor's parents), the 'settlor charge' would *not* apply.

From 2017/18, the 'settlor charge' rules have been extended to non-UK domiciled settlors who later become *deemed domiciled* under the 'long term' UK residence rules (see 17.59A). However, *TCGA 1992, Sch 5, para 5A(1))* prevents such deemed domiciled settlors from incurring a *TCGA 1992, s 86* charge on 'their' overseas trusts if they were created *before 6 April 2017*. However, to obtain the benefit of this protection, certain transitional ('protected settlement') conditions must be satisfied. The key requirements are as follows:

- the tax year is 2017/18 or later;

- the settlor was not domiciled in the UK at the time when the settlement was created;

- during the relevant tax year, the settlor must not be UK domiciled under the general law.

Deemed non-domiciled settlors of pre-6 April 2017 overseas trusts would therefore come within the settlor charging rules if they subsequently acquire a UK domicile of choice.

Furthermore, the 'protected settlement' provisions will cease to apply if further assets are added (directly/indirectly) to the settlement. Consequently if deemed domiciled settlors wish to retain the protection from the settlor charging provisions, they should ensure that no additional assets (widely defined) are transferred to the trust (after 5 April 2017). Similarly, this protection would also be lost if the settlor, spouse and their minor children subsequently received any benefit (however small).

The UK residential property charge

17.58A   Since 6 April 2015, non-resident trusts are liable to UK CGT on the sale of UK residential property at the 'residential property' CGT rate of 28% *(TCGA 1992, s 14B)*. These provisions cover all disposals of UK properties 'used or suitable for use as a dwelling' (unless ATED-related CGT applies in priority) *(TCGA 1992, Sch B1)*.

The trustees must notify HMRC and pay the CGT within 30 days of the sale completing.

However, only gains arising after 5 April 2015 are subject to this direct CGT charge. This is achieved by rebasing the property at its market value at 5 April 2015 for the purposes of calculating the 28% residential property gain charge. Alternatively, the trustees can elect to time apportion the gain over the 'ownership period' and pay the 28% CGT charge on the post-5 April 2015 element of the gain (or on the total gain if this is more advantageous).

Most double tax agreements will enable the 28% UK CGT charge to be credited against any corresponding overseas tax.

The 28% 'residential property' CGT charge takes priority over the other non-resident trust CGT rules. Thus, any part of the gain *not* caught by the special 28% CGT rule will either be taxed under the UK settlor charging rules (see 17.58) or be included in the 'pooled' trust gains for the purposes of the beneficiary charge (see 17.59).

Capital losses arising on the sale of UK residential property are 'ring-fenced' and can only be offset against gains generated on UK residential properties in the same or future tax years. Any unused ring-fenced capital losses would become available for set-off against all types of gains if the trust becomes UK resident.

The special CGT charge for UK residential property also applies where the non-resident trust holds the relevant property indirectly via an overseas company. However, in this case, the overseas company pays the tax charge at the prevailing UK corporation tax (and with the benefit of indexation relief in calculating the gain).

The UK beneficiaries charge

17.59   If the non-resident trust gains are *not* taxed on the settlor (under the above rules), they are then counted as 'trust gains' – which are calculated under the normal CGT rules. Since 6 April 2015, gains arising on disposals of UK residential property incur a direct UK CGT charge of 28% (see 17.58A). Only the post-5 April 2015 gain is taxed at this special rate, with the balance being added to the pool of trust gains.

The 'pooled' trust gains are then subject to CGT when they are distributed as a capital payment to a UK resident (and UK domiciled) beneficiary [*TCGA 1992, s 87*]. A `capital payment` is widely defined and includes not only direct payments from a trust but also indirect benefits, such as interest free loans or free use of property received by the beneficiaries. However, payments made under 'arm's length transactions' should not be caught.

Since 6 April 2008, capital payments are also taxed on non-UK domiciled but resident beneficiaries, except where they are sheltered by claiming the remittance basis (see 15.126).

There are special rules for matching *TCGA 1992, s 87* trust gains to capital payments on a 'beneficiary-by-beneficiary' basis. Broadly, trust gains are allocated to the recipient beneficiary up to the amount of any capital payment(s) made to them.

The gains are apportioned to beneficiaries in the proportion of the capital payments they have received from the trust in the same and/or any earlier tax year. Any excess gains (often known as 'stock-piled gains') are carried forward to match with any subsequent capital payments. Since 6 April 2008, capital payments are matched with prior trust gains on a LIFO (last-in first-out basis). Hence the payments would be matched to more recent gains before earlier ones

Similarly, any excess capital payments would be matched with any trust gains made in later years, restricted where appropriate to the trust gain. The matched amounts would be taxed on the relevant beneficiaries.

Since 6 April 2016, 'matched' trust gains are generally taxed at the main 20% CGT rate.

If the gains are not promptly distributed, the CGT is increased by the supplementary charge [*TCGA 1992, s 91*]. The trust must distribute any gains within the same or following tax year to avoid the supplementary charge. The charge is calculated by applying 10% to the CGT for each year starting from 1 December following the tax year in which the gain arose until 30 November after the tax year the (matched) capital payment is made. The charge is effectively limited to a maximum of 60% of the tax.

This generally means that cash can normally be repatriated to UK beneficiaries at a maximum tax cost of 32% (CGT at 20% plus maximum supplementary charge thereon – 60% × 20%). Where the beneficiary has their own gains, the allocated trust gain attracting the supplementary charge can be treated as being taxed as the lowest amount.

Example 11

Allocating non-resident trust gains to beneficiaries (including supplementary charge)

Mr Matty (UK resident and domiciled) set up 'his' company (Etherington Ltd) in 1990. At that time, 20% of the shareholding was placed in 'his' non-resident discretionary trust. The beneficiaries of the trust comprised his father (Matthew), long-time girlfriend/partner (Matilda) and any future children.

The entire share capital of Etherington Ltd was sold for £2 million in 2010/11. The capital gain arising in the non-resident trust (after taking account of incidental disposal costs) was £96,000.

In May 2017, the trustees made a capital payment of £10,000 to Matthew and £40,000 to Matilda. On 1 June 2017, Matilda had realised a chargeable gain of £18,000 in her own right. She was a higher rate taxpayer for 2017/18.

Attributed trust gains	Matthew	Matilda	Total
	£	£	£
Trust gains b/fwd			96,000
2017/18 – Apportioned gain	10,000	40,000	(50,000)
Trust gains c/fwd (to be matched with future capital payments)			46,000

Matilda's CGT position for 2017/18

	£
Allocated trust gain*	40,000
Less: Annual exemption	(11,300)
	28,700
Own gain	18,000
Total chargeable gains	46,700
CGT thereon	
Total CGT 46,700 @ 20%	£9,340

*Trust gain is treated as the lowest part of Matilda's trust gains

Supplementary charge

Matilda would also have to pay a supplementary charge of 60% on the 'trust' CGT, computed as follows:

Relevant period – 1 December 2011 to 30 November 2018	= 7 years
Therefore: 7 years	= 60% (max)
CGT on trust gain (= lowest part)	
28,700 @ 20%	£5,740
Supplementary charge = £5,740 × 60%	£3,444

Matilda will therefore have to pay a total amount of £9,184 (£5,740 + £3,444) in respect of her trust gains.

Non-domiciled settlors/beneficiaries

17.60 HMRC no longer processes the DOM1 forms, which were used to obtain a formal 'ruling' on an individual's domicile status. In future, individuals will have to decide their own domicile status when submitting their tax returns, which HMRC could challenge under the normal enquiry process.

The CGT charges that apply to non-resident settlor-interested trusts where the settlor is UK domiciled (see 17.58) do not apply provided a UK resident settlor is neither non-UK domiciled nor 'deemed UK-domiciled' (see 17.58).

The *F(No 2)A 2017* reforms to non-domiciliaries' taxation have removed the advantages of non-resident trusts for 'long-term' UK residents (who are non-domiciled under common law principles) (see 17.58). Some benefits remain for those 'non-doms' who are not affected by the 'long term' UK resident deeming rules.

Non-resident trusts cannot escape the 28% CGT charge that arises on the sale of UK residential properties (see 17.58A). However, provided the non-domiciled individual can avoid the settlor charge (see 17.58), trust gains on other assets can be sheltered within the non-resident trust provided they are *not* distributed by way of a capital payment.

Under the normal rules, trust gains can only be taxed to the extent they are matched with a capital payment (see 17.59). The 'matched' trust gains are treated as foreign chargeable gains (irrespective of whether the gains arise in foreign or UK-situs assets held by the trust). Thus, provided the capital payment is received offshore and *not* brought to the UK, a 'non-domiciled' beneficiary could avoid the CGT charge if they are a 'remittance basis user'. In most cases, they will qualify as a remittance basis user provided they have opted to pay the remittance basis charge (see 17.59 and 15.126).

In those cases, where a CGT charge arises on a non-domiciled beneficiary, the trustees can opt to apply rebasing on their pre-6 April 2008 trust assets. This effectively means that the relevant assets are 'rebased' at 6 April 2008, enabling the charge to apply only on the post-6 April 2008 element of the 'distributed' gain.

Transferring an existing (valuable) shareholding into a non-resident trust would generally be unattractive as this would trigger a 'dry' tax charge. CGT would be levied on a deemed 'market value' disposal of the shares and it is not possible to hold-over gains on a transfer to a non-resident trust (*TCGA 1992, ss 166* and *261*) (see 13.14).

Having said that, many non-domiciled owner-managers may not wish to enter into such complex arrangements, especially if they are reasonably confident of obtaining the relatively low (10%) ER CGT rate.

There is a specific transitional rule that prevents someone becoming deemed domiciled in a year when they are not UK resident if that *16th year first occurs in 2017/18.* If the individual (not yet deemed domiciled under current law) leaves in the course of 2016/17 and is not resident in the UK for the tax year 2017/18 they will not become deemed domiciled on 6 April 2017 under the new 15 year rule even if they have been UK resident for 16 years or more previously.

As a general rule, the income of an overseas trust (and any underlying entities) is generally attributed and taxed a *UK resident* but non-UK domiciled settlor, where they retain an interest in the offshore trust. This income is taxed on the arising basis, although the remittance basis may be available for foreign source income *(ITTOIA 2005, s 624* and *ITA 2007, s 720).* A detailed examination of these rules is outside the scope of this chapter.

SETTLOR-INTERESTED UK TRUSTS

Income tax

17.61 If the settlor (or their spouse/civil partner) has an interest, even if it is of a discretionary nature, in their (UK-resident) trust, the income arising in the trust will be taxed on the settlor (even though the income is retained within the trust) *(ITTOIA 2005, ss 624* and *625).*

Although the settlor suffers income tax on the trust income, the trustees would initially incur an income tax liability as recipients of the income at the relevant rates appropriate to the type of trust (see 17.73 for interest in possession trusts; see 17.86 for discretionary trusts).

The settlor records the relevant income on their personal tax return (on Form SA 107 Trusts). They can deduct the tax paid by the trust on the relevant income against their personal income tax due on the trust income, which may result in a refund or further payment. The trustees should provide the settlor with a statement showing the amount of tax they have incurred on the income.

This so-called 'settlor-interested' settlement rule also applies where there is no formal trust vehicle. In recent years, HMRC have attempted to use these provisions to challenge the use of 'income-splitting' which involved the payment of tax-efficient dividends to spouses. Whilst the House of Lords found these arrangements to constitute a settlement, the settlor was exempted under the 'outright gifts' exemption in (what is now) *ITTOIA 2005, s 626,* so the dividends were taxed on the spouse (as intended) – see 9.29–9.39 for further commentary.

Parental settlements

17.62 Special anti-avoidance rules also apply to income *paid out* of or made available by trusts created for the benefit of the settlor's unmarried children aged under 18. Such income is deemed to be the settlor's (subject to a *de minimis* limit of £100 for each child every year) [*ITTOIA 2005, s 629*]. (See 17.71 for treatment of bare trusts for minor children.)

However, income arising in a discretionary trust created for the benefit of the *settlor's* children would *not* be taxed on the settlor whilst it is retained by the trust (as the income does not belong to the child). In these cases, the parent is only liable to tax under *ITTOIA 2005, s 629* when the trust pays the income out to the child or applies it for their benefit (for example, by paying their school fees).

There is no equivalent rule for CGT. Consequently, any capital gains arising in the trust therefore belong to the child, who can set their own annual CGT exemption against them. In the case of a bare trust, the child will be able to call for the capital when they reach their 18th birthday.

However, if the trust is properly established by another 'family' member, for example, a grandparent, then any income paid out of the trust can be treated as that of the children (and hence covered by their personal allowances, etc). However, the legislation prevents the use of reciprocal arrangements – for example, if Bobby sets up a trust for the benefit of Hayden's children, with Hayden doing the same for Bobby's children – in such cases, both trusts would be caught by the parent-settlement rules (*ITTOIA 2005, s 620(3)(c)*, previously *ICTA 1988, s 660G(2)*).

A will trust created for the benefit of the settlor's children would *not* be caught.

Capital gains of settlor-interested trust

17.63   Capital gains arising in a (UK resident) settlor-interested trust (ie one in which the settlor or their spouse is able to benefit (even if only potentially)) are taxed in the trust in the normal way.

For post-5 April 2016 disposals, trust gains are normally taxed at 20%. However, a 28% CGT rate applies to gains arising on the disposal of UK residential property.

It is not possible for a settlor to offset their *personal losses* against gains arising in a UK settlor-interested trust.

A settlor charge still applies to *non-resident* trust gains which are within the very widely defined 'settlor interest' rules (see 17.58).

OVERVIEW OF IHT REGIME FOR TRUSTS

17.64   Transfers to an interest in possession trust or discretionary trust are currently both treated as chargeable transfers. Thus, in practice, the amount that can be transferred into trusts is generally restricted to the settlor's 'nil rate' band (currently £325,000) (see also 17.84A). Where an IHT exemption, such as BPR or APR, applies it is often possible to transfer considerably more.

A transfer to a trust in which the settlor is entitled to benefit, is still treated as a chargeable transfer and an IHT charge may arise. This is because there is a loss to settlor's estate – the settlor is *not* deemed to own the trust's assets for IHT purposes. Where it is not intended that the settlor should benefit, care must be taken to ensure the trust deed provides that they are excluded from benefiting (and cannot be added as a beneficiary in future!).

However, since the settlor is still able to benefit from the transferred assets, this will be a gift with reservation of benefit (GROB) (see 17.10A). This means that the trust's assets will be deemed to form part of the settlor's chargeable estate on death (provided the interest or potential interest is still held by them).

However, where the trust assets are subject to the GROB rules, this does not prevent it being 'relevant property' under the IHT trust regime, and hence subject to exit and ten-year charges.

In computing the settlor's IHT on death, the executors will be able to deduct any IHT paid on the original chargeable transfer into the trust (even the extra IHT arising as a result of the settlor's death within seven years of the transfer into trust). As a general rule, two IHT calculations are made and HMRC takes the computation that produces the largest IHT liability (*Inheritance Tax (Double Charges Relief) Regulations 1987, SI 1987/1130*).

The IHT treatment of interests in possession contrasts sharply with the pre-22 March 2006 position which used to treat the life tenants of such trusts as owning the underlying capital supporting the income for IHT purposes. This meant that if the *settlor* was entitled to the interest in possession, ie the income of the trust, there was no transfer of value – the settlor's estate did not suffer a reduction as they were deemed to own the capital value of the trust fund.

Once again, a chargeable transfer arises for IHT when assets are transferred into the trust. A CGT charge may also be triggered, bearing in mind that hold-over relief (under *TCGA 1992, s 165* or *260*) is no longer available in such cases (see 13.14 and 17.67).

CREATING THE TRUST – TAX IMPLICATIONS

Basic CGT rules

17.65 The tax implications of creating a trust (by transferring cash or assets), generally, depends on the nature of the property being transferred and the type of trust.

The transfer of property to a trust is a disposal for CGT purposes, even if the settlor retains some interest as a beneficiary or is a trustee of the trust

[*TCGA 1992, s 70*]. This disposal is deemed to take place at market value (obviously, a cash payment has no CGT effect).

Where the transfer of an asset to any trust produces an allowable loss, this loss can only be used against gains on future disposals to the same trustees [*TCGA 1992, s 18(3)*] – they are 'connected' with the settlor under *TCGA 1992, s 286(3)(a)*.

CGT hold-over reliefs

17.66   Capital assets transferred to a relevant property trust (eg interest in possession or discretionary trusts) after 21 March 2006 are treated as chargeable transfers for IHT purposes (see 17.68).

This means that CGT hold-over relief under *TCGA 1992, s 260* is potentially available to shelter the settlor's capital gain. However, hold-over relief is now denied where the relevant trust is a 'settlor-interested' one. The definition of a settlor-interested trust was substantially widened from 6 April 2006. This wider definition effectively means that hold-over relief would now be denied where the trust's beneficiaries include the settlor's minor (unmarried) children. In such cases, a 'dry' CGT charge may therefore arise on the transfer (see 13.14 and 17.67).

On the other hand, where the trust is not a 'settlor-interested' one, the settlor will normally be able to hold-over the gains under *TCGA 1992 s 260*. (This is because the disposal of assets to the trust will be treated as a chargeable transfer for IHT purposes, even if it falls within the 'nil rate band'. Even where the assets transferred constitute eligible business assets for the purposes of *TCGA 1992, s 165*, the hold-over relief under *TCGA 1992, s 260* takes precedence.)

For treatment of pre-22 March 2006 transfers, see 2013/14 and earlier editions of this book.

For both types of hold-over relief, the settlor must make the formal election (not the trustees) by using the prescribed HMRC form IR 295 [*TCGA 1992, ss 165(1)(b)* and *260(1)(b)*]. The trustees effectively acquire the asset at its original base cost (ie market value less the held-over gain). This may include indexation where the disposal occurred between 31 March 1982 and 6 April 2008. However, it is possible to avoid computing the proper market value of the asset if both parties agree to invoke the 'valuation dispensation' in SP8/92 (see 13.18).

Hold-over relief restriction for settlor-interested trusts

17.67   CGT hold-over relief under *TCGA 1992, s 165* or *260* cannot be claimed where the settlor or their spouse/civil partner has an 'interest' in the trust, even where they are a *potential* beneficiary [*TCGA 1992, s 169C*]. (A 'separated' spouse or widow or widower can be included without prejudicing the relief.)

Since 6 April 2006, the concept of a 'settlor-interested' trust is now extended to include cases where the settlor's minor unmarried children (including step-children) are able to benefit under the trust. This restriction therefore prevents any CGT hold-over relief being claimed on family trusts that benefit the settlor's minor children! (It is possible, however, to prevent the settlor's children from benefiting under a trust whilst they remain under the age of 18 – this type of clause would prevent the trust being a settlor-interested one)

The hold-over restriction also applies where there are 'arrangements' under which a settlor or their spouse could obtain an interest in the trust.

Furthermore, no hold-over relief is given or, where appropriate, any relief previously claimed is clawed-back if any of the above 'settlor-interested criteria' are satisfied within the relevant 'clawback period'.

The 'clawback period' starts from the date of the transfer into trust and ends six years after the end of the tax year in which the transfer was made [*TCGA 1992, s 169B*]. In such cases, the gain would be computed on the basis that the hold-over claim was never made with the trustees having acquired the shares at their market value.

Basic IHT rules

17.68   *FA 2006* provides that the transfer of assets to virtually *any* type of trust during the settlor's lifetime (*after 21 March 2006*) is a *chargeable* transfer for IHT purposes (unless the trust qualifies as a disabled trust). Relevant property trusts include both interests in possession created after 21 March 2006 and discretionary trusts.

Where shares in a qualifying trading company are transferred to a trust, 100% business property relief (BPR) (see 17.19) would normally be available to exempt the transfer from any IHT. However, if the value transferred is not protected by any relief, then the value transferred (in excess of the available nil rate band) will suffer IHT at 20%. In many cases, settlor's will not wish to incur the 'upfront' lifetime IHT charge of 20%, which would normally be involved when creating a substantial trust.

Many settlors are generally unwilling to incur a lifetime IHT charge of 20% and if the value to be transferred exceeds their available nil rate band, will look for ways in which the IHT can be mitigated. It may be possible to shelter the IHT liability under the 100% BPR or 100% Agricultural Property Relief provisions. Where such reliefs are not available, it may be possible to reduce the value transferred into the trust by selling the assets at an under-value. Provided the assets are sold for *no more* than their original cost, the CGT on the gain (based on market value) can still be held-over. However, if the consideration is left outstanding, care would be needed to ensure that the trust does not become settlor-interested (see 17.67 and 17.94A).

It might also be possible for the settlor's spouse to also make a trust in their own right (using their nil rate band) – effectively doubling-up the nil rate bands available. However, any assets passed to the spouse must be made without any stipulation as to their use, otherwise the 'transferor' could still be considered as the 'real' settlor.

The *FA 2006* changes did not alter the treatment of assets transferred to a *discretionary trust*. These have always created a *chargeable* transfer, incurring a 20% IHT charge on the value transferred after the settlor's available nil rate band was exhausted (subject to the annual exemption and any other available reliefs, such as BPR (see 17.19)).

Powers of trustees

17.69 As the main trust asset is likely to be shares in a family or owner-managed company, the trustees should have complete discretion in dealings with the trust assets. The trust deed should normally give the trustees appropriate powers and have regard to the *Trustee Act 2000*. This codifies the trustees' duty of care, which states that trustees must exercise 'such care and skill as is reasonable in the circumstances'. Clearly, a higher standard would be expected of a professional trustee! Trustees would be expected to invest prudently and avoid speculative and risky investments.

The trustees will also generally have a power to appoint income or capital to a nominated beneficiary and possibly a power of advancement enabling them to make a payment or distribution of capital to a beneficiary before they would normally become entitled to it under the trust deed.

The 'Hastings-Bass' principle and ability to set aside 'mistakes'

17.69A Since the *Hastings Bass* principle was laid down in 1974, trustees have been able apply to the court to set aside as void any decision they previously made under their discretionary power which subsequently turned out to have unforeseen or unintended results (*Re Hastings-Bass (deceased)* [1974] STC 211). This principle has often been use by trustees seeking to avoid an unanticipated tax liability that resulted from them receiving incorrect tax advice.

However, in *Pitt v Holt* and *Futter v Futter* [2011] EWCA Civ 197, the Supreme Court now places substantial restrictions the operation of the *Hastings Bass* rule. The Supreme Court decided that a decision taken by trustees within their power will not be voidable where they have taken reasonable steps and relied on professional advice. Of course, the trustees may be able to bring an action for professional negligence against their advisers.

However, the judgment in *Pitt* shows that it may still be possible to set aside a transaction on the grounds of mistake, although each case would depend on its own facts. In such cases, the court should evaluate whether it would be unjust to leave the mistake uncorrected. The Supreme Court was therefore prepared to use equity to set aside the settlement made by Mrs Pitt since she was genuinely mistaken about the tax consequences of making it.

BARE TRUSTS

Tax implications

17.70　As the trust property is, in effect, held by the trustee in a 'nominee' capacity, the income and capital gains of the bare trust are taxed on the underlying beneficial owners. A bare trust can be as simple as a bank account being held in the trustees' name. The tax legislation requires the relevant income and capital gains to be reported on the beneficiary's (ie the beneficial owner's) tax return, unless the income falls to be treated as the settlor's under the 'parental settlement' rules (see below).

Bare trusts have not been affected by the radical changes that were made to the IHT regime for trusts by *FA 2006*. Consequently, bare trusts may be preferred to more traditional trust vehicles. The transfer of assets to a bare trust is effectively treated as being made to the beneficial owner and would therefore be counted as a potentially exempt transfer for IHT purposes (ie completely exempt from IHT if the donor survives the 'seven-year' period). Similarly, the settlor may have a capital gain on any chargeable assets transferred.

From an IHT perspective, property held by a bare trustee is treated as part of the beneficial owner's estate. This point has now been confirmed by HMRC following advice from leading tax counsel. Thus, a lifetime gift for a minor absolutely (irrespective of whether the provisions of *Trustee Act 1925, s 31* are excluded), will be treated as a PET (see 17.10). Furthermore, an absolute trust of this nature is not a settlement for IHT purposes and does not therefore come within the 'relevant property' trust regime.

Bare trusts for minor children

17.71　Bare trusts have tended to be a useful IHT planning device to give cash to children or grandchildren. It is common for bare trusts to hold funds on behalf of minor beneficiaries – the adult trustees would hold the funds until the beneficiary is old enough to give a valid receipt. Once the beneficiary reaches their 18th birthday (or 16th birthday in Scotland), they can insist that their share of the trust assets is transferred into their own name (this is not a taxable event since there is no change in beneficial ownership).

Child beneficiaries will therefore return the 'bare trust' income and gains on their self-assessment return and pay any tax due on the income/gains arising (after the deduction of personal tax allowances or available CGT exemptions) at the relevant tax rates (depending on the type of income).

However, in certain cases, income arising from bare trusts created by parents in favour of their children would be taxed on the parents under the 'parental settlement' rules in *ITTOIA 2005, s 629* (see 17.62). Thus, income from *parental* bare trusts created (or on *amounts added to an existing bare trust*) after 8 March 1999 are taxed in the parent's hands under *ITTOIA 2005, s 629(1)(b)* unless it was below the £100 per child exemption. These issues do not arise where *grandparents* set up bare trusts, since they are *not* subject to the 'parental settlement' rules. In such cases, the income is reported and (beneficially) taxed in the child's hands.

INTEREST IN POSSESSION/LIFE INTEREST TRUSTS

Creation of trust

17.72 An interest in possession (or life interest) trust is now treated as a 'relevant property trust'. Consequently, a post-21 March 2006 transfer of shares, etc to such trusts will be treated as a chargeable transfer. This means that IHT will only be avoided where the transfer is sheltered by 100% BPR, some other relief (see 17.9), or the transferor's available nil rate band. The spouse exemption is *not* available where the life tenant of the trust is the settlor's spouse.

Any amount transferred in excess of the nil rate band will be taxed at 20%. The amount transferred forms part of the settlor's cumulative chargeable transfers for computing IHT on subsequent gifts and transfers. The on-going IHT treatment of an interest in possession trust is summarised in 17.77.

HMRC's view is that the same IHT treatment applies where assets are *added* to an existing interest in possession trust created before 22 March 2006 – the addition is effectively treated as a separate trust and creates an immediate chargeable transfer. The added property becomes 'relevant property' and will therefore need to be separately identified for future IHT calculations.

The disposal is deemed to take place at market value for CGT purposes. Although hold-over relief under *TCGA 1992, s 260* is potentially available (see

17.66), this will not be the case where the trust is a *settlor-interested* one. The wider definition of a 'settlor-interested' trust which applies from 6 April 2006 is likely to deny hold-over relief in many cases (see 17.67).

The IHT treatment of transfers into an interest in possession trust is completely different to that which applied before 22 March 2006. Under the pre-*FA 2006* regime, the transfer was treated as a PET. See 2013/14 and earlier editions of this book, for details of the IHT treatment of transfers to interest in possession trusts before 22 March 2006.

Taxation of income

17.73 Under an interest in possession/life interest trust, the beneficiary/ beneficiaries (life tenant(s)) have the right to receive the trust income as it arises, usually for life, but it can be for a fixed period. The capital would then normally vest in someone else (the 'remainderman').

The trustees must hand over the income (after any expenses and tax) to that beneficiary. The beneficiary is taxed on the *net* income arising in the tax year, irrespective of whether they actually receive it. Where the trust has different sources of income, the trust management expenses are allocated first against dividend income, then interest income, and finally other income.

Where the income is *not* paid direct to the beneficiary (see 17.74A below), the trustees must account for income tax.

The *current* rates (2017/18) of income tax payable by the *trustees* of an interest in possession trust are as follows:

Income	Rate	Notes
Dividends and other distribution income	Dividend ordinary rate of 7.5%	*Since 6 April 2016, dividends do not carry any tax credit. Trustees are not entitled to the £5,000 dividend nil-rate band.*
Distribution on a company purchase of own shares	38.1%	*This special rate is imposed by ITA 2007, s 481(3).*
Savings income	Basic rate of 20%	*Since 6 April 2016, banks and building societies pay interest gross.*
Other income (such as property income, etc)	Basic rate of 20%	

These trusts are not therefore generally exposed to the high income tax rates imposed on discretionary trusts (see 17.86). No personal allowance is given in computing the trust's taxable income. Similarly, there is no relief for any trust expenses, which are therefore met out of post-tax income.

See 2015/16 and earlier editions of this book for pre-6 April 2016 treatment.

17.74   As the income (net of any 'income-related' expenses) must be paid out to the beneficiary/beneficiaries, the 'net' income is taxed in their hands at their normal income tax rates (and would therefore, where appropriate, suffer additional and top rates of income tax).

In such cases, the recipient beneficiary is provided with a form R185 (trust income) showing the trust income (broken down between the relevant income sources and the trust expenses) and the tax deemed to be deducted (ie normally 7.5% or 20% as shown above).

The R185 income is then is taxed at the relevant income tax rates in the beneficiary's hands, with the relevant tax deducted being offset against their tax liability. No tax credit is available to the recipient beneficiary to the extent the income has been used to satisfy the trust expenses.

17.74A   The majority of trusts mandate dividend and other income directly to the beneficiaries. The income would then be taxed at the beneficiary's personal tax rates and the trustees do not have to account for any income tax (as shown in 17.73). HMRC accept that trustees do not have to submit a tax return where the income is mandated direct to a beneficiary/beneficiaries (*HMRC Trusts, Settlements, and Estates Manual para 30400*).

Example 12

Income tax computation for an interest in possession trust

The Slaven Family Trust was set up in 2016 and provides a life interest for Ivana. The income was not mandated to Ivana.

During the year ended 5 April 2018, the trustees received dividends of £20,000 from Lokomotiv Ltd and bank interest of £800. The trustees paid out management expenses of £1,200.

The trust's income tax computation and form R185E for the year ended 5 April 2018 is shown below:

	Savings	Dividend	Total	Tax deducted at source/tax credit
	£	£	£	£
Bank interest	800		800	–
Dividend from Lokomotiv Ltd		20,000	20,000	–
Total	800	20,000	20,800	–
Tax rates	20%	7.5%		
Tax	£160	£1,500	£1,660	
Trust tax liability			£	
Total tax due			1,660	
Less: Tax deducted at source			–	
Trust tax liability			£1,660	
R185E for Ivana				
Net income	£640	£17,300*		

* *£20,000 less tax £1,500 and expenses £1,200*

CGT on trust gains

17.75 Although the life tenant has no right to the capital, the trustees could be given power to pay capital to them or they may become entitled to capital on reaching a specified age.

For 2017/18, trusts normally pay CGT at 20% on their gains, with a 28% CGT rate applying to disposals of UK residential property.

Trusts enjoy an annual exemption equal to one-half of the individual exemption, ie £5,650 (= 1/2 × £11,300) for 2017/18 [*TCGA 1992, Sch 1*]. However, to counter the potential fragmentation of trust assets, if the settlor has created more than one trust (after 6 June 1978), the trust exemption is shared equally between the trusts, subject to a minimum exemption of one-fifth of the normal trust annual exemption. For example, for two trusts created by the same settlor, the annual exemption is £2,825 (£5,650 × 1/2).

Many CGT reliefs can be claimed by the trust in relevant circumstances.

CGT Entrepreneurs' relief for interest in possession trusts

17.76 In limited circumstances trustees may share the life tenant's lifetime Entrepreneurs' relief (ER) allowance to reduce the CGT rate on a disposal of shares to 10% (see 15.33 and 15.35). The relief is only available if a qualifying 'interest in possession' beneficiary is a director or employee of the company (or fellow 'group' company) and holds personally at least 5% of the ordinary share capital and voting rights of the company.

As any relief claimed by the trustees reduces that potentially available to the beneficiary on a future disposal, a joint election by the trustees and the beneficiary must be made. Since the beneficiary may have no right to benefit from the capital of the trust, it may not be in his best interests to make the election.

IHT treatment of post-21 March 2006 life interest trusts

17.77 Under the *FA 2006* rules, a post-21 March 2006 interest in possession trust is *not* treated as if the life tenant had owned the underlying trust assets, as was previously the case. (Such trusts are sometimes referred to as 'non-estate IIPs'.) Hence, the assets of the trust will not therefore be aggregated with the life tenant's estate on death. The death of the life tenant will therefore largely be irrelevant for IHT purposes.

As a relevant property trust, the trust will be liable to the normal 'exit' charge when property leaves the trust (see 17.78) and a 'ten-year' 'periodic' charge on every ten-year anniversary (see 17.79). Because of the way in which these charges are calculated, where an interest in possession trust is set-up within the transferor's nil rate band, it will not incur any exit charges during the first ten years.

Pre-22 March 2006 interest in possession trusts (or estate IIPs) remain subject to the pre-*FA 2006* regime, which broadly treats the beneficiary as owning the underlying capital of the trust (see 17.80).

Exit charge on capital distributions/property leaving the trust during first ten years

17.78 Under the *FA 2006* regime, interest in possession trusts created after 21 March 2006 are subject to an IHT exit charge when the property leaves the trust, typically by way of a capital distribution to a beneficiary.

Where the trust assets are subsequently appointed on discretionary trusts, this is effectively a 'non-event' for IHT purposes and hence no 'exit' charge arises. (This is because discretionary and post-21 March 2006 interest in possession trusts fall within the same 'relevant property' trust regime.)

From a CGT perspective, there is no uplift to market value on the death of the life tenant. However, where the property leaves the trust, this will be a chargeable transfer for IHT purposes. Consequently, CGT hold-over relief should be available under *TCGA 1992, s 260*.

The exit charge is calculated using an effective IHT rate, which is applied to the property leaving the trust. The calculation of the effective IHT rate on an exit event is summarised in Table 1 below. In essence, the trust rate is derived from a deemed transfer by the settlor at the time of the exit charge

Table 1 – Computation of exit charge during first ten years

(a) Take the value of the hypothetical transfer into the trust by the settlor – this is the value actually transferred into the trust (plus any 'same day' additions and property transferred into 'related settlements' made on the same day, typically on death – see 17.79A) (see *IHTA 1984, s 68*).

(b) The IHT liability on the total notional value transferred (in (a)) is found by applying the lifetime rate of 20% to that value. In calculating the charge, the value of any chargeable transfers made in the previous seven years must be taken into account. The total value is reduced by any prevailing 'nil rate' band available to the settlor. The effective rate is the IHT calculated as a percentage of the total notional transfer.

(c) The effective rate is then time apportioned by applying the fraction q/40 where:

  q = the number of complete quarters between the start of the trust and the day before the distribution (special pro-rota rules apply for added-property)

  40 = the number of complete quarters in the ten-year period

(d) The actual IHT rate to apply to the capital distribution is found by taking 30% of the apportioned effective rate in (c).

(e) If 100% business property relief (BPR) applied on the original transfer into the trust (see 17.19) it cannot be used to reduce the value of the shares initially received by the trust. In other words, 100% BPR does not reduce the value of the property (shares) that is transferred into the trust (the legislation provides that BPR reduces the amount chargeable to tax).

  However, once BPR-eligible shares have been held by the trustees for the relevant 'two-year' period, 100% BPR can be applied against the value of the shares subject to a distribution or exit charge.

(f) No exit charge generally arises within the first three months of the start of the trust (or a subsequent ten-year charge).

(g) If the trustees pay the tax, the value of the property leaving the trust has to be 'grossed up' for the relevant IHT.

Note – Many trusts will be set up within the settlor's nil rate band and hence the calculation in (a) above will be nil. This means that no exit charge will generally arise during the first ten years.

Example 13

Calculation of IHT on capital distribution (during first ten years)

On 20 November 2014 Mr Magnusson transferred a 30% shareholding in his property investment company, Magnusson Properties Ltd, to The Magnusson Trust. The trust was primarily for the benefit of his son, Terry (aged 22), who was entitled to the income of the trust. (Note, the gain on the transfer of the shares was held-over under *TCGA 1992, s 260*. Hold-over relief is available since the trust was *not* a settlor-interested one – Mr Magnusson's son is over 18 years old.)

The value of the shares settled into the trust was agreed with HMRC – Shares Valuation at £450,000. At the time of the transfer, Mr Magnusson had made chargeable transfers of £200,000 within the previous seven years.

Assume that on (say) 5 September 2017 the trustees advanced capital of £100,000 to Terry (exercising their power under the trust deed).

The IHT payable on the exit charge would be £1,192, calculated as follows:

5 September 2017 – capital distribution of £100,000	£
Value of hypothetical chargeable transfer	
Value of 30% shareholding at 20 November 2014*	450,000
Total of previous chargeable transfers	200,000
Aggregate chargeable transfer	650,000
IHT at lifetime (half-death) rates	
First £325,000 × 0%	–
Next £325,000 × 20%	65,000
	65,000
Less: Tax on previous chargeable transfers	–
Notional IHT on assumed chargeable transfer	65,000
Effective rate:	
£65,000/£450,000 × 100	14.4444%
No business property relief is available since Magnusson Properties Ltd is an investment company	

Number of complete quarters between start (Nov 2014) and exit (Sept 2017)	11
Settlement rate:	
14.4444% (effective rate) × 11/40 × 30%	1.1916%
IHT payable:	
£100,000 × 1.1916%	<u>£1,192</u>

First ten-year (or periodic) charge

17.79   Interest in possession trusts set up after 21 March 2006 are 'relevant property' trusts and are therefore subject to a ten-year anniversary (or periodic) charge. The ten year anniversary is taken from when the trust started. Where the trust is created under a will, the date of the testator's death is treated as the commencement date.

IHTA 1984, ss 64–66 provides for the calculation of the ten-year charge, which (for charges arising from 6 April 2014) is summarised in Table 2 below. See Example 16 at 17.98 for calculation of a ten-year charge within the first ten years.

Where the owner manager transfers shares qualifying for 100% BPR into a family discretionary trust, these can be retained for many years in the trust without incurring any ten-year charge. If the shares are sold, there is also an added benefit since the relevant proceeds would not fall within the owner manager's estate, thus aiding the IHT planning process.

Table 2 – Computation of ten-year charge

(*a*)   Compute the chargeable amount – this is based on the value of the trust property immediately before the ten-year anniversary.

The trust property includes the capital (and any accumulated and undistributed trust income which has been in the trust for more than five years – calculated on a FIFO basis) and is reduced by any liabilities of the trust. Where the trust property includes shares in an owner-managed company, they are likely to qualify for 100% business property relief (see 17.19) (after two years), which can be deducted in arriving at the chargeable amount.

(*b*)   Calculate the actual rate of tax to apply to the value of the trust in (*a*). This is 30% of the effective IHT payable on a notional transfer consisting of:

    –   the chargeable amount in (*a*)

    –   the (initial) historic value of property held in any other trust created by the settlor on the same date (typically on death);

- the total chargeable transfers made by the settlor of the trust within the seven years before they created the trust;

- the total of any capital distributions that have been subject to an exit charge within the last ten years (before the relevant anniversary).

The actual tax is calculated by reference to the prevailing nil rate band at the relevant ten-year anniversary.

(c) 100% BPR is available provided the trustees satisfy the relevant BPR conditions at the relevant ten-year anniversary date.

(d) If the value of the other trust assets falls within the nil rate band, there will be no ten-year charge (ie those not qualifying for BPR).

(e) The ten-year charge is payable by the trustees (but there is no 'grossing-up').

(f) Where some of the property was not relevant property for the whole of the ten-year period there are special rules to time apportion the charge.

Notes

(1) In many cases, trusts will be established within the settlor's nil rate band. Provided the settlor has no prior chargeable transfers (as will often be the case), the ten year charge will frequently simplify to an IHT rate of 6% (ie 30% × lifetime charge of 20% (in *b*)) being applied to the current value of the trust assets (*after deducting the prevailing nil rate band*).

(2) If qualifying shares are retained in the trust, they will often attract 100% BPR (see 17.19) and hence would be exempted from the taxable value of the trust assets.

Use of Pilot Trusts

17.79A The rules in relation to the taxation of 'pilot trusts' significantly changed on 10 December 2014. Pilot trusts have historically been used for all types of planning and were usually flexible discretionary trusts that lay dormant until further funds are added.

Typically, a settlor would settle a number of pilot trusts with a nominal amount – often £10 on different days. The trusts lay inactive until further funds are added to them, usually on the same day following the death of the settlor funded from life assurance proceeds, pension death benefits or shares from their residuary estate.

Before 10 December 2014, each pilot trust had its own nil rate band and provided each trust did not exceed its own nil rate threshold and the other trusts were established on different days, the trusts were not charged to IHT.

Since 10 December 2014, each of the trusts can still claim its own nil rate band. However, the calculation of the IHT rate takes into account the value of the assets added to the other trusts on the same day (see 17.78, Table 1(a)). This will clearly apply to additions to the 'pilot' trust taking place on the settlor's death. This effectively cancels out the benefits of having multiple nil rate bands.

The new rules do not apply to trusts established before 10 December 2014 provided the settlor has not made further 'same day' additions to them since that date, or if the additions do not exceed £5,000. Furthermore, trusts established under a will created before 10 December 2014 will not be affected if death occurs before 6 April 2017.

IHT treatment of pre-22 March 2006 life interest trusts

17.80   The *FA 2006* retains the pre-existing IHT treatment for existing interest in possession trusts (ie those trusts established before Budget day 2006) whilst the present interest continues.

Under the pre-*FA 2006* regime, life tenants of such trusts are treated as owning the underlying capital of the trust for IHT purposes, even if they are never entitled to receive it [*IHTA 1984, s 49(1)*]. Thus, where a life tenant of an interest in possession trust dies, their IHT liability is calculated by adding their part of the trust fund to their personal estate. The IHT relating to the trust capital is paid by the trustees out of the trust funds.

Any increase in the value of the chargeable assets up to the date of death generally escapes liability to CGT (see 17.81) [*TCGA 1992, s 72(1), (1A)*]. Where a life interest under an existing IIP terminates after 21 March 2006, this will either be:

- a PET, if the settlement comes to an end at that time so the life tenant is treated as making a gift to another individual under *IHTA 1984, s 3A(1A) (c)–(i)* (see 17.10); or

- a chargeable transfer, if the settlement continues – this will generally be a 'relevant property' trust and the life tenant is treated as making a chargeable transfer when the interest is terminated (see 17.68). Furthermore, the life tenant is treated as making a *gift* of the 'no longer possessed' property. This means that there will be a GROB where they retain an interest in or have continuing enjoyment in that property (see 17.100)

CGT on termination of pre-22 March 2006 life interest

17.81   The underlying assets of a pre-22 March 2006 interest in possession (or a TSI) are effectively rebased for capital gains purposes, where that interest terminates on the life tenant's death and the assets pass to the individual(s) becoming absolutely entitled. In such cases, there will be a deemed disposal and reacquisition by the trustees of the shares/other assets at their market value [*TCGA 1992, ss 71–73*]. The deemed disposal does not give rise to any chargeable gain (or allowable loss).

Nevertheless, CGT will crystallise on any held-over gain claimed [*TCGA 1992, s 74*] when the shares, etc were originally transferred into the trust.

Where the shares qualify as a business asset under *TCGA 1992, s 165(2)(b)* (which will often be the case for a trading company), then the crystallised held-over gain can be the subject of a further hold-over claim under *TCGA 1992, s 165* (see 13.14–13.17).

Where a life interest ends (other than on the death of a life tenant, for example, on their re-marriage) with the property remaining in trust, there is no CGT effect.

Protected 'immediate post-death interest' (IPDI) trusts created by will

17.82   The pre-*FA 2006* IHT treatment of interest in possession trusts will continue where the life interest is created through the *settlor's will or intestacy* – referred to an immediate post-death interest (IPDI) trust. In such cases, the life interest commences *immediately* on death. HMRC accept that this test is met where the interest in possession takes effect on death by virtue of the special 'reading back' provisions for deeds of variation (see 17.18) or survivorship clauses (*IHTA 1984, s 92*).

The 'immediate post-death interest' (IPDI) is taxed under the old regime. This means that the life tenant is treated as owning the underlying capital of the trust under *IHTA 1984, s 49A*. It will therefore be included in the life tenant's estate for IHT purposes on their death (see 17.77). Whilst the IPDI continues it will not be treated as a 'relevant property' trust – the life interest is not subject to any exit or periodic charges.

The testator would be eligible for the spouse/civil partner exemption where an IPDI is granted in favour of the testator's spouse (or civil partner) (see also 17.51).

Transitional serial interest (TSIs) trusts

17.83   *IHTA 1984, s 49C* provides special protection for existing life interests (at 22 March 2006) that come to an end between 6 April 2006 and 5 October 2008. These rules apply to pre-22 March 2006 life interest trusts that terminate before 6 October 2008 and on that event, another interest in possession is created.

DISCRETIONARY TRUSTS

Flexibility of discretionary trusts

17.84 Discretionary trusts probably give the greatest flexibility for estate and IHT planning and largely remain unaffected by the *FA 2006* IHT trust changes. Discretionary trusts often play an important asset protection role to safeguard 'family assets' from spendthrift beneficiaries, creditors and so on.

The income (for example, dividends on the shares) and often the capital would be held by the trustees to be dealt with at their discretion. The trustees (normally including the proprietor) will usually have the power to accumulate the income arising in the trust (normally) during the first 21 years and decide which interest each of the children will have in the trust's assets at a later date.

These features should help to make genuine discretionary trusts relatively safe from divorce claims (unless perhaps where there is a regular pattern of income being paid out or where the trust has been formed to 'frustrate' such claims). The beneficiaries are entirely reliant on the trustees' discretion being exercised in their favour. Hence, where there are concerns or fears about their children's marriages or other long-term relationships, parents may prefer to place the company's shares in a discretionary trust rather than give them directly to their children.

Nil rate band trusts

17.84A A transfer to a discretionary trust where the value of the asset transferred is below the settlor's nil-rate band is a tax-efficient way of passing down assets to the next generation without incurring an immediate tax charge.

Although such a transfer is a chargeable lifetime transfer there is no immediate IHT charge provided the value is within the settlor's available nil-rate band. Assuming the settlor then survives seven years, the transfer will fall out of their cumulative transfer calculation and the transfer will then have the same effect as if a potentially exempt transfer (PET) had been made.

Nil-rate band trusts are frequently used where the shares of an owner-managed company currently have low value and are expected to appreciate significantly in value (or be sold).

Where the value of the assets transferred to the trust exceeds the settlor's nil rate band, the 'excess' amount is subject to the 20% lifetime IHT rate. Where the settlor agrees to pay the tax, this increases the loss to their estate. Thus, the value transferred is grossed-up by the 'excess' × 100/80.

Where the settlor dies within seven years, the IHT on the chargeable amount transferred (in excess of the 'nil rate' band) to the trust is recalculated at the 40% 'death' rate. The settlor's available nil rate band is used against the chargeable transfer into trust in priority, thus reducing the amount available to set against their chargeable estate on death. See 17.13 for detailed rules. In practice, an IHT liability would only arise if the value transferred exceeds the nil rate band prevailing at the settlor's death.

Use of exempt transfers

17.84B An owner manager can use 100% business property relief (BPR) to transfer shares in 'their' trading company (provided they are owned for two years etc (see 17.19)) into a family discretionary trust without any entry charge.

Hold-over relief should also be available under *TCGA 1992, s 260*, provided the trust is not a settlor-interested trust (see 17.66 and 17.67). If the settlor dies within seven years of the transfer, BPR should also available on any re-computation of IHT (see 17.84A). However, this will only be possible if the trustees continue to hold the relevant shares etc, and they continue to qualify for BPR at the date of the settlor's death. However, the trustees do not need to have held the shares for two years (*IHTA 1984, s 113A*).

The same rules apply for any other BPR exempt assets and qualifying agricultural property

For those with regular surplus income, consideration should be giving to using the 'normal expenditure out of income' exemption to make annual transfers of income to the trust. In some cases, significant sums can be added to the trust without creating any IHT charge. It is important for records to be retained to demonstrate that the payments to the trust have been made from 'surplus income'. Following the *FA 2006* abolition of the beneficial statutory regime for accumulation and maintenance trusts (see 17.101), discretionary trusts can also play an important role in planning for grandchildren – for example, to provide for school fees. The trustees can assess and monitor the needs of each grandchild and the lump sum(s) transferred into the trust will reduce the value of the grandparent-donor's estate for IHT. Alternatively, outright gifts can be made within the donor's annual £3,000 exemption (see 17.9) each academic year.

Example 14

Using a discretionary trust to transfer shares to adult children

Bobby owns a 75% shareholding in his furnished holiday letting company, Mooro's Holiday Cottages Ltd, which are currently valued at worth £300,000. The company is unlikely to qualify for BPR (see 17.31).

The shares are standing at a gain of some £280,000. Thus, if Bobby were to gift all his shares to his adult son, the gift would rank as a PET but Bobby would pay CGT of £28,000 (ie £280,000 × ER CGT 10%).

Alternatively, Bobby could set up a discretionary trust (in which he did not have any interest) and transfer the shares to 'his' trust. Bobby would be a trustee of the trust along with his professional adviser, Mr Greenwood.

Although the transfer of the shares would be a chargeable transfer, this would be within Bobby's (unused) available nil rate band. Furthermore, he could make an election to hold-over the capital gain of around £280,000 under *TCGA 1992, s 260* (see 17.92–17.95).

Some four years later, the trust's 75% holding in Mooro's Holiday Cottages Ltd are worth some £500,000.

It would be possible for the shares to be appointed to his (adult) son:

- without any IHT charge (since the exit charge during the first ten years is broadly based on the initial value of the trust and not on the value leaving the settlement).

- with no taxable gain, since this could also be held-over (by joint election) under *TCGA 1992, s 260*.

In this way, the shares have now been transferred to Bobby's son without any tax costs.

Income tax payable by discretionary trusts

Self-assessment return

17.85 The trustees are returning the trust's income (and capital gains) on the trust self-assessment return form (SA 900) and paying the relevant income tax under the normal self-assessment timetable. Two equal annual payments on account are made on 31 January (during the tax year) and 31 July (following the end of the tax year). These 'on account' payments are normally based on the trust's income tax liability for the previous year. Where the trust's tax liability for the relevant tax year exceeds the two payments on account, a further balancing payment is due on the 31 January (following the end of the tax year). Similarly, if too much tax has been paid on account, then a repayment is due from HMRC.

Example 15

Income tax SA payments by trust

The Pardew Discretionary Trust made the following tax payments on account of its income tax liability for 2017/18

31 January 2018 – *(50% of 2016/17 liability of £24,000)*	£12,000
31 July 2018 – *(50% of 2016/17 liability of £24,000)*	£12,000

The trust's 2017/18 self-assessment return is completed in January 2019 and the tax liability for 2017/18 is calculated as £27,500. Thus, the total payment due to HMRC by 31 January 2019 would be £17,250, calculated as follows:

Balancing payment due for 2017/18 – *(£27,500 less payments on account of £24,000)*	£3,500
1st payment on account for 2018/19 – *(50% of 2017/18 liability of £27,500)*	£13,750
Total income tax payable	£17,250

RELEVANT TAX RATES

17.86   Since income may be accumulated within discretionary trusts, they are subject to special rules. It is perhaps unfortunate that the former Labour Government sought to unduly penalise many discretionary and accumulation and maintenance trusts.

The penal 'top' income tax rates apply to such trusts irrespective of their income levels (subject to the paltry £1,000 standard rate band!). Where the settlor has created more than one trust, the available standard rate band is shared equally between the trusts subject to a minimum of £200 for each trust [*IHTA 2007, s 492*].

The current relevant trust rates (on income above the £1,000 standard trust rate band) are:

Income	*Trust rates*
Dividends and distributions	38.1% (the 'dividend trust rate)
All other income	45% (the 'trust rate')

The standard trust rate applied to the first £1,000 income is the one which an individual taxpayer would pay on the relevant type of income (*ITA 2007, s 491*). This means dividend income taxed at 7.5% and all other trust income taxed at 20% (*ITA 2007, s 491*). The order of priority for income attracting the standard rate is non-savings income, savings income, and finally dividends.

Currently income (other than dividend income) above the £1,000 standard rate band is taxed at the trust rate of 45%. Dividends received after 5 April 2016 are taxed at 38.1% on the cash amount received (there is no longer any tax credit or gross-up).

The trustees cannot claim the benefit of the personal savings allowance or the dividend 'nil-rate' band. Thus (ignoring trust expenses), the trust will pay extra tax of 25% on income already taxed at 20%. Trust management expenses can be deducted against trust income taxable at the normal trust rate (45%) and dividend trust rate (38.1%) (but not the 20% or 7.5% basic tax rate elements) (*ITA 2007, s 484*) (see 17.88). Trust expenses are set against dividend income before other income (*ITA 2007, s 486*).

Given the high dividend tax rates, it may be appropriate for the trustees to grant (temporary) revocable interests in possession to improve the level of post-tax distributions to beneficiaries. The dividends would then be taxed at the beneficiary's/beneficiaries' dividend tax rates (see 17.74).

In some cases, it may even be appropriate to convert the discretionary trust to an interest in possession trust (which now involves no IHT difficulty since both 'trusts' remain within the 'relevant property' regime for trusts).

17.87 In *Howell v Trippier* [2004] STC 1245, the Court of Appeal held that a stock dividend was chargeable at (what is now) the dividend trust rate. The trustees had argued that the stock dividend (representing shares worth some £15 million) represented capital for trust law purposes. Consequently, they contended that this was *not* 'income which is to be accumulated or payable at the discretion of the trustees' which was taxable under (what is now *IHT 2007, s 479*) but this analysis was rejected. The stock dividend was therefore subject to income tax. In the subsequent case of *Seddon v HMRC* [2015] UKFTT 140 (TC), the First Tier Tribunal determined that the *Howell v Trippier* decision was only restricted to the income tax treatment of stock dividends (see 17.97)

When the income is distributed to the beneficiaries, credit is given for the tax suffered by the trust, thus avoiding double taxation (see 17.91).

Trusts with only a small amount of income (ie below the £1,000 'standard trust rate' band) are likely to avoid payment of the normal trust rate on their income. Their standard rate liability would generally be covered by tax deducted at source/dividend tax credits).

Special rules apply to qualifying trusts with vulnerable beneficiaries (ie defined disabled persons and certain minors). By making an appropriate election, trustees (and the beneficiary) can elect to compute their income tax liability by reference to the individual beneficiary's personal allowances and basic rate band (see *FA 2005, ss 23–45* and *Sch 1*).

Deduction of trust management expenses (TMEs)

17.88 Trustees can deduct trust management expenses (TMEs) that are properly chargeable to income in calculating their taxable income at the 45% trust rate or 38.1% dividend trust rates (but *not* in calculating income taxable at the special *lower* trust rates). This means that the income applied in paying trust expenses would suffer the relevant lower rates of tax.

The expenses of managing a trust can be deducted against the relevant trust income provided they are properly chargeable from trust income. Following the *ITA 2007*, HMRC accepts that trust expenses from 6 April 2007 are deductible from trust income on an accruals basis.

Based on the leading precedent set by *Carver v Duncan* and *Bosanquet v Allen* [1985] STC 356, HMRC's view is that where an expense benefits the entire trust fund, then it should be charged to 'capital' and thus disallowed (even where the expense is recurrent). This was confirmed in *Trustees of Peter Clay Discretionary Trust v R&CC* [2009] STC 928 which considered the treatment of management expenses incurred by a large discretionary trust. Before the Court of Appeal hearing, HMRC agreed that it was possible for the following expenses to be apportioned (generally on a time-spent basis):

- Executive trustee fees' (charged on a time-spent basis);

- Bank charges;

- Custodian fees; and

- Professional fees for accountancy and administration.

Amounts apportioned to income could be deducted by the trust. For example, the time spent by an executive trustee in exercising their judgment in relation to 'income' matters could be properly apportioned to and deducted against income.

The Court of Appeal therefore only had to rule on the treatment of the investment management fees and the non-executive trustee fees':

- Investment management fees were, on the facts, properly chargeable to capital. Once the trustees had decided to accumulate the income, those monies were regarded as capital. Thus, investment advice relating to income that was to be accumulated was for the benefit of the entire trust fund, since the advice determined the best way to make the income into capital

- Fixed fees of non-executive trustees could be apportioned between income and capital where adequate records were kept of the time spent on each part. However, the difficulty in this case was that no such records were maintained. It was therefore difficult for the trustees to establish the time spent addressing matters that were exclusively for the benefit of income.

TMEs should therefore be apportioned between income and capital based on the proportion of the work performed on each element – as well as being required for tax purposes there is also the need to protect the interest of different classes of beneficiaries. Where fixed fees are charged the trustees should ask the service-provider to keep and log appropriate time sheets to support an 'income/capital' split of the fixed fee.

In practice, HMRC will generally allow, for example, the cost of maintaining accounting records and preparing tax returns and certificates (with appropriate apportionment being made between income and capital). On the other hand, expenses relating to changing trustees or seeking investment advice would be classified as capital and would not be admissible deductions. Although investment management charges may be levied on a regular basis, they clearly relate to capital as confirmed by *Carver v Duncan* [1985] STC 928.

TMEs (chargeable against income) are deductible in calculating the trustee's 'additional' income tax (but not their 'lower/basic' rate) (see Example 16 at 17.91). For these purposes, the expenses are matched with the different sources of income in the following order:

(*a*)   Distribution and stock dividend income;

(*b*)   Foreign dividends;

(*c*)   Savings income (for example, bank and building society interest);

(*d*)   Other income (for example, property and trading income).

Income distributed to beneficiaries

17.89   Where income is paid out to the beneficiaries, each beneficiary is given a form R185 (trust income) showing the net amount and the tax credit – the gross amount is the cash distribution currently multiplied by 100/55. While the distribution may contain 'dividend income', this has lost its character in the trust. It cannot therefore be regarded as dividend income in the beneficiary's hands and consequently does not attract personal dividend tax rates or benefit from the dividend nil-rate band.

However, since the trustees are deemed to have suffered the 45% tax on their distributions, they have to ensure that they have suffered this tax (in the current or previous tax year) and account for it under *ITA 2007, s 496*.

In addition to any pre-6 April 2016 tax pool additions, the trustees' tax pool will now consist of:

- Tax on standard rate band income (7.5% for dividends taxed and 20% for other income within standard rate band)

- Tax on dividend income at 38.1%

- Tax on all other income at 45%

The 'lower-rate' tax charged on TMEs does not enter the tax pool.

In prior years, the treatment of dividend tax was different. Although dividends carried a 10% tax credit, this never entered the trustees' tax pool.

Where tax paid in previous tax years has not been used to 'frank' the tax on payments to beneficiaries, the 'excess' amount is carried forward as the trustees' tax pool to the following tax year. The trustees' *ITA 2007, s 496* liability is calculated as follows:

Income tax due under *ITA 2007, s 496*	
Trust distributions × 45/100	A
Less: Trustees tax pool available for the year (ie tax pool b/fwd + tax paid by trust for the relevant tax year*)	(B)
Trustees' *ITA 2007, s 496* tax liability	X
* Excludes lower/basic rate tax on TMEs	

Each beneficiary's share of income is subsequently reported on their personal tax return (using the information supplied on their R185 on 'form SA 107', with credit being given for the 45% tax that is deemed to have been suffered.

Thus, if a beneficiary's income tax liability on their trust distribution is less than the 45% tax deducted at source, an appropriate tax repayment will be made. The deemed 45% deduction applies, irrespective of the underlying tax rate suffered by the trust.

DISTRIBUTION OF TRUST DIVIDEND INCOME

17.90   Distributions paid to beneficiaries out of *dividend* income received by the trust generally suffer an additional layer of tax (unless the trustees already have a sufficient pool of 'tax paid') as shown below:

	£
Cash dividend (2017/18)	100
Tax payable by trust	
Dividend tax @ 38.1% paid to HMRC	38.10
Maximum distribution to beneficiary	
Dividend (= cash)	100.00
Less: Total tax @ 45%	(45.00)
Amount distributed to beneficiary	55.00
Breakdown of tax	
Tax on dividend (see above)	38.10
s 496 additional tax on distribution (£45 less £38.10)	6.90
	45.00
Overall effective rate on cash dividend	*45%*
(£45/£100 × 100%)	

If dividends are continually paid out to beneficiaries, the trustees' pool of tax credits will eventually become depleted, leading to additional tax payable by the trust on the distributions paid out.

Of course, this problem should not arise if little or no (dividend) income is paid out to beneficiaries or funds are paid out as a genuine capital distribution.

In some cases, it may be appropriate for the shares held by the discretionary trust to be re-designated as a separate class of shares (although continuing to rank *pari passu* with the other shares, which would avoid any 'value-shifting' charge). This would build in additional flexibility with regard to future dividend payments enabling, for example, different levels of dividend to be paid out.

Indeed, in some cases, assuming there are no problems under the 'settlement' rules, it may be more efficient for a separate class of shares to be held directly by those 'family' shareholders (who have little or no other taxable income) to enable tax efficient dividends to be paid to them

Many discretionary trusts will have been created to hold shares and similar investments, normally due to the availability of CGT hold-over relief under *TCGA 1992, s 260*. However, an interest in possession trust is a more tax efficient vehicle for holding shares and receiving dividends (since there it does not suffer any additional income tax charge).

Where a discretionary trust receives substantial dividend income, there may be a case for converting it into an interest in possession trust (provided there is no conflict with the settlor's intentions and so on). Since both are 'relevant property' trusts under the *FA 2006* regime, this can be done without triggering any IHT exit charges.

Worked example of trustee's income tax liability

17.91

Example 16

Calculation of income tax payable by discretionary trust

The trustees of The JF Charlton Family 2008 Discretionary Settlement received the following income during the year ended 5 April 2018

	£
Bank interest (received gross)	2,900
Dividends from 20% holding in Preston Ltd	15,000
Net rental income (after deducting property expenses)	24,700
Trust management expenses	(897)

The trustee's income tax liability for 2017/18 is calculated as follows:

	Gross
	£
Rental income	24,700
Bank interest	2,900
UK dividends ((£15,000 – £970 expenses) *(ie £897 × 100/92.5 since expenses are deemed to be paid out of taxed dividend income)*	14,030
	41,630

Tax	£	£
Standard rate – £1,000 @ 20%		200
On balance of trust income after TMEs (£41,630 less £1,000 standard rate band)		
Bank interest and rental income – £26,600 @ 45%		11,970
Dividend income – £14,030 @ 38.1%		5,345
Basic rate tax on TMEs – £970 × 7.5%		73
		17,588
Less tax credits		–
Tax payable		17,588

The trustees' made a distribution of £55,000 to a beneficiary on 31 December 2018. At that date the balance on the trustees' tax pool was £38,000 (including the £17,588 tax added for 2017/18).

The tax credit attributable to the distribution is £45,000 (£55,000 × 45%/55%) and the gross distribution is £100,000.

However, since the balance on the tax pool is only £38,000, the trustees must pay a further £7,000 (£45,000 less £38,000) tax to HMRC under *ITA 2007, s 496*.

Assuming the recipient beneficiary's marginal rate of tax is (say) 40%, they will be able to reclaim a tax repayment of £5,000 (£100,000 × 40% = £40,000 less tax credit of £45,000).

CGT payable by discretionary trust

17.92   Since 6 April 2016, discretionary trusts are generally subject to CGT at the rate of 20%, with a 28% CGT rate applying to disposals of UK residential property. The capital gains are computed with the normal trust exemption in the same way as a life interest/interest in possession trust.

Where chargeable assets are distributed to a beneficiary (or the beneficiary otherwise becomes absolutely entitled to the relevant assets), a deemed disposal at market value arises under *TCGA 1992, s 71*.

Capital gains arising on the distribution of assets to beneficiaries can normally be held over under *TCGA 1992, s 260* (since this is a chargeable transfer for IHT purposes, even if it is at 'nil rate') – see 17.66. It should be noted that *TCGA 1992, s 260* relief takes precedence over *TCGA 1992, s 165* relief (*TCGA 1992, s 165(3)(d)*). Since the disposal is being made from the trust, the trustees must jointly elect with the recipient beneficiary to hold-over the gain.

However, no *TCGA 1992, s 260* hold-over relief is available for assets distributed within the first three months of the trust's life or within the three months following a 'ten-year' anniversary charge (but see 17.48 for *will trusts* after 9 December 2014). Nevertheless, if the asset transferred is a qualifying business asset, such as shares in an unquoted trading company, it will usually be possible to claim hold-over relief under *TCGA 1992, s 165* instead.

IHT/CGT on assets transferred to discretionary trust

17.93   The broad objective of the IHT regime is to treat a discretionary trust (and, following *FA 2006*, most other trusts) as though it were a separate individual. The underlying capital of the trust is not attributed to the beneficiary or beneficiaries. IHT is therefore collected from the trust as though a gift of the property held by it had been made every generation. However, given the need to collect the tax at more regular intervals, each discretionary trust is currently subject to IHT when property leaves the trust and also there is a periodic charge every ten years (at a maximum rate of 6%).

The general view is that these tax costs represent a reasonable toll-charge to pay for the privilege of keeping property in a separate trust as opposed to remaining in an individual's taxable estate. However, in practice, most trusts have tended to pay only modest amounts of IHT or nothing at all. This is largely due to the operation of the 'nil rate' band and/or important reliefs (such as business property relief or agricultural property relief).

17.94   A gift of assets into a discretionary trust has always been a *chargeable transfer* and is not a PET – the same IHT treatment therefore applies both before and after the *FA 2006* changes. Consequently, to avoid a 20% IHT charge, the value transferred should normally be kept within the transferor's nil rate band (allowing for annual exemptions).

In most cases where the transfer is shares in a qualifying trading company, business property relief (BPR) will apply (where the shares have been owned for the requisite 'two-year' period) to avoid any IHT chargeable transfer (see 17.19–17.35).

If the shares do not qualify for BPR, for example, if the company (mainly) carries on an investment business (see 17.26), then a lifetime IHT charge at 20% can only be avoided if the relevant value transferred (see 17.4A) is broadly within the transferor's available nil rate band, preferably allowing some 'headroom' for agreeing the share value(s) with the HMRC Shares Valuation team.

17.94A   If the value of the asset exceeds the available nil rate band (and no IHT exemptions/reliefs are available), the transferor may consider reducing the amount of the chargeable transfer by *selling* the asset to the trustees at an under-value. Thus, for example, shares in an investment company worth £800,000 may be sold to a discretionary trust for (say) £500,000 left outstanding on loan account, resulting in a transfer of value of £300,000 (within the nil rate band).

In such cases, it is important to avoid any risk of the trust becoming settlor-interested (which would, for example, prevent CGT hold-over relief being available) (see 17.67). The amount left outstanding on loan account should therefore be non-interest bearing, and repayable on demand. The 'loan' by the settlor should *not* be on beneficial terms as this is likely to give the settlor an interest in the income of the trust (*Jenkins v CIR* (1944) 26 TC 265).

A sale at undervalue will involve actual consideration, and thus stamp duty or SDLT is likely to be payable on that amount.

There is a potential income tax trap when the loan is repaid. This may trigger an income tax charge to the extent there is undistributed income within the discretionary trust at the time of repayment or next 10 years (*ITTOIA 2005, ss 633–643)*. This problem would not arise on a transfer to an interest in possession trust.

17.95 CGT hold-over relief will normally be available (under *TCGA 1992, s 260*) for the transfer of shares, etc to a discretionary trust, except where relief is denied under the 'settlor-interested' rule (see 17.67 and 17.94A). Hold-over relief under *TCGA 1992, s 260* takes priority over any *TCGA 1992, s 165* hold-over claim for CGT (see 17.66).

However, if the transferor has sold the asset to the trustees at an under-value, there may be a chargeable gain on the 'realised' amount (ie the excess of the actual consideration over the transferor's base cost) due to the restriction in hold-over relief under *TCGA 1992, s 260(5)* (see also 13.19). This restriction would not operate if the asset is sold for no more than the transferor's original CGT base cost.

Capital distributions from 'nil rate band' trusts

17.96 If the shares were originally transferred within the nil rate band, then no IHT arises on a subsequent appointment of the shares to the beneficiaries (or to another trust) within the *first ten years*. The position where the transfer of shares to the trust was made under the protection of BPR is dealt with in 17.78.

Calculating IHT on capital distributions (during first ten years)

17.97 A distribution or exit IHT charge arises on assets (such as shares) or cash distributed to beneficiaries. This is based on a notional transfer of the value of the shares (and any other property in the trust) *immediately after the trust started*, computed at one-half of the death rate ie 20% (taking into account the transferor's nil rate band). That amount is then multiplied by $3/10 \times q/40$ (where q is the number of complete quarters between the start of the trust and the day before the distribution).

No IHT charge arises on property distributed within the *first three months* of the creation of the trust (or ten-year charge) (see also 17.48).

The detailed computational rules for exit charges (during the first ten years) are covered in 17.78. See 17.99 for calculation of IHT on capital distributions made after a ten-year charge.

It should be noted that in *Seddon v HMRC* [2015] UKFTT 140 (TC), the First-Tier Tribunal held that a stock dividend received by the trustees some nine years ago was 'capital' and hence must be taken into account into account in calculating the exit tax charge rate (see 17.78 (Table 1).

The Tribunal decided to follow the earlier Upper Tribunal ruling in *Gilchrist v HMRC* [2014] UKUT 169 (TC), which concluded that the *Howell v Trippier* [2004] STC 1245 decision (see 17.87) was only limited to the income tax treatment of stock dividends and did not provide any wider authority in relation to general trust law. Consequently, where trustees receive a significant stock dividend, this amount will normally treated as a 'capital' addition in the trustee's hands. The *Finance Act 2014* stipulates that accumulated and undistributed income that arises more than five years before a ten-year anniversary, is regarded as relevant trust property for the purposes of calculating the exit charge.

Ten-year or periodic charge

17.98   A discretionary trust is subject to a periodic IHT charge every ten years, which is broadly 30% of the rate applicable to a deemed transfer of the current value of the property held in the trust (taking into account the settlor's total lifetime transfers within the seven years prior to the creation of the trust) [*IHTA 1984, s 66*]. If the relevant trust property had not been held in the trust throughout the ten-year period, the effective rate is reduced by 1/40th for each complete quarter (three months) before the property was transferred into the trust. See 17.79 for detailed rules for calculating the ten-year charge.

The maximum ten-yearly charge is 6% (being 30% × 20%), but is usually lower. This is generally considered to be an acceptable price to pay for the privilege of placing the shares and other assets outside the settlor's and beneficiaries' estates.

Under so-called '*Rysaffe*' planning, it was possible for trusts to be established on different days (known as 'pilot trusts'), with each of these trusts having their own separate nil rate band for the purposes of calculating their ten year charges. However, since 6 April 2015, such planning has been rendered ineffective (see 17.79A for full details).

Example 17

Calculation of a ten-year anniversary charge

The Pompey Family 2006 discretionary trust was set up on 24 June 2007 by Mr Pompey for the benefit of his children and grandchildren.

On that date, Mr Pompey transferred a 49% shareholding in the Fratton Park Property Investment Company Ltd to the trust. Mr Pompey had previously made several PETs, but no chargeable transfers.

The ten-yearly charge for the trust falls to be calculated on 24 June 2017.

Following negotiations with HMRC's Shares Valuation team, the value of a 49% holding at 24 June 2017 is finally agreed at £870,000. This represented the entire value of the trust.

Calculation of the ten-yearly charge

	£
Value of assumed chargeable transfer	
Value of 49% shareholding at 24 June 2017	870,000
Total of previous chargeable transfers	–
Aggregate chargeable transfer	
IHT at lifetime (half-death) rates	870,000
First £325,000 × 0%	–
Next £545,000 × 20%	109,000
	109,000
Less: Tax on previous chargeable transfers	–
Notional IHT on assumed chargeable transfer	109,000
Effective rate:	
£109,000/£870,000 × 100	12.52874%
Settlement rate:	
12.52874% × 30%	3.758621%
IHT payable:	
£870,000 × 3.758621%	£32,700

No BPR is available as the company does not qualify as a trading company for BPR purposes (see 17.19 and 17.78). However, it is possible for the trustees to pay the IHT of £32,700 in ten equal instalments. This is because broadly the underlying trust property represents shares in an unquoted company, the value transferred exceeds £20,000 and the shareholding is more than 10% [*IHTA 1984, ss 227(1)(c), (2)(b) and 228(1)(d), (3)*].

Calculating IHT on capital distributions after a ten-year charge

17.99   Exit charges on capital distributions made after a ten year charge are based on the effective IHT rate at the last ten-year anniversary. However, the rate must be recalculated by reference to the nil rate band prevailing *at the time of the distribution.*

Gifts with reservation of benefit (GROB) rule

17.100 The gift with reservation of benefit rules will apply if the settlor is able to benefit directly or indirectly from the shares transferred into the trust (as an actual or potential beneficiary of the trust (Law Society Gazette, letter of 10 December 1986). On the other hand, if the settlor retains a reversionary interest (ie has an interest subject to some prior right), this is not treated as a reserved benefit (Inland Revenue letter of 18 May 1987).

If a benefit has been reserved, the shares would be treated as remaining within the proprietor's estate for IHT purposes (although BPR may be available) (see also 17.10A). However, this does not alter the IHT status of the original chargeable transfer – any potential 'double' IHT charge is mitigated by the *IHT (Double Charges Relief) Regulations 1981, SI 1987/1130, regs 5* and *8 [FA 1986, s 102]*. The GROB rules only operate for IHT purposes and do not affect the operation of any other taxes – for example, a disposal will arise for CGT purposes in the normal way.

The continued receipt of (favourable) remuneration from the company via arrangements made prior to a gift of shares by a proprietor/trustee might be regarded as a reservation of benefit. However, HMRC accept that this will not be the case where the remuneration received is 'reasonable' (see also 17.46).

ACCUMULATION AND MAINTENANCE TRUSTS

Abolition of the favourable IHT regime for old A&M trusts

17.101 Accumulation and maintenance (A&M) trusts are trusts that were specially created to fall within the privileged IHT treatment. In some ways, it is better to think of A&M trusts in terms of a favoured IHT regime rather than a particular type of trust. A&M trusts were primarily intended for minor children and enabled shares or other assets to be retained within a beneficial IHT regime for a relatively long time.

17.102 Although akin to a discretionary trust, such trusts did not incur any ten-year anniversary charge or exit charges. Furthermore, the transfer of assets to an A&M trust was a PET. However, the tax privileges for A&M trusts were effectively withdrawn by *FA 2006 [FA 2006, Sch 20, paras 2, 3]*. This means that it is likely that few, if any, new A&M trusts will be created – any new A&M trust would be subject to the normal IHT 'relevant property' regime and any assets transferred into them would be chargeable.

17.103 Under special transitional rules, *existing* A&M trusts could retain their IHT advantages until 6 April 2008 (see 17.106 below). At that point, the property held within the trust became subject to the normal 'relevant property' rules (see 17.64).

17.104   Any new trusts set up for the children/grandchildren of a family are now likely to be framed as a discretionary trust, with powers to accumulate the income or apply if for the children's education and/or maintenance.

For detailed coverage of the IHT rules relating to A&M trusts, see 2013/14 and earlier editions of this book.

Existing A&M trusts entering the 'relevant property' regime at 6 April 2008

17.105   Where an existing A&M trust has become subject to the normal 'relevant property' rules on 6 April 2008, it will become subject to (amongst other things) ten-year anniversary charges and exit charges (see 17.78 and 17.79).

The ten-year anniversary charge is computed from the date the trust was created [*IHTA 1984, s 61(1)*] but the IHT rate only reflects the period between 6 April 2008 and the relevant ten-year anniversary date. This means that the tax rate is reduced for each complete quarter from the start of the trust (or, if this was more than ten years ago, the last 'notional' ten-year date) and 6 April 2008.

THE *FA 2006* 'AGE 18 TO 25' TRUST REGIME

Background to the 'Age 18 to 25' IHT trust regime

17.106   The thrust of the original Budget 2006 proposals (particularly in relation to A&M trusts) was to encourage the passing of assets to beneficiaries on their 18th birthday! These plans met with considerable criticism – parents and trustees were aghast at the idea of capital assets passing to 'spendthrift' children at such a young age! The government response was to introduce a compromise solution for those who did not want to release capital outright at 18.

In June 2006, amendments were therefore made to the original *Finance Bill 2006* permitting existing A&M trusts to become (so-called) 'Age 18 to 25 trusts'.

17.107   Such trusts offer partial protection by giving a lower exit charge on assets passing out to a beneficiary after their 18th birthday (provided they vest by the age of 25) and by exempting them from the normal 'ten-year charge'.

Basic *section 71D* conditions

17.108   Assets held within an existing A&M trust can be held on an 'Age 18 to 25 trust' (or *s 71D* trust) where the terms of the trust deed are amended so that the assets pass absolutely to beneficiaries on (or before) their 25th birthday.

In broad terms, *IHTA 1984, s 71D(3)* applies the 'Age 18 to 25' trust regime to an existing A&M trust at 6 April 2008 where:

- the trust holds assets for a beneficiary who has *not* at that time reached the age of 25;

- the beneficiary will become absolutely entitled to the assets (not just an interest in possession) at or before the age of 25 (together with all the trust income that has been accumulated for their benefit).

17.109   Under the 'Age 18 to 25' trust regime, a reduced 'exit' charge applies after the beneficiary's 18th birthday, when the beneficiary:

- becomes absolutely entitled to the trust property;

- has assets applied for their benefit; or

- dies.

The calculation of the 'exit' charge follows the principles in 17.78, but the effective rate is only based on the period after the beneficiary's 18th birthday. This will therefore be a maximum period of seven years – producing a maximum rate of 4.2% (ie 6% × 7/10).

Income and capital gains of 'old' A&M trusts

17.110   Income tax liabilities of A&M trusts are calculated in the same way as those of general discretionary trusts – the rules set out in 17.86–17.89 will therefore apply.

Income currently paid to or for the benefit of the 'young' beneficiaries is deemed to have suffered tax of 45% (after 5 April 2013).

In the case of payments to grandchildren, their personal allowances may completely 'shelter' the payments received from the trust, enabling them to reclaim the 45% tax deducted at source. The repayment claim would normally be made by the parent or guardian. This advantage cannot be obtained on payments to the settlor's *minor children*, as this income is deemed to be the settlor's under the parent-settlement rules in *ITTOIA 2005, s 629*.

Trusts will normally pay CGT at 20% on their gains (after deducting the trust annual exemption). See 17.75 for further details.

ASSETS HELD OUTSIDE THE COMPANY

BPR entitlement

17.111   It is not uncommon for the company's trading property to be owned by the controlling shareholder with the property being let to the company. However, this is detrimental for IHT purposes.

BPR of only 50% is available for land, buildings, machinery or plant used in the company's trade, but held outside the company where the owner of the asset is a controlling shareholder. This means that the owner must be in a position to exercise the majority of the voting rights ('related property' shareholdings are also counted for this purpose) [*IHTA 1984, ss 104(1)(b) and 105(1)(d)*].

If the proprietor is also a first named trustee of a discretionary trust which holds shares in the company, these may also be taken into account on the grounds that (as first named trustee), he would have control of the voting rights (see *Taxation Practitioner*, November 1994).

Thus, where the company's trading property is held outside the company by the proprietor, there is a strong incentive for them to retain a controlling shareholding. It may, of course, be possible for the proprietor to increase the relief on the property to 100% by transferring it to the company by way of gift (under a *TCGA 1992, s 165* business asset hold-over election). 100% BPR will then be available on the value of the shares, which will have been uplifted by the value of the property. This course of action would have to be weighed against the potential commercial disadvantages, such as exposing the property to claims by the company's creditors.

However, if the value of the property was held by the company and was therefore reflected in the value of the company's shares, 100% BPR would be available.

17.112   If the trading property is held by a non-controlling shareholder, no BPR would be available. The property would then be fully chargeable to IHT, even if it was used for the purposes of the company's trade.

17.113   If the property is held by an elderly member of the family (perhaps the founder or founder's widow) and is particularly valuable, consideration might be given to transferring some additional shares to them so as to give a controlling holding, particularly if the shares and property will revert to the next generation on their death. Obviously, a considerable element of trust is required here!

Gifting or selling trading property to the company

17.114   Where it is feasible (and much would depend on the disposition of any other shareholdings), the property could be gifted to the company, with hold-over relief being claimed under *TCGA 1992, s 165*. It should be noted that a gift to a company cannot qualify as a PET (*IHTA 1984, s 3A*), but, if the company is wholly-owned by the transferor, there will be no reduction in value of their estate. However, any gift of property would normally incur an SDLT charge by reference to the market value of the property (*FA 2003, s 53*).

17.115   If the shareholdings are fragmented, then careful consideration will need to be exercised to ascertain the value of the transfer (particularly bearing in mind the discount attaching to minority shareholdings). Alternatively, a transfer of value or gift could probably be avoided by transferring the property in exchange for shares (as there would be no 'donative intent'). However, a CGT liability might arise – business asset gift hold-over relief would not be available as full consideration would be received in shares. SDLT would normally arise on the company's acquisition of the property (see 12.23–12.29).

PRE-OWNED ASSETS – INCOME TAX CHARGE

Outline of pre-owned assets (POA) charge

17.116 Since 2005/06, an income tax charge on certain pre-owned assets (POAs) may be levied in appropriate cases. Given that the POA rules may potentially impact on certain transactions undertaken by owner-managers, the relevant rules are briefly examined here.

The pre-owned asset legislation (in *FA 2004, s 84* and *Sch 15*) is primarily aimed at a number of IHT avoidance arrangements that broadly enable individuals to dispose of their assets (for IHT purposes) whilst retaining the ability to use or have access to them. Such arrangements would generally be structured to avoid the gift with reservation of benefit (or GROB) rules (see 17.10A and 17.100). However, given its wide-ranging nature, the POA legislation could also affect many innocent transactions, sometimes in an unsuspected manner.

Certain types of specialised insurance-based products are available to mitigate IHT in an efficient way. HMRC have confirmed that gift and loan trusts and discounted gift trusts (see 17.44) do not normally attract any POA income tax charge.

In the context of owner-managed companies, it is common for shareholders to take out life insurance policies to provide funds on their death to enable their shares to be purchased by their fellow shareholders/the company. Provided a shareholder is not a beneficiary of their own policy, it will not attract any POA charge.

Please see 2016/17 and earlier editions of this book for a summary of the POA regime.

PLANNING CHECKLIST – SUCCESSION PLANNING AND PASSING ON THE FAMILY OR OWNER-MANAGED COMPANY

Company

- Investment companies or trading companies that hold significant investments potentially give rise to material capital tax liabilities for the shareholders.

Working shareholders

- Succession planning options should be kept open and fluid to deal with changes in personal circumstances and tax law.

- Consider benefits of retaining shares in the family/owner-managed company to obtain complete exemption from IHT on death (donees also inherit shares at market value for CGT).

- Use sensible will drafting to maximise use of available nil rate band, residential nil-rate band, and business property relief (BPR). In many cases, it would be beneficial to leave shares and other assets qualifying for BPR via a will discretionary trust (which could include the surviving spouse as one of the beneficiaries).

- Lifetime transfers of shares in an owner managed 'trading' company to the next generation (which may be necessary to preserve management morale, etc) are usually tax-free, but donee takes on deferred CGT liability.

- It is not possible to hold-over gains on transfers into a trust in which the settlor, their spouse, or dependent children have an actual or discretionary interest.

- Owner managers who sell their companies (where, for example, there is no succession path) must consider their increased IHT exposure (since they will cease to hold exempt 'business property'). Their realisation proceeds will be potentially chargeable to IHT at 40%. They may therefore wish to transfer some of their shareholding to a discretionary trust (well in advance of any proposed sale of the company). The subsequent sale proceeds would therefore be sheltered from IHT. They might also consider using Discounted Gift Trusts as a means of mitigating IHT.

- Trusts are particularly efficient since they can be used to retain control over shares, but enable value and future growth in shares to be transferred outside shareholder's estate.

- Discretionary trusts may offer a degree of protection for assets against subsequent divorce claims brought (for example) by the spouses of the owner-manager's children. They also offer a degree of flexibility and are a particularly useful vehicle for holding at least part of the shareholding in an owner-managed company. With the benefit of business property relief, any IHT charges should be minimal.

- 'Pilot-trusts' established after 10 December 2014 cease to offer any material IHT advantage.

- Since 6 April 2016, trustees will pay 38.1% on dividends without any tax credit, thus making the receipt of dividends more expensive compared to prior years.

- Trustees may wish to consider granting revocable life interests/ interests in possession to beneficiaries before they receive substantial dividends, since the dividends would then only be taxed at the beneficiaries' marginal tax rate. These interests can subsequently be revoked without any IHT consequences.

- In most cases, discretionary trusts will now be used to hold shares for the future benefit of the owner-manager's children and/or grandchildren (but watch 'hold-over' relief restriction where settlor's minor children benefit from the trust).

- Interest in possession trusts tend to be used where the settlor wishes to provide an automatic right to income (but wishes to protect the underlying capital assets from their potentially 'wastrel' children). However, such trusts are now exposed to exit and ten-year IHT charges (subject to any exemption conferred by business property relief or the settlor's nil rate band). However, assets held within interest in possession trusts are protected from the full 40% IHT charge.

- Watch out for the potential application of the gift with reservation of benefit rules for certain family arrangements, particularly those involving the gifting of property that is subsequently occupied by the donor and also for certain settlor-interested trusts.

Other employees

- Key employees should be involved in succession planning or they may become disenchanted and leave.

- If there is strong second-tier management, consider an MBO if there is no obvious succession route.

Non-working shareholders

- Similar considerations apply as for working shareholders.

Index

[All references are to paragraph number]